ELEMENTS OF LITERATURE

FIFTH COURSE

Literature of the United States

The Elements of Literature Program

ELEMENTS OF LITERATURE: First Course

ELEMENTS OF LITERATURE: Second Course

ELEMENTS OF LITERATURE: Third Course

ELEMENTS OF LITERATURE: Fourth Course

ELEMENTS OF LITERATURE: Fifth Course
Literature of the United States

ELEMENTS OF LITERATURE: Sixth Course
Literature of Britain

A Teacher's Manual, Test Book, and Teacher's Resource Organizer are available for each of the above titles.

Robert Anderson is a playwright, novelist, screenwriter, and television writer. His plays include *Tea and Sympathy; Silent Night, Lonely Night; You Know I Can't Hear You When the Water's Running;* and *I Never Sang for My Father.* His screenplays include *The Nun's Story* and *The Sand Pebbles.* Mr. Anderson has taught at the Writer's Workshop at the University of Iowa, the American Theatre Wing Professional Training Program, and the Salzburg Seminar in American Studies. He is a Past President of the Dramatists' Guild, Vice-President of the Author's League of America, and a member of the Theatre Hall of Fame. He makes his home in Connecticut and New York City.

John Malcolm Brinnin, author of six volumes of poetry which have received many prizes and awards, is a member of the American Academy and Institute of Arts and Letters. He is also a critic of poetry and a biographer of poets and was for a number of years Director of New York's famous Poetry Center. His teaching career, begun at Vassar College, included long terms at the University of Connecticut and Boston University, where he succeeded Robert Lowell as Professor of Creative Writing and Contemporary Letters. Mr. Brinnin has written *Dylan Thomas in America: An Intimate Journal* and *Sextet: T. S. Eliot & Truman Capote & Others.* He divides his time between Duxbury, Massachusetts, and Key West, Florida.

John Leggett is an editor, a novelist, and a biographer who went to the Writer's Workshop at the University of Iowa in the spring of 1969, expecting to put in a single semester. In 1970 he assumed temporary charge of the program and was its Director for the next seventeen years. Mr. Leggett's novels include *Wilder Stone, The Gloucester Branch, Who Took the Gold Away, Gulliver House,* and *Making Believe.* He is also the author of the highly acclaimed biography *Ross and Tom: Two American Tragedies.* His short fiction, articles, and reviews have appeared in *Harper's, Esquire, Mademoiselle, The Ladies Home Journal,* and the *Los Angeles Times.* A native New Yorker, Mr. Leggett now lives in San Francisco.

Gary Q. Arpin received his doctorate from the University of Virginia, where he taught for several years before taking a position with Western Illinois University at Macomb. He has written articles on John Berryman and other American poets, and has published a book, *John Berryman: A Reference Guide.* He currently is an editor at the *Reader's Digest* and lives in Katonah, New York.

Susan Allen Toth has written *Blooming: A Small-Town Girlhood,* about her childhood in Ames, Iowa, and a sequel, *Ivy Days: Making My Way Out East,* about her experiences at Smith College in Northampton, Massachusetts. She studied at the University of California at Berkeley and received her doctorate from the University of Minnesota. She currently teaches at Macalaster College in St. Paul, Minnesota. She contributes articles to many periodicals, including *Harper's, Redbook, McCalls,* and *The New York Times.*

ELEMENTS OF LITERATURE

FIFTH COURSE

Literature of the United States

HOLT, RINEHART AND WINSTON, INC.

AUSTIN   NEW YORK   SAN DIEGO   CHICAGO   TORONTO   MONTREAL

Sandra Cisneros has served as Consultant for the program. A graduate of the Writer's Workshop at the University of Iowa, she has written a novel, *The House on Mango Street,* and several collections of poems, including *My Wicked, Wicked Ways.* She has taught at California State University, Chico, and now makes her home in Texas.

Nancy E. Wiseman Seminoff has served as Consultant in Reading and Questioning Strategies for the program. Dr. Seminoff is Dean of the College of Education at Winona State University, Minnesota. She has served as a reading consultant at the secondary level and as a classroom teacher. She has published widely in national and state educational periodicals. Dr. Seminoff lives in Winona, Minnesota.

Richard Zahner assisted in the planning, development, and writing of the Exercises in Critical Thinking and Writing. He also reviewed critically the essays on The American Language. Mr. Zahner is Head of the English Department at Bunnell High School in Stratford, Connecticut. For several years he has been a reader for the Advanced Placement Examinations in English.

ISBN 0-15-717540-5

890123456 041 987654321

Design: Kirchoff / Wohlberg, Inc.
Art Development and Picture Research: Photosearch, Inc.
Cover: *The Mirage* by Thomas Moran (1879). Oil.
Stark Museum of Art, Orange, Texas.
Page v: *Threshing* (detail) by John Stuart Curry (c. 1935). Oil.
The Kennedy Galleries, Inc., New York.

Acknowledgments

Grateful acknowledgment is made to the teachers who reviewed materials in this book, in manuscript or in classroom tests.

Jean Gelsinger
Ruskin Senior High School
Kansas City, Missouri

Delores Obermiller
Corpus Christi Independent School District
Corpus Christi, Texas

Geraldine Pelegano
Mountain View School
Bristol, Connecticut

Eva-Lynn Powell
Dade County Schools
Dade County, Florida

Charles I. Schuster
Seattle, Washington

CONTENTS

THE COLONIAL PERIOD
THE AGE OF FAITH

The Puritan Deacon Samuel Chapin
by Augustus Saint-Gaudens (1899). Bronze.

Private Collection. Photo: The Graham Galleries, New York.

UNIT ONE

For we must consider that we shall be as a city upon a hill, the eyes of all people are upon us. So that if we shall deal falsely with our God in this work we have undertaken, and so cause Him to withdraw His present help from us, we shall be made a story and a by-word through the world: we shall open the mouths of enemies to speak evil of the ways of God and all professors for God's sake; we shall shame the faces of many of God's worthy servants, and cause their prayers to be turned into curses upon us, till we be consumed out of the good land whither we are going.

—from a sermon preached on the way to the New World, spring 1630, by John Winthrop

The Europeans Visit the New World

Christopher Columbus Landing on San Salvador by an unknown artist (19th century). Watercolor.

New York State Historical Association, Cooperstown.

The adventurers came first. They landed their ships on the beaches of the unexplored continent and, sometimes foolheartedly, marched into the wilderness. Some survived to record their adventures. Many never came out alive.

In 1528, only 36 years after Columbus first sighted that flickering fire on the beach of San Salvador, a Spaniard named Alvar Nuñez Cabeza de Vaca landed with an expedition (he was its treasurer) near the entrance to Tampa Bay, on the west coast of what is now called Florida. (De Vaca's curious name, meaning "cow's head," was his mother's. It was bestowed on one of her ancestors by the king of Spain, after the man had guided the king's army through a pass marked with a cow's skull.) De Vaca and others left the ships and marched inland. The fleet waited a year for the expedition to return. When it didn't, the boats turned around and sailed for Mexico, giving the explorers up for dead.

De Vaca and the others were lost in the wilderness, at times held captive by native groups, but they were not dead. De Vaca himself would spend the next eight years walking around what is now Texas, New Mexico, and Arizona, trying to find fellow explorers who might help him get home.

De Vaca's narrative of his incredible hardships is a gripping adventure story; it is also a first-hand account of the habits of the natives of the American wilderness—de Vaca records what the natives ate (very little), how they housed themselves, and what their religious beliefs were. De Vaca also provides the first account of some animals and plants that Europeans had never known existed. The opossum, for example, first enters the historical record with de Vaca's narrative.

Here is part of de Vaca's account of the expedition's experiences with a tribal group in Florida.

Their support is principally roots, of two or three kinds, and they look for them over the face of all the country. The food is poor and gripes the persons who eat it. The roots require roasting two days: many are very bitter, and withal difficult to be dug. They are sought the distance of two or three leagues, and so great is the want these people experience, that they cannot get through the year without them. Occasionally they kill deer, and at times take fish; but the quantity is so small and the famine so great, that they eat spiders and the eggs of ants, worms, lizards, salamanders, snakes, and vipers that kill whom they strike; and they eat earth and wood, and all that there is, the dung of deer, and other things that I omit to mention; and I honestly believe that were there stones in that land they would eat them. They save the bones of the fishes they consume, of snakes and other animals, that they may afterwards beat them together and eat the powder. The men bear no burthens, nor carry anything of weight; such are borne by women and old men who are of the least esteem. . . . The women work very hard, and do a great deal; of the twenty-four hours they have only six of repose; the rest of the night they pass in heating the ovens to bake those roots they eat. At daybreak they begin to dig them, to bring wood and water to their houses and get in readiness other things that may be necessary. . . .

Their houses are of matting, placed upon four hoops. They carry them on the back, and remove every two or three days in search of food. Nothing is planted for support. They are a merry people, considering the hunger they suffer; for they never cease, notwithstanding, to observe their festivities and

Earliest picture of an American bison from Gomara's *Historia General de las Indias* (1554). Woodcut.

Library of Congress.

Spanish Frontier Guard by an unknown artist (17th century). Watercolor.

Archivo de Indias, Seville, Spain.

Florida Coachwhip Snake by William Bartram (1769). Watercolor.

Botanical Library, Museum of Natural History, New York.

areytos [ceremonial songs and dances]. To them the happiest part of the year is the season of eating prickly pears; they have hunger then no longer, pass all the time in dancing, and eat day and night.

It occurred to us many times while we were among this people, and there was no food, to be three or four days without eating, when they . . . would tell us not to be sad, that soon there would be prickly pears when we should eat a plenty and drink of the juice, when our bellies would be very big and we should be content and joyful, having no hunger. From the time they first told us this, to that at which the earliest were ripe enough to be eaten, was an interval of five or six months; so having tarried until the lapse of this period, and the season had come, we went to eat the fruit.

We found mosquitos of three sorts, and all of them abundant in every part of the country. They poison and inflame, and during the greater part of the summer gave us great annoyance. As a protection we made fires, encircling the people with them, burning rotten and wet wood to produce smoke without flame. The remedy brought another trouble, and the night long we did little else than shed tears from the smoke that came into our eyes, besides feeling intense heat from the many fires, and if at any time we went out for repose to the seaside and fell asleep, we were reminded with blows to make up the fires. . . .

They are accustomed also to kill deer by encircling them with fires. The pasturage is taken from the cattle by burning, that necessity may drive them to seek it in places where it is desired they should go. They encamp only where there are wood and water; and sometimes all carry loads of these when they go to hunt deer, which are usually found where neither is to be got. On the day of their arrival, they kill the deer and other animals which they can, and consume all the water and all the wood in cooking and on the fires they make to relieve them of mosquitos. They remain the next day to get something to sustain them on their return; and when they go, such is their state from those insects that they appear to have the affliction of holy Lazarus. In this way do they appease their hunger, two or three times in the year, at the cost I have mentioned. From my own experience, I can state there is no torment known in this world that can equal it.

—Cabeza de Vaca

Florida Alligator by John White (1585). Watercolor.

The British Museum, London.

Interesting and valuable as these explorers' writings are, they were not as important to the development of the American literary tradition as were the writings of the Puritans of the New England colonies. It was the Puritans who most powerfully influenced the course of American literature and the formation of the American imagination. In fact, much of what we now identify as "American" comes from the moral, ethical, and religious convictions of that small group of early New England settlers who landed, in 1620, on the tip of Cape Cod, just before Christmas.

Their voyage from Plymouth in southwestern England to Cape Cod in North America lasted more than two months and was fraught with disaster. The Puritans began in two ships, the *Mayflower* and the *Speedwell,* but they were forced twice to turn back. They finally had to abandon the inaptly named *Speedwell,* which was prone to leaks. A hired sailor on the *Mayflower* who had mocked and cursed the Puritan passengers died of a fever early in the voyage—evidence, wrote William Bradford, of "the just hand of God upon him." Halfway across the Atlantic, the main beam of the *Mayflower* buckled in a storm, and the group almost turned back for good. But the Puritans had brought with them a large iron screw—a sort of heavy-duty jack. They straightened the beam with the screw, discussed the practical details with the captain, "committed themselves to the will of God," as Bradford put it, "and resolved to proceed."

Each of these attitudes, actions, and decisions is absolutely characteristic of the Puritans. They were practical, as shown by their repair of the beam. But they were also single-minded visionaries convinced of the rightness of their cause, as shown by Bradford's comments on the sailor's death. Their real commerce was with heaven, but they were competent in the business of the world as well. The founding of the New World was a business venture as well as a spiritual one—and for the Puritans, as we shall see, the everyday world and the spiritual world were closely intertwined.

Who Were These Puritans?

Puritan is a broad term, referring to any of a number of Protestant sects that sought to "purify" the established Church of England. The English Puritans, who were part of a much larger pattern of Protestant reform sweeping Western Europe, wished to return to the simple forms of worship and church organization as described in the New Testament. Because they refused to conform to the state church's beliefs and practices, the Puritans were also called "Nonconformists" or "Dissenters." Since the time of King Henry VIII (who reigned from 1509 to 1547), the English church had been virtually inseparable from the government; the Puritans thus represented a threat to the political stability of the nation. "I will *make* them conform," King James I had said of the Puritans in 1604, "or I will harry them out of the land." As it turned out, it was in the end the Puritans who harried the royal family out of the land: forty-five years later, they beheaded James's son Charles I and forced Charles II into exile in France.

Even so, many Puritans suffered persecution. Some of them left England, at first for Holland. But fearing that they would lose their identity as English Christians, a small advance group of about a hundred Puritans set sail in 1620 for the New World. There they hoped to realize their dream of building a new secular society patterned after God's word. "As one small candle may light a thousand," William Bradford would write later, "so the light kindled here hath shone unto many, yes, in some sort to our whole nation."

The Puritans in New England: A Spiritual Journey

Matthew Hopkins, an English Puritan.

Rare Book Division, New York Public Library.

Title page of the Bible owned by
William Bradford.

Pilgrim Society, Plymouth, Massachusetts.

Puritan Beliefs

What sort of spiritual and intellectual cargo did the Puritans bring
with them on the *Mayflower*? They were practical, intensely committed, and convinced of the rightness of their purpose. But
strangely enough, at the center of Puritan theology was an uneasy
mixture of certainty and doubt. The certainty was that because of
Adam and Eve's sin of disobedience, most of humanity would be
damned for all eternity. "In Adam's fall," as the Puritan primer
taught, "we sinned all." Yet, though Adam's sin was damning, the
Puritans were certain that God in His mercy sent His son to earth
to allow some to be saved.

Their doubt centered on whether a particular individual was to
be one of the saved or one of the damned. In theory, a person's
fate was *determined* by God; that is, a person could do nothing to
become one of the saved. In practice, though, the Puritans strove
intensely for salvation and led very pious lives. This was in part
because of the consequences of this question: How did you know
if you were saved or damned?

As it turns out, you did not know. A theology that was so clear-
cut in its division of the world between saints and sinners (or the
"elect" and the "unregenerate") was fuzzy when it came to deter-
mining which were which. There were two principal indications of
the state of your soul, neither of them completely certain. You were

1492–1500	1503–1513	1517–1521	1528–1531
Christopher Columbus lands on San Salvador, October 11–14, 1492	In Italy, Leonardo da Vinci paints *Mona Lisa*, 1503	Martin Luther begins Protestant Reformation in Europe, 1517	Cabeza de Vaca lands in Florida, 1528
25 million Indians live in North and South America, 1500	Juan Ponce de Leon discovers Florida, 1513	Aztec Empire falls to Spaniards, 1521	Henry VIII replaces the Pope as Supreme Head of the Church of England, 1531

1605–1607	1611–1612	1619–1620	1626–1630
Shakespeare's *King Lear* and *Macbeth* first performed in London, 1605	King James version of the Bible completed in England, 1611	First Africans arrive in the New World, on Dutch slave ships, 1619	Peter Minuit buys the island of Manhattan from Native American chiefs for about $24 worth of merchandise, 1626
Settlement founded at Jamestown, Virginia, 1607	**Anne Bradstreet born in England, 1612**	*Mayflower* arrives in the New World, November 11, 1620	**William Bradford begins his history, 1630**

1657–1665	1666	1668–1674	1675
William Bradford dies at Plymouth, 1657	**Sarah Kemble Knight born in Boston, 1666**	**Edward Taylor arrives in Boston, 1668**	Metacomet's war on the colonial settlements in Massachusetts, 1675
The Great Plague kills nearly 70,000 people in London, 1665	**Anne Bradstreet's house burns in Andover, 1666**	**Anne Bradstreet dies in Andover, 1672**	**Mary Rowlandson captured by Metacomet's people, 1675**
		William Byrd born in Virginia, 1674	

saved by the grace of God, and you could *feel* this grace arriving, in an intensely emotional fashion. The inner arrival of God's grace was demonstrated by your outward behavior. After receiving grace, you were "reborn" as a member of the community of saints, and you behaved like a saint. People hoping to be among the saved examined their inner lives closely for signs of grace, and they tried to behave in as exemplary a manner as possible. So "idle hands" really were "the devil's playground," and American Puritans came to value the virtues of industriousness, temperance, sobriety, and simplicity. These were, coincidentally, the ideal qualities needed to carve a civilization out of the wilderness.

Religion for the Puritans, then, was first of all a personal, inner experience. They did not believe that the clergy or the Church should or could act as an intermediary between the individual and God. Not all Puritans felt that the state should be distinct from the Church, but most of the New England colonists were strongly against the idea of a national church. Nevertheless, religious attitudes affected the government, for Puritans believed that the sinful state of humanity made governments necessary. They also believed that the foundation of all governmental laws was the inflexible law of God. In the Puritan view, a covenant, or contract, existed between God and humanity. This covenant was a useful model for social organization as well: people should enter freely into agreements concerning their form of political organization. On

1558–1579	1587–1588	1590–1594	1603
Elizabeth, daughter of Henry VIII, becomes Queen of England, 1558	Virginia Dare, first English child born in North America, 1587	**William Bradford born in England, 1590**	Bubonic plague, which would kill 150,000 people, breaks out in London, 1603
John Smith born in England, 1579	The British defeat the Spanish Armada, 1588	Shakespeare's *Romeo and Juliet* first performed in London, 1594	

1635–1636	1639–1640	1642–1643	1649–1650
First public school in America, 1635	First printing press in the New World, 1639	**Edward Taylor born in England, 1642**	King Charles I of England beheaded, 1649
Mary Rowlandson born in England, 1636	First book published in the New World (*Bay Psalm Book*), 1640	English Civil War begins, 1643	**Anne Bradstreet's first book of poetry published in England, 1650**
Harvard College founded 1636			

1690–1692	1703–1728	1741	1740–1745
Slaves held in all English colonies in North America, 1690	**Jonathan Edwards born in Connecticut, 1703**	**Jonathan Edwards preaches "Sinners in the Hands of an Angry God," 1741**	The Great Awakening, 1740–1745, is touched off by a traveling English preacher
Witch trials held in Salem, Massachusetts, 1692	**Mrs. Knight travels to New York, 1704**	Handel's *The Messiah* first performed in Dublin, 1741	
	William Byrd goes on his expedition, 1728		

English church steeple designed by Sir Christopher Wren (1666–1718).

The Wren Society Publications, 1932.

the *Mayflower,* for example, the Puritans composed and signed a compact outlining how they would be governed once they landed. In this and other ways, they prepared the ground for the later growth of American democracy.

The Puritans' Model: The Pilgrim

Every age has at least one figure, or heroic type, that seems to embody its ideas and aspirations. The Puritans who came to America identified so powerfully with one figure that they called themselves by that name: "Pilgrim." A pilgrim is someone who makes a pilgrimage, or journey to a holy place. But for the Puritans, the word *pilgrimage* took on a wider meaning—it was a journey to salvation.

For the Pilgrims, the outward journey of their lives and the specific voyage to America were also inner, spiritual journeys. "A Christian is sailing through this world unto his heavenly country," the poet Anne Bradstreet wrote some years after sailing across the Atlantic to America. "We must, therefore, be here as strangers and pilgrims, that we may plainly declare that we seek a city above." In a way, each Pilgrim was acting out a tale of salvation in which he or she saw outward physical events as having inner, spiritual meaning.

The Pilgrims read their lives the way a literary critic reads a book, examining the significance of each event. John Winthrop, a governor of the Massachusetts Bay Colony, includes an account in his *Diary* of a snake entering the church during a synod, or council meeting. One of the elders "trod upon the head of it," and the snake was killed. It is perhaps not unnatural for a snake to find its way into a country church on a hot August day, but Winthrop saw far more significance in the snake's visit. "The serpent is the devil; the synod, the representative of the churches of Christ in New England. The devil had . . . lately attempted their disturbance, . . . but their faith . . . overcame him and crushed his head."

The Bible in the American Wilderness

The Puritans read the Bible as the story of the creation, fall, wanderings, and rescue of the human race. Within this long and complex narrative, each Puritan could see connections to events in his or her own life or to events in the life of the community. Thus, William Bradford (page 11) compares the experiences of the Pilgrims to the experiences of the Israelites wandering in the wilderness. Mary Rowlandson (page 23) sees countless similarities between her captivity by the Indians and captivities recorded in the Old Testament.

The Puritans believed that the Bible was the literal word of God. Reading the Bible was a necessity for all Puritans, as was the ability to understand closely reasoned theological debates. For these reasons, the Puritans placed great emphasis on education.

But their interest in education was not confined to simple literacy. Many of the New England settlers had enjoyed the benefits of higher education in England, and they wanted the same for their children. Thus, Harvard College was founded in 1636, just six years after the Massachusetts Bay Colony was established and only sixteen years after the first Pilgrims had landed.

Puritan Writings

The Bible was also the foundation upon which Puritan literature was built. In their religious services, Puritans rejected any ceremonies or adornments not mentioned in the Bible—clerical vestments, stained-glass windows, and the use of incense, for example. The same restrictions applied to literature. The Puritans did not object to figures of speech used to drive home a point, but they rejected mere "adornments" such as ornate figures of speech or witty plays on words. The ideal Puritan style was a **plain style**—strong, simple, and logical. It was a literary style that could make explanations of the scriptures accessible to everyone.

Their beliefs required the Puritans to keep a close watch on both the inner and outer events of their lives. This central aspect of the Puritan mind greatly affected their literature. Inner events, such as feelings of despair or great joy, were stages on the road to salvation; external events, like a snake entering a church, con-

John Eliot Preaching to the Indians (19th century). Colored engraving.

Built in the year 1683. Taken down 1744. 45 feet by 40 — 16 in the walls. Scale 20 feet to an inch. It stood where the first Church now stands.

MEETING HOUSE

Drawing of a Plymouth meeting house (1683).

Pilgrim Society, Plymouth, Massachusetts.

tained messages from God. And so diaries and histories were important forms of Puritan literature, because they were records of the workings of God.

Such concerns determined as well what incidents the Puritans chose to write about. They recorded forms of *revelation*. The Puritans believed that God revealed His purpose to humanity in three principal ways: through the Bible, through the natural world, and through Divine Providence, or God's direct intervention in human affairs. Thus the Puritans wrote on Biblical and devotional topics: the first American best seller was Michael Wigglesworth's long poem on the Judgment Day, *The Day of Doom* (1662). They wrote about the spiritual truth they discovered in the natural world: Edward Taylor's poems (page 45) are especially good examples, but you will find this theme in diaries and histories as well. And they wrote about moments of special Providence or events that contained great lessons, such as Anne Bradstreet's poem on the destruction of her house by fire (page 43).

The Puritans were not machines programmed for worship and nothing else, however. Although they cannot be separated from their religion, neither can they be fully contained by it. They were complex and complete human beings who took great joy in their lives and relationships, while facing hardships difficult to imagine today. Anne Bradstreet's poem on the burning of her house, for example, does not simply draw a dry lesson from the event. It records her moments of joy in the house and works through her grief to a spiritual solace. If there had been no complexity in her, no conflict between her love of things of this world and her conviction that the ultimate value lay in the spiritual world, the poem would have been very different. At its best, Puritan literature records not merely the moments when the physical and the spiritual worlds cross but rather the moments when they seem to diverge—when love of things of this world threatens to push out love of eternity.

William Bradford (1590–1657)

William Bradford's life displayed a mixture of the commonplace and the extraordinary that was characteristic of the Puritan experience. Bradford was the son of a prosperous farmer in Yorkshire, England. His father died when William was a baby, and the child was raised by his grandparents and uncles. It was assumed that the young man would take over the family holdings when he came of age; in keeping with this expectation, he received no higher education but instead was taught the practical arts of farming. Despite his lack of formal training (or perhaps because of it), Bradford was to become a successful, longstanding Colonial governor in the New World, dealing out justice and settling disputes of all kinds. He would also write the first history that depicts America as a unique social experiment.

Bradford might have become the prosperous Yorkshire farmer he was prepared to become if he had not taken a radical step when he was twelve years old. Inspired by his reading of the Bible and by the sermons of a Puritan minister, he joined a small group of Nonconformists despite the vehement objections of his family and friends. The group could not worship publicly, so they met furtively in a private house in the nearby town of Scrooby. Seven years later, under increasing pressure of persecution and fearful that they would be imprisoned, the Scrooby group crossed the North Sea to Holland. There, Bradford set up a weaving business. He also married Dorothy May, a young woman who was a fellow emigrant from England, and the couple had a child. In 1620, after ten years in Holland, the group was aided by London profiteers and merchants, who lent them a ship and crew as an investment, and the Nonconformists sailed for the New World.

For Bradford, the hardships of the ocean voyage did not end with the landing at Plymouth. In December, while the *Mayflower* was anchored in Provincetown Bay, Bradford and other men took a small boat ashore to scout for a place to land and build shelter. When they returned, Bradford learned that his young wife had fallen or jumped

First page, *Of Plimoth Plantation* by William Bradford.

Pilgrim Society, Plymouth, Massachusetts.

from the ship and was drowned. The act may well have been suicide. Dorothy Bradford had been on the crowded ship for more than two months, and when land was finally sighted, she did not see the hoped-for green hills of an earthly paradise. Beyond the ship lay only the bleak sand dunes of Cape Cod. That bitter winter, half the settlers were to die of cold, disease, and malnutrition.

The following year, Bradford was elected governor of the plantation at the age of thirty-one. "Had he not been a person of more than ordinary piety, wisdom, and courage," the Puritan preacher Cotton Mather later recorded, "he must have sunk" under the difficulties of governing such a shaky settlement. But, Mather continued, Bradford had been "laying up a treasure of experience, and he had now occasion to use it." Bradford proved an exemplary leader, and he went on to be elected governor of the Colony no fewer than thirty times.

In 1630, Bradford began to write a history of the Plymouth Colony from its beginning. He continued writing an annual account of the settlement until 1647. His record, *Of Plymouth Plantation,* was not composed for immediate publication or to attract more colonists, like many other early Colonial accounts. It was written for posterity, although by the end of his life Bradford's dreams of that posterity had been shattered.

As the years passed, the plantation at Plymouth prospered economically. Beaver pelts from the Indians brought good money in England, and eventually the plantation managed to pay off its debt. But as the group prospered and grew, it also became more diffuse and less pious. Despite Bradford's efforts to hold it together, the Plymouth Colony gradually disintegrated as a religious community. The ideal of the "city on the hill," the Pilgrims' dream of an ideal society founded on religious principles, gradually gave way to the realities of life in the New World. Bradford's record of this grand experiment ends in disappointment. When more fertile areas for settlement were found and when Boston became a more convenient port to England, Plymouth lost much of its population—especially its young people. "Thus was this poor church left," Bradford wrote in 1644, near the conclusion of his history, "like an ancient mother grown old and forsaken of her children. She that had made so many rich became herself poor."

The first nine chapters of Bradford's history were copied into the Plymouth church records, but the entire manuscript was later lost. Most likely it was carried back to England as a souvenir by a British soldier during the Revolutionary War. The soldier might have sold it for a few cents to a bookseller in London. It was almost a century later that Governor Bradford's vellum-bound volume was discovered in the library of the Bishop of London. *Of Plymouth Plantation* was first published in 1856 by the Massachusetts Historical Society. After long negotiations, the manuscript was finally returned to the United States in 1897. It can be seen today in the Statehouse in Boston.

The Mayflower in Plymouth Harbor by W. F. Halsall (1882). Oil.

Pilgrim Society, Plymouth, Massachusetts.

FROM OF PLYMOUTH PLANTATION

The following extracts from Bradford's history describe some celebrated events: the landing at Plymouth, the framing of the Mayflower Compact, the Pilgrims' early encounters with the native inhabitants, and their first Thanksgiving. In the first paragraph, notice how matter-of-fact Bradford is about God's role in their voyage. Look for similar references to Divine Providence in the rest of the history. Note also how outward events contain an inner, spiritual significance.

Chapter 9

Of Their Voyage, and How They Passed the Sea; and of Their Safe Arrival At Cape Cod

September 6 [1620]. These troubles[1] being blown over, and now all being compact together in one ship, they put to sea again with a prosperous wind, which continued divers [many] days together, which was some encouragement unto them; yet, according to the usual manner, many were afflicted with seasickness. And I may not omit here a special work of God's Providence. There was a proud and very profane young man, one of the seamen, of a lusty [energetic], able body, which made him the more haughty; he would always be condemning the poor people in their sickness and cursing them daily with grievous execrations; and did not let to tell them that he hoped to help to cast half of them overboard before they came to their journey's end, and to make merry with what they had; and if he were by any gently reproved, he would curse and swear most bitterly. But it pleased God before they came half seas over, to smite this young man with a grievous disease, of which he died in a desperate manner, and so was himself the first that was thrown overboard. Thus his curses light on his own head, and it was an astonishment to all his fellows, for they noted it to be the just hand of God upon him.

After they had enjoyed fair winds and weather for a season, they were encountered many times with crosswinds and met with many fierce storms, with which the ship was shroudly[2] shaken and her upper works made very leaky; and one of the main beams in the midships was bowed and cracked, which put them in some fear that the ship could not be able to perform the voyage. So some of the chief of the company, perceiving the mariners to fear the sufficiency of the ship, as appeared by their mutterings, they entered into serious consultation with the master and other officers of the ship, to consider in time of the danger, and rather to return than to cast themselves into a desperate and inevitable peril. And truly there was great distraction and difference of opinion amongst the mariners themselves; fain [gladly] would they do what could be done for their wages' sake (being now near half the seas over), and on the other hand they were loath [reluctant] to hazard their lives too desperately. But in examining all opinions, the master and others affirmed they knew the ship to be strong and firm under water; and for the buckling of the main beam, there was a great iron screw the passengers brought out of Holland, which would raise the beam into his place; the which being done, the carpenter and master affirmed that with a post put under it, set firm in the lower deck, and otherways bound, he would make it sufficient. And as for the decks and upper works, they would caulk them as well as they could, and though with the working of the ship they would not long keep staunch [watertight], yet there would otherwise be no great danger, if they did not overpress her with sails. So they committed themselves to the will of God and resolved to proceed.

---

1. **troubles:** the return of the *Speedwell* to England and the transfer of her passengers to the *Mayflower*.

2. **shroudly:** shrewdly, used here in its archaic sense of "wickedly."

In sundry of these storms the winds were so fierce and the seas so high as they could not bear a knot of sail, but were forced to hull[3] for divers days together. And in one of them, as they thus lay at hull in a mighty storm, a lusty young man called John Howland, coming upon some occasion above the gratings, was, with a seele [roll] of the ship, thrown into sea; but it pleased God that he caught hold of the topsail halyards which hung overboard and ran out at length. Yet he held his hold (though he was sundry fathoms under water) till he was hauled up by the same rope to the brim of the water, and then with a boat hook and other means got into the ship again and his life saved. And though he was something ill with it, yet he lived many years after and became a profitable member both in church and commonwealth. In all this voyage there died but one of the passengers, which was William Butten, a youth, servant to Samuel Fuller, when they drew near the coast.

But to omit other things (that I may be brief) after long beating at sea they fell with that land which is called Cape Cod;[4] the which being made and certainly known to be it, they were not a little joyful. After some deliberation had amongst themselves and with the master of the ship, they tacked about and resolved to stand for the southward (the wind and weather being fair) to find some place about Hudson's River[5] for their habitation. But after they had sailed that course about half the day, they fell amongst dangerous shoals and roaring breakers, and they were so far entangled therewith as they conceived themselves in great danger; and the wind shrinking upon them withal, they resolved to bear up again for the Cape and thought themselves happy to get out of those dangers before night overtook them, as by God's good Providence they did. And the next day[6] they got into the Cape Harbor,[7] where they rid in safety. . . .

Being thus arrived in a good harbor, and brought safe to land, they fell upon their knees and blessed the God of Heaven who had brought them over the vast and furious ocean, and delivered them from all the perils and miseries thereof, again to set their feet on the firm and stable earth, their proper element. . . .

But here I cannot but stay and make a pause, and stand half amazed at this poor people's present condition; and so I think will the reader, too, when he well considers the same. Being thus passed the vast ocean, and a sea of troubles before in their preparation (as may be remembered by that which went before), they had now no friends to welcome them nor inns to entertain or refresh their weather-beaten bodies; no houses or much less towns to repair to, to seek for succor [aid]. It is recorded in Scripture[8] as a mercy to the Apostle and his shipwrecked company, that the barbarians showed them no small kindness in refreshing them, but these savage barbarians, when they met with them (as after will appear) were readier to fill their sides full of arrows than otherwise. And for the season it was winter, and they that know the winters of that country know them to be sharp and violent, and subject to cruel and fierce storms, dangerous to travel to unknown places, much more to search an unknown coast. Besides, what could they see but a hideous and desolate wilderness, full of wild beasts and wild men—and what multitudes there might be of them they knew not. Neither could they, as it were, go up to the top of Pisgah[9] to view from this wilderness a more goodly country to feed their hopes; for which way soever they turned their eyes (save upward to the heavens) they could have little solace or content in respect of any outward objects. For summer being done, all things stand upon them with a weather-beaten face, and the whole country, full of woods and thickets, represented a wild and savage hue. If they looked behind them, there was the mighty ocean which they had passed and was now as a main bar and gulf to separate them from all the civil parts of the world. . . .

What could now sustain them but the Spirit of God and His grace? May not and ought not the children of these fathers rightly say: "Our fathers

---

3. **hull:** lay to and drift under short sail.
4. They sighted Cape Cod at daybreak on November 9, 1620.
5. They were trying for Manhattan Island. Henry Hudson had made his voyage in 1609 and had claimed the area for the Dutch, but the English did not recognize the Dutch claim.
6. November 11. The sea voyage from England had taken sixty-five days.
7. Cape Harbor is now Provincetown Harbor.

8. In the Acts of the Apostles (Chapter 28), St. Paul tells how the shipwrecked Christians were helped by the "barbarous people" of Malta.
9. Pisgah was the mountain from which Moses first viewed the Promised Land (Deuteronomy 34:1).

were Englishmen which came over this great ocean, and were ready to perish in this wilderness; but they cried unto the Lord, and He heard their voice and looked on their adversity,"[10] etc? "Let them therefore praise the Lord, because He is good: and His mercies endure forever." "Yea, let them which have been redeemed of the Lord, shew how He hath delivered them from the hand of the oppressor. When they wandered in the desert wilderness out of the way, and found no city to dwell in, both hungry and thirsty, their soul was overwhelmed in them. Let them confess before the Lord His lovingkindness and His wonderful works before the sons of men."[11]

Chapter 10

Showing How They Sought out a Place of Habitation; and What Befell Them Thereabout

[1620] Being thus arrived at Cape Cod the 11th of November, and necessity calling them to look out a place for habitation (as well as the master's and mariners' importunity); they having brought a large shallop[12] with them out of England, stowed in quarters in the ship, they now got her out and set their carpenters to work to trim her up; but being much bruised and shattered in the ship with foul weather, they saw she would be long in mending. Whereupon a few of them tendered themselves to go by land and discover those nearest places, whilst the shallop was in mending; and the rather because as they went into that harbor there seemed to be an opening some two or three leagues[13] off, which the master judged to be a river. It was conceived there might be some danger in the attempt, yet seeing them resolute, they were permitted to go, being sixteen of them well armed under the conduct of Captain Standish,[14] having such instructions given them as was thought meet.

They set forth the 15th of November; and when they had marched about the space of a mile by

the seaside, they espied five or six persons with a dog coming toward them who were savages; but they fled from them and ran up into the woods, and the English followed them, partly to see if they could speak with them and partly to discover if there might not be more of them lying in ambush. But the Indians, seeing themselves thus followed, they again forsook the woods and ran away on the sands as hard as they could, so as they could not come near them but followed them by the track of their feet sundry miles and saw that they had come the same way. So, night coming on, they made their rendezvous and set out their sentinels, and rested in quiet that night; and the next morning followed their track till they had headed a great creek and so left the sands, and turned another way into the woods. But they still followed them by guess, hoping to find their dwellings; but they soon lost both them and themselves, falling into such thickets as were ready to tear their clothes and armor in pieces; but were most distressed for want of drink. But at length they found water and refreshed themselves, being the first New England water they drunk of, and was now in great thirst as pleasant unto them as wine or beer had been in foretimes.

Afterward they directed their course to come to the other shore, for they knew it was a neck of land they were to cross over, and so at length got to the seaside and marched to this supposed river, and by the way found a pond of clear, fresh water, and shortly after a good quantity of clear ground where the Indians had formerly set corn, and some of their graves. And proceeding further they saw new stubble where corn had been set the same year, also they found where lately a house had been, where some planks and a great kettle were remaining, and heaps of sand newly paddled with their hands. Which, they digging up, found in them divers fair Indian baskets filled with corn, and some in ears, fair and good, of divers colors, which seemed to them a very goodly sight (having never seen any such before). This was near the place of that supposed river they came to seek, to which they went and found it to open itself into two arms with a high cliff of sand in the entrance but more like to be creeks of salt water than any fresh, for aught they saw; and that there was good harborage for their shallop, leaving it further to be discovered by their shallop, when she was ready. So, their time limited them being expired, they returned to the ship lest they should be in

---

10. A quotation from Deuteronomy 26:7.
11. The quotations are from Psalm 107.
12. **shallop:** a small, open boat. This one was fitted with oars and a sail.
13. **leagues:** one league is equivalent to about three miles.
14. Myles Standish (1584–1656) was a soldier who had been hired to handle the colonists' military affairs. Not a member of the Puritan congregation, he still became one of their staunchest supporters.

Landing of the Pilgrims at Plymouth by Michele Corne (1803). Oil.

fear of their safety; and took with them part of the corn and buried up the rest. . . .

After this, the shallop being got ready, they set out again for the better discovery of this place, and the master of the ship desired to go himself. So there went some thirty men but found it to be no harbor for ships but only for boats. There was also found two of their houses [the Indians'] covered with mats, and sundry of their implements in them, but the people were run away and could not be seen. Also there was found more of their corn and of their beans of various colors; the corn and beans they brought away, purposing to give them full satisfaction when they should meet with any of them, as about some six months afterward they did, to their good content.

And here is to be noted a special Providence of God, and a great mercy to this poor people, that here they got seed to plant them corn the next year, or else they might have starved, for they had

Pilgrim Society, Plymouth, Massachusetts.

ten of their principal men and some seamen, upon further discovery, intending to circulate that deep bay of Cape Cod. The weather was very cold and it froze so hard as the spray of the sea lighting on their coats; they were as if they had been glazed. Yet that night betimes they got down into the bottom of the bay, and as they drew near the shore they saw some ten or twelve Indians very busy about something. They landed about a league or two from them, and had much ado to put ashore anywhere—it lay so full of flats. Being landed, it grew late and they made themselves a barricado with logs and boughs as well as they could in the time, and set out their sentinel and betook them to rest, and saw the smoke of the fire the savages made that night. When morning was come they divided their company, some to coast along the shore in the boat, and the rest marched through the woods to see the land, if any fit place might be for their dwelling. They came also to the place where they saw the Indians the night before, and found they had been cutting up a great fish like a grampus, being some two inches thick of fat like a hog, some pieces whereof they had left by the way. And the shallop found two more of these fishes dead on the sands, a thing usual after storms in that place, by reason of the great flats of sand that lie off. . . .

From hence they departed and coasted all along but discerned no place likely for harbor; and therefore hasted to a place that their pilot (one Mr. Coppin, who had been in the country before) did assure them was a good harbor, which he had been in, and they might fetch it before night; of which they were glad, for it began to be foul weather.

After some hours' sailing, it began to snow and rain, and about the middle of the afternoon the wind increased and the sea became very rough, and they broke their rudder, and it was as much as two men could do to steer her with a couple of oars. But their pilot bade them be of good cheer, for he saw the harbor; but the storm increasing, and night drawing on, they bore what sail they could to get in while they could see. But herewith they broke their mast in three pieces and their sail fell overboard in a very grown sea, so as they had like to have been cast away. Yet by God's mercy they recovered themselves and, having the flood [the tide] with them, struck into the harbor. But when it came to, the pilot was deceived in the place, and said the Lord be merciful unto them, for his eyes never saw that place before; and he

none nor any likelihood to get any till the season had been past, as the sequel did manifest. Neither is it likely they had had this if the first voyage had not been made, for the ground was now all covered with snow and hard frozen; but the Lord is never wanting unto His in their greatest needs; let His holy name have all the praise.

The month of November being spent in these affairs, and much foul weather falling in, the 6th of December they sent out their shallop again with

and the master's mate would have run her ashore in a cove full of breakers before the wind. But a lusty seaman which steered bade those which rowed, if they were men, about with her or else they were all cast away; the which they did with speed. So he bid them be of good cheer and row lustily, for there was a fair sound before them, and he doubted not but they should find one place or other where they might ride in safety. And though it was very dark and rained sore, yet in the end they got under the lee of a small island and remained there all that night in safety. But they knew not this to be an island till morning, but were divided in their minds; some would keep the boat for fear they might be amongst the Indians; others were so wet and cold they could not endure, but got ashore, and with much ado got fire (all things being so wet); and the rest were glad to come to them, for after midnight the wind shifted to the northwest and it froze hard.

But though this had been a day and night of much trouble and danger unto them, yet God gave them a morning of comfort and refreshing (as usually He doth to His children), for the next day was a fair, sunshining day, and they found themselves to be on an island secure from the Indians, where they might dry their stuff, fix their pieces, and rest themselves; and gave God thanks for His mercies in their manifold deliverances. And this being the last day of the week, they prepared there to keep the Sabbath.

On Monday they sounded the harbor and found it fit for shipping, and marched into the land and found divers cornfields and little running brooks, a place (as they supposed) fit for situation. At least it was the best they could find, and the season and their present necessity made them glad to accept of it. So they returned to their ship again with this news to the rest of their people, which did much comfort their hearts.

On the 15th of December they weighed anchor to go to the place they had discovered, and came within two leagues of it, but were fain to bear up again; but the 16th day, the wind came fair, and they arrived safe in this harbor. And afterward took better view of the place, and resolved where to pitch their dwelling; and the 25th day began to erect the first house for common use to receive them and their goods.[15]

---

15. This text is the only account written by a participant of the famous landing at Plymouth Rock on December 11, 1620.

From

Chapter 11

The Starving Time

[1620–1621] But that which was most sad and lamentable was that in two or three months' time half of their company died, especially in January and February, being the depth of winter, and wanting houses and other comforts; being infected with the scurvy and other diseases which this long voyage and their inaccommodate condition had brought upon them. So as there died sometimes two or three of a day in the foresaid time, that of 100 and odd persons, scarce fifty remained. And of these, in the time of most distress, there was but six or seven sound persons who to their great commendations, be it spoken, spared no pains night nor day, but with abundance of toil and hazard of their own health, fetched them wood, made them fires, dressed them meat, made their beds, washed their loathsome clothes, clothed and unclothed them: in a word, did all the homely and necessary offices for them which dainty and queasy stomachs cannot endure to hear named; and all this willingly and cheerfully, without any grudging in the least, showing herein their true love unto their friends and brethren; a rare example and worthy to be remembered. Two of these seven were Mr. William Brewster, their reverend elder, and Myles Standish, their captain and military commander, to whom myself and many others were much beholden in our low and sick condition. And yet the Lord so upheld these persons as in this general calamity they were not at all infected either with sickness or lameness. And what I have said of these I may say of many others who died in this general visitation, and others yet living; that whilst they had health, yea, or any strength continuing, they were not wanting to any that had need of them. And I doubt not but their recompense is with the Lord.

But I may not here pass by another remarkable passage not to be forgotten. As this calamity fell among the passengers that were to be left here to plant, and were hasted ashore and made to drink water that the seamen might have the more beer, and one[16] in his sickness desiring but a small can of beer, it was answered that if he were their own father he should have none. The disease began to

---

16. This is Bradford himself.

fall amongst them [the seamen] also, so as almost half of their company died before they went away, and many of their officers and lustiest men, as the boatswain, gunner, three quartermasters, the cook, and others. At which the master was something strucken and sent to the sick ashore and told the governor he should send for beer for them that had need of it, though he drank water homeward bound.

But now amongst his [the ship master's] company there was far another kind of carriage in this misery than amongst the passengers. For they that before had been boon companions in drinking and jollity in the time of their health and welfare began now to desert one another in this calamity, saying they would not hazard their lives for them, they should be infected by coming to help them in their cabins; and so, after they came to lie by it, would do little or nothing for them but, "If they died, let them die." But such of the passengers as were yet aboard showed them what mercy they could, which made some of their hearts relent, as the boatswain (and some others), who was a proud young man and would often curse and scoff at the passengers. But when he grew weak, they had compassion on him and helped him; then he confessed he did not deserve it at their hands, he had abused them in word and deed. "Oh!" (saith he) "you, I now see, show your love like Christians indeed one to another, but we let one another lie and die like dogs." Another lay cursing his wife, saying if it had not been for her he had never come this unlucky voyage, and anon cursing his fellows, saying he had done this and that for some of them; he had spent so much and so much amongst them, and they were now weary of him and did not help him, having need. Another gave his companion all he had, if he died, to help him in his weakness; he went and got a little spice and made him a mess of meat once or twice. And because he died not so soon as he expected, he went among his fellows and swore the rogue would cozen [cheat] him, he would see him choked before he made him any more meat; and yet the poor fellow died before morning.

Indian Relations

All this while the Indians came skulking about them, and would sometimes show themselves aloof off, but when any approached near them, they would run away; and once they stole away their tools where they had been at work and were gone to dinner. But about the 16th of March, a certain Indian came boldly amongst them and spoke to them in broken English, which they could well understand but marveled at it. At length they understood, by discourse with him, that he was not of these parts but belonged to the eastern parts where some English ships came to fish, with whom he was acquainted and could name sundry of them by their names, amongst whom he had got his language. He became profitable to them in acquainting them with many things concerning the state of the country in the east parts where he lived, which was afterward profitable unto them; as also of the people here, of their names, number, and strength, of their situation and distance from this place, and who was chief amongst them. His name was Samoset.[17] He told them also of another Indian whose name was Squanto,[18] a native of this place, who had been in England and could speak better English than himself.

Being, after some time of entertainment and gifts, dismissed, a while after he came again, and five more with him, and they brought again all the tools that were stolen away before, and made way for the coming of their great Sachem, called Massasoit.[19] Who, about four or five days after, came with the chief of his friends and other attendance, with the aforesaid Squanto. With whom, after friendly entertainment and some gifts given him, they made a peace with him (which hath now continued this 24 years)[20] in these terms:

1. That neither he nor any of his should injure or do hurt to any of their people.

2. That if any of his did hurt to any of theirs, he should send the offender, that they might punish him.

3. That if anything were taken away from any of theirs, he should cause it to be restored; and they should do the like to his.

4. If any did unjustly war against him, they would aid him; if any did war against them, he should aid them.

5. He should send to his neighbors confederates

---

17. Samoset was an Algonquin from Maine.
18. Squanto was the sole survivor of the Pawtuckets.
19. Massasoit was the sachem (chief) of the Wampanoag and presided from a place called Sowans, the present-day site of Barrington, Rhode Island.
20. The treaty was kept faithfully until the reign of Massasoit's son Metacomet, known as King Philip by the colonists. See Mary Rowlandson's narrative on page 24.

The First Thanksgiving by Jennie Brownscomb (1914). Oil.   Pilgrim Society, Plymouth, Massachusetts.

to certify them of this, that they might not wrong them, but might be likewise comprised in the conditions of peace.

6. That when their men came to them, they should leave their bows and arrows behind them.

After these things he returned to his place, called Sowams, some 40 miles from this place, but Squanto continued with them and was their interpreter and was a special instrument sent of God for their good beyond their expectation. He directed them how to set their corn, where to take fish and to procure other commodities, and was also their pilot to bring them to unknown places for their profit, and never left them till he died. He was a native of this place, and scarce any left alive besides himself. He was carried away with divers others by one Hunt, a master of a ship, who thought to sell them for slaves in Spain. But he got away for England and was entertained by a merchant in London, and employed to Newfoundland and other parts, and lastly brought hither into these parts by one Mr. Dermer, a gentleman employed by Sir Ferdinando Gorges and others for discovery and other designs in these parts. . . .

First Thanksgiving

[1621] They began now to gather in the small harvest they had, and to fit up their houses and dwellings against winter, being all well recovered in health and strength and had all things in good plenty. For as some were thus employed in affairs abroad, others were exercised in fishing, about cod and bass and other fish, of which they took good store, of which every family had their portion. All the summer there was no want; and now began to come in store of fowl, as winter approached, of which this place did abound when they came first (but afterward decreased by degrees). And besides waterfowl there was great store of wild turkeys, of which they took many, besides venison, etc. Besides they had about a peck of meal a week to a person, or now since harvest, Indian corn to that proportion. Which made many afterward write so largely of their plenty here to their friends in England, which were not feigned but true reports.

Responding to the History

Analyzing the History

Identifying Facts

1. Historian Samuel Eliot Morison has said that "Bradford . . . had a constant sense of an unseen hand . . . that seemed to be guiding Puritan policy." What events on the voyage to the New World does Bradford credit to the direct intervention of God?
2. According to the end of Chapter 9, what hardships and dangers still face the settlers after the voyage is over? According to Bradford, what is the one thing that can sustain the group during these trials?
3. The famous entry in Chapter 10 reports in detail on the Pilgrims' first landing in the New World. What events during those first explorations does Bradford credit to God's Providence?
4. Bradford wrote his history of the "Old Comers" in part for the newcomers, the young people who, he hoped, would carry on the Pilgrims' ideals. What acts of charity and kindness during the "Starving Time" (Chapter 11) would remind later Puritans of their uniqueness and their obligations to their community?

Interpreting Meanings

5. Consider the treaty drawn up with Massasoit (page 19), and explain whether or not you feel its terms were equally favorable to both parties. What seems to be Bradford's attitude toward the Indians?
6. There is a certain timelessness in the Pilgrims' story. What practical and ethical problems common to many societies are reflected in their experience? In what ways might this wilderness experience be relevant to contemporary pilgrims or pioneers?
7. One event that Bradford does not describe is the death of his wife, who either fell or jumped overboard in Provincetown Harbor. How would his history have been different if he had included this tragedy? What reasons can you propose for his having omitted it?
8. Using what you have read, comment on the famous painting on page 20. Do you think it is realistic? Or does it idealize the First Thanksgiving?

Writing About the History

A Creative Response

1. **Using Another Point of View.** Retell the events of Chapter 10 from the point of view of one of the Native Americans who came upon the scouts. Narrate only what the observer would see happening and what you imagine he or she might be feeling.

A Critical Response

2. **Contrasting Two Historical Accounts.** Captain John Smith (1579–1631) had led the first permanent English settlement in the New World, at Jamestown, Virginia, in 1607. He hoped to establish another colony in New England, and in order to attract settlers, he wrote a pamphlet. Here is how Smith, somewhat like a contemporary travel agent, attempted to persuade people to join him in the New World:

> Here nature and liberty afford us that freely which in England we want, or it costs us dearly. What pleasure can be more than (being tired with any occasion ashore) in planting vines, fruits, or herbs, in contriving their own grounds, to the pleasure of their own minds, their fields, gardens, orchards, buildings, ships, and other works, etc., to re-create themselves before their own doors, in their own boats upon the sea, where man, woman, and child, with a small hook and line, by angling, may take divers sorts of excellent fish at their pleasures? And is it not pretty sport to pull up two pence, six pence, and twelve pence as fast as you can haul and veer a line? He is a very bad fisher [who] cannot kill in one day with his hook and line one, two, or three hundred cods, which dressed and dried, if they be sold there for ten shillings the hundred [pounds], though in England they will give more than twenty, may not both the servant, the master, and merchant be well content with this gain? If a man work but three days in seven, he may get more than he can spend, unless he will be excessive. . . .
>
> For hunting also, the woods, lakes, and rivers afford not only chase sufficient for any that delight in that kind of toil or pleasure, but such beasts to hunt that besides the delicacy of their bodies for food, their skins are so rich as may well recompense thy daily labor with a captain's pay.
>
> —from "A Description of New England," 1616, John Smith

Write a brief essay in which you contrast John Smith's promises with William Bradford's actual experiences in the New World. Begin by contrasting the **purposes** of the two writers and their intended **audiences.** Then mention at least three idealistic promises Smith makes and contrast these with Bradford's real experiences. You may also want to point out what Smith *omits* from his pamphlet. Finally, describe the different kinds of newcomers each writer was likely to attract, and explain the reasons for your answer.

Primary Sources
The First Thanksgiving

On December 11, 1621, colonist Edward Winslow sent a letter to a friend in England describing the first Thanksgiving in the Colonies. The letter was reprinted in a book called *A Relation or Journall of the Beginning and Proceedings of the English Plantation settled at Plimouth in New England* (1622). The preface is signed "G. Mourt." Edward Winslow's letter is reprinted as follows. The governor is William Bradford.

"Our harvest being gotten in, our governor sent four men on fowling, that so we might after a more special manner rejoice together, after we had gathered the fruit of our labors. They four in one day killed as much fowl as, with a little help besides, served the company almost a week. At which time, amongst other recreations, we exercised our arms, many of the Indians coming among us, and amongst the rest their greatest king, Massasoit, with some 90 men, whom for three days we entertained and feasted. And they went out and killed five deer which they brought to the plantation and bestowed on our governor and upon the captain and others."

—Edward Winslow

The actual day on which the celebration took place was never recorded.

Elements of Literature

THE PLAIN STYLE

At the beginning of his history, Bradford says he will try to unfold his story "in a plain style, with singular regard unto the simple truth in all things." He means that he will not imitate the ornate "high style" that was in fashion in England at the time—a style that used classical allusions, Latin quotations, and elaborate figures of speech. In a sense, Bradford's stylistic preference reflected the division between the Puritans and the Anglicans in matters of worship. A plain writing style was in keeping with the Puritans' preference for plainness in all other things, especially in church ritual.

One of the English writers who used a "high style" was John Donne, the poet and Anglican clergyman. This passage in the "high style" is from a sermon he delivered on Christmas Day in 1629:

First, for the incomprehensibleness of God, the understanding of man hath a limited, a determined latitude; it is an intelligence able to move that sphere which it is fixed to, but could not move a greater: I can comprehend *naturam naturatam,* created nature, but for that *natura naturans,* God himself, the understanding of man cannot comprehend. I can see the sun in a looking glass, but the nature and the whole working of the sun I cannot see in that glass. I can see God in the creature, but the nature, the essence, the secret purposes of God, I cannot see there. There is *defatigatio in intellectualibus,* says the saddest and soundest of the Hebrew Rabbins; the soul may be tired, as well as the body, and the understanding dazzled, as well as the eye.

—John Donne

The Puritans thought that a "plain style" was much more effective in revealing God's truth. The "plain style" imitated the style of the Geneva Bible, published in 1560 and used by the Puritans. (Other English Protestants of the time used the elegant King James translation, published in 1611.)

Bradford's history is plain, but this does not mean it is crude or lacking in art. Biblical quotations and allusions abound in Bradford's story; the Puritans' experiences are continuously related to the experiences of the early Israelites or early Christians.

Bradford imitates the Geneva Bible in another one of his favorite stylistic devices. When he wants to be emphatic, he uses curious combinations of words that mean the same or nearly the same thing: "Firm and stable earth" on page 14 is an example.

Bradford's style is difficult to understand today because his syntax and vocabulary are now archaic, or not in common use. Take the passage that opens Chapter 10 and recast it into plain modern prose. In doing this, have you lost the "Biblical" sound?

Mary Rowlandson (c. 1636–c. 1678)

From June 1675 to August 1676, the Wampanoag chief Metacomet, called King Philip by the colonists, carried out a series of bloody raids on Colonial settlements in what is now called King Philip's war. The Puritans thought of the war as a sign of God's punishment for the sins of the younger generation (young people had taken to dancing and wearing their hair long), but such a conflict was probably inevitable. It was the natural result of growing encroachments by the settlers on tribal land and of the conflict between the two cultures. Despite careful attempts by Colonial leaders to regulate the buying of territory, the New England tribes had been forced into ever more restricted areas. And although the natives had sold the land, they rejected the condition that they could no longer hunt on it. To them, "selling" meant selling the right to share the land with the buyers, not selling its exclusive ownership.

Matters came to a head when Metacomet's former assistant, who had given information to the whites, was killed by his own people. His killers were tried and hanged by the Puritans. This was too much for Metacomet to bear, and two weeks later the most severe war in the history of New England began. Its tragic result was the virtual extinction of tribal life in the region.

Among the war's victims was Mary Rowlandson. Mrs. Rowlandson was the wife of the Congregational minister of Lancaster, a frontier town of about fifty families that was located thirty miles west of Boston. On a February morning, she and her three children were carried away by a raiding party that wanted to trade hostages for money. After eleven weeks and five days of captivity, her ransom was paid. She was to survive for only two more years.

Her captors, it is important to remember, were only slightly better off than their prisoners. Virtually without food, they were chased from camp to camp by Colonial soldiers. Their captives, they thought, were the only currency with which to buy supplies and food. In a graphic passage, Rowlandson describes the lengths to which the Indians were driven by their hunger:

"They would pick up old bones," she wrote, "and cut them to pieces at the joints, and if they were full of worms and maggots, they would scald them over the fire to make the vermin come out, and then boil them, and drink up the liquor . . . They would eat horses' guts, and ears, and all sorts of wild birds which they could catch: also bear, venison, beaver, tortoise, frogs, squirrels, dogs, skunks, rattlesnakes; yea, the very bark of trees . . . I can but stand in admiration," she concluded, "to see the wonderful power of God, in providing for such a vast number of our enemies in the wilderness, where there was nothing to be seen, but from hand to mouth."

Rowlandson's moving tale of survival shows us the ordinary Puritan mind at work in extraordinary circumstances. Through apt quotations from the Bible, she places her experiences in the context of ancient Biblical captivities, such as the enslavement of Moses and the Israelites by the Egyptians. The Puritans regarded such Biblical captivity narratives as allegories representing the Christian's liberation from sin through the intervention of God's grace. Rowlandson viewed her own experiences as a repetition of the same pattern.

Her narrative, then, not only presents a terrifying and moving tale of frontier life but also provides insight into how the Puritans viewed their lives with a characteristic double vision. For Rowlandson, events had both a physical and a spiritual significance. She did not want merely to record her horrifying experience; she wished to demonstrate how it revealed God's purpose. The full title of her narrative illustrates this intention: *The Sovereignty and Goodness of God, Together with the Faithfulness of His Promises Displayed: Being a Narrative of the Captivity and Restoration of Mrs. Mary Rowlandson.*

Mary Rowlandson's *Narrative* was one of the most widely read prose works of the seventeenth century. It was especially popular in England, where people were eager for lurid tales of the native inhabitants of the New World. The popularity of Rowlandson's story even gave rise to a mass of imitations that were often purely fictional. These "captivity" stories might have been entertaining, but they had a tragic side effect: They contributed to the further deterioration of relations between Native Americans and colonists.

FROM A NARRATIVE OF HER CAPTIVITY

In the opening part of her narrative, Mary Rowlandson describes the attack on Lancaster and the assault on her own house, where twelve people were killed and twenty-five taken captive. The first episode here recounts how her captors took her and her wounded child to Princeton, Massachusetts. Watch for the ways Mary Rowlandson links her sufferings with the sufferings of people in the Bible. Look also for indications of how the writer feels about her captors.

The Move to Princeton, Massachusetts (February 11)

But now, the next morning, I must turn my back upon the town and travel with them [her captors] into the vast and desolate wilderness, I knew not whither. It is not my tongue, or pen, can express the sorrows of my heart and bitterness of my spirit that I had at this departure; but God was with me in a wonderful manner, carrying me along and bearing up my spirit, that it did not quite fail. One of the Indians carried my poor wounded babe upon a horse; it went moaning all along, "I shall die, I shall die." I went on foot after it, with sorrow that cannot be expressed. At length I took it off the horse and carried it in my arms till my strength failed, and I fell down with it. Then they set me upon a horse with my wounded child in my lap, and there being no furniture upon the horse's back, as we were going down a steep hill we both fell over the horse's head. . . . But the Lord renewed my strength still and carried me along, that I might see more of His power; yea, so much that I could never have thought of had I not experienced it.

After this it quickly began to snow, and when night came on, they stopped, and now down I must sit in the snow, by a little fire, and a few boughs behind me, with my sick child in my lap; and calling much for water, being now (through the wound) fallen into a violent fever. My own wound [was] also growing so stiff that I could scarce sit down or rise up; yet so it must be, that I must sit all this cold winter night upon the cold snowy ground, with my sick child in my arms, looking that every hour would be the last of its life; and having no Christian friend near me, either to comfort or help me. Oh, I may see the wonderful power of God, that my spirit did not utterly sink under my affliction: still the Lord upheld me with His gracious and merciful spirit, and we were both alive to see the light of the next morning.

The Move to an Indian Village on the Ware River, Near Braintree (February 12–27)

The morning being come, they prepared to go on their way. One of the Indians got up upon a horse, and they set me up behind him, with my poor sick babe in my lap. A very wearisome and tedious day I had of it, what with my own wound and my child's being so exceeding sick and in a lamentable condition with her wound. It may be easily judged what a poor feeble condition we were in, there being not the least crumb of refreshing that came within either of our mouths from Wednesday night to Saturday night, except only a little cold water. This day in the afternoon, about an hour by sun, we came to the place where they intended, viz., an Indian town, called Wenimesset, northward of Quabaug. . . . I sat much alone with a poor wounded child in my lap, which moaned night and day, having nothing to revive the body or cheer the spirits of her, but instead of that, sometimes one Indian would come and tell me one hour that "your master will knock your child in the head," and then a second, and then a third, "Your master will quickly knock your child in the head."

Portrait of Ninigret II, Chief of the Niantic Indians.
Anonymous (c.1681). Oil.

Mary Rowlandson   25

Algonquin Indian Encampment by Thomas Davies (1788). Watercolor. The National Gallery of Canada, Ottawa.

This was the comfort I had from them, miserable comforters are ye all, as he[1] said. Thus nine days I sat upon my knees, with my babe in my lap, till my flesh was raw again; my child being even ready to depart this sorrowful world, they bade me carry it out to another wigwam (I suppose because they would not be troubled with such spectacles), whither I went with a very heavy heart, and down I sat with the picture of death in my lap. About two hours in the night, my sweet babe like a lamb departed this life on February 18, 1675, it being about six years and five months old. It was nine days from the first wounding, in this miserable condition, without any refreshing of one nature or other, except a little cold water. I cannot but take notice how at another time I could not bear to be in the room where any dead person was, but now the case is changed; I must and could lie down by my dead babe, side by side all the night after. I have thought since of the wonderful goodness of God to me in preserving me in the use of my reason and senses in that distressed time, that I did not use wicked and violent means to end my own miserable life. In the morning, when they understood that my child was dead, they sent for me home to my master's wigwam (by my master in this writing must be understood Quanopin, who was a Sagamore,[2] and married King Philip's wife's sister; not that he first took me, but I was sold to him by another Narragansett Indian, who took me when first I came out of the garrison). I went to take up my dead child in my arms to carry it with me, but they bid me let it alone; there was no resisting, but go I must and

---

1. **he:** the Biblical allusion is to Job 16:2. In the passage cited, Job addresses those who try to console him in his afflictions. God had severely tested Job's faith: He lost his children and his money, and broke out in boils all over his body.

2. **Sagamore:** a subordinate chief in the Algonquin hierarchy.

leave it. When I had been at my master's wigwam, I took the first opportunity I could get to go look after my dead child. When I came. I asked them what they had done with it; then they told me it was upon the hill. Then they went and showed me where it was, where I saw the ground was newly digged, and there they told me they had buried it. There I left that child in the wilderness, and must commit it, and myself also in this wilderness condition, to Him who is above all. God having taken away this dear child, I went to see my daughter Mary, who was at this same Indian town, at a wigwam not very far off, though we had little liberty or opportunity to see one another. She was about ten years old, and taken from the door at first by a Praying Ind. and afterward sold for a gun. When I came in sight, she would fall aweeping; at which they were provoked, and would not let me come near her, but bade me be gone; which was a heart-cutting word to me. I had one child dead, another in the wilderness, I knew not where, the third they would not let me come near to: "Me (as he said) have ye bereaved of my Children, Joseph is not, and Simeon is not, and ye will take Benjamin also, all these things are against me."[3] I could not sit still in this condition, but kept walking from one place to another. And as I was going along, my heart was even overwhelmed with the thoughts of my condition, and that I should have children, and a nation which I knew not ruled over them. Whereupon I earnestly entreated the Lord, that He would consider my low estate and show me a token for good and, if it were His blessed will, some sign and hope of some relief. And indeed quickly the Lord answered, in some measure, my poor prayers; for as I was going up and down mourning and lamenting my condition, my son came to me and asked me how I did. I had not seen him before, since the destruction of the town, and I knew not where he was till I was informed by himself that he was among a smaller parcel of Indians, whose place was about six miles off. With tears in his eyes, he asked me whether his sister Sarah was dead; and told me he had seen his sister Mary; and prayed me that I would not be troubled in reference to himself. . . . I cannot

but take notice of the wonderful mercy of God to me in those afflictions, in sending me a Bible. One of the Indians that came from [the] Medfield fight had brought some plunder, came to me and asked me if I would have a Bible, he had got one in his basket. I was glad of it and asked him whether he thought the Indians would let me read. He answered, yes. So I took the Bible, and in that melancholy time, it came into my mind to read first the 28th chapter of Deuteronomy,[4] which I did, and when I had read it, my dark heart wrought on this manner: that there was no mercy for me, that the blessings were gone, and the curses come in their room, and that I had lost my opportunity. But the Lord helped me still to go on reading till I came to Chapter 30, the seven first verses, where I found there was mercy promised again, if we would return to Him by repentance; and though we were scattered from one end of the earth to the other, yet the Lord would gather us together and turn all those curses upon our enemies. I do not desire to live to forget this Scripture, and what comfort it was to me. . . .

Crossing the Bacquaug (now Miller's) River, in Orange, Massachusetts (March 3–5)

The occasion (as I thought) of their moving at this time was the English Army,[5] it being near and following them. For they [the Indians] went as if they had gone for their lives, for some considerable way, and then they made a stop, and chose some of their stoutest men, and sent them back to hold the English Army in play while the rest escaped. And then, like Jehu,[6] they marched on furiously, with their old and with their young: some carried their old decrepit mothers, some carried one, and some another. Four of them carried a great Indian upon a bier; but going through a thick wood with him, they were hindered and could make no haste, whereupon they took him upon their backs and carried him, one at a time,

---

3. Rowlandson quotes Jacob's lament in Genesis 42:36. All of Jacob's sons had left the country, and he had only the youngest, Benjamin, at home.

4. In Deuteronomy 28, Moses warns that God will bless those who obey Him and curse those who do not.
5. **the English Army:** the Massachusetts and Connecticut forces, led by Thomas Savage.
6. **Jehu:** the Israelite king who led his armies against King Ahab and slew Ahab and all his men (2 Kings 9–10).

till they came to Bacquaug River. Upon a Friday, a little after noon, we came to this river. When all the company was come up and were gathered together, I thought to count the number of them, but they were so many, and being somewhat in motion, it was beyond my skill. In this travel, because of my wound, I was somewhat favored in my load; I carried only my knitting work and two quarts of parched meal. Being very faint, I asked my mistress to give me one spoonful of the meal, but she would not give me a taste. They quickly fell to cutting dry trees, to make rafts to carry them over the river; and soon my turn came to go over. By the advantage of some brush which they had laid upon the raft to sit upon, I did not wet my foot (which many of themselves at the other end were mid-leg deep), which cannot but be acknowledged as a favor of God to my weakened body, it being a very cold time. I was not before acquainted with such kind of doings or dangers. "When thou passeth through the waters I will be with thee, and through the rivers they shall not overflow thee" (Isaiah 43.2). A certain number of us got over the river that night, but it was the night after the sabbath before all the company was got over. On the Saturday they boiled an old horse's leg which they had got, and so we drank of the broth as soon as they thought it was ready, and when it was almost all gone, they filled it up again.

The first week of my being among them I hardly ate anything; the second week I found my stomach grow very faint for want of something; and yet it was very hard to get down their filthy trash; but the third week, though I could think how formerly my stomach would turn against this or that, and I could starve and die before I could eat such things, yet they were sweet and savory to my taste. . . .

The Move to Coasset, Vermont

. . . We traveled on till night; and in the morning, we must go over the river to Philip's crew. When I was in the canoe, I could not but be amazed at the numerous crew of pagans that were on the bank on the other side. When I came ashore, they gathered all about me, I sitting alone in the midst. I observed they asked one another questions, and laughed, and rejoiced over their gains and victories. Then my heart began to fail; and I fell aweeping, which was the first time to my remembrance that I wept before them. Although I had met with so much affliction, and my heart was many times ready to break, yet could I not shed one tear in their sight; but rather had been all this while in a maze and like one astonished. But now I may say as Psalm 137.1, "By the Rivers of Babylon, there we sate down: yea, we wept when we remembered Zion." There one of them asked me why I wept. I could hardly tell what to say; yet I answered, they would kill me. "No," said he, "none will hurt you." Then came one of them and gave me two spoonfuls of meal to comfort me, and another gave me half a pint of peas; which was more worth than many bushels at another time. Then I went to see King Philip. He bade me come in and sit down, and asked me whether I would smoke it (a usual compliment nowadays among saints and sinners), but this no way suited me. For though I had formerly used tobacco, yet I had left it ever since I was first taken. It seems to be a bait the devil lays to make men lose their precious time. I remember with shame how formerly, when I had taken two or three pipes, I was presently ready for another, such a bewitching thing it is. But I thank God, He has now given me power over it; surely there are many who may be better employed than to lie sucking a stinking tobacco pipe.

Now the Indians gather their forces to go against Northhampton. Over night one went about yelling and hooting to give notice of the design. Whereupon they fell to boiling of groundnuts and parching of corn (as many as had it) for their provision; and in the morning away they went. During my abode in this place, Philip spoke to me to make a shirt for his boy, which I did, for which he gave me a shilling. I offered the money to my master, but he bade me keep it; and with it I bought a piece of horseflesh. Afterward he asked me to make a cap for his boy, for which he invited me to dinner. I went, and he gave me a pancake, about as big as two fingers. It was made of parched wheat, beaten, and fried in bear's grease, but I thought I never tasted pleasanter meat in my life. There was a squaw who spake to me to make a shirt for her *sannup* [husband], for which she gave me a piece of bear. Another asked me to knit a pair of stockings, for which she gave me a quart of peas. I boiled my peas and bear together, and invited my master and mistress to dinner; but the proud gossip [old woman], because I served them both in one dish, would eat nothing, except one bit that he gave her upon the point of his knife. . . .

The Move to the Ashuelot Valley, New Hampshire

But instead of going either to Albany or homeward, we must go five miles up the river and then go over it. Here we abode [stayed] awhile. Here lived a sorry Indian, who spoke to me to make him a shirt. When I had done it, he would pay me nothing. But he living by the riverside, where I often went to fetch water, I would often be putting of him in mind and calling for my pay. At last he told me if I would make another shirt, for a papoose not yet born, he would give me a knife, which he did when I had done it. I carried the knife in, and my master asked me to give it him, and I was not a little glad that I had anything that they would accept of and be pleased with. When we were at this place, my master's maid came home; she had been gone three weeks into the Narragansett country to fetch corn, where they had stored up some in the ground. She brought home about a peck and a half of corn. This was about the time that their great captain, Naananto, was killed in the Narragansett country. My son being now about a mile from me, I asked liberty to go and see him; they bade me go, and away I went but quickly lost myself, traveling over hills and through swamps, and could not find the way to him. And I cannot but admire at the wonderful power and goodness of God to me in that, though I was gone from home, and met with all sorts of Indians, and those I had no knowledge of, and there being no Christian soul near me, yet not one of them offered the least imaginable miscarriage to me. I turned homeward again and met with my master. He showed me the way to my son. . . .

But I was fain to go and look after something to satisfy my hunger, and going among the wigwams, I went into one and there found a squaw who showed herself very kind to me and gave me a piece of bear. I put it into my pocket and came home, but could not find an opportunity to broil it, for fear they would get it from me, and there it lay all that day and night in my stinking pocket. In the morning I went to the same squaw, who had a kettle of groundnuts boiling. I asked her to let me boil my piece of bear in her kettle, which she did, and gave me some groundnuts to eat with it; and I cannot but think how pleasant it was to me. I have sometimes seen bear baked very handsomely among the English, and some like it, but the thought that it was bear made me tremble. But now that was savory to me that one would think was enough to turn the stomach of a brute creature.

One bitter cold day I could find no room to sit down before the fire. I went out and could not tell what to do, but I went in to another wigwam, where they were also sitting round the fire, but the squaw laid a skin for me, and bid me sit down, and gave me some groundnuts, and bade me come again; and told me they would buy me, if they were able, and yet these were strangers to me that I never saw before. . . .

A
NARRATIVE
OF THE
CAPTIVITY, SUFFERINGS AND REMOVES
OF
Mrs. *Mary Rowlandson,*

Who was taken Prisoner by the INDIANS with several others, and treated in the most barbarous and cruel Manner by those vile Savages : With many other remarkable Events during her TRAVELS.

Written by her own Hand, for her private Use, and now made public at the earnest Desire of some Friends, and for the Benefit of the afflicted.

BOSTON
Printed and Sold at JOHN BOYLE's Printing-Office, next Door to the *Three Doves* in Marlborough-Street. 1773.

Responding to the Journal

Analyzing the Journal

Identifying Facts

1. In the first extract, what does Rowlandson tell us about how she was treated? What details in the narrative reveal how her religious faith helped her survive?
2. Find the details in Rowlandson's later diary entries that reveal that her captors themselves are desperate to find food.
3. What jobs does Rowlandson do to earn her food? How does her attitude toward food change while she is a captive?
4. Identify at least three occasions during her captivity in which Rowlandson is able to see Divine Providence at work.

Interpreting Meanings

5. Despite her efforts to be accurate, Rowlandson's journal is full of **subjective reporting**. Select any extract from the journal and find the words that reveal her **attitude** toward her captors—words that a detached historian would not use.
6. What instances of kindness does Rowlandson mention in her later entries? Does she reveal any conflicting attitudes toward her captors? Do you think her attitude changes? Explain.
7. The Puritans' habit of seeing specific allegorical meaning in their experiences helped them find significance in even very minor events. In an **allegory**, events, characters, and setting possess both a literal and a symbolic meaning. Describe at least two events of Rowlandson's captivity that she sees as allegories of Biblical stories. Identify the specific ways in which each of these Biblical stories resembles Rowlandson's.
8. What personal characteristics do you think helped Rowlandson survive her experience? Do you think personal courage or religious faith was more significant? Explain.
9. This captivity account was enormously popular in England. What reasons can you propose for its popularity? What aspects of Rowlandson's journal would promote stereotyped (and hostile) views toward Native Americans?
10. Are "captivity stories" still popular today? In what ways are contemporary captivity stories different from Rowlandson's? In what ways are they similar to her account?

Writing About the Journal

A Creative Response

1. **Using Another Point of View.** Write a journal entry in which you explain the situation of the Wampanoag people who captured Rowlandson. Try to account for the causes of the attack on the settlement and for the natives' desperate conditions. Use history texts or encyclopedias for your sources. You will find information under "King Philip's War" and "Metacomet." Write your entry from the point of view of a member of the Wampanoag tribe.

A Critical Response

2. **Explaining an Allusion.** On page 28, Mary Rowlandson alludes to Psalm 137, which is a well-known "captivity" psalm. It was composed when the Israelites were held captive in Babylon by King Nebuchadnezzar. Here is the whole psalm:

> By the rivers of Babylon, there we sat down; yea, we wept, when we remembered Zion.
> We hanged our harps upon the willows in the midst thereof.
> For there they that carried us away captive required of us a song; and they that wasted us required of us mirth, saying, Sing us one of the songs of Zion.
> How shall we sing the Lord's song in a strange land?
> If I forget thee, O Jerusalem, let my right hand forget her cunning.
> If I do not remember thee, let my tongue cleave to the roof of my mouth; if I prefer not Jerusalem above my chief joy.
> Remember, O Lord, the children of Edom in the day of Jerusalem; who said, Raze it, raze it, even to the foundation thereof.
> O daughter of Babylon, who art to be destroyed; happy shall he be, that rewardeth thee as thou hast served us.
> Happy shall he be, that taketh and dasheth thy little ones against the stones.
>
> —Psalm 137

In a brief essay, explain why Rowlandson thought of this psalm at a certain point in her sufferings. What parallel would she see between her experience and that of the psalmist? In her mind, what would "Babylon" be?

Sarah Kemble Knight (1666–1727)

Sarah Kemble Knight's husband, a sea captain and the London representative for an American company, was frequently abroad. In his absence, the capable and energetic Mrs. Knight ran a boardinghouse in Boston. She also taught school (Benjamin Franklin is reputed to have been one of her pupils), gave handwriting lessons, and assisted people with legal matters. It was in this last capacity that she journeyed from Boston to New York in the fall of 1704, to settle a family estate.

In Colonial America, it was almost unheard of for a woman to travel such a long distance with only guides as company. Overland travel was unsafe and far from comfortable, as Knight's account makes clear. A trip that today might be made by plane in an hour, or by train in four, took Knight about two weeks on horseback. But those two weeks were hardly wasted time. Knight's shorthand diary of the journey, kept for her own pleasure and not published until the nineteenth century, gives a lively and accurate portrait of life "on the road" in early eighteenth-century America. It also offers a nice secular contrast to the religious tenor of much Colonial writing. At the same time, it puts us in the company of a most interesting traveling companion. Knight's shrewd observations, her personal strength, and her no-nonsense attitude are qualities especially appealing to modern readers. Like many travelers today, she complains about the food: A Frenchman's fricassee was "so contrary" to her notion of cookery that she went to bed supperless. The beds were bad: "my poor bones complained bitterly." And the prices were too high, "as dear as if we had had far better fare." The feisty Sarah Knight has more in common with Ben Franklin than with many early Puritans. Her point of view is practical rather than theological, and she is more apt to allude to classical literature than to the Bible. To this extent, her diary suggests how Puritan culture was changing. Knight looks forward to the country's future rather than backward to its origins.

A few years after Knight's journey, her husband apparently died: After 1706, there is no further reference to him in her diaries. In 1714, she moved to New London, Connecticut, with her married daughter. There she ran a shop and an inn and made a number of investments in property that—as we might expect—were extremely profitable.

Ferry Scene on the Susquehanna at Wright's Ferry, near Havre de Grace by Petrus Svinin (1811). Watercolor.

The Metropolitan Museum of Art, New York. Rogers Fund, 1942.

FROM THE JOURNAL OF MADAM KNIGHT
A JOURNEY FROM BOSTON TO NEW YORK

As you read Knight's journal, try to form a precise idea of the writer's *tone*, or attitude toward her material. How does this tone contrast with what you might have expected from a Puritan writer? What does the tone reveal about the writer's personality?

Tuesday, October 3, 1704

About eight in the morning, I with the post proceeded forward without observing anything remarkable; and about two, afternoon, arrived at the post's second stage, where the western post met him and exchanged letters.[1] Here, having called for something to eat, the woman brought in a twisted thing like a cable, but something [somewhat] whiter; and laying it on the board, tugged for life to bring it into a capacity to spread; which having with great pains accomplished, she served in a dish of pork and cabbage, I suppose the remains of dinner. The sauce was of a deep purple, which I thought was boiled in her dye kettle; the bread was Indian, and everything on the table service agreeable to these. I, being hungry, got a little down; but my stomach was soon cloyed [filled], and what cabbage I swallowed served me for a cud the whole day after.

Having here discharged the ordinary[2] for self and guide (as I understood was the custom), about three, afternoon, went on with my [second] guide, who rode very hard; and having crossed Providence ferry, we came to a river which they generally ride through. But I dared not venture; so the post got a lad and canoe to carry me to t'other side, and he rode through and led my horse. The canoe was very small and shallow, so that when we were in, she seemed ready to take in water, which greatly terrified me and caused me to be very circumspect, sitting with my hands fast on each side, my eyes steady, not daring so much as to lodge my tongue a hairbreadth more on one side of my mouth than t'other nor so much as think on Lot's wife,[3] for a wry thought would have overset our wherry [small boat]; but was soon put out of this pain by feeling the canoe on shore, which I as soon almost saluted with my feet; and rewarding my sculler, again mounted and made the best of our way forward. The road here was very even and the day pleasant, it being now near sunset. But the post told me we had near fourteen miles to ride to the next stage (where we were to lodge). I asked him of the rest of the road, foreseeing we must travail in the night. He told me that there was a bad river we were to ride through, which was so very fierce a horse could sometimes hardly stem it; but it was but narrow, and we should soon be over. I cannot express the concern of mind this relation set me in: no thoughts but those of the dangerous river could entertain my imagination, and they were as formidable as various, still tormenting me with blackest ideas of my approaching fate—sometimes seeing myself

---

1. Knight is traveling on horseback in the company of mail carriers. They have reached a stop where two carriers exchange pouches of mail.
2. **discharged the ordinary:** paid for the meal. "Ordinary" referred both to a meal bought in a public house (as it does here) and to a public house itself (as it does later in Mrs. Knight's account).

3. **Lot's wife:** Lot's wife was turned into a pillar of salt when she turned to look back at Sodom, the city she and her family were fleeing (Genesis 19:28).

American Stage Wagon (1798). Colored engraving.

drowning, otherwhiles drowned, and at the best, like a holy sister just come out of a spiritual bath in dripping garments.

Now was the glorious luminary with his swift coursers arrived at his stage,[4] leaving poor me with the rest of this part of the lower world in darkness, with which we were soon surrounded. The only glimmering we now had was from the spangled skies, whose imperfect reflections rendered every object formidable. Each lifeless trunk, with its shattered limbs, appeared an armed enemy; and every little stump like a ravenous de-

vourer. Nor could I so much as discern my guide, when at any distance, which added to the terror.

Thus, absolutely lost in thought, and dying with the very thoughts of drowning, I come up with the post, who I did not see 'til even with his horse; he told me he stopped for me, and we rode on very deliberately a few paces, when we entered a thicket of trees and shrubs, and I perceived by the horse's going we were on the descent of a hill, which, as we come nearer the bottom, 'twas totally dark with the trees that surrounded it. But I knew by the going of the horse we had entered the water, which my guide told me was the hazardous river he had told me of; and he, riding up close to my side, bid me not fear—we should be over immediately. I now rallied all the courage I was mistress of, knowing that I must either ven-

4. That is, the sun had set. The reference is to Apollo, the sun god in Greek mythology. The Greeks believed that he pulled the sun as he rode across the sky in a chariot drawn by "courses," or horses.

ture my fate of drowning or be left like the children in the wood.[5] So, as the post bid me, I gave reins to my nag; and sitting as steady as just before in the canoe, in a few minutes got safe to the other side, which he told me was the Narragansett country. . . .

Being come to Mr. Havens',[6] I was very civilly received, and courteously entertained, in a clean comfortable house; and the good woman was very active in helping off my riding clothes, and then asked what I would eat. I told her I had some chocolate, if she would prepare it; which with the help of some milk, and a little clean brass kettle, she soon effected to my satisfaction. I then betook me to my apartment, which was a little room parted from the kitchen by a single board partition; where, after I had noted the occurrences of the past day, I went to bed, which, though pretty hard, [was] yet neat and handsome. But I could get no sleep, because of the clamor of some of the town topers in next room, who were entered into a strong debate concerning the signification of the name of their country (*viz.*), *Narragansett*. One said it was named so by the Indians, because there grew a brier there of a prodigious height and bigness, the like hardly ever known, called by the Indians narragansett; and quotes an Indian of so barbarous a name for his author that I could not write it. His antagonist replied no—it was from a spring it had its name, which he well knew where it was, which was extreme cold in summer, and as hot as could be imagined in the winter, which was much resorted to by the natives, and by them called Narragansett (hot and cold), and that was the original of their place's name—with a thousand impertinences not worth notice, which he uttered with such a roaring voice and thundering blows with the fist of wickedness on the table that it pierced my very head. I heartily fretted, and wished 'um tongue-tied; but with as little success as a friend of mine once, who was (as she said) kept a whole night awake, on a journey, by a country left, and a sergeant insigne,[7] and a deacon, contriving how to bring a triangle into a square. They kept calling for t'other gill,[8] which

5. The phrase "children in the wood," or "babes in the woods," refers to a ballad in which two children are taken out to be murdered and instead are left in the woods, where they die during the night.
6. **Mr. Havens':** the public house where they are to stay.
7. **left . . . insigne:** a lieutenant and an ensign, low-level military officers.
8. **gill:** measure of wine or liquor. A gill is four ounces.

while they were swallowing, was some intermission; but presently, like oil to fire, increased the flame. I set my candle on a chest by the bedside, and setting up, fell to my old way of composing my resentments, in the following manner:

I ask thy aid, O potent rum!
To charm these wrangling topers dumb.
Thou hast their giddy brains possessed—
The man confounded with the beast—
And I, poor I, can get no rest.
Intoxicate them with thy fumes:
O still their tongues 'til morning comes!

And I know not but my wishes took effect; for the dispute soon ended with t'other dram. And so good night!

Friday, October 6

I got up very early, in order to hire somebody to go with me to New Haven, being in great perplexity at the thoughts of proceeding alone; which my most hospitable entertainer observing, himself went, and soon returned with a young gentleman of the town, who he could confide in to go with me; and about eight this morning, with Mr. Joshua Wheeler my new guide, taking leave of this worthy gentleman, we advanced on toward Seabrook. The roads all along this way are very bad, encumbered with rocks and mountainous passages, which were very disagreeable to my tired carcass; but we went on with a moderate pace which made the journey more pleasant. But after about eight miles riding, in going over a bridge under which the river run very swift, my horse stumbled and very narrowly escaped falling over into the water; which extremely frightened me. But through God's goodness I met with no harm, and mounting again, in about half a mile's riding, come to an ordinary, were well entertained by a woman of about seventy and vantage [more], but of as sound intellectuals as one of seventeen. She entertained Mr. Wheeler with some passages of a wedding awhile ago at a place hard by, the brides-groom being about her age or something above, saying his children was dreadfully against their father's marrying, which she condemned them extremely for.

From hence we went pretty briskly forward and arrived at Saybrook ferry about two of the clock afternoon; and crossing it, we called at an inn to bait[9] (foreseeing we should not have such another opportunity 'til we come to Killingsworth). Landlady come in, with her hair about her ears and hands at full pay [busily] scratching. She told us

---

9. **bait:** stop for food and rest.

she had some mutton which she would broil, which I was glad to hear; but I suppose [she] forgot to wash her scratches; in a little time she brought it in; but it being pickled, and my guide said it smelled strong of head sauce [cheese sauce], we left it, and paid sixpence a piece for our dinners, which was only smell. . . .

Responding to the Journal

Analyzing the Journal

Identifying Facts

1. Name at least five facts that you learned from Knight's diary about daily life in early eighteenth-century America—facts about food, inns, and travel.
2. Identify the "twisted thing like a cable" that is spread on the table before lunch (page 32).
3. Find at least three details in the journal that indicate that Knight's grammar and syntax were different from today's standard English.

Interpreting Meanings

4. Find at least three details in the entry for October 3 that show Knight's talent for wry humor and comic comparisons.
5. Explain the comparison implied in the **metaphor** describing the sunset on October 3. Is this stylistic device different from what you might have found in William Bradford's or Mary Rowlandson's writings? Explain.
6. How does Knight's journal differ in **tone** from the writings of William Bradford and Mary Rowlandson?
7. What did you like or dislike about Sarah Knight's journal? How does it compare with travel literature written today?

Tavern sign from New London, Connecticut (c. 1750).

Morgan B. Brainard Collection, Connecticut Historical Society.

Writing About the Journal

A Creative Response

1. **Writing a Journal Entry.** Write a journal entry in which you narrate a trip you have taken recently. To dramatize the differences—and the similarities—between travel today and travel in the early eighteenth century, consider these topics: method of travel; length of trip; discomforts or dangers; food; motel or hotel accommodations. Before you write, decide what **tone** you want to take toward the trip: Humorous? Self-mocking? Satirical? Serious?

A Critical Response

2. **Analyzing Character.** You have read selections by two remarkable women who lived in Colonial America. The experiences they describe are vastly different. But can you detect any similarities in their characters or personalities? Write an essay in which you discuss the characters of Mary Rowlandson and Sarah Kemble Knight. In your essay, consider these points: their response to danger; their ability to surmount difficulties, even terrible sufferings; their attitude toward food; what they reveal about their religious convictions. Quote from both journals to support what you say.

Jonathan Edwards (1703–1758)

Jonathan Edwards is known today principally as the author of the great sermon, "Sinners in the Hands of an Angry God." Despite his fire-and-brimstone imagery, Edwards was not merely a stern, zealous preacher. He was a brilliant, thoughtful, and complicated man whose accomplishments and failures deserve our interest and study. Born eighty years after the Puritans landed in New England and only three years before the birth of Benjamin Franklin, Edwards stood between Puritan America and modern America. Tragically, he fit into neither world.

Edwards's grandfather, Solomon Stoddard, was pastor of the Congregational Church in Northampton, Massachusetts. Stoddard was so powerful a figure in religious affairs that he was known as the "Pope of the Connecticut Valley." His grandson's abilities were recognized early; even in his teens Jonathan was being groomed to succeed his grandfather. The boy entered Yale in 1716, when he was only thirteen. A few years after his graduation, he was made senior tutor of the college—a significant achievement for one so young. In 1726, Jonathan became his grandfather's co-pastor. When Stoddard died three years later, his grandson succeeded him.

Edwards was a strong-willed and charismatic pastor. His formidable presence and brilliant sermons helped to bring about the religious revival known as the "Great Awakening." This revival began in Northampton in the 1730's and during the next fifteen years spread throughout the Eastern Seaboard. The Great Awakening was marked by waves of conversions that spread from congregation to congregation—conversions so intensely emotional as to amount at times to mass hysteria.

The Great Awakening began at a time when enthusiasm for the old Puritan religion was declining. To offset the losses in their congregations, churches had been accepting increasing numbers of "unregenerate" Christians. These were people who accepted church doctrine and lived upright lives but who had not confessed they had been "born again" in God's grace. Thus they were not considered to be saved. In

Jonathan Edwards by Charles Wilson Peale. Oil.

their sermons, Edwards and other pastors strove to make these "sinners" understand the precariousness of their situation by helping them actually to *feel* the horror of their sinful state.

"Sinners in the Hands of an Angry God" is the greatest and best-known example of these sermons. Edwards's methods in the sermon were influenced by the work of the English philosopher John Locke (1632–1704). Locke believed that everything we know comes from experience, and he emphasized that understanding and feeling were two distinct kinds of knowledge. (To Edwards, the difference between these two kinds of knowledge was like the difference between reading the word *fire* and actually being burned.) Edwards preached his famous sermon in Enfield, Massachusetts, in July of 1741. Although he read it in his usual straightforward, unemotional manner, it had such a powerful effect on the congregation that the minister had to pause several times to ask for quiet.

Intellectually, Edwards straddled two ages: the modern, secular world exemplified by such men as Benjamin Franklin, and the religious world of his zealous Puritan ancestors. Edwards could draw on the ideas of philosophers such as John Locke, but he used those ideas to achieve a vision compatible with that of older Puritans such as William Bradford. Science, reason, and observation of the physical world only confirmed Edwards's vision of a universe filled with the presence of God. As he explained in his autobiography (see page 41), his sense of God was formed not only by his reading of the Bible but also by his close examination of nature. "God's excellency," he wrote, "seemed to appear in everything: in the sun, moon, and stars; in the clouds and blue sky; in the grass, flowers, and trees; in the water, and all nature."

Edwards became known for his extremism as a pastor. In his sermons, he didn't hesitate to accuse prominent church members, by name, of relapsing into sin. He was also unbending in his refusal to accept the "unregenerate" into his church. Such attitudes eventually lost him the support of his congregation. In 1750, he was voted out of his prestigious position in Northampton and sent to the then remote and raw Mohican Indian community of Stockbridge, Massachusetts. After eight years of missionary work in this lonely exile, Edwards was "rescued" and named president of the College of New Jersey (which later became Princeton University). Three months after assuming his position, he died of a smallpox inoculation—a modern medical procedure that had been promoted by the old-style Puritan Cotton Mather (see page 66).

SINNERS IN THE HANDS OF AN ANGRY GOD
FROM A SERMON DELIVERED ON JULY 8, 1741

The first two paragraphs of Edwards's sermon contain clues about the audience he was especially trying to awaken and persuade: "natural men" (people in the congregation who were not "reborn"); or those who were "out of Christ" (those who had not specifically confessed Christ as their only Savior). Although Edwards's warnings may strike you as harsh, remember that the Puritans had a vivid sense of divine wrath and an unwavering belief in the sinfulness of the human race. As you read, be aware of the vivid imagery and of how it would affect a member of Edwards's congregation.

So that thus it is that natural men are held in the hand of God, over the pit of hell; they have deserved the fiery pit, and are already sentenced to it; and God is dreadfully provoked, his anger is as great toward them as to those that are actually suffering the executions of the fierceness of his wrath in hell, and they have done nothing in the least to appease or abate that anger, neither is God in the least bound by any promise to hold them up one moment; the devil is waiting for them, hell is gaping for them, the flames gather and flash about them, and would fain lay hold on them, and swallow them up; the fire pent up in their own hearts is struggling to break out; and they have no interest in any Mediator, there are no means within reach that can be any security to them. In short, they have no refuge, nothing to take hold of; all that preserves them every moment is the mere arbitrary will, and uncovenanted, unobliged forbearance of an incensed God.

The use of this awful subject may be for awakening unconverted persons in this congregation. This that you have heard is the case of every one of you that are out of Christ. That world of misery, that lake of burning brimstone, is extended abroad under you. There is the dreadful pit of the glowing flames of the wrath of God; there is hell's wide gaping mouth open; and you have nothing to stand upon, nor anything to take hold of; there is nothing between you and hell but the air; it is only the power and mere pleasure of God that holds you up.

You probably are not sensible of this; you find you are kept out of hell, but do not see the hand of God in it; but look at other things, as the good state of your bodily constitution, your care of your own life, and the means you use for your own preservation. But indeed these things are nothing; if God should withdraw his hand, they would avail no more to keep you from falling than the thin air to hold up a person that is suspended in it.

The Progress of Sin (1744). Woodcut.

Your wickedness makes you as it were heavy as lead, and to tend downward with great weight and pressure toward hell; and if God should let you go, you would immediately sink and swiftly descend and plunge into the bottomless gulf, and your healthy constitution, and your own care and prudence, and best contrivance, and all your righteousness, would have no more influence to uphold you and keep you out of hell than a spider's web would have to stop a fallen rock. . . .

The wrath of God is like great waters that are dammed for the present; they increase more and more, and rise higher and higher, till an outlet is given; and the longer the stream is stopped, the more rapid and mighty is its course when once it is let loose. It is true, that judgment against your evil works has not been executed hitherto; the floods of God's vengeance have been withheld; but your guilt in the meantime is constantly increasing, and you are every day treasuring up more wrath; the waters are constantly rising, and waxing more and more mighty; and there is nothing but the mere pleasure of God that holds the waters back, that are unwilling to be stopped, and press hard to go forward. If God should only withdraw his hand from the floodgate, it would immediately fly open, and the fiery floods of the fierceness and wrath of God would rush forth with inconceivable fury, and would come upon you with omnipotent power; and if your strength were ten thousand times greater than it is, yea, ten thousand times greater than the strength of the stoutest, sturdiest devil in hell, it would be nothing to withstand or endure it.

The bow of God's wrath is bent, and the arrow made ready on the string, and justice bends the arrow at your heart, and strains the bow, and it is nothing but the mere pleasure of God, and that of an angry God, without any promise or obligation at all, that keeps the arrow one moment from being made drunk with your blood. Thus all you that never passed under a great change of heart, by the mighty power of the Spirit of God upon your souls; all you that were never born again, and made new creatures, and raised from being dead in sin, to a state of new, and before altogether unexperienced light and life, are in the hands of an angry God. However you may have reformed your life in many things, and may have had religious affections,[1] and may keep up a form of re-

1. **affections:** feelings.

ligion in your families and closets,[2] and in the house of God, it is nothing but his mere pleasure that keeps you from being this moment swallowed up in everlasting destruction. However unconvinced you may now be of the truth of what you hear, by and by you will be fully convinced of it. Those that are gone from being in the like circumstances with you see that it was so with them; for destruction came suddenly upon most of them; when they expected nothing of it, and while they were saying, Peace and safety: now they see that those things on which they depended for peace and safety were nothing but thin air and empty shadows.

The God that holds you over the pit of hell, much as one holds a spider, or some loathsome insect over the first, abhors you, and is dreadfully provoked: his wrath toward you burns like fire; he looks upon you as worthy of nothing else but to be cast into the fire; he is of purer eyes than to bear to have you in his sight; you are ten thousand times more abominable in his eyes than the most hateful venomous serpent is in ours. You have offended him infinitely more than ever a stubborn rebel did his prince; and yet it is nothing but his hand that holds you from falling into the fire every moment. It is to be ascribed to nothing else, that you did not go to hell the last night; that you was suffered to awake again in this world, after you closed your eyes to sleep. And there is no other reason to be given why you have not dropped into hell since you arose in the morning, but that God's hand has held you up. There is no other reason to be given why you have not gone to hell, since you have sat here in the house of God, provoking his pure eyes by your sinful wicked manner of attending his solemn worship. Yea, there is nothing else that is to be given as a reason why you do not this very moment drop down into hell!

O sinner! Consider the fearful danger you are in: it is a great furnace of wrath, a wide and bottomless pit, full of the fire of wrath, that you are held over in the hand of that God, whose wrath is provoked and incensed as much against you as against many of the damned in hell. You hang by a slender thread, with the flames of divine wrath flashing about it, and ready every moment to singe it, and burn it asunder; and you have no interest in any Mediator, and nothing to lay hold of to save yourself, nothing to keep off the flames of wrath,

nothing of your own, nothing that you ever have done, nothing that you can do, to induce God to spare you one moment. . . .

It is *everlasting* wrath. It would be dreadful to suffer this fierceness and wrath of Almighty God one moment; but you must suffer it to all eternity. There will be no end to this exquisite horrible misery. When you look forward, you shall see a long forever, a boundless duration before you, which will swallow up your thoughts and amaze your soul; and you will absolutely despair of ever having any deliverance, any end, any mitigation, any rest at all. You will know certainly that you must wear out long ages, millions of millions of ages, in wresting and conflicting with this almighty merciless vengeance; and then when you have so done, when so many ages have actually been spent by you in this manner, you will know that all is but a point to what remains. So that your punishment will indeed be infinite. Oh, who can express what the state of a soul in such circumstances is! All that we can possibly say about it gives but a very feeble, faint representation of it; it is inexpressible and inconceivable: For "who knows the power of God's anger?"

How dreadful is the state of those that are daily and hourly in the danger of this great wrath and infinite misery! But this is the dismal case of every soul in this congregation that has not been born again, however moral and strict, sober and religious, they may otherwise be. Oh, that you would consider it, whether you be young or old! There is reason to think, that there are many in this congregation now hearing this discourse that will actually be the subjects of this very misery to all eternity. We know not who they are, or in what seats they sit, or what thoughts they now have. It may be they are now at ease, and hear all these things without much disturbance, and are now flattering themselves that they are not the persons, promising themselves that they shall escape. If we knew that there was one person, and but one, in the whole congregation that was to be the subject of this misery, what an awful thing would it be to think of! If we knew who it was, what an awful sight would it be to see such a person! How might all the rest of the congregation lift up a lamentable and bitter cry over him! But, alas! Instead of one, how many is it likely will remember this discourse in hell? And it would be a wonder if some that are now present should not be in hell in a very short time, even before this year is out. And it would

---

2. **closets:** rooms for meditation (such as studies).

be no wonder if some persons that now sit here, in some seats of this meetinghouse, in health, quiet, and secure, should be there before tomorrow morning. Those of you that finally continue in a natural condition, that shall keep out of hell longest, will be there in a little time! Your damnation does not slumber; it will come swiftly and, in all probability, very suddenly upon many of you. You have reason to wonder that you are not already in hell. It is doubtless the case of some whom you have seen and known that never deserved hell more than you, and that heretofore appeared as likely to have been now alive as you. Their case is past all hope; they are crying in extreme misery and perfect despair. But here you are in the land of the living and in the house of God, and have an opportunity to obtain salvation. What would not those poor damned hopeless souls give for one day's opportunity such as you now enjoy!

And now you have an extraordinary opportunity, a day wherein Christ has thrown the door of mercy wide open, and stands in calling and crying with a loud voice to poor sinners; a day wherein many are flocking to him, and pressing into the kingdom of God. Many are daily coming from the east, west, north, and south; many that were very lately in the same miserable condition that you are in are now in a happy state, with their hearts filled with love to him who has loved them and washed them from their sins in his own blood, and rejoicing in hope of the glory of God. How awful is it to be left behind at such a day! To see so many others feasting, while you are pining and perishing! To see so many rejoicing and singing for joy of heart, while you have cause to mourn for sorrow of heart, and howl for vexation of spirit! How can you rest one moment in such a condition? . . .

Responding to the Sermon

Analyzing the Sermon

Identifying Facts

1. Where does Edwards declare his **purpose**?
2. There are three famous **figures of speech** in Edwards's sermon: the images of the dam, the bow and arrow, and the spider. To what does Edwards compare these familiar, ordinary things? In each case, how does Edwards extend the figure of speech?
3. In the sixth paragraph, where does Edwards remind his audience of what action they must take to escape God's wrath? What behavior does he say is useless to prevent their everlasting destruction?

Interpreting Meanings

4. What does Edwards mean when he says at the end of his sermon that the "door of mercy" is wide open? Does he talk of God's mercy elsewhere in the sermon?
5. Edwards is directing his sermon to what he calls "natural men," those members of his congregation who have not been "reborn." He wants to make these people *feel* the truth of his statements, as direct experience. He does not want them simply to understand his sermon abstractly. What **images** in the first four paragraphs do you think helped his listeners to feel the peril of their unregenerate condition?

6. Why does Edwards want his listeners to feel or experience what eternity is? What does he say to help them experience this difficult concept? Did you find his description effective?
7. During Edwards's sermon, some members of the congregation were said to have cried out and fainted in terror. Identify the parts of the sermon that you think would have called forth such emotional responses.
8. Literature offers several examples of "hellfire" sermons. (Another famous one is found in James Joyce's novel *Portrait of the Artist as a Young Man.)* Think of orations you might hear today. Do they exhibit the imagery and emotional appeals of Edwards's sermon?
9. Compare Edwards's idea of God in the sermon with the ideas expressed in his autobiography (page 41).

Writing About the Sermon

A Creative Response

1. **Adapting the Sermon.** Consider the differences between Edwards's audience and present-day Americans. Then select any two paragraphs from the sermon. Rewrite the paragraphs as Edwards might deliver them today.
2. **Using Another Point of View.** Write a paragraph from the point of view of a member of Edwards's congregation, describing the sermon's effect.

Primary Sources
Journals

When Jonathan Edwards was twenty years old, he wrote this tribute to Sarah Pierrepont, who was then only thirteen. Jonathan married Sarah four years later.

"They say there is a young lady in [New Haven] who is beloved of that Great Being, who made and rules the world, and that there are certain seasons in which this Great Being, in some way or other invisible, comes to her and fills her mind with exceeding sweet delight, and that she hardly cares for anything, except to meditate on Him—that she expects after a while to be received up where He is, to be raised up out of the world and caught up into heaven; being assured that He loves her too well to let her remain at a distance from Him always. There she is to dwell with Him, and to be ravished with His love and delight forever. Therefore, if you present all the world before her, with the richest of its treasures, she disregards it and cares not for it, and is unmindful of any pain or affliction. She has a strange sweetness in her mind, and singular purity in her affections; is most just and conscientious in all her conduct; and you could not persuade her to do anything wrong or sinful, if you would give her all the world, lest she should offend this Great Being. She is of a wonderful sweetness, calmness, and universal benevolence of mind; especially after this Great God has manifested Himself to her mind. She will sometimes go about from place to place, singing sweetly; and seems to be always full of joy and pleasure; and no one knows for what. She loves to be alone, walking in the fields and groves, and seems to have someone invisible always conversing with her."

—Jonathan Edwards

Edwards began an autobiography but did not write anything after 1740. His contemporary Benjamin Franklin also began an autobiography (page 74), but where Franklin describes his wordly success, Edwards records his spiritual experience. In the following selection he is a young man walking alone after a talk with his father:

". . . And as I was walking there, and looking up on the sky and clouds, there came into my mind so sweet a sense of the glorious *majesty* and *grace* of God, that I know not how to express. I seemed to see them both in a sweet conjunction; majesty and meekness joined together; it was a sweet, and gentle, and holy majesty; and also a majestic meekness; an awful sweetness; a high, and great, and holy gentleness.

"After this my sense of divine things gradually increased, and became more and more lively, and had more of that inward sweetness. The appearance of every thing was altered; there seemed to be, as it were, a calm, sweet cast, or appearance of divine glory, in almost every thing. God's excellency, his wisdom, his purity, and love, seemed to appear in every thing; in the sun, moon, and stars; in the clouds, and blue sky; in the grass, flowers, trees; in the water, and all nature; which used greatly to fix my mind. I often used to sit and view the moon for continuance; and in the day, spent much time in viewing the clouds and sky, to behold the sweet glory of God in these things; in the meantime, singing forth, with a low voice, my contemplations of the Creator and Redeemer. And scarce any thing, among all the works of nature, was so sweet to me as thunder and lightning; formerly, nothing had been so terrible to me. Before, I used to be uncommonly terrified with thunder, and to be struck with terror when I saw a thunderstorm rising; but now, on the contrary, it rejoiced me. I felt God, so to speak, at the first appearance of a thunderstorm; and used to take the opportunity, at such times, to fix myself in order to view the clouds, and see the lightnings play, and hear the majestic and awful voice of God's thunder, which oftentimes was exceedingly entertaining, leading me to sweet contemplations of my great and glorious God."

—Jonathan Edwards

This journal entry was written by Jonathan Edwards's daughter Esther, who died in 1755, when she was only twenty-three years old. Esther's son, Aaron Burr, became the Vice President of the United States.

"*May 1* [1742] I have just come back from a wonderful ride with my honored father, Mr. Edwards, through the spring woods. He usually rides alone. But today he said he had something he wanted to show me. The forests between our house and the full-banked river were very beautiful. The wild cherry and the dogwood were in full bloom. The squirrels were leaping from tree to tree, and the birds were making a various melody. Though father is usually taciturn or preoccupied—my mother will call these large words—even when he takes one of us children with him, today he discoursed to me of the awful sweetness of walking with God in Nature. He seems to feel God in the woods, the sky, and the grand sweep of the river which winds so majestically through the woody silences here."

—Esther Edwards

Anne Bradstreet (1612–1672)

One of the most notable characteristics of American literature is the distinction of its women writers, particularly in poetry. The first accomplished poet on American soil, of *either* sex, was Anne Bradstreet. Who could have guessed that the poet who would begin the history of our literature would be an immigrant teen-aged bride? The question becomes less far-fetched when we know something of the life of the young woman who came to America when its claims to civilization were no more than a few muddy villages precariously perched between the ocean and the wilderness. Young as she was, Anne Bradstreet brought civilization with her.

Educated by tutors in her native England, she was immersed in the Bible. She also had access to the large library of the Earl of Lincoln, who employed her father, Thomas Dudley, as his estate manager. Shakespeare was still alive when Anne was born and, like many budding poets, she found in Shakespeare, and in other great poets of England, sources of inspiration and technique that would one day run like threads of gold through the fabric of her own work.

However, what most determined the course of her life was not a poetic influence but a religious one. Anne Bradstreet was born into a family of Puritans. Accepting their reformist views as naturally as most children accept the religious teachings of a parent, Anne married, at the age of sixteen, a well-educated and zealous young Puritan by the name of Simon Bradstreet. Two years later, in 1630, Simon brought his wife across the Atlantic to the part of New England around Salem that would become known as the Massachusetts Bay Colony. There, while her husband rose to prominence (he became a governor of the colony), Anne Bradstreet kept house in Cambridgeport and Ipswich. She raised four boys and four girls and, without seeking an audience or publication, found the time to write poems. These might never have come to light had it not been for John Woodbridge, her brother-in-law and a minister in Andover. He went to England in 1647 and there, in 1650, without consulting the author herself, published her poems under the title *The Tenth Muse Lately Sprung Up in America * * * By a Gentlewoman of Those Parts.*

In one stroke, an obscure housewife from the meadows of New England was placed among the nine Muses of art and learning sacred to the ancient Greeks. In itself, this was embarrassing enough. But in the middle of the seventeenth century, the real arrogance was that a woman would aspire to a place among the august company of established male poets. Conscious of the boldness she might be charged with, Bradstreet was resigned to criticism. "If what I do prove well," she wrote, "it won't advance; / They'll say it's stol'n, or else it was by chance." But *The Tenth Muse* fared better with critics and the public than she expected, and she felt encouraged to write for the rest of her life.

Today, Anne Bradstreet is remembered not for her elaborate earlier poems but for a few simple lyrics about the birth of children, the death of grandchildren, her love for her husband, her son's sailing to England, her own illnesses.

The following poem is about the burning of her home. Though she does not say so, 800 books were lost in this fire, a considerable library for a home in a raw New World. Destroyed also were all of Anne Bradstreet's papers and all her unpublished poems.

A cradle brought to Plymouth on the *Mayflower.*

Pilgrim Society, Plymouth, Massachusetts.

This poem is filled with *inversions,* a device especially common in English poetry written in earlier centuries. In an inversion, the words are wrenched out of the normal order of an English sentence. Poets used to use inversions frequently, to accommodate the demands of meter or rhyme. The second line here, for example, would normally be written:

I did not look for sorrow near

After you have read the poem, read it over a second time and look for the inverted word order. Once you rearrange the inverted sentences, you'll find the poem much easier to understand.

The poem portrays an internal debate, a type of dialogue between self and soul. As you read, note the points at which the speaker questions her own thoughts and emotions. What answers does she give to these questions? What conclusions does she reach? Note also your own responses: How would you "deal with" the destruction of a home?

Here Follow Some Verses upon the Burning of Our House, July 10, 1666

In silent night when rest I took
For sorrow near I did not look
I wakened was with thund'ring noise
And piteous shrieks of dreadful voice.
5 That fearful sound of "Fire!" and "Fire!"
Let no man know is my desire.
I, starting up, the light did spy,
And to my God my heart did cry
To strengthen me in my distress
10 And not to leave me succorless.°
Then, coming out, beheld a space
The flame consume my dwelling place.
And when I could no longer look,
I blest His name that gave and took,°
15 That laid my goods now in the dust.
Yea, so it was, and so 'twas just.
It was His own, it was not mine,
Far be it that I should repine;
He might of all justly bereft
20 But yet sufficient for us left.
When by the ruins oft I past
My sorrowing eyes aside did cast,
And here and there the places spy
Where oft I sat and long did lie:
25 Here stood that trunk, and there that chest,
There lay that store I counted best.
My pleasant things in ashes lie,

And them behold no more shall I.
Under thy roof no guest shall sit,
30 Nor at thy table eat a bit.
No pleasant tale shall e'er be told,
Nor things recounted done of old.
No candle e'er shall shine in thee,
Nor bridegroom's voice e'er heard shall be.
35 In silence ever shall thou lie,
Adieu, adieu, all's vanity.
Then straight I 'gin my heart to chide,
And did thy wealth on earth abide?
Didst fix thy hope on mold'ring dust?
40 The arm of flesh didst make thy trust?
Raise up thy thoughts above the sky
That dunghill mists away may fly.
Thou hast a house on high erect,
Framed by that mighty Architect,
45 With glory richly furnished,
Stands permanent though this be fled.
It's purchased and paid for too
By Him who hath enough to do.
A price so vast as is unknown
50 Yet by His gift is made thine own;
There's wealth enough, I need no more,
Farewell, my pelf,° farewell my store.
The world no longer let me love,
My hope and treasure lies above.

---

10. **succorless:** without aid or assistance; helpless.
14. "The Lord gave, and the Lord hath taken away; blessed be the name of the Lord," (Job 1:21).

52. **pelf:** worldly goods.

A Comment on the Poem

The poet first narrates an incident, then draws some conclusions from it. The incident is clear enough, but the conclusions are comprehensible only when we realize that they reflect an absolute faith in, and absolute submission to, the will of God. In fact, this poem reveals a typical pattern of Puritan thought. It is a series of steps that at first seem to be going anywhere the author chooses, but in the end, these steps always lead to the same affirmation—of the rightness of God's will and of the waywardness of human desires. In this poem, the speaker's anguish is unmistakable, and why not? Before her eyes, her house and all her beloved possessions are going up in flame. Like many people faced with calamity,

she calls on God to give her the strength to endure and not to leave her without help. But she does not curse her bad luck. Instead almost at once she blesses God, who chose to inflict the anguish upon her. In doing this, she puts herself in the shoes of the Biblical figure of Job. In all his misery, Job was still able to say: "The Lord gave, and the Lord hath taken away; blessed be the name of the Lord."

This is the turning point of the poem, the point at which the speaker begins to scold herself for putting such value on the things of this world. It is the point at which she resigns herself to misfortune and embraces the test of faith that misfortune represents.

Responding to the Poem

Analyzing the Poem

Identifying Details

1. What are some of the specific losses that Bradstreet dwells on in the first half of the poem?
2. Bradstreet speaks of another "house" in an **extended metaphor** at the end of the poem. What is this house, who is its architect, and how is it more perfect than the house she has lost?

Interpreting Meanings

3. *Pelf*—a word designating riches or worldly goods—is usually used only when the riches or goods are considered to be slightly tainted, ill-gotten, or stolen. Why do you suppose Bradstreet uses such a bitter word in line 52 to describe her own cherished treasures?
4. At the very end of the poem, are you convinced that the speaker means what she says? Some readers have felt that, by so lovingly enumerating her losses, Bradstreet is "crying to heaven" in a way that, unconsciously, reveals more attachment to her earthly possessions than she would admit to. Do you think these readers have a point? Explain.

Writing About the Poem

A Critical Response

Analyzing the Writer's Attitude. Twice Bradstreet checks herself from mourning over the loss of her beloved possessions. The first instance is in lines 14–20; the second

begins with line 37. Paraphrase lines 14–20; that is, restate each line in your own words. Then write a paragraph explaining what these lines reveal about Bradstreet's attitude toward earthly suffering and the Providence of God. Explain how such faith might have helped these first immigrants face a wilderness in a new world.

Analyzing Language and Style

The "Poetic" Style

During the time Anne Bradstreet wrote, and for many years after, people expected poetry to conform to a basic **meter,** or pattern of stressed and unstressed syllables. Most readers also looked for rhymes. Bradstreet's poem is rhymed in **couplets** and written in **iambic tetrameter.** This means that each line contains four iambs, an **iamb** being an unstressed syllable followed by a stressed syllable. Here is how the first line would be scanned:

In silent night when rest I took

You'll also see that to accommodate her meter, the poet often inverts words. In normal English word order, this sentence would read:

In [the] silent night when I took [my] rest

Continue scanning the poem to see how faithful, even slavish, Bradstreet has been to her basic beat. Then rewrite the lines to get rid of the inversions. What happens to the beat?

Edward Taylor
(c. 1642–1729)

The publication in 1939 of *The Poetical Works of Edward Taylor* was the third important instance in American literature of the discovery of buried poetic treasure. The first discovery occurred when Anne Bradstreet's brother-in-law carried her "private" poems to England and, without her consent, had them printed. The second occurred in 1890, when the heirs of Emily Dickinson decided to ignore her wishes and publish the poems she had carefully saved in little packets but that she expected would be destroyed after her death. (See Unit Five.)

Of these discoveries, the case of Edward Taylor is perhaps the most remarkable. For more than two hundred years, his brilliant poems simply moldered in the archives of the Yale College library. Then, once again, a body of work that the author had ordered his heirs never to publish came to light—in this case, with such compelling force as to cause the history of early poetry in America to be rewritten.

When scholars—particularly a man named Thomas H. Johnson—confronted this crucial addition to Colonial literature, they easily deduced Taylor's literary and religious background from the poems. But they had only a few meager clues to the personal life of the man himself, a life that spanned more than eighty years.

Edward Taylor was born in Leicestershire, England, near the town of Coventry. Like Anne Bradstreet, he was raised in a family that held dissenting views about many of the practices of the Church of England. Feeling more and more uncomfortable in the religious climate of his own country, where a royal Act of Uniformity had caused Puritans to be persecuted, he determined to seek the freedom that other Nonconformists before him had found in the New World. And so, in 1668, Edward Taylor sailed for Boston.

Gravestone rubbing of the Reverend Silas Biglow, Paxton, Massachusetts (1769).

Collection of Avon Neal and Ann Parker.

Friends had equipped Taylor with letters of introduction to some of the established Colonial leaders, among them the great Puritan minister Increase Mather (1639–1723). Impressed with the young man's credentials and charmed by his personality, Mather and other influential people eased the way toward Taylor's enrollment in Harvard College.

After training for the ministry, Taylor in 1671 accepted a call to become the pastor of a church in Westfield, Massachusetts. This town was one of the growing communities of settlers who had left the coastal towns of New England for richer farmlands in the Connecticut River valley. Taylor stayed in Westfield for the rest of his life. During those fifty-eight years in this frontier town, he faithfully tended to the spiritual needs of his flock. Taylor himself increased the flock by fourteen members—he had eight children by his first wife and six by his second. By the time he died in 1729, Taylor had outlived a number of his children. He could have had little notion that the poems he had scrupulously put away would outlive him with a radiance bright enough to penetrate the darkness of two centuries of obscurity.

THE CONCEIT

In discussions of poetry, the term *conceit* does not mean an inflated opinion of oneself. In poetry, a **conceit** is a startling metaphor or other figure of speech—a surprising connection made between two different things. This connection may be especially witty, strange, exaggerated, or cleverly elaborated. The word *conceit* comes from the Italian *concetto,* meaning "bright idea," and this might be a good way to think about this special kind of figurative language.

In his poem about the spider and the fly, Edward Taylor ends with a little conceit, a clever and even shocking comparison between two things that seem to have nothing at all in common. First, he identifies the spider and its

web with Satan and his web, which ensnares and entangles human beings. So far, the metaphor is not startling; it seems reasonable to associate a natural predator with Satan. But as Edwards continues, he creates an unusual metaphor. When the Lord breaks Satan's cords and Adam's race enters the gate to a state of glory, what is there but a *cage*! Most of us would never associate the idea of salvation with a cage, or with any kind of confinement.

Here we have a **conceit.** In this case, the conceit is based on a **paradox**—a statement that seems to contradict itself. If, in being saved, we are free from Satan, how is it that we are in a cage? But, like other paradoxes, this one reveals a complex truth, at least as the poet sees it. In order to be truly free, we must be protected, or "caged" by God and his glory. And if salvation is identified as a cage, it is a glorious cage—a cage that holds not dead flies, but joyfully singing nightingales.

Suppose a poet compares the evening sky to a transparent pink curtain: The poet has created a metaphor. The twentieth-century poet T. S. Eliot wrote that the evening was "spread out against the sky / Like a patient etherized upon a table." This is a simile so startling that we could call it a conceit. The nineteenth-century poet Emily Dickinson created another conceit when she compared the setting sun to a housewife sweeping up the sky with multicolored brooms and carelessly dropping shreds behind her.

Conceits, then, are startling figures of speech that are often extended as far as the poet can take them. They are exercises of the imagination, devices for making us see connections between vastly different things in the world. Conceits often give playful turns to common expressions so that they mean not only what they say on the surface, but something else as well, usually something much more profound.

Taylor's poems, full of conceits and elaborate imagery, are hardly the kinds of poems we might expect from a Puritan minister writing by candlelight in a pioneer village on the edge of a forest. But Edward Taylor, like all poets, was a product of his times. In poetry, he accepted the examples of the established English poets who immediately preceded him. The greatest among them—John Donne, George Herbert, and Richard Crashaw—were all masters of the poetical conceit. They saw no conflict in uniting religious devotion with a playful use of language that was sometimes so outrageous that it might seem to flirt with blasphemy.

Make up an original conceit. Begin by thinking of ordinary comparisons. Then try to match one half of a comparison with something no one is likely to have thought of before. Write your conceit in this format:

_____ is like _____.

These lines are from the "Preface" to a long series of poems that deal with the struggle between God and Satan for those human beings whom God has elected to save. The first nineteen lines contain a series of questions beginning with *Who*.

All these questions have the same answer, given in line 20, and elaborated on in the lines that follow it. In line 1, Taylor uses the word *infinity* to refer to God. What work is God doing in the first four lines of the poem?

from God's Determinations Touching His Elect

Preface

Infinity, when all things it beheld
In nothing, and of nothing all did build,
Upon what base was fixed the lathe,° wherein
He turned this globe, and riggaled° it so trim?
5 Who blew the bellows of His furnace vast?
Or held the mold wherein the world was cast?
Who laid its cornerstone? Or whose command?
Where stand the pillars upon which it stands?
Who laced and filleted° the earth so fine,
10 With rivers like green ribbons smaragdine?°
Who made the seas its selfedge,° and its locks
Like a quilt ball within a silver box?
Who spread its canopy? Or curtains spun?
Who in this bowling alley bowled the sun?
15 Who made it always when it rises set
To go at once both down, and up to get?
Who the curtain rods made for this tapestry?
Who hung the twinkling lanthorns in the sky?
Who? Who did this? Or who is He? Why, know
20 It's only Might Almighty this did do.
His hand hath made this noble work which stands,
His glorious handiwork not made by hands.
Who spake all things from nothing; and with ease
Can speak all things to nothing, if He please.
25 Whose little finger at his pleasure can
Out mete ten thousand worlds with half a span:
Whose Might Almighty can by half a looks
Root up the rocks and rock the hills by the roots
Can take this mighty world up in his hand
30 And shake it like a squitchen° or a wand.
Whose single frown will make the Heavens shake
Like as an aspen leaf the wind makes quake.
Oh! what a might is this whose single frown
Doth shake the world as it would shake it down?
35 Which all from nothing fet,° from nothing, all:
Hath all on nothing set, lets nothing fall.
Gave all to nothing man indeed, whereby

3. **lathe:** a circular disk used by a potter.
4. **riggaled:** applied markings on the pot.

9. **filleted:** netted, meshed.
10. **smaragdine:** an emerald-green jewel.
11. **selfedge:** the finished edge of woven cloth.

30. **squitchen:** probably a switch.

35. **fet:** fetched.

New England church (detail) (late 18th century). Applique quilt with embroidery.

Henry Ford Museum, Dearborn, Michigan.

Through nothing man all might him glorify.
In nothing then imbossed the brightest gem
More precious than all preciousness in them.
But nothing man did throw down all by sin:
And darkened that lightsome gem in him.
That now his brightest diamond is grown
Darker by far than any coalpit stone.

40

Responding to the Poem

Analyzing the Poem

Identifying Details

1. According to the first two lines, what was the whole world built from?
2. The poet draws **images** from human life—specifically from life in a Puritan village—to talk about the act of creation, something that is impossible for human beings to imagine. Identify the various crafts and practical occupations that the poet refers to.
3. Find the lines in which the poet conveys to us the terrifying power of God, a power far greater than that of any human artisan.
4. According to lines 37–38, what is the purpose of human existence in God's world?

Interpreting Meanings

5. What is the "gem" that God sets in "nothing" (line 39)? In the last image of the poem, what has become of this gem? What Biblical event might the poet be referring to here?
6. The first part of the poem is a series of questions. How does Taylor answer his own questions? What feelings about God is this series of questions designed to create?
7. Taylor often uses **puns,** or plays on words, and **paradoxes,** or expressions that seem to be contradictory. What paradox do you find in line 36? What pun does the poet use in line 28?
8. It is possible that Taylor used this poem in one of his sermons. What effect do you think it would have had on a congregation?

Writing About the Poem

A Critical Response

Comparing the Poem with Job. The series of dramatic questions in Edward Taylor's "Preface" echoes a famous passage from the Book of Job, where God speaks to Job from a whirlwind. Job has asked why he has had to suffer so grievously at God's hands. God answers Job with questions of his own:

> Where wast thou when I laid the foundations of the earth? Declare, if thou hast understanding.
> Who hath laid the measures thereof, if thou knowest? Or who hath stretched the line upon it?
> Whereupon are the foundations thereof fastened? Or who laid the corner stone thereof;
> When the morning stars sang together, and all the sons of God shouted for joy?
> Or who shut up the sea with doors, when it brake forth, as if it had issued out of the womb? . . .
>
> —Job 38:4–8

Refer to the Book of Job, Chapters 38–41, for the rest of God's answer. Then write an essay in which you compare the text from Job with Taylor's poem. Before you write, consider these questions and organize your essay around the answers to them: What structure do the two passages have in common that makes them sound so much alike? What are the answers to the questions in each passage? How do both writers use familiar, homely images and metaphors to describe the unimaginable act of creation? What does each passage suggest about the significance of human beings in relation to the might of God?

Analyzing Language and Style

Imagery

Edwards's poetic nourishment came not from the spare plain style of Puritan writers like William Bradford, but from the great English poets of the seventeenth century. To get an idea of the richness of his imagery, make a list of all the **sights** you see in this poem. Are all the images connected with the sense of sight? Or do some reproduce **sounds,** or the feel of **textures**?

Of all the elaborate images in this poem, which one do you think is most fantastic and most successful in describing the world and its creation?

Edwards draws his imagery from the practical concerns of a simple Puritan village. Suppose he were writing this poem today. What crafts and occupations might he use to describe this indescribable act of creation?

The Southern Planters

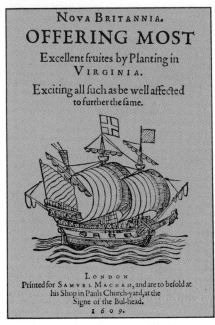

Nova Britannia Offering Most Excellent Fruites by Planting in Virginia, London (1609). Woodcut.

Rare Book Division, New York Public Library.

In addition to the Puritans of New England, there was another literary tradition in the New World. This literature came from the Southern planters, a group of people whose background and social views varied considerably from those of the Puritans.

Many reasons can be suggested for the differences. One factor may have been climate. The Southern climate was kinder; it was warm and soft and the land was enormously fertile. The Northern climate was harsh; springs and summers were brief and winters were long and cold. Even the land in New England was hard; its outcroppings of granite and bedrock broke plows and made farming difficult.

But economic and religious factors were even more important. The land holdings in New England were small for the most part; many colonists were small farmers or tradesmen who lived in villages and owned very little land. But the Southern planter was an aristocrat and the virtual ruler of a huge territory. He maintained this area by keeping a large number of slaves (though there were slaves in New England in those days too).

In religion, most Southerners belonged to the Church of England. In general, they were much more interested in the outside world—in literature, music, art, politics, and the world of nature—than they were in the scrupulous examination of their own souls. But the Puritans, who had rejected the established church, were constantly looking inward and questioning themselves. Where the Southerner saw the world as something to be conquered and enjoyed, the Puritan—who loved the world as much as anyone else did—feared that its beauties were lures and sources of temptation.

The Southern planters shared the world view of the English Renaissance, with its emphasis on classical literature and the growing spirit of scientific inquiry. Thus, when the Southerners wrote about the New World, they were apt to write about it in traditional ways. Characteristically, the first purely literary work of the South was a translation of a Latin classic, Ovid's collection of myths called the *Metamorphoses.* Even a work as original as *The Sotweed Factor* (1708), Ebenezer Cooke's humorous tale of a tobacco merchant, was written in bouncy couplets, the popular form for satirical verse in England.

In many ways, William Byrd is a representative figure for the Southern writers of the Colonial Period. Born in Virginia more than fifty years after the Pilgrims landed on Plymouth, Byrd was truly a Renaissance man in the New World. He translated Greek and Latin works, composed original poetry (mostly satiric verse), and wrote about mathematics and medicine. Writing a generation before Thomas Jefferson, Byrd displayed the same intellectual curiosity that his fellow Virginian would so strongly exemplify later.

Byrd described the pleasures of the life of the Southern planter: "I have a large family of my own, and my doors are open to everybody, yet I have no bills to pay. . . . I live in a kind of independence of everyone but Providence. . . . I must take care to keep all my people to their duty. . . . But then 'tis an amusement in this silent country."

William Byrd
(1674–1744)

It is worth remembering that Jamestown, Virginia, was named for James I, the king who vowed to harry the Puritans out of England. Virginia itself was named for Elizabeth I, the "Virgin Queen." These place names—and many others in the South—remind us of an important difference between Virginia and the colonies of New England. New England was settled largely by those in conflict with British intellectual, theological, and social life; Virginia was settled by those in harmony with that life. By and large, the fervent, short-haired puritanical Roundheads went to New England; the aristocratic, long-haired, worldly Cavaliers went to Virginia.

William Byrd, a man of exceptional intellect and accomplishments, was a thorough Cavalier—worldly, sophisticated, and gentlemanly. Byrd was born in Virginia, the son of a wealthy landowner and merchant, but he was educated in England, where he spent half his life. In London, he acquired a passion for the theater, which the Puritans had once outlawed as immoral. Byrd had many scientific interests: He was even a member of the Royal Society, that pillar of the British scientific establishment.

Byrd alternated between living in England and Virginia. He preferred London, with its elegant homes, witty conversation, and gambling tables. During his visits to Westover, his 26,000-acre home in Virginia, he tried to keep alive both his social and intellectual life. Westover's gardens are still renowned, and its library of 3,600 volumes was rivaled in Byrd's time only by Cotton Mather's library in New England.

Byrd had little in common with the New Englanders. The contrasts between Byrd and the Puritans are instructive. For example, Byrd kept a diary, as many Puritans did. But the Puritans' diaries are primarily records of spiritual examination. Byrd's diary records the pleasures and practical concerns of a man of the world. Dinners, flirtations with women, literature, and natural science were of greater interest to him than matters of the spirit. In London in 1719, for example, he recorded a typical day:

William Byrd by Sir Godfrey Kneller.

May 28. I rose about 7 o'clock and read a chapter in Hebrew and some Greek. I neglected my prayers, but had milk for breakfast. The weather was still warm and clear and very dry, the wind north. About eleven came Annie Wilkinson but I would not speak with her. I was disappointed in the [absence] of Mrs. B—s who wrote me word she would come and breakfast with me, so I read some English and ate some bread and butter because I was to dine late and about 3 o'clock went to dine with Sir Wilfred Lawson and ate some mutton. After dinner we talked a little and about 6 o'clock went to Kensington in Sir Wilfred's coach where there was a ball in the gardens and several ladies and among the rest Miss Perry whom I stuck most to and she complained I squeezed her hand. Here I stayed till 1 o'clock and then came home and neglected my prayers.

In 1728, Byrd joined a survey expedition of the disputed boundary line between Virginia and North Carolina. *The History of The Dividing Line* is far more than a simple record of that expedition. Witty and elegantly written, it is filled with philosophical observations and barbed comments on American Colonial life.

FROM THE HISTORY OF THE DIVIDING LINE

In the first extract from the *History,* Byrd ironically describes the "modish frenzy" of early travelers to America, a fashionable craze which he compares to a "distemper" or illness. Notice immediately how Byrd's *tone* differs from Bradford's, even though both men were writing about the same topic. Which writer do you think sounds more "modern"?

Early Virginia Colonies

As it happened some ages before to be the fashion to saunter to the Holy Land and go upon other Quixote adventures,[1] so it was now grown the humor to take a trip to America. The Spaniards had lately discovered rich mines in their part of the West Indies, which made their maritime neighbors eager to do so too. This modish frenzy, being still more inflamed by the charming account given of Virginia by the first adventurers, made many fond of removing to such a Paradise.

Happy was he, and still happier she, that could get themselves transported, fondly expecting their coarsest utensils in that happy place would be of massy silver.

This made it easy for the Company to procure as many volunteers as they wanted for their new Colony, but, like most other undertakers who have no assistance from the public, they starved the design by too much frugality; for, unwilling to launch out at first into too much expense, they shipped off but few people at a time, and those but scantily provided. The adventurers were, besides, idle and extravagant and expected they might live without work in so plentiful a country.

These wretches were set ashore not far from Roanoke Inlet, but by some fatal disagreement or laziness were either starved or cut to pieces by the Indians.

Several repeated misadventures of this kind did for some time allay the itch of sailing to the new world, but the distemper broke out again about the year 1606. Then it happened that the Earl of Southampton and several other persons eminent for their quality and estates were invited into the Company who applied themselves once more to people the then almost abandoned Colony. For this purpose they embarked about a hundred men, most of them reprobates[2] of good families and related to some of the Company who were men of quality and fortune.

The ships that carried them made a shift to find a more direct way to Virginia and ventured through the capes into the Bay of Chesapeake. The same night they came to an anchor at the mouth of Powhatan, the same as James River, where they built a small fort at a place called Point Comfort.

This settlement stood its ground from that time forward, in spite of all the blunders and disagreement of the first adventurers and the many calamities that befell the Colony afterward. The six gentlemen who were first named of the Company by the Crown and who were empowered to choose an annual president from among themselves were always engaged in factions and quarrels, while the rest detested work more than famine. At this rate the Colony must have come to nothing had it not been for the vigilance and bravery of Captain Smith,[3] who struck a terror into all the Indians round about. This gentleman took some pains to persuade the men to plant Indian corn, but they

---

1. **Quixote adventures:** foolish adventures, after the madcap hero of Cervantes's novel, *Don Quixote* (1605–1615).

2. **reprobates** (rep′rə·bāts): people lost to all sense of duty or decency.
3. **Captain Smith:** John Smith (1579–1631), founder of Virginia.

Map of Virginia by Theodore de Bry (1590). Colored engraving.   Rare Book Division, New York Public Library.

looked upon all labor as a curse. They chose rather to depend upon the musty provisions that were sent from England; and when they failed, they were forced to take more pains to seek for wild fruits in the woods than they would have taken in tilling the ground. Besides, this exposed them to be knocked in the head by the Indians and gave them fluxes [dysentery] into the bargain, which thinned the plantation very much. To supply this mortality, they were reinforced the year following with a greater number of people, along which were fewer gentlemen and more laborers, who, however, took care not to kill themselves with work. These found the first adventurers in a very starving condition but relieved their wants with the fresh supply they brought with them. From Kecoughtan[4] they extended themselves as far as Jamestown, where, like true Englishmen, they built a church that cost no more than fifty pounds and a tavern that cost five hundred.

---

4. **Kecoughtan:** New Hampton, Virginia.

As the Colony grew, violence frequently erupted between the settlers and the Indians. Byrd offered his solution to the conflicts between the two cultures.

Intermarriage

They had now made peace with the Indians, but there was one thing wanting to make that peace lasting. The natives could by no means persuade themselves that the English were heartily their friends so long as they disdained to intermarry with them. And, in earnest, had the English consulted their own security and the good of the Colony, had they intended either to civilize or convert these gentiles, they would have brought their stomachs to embrace this prudent alliance.

The Indians are generally tall and well proportioned, which may make full amends for the darkness of their complexions. Add to this that they are healthy and strong, with constitutions untainted by lewdness and not enfeebled by luxury. Besides, morals and all considered, I cannot think the Indians were much greater heathens than the first adventurers, who, had they been good Christians, would have had the charity to take this only method of converting the natives to Christianity. For after all that can be said, a sprightly lover is the most prevailing missionary that can be sent among these or any other infidels.

Besides, the poor Indians would have had less reason to complain that the English took away their land if they had received it by way of a portion with their daughters. Had such affinities been contracted in the beginning, how much bloodshed had been prevented and how populous would the country have been, and, consequently, how considerable! Nor would the shade of the skin have been any reproach at this day, for if a Moor may be washed white in three generations, surely an Indian might have been blanched.

The French, for their parts, have not been so squeamish in Canada, who upon trial find abundance of attraction in the Indians. Their late grand monarch thought it not below even the dignity of a Frenchman to become one flesh with this people and therefore ordered 100 livres for any of his subjects, man or woman, that would intermarry with a native.

By this piece of policy we find the French interest very much strengthened among the savages and their religion, such as it is, propagated just as far as their love. And I heartily wish this well-concerted scheme doesn't hereafter give the French an advantage over His Majesty's good subjects on the northern continent of America.

Byrd's History touches on other colonies besides Virginia. Here he presents a Cavalier's view of the Puritans of the northern colonies.

The New England Colonies

About the same time New England was pared off from Virginia by letters patent bearing [the] date April 10, 1608. Several gentlemen of the town and neighborhood of Plymouth obtained this grant, with the Lord Chief Justice Popham at their head.

Their bounds were specified to extend from 38 to 45 degrees of northern latitude, with a breadth of one hundred miles from the seashore. The first fourteen years this company encountered many difficulties and lost many men, though, far from being discouraged, they sent over numerous recruits of Presbyterians every year, who for all that

Hunting Party (late 17th century). Oil on wood overmantel.   Collection of Mr. and Mrs. Samuel Schwartz.

had much ado to stand their ground, with all their fighting and praying.

But about the year 1620 a large swarm of dissenters fled thither from the severities of their stepmother, the church. These saints [the Puritan dissenters], conceiving the same aversion to the copper complexion of the natives as that of the first adventurers to Virginia, would on no terms contract alliances with them, afraid, perhaps, like the Jews of old, lest they might be drawn into idolatry by those strange women.

Whatever disgusted them I can't say, but this false delicacy, creating in the Indians a jealousy that the English were ill affected toward them, was the cause that many of them were cut off and the rest exposed to various distresses.

This reinforcement was landed not far from Cape Cod, where for their greater security they built a fort and near it a small town, which, in honor of the proprietors, was called New Plymouth. But they still had many discouragements to struggle with, though by being well supported from home they by degrees triumphed over them all.

Their brethren, after this, flocked over so fast that in a few years they extended the settlement one hundred miles along the coast, including Rhode Island and Martha's Vineyard.

Thus the Colony throve apace and was thronged with large detachments of Independents and Presbyterians who thought themselves persecuted at home.

Byrd's surveying party is guided by an Indian named Bearskin. Here, Byrd records Bearskin's religious beliefs.

The Native Religion

In the evening we examined our friend Bearskin concerning the religion of his country, and he explained it to us without any of that reserve to which his nation is subject. He told us he believed there was one supreme god, who had several subaltern[5] deities under him. And that this master god made the world a long time ago. That he told the sun, the moon, and stars their business in the beginning, which they, with good looking after,

have faithfully performed ever since. That the same power that made all things at first has taken care to keep them in the same method and motion ever since. He believed that God had formed many worlds before he formed this, but that those worlds either grew old and ruinous or were destroyed for the dishonesty of the inhabitants. That God is very just and very good, ever well pleased with those men who possess those godlike qualities. That he takes good people into his safe protection, makes them very rich, fills their bellies plentifully, preserves them from sickness and from being surprised or overcome by their enemies. But all such as tell lies and cheat those they have dealings with he never fails to punish with sickness, poverty, and hunger and, after all that, suffers them to be knocked on the head and scalped by those that fight against them.

He believed that after death both good and bad people are conducted by a strong guard into a great road, in which departed souls travel together for some time till at a certain distance this road forks into two paths, the one extremely level and the other stony and mountainous. Here the good are parted from the bad by a flash of lightning, the first being hurried away to the right, the other to the left. The right-hand road leads to a charming, warm country, where the spring is everlasting and every month is May; and as the year is always in its youth, so are the people, and particularly the women are bright as stars and never scold. That in this happy climate there are deer, turkeys, elks, and buffaloes innumerable, perpetually fat and gentle, while the trees are loaded with delicious fruit quite throughout the four seasons. That the soil brings forth corn spontaneously, without the curse of labor, and so very wholesome that none who have the happiness to eat of it are ever sick, grow old, or die. Near the entrance into this blessed land sits a venerable old man on a mat richly woven, who examines strictly all that are brought before him, and if they have behaved well, the guards are ordered to open the crystal gate and let them enter into the land of delight.

The left-hand path is very rugged and uneven, leading to a dark and barren country where it is always winter. The ground is the whole year round covered with snow, and nothing is to be seen upon the trees but icicles. All the people are hungry yet have not a morsel of anything to eat except a bitter kind of potato, that gives them the dry gripes [heaves] and fills their whole body with loathsome

---

5. **subaltern** (səb·ôl′tərn): subordinate; lower; of inferior rank or position.

ulcers that stink and are insupportably painful. Here all the women are old and ugly, having claws like a panther with which they fly upon the men that slight their passion. For it seems these haggard old furies[6] are intolerably fond and expect a vast deal of cherishing. They talk much and exceedingly shrill, giving exquisite pain to the drum of the ear, which in that place of the torment is so tender that every sharp note wounds it to the quick. At the end of this path sits a dreadful old woman on a monstrous toadstool, whose head is covered with rattlesnakes instead of tresses, with glaring white eyes that strike a terror unspeakable into all that behold her. This hag pronounces sentence of woe upon all the miserable wretches that hold up their hands at her tribunal. After this they are delivered over to huge turkey buzzards, like harpies,[7] that fly away with them to the place above-mentioned. Here, after they have been tormented a certain number of years according to their several degrees of guilt, they are driven back into this world to try if they will mend their manners and merit a place the next time in the regions of bliss.

This was the substance of Bearskin's religion and was as much to the purpose as could be expected from a mere state of nature, without one glimpse of revelation or philosophy. It contained, however, the three great articles of natural religion: the belief of a god, the moral distinction between good and evil, and the expectation of rewards and punishments in another world. . . .

---

6. **furies:** in Greek and Roman mythology, fierce avenging goddesses.

7. **harpies:** in Greek and Roman mythology, filthy, evil creatures with women's heads and birds' bodies.

Responding to the History

Analyzing the History

Identifying Facts

1. What reasons does Byrd suggest for the failure of the first Virginia settlement?
2. According to Byrd, did the first colonists have realistic expectations of life in the New World? Explain his point of view.
3. For what reasons is Byrd in favor of intermarriage with Native Americans? Are his interests here primarily moral or primarily practical? Explain.

Interpreting Meanings

4. Like many English writers of his time, Byrd excels at **satire,** the use of ridicule to expose the faults or weaknesses of people or institutions. From his scathing portrait of the early settlers of Virginia in the first passage of this selection, what personal qualities do you think Byrd admired?
5. What is Byrd's attitude toward the Puritans of New England? Tell how his **diction,** or choice of words, reveals this attitude.
6. According to his description of the native religion, what "articles," or elements, of religion does Byrd consider most important? Consider Byrd's attitudes toward religion as revealed in his remarks on intermarriage, on the New England colonists, and on Native American theology. How closely do his views accord with those expressed by Mary Rowlandson (page 24)?
7. Did you find Byrd a more or less interesting writer than the other Colonials? Support your position with references to the selections you have read.

Writing About the History

A Critical Response

1. **Contrasting Two Histories.** In a brief essay, contrast the selection from Byrd's *History of the Dividing Line* with William Bradford's account of the Puritan landing at Plymouth (pages 17–18). In your essay, consider specifically how the two accounts differ in purpose, tone, and style.
2. **Analyzing the History.** Examine the references to women in this selection from Byrd's history. In a paragraph or two, mention the references and discuss what they reveal about the position of women in Byrd's world.

THE AMERICAN LANGUAGE

The first permanent English settlements in the New World were founded at Jamestown, Virginia, in 1607 and at Plymouth, Massachusetts, in 1620. When was the first loan word from an American Indian language recorded in English? The word, somewhat ominously, was *cannibal*. It appeared in a description of Columbus's voyages published in England in 1553. The word came to English through Spanish from the language of a West Indian Arawak tribe; literally, it meant "strong man," but it was used by the natives to describe a man-eating tribe. (It was believed that one assumed the strength of another man by eating his flesh.) Columbus had difficulty understanding the word's pronunciation. He heard it once as *caniba* and another time as *carib*. *Caribal* became a word for the region, the Caribbean. We all know the fate of the word *cannibal*.

The next recorded loan words, *maize, canoe,* and *hurricane,* also came from West Indian tribes. Like *cannibal,* they were part of the booty that Columbus brought back with him. In 1601, in his play *Troilus and Cressida,* Shakespeare used the word *hurricane,* then still fairly new, to mean "a waterspout." Ten years later, in *The Tempest,* he named his famous brute Caliban, a variant of the word *cannibal.* How strange such words must have seemed then!

Another now-familiar word, this one from the Taino tribe of the West Indies, is *barbecue.* The word seems to have referred to a latticelike arrangement of sticks used in sleeping platforms, in fish traps, and in devices to dry and roast meat. *Potato* also came into English through Spanish from Taino (*batata*), although the word referred originally to a sweet potato. Other words that entered English from Caribbean languages by way of Spanish include *pawpaw, hammock,* and *tobacco,* which in Taino meant something like "cigar."

The kinds of words the early explorers brought back with them from the Caribbean are characteristic of the kinds of words American English would adapt from Native American tongues in general. They all name a person, place, or thing. We can easily imagine them as the answer to that basic question, which must have been asked thousands of times: "What's that?"

Learning the Native Language

The colonists who settled at Jamestown and Plymouth, and those who came later, faced enormous difficulties with language. Their situation was not at all like the situation faced by a German coming to London today, say, and being confronted with a language that shares common roots with German. This German traveler would

Native American Languages

Tobacco plant.

Rare Book Division, New York Public Library.

Pumpkin.

also have books, especially dictionaries, from which to learn. But Native American languages have no relationship with English or with any European language. At the time the colonists came to the New World, the native languages were totally oral. Moreover, they had complex sound systems very different from those of European languages. Sikwayi, the Cherokee, whose name was later given to the giant redwood trees of the West (Sequoia), devised a Cherokee alphabet that required eighty-five symbols.

The unfamiliarity and complexity of the native languages were not the only difficulties for English speakers. In North America at this time, there were fifty-eight different language families and roughly a thousand languages. Most of the native languages in eastern North America belonged to the Algonquian family, which included (in addition to Algonquian) Cree, Cheyenne, Mahican, and Shawnee, among others. But this did not necessarily make things any easier. When a colonist in Algonquian territory pointed to an animal and asked, "What's that?" he might receive the answer *skekakwa* one time and the answer *squnk* another time.

A few factors, though, did make things easier. One is that a number of Native Americans learned English and served as translators and teachers. Among the first natives the settlers met when they landed at Jamestown and Plymouth were some who had learned English from their previous contact with explorers. A second factor was that, among the Puritans at least, there was great zeal to learn native languages in order to translate the Bible into these languages and thus to save the natives' souls. The first of these Bibles to appear was John Eliot's translation into the language of the Massachusetts tribes in 1661. A third factor is that many of the borrowed words did not really need to be understood; these were the thousands of proper names, from Winnipesaukee to Wisconsin, that came to dot our landscape.

All Native American languages contained sounds that were completely unfamiliar to Europeans. This unfamiliarity of another sound system is an obstacle to learning any language; it is even an obstacle to repeating a word. Because the sounds in native languages could be so different from English sounds, words taken into English from these languages were inevitably changed. What was spoken by the Native American would *not* be what was heard and then repeated by the Englishman. The same word would sometimes be recorded in a number of forms, which is what happened with *caribal* and *cannibal*.

Here is an example of this difficulty: In 1608, Captain John Smith wrote the name of an animal he encountered as *rahaugcum* and *raugroughcum*. In 1624, he spelled it *rarowcun*. Another writer, in 1612, spelled it *aracoune*. The name of this animal was not recorded as *raccoon* until 1672. Sometimes a Native American word would be changed into an English word that sounded similar, a process that is called folk etymology. Thus, the Cree word *wisketjan*, "blue jay," became *Whiskey-John* to English speakers. A similar transformation was worked on *wejak*, which became *woodchuck*, despite the fact that the creature had nothing to do with wood or with chuck (a cut of beef).

Moving West

As the settlers moved west, they met people from language families other than the Algonquian, and loan words multiplied. The first Native American word for "dwelling" to enter English was the Algonquian word *wigwam*. In the Great Plains area of the Midwest the Sioux family of languages called a dwelling a *tepee,* but this word didn't come into English use until the 1830's. As settlers moved farther west, they came into the territory of the Na-Dene family of languages and found that the Navaho called their dwellings *qughan* (*hogan*). To further complicate matters, the French used their word *loge* ("hut") for Indian dwellings, from which we got the phrase *Indian lodge,* or simply *lodge.*

A number of words came into English from South American languages as well, and these became more familiar as Americans moved west. Most of these came via Spanish from Nahuatl, the principal Aztec tongue, and many were in use in Britain before they came to America. *Chocolate* and *chili* are two of these. Both appeared in England in the early seventeenth century and were later re-imported to America. *Chocolate,* like tobacco an instant success in Europe, comes from the Aztec word *xocolatl,* which means "bitter water." John Smith described the Indian dish *tamale* (from the Nahuatl *tamal*) in 1612. *Coyote, tomato,* and *mesquite* came into American English after settlers started pushing west.

The Romance of Native Place Names

The greatest number of Native American words entering American English did so as place names. Walt Whitman was especially enthusiastic about Indian names because of their ancient connection with the land and their euphony. *"Mississippi!"* he wrote. "The word winds with chutes—it rolls a stream three thousand miles long . . . *Monongahela* . . . rolls with venison richness upon the palate." Whitman proposed (unsuccessfully) to substitute Native American names for all of our place names. In his poetry, he preferred *Manahatta* to New York, as being more genuine, and Long Island he called *Paumonok.* This drive to rename our landscape was extreme, especially when one considers the many difficult native names that already confused travelers and local inhabitants alike. (Lake Winnipesaukee in New Hampshire is a beautiful name, but it has had 132 different spellings in its history.) Nevertheless, Whitman's enthusiasm was understandable, and it was characteristic of the American love for Indian place names. If Whitman failed to get us to call Long Island *Paumonok,* the Native American heritage is nevertheless well represented on that island by such names as Montauk, Setauket, Amagansett, and Quogue.

Around the country, thousands of rivers, mountains, and towns bear Native American names. In many cases, the derivations of the words have been lost or are in dispute. Linguists agree, for example, that *Milwaukee* comes from an Indian word, but they

Corn plant.

disagree on which word it might be: *Milioke* ("good earth"), *Mahnah-wauk-seepe* ("a riverside council ground"), or *man-a-wau-kee* ("a place where Indians harvested *man-wau,* a medicinal herb"). Since so many native languages have disappeared, we will probably never know the answer to these and other problematical derivations. The origins of other names, however, are clear. *Mohave* means "three mountains" and refers to three mountains near Needles, California. *Shenandoah* means "spruce stream," and *Miami* (Florida) means "people of the peninsula." Native American names are romantic to most Americans, as they were to poets such as Whitman and Longfellow, and often for good reason. At times, though, we have over-romanticized such names. Generations of Americans have thought that *Mississippi* meant "father of the waters." It is a cruel disappointment to learn that it is simply a combination of the Chippewa words for "big" (*mici*) and "river" (*sibi*). Some legends are better left unspoiled.

Analyzing Language

1. Each of the following states has a name that originated with a Native American tribe. Chose any five state names. Use a dictionary to find out what language each name comes from, and what the name means.

Alabama	Mississippi
Arizona	Missouri
Arkansas	Nebraska
Connecticut	North Dakota
Idaho	Ohio
Illinois	Oklahoma
Iowa	South Dakota
Kansas	Tennessee
Kentucky	Texas
Massachusetts	Utah
Michigan	Wisconsin
Minnesota	Wyoming

2. Use a dictionary to trace the origins of the following words. What does each word mean in contemporary American usage?

bayou	podunk	toboggan
caucus	poke	totem
mackinaw		

3. The names of animals and plants were among the first words borrowed from native languages. Most of these words came from the Algonquian family of languages, the family to which most languages spoken in the Eastern half of the United States belonged. Use a good dictionary to locate the original meanings of these words:

opossum	caribou	pecan
moose	tobacco	hominy grits
chipmunk	squash	

4. In his novel *The Last of the Mohicans,* James Fenimore Cooper has a character try to adopt "the figurative language of the natives." Here are some American cities and features whose names were adopted from Native American languages. Using a dictionary, tell what language each name came from and what it translates into. From your research, explain why Cooper called the Indian languages "figurative."

Chattahoochee River	Omaha
Cheyenne	Minneapolis
Erie	Missouri
Lake Mohawk	Potomac River
Nantucket	Spokane
Okefenokee Swamp	Tacoma

5. These lines are from a ritual song of "the sky loom." What figures of speech do they contain?

May the warp be the white light of morning
May the weft be the red light of evening
May the fringes be the falling rain
May the border be the standing rainbow
Weave for us this bright garment that we
may walk where birds sing
where grass is green
O our mother the Earth O our Father the Sky

—Tewa traditional

DETERMINING THE PRECISE MEANINGS OF WORDS

Writing Assignment

Write a brief essay in which you discuss the precise meanings of two italicized words or phrases from one of the passages that follow on page 64.

Background

Understanding what you read and hear is the first necessity in developing critical thinking skills. We use language to communicate with one another, but language sometimes sets up obstacles to understanding. Remember that words are symbols. The word *ship* is not the reality ship. In fact, other languages use different groups of sounds to communicate the same reality (*vaisseau, bastimento*). Remembering that words are symbols, consider the following ways in which language is an imprecise tool for communication:

1. **Words are inexact.** Ask five people to describe very exactly the mental picture they get when they hear the word *ship*. Do any two people have the exact same mental image?
2. **Words have multiple meanings.** The word *ship* has at least twelve different meanings. It can refer to any number of seagoing vessels, an airplane, or a spacecraft. It can be a noun or a verb, and it is spelled the same as the suffix in such words as *friendship* and *leadership*.
3. **Many words name intangible, abstract ideas.** When you say someone is "freckled," you are referring to a physical quality that can be proved by sensory evidence. When you say someone is "proud," however, you are referring to a quality that cannot be perceived by the senses. Words such as *pride* and *justice* involve value judgments, and people can disagree widely on them.
4. **Words and meanings change.** As long as English is used, it will continue to change. Reading something written hundreds of years ago often requires special effort because some of the words and meanings have become **archaic,** or obsolete.

Prewriting

When a regular dictionary does not cover the meaning of a word, particularly if it's from a passage written long ago, you should use an unabridged dictionary. The best sources are *Webster's Third New International Dictionary, Unabridged,* and the *Oxford English Dictionary (OED)*. These dictionaries give complete lists of definitions and example sentences for each meaning; the *OED* also gives the dates the meanings were first recorded. Here is what *Webster's* says in part about *proud*:

---

proud \'praud\ *adj* -ER/-EST [ME, fr. OE *prūd, prūt,* prob. fr. OF *prod, prud, prut, prou* good, capable, brave, fr. LL *prode* advantageous, advantage, fr. L *prodesse* to be useful, be beneficial, fr. *prod-* (var. of *pro-* before, forward) + *esse* to be—more at PRO-, IS] **1** : feeling or showing pride: as **a** : having or displaying inordinate self-esteem <goaded the ~ baronage—J. R. Green> <his cold and ~ nature—A. Conan Doyle> **b** : highly satisfied or pleased : deeply gratified : ELATED, EXULTANT <~ to have such men—Sherwood Anderson> <a ~ boy . . . he has made something with his own hands—*Better Homes & Gardens*>—often used with *of* <~ of his success> <a record to be ~ of> **c** *chiefly Midland* : GLAD, DELIGHTED <we'd be ~ to have you stay for supper> **d** : marked by a proper or becoming self-respect <too ~ to fight—Woodrow Wilson> <brought a ~ . . . efficiency to everything she did—Fred Majdalany> **2 a** : marked by stateliness or magnificence : SPLENDID <~ princes and humble peasants—Vicki Baum> <~ old castles—E. O. Hauser> **b** : giving reason or occasion for pride : GLORIOUS <a ~ heritage> <our ~est feat—Joyce Cary> <his ~est moment—Paul Pickrel> **3** : marked by great vitality or power : VIGOROUS, EXUBERANT: as **a** *of an animal* : full of spirit : METTLESOME <a ~ steed> **b** *of a body of water* : overflowing its banks : SWOLLEN <the ~ stream> **c** *of granulation tissue* : growing exuberantly <~ growth in an old wound>

Choose one of the following passages. Use an unabridged dictionary to investigate the meanings of each word in italics. Then, for each word, fill out a chart like the one on the next page.

1.

He told me there was a bad river we were to ride through, which was so very fierce a horse could sometimes hardly *stem* it: but it was but narrow, and we should soon be over. I cannot express the concern of mind this *relation* set me in. . . .

—Sarah Kemble Knight

2.

I then *betook* me to my *apartment*, which was a little room parted from the kitchen by a single board partition; where, after I had noted the occurrences of the past day, I went to bed, which, though pretty hard, yet neat and *handsome*. But I could get no sleep, because of the clamor of some of the town *topers* in next room, who were entered into a strong debate concerning the signification of the name of their country (viz.), Narragansett.

—Sarah Kemble Knight

3.

As it happened some ages before to be the fashion to *saunter* to the Holy Land and go upon other Quixote adventures, so it was now *grown* the *humor* to take a trip to America. . . . This modish frenzy, being still more inflamed by the charming account given of Virginia by the first adventurers, made many fond of *removing to* such a Paradise. . . .

This made it easy for the Company to procure as many volunteers as they wanted for their new colony, but, like most other *undertakers* who have no assistance from the public, they starved the design by too much frugality. . . .

—William Byrd

Word _____	
Word's etymology	
Meaning in this context	
Is meaning still in use?	
Is word still in use?	
Other common meanings	
Does word imply a value judgment? If so, what evidence supports it?	
Dictionary (or dictionaries) used	

Writing

Choose two of the words from your Prewriting chart, and discuss each word in a separate paragraph. Include all the information you have learned in your research about the word.

Here is a sample paragraph from one writer's essay on the word *proud* as William Bradford uses it in the passage from his *History* (page 13).

> The word *proud* is from an Old English word *prūd*, from an Old French word meaning "good, capable, or brave," which ultimately comes from a Latin word *prodesse*, "to be useful or beneficial." In his comment about the lusty seaman who dies on the journey, Bradford uses the word *proud* in an unfavorable sense to mean "having inordinate self-esteem"; the seaman thinks of himself as superior to the *Mayflower*'s passengers. We would still use the word *proud* to describe someone like the seaman, who has too high an opinion of himself. *Proud* can also mean "highly satisfied or pleased," as in "proud to have such men" (Sherwood Anderson). It can also mean "proper or becoming self-respect," as in "too proud to fight" (Woodrow Wilson). *Proud* is a word implying a value judgment on the part of the user. Bradford cites four or five examples of nasty behavior—specific incidents—to support his own judgment against the unfortunate sailor. He notes that the sailor scorned the passengers when they were sick; he cursed them daily; he told them he hoped to cast half of them overboard before the journey ended (as corpses, I presume) and to make merry with their money. I think Bradford means the word *proud* to contrast with the word *humble*, which would describe the kind of person a Puritan would hope to be: one who served others. To the Puritans, pride would be one of the seven deadly sins. It is interesting that none of the word's original meanings is negative. This information on *proud* comes from *Webster's Third International Dictionary, Unabridged.*

Revising and Proofreading

Use the guidelines in the section at the back of this book, called **Writing About Literature,** to revise and proofread your essay.

THE REVOLUTIONARY PERIOD
THE AGE OF REASON

The Spirit of the Colonists by Frank Schoonover. From *Washington* by Lucy Madison, Penn Publishing Company, 1925.

Collection of Harry Lynch, Wilmington, Delaware.

UNIT TWO

FROM THE AUTOBIOGRAPHY

Franklin was apprenticed to his older brother James, who printed the *New England Courant,* a Boston newspaper. As an apprentice, Ben was treated more harshly than he thought was just. His brother's "tyrannical treatment," Franklin wrote, inspired "that aversion to arbitrary power that has stuck to me through my whole life." Following a dispute with the Massachusetts Assembly about something he had printed, James was imprisoned for a month and forbidden to publish his newspaper. In order to get around this order, James released Ben from his indenture, or contract of service, and made him the publisher, but he forced Ben to sign another, secret indenture. The newspaper was printed under Ben's name for a few months, until, in the fall of 1723, a new dispute arose between the brothers. Watch for the ways Franklin examines his actions and motives. Do you find such evaluations in autobiography today?

Leaving Boston

At length, a fresh difference arising between my brother and me, I took upon me to assert my freedom, presuming that he would not venture to produce the new indentures. It was not fair in me to take this advantage, and this I therefore reckon one of the first errata[1] of my life. But the unfairness of it weighed little with me, when under the *impressions of* resentment, for the blows his passion too often urged him to bestow upon me; though he was otherwise not an ill-natured man. Perhaps I was too saucy and provoking.

When he found I would leave him, he took care to prevent my getting employment in any other printing house of the town, by going round and speaking to every master, who accordingly refused to give me work. I then thought of going to New York as the nearest place where there was a printer; and I was the rather inclined to leave Boston when I reflected that I had already made myself a little obnoxious to the governing party; and from the arbitrary proceedings of the Assembly in my brother's case, it was likely I might if I stayed soon bring myself into scrapes; and farther that my indiscreet disputations about religion began to make me pointed at with horror by good people, as an infidel or atheist; I determined on the point; but my father now siding with my brother, I was sensible that if I attempted to go openly, means would be used to prevent me. My friend Collins therefore undertook to manage a little for me. He agreed with the captain of a New York sloop for my passage, under the notion of my being a young acquaintance of his that had got a naughty girl with child, whose friends would compel me to marry her, and therefore I could not appear or come away publicly. So I sold some of my books to raise a little money, was taken on board privately, and, as we had a fair wind, in three days I found myself in New York near 300 miles from home, a boy of but 17, without the least recommendation to or knowledge of any person in the place, and with very little money in my pocket.

My inclinations for the sea were by this time worn out, or I might now have gratified them. But having a trade, and supposing myself a pretty good workman, I offered my service to the printer of the place, old Mr. William Bradford.[2] He could give me no employment, having little to do and help enough already. But, says he, my son at Philadelphia has lately lost his principal hand, Aquila Rose, by death. If you go thither I believe he may employ you. Philadelphia was 100 miles farther. I set out, however, in a boat for Amboy,[3] leaving my chest and things to follow me round by sea.

---

1. **errata** (e·rät′ə): Latin for "errors," a printer's term.

2. **William Bradford:** one of the first American printers.
3. **Amboy:** Perth Amboy, New Jersey.

Second Street North from Market Street with Christ Church,
Philadelphia by William Birch (1799). Colored line engraving.

Historical Society of Pennsylvania.

Responding to the Autobiography

Analyzing the Autobiography

Identifying Facts

1. Why did Franklin decide to leave Boston secretly? How did he raise some money for the journey from Boston to New York?
2. What method of writing in John Bunyan's *Pilgrim's Progress* does Franklin single out for praise?
3. Franklin's arrival in Philadelphia has become a favorite American anecdote. At the time he wrote this part of his life story, Franklin was living in England and was already one of the most famous Americans of his century. In contrast, what was Franklin's condition in life when he arrived in Philadelphia?
4. What virtue does Franklin place first on his list for achieving moral perfection? Why?

Interpreting Meanings

5. Though Franklin discusses his own character at length in his autobiography, many of his personality traits are revealed not through direct statements but through his actions. Explain what the events of the difficult journey from Boston to Philadelphia disclose about the **character** of the young Franklin. Do you feel Franklin is being honest, or is he trying to make himself look good?
6. What does Franklin's scheme for achieving moral perfection reveal about his views of human nature? What does it suggest about his attitudes toward education? What is your opinion of these views?
7. Franklin ends his list of virtues with humility. Did you find evidence of pride—the opposite of humility—in his history, and if so, where?
8. Which virtue on his list do you consider most important? Which is least important? Why?
9. How does Franklin's scheme for arriving at moral perfection compare with the self-help books available today?

Writing About the Autobiography

A Critical Response

1. **Comparing and Contrasting Two Writers.** Reread the selections from Jonathan Edwards (page 37), and write a brief essay in which you compare and contrast the Puritan preacher with Ben Franklin. Before you write, consider these points: each man's aims in life; his reasons for having them; and the means each man finds to achieve those aims. You quickly will be able to identify differences between the two men. But be sure to cite at least one way in which these two Americans, both heirs of the Puritan tradition, are alike.

2. **Responding to Critical Comments.** Reactions to Franklin's *Autobiography* have often been negative. Here is the response of a famous writer of a later period. Read this response and use a dictionary for any words you don't understand. Then write an essay about Twain's comments. In your first paragraph, restate in your own words how Twain feels about Franklin, and why. In your second paragraph, describe Twain's **tone**. In your third paragraph, give your own reaction to Twain's assessment of Franklin.

> [Franklin had] a malevolence which is without parallel in history; he would work all day and then sit up nights and let on to be studying algebra by the light of a smoldering fire, so that all other boys might have to do that also or else have Benjamin Franklin thrown up to them. Not satisfied with these proceedings, he had a fashion of living wholly on bread and water, and studying astronomy at meal time—a thing which has brought affliction to millions of boys since, whose fathers had read Franklin's pernicious biography.
>
> —Mark Twain

Analyzing Language and Style

American English

Franklin has some trouble communicating with the baker in Philadelphia. Finally, not knowing the names Philadelphians had for bread, he asks for three cents worth of any sort of bread at all. Franklin's troubles might be met by any traveler today.

1. People in different areas mean something different when they order a "roll," "coffee cake," "cinnamon bun," "crumb cake," "muffin," or "biscuit." What would you get in your area if you ordered these in a diner?
2. Use an unabridged dictionary to find out what you would get in England if you asked for a "biscuit."
3. Franklin uses the word *creek* to describe the waterway they pulled into one night. In England, the word meant "an arm of the sea." In America, people changed the word to mean "a shallow feeder of a river." Do you pronounce the word krēk or krik? Is the word used in your area, or do you say *brook, stream,* or *run*?

REMARKS CONCERNING THE SAVAGES OF NORTH AMERICA

Franklin wrote the following essay in 1784, while he was the American representative to France. He was seventy-eight at the time, but, still eager to improve himself, he composed this (and other pieces) in French as an exercise in French composition. He then translated the essay into English. Before you read, think about the word *savages* in the title. Write a list of words or phrases that this word brings to your mind. According to Franklin, why do people use the word *savages*?

Savages we call them, because their manners differ from ours, which we think the perfection of civility; they think the same of theirs.

Perhaps, if we could examine the manners of different nations with impartiality, we should find no people so rude, as to be without any rules of politeness; nor any so polite, as not to have some remains of rudeness.

The Indian men, when young, are hunters and warriors; when old, counselors; for all their government is by counsel of the sages; there is no force, there are no prisons, no officers to compel obedience, or inflict punishment. Hence they generally study oratory, the best speaker having the most influence. The Indian women till the ground, dress the food, nurse and bring up the children, and preserve and hand down to posterity the memory of public transactions. These employments of men and women are accounted natural and honorable. Having few artificial wants, they have abundance of leisure for improvement by conversation. Our laborious manner of life, compared with theirs, they esteem slavish and base; and the learning, on which we value ourselves, they regard as frivolous and useless. An instance of this occurred at the Treaty of Lancaster, in Pennsylvania, *anno* 1744, between the government of Virginia and the Six Nations.[1] After the principal business was settled, the commissioners from Virginia acquainted the Indians by a speech, that there was at Williamsburg a college, with a fund for educating Indian youth; and that, if the Six Nations would send down half a dozen of their young lads to that college, the government would take care that they should be well provided for, and instructed in all the learning of the white people. It is one of the Indian rules of politeness not to answer a public proposition the same day that it is made; they think it would be treating it as a light matter, and that they show it respect by taking time to consider it, as of a matter important. They therefore deferred their answer till the day following when their speaker began, by expressing their deep sense of the kindness of the Virginia government, in making them that offer; "for we know," says he, "that you highly esteem the kind of learning being taught in those colleges, and that the maintenance of our young men, while with you, would be very expensive to you. We are convinced, therefore, that you mean to do us good by your proposal; and we thank you heartily. But you, who are wise, must know that different nations have different conceptions of things; and you will therefore not take it amiss, if our ideas of this kind of education happen not to be the same with yours. We have had some experience of it; several of our young people were formerly brought up at the colleges of the northern provinces; they were instructed in all your sciences; but, when they came back to us, they were bad runners, ignorant of every means of living in the woods, unable to bear either cold or hunger, knew neither how to build a cabin, take a deer, or kill an enemy, spoke our language imperfectly, were therefore neither

1. **Six Nations:** a confederation of six Iroquois tribes.

Young Omaha, War Eagle, Little Missouri, and Pawnee
by Charles Bird King (1822). Oil.

Smithsonian Institution, Washington, D.C.

fit for hunters, warriors, nor counselors; they were totally good for nothing. We are, however, not the less obliged by your kind offer, though we decline accepting it; and, to show our grateful sense of it, if the gentlemen of Virginia will send us a dozen of their sons, we will take great care of their education, instruct them in all we know, and make *men* of them."

Having frequent occasions to hold public councils, they have acquired great order and decency in conducting them. The old men sit in the foremost ranks, the warriors in the next, and the women and children in the hindmost. The business of the women is to take exact notice of what passes, imprint it in their memories (for they have no writing), and communicate it to their children. They are the records of the council, and they preserve traditions of the stipulations in treaties 100 years back; which, when we compare with our writings, we always find exact. He that would speak, rises. The rest observe a profound silence. When he has finished and sits down, they leave him five or six minutes to recollect, that, if he has omitted anything he intended to say, or has anything to add, he may rise again and deliver it. To interrupt another, even in common conversation, is reckoned highly indecent. How different this

from the conduct of a polite British House of Commons, where scarce a day passes without some confusion, that makes the speaker hoarse in calling *to order;* and how different from the mode of conversation in many polite companies of Europe, where, if you do not deliver your sentence with great rapidity, you are cut off in the middle of it by the impatient loquacity of those you converse with, and never suffered to finish it!

The politeness of these savages in conversation is indeed carried to excess, since it does not permit them to contradict or deny the truth of what is asserted in their presence. By this means they indeed avoid disputes; but then it becomes difficult to know their minds, or what impression you make upon them. The missionaries who have attempted to convert them to Christianity all complain of this as one of the great difficulties of their mission. The Indians hear with patience the truths of the Gospel explained to them, and give their usual tokens of assent and approbation; you would think they were convinced. No such matter. It is mere civility.

A Swedish minister, having assembled the chiefs of the Susquehanna Indians, made a sermon to them, acquainting them with the principal historical facts on which our religion is founded; such as the fall of our first parents by eating an apple, the coming of Christ to repair the mischief, His miracles and suffering, &c. When he had finished, an Indian orator stood up to thank him. "What you have told us," says he, "is all very good. It is indeed bad to eat apples. It is better to make them all into cider. We are much obliged by your kindness in coming so far, to tell us these things you have heard from your mothers. In return, I will tell you some of those we have heard from ours. In the beginning, our fathers had only the flesh of animals to subsist on; and if their hunting was unsuccessful, they were starving. Two of our young hunters, having killed a deer, made a fire in the woods to broil some part of it. When they were about to satisfy their hunger, they beheld a beautiful young woman descend from the clouds, and seat herself on that hill, which you see yonder among the blue mountains. They said to each other, it is a spirit that has smelled our broiling venison, and wishes to eat of it; let us offer some to her. They presented her with the tongue; she was pleased with the taste of it, and said, 'Your kindness shall be rewarded; come to this place after thirteen moons, and you shall find something that will be of great benefit in nourishing you and your children to the latest generations.' They did so, and, to their surprise, found plants they had never seen before; but which, from that ancient time, have been constantly cultivated among us, to our great advantage. Where her right hand had touched the ground, they found maize; where her left hand had touched it, they found kidney beans; and where her backside had sat on it, they found tobacco." The good missionary, disgusted with this idle tale, said, "What I delivered to you were sacred truths; but what you tell me is mere fable, fiction, and falsehood." The Indian, offended, replied, "My brother, it seems your friends have not done you justice in your education; they have not well instructed you in the rules of common civility. You saw that we, who understand and practice those rules, believed all your stories; why do you refuse to believe ours?"

Responding to the Essay

Analyzing the Essay

Identifying Facts

1. Like many of Franklin's writings, this essay is **satirical;** it holds certain attitudes up to ridicule. In his opening paragraph, how does Franklin immediately mock the settlers for the name they have given the native inhabitants of North America?
2. Explain how the "savages" differ from the English and the Europeans in their government, education, courtesy, division of labor, and values.
3. Franklin uses a common satirical device in this essay when he reverses certain traditional roles. Such reversals occur when a country bumpkin turns out to be smarter than a city slicker, or when a child turns out to be wiser than a professor. In what ways do the so-called "savages" turn the tables on the "civilized" settlers?

Interpreting Meanings

4. How effective do you think this role-reversal is?
5. According to Franklin, who might be the real savages of North America? Why?
6. What relevance, if any, might this essay have to the world today?

Analyzing Language and Style

Loaded Words

Many words are loaded with emotional overtones called **connotations.** The verb *stink,* for example, suggests a much more vile odor than *smell,* though both words mean more or less the same thing. The words a writer chooses tells us a great deal about his or her attitudes toward a subject; often a writer can convey an attitude through word choice alone, without ever making a direct statement.

What is Franklin's attitude toward the savages and toward the white people? Does he ever say directly? What words suggest the way he feels about both groups?

1. He says the savages see the life of white people as "slavish" and "base." Would the effect have been the same if Franklin had used the word "restricted"?
2. On page 82, the Indians say that they will make "men" of the sons of the Virginia gentlemen. What does this statement suggest about the way the Indians view the white people's education?
3. Reread the paragraph beginning "Having frequent occasions" (page 82). Find examples of words here, describing the Indians and the British, that reveal Franklin's feelings for each group.

SAYINGS OF POOR RICHARD

In 1732, Franklin wanted another income, and he turned to the business of publishing a yearly almanac. Almanacs were sure sellers: every house had one. An almanac was not only a calendar; it also calculated the tides and the phases of the moon, claimed to forecast the weather for the next year, and even provided astrological advice for those who believed in it. Many almanacs also supplied recipes, jokes, poems, and maxims.

Poor Richard's Almanack was Franklin's biggest publishing success, and it continued to appear for over twenty-five years. "Poor Richard" was an imaginary astrologer, who had a wife named Bridget. Over the years, a running dispute took place between Richard and the critical Bridget. One year, Bridget wrote the maxims, to answer those her husband had written the year before on female idleness. Once, Bridget went through the whole almanac and included better weather forecasts so that women would know the good days for drying their clothes.

Franklin took Poor Richard's wit and widsom where he found it—from old sayings in other languages, from other writers, from popular adages. He never hesitated to rework the texts to suit his own purposes. For example, for the 1758 almanac, Franklin skimmed all his previous editions to compose a single speech on economy. Poor Richard claimed to have heard an old man, Father Abraham, deliver the speech at an auction. This speech, called "The Way to Wealth," has become one of the best known of Franklin's works. It has been mistakenly believed to be representative of Poor Richard's wisdom. Poor Richard often called for prudence and thrift, but he just as often favored extravagance.

1. Love your neighbor; yet don't pull down your hedge.

2. If a man empties his purse into his head, no man can take it away from him. An investment in knowledge always pays the best interest.

3. Three may keep a secret if two of them are dead.

4. Tart words make no friends; a spoonful of honey will catch more flies than a gallon of vinegar.

5. Glass, china, and reputation are easily cracked and never well mended.

6. Fish and visitors smell in three days.

7. He that lieth down with dogs shall rise up with fleas.

8. One today is worth two tomorrows.

9. A truly great man will neither trample on a worm nor sneak to an emperor.

10. A little neglect may breed mischief; for want of a nail the shoe was lost; for want of a shoe the horse was lost; for want of a horse the rider was lost; for want of the rider the battle was lost.

11. If you would know the value of money, go and try to borrow some; he that goes a-borrowing goes a-sorrowing.

12. He that composes himself is wiser than he that composes books.

13. He that is of the opinion that money will do everything may well be suspected of doing everything for money.

14. If a man could have half his wishes, he would double his troubles.

15. 'Tis hard for an empty bag to stand upright.

16. A small leak will sink a great ship.

17. A plowman on his legs is higher than a gentleman on his knees.

18. None preaches better than the ant, and she says nothing.

19. There are no ugly loves nor handsome prisons.

20. Keep your eyes wide open before marriage, but shut afterward.

21. Nothing brings more pain than too much pleasure; nothing more bondage than too much liberty.

Dost thou love life? then do not squander time, for that is the stuff life is made of.

The sleeping fox catches no poultry. There will be sleeping enough in the grave.

Illustration from *Poor Richard's Almanack*. Engraving.

Yale University Library, New Haven, Connecticut.

Responding to the Maxims

Analyzing the Maxims

Interpreting Meanings

1. The sharpness of these sayings is partly due to Franklin's **ironic** view of human nature and human relationships. People, he implies, are not always what they would like to be (or what they think they are). Which of these sayings reflect this attitude?
2. Franklin is sometimes criticized for equating virtue with wealth and success. Which of these sayings support that criticism? Which do not?
3. A character in a story by Nathaniel Hawthorne says that he does not like Franklin's proverbs because "they are all about getting money or saving it." Hawthorne thought that the proverbs taught people only a very small proportion of their duties. What sorts of duties do you think Hawthorne felt were omitted from Poor Richard's sayings? Do you agree?
4. Take at least five of these maxims and apply each to a situation in contemporary life—to politics, society, family life, social and private morality, or business.

Writing About the Maxims

A Creative Response

Analyzing Contemporary Maxims. Contemporary Americans are still fond of maxims. Make a list of ten popular sayings or slogans; you'll find some on bumper stickers, some on tee shirts, and some in advertisements on TV and in magazines. Then make up at least three maxims of your own.

Primary Sources
A Letter to Samuel Mather

Samuel Mather was Cotton Mather's son and the last of the Mather Dynasty, which comprised four generations of famous New England ministers and theologians. Samuel Mather was born the same year as Franklin, and both are believed to have studied penmanship under Mrs. Sarah Kemble Knight (see page 31). The occasion for this letter was Samuel Mather's gift to Franklin of his last book, *The Dying Legacy.* Franklin writes from his post in France.

". . . When I was a boy, I met with a book entitled *Essays to do Good,* which I think was written by your father. It had been so little regarded by a former possessor that several leaves of it were torn out; but the remainder gave me such a turn of thinking, as to have an influence on my conduct through life; for I have always set a greater value on the character of a *doer of good* than on any other kind of reputation; and if I have been, as you seem to think, a useful citizen, the public owes the advantage of it to that book.

"You mention your being in your 78th year; I am in my 79th; we are grown old together. It is now more than 60 years since I left Boston, but I remember well both your father and grandfather, having heard them both in the pulpit, and seen them in their houses. The last time I saw your father was in the beginning of 1724, when I visited him after my first trip to Pennsylvania. He received me in his library, and on my taking leave showed me a shorter way out of the house through a narrow passage, which was crossed by a beam overhead. We were still talking as I withdrew, he accompanying me behind, and I turning partly toward him, when he said hastily, 'Stoop, stoop!' I did not understand him, till I felt my head hit against the beam. He was a man that never missed any occasion to giving instruction, and upon this he said to me, 'You are young, and have the world before you; stoop as you go through it, and you will miss many hard thumps.' This advice, thus beat into my head, has frequently been of use to me; and I often think of it, when I see pride mortified, and misfortunes brought upon people by their carrying their heads too high.

"I long much to see again my native place, and to lay my bones there. I left it in 1723; I visited it in 1733, 1743, 1753, and 1763. In 1773 I was in England; in 1775 I had a sight of it, but could not enter, it being in possession of the enemy. I did hope to have been there in 1783, but could not obtain my dismissal from this employment here; and now I fear I shall never have that happiness. My best wishes however attend my dear country. *Esto perpetua* [May she endure forever]. It is now blest with an excellent constitution; may it last forever! . . ."

—B. Franklin

View of the Long Wharf and Part of Boston
by Lt. Richard Byron (1764). Watercolor.

The Bostonian Society, Boston.

Patrick Henry
(1736–1799)

Patrick Henry's impressive oratorical powers made him famous in the public life of Virginia and the Colonies. Born in a frontier region of Virginia, Henry was raised in a cultured although modest environment. During his youth, the country was undergoing the religious revival known as the Great Awakening, and young Henry often accompanied his mother to hear the sermons of the great traveling preachers.

As a young man, Henry made several unsuccessful stabs at farming and merchant life before discovering his true calling: the law. In 1765, when he was twenty-nine, he was chosen to represent his region in the Virginia House of Burgesses. His first great speech was a declaration of resistance to the Stamp Act of that year, a form of taxation passed by the British Parliament that required stamps to be used on all newspapers and public documents. William Wirt, Henry's admirer and biographer, described the dramatic climax of this speech:

> [Henry] exclaimed, in a voice of thunder, and with the look of a god, "Caesar had his Brutus—Charles I, his Cromwell—and George III—" ("Treason," cried the speaker—"treason, treason," echoed from every part of the house. It was one of those trying moments which is decisive of character. Henry faltered not for an instant; but rising to a loftier attitude, and fixing on the speaker an eye of the most determined fire, he finished his sentence with the firmest emphasis)—"may profit by their example. If this be treason, make the most of it."

This speech was so successful that Patrick Henry's political fortunes were secured. For the next ten years, he was one of the most powerful figures in Virginia politics.

Henry was tall and lank, "with a dark sour look," as the historian Gary Wills has written, "which his preacher's clothes made more intriguing. . . . He had the actor's trick, in his oratory, of lifting his whole body up toward climaxes, along with his voice, as if he could add cubits by wanting to. . . . No one who be-

Patrick Henry by an unknown artist (early 19th century). Oil.

The Shelburne Museum, Shelburne, Vermont.

held him incandescent with a Cause ever forgot the experience . . ."

His famous "liberty or death" speech was made in 1775, when the Colonies were nearing the breaking point. Following the Boston Tea Party in December of 1773, the British had closed the port of Boston and inaugurated other harsh measures referred to by the colonists as the "Intolerable Acts." When the First Continental Congress protested these acts, the British Crown relieved the Colonies of taxation on a number of conditions. One condition was that the colonists fully support British rule and contribute toward the maintenance of British troops in America, whose numbers were increasing greatly. On March 20, 1775, the Virginia House of Burgesses held a convention in St. John's Episcopal Church in Richmond to decide how to respond to the growing British military threat. George Washington and Thomas Jefferson were both present.

On March 23, after several speeches in favor

of compromise with the British, Patrick Henry rose to defend his resolution to take up arms against the British. A clergyman who was present later recalled that during Henry's speech he felt "sick with excitement." As the speech reached its climax, Patrick Henry is said to have grabbed an ivory letter opener and plunged it toward his breast with the word *Death*.

Henry persuaded the delegation. The Virginia Convention voted to arm its people against England. A few weeks later, on April 19, the battle of Lexington, in Massachusetts, ignited the Revolutionary War. By June 15, the Revolution had been formalized by the raising of an army under General George Washington. On July 4 of the following year, the Declaration of Independence was adopted in Philadelphia.

Although this speech is one of the most famous in all American oratory, no manuscript of it exists. The traditionally accepted text was pieced together by Henry's biographer, William Wirt, forty years after the speech was given.

SPEECH TO THE VIRGINIA CONVENTION

As you read Henry's speech, try to envision the physical surroundings of its delivery: an eighteenth-century church in Richmond, Virginia. What elements in the speech remind you of the methods used by preachers such as Jonathan Edwards and his contemporaries, whom Henry himself may have heard as a boy? Are these features still current today in the speeches of preachers and politicians? What kind of effect are they intended to have on an audience?

Mr. President: No man thinks more highly than I do of the patriotism, as well as abilities, of the very worthy gentlemen who have just addressed the House. But different men often see the same subject in different lights; and, therefore, I hope that it will not be thought disrespectful to those gentlemen, if, entertaining as I do, opinions of a character very opposite to theirs, I shall speak forth my sentiments freely and without reserve. This is no time for ceremony. The question before the House is one of awful moment to this country. For my own part I consider it as nothing less than a question of freedom or slavery; and in proportion to the magnitude of the subject ought to be the freedom of the debate. It is only in this way that we can hope to arrive at truth, and fulfill the great responsibility which we hold to God and our country. Should I keep back my opinions at such a time, through fear of giving offense, I should consider myself as guilty of treason toward my country, and of an act of disloyalty toward the majesty of heaven, which I revere above all earthly kings.

Mr. President, it is natural to man to indulge in the illusions of hope. We are apt to shut our eyes against a painful truth, and listen to the song of that siren, till she transforms us into beasts. Is this the part of wise men, engaged in a great and arduous struggle for liberty? Are we disposed to be of the number of those who, having eyes, see not, and having ears, hear not, the things which so nearly concern their temporal salvation? For my part, whatever anguish of spirit it may cost, I am willing to know the whole truth; to know the worst and to provide for it.

I have but one lamp by which my feet are guided; and that is the lamp of experience. I know of no way of judging of the future but by the past. And judging by the past, I wish to know what there has been in the conduct of the British ministry for the last ten years, to justify those hopes with which gentlemen have been pleased to solace

*Patrick Henry Speaking Against the Stamp Act in the
Virginia House of Burgesses in 1765* by F. Rothermel (1851).

Patrick Henry Memorial Foundation,
Brookneal, Virginia.

themselves and the House? Is it that insidious smile with which our petition[1] has been lately received? Trust it not, sir; it will prove a snare to your feet. Suffer not yourselves to be betrayed with a kiss. Ask yourselves how this gracious reception of our petition comports with these warlike preparations which cover our waters and darken our land. Are fleets and armies necessary to a work of love and reconciliation? Have we shown ourselves so unwilling to be reconciled, that force must be called in to win back our love? Let us not deceive ourselves, sir. These are the implements of war and subjugation; the last arguments to which kings resort.

I ask gentlemen, sir, what means this martial array, if its purpose be not to force us to submission? Can gentlemen assign any other possible motives for it? Has Great Britain any enemy, in this quarter of the world, to call for all this accumulation of navies and armies? No, sir, she has none. They are meant for us; they can be meant for no other. They are sent over to bind and rivet upon us those chains which the British ministry have been so long forging. And what have we to oppose to them? Shall we try argument? Sir, we have been trying that for the last ten years. Have we anything new to offer on the subject? Nothing. We have held the subject up in every light of which it is capable; but it has been all in vain. Shall we resort to entreaty and humble supplication? What terms shall we find which have not been already exhausted? Let us not, I beseech you, sir, deceive ourselves longer. Sir, we have done everything that could be done, to avert the storm which is now coming on. We have petitioned; we have remonstrated; we have supplicated; we have prostrated ourselves before the throne, and have implored its interposition to arrest the tyrannical hands of the ministry and Parliament. Our petitions have been slighted; our remonstrances have produced additional violence and insult; our supplications have been disregarded; and we have been spurned, with contempt, from the foot of the throne. In vain, after these things, may we indulge the fond hope of peace and reconciliation. There is no longer any room for hope. If we wish to be free—if we mean to preserve inviolate those inestimable privileges for which we have been so long contending—if we mean not basely to abandon the noble struggle in which we have been so long engaged, and which we have pledged ourselves never to abandon until the glorious object of our contest shall be obtained, we must fight! I repeat it, sir, we must fight! An appeal to arms and to the God of Hosts is all that is left us!

They tell us, sir, that we are weak; unable to cope with so formidable an adversary. But when shall we be stronger? Will it be the next week, or the next year? Will it be when we are totally disarmed, and when a British guard shall be stationed in every house? Shall we gather strength by irresolution and inaction? Shall we acquire the means of effectual resistance, by lying supinely on our backs, and hugging the delusive phantom of hope, until our enemies shall have bound us hand and foot? Sir, we are not weak, if we make proper use of the means which the God of nature hath placed in our power. Three millions of people, armed in the holy cause of liberty, and in such a country as that which we possess, are invincible by any force which our enemy can send against us. Besides, sir, we shall not fight our battles alone. There is a just God who presides over the destinies of nations; and who will raise up friends to fight our battles for us. The battle, sir, is not to the strong alone; it is to the vigilant, the active, the brave. Besides, sir, we have no election.[2] If we were base enough to desire it, it is now too late to retire from the contest. There is no retreat, but in submission and slavery! Our chains are forged! Their clanking may be heard on the plains of Boston! The war is inevitable—and let it come! I repeat it, sir, let it come!

It is in vain, sir, to extenuate the matter. Gentlemen may cry peace, peace—but there is no peace. The war is actually begun! The next gale that sweeps from the north will bring to our ears the clash of resounding arms! Our brethren are already in the field! Why stand we here idle? What is it that gentlemen wish? What would they have? Is life so dear, or peace so sweet, as to be purchased at the price of chains and slavery? Forbid it, Almighty God! I know not what course others may take; but as for me, give me liberty, or give me death!

---

1. **our petition:** Henry refers to the First Continental Congress's protest against new taxation laws, which led King George III to retract those laws conditionally.

2. **election:** choice.

Responding to the Speech

Analyzing the Speech

Identifying Facts

1. According to the first two paragraphs of this speech, why is Henry speaking out?
2. Countering the arguments of opponents is essential to any persuasive speech or essay. How does Henry deal with the fact that the British have yielded somewhat to the Continental Congress's petition?
3. According to Henry, why do the colonists have no choice but to go to war?

Interpreting Meanings

4. State in your own words the **main idea** of Henry's impassioned speech.
5. Throughout his speech, Henry uses **metaphors** to seize his listeners' feelings and at the same time to advance his arguments. In paragraph four, what metaphor does he use to describe the coming war?
6. Perhaps like the preachers whose sermons he heard as a child, Patrick Henry makes use of a time-honored device in this speech: the **rhetorical question.** This is a question for which no answer is provided because the answer is obvious. Find a series of rhetorical questions in the fifth paragraph of this speech. What is the answer to each question? Why do you think the speaker makes these points in the form of rhetorical questions rather than in the form of straightforward statements?
7. Because Henry's audience knew classical mythology and, especially, the Bible, the orator knew he could count on certain **allusions** to have emotional effects. Look up the classical and Biblical passages alluded to in each of the following statements. How would each one relate to the conflict in Virginia in 1775? Could any of them relate to life today?

   a. "We are apt to . . . listen to the song of that siren, till she transforms us into beasts." (*Odyssey,* Books 10 and 12)

   b. "Are we disposed to be of the number of those who, having eyes, see not, and having ears, hear not the things which so nearly concern their temporal salvation?" (Ezekiel 12:2)

   c. "Suffer not yourselves to be betrayed with a kiss." (Luke 22:47–48)

8. What contemporary people—individuals or groups—can you name who might use Henry's closing sentence as a slogan?

Writing About the Speech

A Creative Response

1. **Reporting on the Speech.** Pretend you are a reporter who listened to Henry's speech. Write a newspaper article about the event.

A Critical Response

2. **Comparing and Contrasting Speeches.** Compare and contrast Henry's speech with Jonathan Edwards's 1741 sermon "Sinners in the Hands of an Angry God" (see page 37). In your essay, consider the specific ways the speeches are similar and dissimilar. A chart like the following will help you organize your material.

	Edwards	Henry
Speaker's purpose		
Audience		
Metaphors and allusions		
Appeals to emotion		
Appeals to reason		
Use of rhetorical questions and repetition		
Main idea		

PERSUASION

Persuasion is a form of speaking or writing that aims to move a particular audience to take action. The goal of persuasion is not merely to win the audience's agreement but also to make the audience *act*. One of the most powerful examples of persuasion in American literature is Patrick Henry's "Give me liberty, or give me death!" speech. Jonathan Edwards's sermon on page 37 is another excellent example of persuasion. With that sermon, Edwards wanted to persuade his congregation to take the action necessary to save themselves from plummeting into the pit of hell. Patrick Henry wanted the Virginia legislators to put their state in a position of armed defense.

A persuasive speech or essay generally includes: (1) a call to action; (2) proof supporting the speaker's position and motives for taking the action; (3) a heightened style intended to move the audience emotionally. Here is what two critics have said about the style of persuasion. As you read their analysis, consider how well you think it applies to Patrick Henry's speech.

> Along with the emphasis on action and the fusion of proof and motive, the third characteristic stressed in persuasion is the emotional and imaginative appeal of the style. An old axiom states that you cannot move another person to laughter or to tears unless you first laugh or weep yourself. If you wish to excite an audience, you are probably going to be excited yourself, and accordingly you will adopt an exciting style. A plain unemotional style befits an exposition of facts, such as the working of a gasoline engine, and will be adopted just as naturally.
>
> Persuasion, then, is notable for its emphasis on action, the coherence of proof and motive, and a heightened emotional and imaginative style. These are the three essential elements, and they point to other important characteristics. Because persuasion often aims at a specific audience, it is a more personal and direct form of discourse than exposition and argument. A persuasive writer speaks not only from mind to mind, but from heart to heart. In the final analsysis an audience is won over not only by the speaker's arguments and explanations but by the speaker's personality. We do not judge persuasion by the morals of the writer, but we do judge the moral meaning of the speech. This means simply that we respond to ideas that appeal to our sense of honor, justice, and integrity, especially when those ideas are uttered in a manner that is appropriate to the importance of the subject, the dignity of the occasion, and the respect that a speaker owes to the opinions of mankind. At bottom we submit to a legitimate ethical appeal, the morality of mind, in the persuasive effort. No trick of style, no demagogic cleverness, no learning however wide can impart moral character to persuasion. This moral character stems from the writer's own reasoned conviction and passionate belief.
>
> —Francis Connolly and Gerald Levin

Identify at least five examples of Patrick Henry's "heightened style." Look for expressions that don't sound as though they would have occurred to him in a casual conversation.

Eagle and snake sternboard attributed to Skillin Shop, Boston (1790). Gilded wood, metal, and glass.

Collection of Dr. William Greenspon. Photo: Whitney Museum of American Art.

Thomas Paine
(1737–1809)

One of the most popular exponents of the Age of Reason—the most persuasive writer of the American Revolution—came from an unlikely background. The poorly educated son of a corset maker, Thomas Paine was born in England. He spent the first thirty-seven years of his life drifting through a number of occupations: corset maker, grocer, tobacconist, schoolteacher, and excise man (a government employee who examined goods and levied excise taxes on them). In 1774, Paine was dismissed from the excise for attempting to organize the employees in a demand for higher wages (an unusual activity in those days). Like many others at that time and since, he came to America to make a new start.

With a letter of introduction from Ben Franklin, whom he had met in London, Paine went to Philadelphia, where he worked as a journalist. In the disagreement between England and the Colonies, he instantly identified with the cause of the underdog. In January of 1776, he published the most important pamphlet in support of American independence: *Common Sense.*

In this forty-seven-page pamphlet, Paine denounced King George III as a "royal brute" and asserted that a continent should not remain tied to an island. The pamphlet sold half a million copies—in a country whose total population was roughly two and a quarter million.

That same year—1776—Paine joined the Continental Army as it retreated across New Jersey to Philadelphia. During the journey, he began writing what would be a series of sixteen pamphlets called *The American Crisis.* In these, he commented on the course of the war and urged his countrymen not to give up the fight. The first of these pamphlets was read to Washington's troops in December of 1776, a few days before they recrossed the Delaware River to attack Trenton.

After the Revolution, Paine lived peacefully in New York and New Jersey until 1787, when he returned to Europe. There he became involved once more in radical revolutionary politics.

Revolutionary times were over in America, but they were just beginning in France. On July

Thomas Paine by James Watson after Charles Wilson Peale (late 18th century). Colored mezzotint.

14, 1789, the French Revolution began in Paris with the storming of the Bastille by an angry mob. Paine, who considered himself a citizen of the world, soon found a platform for his ideas. In France in 1791, he composed *The Rights of Man,* a reply to the English statesman Edmund Burke's condemnation of the French Revolution.

The Rights of Man was an impassioned defense of republican government and a call to the English people to overthrow their king. Although he was outside the country, Paine was tried for treason and outlawed from England. Safe in France from English law, he was briefly celebrated as a hero of the French Revolution but soon imprisoned for being a citizen of an enemy nation (England). James Monroe, the American minister to France at the time, secured Paine's release in 1794 by insisting that Paine was an American citizen.

The first part of Paine's last great work, *The Age of Reason,* appeared that year; the second part was published two years later. *The Age of Reason* was Paine's statement of belief and an explanation of the principles of deism (see page 69). The book was controversial in America, where it was not fully understood and was thought to be atheistic.

When the author of the book finally returned to America in 1802, he found himself an outcast.

He had been stripped of his right to vote, he had no money, and he was continually harassed as a dangerous radical and atheist. When he died in New York, Paine was denied burial in consecrated ground. His body was buried in a corner of the farm he owned in New Rochelle.

Even in death, though, Thomas Paine was not allowed to rest. In 1819, an English sympathizer dug up Paine's body and removed it and the coffin to England, intending to erect a monument to the author of *The Rights of Man*. But no monument was ever built. The last record of Paine's remains shows that the coffin and the bones were acquired by a furniture dealer in England in 1844.

THE CRISIS, NO. 1

Patrick Henry's words were composed to be heard by an audience, but Thomas Paine wrote his pamphlets to be read. Nevertheless, parts of *The American Crisis* use vivid imagery and rhetorical techniques. You can better appreciate Paine's forceful style by trying an experiment. Read the first paragraph aloud, as if you were addressing a live audience.

These are the times that try men's souls. The summer soldier and the sunshine patriot will, in this crisis, shrink from the service of their country; but he that stands it now deserves the love and thanks of man and woman. Tyranny, like hell, is not easily conquered; yet we have this consolation with us, that the harder the conflict, the more glorious the triumph. What we obtain too cheap, we esteem too lightly: it is dearness only that gives everything its value. Heaven knows how to put a proper price upon its goods; and it would be strange indeed if so celestial an article as freedom should not be highly rated. Britain, with an army to enforce her tyranny, has declared that she has a right (not only to tax) but "to bind us in all cases whatsoever,"[1] and if being bound in that manner is not slavery, then is there not such a thing as slavery upon earth. Even the expression is impious; for so unlimited a power can belong only to God.

Whether the independence of the continent was declared too soon, or delayed too long, I will not now enter into as an argument; my own simple opinion is, that had it been eight months earlier, it would have been much better. We did not make a proper use of last winter, neither could we, while we were in a dependent state. However, the fault, if it were one, was all our own; we have none to blame but ourselves. But no great deal is lost yet. All that Howe[2] has been doing for this month past is rather a ravage than a conquest, which the spirit of the Jerseys,[3] a year ago, would have quickly repulsed, and which time and a little resolution will soon recover.

I have as little superstition in me as any man living, but my secret opinion has ever been, and still is, that God Almighty will not give up a people to military destruction, or leave them unsupportedly to perish, who have so earnestly and so repeatedly sought to avoid the calamities of war, by every decent method which wisdom could invent. Neither have I so much of the infidel in me as to suppose that He has relinquished the government of the world, and given us up to the care of devils; and as I do not, I cannot see on what grounds the King of Britain can look up to heaven for help against us: a common murderer, a highwayman, or a housebreaker has as good a pretense as he.

---

1. **"to bind . . . whatsoever"**: Part of the British Parliament's response to Colonial protest over the "Intolerable Acts" was to rescind taxes while retaining the right to tax and "to bind [the Colonies] in all cases whatsoever."

2. **Howe:** Lord William Howe, commander of the British forces in America.
3. **Jerseys:** New Jersey was divided into East and West Jersey at the time.

'Tis surprising to see how rapidly a panic will sometimes run through a country. All nations and ages have been subject to them: Britain has trembled like an ague[4] at the report of a French fleet of flat-bottomed boats; and in the fourteenth century the whole English army, after ravaging the kingdom of France, was driven back like men petrified with fear; and this brave exploit was performed by a few broken forces collected and headed by a woman, Joan of Arc. Would that heaven might inspire some Jersey maid to spirit up her countrymen, and save her fair fellow sufferers from ravage and ravishment! Yet panics, in some cases, have their uses; they produce as much good as hurt. Their duration is always short; the mind soon grows through them, and acquires a firmer habit than before. But their peculiar advantage is that they are the touchstones of sincerity and hypocrisy, and bring things and men to light, which might otherwise have lain forever undiscovered. In fact, they have the same effect on secret traitors, which an imaginary apparition would have upon a private murderer. They sift out the hidden thoughts of man, and hold them up in public to the world. Many a disguised Tory[5] has lately shown his head, that shall penitentially solemnize with curses the day on which Howe arrived upon the Delaware.

As I was with the troops at Fort Lee, and marched with them to the edge of Pennsylvania, I am well acquainted with many circumstances, which those who live at a distance know but little or nothing of. Our situation there was exceedingly cramped, the place being a narrow neck of land between the North River[6] and the Hackensack. Our force was inconsiderable, being not one fourth so great as Howe could bring against us. We had no army at hand to have relieved the garrison, had we shut ourselves up and stood on our defense. Our ammunition, light artillery, and the best part of our stores had been removed on the apprehension that Howe would endeavor to penetrate the Jerseys, in which case Fort Lee could be of no use to us; for it must occur to every thinking man, whether in the army or not, that these kind of field forts are only for temporary purposes, and last in use no longer than the enemy directs his force against the particular object, which such forts are raised to defend. Such was our situation and condition at Fort Lee on the morning of the 20th of November, when an officer arrived with information that the enemy with 200 boats had landed about seven miles above. Major General Green, who commanded the garrison, immediately ordered them under arms, and sent express to General Washington at the town of Hackensack, distant, by the way of the ferry, six miles. Our first object was to secure the bridge over the Hackensack, which laid up the river between the enemy and us, about six miles from us, and three from them. General Washington arrived in about three quarters of an hour, and marched

Title page of the first edition of
Common Sense (1776).

The Library of Congress.

---

4. **ague:** fit of shivering.
5. **Tory:** supporter of British rule.
6. **North River:** the Hudson River.

at the head of the troops toward the bridge, which place I expected we should have a brush for; however, they did not choose to dispute it with us, and the greatest part of our troops went over the bridge, the rest over the ferry, except some which passed at a mill on a small creek, between the bridge and the ferry, and made their way through some marshy grounds up to the town of Hackensack, and there passed the river. We brought off as much baggage as the wagons could contain; the rest was lost. The simple object was to bring off the garrison, and march them on till they could be strengthened by the Jersey or Pennsylvania militia, so as to be enabled to make a stand. We stayed four days at Newark, collected our outposts with some of the Jersey militia, and marched out twice to meet the enemy, on being informed that they were advancing, though our numbers were greatly inferior to theirs. Howe, in my little opinion, committed a great error in generalship in not throwing a body of forces off from Staten Island through Amboy,[7] by which means he might have seized all our stores at Brunswick, and intercepted our march into Pennsylvania; but if we believe the power of hell to be limited, we must likewise believe that their agents are under some providential control.

I shall not now attempt to give all the particulars of our retreat to the Delaware; suffice it for the present to say, that both officers and men, though greatly harassed and fatigued, frequently without rest, covering, or provision, the inevitable consequences of a long retreat, bore it with a manly and martial spirit. All their wishes centered in one, which was that the country would turn out and help them to drive the enemy back. Voltaire[8] has remarked that King William[9] never appeared to full advantage but in difficulties and in action; the same remark may be made on General Washington, for the character fits him. There is a natural firmness in some minds which cannot be unlocked by trifles, but which, when unlocked, discovers a cabinet of fortitude; and I reckon it among those kind of public blessings, which we do not immediately see, that God hath blessed him with uninterrupted health, and given him a mind that can even flourish upon care.

---

7. **Amboy:** Perth Amboy, New Jersey.
8. **Voltaire:** French philosopher and writer (1694–1778), who had a great influence on Revolutionary thinkers.
9. **King William:** William III of England (reigned 1689–1702).

I shall conclude this paper with some miscellaneous remarks on the state of our affairs; and shall begin with asking the following question: Why is it that the enemy have left the New England provinces, and made these middle ones the seat of war? The answer is easy: New England is not infested with Tories, and we are. I have been tender in raising the cry against these men, and used numberless arguments to show them their danger, but it will not do to sacrifice a world either to their folly or their baseness. The period is now arrived, in which either they or we must change our sentiments, or one or both must fall. And what is a Tory? Good God! What is He? I should not be afraid to go with a hundred Whigs against a thousand Tories, were they to attempt to get into arms. Every Tory is a coward; for servile, slavish, self-interested fear is the foundation of Toryism; and a man under such influence, though he may be cruel, never can be brave.

But, before the line of irrecoverable separation be drawn between us, let us reason the matter together: Your conduct is an invitation to the enemy, yet not one in a thousand of you has heart enough to join him. Howe is as much deceived by you as the American cause is injured by you. He expects you will take up arms, and flock to his standard, with muskets on your shoulders. Your opinions are of no use to him, unless you support him personally, for 'tis soldiers, and not Tories, that he wants.

I once felt all that kind of anger, which a man ought to feel, against the mean principles that are held by the Tories: a noted one, who kept a tavern at Amboy, was standing at his door, with as pretty a child in his hand, about eight or nine years old, as I ever saw, and after speaking his mind as freely as he thought was prudent, finished with this unfatherly expression, "Well! Give me peace in my day." Not a man lives on the continent but fully believes that a separation must sometime or other finally take place, and a generous parent should have said, "If there must be trouble, let it be in my day, that my child may have peace;" and this single reflection, well applied, is sufficient to awaken every man to duty. Not a place upon earth might be so happy as America. Her situation is remote from all the wrangling world, and she has nothing to do but to trade with them. A man can distinguish himself between temper and principle, and I am as confident, as I am that God governs the world, that America will never be happy till she gets clear of foreign dominion. Wars, without ceasing, will break out till that period arrives, and the continent must in the end be conqueror; for though the flame of liberty may sometimes cease to shine, the coal can never expire.

America did not, nor does not, want[10] force; but she wanted a proper application of that force. Wisdom is not the purchase of a day, and it is no wonder that we should err at the first setting off. From an excess of tenderness, we were unwilling to raise an army, and trusted our cause to the temporary defense of a well-meaning militia. A summer's experience has now taught us better; yet with those troops, while they were collected, we were able to set bounds to the progress of the enemy, and thank God! They are again assembling. I always considered militia as the best troops in the world for a sudden exertion, but they will not do for a long campaign. Howe, it is probable, will make an attempt on this city [Philadelphia], should he fail on this side the Delaware, he is ruined; if he succeeds, our cause is not ruined. He stakes all on his side against a part on ours; admitting he succeeds, the consequences will be that armies from both ends of the continent will march to assist their suffering friends in the middle states; for he cannot go everywhere: it is impossible. I consider Howe as the greatest enemy the Tories have; he is bringing a war into their country, which, had it not been for him and partly for themselves, they had been clear of. Should he now be expelled, I wish with all the devotion of a Christian that the names of Whig and Tory may never more be mentioned; but should the Tories give him encouragement to come, or assistance if he come, I as sincerely wish that our next year's arms may expel them from the continent, and the Congress appropriate their possessions to the relief of those who have suffered in well-doing. A single successful battle next year will settle the whole. America could carry on a two years' war by the confiscation of the property of disaffected persons, and be made happy by their expulsion. Say not that this is revenge; call it rather the soft resentment of a suffering people, who, having no object in view but the good of all, have staked their own all upon a seemingly doubtful event. Yet it is folly to argue against determined hardness; eloquence may strike the ear, and the language of sorrow draw forth the tear of compassion, but

nothing can reach the heart that is steeled with prejudice.

Quitting this class of men, I turn with the warm ardor of a friend to those who have nobly stood, and are yet determined to stand the matter out. I call not upon a few, but upon all; not on this state or that state, but on every state: Up and help us; lay your shoulders to the wheel; better have too much force than too little, when so great an object is at stake. Let it be told to the future world that in the depth of winter, when nothing but hope and virtue could survive, that the city and the country, alarmed at one common danger, came forth to meet and to repulse it. Say not that thousands are gone, turn out your tens of thousands;[11] throw not the burden of the day upon Providence, but "show your faith by your works"[12] that God may bless you. It matters not where you live, or what rank of life you hold, the evil or the blessing will reach you all. The far and the near, the home counties and the back,[13] the rich and poor will suffer or rejoice alike. The heart that feels not now is dead: the blood of his children will curse his cowardice who shrinks back at a time when a little might have saved the whole, and made them happy. I love the man that can smile in trouble, that can gather strength from distress, and grow brave by reflection. 'Tis the business of little minds to shrink; but he whose heart is firm, and whose conscience approves his conduct, will pursue his principles unto death. My own line of reasoning is to myself as straight and clear as a ray of light. Not all the treasures of the world, so far as I believe, could have induced me to support an offensive war, for I think it murder; but if a thief breaks into my house, burns and destroys my property, and kills or threatens to kill me, or those that are in it, and to "bind me in all cases whatsoever" to his absolute will, am I to suffer it? What signifies it to me, whether he who does it is a king or a common man; my countryman or not my countryman; whether it be done by an individual villain or an army of them? If we reason to the root of things we shall find no difference; neither can any just cause be assigned why we should punish in the one case and pardon in the other. Let them call me rebel, and welcome, I feel no

---

10. **want:** lack.

11. **thousands:** "Saul hath slain his thousands, and David his ten thousands" (1 Samuel 18:7).
12. **"show . . . works":** "Show me thy faith without thy works, and I will show thee my faith by my works" (James 2:18).
13. **back:** the back counties, or backwoods.

The Battle of Princeton, New Jersey
by William Mercer (1777). Oil.

concern from it; but I should suffer the misery of devils were I to make a whore of my soul by swearing allegiance to one whose character is that of a sottish, stupid, stubborn, worthless, brutish man. I conceive likewise a horrid idea in receiving mercy from a being, who at the last day shall be shrieking to the rocks and mountains to cover him, and fleeing with terror from the orphan, the widow, and the slain of America.

There are cases which cannot be overdone by language, and this is one. There are persons, too, who see not the full extent of the evil which threatens them; they solace themselves with hopes that the enemy, if he succeeds, will be merciful. It is the madness of folly to expect mercy from those who have refused to do justice; and even mercy, where conquest is the object, is only a trick of war; the cunning of the fox is as murderous as the violence of the wolf, and we ought to guard equally against both. Howe's first object is, partly by threats and partly by promises, to terrify or seduce the people to deliver up their arms and receive mercy. The ministry recommended the same plan to Gage,[14] and this is what the Tories call making their peace, "a peace which passeth all understanding"[15] indeed! A peace which would be the immediate forerunner of a worse ruin than any we have yet thought of. Ye men of Pennsylvania, do reason upon these things! Were the back counties to give up their arms, they would fall an easy prey to the Indians, who are all armed: this perhaps is what some Tories would not be sorry for. Were the home counties to deliver up their arms, they would be exposed to the resentment of the back counties, who would then have it in their power to chastise their defection at pleasure. And were any one state to give up its arms, that state must be garrisoned by all Howe's army of Britons and Hessians[16] to preserve it from the anger of the rest. Mutual fear is the principal link in the chain of mutual love, and woe be to that state that breaks the compact. Howe is mercifully inviting you to barbarous destruction, and men must be either rogues or fools that will not see it. I dwell not upon the vapors of imagination: I bring reason to your ears, and, in language as plain as A,B,C, hold up truth to your eyes.

I thank God that I fear not. I see no real cause for fear. I know our situation well, and can see the way out of it. While our army was collected, Howe dared not risk a battle; and it is no credit to him that he decamped from the White Plains,[17] and waited a mean opportunity to ravage the defenseless Jerseys; but it is great credit to us, that with a handful of men, we sustained an orderly retreat for near a hundred miles, brought off our ammunition, all our field pieces, the greatest part of our stores, and had four rivers to pass.

---

14. **Gage:** General Thomas Gage, Howe's predecessor.
15. **"a peace . . . understanding":** an ironic echo of St. Paul's Epistle to the Philippians 4:7.

16. **Hessians:** German mercenary troops from the region of Hesse and elsewhere who fought on the British side.
17. **White Plains:** Howe had defeated Washington at White Plains, New York, but had failed to press his advantage.

None can say that our retreat was precipitate, for we were near three weeks in performing it, that the country[18] might have time to come in. Twice we marched back to meet the enemy, and remained out till dark. The sign of fear was not seen in our camp, and had not some of the cowardly and disaffected inhabitants spread false alarms through the country, the Jerseys had never been ravaged. Once more we are again collected and collecting; our new army at both ends of the continent is recruiting fast, and we shall be able to open the next campaign with sixty thousand men, well armed and clothed. This is our situation, and who will may know it. By perseverance and fortitude, we have the prospect of a glorious issue; by cowardice and submission, the sad choice of a variety of evils—a ravaged country—a depopulated city—habitations without safety, and slavery without hope—our homes turned into barracks and bawdy houses for Hessians, and a future race to provide for, whose fathers we shall doubt of. Look on this picture and weep over it! And if there yet remains one thoughtless wretch who believes it not, let him suffer it unlamented.

Common Sense
1776

18. **country:** local volunteers.

Responding to the Pamphlet

Analyzing the Pamphlet

Identifying Facts

1. What reasons does Paine give for his confidence that Divine help will be given to the Americans and not to the British?
2. Washington's march across New Jersey to the Delaware was actually a retreat from General Howe's British forces. Explain how Paine makes the event seem positive, even heroic. How does he link the results of the retreat to Divine Providence?
3. Find details in the middle of the essay that identify at least part of Paine's audience. What **arguments** does he use to persuade these listeners of their errors?
4. Explain Paine's point in telling the anecdote about the Tory tavern keeper and his child.
5. What powerful emotional appeal does Paine make in the conclusion of his essay to sum up the choice facing the colonists? List the descriptive details that make this appeal especially vivid.

Interpreting Meanings

6. What is Paine's **main idea**? What are his chief supporting details?
7. The pamphlet opens with an emotional statement that is now famous, and it continues with two equally famous **images**. What kinds of people does Paine identify with summer and sunshine? Why are these images appropriate?
8. Explain the meaning of Paine's **metaphor**, "Mutual fear is the principal link in the chain of mutual love." Do you agree or disagree with this idea, and why?
9. An **analogy** is a comparison between two things that are alike in certain respects. Analogies are used often in argument and persuasion to demonstrate the logic of one idea by showing how it is similar to another, accepted idea. Analogies can be tricky, because few ideas or situations are completely alike in all aspects. What analogy does Paine draw when he talks about the thief (page 97)? What point is he making, and how might an opponent answer?
10. How do you think people today would respond to Paine's pamphlet? Are any of his arguments applicable to contemporary political situations? Explain.

Writing About the Pamphlet

A Creative Response

1. **Writing a Firsthand Account.** Imagine you are one of the volunteers who listened to this pamphlet being read a few days before Christmas 1776, just before you were to cross the frozen Delaware River and attack General Howe in Trenton. In a paragraph, explain how you felt while the pamphlet was being read, and describe the responses of the people around you.

A Critical Response

2. **Evaluating a Generalization.** "Not a place upon earth might be so happy as America. Her situation is remote from all the wrangling world, and she has nothing to do but to trade with them. . . . I am . . . confident . . . that America will never be happy till she gets clear of foreign dominion." In a brief essay, explain your evaluation of these words. How would you reply to Paine, in terms of the world as it exists today?

Thomas Jefferson (1743–1826)

Architect, botanist, paleontologist, linguist, musician, and statesman, Thomas Jefferson displayed the wide range of interests that we associate with the eighteenth-century mind at its best. President John F. Kennedy reminded listeners of this once at an official dinner honoring winners of the Nobel Prize. Kennedy said that the White House had not seen such a great collection of talent since Thomas Jefferson dined there alone. Like Benjamin Franklin, Jefferson longed for time for his own research; also like Franklin, he was too valuable to his country to be spared such time for very long.

Jefferson was born in the red-clay country of what is now Albemarle County, Virginia, on 400 acres of land that his father had acquired for a bowl of punch. (Like many Virginians, Jefferson's father was land-hungry. When he died, he left his son more than 5,000 acres.) The elder Jefferson, a surveyor and magistrate, died when Thomas was fourteen. But he had provided his son with an excellent classical education and encouraged the many scientific interests that would occupy Jefferson for the rest of his life.

After attending the College of William and Mary, Jefferson became a lawyer. Soon he was a member of the Virginia House of Burgesses, where he established friendships with other young public servants, such as Patrick Henry. He was a spokesman for the rights of personal liberty and religious freedom, and a vocal opponent of institutions that infringed on those rights. In 1774, he wrote a pamphlet called *A Summary View of the Rights of British America,* in which he urged the rejection of all British Parliamentary authority over the Colonies. The House of Burgesses considered the pamphlet's proposals too radical, but *A Summary View* established Jefferson's reputation as a writer and a thinker. Two years later, when he was thirty-three, his fame as a writer brought him an extraordinary opportunity. The Continental Congress elected him one of the authors of the Declaration of Independence.

Four other writers worked with him on the wording of the Declaration that was submitted to

Thomas Jefferson by Charles Wilson Peale (late 18th century).

Independence National Historical Park Collection.

the Congress: John Adams of Massachusetts; Roger Sherman of Connecticut; Robert L. Livingston of New York; and Benjamin Franklin of Pennsylvania. Few changes were made by these other writers, but the Congress insisted on several major alterations. Jefferson was upset by what he called "mutilations" of his document.

During the Revolution, Jefferson served for a time as governor of Virginia. When the British invaded Virginia, he retired to Monticello, the home he had designed himself. There he devoted himself to the pleasures of family life and to scientific research. He composed most of his *Notes on the State of Virginia* during this period.

Jefferson's second wife died in 1782. A year later he returned to public life, in part as an escape from private grief. He served as minister to France and, with Benjamin Franklin, helped to negotiate the treaty that formally ended the Revolutionary War in 1783. He later became George Washington's secretary of state. After losing the 1796 presidential election to John Adams, he served as Adams's vice-president (a post that, at that time, was awarded to the loser in the presidential contest).

In 1800, Jefferson was elected America's third president. A determined opponent of federal power, Jefferson was nevertheless responsible for one of the most sweeping federal actions of his age—the Louisiana Purchase. The acquisition from France of more than 820,000 square miles of western land would later be divided into thirteen states.

After his presidency ended in 1809, Jefferson retired once again to Monticello. Much of his energy during these years of retirement was devoted to establishing the University of Virginia. Jefferson helped to plan its courses of study and designed many of its buildings.

In 1826, both Jefferson (at eighty-three) and John Adams (at ninety) became gravely ill. Both hoped to live to see the fiftieth anniversary of the independence they had done so much to ensure. Jefferson died on the morning of July 4, several hours before Adams (whose last words were, "Thomas Jefferson still survives"). The epitaph Jefferson composed for himself clearly states which of his many accomplishments he considered most important:

Here was buried Thomas Jefferson, Author of the Declaration of Independence, of the Statute of Virginia for religious freedom, and Father of the University of Virginia.

FROM THE AUTOBIOGRAPHY

In this extract from his *Autobiography,* Jefferson offers a fascinating glimpse of how the most celebrated document in American history was put together. The underlined passages in the Declaration show the parts omitted by Congress. The words added by Congress are in the margins. As you read, think about why Congress may have made the changes it did in the original draft.

The Declaration of Independence

Congress proceeded the same day to consider the Declaration of Independence, which had been reported and lain on the table the Friday preceding, and on Monday referred to a committee of the whole. The pusillanimous[1] idea that we had friends in England worth keeping terms with, still haunted the minds of many. For this reason, those passages which conveyed censures on the people of England were struck out, lest they should give them offense. The clause too, reprobating the enslaving the inhabitants of Africa, was struck out in complaisance to South Carolina and Georgia, who had never attempted to restrain the importation of slaves, and who, on the contrary, still wished to continue it.

Our northern brethren also, I believe, felt a little tender under those censures; for though their people had very few slaves themselves, yet they had been pretty considerable carriers of them to others. The debates, having taken up the greater parts of the 2nd, 3rd, and 4th days of July, were, on the evening of the last, closed; the Declaration was reported by the committee, agreed to by the House, and signed by every member present, except Mr. Dickinson.[2] As the sentiments of men are known not only by what they receive, but what they reject also, I will state the form of the Declaration as originally reported. The parts struck out by Congress shall be distinguished by a black line drawn under them, and those inserted by them shall be placed in the margin, or in a concurrent column.

---

1. **pusillanimous** (pyo͞o's'l·an'ə·məs): cowardly.

2. **Mr. Dickinson:** John Dickinson of Pennsylvania, who opposed the Declaration.

A Declaration by the Representatives of the United States of America, in General Congress Assembled

When, in the course of human events, it becomes necessary for one people to dissolve the political bands which have connected them with another, and to assume among the powers of the earth the separate and equal station to which the laws of nature and of nature's God entitle them, a decent respect to the opinions of mankind requires that they should declare the causes which impel them to the separation.

We hold these truths to be self evident: that all men are created equal; that they are endowed by their Creator with inherent and inalienable rights; that among these are life, liberty, and the pursuit of happiness; that to secure these rights, governments are instituted among men, deriving their just powers from the consent of the governed; that whenever any form of government becomes destructive of these ends, it is the right of the people to alter or to abolish it, and to institute new government, laying its foundation on such principles, and organizing its powers in such form, as to them shall seem most likely to effect their safety and happiness. Prudence, indeed, will dictate that governments long established should not be changed for light and transient causes; and accordingly all experience hath shown that mankind are more disposed to suffer while evils are sufferable, than to right themselves by abolishing the forms to which they are accustomed. But when a long train of abuses and usurpations, begun at a distinguished[3] period and pursuing invariably the same object, evinces a design to reduce them under absolute despotism, it is their right, it is their duty to throw off such government, and to provide new guards for their future security. Such has been the patient sufferance of these colonies; and such is now the necessity which constrains them to expunge their former systems of government. The history of the present king of Great Britain is a history of unremitting injuries and usurpations, among which appears no solitary fact to contradict the uniform tenor of the rest, but all have in direct object the establishment of an absolute tyranny over these states. To prove this, let facts be submitted to a candid world for the truth of which we pledge a faith yet unsullied by falsehood.

He has refused his assent to laws the most wholesome and necessary for the public good.

He has forbidden his governors to pass laws of immediate and pressing importance, unless suspended in their operation till his assent should be obtained; and, when so suspended, he has utterly neglected to attend to them.

He has refused to pass other laws for the accommodation of large districts of people, unless those people would relinquish

(margin notes:) certain · alter · repeated · all having

---

3. **distinguished:** discernible.

The Declaration of Independence (detail)
by John Trumbull (1786–1794). Oil.

Yale University Art Gallery, New Haven, Connecticut.

Primary Sources
A Letter from Jefferson to His Daughter

In 1784, Jefferson was sent to Paris to work out the treaty ending the Revolutionary War. The next year he succeeded Benjamin Franklin as minister to France. He stayed in France for five years. His daughter Martha was with him, but his "dear Patsy" stayed at home. (The wrist Jefferson complains of had been injured years before in a fall from his horse.)

Aix-en-Provence, March 28, 1787

"I was happy, my dear Patsy, to receive, on my arrival here, your letter, informing me of your good health and occupations. I have not written you sooner because I have been almost constantly on the road. My journey hitherto has been a very pleasing one. It was undertaken with the hope that the mineral waters of this place might restore strength to my wrist. Other considerations also concurred, instruction, amusement, and abstraction from business, of which I had too much at Paris. I am glad to learn that you are employed in things new and good, in your music and drawing. You know what have been my fears for some time past—that you do not employ yourself so closely as I could wish. You have promised me a more assiduous attention, and I have great confidence in what you promise. It is your future happiness which interests me, and nothing can contribute more to it (moral rectitude always excepted) than the contracting a habit of industry and activity. Of all the cankers of human happiness none corrodes with so silent, yet so baneful a tooth as indolence. . . . It is while we are young that the habit of industry is formed. If not then, it never is afterward. The fortune of our lives, therefore, depends on employing well the short period of youth. If at any moment, my dear, you catch yourself in idleness, start from it as you would from the precipice of a gulf. You are not, however, to consider yourself as unemployed while taking exercise. That is necessary for your health, and health is the first of all objects. For this reason, if you leave your dancing master for the summer, you must increase your other exercise.

"I do not like your saying that you are unable to read the ancient print of your Livy,[1] but [except] with the aid of your master. We are always equal to what we undertake with resolution. A little degree of this will enable you to decipher your Livy. If you always lean on your master, you will never be able to proceed without him. It is a part of the American character to consider nothing as desperate—to surmount every difficulty by resolution and contrivance. In Europe there are shops for every want: its inhabitants therefore have no idea that their wants can be furnished otherwise. Remote from all other aid, we are obliged to invent and to execute; to find means within ourselves, and not to lean on others. Consider, therefore, the conquering your Livy as an exercise in the habit of surmounting difficulties; a habit which will be necessary to you in the country where you are to live, and without which you will be thought a very helpless animal, and less esteemed. . . .

"You ask me to write you long letters. I will do it, my dear, on condition you will read them from time to time, and practice what they will inculcate. Their precepts will be dictated by experience, by a perfect knowledge of the situation in which you will be placed, and by the fondest love for you. This it is which makes me wish to see you more qualified than common. My expectations from you are high—yet not higher than you may attain. Industry and resolution are all that are wanting. Nobody in this world can make me so happy, or so miserable, as you. Retirement from public life will ere long become necessary for me. To your sister and yourself I look to render the evening of my life serene and contented. Its morning has been clouded by loss after loss, till I have nothing left but you. I do not doubt either your affection or dispositions. But great exertions are necessary, and you have little time to make them. Be industrious, then, my dear child. Think nothing unsurmountable by resolution and application and you will be all that I wish you to be.

". . . Continue to love me with all the warmth with which you are beloved . . . my dear Patsy."

---

1. **Livy:** Roman historian (59 B.C.–A.D. 17).

THE AMERICAN LANGUAGE

In the years following the settlement of the New World, American English continued to develop, and differences between British and American usage became more and more apparent. British travelers to the New World noticed that Americans spoke with a nasality that was disagreeable to their British ears. The visitors also noticed what they thought of as "corruptions" of the language: words were being used in "barbarous" ways, and brand-new words were being coined.

Some of the differences between British and American English were caused by the simple fact of physical separation. Differences in pronunciation, for example, became marked as the accents of speakers on both sides of the ocean gradually changed. Differences are still apparent; for one example, British speakers omit the vowel before the second *r* in words like *secretary* and *laboratory,* but Americans deliberately pronounce all the syllables in such words.

Besides pronunciation, differences in usage also may result from physical separation. In the New World, for example, and especially in New England, it was (and is) common to hear someone speak of throwing a *rock*. In Britain, however, *rock* continued to refer only to a massive stone, such as Plymouth Rock. Throwing a rock would have seemed as odd to a British person as tossing a boulder.

Sometimes the meaning or usage of a word would change in England while Americans retained its older meaning. The American usage of *guess* to mean "suppose" is an example of this. In the eighteenth and nineteenth centuries, "I guess" sounded odd to British visitors, who would have said, "I suppose." But these visitors were unaware that "I guess" had been common in England until the eighteenth century. It even appears in the writings of Chaucer and Shakespeare. The British also criticized Americans for saying *fall* instead of *autumn,* apparently unaware that *fall* had been used in England until around 1750.

Americanisms and Their Critics

The word *Americanism* came into use to describe a word or expression that originated in the United States, or that was peculiar to the States. The word was first used in print in 1781 by the Reverend John Witherspoon, a Scottish clergyman who had come to this country in 1768 to become president of Princeton University. Witherspoon traveled a good deal and recorded words and phrases that were peculiar to the United States. Many of these words are so common today that it is hard to imagine a time when they might have been unusual. Among the Americanisms recorded by Witherspoon were *to notify,* meaning "to inform"; *mad,* in the sense of "angry"; *chunks,* to describe big pieces of wood; *spell,*

"Revolutionary" English

An English hornbook (17th century). A thin, transparent layer of horn protected the sheet of parchment. This was used as a child's textbook.

Continue to outline Henry's arguments in paragraphs 5–8 in this same way. Write your own comments, questions, and responses beside the outline. Then evaluate the argument. Tell how effective you think the argument is, and why. Be sure to give reasons and examples to back up your evaluation.

Guidelines for Evaluating an Argument

1. What does the writer want me to do or think? (In other words, what is the writer's **purpose**?)
2. Does the writer **assume** (take for granted) anything that I don't think is true? If so, what are these assumptions?
3. What **reasons** does the writer give to try to convince me? (Outline the argument paragraph by paragraph.)
4. Are the reasons **opinions**, or are they provable **facts**? Are the reasons supported by specific **evidence** (incidents, examples, statistics)?
5. Are the writer's conclusions **logical**? That is, do they follow from the statements made?

Writing

Now write your essay analyzing and evaluating the logic of Patrick Henry's speech. You might follow this plan:

1. **Paragraph 1:** Introduction identifying the title, the writer, and the writer's purpose. Give background information, if necessary. Include a **thesis statement** that gives your overall evaluation of the logic of the speech.
2. **Paragraphs 2–4:** Your **paraphrase** of Henry's main arguments along with your evaluation of the logic of each argument. (Are the reasons strong or weak? Is there sufficient evidence or not enough? Does the argument contain any fallacies?)
3. **Paragraph 5:** Concluding paragraph, summarizing your main points and stating your general response to the speech.

Here is one writer's introductory paragraph. Remember that your evaluation may be entirely different. Just be sure that you give specific evidence to support it.

When Patrick Henry stood up to make his speech to the Virginia Convention on March 23, 1775, his audience didn't know they were about to hear one of the all-time best examples of persuasive speaking. Henry's purpose was to persuade the delegates to the Convention that they must vote to arm the citizens and prepare for war with Britain. His speech was extremely effective because of its appeals to emotion, not because of its logic. In fact, some of Patrick Henry's logical arguments could be challenged.

Cites author, title, and date of speech.

Cites purpose of speech.

Ends with thesis statement.

Revising and Proofreading

Use the guidelines in the section at the back of this book, called **Writing About Literature,** to revise and proofread your essay.

AMERICAN ROMANTICISM

View of the White Mountains (detail)
by Thomas Cole (1827). Oil.

UNIT THREE

Broadway at Spring Street by
Hyppolite Sebron (1855). Oil.

Graham and Schweitzer Gallery,
Whitney Museum of American Art,
New York.

The Romantic Sensibility

journey from civilization begins in a familiar mountain landscape
that soon becomes mysterious. Rip is given something to drink by
a ghostly crew of Dutchmen, and he falls asleep. He wakes up
twenty years later to discover that his wife is dead, that the American Revolution has taken place, and that he is, both literally and
symbolically, a free man.

Irving's story is a whimsical fairy tale, much of it borrowed from
a German source. But "Rip Van Winkle" contains a number of the
attitudes and tendencies associated with American Romanticism:
a distrust of "civilization," a nostalgia for the past, a concern with
individual freedom, an interest in the supernatural, and a profound
love for the beauties of the natural landscape.

The Romantic sensibility is not easy to define, because Romanticism was a movement that went beyond national,
chronological, and artistic boundaries. Its first stirrings
were felt in Germany in the second half of the eighteenth century.
Romanticism had a strong influence on literature, music, and
painting in Europe and England well into the nineteenth century.
Romanticism came relatively late to America, and, as you will see
in this unit and in the units that follow, took different forms.

What is Romanticism? Because it is no single thing, it is not
easy to define in capsule form. In general, though, *Romanticism*
is the name given to those schools of thought that consider the
rational inferior to the intuitive. For the Romantics, the imagina-

tion, spontaneity, individual feelings, and nature were of greater value than reason, logic, planning, and cultivation. Romanticism developed in part as a reaction against rationalism, as people realized the limits of reason. The Romantics believed that the imagination was able to discover truths that reason could not reach, truths usually accompanied by powerful emotion and associated with beauty. The Romantics did not flatly reject logical thought as invalid for all purposes. But for the purpose of art, they placed a new premium on nonrational experience.

Poetry was the highest work of the imagination for the Romantics. They often contrasted it with science, which was seen as destroying the very truth it claimed to seek. Edgar Allan Poe, for example, accused "science" of being a vulture:

> Who alterest all things with thy peering eyes!
> Why preyest thou thus upon the poet's heart,
> Vulture! Whose wings are dull realities!

The Romantic sensibility sought to rise above "dull realities" to a realm of higher truth. It would do this in two principal ways: first, by exploring exotic settings in the more "natural" past or in a world far removed from our sooty and noisy industrial age; second, by contemplating the natural world until dull reality falls away to reveal underlying beauty and truth.

The Gothic novel, with its wild landscapes and mysterious castles, is one example of the first approach. Samuel Taylor Coleridge's poem "Kubla Khan" (1797) is a striking expression of this impulse to escape to a mysterious and magical landscape:

> In Xanadu did Kubla Khan
> A stately pleasure dome decree,
> Where Alph, the sacred river, ran
> Through caverns measureless to man
> Down to a sunless sea.

The second Romantic approach, the contemplation of the natural world, is evident in many lyric poems. In these, the poet views a commonplace object or event. A flower found by a stream or a waterfowl flying overhead brings the poet to some important, deeply felt insight, which is then recorded in the poem. In William Cullen Bryant's "To a Waterfowl" (see page 139), the lesson the poet takes from nature is clearly expressed in the final stanzas:

> He who, from zone to zone,
> Guides through the boundless sky thy certain flight,
> In the long way that I must tread alone
> Will lead my steps aright.

This contemplative process is similar to the Puritans' habit of drawing moral lessons from nature (see page 6). The difference is one of emphasis and goal. The Puritans' lessons were limited by their religion. They found in nature the God they knew from the Bible. The Romantics found in nature a far less clearly defined divinity; their experience is usually recorded as a more generalized emotional and intellectual awakening.

White Pine Tree by Thomas Cole (c. 1840). Wash drawing.

Museum of Fine Arts, Boston.

the trees, just where the blue tints of the upland melt away into the fresh green of the nearer landscape. It is a little village, of great antiquity, having been founded by some of the Dutch colonists in the early times of the province, just about the beginning of the government of the good Peter Stuyvesant[3] (may he rest in peace!), and there were some of the houses of the original settlers standing within a few years, built of small yellow bricks brought from Holland, having latticed windows and gable fronts, surmounted with weathercocks.

In that same village, and in one of these very houses (which, to tell the precise truth, was sadly timeworn and weather-beaten), there lived, many years since, while the country was yet a province of Great Britain, a simple, good-natured fellow of the name of Rip Van Winkle. He was a descendant of the Van Winkles who figured so gallantly in the chivalrous days of Peter Stuyvesant, and accompanied him to the siege of Fort Christina.[4] He inherited, however, but little of the martial character of his ancestors. I have observed that he was a simple, good-natured man; he was, moreover, a kind neighbor, and an obedient, henpecked husband. Indeed, to the latter circumstance might be owing that meekness of spirit which gained him such universal popularity; for those men are most apt to be obsequious and conciliating abroad, who are under the discipline of shrews at home. Their tempers, doubtless, are rendered pliant and malleable in the fiery furnace of domestic tribulation; and a curtain lecture[5] is worth all the sermons in the world for teaching the virtues of patience and long-suffering. A termagant[6] wife may, therefore, in some respects be considered a tolerable blessing; and if so, Rip Van Winkle was thrice blessed.

Certain it is that he was a great favorite among all the good wives of the village, who, as usual with the amiable sex, took his part in all family squabbles; and never failed, whenever they talked those matters over in their evening gossipings, to lay all the blame on Dame Van Winkle. The children of the village, too, would shout with joy whenever he approached. He assisted at their sports, made their playthings, taught them to fly kites and shoot marbles, and told them long stories of ghosts, witches, and Indians. Whenever he went dodging about the village, he was surrounded by a troop of them, hanging on his skirts, clambering on his back, and playing a thousand tricks on him with impunity; and not a dog would bark at him throughout the neighborhood.

The great error in Rip's composition was an insuperable aversion to all kinds of profitable labor. It could not be from the want of assiduity[7] or perseverance; for he would sit on a wet rock, with a rod as long and heavy as a Tartar's lance, and fish all day without a murmur, even though he should not be encouraged by a single nibble. He would carry a fowling-piece on his shoulder for hours together, trudging through woods and swamps, and up hill and down dale, to shoot a few squirrels or wild pigeons. He would never refuse to assist a neighbor even in the roughest toil, and was a foremost man at all country frolics for husking Indian corn, or building stone fences; the women of the village, too, used to employ him to run their errands, and to do such little odd jobs as their less obliging husbands would not do for them. In a word, Rip was ready to attend to anybody's business but his own; but as to doing family duty, and keeping his farm in order, he found it impossible.

In fact, he declared it was of no use to work on his farm; it was the most pestilent little piece of ground in the whole country; everything about it went wrong, and would go wrong, in spite of him. His fences were continually falling to pieces; his cow would either go astray or get among the cabbages; weeds were sure to grow quicker in his fields than anywhere else; the rain always made a point of setting in just as he had some outdoor work to do; so that though his patrimonial estate had dwindled away under his management, acre by acre, until there was little more left than a mere patch of Indian corn and potatoes, yet it was the worst conditioned farm in the neighborhood.

His children, too, were as ragged and wild as if they belonged to nobody. His son Rip, an urchin

---

3. **Peter Stuyvesant:** governor of New Amsterdam, 1646–1664.
4. **Fort Christina:** on the Delaware River, captured by Stuyvesant from the Swedes in 1655.
5. **curtain lecture:** reprimand given by a wife to her husband, originally delivered behind the curtains of one those old-fashioned beds.
6. **termagant** (tur′mə·gənt): violently abusive.

7. **assiduity** (əs·ə·dyo͞o′ə·tē): close and continuous application of effort.

Title page of ''Rip Van Winkle'' by Washington Irving.
Illustration by N. C. Wyeth (1921). Lithograph.

David McKay Co. Inc.

a quaint, outlandish fashion; some wore short doublets,[13] others jerkins, with long knives in their belts, and most of them had enormous breeches, of similar style with that of the guide's. Their visages, too, were peculiar; one had a large beard, broad face, and small piggish eyes; the face of another seemed to consist entirely of nose, and was surmounted by a white sugar-loaf hat, set off with a little red cock's tail. They all had beards, of various shapes and colors. There was one who seemed to be the commander. He was a stout old gentleman, with a weather-beaten countenance; he wore a laced doublet, broad belt and hanger,[14] high crowned hat and feather, red stockings, and high-heeled shoes, with roses[15] in them. The whole group reminded Rip of the figures in an old Flemish painting, in the parlor of Dominie Van Shaick, the village parson, and which had been brought over from Holland at the time of the settlement.

What seemed particularly odd to Rip was that, though these folks were evidently amusing themselves, yet they maintained the gravest faces, the most mysterious silence, and were, withal, the most melancholy party of pleasure he had ever witnessed. Nothing interrupted the stillness of the scene but the noise of the balls, which, whenever they were rolled, echoed along the mountains like rumbling peals of thunder.

As Rip and his companion approached them, they suddenly desisted from their play, and stared at him with such fixed, statue-like gaze, and such strange, uncouth, lackluster countenances, that his heart turned within him, and his knees smote together. His companion now emptied the contents of the keg into large flagons,[16] and made signs to him to wait upon the company. He obeyed with fear and trembling; they quaffed the liquor in profound silence, and then returned to their game.

By degrees Rip's awe and apprehension subsided. He even ventured, when no eye was fixed upon him, to taste the beverage, which he found had much of the flavor of excellent Hollands [Dutch gin]. He was naturally a thirsty soul, and was soon tempted to repeat the draft. One taste provoked another; and he reiterated his visits to the flagon so often that at length his senses were overpowered, his eyes swam in his head, his head gradually declined, and he fell into a deep sleep.

On waking, he found himself on the green knoll whence he had first seen the old man of the glen. He rubbed his eyes—it was a bright sunny morning. The birds were hopping and twittering among the bushes, and the eagle was wheeling aloft and breasting the pure mountain breeze. "Surely," thought Rip, "I have not slept here all night." He recalled the occurrences before he fell asleep. The strange man with a keg of liquor, the mountain ravine, the wild retreat among the rocks, the woebegone party at ninepins, the flagon—"Oh! that flagon! that wicked flagon!" thought Rip. "What excuse shall I make to Dame Van Winkle?"

He looked round for his gun, but in place of the clean, well-oiled fowling-piece, he found an old firelock lying by him, the barrel incrusted with rust, the lock falling off, and the stock worm-eaten. He now suspected that the grave roisters of the mountain had put a trick upon him, and, having dosed him with liquor, had robbed him of his gun. Wolf, too, had disappeared, but he might have strayed away after a squirrel or partridge. He whistled after him, and shouted his name, but all in vain; the echoes repeated his whistle and shout, but no dog was to be seen.

He determined to revisit the scene of the last evening's gambol, and if he met with any of the party, to demand his dog and gun. As he rose to walk, he found himself stiff in the joints, and wanting in his usual activity. "These mountain beds do not agree with me," thought Rip, "and if this frolic should lay me up with a fit of the rheumatism, I shall have a blessed time with Dame Van Winkle." With some difficulty he got down into the glen: he found the gully up which he and his companion had ascended the preceding evening; but to his astonishment a mountain stream was now foaming down it, leaping from rock to rock, and filling the glen with babbling murmurs. He, however, made shift to scramble up its sides, working his toilsome way through thickets of birch, sassafras, and witchhazel, and sometimes tripped up or entangled by the wild grapevines that twisted their coils or tendrils from tree to tree, and spread a kind of network in his path.

At length he reached to where the ravine had opened through the cliffs to the amphitheater; but no traces of such opening remained. The rocks presented a high, impenetrable wall, over which

---

13. **doublets:** close-fitting jackets.
14. **hanger:** small, curved sword worn at the waist.
15. **roses:** rosettes.
16. **flagons:** large drinking vessels.

the torrent came tumbling in a sheet of feathery foam, and fell into a broad deep basin, black from the shadows of the surrounding forest. Here, then, poor Rip was brought to a stand. He again called and whistled after his dog; he was only answered by the cawing of a flock of idle crows, sporting high in the air about a dry tree that overhung a sunny precipice; and who, secure in their elevation, seemed to look down and scoff at the poor man's perplexities. What was to be done? The morning was passing away, and Rip felt famished for want of his breakfast. He grieved to give up his dog and gun; he dreaded to meet his wife; but it would not do to starve among the mountains. He shook his head, shouldered the rusty firelock, and, with a heart full of trouble and anxiety, turned his steps homeward.

As he approached the village he met a number of people, but none whom he knew, which somewhat surprised him, for he had thought himself acquainted with everyone in the country round. Their dress, too, was of a different fashion from that to which he was accustomed. They all stared at him with equal marks of surprise, and whenever they cast their eyes upon him, invariably stroked their chins. The constant recurrence of this gesture induced Rip, involuntarily, to do the same, when, to his astonishment, he found his beard had grown a foot long!

He had now entered the skirts of the village. A troop of strange children ran at his heels, hooting after him, and pointing at his gray beard. The dogs, too, not one of which he recognized for an old acquaintance, barked at him as he passed. The very village was altered; it was larger and more populous. There were rows of houses which he had never seen before, and those which had been his familiar haunts had disappeared. Strange names were over the doors, strange faces at the windows—everything was strange. His mind now misgave him; he began to doubt whether both he and the world around him were not bewitched. Surely this was his native village, which he had left but the day before. There stood the Kaatskill Mountains, there ran the silver Hudson at a distance, there was every hill and dale precisely as it had always been. Rip was sorely perplexed. "That flagon last night," thought he, "has addled my poor head sadly!"

It was with some difficulty that he found the way to his own house, which he approached with silent awe, expecting every moment to hear the shrill voice of Dame Van Winkle. He found the house gone to decay—the roof fallen in, the windows shattered, and the doors off the hinges. A half-starved dog that looked like Wolf was skulking about it. Rip called him by name, but the cur snarled, showed his teeth, and passed on. This was an unkind cut indeed. "My very dog," sighed poor Rip, "has forgotten me!"

He entered the house, which, to tell the truth, Dame Van Winkle had always kept in neat order. It was empty, forlorn, and apparently abandoned. This desolateness overcame all his connubial fears; he called loudly for his wife and children— the lonely chambers rang for a moment with his voice, and then all again was silence.

He now hurried forth, and hastened to his old resort, the village inn—but it too was gone. A large, rickety, wooden building stood in its place, with great gaping windows, some of them broken and mended with old hats and petticoats, and over the door was painted, "The Union Hotel, by Jonathan Doolittle." Instead of the great tree that used to shelter the quiet little Dutch inn of yore, there now was reared a tall naked pole, with something on the top that looked like a red nightcap,[17] and from it was fluttering a flag, on which was a singular assemblage of stars and stripes; all this was strange and incomprehensible. He recognized on the sign, however, the ruby face of King George, under which he had smoked so many a peaceful pipe; but even this was singularly metamorphosed.[18] The red coat was changed for one of blue and buff, a sword was held in the hand instead of a scepter, the head was decorated with a cocked hat, and underneath was painted in large characters, GENERAL WASHINGTON.

There was, as usual, a crowd of folk about the door, but none that Rip recollected. The very character of the people seemed changed. There was a busy, bustling, disputatious tone about it, instead of the accustomed phlegm and drowsy tranquillity. He looked in vain for the sage Nicholas Vedder, with his broad face, double chin, and fair long pipe, uttering clouds of tobacco smoke instead of idle speeches; or Van Bummel, the schoolmaster, doling forth the contents of an ancient newspaper. In place of these, a lean, bilious-looking fellow, with his pockets full of handbills,

---

17. **a red nightcap:** a "liberty cap," worn as a symbol of independence.
18. **metamorphosed** (met·ə·môr′fōzd): transformed.

The Return of Rip Van Winkle by John Quidor (1829). Oil.

National Gallery of Art, Washington, D.C.

was haranguing vehemently about rights of citizens, elections, members of Congress, liberty, Bunker's Hill, heroes of Seventy-six, and other words which were a perfect Babylonish[19] jargon to the bewildered Van Winkle.

The appearance of Rip, with his long, grizzled beard, his rusty fowling-piece, his uncouth dress, and an army of women and children at his heels, soon attracted the attention of the tavern-politicians. They crowded round him, eyeing him from head to foot with great curiosity. The orator bustled up to him, and, drawing him partly aside, inquired "On which side he voted?" Rip stared in vacant stupidity. Another short but busy little fellow pulled him by the arm, and, rising on tiptoe, inquired in his ear, "Whether he was Federal or Democrat?" Rip was equally at a loss to comprehend the question; when a knowing, self-important old gentleman, in a sharp cocked hat, made his way through the crowd, putting them to the right and left with his elbows as he passed, and planting himself before Van Winkle, with one arm akimbo, the other resting on his cane, his keen eyes and sharp hat penetrating, as it were, into his very soul, demanded, in an austere tone, "What brought him to the election with a gun on his shoulder, and a mob at his heels; and whether he meant to breed a riot in the village?"—"Alas! gentlemen," cried Rip, somewhat dismayed, "I am a poor quiet man, a native of the place, and a loyal subject of the King, God bless him!"

Here a general shout burst from the bystanders—"A Tory! a Tory! a spy! a refugee! hustle him! away with him!" It was with great difficulty that the self-important man in the cocked hat restored order; and, having assumed a tenfold austerity of brow, demanded again of the unknown culprit, what he came there for, and whom he was seeking. The poor man humbly assured him that he meant no harm, but merely came there in search of some of his neighbors, who used to keep about the tavern.

"Well, who are they? Name them."

Rip bethought himself a moment, and inquired, "Where's Nicholas Vedder?"

There was a silence for a little while, when an old man replied, in a thin piping voice, "Nicholas Vedder! Why, he is dead and gone these eighteen years! There was a wooden tombstone in the

---

19. **Babylonish:** confusing (a confusion of languages occurred at the building of the Tower of Babel in the Book of Genesis).

All day thy wings have fanned,
At that far height, the cold, thin atmosphere,
Yet stoop not, weary, to the welcome land,
20   Though the dark night is near.

And soon that toil shall end;
Soon shalt thou find a summer home, and rest,
And scream among thy fellows; reeds shall bend,
Soon, o'er thy sheltered nest.

25   Thou'rt gone, the abyss of heaven
Hath swallowed up thy form; yet, on my heart
Deeply hath sunk the lesson thou hast given,
And shall not soon depart.

He who, from zone to zone,
30   Guides through the boundless sky thy certain flight,
In the long way that I must tread alone
Will lead my steps aright.

Responding to the Poem

Analyzing the Poem

Identifying Details

1. What danger to the bird is mentioned in the second stanza?
2. According to the speaker, what guides the waterfowl in its flight? Describe how the speaker envisions the end of the bird's "toil" in the sixth stanza.
3. The third stanza contains examples of **onomatopoeia,** or words that actually imitate the sounds of the things they refer to. Name these words.

Interpreting Meanings

4. In line 27, the point toward which the poem is building becomes explicit with the word *lesson.* In your own words, what is that lesson? Who is "He" in line 29? What are the "zones"?
5. The phrase "to do thee wrong" (line 6) is a curious way of describing what the fowler, or hunter, wants to do to the bird. What do you think Bryant intends the fowler to **symbolize,** other than just someone who is hunting birds?
6. Throughout the poem, certain words and phrases emphasize that the waterfowl is a migratory bird. What are some of these? What does the idea of a *lonely* migration contribute to the **theme** of the poem?

7. In the eighteenth century, rationalist thinkers had perceived the operations of nature as a "clockwork universe." They saw the universe as governed by "natural law," under which the stars and the seasons moved and rotated with mechanical precision. In their view, the creator of this mechanism did not control its workings but remained merely an indifferent spectator. In what way is this Romantic poem a rejection of that rationalist view?
8. Do you believe the lesson the speaker learns is a useful one? Explain.
9. Can Nature still present "lessons" to people today? How would you describe the way most people today view the natural world?

Writing About the Poem

A Critical Response

Analyzing the Poem. Do you think Bryant's main intention *was* to teach a lesson? If so, why does he spend so much time coming to the point? What does his extended description of the bird in flight do for you, as a reader, that a simple statement of his belief in Divine guidance would not have done? In a paragraph, explain your answers to these questions.

Thanatopsis is a word Bryant coined by joining two Greek words, *thanatos* ("death") and *opsis* ("seeing"). The word is defined by the poem: a way of looking at death and a way of thinking about it. There are two speaking voices in the poem. The poet speaks the introduction. Then, beginning with "Yet a few days" (line 17), the "still voice" of nature speaks. In line 73, the poet's voice resumes with the words "So live. . . ."

In reading the poem, look for complete sentences. Remember that sometimes the subject is not at the beginning of a sentence. Do not stop at the end of a line if there is no punctuation mark. This poem uses many, many "run-on lines"; this means you have to "run-on" to the next line in order to complete the thought. (Notice that the first twelve lines are all run-on lines.) You'll find that many sentences will end in mid-line, indicating that you should pause there. If you read the poem aloud, you'll see how the run-on lines and the mid-line pauses (called *caesuras*) prevent the poem from having a sing-song rhythm.

Thanatopsis

To him who in the love of Nature holds
Communion with her visible forms, she speaks
A various language: for his gayer hours
She has a voice of gladness, and a smile
5   And eloquence of beauty; and she glides
Into his darker musings with a mild
And healing sympathy that steals away
Their sharpness ere he is aware. When thoughts
Of the last bitter hour come like a blight
10   Over thy spirit, and sad images
Of the stern agony and shroud and pall°
And breathless darkness and the narrow house
Make thee to shudder and grow sick at heart,
Go forth under the open sky and list°
15   To Nature's teachings, while from all around—
Earth and her waters and the depths of air—
Comes a still voice—Yet° a few days, and thee
The all-beholding sun shall see no more
In all his course; nor yet in the cold ground,
20   Where thy pale form was laid with many tears,
Nor in the embrace of ocean, shall exist
Thy image. Earth, that nourished thee, shall claim
Thy growth, to be resolved to earth again,
And, lost each human trace, surrendering up
25   Thine individual being, shalt thou go
To mix forever with the elements,
To be a brother to the insensible rock
And to the sluggish clod, which the rude swain°
Turns with his share° and treads upon; the oak
30   Shall send his roots abroad and pierce thy mould.

Yet not to thine eternal resting place
Shalt thou retire alone, nor couldst thou wish
Couch more magnificent. Thou shalt lie down
With patriarchs of the infant world, with kings,
35   The powerful of the earth, the wise, the good,

11. **pall:** coffin cover.

14. **list:** listen.

17. Here begins the voice of nature.

28. **rude swain:** country man, or farmer.
29. **share:** plow.

Fawn's Leap, Catskill, New York by John W. Hill (1868). Oil.

Kennedy Galleries, Inc., New York.

Fair forms, and hoary seers° of ages past,
All in one mighty sepulcher.° The hills
Rock-ribbed and ancient as the sun; the vales
Stretching in pensive quietness between;
40 The venerable woods, rivers that move
In majesty, and the complaining brooks
That make the meadows green; and, poured round all,
Old Ocean's gray and melancholy waste—
Are but the solemn decorations all
45 Of the great tomb of man. The golden sun,
The planets, all the infinite host of heaven,
Are shining on the sad abodes of death,
Through the still lapse of ages. All that tread
The globe are but a handful to the tribes
50 That slumber in its bosom. Take the wings
Of morning,° pierce the Barcan wilderness,°
Or lose thyself in the continuous woods
Where rolls the Oregon,° and hears no sound
Save his own dashings; yet the dead are there,
55 And millions in those solitudes, since first

36. **hoary seers:** white-haired prophets.
37. **sepulcher:** tomb.

51. "Take the wings of morning" is an allusion to Psalm 139; **Barcan wilderness:** a vast desert in Libya.
53. **Oregon:** early name for the Columbia River.

Then a homestead among farms,
And a woman with bare arms
   Drawing water from a well;
As the bucket mounts apace,°

35   With it mounts her own fair face,
   As at some magician's spell.

Then an old man in a tower,
Ringing loud the noontide hour,
   While the rope coils round and round
40   Like a serpent at his feet,
And again, in swift retreat,
   Nearly lifts him from the ground.

Then within a prison yard,
Faces fixed, and stern, and hard,
45   Laughter and indecent mirth;
Ah! it is the gallows tree!°
Breath of Christian charity,
   Blow, and sweep it from the earth!

46. **gallows tree:** a simple structure of two posts and a crossbar on which criminals were once executed by hanging.

The Ropewalk by Charles Bird King (1830). Oil.

Bayley Museum of the University of Virginia, Charlottesville, Virginia.

Then a schoolboy, with his kite
50 Gleaming in a sky of light,
       And an eager, upward look;
    Steeds pursued through lane and field;
    Fowlers with their snares concealed;
       And an angler by a brook.

55 Ships rejoicing in the breeze,
    Wrecks that float o'er unknown seas,
       Anchors dragged through faithless sand;
    Sea fog drifting overhead,
    And, with lessening line and lead,°
60   Sailors feeling for the land.

    All these scenes do I behold,
    These, and many left untold,
       In that building long and low;
    While the wheel goes round and round,
65 With a drowsy, dreamy sound.
       And the spinners backward go.

59. **lead:** a nautical term for a weight used by sailors to take soundings to measure the water's depth.

Responding to the Poem

Analyzing the Poem

Identifying Details

1. In the first stanza, Longfellow uses a **simile**. What is the factory compared to?
2. By the end of stanza 3, the poet has presented a series of **images** of the factory and of the spinners at work. Describe what the workers are doing. What are the "cobwebs" mentioned at the end of this stanza?
3. Beginning with stanza 4, Longfellow takes an imaginary "ropewalk" and gives us a succession of pictures in which some kind of rope or cord plays a part. Briefly describe each of these scenes.

Interpreting Meanings

4. New England factories of the nineteenth century often were unpleasant places with working conditions that would be regarded as intolerable today. What is the implication of the **metaphor** comparing the factory workers to spiders?
5. Describe the changes of **tone** as the poet imagines scene after scene. What opposing aspects of human life is the poet holding "in balance"? How do you think he feels about the "human spiders"?
6. Can you think of any occupations today in which the workers could be compared to insects or animals?

Writing About the Poem

A Creative Response

Describing an Idyllic Scene. The famous printmakers Currier & Ives depicted rural nineteenth-century American scenes so charmingly and idealistically that we still find examples of their work on contemporary greeting cards as well as in art museums. Which idyllic scenes in "The Ropewalk" would you recommend to the attention of the printmakers? State your preference and describe the scene and its mood in a paragraph. Which scenes are definitely *not* Currier & Ives subjects?

Analyzing Language and Style

Trochaic Meter

The unusual sense of physical movement in this poem was not achieved by accident. Longfellow obviously wanted to give a bouncy spring to both his real ropewalk and his imaginary one, and so he decided on a rhythm based on the use of the *trochee*.

   Trochaic meter is the exact opposite of iambic meter: Instead of the iambic da-DAH, the sound of trochaic meter is DAH-da. Once Longfellow has established his count of four of these trochees per line, does he faithfully repeat it from the first line to the last?

Read this poem aloud to hear how rhythm and sound effects contribute to a particular atmosphere. How do the first two lines even imitate the rhythmic rise and fall of the tide itself?

The Tide Rises, the Tide Falls

The tide rises, the tide falls,
The twilight darkens, the curlew° calls;
Along the sea sands damp and brown
The traveler hastens toward the town,
5   And the tide rises, the tide falls.

Darkness settles on roofs and walls,
But the sea, the sea in the darkness calls;
The little waves, with their soft, white
    hands,
Efface the footprints in the sands,
10   And the tide rises, the tide falls.

The morning breaks; the steeds in their
    stalls
Stamp and neigh, as the hostler° calls;
The day returns, but nevermore
Returns the traveler to the shore,
15   And the tide rises, the tide falls.

---

2. **curlew:** large, brown wading bird.
12. **hostler:** stable hand.

Sunlight on the Coast by Winslow Homer (1890). Oil.

Toledo Museum of Art, Toledo, Ohio.

Responding to the Poem

Analyzing the Poem

Identifying Details

1. How does the division into stanzas reflect the passage of time in the poem?

Interpreting Meanings

2. "Footsteps on the sands of time" is a common expression referring to mortality and the passing of time. What do you think is implied about the fate of the traveler when his footprints are washed away in the second stanza?

3. What feeling is suggested by the stamping and neighing of the horses the next morning? What contrasting feeling is suggested by what we are told about the traveler in this stanza?

4. **Onomatopoeia** is a poetic technique in which the sounds of words are used to echo their sense. If you have ever heard the call of a shore bird, you know that the words "curlew calls" in line 2 echo the sound the bird itself makes. (Its cry is particularly mournful when heard at dusk.) What sound do you think dominates this poem? What atmosphere or feeling does it suggest? How does the rhythm of the poem reflect the movement of the tides?

5. The waves are **personified** in stanza 2 as having "soft, white hands." This is an example of Longfellow's poetic style that some readers think is too cute, or too sentimental, to be effective. Do you think the personification is justified here? Why or why not?

6. Do you think this is a poem about one specific traveler? Or could it be seen as a "drama" about everyone's life? What do you think is suggested by the tide's continuing to rise and fall, despite the fact that the human traveler is gone?

Writing About the Poem

A Critical Response

Comparing and Contrasting Poems. Alfred, Lord Tennyson, a British contemporary of Longfellow, wrote poetry that rivaled even Longfellow's in popularity. Read the following poem by Tennyson. Then, in a brief essay, compare and contrast this lyric with Longfellow's "The Tide Rises, the Tide Falls." Before you write, you might fill out a chart like the one following the poem.

Break, Break, Break

Break, break, break,
   On thy cold gray stones, O Sea!
And I would that my tongue could utter
   The thoughts that arise in me.

5 O, well for the fisherman's boy,
   That he shouts with his sister at play!
O, well for the sailor lad,
   That he sings in his boat on the bay!

And the stately ships go on
10 To their haven under the hill;
But O for the touch of a vanish'd hand,
   And the sound of a voice that is still!

Break, break, break,
   At the foot of thy crags, O Sea!
15 But the tender grace of a day that is dead
   Will never come back to me.

       —Alfred, Lord Tennyson

	Longfellow	Tennyson
What the sea represents		
Mood of the poem		
Message of the poem		
Sounds of the poem (rhymes and meter)		

The Cross of Snow.

In the long, sleepless watches of the night,
A gentle face,—the face of one long dead,—
Looks at me from the wall, where round its head
The night-lamp casts a halo of pale light.
Here in this room she died; and soul more white
Never through martyrdom of fire was led
To its repose; nor can in books be read
The legend of a life more benedight.
There is a mountain in the distant West
That, sun-defying, in its deep ravines
Displays a cross of snow upon its side.
Such is the cross I wear upon my breast
These eighteen years, through all the changing scenes
And seasons, changeless since the day she died.

July 10. 1879.

Primary Sources
Visiting Mr. Longfellow

"These were distinguished visitors, but they did not outnumber the succession of simple, often touching, and sometimes afflicting callers, mostly Americans, who came to constitute a serious problem for Longfellow, but who were invariably received with courtesy and consideration—though some of them belonged in that category of 'books, bores, and beggars' which even he came to count as one of the principal vexations of daily life. Fortunately his humor was usually equal to the occasion, and he could describe some of his guests with characteristic good nature. There was the Englishman who remarked that, in other countries, you know, we go to see ruins and all that—'but you have no ruins in your country, and I thought I would call and see *you*.' There was the young Westerner who asked Longfellow how old he was, and when the poet answered, 'Seventy,' rejoined, 'I have seen a good many men of your age who looked much younger than you.' A German woman, with a strong accent, called to talk with him about 'The Building of the Ship,' which she was planning to read in public, and which she called 'The Lunch of the Sheep.' As he was standing at the front door one August morning, a woman in black came up to him and inquired whether this was the house in which Longfellow had been born; when he explained that it was not, she went on to ask, 'Did he die here?' "

—from *Longfellow: His Life and Work,*
Newton Arvin

Craigie House, Longfellow's home in Cambridge, Massachusetts.

John Greenleaf Whittier (1807–1892)

Whittier's poetic subjects and many of the qualities of his verse led him to be included in the group known as the Fireside Poets. But unlike Longfellow, Lowell, and Holmes, who were raised in privilege and enjoyed a distinguished education, Whittier was born into a poor Quaker family and had little formal schooling. He started to write poetry as an adolescent, heavily influenced by the popular Scottish poet Robert Burns (1759–1796). Burns had revived the Scottish literary heritage and written memorably of rural life. Significantly, the ballad and the song, two of Burns's favorite forms, were to remain favorites of Whittier's as well.

With the assistance of the abolitionist William Lloyd Garrison (1805–1879), the young Whittier found work in Boston as a newspaper editor. In 1831, he published his first book, *Legends of New-England in Prose and Verse,* a collection of pieces on local Massachusetts history. But he soon immersed himself in current affairs, in total support of the antislavery cause.

In 1835, Whittier was elected to the state legislature. For the next quarter of a century, until the outbreak of the Civil War, Whittier never stopped working for the abolition of slavery. He contributed poems and articles to the *National Era,* which he also edited from 1847 to 1860. (It was this weekly newspaper that published Harriet Beecher Stowe's novel, *Uncle Tom's Cabin,* in installments during 1851–1852.)

Although much of Whittier's writing during this period was overtly political, he also produced a long work of fiction on the Salem witch trials and several books of nature poetry. ''Barbara Frietchie,'' perhaps Whittier's best-known ballad, appeared in a collection called *In War Time and Other Poems,* published in 1864.

After the Civil War, Whittier turned again to nature for many of his subjects. In 1866, he completed *Snow-Bound,* a long poem (759 lines) which many critics consider his masterpiece and which made Whittier famous. Advancing age did not reduce his output; until he was well into his eighties, Whittier continued to publish poetry on homely incidents from rural life, episodes from

Colonial history, and the humanitarian ideals of justice, religious faith, and tolerance. As much as his poetry, his humane convictions and moral example left a mark for good on his time.

In *Snow-Bound,* Whittier looks back fondly on the life he spent as a boy in the farmhouse in Haverhill, Massachusetts, where his family had lived since 1688. Whittier remembers what we would call ''an extended family,'' a gathering under one roof of eight to nine related people of varying ages, along with the male boarder who taught school nearby. Imprisoned by the storm, these people had to live for days without news of the outside world. Their rooms were dimly lighted by candles, or perhaps by lamps that burned the whale oil called macassar. Their food was stored in crocks and barrels and briny vats and kept in the cellar. Water came from a pump in the kitchen or a well in the yard. The bathroom as we know it today did not exist. For heat and cooking, they burned wood. Life, in a word, was hard. But like many people, Whittier found in his past a kind of benediction.

To be snowbound in the early 1800's, when this poem takes place, was quite different from being snowbound today. But for all of the hardships, being snowbound was something of an adventure, an interruption of the course of ordinary life. When snowbound, people became thoughtful, more deeply aware of one another and of the privileges of their security. Perhaps the main source of the poem's charm is the richness of its details— the lively reporting of Whittier's eye and the simple language by which he describes exactly what he sees. As you read, try to put yourself "there." (An *idyll* is a work describing a simple, pleasant rural scene, or a peaceful domestic setting.)

from Snow-Bound: A Winter Idyll

To the memory of the household it describes,
this poem is dedicated by the author

The sun that brief December day
Rose cheerless over hills of gray,
And, darkly circled, gave at noon
A sadder light than waning moon.
5 Slow tracing down the thickening sky
Its mute and ominous prophecy,
A portent seeming less than threat,
It sank from sight before it set.
A chill no coat, however stout,
10 Of homespun stuff could quite shut out,
A hard, dull bitterness of cold,
That checked, mid-vein, the circling race
Of lifeblood in the sharpened face,
The coming of the snowstorm told.
15 The wind blew east; we heard the roar
Of Ocean on his wintry shore,
And felt the strong pulse throbbing there
Beat with low rhythm our inland air.

Meanwhile we did our nightly chores—
20 Brought in the wood from out of doors,
Littered the stalls, and from the mows°
Raked down the herd's grass for the cows:
Heard the horse whinnying for his corn;
And, sharply clashing horn on horn,
25 Impatient down the stanchion° rows
The cattle shake their walnut bows;°
While, peering from his early perch
Upon the scaffold's pole of birch,
The cock his crested helmet bent
30 And down his querulous challenge sent.

Unwarmed by any sunset light
The gray day darkened into night,
A night made hoary° with the swarm
And whirl-dance of the blinding storm,
35 As zigzag, wavering to and fro,
Crossed and recrossed the wingëd snow:
And ere the early bedtime came
The white drift piled the window frame,
And through the glass the clothesline posts
40 Looked in like tall and sheeted ghosts.

So all night long the storm roared on:
The morning broke without a sun;
In tiny spherule° traced with lines
Of Nature's geometric signs,
45 In starry flake, and pellicle,°
All day the hoary meteor fell;
And, when the second morning shone,
We looked upon a world unknown,
On nothing we could call our own.
50 Around the glistening wonder bent
The blue walls of the firmament,
No cloud above, no earth below—
A universe of sky and snow!

The old familiar sights of ours
55 Took marvelous shapes; strange domes and towers
Rose up where sty or corncrib stood,
Or garden wall, or belt of wood;
A smooth white mound the brush pile showed,
A fenceless drift what once was road;
60 The bridle post an old man sat

---

21. **mows:** storage for feed.
25. **stanchion:** stall.
26. **walnut bows:** wooden yokes.

33. **hoary:** white, as with age or frost.
43. **spherule:** sphere.
45. **pellicle:** a coat or film.

Winter Landscape with Houses by
Charles Burchfield (1916). Watercolor.

Kennedy Galleries, Inc., New York.

With loose-flung coat and high cocked hat;
The well-curb° had a Chinese roof;
And even the long sweep,° high aloof,
In its slant splendor, seemed to tell
65 Of Pisa's leaning miracle.°

A prompt, decisive man, no breath
Our father wasted: "Boys, a path!"
Well pleased (for when did farmer boy
Count such a summons less than joy?),
70 Our buskins° on our feet we drew;
With mittened hands, and caps drawn low,
To guard our necks and ears from snow,
We cut the solid whiteness through.
And, where the drift was deepest, made
75 A tunnel walled and overlaid
With dazzling crystal: we had read
Of rare Aladdin's° wondrous cave,
And to our own his name we gave,
With many a wish the luck were ours
80 To test his lamp's supernal powers.
We reached the barn with merry din,
And roused the prisoned brutes within.
The old horse thrust his long head out,
And grave with wonder gazed about;
85 The cock his lusty greeting said,
And forth his speckled harem led;
The oxen lashed their tails, and hooked,
And mild reproach of hunger looked;
The hornèd patriarch of the sheep,
90 Like Egypt's Amun° roused from sleep,
Shook his sage head with gesture mute,
And emphasized with stamp of foot.

All day the gusty north wind bore
The loosening drift its breath before;
95 Low circling round its southern zone,
The sun through dazzling snow mist shone.
No church bell lent its Christian tone
To the savage air, no social smoke
Curled over woods of snow-hung oak.
100 A solitude made more intense
By dreary-voicèd elements,

The shrieking of the mindless wind,
The moaning tree boughs swaying blind,
And on the glass the unmeaning beat
105 Of ghostly fingertips of sleet.
Beyond the circle of our hearth
No welcome sound of toil or mirth
Unbound the spell, and testified
Of human life and thought outside.
110 We minded° that the sharpest ear
The buried brooklet could not hear,
The music of whose liquid lip
Had been to us companionship,
And, in our lonely life, had grown
115 To have an almost human tone.

As night drew on, and, from the crest
Of wooded knolls that ridged the west,
The sun, a snow-blown traveler, sank
From sight beneath the smothering bank,
120 We piled, with care, our nightly stack
Of wood against the chimney back—
The oaken log, green, huge, and thick,
And on its top the stout back stick;
The knotty forestick laid apart,
125 And filled between with curious art
The ragged brush; then hovering near,
We watched the first red blaze appear,
Heard the sharp crackle, caught the gleam
On whitewashed wall and sagging beam,
130 Until the old, rude-furnished room
Burst, flower-like, into rosy bloom;
While radiant with a mimic flame
Outside the sparkling drift became,
And through the bare-boughed lilac tree
135 Our own warm hearth seemed blazing free.
The crane and pendent trammels° showed,
The Turks' heads° on the andirons glowed;
While childish fancy, prompt to tell
The meaning of the miracle,
140 Whispered the old rhyme: "*Under the tree,
When fire outdoors burns merrily,
There the witches are making tea.*"

---

62. **well-curb:** enclosing frame over a well.
63. **sweep:** a pole with a bucket attached to the end, used for dipping water from a well.
65. **Pisa's miracle:** a reference to the leaning tower of Pisa in Italy. Whittier refers to it as a miracle because it looks as if it should fall over.
70. **buskins:** high boots of leather.
77. **Aladdin:** a young man in the *Arabian Nights* who discovers treasure in a cave by means of a miraculous lamp.
90. **Amun:** an Egyptian god usually represented as a ram.

110. **minded:** understood.
136. **trammels:** the iron hooks that held cooking pots over a grate fire on a swinging arm (crane).
137. **Turks' heads:** the tops of the andirons resembled turbans.

The moon above the eastern wood
Shone at its full; the hill range stood
145 Transfigured in the silver flood,
Its blown snows flashing cold and keen,
Dead white, save where some sharp ravine
Took shadow, or the somber green
Of hemlocks turned to pitchy black
150 Against the whiteness at their back
For such a world and such a night
Most fitting that unwarming light,
Which only seemed where'er it fell
To make the coldness visible.

155 Shut in from all the world without,
We sat the clean-winged° hearth about,
Content to let the north wind roar
In baffled rage at pane and door,

While the red logs before us beat
160 The frost line back with tropic heat;
And ever, when a louder blast
Shook beam and rafter as it passed,
The merrier up its roaring draft
The great throat of the chimney laughed;
165 The house dog on his paws outspread
Laid to the fire his drowsy head,
The cat's dark silhouette on the wall
A couchant° tiger's seemed to fall;
And, for the winter fireside meet,
170 Between the andirons' straddling feet,
The mug of cider simmered slow,
The apples sputtered in a row,
And, close at hand, the basket stood
With nuts from brown October's wood.

---

156. **clean-winged:** turkey wings were used to brush ashes from the hearth.

168. **couchant:** reclining.

Responding to the Poem

Analyzing the Poem

Identifying Details

1. The first eighteen lines of the poem create a mood of foreboding and expectation. List the **images** that help build this suspenseful mood.
2. Cite the **images** of sound in lines 100–105 that help you imagine the storm outside the house. In lines 110–115, what details help you imagine the isolated quality of farm life in the nineteenth century?
3. In lines 155–174, what **images** show how the threatening situation outside is turned into a cozy and pleasant situation inside?

Interpreting Meanings

4. The poet emphasizes the fabulous nature of the snowbound world. What **images** help us see his farmyard as if it's an exotic sight from another world?
5. Another reference to folklore and to the fabulous occurs in the lines describing the crystal cave. In line 80, what do the boys wish they could do? What other details in the poem connect the fabulous or the imaginary with the snowbound farmhouse?
6. How might a realistic writer describe this storm?

Writing About the Poem

A Critical Response

Analyzing the Poem's Appeal. When *Snow-Bound* was published, it was an immediate best seller, and it continued to be reprinted well into the twentieth century. By then, the kind of life it pictures had all but vanished. In one paragraph or more, explain how you would account for this poem's continuing appeal. Consider whether such appeal to a "romantic past" is also made today in movies, books, and TV shows.

Analyzing Language and Style

Allusions

Snow-Bound was an enormously popular poem, and up until a few decades ago, parts of it could be recited by almost every schoolchild in America. However, *Snow-Bound* is not necessarily "easy"; what makes it difficult for some readers are its allusions. Go over the poem and find allusions to (1) architecture, (2) literature, and (3) history. What do these allusions tell you about the kind of education Whittier assumed his readers would have?

Oliver Wendell Holmes (1809–1894)

Oliver Wendell Holmes by Mathew Brady.

One of the most dynamic men of his time, Oliver Wendell Holmes pursued two careers simultaneously—medicine and literature—and he made lasting contributions to each. A descendant of Anne Bradstreet, Holmes was born into an already distinguished family in Cambridge, Massachusetts—the town across the Charles River from Boston and the seat of Harvard College. Quite naturally, he assumed membership in that unofficial social order of "Boston Brahmins," a name taken from the high priests of the Hindu religion and humorously applied to Boston's upper classes. Their odd mixture of philosophical conservatism and intellectual boldness made these prominent Bostonians—Longfellow, Holmes, Lowell, Charles Eliot Norton, and others—part of an American legend extending into the twentieth century.

Before turning to medicine, Holmes had graduated from Harvard and had studied law there, a subject he found "cold and cheerless." He was still a law student when the government's plan to destroy the American warship *Constitution* inspired him to write a poem that saved the ship and made him famous. This poem was the emotional "Old Ironsides," one of the most enduring pieces of verse in American literature.

In spite of this taste of literary glory, Holmes decided that he would become a physician—a profession he chose because it could teach him about humankind. He studied medicine at Harvard for three years. He followed that with three years of further work in Paris hospitals, where the world's best doctors were said to work. He was twenty-seven when, almost at the same time, he published his first book of poetry and was awarded a medical degree from Harvard. Combining poetry and medicine did not seem unusual to Dr. Holmes, who was said to hear poetic meter in the rhythm of the heart.

Practicing medicine proved less interesting to Holmes than teaching medical students. After two years as professor of anatomy at Dartmouth College, he returned to Harvard, and there began a career in medical education that would continue for over three decades.

One of the founders of the *Atlantic Monthly* magazine, Holmes gained his national reputation from a series of chatty, urbane, and sometimes irreverently witty essays. These were eventually collected under the title *The Autocrat of the Breakfast Table* (1858), in which the leading character (recognizable to most readers as the author himself) presided over the spirited table-talk at an imaginary Boston boarding house.

Holmes's poetry was, for the most part, light and even comic. It commented on the social and intellectual shortcomings of his contemporaries, particularly those who aspired to higher forms of verse than he himself dared to write. But, on the evidence of his serious poems such as "The Chambered Nautilus," Holmes had earned the right to judge, not from an envious spirit but in the confidence of an equal talent.

Today, Holmes is perhaps remembered more as a phenomenon—an aristocrat with the common touch, an artist with a passion for science—than as a poet. The sort of wit that made *The Autocrat of the Breakfast Table* and its sequels the equivalents of modern best sellers has long become outdated, but the benign figure of Oliver Wendell Holmes remains. It is impossible to forget the gentleness and humor of a man who, beginning his practice as a young physician, hung out a sign saying: "Grateful for Small Fevers."

In 1830, the 44-gun American warship *Constitution*, which had defeated the British warship *Guerrière* in the War of 1812, was scheduled to be scrapped. Holmes sent this poem to the Boston *Advertiser* in protest.

Suppose that a historic ship or building or site were about to be destroyed today. What sort of letters might come into the newspapers protesting the destruction?

Old Ironsides

    Ay, tear her tattered ensign down!
      Long has it waved on high,
    And many an eye has danced to see
      That banner in the sky;
5   Beneath it rung the battle shout,
      And burst the cannon's roar—
    The meteor of the ocean air
      Shall sweep the clouds no more.

    Her deck, once red with heroes' blood,
10   Where knelt the vanquished foe,
    Where winds were hurrying o'er the flood,
      And waves were white below,
    No more shall feel the victor's tread,
      Or know the conquered knee—
15   The harpies° of the shore shall pluck
      The eagle of the sea!

    Oh, better that her shattered hulk
      Should sink beneath the wave;
    Her thunders shook the mighty deep,
20   And there should be her grave;
    Nail to the mast her holy flag,
      Set every threadbare sail,
    And give her to the god of storms,
      The lightning and the gale!

---

15. **harpies:** an allusion to predatory flying creatures in Greek mythology, which have bodies of vultures and heads of women. The name meant "snatchers" or "robbers." Later, the harpies came to symbolize any creatures that prey on helpless victims.

"Old Ironsides" in Boston harbor today.

Responding to the Poem

Analyzing the Poem

Identifying Details

1. What **metaphors** does Holmes use to describe the ship in stanzas 1 and 2?
2. What proposal concludes the poem?

Interpreting Meanings

3. In simple terms, what message does the first stanza present? What is **ironic** about the way Holmes states his message?
4. When a ship is broken up in the dockyards, she is said to be scrapped—that is, stripped of everything valuable or reusable. Is Holmes comparing the directors of the scrapping business to harpies in stanza 2, or is his scorn directed at someone else? Explain.
5. What do you think the poet wants the ship to **symbolize**?
6. In many circumstances where poets have seen things they love threatened by "progress," they have composed prayers or made petitions. How does Holmes's response differ from a prayer or a petition?
7. If, next year, Old Ironsides should be found to be in danger of sinking at her dock, do you think most Americans would let her go?
8. Do you think other historical relics like this old ship should be preserved? Or do you think they should be destroyed? Why?

Writing About the Poem

A Creative Response

1. **Applying the Poem to Other Situations.** In a paragraph, tell how this poem might be read to apply to a situation involving a human being. In your paragraph, explain what the ship's parts might symbolize in human terms: her flag, her deck red with blood, her shattered hulk, her thunders, her threadbare sails.

A Critical Response

2. **Finding Contemporary Parallels.** Specifically, this poem is an expression of outrage at the thought of a ship that has become a national treasure and a reminder of past glory being regarded as nothing more than an object to be dismantled and sold at a profit. More broadly, however, the poem can be read as a call to honor the past. In a brief essay, explain how that same appeal is sometimes made today. What are some specific issues that have inspired such appeals? Are these appeals still made in the form of poetry? What other forms of expression have contemporary patriots and lovers of the past found effective?

Analyzing Language and Style

Connotations

With his poem, Holmes wanted to persuade people to do something, so he deliberately chose words for their emotional overtones and associations. These emotional shadings that are attached to some words are called **connotations**. For example, in line 1, Holmes describes the ship's flag as a "tattered ensign." *Tattered* suggests many months facing the lashing gale of winds, perhaps in the line of duty. The image of a "tattered flag" (ensign) is likely to stir our hearts. But suppose instead he had called it a "rotting flag" or a "ragged flag" or just a "worn-out flag"? How would the emotional content of the line change?

Suggest substitute wording for each of these lines from the poem, to call forth completely different emotional responses from a reader:

1. meteor of the ocean air
2. red with heroes' blood
3. harpies of the shore
4. eagle of the sea
5. shattered hulk
6. holy flag
7. threadbare sail

A nautilus is a creature that lives in a seashell, one of those mollusks that grow year by year, from the size of a tiny bead to the size of a pumpkin. In Holmes's own description, the nautilus shell is composed of a "series of enlarging compartments successively dwelt in by the animal that inhabits the shell, which is built in a widening spiral." The word *nautilus* comes from the Greek word for "sailor," reminding us that the Greeks thought this shell could actually move on the surface of the water, using a membrane as its sail. Ancient drawings often represent the nautilus as a little boat with its sail billowing in the wind, blown by one of those fat-cheeked figures on the "four corners" of the earth. The nautilus is one of the most beautiful objects in nature and one of the most fragile of life-containing vessels.

The first three stanzas of the poem are a meditation upon the life and death of the shell. In the next-to-last stanza, the poet begins an apostrophe (a direct address to an object or to someone who is not present). The visual description here is like the scene in Shakespeare's *Hamlet* (Act V) in which a gravedigger unearths the skull of a man Hamlet knew. Hamlet holds the skull up to the light and speaks words about life and destiny that the skull evokes for him. In "The Chambered Nautilus," the poet might be pictured holding the shell before him and speaking.

Like most poems written in the 1800's, "The Chambered Nautilus" contains some words that are now archaic, or not in common use. When you come to a word you don't know, stop and think about it; try to use the context to figure out its meaning if a dictionary isn't handy. Remember to pause in reading the poem only when you come to a comma, period, or other mark of punctuation.

The Chambered Nautilus

This is the ship of pearl, which poets feign,°
   Sails the unshadowed main—
   The venturous bark that flings
On the sweet summer wind its purpled wings
5   In gulfs enchanted, where the siren° sings,
     And coral reefs lie bare,
Where the cold sea maids rise to sun their streaming
     hair.

Its webs of living gauze no more unfurl;
   Wrecked is the ship of pearl!
10   And every chambered cell,
Where its dim dreaming life was wont to dwell,
As the frail tenant shaped his growing shell,
   Before thee lies revealed—
Its irised° ceiling rent,° its sunless crypt unsealed!

15   Year after year beheld the silent toil
    That spread his lustrous coil;
    Still, as the spiral grew,
He left the past year's dwelling for the new,
Stole with soft step its shining archway through,
20   Built up its idle door,
Stretched in his last-found home, and knew the old no
    more.

1. **feign:** imagine.

5. **siren:** an allusion to a mythical sea maiden. The sirens' songs were so seductive that sailors would wreck their ships on the rocks in order to hear them.

14. **irised:** iridescent; from Iris, goddess of the rainbow; **rent:** torn.

Thanks for the heavenly message brought by thee,
   Child of the wandering sea,
   Cast from her lap, forlorn!
25 From thy dead lips a clearer note is born
Than ever Triton blew from wreathéd horn!°
   While on mine ear it rings,
Through the deep caves of thought I hear a voice that
   sings—

Build thee more stately mansions, O my soul,
30   As the swift seasons roll!
   Leave thy low-vaulted past!
Let each new temple, nobler than the last,
Shut thee from heaven with a dome more vast,
   Till thou at length art free,
35 Leaving thine outgrown shell by life's unresting sea!

26. This line echoes a famous line from "The World Is Too Much with Us," a sonnet by William Wordsworth: "Or hear old Triton blow his wreathéd horn." Triton was a mythical sea god, often represented as blowing a conch-shell horn.

When James Russell Lowell's first child, Blanche, was only four months old, the poet was so pleased with the lively infant that he could not resist boasting about her. As he wrote to a friend, "Miss Blanche Lowell, in the freshness of her morning spirits, is, in my opinion, a sight well worth a journey from Philadelphia to look upon. Why, she laughs all over. You can see it through her clothes. The very tips of her toes twinkle for joy. . . . She has another grace which I might in modesty omit, but I love truth! She is exceedingly fond of her father!"

Less than a year later, the infant who had been the joy of his life was dead. It took Lowell many months to find words for his grief. When they came, he produced a short elegiac lyric that, in its purity and simplicity, stands apart from the bulk of his collected works.

She Came and Went

As a twig trembles, which a bird
   Lights on to sing, then leaves unbent,
So is my memory thrilled and stirred—
   I only know she came and went.

5 As clasps some lake, by gusts unriven,
   The blue dome's measureless content,
So my soul held that moment's heaven—
   I only know she came and went.

As, at one bound, our swift spring heaps
10   The orchards full of bloom and scent,
So clove her May my wintry sleeps—
   I only know she came and went.

An angel stood and met my gaze,
   Through the low doorway of my tent;
15 The tent is struck, the vision stays—
   I only know she came and went.

Oh, when the room grows slowly dim,
   And life's last oil is nearly spent,
One gush of light these eyes will brim,
20   Only to think she came and went.

Responding to the Poem

Analyzing the Poem

Identifying Details

1. Each of the first three stanzas makes a comparison that describes the effect Lowell's daughter has had on his life. Restate these three **similes** in your own words.
2. What time of life does the last stanza refer to? What does the poet say will happen when this time of his life arrives?

Interpreting Meanings

3. What words and **images** in the poem emphasize the brevity of the daughter's life? What words and images express the joy she gave her father?
4. How would you **paraphrase** the **refrain**?

5. This is a very personal poem. Do you think the ideas Lowell expresses apply only to his own personal tragedy? Or does the poem's meaning transcend the limits of this one personal experience—and, if so, what other experiences might the poem speak for?

Writing About the Poem

A Critical Response

Comparing Two Poems on the Same Theme. In a brief essay, compare and contrast Lowell's "She Came and Went" with Longfellow's "The Cross of Snow" (page 147). What image does each poet use to evoke the emotion of grief? How do the poems differ in structure? Which lyric do you think evokes a more vivid picture of the loved one who was lost?

Mother and Child by Mary Cassatt
(1890's). Oil.

Private Collection.

THE AMERICAN LANGUAGE

"Noah's Ark": Webster's Dictionary

John Adams's proposal to establish an American Academy to guard the language from corruption (see page 111) was a response to a problem of increasing importance—the need many Americans felt to have some kind of authority governing matters of usage.

In England, linguistic authority had traditionally rested in literature and in the aristocracy. The English felt that words should be used the way great writers and the nobility used them. The ultimate authority was royal—the King's English (though one king, the German George I, could not speak English at all). This was beginning to change in England in the eighteenth century, however; and of course in America matters were very different. In America, up until the mid-nineteenth century, there was very little literature and, needless to say, a good deal of disagreement about the scope of royal authority.

Why was an authority necessary at all? People had not always felt the need for one. The Roman poet Horace wrote that "usage is the law and rule of speech." Horace meant that the *speakers* of a language determine matters of usage by common agreement. In a relatively stable social structure, this is what happens: People of a particular class will speak exactly the way their friends and associates speak, and matters of right and wrong won't even be raised. But in societies where social structure is fluid, the matter becomes more complex.

Imagine that you are a baker in London in the eighteenth century. Your cakes and pastries suddenly become very popular, and in a few years you have become a moderately wealthy member of a growing middle class. But your own speech patterns reveal your humbler origins, just as clearly as a caste mark would. Now, how about your children? Well, what you want for your children is a different matter.

In fact, hundreds of eighteenth-century English found themselves in this situation, and they did what you might expect them to do. They sent their children to newly founded schools that, among other things, taught the children for the first time the language habits of the class they wanted to imitate. English grammar now became a subject to be taught to youngsters. Before this, children would be taught Latin and Greek; it was assumed they could speak their own language and needed no instruction in it. The teachers in these new schools were probably not from the nobility and thus did not come by upper-class language usage naturally; but they had *books*. In this way, written grammars dictating English usage became popular in England, and schoolmasters began to take over authority in matters of English language usage. What one writer has called "the schoolmastering of English" had begun.

The teaching of English arose for similar reasons in America. Before the Revolution, it would have been difficult to find an "English School" in the Colonies—that is, a school that taught English grammar rather than Latin grammar. Benjamin Franklin tried to establish a school to teach English in Philadelphia in the 1750's, but his Latin School overwhelmed it, and the English school went out of business. After the Revolution, though, regular instruction in English grammar became common in the public schools. However, the only available textbooks came from England. This was clearly an awkward situation for a new nation that wanted to establish linguistic independence and justify its use of language to carping British critics.

An American Spelling Book

Enter Noah Webster, a young schoolmaster from Connecticut. Webster was looking for a way to finance his legal education, and he was also passionately dedicated to the cause of American English. To help advance these two causes, Webster wrote a spelling book, which he first published in 1783, when he was twenty-five. The spelling book turned out to be a major force in the drive for American linguistic independence. Over the generations, *The American Spelling Book* was used in numerous editions, and over a hundred million copies of it were sold.

Webster believed that "a national language is a band of national union," and he prepared his speller and his later textbooks for a purpose:

> . . . to reform the abuses and corruption which . . . tincture the conversation of the polite part of Americans . . . and especially to render the pronunciation . . . accurate and uniform by demolishing those obvious distinctions of provincial dialects.

Webster reasoned that accurate and uniform American spelling would lead to uniform American speech, and that uniformity in speech would "reconcile the people of America to each other."

The whole idea of consistency in spelling was fairly new in Webster's time and was directly related to the increasing use of the printing press. Until the 1700's, people followed rather flexible rules of spelling, and in fact some letters of the alphabet were not completely fixed: *i, j,* and *y,* and *u, v,* and *w* were not yet distinct letters. Sometimes a word would be written with an *e* at the end and sometimes not. Thus, *join* might be written *ioyn* or *joyne* or *ioyne.* The word *the* was frequently written *ye,* the *y* in this case being a form of a Middle English letter that stood for the sound *th* and that had disappeared. (These spellings are now used by some store owners who want to give an old-fashioned appearance to their store's name; for example, Ye Olde Noveltie Shoppe.)

In 1755, in England, Samuel Johnson's great *Dictionary of the English Language* was published. Dr. Johnson also wished to reg-

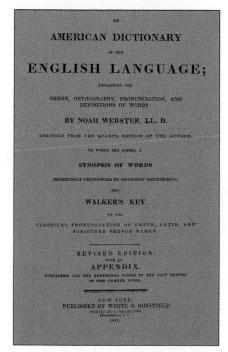

Title page, *The American Spelling Book* by Noah Webster (1790). Printed by Isaiah Thomas, Boston, Massachusetts.

Rare Book Division, New York Public Library.

bär, fall, whạt, prey, marine, pin, bïrd, möve.

THE SQUIRREL.

The squirrel is a beautiful little animal. The gray and black squirrels live in the forest and make a nest of leaves and sticks on the high branches. It is amusing to see the nimble squirrel spring from branch to branch, or run up and down the stem of a tree, and dart behind it to escape from sight. Little ground squirrels burrow in the earth. They subsist on nuts, which they hold in their paws, using them as little boys use their hands.

FABLE I.

Of the Boy that stole Apples.

An old man found a rude boy upon one of his trees stealing apples, and desired him to come down ; but the young sauce-box told him plainly he would not. Won't you? said the old man, then I will fetch you down ; so he pulled up

The American Spelling Book by Noah Webster (1783). Engraving (from 1793 edition).

Rare Book Division, New York Public Library.

ularize spelling, and Webster's attempts to regularize American spelling were partly an attempt to refine Johnson's methods. Early editions of Webster's American speller were quite conservative—that is, most of the spellings were consistent with Johnson's English spellings. The main exception was Webster's omission of the *k* in words ending in -*ck.* Where Johnson's dictionary had *publick* and *musick,* Webster's speller had *public* and *music.* By 1789, though, Webster's more radical ideas regarding spelling had aroused a great deal of mocking resistance, even in his own country. His proposals resulted in spellings that were too different from common usage to be acceptable to many people.

Webster's first principle was the "omission of all superfluous or silent letters"—such as the *k* in *musick* and all silent vowels and consonants. *Bread, give, friend, programme, travelled,* and *built* thus became *bred, giv, frend, program, traveled,* and *bilt.*

Webster's second principle was to regularize spelling and sound. For example, *grieve* and *mean* contain the same vowel sounds spelled differently. Webster used *ee* for both as well as anywhere that sound occurred—*greev* and *meen,* and also *pleez* and *bleet.* Similarly, *laugh* and *draught* became *laf* and *draft, plough* became *plow,* and *women* became *wimmin.*

Webster's batting average was not very high, as these examples show, and he gradually yielded to public pressure and modified his more radical spellings. Still, he had some successes, and virtually all of the present differences between British and American spelling were advocated by Webster.

Webster's Dictionary

Webster's first dictionary, published in 1806, contained all of these spellings and others. Readers no doubt experienced a good deal of surprise when they came across words like *tung, fether, soop,* and *definit.*

Many of Webster's recommended pronunciations must have been surprising as well. Webster disliked fashionable and urban people and manners almost as much as he disliked British ways. At times, in fact, his praise of the common people and their simple ways sounded Whitmanesque, years before Whitman was born. He praised "the great body of farmers and mechanics" in the United States, writing in 1789:

> A man of great soul would sooner imitate the virtues of a cottage than the vices of a court; would deem it more honorable to gain one useful idea from the humble laborer, than to copy the vicious pronunciation of a splendid court.

These words didn't simply express an opinion; they launched a crusade. Any pronunciation that smacked of being affected or too fashionable was hateful to Webster. He rejected the *yu* sound in words such as *lecture, nature, figure,* and *tenure* as affectations. He recommended that they be pronounced *lecter, nater, figger,* and *tenor.*

Webster was an odd mixture of conservative and radical. In matters of spelling and pronunciation, he laid down stern rules; and yet in matters of grammar and usage, he was often willing to bow to the usage of the common people. The single thread running through these two contradictory attitudes was Webster's democratic desire for a common, regular American language.

Many of Webster's spelling reforms and odd pronouncements make him appear to be a crackpot, and there is no question that there was something of the crackpot about him. He had a degree from Yale, but as a linguist he was self-taught. Like many self-taught people he had odd gaps in his learning. As a result, his etymologies, or word derivations, were frequently incorrect.

Despite the fact that his enthusiasms and spotty knowledge led him astray, Webster was no fool, and he was enormously energetic. *The American Dictionary of the English Language* was an incredible accomplishment for one person. His 1806 dictionary had defined 28,000 words and indicated their pronunciation. The 1828 dictionary defined 70,000 words and provided etymologies as well as pronunciations. This was the first dictionary to include Americanisms such as *lot, to spell* ("to relieve someone at work"), and *clever* ("good-natured"). "Such local terms exist," he had written some years before, "in spite of lexicographers and critics. Is this *my* fault? And if local terms exist, why not explain them? . . . How are such words to be understood without the aid of a dictionary?"

The *American Dictionary* also included the new American meanings of older English words such as *congress, court,* and *plantation,* and settled for all time the changes in word endings that distinguish American from British usage: *-er* for *-re* (*center* rather than *centre*); *-or* for *-our* (*favor* rather than *favour*); *-c* for *-ck* (*music* rather than *musick*); *-ck* for *-que* (*check* rather than *cheque*); *-ize* for *-ise* (*legalize* rather than *legalise*); and *-ler* for *-ller* (*traveler* rather than *traveller*). The 1828 dictionary decided firmly that Americans would spell and pronounce the name of the newly produced metal *aluminum* (the British favored *aluminium,* like *sodium* and *potassium*). We say *skedule* rather than *shedule* because Webster thought the pronunciation of *schedule* should follow the example of *school.*

"Noah's Ark"

For all of its eccentricities, then, the *American Dictionary* was a landmark in the development of American English. When Webster had announced, early in the 1800's, that he was preparing a dictionary that would include American words and usages, he was attacked by purists. One wrote in the *New England Palladium:*

> If the Connecticut Lexicographer considers retaining the English language as a badge of slavery, let him not give us a Babylonish dialect in its stead, but adopt at once the language of the aborigines . . . . Let, then, the projected volume of *foul* and *unclean* things bear his own Christian name, and be called—Noah's Ark.

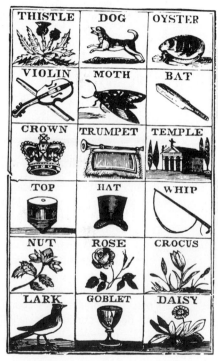

Picture Lessons, a nineteenth-century teaching aid. Engraving.

Despite such criticism, the foul Americanisms found their way aboard Noah's Ark and gained thereby a legitimacy they would otherwise not have had. And Webster's pronouncements, even when they had little sound linguistic reasoning behind them, settled the uncertainties about authority in American English. Generations of Americans decided on the correctness of a word or a usage or a spelling by "looking it up in Webster's," and every household had to have a copy of Webster's dictionary next to the Bible.

Early in his career, Webster had been one of those who thought that American English would become as distinct from British English as Dutch is from German. By 1828, although his patriotism had not diminished, his views of the development of American English had moderated. "The body of the language is the same as in England," he wrote in the Preface to the *American Dictionary,* "and it is desirable to perpetuate that sameness." In the same Preface, though, he pointed proudly at the burgeoning American literature as a source of richness and at the growth of the language as a source of pride. He would have been pleased to have seen the fruits of his labors.

Analyzing Language

1. One of the reasons Webster advocated spelling reform was to provide consistency. He thought that words that sounded the same should be spelled the same. This was not as easy as it seemed, though. Here is a selection written by Webster in his reformed spelling. Read it carefully, then find the places where he was inconsistent. Consider these inconsistencies: the use of *r* instead of *wr* to indicate an *r* sound; the use of *s* instead of *c* to indicate an *s* sound; elimination of unsounded double consonants; elimination of silent letters.

In the essays, ritten within the last year, a considerable change of spelling iz introduced by way of experiment. The liberty waz taken by the writers before the age of Queen Elizabeth, and to this we are indeted for the preference of modern spelling over that of Gower and Chaucer. The man who admits that the change of *hous-bonde, mynde, ygone, moneth* into *husband, mind, gone, month,* iz an improovment, must acknowledge also the riting of *helth, breth, rong, tung, munth,* to be an improovment. There iz no alternativ. Every possible reezon that could ever be offered for altering the spelling of *wurds,* stil exists in full force; and if a gradual reform should not be made in our language, it wil proov that we are less under the influence of reezon than our ancestors.

2. Make a list of words in which the sounds represented by the letters *a, e,* and *i* are very different. (For example, the letter *a* represents three different sounds in the words *mate, mat,* and *all.*)

3. Most efforts at spelling reform have been failures, and we find inconsistencies in English spelling still with us. List pairs of words that are still spelled in similar ways but that are pronounced differently (such as *tough* and *bough*). Then list pairs of words that are still spelled differently but that are pronounced the same (such as *dead* and *bed*).

4. Webster's simplified spelling never completely succeeded, but nonstandard forms of simplified spelling have flourished in product names, in advertising signs ("All-Nite Diner"), and in road signs ("Thruway North"). Make a list of five such simplified spellings from examples you have seen. Explain whether or not you think they are useful.

5. Make a list of school subjects or jobs that you think could be spelled more simply. Next to each word, write its simpler spelling. Then use the words in a paragraph, in their simpler forms, and exchange your paragraphs in class. Does everyone understand the new simplified spellings?

RESPONDING TO LITERATURE

Writing Assignment

Write an essay of at least four paragraphs, in which you discuss your response to the lines from Phyllis Wheatley's poem "To the Right Honorable William, Earl of Dartmouth . . ." which follow. Consider in your resonse the facts of Wheatley's life, which follow the poem.

From **To the Right Honorable William, Earl of Dartmouth, His Majesty's Principal Secretary of State for North America, etc.**

Should you, my lord, while you pursue my song
Wonder from whence my love of *Freedom* sprung,
Whence flow these wishes for the common good,
By feeling hearts alone best understood,
I, young in life, by seeming cruel fate
Was snatched from *Afric's* fancied happy seat:
What pangs excruciating must molest,
What sorrows labor in my parent's breast?
Steeled was the soul and by no misery moved
That from a father seized his babe beloved
Such, such my case. And can I then but pray
Others may never feel tyrannic sway?

For favors past, great Sir, our thanks are due,
And thee we ask thy favors to renew,
Since in thy power, as in thy will before,
To soothe the griefs, which thou didst once deplore.
May heav'nly grace the sacred sanction give
To all thy works, and thou forever live
Not only on the wings of fleeting *Fame,*
Though praise immortal crowns the patriot's name,
But to conduct to heav'ns refulgent fane,
May fiery coursers sweep th' ethereal plain,
And bear thee upwards to that blest abode,
Where, like the prophet, thou shalt find thy God.

—Phyllis Wheatley

Phyllis Wheatley was born in Africa, probably in what is now Senegal or Ghana. She arrived on a slave ship in Boston in 1761 and was purchased by John Wheatley. She was probably only about seven years old at the time (there is a reference to the loss of her baby teeth). She became Mrs. Wheatley's servant. Named Phyllis, and assuming her owners' surname, the young girl showed tremendous precocity. She learned not only English but also Latin, and she often read the Bible and the English poets popular in her time. In 1773 her only book of poetry was published with much fanfare in England. After the Wheatleys died, Phyllis was freed, and she married John Peters, a free man. But all the attention lavished on her in her early life dried up the moment she was on her own. She died destitute when she was only about thirty-five years old.

Wheatley's style is like the style popular in poetry of her time: She uses a Latinate vocabulary, inversions, and elevated diction. Here she addresses a man who had just been appointed secretary in charge of the American Colonies (1772). Dartmouth, she hoped, would be more open to the Colonists' grievances.

Background

Whenever you read something, you respond in some personal way. Your response might be "Terrific!" or "This is boring," or "This character reminds me of my Uncle Paul."

Personal responses are not necessarily based on objective criteria, or standards. For that reason, there are no "right" or "wrong" responses to a piece of writing. Your reactions are as valid as anyone else's.

In planning an essay of response, you might want to consider the following questions.

1. **Enjoyment.** Did you like reading the selection, or not? Can you determine why?
2. **Emotions.** How did the selection make you feel? What did the writer do to evoke these feelings?
3. **Similarity to Your Experience.** Did the characters, scenes, or situations remind you of anything you have experienced or heard about? Did they seem credible? Why or why not?
4. **Style.** How would you describe the writer's style—that is, his or her diction, or word choice; sentence structure; and clarity of expression? How did the style affect your response?
5. **Meanings.** Beyond the surface details of the selection, what is the writer's meaning or **purpose**? (If you aren't sure, say so in your essay.) How effectively is this meaning conveyed? Do you agree with the writer's message? Did the selection make you think about something that had not occurred to you before?

Prewriting

The first step in writing an essay of response is to read the selection carefully. While you read, you should make comments and ask questions. Because you will eventually write about your response, you should write out these comments and questions, so you can make use of them later.

Here is an example of one reader's responses to the first few lines of the poem. They may or may not be similar to your own responses.

> **Lines 1–2:** The first thing I have to do is figure out these archaic words: "Should you . . . wonder from whence my love of *Freedom* sprung." Right away I can say that the style is very old-fashioned.

Frontispiece for *Poems on Various Subjects, Religious and Moral* by Phyllis Wheatley (c. 1772). Engraving.

American Antiquarian Society, Worcester, Massachusetts.

After you have written your comments and questions about the rest of the poem, look again at the five sets of questions under **Background.** Apply those questions to Wheatley's poem.

Sort through your questions and comments. Think about how you reacted to the poem. Then write a **topic statement** that expresses your overall response. (The topic statement can consist of more than one sentence.)

Writing

Here is the first paragraph of one reader's response to Wheatley's poem. You might use it as a model for your own opening paragraph. Then complete your essay with further information on how you responded to the poem. Notice that the first paragraph summarizes very generally the writer's response. Subsequent paragraphs should develop specific aspects of the response.

> When I first read it, I thought Phyllis Wheatley's poem "To the Right Honorable William, Earl of Dartmouth . . ." took a long time to say very little. I thought her style was really tough and old-fashioned and hard to understand. After each additional reading, however, I came to find the poem easier, and I liked it more. The message is made clear and so are the poet's feelings. I was moved by her feelings about tyranny. People may ask: How would you feel about the poem if you knew nothing about the writer? I'm not interested in that question. I'm interested in this one: What would Phyllis Wheatley have written if she'd felt free to be personal?

Revising and Proofreading

Use the guidelines in the section at the back of this book, called **Writing About Literature,** to revise and proofread your essay.

THE AMERICAN RENAISSANCE
FIVE MAJOR WRITERS

Geraniums by Andrew Wyeth (1960). Drybrush watercolor.　　Private collection.

UNIT FOUR

Five Famous Writers

On August 5, 1850, a remarkable party took place in Stockbridge, Massachusetts, at the home of an attorney named David Dudley Field. Among those attending were the Boston publisher, James Fields; two of his authors, Oliver Wendell Holmes and Nathaniel Hawthorne; the New York editor and publisher, Evert Duyckinck; and two of *his* authors, Cornelius Mathews and Herman Melville. The party began in the morning with a climb up Monument Mountain, a peak in the Berkshires made famous by William Cullen Bryant's poem "The Story of an Indian Girl." Although several members of the party had never met before, the group was in good humor—perhaps, in part, because of a champagne picnic lunch. During the climb, Melville, the bravest of the group, leaned out over precipices to demonstrate how sailors took in sail; Hawthorne, usually the most restrained of men, loosened up enough to look wildly about for the great carbuncle (a deep-red gem), the subject of a tale, based on a local legend, which he had written many years before.

The afternoon continued with a long, wine-filled dinner at Field's house. The conversation turned, not surprisingly, to American literature. In response to a mischievous statement by Holmes in praise of English writers, Melville vigorously defended American writers. The question of whether there would ever be an American writer as great as Shakespeare provoked a heated discussion, with Melville again firmly supporting the American side. Hawthorne found himself agreeing with Melville, whom he had never met before, and who, he discovered, was currently living in Pittsfield, not far from Hawthorne's own home in Lenox.

Melville and Hawthorne: An Unlikely Friendship

The possibility of a friendship between these two celebrated writers would have seemed highly unlikely. Herman Melville (see page 294) was a sociable ex-sailor, best known at this time for having lived among cannibals in the South Seas and for having written a remarkable first novel, *Typee* (1846), about the experience. Since the publication of that novel, he had written three moderately successful short novels about the sea. He had also written one immensely long, "experimental" novel, *Mardi,* about . . . well, no one had been quite sure what it was about. At the time of Field's party, Melville was at work on his fifth novel, which, it appeared, was also going to be fairly long.

Nathaniel Hawthorne (see page 263) was fifteen years older than Melville. He had had a slightly more conventional career as a writer of fiction, especially of short tales that had been published

Illustration (detail) by
Mead Shaeffer for *Typee* (1920) by
Herman Melville.

Columbia University Library, New York.

in a variety of magazines. Magazines, and the short stories required to fill them, had become very popular with a growing audience of prosperous and educated readers. Hawthorne had already collected two volumes of his stories in book form. His recently published novel, *The Scarlet Letter,* displayed his fascination with the dark side of New England's Puritan past. And he was at work on another novel, *The House of the Seven Gables.*

Hawthorne was reserved and little given to social activity of any kind. But despite the differences in the two writers' temperaments and interests, a friendship sprang up between them. "I met Melville the other day," Hawthorne wrote to a friend, "and liked him so much that I have asked him to spend a few days with me before leaving these parts." This was the beginning of a remarkable association that came at a critical point in Melville's life, when he was hard at work on *Moby-Dick.* Melville was exposed to what he called the power of darkness in Hawthorne's work, which he began to read avidly following their meeting. This exposure had a powerful effect on what would become the greatest novel written by an American in the nineteenth century.

A Declaration of Literary Independence

The immediate result of this meeting was a magazine essay Melville wrote two weeks later. In addition to extravagant praise of its subject, the essay contained a stirring defense of American literature over English literature. Stating that "England, after all, is, in many things, an alien to us," Melville urged American readers to "prize and cherish her [America's] writers." He claimed that in Hawthorne, America was very close to producing her own Shakespeare, and he went on to add in a burst of literary patriotism that "even if there were no Hawthorne, no Emerson, no Whittier, no Irving, no Bryant, no Dana, no Cooper . . . nevertheless, let America first praise mediocrity, even, in her own children, before she praises . . . the best excellence in the children of any other land."

This was only the latest expression of a common theme that went back to the earliest days of the Republic. As Noah Webster had put it in 1783, "America must be as independent in *literature* as she is in *politics,* as famous for *arts* as for *arms.*" The difference now was that the high expectations for an American literature of the first rank were finally justified. The members of that party in the Berkshires were themselves proof that America did, in fact, finally possess a powerful class of imaginative writers.

Melville's hornblowing for American literature coincided with the beginning of an extraordinary explosion of American literary genius. It was a time when the American landscape and American culture would finally find their place in a native and original literature. Writers of the time were aware of this, and they sometimes used the word *renaissance* to describe the phenomenon.

The American Renaissance was not literally a "rebirth"; rather, it was an equivalent to the earlier European Renaissance, in the sense that it marked the arrival of cultural maturity. "There is a

Puritan children averting their eyes from Hester Prynne. From *The Scarlet Letter* by Nathaniel Hawthorne. Engraving after a painting by George Boughton (mid 19th century).

moment in the history of every nation," Emerson wrote, "when, proceeding out of . . . brute youth, the perceptive powers reach their ripeness . . . so that man, at that instant, extends across the entire scale and, with his feet still planted on the immense forces of night, converses by his eyes and brain with solar and stellar creation. That is the moment of adult health, the culmination of power."

This was the moment America had reached, at least in its literature. The confidence these writers felt in the vitality of their time is evidenced in the remarkable body of work they produced. In the period from 1849 to 1855, the following works were published: Emerson's *Representative Men,* Hawthorne's *The Scarlet Letter* and *The House of the Seven Gables,* Melville's *Moby-Dick* and *Pierre,* Thoreau's *Walden,* and Whitman's *Leaves of Grass* (see page 331)—enough masterpieces for any national literature. How had this come about?

The Intellectual and Social Life of New England

One of the most important reasons for the rise of American literature in the mid-nineteenth century was the intellectual and social ferment in New England. This region had been traditionally noted for its interests in self-improvement and in intellectual pursuits; the prosperity of the century's early decades created an especially fertile soil for their growth.

Lyceum Lecture by James Pollard Espy at Clinton Hall by an unknown artist (1841). Pen and ink.

Museum of the City of New York.

These interests found expression in the Lyceum movement, which was founded in 1826 to improve American education. The Lyceum organizations were named for the school of the Greek philosopher Aristotle. They had a number of goals, ranging from training teachers to establishing museums. One part of the Lyceum program was a course of winter lectures, which became immensely popular in New England and throughout the Midwest. The topics ranged from the practical ("The Honey Bee") to the educational ("The Life and Times of Oliver Cromwell") to the inspirational

("The Capacity of the Human Mind for Culture and Improvement"). One of the most popular speakers in this lecture, from the 1830's to the 1870's, was Ralph Waldo Emerson (see page 187).

"There is something about this familial innocent chapter in American life," the twentieth-century critic Alfred Kazin has written of these times, "that suddenly takes one back to the classic, the prophetic beginning of nations. Emerson was on a mission to his own people; he was preaching now to the whole American congregation. To recall these village lyceums, these rude country halls, evening meetings in odd churches, barns, schools, and banquet rooms, tents spread in preparation for the idyllic summer's opening of the college year. . . is to imagine a time when people still looked to literary men for guidance. . . . Emerson made a thousand appearances, crossed the Mississippi on ice in dead winter to deliver a lecture in Iowa, was bumped, jostled, frozen in wagons, carriages, flatboats, steamboats, trains (where he felt so solitary that he vowed he would go over to any man reading a book and hug him)."

Emerson's School of Philosophy, called "Sylvan," in Concord, Massachusetts.

This was a time of social improvement in other ways as well. New England was a center of numerous reform movements. Horace Mann and others were dedicated to improving public education; Dorothea Dix devoted herself to alleviating the horrible conditions in insane asylums; others addressed themselves to the problems of the blind and the deaf. Abolitionist groups led by the radical William Lloyd Garrison sought the immediate abolition of slavery. Feminists such as Elizabeth Peabody, Margaret Fuller, and Emma Willard campaigned for women's rights. (Women were still not allowed to vote, and their other legal rights were greatly limited.)

Southerners called New England the home of "isms," and they were right—social causes, both reasonable and crackpot, abounded. Numerous utopian projects aimed at reforming society completely. In 1840, Emerson wrote to the British writer Thomas Carlyle that "not a reading man but has a draft [plan] of a new community in his waistcoat pocket." Emerson was speaking from personal experience, for the most influential of these utopian groups had been meeting in his own home since 1836.

The Transcendentalists

Emerson's friend, Dr. Frederic Hedge, had first proposed the group, which called itself "Hedge's Club" or "The Symposium." But to outsiders it quickly became known as "The Transcendental Club." The term **transcendental** came from the German Romantic philosopher Immanuel Kant. The word referred to the idea that matters of ultimate reality—God, the cosmos, the self—transcend, or go beyond, human experience.

For Emerson, Transcendentalism was not a new idea but, as he wrote in 1842, "the very oldest of thoughts cast into the mold of these new times." That "oldest of thoughts" was Idealism, which originated with Plato in ancient Greece. Idealism asserted that the true reality was spiritual or "ideal," rather than physical. The

Transcendentalists were Idealists in this philosophical sense. They sought the permanent spiritual reality that lay behind transitory physical appearances. They were also idealists in a broader sense. They optimistically believed in the perfectibility of man, and they were often engaged in projects intended to make this ideal a reality.

The club that met in Emerson's house comprised a wide range of members and beliefs. There were a number of ministers, including George Ripley, founder of *The Dial,* the Transcendentalists' periodical, and of Brook Farm, a self-governing, experimental community. (Brook Farm survived for six years and became the setting for Hawthorne's *Blithedale Romance.* Hawthorne lived at the Farm for a few months but could not stand all the elevated conversation.) There were radical educators like Bronson Alcott (the father of Louisa May Alcott), who ran the Temple School in Boston. Alcott also founded an experimental community, Fruitlands, a vegetarian group that lasted only seven months. Another member was Margaret Fuller, a feminist and an influential critic, who edited *The Dial* for several years.

These were powerful and independent thinkers, not so much under Emerson's influence as in his circle. When we think of Transcendentalism today, we think almost automatically of Emerson. But in fact, Transcendentalist ideas were as wide-ranging as these minds; they were educational, practical, mystical, poetical, and political. The Transcendentalists shared an idealism and a commitment to the spiritual and the hopeful, but that commitment took many forms.

Emerson and Transcendentalism: The American Roots

Emerson himself remained skeptical of many of the Transcendentalists' ideas and projects. Although he edited *The Dial* for two years, both Brook Farm and Fruitlands were founded (and collapsed) without his participation. Nevertheless, he was the most influential and well known of the Transcendentalists, largely because of his lectures and books.

Transcendental thought was most clearly and forcefully expressed in Emerson's writings and in those of his disciple, Henry David Thoreau (see page 204). As developed by Emerson, Transcendentalism grafted ideas from Europe and the Far East onto a native American philosophical stem. Perhaps the best way of viewing this school of thought is by examining its American roots, especially the ideas about the relations between God, humanity, and nature held by Emerson's New England ancestors.

For the Puritans, there were basically two ways in which God was revealed to people. The first was through the Bible, the word of God. The second was through the physical world; to William Bradford, for example, the death of a scoffing sailor on the *Mayflower* was the direct action of God in the human world. God existed in a less clearly defined way for some other Puritans. Jonathan Edwards found God's "excellency, His wisdom, His purity and love

Ralph Waldo Emerson's home, Concord, Massachusetts.

. . . in the sun, moon, and stars . . . in the grass, flowers, trees; in the water, and all nature." This native mysticism—which was typical as well of Romanticism—would reappear in Emerson's thought.

A rational thinker like Benjamin Franklin, on the other hand, saw nature differently. Far from recognizing in nature any direct manifestation of God, he viewed it as something to be examined scientifically and to be used for the betterment of humanity.

For Emerson, both of these ways of viewing the world around us were important; but the mystical outlook was "higher" than the practical one. The mystical view did not spring from logic; it came, rather, from intuition. It was spontaneous and emotional, not deliberate and rational.

Emerson followed in the Romantic tradition of William Cullen Bryant (see page 138) by holding that the physical facts of the natural world were the doorway to the spiritual or ideal world. Like Jonathan Edwards, he found God's presence in the world around him. Alone in nature, the logical part of his mind gave way, to allow direct, visionary contact with the world of the spirit. Emerson gave memorable expression to this moment: "Standing on the bare ground, all mean egotism vanishes. I become a transparent eyeball. I am nothing. I see all. The currents of the Universal Being circulate through me; I am part or parcel of God."

One product of Emerson's conviction that we can find God directly in nature was a profound optimism. God is good, and God works through nature. Therefore, even the natural events that seem most tragic—pestilence, death, disaster—can be explained on a spiritual level. Death is simply a part of the cycle of life. To the extent that we are separated from a direct, intuitive knowledge of God, we are capable of evil. But if we simply trust ourselves—that is, trust in the power each of us has to know God directly—then we will realize that each of us is also part of the Divine Soul, the source of all good. "That is always best which gives me to myself," Emerson wrote in an address to the Harvard Divinity School. "That which shows God in me, fortifies me. That which shows God out of me, makes me a wart and a wen [cyst]."

Emerson's optimism struck a sympathetic chord with audiences that might have had difficulty with the more complex aspects of his thought. Your condition today, he seemed to tell his readers and listeners, may be mean, dull, and routine, but it need not be. All we need do is discover the god within each of us, he suggested, and our lives will partake of the grandeur of the universe.

Melville, Hawthorne, and Poe: The Power of Darkness

Emerson's idealism was exciting stuff for his audiences, but not all the writers and thinkers of the time were in agreement with Transcendentalist thought. "To one who has weathered Cape Horn as a common sailor," Herman Melville wrote of Emerson's ideas, "what stuff all this is."

An illustration from a French translation of Poe's "The Masque of the Red Death," by Lobel-Riche.

too broad. The best term, perhaps, is *poet,* not in the sense of *versifier,* but in the sense Melville intended when he wrote that Benjamin Franklin was "everything but a poet." (See page 73.)

"I am a poet," Emerson wrote to his fiancée, Lydia Jackson, in 1835, "of a low class without doubt but yet a poet. That is my nature & vocation. My singing be sure is very 'husky,' & is for the most part in prose. Still am I a poet in the sense of a perceiver & dear lover of the harmonies that are in the soul & in matter. . . . ."

This poet was born in Boston in 1803 to a family that was cultured, but poor. When he was only eight years old, his father, a Unitarian minister, died of tuberculosis. His mother was left with four growing boys to care for. A fifth son was mentally retarded and raised by relatives. Mrs. Emerson opened a boardinghouse and depended on the generosity of the Church.

The father's place in the lives of the Emerson children was taken by their aunt. Mary Moody Emerson was a strict Calvinist whose rigid piety emphasized self-sacrifice and whose enormous energy drove the Emerson boys to achievement. "She had the misfortune," Emerson later wrote, "of spinning with a greater velocity than any of the other tops."

Despite Aunt Mary's example of self-reliance in the family, every step of Emerson's own life had been laid out for him from an early age. He was to go to Harvard and become a minister like his father and the seven generations of Emersons before him. Emerson uncomfortably obeyed. His life consisted of a series of attempts to establish his own identity against this background of expectation.

When he was fourteen, Emerson entered Harvard. He was an indifferent student, especially weak at science and mathematics, but he read widely in philosophy and theology. The most significant events of his college career occurred during his junior year. He dropped the name Ralph, a gesture toward establishing his identity, and he began keeping a journal. Eventually reaching monumental proportions (the published version consists of fourteen volumes), that journal would be the source of Emerson's lectures and essays for the rest of his life.

Emerson's academic record at Harvard was so weak that upon graduation he failed to get a teaching post in the prestigious Boston Public Latin School. Instead, he took a teaching job at a school run by his uncle, and he prepared himself, with many doubts, for the Unitarian ministry. In 1826, he was licensed to preach. Three years later, at the age of twenty-six, he accepted a post at Boston's Second Church, which had been Cotton Mather's church a century before. That year, he married Ellen Tucker, a beautiful but fragile seventeen-year-old already in the early stages of tuberculosis, that curse of nineteenth-century life. Sixteen months later Ellen died.

Emerson's grief coincided with a growing disbelief in some of the central doctrines of his religion. As a result, he distrusted his own vocation as a minister. In June of 1832, he shocked his congregation by resigning the ministry and setting off for an extended tour of Europe.

Long influenced by European thinkers, Emerson had read the work of German philosopher Immanuel Kant and admired the writings of British historian Thomas Carlyle, who was in Scotland thundering out calls for individual greatness and denouncing the evils of modern society. Emerson had also read the Romantic poets William Wordsworth and Samuel Taylor Coleridge. From Kant he would adopt the term *transcendentalism;* from Coleridge he would take up the crucial distinction between logical thought and intuition, a poetic form of thought that enables us to see the correspondences between the physical world and spiritual reality. In Europe Emerson met and conversed with Coleridge and Wordsworth, and he visited Carlyle at his remote farmhouse.

When he returned to America in 1834, Emerson settled in Concord, Massachusetts, and soon married Lydia Jackson. He began to supplement his meager income by giving lectures. In fact, he found in the lectern "a second pulpit," as he wrote Carlyle. After a short time, the major works by which we have come to know Emerson's thought began to appear.

The announced subject of Emerson's first series of lectures was the philosophy of history. Emerson's view was distinctively American, in that he denied the importance of the past. "The ancients are dead," he said in one of these early lectures, "but for us the earth is new today and heaven is raining influences. Let us unfetter ourselves of our historical associations and find a pure standard in the idea of man."

The last phrase points to Emerson's focus on

Ralph Waldo Emerson and his family.

the nature of our humanity—a subject that really interested him more in these lectures than any philosophy of history. Individual men and women were part of this "idea of man" in the same way that individual souls were part of a larger entity, which Emerson would later call the "Over-Soul."

The idea of nature corresponded to the idea of man—both were part of a universal whole. "There is in nature," he wrote in the "Humanity of Science," "a parallel unity, which corresponds to this unity in the mind, and makes it available. . . . Not only man puts things in a row, but things belong in a row."

In 1836, there occurred three major events in Emerson's life: the publication of *Nature,* the most complete exposition of his philosophy; the birth of his son Waldo, who would become the center of Emerson's life; and the first meeting of a conversation group of like-minded thinkers in Emerson's drawing room, which would come to be called "The Transcendental Club."

Over the following years, Emerson's influence as a lecturer and an intellectual leader continued to grow. In 1837, he excited his student audience at Harvard with the lecture now known as "The American Scholar." Oliver Wendell Holmes (see page 161) called this speech "our intellectual Declaration of Independence." In the speech, Emerson demanded that American scholars free themselves from the shackles of the past. "Our day of dependence," Emerson declared, "our long apprenticeship to the learning of other lands, draws to a close." He reminded scholars of the importance of the present and of things that were apparently insignificant. Since all things are part of a larger whole, even the commonest matters could open a door to the eternal.

A year later, in 1838, he was invited back to Harvard by a small group of divinity students to speak to them on the eve of their graduation. His speech—"The Divinity School Address"—called for a rejection of institutional religion in favor of a personal relation with God. Religious

"Standing on the bare ground, — my head bathed by the blithe air, & uplifted into infinite space, — all mean egotism vanishes. I become a transparent Eyeball." *Nature, p. 13.*

A caricature by Christopher Pearce Cranch from *Illustrations of the New Philosophy.*

Houghton Library, Harvard University, Cambridge.

truth, Emerson said, was "an intuition. It cannot be received at second hand." Like the scholar's books, the pulpit was for inspiration, not indoctrination. Emerson called upon the young divinity students before him to "cast behind . . . all conformity, and acquaint men at first hand with the Deity." This lecture so outraged Harvard authorities (who seized on what they thought was its denial of the divinity of Christ) that three decades passed before Emerson was allowed to speak there again.

By this time, Emerson's life had settled into a consistent pattern: an ever-widening series of lecture tours, punctuated by the publication of his lectures in essay form. *Essays* appeared in 1841; *Essays: Second Series* in 1844; *Represen-*tative *Men* in 1850. There was something for everyone in his lectures and essays, but especially for the legions of people who were disappointed with the narrowing material or spiritual condition of their lives.

It was to these people, perhaps, that Emerson spoke most intensely. Concord became a kind of Mecca to a rising class of disaffected and truth-seeking young. They sought out Emerson as a kind of guru. But Emerson's genius was such that he appealed to a broad spectrum of American society. Intellectuals responded to his philosophy, his ideas about the relations between humanity, nature, and God; the young responded to his hope, his declarations that they were on the verge of a great new age; while society at large responded to his optimism, his claims that all was really for the best.

That optimism was dealt a severe blow in 1842 when Emerson's son Waldo died at the age of six from scarlet fever. Emerson was profoundly moved. By nature a rather cold, restrained man, he had found in Waldo someone to whom he could demonstrate his love directly and unaffectedly. At the child's death, Emerson shrank back into an emotional shell from which he never reemerged. "How can I hope for a friend," he wrote in his journal during his middle years, "who have never been one?"

In his later years, Emerson suffered from a severe loss of memory and had difficulty recalling the most ordinary words. This affliction resulted in his increasing public silence, and when he did appear in public, he read from notes. Near the end of his life, agreeing to such a performance, he remarked, "A queer occasion it will be—a lecturer who has no idea of what he is lecturing about, and an audience who don't know what he *can* mean."

In the autumn of 1881, Walt Whitman paid Emerson a visit of respect and was asked to dinner. In Whitman's report of this "blessed evening with Emerson," he wrote that Emerson "seated himself in his chair, a trifle pushed back, and, though a listener and apparently an alert one, remained silent through the whole talk and discussion. A lady friend [Louisa May Alcott] quietly took a seat next to him, to give special attention. A good color in his face, eyes clear, with the well-known expression of sweetness, and the old clear-peering aspect quite the same." Six months later, Emerson was dead.

FROM NATURE

In his introduction to the book *Nature,* from which the following chapter is taken, Emerson offers a clue to the underlying purpose of his work when he encourages us, his contemporaries, to look directly at Nature:

"Our age is retrospective. It builds the sepulchres of the fathers. It writes biographies, histories, and criticism. The foregoing generations beheld God and nature face to face; we, through their eyes. Why should we not also enjoy an original relation to the universe? Why should we not have a poetry and philosophy of insight and not of tradition, and a religion by revelation to us, and not the history of theirs?"

As you read this first chapter from *Nature,* think about whether people can still achieve this mystical relationship with natural universe. Since 1836, when the essay was first published, how has the natural world changed? What has happened to "the plantations of God"?

To go into solitude, a man needs to retire as much from his chamber [room] as from society. I am not solitary while I read and write, though nobody is with me. But if a man would be alone, let him look at the stars. The rays that come from those heavenly worlds will separate between him and what he touches. One might think the atmosphere was made transparent with this design, to give man, in the heavenly bodies, the perpetual presence of the sublime. Seen in the streets of cities, how great they are! If the stars should appear one night in a thousand years, how would men believe and adore; and preserve for many generations the remembrance of the city of God which had been shown! But every night come out these envoys of beauty, and light the universe with their admonishing smile.

The stars awaken a certain reverence, because though always present, they are inaccessible; but all natural objects make a kindred impression, when the mind is open to their influence. Nature never wears a mean appearance. Neither does the wisest man extort her secret, and lose his curiosity by finding out all her perfection. Nature never became a toy to a wise spirit. The flowers, the animals, the mountains, reflected the wisdom of his best hour, as much as they had delighted the simplicity of his childhood.

When we speak of nature in this manner, we have a distinct but most poetical sense in the mind. We mean the integrity of impression made by manifold natural objects. It is this which distinguishes the stick of timber of the woodcutter from the tree of the poet. The charming landscape which I saw this morning is indubitably made up of some twenty or thirty farms. Miller owns this field, Locke that, and Manning the woodland beyond. But none of them owns the landscape. There is a property in the horizon which no man has but he whose eye can integrate all the parts, that is, the poet. This is the best part of these men's farms, yet to this their warranty deeds give no title.

To speak truly, few adult persons can see nature. Most persons do not see the sun. At least they have a very superficial seeing. The sun illuminates only the eye of the man, but shines into the eye and the heart of the child. The lover of nature is he whose inward and outward senses are still truly adjusted to each other; who has retained the spirit of infancy even into the era of manhood. His intercourse with heaven and earth becomes part of his daily food. In the presence of nature, a wild delight runs through the man, in spite of real sorrows. Nature says—he is my creature, and maugre [despite] all his impertinent griefs, he shall be glad with me. Not the sun or the summer alone, but every hour and season yields its tribute of delight; for every hour and change corresponds to and authorizes a different state of the mind, from breathless noon to grimmest midnight.

Nature is a setting that fits equally well a comic or a mourning piece. In good health, the air is a cordial of incredible virtue. Crossing a bare common, in snow puddles, at twilight, under a clouded sky, without having in my thoughts any occurrence of special good fortune, I have enjoyed a perfect exhilaration. I am glad to the brink of fear.

In the woods, too, a man casts off his years, as the snake his slough, and at what period soever of life, is always a child. In the woods is perpetual youth. Within these plantations of God, a decorum and sanctity reign, a perennial festival is dressed, and the guest sees not how he should tire of them in a thousand years. In the woods, we return to reason and faith. There I feel that nothing can befall me in life—no disgrace, no calamity (leaving me my eyes), which nature cannot repair. Standing on the bare ground—my head bathed by the blithe air, and uplifted into infinite space—all mean egotism vanishes. I become a transparent eyeball; I am nothing; I see all; the currents of the Universal Being circulate through me; I am part or parcel of God. The name of the nearest friend sounds then foreign and accidental: to be brothers, to be acquaintances, master, or servant, is then a trifle and a disturbance. I am the lover of uncontained and immortal beauty. In the wilderness, I find something more dear and connate [inborn] than in streets or villages. In the tranquil landscape, and especially in the distant line of the horizon, man beholds somewhat [something] as beautiful as his own nature.

The greatest delight which the fields and woods

The Notch of the White Mountains by Thomas Cole (1893). Oil.

National Gallery of Art, Washington, D.C.

minister is the suggestion of an occult relation between man and the vegetable. I am not alone and unacknowledged. They nod to me, and I to them. The waving of the boughs in the storm is new to me and old. It takes me by surprise, and yet is not unknown. Its effect is like that of a higher thought or a better emotion coming over me, when I deemed I was thinking justly or doing right.

Yet it is certain that the power to produce this delight does not reside in nature, but in man, or in a harmony of both. It is necessary to use these pleasures with great temperance. For nature is not always tricked [dressed] in holiday attire, but the same scene which yesterday breathed perfume and glittered as for the frolic of the nymphs, is overspread with melancholy today. Nature always wears the colors of the spirit. To a man laboring under calamity, the heat of his own fire hath sadness in it. Then there is a kind of contempt of the landscape felt by him who has just lost by death a dear friend. The sky is less grand as it shuts down over less worth in the population.

Responding to the Essay

Analyzing the Essay

Identifying Facts

1. Emerson wants his audience to look at some of the commonest elements of their lives—the natural environment that they see every day—in a new way. How would our attitude toward the stars change if they appeared only once every thousand years?
2. The second paragraph makes clear that Emerson is using the stars as an attention-getting example for a point about nature. What point is he making?
3. "To speak truly," Emerson says, "few adult persons can see nature." He says that children somehow have the advantage over adults in this matter. Read carefully the paragraph that begins with that sentence. What do adults seem to lose as they grow older?

Interpreting Meanings

4. What do you think Emerson means by a "poetical sense" of looking at nature? What **images** illustrate the distinction between nature used for practical benefits and nature viewed in this poetic way?
5. The most famous passage in *Nature,* and perhaps in all of Emerson's work, begins, "Standing on the bare ground . . . " and ends, "I am part or parcel of God." In what way is the **image** of a "transparent eyeball" a description of a visionary experience of God? Describe the relation presented here between people, nature, and God. According to Emerson, is God to be found only in nature, only in people, or in some common element that they both share?
6. Describe your response to Emerson's essay. Cite the passages you found yourself agreeing with and those you are doubtful about.

Writing About the Essay

A Critical Response

Comparing Two Descriptions. One of the roots of Emerson's Transcendentalist thought is to be found in the Puritan view of the relations between God, people, and nature. Reread Jonathan Edwards's description of his experience of a thunderstorm (page 41), and in a brief essay compare it to Emerson's description of nature. What similarities do you find? What differences?

Analyzing Language and Style

Paradoxes

Emerson's epigrammatic sentences are justly famous. One aspect of his style that is often overlooked, though, is his use of **paradox**, the linking of seemingly contradictory elements (as in the expression from *Romeo and Juliet*: "Parting is such sweet sorrow"). Read the following sentences from *Nature* and discuss their use of paradox. How would you express each statement in your own words?

1. "I am not solitary while I read and write, though nobody is with me."
2. "But every night come out these envoys of beauty, and light the universe with their admonishing smile."
3. "Most persons do not see the sun."
4. "I am glad to the brink of fear."

FROM SELF-RELIANCE

In an essay published in 1841, Emerson addressed one of the central characteristics of the American sensibility: individualism. Before you read, think about your own definition of "self-reliance."

There is a time in every man's education when he arrives at the conviction that envy is ignorance; that imitation is suicide; that he must take himself for better, for worse, as his portion; that though the wide universe is full of good, no kernel of nourishing corn can come to him but through his toil bestowed on that plot of ground which is given to him to till. The power which resides in him is new in nature, and none but he knows what that is which he can do, nor does he know until he has tried. Not for nothing one face, one character, one fact makes much impression on him, and another none. It is not without preestablished harmony, this sculpture in the memory. The eye was placed where one ray should fall, that it might testify of that particular ray. Bravely let him speak the utmost syllable of his confession. We but half express ourselves, and are ashamed of that divine idea which each of us represents. It may be safely trusted as proportionate and of good issues, so it be faithfully imparted, but God will not have his work made manifest by cowards. It needs a divine man to exhibit any thing divine. A man is relieved and gay when he has put his heart into his work and done his best; but what he has said or done otherwise, shall give him no peace. It is a deliverance which does not deliver. In the attempt his genius deserts him; no muse befriends; no invention, no hope.

Trust thyself: every heart vibrates to that iron string. Accept the place the divine Providence has found for you; the society of your contemporaries, the connection of events. Great men have always done so and confided themselves childlike to the genius of their age, betraying their perception that the Eternal was stirring at their heart, working through their hands, predominating in all their being. And we are now men, and must accept in the highest mind the same transcendent destiny; and not pinched in a corner, not cowards fleeing before a revolution, but redeemers and benefactors, pious aspirants to be noble clay plastic under the Almighty effort, let us advance and advance on Chaos and the Dark. . . .

These are the voices which we hear in solitude, but they grow faint and inaudible as we enter into the world. Society everywhere is in conspiracy against the manhood of every one of its members. Society is a joint-stock company in which the members agree for the better securing of his bread to each shareholder, to surrender the liberty and culture of the eater. The virtue in most request is conformity. Self-reliance is its aversion. It loves not realities and creators, but names and customs.

Whoso would be a man must be a nonconformist. He who would gather immortal palms must not be hindered by the name of goodness, but must explore if it be goodness. Nothing is at last sacred but the integrity of our own mind. Absolve you to yourself, and you shall have the suffrage of the world. . . .

A foolish consistency is the hobgoblin of little minds, adored by little statesmen and philosophers and divines. With consistency a great soul has simply nothing to do. He may as well concern himself with his shadow on the wall. Out upon your guarded lips! Sew them up with packthread, do. Else, if you would be a man, speak what you think today in words as hard as cannon balls, and tomorrow speak what tomorrow thinks in hard words again, though it contradict every thing you said today. Ah, then, exclaim the aged ladies, you shall be sure to be misunderstood. Misunderstood! It is a right fool's word. Is it so bad then to be misunderstood? Pythagoras was misunderstood, and Socrates, and Jesus, and Luther, and Copernicus, and Galileo, and Newton, and every pure and wise spirit that ever took flesh. To be great is to be misunderstood.

Responding to the Essay

Analyzing the Essay

Identifying Facts

1. According to the first sentence, what does every person realize at some moment in his or her education?
2. According to the second paragraph, what is the destiny of every human being?
3. Explain what Emerson thinks of society as a whole, according to the third paragraph.
4. What is the opposite of "self-reliance," according to the third paragraph?
5. In the fourth paragraph, what does Emerson see as the most sacred aspect of a person?
6. What does Emerson think of people who call for consistency in thought and action and who fear being misunderstood?

Interpreting Meanings

7. What do you think Emerson means by "the divine idea which each of us represents" (paragraph 1)?
8. How do you think self-reliance differs from selfishness or self-centeredness?
9. Suppose this essay were to be delivered as a major political address during a Presidential campaign today. How do you think people would respond?

Writing About the Essay

A Creative Response

1. **Writing an Essay.** Take one of these statements and write your own essay. Remember that an essayist expresses personal views on some limited topic.

   a. "Envy is ignorance."
   b. "God will not have His work made manifest by cowards."
   c. "Trust thyself: every heart vibrates to that iron string."
   d. "A foolish consistency is the hobgoblin of little minds."
   e. "To be great is to be misunderstood."

A Critical Response

2. **Writing a Response.** In at least three paragraphs, write an essay called "On Emerson's Self-Reliance." Explain your own responses to Emerson's views on self-reliance. Which of his ideas are most significant today? Are any of his ideas dated? Some readers find nineteenth-century writers are frequently condescending to women; what do you think?

Analyzing Language and Style

Figurative Language

Emerson makes many of his points through a series of **figures of speech**—comparisons between two things that are basically unlike.

1. In "Self-Reliance," what does he compare with these ordinary things and events:

   a. planting corn
   b. an iron string
   c. clay
   d. a stock-company
   e. cannon balls

2. What do you think is the significance of the word *iron* to describe the string? How would the effect and meaning differ if the string were described as silken, golden, or silver?
3. The most famous **metaphor** in "Self-Reliance" is the one that opens the final paragraph. How would you explain what Emerson means by this metaphor? What exactly is a hobgoblin? What is a "little mind"? What would be a "wise" consistency? What would be a "foolish" consistency?

Pat Lyon at the Forge by John Neagle (1829). Oil.

Pennsylvania Academy of Fine Arts, Philadelphia.

The "Concord Hymn" is an example of *occasional poetry,* poetry written to commemorate an "occasion" of historical or local importance. This poem was written for the commemoration of a monument to the Minutemen, the colonial farmers who, on April 19, 1775, routed the red-coated ranks of the British Militia and signaled the start of the Revolutionary War. Over the generations, millions of Americans have made their pilgrimage to the monument at Concord. This poem was sung at the ceremonies to the tune of "Old Hundredth" ("Praise God, from whom all blessings flow . . .")

Concord Hymn

Sung at the Completion of the Battle Monument, July 4, 1837

By the rude° bridge that arched the flood,
    Their flag to April's breeze unfurled,
Here once the embattled farmers stood
    And fired the shot heard round the world.

5 The foe long since in silence slept;
    Alike the conqueror silent sleeps;
And Time the ruined bridge has swept
    Down the dark stream which seaward creeps.

On this green bank, by this soft stream,
10   We set today a votive stone;°
That memory may their deed redeem,
    When, like our sires, our sons are gone.

Spirit, that made those heroes dare
    To die, and leave their children free,
15 Bid Time and Nature gently spare
    The shaft° we raise to them and thee.

1. **rude:** crude, or roughly built.

10. **votive stone:** a marker made of stone, which fulfills a promise or a pledge.

16. **shaft:** column; here, the monument.

Responding to the Poem

Analyzing the Poem

Identifying Details

1. Identify the "foe" and the "conqueror" mentioned in the second stanza. What has happened to them and to the bridge?
2. According to Stanza 3, why are they putting up a monument here?
3. According to Stanza 4, why did the heroes die?
4. What does the speaker ask of the Spirit in Stanza 4?

Interpreting Meanings

5. The poem ends in an **apostrophe**—words spoken to a person or object who cannot or does not answer. How would you define the Spirit addressed in line 13?
6. To say that the shot of the Minutemen was "heard round the world" is, on a literal level, to indulge in **hyperbole,** or exaggeration for effect. On a **figurative** level, how is this statement true? What other "shots" can you think of that might be said to have been heard around the world?

7. What other monuments have been erected to the dead so that "memory may their deed redeem"? Do you believe that memory actually *can* "redeem" or recover the dead? Explain.

8. Could any stanzas of this hymn be sung at other war memorials erected in the years since 1837?

Writing About the Poem

A Creative Response

1. **Writing a Letter.** Imagine that you are an aged veteran of the battle described in the poem. Write a letter to a friend, describing your reaction to hearing the poem sung at the dedication.

A Critical Response

2. **Paraphrasing the Poem.** Paraphrase—state in your own words—the text of this poem, taking it line by line.

   a. Substitute simpler, modern words for the archaic or old-fashioned ones.
   b. Provide any missing words.
   c. Put the inverted (or reversed) words in standard English word order.
   d. Rephrase the figures of speech, using plain, literal language.

Paraphrase the poem as if you are doing it for someone who does not understand it at all—perhaps for someone who is much younger than you are.

Like the Romantics, the Transcendentalists saw in nature signs of divinity and answers to questions about the meaning of life.

"Whence is the flower?" means "Where did the flower come from?" How would most people answer this question?

The Rhodora:

On Being Asked, Whence Is the Flower?

In May, when sea winds pierced our solitudes,
I found the fresh Rhodora in the woods,
Spreading its leafless blooms in a damp nook,
To please the desert and the sluggish brook.
5   The purple petals, fallen in the pool,
Made the black water with their beauty gay;
Here might the redbird come his plumes to cool,
And court the flower that cheapens his array.
Rhodora! if the sages ask thee why
10   This charm is wasted on the earth and sky,
Tell them, dear, that if eyes were made for seeing,
Then Beauty is its own excuse for being:
Why thou wert there, O rival of the rose!
I never thought to ask, I never knew;
15   But, in my simple ignorance, suppose
The selfsame Power that brought me there brought you.

Responding to the Poem

Analyzing the Poem
Identifying Details

1. Describe where the poet comes upon the rhodora. Until then, whom or what had the flower been pleasing with its beauty?
2. In line 9, who might the "sages" be? What is their question, and how does the poet answer it?
3. There are several instances of **personification** in the poem. Identify and explain at least three of these.
4. Part of this poem is an **apostrophe**—a direct address to something that cannot answer. Where is the apostrophe?

Interpreting Meanings

5. How does Emerson say he is like the rhodora?
6. Line 12 is the key to the poem's meaning and one of Emerson's most famous sayings. How would you rephrase the line in your own words? Do you agree with its statement?
7. Do you think everything in the world, including beauty, has to have a utilitarian purpose? Do many people behave as if they believe that usefulness is more important than beauty? Explain.
8. The poet indicates in his subtitle that someone has asked him where the rhodora came from. What is the poet's answer? If you were the questioner, would this answer satisfy you? How would you have answered the question?
9. What do you think the poet means by "Power" in the last line?
10. How might a rationalist writer like Benjamin Franklin have answered the question "Whence is the flower?"

Writing About the Poem
A Critical Response

1. **Analyzing the Poem.** A poem written in **iambic pentameter** has five iambs in a line: that is, the poem has five groups of syllabic pairs in which an unstressed syllable alternates with a stressed syllable (daDUM, daDUM, daDUM, daDUM, daDUM). If you were scanning this poem, you might mark the first line like this:

   ˘ ´ ˘ ´ ˘ ´ ˘ ´ ˘ ´
   In May, when sea winds pierced our solitudes

   In a brief essay, analyze the poem's metrical structure and rhyme scheme. Is it written entirely in iambic pentameter? Does every line rhyme with another line? At the end of your essay, describe your response to Emerson's rhymes and metrics.

2. **Comparing Philosophies.** In Act III, Scene 1, of Shakespeare's *As You Like It*, a character speaks of the compensations he finds in his forest life:

   > . . . this our life, exempt from public haunt,
   > Finds tongues in trees, books in the running brooks,
   > Sermons in stones, and good in every thing.
   > —from *As You Like It*,
   > William Shakespeare

   In an essay, tell whether this philosophy of nature is like Emerson's. Emerson's simplicity in "The Rhodora" opens him to intuition and to a sense of the presence of God. Is there any hint that nature contains signs of divinity in the Shakespeare quotation?

Analyzing Language and Style
Inversions

Inversions are "reversals." Emerson frequently inverts or reverses the normal English word order of a sentence in order to accommodate his meters and rhymes. Lines 5–8 are one complete sentence. What words are wrenched out of their normal order to make the rhymes and meter "come out right"?

Rewrite this sentence in normal English word order. To do this, you have to be sure you know exactly what word or phrase each modifier refers to.

If you have ever witnessed a heavy snow, you will understand at once the message of this poem—which is about the ways that art imitates nature. Emerson probably wrote the poem in 1834, the year after a particularly heavy snow hit Concord. Note again how Emerson sees a correspondence between nature and human life.

The Snow-Storm

Announced by all the trumpets of the sky,
Arrives the snow, and, driving o'er the fields,
Seems nowhere to alight: the whited air
Hides hills and woods, the river, and the heaven,

5   And veils the farmhouse at the garden's end.
The sled and traveler stopped, the courier's feet
Delayed, all friends shut out, the housemates sit
Around the radiant fireplace, enclosed
In a tumultuous privacy of storm.

10   Come see the north wind's masonry.
Out of an unseen quarry evermore
Furnished with tile, the fierce artificer
Curves his white bastions with projected roof
Round every windward stake, or tree, or door.
15   Speeding, the myriad-handed, his wild work
So fanciful, so savage, naught cares he
For number or proportion. Mockingly,
On coop or kennel he hangs Parian° wreaths;
A swanlike form invests the hidden thorn;
20   Fills up the farmer's lane from wall to wall,
Maugre° the farmer's sighs; and at the gate
A tapering turret overtops the work.
And when his hours are numbered, and the world
Is all his own, retiring, as he were not,
25   Leaves, when the sun appears, astonished Art
To mimic in slow structures, stone by stone,
Built in an age, the mad wind's night work,
The frolic architecture of the snow.

18. **Parian:** fine marble from the island of Paros in Greece.

21. **Maugre:** despite.

Responding to the Poem

Analyzing the Poem

Identifying Details

1. What precedes the snow, according to line 1?
2. Name some of the things and people that the snow affects in lines 1—9. Where do the people inside the house sit?
3. The second part of the poem (lines 10—28) is a lengthy **personification.** What type of person is the north wind personified as? Point out at least three details that extend the personification.
4. The final adjective applied to the north wind is "mad" in line 27. How has that "madness" been demonstrated? What details in the poem suggest that this madness is also imaginative and joyful?

Interpreting Meanings

5. Explain how the meanings of the words "tumultuous privacy" (line 9) make this a startling and vivid phrase.

6. According to the last four lines, human art only mimics the work of nature. Why do you think Art's structures are described as "slow" (line 26)?
7. Art is **personified** in this poem as "astonished." What is Art, or human work and creation, astonished at? What overall idea about nature and human work is suggested by the poem?
8. Could artists, writers, and composers also be called "fierce artificers"? Explain.
9. Can you think of other instances where art "mimics" nature?

Writing About the Poem

A Critical Response

Comparing Poems. Compare the transformations of outdoor and indoor worlds in Emerson's "The Snow-Storm" and Whittier's "Snow-Bound" (page 157). In particular, explain how **figurative** and **sensory language** contribute to the mood of each poem.

EMERSON'S APHORISMS

An *aphorism* is a short statement that expresses a wise or clever observation about life. (Aphorisms might also be called "maxims," "adages," or just "sayings.") Try paraphrasing these aphorisms in your own words: you'll see how much meaning the writer has packed into a few words. That, of course, is what makes an aphorism memorable.

I confess I am a little cynical on some topics, and when a whole nation is roaring Patriotism at the top of its voice, I am fain [inclined] to explore the cleanness of its hands and purity of its heart. I have generally found the gravest and most useful citizens are not the easiest provoked to swell the noise, though they may be punctual at the polls.

—*Journals,* 1824

Don't trust children with edge tools. Don't trust man, great God, with more power than he has, until he has learned to use that little better. What a hell should we make of the world if we could do what we would! Put a button on the foil [sword] till the young fencers have learned not to put each other's eyes out.

—*Journals,* 1832

The maker of a sentence, like the other artist, launches out into the infinite and builds a road into Chaos and old Night, and is followed by those who hear him with something of wild, creative delight.

—*Journals,* 1834

Poetry must be as new as foam, and as old as the rock.

—*Journals,* 1844

The invariable mark of wisdom is to see the miraculous in the common.

—*Nature*

A man is a god in ruins.

—*Nature*

Nothing can bring you peace but yourself. Nothing can bring you peace but the triumph of principles.

—"Self-Reliance"

. . . prayer as a means to effect a private end is meanness and theft. It supposes dualism and not a unity in nature and consciousness. As soon as the man is at one with God, he will not beg. He will then see prayer in all action.

—"Self-Reliance"

This time, like all times, is a very good one, if we but know what to do with it.

—"The American Scholar"

Books are the best of things, well used; abused, among the worst.

—"The American Scholar"

Public and private avarice make the air we breathe thick and fat.

—"The American Scholar"

Primary Sources
Hawthorne Talks About Emerson

Emerson, who thought of sin as merely a child's case of measles on the world, and Hawthorne, who plumbed the nature of evil, could never talk together. Hawthorne did live at Brook Farm for a few months, but he left, finding the high-minded discussions stifling. He then lived for a time in a house called the Old Manse in Concord, the same house where Emerson had written his first book, *Nature.* Here, in a passage from his essay called "The Old Manse," Hawthorne talks about Emerson and the "hobgoblins" who came to Concord seeking answers to the riddle of the world.

"These hobgoblins of flesh and blood were attracted thither by the widespreading influence of a great original thinker, who had his earthly abode at the opposite extremity of our village. His mind acted upon other minds of a certain constitution with wonderful magnetism, and drew many men upon long pilgrimages to speak with him face to face. Young visionaries—to whom just so much of insight had been imparted as to make life all a labyrinth [maze] around them—came to seek the clue that should guide them out of their self-involved bewilderment. Gray-headed theorists—whose systems, at first air, had finally imprisoned them in an iron framework—traveled painfully to his door, not to ask deliverance, but to invite the free spirit into their own thraldom [servitude]. People that had lighted on a new thought, or a thought that they fancied new, came to Emerson, as the finder of a glittering gem hastens to a lapidary [gem dealer], to ascertain its quality and value. Uncertain, troubled, earnest wanderers through the midnight of the moral world beheld his intellectual fire as a beacon burning on a hilltop, and, climbing the difficult ascent, looked forth into the surrounding obscurity more hopefully than hitherto. The light revealed objects unseen before—mountains, gleaming lakes, glimpses of a creation among the chaos; but also, as was unavoidable, it attracted bats and owls and the whole host of night birds, which flapped their dusky wings against the gazer's eyes, and sometimes were mistaken for fowls of angelic feather. Such delusions always hover nigh whenever a beacon fire of truth is kindled.

"For myself, there had been epochs of my life when I, too, might have asked of this prophet the master word that should solve me the riddle of the universe; but now, being happy, I felt as if there were no question to be put, and therefore admired Emerson as a poet of deep beauty and austere tenderness, but sought nothing from him as a philosopher. It was good, nevertheless, to meet him in the wood paths, or sometimes in our avenue, with that pure intellectual gleam diffused about his presence like the garment of a shining one; and he so quiet, so simple, so without pretension, encountering each man alive as if expecting to receive more than he could impart. And, in truth, the heart of many an ordinary man had, perchance, inscriptions which he could not read. But it was impossible to dwell in his vicinity without inhaling more or less the mountain atmosphere of his lofty thought, which, in the brains of some people, wrought a singular giddiness— new truth being as heady as new wine. Never was a poor little country village infested with such a variety of queer, strangely dressed, oddly behaved mortals, most of whom took upon themselves to be important agents of the world's destiny, yet were simply bores of a very intense water. . . ."

—from "The Old Manse,"
Nathaniel Hawthorne

"The Old Manse," the home of Nathaniel Hawthorne in Concord, Massachusetts.

Henry David Thoreau (1817–1862)

On July 4, 1845 (the date was deliberately chosen), a young man ended a three-year stay at the house of a friend and moved to a cabin on the shores of Walden Pond in Massachusetts. He was twenty-eight years old and, to all appearances, a failure. He had lasted only two weeks as a schoolteacher (he refused to whip a child, then a mandatory form of punishment); his public lectures had been uninspiring; the woman to whom he had proposed marriage had turned him down; he had little interest in the family business. Despite his impressive Harvard education, he had not realized his literary ambitions.

The pattern of his life had been, and would continue to be, precisely the opposite of the great American success story of the self-made man. If ever a person looked like a self-*un*made man, a man who had squandered the advantages of intelligence, education, and the friendship of brilliant and successful people, it was Henry David Thoreau. On top of all his other problems, Thoreau was difficult to get along with. He was admired, but from a distance—for he kept people at a distance. Three days before Thoreau went to Walden, Hawthorne wrote to a New York publisher that Thoreau was "tedious, tiresome, and intolerable." And yet, Hawthorne added, "he has great qualities of intellect and character."

Even his closest friends had doubts about Thoreau. "He seemed born for great enterprise and for command," Emerson said years later at Thoreau's funeral, "and I so much regret the loss of his rare powers of action, that I cannot help counting it a fault in him that he had no ambition. Wanting [lacking] this, instead of engineering for all America, he was the captain of a huckleberry party."

What Emerson failed to see, and what Thoreau knew (or at least hoped) all along, was that by leading a berry-picking party on a jaunt in the woods he could "engineer for all America" in the most profound way. This paradox is at the center of Thoreau's life and work.

He was born David Henry Thoreau in Concord, Massachusetts, in 1817. (He changed the order of his names after graduating from college.) His father was a moderately successful manufacturer of pencils. His mother took in boarders, among them the sister of Emerson's wife, thus establishing the relationship between the two families. As a boy, Thoreau tramped the woods and fields around Concord, often with a fishing rod, seldom with a gun. No one knew Concord as well as he did, and his attachment to this region was established early in his life.

Thoreau entered Harvard in 1833 and graduated four years later (without any literary distinction). Independent and eccentric even then, he attended chapel in a green coat, "because," he wrote, "the rules required black." He never ranked higher than the middle of his class, but he was extremely well read. At Harvard, mostly on his own, he became thoroughly familiar with English literature and with the German philosophers who provided much of the underpinnings of Transcendentalism.

After graduation, Thoreau went to New York, but he pined after his hometown. ("Am I not made of Concord dust?" he wrote to Emerson's wife.) After a year of struggling, he gave up and came home. Thoreau appeared to be floundering. But, in fact, he knew what he was doing; at least he knew that internally he was heading in the right direction, even if his external navigation looked aimless. A friend proposed that Henry and he sail to Europe and work their way across the continent, but Henry turned him down emphatically:

> I have been surprised when one has with confidence proposed to me, a grown man, to embark in some enterprise of his, as if I had absolutely nothing to do, my life having been a complete failure hitherto. What a doubtful compliment this to pay me! As if he had met me halfway across the ocean beating up against the wind, but bound nowhere, and proposed to me to go along with him! . . . No, no! I am not without employment at this stage of the voyage. To tell the truth, I saw an advertisement for able-bodied seamen, when I was a boy, sauntering in my native port, and as soon as I came of age I embarked.

That last sentence, in what would become Thoreau's typically metaphoric style, expressed the real truth: Thoreau knew where he was going. His voyage would be inward, and it would depart from Walden Pond, where Emerson had offered him the use of some land.

The experiment at Walden Pond was an attempt to rediscover the grandeur and heroism inherent in a simple life led close to Nature. The fact that Thoreau's cabin was only two miles from town—that he had really only set himself up in the suburbs of Concord, to which he commuted almost daily—was not really the point. Walden offered a focus for his contemplative urge. "I wish to meet the facts of life," he wrote in his journal, "the vital facts, which are the phenomena or actuality the gods meant to show us . . . and so I came down here."

This private confrontation was to Thoreau's mind the truly heroic enterprise of his time. "I am glad to remember as I sit by my door tonight," he wrote on the evening of July 7, "that I too am at least a remote descendant of that heroic race of men of whom there is a tradition. I too sit here on the shore of my Ithaca, a fellow wanderer and survivor of Ulysses." Again and again in *Walden*, Thoreau would return to these same images drawn from the Greek and Latin epics, asserting the essential brotherhood between the adventurers of the mythic past and the truth-seeking voyager of the present.

"The mass of men," as one of the most famous sentences in *Walden* puts it, "lead lives of quiet desperation." When he looked toward

Thoreau at Walden by N. C. Wyeth (1936). Tempera on wood.

Brandywine River Museum,
Brandywine, Pennsylvania.

town, Thoreau saw his prosperous fellow citizens so caught up in the material pursuits of making a living that they had become one-dimensional. When he looked along the site of the Fitchburg railway under construction within view of his cabin, he saw Irish railway workers in shanties living desperately poor lives, materially and spiritually. He hoped to wake them all up and show them that the heroic enterprise of confronting the "vital facts of life" lay literally in their own back yards.

Walden—one of the greatest works ever produced in America—owes much of its artistic success to Thoreau's successful blending of style and content. He looked to Nature, rather than to the stylists of the past, for a model. His style would be simple—at least on the surface. "Nature never indulges in exclamations," he wrote, "never says ah! or alas! She is not French. She is a plain writer, uses few gestures, does not add to her verbs, uses few adverbs, no expletives."

For Thoreau, as for Emerson and the Romantics who had preceded them, Nature itself was a form of language; behind its outward appearance, Nature contained spiritual reality. Nature spoke to us, if we could but understand the messages about those "vital facts" which "the gods meant to show us." A style that imitated Nature would also speak fundamental truths. Thoreau wished to write sentences "which lie like boulders on the page, up and down or across; which contain the seed of other sentences, not mere repetition, but creation; which a man might sell his grounds and castles to build."

Such a style rewards careful reading. Its paradoxes are not mere playfulness, but point to what Thoreau sees as a higher truth. A phrase like "I have traveled a good deal in Concord" contains in its apparent paradox the seeds of much of the book.

It was while he was at Walden that Thoreau's other famous act took place. As a protest against the Mexican War, which he and many others saw as an attempt to extend American slave-owning territory, Thoreau refused to pay his poll tax. He then spent a night in jail before someone paid the tax for him. Thoreau was vocally and radically opposed to slavery. While at Walden, and again in 1851 (after the Fugitive Slave Act had been passed), he helped fugitive slaves make their way to Canada. Near the end of his life, in 1859, he was one of the first defenders of John Brown, the radical abolitionist who staged a famous raid on the Federal arsenal at Harpers Ferry in Virginia.

Thoreau remained at Walden for a little more than two years. In 1847, he left the cabin and moved back into the Emersons' house, where he had received room and board before, in exchange for a few hours a day of odd jobs and gardening. During the next few years, he worked on *Walden* and "Resistance to Civil Government," which was delivered as a lecture in 1848 and published in 1849. Later called "Civil Disobedience," this essay asserted the primacy of the individual conscience and the need for action in keeping with that conscience. It had little immediate influence, but few essays have had such an overwhelming, long-range effect on human history. It was especially important in helping to inspire the form of passive resistance used by Mahatma Gandhi in India and, later, by Martin Luther King, Jr., in the United States.

Thoreau moved back into his father's house in 1849 and lived there the rest of his life. He supported himself by making pencils, taking odd jobs—he was an excellent carpenter, mason, and gardener—and doing survey work on the land around Concord that he knew so well. He became a kind of Concord recordkeeper, a fount of local knowledge about the amount of rainfall and snowfall and the first days of frost. He could predict to the day when each wildflower in the area would bloom.

Walden was published in 1854 and was well enough received to expand Thoreau's reputation. His most widely read works, though, were his antislavery tract, "Slavery in Massachusetts," and "A Plea for Captain John Brown" (1860).

In 1861, Thoreau caught a cold, and it soon became clear that beneath the cold lay incurable tuberculosis. He traveled that year to the Midwest in hopes that the change of air would help, but it did not. When he returned to Concord, he began working feverishly to put his work in final shape. He faced his coming death with great calm. The town constable, Sam Staples (who had jailed him for refusing to pay his poll tax), told Emerson that he "never saw a man dying with so much pleasure and peace."

"Henry, have you made your peace with God?" his aunt is said to have asked him toward his end. "Why, Aunt," he replied, "I didn't know we had ever quarreled."

WALDEN, OR LIFE IN THE WOODS

A photograph from the Walden Pond series by
Edward Steichen (early 20th century).

George Eastman House, Rochester, New York.

A temporary move to a site on a large pond in Concord, Massachusetts, resulted in a work of literature that was to become an American classic. Thoreau moved to Walden because he wanted to find out what life is. That is a question people still ask; it is something people the world over have always asked, when they have had the leisure to think about it. As you read, imagine yourself in the woods near this pond. How would you have responded to a life that offered little more in excitement than a battle between ants, little more in company than the visit of a bird?

I do not propose to write an ode to dejection, but to brag as lustily as chanticleer in the morning, standing on his roost, if only to wake my neighbors up.

From
Economy

When I wrote the following pages, or rather the bulk of them, I lived alone, in the woods, a mile from any neighbor, in a house which I had built myself, on the shore of Walden Pond, in Concord, Massachusetts, and earned my living by the labor of my hands only. I lived there two years and two months. At present I am a sojourner in civilized life again.

I should not obtrude my affairs so much on the notice of my readers if very particular inquiries had not been made by my townsmen concerning my mode of life, which some would call impertinent, though they do not appear to me at all impertinent, but, considering the circumstances, very natural and pertinent. Some have asked what I got to eat; if I did not feel lonesome; if I was not afraid; and the like. Others have been curious to learn what portion of my income I devoted to charitable purposes; and some, who have large families, how many poor children I maintained. I will therefore ask those of my readers who feel no particular interest in me to pardon me if I undertake to answer some of these questions in this book. In most books, the *I,* or first person, is omitted; in this it will be retained; that, in respect to egotism, is the main difference. We commonly do not remember that it is, after all, always the first person that is speaking. I should not talk so much about myself if there were anybody else whom I knew as well. Unfortunately, I am confined to this theme by the narrowness of my experience. Moreover, I, on my side, require of every writer, first or last, a simple and sincere account of his own life, and not merely what he has heard of other men's lives; some such account as he would send to his kindred from a distant land; for if he has lived sincerely, it must have been in a distant land to me. Perhaps these pages are more particularly addressed to poor students. As for the rest of my readers, they will accept such portions as apply to them. I trust that none will stretch the seams in putting on the coat, for it may do good service to him whom it fits. . . .

By the middle of April, for I made no haste in my work, but rather made the most of it, my house was framed and ready for the raising. I had already bought the shanty of James Collins, an Irishman who worked on the Fitchburg Railroad, for boards. James Collins' shanty was considered an uncommonly fine one. When I called to see it, he was not at home. I walked about the outside, at first unobserved from within, the window was so deep and high. It was of small dimensions, with a peaked cottage roof, and not much else to be seen, the dirt being raised five feet all around as if it were a compost heap. The roof was the soundest part, though a good deal warped and made brittle by the sun. Doorsill there was none, but a perennial passage for the hens under the door board. Mrs. C. came to the door and asked me to view it from the inside. The hens were driven in by my approach. It was dark, and had a dirt floor for the most part, dank, clammy, and aguish,[1] only here a board and there a board which would not bear removal. She lighted a lamp to show me the inside of the roof and the walls, and also that the board floor extended under the bed, warning me not to step into the cellar, a sort of dust hole two feet deep. In her own words, they were "good boards overhead, good boards all around, and a good window"—of two whole squares originally, only the cat had passed out that way lately. There was a stove, a bed, and a place to sit an infant in the house where it was born, a silk parasol, gilt-framed looking glass, and a patent new coffee mill nailed to an oak sapling, all told. The bargain was

---

1. **aguish:** likely to cause ague, or fever and chills.

soon concluded, for James had in the meanwhile returned. I to pay four dollars and twenty-five cents tonight, he to vacate at five tomorrow morning, selling to nobody else meanwhile: I to take possession at six. It were well, he said, to be there early; and anticipate certain indistinct but wholly unjust claims on the score of ground rent and fuel. This he assured me was the only encumbrance. At six I passed him and his family on the road. One large bundle held their all—bed, coffee mill, looking glass, hens—all but the cat; she took to the woods and became a wild cat, and, as I learned afterward, trod in a trap set for woodchucks, and so became a dead cat at last.

I took down this dwelling the same morning, drawing the nails, and removed it to the pond-side by small cartloads, spreading the boards on the grass there to bleach and warp back again in the sun. One early thrush gave me a note or two as I drove along the woodland path. I was informed treacherously by a young Patrick that neighbor Seeley, an Irishman, in the intervals of the carting, transferred the still tolerable, straight, and drivable nails, staples, and spikes to his pocket, and then stood when I came back to pass the time of day, and look freshly up, unconcerned, with spring thoughts, at the devastation; there being a dearth of work, as he said. He was there to represent spectatordom, and help make this seemingly insignificant event one with the removal of the gods of Troy.[2]

I dug my cellar in the side of a hill sloping to the south, where a woodchuck had formerly dug his burrow, down through sumach and blackberry roots, and the lowest stain of vegetation, six feet square by seven deep, to a fine sand where potatoes would not freeze in any winter. The sides were left shelving, and not stoned; but the sun having never shone on them, the sand still keeps its place. It was but two hours' work. I took particular pleasure in this breaking of ground, for in almost all latitudes men dig into the earth for an equable temperature. Under the most splendid house in the city is still to be found the cellar where they store their roots as of old, and long after the superstructure has disappeared posterity remark its dent in the earth. The house is still but a sort of porch at the entrance of a burrow.

At length, in the beginning of May, with the help of some of my acquaintances, rather to improve so good an occasion for neighborliness than from any necessity, I set up the frame of my house. No man was ever more honored in the character of his raisers[3] than I. They are destined, I trust, to assist at the raising of loftier structures one day. I began to occupy my house on the 4th of July, as soon as it was boarded and roofed, for the boards were carefully feather-edged and lapped,[4] so that it was perfectly impervious to rain; but before boarding I laid the foundation of a chimney at one end, bringing two cartloads of stones up the hill from the pond in my arms. I built the chimney after my hoeing in the fall, before a fire became necessary for warmth, doing my cooking in the meanwhile out of doors on the ground, early in the morning: which mode I still think is in some respects more convenient and agreeable than the usual one. When it stormed before my bread was baked, I fixed a few boards over the fire, and sat under them to watch my loaf, and passed some pleasant hours in that way. In those days, when my hands were much employed, I read but little, but the least scraps of paper which lay on the ground, my holder, or tablecloth, afforded me as much entertainment, in fact answered the same purpose as the *Iliad*.[5]

It would be worth the while to build still more deliberately than I did, considering, for instance, what foundation a door, a window, a cellar, a garret, have in the nature of man, and perchance never raising any superstructure until we found a better reason for it than our temporal necessities even. There is some of the same fitness in a man's building his own house that there is in a bird's building its own nest. Who knows but if men constructed their dwellings with their own hands, and provided food for themselves and families simply and honestly enough, the poetic faculty would be universally developed, as birds universally sing when they are so engaged? But alas! we do like cowbirds and cuckoos, which lay their eggs in

---

2. **the gods of Troy:** the household gods of Aeneas, which he took with him after the fall of Troy (Virgil's *Aeneid,* Book II).

3. **raisers:** Thoreau's helpers included Emerson and the Transcendentalist writers Bronson Alcott and William Ellery Channing. Hence the pun in the next sentence.
4. **feather-edged and lapped:** the edges were cut at a 45-degree angle and overlapped.
5. **the *Iliad*:** Homer's epic about the Greek siege of Troy.

Photograph taken by Eliot Porter to illustrate
the writings of Thoreau, 1962.

nests which other birds have built, and cheer no
traveler with their chattering and unmusical notes.
Shall we forever resign the pleasure of construction to the carpenter? What does architecture
amount to in the experience of the mass of men?
I never in all my walks came across a man engaged
in so simple and natural an occupation as building
his house. . . .

Before winter I built a chimney and shingled the
sides of my house, which were already impervious

to rain, with imperfect and sappy shingles made
of the first slice of the log, whose edges I was
obliged to straighten with a plane.

I have thus a tight-shingled and plastered
house, ten feet wide by fifteen long, and eight-feet
posts, with a garret and a closet, a large window
on each side, two trapdoors, one door at the end,
and a brick fireplace opposite. The exact cost of
my house, paying the usual price for such materials as I used, but not counting the work, all of
which was done by myself, was as follows; and I

give the details because very few are able to tell exactly what their houses cost, and fewer still, if any, the separate cost of the various materials which compose them:

Boards,	$8 03½	Mostly shanty boards
Refuse shingles for roof and sides,	4 00	
Laths,	1 25	
Two secondhand windows with glass,	2 43	
One thousand old brick,	4 00	
Two casks of lime,	2 40	That was high
Hair,	0 31	More than I needed
Mantle-tree iron,	0 15	
Nails,	3 90	
Hinges and screws,	0 14	
Latch,	0 10	
Chalk,	0 01	
Transportation,	1 40	I carried a good
In all,	$28 12½	part on my back

. . . Before I finished my house, wishing to earn ten or twelve dollars by some honest and agreeable method, in order to meet my unusual expenses, I planted about two acres and a half of light and sandy soil near it chiefly with beans, but also a small part with potatoes, corn, peas, and turnips. The whole lot contains eleven acres, mostly growing up to pines and hickories, and was sold the preceding season for eight dollars and eight cents an acre. One farmer said that it was "good for nothing but to raise cheeping squirrels on." I put no manure on this land, not being the owner, but merely a squatter, and not expecting to cultivate so much again, and I did not quite hoe it all once. I got out several cords of stumps in plowing, which supplied me with fuel for a long time, and left small circles of virgin mold, easily distinguishable through the summer by the greater luxuriance of the beans there. The dead and for the most part unmerchantable wood behind my house, and the driftwood from the pond, have supplied the remainder of my fuel. I was obliged to hire a team and a man for the plowing, though I held the plow myself. My farm outgoes for the first season were, for implements, seed, work,

&c., $14.72½. The seed corn was given me. This never costs anything to speak of, unless you plant more than enough. I got twelve bushels of beans, and eighteen bushels of potatoes, beside some peas and sweet corn. The yellow corn and turnips were too late to come to anything. My whole income from the farm was

	$23 44,
Deducting the outgoes,	14 72½
there are left,	$ 8 71½

beside produce consumed and on hand at the time this estimate was made of the value of $4.50—the amount on hand much more than balancing a little grass which I did not raise. All things considered, that is, considering the importance of a man's soul and of today, notwithstanding the short time occupied by my experiment, nay, partly even because of its transient character, I believe that that was doing better than any farmer in Concord did that year. . . .

From
Where I Lived and What I Lived For

I went to the woods because I wished to live deliberately, to front only the essential facts of life, and see if I could not learn what it had to teach, and not, when I came to die, discover that I had not lived. I did not wish to live what was not life, living is so dear; nor did I wish to practice resignation, unless it was quite necessary. I wanted to live deep and suck out all the marrow of life, to live so sturdily and Spartan-like as to put to rout all that was not life, to cut a broad swath and shave close, to drive life into a corner, and reduce it to its lowest terms, and, if it proved to be mean, why then to get the whole and genuine meanness of it, and publish its meanness to the world; or if it were sublime, to know it by experience, and be able to give a true account of it in my next excursion. For most men, it appears to me, are in a strange uncertainty about it, whether it is of the devil or of God, and have *somewhat hastily* concluded that it is the chief end of man here to "glorify God and enjoy Him forever."[6]

---

6. **"glorify . . . forever"**: the answer to the question, Why did God make us?, from the *New England Primer*.

Still we live meanly, like ants; though the fable tells us that we were long ago changed into men;[7] like pygmies we fight with cranes; it is error upon error, and clout upon clout, and our best virtue has for its occasion a superfluous and evitable wretchedness. Our life is frittered away by detail. An honest man has hardly need to count more than his ten fingers, or in extreme cases he may add his ten toes, and lump the rest. Simplicity, simplicity, simplicity! I say, let your affairs be as two or three, and not a hundred or a thousand; instead of a million count half a dozen, and keep your accounts on your thumbnail. In the midst of this chopping sea of civilized life, such are the clouds and storms and quicksands and thousand-and-one items to be allowed for, that a man has to live, if he would not founder and go to the bottom and not make his port at all, by dead reckoning, and he must be a great calculator indeed who succeeds. Simplify, simplify. Instead of three meals a day, if it be necessary eat but one; instead of a hundred dishes, five; and reduce other things in proportion. Our life is like a German Confederacy[8] made up of petty states, with its boundary forever fluctuating, so that even a German cannot tell you how it is bounded at any moment. The nation itself, with all its so-called internal improvements, which, by the way, are all external and superficial, is just such an unwieldy and overgrown establishment, cluttered with furniture and tripped up by its own traps, ruined by luxury and heedless expense, by want of calculation and a worthy aim, as the million households in the land; and the only cure for it as for them is in a rigid economy, a stern and more than Spartan simplicity of life and elevation of purpose. It lives too fast. Men think that it is essential that the *Nation* have commerce, and export ice, and talk through a telegraph, and ride thirty miles an hour, without a doubt, whether *they* do or not; but whether we should live like baboons or like men, is a little uncertain. If we do not get out sleepers,[9] and forge rails, and devote days and nights to the work, but go to tinkering upon our *lives* to improve *them,* who will build railroads? And if railroads are not built, how shall we get to heaven in season? But if we stay at home and mind our business, who will want railroads? We do not ride on the railroad; it rides upon us. Did you ever think what those sleepers are that underlie the railroad? Each one is a man, an Irishman, or a Yankee man. The rails are laid on them, and they are covered with sand, and the cars run smoothly over them. They are sound sleepers, I assure you. And every few years a new lot is laid down and run over; so that, if some have the pleasure of riding on a rail, others have the misfortune to be ridden upon. And when they run over a man that is walking in his sleep, a supernumerary sleeper in the wrong position, and wake him up, they suddenly stop the cars, and make a hue and cry about it, as if this were an exception. I am glad to know that it takes a gang of men for every five miles to keep the sleepers down and level in their beds as it is, for this is a sign that they may sometime get up again.

From
Solitude

Some of my pleasantest hours were during the long rainstorms in the spring or fall, which confined me to the house for the afternoon as well as the forenoon, soothed by their ceaseless roar and pelting; when an early twilight ushered in a long evening in which many thoughts had time to take root and unfold themselves. In those driving northeast rains which tried the village houses so, when the maids stood ready with mop and pail in front entries to keep the deluge out; I sat behind my door in my little house, which was all entry, and thoroughly enjoyed its protection. In one heavy thundershower the lightning struck a large pitch pine across the pond, making a very conspicuous and perfectly regular spiral groove from top to bottom, an inch or more deep, and four or five inches wide, as you would groove a walking stick. I passed it again the other day, and was struck with awe on looking up and beholding that mark, now more distinct than ever, where a terrific and resistless bolt came down out of the harmless sky eight years ago. Men frequently say to me, "I should think you would feel

---

7. **the fable . . . men:** in a Greek fable, Zeus changed ants into men. In the *Iliad,* Homer compares the Trojans to cranes fighting with pygmies.
8. **German Confederacy:** at the time Thoreau was writing, Germany was not yet a unified nation.
9. **sleepers:** railroad ties, so called because they lie flat.

lonesome down there, and want to be nearer folks, rainy and snowy days and nights especially.'' I am tempted to reply to such—This whole earth which we inhabit is but a point in space. How far apart, think you, dwell the two most distant inhabitants of yonder star, the breadth of whose disk cannot be appreciated by our instruments? Why should I feel lonely? is not our planet in the Milky Way? This which you put seems to me not to be the most important question. What sort of space is that which separates a man from his fellows and makes him solitary? I have found that no exertion of the legs can bring two minds much nearer to one another. What do we want most to dwell near to? Not to many men surely, the depot, the post office, the barroom, the meetinghouse, the school-house, the grocery, Beacon Hill, or the Five Points,[10] where men most congregate, but to the perennial source of our life, whence in all our experience we have found that to issue; as the willow stands near the water and sends out its roots in that direction. This will vary with different natures, but this is the place where a wise man will dig his cellar. . . .

From
The Bean-Field

Meanwhile my beans, the length of whose rows, added together, was seven miles already planted, were impatient to be hoed, for the earliest had grown considerably before the latest were in the ground; indeed they were not easily to be put off. What was the meaning of this so steady and self-respecting, this small Herculean labor, I knew not. I came to love my rows, my beans, though so many more than I wanted. They attached me to the earth, and so I got strength like Antæus.[11] But why should I raise them? Only Heaven knows. This was my curious labor all summer—to make this portion of the earth's surface, which had yielded only cinquefoil, blackberries, johnswort, and the like, before,

sweet wild fruits and pleasant flowers, produce instead this pulse.[12] What shall I learn of beans or beans of me? I cherish them, I hoe them, early and late I have an eye to them; and this is my day's work. It is a fine broad leaf to look on. My auxiliaries are the dews and rains which water this dry soil, and what fertility is in the soil itself, which for the most part is lean and effete. My enemies are worms, cool days, and most of all woodchucks. The last have nibbled for me a quarter of an acre clean. But what right had I to oust johnswort and the rest, and break up their ancient herb garden? Soon, however, the remaining beans will be too tough for them, and go forward to meet new foes. . . .

It was a singular experience that long acquaintance which I cultivated with beans, what with planting, and hoeing, and harvesting, and threshing, and picking over, and selling them—the last was the hardest of all—I might add eating, for I did taste. I was determined to know beans. When they were growing, I used to hoe from five o'clock in the morning till noon, and commonly spent the rest of the day about other affairs. Consider the intimate and curious acquaintance one makes with various kinds of weeds—it will bear some iteration in the account, for there was no little iteration in the labor—disturbing their delicate organizations so ruthlessly, and making such invidious distinctions with his hoe, leveling whole ranks of one species, and sedulously cultivating another. That's Roman wormwood, that's pigweed, that's sorrel, that's pipergrass—have at him, chop him up, turn his roots upward to the sun, don't let him have a fiber in the shade; if you do he'll turn himself t'other side up and be as green as a leek in two days. A long war, not with cranes, but with weeds, those Trojans who had sun and rain and dews on their side. Daily the beans saw me come to their rescue armed with a hoe, and thin the ranks of their enemies, filling up the trenches with weedy dead. Many a lusty, crest-waving Hector,[13] that towered a whole foot above his crowding comrades, fell before my weapon and rolled in the dust. . . .

---

10. **Beacon Hill . . . Five Points:** well-known busy areas of nineteenth-century Boston and New York.
11. **Antaeus** (an·tē'əs): in Greek mythology, the giant who drew strength from the earth, his mother.

12. **pulse:** beans, peas, and other legumes.
13. **Hector:** in the *Iliad,* Hector was the Trojan prince killed by the Greek hero Achilles.

than that. How surprised must the fishes be to see this ungainly visitor from another sphere speeding his way amid their schools! Yet he appeared to know his course as surely under water as on the surface, and swam much faster there. Once or twice I saw a ripple where he approached the surface, just put his head out to reconnoiter, and instantly dived again. I found that it was as well for me to rest on my oars and wait his reappearing as to endeavor to calculate where he would rise; for again and again, when I was straining my eyes over the surface one way, I would suddenly be startled by his unearthly laugh behind me. But why, after displaying so much cunning, did he invariably betray himself the moment he came up by that loud laugh? Did not his white breast enough betray him? He was indeed a silly loon, I thought. I could commonly hear the plash of the water when he came up, and so also detected him. But after an hour he seemed as fresh as ever, dived as willingly and swam yet farther than at first. It was surprising to see how serenely he sailed off with unruffled breast when he came to the surface, doing all the work with his webbed feet beneath. His usual note was this demoniac laughter, yet somewhat like that of a waterfowl; but occasion-

On the Concord Banks, a River Boat, and American Bittern, a photograph by Herbert W. Gleason (early 20th century).

Concord Public Library, Concord, Massachusetts.

ally, when he had balked me most successfully and come up a long way off, he uttered a long-drawn unearthly howl, probably more like that of a wolf than any bird; as when a beast puts his muzzle to the ground and deliberately howls. This was his looning—perhaps the wildest sound that is ever heard here, making the woods ring far and wide. I concluded that he laughed in derision of my efforts, confident of his own resources. Though the sky was by this time overcast, the pond was so smooth that I could see where he broke the surface when I did not hear him. His white breast, the stillness of the air, and the smoothness of the water were all against him. At length, having come up fifty rods off, he uttered one of those prolonged howls, as if calling on the god of loons to aid him, and immediately there came a wind from the east and rippled the surface, and filled the whole air with misty rain, and I was impressed as if it were the prayer of the loon answered, and his god was angry with me; and so I left him disappearing far away on the tumultuous surface.

From
Conclusion

I left the woods for as good a reason as I went there. Perhaps it seemed to me that I had several more lives to live, and could not spare any more time for that one. It is remarkable how easily and insensibly we fall into a particular route, and make a beaten track for ourselves. I had not lived there a week before my feet wore a path from my door to the pond-side; and though it is five or six years since I trod it, it is still quite distinct. It is true, I fear that others may have fallen into it, and so helped to keep it open. The surface of the earth is soft and impressible by the feet of men; and so with the paths which the mind travels. How worn and dusty, then, must be the highways of the world, how deep the ruts of tradition and conformity! I did not wish to take a cabin passage, but rather to go before the mast and on the deck of the world, for there I could best see the moonlight amid the mountains. I do not wish to go below now.

I learned this, at least, by my experiment; that if one advances confidently in the direction of his dreams, and endeavors to live the life which he has imagined, he will meet with a success unex-pected in common hours. He will put some things behind, will pass an invisible boundary; new, universal, and more liberal laws will begin to establish themselves around and within him; or the old laws be expanded, and interpreted in his favor in a more liberal sense, and he will live with the license of a higher order of beings. In proportion as he simplifies his life, the laws of the universe will appear less complex, and solitude will not be solitude, nor poverty poverty, nor weakness weakness. If you have built castles in the air, your work need not be lost; that is where they should be. Now put the foundations under them. . . .

Some are dinning in our ears that we Americans, and moderns generally, are intellectual dwarfs compared with the ancients, or even the Elizabethan men. But what is that to the purpose? A living dog is better than a dead lion.[21] Shall a man go and hang himself because he belongs to the race of pygmies, and not be the biggest pygmy that he can? Let everyone mind his own business, and endeavor to be what he was made.

Why should we be in such desperate haste to succeed, and in such desperate enterprises? If a man does not keep pace with his companions, perhaps it is because he hears a different drummer. Let him step to the music which he hears, however measured or far away. It is not important that he should mature as soon as an apple tree or an oak. Shall he turn his spring into summer? If the condition of things which we were made for is not yet, what were any reality which we can substitute? We will not be shipwrecked on a vain reality. Shall we with pains erect a heaven of blue glass over ourselves, though when it is done we shall be sure to gaze still at the true ethereal heaven far above, as if the former were not? . . .

The life in us is like the water in the river. It may rise this year higher than man has ever known it, and flood the parched uplands; even this may be the eventful year, which will drown out all our muskrats. It was not always dry land where we dwell. I see far inland the banks which the stream anciently washed, before science began to record its freshets. Everyone has heard the story which has gone the rounds of New England, of a strong and beautiful bug which came out of the dry leaf of an old table of apple-tree wood, which had

---

21. **living dog . . . dead lion:** from Ecclesiastes 9:4.

stood in a farmer's kitchen for sixty years, first in Connecticut, and afterward in Massachusetts—from an egg deposited in the living tree many years earlier still, as appeared by counting the annual layers beyond it; which was heard gnawing out for several weeks, hatched perchance by the heat of an urn. Who does not feel his faith in a resurrection and immortality strengthened by hearing of this? Who knows what beautiful and winged life, whose egg has been buried for ages under many concentric layers of woodenness in the dead, dry life of society, deposited at first in the alburnum[22] of the green and living tree, which has been gradually converted into the semblance of its well-seasoned tomb—heard perchance gnawing out now for years by the astonished family of man, as they sat round the festive board—may unexpectedly come forth from amid society's most trivial and handselled[23] furniture, to enjoy its perfect summer life at last!

I do not say that John or Jonathan[24] will realize all this; but such is the character of that morrow which mere lapse of time can never make to dawn. The light which puts out our eyes is darkness to us. Only that day dawns to which we are awake. There is more day to dawn. The sun is but a morning star.

THE END

---

22. **alburnum:** sapwood.

23. **handselled:** given as a mere token of good wishes; hence, of no great value in itself.
24. **John or Jonathan:** John Bull and Brother Jonathan were traditional personifications of Britain and the United States.

Responding to the Essays

Analyzing the Essays

Identifying Facts

1. According to the second paragraph in "Economy," why has Thoreau decided to write about his life? How does he justify talking primarily about himself?
2. What does Thoreau think would happen if we made our houses with our own hands?
3. How does Thoreau answer the questions implied in the title "Where I Lived and What I Lived For"?
4. What arguments does Thoreau present in "Solitude" to demonstrate that he is not lonely in his isolated situation? What kind of space does he suggest *really* isolates human beings?
5. What satisfactions does Thoreau find in the labor of raising beans (in "The Bean-Field")? How does he find humor and whimsy even in the task of weeding?
6. In his "Conclusion," what does Thoreau say he learned from his experiment?

Interpreting Meanings

7. Why do you think Thoreau goes to the trouble of itemizing the exact cost of his house? What might he have wanted to prove to his Concord neighbors?
8. What does Thoreau mean when he says "Simplify, simplify" (page 212)? Do you think he has a valid point here? Explain.
9. How would you summarize Thoreau's ideas on progress, as exemplified by what he says about the railroad and other forms of new technology? Do you argree with him? Why or why not?
10. Thoreau was a great observer of nature, though he was not a scientist. Compare Thoreau's description of the war between the ants and his game with the loon in "Brute Neighbors." In each case, what does he find in the natural occurrence that is remarkable or valuable?
11. What do you think is the lesson of the fable of the apple-wood table at the conclusion of *Walden*?
12. Do you see evidences of the Romantic point of view in *Walden*—the emphasis on intuition, on the power in nature, and on human emotions? Explain.
13. What do you think Thoreau means in his final paragraph by the words, "Only that day dawns to which we are awake"?
14. Find at least two passages from these essays that you think pertain to life today. Describe the situations or the people each quotation might apply to or appeal to.
15. Suppose a Puritan, like William Bradford (page 11), Mary Rowlandson (page 23), Jonathan Edwards (page 36), or Anne Bradstreet (page 42), had spent time in Walden and were recording these same experiences. How might their journal entries differ from Thoreau's?

Writing About the Essays

A Creative Response

1. **Writing a Journal Entry.** *Walden* does not record monumental events; it records the day-to-day ordinary events that most people would let pass by unnoticed. But in these events, Thoreau can find something interesting. Try to think like Thoreau for a day: At the end of the day, record in a journal what you saw, what you heard, and what you thought. Did anything remind you of books you have read? Did anything convey a lesson? Did you find a message in any event?

2. **Writing from Another Point of View.** Suppose Benjamin Franklin (see page 72) had lived at Walden Pond for a time. Write an entry that Franklin might have recorded in his journal. What lessons or morals might the rationalist Franklin have found in his experience?

A Critical Response

3. **Developing a Topic.** "The invariable mark of wisdom," Emerson wrote, "is to find the miraculous in the common." Using Emerson's statement as your topic sentence, choose a scene from *Walden* and discuss how Thoreau finds "the miraculous in the common."

4. **Comparing a Poem with Walden.** The Irish poet William Butler Yeats (1865–1939) was supposed to have based one of his famous poems on Thoreau's *Walden,* specifically on the entry about the bean-fields. (When he was a little boy, Yeats listened to his father read Thoreau aloud.) Here is Yeats's poem. In an essay, tell how it compares with Thoreau's writings in terms of **imagery, tone,** and **subject matter.**

The Lake Isle of Innisfree

I will arise and go now, and go to Innisfree,
And a small cabin build there, of clay and wattles
    made:
Nine bean-rows will I have there, a hive for the
    honeybee,
And live alone in the bee-loud glade.

And I shall have some peace there, for peace comes
    dropping slow,
Dropping from the veils of the morning to where the
    cricket sings;
There midnight's all a glimmer, and noon a purple
    glow,
And evening full of the linnet's wings.

I will arise and go now, for always night and day
I hear lake water lapping with low sounds by the shore;
While I stand on the roadway, or on the pavements
    gray,
I hear it in the deep heart's core.

              —William Butler Yeats

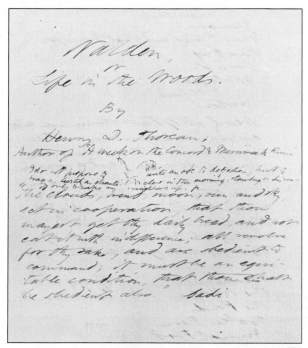

Henry Huntington Library, San Marino, California.

Analyzing Language and Style

A Metaphorical Style

Walden is not a simple book; Thoreau's typical style is metaphorical. For each passage that follows, identify the **metaphor** or **simile** and explain what is being compared with what. (Notice how visual each figure of speech is.) How would you express each idea in your own words?

1. "As for the rest of my readers, they will accept such portions as apply to them. I trust that none will stretch the seams in putting on the coat, for it may do good service to him whom it fits." (Page 208)

2. "I wanted to live deep and suck out all the marrow of life. . . ." (Page 211)

3. "Our life is like a German Confederacy, made up of petty states, with its boundary forever fluctuating. . . ." (Page 212)

4. "I did not wish to take a cabin passage, but rather to go before the mast and on the deck of the world, for there I could best see the moonlight amid the mountains. I do not wish to go below now." (Page 217)

5. "If a man does not keep pace with his companions, perhaps it is because he hears a different drummer. Let him step to the music which he hears, however measured or far away." (Page 217)

6. "The life in us is like the water in the river. It may rise this year higher than man has ever known it, and flood the parched uplands; even this may be the eventful year, which will drown out all our muskrats." (Page 217)

FROM RESISTANCE TO CIVIL GOVERNMENT

In July of 1846, Thoreau's stay at Walden Pond was interrupted by a night in jail. Thoreau was arrested because he refused, on principle, to pay a tax to the state. He refused primarily because he was opposed to the government's support of slavery. The police in Concord offered to pay the tax for Thoreau, but he refused that also. He was forced, therefore, to spend the night in jail, and he might have spent more time there, except that someone, probably his aunt, paid the tax for him.

This night in jail was the inspiration for the essay known as "Resistance to Civil Government" or "Civil Disobedience." Some people have suggested that the essay shows that Thoreau merely wanted to withdraw from life and all its hard questions. Others see Thoreau's position as the only one he could logically take to justify his stand. You will have to decide for yourself how the essay affects you.

John Brown Going to His Hanging
by Horace Pippin (1942). Oil.

Pennsylvania Academy of Fine Arts, Philadelphia.

I heartily accept the motto—"That government is best which governs least;"[1] and I should like to see it acted up to more rapidly and systematically. Carried out, it finally amounts to this, which also I believe—"That government is best which governs not at all;" and when men are prepared for it, that will be the kind of government which they will have. Government is at best but an expedient; but most governments are usually, and all governments are sometimes, inexpedient. The objections which have been brought against a standing army, and they are many and weighty, and deserve to prevail, may also at last be brought against a standing government. The standing army is only an arm of the standing government. The government itself, which is only the mode which the people have chosen to execute their will, is equally liable to be abused and perverted before the people can act through it. Witness the present Mexican war, the work of comparatively a few individuals using the standing government as their tool; for, in the outset, the people would not have consented to this measure.[2]

This American government—what is it but a tradition, though a recent one, endeavoring to transmit itself unimpaired to posterity, but each instant losing some of its integrity? It has not the vitality and force of a single living man; for a single man can bend it to his will. It is a sort of wooden gun to the people themselves; and, if ever they should use it in earnest as a real one against each other, it will surely split. But it is not the less necessary for this; for the people must have some complicated machinery or other, and hear its din, to satisfy that idea of government which they have. Governments show thus how successfully men can be imposed on, even impose on themselves, for their own advantage. It is excellent, we must all allow; yet this government never of itself furthered any enterprise, but by the alacrity with which it got out of its way. *It* does not keep the country free. *It* does not settle the West. *It* does not educate. The character inherent in the American people has done all that has been accomplished; and it would have done somewhat more, if the government had not sometimes got in its way. For government is an expedient by which men would fain[3] succeed in letting one another alone; and, as has been said, when it is most expedient, the governed are most let alone by it. Trade and commerce, if they were not made of India rubber, would never manage to bounce over the obstacles which legislators are continually putting in their way; and, if one were to judge these men wholly by the effects of their actions, and not partly by their intentions, they would deserve to be classed and punished with those mischievous persons who put obstructions on the railroads.

But, to speak practically and as a citizen, unlike those who call themselves no-government men, I ask for, not at once no government, but *at once* a better government. Let every man make known what kind of government would command his respect, and that will be one step toward obtaining it.

After all, the practical reason why, when the power is once in the hands of the people, a majority are permitted, and for a long period continue, to rule, is not because they are most likely to be in the right, nor because this seems fairest to the minority, but because they are physically the strongest. But a government in which the majority rule in all cases cannot be based on justice, even as far as men understand it. Can there not be a government in which majorities do not virtually decide right and wrong, but conscience?— in which majorities decide only those questions to which the rule of expediency is applicable? Must the citizen ever for a moment, or in the least degree, resign his conscience to the legislator? Why has every man a conscience, then? I think that we should be men first, and subjects afterward. It is not desirable to cultivate a respect for the law, so much as for the right. The only obligation which I have a right to assume, is to do at any time what I think right. . . .

It is not a man's duty, as a matter of course, to devote himself to the eradication of any, even the most enormous wrong; he may still properly have other concerns to engage him; but it is his duty, at least, to wash his hands of it, and, if he gives it no thought longer, not to give it practically his support. If I devote myself to other pursuits and

---

1. **"That . . . least"**: this Jeffersonian statement was the motto of the New York *Democratic Review,* which had published two of Thoreau's essays.
2. **this measure:** President Polk initiated hostilities against Mexico without a Congressional declaration of war.

3. **fain:** willingly.

THE MASQUE OF THE RED DEATH

The word *masque* in the title refers to a masked ball, an entertainment that was popular in Europe during the fourteenth and fifteenth centuries. It also refers to a mask that disguises the face. To understand what is happening on a literal level in this story, think about the Black Death, or bubonic plague, an epidemic that killed seventy-five percent of Europe's population during the fourteenth century. The plague lasted twenty years and was spread by fleas that lived on humans and rats. Some critics think the specific source of this story was a news article about a masked ball that was held in Paris in 1832 while a cholera epidemic raged in the city.

The "Red Death" had long devastated the country. No pestilence had ever been so fatal, or so hideous. Blood was its avatar[1] and its seal—the redness and the horror of blood. There were sharp pains, and sudden dizziness, and then profuse bleeding at the pores, with dissolution. The scarlet stains upon the body and especially upon the face of the victim, were the pest ban which shut him out from the aid and from the sympathy of his fellow men. And the whole seizure, progress, and termination of the disease, were the incidents of half an hour.

But the Prince Prospero was happy and dauntless and sagacious. When his dominions were half depopulated, he summoned to his presence a thousand hale and lighthearted friends from among the knights and dames of his court, and with these retired to the deep seclusion of one of his castellated[2] abbeys. This was an extensive and magnificent structure, the creation of the prince's own eccentric yet august taste. A strong and lofty wall girdled it in. This wall had gates of iron. The courtiers, having entered, brought furnaces and massy hammers and welded the bolts. They resolved to leave means neither of ingress or egress to the sudden impulses of despair or of frenzy from within. The abbey was amply provisioned. With such precautions the courtiers might bid defiance to contagion. The external world could take care of itself. In the meantime it was folly to grieve, or to think. The prince had provided all the appliances of pleasure. There were buffoons, there were improvisatori,[3] there were ballet dancers, there were musicians, there was Beauty, there was wine. All these and security were within. Without was the "Red Death."

It was toward the close of the fifth or sixth month of his seclusion, and while the pestilence raged most furiously abroad, that the Prince Prospero entertained his thousand friends at a masked ball of the most unusual magnificence.

It was a voluptuous scene, that masquerade. But first let me tell of the rooms in which it was held. There were seven—an imperial suite. In many palaces, however, such suites form a long and straight vista, while the folding doors slide back nearly to the walls on either hand, so that the view of the whole extent is scarcely impeded. Here the case was very different; as might have been expected from the duke's love of the bizarre. The apartments were so irregularly disposed that the vision embraced but little more than one at a time. There was a sharp turn at every twenty or thirty yards, and at each turn a novel effect. To the right and left, in the middle of each wall, a tall and narrow Gothic window looked out upon a closed corridor which pursued the windings of the suite. These windows were of stained glass whose color varied in accordance with the prevailing hue of the decorations of the chamber into which it opened. That at the eastern extremity was hung, for example, in blue—and vividly blue were its

---

1. **avatar:** embodiment, or concrete form.
2. **castellated:** built with turrets and battlements, like a castle.

3. **improvisatori:** performers who improvise their acts.

The Great Plague of London (1665). Colored woodcut.

windows. The second chamber was purple in its ornaments and tapestries, and here the panes were purple. The third was green throughout, and so were the casements. The fourth was furnished and lighted with orange—the fifth with white—the sixth with violet. The seventh apartment was closely shrouded in black velvet tapestries that hung all over the ceiling and down the walls, falling in heavy folds upon a carpet of the same material and hue. But in this chamber only, the color of the windows failed to correspond with the decorations. The panes here were scarlet—a deep blood color. Now in no one of the seven apartments was there any lamp or candelabrum, amid the profusion of golden ornaments that lay scattered to and fro or depended from the roof. There was no light of any kind emanating from lamp or candle within the suite of chambers. But in the corridors that followed the suite, there stood, opposite to each window, a heavy tripod, bearing a brazier of fire that projected its rays through the tinted glass and so glaringly illumined the room. And thus were produced a multitude of gaudy and fantastic appearances. But in the western or black chamber the effect of the firelight that streamed upon the dark hangings through the blood-tinted panes, was ghastly in the extreme, and produced so wild a look upon the countenances of those who entered, that there were few of the company bold enough to set foot within its precincts at all.

It was in this apartment, also, that there stood against the western wall, a gigantic clock of ebony. Its pendulum swung to and fro with a dull, heavy, monotonous clang; and when the minute hand made the circuit of the face, and the hour was to be stricken, there came from the brazen lungs of the clock a sound which was clear and loud and deep and exceedingly musical, but of so peculiar a note and emphasis that, at each lapse of an hour, the musicians of the orchestra were constrained to pause, momentarily, in their performance, to hearken to the sound; and thus the waltzers perforce ceased their evolutions; and there was a brief disconcert[4] of the whole gay company; and, while the chimes of the clock yet rang, it was observed that the giddiest grew pale, and the more aged and sedate passed their hands over their brows as if in confused reverie or meditation. But when the echoes had fully ceased, a light laughter at once pervaded the assembly; the musicians looked at each other and smiled as if at their own nervousness and folly, and made whispering vows, each to the other, that the next chiming of the clock should produce in them no similar emotion; and then, after the lapse of sixty minutes (which embrace three thousand and six hundred seconds of the Time that flies), there came yet another chiming of the clock, and then were the same disconcert and tremulousness and meditation as before.

But, in spite of these things, it was a gay and magnificent revel. The tastes of the duke were peculiar. He had a fine eye for colors and effects. He disregarded the *decora*[5] of mere fashion. His plans were bold and fiery, and his conceptions glowed with barbaric luster. There are some who would have thought him mad. His followers felt that he was not. It was necessary to hear and see and touch him to be *sure* that he was not.

He had directed, in great part, the moveable embellishments of the seven chambers, upon occasion of this great *fête;*[6] and it was his own guiding taste which had given character to the masqueraders. Be sure they were grotesque. There were much glare and glitter and piquancy and phantasm—much of what has been since seen in *Hernani.*[7] There were arabesque figures with unsuited limbs and appointments. There were delirious fancies such as the madman fashions. There was much of the beautiful, much of the wanton, much of the bizarre, something of the terrible, and not a little of that which might have excited disgust. To and fro in the seven chambers there stalked, in fact, a multitude of dreams. And these—the dreams—writhed in and about, taking hue from the rooms, and causing the wild music of the orchestra to seem as the echo of their steps.

And, anon,[8] there strikes the ebony clock which stands in the hall of the velvet. And then, for a moment, all is still, and all is silent save the voice of the clock. The dreams are stiff-frozen as they stand. But the echoes of the chime die away—they have endured but an instant—and a light, half-subdued laughter floats after them as they depart. And now again the music swells, and the dreams live, and writhe to and fro more merrily than ever, taking hue from the many-tinted windows through which stream the rays from the tripods. But to the chamber which lies most westwardly of the seven, there are now none of the maskers who venture; for the night is waning away; and there flows a ruddier light through the blood-colored panes; and the blackness of the sable drapery appalls; and to him whose foot falls upon the sable carpet, there comes from the near clock of ebony a muffled peal more solemnly emphatic than any which reaches *their* ears who indulge in the more remote gaieties of the other apartments.

But these other apartments were densely crowded, and in them beat feverishly the heart of life. And the revel went whirlingly on, until at length there commenced the sounding of midnight upon the clock. And then the music ceased, as I have told; and the evolutions of the waltzers were quieted; and there was an uneasy cessation of all things as before. But now there were twelve strokes to be sounded by the bell of the clock; and thus it happened, perhaps, that more of thought crept, with more of time, into the meditations of the thoughtful among those who reveled. And thus, too, it happened, perhaps, that before the last echoes of the last chime had utterly sunk into silence, there were many individuals in the crowd who had found leisure to become aware of the presence of a masked figure which had arrested the attention of no single individual before. And the rumor of this new presence having spread itself whisperingly around, there arose at length from the whole company a buzz, or murmur, expressive of disapprobation and surprise—then, finally, of terror, of horror, and of disgust.

In an assembly of phantasms such as I have painted, it may well be supposed that no ordinary

---

4. **disconcert:** embarrassment, confusion.
5. *decora:* here, proper good taste.
6. *fête* (fāt): French for party.
7. *"Hernani"*: a romantic play by the French writer Victor Hugo (1802–1885), first presented in 1830.

8. **anon:** soon.

appearance could have excited such sensation. In truth the masquerade license of the night was nearly unlimited; but, the figure in question had out-Heroded Herod,[9] and gone beyond the bounds of even the prince's indefinite decorum. There are chords in the hearts of the most reckless which cannot be touched without emotion. Even with the utterly lost, to whom life and death are equally jests, there are matters of which no jest can be made. The whole company, indeed, seemed now deeply to feel that in the costume and bearing of the stranger neither wit nor propriety existed. The figure was tall and gaunt, and shrouded from head to foot in the habiliments[10] of the grave. The mask which concealed the visage was made so nearly to resemble the countenance of a stiffened corpse that the closest scrutiny must have had difficulty in detecting the cheat. And yet all this might have been endured, if not approved, by the mad revelers around. But the mummer[11] had gone so far as to assume the type of the Red Death. His vesture was dabbled in *blood*—and his broad brow, with all the features of the face, was besprinkled with the scarlet horror.

When the eyes of Prince Prospero fell upon this spectral image (which with a slow and solemn movement, as if more fully to sustain its role, stalked to and fro among the waltzers), he was seen to be convulsed, in the first moment with a strong shudder either of terror or distaste; but, in the next, his brow reddened with rage.

"Who dares?" he demanded hoarsely of the courtiers who stood near him—"who dares insult us with this blasphemous mockery? Seize him and unmask him—that we may know whom we have to hang at sunrise, from the battlements!"

It was in the eastern or blue chamber in which stood the Prince Prospero as he uttered these words. They rang throughout the seven rooms loudly and clearly—for the prince was a bold and robust man, and the music had become hushed at the waving of his hand.

It was in the blue room where stood the prince, with a group of pale courtiers by his side. At first, as he spoke, there was a slight rushing movement of this group in the direction of the intruder, who at the moment was also near at hand, and now, with deliberate and stately step, made closer approach to the speaker. But from a certain nameless awe with which the mad assumptions of the mummer had inspired the whole party, there were found none who put forth hand to seize him; so that, unimpeded, he passed within a yard of the prince's person; and, while the vast assembly, as if with one impulse, shrank from the centers of the rooms to the walls, he made his way uninterruptedly, but with the same solemn and measured step which had distinguished him from the first, through the blue chamber to the purple—through the purple to the green—through the green to the orange—through this again to the white—and even thence to the violet, ere a decided movement had been made to arrest him. It was then, however, that the Prince Prospero, maddening with rage and the shame of his own momentary cowardice, rushed hurriedly through the six chambers, while none followed him on account of a deadly terror that had seized upon all. He bore aloft a drawn dagger, and had approached, in rapid impetuosity, to within three or four feet of the retreating figure, when the latter, having attained the extremity of the velvet apartment, turned suddenly and confronted his pursuer. There was a sharp cry—and the dagger dropped gleaming upon the sable carpet, upon which, instantly afterward, fell prostrate in death the Prince Prospero. Then, summoning the wild courage of despair, a throng of the revelers at once threw themselves into the black apartment, and seizing the mummer, whose tall figure stood erect and motionless within the shadow of the ebony clock, gasped in unutterable horror at finding the grave-cerements[12] and corpselike mask which they handled with so violent a rudeness, untenanted by any tangible form.

And now was acknowledged the presence of the Red Death. He had come like a thief in the night. And one by one dropped the revelers in the blood-bedewed halls of their revel, and died each in the despairing posture of his fall. And the life of the ebony clock went out with that of the last of the gay. And the flames of the tripods expired. And Darkness and Decay and the Red Death held illimitable dominion over all.

---

9. **Herod:** the Biblical king responsible for the massacre of innocent children in his attempt to kill the infant Jesus. To "out-Herod Herod" is to be more evil than the expert.
10. **habiliments:** clothing.
11. **mummer:** masked person.

---

12. **grave-cerements:** shrouds, cloths that cover a body.

Responding to the Story

Analyzing the Story

Identifying Facts

1. According to the first paragraph, what characteristics of the "Red Death" make it a horrifying disease?
2. Describe Prospero's plan for surviving the epidemic.
3. Poe gives a great deal of space in the story to the palace plans and decorations, providing us with textures and colors in profusion. What are some of the sensory **images** that create a vivid, concrete impression of Prince Prospero's hall?
4. What happens at the **climax** of the story?
5. The story concludes, "And Darkness and Decay and the Red Death held illimitable dominion over all." List the specific **images** of darkness, decay, and death in the final paragraph.

Interpreting Meanings

6. What do the ebony clock and its arresting chimes add to the plot? Can you think of any **symbolic** value the clock might have?
7. What **symbolic** significance can you find in Poe's use of numbers? In his use of colors, especially the black and the scarlet in the seventh room? In the movement from east to west in the sequence of rooms?
8. Poe's story is clearly not meant to be realistic; instead, it is a masterpiece of imaginative atmosphere that may be read as an **allegory**—a story in which characters, objects, and events symbolize various ideas and qualities. The mysterious guest, for example, turns out not to be a real person, but the embodiment of the Red Death. What, in a still larger sense, might this figure symbolize? What attitudes toward life and death do you think the Prince and his party-goers might symbolize?
9. In the last paragraph, Poe **alludes** to a prophecy from the Bible: "For yourselves know perfectly that the Day of the Lord so cometh as a thief in the night." (1 Thessalonians 5:2) "The Day of the Lord" is a way of referring to the last day of the world, or Judgment Day. Explain how the allusion adds a layer of meaning to Poe's story.
10. How would you state the **theme** of this story—the main idea about human behavior that is revealed by the fictional events? How do you feel about this theme—is it a valid one, in your experience?
11. Poe felt strongly that the main concern of any story was its **psychological effect.** He believed that neither narrative nor characterization was as important as the reader's emotional response. What emotional effect did the first paragraph of this story have on you? How does Poe produce this effect?

Writing About the Story

A Creative Response

1. **Staging the Story.** Suppose you were planning a movie or stage adaptation of "The Masque of the Red Death." Write a brief description of the first thing the audience would see. What would they hear?
2. **Writing an Opening Sentence.** In a review of Nathaniel Hawthorne's *Twice-Told Tales,* Poe said that the very first sentence in a story should create a particular effect. Reread the first sentence of this story. Then write three original sentences that you think would be good story openers. What effect do you want to create by each sentence?

A Critical Response

3. **Commenting on a Criticism.** Richard Wilbur, an American poet and an authority on Poe, has said this about "The Masque of the Red Death":

> Prince Prospero's flight from the Red Death is the poetic imagination's flight from temporal and worldly consciousness into dream. The thousand dancers of Prince Prospero's costume ball are just what Poe says they are—"dreams" or "phantasms," veiled and vivid creatures of Prince Prospero's rapt imagination. Whenever there is a feast, or carnival, or costume ball in Poe, we may be sure that a dream is in progress.
>
> —Richard Wilbur

Write an essay commenting on this remark. If you agree with it, explain what the events of the story suggest about the conflict between the dream world and the temporal world, or between illusion and reality. If you disagree, explain why.

Analyzing Language and Style

Emotional Effects

Poe was a master at finding words that created specific emotional effects. In this story, perhaps the most prominent word is *blood.* In his third sentence, Poe names the emotion he associates with blood: horror.

1. Find at least three passages in which blood is used to describe the color red. Think of at least one other descriptive word that might have been used in each case to create a different emotional effect. (For example, would "tomato red" make you feel horror?)

2. Given the nature of the enemy in the story, why do you think Poe keeps using the word *blood* as he does?

3. Poe uses the French word *bizarre* twice. *Bizarre* means "strange, odd, eccentric, outrageous, grotesque." Here are the two passages in which *bizarre* is used. Read each passage in context and suggest another word that could have been used to suggest a completely different emotional effect:

   a. ". . . the duke's love of the bizarre." (Page 228)
   b. "There was much of the . . . bizarre. . . ." (Page 230)

4. "There were delirious fancies such as the madman fashions. There was much of the beautiful, much of the wanton, much of the bizarre, something of the terrible, and not a little of that which might have excited disgust." Define the words in this passage, besides *bizarre,* that create a particular emotional tone. How would you describe that tone? What effect is Poe looking for?

5. Reread the very last sentence of the story. What is its emotional effect? What things do you associate with the word *decay?* What word means the opposite of decay?

Primary Sources
A Visit to the Poes

Mrs. Gove Nichols visited Poe's cottage in New York and recorded her impressions.

"The cottage had an air of gentility that must have been lent to it by the presence of its inmates. So neat, so poor, so unfurnished, and yet so charming a dwelling I never saw. The floor of the kitchen was white as wheaten flour. A table, a chair, and a little stove it contained seemed to furnish it completely. The sitting room was laid with check matting; four chairs, a light stand, and a hanging bookshelf completed its furniture. There were pretty presentation copies of books on the little shelves, and the Brownings had posts of honor on the stand. With quiet exultation Poe drew from his inside pocket a letter he had recently received from Elizabeth Barrett Browning. He read it to us. It was very flattering. . . . On the bookshelf there lay a volume of Poe's poems. He took it down, wrote my name in it and gave it to me. . . . He was at this time greatly depressed. Their extreme poverty, the sickness of his wife, and his own inability to write sufficiently accounted for this. We spent half an hour in the house, when some more company came, which included ladies, and then we all went to walk.

"We strolled away into the woods, and had a very cheerful time, till someone proposed a game at leaping. I think it must have been Poe, as he was expert in the exercise. Two or three gentlemen agreed to leap with him, and though one of them was tall and had been a hunter in times past, Poe still distanced them all. But alas! his gaiters [cloth or leather coverings that went over the shoes and covered the ankle], long worn and carefully kept, were both burst in the grand leap that made him victor. . . . I was certain he had no other shoes, boots, or gaiters. Who among us could offer him money to buy a new pair?

. . . When we reached the cottage, I think all felt that we must not go in, to see the shoeless unfortunate sitting or standing in our midst. I had an errand, however—and I entered the house to get it. The poor old mother looked at his feet with a dismay that I shall never forget. 'Oh, Eddie!' said she, 'how did you burst your gaiters?' Poe seemed to have come into a semi-torpid state as soon as he saw his mother. 'Do answer Muddie,' now said she coaxingly—I related the cause of the mishap, and she drew me into the kitchen.

" 'Will you speak to Mr. _____ [an editor],' she said, 'about Eddie's last poem? . . . If he will only take the poem, Eddie can have a pair of shoes. He has it—I carried it last week, and Eddie says it is his best. You will speak to him about it, won't you?'

"We had already read the poem in conclave, and Heaven forgive us, we could not make head or tail of it. It might as well have been in any of the lost languages, for any meaning we could extract from its melodious numbers. I remember saying that I believed it was only a hoax that Poe was passing off for poetry, to see how far his name would go in imposing upon people. But here was a situation. The reviewer had been actively instrumental in the demolition of the gaiters.

" 'Of course, they will publish the poem,' said I, 'and I will ask C_____ to be quick about it.'

"The poem was paid for at once and published soon after. I presume it is regarded as genuine poetry in the collected poems of its author, but then it bought the poet a pair of gaiters, and twelve shillings over."

—from *Israfel: The Life and Times of Edgar Allan Poe,* Hervey Allen

THE FALL OF THE HOUSE OF USHER

"The Fall of the House of Usher" is probably Poe's best and most famous story. The story exhibits so many trappings of the Gothic tale that a list of them would stretch to the bottom of the page. We have a mysterious setting, mysterious illnesses, mysterious sounds in the night, the possibility of live burial, and the suggestion of the supernatural at work. But despite all its Gothic touches, the story aims for much more than mere thrills. The narrator's journey to the House of Usher has been seen as a symbolic psychological journey out of the world of reason and sanity into the unexplored world of the human mind.

Notice how Poe begins by establishing the mood of his story. Which words and phrases in the opening paragraph make you aware that the narrator is leaving one region and entering another, uncertain one?

Son cœur est un luth suspendu;
Sitôt qu'on le touche il résonne.[1]
—*De Béranger.*

During the whole of a dull, dark, and soundless day in the autumn of the year, when the clouds hung oppressively low in the heavens, I had been passing alone, on horseback, through a singularly dreary tract of country; and at length found myself, as the shades of the evening drew on, within view of the melancholy House of Usher. I know not how it was—but, with the first glimpse of the building, a sense of insufferable gloom pervaded my spirit. I say insufferable; for the feeling was unrelieved by any of that half-pleasurable, because poetic, sentiment, with which the mind usually receives even the sternest natural images of the desolate or terrible. I looked upon the scene before me—upon the mere[2] house, and the simple landscape features of the domain—upon the bleak walls—upon the vacant eyelike windows—upon a few rank sedges[3]—and upon a few white trunks of decayed trees—with an utter depression of soul which I can compare to no earthly sensation more properly than to the after-dream of the reveler upon opium—the bitter lapse into everyday life—the hideous dropping off of the veil. There was an iciness, a sinking, a sickening of the heart—an unredeemed dreariness of thought which no goading of the imagination could torture into aught[4] of the sublime. What was it—I paused to think—what was it that so unnerved me in the contemplation of the House of Usher? It was a mystery all insoluble; nor could I grapple with the shadowy fancies that crowded upon me as I pondered. I was forced to fall back upon the unsatisfactory conclusion, that while, beyond doubt, there *are* combinations of very simple natural objects which have the power of thus affecting us, still the analysis of this power lies among considerations beyond our depth. It was possible, I reflected, that a mere different arrangement of the particulars of the scene, of the details of the picture, would be sufficient to modify, or perhaps to annihilate its capacity for sorrowful impression; and, acting upon this idea, I reined my horse to the precipitous brink of a black and lurid tarn[5] that lay in unruffled luster by the dwelling, and gazed down—but with a shudder even more thrilling than before—upon the remodeled and inverted images of the gray sedge, and the ghastly tree stems, and the vacant and eyelike windows.

Nevertheless, in this mansion of gloom I now

---

1. *Son coeur . . . il résonne:* "His heart is a suspended lute; / Whenever one touches it, it resounds." From "Le Refus" ("The Refusal") by Pierre Jean de Béranger (1780–1857).
2. **mere:** lake.
3. **sedges:** grasslike plants that grow in watery ground.
4. **aught:** anything.
5. **tarn:** small mountain lake or pond with dark waters.

Illustration of a scene from ''The Fall of the House
of Usher'' by Arthur Rackham (1935).

proposed to myself a sojourn of some weeks. Its proprietor, Roderick Usher, had been one of my boon companions in boyhood; but many years had elapsed since our last meeting. A letter, however, had lately reached me in a distant part of the country—a letter from him—which, in its wildly importunate nature, had admitted of no other than a personal reply. The MS.[6] gave evidence of nervous agitation. The writer spoke of acute bodily illness—of a mental disorder which oppressed him—and of an earnest desire to see me, as his best, and indeed his only personal friend, with a view of attempting, by the cheerfulness of my society, some alleviation of his malady. It was the manner in which all this, and much more, was said—it was the apparent *heart* that went with his request—which allowed me no room for hesitation; and I accordingly obeyed forthwith what I still considered a very singular summons.

Although, as boys, we had been even intimate associates, yet I really knew little of my friend. His reserve had been always excessive and habitual. I was aware, however, that his very ancient family had been noted, time out of mind, for a peculiar sensibility of temperament, displaying itself, through long ages, in many works of exalted art, and manifested, of late, in repeated deeds of munificent yet unobtrusive charity, as well as in a passionate devotion to the intricacies, perhaps even more than to the orthodox and easily recognizable beauties, of musical science. I had learned, too, the very remarkable fact, that the stem of the Usher race, all time-honored as it was, had put forth, at no period, any enduring branch; in other words, that the entire family lay in the direct line of descent, and had always, with very trifling and very temporary variation, so lain. It was this deficiency, I considered, while running over in thought the perfect keeping of the character of the premises with the accredited character of the people, and while speculating upon the possible influence which the one, in the long lapse of centuries, might have exercised upon the other— it was this deficiency, perhaps, of collateral issue,[7] and the consequent undeviating transmission, from sire to son, of the patrimony with the name, which had at length, so identified the two as to merge the original title of the estate in the quaint and equivocal appellation of the "House of Usher"—an appellation which seemed to include, in the minds of the peasantry who used it, both the family and the family mansion.

I have said that the sole effect of my somewhat childish experiment—that of looking down within the tarn—had been to deepen the first singular impression. There can be no doubt that the consciousness of the rapid increase of my superstition—for why should I not so term it?—served mainly to accelerate the increase itself. Such, I have long known, is the paradoxical law of all sentiments having terror as a basis. And it might have been for this reason only, that, when I again uplifted my eyes to the house itself, from its image in the pool, there grew in my mind a strange fancy—a fancy so ridiculous, indeed, that I but mention it to show the vivid force of the sensations which oppressed me. I had so worked upon my imagination as really to believe that about the whole mansion and domain there hung an atmosphere peculiar to themselves and their immediate vicinity—an atmosphere which had no affinity with the air of heaven, but which had reeked up from the decayed trees, and the gray wall, and the silent tarn—a pestilent and mystic vapor, dull, sluggish, faintly discernible, and leaden-hued.

Shaking off from my spirit what *must* have been a dream, I scanned more narrowly the real aspect of the building. Its principal feature seemed to be that of an excessive antiquity. The discoloration of ages had been great. Minute fungi overspread the whole exterior, hanging in a fine tangled webwork from the eaves. Yet all this was apart from any extraordinary dilapidation. No portion of the masonry had fallen; and there appeared to be a wild inconsistency between its still perfect adaptation of parts, and the crumbling condition of the individual stones. In this there was much that reminded me of the specious totality of old woodwork which has rotted for long years in some neglected vault, with no disturbance from the breath of the external air. Beyond this indication of extensive decay, however, the fabric gave little token of instability. Perhaps the eye of a scrutinizing observer might have discovered a barely perceptible fissure, which, extending from the roof of the building in front, made its way down the wall in a zigzag direction, until it became lost in the sullen waters of the tarn.

Noticing these things, I rode over a short causeway to the house. A servant-in-waiting took my horse, and I entered the Gothic archway of the

---

6. **MS.:** an abbreviation of the word *manuscript*.
7. **collateral issue:** descendants.

hall.[8] A valet, of stealthy step, thence conducted me, in silence, through many dark and intricate passages in my progress to the *studio* of his master. Much that I encountered on the way contributed, I know not how, to heighten the vague sentiments of which I have already spoken. While the objects around me—while the carvings of the ceilings, the somber tapestries of the walls, the ebon blackness of the floors, and the phantasmagoric[9] armorial trophies which rattled as I strode, were but matters to which, or to such as which, I had been accustomed from my infancy—while I hesitated not to acknowledge how familiar was all this—I still wondered to find how unfamiliar were the fancies which ordinary images were stirring up. On one of the staircases, I met the physician of the family. His countenance, I thought, wore a mingled expression of low cunning and perplexity. He accosted me with trepidation and passed on. The valet now threw open a door and ushered me into the presence of his master.

The room in which I found myself was very large and lofty. The windows were long, narrow, and pointed, and at so vast a distance from the black oaken floor as to be altogether inaccessible from within. Feeble gleams of encrimsoned light made their way through the trellised panes, and served to render sufficiently distinct the more prominent objects around; the eye, however, struggled in vain to reach the remoter angles of the chamber, or the recesses of the vaulted and fretted[10] ceiling. Dark draperies hung upon the walls. The general furniture was profuse, comfortless, antique, and tattered. Many books and musical instruments lay scattered about, but failed to give any vitality to the scene. I felt that I breathed an atmosphere of sorrow. An air of stern, deep, and irredeemable gloom hung over and pervaded all.

Upon my entrance, Usher arose from a sofa on which he had been lying at full length, and greeted me with a vivacious warmth which had much in it, I at first thought, of an overdone cordiality—of the constrained effort of the *ennuyé*[11] man of the world. A glance, however, at his countenance, convinced me of his perfect sincerity. We sat down; and for some moments, while he spoke not, I gazed upon him with a feeling half of pity, half of awe. Surely, man had never before so terribly altered, in so brief a period, as had Roderick Usher! It was with difficulty that I could bring myself to admit the identity of the wan being before me with the companion of my early boyhood. Yet the character of his face had been at all times remarkable. A cadaverousness[12] of complexion, an eye large, liquid, and luminous beyond comparison; lips somewhat thin and very pallid, but of a surpassing beautiful curve; a nose of a delicate Hebrew model, but with a breadth of nostril unusual in similar formations; a finely molded chin, speaking, in its want of prominence, of a want of moral energy; hair of a more than weblike softness and tenuity;[13] these features, with an inordinate expansion above the regions of the temple, made up altogether a countenance not easily to be forgotten. And now in the mere exaggeration of the prevailing character of these features, and of the expression they were wont to convey, lay so much of change that I doubted to whom I spoke. The now ghastly pallor of the skin, and the now miraculous luster of the eye, above all things startled and even awed me. The silken hair, too, had been suffered to grow all unheeded, and as, in its wild gossamer texture, it floated rather than fell about the face, I could not, even with effort, connect its Arabesque[14] expression with any idea of simple humanity.

In the manner of my friend I was at once struck with an incoherence—an inconsistency; and I soon found this to arise from a series of feeble and futile struggles to overcome a habitual trepidancy—an excessive nervous agitation. For something of this nature I had indeed been prepared, no less by his letter, than by reminiscences of certain boyish traits, and by conclusions deduced from his peculiar physical conformation and temperament. His action was alternately vivacious and sullen. His voice varied rapidly from a tremulous indecision (when the animal spirits seemed utterly in abeyance) to that species of energetic concision—that abrupt, weighty, unhurried, and

---

8. The archway looked like a doorway in a Gothic cathedral—high, pointed, and elaborately carved.
9. **phantasmagoric** (fan·taz·mə·gor′ik): dreamlike, bizarre.
10. **fretted:** carved in an intricate pattern.
11. *ennuyé* (än·nwē′ā): a French word meaning "bored" or "jaded."

12. **cadaverousness** (kə·dav′ər·əs·nes): corpselike quality.
13. **tenuity** (tə·nōō′ə·tē): thinness, fineness.
14. **Arabesque:** elaborately intricate, as in Moorish or Arabic ornamentation.

hollow-sounding enunciation—that leaden, self-balanced, and perfectly modulated guttural utterance, which may be observed in the lost drunkard, or the irreclaimable eater of opium, during the periods of his most intense excitement.

It was thus that he spoke of the object of my visit, of his earnest desire to see me, and of the solace he expected me to afford him. He entered, at some length, into what he conceived to be the nature of his malady. It was, he said, a constitutional and a family evil, and one for which he despaired to find a remedy—a mere nervous affection,[15] he immediately added, which would undoubtedly soon pass off. It displayed itself in a host of unnatural sensations. Some of these, as he detailed them, interested and bewildered me; although, perhaps, the terms, and the general manner of the narration had their weight. He suffered much from a morbid acuteness of the senses; the most insipid food was alone endurable; he could wear only garments of certain texture; the odors of all flowers were oppressive; his eyes were tortured by even a faint light; and there were but peculiar sounds, and these from stringed instruments, which did not inspire him with horror.

To an anomalous[16] species of terror I found him a bounden slave. "I shall perish," said he, "I *must* perish in this deplorable folly. Thus, thus, and not otherwise, shall I be lost. I dread the events of the future, not in themselves, but in their results. I shudder at the thought of any, even the most trivial, incident, which may operate upon this intolerable agitation of soul. I have, indeed, no abhorrence of danger, except in its absolute effect—in terror. In this unnerved—in this pitiable condition—I feel that the period will sooner or later arrive when I must abandon life and reason together, in some struggle with the grim phantasm, FEAR."

I learned, moreover, at intervals, and through broken and equivocal hints, another singular feature of his mental condition. He was enchained by certain superstitious impressions in regard to the dwelling which he tenanted, and whence, for many years, he had never ventured forth—in regard to an influence whose supposititious[17] force was conveyed in terms too shadowy here to be restated—an influence which some peculiarities in the mere form and substance of his family mansion, had, by dint of long sufferance, he said, obtained over his spirit—an effect which the *physique* of the gray walls and turrets, and of the dim tarn into which they all looked down, had, at length, brought about upon the *morale* of his existence.

He admitted, however, although with hesitation, that much of the peculiar gloom which thus afflicted him could be traced to a more natural and far more palpable origin—to the severe and long-continued illness—indeed to the evidently approaching dissolution—of a tenderly beloved sister—his sole companion for long years—his last and only relative on earth. "Her decease," he said, with a bitterness which I can never forget, "would leave him (him the hopeless and the frail) the last of the ancient race of the Ushers." While he spoke, the lady Madeline (for so was she called) passed slowly through a remote portion of the apartment, and, without having noticed my presence, disappeared. I regarded her with an utter astonishment not unmingled with dread—and yet I found it impossible to account for such feelings. A sensation of stupor oppressed me, as my eyes followed her retreating steps. When a door, at length, closed upon her, my glance sought instinctively and eagerly the countenance of the brother—but he had buried his face in his hands, and I could only perceive that a far more than ordinary wanness had overspread the emaciated fingers through which trickled many passionate tears.

The disease of the lady Madeline had long baffled the skill of her physicians. A settled apathy, a gradual wasting away of the person, and frequent although transient affections of a partially cataleptical[18] character, were the unusual diagnosis. Hitherto she had steadily borne up against the pressure of her malady, and had not betaken herself finally to bed; but, on the closing in of the evening of my arrival at the house, she succumbed (as her brother told me at night with inexpressible agitation) to the prostrating power of the destroyer; and I learned that the glimpse I had obtained of her person would thus probably be the last I should obtain—that the lady, at least while living, would be seen by me no more.

---

15. **affection:** here, affliction.
16. **anomalous:** abnormal.
17. **supposititious:** supposed.

18. **cataleptical:** in catalepsy, the victim loses sensation and the ability to move the limbs, or even the entire body. In a cataleptic attack, Madeline could be as stiff as a corpse.

The Dead Wife by George Lambdin (late 19th century). Oil. North Carolina Museum of Art, Raleigh.

For several days ensuing, her name was un-mentioned by either Usher or myself: and during this period I was busied in earnest endeavors to alleviate the melancholy of my friend. We painted and read together; or I listened, as if in a dream, to the wild improvisations of his speaking guitar. And thus, as a closer and still closer intimacy admitted me more unreservedly into the recesses of his spirit, the more bitterly did I perceive the futility of all attempt at cheering a mind from which darkness, as if an inherent positive quality, poured forth upon all objects of the moral and physical universe, in one unceasing radiation of gloom.

I shall ever bear about me a memory of the many solemn hours I thus spent alone with the master of the House of Usher. Yet I should fail in any attempt to convey an idea of the exact char-acter of the studies, or of the occupations, in which he involved me, or led me the way. An excited and highly distempered ideality[19] threw a sulfureous[20] luster over all. His long, improvised dirges will ring forever in my ears. Among other things, I hold painfully in mind a certain singular perversion and amplification of the wild air of the

19. **distempered ideality:** disturbed or disordered idea.
20. **sulfureous:** yellowish, like sulfur.

last waltz of Von Weber.[21] From the paintings over which his elaborate fancy brooded, and which grew, touch by touch, into vaguenesses at which I shuddered the more thrillingly, because I shuddered knowing not why—from these paintings (vivid as their images now are before me) I would in vain endeavor to educe more than a small portion which should lie within the compass of merely written words. By the utter simplicity, by the nakedness of his designs, he arrested and overawed attention. If ever mortal painted an idea, that mortal was Roderick Usher. For me at least—in the circumstances then surrounding me—there arose out of the pure abstractions which the hypochondriac contrived to throw upon his canvas, an intensity of intolerable awe, no shadow of which felt I ever yet in the contemplation of the certainly glowing yet too concrete reveries of Fuseli.[22]

One of the phantasmagoric conceptions of my friend, partaking not so rigidly of the spirit of abstraction, may be shadowed forth, although feebly, in words. A small picture presented the interior of an immensely long and rectangular vault or tunnel, with low walls, smooth, white, and without interruption or device. Certain accessory points of the design served well to convey the idea that this excavation lay at an exceeding depth below the surface of the earth. No outlet was observed in any portion of its vast extent, and no torch, or other artificial source of light was discernible; yet a flood of intense rays rolled throughout, and bathed the whole in a ghastly and inappropriate splendor.

I have just spoken of that morbid condition of the auditory nerve which rendered all music intolerable to the sufferer, with the exception of certain effects of stringed instruments. It was, perhaps, the narrow limits to which he thus confined himself upon the guitar, which gave birth, in great measure, to the fantastic character of his performances. But the fervid *facility* of his *impromptus*[23] could not be so accounted for. They must have been, and were, in the notes, as well as in the words of his wild fantasias (for he not unfrequently accompanied himself with rhymed verbal improvisations), the result of that intense mental collectedness and concentration to which I have previously alluded as observable only in particular moments of the highest artificial excitement. The words of one of these rhapsodies I have easily remembered. I was, perhaps, the more forcibly impressed with it, as he gave it, because, in the under or mystic current of its meaning, I fancied that I perceived, and for the first time, a full consciousness on the part of Usher, of the tottering of his lofty reason upon her throne. The verses, which were entitled ''The Haunted Palace,'' ran very nearly, if not accurately, thus:

I

In the greenest of our valleys,
  By good angels tenanted,
Once a fair and stately palace—
  Radiant palace—reared its head.
In the monarch Thought's dominion—
  It stood there!
Never seraph spread a pinion[24]
  Over fabric half so fair.

II

Banners yellow, glorious, golden,
  On its roof did float and flow;
(This—all this—was in the olden
  Time long ago)
And every gentle air that dallied,
  In that sweet day,
Along the ramparts plumed and pallid,
  A winged odor went away.

III

Wanderers in that happy valley
  Through two luminous windows saw
Spirits moving musically
  To a lute's well-tuned law,
Round about a throne, where sitting
  (Porphyrogene!)[25]
In state his glory well befitting,
  The ruler of the realm was seen.

---

21. **Von Weber:** Carl Maria von Weber (1786–1826), a German composer of Romantic music.
22. **Fuseli:** Johann Heinrich Fuseli, a Swiss painter (1741–1825) who lived in England and illustrated the epics of Milton and the tragedies of Shakespeare. He often painted scenes of horror and the supernatural.
23. *impromptus:* improvised performances.

24. **pinion** (pin′yən): wing (a seraph is an angel).
25. **Porphyrogene:** someone ''born to the purple,'' or of royal blood. Porphyry was a purple dye reserved for royalty. (Poe coined the word *Porphyrogene*.)

IV

And all with pearl and ruby glowing
 Was the fair palace door,
Through which came flowing, flowing, flowing
 And sparkling evermore,
A troop of Echoes whose sweet duty
 Was but to sing,
In voices surpassing beauty,
 The wit and wisdom of their king.

V

But evil things, in robes of sorrow,
 Assailed the monarch's high estate;
(Ah, let us mourn, for never morrow
 Shall dawn upon him, desolate!)
And, round about his home, the glory
 That blushed and bloomed
Is but a dim-remembered story
 Of the oldtime entombed.

VI

And travelers now within that valley,
 Through the red-litten[26] windows, see
Vast forms that move fantastically
 To a discordant melody;
While, like a rapid ghastly river,
 Through the pale door,
A hideous throng rush out forever,
 And laugh—but smile no more.

I well remember that suggestions arising from this ballad led us into a train of thought wherein there became manifest an opinion of Usher's which I mention not so much on account of its novelty (for other men have thought thus); as on account of the pertinacity with which he maintained it. This opinion, in its general form, was that of the sentience[27] of all vegetable things. But, in his disordered fancy, the idea had assumed a more daring character, and trespassed, under certain conditions, upon the kingdom of inorganization.[28] I lack words to express the full extent, of the earnest *abandon* of his persuasion. The belief, however, was connected (as I have previously hinted) with the gray stones of the home of his forefathers. The conditions of the sentience had been here, he imagined, fulfilled in the method of collocation of these stones—in the order of their arrangement, as well as in that of the many *fungi* which overspread them, and of the decayed trees which stood around—above all, in the long undisturbed endurance of this arrangement, and in its reduplication in the still waters of the tarn. Its evidence—the evidence of the sentience—was to be seen, he said (and I here started as he spoke), in the gradual yet certain condensation of an atmosphere of their own about the waters and the walls. The result was discoverable, he added, in that silent, yet importunate and terrible influence which for centuries had molded the destinies of his family, and which made *him* what I now saw him—what he was. Such opinions need no comment, and I will make none.

Our books—the books which, for years, had formed no small portion of the mental existence of the invalid—were, as might be supposed, in strict keeping with this character of phantasm. We pored together over such works as the Ververt et Chartreuse[29] of Gresset; the Belphegor of Machiavelli; the Heaven and Hell of Swedenborg; the Subterranean Voyage of Nicholas Klimm by Holberg; the Chiromancy of Robert Flud, of Jean D'Indaginé, and of De la Chambre; the Journey into the Blue Distance of Tieck; and the City of the Sun of Campanella. One favorite volume was a small octavo edition of the *Directorium Inquisitorum,* by the Dominican Eymeric de Gironne; and there were passages in Pomponius Mela, about the old African Satyrs and Ægipans, over which Usher would sit dreaming for hours. His chief delight, however, was found in the perusal of an exceedingly rare and curious book in quarto Gothic—the manual of a forgotten church—the *Vigiliæ Mortuorum secundum Chorum Ecclesiæ Maguntinæ.*[30]

I could not help thinking of the wild ritual of this work, and of its probable influence upon the hypochondriac, when, one evening, having informed me abruptly that the lady Madeline was no more, he stated his intention of preserving her corpse for a fortnight (previously to its final interment), in one of the numerous vaults within the

---

26. **red-litten:** red-lighted.
27. **sentience** (sen′shəns): consciousness.
28. **kingdom of inorganization:** the world of inorganic objects.

29. **Ververt et Chartreuse,** etc.: the books listed include works of mysticism, of magic, or of horror. Most of them foreshadow what is to happen to Madeline Usher.
30. *Vigiliae Mortuorum* means "vigil of the dead."

main walls of the building. The worldly reason, however, assigned for this singular proceeding, was one which I did not feel at liberty to dispute. The brother had been led to his resolution (so he told me) by consideration of the unusual character of the malady of the deceased, of certain obtrusive and eager inquiries on the part of her medical men, and of the remote and exposed situation of the burial ground of the family. I will not deny that when I called to mind the sinister countenance of the person whom I met upon the staircase,[31] on the day of my arrival at the house, I had no desire to oppose what I regarded as at best but a harmless, and by no means an unnatural, precaution.[32]

At the request of Usher, I personally aided him in the arrangements for the temporary entombment. The body having been encoffined, we two alone bore it to its rest. The vault in which we placed it (and which had been so long unopened that our torches, half smothered in its oppressive atmosphere, gave us little opportunity for investigation) was small, damp, and entirely without means of admission for light; lying, at great depth, immediately beneath that portion of the building in which was my own sleeping apartment. It had been used, apparently, in remote feudal times, for the worst purposes of a dungeon-keep,[33] and, in later days, as a place of deposit for powder, or some other highly combustible substance, as a portion of its floor, and the whole interior of a long archway through which we reached it, were carefully sheathed with copper. The door, of massive iron, had been, also, similarly protected. Its immense weight caused an unusually sharp grating sound, as it moved upon its hinges.

Having deposited our mournful burden upon tressels within this region of horror, we partially turned aside the yet unscrewed lid of the coffin, and looked upon the face of the tenant. A striking similitude between the brother and sister now first arrested my attention; and Usher, divining, perhaps, my thoughts, murmured out some few words from which I learned that the deceased and himself had been twins, and that sympathies of a scarcely intelligible nature had always existed between them. Our glances, however, rested not long upon the dead—for we could not regard her unawed. The disease which had thus entombed the lady in the maturity of youth, had left, as usual in all maladies of a strictly cataleptical character, the mockery of a faint blush upon the bosom and the face, and that suspiciously lingering smile upon the lip which is so terrible in death. We replaced and screwed down the lid, and, having secured the door of iron, made our way, with toil, into the scarcely less gloomy apartments of the upper portion of the house.

And now, some days of bitter grief having elapsed, an observable change came over the features of the mental disorder of my friend. His ordinary manner had vanished. His ordinary occupations were neglected or forgotten. He roamed from chamber to chamber with hurried, unequal, and objectless step. The pallor of his countenance had assumed, if possible, a more ghastly hue—but the luminousness of his eye had utterly gone out. The once occasional huskiness of this tone was heard no more; and a tremulous quaver, as if of extreme terror, habitually characterized his utterance. There were times, indeed, when I thought his unceasingly agitated mind was laboring with some oppressive secret, to divulge which he struggled for the necessary courage. At times, again, I was obliged to resolve all into the mere inexplicable vagaries[34] of madness, for I beheld him gazing upon vacancy for long hours, in an attitude of the profoundest attention, as if listening to some imaginary sound. It was no wonder that his condition terrified—that it infected me. I felt creeping upon me, by slow yet certain degrees, the wild influences of his own fantastic yet impressive superstitions.

It was, especially, upon retiring to bed late in the night of the seventh or eighth day after the placing of the lady Madeline within the dungeon, that I experienced the full power of such feelings. Sleep came not near my couch—while the hours waned and waned away. I struggled to reason off the nervousness which had dominion over me. I endeavored to believe that much, if not all of what I felt, was due to the bewildering influence of the gloomy furniture of the room—of the dark and tattered draperies, which, tortured into motion by the breath of a rising tempest, swayed fitfully to

---

31. This person is the doctor.
32. Usher wishes to be sure his sister's body will not be dissected by doctors. At the time, bodies were often stolen and sold to medical students.
33. **dungeon-keep:** dungeon.

34. **vagaries:** whims.

and fro upon the walls, and rustled uneasily about the decorations of the bed. But my efforts were fruitless. An irrepressible tremor gradually pervaded my frame; and, at length, there sat upon my very heart an incubus[35] of utterly causeless alarm. Shaking this off with a gasp and a struggle, I uplifted myself upon the pillows, and, peering earnestly within the intense darkness of the chamber, hearkened—I know not why, except that an instinctive spirit prompted me—to certain low and indefinite sounds which came, through the pauses of the storm, at long intervals, I knew not whence. Overpowered by an intense sentiment of horror, unaccountable yet unendurable, I threw on my clothes with haste (for I felt that I should sleep no more during the night), and endeavored to arouse myself from the pitiable condition into which I had fallen, by pacing rapidly to and fro through the apartment.

I had taken but few turns in this manner, when a light step on an adjoining staircase arrested my attention. I presently recognized it as that of Usher. In an instant afterward he rapped, with a gentle touch, at my door, and entered, bearing a lamp. His countenance was, as usual, cadaverously wan—but, moreover, there was a species of mad hilarity in his eyes—an evidently restrained *hysteria* in his whole demeanor. His air appalled me—but anything was preferable to the solitude which I had so long endured, and even welcomed his presence as a relief.

"And you have not seen it?" he said abruptly, after having stared about him for some moments in silence—"you have not then seen it?—but, stay! you shall." Thus speaking, and having carefully shaded his lamp, he hurried to one of the casements, and threw it freely open to the storm.

The impetuous fury of the entering gust nearly lifted us from our feet. It was, indeed, a tempestuous yet sternly beautiful night, and one wildly singular in its terror and its beauty. A whirlwind had apparently collected its force in our vicinity; for there were frequent and violent alterations in the direction of the wind; and the exceeding density of the clouds (which hung so low as to press upon the turrets of the house) did not prevent our perceiving the lifelike velocity with which they flew careering from all points against each other, without passing away into the distance. I say that even their exceeding density did not prevent our perceiving this—yet we had no glimpse of the moon or stars—nor was there any flashing forth of the lightning. But the under surfaces of the huge masses of agitated vapor, as well as all terrestrial objects immediately around us, were glowing in the unnatural light of a faintly luminous and distinctly visible gaseous exhalation which hung about and enshrouded the mansion.

"You must not—you shall not behold this!" said I, shudderingly, to Usher, as I led him, with a gentle violence, from the window to a seat. "These appearances, which bewilder you, are merely electrical phenomena not uncommon—or it may be that they have their ghastly origin in the rank miasma[36] of the tarn. Let us close this casement—the air is chilling and dangerous to your frame. Here is one of your favorite romances. I will read, and you shall listen—and so we will pass away this terrible night together."

The antique volume which I had taken up was the *Mad Trist* of Sir Launcelot Canning;[37] but I called it a favorite of Usher's more in sad jest than in earnest; for, in truth, there is little in its uncouth and unimaginative prolixity[38] which could have had interest for the lofty and spiritual ideality of my friend. It was, however, the only book immediately at hand; and I indulged a vague hope that the excitement which now agitated the hypochondriac, might find relief (for the history of mental disorder is full of similar anomalies) even in the extremeness of the folly which I should read. Could I have judged, indeed, by the wild, overstrained air of vivacity with which he hearkened, or apparently hearkened, to the words of the tale, I might well have congratulated myself upon the success of my design.

I had arrived at that well-known portion of the story where Ethelred, the hero of the Trist, having sought in vain for peaceable admission into the dwelling of the hermit, proceeds to make good an entrance by force. Here, it will be remembered, the words of the narrative run thus:

"And Ethelred, who was by nature of a doughty[39] heart, and who was now mighty withal,

---

35. **incubus** (in′kyə·bəs): nightmare. At one time, people believed nightmares were caused by demons who lay on top of sleeping persons.

36. **rank miasma:** marsh gas, arising from rotting vegetable or animal matter.
37. ***Mad Trist* of Sir Launcelot Canning:** an invented book.
38. **prolixity:** wordiness.
39. **doughty** (dout′ē): courageous.

on account of the powerfulness of the wine which he had drunken, waited no longer to hold parley with the hermit, who, in sooth, was of an obstinate and maliceful turn, but, feeling the rain upon his shoulders, and fearing the rising of the tempest, uplifted his mace outright, and, with blows, made quickly room in the plankings of the door for his gauntleted hand; and now pulling therewith sturdily, he so cracked, and ripped, and tore all asunder, that the noise of the dry and hollow-sounding wood alarmed and reverberated throughout the forest.''

At the termination of this sentence I started, and for a moment, paused; for it appeared to me (although I at once concluded that my excited fancy had deceived me)—it appeared to me that, from some very remote portion of the mansion, there came, indistinctly, to my ears, what might have been, in its exact similarity of character, the echo (but a stifled and dull one certainly) of the very cracking and ripping sound which Sir Launcelot had so particularly described. It was, beyond doubt, the coincidence alone which had arrested my attention; for, amid the rattling of the sashes of the casements, and the ordinary commingled noises of the still increasing storm, the sound, in itself, had nothing, surely which should have interested or disturbed me. I continued the story:

"But the good champion Ethelred, now entering within the door, was sore enraged and amazed to perceive no signal of the maliceful hermit; but, in the stead thereof, a dragon of a scaly and prodigious demeanor, and of a fiery tongue, which sat in guard before a palace of gold, with a floor of silver; and upon the wall there hung a shield of shining brass with this legend enwritten—

Who entereth herein, a conqueror hath bin;
Who slayeth the dragon, the shield he shall win;

And Ethelred uplifted his mace, and struck upon the head of the dragon, which fell before him, and gave up his pesty breath, with a shriek so horrid and harsh, and withal so piercing, that Ethelred had fain to close his ears with his hands against the dreadful noise of it, the like whereof was never before heard.''

Here again I paused abruptly, and now with a feeling of wild amazement—for there could be no doubt whatever that, in this instance, I did actually hear (although from what direction it proceeded I found it impossible to say) a low and apparently distant, but harsh, protracted, and most unusual screaming or grating sound—the exact counterpart of what my fancy had already conjured up for the dragon's unnatural shriek as described by the romancer.

Oppressed, as I certainly was, upon the occurrence of the second and most extraordinary coincidence, by a thousand conflicting sensations, in which wonder and extreme terror were predominant, I still retained sufficient presence of mind to avoid exciting, by any observation, the sensitive nervousness of my companion. I was by no means certain that he had noticed the sounds in question; although, assuredly, a strange alteration had, during the last few minutes, taken place in his demeanor. From a position fronting my own, he had gradually brought round his chair, so as to sit with his face to the door of the chamber; and thus I could but partially perceive his features, although I saw that his lips trembled as if he were murmuring inaudibly. His head had dropped upon his breast—yet I knew that he was not asleep, from the wide and rigid opening of the eye as I caught a glimpse of it in profile. The motion of his body, too, was at variance with this idea—for he rocked from side to side with a gentle yet constant and uniform sway. Having rapidly taken notice of all this, I resumed the narrative of Sir Launcelot, which thus proceeded:

"And now, the champion, having escaped from the terrible fury of the dragon, bethinking himself of the brazen shield, and of the breaking up of the enchantment which was upon it, removed the carcass from out of the way before him, and approached valorously over the silver pavement of the castle to where the shield was upon the wall; which in sooth tarried not for his full coming, but fell down at his feet upon the silver floor, with a mighty great and ringing sound.''

No sooner had these syllables passed my lips, than—as if a shield of brass had indeed, at the moment, fallen heavily upon a floor of silver—I became aware of a distinct, hollow, metallic, and clangorous, yet apparently muffled reverberation. Completely unnerved, I leaped to my feet; but the measured rocking movement of Usher was undisturbed. I rushed to the chair in which he sat. His eyes were bent fixedly before him, and throughout his whole countenance there reigned a stony rigidity. But, as I placed my hand upon his shoulder, there came a strong shudder over his whole person; a sickly smile quivered about his lips; and I saw that he spoke in a low, hurried, and gibbering murmur, as if unconscious of my presence. Bending closely over him, I at length drank in the hideous import of his words.

"Not hear it?—yes, I hear it, and *have* heard it. Long—long—long—many minutes, many hours, many days, have I heard it—yet I dared not—oh, pity me, miserable wretch that I am!—I dared not—I *dared* not speak! *We have put her living in the tomb!* Said I not that my senses were acute? I *now* tell you that I heard her first feeble movements in the hollow coffin. I heard them—many, many days ago—yet I dared not—*I dared not speak!* And now—tonight—Ethelred—ha! ha!—the breaking of the hermit's door, and the death-cry of the dragon, and the clangor of the shield!—say, rather, the rending of her coffin, and the grating of the iron hinges of her prison, and her struggles within the coppered archway of the vault! Oh whither shall I fly? Will she not be here anon? Is she not hurrying to upbraid me for my haste? Have I not heard her footstep on the stair? Do I not distinguish that heavy and horrible beating of her heart? MADMAN!" here he sprang furiously to his feet, and shrieked out his syllables, as if in the effort he were giving up his soul— "MADMAN! I TELL YOU THAT SHE NOW STANDS WITHOUT THE DOOR!"

As if in the superhuman energy of his utterance there had been found the potency of a spell—the huge antique panels to which the speaker pointed, threw slowly back, upon the instant, their ponderous and ebony jaws. It was the work of the rushing gust—but then without those doors there DID stand the lofty and enshrouded figure of the lady Madeline of Usher. There was blood upon her white robes, and the evidence of some bitter struggle upon every portion of her emaciated frame. For a moment she remained trembling and reeling to and fro upon the threshold, then, with a low, moaning cry, fell heavily inward upon the person of her brother, and in her violent and now final death-agonies, bore him to the floor a corpse, and a victim to the terrors he had anticipated.

From that chamber, and from that mansion, I fled aghast. The storm was still abroad in all its wrath as I found myself crossing the old causeway. Suddenly there shot along the path a wild light, and I turned to see whence a gleam so unusual could have issued; for the vast house and its shadows were alone behind me. The radiance was that of the full, setting, and blood-red moon which now shone vividly through the once barely discernible fissure of which I have before spoken as extending from the roof of the building, in a zigzag direction, to the base. While I gazed, this fissure rapidly widened—there came a fierce breath of the whirlwind—the entire orb of the satellite burst at once upon my sight—my brain reeled as I saw the mighty walls rushing asunder—there was a long tumultuous shouting sound like the voice of a thousand waters—and the deep and dank tarn at my feet closed sullenly and silently over the fragments of the "HOUSE OF USHER."

A Comment on the Story

Nature seems to have provided us with an emotional circuit for the registering of fright. Presumably, it is an alarm system that will send us flying toward a less threatening environment. It might be the need to flush out that fright system under controlled circumstances that sends us to scary movies and terrifying stories. Imagine yourself seated in a dark theater watching a scene take place on stage. An innocent young woman is brushing her hair at a mirror as she prepares for bed. Suddenly we see, although she does not, a sinister face appear at her window. What would be the impact on you at the time? What would it be after you had left the theater and begun your long walk home in the dark?

It must have been some knowledge of this human susceptibility that led Edgar Allan Poe to explore the uses of the horror tale, a story that exploits our subconscious fears. Although we each have different furnishings for our nightmares, we all respond the same way to such universal images as remote, crumbling houses set in the midst of swamps or lonely moors; stormy skies; thick mists; eerie sounds; characters who are sick in mind and body, who speak little and never hum or whistle.

It is the relationship of Roderick and Madeline that first claims our attention in this story. Twins united by sensibility and temperament, they suffer from similar illnesses (hers physical, his mental); at the end of the story, they embrace a common fate. But it may gradually dawn on us that the relationship of Roderick and the narrator may be even more fascinating, and ominous. The unnamed storyteller seems to be a relatively detached observer at the beginning. He goes out of his way to tell us that he "really knew little" of his friend. Gradually, however, we discover that the narrator is not only fascinated by Usher's mental degeneration; he also finds himself participating in it. The first-person point of view in the story becomes not only a technical device, but also part of its very theme.

In describing the narrator's deteriorating mental state, Poe seems to recognize the fact that we are fascinated by tales of horror because, below the surface, the forces of chaos bubble in all of us. Like the narrator, we enjoy approaching the brink—and then drawing back. The problem, of course, is that we may withdraw too late from a glimpse of the dark elements of human nature—elements which we may imagine exist in ourselves as well. Usher, who enjoyed confronting his own extremes, was condemned to madness and death. The narrator, whom

Poe may have intended to represent "normal" people, watched in fascination and then "fled aghast," just in time, with the "deep and dank tarn" at his feet.

In some sense, then, the narrator of Poe's tale has followed our emotional course as we read a horror story. At first disclaiming any identification or sympathy, Poe's storyteller is inexorably drawn into the situation. He is both observer and participant. As if to underline his ambiguous status, this narrator indulges repeatedly in paradoxical expressions, such as "sad jest," "gentle violence," and "[a night] wildly singular for its terror and its beauty." Terror is repellent; it is also, in some guises, fascinating and pleasurable. Just in the nick of time, the narrator escapes. In the same way, we the readers, after taking pleasure in a tale that is discomforting and even terrifying, can close our books with the thought that "it's all only a story after all."

Responding to the Story

Analyzing the Story

Identifying Facts

1. As the story opens, how does the narrator respond to his first sight of the House of Usher? What **images** help you to see and hear this **setting**?
2. Explain why the narrator has come to this house.
3. Describe the symptoms of Roderick Usher's illness. What are his sister Madeline's symptoms?
4. Summarize what happens during the narrator's visit to the House of Usher.

Interpreting Meanings

5. What do you think Roderick's artistic efforts—his guitar solo, his painting, and his poem "The Haunted Palace"—reveal about his state of mind?
6. Why do you think Poe had Roderick and Madeline be *twins* instead of merely brother and sister?
7. The story is presented from the **point of view** of a typical Poe narrator—a character who claims to provide an objective, rational view of events, but whose rationality becomes suspect during the course of the tale. What evidence can you find suggesting that the narrator's state of mind may be approaching that of his friend Roderick? How does this uncertainty about the narrator's objectivity affect your response to the events of the plot?
8. What do you think is happening at the end of the story, when Madeline Usher appears? Is she a hallucination of the narrator? Is she a ghost? Or is she

a real, living person who has been buried alive? How do you interpret Madeline's appearance?

9. Poe wrote of the poem within the story, ". . . by the Haunted Palace I mean to imply a mind haunted by phantoms—a disordered brain." How might the whole story be seen as an **allegory** of a journey into the human mind in its conscious and unconscious states? In this light, what, for example, would the final *fall* of the house represent?

10. Do you think a filmed version of Poe's story would be popular today? Why?

Writing About the Story

A Creative Response

1. **Using Another Point of View.** Select one incident from the story. Retell the incident from Madeline's point of view.

A Critical Response

2. **Analyzing the Story's Effect.** Poe wrote that a skillful literary artist fashions a tale to achieve

> a certain unique or single *effect*. . . . In the whole composition there should be no word written, of which the tendency, direct or indirect, is not to the one pre-established design.
>
> —Edgar Allan Poe

Analyze "The Fall of the House of Usher" to show whether or not every detail builds and heightens the story's mood of terror.

3. **Comparing Two Stories.** In an essay, compare the **themes** of "The Masque of the Red Death" and "The Fall of the House of Usher." In particular, consider how each story might be about the impossibility of achieving the Romantic ideal—that is, the transcendence of imagination over reality.

4. **Analyzing the Story's Meaning.** In a brief essay, develop one of the following statements about the meaning of "The Fall of the House of Usher." Quote from the story to support your position.

   a. The narrator becomes insane under the influence of Roderick, and at the end of the story he is hallucinating.

   b. The story is symbolic. Roderick is identified with the house, and both are ruined when the story ends as Madeline gets her revenge.

   c. The story is about an artist who leaves the real world and journeys through the underside of the human mind.

Analyzing Language and Style

Suggestive Words

1. Reread the famous first paragraph of this story and list all the words that suggest decay, sterility, finality, and emptiness.

2. What sound do you hear repeated in this paragraph? What might this repeated sound remind you of?

3. Which words in this description do you think characterize the mind of the narrator? Which adverbs and adjectives reveal his feelings?

4. What details in this first paragraph suggest that the house and its occupants are tied together? (Look for details that **personify** the house.)

5. How would your feelings about the house have been different if the narrator had come upon it on a sunny morning in springtime?

6. Rewrite the first sentence, and change the time of day, the time of year, the weather, and the adjectives and adverbs that suggest the narrator's feelings rather than actuality. Can you change the sentence's emotional effect?

Elements of Literature

SYMBOLS

A **symbol** in literature is a concrete object, person, place, or action that operates on at least two levels of meaning: It functions as itself, and it stands for a larger meaning or quality.

Certain symbols are so well known and their meanings so broadly agreed upon, that they may be called conventional. For example, most people accept the flag of their nation as a symbol of unity and patriotism. In Western cultures, the rose is a conventional symbol of beauty or love, the color white of purity or innocence, and the color green of hope.

The underlying meanings of other symbols arise from the context that writers create. In Poe's "The Fall of the House of Usher," for example, the opening description of Roderick's decaying mansion inspires certain responses in both the narrator and the reader. However, it is not until later in the story, when Roderick mentions his strange theory of the "sentience" of the building's stones (page 241), that we realize that the decaying house also symbolizes the degeneration of Usher's own mind. At the end of the story, Poe further emphasizes this symbolic meaning with a stroke of fantasy: immediately after Roderick and Madeline collapse in death, the horrified narrator watches the house itself collapse into the tarn.

Symbolism in literature is often more complex than this example would suggest. In fact, the most interesting symbols may be those that provoke different, sometimes conflicting interpretations. For instance, does Poe hint in this story that Roderick and Madeline, as twins who suffer from similar maladies, are symbolic of two halves of the same mind? Or does he suggest, through the narrator's growing apprehension, that the narrator sees the dark side of his own mind symbolized in Usher? Is the narrator's situation in the story unique and grotesque? Or is it indirectly symbolic of a universal fascination with evil? And exactly what is suggested in the story by Roderick's use of the arts of painting and music? If there were one, definitive, undeniable answer to each of these questions, much of the mysterious power of the story's symbolism might disappear.

Symbols are as old as literature itself. Folk tales, parables, and allegories have always depended on the use of symbols. But there is no point in trying to squeeze symbolic meaning out of everything we read. To convey several levels of abstract meaning successfully, symbols must be supported by a context that sparks our imagination. In their ability to evoke responses from our unconscious emotions, symbols can be a writer's most effective tools.

Did you find other symbols in the story of the House of Usher that have not been mentioned? Can you justify your responses?

El Dorado is Spanish for "the gilded one" or "the man of gold," from the Spanish word for gold, *oro*. The term is associated with the conquistadors, who had heard repeatedly about a ruler who lived in what is now Colombia. Every year, the ruler would be covered in gold which would then be rinsed from his body in Lake Guatavitá. During the ceremony, emeralds and other precious stones would be sacrificially washed into the depths of the lake. The conquistadors became convinced that, if only they could find it, a country of vast riches would be theirs. "Eldorado" was never found. But in 1849, the year in which this poem was written, Eldorado took on a new meaning.

The discovery of gold in California convinced thousands of Americans that a land of golden opportunity was at hand. Thus began the great rush that would take the gold seekers to the vicinity of Sutter's Mill and the muddy streets of San Francisco.

Behind this poem, then, lie both the legend passed on by the frustrated conquistadors and the reality reported in the daily papers. Yet for Poe, Eldorado was predominantly an idea, as it remains for us today. "El Dorado" speaks to our hopes that somewhere lies a great good place, the land of our heart's desire.

Eldorado

Gaily bedight,°
A gallant knight,
In sunshine and in shadow,
Had journeyed long,
5   Singing a song,
In search of Eldorado.

But he grew old—
This knight so bold—
And o'er his heart a shadow
10   Fell as he found
No spot of ground
That looked like Eldorado.

And, as his strength
Failed him at length,
15   He met a pilgrim shadow—
"Shadow," said he,
"Where can it be—
This land of Eldorado?"

"Over the Mountains
20   Of the Moon,°
Down the Valley of the Shadow,°
Ride, boldly ride,"
The shade replied,
"If you seek for Eldorado!"

1. **bedight:** bedecked (dressed).

20. **Mountains of the Moon:** the legendary source of the Nile River.
21. **Valley of the Shadow:** the "valley of the shadow of death" is mentioned in Psalm 23.

Responding to the Poem

Analyzing the Poem

Identifying Details

1. Describe what happens to the knight in the course of the first two stanzas.
2. What directions does the shadow give him?

Interpreting Meanings

3. What adjective does Poe use to describe the shadow the knight meets? What do you think this word suggests about the nature of the shadow?
4. Describe the **meter** of the poem. Do you think the poem's beat is appropriate to its subject? Explain.

5. The words *Eldorado* and *shadow* are rhymed in each stanza, creating a pleasant echo throughout the poem. How do the meaning and the **connotations** of the word *shadow* change from stanza to stanza? How do these changes reflect a gradual change in the poem's **tone**?
6. The characters of the knight and the shadow have a **symbolic** meaning. What types of people, attitudes, or concepts might these two characters represent?
7. The response the shadow makes to the knight's question is open to interpretation. Explain what *you* think the shadow's answer means.
8. Name some "Eldorados" that contemporary people might search for. Would the shadow's advice pertain to these quests?

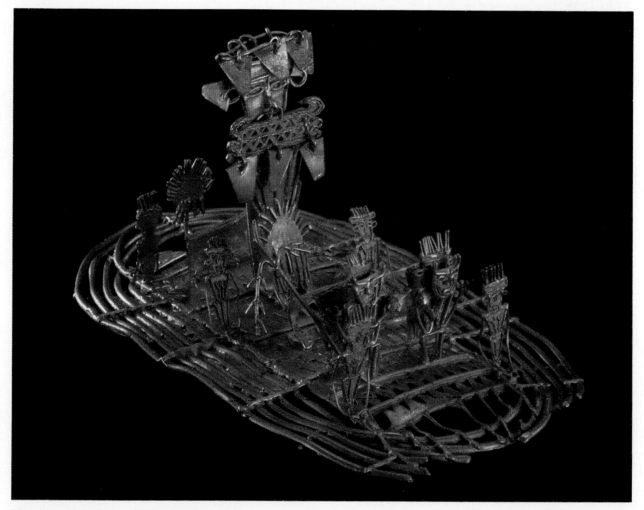

The raft of El Dorado. Pre-Columbian gold (late 16th century).

Museo del Oro, Bogota, Colombia.

Not long before his own death, Poe wrote this poem about the death of his wife Virginia. Like other fairy tales, the poem is set far away and long ago. Its details nevertheless reflect some of the actual circumstances of Virginia's life and death. When barely an adult, she contracted tuberculosis, a disease for which there was then no known cure. Slowly wasting away, she managed to live a fairly normal life until the fatal stage of her illness became apparent. In the midst of singing a song for a family gathering, she lost her voice as blood came gushing from her mouth. Lingering for months as an invalid, she died near the end of 1847. Her body was placed in a burial vault—if not exactly "by the sea," at least close to the Hudson River at a point where it approaches the Atlantic Ocean. Read the poem aloud to hear its rhymes and feel its rhythm.

Annabel Lee

It was many and many a year ago,
   In a kingdom by the sea,
That a maiden there lived whom you may know
   By the name of Annabel Lee;
5 And this maiden she lived with no other thought
   Than to love and be loved by me.

I was a child and *she* was a child,
   In this kingdom by the sea,
But we loved with a love that was more than love—
10 I and my Annabel Lee—
With a love that the wingèd seraphs of Heaven
   Coveted her and me.

And this was the reason that, long ago,
   In this kingdom by the sea,
15 A wind blew out of a cloud, chilling
   My beautiful Annabel Lee;
So that her highborn kinsmen° came
   And bore her away from me,
To shut her up in a sepulcher
20 In this kingdom by the sea.

The angels, not half so happy in Heaven,
   Went envying her and me:—
Yes!—all that was the reason (as all men know,
   In this kingdom by the sea)
25 That the wind came out of the cloud by night,
   Chilling and killing my Annabel Lee.

But our love it was stronger by far than the love
   Of those who were older than we—
   Of many far wiser than we—
30 And neither the angels in Heaven above,
   Nor the demons down under the sea,
Can ever dissever my soul from the soul
   Of the beautiful Annabel Lee:—

17. **highborn kinsmen:** angels.

Sissy, a drawing by Edgar Allan Poe.
Sissy was a nickname for Poe's wife, Virginia.

Valentine Museum, Richmond.

For the moon never beams, without bringing me dreams
35   Of the beautiful Annabel Lee;
And the stars never rise, but I feel the bright eyes
    Of the beautiful Annabel Lee:
And so, all the nighttide, I lie down by the side
Of my darling—my darling—my life and my bride,
40   In the sepulcher there by the sea—
    In her tomb by the sounding sea.

A Comment on the Poem

The relationship between fact and imagination is a minor part of this poem. Its larger concern is with the spiritual qualities of love that endure even beyond death. In Poe's conception, the love he shared was "more than love." It was not only love between a man and a woman, but a kind of love that transcends mortal considerations because it is part of the God-given innocence of childhood. This is the love possible in that state of being which William Wordsworth wrote about:

> Not in entire forgetfulness,
> And not in utter nakedness,
> But trailing clouds of glory do we come
> From God, who is our home;
> Heaven lies about us in our infancy!
> —from "Intimations of Immortality,"
> William Wordsworth

By transforming his child bride, Virginia Clemm, into the fantasy of Annabel Lee, Poe created a fable in which an actual person becomes a character unrelated to a particular place or time. Annabel Lee is one of many figures in the imaginative history of love and loss.

A Vision of Dead Desire by Clarence John Laughlin (1954). Photograph.

The Robert Miller Gallery, New York.

Responding to the Poem

Analyzing the Poem

Identifying Details

1. What explanation does the narrator give for Annabel Lee's death?
2. In Stanza 5, how does the speaker defy both the angels and the demons who succeed in separating him from his beloved? In Stanza 6, how does he attempt to show that loving memory can defeat death and absence?
3. Describe the pattern of **end rhymes** in the poem. How many **internal rhymes**—rhymes within lines—can you find?

Interpreting Meanings

4. The poem's singsong **meter**, together with its **rhymes** and **repetition**, give it the effect of an old ballad. Some critics have felt that Poe was more concerned with the music of his composition than with the story it tells or the emotion it expresses. Do you feel that the poem is primarily memorable as "word music," or that it is primarily a haunting story of lost love? Give reasons for your opinion.
5. Grief is one kind of emotion; sadness is another. Which emotion do you think this poem more effectively expresses?

Writing About the Poem

A Creative Response

1. **Imitating the Poem.** Write at least one stanza—about any topic—imitating the meter and rhyme scheme of "Annabel Lee." Begin with Poe's first line.

A Critical Response

2. **Comparing Poems.** In one paragraph, cite a way in which Poe's "Annabel Lee" is like the lines from Wordsworth's "Intimations of Immortality." In a second paragraph, tell how "Annabel Lee" is different: in other words, what does Poe go on to imagine that is not mentioned by Wordsworth?

This poem is addressed to a woman, but whether it is a real woman or an idealized woman no one knows. The poem is filled with allusions; read it once, aloud, and then, after you have read the comment following it, read it again. Is "Helen" real, or is she an ideal? Or is she a beautiful statue the poet is looking at?

To Helen

Helen, thy beauty is to me
    Like those Nicéan barks of yore,
That gently, o'er a perfumed sea,
    The weary, way-worn wanderer bore
5   To his own native shore.

On desperate seas long wont to roam,
    Thy hyacinth hair, thy classic face,
Thy Naiad airs have brought me home
    To the glory that was Greece,
10   And the grandeur that was Rome.

Lo! in yon brilliant window-niche
    How statue-like I see thee stand,
The agate lamp within thy hand!
    Ah, Psyche, from the regions which
15   Are Holy Land!

Funeral Stele of a Young Girl (5th century B.C.)
Greek sculpture.

Museo Nazionale, Athens.

The Raven III by Antonio Frasconi (1959). Colored woodcut.

5.

25 Deep into that darkness peering, long I stood there wondering, fearing,
Doubting, dreaming dreams no mortal ever dared to dream before;
But the silence was unbroken, and the stillness gave no token,
And the only word there spoken was the whispered word, "Lenore?"
This I whispered, and an echo murmured back the word "Lenore!"
30   Merely this and nothing more.

6.

Back into the chamber turning, all my soul within me burning,
Soon again I heard a tapping somewhat louder than before.
"Surely," said I, "surely that is something at my window lattice;
Let me see, then, what thereat is, and this mystery explore—
35 Let my heart be still a moment and this mystery explore—
                            'Tis the wind and nothing more!"

7.

Open here I flung the shutter, when, with many a flirt and flutter,
In there stepped a stately Raven of the saintly days of yore;°
Not the least obeisance made he; not a minute stopped or stayed he;
40 But, with mien of lord or lady, perched above my chamber door—
Perched upon a bust of Pallas° just above my chamber door—
                          Perched, and sat, and nothing more.

8.

Then this ebony bird beguiling my sad fancy into smiling,
By the grave and stern decorum of the countenance it wore,
45 "Though thy crest be shorn and shaven, thou," I said, "art sure no craven,
Ghastly grim and ancient Raven wandering from the Nightly shore—
Tell me what thy lordly name is on the Night's Plutonian shore!"°
                          Quoth the Raven, "Nevermore."

9.

Much I marveled this ungainly fowl to hear discourse so plainly,
50 Though its answer little meaning—little relevancy bore;
For we cannot help agreeing that no living human being
Ever yet was blessed with seeing bird above his chamber door—
Bird or beast upon the sculptured bust above his chamber door,
                          With such name as "Nevermore."

---

38. In early Christian legends, holy men who withdrew from the world and lived in isolation in the desert were visited by ravens who brought them bread in their beaks. (*Of yore* means "of time long past.")
41. **Pallas:** Pallas Athena, the Greek goddess of wisdom.
47. **Plutonian shore:** Pluto was the Greek god of the underworld—the land of darkness. The underworld, also called Hades, was surrounded by the River Styx: hence the mention of a shore.

He emerged from this seclusion in 1837 to publish a collection of stories with the unassuming title, *Twice-Told Tales*. If they were conventionally presented, they nonetheless offered a unique foretaste of Hawthorne's singular vision, that of the human heart as a lurking place for the secrets of past violence. The book was favorably reviewed by his friend Longfellow and, in a later edition, by Poe. Hawthorne had achieved just enough success to encourage further work.

In 1839, he became engaged to Sophia Peabody, but the couple heeded traditional warnings against hasty marriage. Meanwhile, Hawthorne went off to West Roxbury to join the utopian experiment in communal living at Brook Farm. It did not suit him. Neither the shoveling of manure nor the endless, lofty discussions of the Transcendentalists appealed to him (see page 183). Although he left after a few months, he made good use of the experience later, in his novel, *The Blithedale Romance* (1852).

When they were married in 1842, Hawthorne and his wife moved into the Old Manse in Concord, where Emerson had lived before them. Concord was the home of many prominent writers, and we might imagine that Hawthorne would have found it more congenial than Brook Farm. However, although he often walked with Thoreau and Emerson, neither creativity nor warm friendship came from these relationships.

Since he was making only the barest living from his stories, Hawthorne had to accept a political appointment as surveyor to the Salem customhouse in 1846. This appointment freed him from financial worry for three years, but in 1849 he lost the job. Despite this loss and the simultaneous death of his mother, he somehow found the energies for his masterwork, *The Scarlet Letter*. It was, he said, "a particularly hell-fired story into which I found it almost impossible to throw a cheering light."

The Scarlet Letter is set in Puritan Boston during the mid-seventeenth century. The title refers to a cloth letter, *A,* which the narrator finds in a customhouse, along with documents outlining the tragic story of Hester Prynne, who bore an illegitimate child. Refusing to name its father, she was sentenced to wear the scarlet *A* (for adultery) on her breast. The story is about sin and redemption, and the tragic consequences of hypocrisy and concealed guilt.

When *The Scarlet Letter* was published in 1850, it brought Hawthorne wide acclaim, some money, and the admiration and friendship of Herman Melville. This success continued. Another novel, *The House of the Seven Gables,* appeared the following year, as well as another collection of stories, *The Snow-Image.*

In 1853, Hawthorne's friend Franklin Pierce became President and offered Hawthorne the post of United States consul at Liverpool. Hawthorne accepted willingly. He and his family lived in Europe for seven years. Hawthorne wrote, traveled, filled his notebooks, and worked on an ambitious novel, *The Marble Faun,* a romance set in Italy and published in 1860, when he returned to America.

As an exile, however, Hawthorne found his creativity dwindling, and he had become inexplicably dejected. Arriving back in America, he was further discouraged by his own judgment of *The Marble Faun,* which he decided was a failure. Even his return home was oddly cheerless. After his years abroad, he was disenchanted with both the Europe where he had been and the America from which he now felt estranged. His old friend Pierce, for whom he had written a campaign biography in 1852, had been defeated for reelection. Abraham Lincoln was in the White House, and with the onset of the Civil War, Hawthorne felt entirely out of harmony with his times.

Back in Concord, he did manage to convert his English journals into the book *Our Old Home* (1863); but he found himself unable to complete the several fiction projects he had promised his publisher. His health declined. Glimpsing Hawthorne at a social gathering (which he hated), the elder Henry James noted that he had the look "of a rogue who suddenly finds himself in the company of detectives." On the night of May 18, 1864, while on a trip with Franklin Pierce, Hawthorne died in a New Hampshire hotel room.

Emerson felt that Hawthorne, no longer able to endure his painful solitude, "died of it." Emerson also noted in his journal, after attending Hawthorne's funeral, that he was sorry he hadn't known Hawthorne better. And he recorded this sadly ironic anecdote: "One day, when I found him on the top of his hill, in the woods, he paced back the path to his house, and said, *'This path is the only remembrance of me that will remain.'*"

THE MINISTER'S BLACK VEIL

Winter Sunday in Norway, Maine, by an unknown artist (c. 1860). Oil.

New York State Historical Association, Cooperstown.

sober-minded man like myself. The black veil, though it covers only our pastor's face, throws its influence over his whole person, and makes him ghostlike from head to foot. Do you not feel it so?''

''Truly do I,'' replied the lady, ''and I would not be alone with him for the world. I wonder he is not afraid to be alone with himself!''

''Men sometimes are so,'' said her husband.

The afternoon service was attended with similar circumstances. At its conclusion, the bell tolled for the funeral of a young lady. The relatives and friends were assembled in the house, and the more distant acquaintances stood about the door, speaking of the good qualities of the deceased, when their talk was interrupted by the appearance of Mr. Hooper, still covered with his black veil. It was now an appropriate emblem. The clergyman stepped into the room where the corpse was laid, and bent over the coffin, to take a last farewell of his deceased parishioner. As he stooped, the veil hung straight down from his forehead, so that, if her eyelids had not been closed forever, the dead maiden might have seen his face. Could Mr. Hooper be fearful of her glance, that he so hastily caught back the black veil? A person who watched the interview between the dead and living scrupled[4] not to affirm that, at the instant when the clergyman's features were disclosed, the corpse had slightly shuddered, rustling the shroud and muslin cap, though the countenance retained the composure of death. A superstitious old woman was the only witness of this prodigy. From the coffin Mr. Hooper passed into the chamber of the mourners, and thence to the head of the staircase, to make the funeral prayer. It was a tender and heart-dissolving prayer, full of sorrow, yet so imbued with celestial hopes that the music of a heavenly harp, swept by the fingers of the dead, seemed faintly to be heard among the saddest accents of the minister. The people trembled, though they but darkly understood him when he prayed that they, and himself, and all of mortal race, might be ready, as he trusted this young maiden had been, for the dreadful hour that should snatch the veil from their faces. The bearers went heavily forth, and the mourners followed, saddening all the street, with the dead before them, and Mr. Hooper in his black veil behind.

''Why do you look back?'' said one in the procession to his partner.

''I had a fancy,'' replied she, ''that the minister and the maiden's spirit were walking hand in hand.''

''And so had I, at the same moment,'' said the other.

That night, the handsomest couple in Milford village were to be joined in wedlock. Though reckoned a melancholy man, Mr. Hooper had a placid cheerfulness for such occasions, which often excited a sympathetic smile where livelier merriment would have been thrown away. There was no quality of his disposition which made him more beloved than this. The company at the wedding awaited his arrival with impatience, trusting that the strange awe which had gathered over him throughout the day would now be dispelled. But such was not the result. When Mr. Hooper came, the first thing that their eyes rested on was the same horrible black veil, which had added deeper gloom to the funeral, and could portend nothing but evil to the wedding. Such was its immediate effect on the guests that a cloud seemed to have rolled duskily from beneath the black crape, and dimmed the light of the candles. The bridal pair stood up before the minister. But the bride's cold fingers quivered in the tremulous hand of the bridegroom, and her deathlike paleness caused a whisper that the maiden who had been buried a few hours before was come from her grave to be married. If ever another wedding were so dismal, it was that famous one where they tolled the wedding knell.[5] After performing the ceremony, Mr. Hooper raised a glass of wine to his lips, wishing happiness to the new-married couple in a strain of mild pleasantry that ought to have brightened the features of the guests, like a cheerful gleam from the hearth. At that instant, catching a glimpse of his figure in the looking glass, the black veil involved his own spirit in the horror with which it overwhelmed all others. His frame shuddered, his lips grew white, he spilled the untasted wine upon the carpet, and rushed forth into the darkness. For the earth, too, had on her Black Veil.

The next day, the whole village of Milford talked of little else than Parson Hooper's black veil. That, and the mystery concealed behind it, supplied a topic for discussion between acquaint-

---

4. **scrupled:** here, refrained.

5. **If . . . knell:** a reference to Hawthorne's story, ''The Wedding Knell.'' A *knell* is the ringing of a bell.

ances meeting in the street, and good women gossiping at their open windows. It was the first item of news that the tavern keeper told to his guests. The children babbled of it on their way to school. One imitative little imp covered his face with an old black handkerchief, thereby so frightening his playmates that the panic seized himself, and he well-nigh lost his wits by his own waggery.

It was remarkable that of all the busybodies and impertinent people in the parish, not one ventured to put the plain question to Mr. Hooper, wherefore he did this thing. Hitherto, whenever there appeared the slightest call for such interference, he had never lacked advisers, nor shown himself averse to be guided by their judgment. If he erred at all, it was by so painful a degree of self-distrust that even the mildest censure would lead him to consider an indifferent action as a crime. Yet, though so well acquainted with this amiable weakness, no individual among his parishioners chose to make the black veil a subject of friendly remonstrance. There was a feeling of dread, neither plainly confessed nor carefully concealed, which caused each to shift the responsibility upon another, till at length it was found expedient to send a deputation of the church, in order to deal with Mr. Hooper about the mystery, before it should grow into a scandal. Never did an embassy so ill discharge its duties. The minister received them with friendly courtesy, but became silent, after they were seated, leaving to his visitors the whole burden of introducing their important business. The topic, it might be supposed, was obvious enough. There was the black veil swathed round Mr. Hooper's forehead, and concealing every feature above his placid mouth, on which, at times, they could perceive the glimmering of a melancholy smile. But that piece of crape, to their imagination, seemed to hang down before his heart, the symbol of a fearful secret between him and them. Were the veil but cast aside, they might speak freely of it, but not till then. Thus they sat a considerable time, speechless, confused, and shrinking uneasily from Mr. Hooper's eye, which they felt to be fixed upon them with an invisible glance. Finally, the deputies returned abashed to their constituents, pronouncing the matter too weighty to be handled, except by a council of the churches, if, indeed, it might not require a general synod.[6]

But there was one person in the village unappalled by the awe with which the black veil had impressed all beside herself. When the deputies returned without an explanation, or even venturing to demand one, she, with the calm energy of her character, determined to chase away the strange cloud that appeared to be settling round Mr. Hooper, every moment more darkly than before. As his plighted wife,[7] it should be her privilege to know what the black veil concealed. At the minister's first visit, therefore, she entered upon the subject with a direct simplicity, which made the task easier both for him and her. After he had seated himself, she fixed her eyes steadfastly upon the veil, but could discern nothing of the dreadful gloom that had so overawed the multitude: it was but a double fold of crape, hanging down from his forehead to his mouth, and slightly stirring with his breath.

"No," said she aloud, and smiling, "there is nothing terrible in this piece of crape, except that it hides a face which I am always glad to look upon. Come, good sir, let the sun shine from behind the cloud. First lay aside your black veil; then tell me why you put it on."

Mr. Hooper's smile glimmered faintly.

"There is an hour to come," said he, "when all of us shall cast aside our veils. Take it not amiss, beloved friend, if I wear this piece of crape till then."

"Your words are a mystery, too," returned the young lady. "Take away the veil from them, at least."

"Elizabeth, I will," said he, "so far as my vow may suffer me. Know, then, this veil is a type and a symbol, and I am bound to wear it ever, both in light and darkness, in solitude and before the gaze of multitudes, and as with strangers, so with my familiar friends. No mortal eye will see it withdrawn. This dismal shade must separate me from the world: even you, Elizabeth, can never come behind it!"

"What grievous affliction hath befallen you," she earnestly inquired, "that you should thus darken your eyes forever?"

"If it be a sign of mourning," replied Mr. Hooper, "I, perhaps, like most other mortals, have sorrows dark enough to be typified by a black veil."

"But what if the world will not believe that it

6. **synod** (sin′əd): a council of churches.

7. **plighted wife:** intended wife.

Illustration for "The Minister's Black Veil" from *Tales*
by Nathaniel Hawthorne, published by Dodd, Mead & Co., 1964.

is the type of an innocent sorrow?'' urged Elizabeth. ''Beloved and respected as you are, there may be whispers that you hide your face under the consciousness of secret sin. For the sake of your holy office, do away with this scandal!''

The color rose into her cheeks as she intimated the nature of the rumors that were already abroad in the village. But Mr. Hooper's mildness did not foresake him. He even smiled again—that same sad smile, which always appeared like a faint glimmering of light, proceeding from the obscurity beneath the veil.

''If I hide my face for sorrow, there is cause enough,'' he merely replied; ''and if I cover it for secret sin, what mortal might not do the same?''

And with this gentle but unconquerable obstinacy did he resist all her entreaties. At length Elizabeth sat silent. For a few moments she appeared lost in thought, considering, probably, what new methods might be tried to withdraw her lover from so dark a fantasy, which, if it had no other meaning, was perhaps a symptom of mental disease. Though of a firmer character than his own, the tears rolled down her cheeks. But, in an instant, as it were, a new feeling took the place of sorrow: her eyes were fixed insensibly on the black veil, when, like a sudden twilight in the air, its terrors fell around her. She arose, and stood trembling before him.

"And do you feel it then, at last?" said he mournfully.

She made no reply, but covered her eyes with her hand, and turned to leave the room. He rushed forward and caught her arm.

"Have patience with me, Elizabeth!" cried he, passionately. "Do not desert me, though this veil must be between us here on earth. Be mine, and hereafter there shall be no veil over my face, no darkness between our souls! It is but a mortal veil—it is not for eternity! Oh! you know not how lonely I am, and how frightened, to be alone behind my black veil. Do not leave me in this miserable obscurity forever!"

"Lift the veil but once, and look me in the face," said she.

"Never! It cannot be!" replied Mr. Hooper.

"Then farewell!" said Elizabeth.

She withdrew her arm from his grasp, and slowly departed, pausing at the door, to give one long, shuddering gaze, that seemed almost to penetrate the mystery of the black veil. But, even amid his grief, Mr. Hooper smiled to think that only a material emblem had separated him from happiness, though the horrors which it shadowed forth must be drawn darkly between the fondest of lovers.

From that time no attempts were made to remove Mr. Hooper's black veil, or, by a direct appeal, to discover the secret which it was supposed to hide. By persons who claimed a superiority to popular prejudice, it was reckoned merely an eccentric whim, such as often mingles with the sober actions of men otherwise rational, and tinges them all with its own semblance of insanity. But with the multitude, good Mr. Hooper was irreparably a bugbear.[8] He could not walk the street with any peace of mind, so conscious was he that the gentle and timid would turn aside to avoid him, and that others would make it a point of hardihood to throw themselves in his way. The impertinence of the latter class compelled him to give up his customary walk at sunset to the burial ground; for when he leaned pensively over the gate, there would always be faces behind the

---

8. **bugbear:** source of fears, often groundless ones.

gravestones, peeping at his black veil. A fable went the rounds that the stare of the dead people drove him thence. It grieved him, to the very depth of his kind heart, to observe how the children fled from his approach, breaking up their merriest sports, while his melancholy figure was yet afar off. Their instinctive dread caused him to feel more strongly than aught else that a preternatural horror was interwoven with the threads of the black crape. In truth, his own antipathy to the veil was known to be so great that he never willingly passed before a mirror, nor stooped to drink at a still fountain, lest, in its peaceful bosom, he should be affrighted by himself. This was what gave plausibility to the whispers that Mr. Hooper's conscience tortured him for some great crime too horrible to be entirely concealed, or otherwise than so obscurely intimated. Thus, from beneath the black veil, there rolled a cloud into the sunshine, an ambiguity of sin or sorrow, which enveloped the poor minister, so that love or sympathy could never reach him. It was said that ghost and fiend consorted with him there. With self-shudderings and outward terrors, he walked continually in its shadow, groping darkly within his own soul, or gazing through a medium that saddened the whole world. Even the lawless wind, it was believed, respected his dreadful secret, and never blew aside the veil. But still good Mr. Hooper sadly smiled at the pale visages of the wordly throng as he passed by.

Among all its bad influences, the black veil had the one desirable effect of making its wearer a very efficient clergyman. By the aid of his mysterious emblem—for there was no other apparent cause—he became a man of awful power over souls that were in agony for sin. His converts always regarded him with a dread peculiar to themselves, affirming, though but figuratively, that before he brought them to celestial light, they had been with him behind the black veil. Its gloom, indeed, enabled him to sympathize with all dark affections. Dying sinners cried aloud for Mr. Hooper, and would not yield their breath till he appeared; though ever, as he stooped to whisper consolation, they shuddered at the veiled face so near their own. Such were the terrors of the black veil, even when Death had bared his visage! Strangers came long distances to attend service at his church, with the mere idle purpose of gazing at his figure, because it was forbidden them to behold his face. But many were made to quake ere they departed! Once, during Governor Belcher's[9] administration, Mr. Hooper was appointed to preach the election sermon. Covered with his black veil, he stood before the chief magistrate, the council, and the representatives, and wrought so deep an impression that the legislative measures of that year were characterized by all the gloom and piety of our earliest ancestral sway.

In this manner Mr. Hooper spent a long life, irreproachable in outward act, yet shrouded in dismal suspicions; kind and loving, though unloved, and dimly feared; a man apart from men, shunned in their health and joy, but ever summoned to their aid in mortal anguish. As years wore on, shedding their snows above his sable veil, he acquired a name throughout the New England churches, and they called him Father Hooper. Nearly all his parishioners who were of mature age when he was settled had been borne away by many a funeral: he had one congregation in the church, and a more crowded one in the churchyard; and having wrought so late into the evening, and done his work so well, it was now good Father Hooper's turn to rest.

Several persons were visible by the shaded candlelight, in the death chamber of the old clergyman. Natural connections he had none. But there was the decorously grave, though unmoved physician, seeking only to mitigate the last pangs of the patient whom he could not save. There were the deacons, and other eminently pious members of his church. There, also, was the Reverend Mr. Clark, of Westbury, a young and zealous divine, who had ridden in haste to pray by the bedside of the expiring minister. There was the nurse, no hired handmaiden of death, but one whose calm affection had endured thus long in secrecy, in solitude, amid the chill of age, and would not perish, even at the dying hour. Who, but Elizabeth! And there lay the hoary head of good Father Hooper upon the death pillow, with the black veil still swathed about his brow, and reaching down over his face, so that each more difficult gasp of his faint breath caused it to stir. All through life that piece of crape had hung between him and the world: it had separated him from cheerful brotherhood and woman's love, and kept him in that saddest of all prisons, his own heart; and still it lay upon his face, as if to deepen the gloom of his

---

9. **Governor Belcher:** Jonathan Belcher was governor of the Massachusetts Bay Colony from 1730 to 1741.

darksome chamber, and shade him from the sunshine of eternity.

For some time previous, his mind had been confused, wavering doubtfully between the past and the present, and hovering forward, as it were, at intervals, into the indistinctness of the world to come. There had been feverish turns, which tossed him from side to side, and wore away what little strength he had. But in his most convulsive struggles, and in the wildest vagaries of his intellect, when no other thought retained its sober influence, he still showed an awful solicitude lest the black veil should slip aside. Even if his bewildered soul could have forgotten, there was a faithful woman at his pillow, who, with averted eyes, would have covered that aged face, which she had last beheld in the comeliness of manhood. At length the death-stricken old man lay quietly in the torpor of mental and bodily exhaustion, with an imperceptible pulse, and breath that grew fainter and fainter, except when a long, deep, and irregular inspiration seemed to prelude the flight of his spirit.

The minister of Westbury approached the bedside.

"Venerable Father Hooper," said he, "the moment of your release is at hand. Are you ready for the lifting of the veil that shuts in time from eternity?"

Father Hooper at first replied merely by a feeble motion of his head; then, apprehensive, perhaps, that his meaning might be doubtful, he exerted himself to speak.

"Yea," said he, in faint accents, "my soul hath a patient weariness until that veil be lifted."

"And is it fitting," resumed the Reverend Mr. Clark, "that a man so given to prayer, of such a blameless example, holy in deed and thought, so far as mortal judgment may pronounce; is it fitting that a father in the church should leave a shadow on his memory that may seem to blacken a life so pure? I pray you, my venerable brother, let not this thing be! Suffer us to be gladdened by your triumphant aspect as you go to your reward. Before the veil of eternity be lifted, let me cast aside this black veil from your face!"

And thus speaking, the Reverend Mr. Clark bent forward to reveal the mystery of so many years. But, exerting a sudden energy, that made all the beholders stand aghast, Father Hooper snatched both his hands from beneath the bedclothes, and pressed them strongly on the black veil, resolute to struggle, if the minister of Westbury would contend with a dying man.

"Never!" cried the veiled clergyman. "On earth, never!"

"Dark old man!" exclaimed the frightened minister, "with what horrible crime upon your soul are you now passing to the judgment?"

Father Hooper's breath heaved; it rattled in his throat; but, with a mighty effort, grasping forward with his hands, he caught hold of life, and held it back till he should speak. He even raised himself in bed; and there he sat, shivering with the arms of death around him, while the black veil hung down, awful at that last moment, in the gathered terrors of a lifetime. And yet the faint, sad smile, so often there, now seemed to glimmer from its obscurity, and linger on Father Hooper's lips.

"Why do you tremble at me alone?" cried he, turning his veiled face round the circle of pale spectators. "Tremble also at each other! Have men avoided me, and women shown no pity, and children screamed and fled, only for my black veil? What, but the mystery which it obscurely typifies, has made this piece of crape so awful? When the friend shows his inmost heart to his friend; the lover to his best beloved; when man does not vainly shrink from the eye of his Creator, loathsomely treasuring up the secret of his sin; then deem me a monster, for the symbol beneath which I have lived, and die! I look around me, and, lo! on every visage a Black Veil!"

While his auditors shrank from one another, in mutual fright, Father Hooper fell back upon his pillow, a veiled corpse, with a faint smile lingering on the lips. Still veiled, they laid him in his coffin, and a veiled corpse they bore him to the grave. The grass of many years has sprung up and withered on that grave, the burial stone is moss-grown, and good Mr. Hooper's face is dust; but awful is still the thought that it moldered beneath the Black Veil!

A Comment on the Story

About a century before Hawthorne wrote this story, the fiery Jonathan Edwards reminded his congregation of their "sinful, wicked manner of attending [God's] solemn worship." Those who listened to Edward's famous sermon, "Sinners in the Hands of an Angry God" (see page 37), heard their preacher's powerful images of God's anger: it was "great waters that are dammed for the present"; it was a bow that was already bent to pierce them with the arrow of justice; it was the fire into which a spider or loathsome insect would be cast. It did not take the citizens of Northampton, Massachusetts, long to decide that Edward's theology was overly harsh, and he was soon dismissed from his post.

In "The Minister's Black Veil," the kindly and gentle Hooper might at first seem the very opposite of Edwards. But it is soon clear that Hooper's actions, perhaps even more effectively than Edward's words, inspired his congregation with dread. It is Hooper's sermon, outwardly mild but profoundly disturbing, that provides the best clue to the black veil's symbolic meaning. By wearing the veil, Hooper physically declares his kinship with all human beings as secret sinners. Instead of denouncing, as Edwards did, our illusion that we can somehow hide our wickedness from God, Hawthorne's hero humbly wears a visual reminder to all of his own guilt.

Paradoxically, the minister's symbolic confession that he too is a secret sinner has the opposite effect from what he intended; his parishioners, unwilling to face an uncomfortable truth about themselves, are alienated from him. It does not occur to them that the black veil could represent a general truth about human nature; they prefer to speculate instead on Hooper's sanity and on his guilt for some mysterious past crime. Only sinners who must confront death seem to find comfort in his ministry. Instead of dismissal, Hooper lives out his life suffering a harsher fate: though grudgingly respected, he must bear isolation, mockery, and "dismal suspicions."

In the note on page 266, Hawthorne reveals that he knew of a clergyman in Maine who had worn a black veil as a symbol of his sorrow and penance for having accidentally killed a friend. At the same time, by pointedly describing his own tale as a "parable," Hawthorne emphasizes his own distance from realism and his story's significance as a moral tale. We know that very few clergymen in real life would go to the extreme of Parson Hooper. Nevertheless, Hawthorne's story, precisely attuned to the American Puritan past, remains a haunting exploration of the nature of evil and of the Puritan's need to satisfy the demands of a hidden, ungraspable God.

Responding to the Story

Analyzing the Story

Identifying Facts

1. Describe the congregation's response to their first sight of Mr. Hooper's black veil.
2. Briefly describe Hooper's **character**, based on the picture of him offered in the story's opening paragraphs. What does the congregation's attitude toward him seem to have been up to this point?
3. In a single afternoon, Hooper presides at both a funeral and a wedding. Explain how the veil is responsible for a shudder and a general heightening of mood at each event.
4. Elizabeth, Hooper's fiancée, demands to know why he must wear the veil. Locate the passage that gives Hooper's explanation. What arguments against the veil does Elizabeth make?
5. Does the black veil have any positive effects throughout Hooper's long ministry? Explain.

Interpreting Meanings

6. Why do you think the villagers bury Hooper without removing the veil?
7. Poe said that Hooper wore the veil because:

> . . . a crime of dark dye (having reference to the "young lady") has been committed . . .
>
> —Edgar Allan Poe

What do you think Poe refers to? What is your response to this explanation for the veil?
8. Describe Elizabeth's first response to the sight of her fiancé's veil, and tell how her reaction changes. How would you explain her sudden change of attitude?
9. From his deathbed, Hooper makes it clear that he is not the only wearer of the veil, but that he sees similar veils all around him. Explain what you think the minister means by this deathbed statement. What does the veil **symbolize**, in your opinion?
10. Would you describe the narrator's **tone** as neutral or emotional? Explain how the words the narrator chooses in referring to the veil affect the story's tone.
11. On page 272, the narrator remarks that the "saddest of all prisons" is a person's "own heart." What does this mean? Do you agree? Explain your response.
12. What do you think is this story's **theme,** or main idea? In your answer, consider that Hawthorne subtitled the story "A Parable" and that a **parable** is a short, usually simple story from which a moral or religious lesson can be drawn.

Writing About the Story

A Creative Response

1. **Using Another Point of View.** This story would be very different if we were to hear it told from Reverend Hooper's point of view. Write a paragraph of the story as it might be told by Reverend Hooper himself. Let Hooper explain the significance of the veil, and how he first thought of wearing it. Let him describe how he feels wearing it all the time.

A Critical Response

2. **Comparing the Story to a Sermon.** In an essay, compare Hawthorne's story to Jonathan Edwards's sermon "Sinners in the Hands of an Angry God" (page 37). Consider the attitude toward sin revealed in each selection, the attitude toward hypocrisy, and the conditions needed for salvation. If you think the two selections are radically different, then construct your essay as a series of contrasts.
3. **Comparing the Story to an Essay.** On page 192, in *Nature,* Emerson says that we are "part or parcel of God," and that in the beauties of nature we can behold something "as beautiful as our own nature." In an essay, explain how Emerson's views of human nature compare or contrast with Hawthorne's. Cite specific passages from both writers to support what you say. Do you agree with either writer?

Analyzing Language and Style

Archaic and Old-Fashioned Words

Hawthorne's story, though symbolic and ambiguous in meaning, is told in a plain, accessible style. If modern readers have trouble with Hawthorne, it is with his archaic or old-fashioned language. Context clues should help you figure out any language that is strange. Which word or words in each of the following passages from the story are rarely used today? How would you rephrase each passage in a modern idiom? Are any of these words used today in different senses?

1. "On a nearer view it seemed to consist of two folds of crape. . . ." (Page 266)
2. "A superstitious old woman was the only witness of this prodigy." (Page 268)
3. ". . . he well-nigh lost his wits from his own waggery." (Page 269)
4. ". . . having wrought so late into the evening. . . ." (Page 272)

RAPPACCINI'S DAUGHTER

This story reflects Hawthorne's ideas about scientific experimentation. Science had taken a strong hold on people's imaginations in his time: Here he describes a perversion of the art. Watch for hints in the story that Hawthorne imagines Rappaccini's garden as another Eden, with an Adam, an Eve, and a serpent. Given Hawthorne's concerns, what would you predict his attitude would be toward a scientist who misuses his powers?

A young man, named Giovanni Guasconti,[1] came, very long ago, from the more southern region of Italy, to pursue his studies at the University of Padua. Giovanni, who had but a scanty supply of gold ducats in his pocket, took lodgings in a high and gloomy chamber of an old edifice which looked not unworthy to have been the palace of a Paduan noble, and which, in fact, exhibited over its entrance the armorial bearings of a family long since extinct. The young stranger, who was not unstudied in the great poem of his country, recollected that one of the ancestors of this family, and perhaps an occupant of this very mansion, had been pictured by Dante as a partaker of the immortal agonies of his Inferno.[2] These reminiscences and associations, together with the tendency to heartbreak natural to a young man for the first time out of his native sphere, caused Giovanni to sigh heavily as he looked around the desolate and ill-furnished apartment.

"Holy Virgin, signor!" cried old Dame Lisabetta, who, won by the youth's remarkable beauty of person, was kindly endeavoring to give the chamber a habitable air, "what a sigh was that to come out of a young man's heart! Do you find this old mansion gloomy? For the love of Heaven, then, put your head out of the window, and you will see as bright sunshine as you have left in Naples."

Guasconti mechanically did as the old woman advised, but could not quite agree with her that the Paduan sunshine was as cheerful as that of southern Italy. Such as it was, however, it fell upon a garden beneath the window and expended its fostering influences on a variety of plants, which seemed to have been cultivated with exceeding care.

"Does this garden belong to the house?" asked Giovanni.

"Heaven forbid, signor, unless it were fruitful of better pot herbs than any that grow there now," answered old Lisabetta. "No, that garden is cultivated by the own hands of Signor Giacomo Rappaccini,[3] the famous doctor, who, I warrant him, has been heard of as far as Naples. It is said that he distills these plants into medicines that are as potent as a charm. Oftentimes you may see the signor doctor at work, and perchance the signora,[4] his daughter, too, gathering the strange flowers that grow in the garden."

The old woman had now done what she could for the aspect of the chamber; and, commending the young man to the protection of the saints, took her departure.

Giovanni still found no better occupation than to look down into the garden beneath his window. From its appearance, he judged it to be one of those botanic gardens which were of earlier date in Padua than elsewhere in Italy or in the world. Or, not improbably, it might once have been the pleasure place of an opulent family; for there was the ruin of a marble fountain in the center, sculptured with rare art, but so woefully shattered that it was impossible to trace the original design from the chaos of remaining fragments. The water, however, continued to gush and sparkle into the

---

1. **Giovanni Guasconti** (jô·vän′nē gwä·skôn′ tē).
2. **Dante . . . Inferno:** the *Inferno* is the first of the three major sections of *The Divine Comedy,* the great Italian epic poem written by Dante Alighieri (1265–1321). The *Inferno* describes the souls in Hell, many of whom are real people of Dante's day.

3. **Signor Giacomo Rappaccini** (sē·nyôr′ jä′kô·mô rap·a·chē′ nē).
4. **signora** (sē·nyô′rä): a title of respect for a lady.

sunbeams as cheerfully as ever. A little gurgling sound ascended to the young man's window, and made him feel as if the fountain were an immortal spirit that sung its song unceasingly and without heeding the vicissitudes around it, while one century embodied it in marble and another scattered the perishable garniture on the soil. All about the pool into which the water subsided grew various plants, that seemed to require a plentiful supply of moisture for the nourishment of gigantic leaves, and, in some instances, flowers gorgeously magnificent. There was one shrub in particular, set in a marble vase in the midst of the pool, that bore a profusion of purple blossoms, each of which had the luster and richness of a gem; and the whole together made a show so resplendent that it seemed enough to illuminate the garden, even had there been no sunshine. Every portion of the soil was peopled with plants and herbs, which, if less beautiful, still bore tokens of assiduous care, as if all had their individual virtues, known to the scientific mind that fostered them. Some were placed in urns, rich with old carving, and others in common garden pots; some crept serpentlike along the ground or climbed on high, using whatever means of ascent was offered them. One plant had wreathed itself round a statue of Vertumnus,[5] which was thus quite veiled and shrouded in a drapery of hanging foliage, so happily arranged that it might have served a sculptor for a study.

While Giovanni stood at the window, he heard a rustling behind a screen of leaves, and became aware that a person was at work in the garden. His figure soon emerged into view, and showed itself to be that of no common laborer, but a tall, emaciated, sallow, and sickly looking man, dressed in a scholar's garb of black. He was beyond the middle term of life, with gray hair, a thin, gray beard, and a face singularly marked with intellect and cultivation, but which could never, even in his more youthful days, have expressed much warmth of heart.

Nothing could exceed the intentness with which this scientific gardener examined every shrub which grew in his path: it seemed as if he was looking into their inmost nature, making observations in regard to their creative essence, and discovering why one leaf grew in this shape and another in that, and wherefore such and such flowers differed among themselves in hue and

perfume. Nevertheless, in spite of this deep intelligence on his part, there was no approach to intimacy between himself and these vegetable existences. On the contrary, he avoided their actual touch or the direct inhaling of their odors with a caution that impressed Giovanni most disagreeably; for the man's demeanor was that of one walking among malignant influences, such as savage beasts, or deadly snakes, or evil spirits, which, should he allow them one moment of license, would wreak upon him some terrible fatality. It was strangely frightful to the young man's imagination to see this air of insecurity in a person cultivating a garden, that most simple and innocent of human toils, and which had been alike the joy and labor of the unfallen parents of the race. Was this garden, then, the Eden of the present world? And this man, with such a perception of harm in what his own hands caused to grow—was he the Adam?

The distrustful gardener, while plucking away the dead leaves or pruning the too luxuriant growth of the shrubs, defended his hands with a pair of thick gloves. Nor were these his only armor. When, in his walk through the garden, he came to the magnificent plant that hung its purple gems beside the marble fountain, he placed a kind of mask over his mouth and nostrils, as if all this beauty did but conceal a deadlier malice; but, finding his task still too dangerous, he drew back, removed the mask, and called loudly, but in the infirm voice of a person affected with inward disease:

"Beatrice! Beatrice!"

"Here am I, my father. What would you?" cried a rich and youthful voice from the window of the opposite house—a voice as rich as a tropical sunset, and which made Giovanni, though he knew not why, think of deep hues of purple or crimson and of perfumes heavily delectable. "Are you in the garden?"

"Yes, Beatrice," answered the gardener, "and I need your help."

Soon there emerged from under a sculptured portal the figure of a young girl, arrayed with as much richness of taste as the most splendid of the flowers, beautiful as the day, and with a bloom so deep and vivid that one shade more would have been too much. She looked redundant with life, health, and energy; all of which attributes were bound down and compressed, as it were, and girdled tensely, in their luxuriance, by her virgin

---

5. **Vertumnus:** Roman god of gardens and orchards.

Isabella and the Pot of Basil
by John White Alexander (1897). Oil.

Museum of Fine Arts, Boston.

between the beautiful girl and the gorgeous shrub that hung its gemlike flowers over the fountain—a resemblance which Beatrice seemed to have indulged a fantastic humor in heightening, both by the arrangement of her dress and the selection of its hues.

Approaching the shrub, she threw open her arms, as with a passionate ardor, and drew its branches into an intimate embrace—so intimate that her features were hidden in its leafy bosom and her glistening ringlets all intermingled with the flowers.

"Give me thy breath, my sister," exclaimed Beatrice, "for I am faint with common air. And give me this flower of thine, which I separate with gentlest fingers from the stem and place it close beside my heart."

With these words, the beautiful daughter of Rappaccini plucked one of the richest blossoms of the shrub, and was about to fasten it in her bosom. But now, unless Giovanni's draughts of wine had bewildered his senses, a singular incident occurred. A small orange-colored reptile, of the lizard or chameleon species, chanced to be creeping along the path, just at the feet of Beatrice. It appeared to Giovanni—but, at the distance from which he gazed, he could scarcely have seen anything so minute—it appeared to him, however, that a drop or two of moisture from the broken stem of the flower descended upon the lizard's head. For an instant the reptile contorted itself violently, and then lay motionless in the sunshine. Beatrice observed this remarkable phenomenon, and crossed herself, sadly, but without surprise; nor did she therefore hesitate to arrange the fatal flower in her bosom. There it blushed, and almost glimmered with the dazzling effect of a precious stone, adding to her dress and aspect the one appropriate charm which nothing else in the world could have supplied. But Giovanni, out of the shadow of his window, bent forward and shrank back, and murmured and trembled.

"Am I awake? Have I my senses?" said he to himself. "What is this being? Beautiful shall I call her, or inexpressibly terrible?"

Beatrice now strayed carelessly through the garden, approaching closer beneath Giovanni's window, so that he was compelled to thrust his head quite out of its concealment in order to gratify the intense and painful curiosity which she excited. At this moment, there came a beautiful insect over the garden wall; it had, perhaps, wandered through the city, and found no flowers or verdure among those antique haunts of men until the heavy perfumes of Dr. Rappaccini's shrubs had lured it from afar. Without alighting on the flowers, this winged brightness seemed to be attracted by Beatrice, and lingered in the air and fluttered about her head. Now, here it could not be but that Giovanni Guasconti's eyes deceived him. Be that as it might, he fancied that, while Beatrice was gazing at the insect with childish delight, it grew faint and fell at her feet; its bright wings shivered; it was dead—from no cause that he could discern, unless it were the atmosphere of her breath. Again Beatrice crossed herself and sighed heavily as she bent over the dead insect.

An impulsive movement of Giovanni drew her eyes to the window. There she beheld the beautiful head of the young man—rather a Grecian than an Italian head, with fair, regular features, and a glistening of gold among his ringlets—gazing down upon her like a being that hovered in midair. Scarcely knowing what he did, Giovanni threw down the bouquet which he had hitherto held in his hand.

"Signora," said he, "these are pure and healthful flowers. Wear them for the sake of Giovanni Guasconti."

"Thanks, signor," replied Beatrice, with her rich voice, that came forth as it were like a gush of music, and with a mirthful expression half childish and half womanlike. "I accept your gift, and would fain recompense it with this precious purple flower; but if I toss it into the air, it will not reach you. So Signor Guasconti must even content himself with my thanks."

She lifted the bouquet from the ground, and then, as if inwardly ashamed at having stepped aside from her maidenly reserve to respond to a stranger's greeting, passed swiftly homeward through the garden. But few as the moments were, it seemed to Giovanni, when she was on the point of vanishing beneath the sculptured portal, that his beautiful bouquet was already beginning to wither in her grasp. It was an idle thought; there could be no possibility of distinguishing a faded flower from a fresh one at so great a distance.

For many days after this incident, the young man avoided the window that looked into Dr. Rappaccini's garden, as if something ugly and monstrous would have blasted his eyesight had he been betrayed into a glance. He felt conscious of having put himself, to a certain extent, within the influence of an unintelligible power by the communication which he had opened with Beatrice. The wisest course would have been, if his heart were in any real danger, to quit his lodgings and Padua itself at once; the next wiser, to have accustomed himself, as far as possible, to the familiar and daylight view of Beatrice—thus bringing her rigidly and systematically within the limits of ordinary experience. Least of all, while avoiding her sight, ought Giovanni to have remained so near this extraordinary being that the proximity and possibility even of intercourse should give a kind of substance and reality to the wild vagaries which his imagination ran riot continually in producing. Guasconti had not a deep heart—or, at all events, its depths were not sounded now; but he had a quick fancy, and an ardent southern temperament, which rose every instant to a higher fever pitch. Whether or no Beatrice possessed those terrible attributes, that fatal breath, the affinity with those so beautiful and deadly flowers which were indicated by what Giovanni had witnessed, she had at least instilled a fierce and subtle poison into his system. It was not love, although her rich beauty was a madness to him; nor horror, even while he fancied her spirit to be imbued with the same baneful essence that seemed to pervade her physical frame; but a wild offspring of both love and horror that had each parent in it, and burned like one and shivered like the other. Giovanni knew not what to dread; still less did he know what to hope; yet hope and dread kept a continual warfare in his breast, alternately vanquishing one another and starting up afresh to renew the contest. Blessed are all simple emotions, be they dark or bright! It is the lurid intermixture of the two that produces the illuminating blaze of the infernal regions.

Sometimes he endeavored to assuage the fever of his spirit by a rapid walk through the streets of Padua or beyond its gates: his footsteps kept time with the throbbings of his brain, so that the walk was apt to accelerate itself to a race. One day he found himself arrested; his arm was seized by a portly personage, who had turned back on recognizing the young man and expended much breath in overtaking him.

"Signor Giovanni! Stay, my young friend!" cried he. "Have you forgotten me? That might well be the case if I were as much altered as yourself."

It was Baglioni, whom Giovanni had avoided ever since their first meeting, from a doubt that the professor's sagacity would look too deeply into his secrets. Endeavoring to recover himself, he stared forth wildly from his inner world into the outer one and spoke like a man in a dream.

"Yes, I am Giovanni Guasconti. You are Professor Pietro Baglioni. Now let me pass!"

"Not yet, not yet, Signor Giovanni Guasconti," said the professor, smiling, but at the same time scrutinizing the youth with an earnest glance. "What! did I grow up side by side with your father, and shall his son pass me like a stranger in these old streets of Padua? Stand still, Signor Giovanni; for we must have a word or two before we part."

"Speedily, then, most worshipful professor, speedily," said Giovanni, with feverish impatience. "Does not your worship see that I am in haste?"

Now, while he was speaking, there came a man in black along the street, stooping and moving feebly like a person in inferior health. His face was all overspread with a most sickly and sallow hue, but yet so pervaded with an expression of piercing and active intellect that an observer might easily have overlooked the merely physical attributes and have seen only this wonderful energy. As he passed, this person exchanged a cold and distant salutation with Baglioni, but fixed his eyes upon Giovanni with an intentness that seemed to bring out whatever was within him worthy of notice. Nevertheless, there was a peculiar quietness in the look, as if taking merely a speculative, not a human, interest in the young man.

"It is Dr. Rappaccini!" whispered the professor when the stranger had passed. "Has he ever seen your face before?"

"Not that I know," answered Giovanni, starting at the name.

"He *has* seen you! he must have seen you!" said Baglioni, hastily. "For some purpose or other, this man of science is making a study of you. I know that look of his! It is the same that coldly illuminates his face as he bends over a bird, a mouse, or a butterfly, which, in pursuance of some experiment, he has killed by the perfume of a flower; a look as deep as Nature itself, but without Nature's warmth of love. Signor Giovanni, I will stake my life upon it, you are the subject of one of Rappaccini's experiments!''

"Will you make a fool of me?'' cried Giovanni, passionately. "*That,* signor professor, was an untoward experiment.''

"Patience! patience!'' replied the imperturbable professor. "I tell thee, my poor Giovanni, that Rappaccini has a scientific interest in thee. Thou hast fallen into fearful hands! And the Signora Beatrice—what part does she act in this mystery?''

But Guasconti, finding Baglioni's pertinacity intolerable, here broke away, and was gone before the professor could again seize his arm. He looked after the young man intently and shook his head.

"This must not be,'' said Baglioni to himself. "The youth is the son of my old friend, and shall not come to any harm from which the arcana[6] of medical science can preserve him. Besides, it is too insufferable an impertinence in Rappaccini, thus to snatch the lad out of my own hands, as I may say, and make use of him for his infernal experiments. This daughter of his! It shall be looked to. Perchance, most learned Rappaccini, I may foil you where you little dream of it!''

Meanwhile Giovanni had pursued a circuitous route, and at length found himself at the door of his lodgings. As he crossed the threshold, he was met by old Lisabetta, who smirked and smiled, and was evidently desirous to attract his attention; vainly, however, as the ebullition of his feelings had momentarily subsided into a cold and dull vacuity. He turned his eyes full upon the withered face that was puckering itself into a smile, but seemed to behold it not. The old dame, therefore, laid her grasp upon his cloak.

"Signor! signor!'' whispered she, still with a smile over the whole breadth of her visage, so that it looked not unlike a grotesque carving in wood, darkened by centuries. "Listen, signor! There is a private entrance into the garden!''

"What do you say?'' exclaimed Giovanni, turning quickly about, as if an inanimate thing should start into feverish life. "A private entrance into Dr. Rappaccini's garden?''

"Hush! hush! not so loud!'' whispered Lisabetta, putting her hand over his mouth. "Yes, into the worshipful doctor's garden, where you may see all his fine shrubbery. Many a young man in

---

6. **arcana** (är·kā′nə): secret or hidden knowledge.

Padua would give gold to be admitted among those flowers.''

Giovanni put a piece of gold into her hand.

"Show me the way,'' said he.

A surmise, probably excited by his conversation with Baglioni, crossed his mind that this interposition of old Lisabetta might perchance be connected with the intrigue, whatever was its nature, in which the professor seemed to suppose that Dr. Rappaccini was involving him. But such a suspicion, though it disturbed Giovanni, was inadequate to restrain him. The instant that he was aware of the possibility of approaching Beatrice, it seemed an absolute necessity of his existence to do so. It mattered not whether she was angel or demon; he was irrevocably within her sphere, and must obey the law that whirled him onward, in ever lessening circles, toward a result which he did not attempt to foreshadow; and yet, strange to say, there came across him a sudden doubt whether this intense interest on his part was not delusory; whether it was really of so deep and positive a nature as to justify him in now thrusting himself into an incalculable position; whether it was not merely the fantasy of a young man's brain, only slightly or not at all connected with his heart.

He paused, hesitated, turned half about, but again went on. His withered guide led him along several obscure passages, and finally undid a door, through which, as it was opened, there came the sight and sound of rustling leaves, with the broken sunshine glimmering among them. Giovanni stepped forth, and, forcing himself through the entanglement of a shrub that wreathed its tendrils over the hidden entrance, stood beneath his own window in the open area of Dr. Rappaccini's garden.

How often is it the case that, when impossibilities have come to pass and dreams have condensed their misty substance into tangible realities, we find ourselves calm, and even coldly self-possessed, amid circumstances which it would have been a delirium of joy or agony to anticipate! Fate delights to thwart us thus. Passion will choose his own time to rush upon the scene, and lingers sluggishly behind when an appropriate adjustment of events would seem to summon his appearance. So was it now with Giovanni. Day after day, his pulses had throbbed with feverish blood at the improbable idea of an interview with

Beatrice, and of standing with her, face to face, in this very garden, basking in the Oriental sunshine of her beauty, and snatching from her full gaze the mystery which he deemed the riddle of his own existence. But now there was a singular and untimely equanimity within his breast. He threw a glance around the garden to discover if Beatrice or her father was present, and, perceiving that he was alone, began a critical observation of the plants.

The aspect of one and all of them dissatisfied him; their gorgeousness seemed fierce, passionate, and even unnatural. There was hardly an individual shrub which a wanderer, straying by himself through a forest, would not have been startled to find growing wild, as if an unearthly face had glared at him out of the thicket. Several also would have shocked a delicate instinct by an appearance of artificialness indicating that there had been such commixture and, as it were, adultery of various vegetable species that the production was no longer of God's making, but the monstrous offspring of man's depraved fancy, glowing with only an evil mockery of beauty. They were probably the result of experiment, which in one or two cases had succeeded in mingling plants individually lovely into a compound possessing the questionable and ominous character that distinguished the whole growth of the garden. In fine, Giovanni recognized but two or three plants in the collection, and those of a kind that he well knew to be poisonous. While busy with these contemplations, he heard the rustling of a silken garment, and, turning, beheld Beatrice emerging from beneath the sculptured portal.

Giovanni had not considered with himself what should be his deportment; whether he should apologize for his intrusion into the garden, or assume that he was there with the privity,[7] at least, if not by the desire, of Dr. Rappaccini or his daughter; but Beatrice's manner placed him at his ease, though leaving him still in doubt by what agency he had gained admittance. She came lightly along the path and met him near the broken fountain. There was surprise in her face, but brightened by a simple and kind expression of pleasure.

"You are a connoisseur in flowers, signor," said Beatrice, with a smile, alluding to the bouquet which he had flung her from the window. "It is

---

7. **privity:** private knowledge.

no marvel, therefore, if the sight of my father's rare collection has tempted you to take a nearer view. If he were here, he could tell you many strange and interesting facts as to the nature and habits of these shrubs; for he has spent a lifetime in such studies, and this garden is his world."

"And yourself, lady," observed Giovanni, "if fame says true, you likewise are deeply skilled in the virtues indicated by these rich blossoms and these spicy perfumes. Would you deign to be my instructress, I should prove an apter scholar than if taught by Signor Rappaccini himself."

"Are there such idle rumors?" asked Beatrice, with the music of a pleasant laugh. "Do people say that I am skilled in my father's science of plants? What a jest is there! No, though I have grown up among these flowers, I know no more of them than their hues and perfume; and sometimes methinks I would fain rid myself of even that small knowledge. There are many flowers here, and those not the least brilliant, that shock and offend me when they meet my eye. But pray, signor, do not believe these stories about my science. Believe nothing of me save what you see with your own eyes."

"And must I believe all that I have seen with my own eyes?" asked Giovanni, pointedly, while the recollection of former scenes made him shrink. "No, signora; you demand too little of me. Bid me believe nothing save what comes from your own lips."

It would appear that Beatrice understood him. There came a deep flush to her cheek; but she looked full into Giovanni's eyes, and responded to his gaze of uneasy suspicion with a queenlike haughtiness.

"I do so bid you, signor," she replied. "Forget whatever you may have fancied in regard to me. If true to the outward senses, still it may be false in its essence; but the words of Beatrice Rappaccini's lips are true from the depths of the heart outward. Those you may believe."

A fervor glowed in her whole aspect and beamed upon Giovanni's consciousness like the light of truth itself; but while she spoke, there was a fragrance in the atmosphere around her, rich and delightful, though evanescent, yet which the young man, from an indefinable reluctance, scarcely dared to draw into his lungs. It might be the odor of the flowers. Could it be Beatrice's breath which thus embalmed her words with a

Orchids, Passion Flowers, and Hummingbird
by Martin Johnson Heade (1865). Oil.

The Whitney Museum of American Art, New York.
Gift of Mrs. Robert Graham.

strange richness, as if by steeping them in her heart? A faintness passed like a shadow over Giovanni and flitted away; he seemed to gaze through the beautiful girl's eyes into her transparent soul, and felt no more doubt or fear.

The tinge of passion that had colored Beatrice's manner vanished; she became gay, and appeared to derive a pure delight from her communion with the youth not unlike what the maiden of a lonely island might have felt conversing with a voyager from the civilized world. Evidently her experience of life had been confined within the limits of that garden. She talked now about matters as simple as the daylight or summer clouds, and now asked questions in reference to the city, or Giovanni's distant home, his friends, his mother, and his sisters—questions indicating such seclusion, and such lack of familiarity with modes and forms, that Giovanni responded as if to an infant. Her spirit gushed out before him like a fresh rill that was just catching its first glimpse of the sunlight and wondering at the reflections of earth and sky which were flung into its bosom. There came thoughts, too, from a deep source, and fantasies of a gemlike brilliancy, as if diamonds and rubies sparkled upward among the bubbles of the fountain. Ever and anon there gleamed across the young man's mind a sense of wonder that he should be walking side by side with the being who had so wrought upon his imagination, whom he had idealized in such hues of terror, in whom he had positively witnessed such manifestations of dreadful attributes—that he should be conversing with Beatrice like a brother, and should find her so human and so maidenlike. But such reflections were only momentary; the effect of her character was too real not to make itself familiar at once.

In this free intercourse, they had strayed through the garden, and now, after many turns among its avenues, were come to the shattered fountain, beside which grew the magnificent shrub, with its treasury of glowing blossoms. A fragrance was diffused from it which Giovanni recognized as identical with that which he had attributed to Beatrice's breath, but incomparably more powerful. As her eyes fell upon it, Giovanni beheld her press her hand to her bosom as if her heart were throbbing suddenly and painfully.

"For the first time in my life," murmured she, addressing the shrub, "I had forgotten thee."

"I remember, signora," said Giovanni, "that you once promised to reward me with one of these living gems for the bouquet which I had the happy boldness to fling to your feet. Permit me now to pluck it as a memorial of this interview."

He made a step toward the shrub with extended hand; but Beatrice darted forward, uttering a shriek that went through his heart like a dagger. She caught his hand and drew it back with the whole force of her slender figure. Giovanni felt her touch thrilling through his fibers.

"Touch it not!" exclaimed she, in a voice of agony. "Not for thy life! It is fatal!"

Then, hiding her face, she fled from him and vanished beneath the sculptured portal. As Giovanni followed her with his eyes, he beheld the emaciated figure and pale intelligence of Dr. Rappaccini, who had been watching the scene, he knew not how long, within the shadow of the entrance.

No sooner was Guasconti alone in his chamber than the image of Beatrice came back to his passionate musings, invested with all the witchery that had been gathering around it ever since his first glimpse of her, and now likewise imbued with a tender warmth of girlish womanhood. She was human; her nature was endowed with all gentle and feminine qualities; she was worthiest to be worshiped; she was capable, surely, on her part, of the height and heroism of love. Those tokens which he had hitherto considered as proofs of a frightful peculiarity in her physical and moral system were now either forgotten, or, by the subtle sophistry[8] of passion, transmitted into a golden crown of enchantment, rendering Beatrice the more admirable by so much as she was the more unique. Whatever had looked ugly was now beautiful; or, if incapable of such a change, it stole away and hid itself among those shapeless half ideas which throng the dim region beyond the daylight of our perfect consciousness. Thus did he spend the night, nor fell asleep until the dawn had begun to awake the slumbering flowers in Dr. Rappaccini's garden, whither Giovanni's dreams doubtless led him. Up rose the sun in his due season, and, flinging his beams upon the young man's eyelids, awoke him to a sense of pain. When thoroughly aroused, he became sensible of a burning and tingling agony in his hand—in his right hand—the very hand which Beatrice had grasped in her own when he was on the point of plucking one of the gemlike flowers. On the back

---

8. **sophistry** (säf'is·trē): clever but unsound arguments.

of that hand there was now a purple print like that of four small fingers, and the likeness of a slender thumb upon his wrist.

Oh, how stubbornly does love—or even that cunning semblance of love which flourishes in the imagination, but strikes no depth of root into the heart—how stubbornly does it hold its faith until the moment comes when it is doomed to vanish into thin mist! Giovanni wrapped a handkerchief about his hand and wondered what evil thing had stung him, and soon forgot his pain in a reverie of Beatrice.

After the first interview, a second was in the inevitable course of what we call fate. A third; a fourth; and a meeting with Beatrice in the garden was no longer an incident in Giovanni's daily life, but the whole space in which he might be said to live; for the anticipation and memory of that ecstatic hour made up the remainder. Nor was it otherwise with the daughter of Rappaccini. She watched for the youth's appearance, and flew to his side with confidence as unreserved as if they had been playmates from early infancy—as if they were such playmates still. If, by any unwonted chance, he failed to come at the appointed moment, she stood beneath the window and sent up the rich sweetness of her tones to float around him in his chamber and echo and reverberate throughout his heart: "Giovanni! Giovanni! Why tarriest thou? Come down!" And down he hastened into that Eden of poisonous flowers.

But, with all this intimate familiarity, there was still a reserve in Beatrice's demeanor, so rigidly and invariably sustained that the idea of infringing it scarcely occurred to his imagination. By all appreciable signs, they loved; they had looked love with eyes that conveyed the holy secret from the depths of one soul into the depths of the other, as if it were too sacred to be whispered by the way; they had even spoken love in those gushes of passion when their spirits darted forth in articulated breath like tongues of long-hidden flame; and yet there had been no seal of lips, no clasp of hands, nor any slightest caress such as love claims and hallows. He had never touched one of the gleaming ringlets of her hair; her garment—so marked was the physical barrier between them—had never been waved against him by a breeze. On the few occasions when Giovanni had seemed tempted to overstep the limit, Beatrice grew so sad, so stern, and withal wore such a look of desolate separation, shuddering at itself, that not

a spoken word was requisite to repel him. At such times, he was startled at the horrible suspicions that rose, monsterlike, out of the caverns of his heart and stared him in the face; his love grew thin and faint as the morning mist; his doubts alone had substance. But, when Beatrice's face brightened again after the momentary shadow, she was transformed at once from the mysterious, questionable being whom he had watched with so much awe and horror; she was now the beautiful and unsophisticated girl whom he felt that his spirit knew with a certainty beyond all other knowledge.

A considerable time had now passed since Giovanni's last meeting with Baglioni. One morning, however, he was disagreeably surprised by a visit from the professor, whom he had scarcely thought of for whole weeks, and would willingly have forgotten still longer. Given up as he had long been to a pervading excitement, he could tolerate no companions except upon condition of their perfect sympathy with his present state of feeling. Such sympathy was not to be expected from Professor Baglioni,

The visitor chatted carelessly for a few moments about the gossip of the city and the university, and then took up another topic.

"I have been reading an old classic author lately," said he, "and met with a story that strangely interested me. Possibly you may remember it. It is of an Indian prince, who sent a beautiful woman as a present to Alexander the Great. She was as lovely as the dawn and gorgeous as the sunset, but what especially distinguished her was a certain rich perfume in her breath—richer than a garden of Persian roses. Alexander, as was natural to a youthful conqueror, fell in love at first sight with this magnificent stranger; but a certain sage physician, happening to be present, discovered a terrible secret in regard to her."

"And what was that?" asked Giovanni, turning his eyes downward to avoid those of the professor.

"That this lovely woman," continued Baglioni, with emphasis, "had been nourished with poisons from her birth upward, until her whole nature was so imbued with them that she herself had become the deadliest poison in existence. Poison was her element of life. With that rich perfume of her breath she blasted the very air. Her love would have been poison—her embrace death. Is not this a marvelous tale?"

"A childish fable," answered Giovanni, nervously starting from his chair. "I marvel how your worship finds time to read such nonsense among your graver studies."

"By the by," said the professor, looking uneasily about him, "what singular fragrance is this in your apartment? Is it the perfume of your gloves? It is faint, but delicious; and yet, after all, by no means agreeable. Were I to breathe it long, methinks it would make me ill. It is like the breath of a flower, but I see no flowers in the chamber."

"Nor are there any," replied Giovanni, who had turned pale as the professor spoke, "nor, I think, is there any fragrance except in your worship's imagination. Odors, being a sort of element combined of the sensual and the spiritual, are apt to deceive us in this manner. The recollection of a perfume, the bare idea of it, may easily be mistaken for a present reality."

"Ay, but my sober imagination does not often play such tricks," said Baglioni, "and, were I to fancy any kind of odor, it would be that of some vile apothecary drug wherewith my fingers are likely enough to be imbued. Our worshipful friend Rappaccini, as I have heard, tinctures his medicaments with odors richer than those of Araby. Doubtless, likewise, the fair and learned Signora Beatrice would minister to her patients with draughts as sweet as a maiden's breath; but woe to him that sips them."

Giovanni's face evinced many contending emotions. The tone in which the professor alluded to the pure and lovely daughter of Rappaccini was a torture to his soul; and yet the intimation of a view of her character opposite to his own gave instantaneous distinctness to a thousand dim suspicions, which now grinned at him like so many demons. But he strove hard to quell them and to respond to Baglioni with a true lover's perfect faith.

"Signor professor," said he, "you were my father's friend; perchance, too, it is your purpose to act a friendly part toward his son. I would fain feel nothing toward you save respect and deference; but I pray you to observe, signor, that there is one subject on which we must not speak. You know not the Signora Beatrice. You cannot, therefore, estimate the wrong—the blasphemy, I may even say—that is offered to her character by a light or injurious word."

"Giovanni! my poor Giovanni!" answered the professor, with a calm expression of pity, "I know this wretched girl far better than yourself. You shall hear the truth in respect to the poisoner Rappaccini and his poisonous daughter; yes, poisonous as she is beautiful. Listen; for, even should you do violence to my gray hairs, it shall not silence me. That old fable of the Indian woman has become a truth by the deep and deadly science of Rappaccini and in the person of the lovely Beatrice."

Giovanni groaned and hid his face.

"Her father," continued Baglioni, "was not restrained by natural affection from offering up his child in this horrible manner as the victim of his insane zeal for science; for, let us do him justice, he is as true a man of science as ever distilled his own heart in an alembic.[9] What, then, will be your fate? Beyond a doubt you are selected as the material of some new experiment. Perhaps the result is to be death; perhaps a fate more awful still. Rappaccini, with what he calls the interest of science before his eyes, will hesitate at nothing."

"It is a dream," muttered Giovanni to himself. "Surely it is a dream."

"But," resumed the professor, "be of good cheer, son of my friend. It is not yet too late for the rescue. Possibly we may even succeed in bringing back this miserable child within the limits of ordinary nature, from which her father's madness has estranged her. Behold this little silver vase! It was wrought by the hands of the renowned Benvenuto Cellini,[10] and is well worthy to be a love gift to the fairest dame in Italy. But its contents are invaluable. One little sip of this antidote would have rendered the most virulent poisons of the Borgias[11] innocuous. Doubt not that it will be as efficacious against those of Rappaccini. Bestow the vase, and the precious liquid within it, on your Beatrice, and hopefully await the result."

Baglioni laid a small, exquisitely wrought silver vial on the table and withdrew, leaving what he had said to produce its effect upon the young man's mind.

"We will thwart Rappaccini yet," thought he, chuckling to himself, as he descended the stairs. "But, let us confess the truth of him, he is a wonderful man—a wonderful man indeed; a vile empiric,[12] however, in his practice, and therefore

---

9. **alembic:** an apparatus made of glass or metal.
10. **Benvenuto Cellini:** sculptor and goldsmith (1500–1571).
11. **Borgias:** an aristocratic Italian family of the Renaissance; many Borgias were accused of poisoning their enemies.
12. **empiric:** charlatan or quack.

both exploit his whaling experience and, on a far more ambitious plane, seek the ultimate truth of human existence. That truth, and the mystery of whether it is benign or evil in nature, is embodied in Moby-Dick, the great white whale that gives the book its title and central symbol.

Melville found the perfect narrator for his whale story in a young man named Ishmael, who has a keen eye and a questioning voice. Moreover, he saw his main character clearly: Captain Ahab, standing on the *Pequod*'s quarter-deck with his peg leg jammed into that accommodating hole and his heart full of brooding vengeance. In Ahab, Melville created a giant of a character, one with very few equals in American literature.

When he finished *Moby-Dick* in July of 1851, Melville sensed that he had taken a great risk and won, that he had written a sublime novel. He dedicated it to Hawthorne and wrote him, ''I have written a wicked book but I feel spotless as a lamb.''

Yet for all his bright expectations, *Moby-Dick* was a failure. Critics and readers alike were either puzzled or indifferent, and Melville finally had to admit that his literary career had foundered. He wrote to Hawthorne:

> The calm, the coolness, the silent, grass-growing mood in which a man *ought* always to compose—that, I fear can seldom be mine. Dollars damn me; and the malicious Devil is forever grinning in upon me, holding the door ajar. My dear Sir, a presentiment [feeling of fear about the future] is on me—I shall at last be worn out and perish . . . What I feel most moved to write, that is banned—it will not pay. Yet, altogether, write the other way I cannot. So the product is a final hash, and all my books are botches.

He was in debt, unable to meet the needs of his family, and in ill health, quite possibly falling toward the mental derangement that had ended his father's life. However, he continued to hope for a change in his fortunes. He published the poorly-received novels *Pierre* in 1852, *Israel Potter* in 1855, and *The Confidence Man* in 1857.

In 1856, he scraped together enough money for a trip to Europe, visiting Hawthorne in England and going on to Italy and Palestine. He returned home feeling somewhat restored by his travels, but he still could find no way out of the hopeless, impoverished life that had been thrust upon him. This same year he published a collection of stories, entitled *The Piazza Tales,* which included one of his finest short pieces of fiction, ''Bartleby the Scrivener.'' It is tempting to see in the stubborn pathos of the title character something of Melville's own bitterly stung emotions.

In 1866, he found a job, much as Hawthorne had, with the customhouse. As an inspector, he visited the North River steamship piers each day to examine the incoming freight and passenger luggage. But if the customhouse gave him the financial security he yearned for, the ''grass-growing'' peace of mind was still denied him. A different kind of tragedy hit the following year, when his son Malcolm took to his room and killed himself with a pistol.

Nevertheless, during this dark period—during the twenty years in which he worked at the most routine of jobs—Melville never stopped writing, producing in particular a number of notable poems. Almost none of his work found a publisher, and he was obliged to bring it out in private editions of only a few copies. To end this period in Melville's life, there was further tragedy. In 1886, his son Stanwix, always an unstable wanderer, died in San Francisco.

At about the same time, Lizzie Melville came into a small inheritance which allowed her husband, at the age of sixty-seven, to retire from the customhouse and begin work on a book that would become another masterpiece. This was *Billy Budd.* When Melville died on September 28, 1891, the novella lay unwanted in his desk drawer. In 1924, thirty-three years later, it was published and acclaimed. Near the desk where Melville had composed it, a note was found. It read, ''Be true to the dreams of thy youth.''

FROM **MOBY-DICK**

"Now the Lord had prepared a great fish to swallow up Jonah."
—The Book of Jonah

*"Whales in the sea
God's voice obey."*
—The New England Primer

Whaleboat Comes to Grief (detail) after a painting by
Ambrose Garneray (mid-19th century). Lithograph.

Shelburne Museum, Vermont.

Sailor (detail) by John Cranch (mid 19th century). Oil on wood panel.

able you to grin and bear it. But even this wears off in time.

What of it, if some old hunks of a sea captain orders me to get a broom and sweep down the decks? What does that indignity amount to, weighed, I mean, in the scales of the New Testament? Do you think the archangel Gabriel thinks anything the less of me, because I promptly and respectfully obey that old hunks in that particular instance? Who ain't a slave? Tell me that. Well, then, however the old sea captains may order me about—however they may thump and punch me about, I have the satisfaction of knowing that it is all right; that everybody else is one way or other served in much the same way—either in a physical or metaphysical point of view, that is; and so the universal thump is passed round, and all hands should rub each other's shoulderblades, and be content.

Again, I always go to sea as a sailor, because they make a point of paying me for my trouble, whereas they never pay passengers a single penny that I ever heard of. On the contrary, passengers themselves must pay. And there is all the difference in the world between paying and being paid.

The act of paying is perhaps the most uncomfortable infliction that the two orchard thieves[9] entailed upon us. But *being paid*—what will compare with it? The urbane activity with which a man receives money is really marvelous, considering that we so earnestly believe money to be the root of all earthly ills, and that on no account can a monied man enter heaven. Ah! how cheerfully we consign ourselves to perdition!

Finally, I always go to sea as a sailor, because of the wholesome exercise and pure air of the forecastle deck. For as in this world, head winds are far more prevalent than winds from astern (that is, if you never violate the Pythagorean maxim), so for the most part the Commodore on the quarter-deck[10] gets his atmosphere at second hand from the sailors on the forecastle. He thinks he breathes it first; but not so. In much the same way do the commonalty lead their leaders in many other things, at the same time that the leaders little suspect it. But wherefore it was that after having

---

9. **the two orchard thieves:** Adam and Eve.
10. **quarter-deck:** a part of the upper deck normally reserved for officers.

repeatedly smelled the sea as a merchant sailor, I should now take it into my head to go on a whaling voyage; this the invisible police officer of the Fates, who has the constant surveillance of me, and secretly dogs me, and influences me in some unaccountable way—he can better answer than anyone else. And, doubtless, my going on this whaling voyage, formed part of the grand program of Providence that was drawn up a long time ago. It came in as a sort of brief interlude and solo between more extensive performances. I take it that this part of the bill must have run something like this:

Grand Contested Election for the Presidency of the United States.
WHALING VOYAGE BY ONE ISHMAEL.
BLOODY BATTLE IN AFFGHANISTAN.

Though I cannot tell why it was exactly that those stage managers, the Fates, put me down for this shabby part of a whaling voyage, when others were set down for magnificent parts in high tragedies, and short and easy parts in genteel comedies, and jolly parts in farces—though I cannot tell why this was exactly; yet, now that I recall all the circumstances, I think I can see a little into the springs and motives which being cunningly presented to me under various disguises, induced me to set about performing the part I did, besides cajoling me into the delusion that it was a choice resulting from my own unbiased free will and discriminating judgment.

Chief among these motives was the overwhelming idea of the great whale himself. Such a portentous and mysterious monster roused all my curiosity. Then the wild and distant seas where he rolled his island bulk; the undeliverable, nameless perils of the whale; these, with all the attending marvels of a thousand Patagonian[11] sights and sounds, helped to sway me to my wish. With other men, perhaps, such things would not have been inducements; but as for me, I am tormented with an everlasting itch for things remote. I love to sail forbidden seas, and land on barbarous coasts. Not ignoring what is good, I am quick to perceive a horror, and could still be social with it—would they let me—since it is but well to be on friendly terms with all the inmates of the place one lodges in.

By reason of these things, then, the whaling voyage was welcome; the great floodgates of the wonder-world swung open, and in the wild conceits that swayed me to my purpose, two and two there floated into my inmost soul, endless processions of the whale, and, midmost of them all, one grand hooded phantom, like a snow hill in the air.

---

11. **Patagonian:** Patagonia is a region east of the Andes mountains, covering the southern parts of Argentina and Chile. *Patagonian* suggested a place very exotic and far away.

Responding to the Novel

Analyzing the Novel

Identifying Facts

1. What **point of view** will the novel be told from? What does the narrator tell us about himself and the mood that moves him to go to sea?
2. What details does the narrator offer to prove that waters and oceans hold a mysterious allure for humanity?
3. What details in the final paragraph **foreshadow** the fact that Ishmael's quest will be for the white whale?

Interpreting Meanings

4. Ishmael prefers the lowliest of shipboard roles. What reasons does he give for this choice? What does this choice suggest about his **character**?

5. What role does the idea of the whale play in Ishmael's decision? What does this information contribute to our knowledge of Ishmael's **character**?
6. Ishmael wonders whether leaving the comparative safety of the merchant fleet for a whaling voyage was decided by fate or by his own free will. Why would this be a matter of importance to him? Or to us as readers?
7. What does Ishmael mean by the whale's "island bulk" (page 301)?
8. Ishmael calls us all "water-gazers"; he says we are fixed in "ocean reveries." Do you agree? What reasons can you suggest for our fascination with the ocean? Why do you think the sea and the large creatures that inhabit it are so often used to symbolize evil or destructiveness?

Ishmael leaves New York for the Massachusetts seaport of New Bedford. At an inn there, he makes the acquaintance of a South Sea islander named Queequeg, and the two become friends. The would-be sailors journey next to Nantucket, Massachusetts, where they sign on for a three-year voyage on the whaling ship, the Pequod, *under the command of a mysterious Captain Ahab. The ship sets sail on an icy Christmas Day; she is weirdly decorated with whale bones, and her crew is an assortment of officers and men from all over the world. It is not until the voyage is under way for several days, however, that we first glimpse the mysterious, forbidding figure of the captain.*

Ahab

For several days after leaving Nantucket, nothing above hatches was seen of Captain Ahab. The mates regularly relieved each other at the watches, and for aught that could be seen to the contrary, they seemed to be the only commanders of the ship; only they sometimes issued from the cabin with orders so sudden and peremptory, that after all it was plain they but commanded vicariously.[1] Yes, their supreme lord and dictator was there, though hitherto unseen by any eyes not permitted to penetrate into the now sacred retreat of the cabin.

Every time I ascended to the deck from my watches below, I instantly gazed aft to mark if any strange face was visible; for my first vague disquietude touching the unknown captain, now in the seclusion of the sea, became almost a perturbation. This was strangely heightened at times by the ragged Elijah's diabolical incoherences uninvitedly recurring to me,[2] with a subtle energy I could not have before conceived of. But poorly could I withstand them, much as in other moods I was almost ready to smile at the solemn whimsicalities of that outlandish prophet of the wharves. But whatever it was of apprehensiveness or uneasiness—to call it so—which I felt, yet whenever I came to look about me in the ship, it

seemed against all warranty to cherish such emotions. For though the harpooneers, with the great body of the crew, were a far more barbaric, heathenish, and motley set than any of the tame merchant-ship companies which my previous experiences had made me acquainted with, still I ascribed this—and rightly ascribed it—to the fierce uniqueness of the very nature of that wild Scandinavian vocation in which I had so abandonedly embarked. But it was especially the aspect of the three chief officers of the ship, the mates, which was most forcibly calculated to allay these colorless misgivings, and induce confidence and cheerfulness in every presentment[3] of the voyage. Three better, more likely sea officers and men, each in his own different way, could not readily be found, and they were every one of them Americans: a Nantucketer, a Vineyarder, a Cape man. Now, it being Christmas when the ship shot from out her harbor, for a space we had biting Polar weather, though all the time running away from it to the southward; and by every degree and minute of latitude which we sailed, gradually leaving that merciless winter, and all its intolerable weather behind us. It was one of those less lowering, but still gray and gloomy enough mornings of the transition, when with a fair wind the ship was rushing through the water with a vindictive sort of leaping and melancholy rapidity, that as I mounted to the deck at the call of the forenoon watch, so soon as I leveled my glance toward the taffrail,[4] foreboding shivers ran over me. Reality outran apprehension: Captain Ahab stood upon his quarter-deck.

There seemed no sign of common bodily illness about him, nor of the recovery from any. He looked like a man cut away from the stake, when the fire has overrunningly wasted all the limbs without consuming them, or taking away one particle from their compacted, aged robustness. His whole high, broad form, seemed made of solid bronze, and shaped in an unalterable mold, like Cellini's cast Perseus.[5] Threading its way out from among his gray hairs, and continuing right down one side of his tawny scorched face and neck, till it disappeared in his clothing, you saw a slender

---

1. **vicariously:** as substitutes for another (in this case, for Captain Ahab).
2. Before the *Pequod* sailed, an old man named Elijah had asked Ishmael how much he knew about Ahab. "Look ye," Elijah had said ominously, "when Captain Ahab is all right, then this left arm of mine will be all right."

3. **presentment:** here, prediction.
4. **taffrail:** the rail around a ship's stern.
5. **Cellini's cast Perseus:** Benvenuto Cellini (1500–1571), famous Italian sculptor, created an imposing bronze statue of Perseus, a hero of Greek mythology.

Leonard's Candeleworks by William Wall (1855). Oil.

New Bedford Whaling Museum,
New Bedford, Massachusetts.

rodlike mark, lividly whitish. It resembled that perpendicular seam sometimes made in the straight, lofty trunk of a great tree, when the upper lightning tearingly darts down it, and without wrenching a single twig, peels and grooves out the bark from top to bottom, ere running off into the soil, leaving the tree still greenly alive, but branded. Whether that mark was born with him, or whether it was the scar left by some desperate wound, no one could certainly say. By some tacit consent, throughout the voyage little or no allusion was made to it, especially by the mates. But once Tashtego's senior, an old Gay-Head Indian[6] among the crew, superstitiously asserted that not till he was full forty years old did Ahab become that way branded, and then it came upon him, not in the fury of any mortal fray, but in an elemental strife at sea. Yet, this wild hint seemed inferentially negatived, by what a gray Manxman[7] insinuated, an old sepulchral man, who, having never before sailed out of Nantucket, had never ere this laid eye upon wild Ahab. Nevertheless, the old

sea traditions, the immemorial credulities, popularly invested this old Manxman with preternatural powers of discernment. So that no white sailor seriously contradicted him when he said that if ever Captain Ahab should be tranquilly laid out—which might hardly come to pass, so he muttered—then, whoever should do that last office for the dead, would find a birthmark on him from crown to sole.

So powerfully did the whole grim aspect of Ahab affect me, and the livid branch which streaked it, that for the first few moments I hardly noted that not a little of this overbearing grimness was owing to the barbaric white leg upon which he partly stood. It had previously come to me that this ivory leg had at sea been fashioned from the polished bone of the sperm whale's jaw. "Aye, he was dismasted off Japan," said the old Gay-Head Indian once; "but like his dismasted craft, he shipped [8] another mast without coming home for it. He has a quiver of 'em."

I was struck with the singular posture he main-

---

6. **Gay-Head Indian:** an Indian from the town of Gay-Head, Massachusetts.
7. **Manxman:** a man from the Isle of Man, one of the islands located between Northern Ireland and England.

8. **shipped:** took aboard.

tained. Upon each side of the Pequod's quarter-deck, and pretty close to the mizen shrouds,[9] there was an auger-hole, bored about half an inch or so, into the plank. His bone leg steadied in that hole; one arm elevated, and holding by a shroud; Captain Ahab stood erect, looking straight out beyond the ship's ever-pitching prow. There was an infinity of firmest fortitude, a determinate, unsurrenderable willfulness, in the fixed and fearless, forward dedication of that glance. Not a word he spoke; nor did his officers say aught to him; though by all their minutest gestures and expressions, they plainly showed the uneasy, if not painful, consciousness of being under a troubled master-eye. And not only that, but moody, stricken Ahab stood before them with a crucifixion in his face; in all the nameless, regal, overbearing dignity of some mighty woe.

Ere long, from his first visit in the air, he withdrew into his cabin. But after that morning, he was every day visible to the crew; either standing in his pivot-hole, or seated upon an ivory stool he had; or heavily walking the deck. As the sky grew less gloomy, indeed, began to grow a little genial, he became still less and less a recluse; as if, when the ship had sailed from home, nothing but the

dead, wintry bleakness of the sea had then kept him so secluded. And, by and by, it came to pass, that he was almost continually in the air; but, as yet, for all that he said, or perceptibly did, on the at last sunny deck, he seemed as unnecessary there as another mast. But the Pequod was only making a passage now; not regularly cruising; nearly all whaling preparatives needing supervision the mates were fully competent to, so that there was little or nothing, out of himself to employ or excite Ahab, now; and thus chase away, for that one interval, the clouds that layer upon layer were piled upon his brow, as ever all clouds choose the loftiest peaks to pile themselves upon.

Nevertheless, ere long, the warm, warbling persuasiveness of the pleasant holiday weather we came to seemed gradually to charm him from his mood. For, as when the red-cheeked, dancing girls, April and May, trip home to the wintry, misanthropic woods, even the barest, ruggedest, most thunder-cloven old oak will at least send forth some few green sprouts, to welcome such glad-hearted visitants; so Ahab did, in the end, a little respond to the playful allurings of that girlish air. More than once did he put forth the faint blossom of a look, which, in any other man, would have soon flowered out in a smile.

---

9. **mizen shrouds:** the sails on the mast closest to the stern.

Responding to the Novel

Analyzing the Novel

Identifying Facts

1. Even before Ahab makes his first appearance on deck, what evidence of his presence does Ishmael observe?
2. Apprehensions regarding the mysterious captain make Ishmael uneasy. By contrast, why does he find the presence of the rest of the ship's company reassuring?
3. Describe Ahab's "brand," or scar. What superstitions surround the scar?
4. Describe the "posture" Ahab maintains on the quarter-deck.
5. In the final paragraph, what hint is offered that Ahab's personality may have a gentler side? Find the examples of **figurative language** in this paragraph that help make this point about Ahab's character.

Interpreting Meanings

6. Find the three **similes** that describe Ahab's appearance as he stands on the quarter-deck. What do you think each simile implies about Ahab's **character**?
7. Ishmael's first impression of Ahab is of terrifying grimness, in part because of Ahab's "barbaric white leg," crafted from the jawbone of a sperm whale. What additional feelings about Ahab are suggested by Ishmael's description of the captain at his post?
8. The old Gay-Head Indian says that Ahab "was dismasted off Japan" (see page 303). What **figure of speech** is implied in the word *dismasted*? (What is the Indian comparing to a mast?) What other figures of speech does the Indian use in this speech to describe Ahab's affliction? Why are his figures of speech particularly suitable?

Stubb and Ahab quarrel violently, and an ominous dream suggests to the mate that he had better beware of the captain's anger. Hinting at the true nature of his quest over the oceans of the world, Ahab orders the crew to be on the lookout for a great white whale. Notice that, as the narrative gathers dramatic momentum, Melville introduces several chapters, like this one, with stage directions.

The Quarter-Deck

(Enter Ahab: Then, all.)

It was not a great while after the affair of the pipe,[1] that one morning shortly after breakfast, Ahab, as was his wont, ascended the cabin-gangway to the deck. There most sea captains usually walk at that hour, as country gentlemen, after the same meal, take a few turns in the garden.

Soon his steady, ivory stride was heard, as to and fro he paced his old rounds, upon planks so familiar to his tread, that they were all over dented, like geological stones, with the peculiar mark of his walk. Did you fixedly gaze, too, upon that ribbed and dented brow, there also, you would see still stranger footprints—the footprints of his one unsleeping, ever-pacing thought.

But on the occasion in question, those dents looked deeper, even as his nervous step that morning left a deeper mark. And, so full of his thought was Ahab, that at every uniform turn that he made, now at the main-mast and now at the binnacle,[2] you could almost see that thought turn in him as he turned, and pace in him as he paced; so completely possessing him, indeed, that it all but seemed the inward mold of every outer movement.

"D'ye mark him, Flask?" whispered Stubb, "the chick that's in him pecks the shell. 'Twill soon be out."

The hours wore on—Ahab now shut up within his cabin; anon, pacing the deck, with the same intense bigotry of purpose[3] in his aspect.

It drew near the close of day. Suddenly he came to a halt by the bulwarks, and inserting his bone leg into the auger-hole there, and with one hand grasping a shroud, he ordered Starbuck to send everybody aft.

"Sir!" said the mate, astonished at an order seldom or never given on shipboard except in some extraordinary case.

"Send everybody aft," repeated Ahab. "Mastheads, there! come down!"

When the entire ship's company were assembled, and with curious and not wholly unapprehensive faces, were eyeing him, for he looked not unlike the weather horizon when a storm is coming up, Ahab, after rapidly glancing over the bulwarks, and then darting his eyes among the crew, started from his stand-point; and as though not a soul were nigh him resumed his heavy turns upon the deck. With bent head and half-slouched hat he continued to pace, unmindful of the wondering whispering among the men; till Stubb cautiously whispered to Flask that Ahab must have summoned them there for the purpose of witnessing a pedestrian feat. But this did not last long. Vehemently pausing, he cried—

"What do ye do when ye see a whale, men?"

"Sing out for him!" was the impulsive rejoinder from a score of clubbed voices.

"Good!" cried Ahab, with a wild approval in his tones; observing the hearty animation into which his unexpected question had so magnetically thrown them.

"And what do ye next, men?"

"Lower away, and after him!"

"And what tune is it ye pull to, men?"

"A dead whale or a stove[4] boat!"

More and more strangely and fiercely glad and approving, grew the countenance of the old man at every shout; while the mariners began to gaze curiously at each other, as if marveling how it was that they themselves became so excited at such seemingly purposeless questions.

But, they were all eagerness again, as Ahab, now half-revolving in his pivot-hole, with one hand reaching high up a shroud, and tightly, almost convulsively grasping it, addressed them thus—

---

1. Ahab had thrown his pipe overboard one evening, when he realized that he had no business "with the thing that is meant for sereneness."
2. **binnacle:** case containing the compass.
3. **bigotry of purpose:** intense single-mindedness (bigotry suggests narrowness or exclusion of other ideas).

4. **stove:** with a hole smashed in it.

Following the ritual on the quarter-deck, when Ahab baptized the harpoons in liquor and revealed the object of his chase, we hear three characters privately reflect on their journey's goal. Ahab recognizes himself as a driven man; Starbuck reflects on what he sees as the captain's insanity; and Stubb fatalistically resigns himself to whatever destiny may bring. That night a squall threatens to strike the ship, and the crew become tense. Now at last, however, we are about to meet the object of Ahab's obsession—the white whale, Moby-Dick.

Moby-Dick

I, Ishmael, was one of that crew; my shouts had gone up with the rest; my oath had been welded with theirs; and stronger I shouted, and more did I hammer and clinch my oath, because of the dread in my soul. A wild, mystical, sympathetical feeling was in me; Ahab's quenchless feud seemed mine. With greedy ears I learned the history of that murderous monster against whom I and all the others had taken our oaths of violence and revenge.

For some time past, though at intervals only, the unaccompanied, secluded White Whale had haunted those uncivilized seas mostly frequented by the Sperm Whale fishermen. But not all of them knew of his existence; only a few of them, comparatively, had knowingly seen him; while the number who as yet had actually and knowingly given battle to him, was small indeed. For, owing to the large number of whale-cruisers; the disorderly way they were sprinkled over the entire watery circumference, many of them adventurously pushing their quest along solitary latitudes, so as seldom or never for a whole twelvemonth or more on a stretch, to encounter a single news-telling sail of any sort; the inordinate length of each separate voyage; the irregularity of the times of sailing from home; all these, with other circumstances, direct and indirect, long obstructed the spread through the whole worldwide whaling-fleet of the special individualizing tidings concerning Moby-Dick. It was hardly to be doubted that several vessels reported to have encountered, at such or such a time, or on such or such a meridian, a Sperm Whale of uncommon magnitude and malignity,[1]

which whale, after doing great mischief to his assailants, had completely escaped them; to some minds it was not an unfair presumption, I say, that the whale in question must have been no other than Moby-Dick. Yet as of late the Sperm Whale fishery had been marked by various and not unfrequent instances of great ferocity, cunning, and malice in the monster attacked; therefore it was, that those who by accident ignorantly gave battle to Moby-Dick; such hunters, perhaps, for the most part, were content to ascribe the peculiar terror he bred, more, as it were, to the perils of the Sperm Whale fishery at large, than to the individual cause. In that way, mostly, the disastrous encounter between Ahab and the whale had hitherto been popularly regarded.

And as for those who, previously hearing of the White Whale, by chance caught sight of him, in the beginning of the thing they had every one of them, almost, as boldly and fearlessly lowered for him, as for any other whale of that species. But at length, such calamities did ensue in these assaults—not restricted to sprained wrists and ankles, broken limbs, or devouring amputations—but fatal to the last degree of fatality; those repeated disastrous repulses, all accumulating and piling their terrors upon Moby-Dick; those things had gone far to shake the fortitude of many brave hunters, to whom the story of the White Whale had eventually come.

Nor did wild rumors of all sorts fail to exaggerate and still the more horrify the true histories of these deadly encounters. For not only do fabulous rumors naturally grow out of the very body of all surprising terrible events—as the smitten tree gives birth to its fungi—but, in maritime life, far more than in that of terra firma, wild rumors abound, wherever there is any adequate reality for them to cling to. And as the sea surpasses the land in this matter, so the whale fishery surpasses every other sort of maritime life, in the wonderfulness and fearfulness of the rumors which sometimes circulate there. For not only are whalemen as a body unexempt from that ignorance and superstitiousness hereditary to all sailors; but of all sailors, they are by all odds the most directly brought into contact with whatever is appallingly astonishing in the sea; face to face they not only eye its greatest marvels, but, hand to jaw, give battle to them. Alone, in such remotest waters, that though you sailed a thousand miles, and passed a thousand shores, you would not come to

---

1. **malignity:** intense ill will.

any chiseled hearthstone, or aught hospitable beneath that part of the sun; in such latitudes and longitudes, pursuing too such a calling as he does, the whaleman is wrapped by influences all tending to make his fancy pregnant with many a mighty birth.

No wonder, then, that ever gathering volume from the mere transit over the widest watery spaces, the outblown rumors of the White Whale did in the end incorporate with themselves all manner of morbid hints and half-formed fetal suggestions of supernatural agencies, which eventually invested Moby-Dick with new terrors unborrowed from anything that visibly appears. So that in many cases such a panic did he finally strike, that few who by those rumors, at least, had heard of the White Whale, few of those hunters were willing to encounter the perils of his jaw.

But there were still other and more vital practical influences at work. Not even at the present day has the original prestige of the Sperm Whale, as fearfully distinguished from all other species of the leviathan,[2] died out of the minds of the whalemen as a body. There are those this day among them, who, though intelligent and courageous enough in offering battle to the Greenland or Right whale, would perhaps—either from professional inexperience, or incompetency, or timidity, decline a contest with the Sperm Whale; at any rate, there are plenty of whalemen, especially among those whaling nations not sailing under the American flag, who have never hostilely encountered the Sperm Whale, but whose sole knowledge of the leviathan is restricted to the ignoble monster primitively pursued in the North; seated on their hatches, these men will hearken with a childish fireside interest and awe, to the wild, strange tales of Southern whaling. Nor is the preeminent tremendousness of the great Sperm Whale anywhere more feelingly comprehended than on board of those prows which stem him. . . .

So that overawed by the rumors and portents concerning him, not a few of the fishermen recalled, in reference to Moby-Dick, the earlier days of the Sperm Whale fishery, when it was oftentimes hard to induce long-practiced Right whalemen to embark in the perils of this new and daring warfare; such men protesting that although other leviathans

might be hopefully pursued, yet to chase and point lance at such an apparition as the Sperm Whale was not for mortal man. That to attempt it, would be inevitably to be torn into a quick eternity. On this head, there are some remarkable documents that may be consulted.

Nevertheless, some there were, who even in the face of these things, were ready to give chase to Moby-Dick; and a still greater number who, chancing only to hear of him distantly and vaguely, without the specific details of any certain calamity, and without superstitious accompaniments, were sufficiently hardy not to flee from the battle if offered.

One of the wild suggestions referred to, as at last coming to be linked with the White Whale in the minds of the superstitiously inclined, was the unearthly conceit that Moby-Dick was ubiquitous; that he had actually been encountered in opposite latitudes at one and the same instant of time.

Nor, credulous as such minds must have been, was this conceit altogether without some faint show of superstitious probability. For as the secrets of the currents in the seas have never yet been divulged, even to the most erudite research, so the hidden ways of the Sperm Whale when beneath the surface remain, in great part, unaccountable to his pursuers; and from time to time have originated the most curious and contradictory speculations regarding them, especially concerning the mystic modes whereby, after sounding to a great depth, he transports himself with such vast swiftness to the most widely distant points.

It is a thing well known to both American and English whaleships, and also a thing placed upon authoritative record years ago by Scoresby, that some whales have been captured far north in the Pacific, in whose bodies have been found the barbs of harpoons darted in the Greenland seas. Nor is it to be gainsaid, that in some of these instances it has been declared that the interval of time between the two assaults could not have exceeded very many days. Hence, by inference, it has been believed by some whalemen, that the Nor' West Passage,[3] so long a problem to man, was never a problem to the whale. . . .

Forced into familiarity, then, with such prodigies as these, and knowing that after repeated, intrepid

---

2. **leviathan** (lə·vī′ə·thən): huge sea monster.

3. **Nor' West Passage:** sailors long hoped to discover a river joining the Atlantic and Pacific oceans through Canada.

assaults, the White Whale had escaped alive, it cannot be much matter of surprise that some whalemen should go still further in their superstitions, declaring Moby-Dick not only ubiquitous, but immortal (for immortality is but ubiquity in time); that though groves of spears should be planted in his flanks, he would still swim away unharmed; or if indeed he should ever be made to spout thick blood, such a sight would be but a ghastly deception; for again in unensanguined[4] billows hundreds of leagues away, his unsullied jet would once more be seen.

But even stripped of these supernatural surmisings, there was enough in the earthly make and incontestable character of the monster to strike the imagination with unwonted power. For, it was not so much his uncommon bulk that so much distinguished him from other sperm whales, but, as was elsewhere thrown out—a peculiar snow-white, wrinkled forehead, and a high, pyramidical white hump. These were his prominent features; the tokens whereby, even in the limitless, uncharted seas, he revealed his identity, at a long distance, to those who knew him.

The rest of his body was so streaked, and spotted, and marbled with the same shrouded hue, that, in the end, he had gained his distinctive appellation of the White Whale; a name, indeed, literally justified by his vivid aspect, when seen gliding at high noon through a dark blue sea, leaving a milky-way wake of creamy foam, all spangled with golden gleamings.

Nor was it his unwonted magnitude, nor his remarkable hue, nor yet his deformed lower jaw, that so much invested the whale with natural terror, as that unexampled, intelligent malignity which, according to specific accounts, he had over and over again evinced in his assaults. More than all, his treacherous retreats struck more of dismay than perhaps aught else. For, when swimming before his exulting pursuers, with every apparent symptom of alarm, he had several times been known to turn round suddenly, and, bearing down upon them, either stave[5] their boats to splinters, or drive them back in consternation to their ship.

Already several fatalities had attended his chase. But though similar disasters, however little bruited[6] ashore, were by no means unusual in the

Capturing the Sperm Whale after Ambrose Garneray (c. 1850). Colored lithograph.

---

4. **unensanguined:** unbloodied.
5. **stave:** smash.
6. **bruited:** reported.

Forging the Shaft: A Welding Heat (1877). Oil.

This famous lyric appears in the front of *Leaves of Grass* and serves to introduce one of the poet's major themes. The poem celebrates work. In a truly American epic, what sort of work would you expect to be celebrated?

I Hear America Singing

I hear America singing, the varied carols I hear,
Those of mechanics, each one singing his as it should be blithe
    and strong,
The carpenter singing his as he measures his plank or beam,
The mason singing his as he makes ready for work, or leaves off
    work,
The boatman singing what belongs to him in his boat, the deck-
5   hand singing on the steamboat deck,
The shoemaker singing as he sits on his bench, the hatter singing
    as he stands,
The wood-cutter's song, the ploughboy's on his way in the
    morning, or at noon intermission or at sundown,
The delicious singing of the mother, or of the young wife at work,
    or of the girl sewing or washing,
Each singing what belongs to him or her and to none else,
The day what belongs to the day—at night the party of young
10   fellows, robust, friendly,
Singing with open mouths their strong melodious songs.

Responding to the Poem

Analyzing the Poem

Identifying Details

1. Name the people whom the poet hears in lines 2–8. What does each person sing, according to line 9?
2. Most of the poem describes the songs of the day. What is the setting for the songs of the night in the concluding lines?

Interpreting Meanings

3. What Whitman has in mind here are not the actual work songs once associated with various trades and kinds of physical labor, but something more subtle. What would you say this poem is really about?

4. A feeling of acceptance, even of contentment, runs through the sounds of these many voices. Remembering the long hours and small pay of tradespeople and manual laborers in the nineteenth century, would you say that the poet is romanticizing or idealizing their lot? Or would you say that the songs he hears are expressions of independence and joy in life? Explain your response, and support it with specific references to the poem.
5. If the poet of *Leaves of Grass* were alive today, what kinds of singing do you think he would hear? In what ways would these "songs" be different from those he heard in his own time? In what ways would they be the same as what Whitman heard? Explain your answers with references to Whitman's poems.

The speaker introduces this selection by telling us what *he* is going to do—*we* must stay with him and, like Whitman, "do nothing but listen." Whitman's allusion to Uranus in line 23 serves him well, since it refers to a remote planet with a broad orbit. The word *fakes* in line 27 shows his knowledge of nautical terms: A *fake* is a loop of coiled rope, especially the kind of "running" rope used on cargo ships. In reading this "song," you will have to hear the sounds that are evoked by the images.

26.

Now I will do nothing but listen,
To accrue what I hear into this song, to let sounds contribute
    toward it.

I hear bravuras of birds, bustle of growing wheat, gossip of
    flames, clack of sticks cooking my meals.
I hear the sound I love, the sound of the human voice,
5   I hear all sounds running together, combined, fused or following,
Sounds of the city and sounds out of the city, sounds of the day
    and night,
Talkative young ones to those that like them, the loud laugh of
    work-people at their meals,
The angry base of disjointed friendship, the faint tones of the
    sick,
The judge with hands tight to the desk, his pallid lips pronoun-
    cing a death-sentence,
The heave'e'yo of stevedores unlading ships by the wharves,
10   the refrain of the anchor-lifters,

The Terminal by Alfred Stieglitz (1892). Photogravure.

The Museum of Modern Art, New York.
Gift of Georgia O'Keeffe.

This famous lyric appears in the front of *Leaves of Grass* and serves to introduce one of the poet's major themes. The poem celebrates work. In a truly American epic, what sort of work would you expect to be celebrated?

I Hear America Singing

I hear America singing, the varied carols I hear,
Those of mechanics, each one singing his as it should be blithe
    and strong,
The carpenter singing his as he measures his plank or beam,
The mason singing his as he makes ready for work, or leaves off
    work,
The boatman singing what belongs to him in his boat, the deck-
5   hand singing on the steamboat deck,
The shoemaker singing as he sits on his bench, the hatter singing
    as he stands,
The wood-cutter's song, the ploughboy's on his way in the
    morning, or at noon intermission or at sundown,
The delicious singing of the mother, or of the young wife at work,
    or of the girl sewing or washing,
Each singing what belongs to him or her and to none else,
The day what belongs to the day—at night the party of young
10   fellows, robust, friendly,
Singing with open mouths their strong melodious songs.

Responding to the Poem

Analyzing the Poem

Identifying Details

1. Name the people whom the poet hears in lines 2–8. What does each person sing, according to line 9?
2. Most of the poem describes the songs of the day. What is the setting for the songs of the night in the concluding lines?

Interpreting Meanings

3. What Whitman has in mind here are not the actual work songs once associated with various trades and kinds of physical labor, but something more subtle. What would you say this poem is really about?

4. A feeling of acceptance, even of contentment, runs through the sounds of these many voices. Remembering the long hours and small pay of tradespeople and manual laborers in the nineteenth century, would you say that the poet is romanticizing or idealizing their lot? Or would you say that the songs he hears are expressions of independence and joy in life? Explain your response, and support it with specific references to the poem.

5. If the poet of *Leaves of Grass* were alive today, what kinds of singing do you think he would hear? In what ways would these "songs" be different from those he heard in his own time? In what ways would they be the same as what Whitman heard? Explain your answers with references to Whitman's poems.

The varied subjects of these selections from Whitman's boldly entitled poem reveal the mind and character of the poet whose sensibilities hold the "song" together. "Song of Myself" employs a form so rarely practiced in Whitman's time that it did not even have a name. Today we know it as *free verse*—a kind of expression that ignores the many available forms of meter and the music of rhyme in favor of cadences meant to imitate the natural flow of thought and feeling.

The first poem—number 1 of the 52 that make up "Song of Myself"—is a kind of opening prayer. It answers three questions: Who is the speaker? What are his intentions? How will he compose his "song"?

Song of Myself

1.

I celebrate myself, and sing myself,
And what I assume you shall assume,
For every atom belonging to me as good belongs to you.

I loaf and invite my soul,
5   I lean and loaf at my ease observing a spear of summer grass.

My tongue, every atom of my blood, formed from this soil, this
    air,
Born here of parents born here from parents the same, and their
    parents the same,
I, now thirty-seven years old in perfect health begin,
Hoping to cease not till death.

10   Creeds and schools in abeyance,
Retiring back a while sufficed at what they are, but never
    forgotten,
I harbor for good or bad, I permit to speak at every hazard,
Nature without check with original energy.

Responding to the Poem

Analyzing the Poem

Identifying Details

1. Who is "you" in lines 2 and 3?
2. What autobiographical facts does the speaker reveal in lines 7–9?

Interpreting Meanings

3. What is the connection between the "soul" and "a spear of summer grass" (lines 4–5)? How is this speaker's "loafing" more than mere idleness?

4. What other terms could you substitute for "creeds" and "schools" in line 10? For what purpose does the speaker hold these "in abeyance"?
5. In Whitman's time, as never before, nature was being explored, analyzed, harnessed, exploited, and otherwise "used" to serve humankind. How is this poet going to "use" nature? How could this statement be seen as a description of the poet's style?
6. What lines of this poem show that the speaker wants to share his being or individuality with all of the natural world? What do you think of the idea expressed in line 3?

FREE VERSE

Today we are so used to poetry written in free verse that we take it for granted. But in Whitman's time, Americans preferred poetry that was just like the poetry being written in England; they expected a poem to show the very strictest concern for meter and rhyme. Thus, Whitman's sprawling lines were revolutionary, as was his daring use of American slang, of foreign words, or of words he simply made up to suit his purpose. Whitman's "free verse" is said to have been inspired by the roll and sweep of passages from the Bible and even by the measured cadences of Emerson's essays (see page 191).

Free verse is poetry that is written without concern for regular rhyme schemes and meter. But free verse is not really free at all. Whitman abandoned meter and regular rhyme schemes, but he made full use of these other poetic elements:

1. **Assonance:** the repetition of similar vowel sounds.
2. **Alliteration:** the repetition of similar sounds, usually consonants.
3. **Onomatopoeia:** the use of words whose sounds echo their sense (such as *buzz*).
4. **Parallel structure:** the repetition of similarly constructed phrases or clauses or sentences, one after the other.
5. **Imagery:** the use of language to evoke visual images, as well as sensations of smell, hearing, taste, and touch.

What you hear when you read Whitman's lines aloud is **cadence**—the run of words that rise and fall in emphasis when he has a particular point to make and measures his lines to make it. As you can see from Whitman's poems, cadence does not depend on any strict count of stressed syllables. In traditional poetry, line length is determined by the demands of the meter.

For example, look at *The Song of Hiawatha,* an epic poem by Henry Wadsworth Longfellow (see page 146), which was published in the same year as Whitman's epic, *Leaves of Grass* (1855). Longfellow's poem, which was far more popular than Whitman's, is written in strict **trochaic tetrameter;** that is, each line has four trochees. A **trochee** is an accented syllable followed by an unaccented syllable (DAH da). Read aloud these lines from *The Song of Hiawatha,* to hear how different they sound from the opening lines of "Song of Myself":

By the shores of Gitche Gumee,
By the shining Big-Sea-Water,
Stood the wigwam of Nokomis,
Daughter of the moon, Nokomis.

In Whitman's poetry, lines can be any length at all—three syllables or thirty syllables, depending on the emphasis he wants. In the same poem, Whitman can write in one line

Now I will do nothing but listen

and in a subsequent line

I hear the bravuras of birds, bustle of growing wheat, gossip of flames, clack of sticks cooking my meals

Poets, who, like Whitman, choose to write in cadence have nothing but their own sense of balance and proportion to tell them when a line should end and when it should go on. With no meter to work against, and no other count to give their poems a semblance of order, they are, so to speak, on their own. They must rely completely on their own sense of spacing and timing, on their own feelings as to the "rightness" of sound and movement in every poem.

Traditional poets have found this freedom to be a handicap. Robert Frost has said that writing in this manner is "like playing tennis with the net down." Frost meant that the net on the tennis court is like the meter in poetry—the essential thing that the player and the poet must both respect and overcome. But in the twentieth century, poets have more and more accepted the challenge of writing in cadence. Instead of conforming to a chosen meter or a count of stressed syllables, they write in cadences which follow "curves of thought" or "shapes of speech." They are trusting that their own sense of balance and measure will lead to poems as well-composed as any written in meter. A poem written in regular meter might be compared to a metronome, which keeps a predictable, mechanical beat. Free verse, on the other hand, might be compared to the style of a jazz drummer, who varies the beat throughout a performance.

To hear Whitman's cadences, you must read his poems aloud. In the short opening passage (number 1), you should hear no fewer than thirty-three occurrences of the same consonant sound. What sound is it? What other examples of repetition (including parallel sentence constructions) help create the rhythms and music in this supposedly "free" verse?

Here we have the poet as both observer and participant. In these movie-like glimpses into the broad American scene, he sees what he knows. The poet speaks as though he were not only the cameraman who shoots the pictures but also the director behind each scene who "arranges" just what it will look like. As you read, try to form mental pictures of each of these scenes.

10.

Alone far in the wilds and mountains I hunt,
Wandering amazed at my own lightness and glee,
In the late afternoon choosing a safe spot to pass the night,
Kindling a fire and broiling the fresh-killed game,
5   Falling asleep on the gathered leaves with my dog and gun by
    my side.

The Yankee clipper is under her sky-sails, she cuts the sparkle
    and scud,
My eyes settle the land, I bend at her prow or shout joyously
    from the deck.

The boatmen and clam-diggers arose early and stopped for me,
I tucked my trowser-ends in my boots and went and had a good
    time;
10 You should have been with us that day round the chowder-kettle.

I saw the marriage of the trapper in the open air in the far west,
    the bride was a red girl,
Her father and his friends sat near cross-legged and dumbly
    smoking, they had moccasins to their feet and large thick
    blankets hanging from their shoulders,
On a bank lounged the trapper, he was dressed mostly in skins,
    his luxuriant beard and curls protected his neck, he held
    his bride by the hand.
She had long eyelashes, her head was bare, her coarse straight
    locks descended upon her voluptuous limbs and reached
    to her feet.

15 The runaway slave came to my house and stopped outside,
I heard his motions crackling the twigs of the woodpile,
Through the swung half-door of the kitchen I saw him limpsy
    and weak,
And went where he sat on a log and led him in and assured him,
And brought water and filled a tub for his sweated body and
    bruised feet,
And gave him a room that entered from my own, and gave him
20   some coarse clean clothes,
And remember perfectly well his revolving eyes and his awk-
    wardness,
And remember putting plasters on the galls° of his neck and
    ankles;
He staid with me a week before he was recuperated and passed
    north,
I had him sit next me at table, my fire-lock leaned in the corner.

22. **galls:** sores.

Hunter in the Adirondacks by Winslow Homer (1892). Watercolor.

Fogg Art Museum, Cambridge, Massachusetts.

Responding to the Poem

Analyzing the Poem

Identifying Details

1. In the five stanzas of this poem, the speaker observes and participates in five far-ranging American scenes. Identify the "scene" in each stanza.
2. What **images** of sight, touch, and sound bring the reader into each of these scenes?
3. What repetitions of sentence patterns help create a sense of **cadence** in this poem—a rhythmic rise and fall of your voice as the lines are spoken aloud?
4. To read poetry, you need to keep a dictionary handy. What is the meaning of a "Yankee Clipper" and of "scud" (line 6)? Does "dumbly" in line 12 mean "stupidly" or "mutely"? What do you guess "limpsy" is in line 17? What are "revolving eyes" (line 21) and "galls" (line 22)?

Interpreting Meanings

5. In the first scene, the speaker says that he was "amazed" at his own "lightness and glee." In the second scene, he shouts "joyously from the deck." In the third, he "went and had a good time." In the fourth and fifth scenes, such expressions of personal delight are absent. What is the **tone** of these scenes? How do you account for this?
6. In the last scene, the "runaway slave" is one of thousands who entrusted their lives to the compassion of men and women who might feed and clothe them and otherwise assist their attempts to escape bondage. With this fact in mind, what do you think the stanza—especially the last line—shows about the speaker's character?
7. How would you describe the speaker's **attitude** toward the red girl and the runaway slave?

The speaker introduces this selection by telling us what *he* is going to do—*we* must stay with him and, like Whitman, "do nothing but listen." Whitman's allusion to Uranus in line 23 serves him well, since it refers to a remote planet with a broad orbit. The word *fakes* in line 27 shows his knowledge of nautical terms: A *fake* is a loop of coiled rope, especially the kind of "running" rope used on cargo ships. In reading this "song," you will have to hear the sounds that are evoked by the images.

26.

Now I will do nothing but listen,
To accrue what I hear into this song, to let sounds contribute
    toward it.

I hear bravuras of birds, bustle of growing wheat, gossip of
    flames, clack of sticks cooking my meals.
I hear the sound I love, the sound of the human voice,
5   I hear all sounds running together, combined, fused or following,
Sounds of the city and sounds out of the city, sounds of the day
    and night,
Talkative young ones to those that like them, the loud laugh of
    work-people at their meals,
The angry base of disjointed friendship, the faint tones of the
    sick,
The judge with hands tight to the desk, his pallid lips pronoun-
    cing a death-sentence,
The heave'e'yo of stevedores unlading ships by the wharves,
10   the refrain of the anchor-lifters,

The Terminal by Alfred Stieglitz (1892). Photogravure.

The Museum of Modern Art, New York.
Gift of Georgia O'Keeffe.

The ring of alarm-bells, the cry of fire, the whirr of swift-streak-
    ing engines and hose-carts with premonitory tinkles and
    colored lights,
The steam-whistle, the solid roll of the train of approaching cars,
The slow march played at the head of the association marching
    two and two,
(They go to guard some corpse, the flag-tops are draped with
    black muslin.)
15   I hear the violincello ('tis the young man's heart's complaint),
I hear the keyed cornet, it glides quickly in through my ears,
It shakes mad-sweet pangs through my belly and breast.

I hear the chorus, it is a grand opera,
Ah this indeed is music—this suits me.

20   A tenor large and fresh as the creation fills me,
The orbic flex of his mouth is pouring and filling me full.

I hear the trained soprano (what work with hers is this?)
The orchestra whirls me wider than Uranus flies,
It wrenches such ardors from me I did not know I possessed
    them,
It sails me, I dab with bare feet, they are licked by the indolent
25   waves,
I am cut by bitter and angry hail, I lose my breath,
Steeped amid honeyed morphine, my windpipe throttled in fakes
    of death,
At length let up again to feel the puzzle of puzzles,
And that we call Being.

Responding to the Poem

Analyzing the Poem

Identifying Details

1. The speaker says in line 2 that he will let sounds "contribute" to his own song. How does he *describe* the sounds he hears in line 3?
2. What is the sound that the speaker says he loves?
3. What is "honeyed morphine" (line 27)?
4. The sounds in this poem tend to fall into categories. Break Whitman's long **catalogue**—or list—of sounds into these categories: sounds of joy, sorrow, work, art, and nature.
5. How many examples of **parallel sentence construction** can you find in this poem of 29 lines?
6. What sound in line 3 is an example of **onomatopoeia**—the use of a word with a sound that echoes its sense? What open vowel sounds contribute to the majestic sounds of the last three stanzas?

Interpreting Meanings

7. Whitman's lines are not long or short by accident. He had a reason for stopping each line as he did, or for extending it as long as he did. What long lines suggest a medley of many different sounds? What does the poet gain by making the last line so short?
8. Whitman had a great love for grand opera, especially Italian opera. In opera, many different characters may sing simultaneously of their own emotions. What makes the mention of an operatic chorus particularly appropriate at lines 18–19?
9. Why do you think the speaker calls "Being" the "puzzle of puzzles" in the last two lines?
10. In the final section of this selection, the speaker describes the physical effect that operatic singing has upon him, and he attempts to suggest its spiritual effect. What is the physical effect? What would you say the spiritual effect is?

In this excerpt from the thirty-third section of "Song of Myself," we come upon one of the poet's most famous lines: "I am the man, I suffered, I was there." The line not only shows the poet as a man of sympathetic disposition, but as one capable of *empathy*—the ability to project one's own feelings into the consciousness of others. A great part of Whitman's work is distinguished by his attempts to erase the line between observer and object. Whitman does this in order that, imaginatively speaking, he might *become* the thing or person he is talking about. This is why his poems strike even his most resistant readers with an urgency they cannot ignore.

From 33.

I understand the large hearts of heroes,
The courage of present times and all times,
How the skipper saw the crowded and rudderless wreck of the
    steam-ship, and Death chasing it up and down the storm,
How he knuckled tight and gave not back an inch, and was
    faithful of days and faithful of nights,
And chalked in large letters on a board, *Be of good cheer, we*
5   *will not desert you;*
How he followed with them and tacked with them three days
    and would not give it up.
How he saved the drifting company at last.
How the lank loose-gowned women looked when boated from
    the side of their prepared graves,
How the silent old-faced infants and the lifted sick, and the
    sharp-lipped unshaved men;
10   All this I swallow, it tastes good, I like it well, it becomes mine,
I am the man, I suffered, I was there.

The disdain and calmness of martyrs,
The mother of old, condemned for a witch, burnt with dry
    wood, her children gazing on,
The hounded slave that flags in the race, leans by the fence,
    blowing, covered with sweat,
The twinges that sting like needles his legs and neck, the
15   murderous buckshot and the bullets,
All these I feel or am.

I am the hounded slave, I wince at the bite of the dogs,
Hell and despair are upon me, crack and again crack the
    marksmen,
I clutch the rails of the fence, my gore dribs, thinned with the
    ooze of my skin,
20 I fall on the weeds and stones,
The riders spur their unwilling horses, haul close,
Taunt my dizzy ears and beat me violently over the head with
    whip-stocks.

Agonies are one of my changes of garments.
I do not ask the wounded person how he feels, I myself become
    the wounded person,
25 My hurts turn livid upon me as I lean on a cane and observe.
I am the mashed fireman with breast-bone broken,

Slaves Escaping Through the Swamps
by Thomas Moran (c. 1870). Oil.

Philbrook Art Center, Tulsa, Oklahoma.

Tumbling walls buried me in their debris,
Heat and smoke I inspired, I heard the yelling shouts of my
    comrades,
I heard the distant click of their picks and shovels,
30   They have cleared the beams away, they tenderly lift me forth.

I lie in the night air in my red shirt, the pervading hush is for
    my sake,
Painless after all I lie exhausted but not so unhappy.
White and beautiful are the faces around me, the heads are
    bared of their fire-caps,
The kneeling crowd fades with the light of the torches.

35   Distant and dead resuscitate,
They show as the dial or move as the hands of me, I am the
    clock myself.

I am an old artillerist, I tell of my fort's bombardment,
I am there again.

Again the long roll of the drummers,
40   Again the attacking cannon, mortars,
Again to my listening ears the cannon responsive.

I take part, I see and hear the whole,
The cries, curses, roar, the plaudits for well-aimed shots,
The ambulanza slowly passing trailing its red drip.
45   Workmen searching after damages, making indispensable repairs,
The fall of grenades through the rent roof, the fan-shaped
    explosion,
The whiz of limbs, heads, stone, wood, iron, high in the air.

Again gurgles the mouth of my dying general, he furiously
    waves with his hand,
He gasps through the clot *Mind not me—mind—the entrenchments.*

Responding to the Poem

Analyzing the Poem

Identifying Details

1. "The large hearts of heroes" is the keynote for this passage. What kinds of heroism does the speaker describe here? List the people he identifies with.
2. At what moments does the speaker restate the point of "I am the man, I suffered, I was there"?
3. Remembering the historical background against which this poem was written, how would you explain the incident described in lines 17–22? What conflict is the poet describing in the account of the old artillerist in lines 37–49?

4. What does "mind" mean in the last line?
5. Find at least five **sentence structures** that Whitman repeats in this poem to create his **rhythm**.
6. The poet wants us to share his empathy. What **images** of sight and sound help us feel we also "are there"?

Interpreting Meanings

7. How would you describe the speaker's **tone** in this passage—what are his feelings for these "heroes"?
8. Notice the alternation of very long lines and very short lines. Can you see the reason for each short line? How would you use your voice in reading each short line aloud?

The final poem of "Song of Myself" is a *coda*—a brief restatement and summing up of the themes of the entire song. Since none of these themes is more insistently present throughout the poem than the mind and spirit of the speaker himself, the passage is highly personal. True to his nature, the poet mocks his own egotism; but, just as true to his confidence in himself, he proclaims his importance—and his inescapability. What is happening to the speaker in this famous passage?

52.

The spotted hawk swoops by and accuses me, he complains
    of my gab and my loitering.

I too am not a bit tamed, I too am untranslatable,
I sound my barbaric yawp over the roofs of the world.

The last send of day holds back for me,
It flings my likeness after the rest and true as any on the
5   shadowed wilds,
It coaxes me to the vapor and the dusk.

I depart as air, I shake my white locks at the runaway sun,
I effuse my flesh in eddies, and drift it in lacy jags.

I bequeath myself to the dirt to grow from the grass I love,
10   If you want me again look for me under your boot-soles.

You will hardly know who I am or what I mean,
But I shall be good health to you nevertheless,
And filter and fiber your blood.

Failing to fetch me at first keep encouraged,
15   Missing me one place search another,
I stop somewhere waiting for you.

Responding to the Poem

Analyzing the Poem

Identifying Details

1. What qualities does the speaker say he shares with the spotted hawk?
2. Beginning with line 9, the speaker makes one of his most direct addresses to his readers. What, in your own words, is his parting message?

Interpreting Meanings

3. Considering what you know of the work of poets who preceded him, what does the poet mean when he describes his own poetry as "barbaric yawp"? Do you agree? Describe your response to Whitman's language. Do you think its effect on people has changed with the passage of time?
4. Could Whitman also be using the phrase "barbaric yawp" to refer to the way the Old World might have regarded the experiment of democracy itself? Explain your answer.
5. What do you think the poet means when he says, in line 10, "If you want me again look for me under your boot-soles"?
6. The first line of "Song of Myself" is "I celebrate myself, and sing myself"; the last line is "I stop somewhere waiting for you." Taking into account all that you have learned of the poet's character and the range of his poem, tell what you think the last words in the poem reveal about Whitman's overall **purpose** in writing the poem.
7. What tense does the poet use in these selections from "Song of Myself"? How would the effect have differed if he had spoken in the past tense?

Writing About "Song of Myself"

A Creative Response

1. **Writing an Essay as a Poem.** Whitman is said to have been influenced by the rolling cadences of Emerson's essays. Take a paragraph from one of Emerson's essays, and write it in the shape of a poem. Pay special attention to where you will break the lines: Which lines will you run long and which will you run short?

A Critical Response

2. **Comparing Whitman to Emerson.** In a brief essay, compare these selections from "Song of Myself" with Emerson's essay "Nature" (page 191). First, compare Whitman's message about people and their relationship to nature with Emerson's views on the same subject. Second, compare the style and diction of the writings. Quote from the poems and the essay to support what you say.
3. **Comparing a Poem to a Psalm.** Whitman knew his Bible very well. In a brief essay, tell whether or not you detect similarities between Song 33 and Psalm 22. Quote from the psalm and the poem to support your opinions. Fill out a chart like the following one before you write.

	Psalm 22	Song 33
Parallel structures		
Cadences		
Message		
Tone		

Evening Storm, Schoodic, Maine by Marsden Hartley (1942). Oil.

The Museum of Modern Art, New York.

On the Beach at Night

On the beach at night,
Stands a child with her father,
Watching the east, the autumn sky.

Up through the darkness,
While ravening clouds, the burial clouds, in black masses
5   spreading,
Lower sullen and fast athwart and down the sky,
Amid a transparent clear belt of ether° yet left in the east,
Ascends large and calm the lord-star Jupiter,
And nigh at hand, only a very little above,
10   Swim the delicate sisters the Pleiades.°

7. **ether:** sky.

10. **Pleiades** (plē'ə·dēz): a cluster of seven stars in the constellation Taurus, imagined to be seven sisters.

From the beach the child holding the hand of her father,
Those buried clouds that lower victorious soon to
    devour all,
Watching, silently weeps.

Weep not, child,
15   Weep not, my darling,
With these kisses let me remove your tears,
The ravening clouds shall not long be victorious,
They shall not long possess the sky, they devour the
    stars only in apparition,
Jupiter shall emerge, be patient, watch again another
    night, the Pleiades shall emerge,
They are immortal, all those stars both silvery and
20   golden shall shine out again,
The great stars and the little ones shall shine out again,
    they endure,
The vast immortal suns and the long-enduring pensive
    moons shall again shine.

Then dearest child mournest thou only for Jupiter?
Considerest thou alone the burial of the stars?
25   Something there is,
(With my lips soothing thee, adding I whisper,
I give thee the first suggestion, the problem and indirec-
    tion),
Something there is more immortal even than the stars,
(Many the burials, many the days and nights, passing
    away),
Something that shall endure longer even than lustrous
30   Jupiter,
Longer than sun or any revolving satellite,
Or the radiant sisters the Pleiades.

Responding to the Poem

Analyzing the Poem

Identifying Details

1. What does *ravening* mean in lines 5 and 17?
2. Why does the child weep silently in lines 11–13?
3. How does the poet reassure the child in the fourth stanza?

Interpreting Meanings

4. The last stanza implies that the poem is intended to be read on a **symbolic,** as well as on a literal, level. What do you think the "ravening clouds" might symbolize? What might Jupiter and the "immortal stars" symbolize?

5. When the poet says in line 27 that he is giving "the first suggestion, the problem and indirection," it is as if he were teaching the child her first lesson on an important, and possibly difficult subject. What do you think the subject is, and what is the lesson the poet wants to teach the child?
6. What specific **images** help you to visualize what is happening in the sky? How do the two figures on the beach contrast with these distant sky images? How is this contrast important to the poem?
7. What do you think he means by the "something" in the last stanza—the "something" that is immortal and will endure? Do you think the lesson he intends for the child is clear? How would you respond to Whitman's main point in this poem?

"Even as a boy," wrote Whitman in his *Specimen Days* (see page 350), "I had the fancy, the wish, to write a piece, perhaps a poem, about the sea-shore—that suggesting, dividing line, contact, junction, the solid marrying the liquid . . . blending the real and ideal, and each made portion of the other. Hours, days, in my Long Island youth and early manhood, I haunted the shores of Rockaway or Coney Island, or away east to the Hamptons or Montauk. Once, at the latter place (by the old lighthouse, nothing but sea-tossings in sight in every direction as far as the eye could reach), I remember well, I felt that I must one day write a book expressing this liquid, mystic theme."

On the Beach at Night Alone

On the beach at night alone,
As the old mother sways her to and fro singing her husky song,
As I watch the bright stars shining, I think a thought of the clef
    of the universes and of the future.
A vast similitude interlocks all,
5   All spheres, grown, ungrown, small, large, suns, moons, planets,
All distances of place however wide,
All distances of time, all inanimate forms,
All souls, all living bodies though they be ever so different, or in
    different worlds,
All gaseous, watery, vegetable, mineral processes, the fishes, the
    brutes,
10   All nations, colors, barbarisms, civilizations, languages,
All indentities that have existed or may exist on this globe, or
    any globe
All lives and deaths, all of the past, present, future,
This vast similitude spans them, and always has spanned,
And shall forever span them and compactly hold and enclose
    them.

Responding to the Poem

Analyzing the Poem

Identifying Details

1. Who is the "old mother"? (The title gives you the clue.) What is her "to and fro"?
2. What is the old mother's "husky song"?
3. How would you define "similitude"?

Interpreting Meanings

4. What in human life might the old mother's "to and fro" be compared with?
5. What does the poet mean by a "vast similitude" that "interlocks" all? The **catalogue** that Whitman cites includes many categories. Name some of them.

6. What distinction can you make between a "vast similitude" that "*interlocks* all" and a "vast similitude" that "*spans* them"? Do the verbs merely suggest two aspects of the same phenomenon? Explain.
7. Why do you think thoughts like these came to the poet while he was on the beach?

Writing About the Poem

A Critical Response

Comparing the Poem to "Thanatopsis." In a brief essay, explain whether or not you think Whitman's "vast similitude" has anything in common with the view of the universe expressed in "Thanatopsis" (see page 142).

The Laboratory of Thomas Price
by Henry Alexander (c. 1885). Oil.

The Metropolitan Museum of Art, New York.

This poem, made up of a single sentence, moves with sure steps from its quiet opening line to its abrupt, yet carefully calculated, conclusion.

To place the poem in its time—and to anticipate Whitman's attitude toward its subject—remember that astronomy was of great interest to many nineteenth-century Americans, who followed scientific lectures and debates as eagerly as their great-grandchildren would follow television serials.

When I Heard the Learned Astronomer

When I heard the learned astronomer,
When the proofs, the figures, were ranged in columns before me,
When I was shown the charts and diagrams, to add, divide, and
   measure them,
When I sitting heard the astronomer where he lectured with much
   applause in the lecture-room,
How soon unaccountable I became tired and sick,
Till rising and gliding out I wandered off by myself,
In the mystical moist night air, and from time to time,
Looked up in perfect silence at the stars.

Responding to the Poem

Analyzing the Poem

Identifying Details

1. How does the audience's reaction to the astronomer's lecture differ from the speaker's reaction?

Interpreting Meanings

2. Listening to a lecture that he had obviously wanted to attend, the speaker finds it puzzling—"unaccountable"—that he "became tired and sick." What do you think might have been the reason for such an unexpected reaction? How is this reaction typical of the Romantic attitude toward a scientific dissection of nature?

3. In terms of the conflict of reality versus imagination, of science versus art, what is the significance of the poem's final line? What do you think the poet gained from watching the stars in "perfect silence" that he couldn't get from the astronomer?

Writing About the Poem

A Critical Response

Comparing Poems. In "On the Beach at Night" (page 343), the poet also uses the stars. In a brief essay, explain how that speaker's way of looking at the stars in that poem is different from the method used by the learned astronomer.

During the Civil War, Whitman spent several years as a volunteer assistant to the staffs of hospitals and medical field units of the Union army. Without an official position or title, he came to know the wounded as persons, rather than as casualties or "cases"—an experience that profoundly affected his life and work. His association with dying men, whom he tried to comfort with words, little gifts, and offers to write letters, brought a wider dimension of tragedy into his thinking. In his poetry, a gentle poignancy began to balance his bluster.

A Sight in Camp in the Daybreak Gray and Dim

A sight in camp in the daybreak gray and dim,
As from my tent I emerge so early sleepless,
As slow I walk in the cool fresh air the path near by the hospital
    tent,
Three forms I see on stretchers lying, brought out there untended
    lying,
5   Over each the blanket spread, ample brownish woolen blanket,
Gray and heavy blanket, folding, covering all.

Curious I halt and silent stand,
Then with light fingers I from the face of the nearest the first just
    lift the blanket;
Who are you elderly man so gaunt and grim, with well-grayed hair,
    and flesh all sunken about the eyes?
10   Who are you my dear comrade?

Then to the second I step—and who are you my child and darling?
Who are you sweet boy with cheeks yet blooming?

Then to the third—a face nor child nor old, very calm, as of
    beautiful yellow-white ivory;
Young man I think I know you—I think this face is the face of the
    Christ himself,
15   Dead and divine and brother of all, and here again he lies.

Burial place for the Civil War dead,
Fredericksburg, Virginia, May 12, 1861.

Photograph by Timothy O'Sullivan.

Responding to the Poem

Analyzing the Poem

Identifying Details

1. Find the details that identify the **setting** of the poem.
2. What is the sight that the speaker sees in the daybreak? Describe the three faces he sees.

Interpreting Meanings

3. The poem moves from anonymity to identity, from mere "forms," each hidden by an "ample brownish woolen blanket," to individuals with particular physical features. One of these strikes the speaker as having the features of "the Christ himself." Why, given the circumstances of this particular war, might the poet have seen this face on one of the dead soldiers?
4. The point of the poem is never openly stated; that is, it remains implicit. How would you make the poet's **message** explicit? Is there any significance to the fact that the "forms" who become persons in the eyes of the speaker are a trio? Explain.
5. Whitman's poetry, technically speaking, is all of a piece—a body of work easily identified by rolling **ca-**

dences, by **catalogues** of things and activities, and by self-assertive expostulations. What most distinguishes one of his poems from another lies in the **tone:** in modulations of voice that indicate his attitude toward different subjects, and in a kind of timing that suggests that the reader is overhearing a man's conversation with himself. How would you describe the tone of this poem? What are the main elements that support your description?

The Poems as a Whole

1. Describe your own response to Whitman's poetry. How do you respond to his **rhythms, diction, catalogues, subject matter,** and **tone?**
2. Whitman's biographer Paul Zweig says that Whitman had a genius for the single line, "the verbal snapshot." Find at least five **images** from the poems that you think make particularly unusual and evocative "verbal snapshots."
3. Suppose you had to select a line or word from Whitman's own works to characterize him. Which line or lines from these poems would you select, and why?

Writing About the Poems

A Creative Response

1. **Writing a Free-Verse Poem.** Write a free-verse poem, beginning with one of Whitman's openers.

> I was there . . .
> You will hardly know who I am . . .
> I hear America singing . . .
> On the beach . . .

In free verse, you are not restricted to the use of rhymes and regular meters, but you will want to use imagery and sound effects, including alliteration, parallel structures, and other forms of repetition.

A Critical Response

2. **Analyzing the Ideas in the Poems.** In a brief essay, show how Whitman expresses the following ideas in the poems you have read.

   a. The notion of "similitudes."
   b. The notion that the poet is "with us" or "is there."
   c. The notion that imagination can discover truths not necessarily accessible to reason.

3. **Explaining the Poet's Statement.** In an essay, explain how the poems you have read here can be used to illustrate and justify the following statement by Whitman.

> I know very well that my "Leaves" could not possibly have emerged . . . from . . . any other land than democratic America.
>
> —Walt Whitman

4. **Contrasting Whitman with a Fireside Poet.** In an essay, contrast Whitman's subject matter and style with those of one of the Fireside Poets (see pages 146–171). Use the following statement by Whitman as your thesis statement.

> For grounds for "Leaves of Grass," as a poem, I abandoned conventional themes, which do not appear in it; none of the stock ornamentation or choice plots of love or war, or high, exceptional personages of Old World song . . . no legend, or myth, or romance, nor euphemism, nor rhyme.
>
> —Walt Whitman

5. **Comparing Whitman to Taylor and Emerson.** You have seen that it was a habit of the Puritans to "read" nature for signs of divinity. You have also seen how the Transcendentalists "read" nature. In an essay, compare and contrast Whitman's "reading" of nature with that of Edward Taylor (see page 45) and Ralph Waldo Emerson (see page 187).

6. **Analyzing the Prose.** Some samples of Whitman's prose writings follow (see "Primary Sources"). In a brief essay, compare the prose with the poems you have read. Before you write, collect your data on a chart such as the following:

	Prose	Poetry
Tone		
Democratic feelings		
Use of list and catalogues		
Use of vigorous language		

Primary Sources
From Specimen Days

The following extracts are from Whitman's "memoranda book," which he called *Specimen Days*.

The Inauguration

"March 4, 1865—The President[1] very quietly rode down to the capitol in his own carriage, by himself, on a sharp trot, about noon, either because he wished to be on hand to sign bills, or to get rid of marching in line with the absurd procession, the muslin temple of liberty, and pasteboard monitor. I saw him on his return, at three o'clock, after the performance was over. He was in his plain two-horse barouche,[2] and looked very much worn and tired; the lines, indeed, of vast responsibilities, intricate questions, and demands of life and death, cut deeper than ever upon his dark brown face; yet all the old goodness, tenderness, sadness, and canny shrewd-

---

1. **The President:** Abraham Lincoln. He would be assassinated in April, just a month after Whitman wrote this.

2. **barouche** (bə·rōosh'): four-wheeled, horse-drawn carriage.

ness, underneath the furrows. (I never see that man without feeling that he is one to become personally attached to, for his combination of purest, heartiest tenderness, and native western form of manliness.) By his side sat his little boy, of ten years. There were no soldiers, only a lot of civilians on horseback, with huge yellow scarfs over their shoulders, riding around the carriage. (At the inauguration four years ago, he rode down and back again surrounded by a dense mass of armed cavalrymen eight deep, with drawn sabres; and there were sharpshooters stationed at every corner on the route.) I ought to make mention of the closing levee[3] of Saturday night last. Never before was such a compact jam in front of the White House—all the grounds filled, and away out to the spacious sidewalks. I was there, as I took a notion to go—was in the rush inside with the crowd—surged along the passage-ways, the blue and other rooms, and through the great east room. Crowds of country people, some very funny. Fine music from the Marine band, off in a side place. I saw Mr. Lincoln, dressed all in black, with white kid gloves and a claw-hammer coat, receiving, as in duty bound, shaking hands, looking very disconsolate, and as if he would give anything to be somewhere else."

The Real War Will Never Get in the Books

"And so goodbye to the war. I know not how it may have been, or may be, to others—to me the main interest I found (and still, on recollection, find), in the rank and file of the armies, both sides, and in those specimens amid the hospitals, and even the dead on the field. To me the points illustrating the latent personal character and eligibilities of these States, in the two or three millions of American young and middle-aged men, North and South, embodied in those armies—and especially the one-third or one-fourth of their number, stricken by wounds or disease at some time in the course of the contest—were of more significance even than the political interests involved. (As so much of a race depends on how it faces death, and how it stands personal anguish and sickness. As, in the glints of emotions under emergencies, and the indirect traits and asides in Plutarch, we get far profounder clues to the antique world than all its more formal history.)

"Future years will never know the seething hell and the black infernal background of countless minor scenes and interiors (not the official surface-courteousness of the Generals, not the few great battles) of the Secession war; and it is best they should not—the real war will never get in the books. In the mushy influences of current times, too, the fervid atmosphere and typical events of those years are in danger of being totally forgotten. I have at night watched by the side of a sick man in the hospital, one who could not live many hours. I have seen his eyes flash and burn as he raised himself and recurred to the cruelties on his surrendered brother, and mutilations of the corpse afterward. (See, in the preceding pages, the incident at Upperville—the seventeen killed as in the description, were left there on the ground. After they dropped dead, no one touched them—all were made sure of, however. The carcasses were left for the citizens to bury or not, as they chose.)

"Such was the war. It was not a quadrille[4] in a ballroom. Its interior history will not only never be written—its practicality, minutiae of deeds and passions, will never be even suggested. The actual soldier of 1862–'65, North and South, with all his ways, his incredible dauntlessness, habits, practices, tastes, language, his fierce friendship, his appetite, rankness, his superb strength and animality, lawless gait, and a hundred unnamed lights and shades of camp, I say, will never be written—perhaps must not and should not be.

"The preceding notes may furnish a few stray glimpses into that life, and into those lurid interiors, never to be fully conveyed to the future. The hospital part of the drama from '61 to '65, deserves indeed to be recorded. Of that many-threaded drama, with its sudden and strange surprises, its confounding of prophecies, its moments of despair, the dread of foreign interference, the interminable campaigns, the bloody battles, the mighty cumbrous and green armies, the drafts and bounties—the immense money expenditure, like a heavy-pouring constant rain—with, over the whole land, the last three years of the struggle, an unending, universal mourning-wail of women, parents, orphans—the marrow of the tragedy concentrated in those Army Hospitals—(it seemed sometimes as if the whole interest of the land, North and South, was one vast central hospital, and all the rest of the affair but flanges)—those forming the untold and unwritten history of the war—infinitely greater (like life's) than the few scraps and distortions that are ever told or written. Think how much, and of importance, will be—how much, civic and military, has already been—buried in the grave, in eternal darkness."

—Walt Whitman

---

3. **levee:** reception.

4. **quadrille** (kwə·dril′): a French dance for four couples.

Emily Dickinson (1830–1886)

A brief outline of Emily Dickinson's life reads like the plot of a story destined to become a legend. Once upon a time there was born to a religious and well-to-do New England family a daughter they named Emily. As a child she was lively, well-behaved, and obedient; she took pleasure in the busy household of which she was a part and in the seasonal games, parties, and outings of a village snowy cold in winter and brilliantly green and flowering in the summer.

At home she learned to cook and sew. When she was old enough, she was sent to a school where strict rules did not keep Emily and the other girls from displaying their high spirits as they enjoyed the entertainments of boarding-school life. Emily took part in these, but not always with as much enthusiasm as she might have. As she said many years later, something sad and reserved in her nature made her "a mourner among the children."

To her family and friends, everything about the young Dickinson seemed normal. No one doubted that she would grow gracefully into womanhood, make a good marriage, and settle into a village life of churchgoing, holiday gatherings, and neighborly harmony. But something happened in her life that has been the subject of speculation for decades.

When Dickinson was twenty-three years old, her father, who had become a United States congressman, took her with him to Washington, D.C., and then on to Philadelphia. The journey seems to have marked the start of the turning point of her existence. Her father may have taken her with him because she had fallen in love with someone she could never marry. This was a married lawyer, older than Emily, a man who would die that year of tuberculosis.

Whatever happened, it seems likely that in the course of the journey, Emily fell in love with someone else. This was Charles Wadsworth, who was also married and who was pastor of the Arch Street Presbyterian Church in Philadelphia. Letters to the Reverend Wadsworth show that Dickinson saw him as a "muse," someone who could help her with her feelings and her writings,

The only authentic photograph of Emily Dickinson. She is about seventeen years old here.

someone she could love passionately in her imagination.

But in 1861 Wadsworth took up a new assignment in San Francisco. His leaving seems to have caused the great crisis in Dickinson's life: "I sing," she wrote around this time, "as the boy does by the burying ground, because I am afraid."

The young woman quietly and abruptly withdrew from all social life except that involving her immediate family. Within a few years, dressed always in white—like the bride she would never become—she had gone into a state of seclusion. Her only activities were household tasks and the writing of poems that she either kept to herself or sent out as valentines, birthday greetings, or notes to go with the gift of a cherry pie or a batch of cookies.

Around the time that Wadsworth was preparing to move to California, Dickinson sent a few of her poems to Thomas Wentworth Higginson. (Her letter is on page 372.) As editor of the *Atlantic Monthly,* Higginson had been encouraging the work of younger poets. Higginson never became a substitute for Wadsworth, but he was kindly, and he did serve as a distant "teacher" and "mentor." Eventually, Dickinson gave up hope of ever finding a wider audience than her few friends and relatives. About 1861, she wrote "I'm Nobody! Who are you?/Are you—Nobody—too?"

During her lifetime, Emily Dickinson published no more than a handful of her typically brief poems. She seemed to lack all concern for an audience, and she went so far as to instruct her family to destroy any poems she might leave behind. Still, she saw to it that bundles of handwritten poems were carefully wrapped and put away in places where friendly, appreciative, and, finally, astonished eyes would find them. The poems were assembled and edited by different members of her family and friends; they were then published in installments so frequent that readers began to wonder when they would ever end.

Then, in 1955, a collection called *The Poems of Emily Dickinson* was finally made available. This was the devoted work of Thomas H. Johnson, a scholar who, unlike Dickinson's earlier editions, refrained from making "presentable" entities of poems whose punctuation, rhyme schemes, syntax, and word choice were frequently baffling.

As a result of Johnson's research, whole generations of readers who had grown up on Dickinson poems were faced with new versions of poems that sometimes "rescued" meanings from the tamperings of her first editors. And sometimes, these originals made emphases which, in the interests of "smoothness," those editors had overlooked. Yet, at other times, comparisons also revealed that Dickinson's first editors had often served her well—in spirit, if not always in the way demanded by scholarship.

Here is an example of how one stanza was changed by the original editors. Johnson's version is first:

We passed the School, where Children strove
At Recess—in the Ring—
We passed the Fields of Gazing Grain—
We passed the Setting Sun—

And this is how the early editor changed it:

We passed the school where children played
Their lessons scarcely done;
We passed the fields of gazing grain,
We passed the setting sun.

When Dickinson died at the age of fifty-six, hardly anyone knew that the strange, shy woman in their midst, the perpetual bride who never crossed her own doorstep, was a poet whose sharp and delicate voice would echo for generations to come. Some eighty years after her death, when the quarrels among her relatives who had inherited her manuscripts had died down and all of her work was finally published, she was recognized as one of the greatest poets America, and perhaps the world, had produced.

The self-imposed restrictions of Dickinson's actual life were more than matched by her ability to see the universal in the particular, and vice versa. She perceived the relationship between a drop of dew and a flood, between a desert and a grain of sand. These perceptions helped her to make metaphors that embraced experiences far beyond the limited compass of Amherst village life.

Yet, no matter how far her imagination ranged, Dickinson never denied those experiences their truth as aspects of a cycle of existence important in itself. When an Amherst neighbor's barn caught fire and lit up the sky, it was a real barn at the edge of a real pasture, and its loss became a matter of local anguish. But these local actualities did not prevent Dickinson from regarding the incident as a reminder of ultimate doom, of the Biblical prophecies of destruction of the earth by fire.

Behind the now famous legend of Emily Dickinson, and the plays and novels that have romanticized and sentimentalized her life is a woman whose genius made its own rules, followed its own commands, and found its own fulfillment. Tears for the once cheerful young woman whose supposed broken heart drove her into self-imposed exile do not apply. Emily Dickinson's life as a recluse was richer, more varied and—in the satisfactions that come with the exercise of God-given talent—even happier than the lives of those around her. In the prospect of history, we can see that the untold secret of Emily Dickinson's emotional life is secondary to the great secret of her genius, the one that destiny would not let her keep.

The Girl I Left Behind Me
by Eastman Johnson (1907). Oil.

Sotheby Parke-Bernet Galleries, Inc., New York.

The poems are reprinted here exactly as the poet wrote them. After Dickinson died, her sister Lavinia and a family friend took forty-nine packets of poems, all carefully tied with thread so that they looked like little "books," and worked for several years to prepare them for publication. In the process, the editors changed some of Dickinson's words and her unusual punctuation and capitalization. Only recently have we been able to read Dickinson's poems just as they appear in her manuscript. As you read, be alert to her use of dashes—they indicate a pause in thought or rhythm.

Here we have Emily Dickinson's version of the old story of unrequited love—or of love that is impossible because of the circumstances of the potential lovers. The substance of the poem is conflict: between will and emotion, between the thinking mind and the feeling heart. Which of these do you think is more powerful—the mind or the heart?

Heart! We will forget him!

Heart! We will forget him!
You and I—tonight!
You may forget the warmth he gave—
I will forget the light!

When you have done, pray tell me
That I may straight begin!
Haste! lest while you're lagging
I remember him!

Responding to the Poem

Analyzing the Poem

Identifying Details

1. Assume that the speaker is the mind. What does it order the heart to do?
2. Which word describes what "he" gave the heart? Which word describes what "he" gave the mind?
3. Exclamation points punctuate this little poem, as if the poem were saying, "Hurry up! We must get this over with!" Why is she in such a hurry?

Interpreting Meanings

4. Why do you think the heart is asked to take the lead in this situation?
5. How would you **paraphrase** what the speaker means by warmth and light?
6. If you wanted to forget someone, would you first try to forget his or her "warmth" or "light"? Why?
7. What feeling or **tone** would you say this lyric expresses?

Dickinson sent this poem along with three others to Higginson in 1862 to ask his advice about publication. It is one of several poems that show Dickinson's concern with fame. Could the feeling expressed here reflect the poet's sense of failure to win an audience for her poems? What kind of endeavor does she use as a concrete illustration of success? What might this illustration suggest about the way she thought of her own struggles with the world?

Success is counted sweetest

Success is counted sweetest
By those who ne'er succeed.
To comprehend a nectar°
Requires sorest° need.

5 Not one of all the purple Host°
Who took the Flag today
Can tell the definition
So clear of Victory

As he defeated—dying—
10 On whose forbidden ear
The distant strains of triumph
Burst agonized and clear!

3. **nectar:** once a name for the drink of the gods of classical literature, now a term applied to any delicious beverage.
4. **sorest:** as used here, "deepest" or "most extreme."
5. **Host:** an archaic word for an army.

Responding to the Poem

Analyzing the Poem

Identifying Details

1. According to the poet, who is likely to count success sweetest?
2. Purple is a color associated with blood shed in battle. What is the "purple Host" in line 5?
3. What example does the poet supply to illustrate her statement about those who know success best?
4. What **image** does the poet present in the last stanza?

Interpreting Meanings

5. Two kinds of desire are balanced in the first stanza. How would you define them? What is their relationship to each other?
6. Why is the ear "forbidden" in line 10?
7. Do you think the feeling expressed in this poem is valid? Is it common? Explain.
8. "Victory" is considered in military terms here. Can you think of other circumstances—perhaps a circumstance in your own life—in which the situation in this poem, and its conclusion, might be repeated?

Memorial to Robert Gould Shaw (detail) by Augustus Saint-Gaudens (1897). Bronze relief.

Boston Common, Boston, Massachusetts.

This poem is about choices and the mysterious instinct that leads each one of us to prefer certain things and cherish certain people above all others. In Emily Dickinson's view, this instinct has less to do with the discriminations of the mind than with the inclinations of that spiritual part of us that we call the soul. When you select friends, do you do it because of what your intellect tells you or because of what your soul prompts you to do?

The Soul selects her own Society

The Soul selects her own Society—
Then—shuts the Door—
To her divine Majority—
Present no more—

5   Unmoved—she notes the Chariots—pausing—
At her low Gate—
Unmoved—an Emperor be kneeling
Upon her Mat—

I've known her—from an ample nation—
10   Choose One—
Then—close the Valves of her attention—
Like Stone—

Responding to the Poem

Analyzing the Poem

Identifying Details

1. In the first stanza, what does the soul do?
2. What words have to be added to lines 3-4 to make a complete sentence?
3. What is the principal **image** of the second stanza?
4. In stanza 2, where does the poet sacrifice correct syntax in order to make her point? How would you put this stanza into conventional English?
5. In the last stanza, what does the soul do?

Interpreting Meanings

6. "Majority" as used here has at least two meanings. It could mean having reached the full legal age, or having "come into one's own"; or it could mean superiority (an obsolete usage); or it could mean "the greater part of something." What do you think it means? What kind of person does the adjective "divine" suggest?
7. Look up the word *valve* in a dictionary. Do you think the phrase "Valves of her attention" is drawn from the world of organic things (the valves of a clamshell)? Or from the world of mechanical things (the valve of a faucet)? What do you picture happening here?
8. The editors changed the word *valves* to the word *lids*. How does this change the **metaphor?** How does it change your **image** of what is happening?
9. Look carefully at the **meter** of lines 10 and 12. How does the rhythmical pattern of these lines differ from the corresponding lines in the first and second stanzas? What is the effect of this difference?
10. What advantage may lie in a "selection" as strict as this "soul" makes? What are its disadvantages?

Writing About the Poem

A Critical Response

Evaluating a Title. Dickinson did not give her poems titles. The editors titled this poem "Exclusion." In a brief essay, give your evaluation of this as the title of the poem. In what ways does it apply? Are there any ways in which it is too limiting? What titles would you suggest?

SLANT RHYME

Not long ago, rhyme was part of every poet's craft. Today it is still the most familiar aspect of sound in poetry; but rhyme has, over the years, fallen out of favor with many poets. This is because these poets feel that almost all the rhymes in English have been used over and over again. Some poets, as a solution, have abandoned rhyme altogether. Other poets, like Dickinson, use slant rhyme.

Exact rhyme is the use of two or more words with identical sounds to their accented syllables and all succeeding syllables. Exact rhymes are found in words like *cat/mat, tarnished/varnished,* and *dreary/weary.*

When the rhyming sound is *not* exact—as in *follow/fellow, morn/spurn,* or *mystery/mastery*—it is called **slant rhyme, off-rhyme,** or **half rhyme.** Slant rhyme makes many readers uncomfortable—in the way that a sharp or flat note on a piano would disturb a listener who wasn't expecting it.

Part of the shock value of Dickinson's poems comes from her use of slant rhyme. In "The Soul selects her own Society," only one perfect rhyme is used: *door/more.* How many slant rhymes can you find? What rhyming sounds were you expecting to hear?

Slant rhyme is a subtle use of sound. It is often used to force our attention onto particular words. For example, the last word in this poem, *stone,* stands out because it doesn't match exactly in sound the word *one.* Why is it important that the word *stone* be emphasized? To hear and understand the difference, imagine that Dickinson had ended her poem with the words "And be done."

Here is a poem that seems to have no message, nothing but an invitation to share an experience in which, step by step, we are guided by the poet's acute observations. Dickinson wrote many poems about nature, but they are always more than simple appreciations of natural beauty. If you had to select the most significant phrase in this poem, which would it be?

A Bird came down the Walk

A Bird came down the Walk—
He did not know I saw—
He bit an Angleworm in halves
And ate the fellow, raw,

5   And then he drank a Dew
From a convenient Grass—
And then hopped sidewise to the Wall
To let a Beetle pass—

He glanced with rapid eyes
10   That hurried all around—
They looked like frightened Beads, I thought—
He stirred his Velvet Head

Like one in danger, Cautious,
I offered him a Crumb
15   And he unrolled his feathers
And rowed him softer home—

Than Oars divide the Ocean,
Too silver for a seam—
Or Butterflies, off Banks of Noon
20   Leap, plashless° as they swim.

20. **plashless:** without splashing.

Responding to the Poem

Analyzing the Poem

Identifying Details

1. What various things does the bird do while the speaker watches?
2. What happens when the speaker tries to be friendly with the bird?
3. The poem is purely descriptive until the third stanza, when one daring **simile** lifts it into the realm of the imagination. What is that simile and what two distinct things is it comparing?
4. The two **figures of speech** in lines 15–20 are also strikingly unusual. What is the bird compared to here?
5. Describe how the actions of the bird in the air contrast with its actions on the ground.

Interpreting Meanings

6. Explain what you think the poet means by "unrolled," "rowed him," "Banks of Noon," and butterflies that "swim." What **images** do these words put in your mind?
7. What kind of ocean do you think would be "Too silver for a seam"?
8. Beginning with line 15, how many "o" sounds can you hear? What other sounds in lines 15–20 do you think help create a soft, "liquid" music?
9. Some readers feel that this poem dramatizes the unbridgeable distance between the human world and the natural world. Do you agree? Explain.
10. When this poem was first published, it was entitled "In the Garden." Do you think this title adds or subtracts from the impact of the poem? Explain.

Head of a Squawking Bird by Louis Agassiz Fuertes (early 20th century). Watercolor and ink on paper.

Sotheby Parke-Bernet Galleries, Inc., New York.

"Beauty is truth, truth beauty"—that is all
Ye know on earth, and all ye need to know.

These concluding lines of John Keats's "Ode on a Grecian Urn" are among the most famous in English poetry. Emily Dickinson knew them, of course, and here she presents her own version of the theme suggested by Keats. Before you read the poem, decide how you would define these two concepts: beauty and truth.

I died for Beauty—but was scarce

I died for Beauty—but was scarce
Adjusted in the Tomb
When One who died for Truth, was lain
In an adjoining Room—

5   He questioned softly "Why I failed?"
"For Beauty," I replied—
"And I—for Truth—Themself are One—
We Bretheren, are," He said—

And so, as Kinsmen, met at Night—
10   We talked between the Rooms—
Until the Moss had reached our lips—
And covered up—our names—

Responding to the Poem

Analyzing the Poem

Identifying Details

1. What situation does the speaker imagine happening in the first stanza? Where is this situation taking place?
2. What do the two speakers have in common that allows one of them to claim that they are "Bretheren," that is, brothers?
3. What event is described in the last two lines of the poem?
4. The **meter** in this poem is so regular and the rhyme arranged so like clockwork that only the use of two **slant rhymes** saves it from a sing-song quality. Where are the slant rhymes? What sound do you *expect* to hear?

Interpreting Meanings

5. How does the **slant rhyme** make the last word stand out? Do you think this is an important word? Why?
6. What are the "rooms" in lines 4 and 10?
7. In the third stanza, "the moss" is real, in the sense that it is a kind of green growth likely to be found in a cemetery, or in any other place of stones and shade. But "the moss" is also a **metaphor.** For what? What is significant in the fact that it covered up the speaker's names?
8. The incident recounted here is imaginary. Nevertheless, Dickinson seems to have a **message** in mind. What would you say that message is? Would you say that it is optimistic or pessimistic?
9. Poetry gives form to feelings. What feelings would you say are expressed in this poem?

written her name on a card, and put it under the shelter of a smaller envelope inclosed in the larger; and even this name was written—as if the shy writer wished to recede as far as possible from view—in pencil, not in ink. The name was Emily Dickinson. Enclosed with the letter were four poems. . . . I remember to have ventured on some criticism which she afterwards called 'surgery,' and on some questions, part of which she evaded, as will be seen, with a naïve skill such as the most experienced and worldly coquette might envy. Her second letter (received April 26, 1862) was as follows:—

Mr. Higginson,—Your kindness claimed earlier gratitude, but I was ill, and write to-day from my pillow.

Thank you for the surgery; it was not so painful as I supposed. I bring you others, as you ask. . . .

You asked how old I was? I made no verse, but one or two, until this winter, sir.

I had a terror since September, I could tell to none; and so I sing, as the boy does by the burying ground, because I am afraid.

You inquire my books. For poets, I have Keats, and Mr. and Mrs. Browning. For prose, Mr. Ruskin, Sir Thomas Browne, and the Revelations. I went to school, but in your manner of the phrase had no education. When a little girl, I had a friend who taught me Immortality; but venturing too near, himself, he never returned. Soon after my tutor died, and for several years my lexicon was my only companion. Then I found one more,[1] but he was not contented I be his scholar, so he left the land.

You ask of my companions. Hills, sir, and the sundown, and a dog large as myself, that my father bought me. They are better than beings because they know, but do not tell; and the noise in the pool at noon excels my piano.

I have a brother and sister; my mother does not care for thought, and father, too busy with his briefs to notice what we do. He buys me many books, but begs me not to read them, because he fears they joggle the mind. They are religious, except me. . . .

But I fear my story fatigues you. I would like to learn. Could you tell me how to grow, or is it unconveyed, like melody or witchcraft?

You speak of Mr. Whitman. I never read his book, but was told that it was disgraceful.

". . . I must soon have written to ask her for her picture, that I might form some impression of my enigmatical

1. Probably Charles Wadsworth.

Manuscript for "I died for Beauty."

Johnson Collection, Harvard University Library, Cambridge, Massachusetts.

correspondent. To this came the following reply, in July, 1862:

Could you believe me without? I had no portrait, now, but am small, like the wren; and my hair is bold like the chestnut bur; and my eyes, like the sherry in the glass, that the guest leaves. Would this do just as well?

It often alarms father. He says death might occur and he has molds [photographs] of all the rest, but has no mold of me. . . .' "

—from "Emily Dickinson,"
Thomas Wentworth Higginson

COMPARING AND CONTRASTING POEMS

Writing Assignment

Write a brief essay in which you compare and contrast Walt Whitman's "Song Number 6" and Emily Dickinson's "This quiet Dust Was Gentlemen and Ladies."

Background

When you **compare** two poems, you point out the ways in which they are alike; when you **contrast** them, you tell how they're different. But first you must be able to *see* the similarities and differences. The easiest way to approach this assignment is to focus on the **elements** of poetry: **subject, figurative language, imagery, sound effects, form,** and **theme.**

When you write a comparison and/or contrast essay, it's important to decide how you're going to present your ideas. Here are three possible ways to organize your essay:

1. **Similarities and differences.** You can discuss all of the ways the poems are similar, then go on to discuss all of the ways they're different.
2. **Block method.** You can discuss all of the elements of one poem first and then discuss all of the elements of the second poem.
3. **Point-by-point method.** You can discuss each element in both poems, one element at a time. For example, you can first deal with the subject in both poems, then figurative language in both poems, etc. Each element might take a single paragraph.

Prewriting

1. Read both poems carefully several times. At least one reading should be aloud so that you can listen to the poems' sound effects.

6

A child said *What is the grass?* fetching it to me with full hands;
How could I answer the child? I do not know what it is anymore than he.

I guess it must be the flag of my disposition, out of hopeful green stuff woven.
Or I guess it is the handkerchief of the Lord,
A scented gift and remembrancer designedly dropt,
Bearing the owner's name someway in the corners, that we may see and remark, and say *Whose?*

Or I guess the grass is itself a child, the produced babe of the vegetation. . . .

And now it seems to me the beautiful uncut hair of graves.

Tenderly will I use you curling grass,
It may be you transpire from the breasts of young men,
It may be if I had known them I would have loved them,
It may be you are from old people, or from offspring taken soon out of their mothers' laps,
And here you are the mothers' laps. . . .

What do you think has become of the young and old men?
And what do you think has become of the women and children?

They are alive and well somewhere,
The smallest sprout shows there is really no death,
And if ever there was it led forward life, and does not wait at the end to arrest it,
And ceased the moment life appeared.

All goes onward and outward, nothing collapses,
And to die is different from what anyone supposed, and luckier.

—from *Song of Myself,*
Walt Whitman

This quiet Dust was Gentlemen and Ladies
And Lads and Girls
Was Laughter and Ability and Sighing
And Frocks and Curls—
This passive place a Summer's nimble Mansion
Where Bloom and Bees
Fulfilled their Oriental Circuit
Then ceased, like these.

—Emily Dickinson

2. Now, for each poem, jot down answers to the following questions. Note line numbers that will serve as examples.

a. What is the poem's **subject?**
b. Does the poem use **figures of speech?** What is the effect of the figures?
c. Does the poem use **imagery?** What is the emotional effect of the imagery?
d. Does the poem use **meter** and **rhyme,** or is it written in **free verse?** What is the effect of the poem's sounds?
e. What is the poet's **tone**—or attitude toward the subject?
f. What is the poet's message, or **theme?**

3. Once you've answered these questions, organize your information into two lists: Similarities and Differences. For example:

Similarities	Differences
a. Both poems are about time and loss.	a. Whitman's poem is in free verse; Dickinson's conforms to meter and uses rhyme.
Etc.	Etc.

4. When you have finished your lists, think of a **thesis statement** which will summarize your main idea. Say whether you think the poems are more alike or more different. Here are two examples:

a. Whitman's poem and Dickinson's poem are totally different in form, but they are similar in subject and tone.
b. Whitman's poem about grass and Dickinson's poem about "quiet dust" may share the same subject matter, but they are as different as two poems can possibly be.

Writing

With your thesis statement and lists in front of you, you're ready to decide on your method of organization. Here is one possible plan:

Paragraph 1: Cite the titles and authors of the two poems. Include your thesis statement.
Paragraph 2: Discuss the poems' similarities. (If you have a lot to say, this may take more than one paragraph.)
Paragraph 3: Discuss the poems' differences. (Again, this may take more than one paragraph.)
Concluding paragraph: State your response to the two poems. Tell which one you liked better, and why.

Remember to cite specific examples (lines, words, or phrases) from the poems to support your points. Whenever you quote directly, use quotation marks, and check the text to make sure you've quoted accurately.

Revision and Proofreading

Don't hand in your first draft. Take the time to revise and proofread your essay, using the guidelines in the section at the back of this book, called **Writing About Literature.**

THE RISE OF REALISM
THE CIVIL WAR AND POST-WAR PERIOD

Shiloh by Edwin Dickinson (1940). Oil.   Commerce Bankshares, Kansas City.

UNIT SIX

A man said to the universe:
"Sir, I exist!"
"However," replied the universe,
"The fact has not created in me
"A sense of obligation."

—Stephen Crane

The Civil War

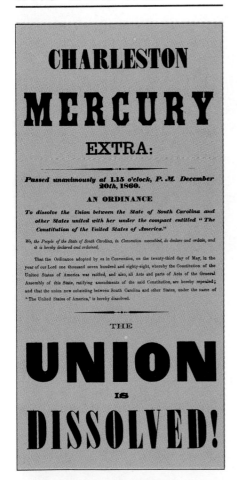

CHARLESTON

MERCURY

EXTRA:

Passed unanimously at 1.15 o'clock, P. M. December 20th, 1860.

AN ORDINANCE

To dissolve the Union between the State of South Carolina and other States united with her under the compact entitled " The Constitution of the United States of America."

We, the People of the State of South Carolina, in Convention assembled, do declare and ordain, and it is hereby declared and ordained,

That the Ordinance adopted by us in Convention, on the twenty-third day of May, in the year of our Lord one thousand seven hundred and eighty-eight, whereby the Constitution of the United States of America was ratified, and also, all Acts and parts of Acts of the General Assembly of this State, ratifying amendments of the said Constitution, are hereby repealed; and that the union now subsisting between South Carolina and other States, under the name of "The United States of America," is hereby dissolved.

THE

UNION

IS

DISSOLVED!

O n the evening of April 13, 1861, Walt Whitman went to the opera at the Academy of Music in Manhattan. After the opera, he was walking down Broadway toward Brooklyn when, as he later wrote, "I heard in the distance the loud cries of the newsboys, who came presently tearing and yelling up the street, rushing from side to side even more furiously than usual. I bought an extra and crossed to the Metropolitan Hotel . . . where the great lamps were still brightly blazing, and, with a crowd of others, who gathered impromptu, read the news, which was evidently authentic."

The news that Whitman and the others read so avidly was of the Confederate attack on Fort Sumter, the opening shots of the Civil War. Thus solemnly began, for one of the few American writers who would witness it firsthand, the greatest cataclysm in United States history.

Responses to the War: Idealism . . .

In Concord, Massachusetts, home of Emerson, Thoreau, Hawthorne, Bronson Alcott, and many other intellectual leaders of the nation, army volunteers met at the bridge that Emerson had immortalized in "The Concord Hymn" (page 196), his famous poem about the beginning of the American Revolution. Emerson had for decades warned that this day would come if slavery were not abolished. Now that the day had arrived, he was filled with patriotic fervor. "Now we have a country again," he had said when he heard of the outbreak of hostilities. He watched the Concord volunteers march to Boston, and he visited a navy yard, declaring that "sometimes gunpowder smells good."

Emerson had great respect for the Southern will to fight, and he suspected, quite rightly, that the war would not be over in a few months as some people had predicted. He expected setbacks during the war, but he would not let them dampen his faith in the Union cause. When the Concord volunteers returned a few months later from the Battle of Bull Run, defeated and disillusioned, many of them unwilling to re-enlist, Emerson maintained his conviction that the war must be pursued. "The war with its defeats and uncertainties," he wrote, "is immensely better than what we lately called the integrity of the Republic, as amputation is better than cancer."

Still, Northern disillusionment after a defeat so early in the war was strong. With a keen eye for the sad details, Whitman recorded the sense of gloomy defeat in Washington at the end of June when Northern troops returned from the disaster of Bull Run:

> The defeated troops commenced pouring into Washington over the Long Bridge at daylight on Monday, 22nd—day drizzling all through with rain. The Saturday and Sunday of the battle (20th, 21st) had been parched and hot to an extreme—the dust, the grime and smoke, in layers, sweated in followed by other layers again sweated in, absorbed by those excited souls—their clothes all saturated with the clay-powder filling the air—stirred up everywhere on the dry roads and trodden fields by the regiments, swarming wagons, artillery, etc.—all the men with this coating of murk and sweat and rain, now recoiling back, pouring over the Long Bridge—a horrible march of twenty miles, returning to Washington baffled, humiliated, panic-struck. Where are the vaunts, and the proud boasts with which you went forth? Where are your banners, and your bands of music, and your ropes to bring back your prisoners? Well, there isn't a band playing—and there isn't a flag but clings ashamed and lank to its staff.
>
> —Walt Whitman

New York's Seventh Regiment marching down Broadway on April 19, 1861, by Thomas Nast (1869). Oil.

Seventh Regiment Armory, New York City.

Late in 1862, Whitman traveled to Virginia to find his brother George, who had been wounded in battle. After George was nursed back to health, Whitman remained in Washington off and on, working part-time and serving as a volunteer hospital visitor, com-

In 1871, with a $10,000 contract to write for the Boston-based *Atlantic Monthly* magazine, Harte left San Francisco. He was at the height of his literary career. His cross-country trip with his family was covered by daily newspapers from California to Boston, where he was the guest of honor at a literary dinner.

The attention Harte received at this dinner—as well as his $10,000 contract—so irritated Mark Twain that it probably triggered the decline of the friendship between the two men. Twain became increasingly outspoken about Harte's failure to pay his debts, his rude behavior, and his heavy drinking.

Harte disappointed the editors of *The Atlantic Monthly,* for his creative ability was a thing of the past. With his marriage foundering, he left his family and accepted an appointment as a diplomat in Germany. By the time he died of cancer in 1902, in London, the public was reading novels by writers who made Harte seem tame and old-fashioned. Few people even remembered him as one of the shapers of the myth of the American West.

THE OUTCASTS OF POKER FLAT

As you read this story, look for the familiar Western "types." Which characters are still around, in almost every Western movie and TV show? Look also for Harte's method of characterization. The first two paragraphs, for example, don't contain a single direct reference to what kind of man John Oakhurst is. In spite of that, the reader gets a pretty clear picture of him. How does Harte manage this?

As Mr. John Oakhurst, gambler, stepped into the main street of Poker Flat on the morning of the twenty-third of November, 1850, he was conscious of a change in its moral atmosphere since the preceding night. Two or three men, conversing earnestly together, ceased as he approached and exchanged significant glances. There was a Sabbath lull in the air, which, in a settlement unused to Sabbath influences, looked ominous.

Mr. Oakhurst's calm, handsome face betrayed small concern in these indications. Whether he was conscious of any predisposing cause was another question. "I reckon they're after somebody," he reflected; "likely it's me." He returned to his pocket the handkerchief with which he had been whipping away the red dust of Poker Flat from his neat boots, and quietly discharged his mind of any further conjecture.

In point of fact, Poker Flat was "after somebody." It had lately suffered the loss of several thousand dollars, two valuable horses, and a prominent citizen. It was experiencing a spasm of virtuous reactions, quite as lawless and ungovernable as any of the acts that had provoked it. A secret committee had determined to rid the town of all improper persons. This was done permanently in regard to two men who were then hanging from the boughs of a sycamore in the gulch, and temporarily in the banishment of certain other objectionable characters. I regret to say that some of these were ladies. It is but due to the sex, however, to state that their impropriety was professional, and it was only in such easily established standards of evil that Poker Flat ventured to sit in judgment.

Mr. Oakhurst was right in supposing that he was included in this category. A few of the com-

When Guns Speak by Charles Russell (1911). Oil.

The Thomas Gilcrease Institute,
Tulsa, Oklahoma.

mittee had urged hanging him as a possible example and a sure method of reimbursing
themselves from his pockets of the sums he had
won from them. "It's agin justice," said Jim
Wheeler, "to let this yer young man from Roaring
Camp—an entire stranger—carry away our
money." But a crude sentiment of equity residing
in the breasts of those who had been fortunate
enough to win from Mr. Oakhurst overruled this
narrower local prejudice.

Mr. Oakhurst received his sentence with philosophic calmness, none the less coolly that he was
aware of the hesitation of his judges. He was too
much of a gambler not to accept fate. With him
life was at best an uncertain game, and he recognized the usual percentage in favor of the dealer.

A body of armed men accompanied the de-
ported wickedness of Poker Flat to the outskirts
of the settlement. Besides Mr. Oakhurst, who was
known to be a coolly desperate man, and for
whose intimidation the armed escort was intended, the expatriated party consisted of a young
woman familiarly known as "The Duchess"; another who had won the title of "Mother Shipton";[1] and "Uncle Billy," a suspected sluice
robber[2] and confirmed drunkard. The cavalcade
provoked no comments from the spectators, nor

---

1. **"Mother Shipton":** an English woman who was accused of
witchcraft.
2. **sluice robber:** Sluices were channels in which gold ore was
washed. Robbing a sluice was a low form of stealing.

was any word uttered by the escort. Only when the gulch which marked the uttermost limit of Poker Flat was reached, the leader spoke briefly and to the point. The exiles were forbidden to return at the peril of their lives.

As the escort disappeared, their pent-up feelings found vent in a few hysterical tears from the Duchess, some bad language from Mother Shipton, and a Parthian[3] volley of expletives from Uncle Billy. The philosophic Oakhurst alone remained silent. He listened calmly to Mother Shipton's desire to cut somebody's heart out, to the repeated statements of the Duchess that she would die in the road, and to the alarming oaths that seemed to be bumped out of Uncle Billy as he rode forward. With the easy good humor characteristic of his class, he insisted upon exchanging his own riding horse, "Five-Spot," for the sorry mule which the Duchess rode. But even this act did not draw the party into any closer sympathy. The young woman adjusted her somewhat draggled plumes with a feeble, faded coquetry; Mother Shipton eyed the possessor of Five-Spot with malevolence, and Uncle Billy included the whole party in one sweeping anathema.

The road to Sandy Bar—a camp that, not having as yet experienced the regenerating influences of Poker Flat, consequently seemed to offer some invitation to the emigrants—lay over a steep mountain range. It was distant a day's severe travel. In that advanced season the party soon passed out of the moist, temperate regions of the foothills into the dry, cold, bracing air of the Sierras. The trail was narrow and difficult. At noon the Duchess, rolling out of her saddle upon the ground, declared her intention of going no farther, and the party halted.

The spot was singularly wild and impressive. A wooded amphitheater, surrounded on three sides by precipitous cliffs of naked granite, sloped gently toward the crest of another precipice that overlooked the valley. It was, undoubtedly, the most suitable spot for a camp, had camping been advisable. But Mr. Oakhurst knew that scarcely half the journey to Sandy Bar was accomplished, and the party were not equipped or provisioned for delay. This fact he pointed out to his companions curtly, with a philosophic commentary on the

folly of "throwing up their hand before the game was played out." But they were furnished with liquor, which in this emergency stood them in place of food, fuel, rest, and prescience. In spite of his remonstrances, it was not long before they were more or less under its influence. Uncle Billy passed rapidly from a bellicose state into one of stupor, the Duchess became maudlin, and Mother Shipton snored. Mr. Oakhurst alone remained erect, leaning against a rock, calmly surveying them.

Mr. Oakhurst did not drink. It interfered with a profession which required coolness, impassiveness, and presence of mind, and, in his own language, he "couldn't afford it." As he gazed at his recumbent fellow exiles, the loneliness begotten of his pariah[4] trade, his habits of life, his very vices, for the first time, seriously oppressed him. He bestirred himself in dusting his black clothes, washing his hands and face, and other acts characteristic of his studiously neat habits, and for a moment forgot his annoyance. The thought of deserting his weaker and more pitiable companions never perhaps occurred to him. Yet he could not help feeling the want of that excitement which, singularly enough, was most conducive to that calm equanimity for which he was notorious. He looked at the gloomy walls that rose a thousand feet sheer above the circling pines around him, at the sky ominously clouded, at the valley below, already deepening into shadow; and, doing so, suddenly he heard his own name called.

A horseman slowly ascended the trail. In the fresh, open face of the newcomer Mr. Oakhurst recognized Tom Simson, otherwise known as "The Innocent," of Sandy Bar. He had met him some months before over a "little game" and had, with perfect equanimity, won the entire fortune—amounting to some forty dollars—of that guileless youth. After the game was finished, Mr. Oakhurst drew the youthful speculator behind the door and thus addressed him: "Tommy, you're a good little man, but you can't gamble worth a cent. Don't try it over again." He then handed him his money back, pushed him gently from the room, and so made a devoted slave of Tom Simson.

There was a remembrance of this in his boyish and enthusiastic greeting of Mr. Oakhurst. He had

---

3. **Parthian:** In ancient times, the Parthians were said to have turned about during their retreats and fired arrows at their enemy.

4. **pariah:** outcast, despised.

started, he said, to go to Poker Flat to seek his fortune. "Alone?" No, not exactly alone; in fact (a giggle), he had run away with Piney Woods. Didn't Mr. Oakhurst remember Piney? She that used to wait on the table at the Temperance House? They had been engaged a long time, but old Jake Woods had objected, and so they had run away, and were going to Poker Flat to be married, and here they were. And they were tired out, and how lucky it was they had found a place to camp, and company. All this the Innocent delivered rapidly, while Piney, a stout, comely damsel of fifteen, emerged from behind the pine tree, where she had been blushing unseen, and rode to the side of her lover.

Mr. Oakhurst seldom troubled himself with sentiment, still less with propriety; but he had a vague idea that the situation was not fortunate. He retained, however, his presence of mind sufficiently to kick Uncle Billy, who was about to say something, and Uncle Billy was sober enough to recognize in Mr. Oakhurst's kick a superior power that would not bear trifling. He then endeavored to dissuade Tom Simson from delaying further, but in vain. He even pointed out the fact that there was no provision, nor means of making a camp. But, unluckily, the Innocent met this objection by assuring the party that he was provided with an extra mule loaded with provisions, and by the discovery of a rude attempt at a log house near the trail. "Piney can stay with Mrs. Oakhurst," said the Innocent, pointing to the Duchess, "and I can shift for myself."

Nothing but Mr. Oakhurst's admonishing foot saved Uncle Billy from bursting into a roar of laughter. As it was, he felt compelled to retire up the canyon until he could recover his gravity. There he confided the joke to the tall pine trees, with many slaps of his leg, contortions of his face, and the usual profanity. But when he returned to the party, he found them seated by a fire—for the air had grown strangely chill and the sky overcast—in apparently amicable conversation. Piney was actually talking in an impulsive girlish fashion to the Duchess, who was listening with an interest and animation she had not shown for many days. The Innocent was holding forth, apparently with equal effect, to Mr. Oakhurst and Mother Shipton, who was actually relaxing into amiability. "Is this yer a d—d[5] picnic?" said Uncle Billy, with inward

scorn, as he surveyed the sylvan group, the glancing firelight, and the tethered animals in the foreground. Suddenly an idea mingled with the alcoholic fumes that disturbed his brain. It was apparently of a jocular nature, for he felt impelled to slap his leg again and cram his fist into his mouth.

As the shadows crept slowly up the mountain, a slight breeze rocked the tops of the pine trees and moaned through their long and gloomy aisles. The ruined cabin, patched and covered with pine boughs, was set apart for the ladies. As the lovers parted, they unaffectedly exchanged a kiss, so honest and sincere that it might have been heard above the swaying pines. The frail Duchess and the malevolent Mother Shipton were probably too stunned to remark upon this last evidence of simplicity, and so turned without a word to the hut. The fire was replenished, the men lay down before the door, and in a few minutes were asleep.

Mr. Oakhurst was a light sleeper. Toward morning he awoke benumbed and cold. As he stirred the dying fire, the wind, which was now blowing strongly, brought to his cheek that which caused the blood to leave it—snow!

He started to his feet with the intention of awakening the sleepers, for there was no time to lose. But, turning to where Uncle Billy had been lying, he found him gone. A suspicion leaped to his brain, and a curse to his lips. He ran to the spot where the mules had been tethered—they were no longer there. The tracks were already rapidly disappearing in the snow.

The momentary excitement brought Mr. Oakhurst back to the fire with his usual calm. He did not waken the sleepers. The Innocent slumbered peacefully, with a smile on his good-humored, freckled face; the virgin Piney slept beside her frailer sisters as sweetly as though attended by celestial guardians; and Mr. Oakhurst, drawing his blanket over his shoulders, stroked his mustaches and waited for the dawn. It came slowly in a whirly mist of snowflakes that dazzled and confused the eye. What could be seen of the landscape appeared magically changed. He looked over the valley and summed up the present and future in two words, "Snowed in!"

A careful inventory of the provisions, which, fortunately for the party, had been stored within the hut, and so escaped the felonious fingers of Uncle Billy, disclosed the fact that with care and prudence, they might last ten days longer. "That

---

5. Harte himself omitted the expletive.

fate. Neither spoke, but Piney, accepting the position of the stronger, drew near and placed her arm around the Duchess's waist. They kept this attitude for the rest of the day. That night the storm reached its greatest fury and, rending asunder the protecting vines, invaded the very hut.

Toward morning they found themselves unable to feed the fire, which gradually died away. As the embers slowly blackened, the Duchess crept closer to Piney and broke the silence of many hours: "Piney, can you pray?" "No, dear," said Piney simply. The Duchess, without knowing exactly why, felt relieved and putting her head upon Piney's shoulder, spoke no more. And so reclining, the younger and purer pillowing the head of her soiled sister upon her virgin breast, they fell asleep.

The wind lulled as if it feared to waken them. Feathery drifts of snow, shaken from the long pine boughs, flew like white-winged birds and settled about them as they slept. The moon through the rifted clouds looked down upon what had been the camp. But all human stain, all trace of earthly travail, was hidden beneath the spotless mantle mercifully flung from above.

They slept all that day and the next, nor did they waken when voices and footsteps broke the silence of the camp. And when pitying fingers brushed the snow from their wan faces, you could scarcely have told from the equal peace that dwelt upon them which was she that had sinned. Even the law of Poker Flat recognized this and turned away, leaving them still locked in each other's arms.

But at the head of the gulch, on one of the largest pine trees, they found the deuce of clubs[11] pinned to the bark with a bowie knife. It bore the following, written in pencil in a firm hand:

> BENEATH THIS TREE
> LIES THE BODY
> OF
> JOHN OAKHURST,
> WHO STRUCK A STREAK OF BAD LUCK
> ON THE 23RD OF NOVEMBER, 1850,
> AND
> HANDED IN HIS CHECKS
> ON THE 7TH DECEMBER, 1850.

And pulseless and cold, with a Derringer by his side and a bullet in his heart, though still calm as in life, beneath the snow lay he who was at once the strongest and yet the weakest of the outcasts of Poker Flat.

---

11. **deuce of clubs:** the two of clubs, the card with the lowest value in the deck.

Responding to the Story

Analyzing the Story

Identifying Facts

1. Who are the outcasts of Poker Flat?
2. Why are Oakhurst and the others forced to leave town?
3. Who are Tom Simson and Piney Woods, and where are they going? Why is Tom so glad to run into Oakhurst?
4. What **complications** result to make the characters' problem difficult to resolve?
5. What has happened to each character by the story's end? Which two might still be alive?

Interpreting Meanings

6. When Piney first reveals herself to the group, Oakhurst has a vague idea that the situation is not "fortunate." What might be unfortunate about having Piney and Tom join them? What is Uncle Billy's reaction?
7. Why doesn't Oakhurst want Piney and Tom to know what Uncle Billy has done?
8. How does each of the outcasts—except for Uncle Billy—change in the course of the story? What causes the changes? What early clues **foreshadow** the fact that Billy might be the one character not to undergo a change?

9. Why does Oakhurst leave the camp with Tom? In what ways is he the strongest of the outcasts? In what way might he be considered the weakest?
10. What does this story reveal about the power of innocence? Do you find what it says believable?
11. How would you state the **theme** of this story? Do you think the story is strongly moralistic? Explain.
12. If this story were being told by a contemporary realist, how do you think it might change?
13. How do you feel about Harte's depiction of the women characters in this story? Can you find any attitudes toward the women that might be labeled sexist today?

Writing About the Story

A Creative Response

1. **Casting a Film.** Imagine that you are the producer of a movie version of "The Outcasts of Poker Flat," being made either for TV or for theatrical release. Imagine further that you have no financial restrictions and can hire any actors you want. Write a list naming the actors you would hire for parts in the story. Then, for each of your choices, write a brief paragraph explaining why that actor would be right for the role.

A Critical Response

2. **Comparing Depictions of the Frontier.** In a library, find another book of fiction about the Old West by one of the following twentieth-century writers. Then write a report in which you compare that writer's characters and themes with Harte's. Does the contemporary writer also perpetuate myths about the Old West? Or is the other story more realistic?

   a. Louis L'Amour
   b. Jack Schaefer
   c. Walter van Tilburg Clark
   d. Dorothy Johnson

Analyzing Language and Style

Euphemisms and Comic Irony

Harte's style is marked by two characteristics: (1) **euphemism**—the use of language to conceal an unpleasant reality, and (2) **irony,** the use of language to contrast appearances with reality. Both stylistic devices account for the humor in the story.

1. "It is but due to the sex, however, to state that their impropriety was professional. . . ." (Page 394)

   a. What does Harte mean by *professional*?
   b. What *is* their "impropriety"?

Poker game (c. 1890).

2. ". . . Sandy Bar—a camp that, not having as yet experienced the regenerating influences of Poker Flat. . . ." (Page 396)

   a. What does *regenerating* mean, and how is the word usually used?
   b. What does Harte really mean here?

3. "Mr. Oakhurst did not drink. It interfered with a profession which required coolness. . . ." (Page 396)

   a. What do we usually mean when we refer to a *profession*?
   b. What is Mr. Oakhurst's real profession?

4. ". . . the virgin Piney slept beside her frailer sisters as sweetly as though attended by celestial guardians. . . ." (Page 397)

   a. In what ways are Mother Shipton and the duchess "frailer" than Piney?
   b. What is ironic about the use of the phrase "celestial guardians" here?

5. ". . . the Duchess directed Piney in the rearrangement of the interior with a taste and tact that opened the blue eyes of that provincial maiden. . . ." (Page 398)

   a. What is actually taking place here?
   b. Why is this description of the Duchess's interior decorating humorously ironic?

6. ". . . something that reddened her [the Duchess's] cheeks through their professional tint. . . ." (Page 398)

   a. What does Harte mean by "professional tint"?
   b. Why is it "professional"?

FROM LIFE ON THE MISSISSIPPI

In *Life on the Mississippi*, Twain offers a sometimes humorous account of his boyhood days in Hannibal, Missouri, and of his adventures as an apprentice pilot on a steamboat on the great river. As a youth, Twain was so fascinated by the riverboats that he persuaded Horace Bixby, the locally famous pilot of the *Paul Jones,* to teach him how to navigate the river between New Orleans and St. Louis (a distance of about seven hundred miles) for five hundred dollars. In the following excerpt, taken from an early chapter called "Frescos from the Past," Twain provides a colorful portrait of life on the river by incorporating a passage intended as part of *The Adventures of Huckleberry Finn,* a novel which he had in progress at the time. The story is told in dialect. For greatest pleasure, you should read it aloud, or listen to an oral reading.

Frescos from the Past: The Raftsmen

Seventy years elapsed after the exploration before the river's borders had a white population worth considering; and nearly fifty more before the river had a commerce. Between La Salle's opening of the river and the time when it may be said to have become the vehicle of anything like a regular and active commerce, seven sovereigns had occupied the throne of England, America had become an independent nation, Louis XIV and Louis XV had rotted and died,[1] the French monarchy had gone down in the red tempest of the Revolution, and Napoleon[2] was a name that was beginning to be talked about. Truly, there were snails in those days.

The river's earliest commerce was in great barges—keelboats, broadhorns.[3] They floated and sailed from the upper rivers to New Orleans, changed cargoes there, and were tediously warped and poled back by hand. A voyage down and back sometimes occupied nine months. In time this commerce increased until it gave employment to hordes of rough and hardy men; rude, uneducated, brave, suffering terrific hardships with sailor-like stoicism; heavy drinkers, coarse frolickers in moral sties like the Natchez-under-the-hill of that day, heavy fighters, reckless fellows, every one, elephantinely jolly, foul-witted, profane, prodigal of their money, bankrupt at the end of the trip, fond of barbaric finery, prodigious braggarts; yet, in the main, honest, trustworthy, faithful to promises and duty, and often picturesquely magnanimous.

By and by the steamboat intruded. Then, for fifteen or twenty years, these men continued to run their keelboats downstream, and the steamers did all of the upstream business, the keelboatmen selling their boats in New Orleans, and returning home as deck-passengers in the steamers.

But after a while the steamboats so increased in number and in speed that they were able to absorb the entire commerce; and then keelboating died a permanent death. The keelboatman became a deckhand, or a mate, or a pilot on the steamer; and when steamer-berths were not open to him, he took a berth on a Pittsburgh coal-flat, or on a pine raft constructed in the forests up toward the sources of the Mississippi.

In the heyday of the steamboating prosperity, the river from end to end was flaked with coal-fleets and timber-rafts, all managed by hand, and employing hosts of the rough characters whom I have been trying to describe. I remember the annual processions of mighty rafts that used to glide by Hannibal when I was a boy—an acre or so of

---

1. **Louis XIV . . . died:** Louis XIV and Louis XV ruled France from 1643 to 1774.
2. **Napoleon:** Napoleon Bonaparte (1769–1821), conquering general and Emperor of France from 1804 to 1814.
3. **broadhorns:** river barges without keels.

white, sweet-smelling boards in each raft, a crew of two dozen men or more, three or four wigwams scattered about the raft's vast level space for storm-quarters—and I remember the rude ways and the tremendous talk of their big crews, the ex-keelboatmen and their admiringly patterning successors; for we used to swim out a quarter or a third of a mile and get on these rafts and have a ride.

By way of illustrating keelboat talk and manners, and that now departed and hardly remembered raft life, I will throw in, in this place, a chapter from a book which I have been working at, by fits and starts, during the past five or six years, and may possibly finish in the course of five or six more. The book is a story which details some passages in the life of an ignorant village boy, Huck Finn, son of the town drunkard of my time out West, there. He has run away from his persecuting father, and from a persecuting good widow who wishes to make a nice, truth-telling, respectable boy of him; and with him a slave of the widow's has also escaped. They have found a fragment of a lumber-raft (it is high water and dead summer-time), and are floating down the river by night, and hiding in the willows by day—bound for Cairo,[4] whence the Negro will seek freedom in the heart of the free states. But, in a fog, they pass Cairo without knowing it. By and by they begin to suspect the truth, and Huck Finn is persuaded to end the dismal suspense by swimming down to a huge raft which they have seen in the distance ahead of them, creeping aboard under cover of the darkness, and gathering the needed information by eavesdropping:

But you know a young person can't wait very well when he is impatient to find a thing out. We talked it over, and by and by Jim said it was such a black night, now, that it wouldn't be no risk to swim down to the big raft and crawl aboard and listen—they would talk about Cairo, because they would be calculating to go ashore there for a spree, maybe; or anyway they would send boats ashore to buy whiskey or fresh meat or something. Jim has a wonderful level head . . . he could most always start a good plan when you wanted one.

I stood up and shook my rags off and jumped into the river, and struck out for the raft's light.

By and by, when I got down nearly to her, I eased up and went slow and cautious. But everything was all right—nobody at the sweeps. So I swum down along the raft till I was most abreast the campfire in the middle, then I crawled aboard and inched along and got in among some bundles of shingles on the weather side of the fire. There was thirteen men there—they was the watch on deck of course. And a mighty rough-looking lot, too. They had a jug, and tin cups, and they kept the jug moving. One man was singing—roaring, you may say; and it wasn't a nice song—for a parlor, anyway. He roared through his nose, and strung out the last word of every line very long. When he was done they all fetched a kind of Injun war-whoop, and then another was sung. It begun:

"There was a woman in our towdn,
  In our towdn did dwed'l [dwell],
She loved her husband dear-i-lee,
  But another man twyste as wed'l.

"Singing too, riloo, riloo, riloo,
  Ri-too, riloo, rilay - - - e,
She loved her husband dear-i-lee,
  But another man twyste as wed'l."

And so on—fourteen verses. It was kind of poor, and when he was going to start on the next verse one of them said it was the tune the old cow died on; and another one said: "Oh, give us a rest!" And another one told him to take a walk. They made fun of him till he got mad and jumped up and began to cuss the crowd, and said he could lam[5] any thief in the lot.

They was all about to make a break for him, but the biggest man there jumped up and says:

"Set whar you are, gentlemen. Leave him to me; he's my meat."

Then he jumped up in the air three times, and cracked his heels together every time. He flung off a buckskin coat that was all hung with fringes, and says, "You lay thar tell the chawin-up's done"; and flung his hat down, which was all over ribbons, and says, "You lay thar tell his sufferin's is over."

Then he jumped up in the air and cracked his heels together again, and shouted out:

"Whoo-oop! I'm the old original iron-jawed, brass-mounted, copper-bellied corpse-maker from

---

4. **Cairo:** town in Southern Illinois, the destination in free territory of many runaway slaves.

5. **lam:** beat, thrash.

The Jolly Flatboatmen in Port by George Caleb Bingham (1857). Oil.

St. Louis Art Museum.

the wilds of Arkansaw! Look at me! I'm the man they call Sudden Death and General Desolation! Sired by a hurricane, dam'd[6] by an earthquake, half-brother to the cholera, nearly related to the smallpox on the mother's side! Look at me! I take nineteen alligators and a bar'l of whiskey for breakfast when I'm in robust health, and a bushel of rattlesnakes and a dead body when I'm ailing. I split the everlasting rocks with my glance, and I squench the thunder when I speak! Whoo-oop! Stand back and give me room according to my strength! Blood's my natural drink, and the wails of the dying is music to my ear. Cast your eye on me, gentlemen! and lay low and hold your breath, for I'm 'bout to turn myself loose!

All the time he was getting this off, he was shaking his head and looking fierce, and kind of swelling around in a little circle, tucking up his wristbands, and now and then straightening up and beating his breast with his fist, saying, "Look at me, gentlemen!" When he got through, he jumped up and cracked his heels together three times, and let off a roaring "Whoo-oop! I'm the bloodiest son of a wildcat that lives!"

Then the man that had started the row tilted his old slouch hat down over his right eye; then he bent stooping forward, with his back sagged and his south end sticking out far, and his fists a-shoving out and drawing in in front of him, and so went around in a little circle about three times, swelling himself up and breathing hard. Then he straightened, and jumped up and cracked his heels together three times before he lit[7] again (that made them cheer), and he began to shout like this:

"Whoo-oop! bow your neck and spread, for the kingdom of sorrow's a-coming! Hold me down to the earth, for I feel my powers a-working! Whoo-oop! I'm a child of sin, *don't* let me get a start! Smoked glass, here, for all! Don't attempt to look at me with the naked eye, gentlemen! When I'm playing I use the meridians of longitude and parallels of latitude for a seine,[8] and drag the Atlantic Ocean for whales! I scratch my head with the lightning and purr myself to sleep with the thunder! When I'm cold, I bile the Gulf of Mexico and bathe in it; when I'm hot I fan myself with an equinoctial storm; when I'm thirsty I reach up and suck a cloud dry like a sponge; when I range the

---

6. **dam'd:** mothered.
7. **lit:** landed.
8. **seine** (sān): a large fishing net.

earth hungry, famine follows in my tracks! Whoo-oop! Bow your neck and spread! I put my hand on the sun's face and make it night in the earth; I bite a piece out of the moon and hurry the seasons; I shake myself and crumble the mountains! Contemplate me through leather—*don't* use the naked eye! I'm the man with a petrified heart and biler-iron bowels! The massacre of isolated communities is the pastime of my idle moments, the destruction of nationalities the serious business of my life! The boundless vastness of the great American desert is my inclosed property, and I bury my dead on my own premises!'' He jumped up and cracked his heels together three times before he lit (they cheered him again), and as he come down he shouted out: ''Whoo-oop! Bow your neck and spread, for the Pet Child of Calamity's a-coming!''

Then the other one went to swelling around and blowing again—the first one—the one they called Bob; next, the Child of Calamity chipped in again, bigger than ever; then they both got at it at the same time, swelling round and round each other and punching their fists into each other's faces, and whooping and jawing . . . , then Bob called the Child names, and the Child called him names back again; next, Bob called him a heap rougher names, and the Child came back at him with the very worst kind of language; next, Bob kicked the Child's hat off, and the Child picked it up and kicked Bob's ribbony hat about six foot; Bob went and got it and said never mind, this warn't going to be the last of this thing, because he was a man that never forgot and never forgive, and so the Child better look out, for there was a time a-coming, just as sure as he was a living man, that he would have to answer to him with the best blood in his body. The Child said no man was willinger than he for that time to come, and he would cross his path again, for he could never rest till he had waded in his blood, for such was his nature, though he was sparing him now on account of his family, if he had one.

Both of them was edging away in different directions, growling and shaking their heads and going on about what they was going to do; but a little black-whiskered chap skipped up and says:

''Come back here, you couple of chicken-livered cowards, and I'll thrash the two of ye!''

And he done it, too. He snatched them, he jerked them this way and that, he booted them around, he knocked them sprawling faster than they could get up. Why, it warn't two minutes till

they begged like dogs—and how the other lot did yell and laugh and clap their hands all the way through, and shout, ''Sail in, Corpse-Maker!'' ''Hi! At him again, Child of Calamity!'' ''Bully for you, little Davy!'' Well, it was a perfect powwow for a while. Bob and the Child had red noses and black eyes when they got through. Little Davy made them own up that they was sneaks and cowards and not fit to eat with a dog . . . ; then Bob and the Child shook hands with each other, very solemn, and said they had always respected each other and was willing to let bygones be bygones. So then they washed their faces in the river; and just then there was a loud order to stand by for a crossing, and some of them went forward to man the sweeps there, and the rest went aft to handle the after sweeps.

I lay still for fifteen minutes, and had a smoke out of a pipe that one of them left in reach; then the crossing was finished, and they stumped back and had a drink around and went to talking and singing again. Next they got out an old fiddle, and one played, and another patted juba,[9] and the rest turned themselves loose on a regular old-fashioned keelboat breakdown. They couldn't keep that up very long without getting winded, so by and by they settled around the jug again.

They sung ''Jolly, Jolly Raftsman's the Life for Me,'' with a rousing chorus, and then they got to talking about differences betwixt hogs, and their different kind of habits; and next about women and their different ways; and next about the ways to put out houses that was afire; and next about what ought to be done with the Indians; and next about what a king had to do, and how much he got; and next about how to make cats fight; and next about what to do when a man has fits; and next about differences betwixt clear-water rivers and muddy-water ones. The man they called Ed said the muddy Mississippi water was wholesomer to drink than the clear water of the Ohio; he said if you let a pint of this yaller Mississippi water settle, you would have about a half to three-quarters of an inch of mud in the bottom, according to the stage of the river, and then it warn't no better than Ohio water—what you wanted to do was to keep it stirred up—and when the river was low, keep mud on hand to put in and thicken the water up the way it ought to be.

---

9. **juba:** a lively Southern black dance, accompanied by hand clapping.

The Child of Calamity said that was so; he said there was nutritiousness in the mud, and a man that drunk Mississippi water could grow corn in his stomach if he wanted to. He says:

"You look at the graveyards; that tells the tale. Trees won't grow worth shucks in a Cincinnati graveyard, but in a Sent Louis graveyard they grow upwards of eight hundred foot high. It's all on account of the water the people drunk before they laid up. A Cincinnati corpse don't richen a soil any."

And they talked about how Ohio water didn't like to mix with Mississippi water. Ed said if you take the Mississippi on a rise when the Ohio is low, you'll find a wide band of clear water all the way down the east side of the Mississippi for a hundred mile or more, and the minute you get out a quarter of a mile from shore and pass the line, it is all thick and yaller the rest of the way across. Then they talked about how to keep tobacco from getting moldy, and from that they went into ghosts and told about a lot that other folks had seen; but Ed says:

"Why don't you tell something that you've seen yourselves? Now let me have a say. Five years ago I was on a raft as big as this, and right along here it was a bright moonshiny night, and I was on watch and boss of the stabboard oar forrard, and one of my pards was a man named Dick Allbright, and he come along to where I was sitting, forrard[10]—gaping and stretching, he was—and stopped down on the edge of the raft and washed his face in the river, and come and set down by me and got out his pipe, and had just got it filled, when he looks up and says:

"'Why looky-here,' he says, 'ain't that Buck Miller's place, over yander in the bend?'

"'Yes,' says I, 'it is—why?' He laid his pipe down and leaned his head on his hand, and says:

"'I thought we'd be furder down.' I says:

"'I thought it, too, when I went off watch'—we was standing six hours on and six off—'but the boys told me,' I says, 'that the raft didn't seem to hardly move, for the last hour,' says I, 'though she's a-slipping along all right now,' says I. He give a kind of a groan, and says:

"'I've seed a raft act so before, along here,' he says, "pears to me the current has most quit above the head of this bend durin' the last two years,' he says.

---

10. **stabboard . . . forrard:** *starboard* (right side) and *forward*.

"Well, he raised up two or three times, and looked away off and around on the water. That started me at it, too. A body is always doing what he sees somebody else doing, though there mayn't be no sense in it. Pretty soon I see a black something floating on the water away off to stabboard and quartering behind us. I see he was looking at it, too. I says:

"'What's that?' He says, sort of pettish:

"'Tain't nothing but an old empty bar'l.'

"'An empty bar'l!' says I, 'why,' says I, 'a spyglass is a fool to *your* eyes. How can you tell it's an empty bar'l?' He says:

"'I don't know; I reckon it ain't a bar'l, but I thought it might be,' says he.

"'Yes,' I says, 'so it might be, and it might be anything else, too; a body can't tell nothing about it, such a distance as that,' I says.

"We hadn't nothing else to do, so we kept on watching it. By and by I says:

"'Why, looky-here, Dick Allbright, that thing's a-gaining on us, I believe.'

"He never said nothing. The thing gained and gained, and I judged it must be a dog that was about tired out. Well, we swung down into the crossing, and the thing floated across the bright streak of the moonshine, and by George, it *was* a bar'l. Says I:

"'Dick Allbright, what made you think that thing was a bar'l, when it was half a mile off?' says I. Says he:

"'I don't know,' Says I:

"'You tell me, Dick Allbright,' Says he:

"'Well, I knowed it was a bar'l; I've seen it before; lots has seen it, they say it's a ha'nted bar'l.'

"I called the rest of the watch, and they come and stood there, and I told them what Dick said. It floated right along abreast, now, and didn't gain any more. It was about twenty foot off. Some was for having it aboard, but the rest didn't want to. Dick Allbright said rafts that had fooled with it had got bad luck by it. The captain of the watch said he didn't believe in it. He said he reckoned the bar'l gained on us because it was in a little better current than what we was. He said it would leave by and by.

"So then we went to talking about other things, and we had a song, and then a breakdown; and after that the captain of the watch called for another song; but it was clouding up now, and the bar'l stuck right thar in the same place, and the song didn't seem to have much warm-up to it, somehow, and so they didn't finish it, and there warn't any cheers, but it sort of dropped flat, and nobody said anything for a minute. Then everybody tried to talk at once, and one chap got off a joke, but it warn't no use, they didn't laugh, and even the chap that made the joke didn't laugh at it, which ain't usual. We all just settled down glum, and watched the bar'l, and was oneasy and oncomfortable. Well, sir, it shut down black and still, and then the wind began to moan around, and next the lightning began to play and the thunder to grumble. And pretty soon there was a regular storm, and in the middle of it a man that was running aft stumbled and fell and sprained his ankle so that he had to lay up. This made the boys shake their heads. And every time the lightning come, there was that bar'l, with the blue lights winking around it. We was always on the lookout for it. But by and by, toward dawn, she was gone. When the day come we couldn't see her anywhere, and we warn't sorry, either.

"But next night about half past nine, when there was songs and high jinks going on, here she comes again, and took her old roost on the stabboard side. There warn't no more high jinks. Everybody got solemn; nobody talked; you couldn't get anybody to do anything but set around moody and look at the bar'l. It begun to cloud up again. When the watch changed, the off watch stayed up, 'stead of turning in. The storm ripped and roared around all night, and in the middle of it another man tripped and sprained his ankle, and had to knock off. The bar'l left toward day, and nobody see it go.

"Everybody was sober and down in the mouth all day. I don't mean the kind of sober that comes of leaving liquor alone—not that. They was quiet, but they all drunk more than usual—not together, but each man sidled off and took it private, by himself.

"After dark the off watch didn't turn in; nobody sung, nobody talked; the boys didn't scatter around, neither; they sort of huddled together, forrard; and for two hours they set there, perfectly still, looking steady in the one direction, and heaving a sigh once in a while. And then, here comes the bar'l again. She took up her old place. She stayed there all night; nobody turned in. The storm come on again, after midnight. It got awful dark; the rain poured down; hail, too; the thunder boomed and roared and bellowed; the wind blowed a hurricane; and the lightning spread over everything in big sheets of glare, and showed the whole raft as plain as day; and the river lashed up white as milk as far as you could see for miles, and there was that bar'l jiggling along, same as ever. The captain ordered the watch to man the after sweeps for a crossing, and nobody would go—no more sprained ankles for them, they said. They wouldn't even *walk* aft. Well, then, just then the sky split wide open, with a crash, and the lightning killed two men of the after watch, and crippled two more. Crippled them how, say you? Why, *sprained their ankles!*

"The bar'l left in the dark betwixt lightnings, toward dawn. Well, not a body eat a bite at breakfast that morning. After that the men loafed around, in twos and threes, and talked low together. But none of them herded with Dick Allbright. They all give him the cold shake. If he come around where any of the men was, they split up and sidled away. They wouldn't man the sweeps with him. The captain had all the skiffs hauled up on the raft, alongside of his wigwam, and wouldn't let the dead men be took ashore to be planted; he didn't believe a man that got ashore would come back, and he was right.

"After night come, you could see pretty plain that there was going to be trouble if that bar'l come again; there was such a muttering going on. A good many wanted to kill Dick Allbright, because he'd seen the bar'l on other trips, and that had an ugly look. Some wanted to put him ashore. Some said: 'Let's all go ashore in a pile, if the bar'l comes again.'

"This kind of whispers was still going on, the men being bunched together forrard watching for the bar'l, when lo and behold you! here she comes again. Down she comes, slow and steady, and settles into her old tracks. You could'a heard a pin drop. Then up comes the captain, and says:

"'Boy's don't be a pack of children and fools; I don't want this bar'l to be dogging us all the way to Orleans, and *you* don't: Well, then, how's the best way to stop it? Burn it up—that's the way. I'm to fetch it aboard,' he says. And before anybody could say a word, in he went.

"He swum to it, and as he come pushing it to the raft, the men spread to one side. But the old man got it aboard and busted in the head, and there was a baby in it! Yes, sir; a stark-naked baby. It was Dick Allbright's baby; he owned up and said so.

" 'Yes,' he says, a-leaning over it, 'yes, it is my own lamented darling, my poor lost Charles William Allbright deceased,' says he—for he could curl his tongue around the bulliest words in the language when he was a mind to, and lay them before you without a jint started anywheres. Yes, he said, he used to live up at the head of this bend, and one night he choked his child, which was crying, not intending to kill it—which was prob'ly a lie—and then he was scared, and buried it in a bar'l, before his wife got home, and off he went, and struck the northern trail and went to rafting; and this was the third year that the bar'l had chased him. He said the bad luck always begun light, and lasted till four men was killed, and then the bar'l didn't come any more after that. He said if the men would stand it one more night—and was a-going on like that—but the men had got enough. They started to get out a boat to take him ashore and lynch him, but he grabbed the little child all of a sudden and jumped overboard with it, hugged up to his breast and shedding tears, and we never see him again in this life, poor old suffering soul, nor Charles William neither."

"*Who* was shedding tears?" says Bob; "was it Allbright or the baby?"

"Why, Allbright, of course; didn't I tell you the baby was dead? Been dead three years—how could it cry?"

"Well, never mind how it could cry—how could it *keep* all that time?" says Davy. "You answer me that."

"I don't know how it done it," says Ed. "It done it, though—that's all I know about it."

"Say—what did they do with the bar'l?" says the Child of Calamity.

"Why, they hove it overboard, and it sunk like a chunk of lead."

"Edward, did the child look like it was choked?" says one.

"Did it have its hair parted?" says another.

"What was the brand on that bar'l, Eddy?" says a fellow they called Bill.

"Have you got the papers for them statistics, Edmund?" says Jimmy.

"Say, Edwin, was you one of the men that was killed by the lightning?" says Davy.

"Him? Oh, no! he was both of 'em," says Bob. Then they all haw-hawed.

"Say, Edward, don't you reckon you'd better take a pill? You look bad—don't you feel pale?" says the Child of Calamity.

Let a Leadsman Cry by Thomas Hart Benton (1944). Lithograph from *Life on the Mississippi* by Mark Twain.

Limited Editions Club, New York City.

"Oh, come, now, Eddy," says Jimmy, "show up; you must'a kept part of that bar'l to prove the thing by. Show us the bunghole—*do*—and we'll all believe you."

"Say, boys," says Bill, "less divide it up. Thar's thirteen of us. I can swaller a thirteenth of the yarn, if you can worry down the rest."

Ed got up mad and said they could all go to some place which he ripped out pretty savage, and then walked off aft, cussing to himself, and they yelling and jeering at him, and roaring and laughing so you could hear them a mile.

"Boys, we'll split a watermelon on that," says the Child of Calamity; and he came rummaging around in the dark amongst the shingle bundles where I was, and put his hand on me. I was warm and soft and naked; so he says "Ouch!" and jumped back.

"Fetch a lantern or a chunk of fire here, boys—there's a snake here as big as a cow!"

So they run there with a lantern, and crowded up and looked in on me.

"Come out of that, you beggar!" says one.

"Who are you?" says another.

"What are you after here? Speak up prompt, or overboard you go."

"Snake him out, boys. Snatch him out by the heels."

I began to beg, and crept out amongst them trembling. They looked me over, wondering, and the Child of Calamity says:

"A cussed thief! Lend a hand and less heave him overboard!"

"No," says Big Bob, "less get out the paint-pot and paint him a sky-blue all over from head to heel, and *then* heave him over."

"Good! that's it. Go for the paint, Jimmy."

When the paint come, and Bob took the brush and was just going to bend, the others laughing and rubbing their hands, I begun to cry, and that sort of worked on Davy, and he says:

"'Vast[11] there. He's nothing but a cub. I'll paint the man that teches him!"

So I looked around on them, and some of them grumbled and growled, and Bob put down the paint, and the others didn't take it up.

"Come here to the fire, and less see what you're up to here," says Davy. "Now set down there and give an account of yourself. How long have you been aboard here?"

"Not over a quarter of a minute, sir," says I.

"How did you get dry so quick?"

"I don't know, sir. I'm always that way, mostly."

"Oh, you are, are you? What's your name?"

I warn't going to tell my name. I didn't know what to say, so I just says:

"Charles William Allbright, sir."

Then they roared—the whole crowd; and I was mighty glad I said that, because, maybe, laughing would get them in a better humor.

When they got done laughing, Davy says:

"It won't hardly do, Charles William. You couldn't have growed this much in five years, and you was a baby when you come out of the bar'l,

you know, and dead at that. Come, now, tell a straight story, and nobody'll hurt you, if you ain't up to anything wrong. What *is* your name?"

"Aleck Hopkins, sir. Aleck James Hopkins."

"Well, Aleck, where did you come from, here?"

"From a trading-scow.[12] She lays up the bend yonder. I was born on her. Pap has traded up and down here all his life; and he told me to swim off here, because when you went by he said he would like to get some of you to speak to a Mr. Jonas Turner, in Cairo, and tell him—"

"Oh, come!"

"Yes, sir, it's as true as the world. Pap he says—"

"Oh, your grandmother!"

They all laughed, and I tried again to talk, but they broke in on me and stopped me.

"Now, looky-here," says Davy; "you're scared, and so you talk wild. Honest, now, do you live in a scow, or is it a lie?"

"Yes, sir, in a trading-scow. She lays up at the head of the bend. But I warn't born in her. It's our first trip."

"Now you're talking! What did you come aboard here for? To steal?"

"No, sir, I didn't. It was only to get a ride on the raft. All boys does that."

"Well, I know that. But what did you hide for?"

"Sometimes they drive the boys off."

"So they do. They might steal. Looky-here; if we let you off this time, will you keep out of these kind of scrapes hereafter?"

"'Deed I will, boss. You try me."

"All right, then. You ain't but little ways from shore. Overboard with you, and don't you make a fool of yourself another time this way. Blast it, boy, some raftsmen would rawhide you till you were black and blue!"

I didn't wait to kiss goodbye, but went overboard and broke for shore. When Jim come along by and by, the big raft was away out of sight around the point. I swum out and got aboard, and was mighty glad to see home again.

The boy did not get the information he was after, but his adventure has furnished the glimpse of the departed raftsman and keelboatman which I desire to offer in this place.

---

11. **vast:** a contraction of *avast,* a cry meaning "Stop!"

12. **trading-scow:** a large, flat-bottomed boat.

Responding to the Story

Analyzing the Story

Identifying Facts

1. What is Twain's purpose in presenting a chapter from his work in progress?
2. Explain why Huck Finn swims to the huge raft. Describe what he observes when he climbs aboard.
3. Describe how the keelboatmen seem to pass their time.

Interpreting Meanings

4. List the words Twain uses to describe the keelboatmen in the opening passage of this selection. How is this litany like Whitman's **catalogue** style? (See page 326.)
5. In ancient epics and romances, the heroes had supernatural powers and were often identified with the forces of nature. Find the **images** and details in the boasts of Bob and the Child of Calamity that show they are the backwoods equivalents of these heroes.
6. What supernatural elements are in the story of Dick Allbright and the baby? How does this combine "gallows humor" (morbid humor) and pathos?
7. In the *Odyssey,* Homer's epic, Odysseus is a prototype of the cunning hero, one who often escapes from tight or dangerous situations by using his wits rather than brute force. Odysseus has been called the master "artificer," meaning that he is a skilled liar. Explain how this boy narrator is also a master "artificer."
8. How would you describe the **characters** of the keelboatmen? Are such character types evident in any occupation in American life today? Explain.

Writing About the Story

A Creative Response

1. **Writing an Exaggerated Boast.** In the shouting contest between Bob and the Child of Calamity each man tries to top the other with boasts and insults. There is a long oral tradition behind such contests, dating back ultimately to the boasts of the heroes in ancient epic poems. For example, Odysseus opens his remarks to the king of the Phaiakians with a kind of boast:

> I am Laertes' son, Odysseus.
>   Men hold me
> formidable for guile in peace and war:
> this fame has gone abroad to the sky's rim.
>
>   —from the *Odyssey,* Book 9,
>   by Homer

In the American South and Southwest, the tradition of boasting continued in its own special way. Speakers would try to top each other with tall tales, jokes, anecdotes, and boastings about their achievements. (See Davy Crockett's speech on page 510.) Write a boast for a speaker who is "vying for supremacy." Give your speaker a name and try to include as much humor in the boast as possible. Open with the words "I am." What **metaphors** will your boaster use to exaggerate his or her achievements and prowess?

2. **Rewriting Dialect.** The dialect in this selection comprises a mixture of regional vernaculars: the backwoodsmen's speech, the dialect of the American Southwest, and the raftsmen's jargon. Choose a speech or an exchange in dialogue from the selection that you find especially colorful, and rewrite it in standard English. Then compare the two versions. What has been lost when standard English is used in this specific context?

Analyzing Language Style

Dialect and Frontier Humor

Twain, who is celebrated for his reproductions of dialect, claims in the introduction to *The Adventure of Huckleberry Finn* that he has used seven dialects in that book (a boast that might have to be taken as a slight exaggeration). Dialect may differ from standard English in vocabulary, in pronunciation, and in grammar. "Frontier humor" uses dialect plus a few humorous devices:

a. **Hyperbole,** or exaggeration for effect
b. Colorful and often comic **metaphors,** which usually create hilarious images through the terms of comparisons
c. **Incongruity,** whereby two opposites—two images or events or elements that seem inappropriately matched—are unexpectedly joined
d. **Boasts**
e. **Digressions** from the point of the story

1. Locate at least five examples of each characteristic of dialect in the selection from *Life on the Mississippi.*
2. Locate at least one example of Twain's use of each of the techniques of frontier humor.
3. Which humorous techniques are most prevalent in this episode from *Life on the Mississippi?*
4. Which of these humorous techniques are used by humorists and comics today? What variations do contemporary comics use to appeal to their particular audiences?

That pleased the old man till he couldn't rest. He said he'd cowhide me till I was black and blue if I didn't raise some money for him. I borrowed three dollars from Judge Thatcher, and Pap took it and got drunk, and went a-blowing around and cussing and whooping and carrying on; and he kept it up all over town, with a tin pan, till most midnight; then they jailed him, and the next day they had him before court, and jailed him again for a week. But he said *he* was satisfied; said he was boss of his son, and he'd make it warm for *him*.

When he got out the new judge said he was a-going to make a man of him. So he took him to his own house, and dressed him up clean and nice, and had him to breakfast and dinner and supper with the family, and was just old pie to him, so to speak. And after supper he talked to him about temperance and such things till the old man cried, and said he'd been a fool, and fooled away his life; but now he was a-going to turn over a new leaf and be a man nobody wouldn't be ashamed of, and he hoped the judge would help him and not look down on him. The judge said he could hug him for them words; so *he* cried, and his wife she cried again; Pap said he'd been a man that had always been misunderstood before, and the judge said he believed it. The old man said that what a man wanted that was down was sympathy, and the judge said it was so; so they cried again. And when it was bedtime the old man rose up and held out his hand, and says:

"Look at it, gentlemen and ladies all; take a-hold of it; shake it. There's a hand that was the hand of a hog; but it ain't so no more; it's the hand of a man that's started in on a new life, and'll die before he'll go back. You mark them words—don't forget I said them. It's a clean hand now; shake it—don't be afeared."

So they shook it, one after the other, all around, and cried. The judge's wife she kissed it. Then the old man he signed a pledge—made his mark. The judge said it was the holiest time on record, or something like that. Then they tucked the old man into a beautiful room, which was the spare room, and in the night some time he got powerful thirsty and clumb out on to the porch roof and slid down a stanchion and traded his new coat for a jug of forty-rod, and clumb back again and had a good old time; and toward daylight he crawled out again, drunk as a fiddler, and rolled off the porch and broke his left arm in two places, and was most

froze to death when somebody found him after sun-up. And when they come to look at that spare room they had to take soundings before they could navigate it.

The judge he felt kind of sore. He said he reckoned a body could reform the old man with a shotgun, maybe, but he didn't know no other way.

Pap Struggles with the Death Angel

Well, pretty soon the old man was up and around again, and then he went for Judge Thatcher in the courts to make him give up that money, and he went for me, too, for not stopping school. He catched me a couple of times and thrashed me, but I went to school just the same, and dodged him or outrun him most of the time. I didn't want to go to school much before, but I reckoned I'd go now to spite Pap. That law trial was a slow business—appeared like they warn't ever going to get started on it; so every now and then I'd borrow two or three dollars off of the judge for him, to keep from getting a cowhiding. Every time he got money he got drunk: and every time he got drunk he raised Cain around town; and every time he raised Cain he got jailed. He was just suited—this kind of thing was right in his line.

He got to hanging around the widow's too much, and so she told him at last that if he didn't quit using around there she would make trouble for him. Well, *wasn't* he mad? He said he would show who was Huck Finn's boss. So he watched out for me one day in the spring, and catched me, and took me up the river about three mile in a skiff, and crossed over to the Illinois shore where it was woody and there warn't no houses but an old log hut in a place where the timber was so thick you couldn't find it if you didn't know where it was.

He kept me with him all the time, and I never got a chance to run off. We lived in that old cabin, and he always locked the door and put the key under his head nights. He had a gun which he had stole, I reckon, and we fished and hunted, and that was what we lived on. Every little while he locked me in and went down to the store, three miles, to the ferry, and traded fish and game for whiskey, and fetched it home and got drunk and had a good time, and licked me. The widow she found out where I was by and by, and she sent a man over to try to get hold of me; but Pap drove him off with the gun, and it warn't long after that till I was used to being where I was, and liked it—all but the cowhide part.

It was kind of lazy and jolly, laying off comfortable all day, smoking and fishing, and no books nor study. Two months or more run along, and my clothes got to be all rags and dirt, and I didn't see how I'd ever got to like it so well at the widow's, where you had to wash, and eat on a plate, and comb up, and go to bed and get up regular, and be forever bothering over a book, and have old Miss Watson pecking at you all the time. I didn't want to go back no more. I had stopped cussing, because the widow didn't like it; but now I took to it again because Pap hadn't no objec-

tions. It was pretty good times up in the woods there, take it all around.

But by and by Pap got too handy with his hick'ry, and I couldn't stand it. I was all over welts. He got to going away so much, too, and locking me in. Once he locked me in and was gone three days. It was dreadful lonesome. I judged he had got drownded, and I wasn't ever going to get out anymore. I was scared. I made up my mind I would fix up some way to leave there. I had tried to get out of that cabin many a time, but I couldn't find no way. There warn't a window to it big enough for a dog to get through. I couldn't get up the chimbly; it was too narrow. The door was thick, solid oak slabs. Pap was pretty careful not to leave a knife or anything in the cabin when he was away; I reckon I had hunted the place over as much as a hundred times; well, I was most all the time at it, because it was about the only way to put in the time. But this time I found something at last; I found an old rusty wood saw without any handle; it was laid in between a rafter and the clapboards of the roof. I greased it up and went to work. There was an old horse blanket nailed against the logs at the far end of the cabin behind the table, to keep the wind from blowing through the chinks and putting the candle out. I got under the table and raised the blanket, and went to work to saw a section of the big bottom log out—big enough to let me through. Well, it was a good long job, but I was getting toward the end of it when I heard Pap's gun in the woods. I got rid of the signs of my work, and dropped the blanket and hid my saw, and pretty soon Pap come in.

Pap warn't in a good humor—so he was his natural self. He said he was downtown, and everything was going wrong. His lawyer said he reckoned he would win his lawsuit and get the money if they ever got started on the trial; but then there was ways to put it off a long time, and Judge Thatcher knowed how to do it. And he said people allowed there'd be another trial to get me away from him and give me to the widow for my guardian, and they guessed it would win this time. This shook me up considerable, because I didn't want to go back to the widow's any more and be so cramped up and civilized, as they called it. Then the old man got to cussing, and cussed everything and everybody he could think of, and then cussed them all over again to make sure he hadn't skipped any, and after that he polished off with a kind of a general cuss all round, including a considerable

it was loaded, and then I laid it across the turnip barrel, pointing towards pap, and set down behind it to wait for him to stir. And how slow and still the time did drag along.

I Fool Pap and Get Away

"Git up! What you 'bout?"

I opened my eyes and looked around trying to make out where I was. It was after sun-up, and I had been sound asleep. Pap was standing over me looking sour—and sick, too. He says:

"What you doin' with this gun?"

I judged he didn't know nothing about what he had been doing, so I says:

"Somebody tried to get in, so I was laying for him."

"Why didn't you roust me out?"

"Well, I tried to, but I couldn't; I couldn't budge you."

"Well, all right. Don't stand there palavering[5] all day, but out with you and see if there's a fish on the lines for breakfast. I'll be along in a minute."

He unlocked the door, and I cleared out up the riverbank. I noticed some pieces of limbs and such things floating down, and a sprinkling of bark; so I knowed the river had begun to rise. I reckoned I would have great times now if I was over at the town. The June rise used to be always luck for me; because as soon as that rise begins here comes cordwood floating down, and pieces of log rafts—

---

5. **palavering** (pə·lav′ər·ing): chatting idly.

sometimes a dozen logs together; so all you have to do is to catch them and sell them to the wood-yards and the sawmill.

I went along up the bank with one eye out for pap and t'other one out for what the rise might fetch along. Well, all at once here comes a canoe; just a beauty, too, about thirteen or fourteen foot long, riding high like a duck. I shot headfirst off of the bank like a frog, clothes and all on, and struck out for the canoe. I just expected there'd be somebody laying down in it, because people often done that to fool folks, and when a chap had pulled a skiff out most to it they'd raise up and laugh at him. But it warn't so this time. It was a drift-canoe sure enough, and I clumb in and paddled her ashore. Thinks I, the old man will be glad when he sees this—she's worth ten dollars. But when I got to shore Pap wasn't in sight yet, and as I was running her into a little creek like a gully, all hung over with vines and willows, I struck another idea: I judged I'd hide her good, and then, 'stead of taking to the woods when I run off, I'd go down the river about fifty mile and camp in one place for good, and not have such a rough time tramping on foot.

It was pretty close to the shanty, and I thought I heard the old man coming all the time; but I got her hid; and then I out and looked around a bunch of willows, and there was the old man down the path a piece just drawing a bead on a bird with his gun. So he hadn't seen anything.

When he got along I was hard at it taking up a "trot" line. He abused me a little for being so slow; but I told him I fell in the river, and that was what made me so long. I knowed he would see I was wet, and then he would be asking questions. We got five catfish off the lines and went home.

While we laid off after breakfast to sleep up, both of us being about wore out, I got to thinking that if I could fix up some way to keep Pap and the widow from trying to follow me, it would be a certainer thing than trusting to luck to get far enough off before they missed me; you see, all kinds of things might happen. Well, I didn't see no way for a while, but by and by Pap raised up a minute to drink another barrel of water, and he says:

"Another time a man comes a-prowling round here you roust me out, you hear? That man warn't here for no good. I'd a shot him. Next time you roust me out, you hear?"

Then he dropped down and went to sleep again; what he had been saying give me the very idea I wanted. I says to myself, I can fix it now so nobody won't think of following me.

About twelve o'clock we turned out and went along up the bank. The river was coming up pretty fast, and lots of driftwood going by on the rise. By and by along comes part of a log raft—nine logs fast together. We went out with the skiff and towed it ashore. Then we had dinner. Anybody but Pap would 'a' waited and seen the day through, so as to catch more stuff; but that warn't Pap's style. Nine logs was enough for one time; he must shove right over to town and sell. So he locked me in and took the skiff, and started off towing the raft about half past three. I judged he wouldn't come back that night. I waited till I reckoned he had got a good start; then I out with my saw, and went to work on that log again. Before he was t'other side of the river I was out of the hole; him and his raft was just a speck on the water away off yonder.

I took the sack of corn meal and took it to where the canoe was hid, and shoved the vines and branches apart and put it in; then I done the same with the side of bacon; then the whiskey jug. I took all the coffee and sugar there was, and all the ammunition; I took the wadding; I took the bucket and gourd; took a dipper and a tin cup, and my old saw and two blankets, and the skillet and the coffee pot. I took fish lines and matches and other things—everything that was worth a cent. I cleaned out the place. I wanted an ax, but there wasn't any, only the one out at the woodpile, and I knowed why I was going to leave that. I fetched out the gun, and now I was done.

I had wore the ground a good deal crawling out of the hole and dragging out so many things. So I fixed that as good as I could from the outside by scattering dust on the place, which covered up the smoothness and the sawdust. Then I fixed the piece of log back into its place, and put two rocks under it and one against it to hold it there, for it was bent up at that place and didn't quite touch ground. If you stood four of five foot away and didn't know it was sawed, you wouldn't never notice it; and besides, this was the back of the cabin, and it warn't likely anybody would go fooling around there.

It was all grass clear to the canoe, so I hadn't left a track. I followed around to see. I stood on the bank and looked out over the river. All safe.

So I took the gun and went up a piece into the woods, and was hunting around for some birds when I see a wild pig; hogs soon went wild in them bottoms after they got away from the prairie-farms. I shot this fellow and took him into camp.

I took the ax and smashed in the door. I beat it and hacked it considerable a-doing it. I fetched the pig in, and took him back nearly to the table and hacked into his throat with the ax, and laid him down on the ground to bleed; I say ground because it *was* ground—hard packed, and no boards. Well, next I took an old sack and put a lot of big rocks in it—all I could drag—and I started it from the pig, and dragged it to the door and through the woods down to the river and dumped it in, and down it sunk, out of sight. You could easy see that something had been dragged over the ground. I did wish Tom Sawyer was there; I knowed he would take an interest in this kind of business, and throw in the fancy touches. Nobody could spread himself like Tom Sawyer in such a thing as that.

Well, last I pulled out some of my hair, and blooded the ax good, and stuck it on the back side, and slung the ax in the corner. Then I took up the pig and held him to my breast with my jacket (so he couldn't drip) till I got a good piece below the house and then dumped him into the river. Now I thought of something else. So I went and got the bag of meal and my old saw out of the canoe, and fetched them to the house. I took the bag to where it used to stand, and ripped a hole in the bottom of it with the saw, for there warn't no knives and forks on the place—Pap done every-

see who was aboard when she come along, because she would come in close, where the bread did. When she'd got pretty well along down towards me, I put out my pipe and went to where I fished out the bread, and laid down behind a log on the bank in a little open place. Where the log forked I could peep through.

By and by she come along, and she drifted in so close that they could 'a' run out a plank and walked ashore. Most everybody was on the boat. Pap, and Judge Thatcher, and Bessie Thatcher, and Joe Harper, and Tom Sawyer, and his old Aunt Polly, and Sid and Mary, and plenty more. Everybody was talking about the murder, but the captain broke in and says:

"Look sharp, now; the current sets in the closest here, and maybe he's washed ashore and got tangled amongst the brush at the water's edge. I hope so, anyway."

I didn't hope so. They all crowded up and leaned over the rails, nearly in my face, and kept still, watching with all their might. I could see them first-rate, but they couldn't see me. Then the captain sung out: "Stand away!" and the cannon let off such a blast right before me that it made me deef with the noise and pretty near blind with the smoke, and I judged I was gone. If they'd 'a' had some bullets in, I reckon they'd 'a' got the corpse they was after. Well, I see I warn't hurt, thanks to goodness. The boat floated on and went out of sight around the shoulder of the island. I could hear the booming now and then, further and further off, and by and by, after an hour, I didn't hear it no more. The island was three mile long. I judged they had got to the foot, and was giving it up. But they didn't yet awhile. They turned around the foot of the island and started up the channel on the Missouri side, under steam, and booming once in a while as they went. I crossed over to that side and watched them. When they got abreast the head of the island they quit shooting and dropped over to the Missouri shore and went home to the town.

I knowed I was all right now. Nobody else would come a-hunting after me. I got my traps out of the canoe and made me a nice camp in the thick woods. I made a kind of a tent out of my blankets to put my things under so the rain couldn't get at them. I catched a catfish and haggled him open with my saw, and towards sundown I started my campfire and had supper. Then I set out a line to catch some fish for breakfast.

When it was dark I set by my campfire smoking, and feeling pretty well satisfied; but by and by it got sort of lonesome, and so I went and set on the bank and listened to the current swashing along, and counted the stars and drift logs and rafts that come down, and then went to bed; there ain't no better way to put in time when you are lonesome; you can't stay so, you soon get over it.

And so for three days and nights. No difference—just the same thing. But the next day I went exploring around down through the island. I was boss of it; it all belonged to me, so to say, and I wanted to know all about it; but mainly I wanted to put in the time. I found plenty strawberries, ripe and prime; and green summer grapes, and green razberries; and the green blackberries was just beginning to show. They would all come handy by and by, I judged.

Well, I went fooling along in the deep woods till I judged I warn't far from the foot of the island. I had my gun along, but I hadn't shot nothing; it was for protection; thought I would kill some game nigh home. About this time I mighty near stepped on a good-sized snake, and it went sliding off through the grass and flowers, and I after it, trying to get a shot at it. I clipped along, and all

By the time it was night I was pretty hungry. So when it was good and dark I slid out from shore before moonrise and paddled over to the Illinois bank—about a quarter of a mile. I went out in the woods and cooked a supper, and I had about made up my mind I would stay there all night when I hear a *plunkety-plunk, plunkety-plunk,* and says to myself, horses coming; and next I hear people's voices. I got everything into the canoe as quick as I could, and then went creeping through the woods to see what I could find out. I hadn't got far when I hear a man say:

"We better camp here if we can find a good place; the horses is about beat out. Let's look around."

I didn't wait, but shoved out and paddled away easy. I tied up in the old place, and reckoned I would sleep in the canoe.

I didn't sleep much. I couldn't, somehow, for thinking. And every time I waked up I thought somebody had me by the neck. So the sleep didn't do me no good. By and by I says to myself, I can't live this way; I'm a-going to find out who it is that's here on the island with me; I'll find it our or bust. Well, I felt better right off.

So I took my paddle and slid out from shore just a step or two, and then let the canoe drop along down amongst the shadows. The moon was shining, and outside of the shadows it made it most as light as day. I poked along well on to an hour, everything still as rocks and sound asleep. Well, by this time I was most down to the foot of the island. A little ripply, cool breeze begun to blow, and that was as good as saying the night was about done. I give her a turn with the paddle and brung her nose to shore; then I got my gun and slipped out and into the edge of the woods. I sat down there on a log, and looked out through the leaves. I see the moon go off watch, and the darkness begin to blanket the river. But in a little while I see a pale streak over the treetops, and knowed the day was coming. So I took my gun and slipped off towards where I had run across that campfire, stopping every minute or two to listen. But I hadn't no luck somehow; I couldn't seem to find the place. But by and by, sure enough, I catched a glimpse of fire away through the trees. I went for it, cautious and slow. By and by I was close enough to have a look, and there

of a sudden I bounded right on to the ashes of a campfire that was still smoking.

My heart jumped up amongst my lungs. I never waited for to look further, but uncocked my gun and went sneaking back on my tiptoes as fast as ever I could. Every now and then I stopped a second amongst the thick leaves and listened, but my breath come so hard I couldn't hear nothing else. I slunk along another piece further, then listened again; and so on, and so on. If I see a stump, I took it for a man; if I trod on a stick and broke it, it made me feel like a person had cut one of my breaths in two and I only got half, and the short half, too.

When I got to camp I warn't feeling very brash, there warn't much sand in my craw; but I says, this ain't no time to be fooling around. So I got all my traps into my canoe again so as to have them out of sight, and I put out the fire and scattered the ashes around to look like an old last-year's camp, and then clumb a tree.

I reckon I was up in the tree two hours; but I didn't see nothing. I didn't hear nothing—I only *thought* I heard and seen as much as a thousand things. Well, I couldn't stay up there forever; so at last I got down, but I kept in the thick woods

for a hundred yards, then, curving, was lost to view. Doubtless there was an outpost farther along. The other bank of the stream was open ground—a gentle acclivity topped with a stockade of vertical tree trunks, loopholed for rifles, with a single embrasure through which protruded the muzzle of a brass cannon commanding the bridge. Midway of the slope between bridge and fort were the spectators—a single company of infantry in line, at "parade rest," the butts of the rifles on the ground, the barrels inclining slightly backward against the right shoulder, the hands crossed upon the stock. A lieutenant stood at the right of the line, the point of his sword upon the ground, his left hand resting upon his right. Excepting the group of four at the center of the bridge, not a man moved. The company faced the bridge, staring stonily, motionless. The sentinels, facing the banks of the stream, might have been statues to adorn the bridge. The captain stood with folded arms, silent, observing the work of his subordinates, but making no sign. Death is a dignitary who when he comes announced is to be received with formal manifestations of respect, even by those most familiar with him. In the code of military etiquette silence and fixity are forms of deference.

The man who was engaged in being hanged was apparently about thirty-five years of age. He was a civilian, if one might judge from his habit, which was that of a planter. His features were good—a straight nose, firm mouth, broad forehead, from which his long, dark hair was combed straight back, falling behind his ears to the collar of his well-fitting frock coat. He wore a mustache and pointed beard, but no whiskers; his eyes were large and dark gray, and had a kindly expression which one would hardly have expected in one whose neck was in the hemp. Evidently this was no vulgar assassin. The liberal military code makes provision for hanging many kinds of persons, and gentlemen are not excluded.

The preparations being complete, the two private soldiers stepped aside and each drew away the plank upon which he had been standing. The sergeant turned to the captain, saluted and placed himself immediately behind that officer, who in turn moved apart one pace. These movements left the condemned man and the sergeant standing on the two ends of the same plank, which spanned three of the cross-ties of the bridge. The end upon

The Red Bridge by Julian Alden Weir (1896). Oil.

The Metropolitan Museum of Art, New York.

which the civilian stood almost, but not quite, reached a fourth. This plank had been held in place by the weight of the captain; it was now held by that of the sergeant. At a signal from the former the latter would step aside, the plank would tilt and the condemned man go down between two ties. The arrangement commended itself to his judgment as simple and effective. His face had not been covered nor his eyes bandaged. He looked a moment at his "unsteadfast footing," then let his gaze wander to the swirling water of the stream racing madly beneath his feet. A piece of dancing driftwood caught his attention and his eyes followed it down the current. How slowly it appeared to move! What a sluggish stream!

He closed his eyes in order to fix his last thoughts upon his wife and children. The water, touched to gold by the early sun, the brooding mists under the banks at some distance down the stream, the fort, the soldiers, the piece of drift— all had distracted him. And now he became conscious of a new disturbance. Striking through the thought of his dear ones was a sound which he could neither ignore nor understand, a sharp, distinct, metallic percussion like the stroke of a blacksmith's hammer upon the anvil; it had the same ringing quality. He wondered what it was, and whether immeasurably distant or near by—it seemed both. Its recurrence was regular, but as slow as the tolling of a death knell. He awaited each stroke with impatience and—he knew not why—apprehension. The intervals of silence grew progressively longer; the delays became maddening. With their greater infrequency the sounds increased in strength and sharpness. They hurt his ear like the thrust of a knife; he feared he would shriek. What he heard was the ticking of his watch.

He unclosed his eyes and saw again the water below him. "If I could free my hands," he thought, "I might throw off the noose and spring into the stream. By diving I could evade the bullets and, swimming vigorously, reach the bank, take to the woods and get away home. My home, thank God, is as yet outside their lines; my wife and little ones are still beyond the invader's farthest advance."

As these thoughts, which have here to be set down in words, were flashed into the doomed man's brain rather than evolved from it the captain nodded to the sargent. The sergeant stepped aside.

II

Peyton Farquhar was a well-to-do planter, of an old and highly respected Alabama family. Being a slave owner and like other slave owners a politician he was naturally an original secessionist and ardently devoted to the Southern cause. Circumstances of an imperious nature, which it is unnecessary to relate here, had prevented him from taking service with the gallant army that had fought the disastrous campaigns ending with the fall of Corinth,[2] and he chafed under the inglorious restraint, longing for the release of his energies, the larger life of the soldier, the opportunity for distinction. That opportunity, he felt, would come, as it comes to all in wartime. Meanwhile he did what he could. No service was too humble for him to perform in aid of the South, no adventure too perilous for him to undertake if consistent with the character of a civilian who was at heart a soldier, and who in good faith and without too much qualification assented to at least a part of the frankly villainous dictum that all is fair in love and war.

One evening while Farquhar and his wife were sitting on a rustic bench near the entrance to his grounds, a gray-clad soldier rode up to the gate and asked for a drink of water. Mrs. Farquhar was only too happy to serve him with her own white hands. While she was fetching the water her husband approached the dusty horseman and inquired eagerly for news from the front.

"The Yanks are repairing the railroads," said the man, "and are getting ready for another advance. They have reached the Owl Creek bridge, put it in order and built a stockade on the north bank. The commandant has issued an order, which is posted everywhere, declaring that any civilian caught interfering with the railroad, its bridges, tunnels, or trains will be summarily hanged. I saw the order."

"How far is it to the Owl Creek bridge?" Farquhar asked.

"About thirty miles."

"Is there no force on this side the creek?"

"Only a picket post half a mile out, on the railroad, and a single sentinel at this end of the bridge."

"Suppose a man—a civilian and student of

2. **Corinth:** General Grant took Corinth, Mississippi, on April 7, 1862, after the Battle of Shiloh.

hanging—should elude the picket post and perhaps get the better of the sentinel," said Farquhar, smiling, "what could he accomplish?"

The soldier reflected. "I was there a month ago," he replied. "I observed that the flood of last winter had lodged a great quantity of driftwood against the wooden pier at this end of the bridge. It is now dry and would burn like tow."

The lady had now brought the water, which the soldier drank. He thanked her ceremoniously, bowed to her husband and rode away. An hour later, after nightfall, he repassed the plantation, going northward in the direction from which he had come. He was a Federal scout.

III

As Peyton Farquhar fell straight downward through the bridge he lost consciousness and was as one already dead. From this state he was awakened—ages later, it seemed to him—by the pain of a sharp pressure upon his throat, followed by a sense of suffocation. Keen, poignant agonies seemed to shoot from his neck downward through every fiber of his body and limbs. These pains appeared to flash along well-defined lines of ramification and to beat with an inconceivably rapid periodicity. They seemed like streams of pulsating fire heating him to an intolerable temperature. As to his head, he was conscious of nothing but a feeling of fullness—of congestion. These sensations were unaccompanied by thought. The intellectual part of his nature was already effaced; he had power only to feel, and feeling was torment. He was conscious of motion. Encompassed in a luminous cloud, of which he was now merely the fiery heart, without material substance, he swung through unthinkable arcs of oscillation, like a vast pendulum. Then all at once, with terrible suddenness, the light about him shot upward with the noise of a loud plash; a frightful roaring was in his ears, and all was cold and dark. The power of thought was restored; he knew that the rope had broken and he had fallen into the stream. There was no additional strangulation; the noose about his neck was already suffocating him and kept the water from his lungs. To die of hanging at the bottom of a river!—the idea seemed to him ludicrous. He opened his eyes in the darkness and saw above him a gleam of light, but how distant, how inaccessible! He was still sinking, for the light

became fainter until it was a mere glimmer. Then it began to grow and brighten, and he knew that he was rising toward the surface—knew it with reluctance, for he was now very comfortable. "To be hanged and drowned," he thought, "that is not so bad; but I do not wish to be shot. No; I will not be shot; that is not fair."

He was not conscious of an effort, but a sharp pain in his wrist apprised him that he was trying to free his hands. He gave the struggle his attention, as an idler might observe the feat of a juggler, without interest in the outcome. What splendid effort!—what magnificent, what superhuman strength! Ah, that was a fine endeavor! Bravo! The cord fell away; his arms parted and floated upward, the hands dimly seen on each side in the growing light. He watched them with a new interest as first one and then the other pounced upon the noose at his neck. They tore it away and thrust it fiercely aside, its undulations resembling those of a water snake. "Put it back, put it back!" He thought he shouted these words to his hands, for the undoing of the noose had been succeeded by the direst pang that he had yet experienced. His neck ached horribly; his brain was on fire; his heart, which had been fluttering faintly, gave a great leap, trying to force itself out at his mouth. His whole body was racked and wrenched with an insupportable anguish! But his disobedient hands gave no heed to the command. They beat the water vigorously with quick, downward strokes, forcing him to the surface. He felt his head emerge; his eyes were blinded by the sunlight; his chest expanded convulsively, and with a supreme and crowning agony his lungs engulfed a great draught of air, which instantly he expelled in a shriek!

He was now in full possession of his physical senses. They were, indeed, preternaturally keen and alert. Something in the awful disturbance of his organic system had so exalted and refined them that they made record of things never before perceived. He felt the ripples upon his face and heard their separate sounds as they struck. He looked at the forest on the bank of the stream, saw the individual trees, the leaves and the veining of each leaf—saw the very insects upon them: the locusts, the brilliant-bodied flies, the gray spiders stretching their webs from twig to twig. He noted the prismatic colors in all the dewdrops upon a million blades of grass. The humming of the gnats that danced above the eddies of the stream, the beating of the dragonflies' wings, the strokes of the water spiders' legs, like oars which had lifted their boat—all these made audible music. A fish slid along beneath his eyes and he heard the rush of its body parting the water.

He had come to the surface facing down the stream; in a moment the visible world seemed to wheel slowly round, himself the pivotal point, and he saw the bridge, the fort, the soldiers upon the bridge, the captain, the sergeant, the two privates, his executioners. They were in silhouette against the blue sky. They shouted and gesticulated, pointing at him. The captain had drawn his pistol, but did not fire; the others were unarmed. Their movements were grotesque and horrible, their forms gigantic.

Suddenly he heard a sharp report and something struck the water smartly within a few inches of his head, spattering his face with spray. He heard a second report, and saw one of the sentinels with his rifle at his shoulder, a light cloud of blue smoke rising from the muzzle. The man in the water saw the eye of the man on the bridge gazing into his own through the sights of the rifle. He observed that it was a gray eye and remembered having read that gray eyes were keenest, and that all famous marksmen had them. Nevertheless, this one had missed.

A counter-swirl had caught Farquhar and turned him half round; he was again looking into the forest on the bank opposite the fort. The sound of a clear, high voice in a monotonous singsong now rang out behind him and came across the water with a distinctness that pierced and subdued all other sounds, even the beating of the ripples in his ears. Although no soldier, he had frequented camps enough to know the dread significance of that deliberate, drawling, aspirated chant; the lieutenant on shore was taking a part in the morning's work. How coldly and pitilessly—with what an even, calm intonation, presaging, and enforcing tranquility in the men—with what accurately measured intervals fell those cruel words:

"Attention, company! . . . Shoulder arms! . . . Ready! . . . Aim! . . . Fire!"

Farquhar dived—dived as deeply as he could. The water roared in his ears like the voice of Niagara, yet he heard the dulled thunder of the volley and, rising again toward the surface, met shining bits of metal, singularly flattened, oscillating slowly downward. Some of them touched him on the face and hands, then fell away, continuing

their descent. One lodged between his collar and neck; it was uncomfortably warm and he snatched it out.

As he rose to the surface, gasping for breath, he saw that he had been a long time under water; he was perceptibly farther down stream—nearer to safety. The soldiers had almost finished reloading; the metal ramrods flashed all at once in the sunshine as they were drawn from the barrels, turned in the air, and thrust into their sockets. The two sentinels fired again, independently and ineffectually.

The hunted man saw all this over his shoulder; he was now swimming vigorously with the current. His brain was as energetic as his arms and legs; he thought with the rapidity of lightning.

"The officer," he reasoned, "will not make this martinet's[3] error a second time. It is as easy to dodge a volley as a single shot. He has probably already given the command to fire at will. God help me, I cannot dodge them all!"

An appalling plash within two yards of him was followed by a loud, rushing sound, *diminuendo*,[4] which seemed to travel back through the air to the fort and died in an explosion which stirred the very river to its deeps! A rising sheet of water curved over him, fell down upon him, blinded him, strangled him! The cannon had taken a hand in the game. As he shook his head free from the commotion of the smitten water he heard the deflected shot humming through the air ahead, and in an instant it was cracking and smashing the branches in the forest beyond.

"They will not do that again," he thought; "the next time they will use a charge of grape.[5] I must keep an eye upon the gun; the smoke will apprise me—the report arrives too late; it lags behind the missile. That is a good gun."

Suddenly he felt himself whirled round and round—spinning like a top. The water, the banks, the forests, the now distant bridge, fort and men— all were commingled and blurred. Objects were represented by their colors only; circular horizontal streaks of color—that was all he saw. He had been caught in a vortex and was being whirled on with a velocity of advance and gyration that made him giddy and sick. In a few moments he was flung upon the gravel at the foot of the left bank

3. **martinet** (mär·t'n·et'): a strict military disciplinarian.
4. *diminuendo* (də·min·yoo·wen'dō): decreasing in loudness.
5. **a charge of grape:** a cannon charge of small iron balls, called grapeshot.

of the stream—the southern bank—and behind a projecting point which concealed him from his enemies. The sudden arrest of his motion, the abrasion of one of his hands on the gravel, restored him, and he wept with delight. He dug his fingers into the sand, threw it over himself in handfuls and audibly blessed it. It looked like diamonds, rubies, emeralds; he could think of nothing beautiful which it did not resemble. The trees upon the bank were giant garden plants; he noted a definite order in their arrangement, inhaled the fragrance of their blooms. A strange, roseate light shone through the spaces among their trunks and the wind made in their branches the music of aeolian harps.[6] He had no wish to perfect his escape—was content to remain in that enchanting spot until retaken.

A whiz and rattle of grapeshot among the branches high above his head roused him from his dream. The baffled cannoneer had fired him a random farewell. He sprang to his feet, rushed up the sloping bank, and plunged into the forest.

All that day he traveled, laying his course by the rounding sun. The forest seemed interminable; nowhere did he discover a break in it, not even a woodsman's road. He had not known that he lived in so wild a region. There was something uncanny in the revelation.

By nightfall he was fatigued, footsore, famishing. The thought of his wife and children urged him on. At last he found a road which led him in what he knew to be the right direction. It was as wide and straight as a city street, yet it seemed untraveled. No fields bordered it, no dwelling anywhere. Not so much as the barking of a dog suggested human habitation. The black bodies of the trees formed a straight wall on both sides, termi-

---

6. **aeolian harps:** stringed instruments that are played by the wind. Aeolus was the king of the winds in Greek mythology.

nating on the horizon in a point, like a diagram in a lesson in perspective. Overhead, as he looked up through this rift in the wood, shone great golden stars looking unfamiliar and grouped in strange constellations. He was sure they were arranged in some order which had a secret and malign significance. The wood on either side was full of singular noises, among which—once, twice, and again—he distinctly heard whispers in an unknown tongue.

His neck was in pain and lifting his hand to it he found it horribly swollen. He knew that it had a circle of black where the rope had bruised it. His eyes felt congested; he could no longer close them. His tongue was swollen with thirst; he relieved its fever by thrusting it forward from between his teeth into the cold air. How softly the turf had carpeted the untraveled avenue—he could no longer feel the roadway beneath his feet!

Doubtless, despite his suffering, he had fallen asleep while walking, for now he sees another scene—perhaps he has merely recovered from a delirium. He stands at the gate of his own home. All is as he left it, and all bright and beautiful in the morning sunshine. He must have traveled the entire night. As he pushes open the gate and passes up the wide white walk, he sees a flutter of female garments; his wife, looking fresh and cool and sweet, steps down from the veranda to meet him. At the bottom of the steps she stands waiting, with a smile of ineffable joy, an attitude of matchless grace and dignity. Ah, how beautiful she is! He springs forward with extended arms. As he is about to clasp her he feels a stunning blow upon the back of the neck; a blinding white light blazes all about him with a sound like the shock of a cannon—then all is darkness and silence!

Peyton Farquhar was dead; his body, with a broken neck, swung gently from side to side beneath the timbers of the Owl Creek bridge.

Responding to the Story

Analyzing the Story

Identifying Facts

1. How much time actually elapses between the opening and closing lines of Part III?
2. Describe the **setting** at the opening of the story. What is Peyton Farquhar's situation?
3. Describe Farquhar's last thoughts. Identify and describe the sound that disturbs the thoughts going through his mind.
4. In the **flashback** of the story's second section, who visits Peyton Farquhar? What plan does Farquhar conceive as a result of this visit?
5. What does Farquhar imagine in the story's last section? Ironically, what is his real fate?

Interpreting Meanings

6. Summarize what you think this story reveals about the psychology of a person facing death. Do you find the psychology believable? Explain.
7. The third part of the story, which occurs within the few seconds before Farquhar dies, is presumably a fantasy. What **point of view** does the writer use here? How does Bierce prepare us for the final outcome of the story?
8. When you discovered Farquhar had not actually escaped but had only imagined it, what were your own emotions? Did you feel that this outcome was more credible and more powerful than the one you had been led to anticipate? Or did you feel cheated by the surprise ending? Explain your response.
9. Do you think the writer tries to enlist your sympathies toward either the Union or the Confederate side? Or does the story seem to be focused on a more general **theme** about the nature of the war? Cite details from the story to support your response.
10. Review the story closely and comment on how Bierce has used a cinematic style, including the following techniques:

    a. close-up shots
    b. group shots
    c. panoramic shots
    d. fast motion
    e. slowed motion
    f. dream sequences
    g. sound effects
    h. quick cuts
    i. moving camera shots

    Discuss how you think the story might be adapted into a movie.

Writing About the Story

A Creative Response

1. **Imitating a Technique.** An outstanding aspect of Bierce's narrative technique in this story is his ability to "slow time down" as he dramatizes, almost second by second, the thoughts that flash through Farquhar's mind immediately before and after he is hanged. Bierce's technique anticipates, at least to some degree, the more modern mode of narration known as "stream-of-consciousness." Imagine that you, or a character you create, are subjected to an extraordinary crisis or moment of pressure. Define the nature of this pressure in a sentence or two. Then write an account, either in the first or third person, of the thoughts inside your character's mind over a very short period of time. Try to imitate Bierce by making this account as varied and as suspenseful as possible.

A Critical Response

2. **Analyzing Suspense.** Bierce is noted for the surprise endings of many of his stories and for his ability to keep the reader uncertain and tense about the outcome. In a brief essay, explain how Bierce increases the reader's suspense in two different ways in the second and the third parts of this story.
3. **Responding to a Critical Comment.** The following comment on Bierce's story was made by two prominent critics:

> The plot that depends on some peculiarity of human psychology—as does "An Occurrence at Owl Creek Bridge"—may give us a shock of surprise, but it does not carry a fictional meaning. The peculiar quirk of psychology—the "case study"—must also involve some significant human evaluation, some broadening or deepening of our human attitudes, if it is to be acceptable as fiction. Fiction involves all kinds of human characters and human experiences, common and uncommon, but it is concerned to do more than make a clinical report, medical or psychological.
>
> —Cleanth Brooks and Robert Penn Warren

In a brief essay, respond to these critical remarks. If you agree that the story is merely a "case study" in psychology and therefore not true fiction, cite details from the story to support your response. If you feel, on the other hand, that the story uses psychology to reveal something important about character or human nature in general, explain your reasons for holding that opinion.

Stephen Crane
(1871–1900)

Stephen Crane was the youngest of the fourteen children of Jonathan Townley Crane, a Methodist minister, and his devout wife Mary. Stephen's frail health as a child was one reason for the family's move from the parsonage in Newark, New Jersey, to Port Jervis in upstate New York. Here the child grew up with a yearning to become a baseball star. He put in a term first at Lafayette College and then at Syracuse University (where he was made captain of the baseball team) before he decided to try earning a living as a writer.

In the spring of 1891 he went to work for his brother Townley's news agency in Asbury Park, New Jersey; he soon caused a scandal in that pious and conservative seaside resort with an ironic story about a workingmen's parade. Later, struggling to make a living as a reporter in New York City, he was drawn to the city's underside. What he called his "artistic education on the Bowery" (the city's skid row) kept him hungry and often ill.

He lived at the Art Students' League on Twenty-third Street, reporting intermittently for the *Herald* and the *Tribune,* exploring the city's slums and saloons, and writing his first significant fiction about his experiences. This was *Maggie: A Girl of the Streets,* a somber, somewhat shocking novel, whose plot involved brutality, alcoholism, prostitution, and suicide.

Crane's subject matter and style in *Maggie* revealed him as a pioneer of naturalism, the literary movement which went beyond realism in its dissection of human instincts and behavior, and of the social environment that was believed to "condition" people to be what they are. Furthermore, *Maggie* broke other new ground; it was one of the first novels to use the city and its all-too-real slums as a setting. *Maggie* was impossibly grim for the popular magazines, and Crane borrowed $700 to have it printed in 1893. The copies of the little yellow paperback lay piled in his rented room for want of readers.

But a literary triumph followed soon after Crane's apparent failure with *Maggie.* In the summer of 1893, he finished a short novel entitled *The Red Badge of Courage.* This story focused on the impressions of Henry Fleming, a young soldier at the Civil War battle of Chancellorsville. As William Dean Howells (see page 382) observed, Crane's genius seemed to "spring to life fully armed" with this book. He had been born well after the end of the Civil War and had had no direct experience with battle. But he had read the popular anthology *Battles and Leaders of the Civil War,* and he had seen Mathew Brady's famous battle photographs. "I have never been in a battle, of course," wrote Crane later, "and I believe that I got my sense of the rage of conflict on the football field. The psychology is the same. The opposing team is an enemy tribe."

Whatever his sources, Crane managed to produce an extraordinary work that not only persuaded the war's veterans of its essential truth but also provided an arresting psychological study of the ordinary man thrust into war. The impressionistic technique used by Crane in the novel would have an important influence on the fiction of the next several decades.

In fiction, **impressionism** is a technique whereby the writer gives us not objective reality, but one character's impression of that reality. In other words, in *The Red Badge of Courage,* we get Henry Fleming's impressions of what he sees and feels and hears of the war, not a description of what is actually happening.

The Red Badge of Courage, published in 1895, sold so widely that in the following year Crane's publishers reissued *Maggie.* The renown of *The Red Badge of Courage* made Crane into a national expert on war, and he was to spend the rest of his short life writing about it for the newspapers. His celebrity was such that he also became the prototype of the adventurous correspondent who not only writes about sensational events but also lives a sensational life, delighting in shocking conservative readers.

One of the fascinating elements of Crane's life was the degree to which he interwove his fiction and his real-life experiences. It was as if he had invented a war in his novel, and then had to pursue the brushfire wars of his own times in order to confirm what he had written. Nor was experience wasted on him. When he sailed from Florida to cover a gun-running operation to Cuba, he was shipwrecked off the Florida coast and endured a fifty-four hour struggle against the sea. The result was his superb story "The Open Boat" (1898).

Before this ill-fated journey, he had stopped off at the Hotel de Dream in Jacksonville, Florida, and taken up with the hostess, Cora Taylor. She soon decided that she would stay with him and become the first female war correspondent. This oddly matched couple later went off to Greece to cover a war. They settled eventually in England, renting a huge, dilapidated, medieval house in Sussex.

All of these adventures were taking their toll on Crane's always delicate health. When he returned to England from another trip to Cuba, this time to cover the Spanish-American War, he was in the last year of his life. Still he continued to write, desperate now to pay for Cora's extravagant domestic life. In his last year he produced his second volume of poems (he called them "lines"), *War Is Kind* (page 508). But tuberculosis was sapping his strength. He suffered a serious hemorrhage in March 1900. After a hurried journey to a sanitarium in the Black Forest of Germany, Stephen Crane died there in May, not quite thirty years old.

THE RED BADGE OF COURAGE
AN EPISODE OF THE AMERICAN CIVIL WAR

Georgia private, Edwin Jennison, who was killed at Malvern Hill, July 1, 1862. Daguerreotype.

This short novel about the Civil War is probably the one piece of literature which Americans associate most closely with the ideas of courage and cowardice, and with the very notion of patriotism and what it may ask of the young.

The lasting impact of *The Red Badge of Courage* derives from the truth it reveals about men at war. The story appears to cut through the romantic illusions about warrior heroes that have been propagated down through the ages. We have been led to believe that the immortal heroes who proved their valor on such famous battlefields as Troy and Agincourt and Waterloo and the Marne were unafraid of danger, that they rejoiced to shed their blood for the honor of their nation or religion.

In the course of Crane's story, which takes an ordinary recruit into battle and out of it, we see dramatic changes take place in a soldier's understanding of war and of himself. These changes are persuasive enough to raise some doubts about our romantic notions of those brave hearts so central to the whole library of patriotic history and historical fiction. *The Red Badge of Courage* reveals the warrior's emotions as the familiar ones: fear, pride, shame, anger, and at least a touch of madness.

The third-person narrator who tells *The Red Badge of Courage* is so close to the hero, Henry Fleming, that we see the vivid, often gorgeous, war-torn landscape, with its fogs and smoke and that famous red sun "pasted in the sky like a wafer," through Henry's innocent eyes alone.

This style, in which the writer allows us to share a character's impressions of experience, is called *impressionism*. The style has been compared to Impressionist paintings, which aim not at mere realism, but at personal impressions of reality. Look for colors, sounds, smells, and other impressions in this story, which, taken all together, form a kind of painting of Henry's experiences with war.

Just as we might expect of a raw army recruit, Henry has no notion of what battle he is in, nor its location, nor who commands the rival forces. Like all footsoldiers, Henry is ignorant of where he is marching or why. He has no understanding of the maneuvers or strategies which propel him; he doesn't even know whether he is taking part in a victory or a defeat.

That is the central irony of Crane's story: that from the footsoldier's point of view, it is hard to tell the difference.

During the first part of the novel, we know the hero only as "the youth." We see him leaving home, enduring his mother's tearful advice—to beware the wickedness common to soldiers, and to change his socks frequently. But Henry dreams of heroism on the battlefield.

His first impressions of warfare are drawn from his comrades-at-arms. When he hears them bragging about courage under fire, Henry becomes suspicious about his own backbone. When the test of battle comes, will he stand and fight? Is it conceivable he might turn from the battle and run? Just what *is* he made of?

Henry's war, no different from other wars, puts him through the ordeal of interminable boredom before it gives him a chance to answer his own questions. As in any war, there is the endless marching and the countermarching, described so eloquently by latter-day infantrymen as "hurry-up and wait."

Just as we despair of ever getting to a battle, we are there, and the process of turning Henry Fleming into a warrior begins. At first he seems to fail the test of bravery, most humiliatingly, and then he seems to have passed it with distinction—but you will be the judge of that.

In any case, the story is filled with vivid, memorable scenes of war—Henry's flight into the cathedral-like woods where he confronts the corpse of a fellow soldier; his joining the column of wounded and his humiliation because his skin is whole; the extraordinary death of the tall soldier, Jim Conklin; Henry's acquisition of his own "red badge" under such surprising circumstances; and finally, Henry's own experience under enemy fire.

The Red Badge of Courage portrays warfare so vividly that we get the very smell of gunpowder and blood. We also realize that, even as limbs are shredded and as sudden death walks alongside them, men will respond with humor, as if laughter were the only island of sanity left.

Perhaps the most surprising aspect of *The Red Badge of Courage* is that its young author, Stephen Crane, was born six years after the Civil War ended. In his early twenties when he wrote the book, he had never seen a battle.

Chapter 1

The cold passed reluctantly from the earth, and the retiring fogs revealed an army stretched out on the hills, resting. As the landscape changed from brown to green, the army awakened, and began to tremble with eagerness at the noise of rumors. It cast its eyes upon the roads, which were growing from long troughs of liquid mud to proper thoroughfares. A river, amber-tinted in the shadow of its banks, purled at the army's feet; and at night, when the stream had become of a sorrowful blackness, one could see across it the red, eyelike gleam of hostile campfires set in the low brows of distant hills.

Once a certain tall soldier developed virtues and went resolutely to wash a shirt. He came flying back from a brook waving his garment bannerlike. He was swelled with a tale he had heard from a reliable friend, who had heard it from a truthful cavalryman, who had heard it from his trustworthy brother, one of the orderlies at division headquarters. He adopted the important air of a herald[1] in red and gold.

"We're goin' t' move t'morrah—sure," he said pompously to a group in the company street. "We're goin' 'way up the river, cut across, an' come around in behint 'em."

To his attentive audience he drew a loud and elaborate plan of a very brilliant campaign. When he had finished, the blue-clothed men scattered into small arguing groups between the rows of squat brown huts. A Negro teamster who had been dancing upon a cracker box with the hilarious encouragement of two score soldiers was deserted. He sat mournfully down. Smoke drifted lazily from a multitude of quaint chimneys.

"It's a lie! that's all it is—a thunderin' lie!" said another private loudly. His smooth face was flushed, and his hands were thrust sulkily into his trousers' pockets. He took the matter as an affront to him. "I don't believe the derned old army's ever going to move. We're set. I've got ready to move eight times in the last two weeks, and we ain't moved yet."

The tall soldier felt called upon to defend the truth of a rumor he himself had introduced. He and the loud one came near to fighting over it.

A corporal began to swear before the assemblage. He had just put a costly board floor in his house, he said. During the early spring he had refrained from adding extensively to the comfort of his environment because he had felt that the army might start on the march at any moment. Of

---

1. **herald:** an officer who carried messages back and forth.

late, however, he had been impressed that they were in a sort of eternal camp.

Many of the men engaged in a spirited debate. One outlined in a peculiarly lucid manner all the plans of the commanding general. He was opposed by men who advocated that there were other plans of campaign. They clamored at each other, numbers making futile bids for the popular attention. Meanwhile, the soldier who had fetched the rumor bustled about with much importance. He was continually assailed by questions.

"What's up, Jim!"

"Th' army's goin' t' move."

"Ah, what yeh talkin' about? How yeh know it is?"

"Well, yeh kin b'lieve me er not, jest as yeh like. I don't care a hang. I tell yeh what I know an' yeh kin take it er leave it. Suit yourselves. It don't make no difference t' me."

There was much food for thought in the manner in which he replied. He came near to convincing them by disdaining to produce proofs. They grew much excited over it.

There was a youthful private who listened with eager ears to the words of the tall soldier and to the varied comments of his comrades. After receiving a fill of discussions concerning marches and attacks, he went to his hut and crawled through an intricate hole that served it as a door. He wished to be alone with some new thoughts that had lately come to him.

He lay down on a wide bunk that stretched across the end of the room. In the other end, cracker boxes were made to serve as furniture. They were grouped about the fireplace. A picture from an illustrated weekly was upon the log walls, and three rifles were paralleled on pegs. Equipments hung on handy projections, and some tin dishes lay upon a small pile of firewood. A folded tent was serving as a roof. The sunlight, without, beating upon it, made it glow a light yellow shade. A small window shot an oblique square of whiter light upon the cluttered floor. The smoke from the fire at times neglected the clay chimney and wreathed into the room, and this flimsy chimney of clay and sticks made endless threats to set ablaze the whole establishment.

The youth was in a little trance of astonishment. So they were at last going to fight. On the morrow, perhaps, there would be a battle, and he would be in it. For a time he was obliged to labor to make himself believe. He could not accept with assurance an omen that he was about to mingle in one of those great affairs of the earth.

He had, of course, dreamed of battles all his life—of vague and bloody conflicts that had thrilled him with their sweep and fire. In visions he had seen himself in many struggles. He had imagined peoples secure in the shadow of his eagle-eyed prowess. But awake he had regarded battles as crimson blotches on the pages of the past. He had put them as things of the bygone with his thought-images of heavy crowns and high castles. There was a portion of the world's history which he had regarded as the time of wars, but it, he thought, had been long gone over the horizon and had disappeared forever.

From his home his youthful eyes had looked upon the war in his own country with distrust. It must be some sort of a play affair. He had long despaired of witnessing a Greeklike struggle. Such would be no more, he had said. Men were better, or more timid. Secular and religious education had effaced the throat-grappling instinct, or else firm finance held in check the passions.

He had burned several times to enlist. Tales of great movements shook the land. They might not be distinctly Homeric, but there seemed to be much glory in them. He had read of marches, sieges, conflicts, and he had longed to see it all. His busy mind had drawn for him large pictures extravagant in color, lurid with breathless deeds.

But his mother had discouraged him. She had affected to look with some contempt upon the quality of his war ardor and patriotism. She could calmly seat herself and with no apparent difficulty give him many hundreds of reasons why he was of vastly more importance on the farm than on the field of battle. She had had certain ways of expression that told him that her statements on the subject came from a deep conviction. Moreover, on her side, was his belief that her ethical motive in the argument was impregnable.

At last, however, he had made firm rebellion against this yellow light thrown upon the color of his ambitions. The newspapers, the gossip of the village, his own picturings, had aroused him to an uncheckable degree. They were in truth fighting finely down there. Almost every day the newspapers printed accounts of a decisive victory.

One night, as he lay in bed, the winds had carried to him the clangoring of the church bell as some enthusiast jerked the rope frantically to tell the twisted news of a great battle. This voice of the people rejoicing in the night had made him shiver in a prolonged ecstasy of excitement. Later, he had gone down to his mother's room and had spoken thus: "Ma, I'm going to enlist."

"Henry, don't you be a fool," his mother had replied. She had then covered her face with the quilt. There was an end to the matter for that night.

Nevertheless, the next morning he had gone to a town that was near his mother's farm and had enlisted in a company that was forming there. When he had returned home his mother was milking the brindle cow. Four others stood waiting. "Ma, I've enlisted," he had said to her diffidently. There was a short silence. "The Lord's will be done, Henry," she had finally replied, and had then continued to milk the brindle cow.

When he had stood in the doorway with his soldier's clothes on his back, and with the light of excitement and expectancy in his eyes almost defeating the glow of regret for the home bonds, he had seen two tears leaving their trails on his mother's scarred cheeks.

Still, she had disappointed him by saying nothing whatever about returning with his shield or on it.[2] He had privately primed himself for a beautiful scene. He had prepared certain sentences which he thought could be used with touching effect. But her words destroyed his plans. She had doggedly peeled potatoes and addressed him as follows: "You watch out, Henry, an' take good care of yerself in this here fighting business—you watch out, an' take good care of yerself. Don't go a-thinkin' you can lick the hull rebel army at the start, because yeh can't. Yer jest one little feller amongst a hull lot of others, and yeh've got to keep quiet an' do what they tell yeh. I know how you are, Henry.

"I've knet yeh eight pair of socks, Henry, and I've put in all yer best shirts, because I want my boy to be jest as warm and comf'able as anybody in the army. Whenever they get holes in 'em, I want yeh to send 'em right-away back to me, so's I kin dern 'em.

"An' allus be careful an' choose yer comp'ny. There's lots of bad men in the army, Henry. The army makes 'em wild, and they like nothing better than the job of leading off a young feller like you, as ain't never been away from home much and has allus had a mother, an' a-learning 'em to drink and swear. Keep clear of them folks, Henry. I don't want yeh to ever do anything, Henry, that yeh would be 'shamed to let me know about. Jest think as if I was a-watchin' yeh. If yeh keep that in yer mind allus, I guess yeh'll come out about right.

"Young fellers in the army get awful careless in their ways, Henry. They're away f'm home and they don't have nobody to look after 'em. I'm

---

2. . . . with his shield or on it: an allusion to the words Spartan women were said to have directed to their sons or husbands as they went into battle: Return with your shield, or on top of it. (Victims of wars were carried home on their huge shields.)

'feared fer yeh about that. Yeh ain't never been used to doing for yerself. So yeh must keep writing to me how yer clothes are lasting.

"Yeh must allus remember yer father, too, child, an' remember he never drunk a drop of licker in his life, and seldom swore a cross oath.

"I don't know what else to tell yeh, Henry, excepting that yeh must never do no shirking, child, on my account. If so be a time comes when yeh have to be kilt or do a mean thing, why, Henry, don't think of anything 'cept what's right, because there's many a woman has to bear up 'ginst sech things these times, and the Lord'll take keer of us all. Don't fergit to send yer socks to me the minute they git holes in 'em, and here's a little Bible I want yeh to take along with yeh, Henry. I don't presume yeh'll be a-setting reading it all day long, child, ner nothin' like that. Many a time, yeh'll fergit yeh got it, I don't doubt. But there'll be many a time, too, Henry, when yeh'll be wanting advice, boy, and all like that, and there'll be nobody round, perhaps, to tell yeh things. Then if yeh take it out, boy, yeh'll find wisdom in it—wisdom in it, Henry—with little or no searching. Don't fergit about the socks and the shirts, child; and I've put a cup of blackberry jam with yer bundle because I know yeh like it above all things. Goodbye, Henry. Watch out, and be a good boy."

He had, of course, been impatient under the ordeal of this speech. It had not been quite what he expected, and he had borne it with an air of irritation. He departed feeling vague relief.

Still, when he had looked back from the gate, he had seen his mother kneeling among the potato parings. Her brown face, upraised, was stained with tears, and her spare form was quivering. He bowed his head and went on, feeling suddenly ashamed of his purposes.

From his home he had gone to the seminary[3] to bid adieu to many schoolmates. They had thronged about him with wonder and admiration. He had felt the gulf now between them and had swelled with calm pride. He and some of his fellows who had donned blue were quite overwhelmed with privileges for all of one afternoon, and it had been a very delicious thing. They had strutted.

A certain light-haired girl had made vivacious fun at his martial spirit, but there was another and darker girl whom he had gazed at steadfastly, and he thought she grew demure and sad at sight of his blue and brass. As he had walked down the path between the rows of oaks, he had turned his

head and detected her at a window watching his departure. As he perceived her, she had immediately begun to stare up through the high tree branches at the sky. He had seen a good deal of flurry and haste in her movements as she changed her attitude. He often thought of it.

On the way to Washington his spirit had soared. The regiment was fed and caressed at station after station until the youth had believed that he must be a hero. There was a lavish expenditure of bread and cold meats, coffee, and pickles and cheese. As he basked in the smiles of the girls and was patted and complimented by the old men, he had felt growing within him the strength to do mighty deeds of arms.

After complicated journeyings with many pauses, there had come months of monotonous life in a camp. He had had the belief that real war was a series of death struggles with small time in between for sleep and meals; but since his regiment had come to the field the army had done little but sit still and try to keep warm.

He was brought then gradually back to his old ideas. Greeklike struggles would be no more. Men were better, or more timid. Secular and religious education had effaced the throat-grappling instinct, or else firm finance held in check the passions.

He had grown to regard himself merely as a part of a vast blue demonstration. His province was to look out, as far as he could, for his personal comfort. For recreation he could twiddle his thumbs and speculate on the thoughts which must agitate the minds of the generals. Also, he was drilled and drilled and reviewed, and drilled and drilled and reviewed.

The only foes he had seen were some pickets along the riverbank. They were a sun-tanned, philosophical lot, who sometimes shot reflectively at the blue pickets. When reproached for this afterward, they usually expressed sorrow, and swore by their gods that the guns had exploded without their permission. The youth, on guard duty one night, conversed across the stream with one of them. He was a slightly ragged man, who spat skillfully between his shoes and possessed a great fund of bland and infantile assurance. The youth liked him personally.

"Yank," the other had informed him, "yer a right dum good feller." This sentiment, floating to him upon the still air, had made him temporarily regret war.

Various veterans had told him tales. Some talked of gray, bewhiskered hordes who were advancing with relentless curses and chewing tobacco with unspeakable valor; tremendous bodies

---

3. **seminary:** here, the local secondary school.

of fierce soldiery who were sweeping along like the Huns.[4] Others spoke of tattered and eternally hungry men who fired despondent powders. "They'll charge through hell's fire an' brimstone t' git a holt on a haversack,[5] an' sech stomachs ain't a-lastin' long," he was told. From the stories, the youth imagined the red, live bones sticking out through slits in the faded uniforms.

Still, he could not put a whole faith in veterans' tales, for recruits were their prey. They talked much of smoke, fire, and blood, but he could not tell how much might be lies. They persistently yelled, "Fresh fish!"[6] at him, and were in no wise to be trusted.

However, he perceived now that it did not greatly matter what kind of soldiers he was going to fight, so long as they fought, which fact no one disputed. There was a more serious problem. He lay in his bunk pondering upon it. He tried to mathematically prove to himself that he would not run from a battle.

Previously he had never felt obliged to wrestle too seriously with this question. In his life he had taken certain things for granted, never challenging his belief in ultimate success, and bothering little about means and roads. But here he was confronted with a thing of moment. It had suddenly appeared to him that perhaps in a battle he might run. He was forced to admit that as far as war was concerned he knew nothing of himself.

A sufficient time before he would have allowed the problem to kick its heels at the outer portals of his mind, but now he felt compelled to give serious attention to it.

A little panic-fear grew in his mind. As his imagination went forward to a fight, he saw hideous possibilities. He contemplated the lurking menaces of the future, and failed in an effort to see himself standing stoutly in the midst of them. He recalled his visions of broken-bladed glory, but in the shadow of the impending tumult he suspected them to be impossible pictures.

He sprang from the bunk and began to pace nervously to and fro. "Good Lord, what's th' matter with me?" he said aloud.

He felt that in this crisis his laws of life were useless. Whatever he had learned of himself was here of no avail. He was an unknown quantity. He saw that he would again be obliged to experiment as he had in early youth. He must accumulate information of himself, and meanwhile he resolved to remain close upon his guard lest those qualities of which he knew nothing should everlastingly disgrace him. "Good Lord!" he repeated in dismay.

After a time the tall soldier slid dexterously through the hole. The loud private followed. They were wrangling.

"That's all right," said the tall soldier as he entered. He waved his hand expressively. "You can believe me or not, jest as you like. All you got to do is to sit down and wait as quiet as you can. Then pretty soon you'll find out I was right."

His comrade grunted stubbornly. For a moment he seemed to be searching for a formidable reply. Finally he said: "Well, you don't know everything in the world, do you?"

"Didn't say I knew everything in the world," retorted the other sharply. He began to stow various articles snugly into his knapsack.

The youth, pausing in his nervous walk, looked down at the busy figure. "Going to be a battle, sure, is there, Jim?" he asked.

"Of course there is," replied the tall soldier. "Of course there is. You jest wait 'til tomorrow, and you'll see one of the biggest battles ever was. You jest wait."

"Thunder!" said the youth.

"Oh, you'll see fighting this time, my boy, what'll be regular out-and-out fighting," added the tall soldier, with the air of a man who is about to exhibit a battle for the benefit of his friends.

"Huh!" said the loud one from a corner.

"Well," remarked the youth, "like as not this story'll turn out jest like them others did."

"Not much it won't" replied the tall soldier, exasperated. "Not much it won't. Didn't the cavalry all start this morning?" He glared about him. No one denied his statement. "The cavalry started this morning," he continued. "They say there ain't hardly any cavalry left in camp. They're going to Richmond, or some place, while we fight all the Johnnies.[7] It's some dodge like that. The regiment's got orders, too. A feller what seen 'em go to headquarters told me a little while ago. And they're raising blazes all over camp—anybody can see that."

"Shucks!" said the loud one.

The youth remained silent for a time. At last he spoke to the tall soldier. "Jim!"

"What?"

"How do you think the reg'ment 'll do?"

"Oh, they'll fight all right, I guess, after they once get into it," said the other with cold judg-

---

4. **Huns:** a tribe of fifth-century barbarians.
5. **haversack:** canvas bag.
6. **"Fresh fish":** a taunt about his lack of experience.

7. **Johnnies:** the name the Union soldiers gave the Confederate soldiers (Johnny Rebel).

ment. He made a fine use of the third person. "There's been heaps of fun poked at 'em because they're new, of course, and all that; but they'll fight all right, I guess."

"Think any of the boys 'll run?" persisted the youth.

"Oh, there may be a few of 'em run, but there's them kind in every regiment, 'specially when they first goes under fire," said the other in a tolerant way. "Of course it might happen that the hull kit-and-boodle might start and run, if some big fighting came first-off, and then again they might stay and fight like fun. But you can't bet on nothing. Of course they ain't never been under fire yet, and it ain't likely they'll lick the hull rebel army all-at-oncet the first time; but I think they'll fight better than some, if worse than others. That's the way I figger. They call the reg'ment 'Fresh fish' and everything; but the boys come of good stock, and most of 'em 'll fight like sin after they oncet git shootin'," he added, with a mighty emphasis on the last four words.

"Oh, you think you know——" began the loud soldier with scorn.

The other turned savagely upon him. They had a rapid altercation, in which they fastened upon each other various strange epithets.

The youth at last interrupted them. "Did you ever think you might run yourself, Jim?" he asked. On concluding the sentence he laughed as if he had meant to aim a joke. The loud soldier also giggled.

The tall private waved his hand. "Well," said he profoundly, "I've thought it might get too hot for Jim Conklin in some of them scrimmages, and if a whole lot of boys started and run, why, I s'pose I'd start and run. And if I once started to run, I'd run like the devil, and no mistake. But if everybody was a-standing and a-fighting, why, I'd stand and fight. Be jiminey, I would. I'll bet on it."

"Huh!" said the loud one.

The youth of this tale felt gratitude for these words of his comrade. He had feared that all of the untried men possessed a great and correct confidence. He now was in a measure reassured.

Chapter 2

The next morning the youth discovered that his tall comrade had been the fast-flying messenger of a mistake. There was much scoffing at the latter by those who had yesterday been firm adherents of his views, and there was even a little sneering by men who had never be-

lieved the rumor. The tall one fought with a man from Chatfield Corners and beat him severely.

The youth felt, however, that his problem was in no wise lifted from him. There was, on the contrary, an irritating prolongation. The tale had created in him a great concern for himself. Now, with the newborn question in his mind, he was compelled to sink back into his old place as part of a blue demonstration.

For days he made ceaseless calculations, but they were all wondrously unsatisfactory. He found that he could establish nothing. He finally concluded that the only way to prove himself was to go into the blaze, and then figuratively to watch his legs to discover their merits and faults. He reluctantly admitted that he could not sit still and with a mental slate and pencil derive an answer. To gain it, he must have blaze, blood, and danger, even as a chemist requires this, that, and the other. So he fretted for an opportunity.

Meanwhile he continually tried to measure himself by his comrades. The tall soldier, for one, gave him some assurance. This man's serene unconcern dealt him a measure of confidence, for he had known him since childhood, and from his intimate knowledge he did not see how he could be capable of anything that was beyond him, the youth. Still, he thought that his comrade might be mistaken about himself. Or, on the other hand, he might be a man heretofore doomed to peace and obscurity, but, in reality, made to shine in war.

The youth would have liked to have discovered another who suspected himself. A sympathetic comparison of mental notes would have been a joy to him.

He occasionally tried to fathom[1] a comrade with seductive sentences. He looked about to find men in the proper mood. All attempts failed to bring forth any statement which looked in any way like a confession to those doubts which he privately acknowledged in himself. He was afraid to make an open declaration of his concern, because he dreaded to place some unscrupulous confidant upon the high plane of the unconfessed from which elevation he could be derided.

In regard to his companions his mind wavered between two opinions, according to his mood. Sometimes he inclined to believing them all heroes. In fact, he usually admitted in secret the superior development of the higher qualities in others. He could conceive of men going very insignificantly about the world bearing a load of courage unseen, and, although he had known many of his comrades through boyhood, he began

---

1. **fathom:** question.

Winter quarters (1861-1864). Photograph by Mathew Brady.

to fear that his judgment of them had been blind. Then, in other moments, he flouted these theories, and assured himself that his fellows were all privately wondering and quaking.

His emotions made him feel strange in the presence of men who talked excitedly of a prospective battle as of a drama they were about to witness, with nothing but eagerness and curiosity apparent in their faces. It was often that he suspected them to be liars.

He did not pass such thoughts without severe condemnation of himself. He dinned reproaches at times. He was convicted by himself of many shameful crimes against the gods of traditions.

In his great anxiety his heart was continually clamoring at what he considered the intolerable slowness of the generals. They seemed content to perch tranquilly on the river bank, and leave him bowed down by the weight of a great problem. He wanted it settled forthwith. He could not long bear such a load, he said. Sometimes his anger at the commanders reached an acute stage, and he grumbled about the camp like a veteran.

One morning, however, he found himself in the ranks of his prepared regiment. The men were whispering speculations and recounting the old rumors. In the gloom before the break of the day their uniforms glowed a deep purple hue. From across the river the red eyes were still peering. In the eastern sky there was a yellow patch like a rug laid for the feet of the coming sun; and against it, black and patternlike, loomed the gigantic figure of the colonel on a gigantic horse.

From off in the darkness came the trampling of feet. The youth could occasionally see dark shadows that moved like monsters. The regiment stood at rest for what seemed a long time. The youth grew impatient. It was unendurable the way these affairs were managed. He wondered how long they were to be kept waiting.

As he looked all about him and pondered upon the mystic gloom, he began to believe that at any moment the ominous distance might be aflare, and the rolling crashes of an engagement come to his ears. Staring once at the red eyes across the river, he conceived them to be growing larger, as the orbs of a row of dragons advancing. He turned toward the colonel and saw him lift his gigantic arm and calmly stroke his mustache.

At last he heard from along the road at the foot of the hill the clatter of a horse's galloping hoofs. It must be the coming of orders. He bent forward, scarce breathing. The exciting clickety-click, as it grew louder and louder, seemed to be beating upon his soul. Presently a horseman with jangling equipment drew rein before the colonel of the regiment. The two held a short, sharp-worded conversation. The men in the foremost ranks craned their necks.

As the horseman wheeled his animal and galloped away he turned to shout over his shoulder, "Don't forget that box of cigars!" The colonel mumbled in reply. The youth wondered what a box of cigars had to do with war.

A moment later the regiment went swinging off into the darkness. It was now like one of those moving monsters wending with many feet. The air was heavy, and cold with dew. A mass of wet grass, marched upon, rustled like silk.

There was an occasional flash and glimmer of steel from the backs of all these huge crawling reptiles. From the road came creakings and grumblings as some surly guns were dragged away.

The men stumbled along still muttering speculations. There was a subdued debate. Once a man fell down, and as he reached for his rifle a comrade, unseeing, trod upon his hand. He of the injured fingers swore bitterly and aloud. A low, tittering laugh went among his fellows.

Presently they passed into a roadway and marched forward with easy strides. A dark regiment moved before them, and from behind also came the tinkle of equipments on the bodies of marching men.

The rushing yellow of the developing day went on behind their backs. When the sunrays at last struck full and mellowingly upon the earth, the youth saw that the landscape was streaked with two long, thin, black columns which disappeared on the brow of a hill in front and rearward vanished in a wood. They were like two serpents crawling from the cavern of the night.

The river was not in view. The tall soldier burst into praises of what he thought to be his powers of perceptions. "I told you so, didn't I?"

Some of the tall one's companions cried with emphasis that they, too, had evolved the same thing, and they congratulated themselves upon it. But there were others who said that the tall one's plan was not the true one at all. They persisted with other theories. There was a vigorous discussion.

The youth took no part in them. As he walked along in careless line he was engaged with his own eternal debate. He could not hinder himself from dwelling upon it. He was despondent and sullen, and threw shifting glances about him. He looked ahead, often expecting to hear from the advance the rattle of firing.

But the long serpents crawled slowly from hill

carried anything but their necessary clothing, blankets, haversacks, canteens, and arms and ammunition. "Yuh kin now eat, drink, sleep, and shoot," said the tall soldier to the youth. "That's all you need. What do you want to do—carry a hotel?" There was sudden change from the ponderous infantry of theory to the light and speedy infantry of practice. The regiment, relieved of a burden, received a new impetus. But there was much loss of valuable knapsacks, and, on the whole, very good shirts.

But the regiment was not yet veteranlike in appearance. Veteran regiments in the army were likely to be very small aggregations of men. Once, when the command had first come to the field, some perambulating veterans, noting the length of their column, had accosted them thus: "Hey, fellers, what brigade is that?" And when the men had replied that they formed a regiment and not a brigade, the older soldiers had laughed, and said, "O Gawd!"

Also, there was too great a similarity in the hats. The hats of a regiment should properly represent the history of headgear for a period of years. And, moreover, there were no letters of faded gold speaking from the colors. They were new and beautiful, and the color bearer habitually oiled the pole.

Presently the army again sat down to think. The odor of the peaceful pines was in the men's nostrils. The sound of monotonous ax blows rang through the forest, and the insects, nodding upon their perches, crooned like old women. The youth returned to his theory of a blue demonstration.

One gray dawn, however, he was kicked in the leg by the tall soldier, and then, before he was entirely awake, he found himself running down a wood road in the midst of men who were panting from the first effects of speed. His canteen banged rhythmically upon his thigh, and his haversack bobbed softly. His musket bounced a trifle from his shoulder at each stride and made his cap feel uncertain upon his head.

He could hear the men whisper jerky sentences: "Say—what's all this—about?" "What th' thunder—we—skedaddlin' this way fer?" "Billie—keep off m' feet. Yeh run—like a cow." And the loud soldier's shrill voice could be heard: "What th' devil they in sich a hurry for?"

The youth thought the dam fog of early morning moved from the rush of a great body of troops. From the distance came a sudden spatter of firing.

He was bewildered. As he ran with his comrades he strenuously tried to think, but all he knew was that if he fell down those coming behind would tread upon him. All his faculties seemed to be needed to guide him over the past obstructions. He felt carried along by a mob.

The sun spread disclosing rays, and, one by one, regiments burst into view like armed men just born of the earth. The youth perceived that the time had come. He was about to be measured. For a moment he felt in the face of his great trial like a babe, and the flesh over his heart seemed very thin. He seized time to look about him calculatingly.

But he instantly saw that it would be impossible for him to escape from the regiment. It inclosed him. And there were iron laws of tradition and law on four sides. He was in a moving box.

As he perceived this fact it occurred to him that he had never wished to come to the war. He had not enlisted of his free will. He had been dragged by the merciless government. And now they were taking him out to be slaughtered.

The regiment slid down a bank and wallowed across a little stream. The mournful current moved slowly on, and from the water, shaded black, some white bubble eyes looked at the men.

As they climbed the hill on the farther side artillery began to boom. Here the youth forgot many things as he felt a sudden impulse of curiosity. He scrambled up the bank with a speed that could not be exceeded by a bloodthirsty man.

He expected a battle scene.

There were some little fields girted and squeezed by a forest. Spread over the grass and in among the tree trunks, he could see knots and waving lines of skirmishers who were running hither and thither and firing at the landscape. A dark battle line lay upon a sunstruck clearing that gleamed orange color. A flag fluttered.

Other regiments floundered up the bank. The brigade was formed in line of battle, and after a pause started slowly through the woods in the rear of the receding skirmishers, who were continually melting into the scene to appear again farther on. They were always busy as bees, deeply absorbed in their little combats.

The youth tried to observe everything. He did not use care to avoid trees and branches, and his forgotten feet were constantly knocking against stones or getting entangled in briers. He was aware that these battalions with their commotions were woven red and startling into the gentle fabric of softened greens and browns. It looked to be a wrong place for a battlefield.

The skirmishers in advance fascinated him. Their shots into thickets and at distant and prominent trees spoke to him of tragedies—hidden, mysterious, solemn.

Once the line encountered the body of a dead

soldier. He lay upon his back staring at the sky. He was dressed in an awkward suit of yellowish brown. The youth could see that the soles of his shoes had been worn to the thinness of writing paper, and from a great rent in one the dead foot projected piteously. And it was as if fate had betrayed the soldier. In death it exposed to his enemies that poverty which in life he had perhaps concealed from his friends.

The ranks opened covertly to avoid the corpse. The invulnerable dead man forced a way for himself. The youth looked keenly at the ashen face. The wind raised the tawny beard. It moved as if a hand were stroking it. He vaguely desired to walk around and around the body and stare; the impulse of the living to try to read in dead eyes the answer to the Question.

During the march the ardor which the youth had acquired when out of view of the field rapidly faded to nothing. His curiosity was quite easily satisfied. If an intense scene had caught him with its wild swing as he came to the top of the bank, he might have gone roaring on. This advance upon Nature was too calm. He had opportunity to reflect. He had time in which to wonder about himself and to attempt to probe his sensations.

Absurd ideas took hold upon him. He thought that he did not relish the landscape. It threatened him. A coldness swept over his back, and it is true that his trousers felt to him that they were no fit for his legs at all.

A house standing placidly in distant fields had to him an ominous look. The shadows of the woods were formidable. He was certain that in this vista there lurked fierce-eyed hosts. The swift thought came to him that the generals did not know what they were about. It was all a trap. Suddenly those close forests would bristle with rifle barrels. Ironlike brigades would appear in the rear. They were all going to be sacrificed. The generals were stupids. The enemy would presently swallow the whole command. He glared about him, expecting to see the stealthy approach of his death.

He thought that he must break from the ranks and harangue his comrades. They must not all be killed like pigs; and he was sure it would come to pass unless they were informed of these dangers. The generals were idiots to send them marching into a regular pen. There was but one pair of eyes in the corps. He would step forth and make a speech. Shrill and passionate words came to his lips.

The line, broken into moving fragments by the ground, went calmly on through fields and woods. The youth looked at the men nearest him, and saw, for the most part, expressions of deep interest, as if they were investigating something that had fascinated them. One or two stepped with overvaliant airs as if they were already plunged into war. Others walked as upon thin ice. The greater part of the untested men appeared quiet and absorbed. They were going to look at war, the red animal—war, the blood-swollen god. And they were deeply engrossed in this march.

As he looked the youth gripped his outcry at his throat. He saw that even if the men were tottering with fear they would laugh at his warning. They would jeer him, and, if practicable, pelt him with missiles. Admitting that he might be wrong, a frenzied declamation of the kind would turn him into a worm.

He assumed, then, the demeanor of one who knows that he is doomed alone to unwritten responsibilities. He lagged, with tragic glances at the sky.

He was surprised presently by the young lieutenant of his company, who began heartily to beat him with a sword, calling out in a loud and insolent voice: "Come, young man, get up into ranks there. No skulking 'll do here." He mended his pace with suitable haste. And he hated the lieutenant, who had no appreciation of fine minds. He was a mere brute.

After a time the brigade was halted in the cathedral light of a forest. The busy skirmishers were still popping. Through the aisles of the wood could be seen the floating smoke from their rifles. Sometimes it went up in little balls, white and compact.

During this halt many men in the regiment began erecting tiny hills in front of them. They used stones, sticks, earth and anything they thought might turn a bullet. Some built comparatively large ones, while others seemed content with little ones.

This procedure caused a discussion among the men. Some wished to fight like duelists, believing it to be correct to stand erect and be, from their feet to their foreheads, a mark. They said they scorned the devices of the cautious. But the others scoffed in reply, and pointed to the veterans on the flanks who were digging at the ground like terriers. In a short time there was quite a barricade along the regimental fronts. Directly, however, they were ordered to withdraw from that place.

This astounded the youth. He forgot his stewing over the advance movement. "Well, then, what did they march us out here for?" he demanded of the tall soldier. The latter with calm faith began a heavy explanation, although he had been compelled to leave a little protection of stones and dirt to which he had devoted much care and skill.

When the regiment was aligned in another position each man's regard for his safety caused another line of small intrenchments. They ate their noon meal behind a third one. They were moved from this one also. They were marched from place to place with apparent aimlessness.

The youth had been taught that a man became another thing in a battle. He saw his salvation in such a change. Hence this waiting was an ordeal to him. He was in a fever of impatience. He considered that there was denoted a lack of purpose on the part of the generals. He began to complain to the tall soldier. "I can't stand this much longer," he cried. "I don't see what good it does to make us wear out our legs for nothin'." He wished to return to camp, knowing that this affair was a blue demonstration; or else to go into a battle and discover that he had been a fool in his doubts, and was, in truth, a man of traditional courage. The strain of present circumstances he felt to be intolerable.

The philosophical tall soldier measured a sandwich of cracker[1] and pork and swallowed it in a nonchalant manner. "Oh, I suppose we must go reconnoitering around the country jest to keep 'em from getting too close, or to develop 'em, or something."

"Huh!" said the loud soldier.

"Well," cried the youth, still fidgeting, "I'd rather do anything 'most than go tramping 'round the country all day doing no good to nobody and jest tiring ourselves out."

"So would I," said the loud soldier. "It ain't right. I tell you if anybody with any sense was a-runnin' this army it—"

"Oh, shut up!" roared the tall private. "You little fool. You little damn' cuss. You ain't had that there coat and them paints on for six months, and yet you talk as if—"

"Well, I wanta do some fighting anyway," interrupted the other. "I didn't come here to walk. I could 'ave walked to home—'round and 'round the barn, if I jest wanted to walk."

The tall one, red-faced, swallowed another sandwich as if taking poison in despair.

But gradually, as he chewed, his face became again quiet and contented. He could not rage in fierce argument in the presence of such sandwiches. During his meals he always wore an air of blissful contemplation of the food he had swallowed. His spirit seemed then to be communing with the viands.

---

1. **cracker:** hard, unleavened bread, standard army rations during the Civil War.

He accepted new environment and circumstance with great coolness, eating from his haversack at every opportunity. On the march he went along with the strike of a hunter, objecting to neither gait nor distance. And he had not raised his voice when he had been ordered away from three little protective piles of earth and stone, each of which had been an engineering feat worthy of being made sacred to the name of his grandmother.

In the afternoon the regiment went out over the same ground it had taken in the morning. The landscape then ceased to threaten the youth. He had been close to it and become familiar with it.

When, however, they began to pass into a new region, his fears of stupidity and incompetence reassailed him, but this time he doggedly let them babble. He was occupied with his problem, and in his desperation he concluded that the stupidity did not greatly matter.

Once he thought he had concluded that it would be better to get killed directly and end his troubles. Regarding death thus out of the corner of his eye, he conceived it to be nothing but rest, and he was filled with a momentary astonishment that he should have made an extraordinary commotion over the mere matter of getting killed. He would die; he would go to some place where he would be understood. It was useless to expect appreciation of his profound and fine senses from such men as the lieutenant. He must look to the grave for comprehension.

The unceasing skirmish-fire increased to a long clattering sound. With it was mingled faraway cheering. A battery spoke.

Directly the youth would see the skirmishers running. They were pursued by the sound of musketry fire. After a time the hot, dangerous flashes of the rifles were visible. Smoke clouds went slowly and insolently across the fields like observant phantoms. The din became crescendo, like the roar of an oncoming train.

The brigade ahead of them and on the right went into action with a rending roar. It was as if it had exploded. And thereafter it lay stretched in the distance behind a long gray wall, that one was obliged to look twice at to make sure that it was smoke.

The youth, forgetting his neat plan of getting killed, gazed spellbound. His eyes grew wide and busy with the action of the scene. His mouth was a little ways open.

Of a sudden he felt a heavy and sad hand laid upon his shoulder. Awakening from his trance of observation he turned and beheld the loud soldier.

"It's my first and last battle, old boy," said the

latter, with intense gloom. He was quite pale and his girlish lip was trembling.

"Eh?" murmured the youth in great astonishment.

"It's my first and last battle, old boy," continued the loud soldier. "Something tells me—"

"What?"

"I'm a gone coon this first time and—and I w-want you to take these here things—to—my—folks." He ended in a quavering sob of pity for himself. He handed the youth a little packet done up in a yellow envelope.

"Why, what the devil—" began the youth again.

But the other gave him a glance as from the depths of a tomb, and raised his limp hand in a prophetic manner and turned away.

Chapter 4

The brigade was halted in the fringe of a grove. The men crouched among the trees and pointed their restless guns out at the fields. They tried to look beyond the smoke.

Out of this haze they could see running men. Some shouted information and gestured as they hurried.

The men of the new regiment watched and listened eagerly, while their tongues ran on in gossip of the battle. They mouthed rumors that had flown like birds out of the unknown.

"They say Perry has been driven in with big loss."

"Yes, Carrott went t' th' hospital. He said he was sick. That smart lieutenant is commanding 'G' Company. Th' boys say they won't be under Carrott no more if they all have t' desert. They allus knew he was a—"

"Hannises' batt'ry is took."

"It ain't either. I saw Hannises' batt'ry off on th' left not more 'n fifteen minutes ago."

"Well—"

"Th' general, he ses he is goin' t' take th' hull cammand of th' 304th when we go inteh action, an' then he ses we'll do sech fightin' as never another one reg'ment done."

"They say we're catchin' it over on th' left. They say th' enemy driv' our line inteh a devil of a swamp an' took Hannises' batt'ry."

"No sech thing. Hannises' batt'ry was 'long here 'bout a minute ago."

"That young Hasbrouck, he makes a good off'cer. He ain't afraid 'a nothin'."

"I met one of th' 148th Maine boys an' he ses his brigade fit th' hull rebel army fer four hours over on th' turnpike road an' killed about five thousand of 'em. He ses one more sech fight as that an' th' war 'll be over."

"Bill wasn't scared either. No sir! It wasn't that. Bill ain't a-gittin' scared easy. He was jest mad, that's what he was. When that feller trod on his hand, he up an' sed that he was willin' t' give his hand t' his country, but he be dumbed if he was goin' t' have every dumb bushwacker[1] in th' kentry walkin' 'round on it. So he went t' th' hospital disregardless of th' fight. Three fingers was crunched. Th' dern doctor wanted t' amputate 'm, an' Bill, he raised a heluva row, I hear. He's a funny feller."

"Hear that what the ol' colonel ses, boys. He ses he'll shoot th' first man what 'll turn an' run."

"He'd better try it. I'd like t' see him shoot at *me*."

"He wants t' look fer his *own* self. *He* don't wanta go 'round talkin' big."

"They say Perry's division's a-givin' 'em thunder."

"Ed Williams over in Company A, he ses the rebs 'll all drop their guns an' run an' holler if we onct give 'em once good lickin'."

"Oh, thunder, Ed Williams, what does he know? Ever since he got shot at on picket he's been runnin' th' war."

"Well, he—"

"Hear th' news, boys? Corkright's crushed th' hull rebel right an' captured two hull divisions. We'll be back in winter quarters by a short cut t'morrah."

"I tell yeh I've been all over that there kentry where th' rebel right is an' it's th' nastiest part th' rebel line. It's all mussed up with hills an' little damn creeks. I'll bet m' shirt Corkright never harmed 'em down there."

"Well he's a fighter an' if they could be licked, he'd lick 'em."

The din in front swelled to a tremendous chorus. The youth and his fellows were frozen to silence. They could see a flag that tossed in the smoke angrily. Near it were the blurred and agitated forms of troops. There came a turbulent stream of men across the fields. A battery changing position at a frantic gallop scattered the stragglers right and left.

A shell screaming like a storm banshee[2] went over the huddled heads of the reserves. It landed in the grove, and exploding redly flung the brown earth. There was a little shower of pine needles.

---

1. **bushwacker:** guerrilla fighter.
2. **banshee:** in Irish folklore, a spirit that wails when someone has died.

Bullets began to whistle among the branches and nip at the trees. Twigs and leaves came sailing down. It was as if a thousand axes, wee and invisible, were being wielded. Many of the men were constantly dodging and ducking their heads.

The lieutenant of the youth's company was shot in the hand. He began to swear so wondrously that a nervous laugh went along the regimental line. The officer's profanity sounded conventional. It relieved the tightened senses of the new men. It was as if he had hit his fingers with a tack hammer at home.

He held the wounded member carefully away from his side so that the blood would not drip upon his trousers.

The captain of the company, tucking his sword under his arm, produced a handkerchief and began to bind with it the lieutenant's wound. And they disputed as to how the binding should be done.

The battle flag in the distance jerked about madly. It seemed to be struggling to free itself from an agony. The billowing smoke was filled with horizontal flashes.

Men running swiftly emerged from it. They grew in numbers until it was seen that the whole command was fleeing. The flag suddenly sank down as if dying. Its motion as it fell was a gesture of despair.

Wild yells came from behind the walls of smoke. A sketch in gray and red dissolved into a moblike body of men who galloped like wild horses.

The veteran regiments on the right and left of the 304th immediately began to jeer. With the passionate song of the bullets and the banshee shrieks of shells were mingled loud catcalls and bits of facetious advice concerning places of safety.

But the new regiment was breathless with horror. "Gawd! Saunders's got crushed!" whispered the man at the youth's elbow. They shrank back and crouched as if compelled to await a flood.

The youth shot a swift glance along the blue ranks of the regiment. The profiles were motionless, carven; and afterward he remembered that the color sergeant was standing with his legs apart, as if he expected to be pushed to the ground.

The following throng went whirling around the flank. Here and there were officers carried along on the stream like exasperated chips. They were striking about them with their swords and with their left fists, punching every head they could reach. They cursed like highwaymen.

A mounted officer displayed the furious anger of a spoiled child. He raged with his head, his arms, and his legs.

Another, the commander of the brigade, was galloping about bawling. His hat was gone and his clothes were awry. He resembled a man who has come from bed to go to a fire. The hoofs of his horse often threatened the heads of the running men, but they scampered with singular fortune. In this rush they were apparently all deaf and blind. They heeded not the largest and longest of the oaths that were thrown at them from all directions.

Frequently over this tumult could be heard the grim jokes of the critical veterans; but the retreating men apparently were not even conscious of the presence of an audience.

The battle reflection that shone for an instant in the faces on the mad current made the youth feel that forceful hands from heaven would not have been able to have held him in place if he could have got intelligent control of his legs.

There was an appalling imprint upon these faces. The struggle in the smoke had pictured an exaggeration of itself on the bleached cheeks and in the eyes wild with one desire.

The sight of this stampede exerted a floodlike force that seemed able to drag sticks and stones and men from the ground. They of the reserves had to hold on. They grew pale and firm, and red and quaking.

The youth achieved one little thought in the midst of this chaos. The composite monster which had caused the other troops to flee had not then appeared. He resolved to get a view of it, and then, he thought he might very likely run better than the best of them.

Chapter 5

There were moments of waiting. The youth thought of the village street at home before the arrival of the circus parade on a day in the spring. He remembered how he had stood, a small, thrillful boy, prepared to follow the dingy lady upon the white horse, or the band in its faded chariot. He saw the yellow road, the lines of expectant people, and the sober houses. He particularly remembered an old fellow who used to sit upon a cracker box in front of the store and feign to despise such exhibitions. A thousand details of color and form surged in his mind. The old fellow upon the cracker box appeared in middle prominence.

Someone cried, "Here they come!"

There was rustling and muttering among the men. They displayed a feverish desire to have every possible cartridge ready to their hands. The boxes were pulled around into various positions, and adjusted with great care. It was as if seven hundred new bonnets were being tried on.

The tall soldier, having prepared his rifle, produced a red handkerchief of some kind. He was engaged in knitting it about his throat with exquisite attention to its position, when the cry was repeated up and down the line in a muffled roar of sound.

"Here they come! Here they come!" Gun locks clicked.

Across the smoke-infested fields came a brown swarm of running men who were giving shrill yells. They came on, stooping and swinging their rifles at all angles. A flag, tilted forward, sped near the front.

As he caught sight of them the youth was momentarily startled by a thought that perhaps his gun was not loaded. He stood trying to rally his faltering intellect so that he might recollect the moment when he had loaded, but he could not.

A hatless general pulled his dripping horse to a stand near the colonel of the 304th. He shook his fist in the other's face. "You've got to hold 'em back!" he shouted, savagely; "you've got to hold 'em back!"

In his agitation the colonel began to stammer. "A-all r'right, General, all right, by Gawd! We-we'll do our—we-we'll d-d-do—do our best, General." The general made a passionate gesture and galloped away. The colonel, perchance to relieve his feelings, began to scold like a wet parrot. The youth, turning swiftly to make sure that the rear was unmolested, saw the commander regarding his men in a highly resentful manner, as if he regretted above everything his association with them.

The man at the youth's elbow was mumbling, as if to himself: "Oh, we're in for it now! Oh, we're in for it now!"

The captain of the company had been pacing excitedly to and fro in the rear. He coaxed in schoolmistress fashion, as to a congregation of boys with primers. His talk was an endless repetition. "Reserve your fire, boys—don't shoot till I tell you—save your fire—wait till they get close up—don't be damned fools—"

Perspiration streamed down the youth's face, which was soiled like that of a weeping urchin. He frequently, with a nervous movement, wiped his eyes with his coat sleeve. His mouth was still a little ways open.

He got the one glance at the foe-swarming field in front of him, and instantly ceased to debate the question of his piece being loaded. Before he was ready to begin—before he had announced to himself that he was about to fight—he threw the obedient, well-balanced, rifle into position and fired a first wild shot. Directly he was working at his weapon like an automatic affair.

He suddenly lost concern for himself, and forgot to look at a menacing fate. He became not a man but a member. He felt that something of which he was a part—a regiment, an army, a cause, or a country—was in a crisis. He was welded into a common personality which was dominated by a single desire. For some moments he could not flee no more than a little finger can commit a revolution from a hand.

If he had thought the regiment was about to be annihilated perhaps he could have amputated himself from it. But its noise gave him assurance. The regiment was like a firework that, once ignited, proceeds superior to circumstances until its blazing vitality fades. It wheezed and banged with a mighty power. He pictured the ground before it as strewn with the discomfited.

There was a consciousness always of the presence of his comrades about him. He felt the subtle battle brotherhood more potent even than the cause for which they were fighting. It was a mysterious fraternity born of the smoke and danger of death.

He was at a task. He was like a carpenter who has made many boxes, making still another box, only there was furious haste in his movements. He, in his thought, was careering off in other places, even as the carpenter who as he works whistles and thinks of his friend or his enemy, his home or a saloon. And these jolted dreams were never perfect to him afterward, but remained a mass of blurred shapes.

Presently he began to feel the effects of the war atmosphere—a blistering sweat, a sensation that his eyeballs were about to crack like hot stones. A burning roar filled his ears.

Following this came a red rage. He developed the acute exasperation of a pestered animal, a well-meaning cow worried by dogs. He had a mad feeling against his rifle, which could only be used against one life at a time. He wished to rush forward and strangle with his fingers. He craved a power that would enable him to make a world-sweeping gesture and brush all back. His impotency appeared to him, and made his rage into that of a driven beast.

Buried in the smoke of many rifles his anger was directed not so much against men whom he knew were rushing toward him as against the swirling battle phantoms which were choking him, stuffing their smoke robes down his parched throat. He fought frantically for respite for his senses, for air, as a babe being smothered attacks the deadly blankets.

There was a blare of heated rage mingled with a certain expression of intentness on all faces. Many of the men were making low-toned noises with their mouths, and these subdued cheers, snarls, imprecations, prayers, made a wild, barbaric song that went as an undercurrent of sound, strange and chantlike with the resounding chords of the war march. The man at the youth's elbow was babbling. In it there was something soft and tender like the monologue of a babe. The tall soldier was swearing in a loud voice. From his lips came a black procession of curious oaths. Of a sudden another broke out in a querulous way like a man who has mislaid his hat. "Well, why don't they support us? Why don't they send supports? Do they think—"

The youth in his battle sleep heard this as one who dozes hears.

There was a singular absence of heroic poses. The men bending and surging in their haste and rage were in every impossible attitude. The steel ramrods clanked and clanged with incessant din as the men pounded them furiously into the hot rifle barrels. The flaps of the cartridge boxes were all unfastened, and bobbed idiotically with each movement. The rifles, once loaded, were jerked to the shoulder and fired without apparent aim into the smoke or at one of the blurred and shifting forms which upon the field before the regiment had been growing larger and larger like puppets under a magician's hand.

The officers, at their intervals, rearward, neglected to stand in picturesque attitudes. They were bobbing to and fro roaring directions and encouragements. The dimensions of their howls were extraordinary. They expended their lungs with prodigal wills. And often they nearly stood upon their heads in the anxiety to observe the enemy on the other side of the tumbling smoke.

The lieutenant of the youth's company had encountered a soldier who had fled screaming at the first volley of his comrades. Behind the lines these two were acting a little isolated scene. The man was blubbering and staring with sheeplike eyes at the lieutenant, who had seized him by the collar and was pommeling him. He drove him back into the ranks with many blows. The soldier went mechanically, dully, with his animal-like eyes upon the officer. Perhaps there was to him a divinity expressed in the voice of the other—stern, hard, with no reflection of fear in it. He tried to reload his gun, but his shaking hands prevented. The lieutenant was obliged to assist him.

The men dropped here and there like bundles. The captain of the youth's company had been killed in an early part of the action. His body lay stretched out in the position of a tired man resting, but upon his face there was an astonished and sorrowful look, as if he thought some friend had done him an ill turn. The babbling man was grazed by a shot that made the blood stream widely down his face. He clapped both hands to his head. "Oh!" he said, and ran. Another grunted suddenly as if he had been struck by a club in the stomach. He sat down and gazed ruefully. In his eyes there was mute, indefinite reproach. Farther up the line a man standing behind a tree had had his knee joint splintered by a ball. Immediately he had dropped his rifle and gripped the tree with both arms. And there he remained, clinging desperately and crying for assistance that he might withdraw his hold upon the tree.

At last an exultant yell went along the quivering line. The firing dwindled from an uproar to a last vindictive popping. As the smoke slowly eddied away, the youth saw that the charge had been repulsed. The enemy were scattered into reluctant groups. He saw a man climb to the top of the fence, straddle the rail, and fire a parting shot. The waves had receded, leaving bits of dark débris upon the ground.

Some in the regiment began to whoop frenziedly. Many were silent. Apparently they were trying to contemplate themselves.

After the fever had left his veins, the youth thought that at last he was going to suffocate. He became aware of the foul atmosphere in which he had been struggling. He was grimy and dripping like a laborer in a foundry. He grasped his canteen and took a long swallow of the warmed water.

A sentence with variations went up and down the line. "Well, we've helt 'em back. We've helt 'em back; derned if we haven't." The men said it blissfully, leering at each other with dirty smiles.

The youth turned to look behind him and off to the right and off to the left. He experienced the joy of a man who at last finds leisure in which to look about him.

Under foot there were a few ghastly forms motionless. They lay twisted in fantastic contortions. Arms were bent and heads were turned in incredible ways. It seemed that the dead men must have fallen from some great height to get into such positions. They looked to be dumped out upon the ground from the sky.

From a position in the rear of the grove a battery was throwing shells over it. The flash of the guns startled the youth at first. He thought they were aimed directly at him. Through the trees he watched the black figures of the gunners as they worked swiftly and intently. Their labor seemed a complicated thing. He wondered how they could remember its formula in the midst of confusion.

The guns squatted in a row like savage chiefs. They argued with abrupt violence. It was a grim powwow. Their busy servants ran hither and thither.

A small procession of wounded men were going drearily toward the rear. It was a flow of blood from the torn body of the brigade.

To the right and to the left were the dark lines of other troops. Far in front he thought he could see lighter masses protruding in points from the forest. They were suggestive of unnumbered thousands.

Once he saw a tiny battery go dashing along the line of the horizon. The tiny riders were beating the tiny horses.

From a sloping hill came the sound of cheerings and clashes. Smoke welled slowly through the leaves.

Batteries were speaking with thunderous oratorical effort. Here and there were flags, the red in the stripes dominating. They splashed bits of warm color upon the dark lines of troops.

The youth felt the old thrill at the sight of the emblem. They were like beautiful birds strangely undaunted in a storm.

As he listened to the din from the hillside, to a deep pulsating thunder that came from afar to the left, and to the lesser clamors which came from many directions, it occurred to him that they were fighting, too, over there, and over there, and over there. Heretofore he had supposed that all the battle was directly under his nose.

As he gazed around him the youth felt a flash of astonishment at the blue, pure sky and the sungleamings on the trees and fields. It was surprising that Nature had gone tranquilly on with her golden process in the midst of so much devilment.

Chapter 6

The youth awakened slowly. He came gradually back to a position from which he could regard himself. For moments he had been scrutinizing his person in a dazed way as if he had never before seen himself. Then he picked up his cap from the ground. He wriggled in his jacket to make a more comfortable fit, and kneeling relaced

Young Soldier by Winslow Homer (1861). Oil.

Cooper Hewitt Museum, The Smithsonian Institution.

his shoe. He thoughtfully mopped his reeking[1] features.

So it was all over at last! The supreme trial had been passed. The red, formidable difficulties of war had been vanquished.

He went into an ecstasy of self-satisfaction. He had the most delightful sensations of his life. Standing as if apart from himself, he viewed that last scene. He perceived that the man who had fought thus was magnificent.

---

1. **reeking:** sweating.

He felt that he was a fine fellow. He saw himself even with those ideals which he had considered as far beyond him. He smiled in deep gratification.

Upon his fellows he beamed tenderness and good will. "Gee! ain't it hot, hey?" he said affably to a man who was polishing his streaming face with his coat sleeves.

"You bet!" said the other, grinning sociably. "I never seen sech dumb hotness." He sprawled out luxuriously on the ground. "Gee, yes! An' I hope we don't have no more fightin' till a week from Monday."

There were some handshakings and deep speeches with men whose features were familiar, but with whom the youth now felt the bonds of tied hearts. He helped a cursing comrade to bind up a wound of the shin.

But, of a sudden, cries of amazement broke out along the ranks of the new regiment. "Here they come ag'in! Here they come ag'in!" The man who had sprawled upon the ground started up and said, "Gosh!"

The youth turned quick eyes upon the field. He discerned forms begin to swell in masses out of a distant wood. He again saw the tilted flag speeding forward.

The shells, which had ceased to trouble the regiment for a time, came swirling again, and exploded in the grass or among the leaves of the trees. They looked to be strange war flowers bursting into fierce bloom.

The men groaned. The luster faded from their eyes. Their smudged countenances now expressed a profound dejection. They moved their stiffened bodies slowly, and watched in sullen mood the frantic approach of the enemy. The slaves toiling in the temple of this god began to feel rebellion at his harsh tasks.

They fretted and complained each to each. "Oh, say, this is too much of a good thing! Why can't somebody send up supports?"

"We ain't never goin' to stand this second banging. I didn't come here to fight the hull damn' rebel army."

There was one who raised a doleful cry. "I wish Bill Smithers had trod on my hand, insteader me treddin' on his'n." The sore joints of the regiment creaked as it painfully floundered into position to repulse.

The youth stared. Surely, he thought, this impossible thing was not about to happen. He waited as if he expected the enemy to suddenly stop, apologize, and retire bowing. It was all a mistake.

But the firing began somewhere on the regimental line and ripped along in both directions. The level sheets of flame developed great clouds of smoke that tumbled and tossed in the mild wind near the ground for a moment, and then rolled through the ranks as through a gate. The clouds were tinged an earthlike yellow in the sun-rays and in the shadow were a sorry blue. The flag was sometimes eaten and lost in this mass of vapor, but more often it projected, sun-touched, resplendent.

Into the youth's eyes there came a look that one can see in the orbs of a jaded horse. His neck was quivering with nervous weakness and the muscles of his arms felt numb and bloodless. His hands, too, seemed large and awkward as if he was wearing invisible mittens. And there was a great uncertainty about his knee joints.

The words that comrades had uttered previous to the firing began to recur to him. "Oh, say, this is too much of a good thing! What do they take us for—why don't they send supports? I didn't come here to fight the hull damned rebel army."

He began to exaggerate the endurance, the skill, and the valor of those who were coming. Himself reeling from exhaustion, he was astonished beyond measure at such persistency. They must be machines of steel. It was very gloomy struggling against such affairs, wound up perhaps to fight until sundown.

He slowly lifted his rifle and catching a glimpse of the thick-spread field he blazed at a cantering cluster. He stopped then and began to peer as best he could through the smoke. He caught changing views of the ground covered with men who were all running like pursued imps and yelling.

To the youth it was an onslaught of redoubtable dragons. He became like the man who lost his legs at the approach of the red and green monster. He waited in a sort of a horrified, listening attitude. He seemed to shut his eyes and wait to be gobbled.

A man near him who up to this time had been working feverishly at his rifle suddenly stopped and ran with howls. A lad whose face had borne an expression of exalted courage, the majesty of he who dares give his life, was, at an instant, smitten abject.[2] He blanched like one who has come to the edge of a cliff at midnight and is suddenly made aware. There was a revelation. He, too, threw down his gun and fled. There was no shame in his face. He ran like a rabbit.

Others began to scamper away through the smoke. The youth turned his head, shaken from his trance by this movement as if the regiment was leaving him behind. He saw the few fleeting forms.

---

2. **smitten abject:** struck down with degrading fear (like a groveling dog).

He yelled then with fright and swung about. For a moment, in the great clamor, he was like a proverbial chicken. He lost the direction of safety. Destruction threatened him from all points.

Directly he began to speed toward the rear in great leaps. His rifle and cap were gone. His unbuttoned coat bulged in the wind. The flap of his cartridge box bobbed wildly, and his canteen, by its slender cord, swung out behind. On his face was all the horror of those things which he imagined.

The lieutenant sprang forward bawling. The youth saw his features wrathfully red, and saw him make a dab with his sword. His one thought of the incident was that the lieutenant was a peculiar creature to feel interested in such matters upon this occasion.

He ran like a blind man. Two or three times he fell down. Once he knocked his shoulder so heavily against a tree that he went headlong.

Since he had turned his back upon the fight his fears had been wondrously magnified. Death about to thrust him between the shoulder blades was far more dreadful than death about to smite him between the eyes. When he thought of it later, he conceived the impression that it is better to view the appalling than to be merely within hearing. The noises of the battle were like stones; he believed himself liable to be crushed.

As he ran on he mingled with others. He dimly saw men on his right and on his left, and he heard footsteps behind him. He thought that all the regiment was fleeing, pursued by these ominous crashes.

In his flight the sound of these following footsteps gave him his one meager relief. He felt vaguely that death must make a first choice of the men who were nearest; the initial morsels for the dragons would be then those who were following him. So he displayed the zeal of an insane sprinter in his purpose to keep them in the rear. There was a race.

As he, leading, went across a little field, he found himself in a region of shells. They hurtled over his head with long wild screams. As he listened he imagined them to have rows of cruel teeth that grinned at him. Once one lit before him and the livid lightning of the explosion effectually barred the way in his chosen direction. He groveled on the ground and then springing up went careering off through some bushes.

He experienced a thrill of amazement when he came within view of a battery in action. The men there seemed to be in conventional moods, altogether unaware of the impending annihilation. The battery was disputing with distant antagonist and the gunners were wrapped in admiration of their shooting. They were continually bending in coaxing postures over the guns. They seemed to be patting them on the back and encouraging them with words. The guns, stolid and undaunted, spoke with dogged valor.

The precise gunners were coolly enthusiastic. They lifted their eyes every chance to the smoke-wreathed hillock from whence the hostile battery addressed them. The youth pitied them as he ran. Methodical idiots! Machinelike fools! The refined joy of planting shells in the midst of the other battery's formation would appear a little thing when the infantry came swooping out of the woods.

The face of a youthful rider, who was jerking his frantic horse with an abandon of temper he might display in a placid barnyard, was impressed deeply upon his mind. He knew that he looked upon a man who would presently be dead.

Too, he felt a pity for the guns, standing, six good comrades, in a bold row.

He saw a brigade going to the relief of its pestered fellows. He scrambled upon a wee hill and watched it sweeping finely, keeping formation in difficult places. The blue of the line was crusted with steel color, and the brilliant flags projected. Officers were shouting.

This sight also filled him with wonder. The brigade was hurrying briskly to be gulped into the infernal mouths of the war god. What manner of men were they, anyhow? Ah, it was some wondrous breed! Or else they didn't comprehend—the fools.

A furious order caused commotion in the artillery. An officer on a bounding horse made maniacal motions with his arms. The teams went swinging up from the rear, the guns were whirled about, and the battery scampered away. The cannon with their noses poked slantingly at the ground grunted and grumbled like stout men, brave but with objections to hurry.

The youth went on, moderating his pace since he had left the place of noises.

Later he came upon a general of division seated upon a horse that pricked its ears in an interested way at the battle. There was a great gleaming of yellow and patent leather about the saddle and bridle. The quiet man astride looked mouse-colored upon such a splendid charger.

A jingling staff was galloping hither and thither. Sometimes the general was surrounded by horsemen and at other times he was quite alone. He looked to be much harassed. He had the appearance of a businessman whose market is swinging up and down.

The youth went slinking around this spot. He went as near as he dared trying to overhear words. Perhaps the general, unable to comprehend chaos, might call upon him for information. And he could tell him. He knew all concerning it. Of a surety the force was in a fix, and any fool could see that if they did not retreat while they had opportunity—why—

He felt that he would like to thrash the general, or at least approach and tell him in plain words exactly what he thought him to be. It was criminal to stay calmly in one spot and make no effort to stay destruction. He loitered in a fever of eagerness for the division commander to apply to him.

As he warily moved about, he heard the general call out irritably: "Tompkins, go over an' see Taylor, an' tell him not t' be in such an all-fired hurry; tell him t' halt his brigade in th' edge of th' woods; tell him t' detach a reg'ment—say I think th' center 'll break if we don't help it out some; tell him t' hurry up."

A slim youth on a fine chestnut horse caught these swift words from the mouth of his superior. He made his horse bound into a gallop almost from a walk in his haste to go upon his mission. There was a cloud of dust.

A moment later the youth saw the general bounce excitedly in his saddle.

"Yes, by heavens, they have!" The officer leaned forward. His face was aflame with excitement. "Yes, by heavens, they've held 'im! They've held 'im!"

He began to blithely roar at his staff: "We'll wallop 'im now. We'll wallop 'im now. We've got 'em sure." He turned suddenly upon an aide: "Here—you—Jones—quick—ride after Tompkins—see Taylor—tell him t' go in—everlastingly—like blazes—anything."

As another officer sped his horse after the first messenger, the general beamed upon the earth like a sun. In his eyes was a desire to chant a paean.[3] He kept repeating, "They've held 'em, by heavens!"

His excitement made his horse plunge, and he merrily kicked and swore at it. He held a little carnival of joy on horseback.

---

3. **paean** (pē′ən): a hymn of thanksgiving or joy.

Responding to the Novel

Analyzing Chapters 1–6

Identifying Facts

1. We don't discover the full name of the main character, Henry Fleming, until long after the opening of the novel. How does the writer usually refer to Henry?
2. What rumor does the tall soldier report at the opening of Chapter 1? How does this news affect Henry?
3. What problem preoccupies Henry in the opening chapters? How does he try to solve this problem?
4. In Chapter 3, why does the youth experience a wave of hatred for the young lieutenant?
5. What does the loud soldier tell Henry at the end of Chapter 3?
6. At the opening of Chapter 6, Henry feels proud. What **ironic reversal** occurs in this chapter?

Interpreting Meanings

7. What general notions of war does Henry have when he enlists? Are they romantic, or realistic? What do you think may be the source of these ideas? Are they typical of young people today as well? If they aren't, what has caused the change?

8. Henry's mother tells him, "Yer jest one little feller amongst a hull lot of others, and yeh've got to keep quiet an' do what they tell yeh." Pick out some passages that stress the notion of the army as a mass, rather than as a collection of individual soldiers. How is this related to Crane's referring to Henry as "the youth," rather than by name? What other soldiers play prominent roles in this part of the novel, and how are they referred to?
9. Crane's **style** pushes realism to such limits that it is often called **impressionistic.** He offers us vivid, fragmented images that correspond with the moment-by-moment impressions of the men on the field. How does Crane's use of vivid **metaphors** contribute to this impressionistic style? Select and discuss some examples of metaphors from the opening chapters.
10. Crane's handling of **dialogue** is also a major feature of his impressionistic style. Why do you think he includes so many snatches of dialogue that are disjointed or fragmented? How does Crane's use of **dialect** affect your reading of the novel?
11. Are the soldiers you have met so far like soldiers in contempory fiction, in movies, and on TV? Are they like real soldiers you know? Explain your answers.

Chapter 7

The youth cringed as if discovered in a crime. By heavens, they had won after all! The imbecile line had remained and become victors. He could hear cheering.

He lifted himself upon his toes and looked in the direction of the fight. A yellow fog lay wallowing on the treetops. From beneath it came the clatter of musketry. Hoarse cries told of an advance.

He turned away amazed and angry. He felt that he had been wronged.

He had fled, he told himself, because annihilation approached. He had done a good part in saving himself, who was a little piece of the army. He had considered the time, he said, to be one in which it was the duty of every little piece to rescue itself if possible. Later the officers could fit the little pieces together again, and make a battle front. If none of the little pieces were wise enough to save themselves from the flurry of death at such a time, why, then, where would be the army? It was all plain that he had proceeded according to very correct and commendable rules. His actions had been sagacious things. They had been full of strategy. They were the work of a master's legs.

Thoughts of his comrades came to him. The brittle blue line had withstood the blows and won. He grew bitter over it. It seemed that the blind ignorance and stupidity of those little pieces had betrayed him. He had been overturned and crushed by their lack of sense in holding the position, when intelligent deliberation would have convinced them that it was impossible. He, the enlightened man who looks afar in the dark, had fled because of his superior perceptions and knowledge. He felt a great anger against his comrades. He knew it could be proved that they had been fools.

He wondered what they would remark when later he appeared in camp. His mind heard howls of derision. Their destiny would not enable them to understand his sharper point of view.

He began to pity himself acutely. He was ill used. He was trodden beneath the feet of an iron injustice. He had proceeded with wisdom and from the most righteous motives under heaven's blue only to be frustrated by hateful circumstances.

A dull, animal-like rebellion against his fellows, war in the abstract, and fate grew within him. He shambled along with bowed head, his brain in a tumult of agony and despair. When he looked loweringly up, quivering at each sound, his eyes had the expression of those of a criminal who thinks his guilt and his punishment great, and knows that he can find no words; who, through his suffering, thinks that he peers into the core of things and sees that the judgment of man is thistledown in wind.

He went from the fields into a thick woods, as if resolved to bury himself. He wished to get out of hearing of the crackling shots which were to him like voices.

The ground was cluttered with vines and bushes, and the trees grew close and spread out like bouquets. He was obliged to force his way with much noise. The creepers, catching against his legs, cried out harshly as their sprays were torn from the barks of trees. The swishing saplings tried to make known his presence to the world. He could not conciliate the forest. As he made his way, it was always calling out protestations. When he separated embraces of trees and vines the disturbed foliages waved their arms and turned their face leaves toward him. He dreaded lest these noisy motions and cries should bring men to look at him. So he went far, seeking dark and intricate places.

After a time the sound of musketry grew faint and the cannon boomed in the distance. The sun, suddenly apparent, blazed among the trees. The insects were making rhythmical noises. They seemed to be grinding their teeth in unison. A woodpecker stuck his impudent head around the side of a tree. A bird flew on lighthearted wing.

Off was the rumble of death. It seemed now that Nature had no ears.

This landscape gave him assurance. A fair field holding life. It was the religion of peace. It would die if its timid eyes were compelled to see blood. He conceived Nature to be a woman with a deep aversion to tragedy.

He threw a pine cone at a jovial squirrel, and he ran with chattering fear. High in a tree top he stopped, and, poking his head cautiously from behind a branch, looked down with an air of trepidation.

The youth felt triumphant at this exhibition. There was the law, he said. Nature had given him a sign. The squirrel, immediately upon recognizing danger, had taken to his legs without ado. He did not stand stolidly baring his furry belly to the missile, and die with an upward glance at the sympathetic heavens. On the contrary, he had fled as fast as his legs could carry him; and he was but an ordinary squirrel, too—doubtless no philosopher of his race. The youth wended, feeling that Nature was of his mind. She reinforced his argument with proofs that lived where the sun shone.

Once he found himself almost into a swamp. He was obliged to walk upon bog tufts and watch his feet to keep from the oily mire. Pausing at one time to look about him he saw, out at some black water, a small animal pounce in and emerge directly with a gleaming fish.

The youth went again into the deep thickets. The brushed branches made a noise that drowned the sounds of cannon. He walked on, going from obscurity into promises of a greater obscurity.

At length he reached a place where the high, arching boughs made a chapel. He softly pushed the green doors aside and entered. Pine needles were a gentle brown carpet. There was a religious half light.

Near the threshold he stopped, horror-stricken at the sight of a thing.

He was being looked at by a dead man who was seated with his back against a columnlike tree. The corpse was dressed in a uniform that once had been blue, but was now faded to a melancholy shade of green. The eyes, staring at the youth, had changed to the dull hue to be seen on the side of a dead fish. The mouth was open. Its red had changed to an appalling yellow. Over the gray skin of the face ran little ants. One was trundling some sort of a bundle along the upper lip.

The youth gave a shriek as he confronted the thing. He was for moments turned to stone before it. He remained staring into the liquid-looking eyes. The dead man and the living man exchanged a long look. Then the youth cautiously put one hand behind him and brought it against a tree. Leaning upon this he retreated, step by step, with his face still toward the thing. He feared that if he turned his back the body might spring up and stealthily pursue him.

The branches, pushing against him, threatened to throw him over upon it. His unguided feet, too, caught aggravatingly in brambles; and with it all he received a subtle suggestion to touch the corpse. As he thought of his hand upon it he shuddered profoundly.

At last he burst the bonds which had fastened him to the spot and fled, unheeding the underbrush. He was pursued by a sight of the black ants swarming greedily upon the gray face and venturing horribly near to the eyes.

After a time he paused, and, breathless and panting, listened. He imagined some strange voice would come from the dead throat and squawk after him in horrible menaces.

The trees about the portals of the chapel moved soughingly in a soft wind. A sad silence was upon the little guarding edifice.

Chapter 8

The trees began softly to sing a hymn of twilight. The sun sank until slanted bronze rays struck the forest. There was a lull in the noises of insects as if they had bowed their beaks and were making a devotional pause. There was silence save for the chanted chorus of the trees.

Then, upon this stillness, there suddenly broke a tremendous clangor of sounds. A crimson roar came from the distance.

The youth stopped. He was transfixed by this terrific medley of all noises. It was as if worlds were being rended. There was the ripping sound of musketry and the breaking crash of the artillery.

His mind flew in all directions. He conceived the two armies to be at each other panther fashion. He listened for a time. Then he began to run in the direction of the battle. He saw that it was an ironical thing for him to be running thus toward that which he had been at such pains to avoid. But he said, in substance, to himself that if the earth and the moon were about to clash, many persons would doubtless plan to get upon the roofs to witness the collision.

As he ran, he became aware that the forest had stopped its music, as if at last becoming capable of hearing the foreign sounds. The trees hushed and stood motionless. Everything seemed to be listening to the crackle and clatter and ear-shaking thunder. The chorus pealed over the still earth.

It suddenly occurred to the youth that the fight in which he had been was, after all, but perfunctory popping. In the hearing of this present din he was doubtful if he had seen real battle scenes. This uproar explained a celestial battle; it was tumbling hordes a-struggle in the air.

Reflecting, he saw a sort of a humor in the point of view of himself and his fellows during the late encounter. They had taken themselves and the enemy very seriously and had imagined that they were deciding the war. Individuals must have supposed that they were cutting the letters of their names deep into everlasting tablets of brass, or enshrining their reputations forever in the hearts of their countrymen, while, as to fact, the affair would appear in printed reports under a meek and immaterial title. But he saw that it was good, else, he said, in battle every one would surely run save forlorn hopes and their ilk.

He went rapidly on. He wished to come to the edge of the forest that he might peer out.

As he hastened, there passed through his mind pictures of stupendous conflicts. His accumulated thought upon such subjects was used to form scenes. The noise was as the voice of an eloquent being, describing.

Sometimes the brambles formed chains and tried to hold him back. Trees, confronting him, stretched out their arms and forbade him to pass. After its previous hostility this new resistance of the forest filled him with a fine bitterness. It seemed that Nature could not be quite ready to kill him.

But he obstinately took roundabout ways, and presently he was where he could see long gray walls of vapor where lay battle lines. The voices of cannon shook him. The musketry sounded in long irregular surges that played havoc with his ears. He stood regardant[1] for a moment. His eyes had an awestruck expression. He gawked in the direction of the fight.

Presently he proceeded again on his forward way. The battle was like the grinding of an immense and terrible machine to him. Its complexities and powers, its grim processes, fascinated him. He must go close and see it produce corpses.

He came to a fence and clambered over it. On the far side, the ground was littered with clothes and guns. A newspaper, folded up, lay in the dirt. A dead soldier was stretched with his face hidden in his arm. Farther off there was a group of four or five corpses keeping mournful company. A hot sun had blazed upon the spot.

In this place the youth felt that he was an invader. This forgotten part of the battleground was owned by the dead men, and he hurried, in the vague apprehension that one of the swollen forms would rise and tell him to be gone.

He came finally to a road from which he could see in the distance dark and agitated bodies of troops, smoke-fringed. In the lane was a blood-stained crowd streaming to the rear. The wounded men were cursing, groaning, and wailing. In the air, always, was a mighty swell of sound that it seemed could sway the earth. With the courageous words of the artillery and the spiteful sentences of the musketry mingled red cheers. And from this region of noises came the steady current of the maimed.

One of the wounded men had a shoeful of blood. He hopped like a schoolboy in a game. He was laughing hysterically.

One was swearing that he had been shot in the arm through the commanding general's mismanagement of the army. One was marching with an air imitative of some sublime drum major.[2] Upon his features was an unholy mixture of merriment

and agony. As he marched he sang a bit of doggerel in a high and quavering voice:

"Sing a song 'a vic'try,
A pocketful 'a bullets,
Five an' twenty dead men
Baked in a—pie."

Parts of the procession limped and staggered to this tune.

Another had the gray seal of death already upon his face. His lips were curled in hard lines and his teeth were clinched. His hands were bloody from where he had pressed them upon his wound. He seemed to be awaiting the moment when he should pitch headlong. He stalked like the specter of a soldier, his eyes burning with the power of a stare into the unknown.

There were some who proceeded sullenly, full of anger at their wounds, and ready to turn upon anything as an obscure cause.

An officer was carried along by two privates. He was peevish. "Don't joggle so, Johnson, yeh fool," he cried. "Think m' leg is made of iron? If yeh can't carry me decent, put me down an' let some one else do it."

He bellowed at the tottering crowd who blocked the quick march of his bearers. "Say, make way there, can't yeh? Make way, dickens take it all."

They sulkily parted and went to the roadsides. As he was carried past they made pert remarks to him. When he raged in reply and threatened them, they told him to be damned.

The shoulder of one of the tramping bearers knocked heavily against the spectral soldier who was staring into the unknown.

The youth joined this crowd and marched along with it. The torn bodies expressed the awful machinery in which the men had been entangled.

Orderlies and couriers occasionally broke through the throng in the roadway, scattering wounded men right and left, galloping on, followed by howls. The melancholy march was continually disturbed by the messengers, and sometimes by bustling batteries that came swinging and thumping down upon them, the officers shouting orders to clear the way.

There was a tattered man, fouled with dust, blood and powder stain from hair to shoes, who trudged quietly at the youth's side. He was listening with eagerness and much humility to the lurid descriptions of a bearded sergeant. His lean features wore an expression of awe and admiration. He was like a listener in a country store to wondrous tales told among the sugar barrels. He eyed

---

1. **regardant:** looking backward.
2. **drum major:** leader of a marching band.

the storyteller with unspeakable wonder. His mouth was agape in yokel fashion.

The sergeant, taking note of this, gave pause to his elaborate history while he administered a sardonic comment. "Be keerful, honey, you'll be a-ketchin' flies," he said.

The tattered man shrank back abashed.

After a time he began to sidle near to the youth, and in different way try to make him a friend. His voice was gentle as a girl's voice and his eyes were pleading. The youth saw with surprise that the soldier had two wounds, one in the head, bound with a blood-soaked rag, and the other in the arm, making that member dangle like a broken bough.

After they had walked together for some time the tattered man mustered sufficient courage to speak. "Was pretty good fight, wa'n't it?" he timidly said. The youth, deep in thought, glanced up at the bloody and grim figure with its lamblike eyes. "What?"

"Was pretty good fight, wa'n't it?"

"Yes," said the youth shortly. He quickened his pace.

But the other hobbled industriously after him. There was an air of apology in his manner, but he evidently thought that he needed only to talk for a time, and the youth would perceive that he was a good fellow.

"Was pretty good fight, wa'n't it?" he began in a small voice, and then he achieved the fortitude to continue. "Dern me if I ever see fellers fight so. Laws, how they did fight! I knowed th' boys 'd like when they onct got square at it. Th' boys ain't had no fair chanct up t' now, but this time they showed what they was. I knowed it 'd turn out this way. Yeh can't lick them boys. No, sir! They're fighters, they be."

He breathed a deep breath of humble admiration. He had looked at the youth for encouragement several times. He received none, but gradually he seemed to get absorbed in his subject.

"I was talkin' 'cross pickets with a boy from Georgie, onct, an' that boy, he ses, 'Your fellers 'll all run like hell when they onct hearn a gun,' he ses. 'Mebbe they will,' I ses, 'but I don't b'lieve none of it,' I ses; 'an b' jiminey,' I ses back t' 'um, 'mebbe your fellers 'll all run like hell when they onct hearn a gun,' I ses. He larfed. Well, they didn't run t'day, did they, hey? No, sir! They fit, an' fit, an' fit."

His homely face was suffused with a light of love for the army which was to him all things beautiful and powerful.

After a time he turned to the youth, "Where yeh hit, ol' boy?" he asked in a brotherly tone.

A field hospital scene at Savage Station, Virginia, during the battle on June 27, 1862. The wounded were brought in by the hundreds. Photograph by Mathew Brady.

The youth felt instant panic at this question, although at first its full import was not borne in upon him.

"What?" he asked.

"Where yeh hit?" repeated the tattered man.

"Why," began the youth, "I—I—that is—why—I—"

He turned away suddenly and slid through the crowd. His brow was heavily flushed, and his fingers were picking nervously at one of his buttons. He bent his head and fastened his eyes studiously upon the button as if it were a little problem.

The tattered man looked after him in astonishment.

Chapter 9

The youth fell back in the procession until the tattered soldier was not in sight. Then he started to walk on with the others.

But he was amid wounds. The mob of men was bleeding. Because of the tattered soldier's question he now felt that his shame could be viewed. He was continually casting sidelong glances to see if the men were contemplating the letters of guilt he felt burned into his brow.

At times he regarded the wounded soldiers in an envious way. He conceived persons with torn bodies to be peculiarly happy. He wished that he, too, had a wound, a little red badge of courage.

The spectral soldier was at his side like a stalking reproach. The man's eyes were still fixed in a stare into the unknown. His gray, appalling face had attracted attention in the crowd, and men, slowing to his dreary pace, were walking with him. They were discussing his plight, questioning him and giving him advice. In a dogged way he repelled them, signing to them to go on and leave him alone. The shadows of his face were deepening and his tight lips seemed holding in check the moan of great despair. There could be seen a certain stiffness in the movements of his body, as if he were taking infinite care not to arouse the passion of his wounds. As he went on, he seemed always looking for a place, like one who goes to choose a grave.

Something in the gesture of the man as he waved the bloody and pitying soldiers away made the youth start as if bitten. He yelled in horror. Tottering forward he laid a quivering hand upon the man's arm. As the latter slowly turned his waxlike features toward him, the youth screamed:

"Gawd! Jim Conklin!"

The tall soldier made a little commonplace smile. "Hello, Henry," he said.

The youth swayed on his legs and glared strangely. He stuttered and stammered. "Oh, Jim—oh, Jim—oh, Jim—"

The tall soldier held out his gory hand. There was a curious red and black combination of new blood and old blood upon it. "Where yeh been, Henry?" he asked. He continued in a monotonous voice, "I thought mebbe yeh got keeled over. There's been thunder t' pay t'day. I was worryin' about it a good deal."

The youth still lamented. "Oh, Jim—oh, Jim—oh, Jim—"

"Yeh know," said the tall soldier, "I was out there." He made a careful gesture. "An', Lord, what a circus! An, b'jiminey, I got shot—I got shot. Yes, b'jiminey, I got shot." He reiterated this fact in a bewildered way, as if he did not know how it came about.

The youth put forth anxious arms to assist him, but the tall soldier went firmly on as if propelled. Since the youth's arrival as a guardian for his friend, the other wounded men had ceased to display much interest. They occupied themselves again in dragging their own tragedies toward the rear.

Suddenly, as the two friends marched on, the tall soldier seemed to be overcome by a terror. His face turned to a semblance of gray paste. He clutched the youth's arm and looked all about him, as if dreading to be overheard. Then he began to speak in a shaking whisper:

"I tell yeh what I'm 'fraid of, Henry—I'll tell yeh what I'm 'fraid of. I'm 'fraid I'll fall down—an' then yeh know—them damned artillery wagons—they like as not 'll run over me. That's what I'm 'fraid of—"

The youth cried out to him hysterically: "I'll take care of yeh, Jim! I'll take care of yeh! I swear t' Gawd I will!"

"Sure—will yeh, Henry?" the tall soldier beseeched.

"Yes—yes—I tell yeh—I'll take care of yeh, Jim!" protested the youth. He could not speak accurately because of the gulpings in his throat.

But the tall soldier continued to beg in a lowly way. He now hung babelike to the youth's arm. His eyes rolled in the wildness of his terror. "I was allus a good friend t' yeh, wa'n't I, Henry? I've allus been a pretty good feller, ain't I? An' it ain't much t' ask, is it? Jest t' pull me along outer th' road? I'd do it fer you, wouldn't I, Henry?"

He paused in piteous anxiety to await his friend's reply.

The youth had reached an anguish where the sobs scorched him. He strove to express his loyalty, but he could only make fantastic gestures.

However, the tall soldier seemed suddenly to

forget all those fears. He became again the grim, stalking specter of a soldier. He went stonily forward. The youth wished his friend to lean upon him, but the other always shook his head and strangely protested. "No—no—no—leave me be—leave me be—"

His look was fixed again upon the unknown. He moved with mysterious purpose, and all of the youth's offers he brushed aside. "No—no—leave me be—"

The youth had to follow.

Presently the latter heard a voice talking softly near his shoulders. Turning he saw that it belonged to the tattered soldier. "Ye'd better take 'im outa th' road, pardner. There's a batt'ry comin' helitywhoop down th' road an' he'll git runned over. He's a goner anyhow in about five minutes—yeh kin see that. Ye'd better take 'im outa th' road. Where th' blazes does he git his stren'th from?"

"Lord knows!" cried the youth. He was shaking his hands helplessly.

He ran forward presently and grasped the tall soldier by the arm. "Jim! Jim!" he coaxed, "come with me."

The tall soldier weakly tried to wrench himself free. "Huh," he said vacantly. He stared at the youth for a moment. At last he spoke as if dimly comprehending. "Oh, inteh th' fields? Oh!"

He started blindly through the grass.

The youth turned once to look at the lashing riders and jouncing guns of the battery. He was startled from this view by a shrill outcry from the tattered man.

"Gawd! He's runnin'!"

Turning his head swiftly, the youth saw his friend running in a staggering and stumbling way toward a little clump of bushes. His heart seemed to wrench itself almost free from his body at this sight. He made a noise of pain. He and the tattered man began a pursuit. There was a singular race.

When he overtook the tall soldier he began to plead with all the words he could find. "Jim—Jim—what are you doing—what makes you do this way—you'll hurt yerself."

The same purpose was in the tall soldier's face. He protested in a dulled way, keeping his eyes fastened on the mystic place of his intentions. "No—no—don't tech me—leave me be—leave me be—"

The youth, aghast and filled with wonder at the tall soldier, began quaveringly to question him. "Where yeh goin', Jim? What you thinking about? Where you going? Tell me, won't you, Jim?"

The tall soldier faced about as upon relentless pursuers. In his eyes there was a great appeal.

"Leave me be, can't yeh? Leave me be fer a minnit."

The youth recoiled. "Why, Jim," he said, in a dazed way, "what's the matter with you?"

The tall soldier turned and, lurching dangerously, went on. The youth and the tattered soldier followed, sneaking as if whipped, feeling unable to face the stricken man if he should again confront them. They began to have thoughts of a solemn ceremony. There was something ritelike in these movements of the doomed soldier. And there was a resemblance in him to a devotee of a mad religion, blood-sucking, muscle-wrenching, bone-crushing. They could not understand. They were awed and afraid. They hung back lest he have at command a dreadful weapon.

At last, they saw him stop and stand motionless. Hastening up, they perceived that his face wore an expression telling that he had at last found the place for which he had struggled. His spare figure was erect; his bloody hands were quietly at his side. He was waiting with patience for something that he had come to meet. He was at the rendezvous. They paused and stood, expectant.

There was a silence.

Finally, the chest of the doomed soldier began to heave with a strained motion. It increased in violence until it was as if an animal was within and was kicking and tumbling furiously to be free.

This spectacle of gradual strangulation made the youth writhe, and once as his friend rolled his eyes, he saw something in them that made him sink wailing to the ground. He raised his voice in a last supreme call.

"Jim—Jim—Jim—"

The tall soldier opened his lips and spoke. He made a gesture. "Leave me be—don't tech me—leave me be—"

There was another silence while he waited.

Suddenly, his form stiffened and straightened. Then it was shaken by a prolonged ague. He stared into space. To the two watchers there was a curious and profound dignity in the firm lines of his awful face.

He was invaded by a creeping strangeness that slowly enveloped him. For a moment the tremor of his legs caused him to dance a sort of hideous hornpipe. His arms beat wildly about his head in expression of implike enthusiasm.

His tall figure stretched itself to its full height. There was a slight rending sound. Then it began to swing forward, slow and straight, in the manner of a falling tree. A swift muscular contortion made the left shoulder strike the ground first.

The body seemed to bounce a little way from the earth. "God!" said the tattered soldier.

Presently the calm head of a forward-going column of infantry appeared in the road. It came swiftly on. Avoiding the obstructions gave it the sinuous movement of a serpent. The men at the head butted mules with their musket stocks. They prodded teamsters indifferent to all howls. The men forced their way through parts of the dense mass by strength. The blunt head of the column pushed. The raving teamsters swore many strange oaths.

The commands to make way had the ring of a great importance in them. The men were going forward to the heart of the din. They were to confront the eager rush of the enemy. They felt the pride of their onward movement when the remainder of the army seemed trying to dribble down this road. They tumbled teams about with a fine feeling that it was no matter so long as their column got to the front in time. This importance made their faces grave and stern. And the backs of the officers were very rigid.

As the youth looked at them the black weight of his woe returned to him. He felt that he was regarding a procession of chosen beings. The separation was as great to him as if they had marched with weapons of flame and banners of sunlight. He could never be like them. He could have wept in his longings.

He searched about in his mind for an adequate malediction[3] for the indefinite cause, the thing upon which men turn the words of final blame. It—whatever it was—was responsible for him, he said. There lay the fault.

The haste of the column to reach the battle seemed to the forlorn young man to be something much finer than stout fighting. Heroes, he thought, could find excuses in that long seething lane. They could retire with perfect self-respect and make excuses to the stars.

He wondered what those men had eaten that they could be in such haste to force their way to grim chances of death. As he watched his envy grew until he thought that he wished to change lives with one of them. He would have liked to have used a tremendous force, he said, throw off himself and become a better. Swift pictures of himself, apart, yet in himself, came to him—a blue desperate figure leading lurid charges with one knee forward and a broken blade high—a blue, determined figure standing before a crimson and steel assault, getting calmly killed on a high place before the eyes of all. He thought of the magnificent pathos of his dead body.

These thoughts uplifted him. He felt the quiver of war desire. In his ears, he heard the ring of victory. He knew the frenzy of a rapid successful charge. The music of the trampling feet, the sharp voices, the clanking arms of the column near him made him soar on the red wings of war. For a few moments he was sublime.

He thought that he was about to start for the front. Indeed, he saw a picture of himself, dust-stained, haggard, panting, flying to the front at the proper moment to seize and throttle the dark, leering witch of calamity.

Then the difficulties of the thing began to drag at him. He hesitated, balancing awkwardly on one foot.

He had no rifle; he could not fight with his hands, said he resentfully to his plan. Well, rifles could be had for the picking. They were extraordinarily profuse.

Also, he continued, it would be a miracle if he found his regiment. Well, he could fight with any regiment.

He started forward slowly. He stepped as if he expected to tread upon some explosive thing. Doubts and he were struggling.

He would truly be a worm if any of his comrades should see him returning thus, the marks of his flight upon him. There was a reply that the intent fighters did not care for what happened rearward saving that no hostile bayonets appeared there. In the battle-blur his face would in a way be hidden, like the face of a cowled man.

But then he said that his tireless fate would bring forth, when the strife lulled for a moment, a man to ask of him an explanation. In imagination he felt the scrutiny of his companions as he painfully labored through some lies.

Eventually, his courage expended itself upon these objections. The debates drained him of his fire.

He was not cast down by this defeat of his plan, for, upon studying the affair carefully, he could not but admit that the objections were very formidable.

Furthermore, various ailments had begun to cry out. In their presence he could not persist in flying high with the wings of war; they rendered it almost impossible for him to see himself in a heroic light. He tumbled headlong.

He discovered that he had a scorching thirst. His face was so dry and grimy that he thought he could feel his skin crackle. Each bone of his body had an ache in it, and seemingly threatened to break with each movement. His feet were like two sores. Also, his body was calling for food. It was more powerful than a direct hunger. There was a dull, weight like feeling in his stomach, and when

---

3. **malediction:** curse.

he tried to walk, his head swayed and he tottered. He could not see with distinctness. Small patches of green mist floated before his vision.

While he had been tossed by many emotions, he had not been aware of ailments. Now they beset him and made clamor. As he was at last compelled to pay attention to them, his capacity for self-hate was multiplied. In despair, he declared that he was not like those others. He now conceded it to be impossible that he would ever become a hero. He was a craven loon. Those pictures of glory were piteous things. He groaned from his heart and went staggering off.

A certain mothlike quality within him kept him in the vicinity of the battle. He had a great desire to see, and to get news. He wished to know who was winning.

He told himself that, despite his unprecedented suffering, he had never lost his greed for a victory, yet, he said, in a half-apologetic manner to his conscience, he could not but know that a defeat for the army this time might mean many favorable things for him. The blows of the enemy would splinter regiments into fragments. Thus, many men of courage, he considered, would be obliged to desert the colors and scurry like chickens. He would appear as one of them. They would be sullen brothers in distress, and he could then easily believe he had not run any farther or faster than they. And if he himself could believe in his virtuous perfection, he conceived that there would be small trouble in convincing all others.

He said, as if in excuse for this hope, that previously the army had encountered great defeats and in a few months had shaken off all blood and tradition of them, emerging as bright and valiant as a new one; thrusting out of sight the memory of disaster, and appearing with the valor and confidence of unconquered legions. The shrilling voices of the people at home would pipe dismally for a time, but various generals were usually compelled to listen to these ditties. He of course felt no compunctions for proposing a general as a sacrifice. He could not tell who the chosen for the barbs might be, so he could center no direct sympathy upon him. The people were afar and he did not conceive public opinion to be accurate at long range. It was quite probable they would hit the wrong man who, after he had recovered from his amazement would perhaps spend the rest of his days in writing replies to the songs of his alleged failure. It would be very unfortunate, no doubt, but in this case a general was of no consequence to the youth.

In a defeat there would be a roundabout vindication of himself. He thought it would prove, in a manner, that he had fled early because of his superior powers of perception. A serious prophet upon predicting a flood should be the first man to climb a tree. This would demonstrate that he was indeed a seer.

A moral vindication was regarded by the youth as a very important thing. Without salve, he could not, he thought, wear the sore badge of his dishonor through life. With his heart continually assuring him that he was despicable, he could not exist without making it, through his actions, apparent to all men.

If the army had gone gloriously on he would be lost. If the din meant that now his army's flags were tilted forward he was a condemned wretch. He would be compelled to doom himself to isolation. If the men were advancing, their indifferent feet were trampling upon his chances for a successful life.

As these thoughts went rapidly through his mind, he turned upon them and tried to thrust them away. He denounced himself as a villain. He said that he was the most unutterably selfish man in existence. His mind pictured the soldiers who would place their defiant bodies before the spear of the yelling battle fiend, and as he saw their dripping corpses on an imagined field, he said that he was their murderer.

Again he thought that he wished he was dead. He believed that he envied a corpse. Thinking of the slain, he achieved a great contempt for some of them, as if they were guilty for thus becoming lifeless. They might have been killed by lucky chances, he said, before they had had opportunities to flee or before they had been really tested. Yet they would receive laurels[4] from tradition. He cried out bitterly that their crowns were stolen and their robes of glorious memories were shams. However, he still said that it was a great pity he was not as they.

A defeat of the army had suggested itself to him as a contrivance[5] turns out buttons. He presently his fall. He considered, now, however, that it was useless to think of such a possibility. His education had been that success for that mighty blue machine was certain; that it would make victories as a contrivance[4] turns out buttons. He presently discarded all his speculations in the other direction. He returned to the creed of soldiers.

When he perceived again that it was not possible for the army to be defeated, he tried to bethink him of a fine tale which he could take back

---

4. **laurels:** crowns (tributes, medals). (In ancient Greece, victors were crowned with laurel leaves.)
5. **contrivance:** machine.

to his regiment, and with it turn the expected shafts of derision.

But, as he mortally feared these shafts, it became impossible for him to invent a tale he felt he could trust. He experimented with many schemes, but threw them aside one by one as flimsy. He was quick to see vulnerable places in them all.

Furthermore, he was much afraid that some arrow of scorn might lay him mentally low before he could raise his protecting tale.

He imagined the whole regiment saying: "Where's Henry Fleming? He run, didn't 'e? Oh, my!" He recalled various persons who would be quite sure to leave him no peace about it. They would doubtless question him with sneers, and laugh at his stammering hesitation. In the next engagement they would try to keep watch of him to discover when he would run.

Wherever he went in camp, he would encounter insolent and lingeringly cruel stares. As he imagined himself passing near a crowd of comrades, he could hear some one say, "There he goes!"

Then, as if the heads were moved by one muscle, all the faces turned toward him with wide, derisive grins. He seemed to hear some one make a humorous remark in a low tone. At it the others all crowed and cackled. He was a slang phrase.

Chapter 12

The column that had butted stoutly at the obstacles in the roadway was barely out of the youth's sight before he saw dark waves of men come sweeping out of the woods and down through the fields. He knew at once that the steel fibers had been washed from their hearts. They were bursting from their coats and their equipments as from entanglements. They charged down upon him like terrified buffaloes.

Behind them blue smoke curled and clouded above the treetops, and through the thickets he could sometimes see a distant pink glare. The voices of the cannon were clamoring in interminable chorus.

The youth was horror-stricken. He stared in agony and amazement. He forgot that he was engaged in combating the universe. He threw aside his mental pamphlets on the philosophy of the retreated and rules for the guidance of the damned. He lost concern for himself.

The fight was lost. The dragons were coming with invincible strides. The army, helpless in the matted thickets and blinded by the overhanging night, was going to be swallowed. War, the red animal, war, the blood-swollen god, would have bloated fill.

Within him something bade to cry out. He had the impulse to make a rallying speech, to sing a battle hymn, but he could only get his tongue to call into the air: "Why—why—what—what's th' matter?"

Soon he was in the midst of them. They were leaping and scampering all about him. Their blanched faces shone in the dusk. They seemed, for the most part, to be very burly men. The youth turned from one to another of them as they galloped along. His incoherent questions were lost. They were heedless of his appeals. They did not seem to see him.

They sometimes gabbled insanely. One huge man was asking of the sky: "Say, where de plank road? Where de plank road!" It was as if he had lost a child. He wept in his pain and dismay.

Presently, men were running hither and thither in all ways. The artillery booming, forward, rearward, and on the flanks made jumble of ideas of direction. Landmarks had vanished into the gathered gloom. The youth began to imagine that he had got into the center of the tremendous quarrel, and he could perceive no way out of it. From the mouths of the fleeing men came a thousand wild questions, but no one made answers.

The youth, after rushing about and throwing interrogations at the heedless bands of retreating infantry, finally clutched a man by the arm. They swung around face to face.

"Why—why—" stammered the youth struggling with his balking tongue.

The man screamed: "Let go me! Let go me!" His face was livid and his eyes were rolling uncontrolled. He was heaving and panting. He still grasped his rifle, perhaps having forgotten to release his hold upon it. He tugged frantically, and the youth being compelled to lean forward was dragged several paces.

"Let go me! Let go me!"

"Why—why—" stuttered the youth.

"Well, then!" bawled the man in a lurid rage. He adroitly and fiercely swung his rifle. It crushed upon the youth's head. The man ran on.

The youth's fingers had turned to paste upon the other's arm. The energy was smitten from his muscles. He saw the flaming wings of lightning flash before his vision. There was a deafening rumble of thunder within his head.

Suddenly his legs seemed to die. He sank writhing to the ground. He tried to arise. In his efforts against the numbing pain he was like a man wrestling with a creature of the air.

There was a sinister struggle.

Sometimes he would achieve a position half erect, battle with the air for a moment, and then fall again, grabbing at the grass. His face was of a clammy pallor. Deep groans were wrenched from him.

At last, with a twisting movement, he got upon his hands and knees, and from thence, like a babe trying to walk, to his feet. Pressing his hands to his temples he went lurching over the grass.

He fought an intense battle with his body. His dulled senses wished him to swoon and he opposed them stubbornly, his mind portraying unknown dangers and mutilations if he should fall upon the field. He went tall soldier fashion. He imagined secluded spots where he could fall and be unmolested. To search for one he strove against the tide of his pain.

Once he put his hand on the top of his head and timidly touched the wound. The scratching pain of the contact made him draw a long breath through his clinched teeth. His fingers were dabbled with blood. He regarded them with a fixed stare.

Around him he could hear the grumble of jolted cannon as the scurrying horses were lashed toward the front. Once, a young officer on a besplashed charger nearly ran him down. He turned and watched the mass of guns, men, and horses sweeping in a wide curve toward a gap in a fence. The officer was making excited motions with a gauntleted[1] hand. The guns followed the teams with an air of unwillingness, of being dragged by the heels.

Some officers of the scattered infantry were cursing and railing like fishwives. Their scolding voices could be heard above the din. Into the unspeakable jumble in the roadway rode a squadron of cavalry. The faded yellow of their facings[2] shone bravely. There was a mighty altercation.[3]

The artillery was assembling as if for a conference.

The blue haze of evening was upon the field.

The lines of forest were long purple shadows. One cloud lay along the western sky partly smothering the red.

As the youth left the scene behind him, he heard the guns suddenly roar out. He imagined them shaking in black rage. They belched and howled like brass devils guarding a gate. The soft air was filled with the tremendous remonstrance.

With it came the shattering peal of opposing infantry. Turning to look behind him, he could see sheets of orange light illumine the shadowy distance. There were subtle and sudden lightnings in the far air. At times he thought he could see heaving masses of men.

He hurried on in the dusk. The day had faded until he could barely distinguish a place for his feet. The purple darkness was filled with men who lectured and jabbered. Sometimes he could see them gesticulating against the blue and somber sky. There seemed to be a great ruck[4] of men and munitions spread about in the forest and in the fields.

The little narrow roadway now lay lifeless. There were overturned wagons like sun-dried boulders. The bed of the former torrent was choked with the bodies of horses and splintered parts of war machines.

It had come to pass that his wound pained him but little. He was afraid to move rapidly, however, for a dread of disturbing it. He held his head very still and took many precautions against stumbling. He was filled with anxiety, and his face was pinched and drawn in anticipation of the pain of any sudden mistake of his feet in the gloom.

His thoughts, as he walked, fixed intently upon his hurt. There was a cool, liquid feeling about it and he imagined blood moving slowly down under his hair. His head seemed swollen to a size that made him think his neck to be inadequate.

The new silence of his wound made much worriment. The little blistering voices of pain that had called out from the scalp were, he thought, definite in their expression of danger. By them he believed that he could measure his plight. But when they remained ominously silent he became frightened and imagined terrible fingers that clutched into his brain.

Amid it he began to reflect upon various incidents and conditions of the past. He bethought him of certain meals his mother had cooked at home, in which those dishes of which he was particularly fond had occupied prominent positions. He saw the spread table. The pine walls of the kitchen were glowing in the warm light from the stove. Too, he remembered how he and his companions used to go from the schoolhouse to the bank of a shaded pool. He saw his clothes in disorderly array upon the grass of the bank. He felt the swash of the fragrant water upon his body.

1. **gauntleted:** gloved.
2. **facings:** trimmings on their coats.
3. **altercation:** argument.

4. **ruck:** crowd.

Campfire by Winslow Homer (1880). Oil. The Metropolitan Museum of Art, New York.

The leaves of the overhanging maple rustled with melody in the wind of youthful summer.

He was overcome presently by a dragging weariness. His head hung forward and his shoulders were stooped as if he were bearing a great bundle. His feet shuffled along the ground.

He held continuous arguments as to whether he should lie down and sleep at some near spot, or force himself on until he reached a certain haven. He often tried to dismiss the question, but his body persisted in rebellion and his senses nagged at him like pampered babies.

At last he heard a cheery voice near his shoulder: "Yeh seem t' be in a pretty bad way, boy?"

The youth did not look up, but he assented with thick tongue. "Uh!"

The owner of the cheery voice took him firmly by the arm. "Well," he said, with a round laugh. "I'm goin' your way. Th' hull gang is goin' your way. An' I guess I kin give yeh a lift." They began to walk like a drunken man and his friend.

As they went along, the man questioned the youth and assisted him with the replies like one manipulating the mind of a child. Sometimes he interjected anecdotes. "What reg'ment do yeh b'long teh? Eh? What's that? Th' 304th N' York? Why, what corps is that in? Oh, it is? Why, I thought they wasn't engaged t'day—they're 'way over in th' center. Oh, they was, eh? Well, pretty nearly everybody got their share 'a fightin' t'day. By dad, I give myself up fer dead any number 'a times. There was shootin' here an' shootin' there, an' hollerin' here an' hollerin' there, in th' damn' darkness, until I couldn't tell t' save m' soul which side I was on. Sometimes I thought I was sure 'nough from Ohier, an' other times I could a' swore I was from th' bitter end of Florida. It was th' most mixed up dern thing I ever see. An' these here hull woods is a reg'lar mess. It'll be a miracle if we find our reg'ments t'night. Pretty soon, though, we'll meet a-plenty of guards an' provost-guards, an' one thing an' another. Ho! there they go with an off'cer, I guess. Look at his hand a-draggin'. He's got all th' war he wants, I bet. He won't be talkin' so big about his reputation an' all when they go t' sawin' off his leg. Poor feller! My brother's got whiskers jest like that. How did yeh git 'way over here, anyhow? Your reg'ment is a long way from here, ain't it? Well, I guess we can find it. Yeh know there was a boy killed in my comp'ny t'day that I thought th' world an' all of. Jack was a nice feller. By ginger, it hurt like thunder t' see ol' Jack jest git knocked flat. We was a-standin' purty peaceable fer a spell, 'though there was men runnin' ev'ry way all 'round us, an' while we was a-standin' like that, 'long come a big fat feller. He began t' peck at Jack's elbow, an' he ses: 'Say, where's th' road t' th' river?' An' Jack, he never paid no attention, an' th' feller kept on a-peckin' at his elbow an' sayin': 'Say, where's th' road t' th' river?' Jack was a-lookin' ahead all th' time tryin' t' see th' Johnnies comin' through th' woods, an' he never paid no attention t' this big fat feller fer a long time, but at last he turned 'round an' he ses: 'Ah, go t' hell an' find th' road t' th' river!' An' jest then a shot slapped him bang on th' side th' head. He was a sergeant, too. Them was his last words. Thunder, I wish we was sure 'a findin' our reg'ments t'night. It's goin' t' be long huntin'. But I guess we kin do it.''

In the search that followed, the man of the cheery voice seemed to the youth to possess a wand of a magic kind. He threaded the mazes of the tangled forest with a strange fortune. In en-counters with guards and patrols he displayed the keenness of a detective and the valor of a gamin.[5] Obstacles fell before him and became of assistance. The youth, with his chin still on his breast, stood woodenly by while his companion beat ways and means out of sullen things.

The forest seemed a vast hive of men buzzing about in frantic circles, but the cheery man conducted the youth without mistakes, until at last he began to chuckle with glee and self-satisfaction. ''Ah, there yeh are! See that fire?''

The youth nodded stupidly.

''Well, there's where your reg'ment is. An' now, goodbye ol' boy, good luck t' yeh.''

A warm and strong hand clasped the youth's languid fingers for an instant, and then he heard a cheerful and audacious whistling as the man strode away. As he who had so befriended him was thus passing out of his life, it suddenly occurred to the youth that he had not once seen his face.

---

5. **gamin:** tough street kid.

Responding to the Novel

Analyzing Chapters 7–12

Identifying Facts

1. How does Henry try to rationalize his flight in Chapter 7? What does the sight of the running squirrel do for Henry's image of himself as a deserter?

2. Why does the talk of the tattered man disturb Henry?

3. What have we learned so far in the novel about Jim Conklin and Henry's relationship to him? How does Henry try to help Jim in Chapter 9?

4. According to the opening paragraphs of Chapter 9, what is the meaning of the novel's **title?**

5. In Chapter 11, Henry experiences renewed anxiety about his flight. How does he hope he might be vindicated?

6. How does Henry acquire his ''red badge''? What is **ironic** about this incident?

7. At the end of Chapter 12, what does Henry suddenly realize about the man with the cheery voice?

Interpreting Meanings

8. Why is the encounter with the dead soldier, toward the end of Chapter 7, a **turning point** for Henry?

9. What are some of the memorable details describing Jim's death? Jim's death is tragic, but some people feel there is humor in the telling of it. What do you think?

10. What is **ironic** about Jim's wish to be alone when he dies? How do you think Jim's wish affects Henry?

11. In his flight, Henry believes that the Union forces are defeated. Why is that important to his self-esteem? How is he affected by the discovery that the general is rejoicing in a victory?

12. Crane often achieves powerful effects with simple, short sentences at the end of an episode or chapter. Analyze and comment on the effect of the following sentences, in context:

   a. ''A sad silence was upon the little guarding edifice.'' (Chapter 7)
   b. ''The red sun was pasted in the sky like a fierce wafer.'' (Chapter 9)
   c. ''He was a slang phrase.'' (Chapter 11)

13. Where in these chapters are you most sympathetic with Henry? Where are you least sympathetic?

Defiance: Inviting a Shot Before Petersburg, Virginia by Winslow Homer (1864). Oil.

The front shifted a trifle to meet it squarely. There was a wait. In this part of the field there passed slowly the intense moments that precede the tempest.

A single rifle flashed in a thicket before the regiment. In an instant it was joined by many others. There was a mighty song of clashes and crashes that went sweeping through the woods. The guns in the rear, aroused and enraged by shells that had been thrown burrlike at them, suddenly involved themselves in a hideous altercation with another band of guns. The battle roar settled to a rolling thunder, which was a single, long explosion.

Chapter 17

This advance of the enemy had seemed to the youth like a ruthless hunting. He began to fume with rage and exasperation. He beat his foot upon the ground, and scowled with hate at the swirling smoke that was approaching like a phantom flood. There was a maddening quality in this seeming resolution of the foe to give him no rest, to give him no time to sit down and think. Yesterday he had fought and had fled rapidly. There had been many adventures. For today he felt that he had earned opportunities for contemplative repose. He could have enjoyed portraying to uninitiated listeners various scenes at which he had been a witness or ably discussing the processes of war with other proved men. Too it was important that he should have time for physical recuperation. He was sore and stiff from his experiences. He had received his fill of all exertions, and he wished to rest.

But those other men seemed never to grow weary; they were fighting with their old speed. He had a wild hate for the relentless foe. Yesterday, when he had imagined the universe to be against him, he had hated it, little gods and big gods; today he hated the army of the foe with the same great hatred. He was not going to be badgered of his life, like a kitten chased by boys, he said. It was not well to drive men into final corners; at those moments they could all develop teeth and claws.

He leaned and spoke into his friend's ear. He menaced the woods with a gesture. "If they keep on chasing us, by Gawd, they'd better watch out. Can't stand *too* much."

The friend twisted his head and made a calm reply. "If they keep on a-chasin' us they'll drive us all inteh th' river."

The youth cried out savagely at this statement. He crouched behind a little tree, with his eyes burning hatefully and his teeth set in a curlike snarl. The awkward bandage was still about his head, and upon it, over his wound, there was a spot of dry blood. His hair was wondrously tousled, and some straggling, moving locks hung over the cloth of the bandage down toward his forehead. His jacket and shirt were open at the throat, and exposed his young bronzed neck. There could be seen spasmodic gulpings at his throat.

His fingers twined nervously about his rifle. He wished that it was an engine of annihilating power. He felt that he and his companions were being taunted and derided from sincere convictions that they were poor and puny. His knowledge of his inability to take vengeance for it made his rage into a dark and stormy specter, that possessed him

Gift of Dexter M. Ferry, Jr., The Detroit Institute of Arts.

In the regiment there was a peculiar kind of hesitation denoted in the attitudes of the men. They were worn, exhausted, having slept but little and labored much. They rolled their eyes toward the advancing battle as they stood awaiting the shock. Some shrank and flinched. They stood as men tied to stakes.

Stephen Crane   487

and made him dream of abominable cruelties. The tormenters were flies sucking insolently at his blood, and he thought that he would have given his life for a revenge of seeing their faces in pitiful plights.

The winds of battle had swept all about the regiment, until the one rifle, instantly followed by others, flashed in its front. A moment later the regiment roared forth its sudden and valiant retort. A dense wall of smoke settled slowly down. It was furiously slit and slashed by the knifelike fire from the rifles.

To the youth the fighters resembled animals tossed for a death struggle into a dark pit. There was a sensation that he and his fellows, at bay, were pushing back, always pushing fierce onslaughts of creatures who were slippery. Their beams of crimson seemed to get no purchase upon the bodies of their foes; the latter seemed to evade them with ease, and come through, between, around, and about with unopposed skill.

When, in a dream, it occurred to the youth that his rifle was an impotent stick, he lost sense of everything but his hate, his desire to smash into pulp the glittering smile of victory which he could feel upon the faces of his enemies.

The blue smoke-swallowed line curled and writhed like a snake stepped upon. It swung its ends to and fro in an agony of fear and rage.

The youth was not conscious that he was erect upon his feet. He did not know the direction of the ground. Indeed, once he even lost the habit of balance and fell heavily. He was up again immediately. One thought went through the chaos of his brain at the time. He wondered if he had fallen because he had been shot. But the suspicion flew away at once. He did not think more of it.

He had taken up a first position behind the little tree, with a direct determination to hold it against the world. He had not deemed it possible that his army could that day succeed, and from this he felt the ability to fight harder. But the throng had surged in all ways, until he lost directions and locations, save that he knew where lay the enemy.

The flames bit him, and the hot smoke broiled his skin. His rifle barrel grew so hot that ordinarily he could not have borne it upon his palms; but he kept on stuffing cartridges into it, and pounding them with his clanking, bending ramrod. If he aimed at some changing form through the smoke, he pulled his trigger with a fierce grunt, as if he were dealing a blow of the fist with all his strength.

When the enemy seemed falling back before him and his fellows, he went instantly forward, like a dog who, seeing his foes lagging, turns and insists upon being pursued. And when he was compelled to retire again, he did it slowly, sullenly, taking steps of wrathful despair.

Once he, in his intent hate, was almost alone, and was firing, when all those near him had ceased. He was so engrossed in his occupation that he was not aware of a lull.

He was recalled by a hoarse laugh and a sentence that came to his ears in a voice of contempt and amazement. "Yeh infernal fool, don't yeh know enough t' quit when there ain't anything t' shoot at? Good Gawd!"

He turned then and, pausing with his rifle thrown half into position, looked at the blue line of his comrades. During this moment of leisure they seemed all to be engaged in staring with astonishment at him. They had become spectators. Turning to the front again he saw, under the lifted smoke, a deserted ground.

He looked bewildered for a moment. Then there appeared upon the glazed vacancy of his eyes a diamond point of intelligence. "Oh," he said, comprehending.

He returned to his comrades and threw himself upon the ground. He sprawled like a man who had been thrashed. His flesh seemed strangely on fire, and the sounds of the battle continued in his ears. He groped blindly for his canteen.

The lieutenant was crowing. He seemed drunk with fighting. He called out to the youth: "By heavens, if I had ten thousand wildcats like you I could tear th' stomach outa this war in less'n a week!" He puffed out his chest with large dignity as he said it.

Some of the men muttered and looked at the youth in awestruck ways. It was plain that as he had gone on loading and firing and cursing without the proper intermission, they had found time to regard him. And they now looked upon him as a war devil.

The friend came staggering to him. There was some fright and dismay in his voice. "Are yeh all right, Fleming? Do yeh feel all right? There ain't nothin' th' matter with yeh, Henry, is there?"

"No," said the youth with difficulty. His throat seemed full of knobs and burrs.

These incidents made the youth ponder. It was revealed to him that he had been a barbarian, a beast. He had fought like a pagan who defends his religion. Regarding it, he saw that it was fine, wild, and, in some ways, easy. He had been a tremendous figure, no doubt. By this struggle he had overcome obstacles which he had admitted to be mountains. They had fallen like paper peaks, and he was now what he called a hero. And he had not been aware of the process. He had slept and, awakening, found himself a knight.

He lay and basked in the occasional stares of his comrades. Their faces were varied in degrees of blackness from the burned powder. Some were utterly smudged. They were reeking with perspiration, and their breaths came hard and wheezing. And from these soiled expanses they peered at him.

"Hot work! Hot work!" cried the lieutenant deliriously. He walked up and down, restless and eager. Sometimes his voice could be heard in a wild, incomprehensible laugh.

When he had a particularly profound thought upon the science of war he always unconsciously addressed himself to the youth.

There was some grim rejoicing by the men. "By thunder, I bet this army'll never see another new reg'ment like us!"

"You bet!

'A dog, a woman, an' a walnut tree,
Th' more yeh beat 'em, th' better they be!'

That's like us."

"Lost a piler men, they did. If an' ol' woman swep' up th' woods she'd git a dustpanful."

"Yes, an' if she'll come around ag'in in 'bout an hour she'll git a pile more."

The forest still bore its burden of clamor. From off under the trees came the rolling clatter of the mustketry. Each distant thicket seemed a strange porcupine with quills of flame. A cloud of dark smoke, as from smoldering ruins, went up toward the sun, now bright and gay in the blue, enameled sky.

Chapter 18

The ragged line had respite for some minutes, but during its pause the struggle in the forest became magnified until the trees seemed to quiver from the firing and the ground to shake from the rushing of the men. The voices of the cannon were mingled in a long and interminable row. It seemed difficult to live in such an atmosphere. The chests of the men strained for a bit of freshness, and their throats craved water.

There was one, shot through the body, who raised a cry of bitter lamentation when came this lull. Perhaps he had been calling out during the fighting also, but at that time no one had heard him. But now the men turned at the woeful complaints of him upon the ground.

"Who is it? Who is it?"

"It's Jimmie Rogers, Jimmie Rogers."

When their eyes first encountered him there was a sudden halt, as if they feared to go near.

He was thrashing about in the grass, twisting his shuddering body into many strange postures. He was screaming loudly. This instant's hesitation seemed to fill him with a tremendous, fantastic contempt, and he damned them in shrieked sentences.

The youth's friend had a geographical illusion concerning a stream, and he obtained permission to go for some water. Immediately canteens were showered upon him. "Fill mine, will yeh?" "Bring me some, too." "And me, too." He departed, laden. The youth went with his friend, feeling a desire to throw his heated body onto the stream, and soaking there, drink quarts.

They made a hurried search for the supposed stream, but did not find it. "No water here," said the youth. They turned without delay and began to retrace their steps.

From their position as they again faced toward the place of the fighting, they could of course comprehend a greater amount of the battle than when their visions had been blurred by the hurling smoke of the line. They could see dark stretches winding along the land, and on one cleared space there was a row of guns making gray clouds, which were filled with large flashes of orange-colored flame. Over some foliage they could see the roof of a house. One window, glowing a deep murder red, shone squarely through the leaves. From the edifice a tall leaning tower of smoke went far into the sky.

Looking over their own troops, they saw mixed masses slowly getting into regular form. The sunlight made twinkling points of the bright steel. To the rear there was a glimpse of a distant roadway as it curved over a slope. It was crowded with retreating infantry. From all the interwoven forest arose the smoke and bluster of the battle. The air was always occupied by a blaring.

Near where they stood shells were flip-flapping and hooting. Occasional bullets buzzed in the air and spanged into tree trunks. Wounded men and other stragglers were slinking through the woods.

Looking down an aisle of the grove, the youth and his companion saw a jangling general and his staff almost ride upon a wounded man, who was crawling on his hands and knees. The general reined strongly at his charger's opened and foamy mouth and guided it with dexterous horsemanship past the man. The latter scrambled in wild and torturing haste. His strength evidently failed him as he reached a place of safety. One of his arms suddenly weakened, and he fell, sliding upon his back. He lay stretched out, breathing gently.

A moment later the small, creaking cavalcade was directly in front of the two soldiers. Another

until an interminable roar was developed. To those in the midst of it it became a din fitted to the universe. It was the whirring and thumping of gigantic machinery, complications among the smaller stars. The youth's ears were filled up. They were incapable of hearing more.

On an incline over which a road wound he saw wild and desperate rushes of men perpetually backward and forward in riotous surges. These parts of the opposing armies were two long waves that pitched upon each other madly at dictated points. To and fro they swelled. Sometimes, one side by its yells and cheers would proclaim decisive blows, but a moment later the other side would be all yells and cheers. Once the youth saw a spray of light forms go in houndlike leaps toward the waving blue lines. There was much howling, and presently it went away with a vast mouthful of prisoners. Again, he saw a blue wave dash with such thunderous force against a gray obstruction that it seemed to clear the earth of it and leave nothing but trampled sod. And always in their swift and deadly rushes to and fro the men screamed and yelled like maniacs.

Particular pieces of fence or secure positions behind collections of trees were wrangled over, as gold thrones or pearl bedsteads. There were desperate lunges at these chosen spots seemingly every instant, and most of them were bandied like light toys between the contending forces. The youth could not tell from the battle flags flying like crimson foam in many directions which color of cloth was winning.

His emaciated regiment bustled forth with undiminished fierceness when its time came. When assaulted again by bullets, the men burst out in a barbaric cry of rage and pain. They bent their heads in aims of intent hatred behind the projected hammers of their guns. Their ramrods clanged loud with fury as their eager arms pounded the cartridges into the rifle barrels. The front of the regiment was a smoke-wall penetrated by the flashing points of yellow and red.

Wallowing in the fight, they were in an astonishingly short time resmudged. They surpassed in stain and dirt all their previous appearances. Moving to and fro with strained exertion, jabbering the while, they were, with their swaying bodies, black faces, and glowing eyes, like strange and ugly fiends jigging heavily in the smoke.

The lieutenant, returning from a tour after a bandage, produced from a hidden receptacle of his mind new and portentous[1] oaths suited to the emergency. Strings of expletives he swung lash-like over the backs of his men, and it was evident that his previous efforts had in nowise impaired his resources.

The youth, still the bearer of the colors, did not feel his idleness. He was deeply absorbed as a spectator. The crash and swing of the great drama made him lean forward, intent-eyed, his face working in small contortions. Sometimes he prattled, words coming unconsciously from him in grotesque exclamations. He did not know that he breathed; that the flag hung silently over him, so absorbed was he.

A formidable line of the enemy came within dangerous range. They could be seen plainly—tall, gaunt men with excited faces running with long strides toward a wandering fence.

At sight of this danger the men suddenly ceased their cursing monotone. There was an instant of strained silence before they threw up their rifles and fired a plumping volley at the foes. There had been no order given; the men, upon recognizing the menace, had immediately let drive their flock of bullets without waiting for word of command.

But the enemy were quick to gain the protection of the wandering line of fence. They slid down behind it with remarkable celerity, and from this position they began briskly to slice up the blue men.

These latter braced their energies for a great struggle. Often, white clinched teeth shone from the dusky faces. Many heads surged to and fro, floating upon a pale sea of smoke. Those behind the fence frequently shouted and yelped in taunts and gibelike[2] cries, but the regiment maintained a stressed silence. Perhaps, at this new assault the men recalled the fact that they had been named mud diggers, and it made their situation thrice bitter. They were breathlessly intent upon keeping the ground and thrusting away the rejoicing body of the enemy. They fought swiftly and with a despairing savageness denoted in their expressions.

The youth had resolved not to budge whatever should happen. Some arrows of scorn that had buried themselves in his heart had generated strange and unspeakable hatred. It was clear to him that his final and absolute revenge was to be achieved by his dead body lying, torn and gluttering,[3] upon the field. This was to be a poignant retaliation upon the officer who had said "mule drivers," and later "mud diggers," for in all the wild graspings of his mind for a unit responsible for his sufferings and commotions he always

---

1. **portentous:** here, frightening.

2. **gibelike:** jeering.
3. **gluttering:** bleeding heavily.

seized upon the man who had dubbed him wrongly. And it was his idea, vaguely formulated, that his corpse would be for those eyes a great and salt reproach.

The regiment bled extravagantly. Grunting bundles of blue began to drop. The orderly sergeant of the youth's company was shot through the cheeks. Its supports being injured, his jaw hung afar down, disclosing in the wide cavern of his mouth a pulsing mass of blood and teeth. And with it all he made attempts to cry out. In his endeavor there was a dreadful earnestness, as if he conceived that one great shriek would make him well.

The youth saw him presently go rearward. His strength seemed in nowise impaired. He ran swiftly, casting wild glances for succor.

Others fell down about the feet of their companions. Some of the wounded crawled out and away, but many lay still, their bodies twisted into impossible shapes.

The youth looked once for his friend. He saw a vehement young man, powder-smeared and frowzled,[4] whom he knew to be him. The lieutenant, also, was unscathed in his position at the rear. He had continued to curse, but it was now with the air of a man who was using his last box of oaths.

For the fire of the regiment had begun to wane and drip. The robust voice, that had come strangely from the thin ranks, was growing rapidly weak.

Chapter 23

The colonel came running along back of the line. There were other officers following him. "We must charge'm!" they shouted. "We must charge'm!" they cried with resentful voices, as if anticipating a rebellion against this plan by the men.

The youth, upon hearing the shouts, began to study the distance between him and the enemy. He made vague calculations. He saw that to be firm soldiers they must go forward. It would be death to stay in the present place, and with all the circumstances to go backward would exalt too many others. Their hope was to push the galling foes away from the fence.

He expected that his companions, weary and stiffened, would have to be driven to this assault, but as he turned toward them he perceived with a certain surprise that they were giving quick and unqualified expressions of assent. There was an ominous, clanging overture to the charge when the shafts of the bayonets rattled upon the rifle barrels. At the yelled words of command the soldiers sprang forward in eager leaps. There was new and unexpected force in the movement of the regiment. A knowledge of its faded and jaded condition made the charge appear like a paroxysm, a display of the strength that comes before a final feebleness. The men scampered in insane fever of haste, racing as if to achieve a sudden success before an exhilarating fluid should leave them. It was a blind and despairing rush by the collection of men in dusty and tattered blue, over a green sward and under a sapphire sky, toward a fence, dimly outlined in smoke, from behind which spluttered the fierce rifles of enemies.

The youth kept the bright colors to the front. He was waving his free arm in furious circles, the while shrieking mad calls and appeals, urging on those that did not need to be urged, for it seemed that the mob of blue men hurling themselves on the dangerous group of rifles were again grown suddenly wild with an enthusiasm of unselfishness. From the many firings starting toward them, it looked as if they would merely succeed in making a great sprinkling of corpses on the grass between their former position and the fence. But they were in a state of frenzy, perhaps because of forgotten vanities, and it made an exhibition of sublime recklessness. There was no obvious questioning, nor figurings, nor diagrams. There was, apparently, no considered loopholes. It appeared that the swift wings of their desires would have shattered against the iron gates of the impossible.

He himself felt the daring spirit of a savage religion-mad. He was capable of profound sacrifices, a tremendous death. He had no time for dissections, but he knew that he thought of the bullets only as things that could prevent him from reaching the place of his endeavor. There were subtle flashings of joy within him that thus should be his mind.

He strained all his strength. His eyesight was shaken and dazzled by the tension of thought and muscle. He did not see anything excepting the mist of smoke gashed by the little knives of fire, but he knew that in it lay the aged fence of a vanished farmer protecting the snuggled bodies of the gray men.

As he ran a thought of the shock of contact gleamed in his mind. He expected a great concussion when the two bodies of troops crashed together. This became a part of his wild battle madness. He could feel the onward swing of the regiment about him and he conceived of a thun-

---

4. **frowzled:** disheveled.

Assault on Marye's Heights by Lt. Frederic Cavada (1862). Oil.

derous, crushing blow that would prostrate the resistance and spread consternation and amazement for miles. The flying regiment was going to have a catapultian effect.[1] This dream made him run faster among his comrades, who were giving vent to hoarse and frantic cheers.

But presently he could see that many of the

men in gray did not intend to abide the blow. The smoke, rolling, disclosed men who ran, their faces still turned. These grew to a crowd, who retired stubbornly. Individuals wheeled frequently to send a bullet at the blue wave.

But at one part of the line there was a grim and obdurate group that made no movement. They were settled firmly down behind posts and rails. A flag, ruffled and fierce, waved over them and their rifles dinned fiercely.

---

1. **catapultian effect:** like a catapult, an ancient military machine that hurled heavy missile-like spears or stones.

Historical Society of Pennsylvania.

the throats of those who stood resisting. The space between dwindled to an insignificant distance.

The youth had centered the gaze of his soul upon that other flag. Its possession would be high pride. It would express bloody minglings, near blows. He had a gigantic hatred for those who made great difficulties and complications. They caused it to be as a craved treasure of mythology, hung amid tasks and contrivances of danger.

He plunged like a mad horse at it. He was resolved it should not escape if wild blows and darings of blows could seize it. His own emblem, quivering and aflare, was winging toward the other. It seemed there would shortly be an encounter of strange beaks and claws, as of eagles.

The swirling body of blue men came to a sudden halt at close and disastrous range and roared a swift volley. The group in gray was split and broken by this fire, but its riddled body still fought. The men in blue yelled again and rushed in upon it.

The youth, in his leapings, saw, as through a mist, a picture of four or five men stretched upon the ground or writhing upon their knees with bowed heads as if they had been stricken by bolts from the sky. Tottering among them was the rival color bearer, whom the youth saw had been bitten vitally by the bullets of the last formidable volley. He perceived this man fighting a last struggle, the struggle of one whose legs are grasped by demons. It was a ghastly battle. Over his face was the bleach of death, but set upon it was the dark and hard lines of desperate purpose. With this terrible grin of resolution he hugged his precious flag to him and was stumbling and staggering in his design to go the way that led to safety for it.

But his wounds always made it seem that his feet were retarded, held, and he fought a grim fight, as with invisible ghouls fastened greedily upon his limbs. Those in advance of the scampering blue men, howling cheers, leaped at the fence. The despair of the lost was in his eyes as he glanced back at them.

The youth's friend went over the obstruction in a tumbling heap and sprang at the flag as a panther at prey. He pulled at it and, wrenching it free, swung up its red brilliancy with a mad cry of exultation even as the color bearer, gasping, lurched over in a final throe and, stiffening convulsively, turned his dead face to the ground. There was much blood upon the grass blades.

At the place of success there began more wild clamorings of cheers. The men gesticulated and bellowed in an ecstasy. When they spoke it was as if they considered their listener to be a mile

The blue whirl of men got very near, until it seemed that in truth there would be a close and frightful scuffle. There was an expressed disdain in the opposition of the little group, that changed the meaning of the cheers of the men in blue. They became yells of wrath, directed, personal. The cries of the two parties were now in sound an interchange of scathing insults.

They in blue showed their teeth; their eyes shone all white. They launched themselves as at

away. What hats and caps were left to them they often slung high in the air.

At one part of the line four men had been swooped upon, and they now sat as prisoners. Some blue men were about them in an eager and curious circle. The soldiers had trapped strange birds, and there was an examination. A flurry of fast questions was in the air.

One of the prisoners was nursing a superficial wound in the foot. He cuddled it, babywise, but he looked up from it often to curse with an astonishing utter abandon straight at the noses of his captors. He consigned them to red regions; he called upon the pestilential wrath of strange gods. And with it all he was singularly free from recognition of the finer points of the conduct of prisoners of war. It was as if a clumsy clod had trod upon his toe and he conceived it to be his privilege, his duty, to use deep, resentful oaths.

Another, who was a boy in years, took his plight with great calmness and apparent good nature. He conversed with the men in blue, studying their faces with his bright and keen eyes. They spoke of battle and conditions. There was an acute interest in all their faces during this exchange of viewpoints. It seemed a great satisfaction to hear voices from where all had been darkness and speculation.

The third captive sat with a morose countenance. He preserved a stoical and cold attitude. To all advances he made one reply without variation, "Ah, go t' hell!"

The last of the four was always silent, and, for the most part, kept his face turned in unmolested directions. From the views of the youth received he seemed to be in a state of absolute dejection. Shame was upon him, and with it profound regret that he was, perhaps, no more to be counted in the ranks of his fellows. The youth could detect no expression that would allow him to believe that the other was giving a thought to his narrowed future, the pictured dungeons, perhaps, and starvations and brutalities, liable to the imagination. All to be seen was shame for captivity and regret for the right to antagonize.

After the men had celebrated sufficiently they settled down behind the old rail fence, on the opposite side to the one from which their foes had been driven. A few shot perfunctorily at distant marks.

There was some long grass. The youth nestled in it and rested, making a convenient rail support the flag. His friend, jubilant and glorified, holding his treasure with vanity, came to him there. They sat side by side and congratulated each other.

Chapter 24

The roarings that had stretched in a long line of sound across the face of the forest began to grow intermittent and weaker. The stentorian[1] speeches of the artillery continued in some distant encounter, but the crashes of the musketry had almost ceased. The youth and his friend of a sudden looked up, feeling a deadened form of distress at the waning of these noises, which had become a part of life. They could see changes going on among the troops. There were marchings this way and that way. A battery wheeled leisurely. On the crest of a small hill was the thick gleam of many departing muskets.

The youth arose. "Well, what now, I wonder?" he said. By his tone he seemed to be preparing to resent some new monstrosity in the way of dins and smashes. He shaded his eyes with his grimy hand and gazed over the field.

His friend also arose and stared. "I bet we're goin' t' git along out of this an' back over the' river," said he.

"Well, I swan!" said the youth.

They waited, watching. Within a little while the regiment received orders to retrace its way. The men got up grunting from the grass, regretting the soft repose. They jerked their stiffened legs, and stretched their arms over their heads. One man swore as he rubbed his eyes. They all groaned "O Lord!" They had as many objections to this change as they would have had to a proposal for a new battle.

They trampled slowly back over the field across which they had run in a mad scamper. The fence, deserted, resumed with its careening posts and disjointed bars, an air of quiet and rural depravity. Beyond it, there lay spread a few corpses. Conspicuous was the contorted body of the color-bearer in gray whose flag the youth's friend was now bearing away.

The regiment marched until it had joined its fellows. The reformed brigade, in column, aimed through a wood at the road. Directly they were in a mass of dust-covered troops, and were trudging along in a way parallel to the enemy's lines as these had been defined by the previous turmoil.

They passed within view of a stolid white house, and saw in front of it groups of their comrades lying in wait behind a neat breastwork. A row of guns were booming at a distant enemy. Shells thrown in reply were raising clouds of dust

---

1. **stentorian:** loud. (Stentor, in the *Iliad*, is a messenger who has a very loud voice.)

and splinters. Horsemen dashed along the line of entrenchments.

As they passed near other commands, men of the dilapidated regiment procured the captured flag from Wilson and, tossing it high into the air cheered tumultuously as it turned, with apparent reluctance, slowly over and over.

At this point of its march the division curved away from the field and went winding off in the direction of the river. When the significance of this movement had impressed itself upon the youth he turned his head and looked over his shoulder toward the trampled and debris-strewed ground. He breathed a breath of new satisfaction. He finally nudged his friend. "Well, it's all over," he said to him.

His friend gazed backward. "B' Gawd, it is," he assented. They mused.

For a time the youth was obliged to reflect in a puzzled and uncertain way. His mind was undergoing a subtle change. It took moments for it to cast off its battleful ways and resume its accustomed course of thought. Gradually his brain emerged from the clogged clouds, and at last was enabled to more closely comprehend himself and circumstance.

He understood then that the existence of shot and countershot was in the past. He had dwelt in a land of strange, squalling upheavals and had come forth. He had been where there was red of blood and black of passion, and he was escaped. His first thoughts were given to rejoicings at this fact.

Later he began to study his deeds, his failures, and his achievements. Thus, fresh from scenes where many of his usual machines of reflection had been idle, from where he had proceeded sheeplike, he struggled to marshal all his acts.

At last they marched before him clearly. From this present viewpoint he was enabled to look at them in spectator fashion and to criticize them with some correctness, for his new condition had already defeated certain sympathies.

His friend, too, seemed engaged with some retrospection, for he suddenly gestured and said: "Good Lord!"

"What?" asked the youth.

"Good Lord!" repeated his friend. "Yeh know Jimmie Rogers? Well, he—gosh, when he was hurt I started t' git some water fer 'im an', thunder, I ain't seen 'im from that time 'til this. I clean forgot what I—say, has anybody seen Jimmie Rogers?"

"Seen 'im? No! He's dead," they told him.

His friend swore.

But the youth, regarding his procession of memory, felt gleeful and unregretting, for in it his public deeds were paraded in great and shining prominence. Those performances which had been witnessed by his fellows marched now in wide purple and gold, having various deflections.[2] They went gaily with music. It was pleasure to watch these things. He spent delightful minutes viewing the gilded images of memory.

He saw that he was good. He recalled with a thrill of joy the respectful comments of his fellows upon his conduct. He said to himself again the sentence of the insane lieutenant: "If I had ten thousand wildcats like you, I could tear th' stomach outa this war in less'n a week." It was a little coronation.

Nevertheless, the ghost of his flight from the first engagement appeared to him and danced. Echoes of his terrible combat with the arrayed forces of the universe came to his ears. There were small shoutings in his brain about these matters. For a moment he blushed, and the light of his soul flickered with shame.

However, he presently procured an explanation and an apology. He said that those tempestuous moments were of the wild mistakes and ravings of a novice who did not comprehend. He had been a mere man railing at a condition, but now he was out of it and could see that it had been very proper and just. It had been necessary for him to swallow swords that he might have a better throat for grapes. Fate had in truth been kind to him; she had stabbed him with benign purpose and diligently cudgeled him for his own sake. In his rebellion, he had been very portentous, no doubt, and sincere, and anxious for humanity, but now that he stood safe, with no lack of blood, it was suddenly clear to him that he had been wrong not to kiss the knife and bow to the cudgel. He had foolishly squirmed.

But the sky would forget. It was true, he admitted, that in the world it was the habit to cry devil at persons who refused to trust what they could not trust, but he thought that perhaps the stars dealt differently. The imperturbable sun shines on insult and worship.

As Fleming was thus fraternizing again with nature, a specter of reproach came to him. There loomed the dogging memory of the tattered soldier—he who, gored by bullets and faint for blood, had fretted concerning an imagined wound in another; he who had loaned his last of strength and intellect for the tall soldier; he who, blind with weariness and pain, had been deserted in the field.

---

2. **deflections:** shadings.

For an instant a wretched chill of sweat was upon him at the thought that he might be detected in the thing. As he stood persistently before his vision, he gave vent to a cry of sharp irritation and agony.

His friend turned. "What's the matter, Henry?" he demanded. The youth's reply was an outburst of crimson oaths.

As he marched along the little branch-hung roadway among his prattling companions this vision of cruelty brooded over him. It clung near him always and darkened his view of these deeds in purple and gold. Whichever way his thoughts turned they were followed by the somber phantom of the desertion in the fields. He looked stealthily at his companions, feeling sure that they must discern in his face evidences of this pursuit. But they were plodding in ragged array, discussing with quick tongues the accomplishments of the late battle.

"Oh, if a man should come up an' ask me, I'd say we got a dum good lickin'."

"Lickin—in yer eye! We ain't licked, sonny. We're going down here aways, swing aroun', an' come in behint 'em."

"Oh, hush, with your comin' in behint 'em. I've seen all 'a that I wanta. Don't tell me about comin' in behint—"

"Bill Smithers, he ses he'd rather been in ten hundred battles than been in that heluva hospital. He ses they got shootin' in th' nighttime, an' shells dropped plum among 'em in th' hospital. He ses sech hollerin' he never see."

"Hasbrouck? He's th' best off'cer in this here reg'ment. He's a whale."

"Didn't I tell yeh we'd come aroun' in behint 'em? Didn't I tell yeh so? We—"

"Oh, shet yer mouth!"

"You make me sick."

"G' home, yeh fool."

For a time this pursuing recollection of the tattered man took all elation from the youth's veins. He saw his vivid error, and he was afraid that it would stand before him all his life. He took no share in the chatter of his comrades, nor did he look at them or know them, save when he felt sudden suspicion that they were seeing his thoughts and scrutinizing each detail of the scene with the tattered soldier.

Yet gradually he mustered force to put the sin at a distance. And then he regarded it with what he thought to be great calmness. At last, he concluded that he saw it in quaint uses. He exclaimed that its importance in the aftertime would be great to him if it even succeeded in hindering the workings of his egotism. It would make a sobering balance. It would become a good part of him. He would have upon him often the consciousness of a great mistake. And he would be taught to deal gently and with care. He would be a man.

This plan for the utilization of a sin did not give him complete joy but it was the best sentiment he could formulate under the circumstances, and when it was combined with his success, or public deeds, he knew that he was quite contented. And at last his eyes seemed to open to new ways. He found that he could look back upon the brass and bombast of his earlier gospels and see them truly. He was gleeful when he discovered that he now despised them.

He was emerged from his struggles, with a large sympathy for the machinery of the universe. With his new eyes, he could see that the secret and open blows which were being dealt about the world with such heavenly lavishness were in truth blessings. It was a deity laying about him with the bludgeon of correction.

His loud mouth against these things had been lost as the storm ceased. He would no more stand upon places high and false, and denounce the distant planets. He beheld that he was tiny but not inconsequent to the sun. In the space-wide whirl of events no grain like him would be lost.

With this conviction came a store of assurance. He felt a quiet manhood, nonassertive but a sturdy and strong blood. He knew that he would no more quail before his guides wherever they should point. He had been to touch the great death, and found that, after all, it was but the great death and was for others. He was a man.

So it came to pass that as he trudged from the place of blood and wrath his soul changed. He came from hot plowshares[3] to prospects of clover tranquilly, and it was as if hot plowshares were not. Scars faded as flowers.

It rained. The procession of weary soldiers became a bedraggled train, despondent and muttering, marching with churning effort in a trough of liquid brown mud under a low, wretched sky. Yet the youth smiled, for he saw that the world was a world for him, though many discovered it to be made of oaths and walking sticks. He had rid himself of the red sickness of battle. The sultry nightmare was in the past. He had been an animal blistered and sweating in the heat and pain of war. He turned now with a lover's thirst to images of tranquil skies, fresh meadows, cool brooks—an existence of soft and eternal peace.

Over the river a golden ray of sun came through the hosts of leaden rain clouds.

---

3. **hot plowshares:** plows that have been melted into swords.

Responding to the Novel

Analyzing Chapters 19–24

Identifying Facts

1. Describe how Henry behaves in the charge. Why does he abandon his rifle to carry the flag?
2. How does Henry feel toward the officer who called him a "mule-driver"?
3. What two extremes of blame and praise does the author present in Chapter 21?
4. Describe the capture of the enemy's flag.
5. How does Henry sum up his experience in the last chapter of the novel? What kind of life does he now look forward to?

Interpreting Meanings

6. Toward the end of Chapter 19, what emotions does the sight of the flag inspire in Henry? To what is the flag compared? How is this incident both a critical **turning point** in the novel and a **symbolic** episode?
7. The heat of battle reaches a **climax** in Chapter 19. Analyze the **imagery** of this chapter closely. What does Crane seem to imply about the men and the physical scene through his choice of images?
8. Explain how Crane uses **synaesthesia** (see page 491) in the following phrases from Chapter 19: (a) "a blue haze of curses"; (b) "the yellow tongues"; (c) "pulsating saliva."
9. Crane prepares us for the general's bitter reproaches when he has Henry perceive the warping of space and time in Chapter 21 (see page 497). What is the **ironic** effect of this paragraph in its context?
10. What do you think is the point of the description of the four enemy captives at the end of Chapter 23? Why is the placement of this description, immediately after the capture of the enemy's flag, especially appropriate?
11. Why do you think Henry is disturbed by the "dogging memory of the tattered soldier" in Chapter 24? Does he finally succeed in putting this memory to rest?
12. Analyze the **image** in the last sentence of the novel. How is this concluding sentence similar to, yet different from, other places we have seen where Crane refers to the sky? What may Crane be **symbolically** suggesting in these few words, about the development of Henry and about the **theme** of the novel as a whole?
13. Do you agree that Henry has, in the end, achieved "a quiet manhood, non-assertive but of sturdy and strong blood"? Or do you think this confidence is only temporary? Explain why or why not.

The Novel as a Whole

1. What *is* the red badge of courage? Did Henry win his red badge? Explain.
2. Is Henry a **hero** in any conventional sense of the word? How is he similar to, or different from, a mythical hero like Odysseus, or a romance hero like King Arthur, or a tragic hero like Antigone? Is Henry like the heroes you see today in films and in other works of contemporary literature?
3. Chapter 24 of *The Red Badge of Courage* appears to imply that Henry has, by hard-won experience, become truly a man. Do you think the overall portrayal of Henry in the novel justifies the protagonist's own view of himself in the last chapter: "He saw that he was good"? Do you believe Henry has undergone a genuine change in character in the course of the novel? Explain.
4. The **setting** of Crane's novel is never precisely specified, but many scholars believe it is based on events that took place at the Battle of Chancellorsville, fought in the opening days of May 1863. In that battle, desite major losses, neither side achieved a clear victory. Read about the actual battle and discuss its similarities to the battle in the novel.
5. Imagine that you are directing a filmed version of *The Red Badge of Courage*. What aspects of the novel do you think would lend themselves especially well to a film adaptation? What features or qualities of Crane's style, and of the work's overall effect, would be especially difficult to capture in a filmed version?
6. In the century since *The Red Badge of Courage* was published, many novels, stories, and movies have been produced about war. How does Crane's story compare with these more recent portrayals of men in battle? You might consider comparing Crane's novel to the following:

   a. Ernest Hemingway, *A Farewell to Arms* (novel)
   b. James Jones, *From Here to Eternity* (novel)
   c. Eric Maria Remarque, *All Quiet on the Western Front* (novel)
   d. Joseph Heller, *Catch-22* (novel)
   e. Leon Uris, *Exodus* (novel)
   f. *Apocalypse Now* (movie)
   g. *Platoon* (movie)
   h. M*A*S*H (TV series)

   Walt Whitman, writing before *The Red Badge* was published, said ". . . the real war will never get in the books" (see page 351). Do you think this is any longer true?

Writing About the Novel

A Creative Response

1. **Imitating the Writer's Style.** You have seen that Crane's vivid, sensuous imagery is one of the most prominent stylistic traits of *The Red Badge of Courage.* Write a short description of a location you know well. In your description, focus on using images that are as vivid and original as you can make them. Try to describe your scene through the impressions of one onlooker.

2. **Extending the Novel.** Write a short concluding chapter to *The Red Badge of Courage,* in which you narrate the homecoming of Henry Fleming. In your sequel, use some of the hints about this event that Crane has provided in the course of the novel.

A Critical Response

3. **Analyzing Theme.** *"They had fallen like paper peaks, and he was now what he called a hero. And he had not been aware of the process. He had slept and, awakening, found himself a knight."* In a brief essay, discuss the significance of this quotation in its context (Chapter 17) and analyze its relationship to the **theme** of the novel as a whole. Because Crane uses the word *knight* here, be sure to analyze the ways in which the novel resembles a quest story. Since Crane is a realist, not a romantic, tell whether or not he relates this quest story with ironic twists. You might want to fill out a chart like the following before you write:

Elements of a Quest Story	The Red Badge of Courage
1. Perilous journey	
2. Goal of the quest	
3. Physical obstacles met on the journey	
4. Psychological obstacles met on the journey	
5. People who aid the quest	
6. Outcome of quest	
7. Glorification of the hero	

4. **Comparing Crane's Poetry and Fiction.** In a brief essay, compare the theme and tone of the following poem by Crane with the theme and tone of *The Red Badge of Courage.* Pay particular attention to Crane's use of **irony.** How does he set human beings in a universe that is indifferent to their needs?

War Is Kind

Do not weep, maiden, for war is kind.
Because your lover threw wild hands toward the sky
And the affrighted steed ran on alone,
Do not weep.
5 War is kind.

Hoarse, booming drums of the regiment,
Little souls who thirst for fight,
These men were born to drill and die.
The unexplained glory flies above them,
10 Great is the battle-god, great, and his kingdom—
A field where a thousand corpses lie.

Do not weep, babe, for war is kind.
Because your father tumbled in the yellow trenches,
Raged at his breast, gulped and died,
15 Do not weep.
War is kind.

Swift blazing flag of the regiment,
Eagle with crest of red and gold,
These men were born to drill and die.
20 Point for them the virtue of slaughter,
Make plain to them the excellence of killing
And a field where a thousand corpses lie.

Mother whose heart hung humble as a button
On the bright splendid shroud of your son,
25 Do not weep.
War is kind.

—Stephen Crane, 1896

The Letter Home by Eastman Johnson (1867). Oil.

Museum of Fine Arts, Boston.

5. Responding to a Critique. Read the following comment on *The Red Badge of Courage:*

What is most notable about *The Red Badge* is that this *illusion* of "control" and confidence—the real theme of the book—is always before the reader. Although the youth learns soon enough that he controls nothing, that he is just another helpless soldier under fire, and becomes sick with fear until he runs away, his actual "desertion" is never noticed. Here is a joke, if you like, at the expense of Henry Fleming's actual cowardice, just as Henry's eventual "courage" will also be treated as a kind of joke, for in this book courage is as mechanical as desertion. Henry is swept back into the battle without any will on his part. Without quite knowing where he is or what he is doing, he becomes hysterically aggressive like his comrades. Performing an act of unintentional heroism (he seizes a Confederate flag from its falling bearer), he is acclaimed at battle's end. He is now, and at last, perfectly satisfied with hmself. He has got through his initiation, his real battle—with his own fear. But the reader who has been following Henry's every sensation from paragraph to paragraph (Crane's greatest feat in the book) knows that this triumph is of no real significance and the youth's satisfaction with himself is a passing phase. War is so mad and terrible that nothing is easier for the actual participant to forget—and to turn into something utterly different from the actual moments of terror and madness.

—Alfred Kazin

In a well-organized essay, discuss your response to opinions in this passage. Support your own position with references from the text.

6. Analyzing Character. In a five-paragraph essay, analyze the character of one of the following figures in the novel. In your essay, discuss the character's function in the novel, and tell whether he is a flat, one-dimensional character, or a fully developed, dynamic character:

a. The youth, Henry Fleming
b. The tall soldier, Jim Conklin
c. The loud soldier, Wilson
d. The tattered man

Analyzing Language and Style

Impressionism

The artistic movement known as *Impressionism* flourished among French painters in the two decades between 1875 and 1895. Deliberately rebelling against the narrative, realistic paintings favored by the preceding generation, the Impressionists aimed at suggestion and the

Rouen Cathedral (façade) by Claude Monet (1894). Oil.

Museum of Fine Arts, Boston.

evocation of a particular atmosphere or mood, rather than at direct statement. Led by such painters as Claude Monet, Pierre-Auguste Renoir, Camille Pissaro, and Paul Cezanne, these artists experimented with light and perspective, which they believed were the essential elements of a painting.

Impressionism is also a style of writing, in which all events and scenes are conveyed to the reader through the senses and mind of one character. A variety of features in Crane's style have been described as impressionistic. You have already examined some of Crane's **imagery,** which often appeals evocatively to more than one sense in the same phrase.

1. In Chapter 4, find the **fragmented quotations** which mirror the moment-by-moment impressions of the men in actual conversation.
2. Like the Impressionist painters, Crane believed that one object or action can be perceived in a multitude of ways, sometimes in conflicting ways. (One of the Impressionists, Claude Monet, painted a series of almost identical views of the Cathedral at Rouen in France, seen in different lights at different times of day.) Can you find a passage that suggests Henry's sharply conflicting, **ambiguous** impressions of battle?
3. Where does Crane use **syntax,** or sentence structure, to suggest the men's psychological disorientation on the battlefield?

In *Two Years Before the Mast* (1840), Richard Henry Dana called *loafer* "the newly invented Yankee word." Four years later, in *Martin Chuzzlewit,* some of which takes place in America, Charles Dickens put *loaf* in quotation marks to show that it was a peculiarly American term. Whitman's use of *loaf* eleven years later proclaimed his Americanness just as surely as if he had called himself a ring-tailed roarer.

The Language of the Stump: Political Coinages

The American vernacular was not only used in literature. It was also being used on the political platform, or "stump." (Candidates for offices would stand on tree stumps to deliver their speeches.) Candidates in the West used Crockett-style language to capture the attention of their rough-hewn audiences. Here is a part of a speech made by an Oregon candidate for office in 1858:

> Fellow-citizens, you might as well try to dry up the Atlantic Ocean with a broomstraw, or draw this 'ere stump from under my feet with a harnessed gadfly, as to convince me that I ain't gwine to be elected this heat [race]. My opponent don't stand a chance; not a sniff. Why, he ain't as intellectual as a common sized shad. . . . If thar's anybody this side of whar the sun begins to blister the yea'th [heath] that can wallop me, let him show himself—I'm ready. Boys, I go in for the American Eagle, claws, stars, stripes, and all; and may I bust my everlastin' button-holes ef I don't knock down, drag out, and gouge everybody as denies me!

This so-called "stump style" is long gone, but many phrases coined by politicians of the period have lasted.

The word *gerrymander* was coined in 1812 after Massachusetts Governor Gerry reorganized the election districts in his state in order to maintain control of the state senate. One of the districts was absurdly long and serpentine, and Gilbert Stuart, noting its resemblance to a salamander, drew a map for a newspaper giving this district a head, wings, and claws. "A Gerrymander," proclaimed the newspaper's editor, and thus the word was born.

Filibuster comes from the Dutch *vribuiter* ("freebooter" or "pirate"). The word was first used in the nineteenth century to refer to attempts by Americans to encourage revolutions in Latin America by running in guns.

The Language of the Press

Newspapers began to flourish in America in the late 1830's, thanks to improved printing methods which made a penny newspaper profitable. Dickens' satirical scene in *Martin Chuzzlewit* gives some indication of the flavor of many newspapers of the day. When Martin Chuzzlewit lands in New York, he is confronted by a mass of newsboys:

A stump-speaking politician.
Drawing by George Caleb Bingham (1853).

St. Louis Art Museum.

"Here's this morning's *New York Sewer!*" cried one. "Here's this morning's *New York Stabber!* Here's the *New York Family Spy!* Here's the *New York Private Listener!* Here's the *New York Peeper!* . . . Here's full particulars of the patriotic loco-foco movement yesterday in which the whigs was so chawed up, and the last Alabama gouging case, and the interesting Arkansas dooel with bowie-knives, and all the political, commercial, and fashionable news!"

—from *Martin Chuzzlewit,*
Charles Dickens

Newspapers tried to attract readers with colorful language. One of the ways they did this was to invent whimsical abbreviations. The earliest recorded use of the most famous Americanism of them all—*OK*—shows that it had its origin in the fad for witty abbreviations. *OK* was first used in a Boston newspaper in 1839, to mean "all correct" ("oll korrect"). But *OK* might never have survived if the New York Democratic Club, during the 1840 presidential election, had not dubbed themselves *The OK Club.* The Democrats intended *OK* to stand for "Old Kinderhook," a nickname for their candidate, President Martin Van Buren, who had been born in Kinderhook, New York. But their opponents claimed that *OK* stood for "oll korrect" and that the letters had been coined by former President Andrew Jackson, who had misspelled "all correct." (This was to remind voters that Van Buren had been Jackson's hand-picked successor and to make fun of Jackson's lack of education.) "OK!" became a Democratic rallying cry during that boisterous election year and from then on came into widespread popular use. But its true derivation—in that Boston newspaper—eluded researchers for over a hundred years.

The Last Edition by George Loring Brown (undated). Oil.

Carnegie Institution, Pittsburgh, Pennsylvania. Gift of Mr. and Mrs. Henry J. Heinz II.

The Influence of the Immigrants

The late 1840's saw a tremendous increase in the number of immigrants to the United States. In 1845, about 100,000 immigrants arrived; in 1854, this number had grown to 500,000. A majority of immigrants during the mid-nineteenth century were either Germans, seeking haven from political disorder, or Irish, fleeing the devastating famine. The influence of Irish words on American English was small—Irish immigrants also spoke English, since their own language had been suppressed by the British. The German influence was stronger, especially in words for foods (*sauerkraut, frankfurter, hamburger, noodle.*) German has also given us *kindergarten* ("garden of children"); *bum* (from *bummeln,* "to waste time"); *dumb,* in the sense of "stupid" (from *dumm*); and *fresh,* meaning "impertinent" (from *frech,* "impudent").

However, the greatest source of loan words in the nineteenth century was Spanish. As Americans moved westward into territory originally settled by the Spanish, they came upon a host of novelties with Spanish names. *Mustang, lasso, ranch, fiesta, plaza, bronco, canyon,* and *patio* are just a few words of Spanish origin.

The Language of the Rails

The rapid growth of the railroad created a unique problem—an urgent need for new place names. Every station had to have a name, and many sparsely settled areas where the railroad stopped were nameless. The responsibility for providing these new names often fell to railroad executives. As historian Daniel Boorstin writes, one executive who was assigned to name thirty-two stations in the state of Washington performed his task in this way:

> By a strenuous exercise of free-association, [the executive] christened the required number of stations with a variety of names ranging from Warden ("after a heavy stockholder"), to Othello ("after the play"), Ralston ("after a health food"), Horlick ("after the malted milk"), Whittier ("after the poet"), and Laconia ("on account of its location at the summit—after what I thought was Laconia in Switzerland located high up among the Alps, but in looking over the Swiss map this morning I am unable to find a place of that name there").
>
> —from *The Americans,* Daniel Boorstin

The executive may have been weak in European geography, but the name he gave the mountain station had its own nobility. If we assume that it required hardy people to live in the Washington mountains, it was appropriate as well, for in ancient Greece, the dominant people of Laconia were the Spartans.

Analyzing Language

1. One characteristic of English that is common in American speech is the fluidity of parts of speech. Americans change nouns into verbs or adjectives, and verbs into nouns or adjectives. These changes are often brought about by the addition of a suffix. The first suffix popularly used in the United States to make new nouns was *-ery*. *Printery* was coined in 1638, *grocery* in 1791. Other suffixes used to change a word's function are *-logy, -ism, -ize,* and *-ish*. Make a list of five words that have been formed by the addition of each of these suffixes. What information is given in the dictionary about each word's origin?

2. Nearly every occupation coins its own special vocabulary, which may then find its way into general usage. Short-order cooks, for example, have developed an imaginative vocabulary for the food they serve. You probably use many of the terms yourself: *BLT* ("bacon, lettuce, and tomato sandwich"), *two eggs sunny side up* ("two eggs fried on one side only"), *one medium burger without* ("one hamburger medium-cooked without onions"). Compile a brief dictionary of the special vocabulary of people in a business or industry you are familiar with (stockbrokers, doctors, lawyers, news reporters, weather forecasters, computer programmers, athletes, singers, and so on). Explain the meaning of each word or phrase and, if you can, cite its derivation. Have any of these words or phrases been picked up and used by people outside the occupation?

3. In his book on language, *Word Play: What Happens When People Talk* (Knopf, 1974), Peter Farb says that "even the menu for an American breakfast emphasizes that English is a patchwork of words borrowed from other languages." Here is a menu for what might be called a typical American breakfast. Use a dictionary to find the language that the name of each breakfast food is borrowed from, and write a paragraph explaining your findings.

> Orange juice or tomato juice
> Cereal
> Waffles with syrup
> Bacon
> Coffee or tea

MAKING INFERENCES AND ANALYZING POINT OF VIEW

Writing Assignment

In a brief essay, analyze the effect of the point of view in "An Occurrence at Owl Creek Bridge" (page 431). Include a discussion of some of the inferences the point of view requires you to make.

Background

Making Inferences

An **inference** is a conclusion based on observation or known information. An inference is not a fact, but an educated guess. One of the most famous "inferrers" is Sherlock Holmes, who solves mysteries using his amazing powers of deduction. Here is an example of his method:

I took the tattered object in my hands and turned it over rather ruefully. It was a very ordinary black hat of the usual round shape, hard and much the worse for wear. The lining had been of red silk, but was a good deal discolored. There was no maker's name; but, as Holmes had remarked, the initials "H.B." were scrawled upon one side. It was pierced in the brim for a hat-securer, but the elastic was missing. For the rest, it was cracked, exceedingly dusty, and spotted in several places, although there seemed to have been some attempt to hide the discolored patches by smearing them with ink.

"I can see nothing," said I, handing it back to my friend.

"On the contrary, Watson, you can see everything. You fail, however, to reason from what you see. You are too timid in drawing your inferences."

"Then, pray tell me what it is that you can infer from this hat?"

He picked it up and gazed at it in the peculiar introspective fashion which was characteristic of him.

"It is perhaps less suggestive than it might have been," he remarked, "and yet there are a few inferences which are very distinct, and a few others which represent at least a strong balance of probability. That the man was highly intellectual is of course obvious upon the face of it, and also that he was fairly well-to-do within the last three years, although he has now fallen upon evil days. He had foresight, but has less now than formerly, pointing to a moral retrogression, which, when taken with the decline of his fortunes, seems to indicate some evil influence, probably drink, at work upon him. This may account also for the obvious fact that his wife has ceased to love him."

"My dear Holmes!"

"He has, however, retained some degree of self-respect," he continued, disregarding my remonstrance. "He is a man who leads a sedentary life, goes out little, is out of training entirely, is middle-aged, has grizzled hair which he has had cut within the last few days, and which he anoints with lime-cream. These are the more patent facts which are to be deduced from his hat. Also, by the way, that it is extremely improbable that he has gas laid on in his house."

"You are certainly joking, Holmes."

"Not in the least. Is it possible that even now, when I give you these results, you are unable to see how they are attained?"

—from "The Adventure of the Blue Carbuncle," Sir Arthur Conan Doyle

Part of the pleasure in reading fiction comes from being able to make guesses. Since writers don't tell us everything directly, most reading involves a constant process of inferring. We often have to infer some of the most important aspects of a story, such as:

1. **Characters' motivation.** (The narrator's questions to the raven in Poe's poem seem designed for self-torture.)
2. **Characters' traits.** (Rip Van Winkle is so passive that most of the townspeople sympathize with him.)
3. **Theme.** (Although Huck thinks of himself as a bad boy, Twain is suggesting that virtue has nothing to do with conventional forms of behavior.)

Analyzing Point of View

The **point of view** from which a story is told will determine the kind and the amount of information a reader will get. Keep in mind the four basic points of view:

1. **First-person.** The narrator, who is a main character in the story, supplies all the information. The narrator's thoughts are the only ones the reader can be sure of. This first-person narrator can be unreliable.
2. **Omniscient.** The word means "all-knowing," and it refers to a narrator who enters into the minds of all the major characters. With this point of view, the narrator may include judgments and evaluations of characters and events. This narrator is not in the story.
3. **Limited third person.** This narrator, who is not in the story either, focuses on the thoughts and responses of one character. Everyone, including the main character, is referred to by the third-person pronoun (as is the case with the omniscient point of view). With this point of view, we feel we are experiencing everything in just the way one character is experiencing it.
4. **Objective or dramatic.** Like a movie camera, this narrator records only speeches and actions, with absolutely no comments on the characters or events. The only things the reader knows directly are those that are spoken about or acted out.

Prewriting

Look over "An Occurrence at Owl Creek Bridge." As you read, take notes with the following questions in mind.

Part I
1. Why is the man being hanged? Who is he?

Part II
2. Why does the Union scout pretend to be a Confederate soldier? Why does he try to get the planter to sabotage the bridge?
3. Exactly what did the planter do? Why did he do it?

Part III
4. The condemned man's escape is described realistically and in great detail. If he really dies of a broken neck while being hanged, why does Bierce include the whole episode of his escape?

5. How is the story structured? What function does each of the three parts have? Why do you think Bierce arranged the parts in this sequence?
6. What point of view does Bierce use? Is the point of view consistent, or does it change?
7. What information does Bierce withhold from the reader? What is the effect of withholding this information?
8. What different points of view might Bierce have used? How would the story and our perception of it have changed if he had used a different point of view? Would it have been more or less effective? Why?

Writing

Use your prewriting notes to write an essay of at least four paragraphs. You may want to follow this plan:

Paragraph 1: Mention the writer and the story title; identify the point of view; tell whether you think the point of view is effective.

Paragraph 2: Discuss alternate points of view and how they might have changed the impact of the story.

Paragraph 3: Discuss some of the inferences you must make; discuss the effect of the author's withholding certain information.

Paragraph 4: Summarize your responses to the point of view used in the story.

Revising and Proofreading

Use the guidelines in the section at the back of this book, called **Writing About Literature,** to revise and proofread your essay.

THE MODERNS
THE AMERICAN
VOICE IN FICTION

Buildings Abstraction, Lancaster 1931
by Charles Demuth. Oil on panel.

The Detroit Institute of
Arts, Detroit, Michigan.

UNIT SEVEN

. . . gradually I became aware of the old island here that flowered once for Dutch sailors' eyes—a fresh, green breast of the new world. Its vanished trees, the trees that had made way for Gatsby's house, had once pandered in whispers to the last and greatest of all human dreams; for a transitory enchanted moment man must have held his breath in the presence of this continent, compelled into an aesthetic contemplation he neither understood nor desired, face to face for the last time in history with something commensurate to his capacity for wonder.

—from *The Great Gatsby,*
F. Scott Fitzgerald

The second element in the American dream is optimism in the future, justified by the ever-expanding opportunity and abundance that we have come to see as our birthright. Most of the time, we Americans have believed in progress—in the fact that our lives are getting better. We tend to view history as a narrative, with a beginning and an end. We conceive of ourselves as moving toward perfection, toward an era of prosperity, justice, and joy that always seems just around the corner.

The third important element in the American dream, and an enduring subject of the American voice, has been a belief in the importance and ultimate triumph of the individual—the independent, self-reliant person.

We can find all three of these elements reflected in American literature from its beginning, especially in the writings of Ralph Waldo Emerson (see page 187), who is given most credit for defining the essence of the American dream. Emerson did not leave the kind of literary monument left by his contemporaries Walt Whitman and Herman Melville; but some of the essays and speeches he produced in the early nineteenth century are arrows in the eye of the target. Emerson championed the individual. Trust the universe and trust yourself, he wrote. "If the single man plant himself indomitable on his instincts and there abide, the huge world will come around to him." Emerson found God in nature, and he radiated a persuasive optimism. He could find "no calamity which nature cannot repair."

The Breakdown of Beliefs and Traditions

It was these inherited ideas of an Edenic land, an optimism in the future, and a faith in individualism that were most heavily damaged by the cannonades of World War I and by the economic crash that followed a decade later. Post-war writers became skeptical of the New England Puritan tradition and the gentility which had been central to the literary ideal. In fact, the center of American literary life now shifted away from New England, which had been the native region of America's most brilliant writers during the nineteenth century. Significantly, the writers you will read in this unit were born in the South, the Midwest, or the West.

As traditional beliefs and values were bombarded by the powerful new philosophies and movements in this post-war period, Americans witnessed something of a breakdown in traditional morality and values. Two of these new "movements" were Marxism and psychoanalysis. In Russia, a Marxist revolution had toppled and even murdered an anointed ruler, the Czar. The socialistic beliefs of Karl Marx that had powered the revolution in Russia were in direct opposition to the American system of capitalism and free enterprise. It didn't help that Russia was so far away; Marxists threatened to export their revolution everywhere. From Moscow, the American writer John Reed sent back the alarming message: "I have seen the future and it works."

In Vienna, there was another unsettling movement. There, the founder of psychoanalysis, Sigmund Freud, had opened the workings of the unconscious mind to general scrutiny and called for a new understanding of human sexuality and the role it plays in our unconscious thoughts. Throughout America, there was a growing interest in this new field of psychology, and a resultant anxiety about the amount of freedom an individual really had. If our actions were influenced by our subconscious, and if we had no control over our subconscious, there seemed to be little room left for "free will."

One literary result of this interest in the psyche was the narrative technique called **stream of consciousness**. This was a writing style that abandoned chronology and attempted to imitate the moment-by-moment flow of a character's perceptions and memories. Irish writer James Joyce radically changed the very concept of the novel itself by using the stream-of-consciousness technique in *Ulysses* (1922), his monumental "odyssey" set in modern-day Dublin. William Faulkner used the stream-of-consciousness technique somewhat later in America. (See page 605.)

Meanwhile, alcohol was singled out as a central social evil. In 1919 the Constitution was amended to prohibit the manufacture and sale of alcoholic beverages. But far from shoring up traditional values, Prohibition ushered in an age that was characterized by the bootlegger, the speakeasy, the cocktail, the short-skirted flapper, the Charleston, the new syncopation of jazz, and the dangerous but lucrative profession of gangster. Recording the 1920's, and making the era a vivid chapter in our history, F. Scott Fitzgerald gave it its name: the Jazz Age.

Fitzgerald was only one of many American writers and artists who abandoned their own shores after the war for the expatriate life in France. After the war, the dollar was the dominant currency abroad. Life was not only cheap in Paris and on the sunny French Riviera; it was also somehow better there, more exotic, more filled with grace and luxury—and there was no need to go down a cellar stairway to get a drink.

Clearly, something had gone wrong with the American dream—with the idea that America was Eden, with the notion of our inherent virtue, with the conviction that America was a land of heroes. The critic H. L. Mencken scoffed at what he saw as the sheep-like quality of most Americans. Their willingness to follow

"Teaching an old dog new tricks" by John Held. Lithograph.

Cover of *Life* Magazine, February 18, 1926.

traditional ways without questioning led him to coin a word to describe the army of consumers that he saw as the American public: "the booboisie" (a take-off on the French word for the middle class, *bourgeoisie*). Mencken's pen seemed to have been dipped in acid.

Disillusionment was a major theme in the fiction of the time. In 1920, Sinclair Lewis (see page 534) lashed out satirically at the parochialism of small-town life in his immensely popular novel, *Main Street.* For Lewis, the widely sentimentalized life of our small towns was actually a narrow-minded, cultural void. In *Babbitt* (1922), Lewis portrayed a middle-class American businessman as profit-driven and small-minded.

In 1925 Theodore Dreiser produced a literary landmark with his prototype of the realistic novel, *An American Tragedy.* The "tragedy" involves the ambitious but luckless Clyde Griffiths, who takes a path that leads him not to the success he seeks, but to the execution chamber. Dreiser sees this path to destruction as an inevitable one, for Clyde does not even question the values American society has thrust upon him. Like the Romantics of an earlier generation, ironically enough, Dreiser placed the seeds of Clyde's destruction in the urban world. Dreiser's story opens and closes within the tall walls of the commerical heart of an American city. *An American Tragedy*—set in a land whose wide-open spaces were once a cause for wonder—is a tragedy of a world enclosed.

1895	1896–1905	1909	1911–1912
Crane publishes *The Red Badge of Courage*, 1895	**Dunbar's poetry published, 1896**	**William Carlos Williams's first collection of poems published, 1909**	**Edith Wharton publishes *Ethan Frome*, 1911**
Final volume of Karl Marx's *Das Kapital* published, 1895	**Jack London publishes *The Call of the Wild*, 1903**	Freud lectures on psychoanalysis in U.S., 1909	*Titanic* sinks, killing 1,513 people, 1912
	Einstein formulates his theory of relativity, 1905		**Ezra Pound founds Imagist Movement, 1912**

1920	1920–1922	1922	1923
Women win the right to vote, 1920	Prohibition of "intoxicating liquors" begins in U.S., 1920	Stock market boom begins in U.S., 1922	George Gershwin's "Rhapsody in Blue" performed, 1923
***Beyond the Horizon* opens and wins Eugene O'Neill the first of four Pulitzer Prizes, 1920**	**Robinson's *Collected Poems* published, 1922**	Mussolini seizes power in Italy, 1922	**Frost wins the first of four Pulitzer Prizes for Poetry, 1923**
		Millay wins the Pulitzer Prize for Poetry, 1922	

1936–1937	1938–1939	1938–1939	1941
Eugene O'Neill wins Nobel Prize for Literature, 1936	**Pearl Buck wins the Nobel Prize for Literature, 1938**	***Our Town* opens and wins Pulitzer Prize, 1938**	Pearl Harbor bombed, December 7, 1941
Steinbeck publishes *Of Mice and Men*, 1937	*The Grapes of Wrath* **is published in 1939 and wins the Pulitzer Prize**	Germany invades Poland, September 1, 1939	America enters the war in Europe, December 11, 1941

A New American Style and "Hero" in Fiction

The most influential of all these post-World War I writers was Ernest Hemingway (see page 566). It was Hemingway who called himself and his generation "the lost generation." (He borrowed the phrase from his friend Gertrude Stein, but then she in turn was reputed to have heard it from her garage mechanic in Paris.) Hemingway is perhaps most famous for his literary style, which affected the style of American prose fiction for several generations. Much in the fashion of the Puritan writers who strove for a "plain style," Hemingway reduced the flamboyance of literary language to a minimum, to the bones of the truth it must express. He is also well remembered for adding a new kind of hero to American fiction, a character many readers embraced as a protagonist and a role model. This Hemingway hero was a man of action, a man of war, and a tough competitor; he had a code of honor, courage, and endurance. He shows, in Hemingway's words, "grace under pressure."

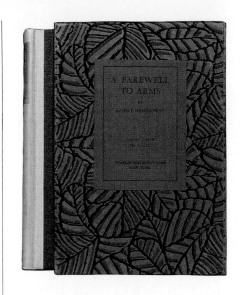

He is Nick Adams of *In Our Times,* Frederick Henry of *A Farewell to Arms,* Jake Barnes of *The Sun Also Rises,* Robert Jordan of *For Whom the Bell Tolls,* and Santiago of *The Old Man and the Sea.* But the most important thing about this Hemingway hero is that he is thoroughly disillusioned, a quality that reflected Hemingway's own outlook.

1913–1915	1915–1916	1917	1917–1920
Frost publishes first book of poetry, 1913 World War I, 1914–1918 **Masters publishes *Spoon River Anthology,* 1915**	British liner *Lusitania* sunk by German U-boats, May 7, 1915 **Sandburg publishes "Chicago," 1916**	**Eliot publishes "The Love Song of J. Alfred Prufrock," 1917** Revolution in Russia topples Czar and establishes socialist government, 1917	U.S. declares war on Germany, April 16, 1917 **Anderson publishes *Winesburg, Ohio,* 1919** Harlem Renaissance begins, 1920

1925–1926	1926–1927	1929–1930	1932–1933
Fitzgerald's *The Great Gatsby* published, 1925 Fascist youth organizations formed in Italy and Germany, 1926	**Wolfe publishes *Look Homeward, Angel,* 1926** Charles Lindbergh makes first solo transatlantic flight, 1927.	U.S. stock market crash, October 24, 1929. Great Depression begins. **Sinclair Lewis wins Nobel Prize for Literature, 1930**	12 million Americans unemployed, 1932 Roosevelt's New Deal begins, 1933 Adolf Hitler appointed German Chancellor, 1933

Hemingway feared, a little like Melville, that at the inscrutable center of creation lay nothing at all.

Nearly a century earlier, Emerson had also sensed a collapse of faith and had told the Class of 1838 at the Harvard Divinity School that the church's hold on people was weakening. Emerson was appalled.

> What greater calamity can fall upon a nation than the lack of worship? Genius leaves the temple to haunt the senate or the market. Literature becomes frivolous. Science is cold. The eye of the youth is not lighted by the hope of other worlds and age is without honor. Society lives to trifles and when men die we do not mention them.
>
> —Ralph Waldo Emerson

Hemingway found his own "answer" in a belief in the self and in such qualities of decency, bravery, competence, and skill as one can summon. He clung to this belief in spite of what he saw as the absolutely unbeatable odds ranged against us all. A further part of the Hemingway code was the importance of recognizing and snatching up the rare, good, rich moments that life offers, before those moments elude us.

Even though Hemingway rejected Emerson's optimism, a belief in self-reliance still persists in Hemingway's work, as the old idea of America as Eden. Hemingway is really telling us about Eden in his *Up in Michigan* stories, where he describes the lakes and streams and woods he knew as a boy and where he extols the restorative power of nature in a way that Emerson might have recognized. This is the same Edenic America that has come down to us through Mark Twain's Mississippi, through Faulkner's Yoknapatawpha County, and through John Steinbeck's Salinas Valley (see page 578).

As we explore this period of American writing—in some respects, the richest period since the flowering of New England in the first half of the nineteenth century—we stand at the threshold of our own time. Though this part of our own century has seen a major change in American attitudes, you'll recognize many concerns that are consistent with concerns of the past. These writers—some of the best that America has produced—experimented boldly with forms and subject matter. But they were also still trying to find the answers to the basic human questions: Who are we? Where are we going? And what values should guide us on that search for our human identity?

Sherwood Anderson (1876–1941)

When the first stories of Sherwood Anderson were published, they were the subjects of heated debate. *Winesburg, Ohio*, Anderson's series of short stories about the people in a small midwestern town, is now an American classic. But when it first appeared, it was called "unclean, filthy," even by Theodore Dreiser, the popular realistic novelist who had helped Anderson bring his first works to the public.

Sherwood Anderson was born on September 13, 1876, in southern Ohio, the third of seven children. His father was a harness-maker, and his trade was being rendered obsolete by mass production. An easygoing man, the elder Anderson was given to telling tall tales and to heavy drinking.

Since Sherwood often had to help out at home, his schooling was spotty. His mother died when he was fourteen, his father drifted out and away from the family forever, and Anderson's formal education virtually came to an end.

Anderson eventually became an advertising copywriter, and in the spirit of the new century and the "new age," he extolled the world of business in his copy. Married and a family man, he bought a paint factory and continued to write copy ennobling the life he had chosen, even though he felt trapped in it. He was, he later said, following an adage often repeated to him: "Get money. Money makes the mare go."

On November 27, 1912, at the age of thirty-seven, Anderson had had enough. On that day, he walked out on his job and on his whole life. He left the factory muttering, leaving his co-workers with the idea that he had lost his mind.

In 1919, Anderson published *Winesburg, Ohio*. The structure and focus of this collection of stories were inspired by Edgar Lee Masters's collection of poems called *Spoon River Anthology* (page 656). Anderson was concerned not with well-crafted plots in the traditional sense, but with revealing the secret needs and longings of twenty-two people from one small town. The stories are unified by their characters, by their setting, and by Anderson's theory of the "grotesque."

According to the introduction to *Winesburg, Ohio*, a *grotesque* is someone who seizes a single truth out of life and lives by that truth alone. Tragically, these single-minded pursuits drive the characters into isolation. The only person the Winesburg "grotesques" can communicate with is George Willard, a writer. Anderson thus uses Willard to dramatize the function of the artist: That function is, as Anderson sees it, to absorb other people's lives and to "become" them.

What made the stories in *Winesburg* shocking was that Anderson also explored the intimate thoughts of his characters. The result was a series of portraits that were honest, unflinching— and, at the time, painful for many to deal with.

Because there are few dramatic events in the Winesburg stories, many readers dismissed them as "non-stories." One member of the Chicago Group felt that the stories were so formless that Anderson should throw them away. The major complaint from readers, however, dealt with the unconventional subject matter, especially with the themes of sexuality and repression. One woman, who had attended a dinner party with Anderson, sent him a letter saying, ". . . having sat beside you and having read your stories, I feel that I should never be clean again."

In his criticism of industry and of the American dream that money will bring happiness, Anderson proposed his own dream of love as happiness. He once wrote:

I began to gather these impressions. There was a thing called happiness toward which men were striving. They never got to it. All of life was amazingly accidental. Love, moments of tenderness and despair, came to the poor and the miserable as to the rich and successful.

It began to seem to me that what was most wanted by all people was love, understanding. Our writers, our storytellers, in wrapping life up into neat little packages, were only betraying life.

As for himself, Anderson kept "escaping" for the rest of his life. Attractive to women, he married four times and traveled as far as Paris, where he met the writer Gertrude Stein who had an important influence on his work. He also met, in Chicago, a young writer who impressed him. It was Anderson who sent the young man—whose name was Ernest Hemingway (page 566)—to Paris with a letter of introduction to Gertrude Stein.

During the Depression and the New Deal that followed it, Anderson's stories became oddly dated and irrelevant. Today, however, a few of Anderson's stories have taken their places as American classics. These include such later stories as "The Egg" from *The Triumph of the Egg* (1921) and "Death in the Woods" and "Brother Death" from *Death in the Woods* (1933).

THE EGG

This story provides a good illustration of Anderson's ability to attack the human condition without attacking the people living in that condition. As you read, keep in mind Anderson's well-known definition of the word *grotesque* (see page 525), which is used in this story in a different sense. Look for clues about how the narrator of the story feels toward his parents.

My father was, I am sure, intended by nature to be a cheerful, kindly man. Until he was thirty-four years old he worked as a farmhand for a man named Thomas Butterworth whose place lay near the town of Bidwell, Ohio. He had then a horse of his own and on Saturday evenings drove into town to spend a few hours in social intercourse with other farmhands. In town he drank several glasses of beer and stood about in Ben Head's saloon—crowded on Saturday evenings with visiting farmhands. Songs were sung and glasses thumped on the bar. At ten o'clock father drove home along a lonely country road, made his horse comfortable for the night and himself went to bed, quite happy in his position in life. He had at that time no notion of trying to rise in the world.

It was in the spring of his thirty-fifth year that father married my mother, then a country schoolteacher, and in the following spring I came wriggling and crying into the world. Something happened to the two people. They became ambitious. The American passion for getting up in the world took possession of them.

It may have been that mother was responsible. Being a schoolteacher she had no doubt read books and magazines. She had, I presume, read of how Garfield, Lincoln, and other Americans rose from poverty to fame and greatness and as I lay beside her—in the days of her lying-in[1]—she may have dreamed that I would some day rule men and cities. At any rate she induced father to give up his place as a farmhand, sell his horse and embark on an independent enterprise of his own. She was a tall silent woman with a long nose and troubled gray eyes. For herself she wanted nothing. For father and myself she was incurably ambitious.

The first venture into which the two people went turned out badly. They rented ten acres of

---

1. **days of her lying-in:** her time spent in bed after giving birth.

The Farmer and His Son by Ben Shahn. Oil.

Hirshhorn Museum and Sculpture Garden,
Smithsonian Institution, Washington, D.C.

poor stony land on Griggs's Road, eight miles from Bidwell, and launched into chicken raising. I grew into boyhood on the place and got my first impressions of life there. From the beginning they were impressions of disaster and if, in my turn, I am a gloomy man inclined to see the darker side of life, I attribute it to the fact that what should have been for me the happy joyous days of childhood were spent on a chicken farm.

One unversed in such matters can have no notion of the many and tragic things that can happen to a chicken. It is born out of an egg, lives for a few weeks as a tiny fluffy thing such as you will see pictured on Easter cards, then becomes hideously naked, eats quantities of corn and meal bought by the sweat of your father's brow, gets diseases called pip, cholera, and other names, stands looking with stupid eyes at the sun, becomes sick and dies. A few hens and now and then a rooster, intended to serve God's mysterious ends, struggle through to maturity. The hens lay eggs out of which come other chickens and the dreadful cycle is thus made complete. It is all unbelievably complex. Most philosophers must have been raised on chicken farms. One hopes for so much from a chicken and is so dreadfully disillusioned. Small chickens, just setting out on the journey of life, look so bright and alert and they are in fact so dreadfully stupid. They are so much like people they mix one up in one's judgments of life. If disease does not kill them they wait until your expectations are thoroughly aroused and then walk under the wheels of a wagon—to go squashed and dead back to their maker. Vermin infest their youth, and fortunes must be spent for curative powders. In later life I have seen how a literature has been built up on the subject of fortunes to be made out of the raising of chickens. It is intended to be read by the gods who have just eaten of the tree of the knowledge of good and evil.[2] It is a hopeful literature and declares that much may be done by simple ambitious people who own a few hens. Do not be led astray by it. It was not written for you. Go hunt for gold on the frozen hills of Alaska, put your faith in the honesty of a politician, believe if you will that the world is daily growing better and that good will triumph over evil, but do not read and believe the literature that is written concerning the hen. It was not written for you.

I, however, digress. My tale does not primarily concern itself with the hen. If correctly told it will center on the egg. For ten years my father and mother struggled to make our chicken farm pay and then they gave up that struggle and began another. They moved into the town of Bidwell, Ohio, and embarked in the restaurant business. After ten years of worry with incubators that did not hatch, and with tiny—and in their own way lovely—balls of fluff that passed on into seminaked pullethood and from that into dead henhood, we threw all aside and packing our belongings on a wagon drove down Griggs's Road toward Bidwell, a tiny caravan of hope looking for a new place from which to start on our upward journey through life.

We must have been a sad-looking lot, not, I fancy, unlike refugees fleeing from a battlefield. Mother and I walked in the road. The wagon that contained our goods had been borrowed for the day from Mr. Albert Griggs, a neighbor. Out of its sides stuck the legs of cheap chairs and at the back of the pile of beds, tables, and boxes filled with kitchen utensils was a crate of live chickens, and on top of that the baby carriage in which I had been wheeled about in my infancy. Why we stuck to the baby carriage I don't know. It was unlikely other children would be born and the wheels were broken. People who have few possessions cling tightly to those they have. That is one of the facts that make life so discouraging.

Father rode on top of the wagon. He was then a bald-headed man of forty-five, a little fat and from long association with mother and the chickens he had become habitually silent and discouraged. All during our ten years on the chicken farm he had worked as a laborer on neighboring farms and most of the money he had earned had been spent for remedies to cure chicken diseases, on Wilmer's White Wonder Cholera Cure or Professor Bidlow's Egg Producer or some other preparations that mother found advertised in the poultry papers. There were two little patches of hair on father's head just above his ears. I remember that as a child I used to sit looking at him when he had gone to sleep in a chair before the stove on Sunday afternoons in the winter. I had at that time already begun to read books and have notions of my own and the bald path that led over the top of his head was, I fancied, something like a broad road, such

---

2. **tree of the knowledge of good and evil:** an allusion to the third chapter of Genesis, and to the tree in Eden that bore the forbidden fruit.

a road as Caesar might have made on which to lead his legions out of Rome and into the wonders of an unknown world. The tufts of hair that grew above father's ears were, I thought, like forests. I fell into a half-sleeping, half-waking state and dreamed I was a tiny thing going along the road into a far beautiful place where there were no chicken farms and where life was a happy eggless affair.

One might write a book concerning our flight from the chicken farm into town. Mother and I walked the entire eight miles—she to be sure that nothing fell from the wagon and I to see the wonders of the world. On the seat of the wagon beside father was his greatest treasure. I will tell you of that.

On a chicken farm where hundreds and even thousands of chickens come out of eggs surprising things sometimes happen. Grotesques are born out of eggs as out of people. The accident does not often occur—perhaps once in a thousand births. A chicken is, you see, born that has four legs, two pairs of wings, two heads or whatnot. The things do not live. They go quickly back to the hand of their maker that has for a moment trembled. The fact that the poor little things could not live was one of the tragedies of life to father. He had some sort of notion that if he could but bring into henhood or roosterhood a five-legged hen or a two-headed rooster his fortune would be made. He dreamed of taking the wonder about to country fairs and of growing rich by exhibiting it to other farmhands.

At any rate he saved all the little monstrous things that had been born on our chicken farm. They were preserved in alcohol and put each in its own glass bottle. These he had carefully put into a box and on our journey into town it was carried on the wagon seat beside him. He drove the horses with one hand and with the other clung to the box. When we got to our destination the box was taken down at once and the bottles removed. All during our days as keepers of a restaurant in the town of Bidwell, Ohio, the grotesques in their little glass bottles sat on a shelf back of the counter. Mother sometimes protested but father was a rock on the subject of his treasure. The grotesques were, he declared, valuable. People, he said, liked to look at strange and wonderful things.

Did I say that we embarked in the restaurant business in the town of Bidwell, Ohio? I exaggerated a little. The town itself lay at the foot of a low hill and on the shore of a small river. The railroad did not run through the town and the station was a mile away to the north at a place called Pickleville. There had been a cider mill and pickle factory at the station, but before the time of our coming they had both gone out of business. In the morning and in the evening buses came down to the station along a road called Turner's Pike from the hotel on the main street of Bidwell. Our going to the out-of-the-way place to embark in the restaurant business was mother's idea. She talked of it for a year and then one day went off and rented an empty store building opposite the railroad station. It was her idea that the restaurant would be profitable. Traveling men, she said, would be always waiting around to take trains out of town and town people would come to the station to await incoming trains. They would come to the restaurant to buy pieces of pie and drink coffee. Now that I am older I know that she had another motive in going. She was ambitious for me. She wanted me to rise in the world, to get into a town school and become a man of the towns.

At Pickleville father and mother worked hard as they always had done. At first there was the necessity of putting our place into shape to be a restaurant. That took a month. Father built a shelf on which he put tins of vegetables. He painted a sign on which he put his name in large red letters. Below his name was the sharp command—"EAT HERE"—that was so seldom obeyed. A showcase was bought and filled with cigars and tobacco. Mother scrubbed the floor and the walls of the room. I went to school in the town and was glad to be away from the farm and from the presence of the discouraged, sad-looking chickens. Still I was not very joyous. In the evening I walked home from school along Turner's Pike and remembered the children I had seen playing in the town schoolyard. A troop of little girls had gone hopping about and singing. I tried that. Down along the frozen road I went hopping solemnly on one leg. "Hippity Hop to the Barber Shop," I sang shrilly. Then I stopped and looked doubtfully about. I was afraid of being seen in my gay mood. It must have seemed to me that I was doing a thing that should not be done by one who, like myself, had been raised on a chicken farm where death was a daily visitor.

Mother decided that our restaurant should remain open at night. At ten in the evening a passenger train went north past our door followed by a local freight. The freight crew had switching to do in Pickleville and when the work was done they came to our restaurant for hot coffee and food. Sometimes one of them ordered a fried egg. In the morning at four they returned northbound and again visited us. A little trade began to grow up. Mother slept at night and during the day tended the restaurant and fed our boarders while father slept. He slept in the same bed mother had occupied during the night and I went off to the town of Bidwell and to school. During the long nights, while mother and I slept, father cooked meats that were to go into sandwiches for the lunch baskets of our boarders. Then an idea in regard to getting up in the world came into his head. The American spirit took hold of him. He also became ambitious.

In the long nights when there was little to do father had time to think. That was his undoing. He decided that he had in the past been an unsuccessful man because he had not been cheerful enough and that in the future he would adopt a cheerful outlook on life. In the early morning he came upstairs and got into bed with mother. She woke and the two talked. From my bed in the corner I listened.

It was father's idea that both he and mother should try to entertain the people who came to eat at our restaurant. I cannot now remember his words, but he gave the impression of one about to become in some obscure way a kind of public entertainer. When people, particularly young people from the town of Bidwell, came into our place, as on very rare occasions they did, bright entertaining conversation was to be made. From father's words I gathered that something of the jolly innkeeper effect was to be sought. Mother must have been doubtful from the first, but she said nothing discouraging. It was father's notion that a passion for the company of himself and mother would spring up in the breasts of the younger people of the town of Bidwell. In the evening bright happy groups would come singing down Turner's Pike. They would troop shouting with joy and laughter into our place. There would be song and festivity. I do not mean to give the impression that father spoke so elaborately of the matter. He was as I have said an uncommunicative man. "They want some place to go. I tell you they want some place to go," he said over and over.

That was as far as he got. My own imagination has filled in the blanks.

For two or three weeks this notion of father's invaded our house. We did not talk much, but in our daily lives tried earnestly to make smiles take the place of glum looks. Mother smiled at the boarders and I, catching the infection, smiled at our cat. Father became a little feverish in his anxiety to please. There was no doubt, lurking somewhere in him, a touch of the spirit of the showman. He did not waste much of his ammunition on the railroad men he served at night but seemed to be waiting for a young man or woman from Bidwell to come in to show what he could do. On the counter in the restaurant there was a wire basket kept always filled with eggs, and it must have been before his eyes when the idea of being entertaining was born in his brain. There was something prenatal about the way eggs kept themselves connected with the development of his idea. At any rate an egg ruined his new impulse in life. Late one night I was awakened by a roar of anger coming from father's throat. Both mother and I sat upright on our beds. With trembling hands she lighted a lamp that stood on a table by her head. Downstairs the front door of our restaurant went shut with a bang and in a few minutes father tramped up the stairs. He held an egg in his hand and his hand trembled as though he was having a chill. There was a half-insane light in his eyes. As he stood glaring at us I was sure he intended throwing the egg at either mother or me. Then he laid it gently on the table beside the lamp and dropped on his knees beside mother's bed. He began to cry like a boy and I, carried away by his grief, cried with him. The two of us filled the little upstairs room with our wailing voices. It is ridiculous, but of the picture we made I can remember only the fact that mother's hand continually stroked the bald path that ran across the top of his head. I have forgotten what mother said to him and how she induced him to tell her of what had happened downstairs. His explanation also has gone out of my mind. I remember only my own grief and fright and the shiny path over father's head glowing in the lamplight as he knelt by the bed.

As to what happened downstairs. For some unexplainable reason I know the story as well as though I had been a witness to my father's discomfiture. One in time gets to know many unexplainable things. On that evening young Joe Kane, son of a merchant of Bidwell, came to Pickleville to meet his father, who was expected on the ten o'clock evening train from the South. The train was three hours late and Joe came into our place to loaf about and to wait for its arrival. The local freight train came in and the freight crew were fed. Joe was left alone in the restaurant with father.

From the moment he came into our place the Bidwell young man must have been puzzled by my father's actions. It was his notion that father was angry at him for hanging around. He noticed that the restaurant keeper was apparently disturbed by his presence and he thought of going out. However, it began to rain and he did not fancy the long walk to town and back. He bought a five-cent cigar and ordered a cup of coffee. He had a newspaper in his pocket and took it out and began to read. "I'm waiting for the evening train. It's late," he said apologetically.

For a long time father, whom Joe Kane had never seen before, remained silently gazing at his visitor. He was no doubt suffering from an attack of stage fright. As so often happens in life he had thought so much and so often of the situation that now confronted him that he was somewhat nervous in its presence.

For one thing, he did not know what to do with his hands. He thrust one of them nervously over the counter and shook hands with Joe Kane. "How-de-do," he said. Joe Kane put his newspaper down and stared at him. Father's eye lighted on the basket of eggs that sat on the counter and he began to talk. "Well," he began hesitatingly, "well, you have heard of Christopher Columbus, eh?" He seemed to be angry. "That Christopher Columbus was a cheat," he declared emphatically. "He talked of making an egg stand on its end. He talked, he did, and then he went and broke the end of the egg."

My father seemed to his visitor to be beside himself at the duplicity of Christopher Columbus. He muttered and swore. He declared it was wrong to teach children that Christopher Columbus was a great man when, after all, he cheated at the critical moment. He had declared he would make an egg stand on end and then when his bluff had been called he had done a trick. Still grumbling at Columbus, father took an egg from the basket on the counter and began to walk up and down. He rolled the egg between the palms of his hands. He smiled genially. He began to mumble words

regarding the effect to be produced on an egg by the electricity that comes out of the human body. He declared that without breaking its shell and by virtue of rolling it back and forth in his hands he could stand the egg on its end. He explained that the warmth of his hands and the gentle rolling movement he gave the egg created a new center of gravity, and Joe Kane was mildly interested. "I have handled thousands of eggs," father said. "No one knows more about eggs than I do."

He stood the egg on the counter and it fell on its side. He tried the trick again and again, each time rolling the egg between the palms of his hands and saying the words regarding the wonders of electricity and the laws of gravity. When after a half hour's effort he did succeed in making the egg stand for a moment he looked up to find that his visitor was no longer watching. By the time he had succeeded in calling Joe Kane's attention to the success of his effort the egg had again rolled over and lay on its side.

Afire with the showman's passion and at the same time a good deal disconcerted by the failure of his first effort, father now took the bottles containing the poultry monstrosities down from their place on the shelf and began to show them to his visitor. "How would you like to have seven legs and two heads like this fellow?" he asked, exhibiting the most remarkable of his treasures. A cheerful smile played over his face. He reached over the counter and tried to slap Joe Kane on the shoulder as he had seen men do in Ben Head's saloon when he was a young farmhand and drove to town on Saturday evenings. His visitor was made a little ill by the sight of the body of the terribly deformed bird floating in the alcohol in the bottle and got up to go. Coming from behind the counter father took hold of the young man's arm and led him back to his seat. He grew a little angry and for a moment had to turn his face away and force himself to smile. Then he put the bottles back on the shelf. In an outburst of generosity he fairly compelled Joe Kane to have a fresh cup of coffee and another cigar at his expense. Then he took a pan and, filling it with vinegar taken from a jug that sat beneath the counter, he declared himself about to do a new trick. "I will heat this egg in this pan of vinegar," he said. "Then I will put it through the neck of a bottle without breaking the shell. When the egg is inside the bottle it will resume its normal shape and the shell will become hard again. Then I will give the bottle with the egg in it to you. You can take it about with you wherever you go. People will want to know how you got the egg in the bottle. Don't tell them. Keep them guessing. That is the way to have fun with this trick."

Father grinned and winked at his visitor. Joe Kane decided that the man who confronted him was mildly insane but harmless. He drank the cup of coffee that had been given him and began to read his paper again. When the egg had been heated in vinegar father carried it on a spoon to the counter and going into a back room got an empty bottle. He was angry because his visitor did not watch him as he began to do his trick, but nevertheless went cheerfully to work. For a long time he struggled, trying to get the egg to go through the neck of the bottle. He put the pan of vinegar back on the stove, intending to reheat the egg, then picked it up and burned his fingers. After a second bath in the hot vinegar the shell of the egg had been softened a little but not enough for his purpose. He worked and worked and a spirit of desperate determination took possession of him. When he thought that at last the trick was about to be consummated the delayed train came in at the station and Joe Kane started to go nonchalantly out at the door. Father made a last desperate effort to conquer the egg and make it do the thing that would establish his reputation as one who knew how to entertain guests who came into his restaurant. He worried the egg. He attempted to be somewhat rough with it. He swore and the sweat stood out on his forehead. The egg broke under his hand. When the contents spurted over his clothes, Joe Kane, who had stopped at the door, turned and laughed.

A roar of anger rose from my father's throat. He danced and shouted a string of inarticulate words. Grabbing another egg from the basket on the counter, he threw it, just missing the head of the young man as he dodged through the door and escaped.

Father came upstairs to mother and me with an egg in his hand. I do not know what he intended to do. I imagine he had some idea of destroying it, of destroying all eggs, and that he intended to let mother and me see him begin. When, however, he got into the presence of mother something happened to him. He laid the egg gently on the table and dropped on his knees by the bed as I have already explained. He later decided to close the restaurant for the night and to come upstairs and get into bed. When he did so he blew out the light and after much muttered conversation both he and mother went to sleep. I suppose I went to sleep also, but my sleep was troubled. I awoke at dawn and for a long time looked at the egg that lay on the table. I wondered why eggs had to be and why from the egg came the hen who again laid the egg. The question got into my blood. It has stayed there, I imagine, because I am the son of my father. At any rate, the problem remains unsolved in my mind. And that, I conclude, is but another evidence of the complete and final triumph of the egg—at least as far as my family is concerned.

Responding to the Story

Analyzing the Story

Identifying Facts

1. What change took place in the attitude of his parents shortly after the narrator was born? What does he suggest as a cause of this change?
2. What tragic facts about chickens caused the narrator to become "a gloomy man inclined to see the darker side of life"?
3. Why does the family move to Pickleville?
4. What are the "grotesques"? Why are they regarded as the family's greatest treasure? What does Joe Kane seem to think of them?

5. What means does the father decide on to increase business at his restaurant? What dreams does the father have about the restaurant and its effect on the townspeople?
6. Describe what happens when the father puts his ideas into practice with Joe Kane.

Interpreting Meanings

7. A **symbol** is something used to stand for itself and also for an idea or a force other than itself. A lamb, for example, often symbolizes innocence, and a serpent often symbolizes evil or duplicity. In the hands of a skillful writer, a symbol can have several layers

of meaning because its several characteristics can stand for several ideas. A bird, for example, could symbolize freedom because it can fly; fragility because it can be easily destroyed by larger animals; and beauty because of its song. What does the egg symbolize in this story? Describe the layers of symbolism you can find in these characteristics of an egg: Life hatches from eggs; the shell is a protective cover; the shell is easily broken.

8. Why does Anderson refer to "the triumph of the egg" at the story's end? How would you state the story's **theme,** considering this phrase and the egg's symbolism?

9. The narrator says of his parents: "The American passion for getting up in the world took possession of them." How does the narrator feel about this passion? How would a Romantic writer feel about the father's dream of getting ahead, and what would probably become of that dream?

10. Think of what you know about the narrator's father before the family moves to Pickleville. What evidence is there that his scheme to increase his business is bound to fail? Does the father remind you of a common character "type" in American literature? Explain.

11. Does the narrator's father fit Anderson's definition of the word *grotesque* (page 525)? Explain.

12. Do you think this story, especially its final scene, is pathetic or comical, or a combination of both? Why?

Writing About the Story

A Creative Response

1. **Using Another Point of View.** Although she is a powerful force in the family, the narrator's mother plays a minor role in this story. Select one section of the story and imagine the mother's thoughts about it. Then write a passage narrating the events of that part of the story from the mother's vantage point. You can use either the first-person point of view or the limited third person.

A Critical Response

2. **Analyzing Conflict.** If conflict is basic to every story, what is the nature of the conflict in this story? Is it external, internal, or both? Write your analysis of the story's conflict in a three-paragraph essay. Be sure to tell how the conflict is resolved.

Primary Sources
"They were not nice little packages . . ."

On August 27, 1938, Anderson wrote this in a letter to George Freitag, who was corresponding with Anderson about the problems of young writers.

"It is so difficult for most of us to realize how fully and completely commercialism enters into the arts. For example, how are you to know that really the opinion of the publisher or the magazine editor in regard to your work, what is a story and what isn't, means nothing? Some of my own stories, for example, that have now become almost American classics, that are put before students in our schools and colleges as examples of good storytelling, were, when first written, when submitted to editors, and when seen by some of the so-called outstanding American critics, declared not stories at all.

"It is true they were not nice little packages, wrapped and labeled in the O. Henry manner. They were obviously written by one who did not know the answers. They were simple little tales of happenings, things observed and felt. There were no cowboys or daring wild game hunters. None of the people in the tales got lost in burning deserts or went seeking the North Pole. In my stories I simply stayed at home, among my own people, wherever I happened to be, people in my own street. I think I must, very early, have realized that this was my milieu, that is to say, common everyday American lives. The ordinary beliefs of the people about me, that love lasted indefinitely, that success meant happiness, simply did not seem true to me."

—Sherwood Anderson

Sinclair Lewis (1885–1951)

Sinclair Lewis, who was known to his friends as "Hal" or "Red," was a man of immense energy, much of which he channeled directly into writing. He produced scores of novels, stories, plays, and poetry. A great deal of this work was hastily composed, shoddy, and forgettable. But during the golden decade of his life, the 1920's, Lewis wrote half a dozen novels which touched a tender nerve in the American consciousness, shocking and delighting an army of readers by his ridicule of primary American values. As a result of their incisive satire, these works have become fixtures of our literature.

Lewis was born in Sauk Centre, Minnesota, the son of Edwin Lewis, a doctor whose disciplined life set an impressive standard for his son. Lewis was only six when his mother died, and while his stepmother treated him kindly, he grew up feeling he was a disappointment to his father. He was an eager reader, but otherwise a dreamy, difficult boy who did not stand out in any way.

In 1903 he entered Yale and did little better there. A skin disease had left him with a pitted complexion, and he felt unattractive. Although he later compensated for this with charm and an outgoing manner, Lewis was not a popular undergraduate; he did not do well either in his studies or in sports.

His first novel was a boy's adventure story, *Hike and the Aeroplane,* written under a pseudonym for his employer, a publisher, in exchange for two months' salary. His second, *Our Mr. Wrenn,* was rejected by several publishers before Harper accepted it. Despite some good reviews, the book sold poorly. This was also true of *The Trail of the Hawk, The Job, The Innocents,* and *Free Air,* traditional novels which Lewis produced over the next five years, along with stories for the *Saturday Evening Post.*

All of these works were written in the optimistic, "genteel" tradition. But Lewis had also begun to conceive a different kind of novel, one which looked back at the complacent village of his childhood with a critical eye. This novel became *Main Street.* The village Lewis depicted was the one he recalled so vividly from a painful childhood as an academy of narrow conformity, materialistic in its values and restrictive of every creative impulse.

The American reading public, which held the "small town" to be a stronghold of virtue, generosity, and the homely joys, was bowled over by Harcourt Brace's publication of *Main Street* in 1920. The book became a huge success, eventually selling millions of copies in the biggest publishing event in American history, and making Lewis a wealthy, international celebrity.

Another triumph followed in 1922 with *Babbitt,* in which Lewis portrayed that traditional hero, the American businessman, as a spiritually impoverished, pathetic figure. The novel provoked a furor over the nation's values.

Lewis next turned his pen upon the medical profession. The publication of *Arrowsmith* in 1925 ignited controversy among doctors and medical associations, further stimulating book sales. In that year, Lewis rejected the Pulitzer Prize for *Arrowsmith* on the grounds that the judges had withheld the honor from *Main Street* and *Babbitt*. However, after the publication of *Elmer Gantry* (1927), Lewis's unflattering portrayal of an evangelist clergyman, and of *Dodsworth* (1929), a more sympathetic portrait of businessman, he became in 1930 the first American to receive the greatest of literary accolades, the Nobel Prize.

Ironically, the prize marked the end of an era in which it seemed that Lewis could do no wrong. His personal life was deteriorating; he divorced his wife to marry Dorothy Thompson, a famous political columnist, only to have this marriage end in divorce as well. He was also drinking heavily, and he was restless, forever on the move.

Nevertheless, he continued to publish. After 1930 he produced nine more novels. Lewis broached important issues in these works: the role of women in social reform, the dangers of fascism, and the evil of race prejudice. But he had lost his satiric bite. Lewis was becoming sentimental, praising some of the traditional values he had once mocked. After a lifetime of exuberance, Lewis became increasingly melancholy—sailing off for Italy in the end, where he died of heart failure in 1951.

FROM BABBITT

Lewis's "non-hero," George F. Babbitt, has given his name not only to the novel in which he appears but to our language as well. A dictionary might define a "babbitt" as a member of the business class whose unquestioning conformity to its ideals have made him narrow-minded and self-satisfied. "Boosterism," another Lewis coinage, is a hidden form of moneymaking, and it is clearly Babbitt's preoccupation. Babbitt finds comfort in every sort of conformity—dress, work, and recreation; he is wary of diverse opinions and of imagination and freedom.

Here Babbitt delivers a speech to the Real Estate Board in his growing hometown of Zenith. Notice how Babbitt, in his emphasis on pep and enthusiasm, seems to yearn for genuine emotion, and how he pretends to find it in his highly conventional life.

His reputation for oratory established, at the dinner of the Zenith Real Estate Board he made the Annual Address. The *Advocate-Times* reported this speech with unusual fullness:

"One of the livest banquets that has recently been pulled off occurred last night in the annual Get-Together Fest of the Zenith Real Estate Board, held in the Venetian Ball Room of the O'Hearn House. Mine host Gil O'Hearn had as usual done himself proud and those assembled feasted on such an assemblage of plates as could be rivaled nowhere west of New York, if there, and washed down the plenteous feed with the cup which inspired but did not inebriate in the shape of cider from the farm of Chandler Mott, president of the board and who acted as witty and efficient chairman.

"As Mr. Mott was suffering from slight infection and sore throat, G. F. Babbitt made the principal talk. Besides outlining the progress of Torrensing real estate titles, Mr. Babbitt spoke in part as follows:

"'In rising to address you, with my impromptu speech carefully tucked into my vest pocket, I am reminded of the story of the two Irishmen, Mike and Pat, who were riding on the Pullman. Both of them, I forgot to say, were sailors in the Navy. It seems Mike had the lower berth and by and by he heard a terrible racket from the upper, and when he yelled up to find out what the trouble was, Pat answered, ''Shure an' bedad an' how can I ever get a night's sleep at all, at all? I been trying to get into this darned little hammock ever since eight bells!''

"'Now, gentlemen, standing up here before

you, I feel a good deal like Pat, and maybe after I've spieled[1] along for a while, I may feel so darn small that I'll be able to crawl into a Pullman hammock with no trouble at all, at all!

"'Gentlemen, it strikes me that each year at this annual occasion when friend and foe get together and lay down the battle-ax and let the waves of good-fellowship waft them up the flowery slopes of amity, it behooves us, standing together eye to eye and shoulder to shoulder as fellow-citizens of the best city in the world, to consider where we are both as regards ourselves and the common weal.

"'It is true that even with our 361,000, or practically 362,000, population, there are, by the last census, almost a score of larger cities in the United States. But, gentlemen, if by the next census we do not stand at least tenth, then I'll be the first to request any knocker to remove my shirt and to eat the same, with the compliments of G. F. Babbitt, Esquire! It may be true that New York, Chicago, and Philadelphia will continue to keep ahead of us in size. But aside from these three cities, which are notoriously so overgrown that no decent white man, nobody who loves his wife and kiddies and God's good out-o'-doors and likes to shake the hand of his neighbor in greeting, would want to live in them—and let me tell you right here and now, I wouldn't trade a high-class Zenith acreage development for the whole length and breadth of Broadway or State Street!—aside from these three, it's evident to any one with a head for facts that Zenith is the finest example of American life and prosperity to be found anywhere.

"'I don't mean to say we're perfect. We've got a lot to do in the way of extending the paving of motor boulevards, for, believe me, it's the fellow with four to ten thousand a year,[2] say, and an automobile and a nice little family in a bungalow on the edge of town, that makes the wheels of progress go round!

"'That's the type of fellow that's ruling America today; in fact, it's the ideal type to which the entire world must tend, if there's to be a decent, well-balanced, Christian, go-ahead future for this little old planet! Once in a while I just naturally sit back and size up this Solid American Citizen, with a whale of a lot of satisfaction.

"'Our Ideal Citizen—I picture him first and foremost as being busier than a bird-dog, not wasting a lot of good time in daydreaming or going to sassiety[3] teas or kicking about things that are none of his business, but putting the zip into some store or profession or art. At night he lights up a good cigar, and climbs into the little old bus, and maybe cusses the carburetor, and shoots out home. He mows the lawn, or sneaks in some practice putting, and then he's ready for dinner. After dinner he tells the kiddies a story, or takes the family to the movies, or plays a few fists of bridge, or reads the evening paper, and a chapter or two of some good lively Western novel if he has a taste for literature, and maybe the folks next door drop in and they sit and visit about their friends and the topics of the day. Then he goes happily to bed, his conscience clear, having contributed his mite to the prosperity of the city and to his own bank account.

"'In politics and religion this Sane Citizen is the canniest man on earth; and in the arts he invariably has a natural taste which makes him pick out the best, every time. In no country in the world will you find so many reproductions of the Old Masters and of well-known paintings on parlor walls as in these United States. No country has anything like our number of phonographs, with not only dance records and comic but also the best operas, such as Verdi, rendered by the world's highest-paid singers.

"'In other countries, art and literature are left to a lot of shabby bums living in attics and feeding on booze and spaghetti, but in America the successful writer or picture-painter is indistinguishable from any other decent business man; and I, for one, am only too glad that the man who has the rare skill to season his message with interesting reading matter and who shows both purpose and pep in handling his literary wares has a chance to drag down his fifty thousand bucks a year, to mingle with the biggest executives on terms of perfect equality, and to show as big a house and as swell a car as any Captain of Industry! But, mind you, it's the appreciation of the Regular Guy who I have been depicting which has made this possible, and you got to hand as much credit to him as to the authors themselves.

"'Finally, but most important, our Standardized Citizen, even if he is a bachelor, is a lover of

---

1. **spieled:** talked.
2. Remember that *Babbit* was written in 1922.

3. **sassiety:** satirical pronunciation of "society."

Salesmen at a meeting, 1925.

the Little Ones, a supporter of the hearthstone which is the basic foundation of our civilization, first, last, and all the time, and the thing that most distinguishes us from the decayed nations of Europe.

"'I have never yet toured Europe—and as a matter of fact, I don't know that I care to such an awful lot, as long as there's our own mighty cities and mountains to be seen—but, the way I figure it out, there must be a good many of our own sort of folks abroad. Indeed, one of the most enthusiastic Rotarians I ever met boosted the tenets of one hundred percent pep in a burr[4] that smacked o'bonny Scutlond and all ye bonny braes o' Bobby

---

4. **burr:** Scottish accent.

Burns. But same time, one thing that distinguishes us from our good brothers, the hustlers over there, is that they're willing to take a lot off the snobs and journalists and politicians, while the modern American business man knows how to talk right up for himself, knows how to make it good and plenty clear that he intends to run the works. He doesn't have to call in some highbrow hired man when it's necessary for him to answer the crooked critics of the sane and efficient life. He's not dumb, like the old-fashioned merchant. He's got a vocabulary and a punch.

"'With all modesty, I want to stand up here as a representative business man and gently whisper, "Here's our kind of folks! Here's the specifications of the Standardized American Citizen!

Here's the new generation of Americans: fellows with hair on their chests and smiles in their eyes and adding machines in their offices. We're not doing any boasting, but we like ourselves first-rate, and if you don't like us, look out—better get under cover before the cyclone hits town!''

'' 'So! In my clumsy way I have tried to sketch the Real He-man, the fellow with Zip and Bang. And it's because Zenith has so large a proportion of such men that it's the most stable, the greatest of our cities. New York also has its thousands of Real Folks, but New York is cursed with unnumbered foreigners. So are Chicago and San Francisco. Oh, we have a golden roster of cities—Detroit and Cleveland with their renowned factories, Cincinnati with its great machine-tool and soap products, Pittsburgh and Birmingham with their steel, Kansas City and Minneapolis and Omaha that open their bountiful gates on the bosom of the oceanlike wheatlands, and countless other magnificent sister-cities, for, by the last census, there were no less than sixty-eight glorious American burgs[5] with a population of over one hundred thousand! And all these cities stand together for power and purity, and against foreign ideas and communism—Atlanta with Hartford, Rochester with Denver, Milwaukee with Indianapolis, Los Angeles with Scranton, Portland, Maine, with Portland, Oregon. A good live wire from Baltimore or Seattle or Duluth is the twin-brother of every like fellow booster from Buffalo or Akron, Fort Worth or Oskaloosa!

'' 'But it's here in Zenith, the home for manly men and womanly women and bright kids, that you find the largest proportion of these Regular Guys, and that's what sets it in a class by itself; that's why Zenith will be remembered in history as having set the pace for a civilization that shall endure when the old time-killing ways are gone forever and the day of earnest efficient endeavor shall have dawned all round the world!

'' 'Some time I hope folks will quit handing all the credit to a lot of moth-eaten, mildewed, out-of-date, old European dumps, and give proper credit to the famous Zenith spirit, that clean fighting determination to win Success that has made the little old Zip City celebrated in every land and clime, wherever condensed milk and pasteboard cartons are known! Believe me, the world has fallen too long for these worn-out countries that aren't producing anything but bootblacks and scenery and booze, that haven't got one bathroom per hundred people, and that don't know a loose-leaf ledger from a slipcover; and it's just about time for some Zenithite to get his back up and holler for a showdown!

'' 'I tell you, Zenith and her sister-cities are producing a new type of civilization. There are many resemblances between Zenith and these other burgs, and I'm darn glad of it! The extraordinary, growing, and sane standardization of stores, offices, streets, hotels, clothes, and newspapers throughout the United States shows how strong and enduring a type is ours.

'' 'I always like to remember a piece that Chum Frink wrote for the newspapers about his lecture-tours. It is doubtless familiar to many of you, but if you will permit me, I'll take a chance and read it. It's one of the classic poems, like ''If'' by Kipling, or Ella Wheeler Wilcox's ''The Man Worth While''; and I always carry this clipping of it in my note-book:

When I am out upon the road, a poet with a peddler's load, I mostly sing a hearty song, and take a chew and hike along, a-handing out my samples fine of Cheero Brand of sweet sunshine, and peddling optimistic pokes and stable lines of japes and jokes to Lyceums and other folks, to Rotarys, Kiwanis' Clubs, and feel I ain't like other dubs. And then old Major Silas Satan, a brainy cuss who's always waitin', he gives his tail a lively quirk, and gets in quick his dirty work. He fills me up with mullygrubs; my hair the backward way he rubs; he makes me lonelier than a hound, on Sunday when the folks ain't round. And then b' gosh, I would prefer to never be a lecturer, a-ridin' round in classy cars and smoking fifty-cent cigars, and never more I want to roam; I simply want to be back home, a-eatin' flapjacks, hash, and ham, with folks who savvy whom I am!

But when I get that lonely spell, I simply seek the best hotel, no matter in what town I be—St. Paul, Toledo, or K.C., in Washington, Schenectady, in Louisville or Albany. And at that inn it hits my dome that I again am right at home. If I should stand a lengthy spell in front of that first-class hotel, that to the drummers[6] loves to cater, across from some big film theayter; if I should look around and buzz, and wonder in what town

<hr />

5. **burgs:** towns.

6. **drummers:** traveling salesmen.

I was, I swear that I could never tell! For all the crowd would be so swell, in just the same fine sort of jeans they wear at home, and all the queens with spiffy bonnets on their beans, and all the fellows standing round a-talkin' always, I'll be bound, the same good jolly kind of guff, 'bout autos, politics and stuff and baseball players of renown that Nice Guys talk in my home town!

Then when I entered that hotel, I'd look around and say, "Well, well!" For there would be the same newsstand, same magazines and candies grand, same smokes of famous standard brand, I'd find at home, I'll tell! And when I saw the jolly bunch come waltzing in for eats at lunch, and squaring up in natty duds to platters large of French Fried spuds, why then I'd stand right up and bawl, "I've never left my home at all!" And all replete I'd sit me down beside some guy in derby brown upon a lobby chair of plush, and murmur to him in a rush, "Hello, Bill, tell me, good old scout, how is your stock a-holdin' out?" Then we'd be off, two solid pals, a-chatterin' like giddy gals of flivvers,[7] weather, home, and wives, lodge-brothers then for all our lives! So when Sam Satan makes you blue, good friend, that's what I'd up and do, for in these States where'er you roam, you never leave your home sweet home.

" 'Yes, sir, these other burgs are our true partners in the great game of vital living. But let's not have any mistake about this. I claim that Zenith is the best partner and the fastest-growing partner of the whole caboodle. I trust I may be pardoned if I give a few statistics to back up my claims. If they are old stuff to any of you, yet the tidings of prosperity, like the good news of the Bible, never become tedious to the ears of a real hustler, no matter how oft the sweet story is told! Every intelligent person knows that Zenith manufactures more condensed milk and evaporated cream, more paper boxes, and more lighting fixtures, than any other city in the United States, if not in the world. But it is not so universally known that we also stand second in the manufacture of package butter, sixth in the giant realm of motors and automobiles, and somewhere about third in cheese, leather findings, tar roofing, breakfast food, and overalls!

" 'Our greatness, however, lies not alone in punchful prosperity but equally in that public spirit, that forward-looking idealism and brotherhood, which has marked Zenith ever since its foundation by the Fathers. We have a right, indeed we have a duty toward our fair city, to announce broadcast[8] the facts about our high schools, characterized by their complete plants and the finest school-ventilating systems in the country, bar none; our magnificent new hotels and banks and the paintings and carved marble in their lobbies; and the Second National Tower, the second highest business building in any inland city in the entire country. When I add that we have an unparalleled number of miles of paved streets, bathrooms, vacuum cleaners, and all the other signs of civilization; that our library and art museum are well supported and housed in convenient and roomy buildings; that our park system is more than up to par, with its handsome driveways adorned with grass, shrubs, and statuary, then I give but a hint of the all-round unlimited greatness of Zenith!

" 'I believe, however, in keeping the best to the last. When I remind you that we have one motor car for every five and seven-eighths persons in the city, then I give a rock-ribbed practical indication of the kind of progress and braininess which is synonymous with the name Zenith!

" 'But the way of the righteous is not all roses. Before I close I must call your attention to a problem we have to face this coming year. The worst menace to sound government is not the avowed socialists but a lot of cowards who work under cover—the long-haired gentry who call themselves "liberals" and "radicals" and "non-partisan" and "intelligentsia" and God only knows how many other trick names! Irresponsible teachers and professors constitute the worst of this whole gang, and I am ashamed to say that several of them are on the faculty of our great State University! The U. is my own Alma Mater, and I am proud to be known as an alumni, but there are certain instructors there who seem to think we ought to turn the conduct of the nation over to hoboes and roustabouts.

" 'Those profs are the snakes to be scotched—they and all their milk-and-water ilk! The American businessman is generous to a fault, but one thing he does demand of all teachers and lecturers and journalists: if we're going to pay them our good money, they've got to help us by selling

---

7. **flivvers:** cars.

8. **broadcast:** used here to mean *publicly.*

efficiency and whooping it up for rational pros-perity! And when it comes to these blab-mouth, fault-finding, pessimistic, cynical University teachers, let me tell you that during this golden coming year it's just as much our duty to bring influence to have those cusses fired as it is to sell all the real estate and gather in all the good shekels[9] we can.

" 'Not till that is done will our sons and daughters see that the ideal of American manhood and culture isn't a lot of cranks sitting around chewing

the rag about their Rights and their Wrongs, but a God-fearing, hustling, successful, two-fisted Regular Guy, who belongs to some church with pep and piety to it, who belongs to the Boosters or the Rotarians or the Kiwanis, to the Elks or Moose or Red Men or Knights of Columbus or any one of a score of organizations of good, jolly, kidding, laughing, sweating, upstanding, lend-a-handing Royal Good Fellows, who plays hard and works hard, and whose answer to his critics is a square-toed boot that'll teach the grouches and smart alecks to respect the He-man and get out and root for Uncle Samuel, U.S.A.!' "

---

9. **shekels:** used here as slang for "money."

Responding to the Speech

Analyzing the Speech

Identifying Facts

1. According to Babbitt's description of what Zenith has to accomplish in order to become "perfect," how would he define a "perfect" city?
2. List the phrases Babbitt uses to describe his ideal citizen. What is his attitude toward women?
3. How would you describe Babbitt's attitude toward European civilization? Toward foreigners? Toward higher education? Toward art and literature?
4. Find details in the speech that reveal Babbitt's overriding concern with conformity.

Interpreting Meanings

5. Although Babbitt pays lip service to friendship and harmony, he reveals a great amount of prejudice and hostility toward certain groups. Who are these groups? Where does Babbitt reveal his bias? Why would a person like Babbitt dislike or distrust these groups?
6. Babbitt delivers this speech sincerely. But Lewis has written it so that we, as readers, feel his mockery of Babbitt. Tell how Babbitt's speech fits the requirements of **satire** (the use of irony or derision to expose folly). In light of the definition of *zenith*, how is the town's name **ironic?**
7. The headnote says that Babbitt really yearns for emotion. Do you agree? Do you find any evidence of this in his speech? Explain.
8. How would you account for Babbitt's values? Why do you think he needs conformity and fears what is "different"? What are your own responses to Babbitt as you read this speech?

Writing About the Speech

A Creative Response

1. **Answering Babbitt.** Suppose Babbitt were running for public office and this were his stock campaign speech. Write a speech prepared by Babbitt's opponent challenging Babbitt's values and visions.
2. **Updating Babbitt.** Maybe you think Babbitt has made some valid points. Update his speech, to show where it might be delivered today.

A Critical Response

3. **Comparing and Contrasting the Speech with "Self-Reliance."** In his essay "Self-Reliance" (page 194), Ralph Waldo Emerson defines the essence of individualism. In an essay, compare and contrast Babbitt's Regular Guy with Emerson's individual. Is Babbitt's hero an extension or a distortion of Emerson's self-reliant individual? Pay particular attention to what Emerson and Babbitt say or suggest about conformity.

Analyzing Language and Style

Clichés

Clichés are stock expressions that have been used so often we hardly think any more about what they really mean. People who accept clichés instead of more complex ideas can be easily manipulated. Find at least five clichés about American ideals or small-town life used here by Babbitt. What stock responses does Babbitt want to elicit from his audience?

Willa Cather
(1873–1947)

Willa Cather was born in rural Virginia, the first of seven children. When she was nine, her father uprooted the family and headed for the untried lands of the West, settling in Webster County, Nebraska. She would later recall that this first encounter with the prairie was so striking that she "felt an erasure of personality."

Nevertheless, Cather had a strong curiosity about life and an ambition to make the most of it. She was stimulated by the hard life of the soil she saw around her, and she absorbed the stories of the immigrant families who were her neighbors. Her grandmother read to her from the Bible and John Bunyan's *Pilgrim's Progress;* she herself also read widely, and she became an outstanding student at the Red Cloud, Nebraska, school. In her boyish clothes and haircut, Willa was an unusual figure, and her teachers recognized in her an adolescent nonconformist, already determined on a career in science.

While a freshman at the University of Nebraska, Cather wrote an essay on Thomas Carlyle, the British philosopher and social critic. She dealt with the artist's commitment, which often requires the sacrifice of love and marriage. (Cather herself never married.) When this piece appeared in a Lincoln newspaper, her own ambitions had already turned toward writing. She became a regular contributor to the newspaper and began to write poetry and stories.

By the time Cather graduated from college in 1895, she had won a statewide reputation for brash, bright reviews. She continued to work as a journalist, moving to Pittsburgh for a decade as editor and reviewer for the *Daily Leader.* In 1903, she published her first book, a collection of verse entitled *April Twilights.* She followed it with *The Troll Garden,* a group of stories.

In 1906, the publisher S. S. McClure persuaded her to move to New York and join the staff of his dynamic, muckraking magazine, *McClure's.* For six years she served as a writer and editor, immersed in the social and political currents of the time; in 1912 she resigned from the magazine to give herself completely to writing fiction.

Cather had met the Maine writer Sarah Orne Jewett in 1908 and had been encouraged by her to write about the themes and settings she knew best: the moral values of the hard-working immigrant families on the Midwestern prairie. It was Cather's view that these pioneers, who had sought to bring the wild, new land under cultivation, were heroic and that their era was the heart of the American dream. She saw these immigrant settlers as contributing a cultural richness and an earthy love of life that were lacking in the pale, self-satisfied native-born Americans who clung to the seaboard cities.

O Pioneers!, a novel whose title Cather borrowed from Walt Whitman, appeared in 1913. The work revealed Cather's love for the Nebraska of her childhood; it also praised the men and women she recalled as survivors of their encounter with the stubborn prairie. When Alexandra Bergson, the novel's Scandinavian heroine, looks out upon the land's glorious expanse, she weeps at the very sight of it.

My Ántonia, appearing in 1918, presents a heroine who struggles to find a fulfilling life on the farm. The narrator of this novel is clearly nostalgic, seeing Ántonia as a fortunate exception to the social currents of her time.

As Cather witnessed the decline of the agrarian ideal, her work became increasingly elegiac about the past and disillusioned with the present. *One of Ours* (1922), which was far from Cather's best novel but which won her the Pulitzer Prize, features as its hero a young farmer who reflects the author's dissatisfaction with the new men and machines who were betraying the pioneer ideal. The protagonist escapes them only through the Great War in Europe.

In later life and later novels, Cather became ever more nostalgic, ever more estranged from her own times. "The world broke in two in 1922 or thereabout," she said, explaining that no one born in the twentieth century could grasp her own vision of America. She had seen her beloved Nebraska devastated by the machine, and she lamented the end of her epic vision of a noble society. She made no secret of her skepticism toward progress. As an Indian character says in *Death Comes for the Archbishop* (1927), her novel about religious missionaries in New Mexico: "Men travel faster now, but I do not know if they go to better things."

It is often observed that social progress is inevitable, and that the changes which each generation brings do not necessarily destroy old values. Nevertheless, we may want to let Cather remind us of the novelist's duty to keep a wary eye on our relation to scientific progress. It was Cather's profound intuition that a science which offers us new comfort, new speed, new security, and longer life will almost surely demand something of our spirit in return.

A WAGNER MATINÉE

As in most of Willa Cather's novels and stories, setting plays a central role in the story that follows. In this case, however, there are really two settings: the rural Nebraska, in which the narrator, like Cather, spent his formative years, is contrasted with the thriving cultural life of Boston, a large city. Although Cather believed that farm life in the Midwest fostered essential values, she was hardly a romantic in underestimating the hardships of that life, or the lost opportunities for some of the people who lived it.

The story's title refers to the German composer Richard Wagner (väg′nər) (1813–1883), the outstanding Romantic operatic composer of the century. A matinée is an afternoon performance of a play or concert.

Cather herself loved music.

I received one morning a letter, written in pale ink on glossy, blue-lined notepaper, and bearing the postmark of a little Nebraska village. This communication, worn and rubbed, looking as though it had been carried for some days in a coat pocket that was none too clean, was from my Uncle Howard and informed me that his wife had been left a small legacy by a bachelor relative who had recently died, and that it would be necessary for her to go to Boston to attend to the settling of the estate. He requested me to meet her at the station and render her whatever services might be necessary. On examining the date indicated as that of her arrival, I found it no later than tomorrow. He had characteristically delayed writing until, had I been away from home for a day, I must have missed the good woman altogether.

The name of my Aunt Georgiana called up not alone her own figure, at once pathetic and grotesque, but opened before my feet a gulf of recollection so wide and deep, that, as the letter dropped from my hand, I felt suddenly a stranger to all the present conditions of my existence, wholly ill at ease and out of place amid the familiar surroundings of my study. I became, in short, the gangling farmer-boy my aunt had known, scourged with chilblains[1] and bashfulness, my hands cracked and sore from the corn husking. I felt the knuckles of my thumb tentatively, as though they were raw again. I sat again before her parlor organ, fumbling the scales with my stiff,

---

1. **chilblains:** an inflammation of the hands and feet caused by exposure to cold and moisture.

red hands, while she, beside me, made canvas mittens for the huskers.

The next morning, after preparing my landlady somewhat, I set out for the station. When the train arrived I had some difficulty in finding my aunt. She was the last of the passengers to alight, and it was not until I got her into the carriage that she seemed really to recognize me. She had come all the way in a day coach; her linen duster had become black with soot and her black bonnet gray with dust during the journey. When we arrived at my boardinghouse the landlady put her to bed at once and I did not see her again until the next morning.

Whatever shock Mrs. Springer experienced at my aunt's appearance, she considerately concealed. As for myself, I saw my aunt's misshapen figure with that feeling of awe and respect with which we behold explorers who have left their ears and fingers north of Franz-Joseph-Land,[2] or their health somewhere along the Upper Congo. My Aunt Georgiana had been a music teacher at the Boston Conservatory, somewhere back in the latter sixties. One summer, while visiting in the little village among the Green Mountains where her ancestors had dwelt for generations, she had kindled the callow fancy of the most idle and shiftless of all the village lads, and had conceived for this Howard Carpenter one of those extravagant passions which a handsome country boy of twenty-one sometimes inspires in an angular, spectacled woman of thirty. When she returned to her duties in Boston, Howard followed her, and the upshot of this inexplicable infatuation was that she eloped with him, eluding the reproaches of her family and the criticisms of her friends by going with him to the Nebraska frontier. Carpenter, who, of course, had no money, had taken a homestead in Red Willow County, fifty miles from the railroad. There they had measured off their quarter section themselves by driving across the prairie in a wagon, to the wheel of which they had tied a red cotton handkerchief, and counting off its revolutions. They built a dugout in the red hillside, one of those cave dwellings whose inmates so often reverted to primitive conditions. Their water they got from the lagoons where the buffalo drank, and their slender stock of provisions was always at the mercy of bands of roving Indians. For thirty years my aunt had not been further than fifty miles from the homestead.

But Mrs. Springer knew nothing of all this, and must have been considerably shocked at what was left of my kinswoman. Beneath the soiled linen duster which, on her arrival, was the most conspicuous feature of her costume, she wore a black stuff[3] dress, whose ornamentation showed that she had surrendered herself unquestioningly into the hands of a country dressmaker. My poor aunt's figure, however, would have presented astonishing difficulties to any dressmaker. Originally stooped, her shoulders were now almost bent together over her sunken chest. She wore no stays, and her gown, which trailed unevenly behind, rose in a sort of peak over her abdomen. She wore ill-fitting false teeth, and her skin was as yellow as a Mongolian's from constant exposure to a pitiless wind and to the alkaline water which hardens the most transparent cuticle into a sort of flexible leather.

I owed to this woman most of the good that ever came my way in my boyhood, and had a reverential affection for her. During the years when I was riding herd for my uncle, my aunt, after cooking the three meals—the first of which was ready at six o'clock in the morning—and putting the six children to bed, would often stand until midnight at her ironing board, with me at the kitchen table beside her, hearing me recite Latin declensions and conjugations,[4] gently shaking me when my drowsy head sank down over a page of irregular verbs. It was to her, at her ironing or mending, that I read my first Shakespeare, and her old text book on mythology was the first that ever came into my empty hands. She taught me my scales and exercises, too—on the little parlor organ, which her husband had bought her after fifteen years, during which she had not so much as seen any instrument, but an accordion that belonged to one of the Norwegian farmhands. She would sit beside me by the hour, darning and counting while I struggled with the "Joyous Farmer," but she seldom talked to me about music, and I understood why. She was a pious woman; she had the consolations of religion and, to her at least, her martyrdom was not wholly

---

2. **Franz-Joseph-Land:** a group of islands in the Arctic Ocean.

3. **stuff:** cloth, usually woolen.
4. **declensions and conjugations:** lists of noun and verb forms, often memorized by beginning students.

Landscape No. 34 by Art Sinsabaugh (1962). Photograph.

sordid. Once when I had been doggedly beating out some easy passages from an old score of *Euryanthe* I had found among her music books, she came up to me and, putting her hands over my eyes, gently drew my head back upon her shoulder, saying tremulously, "Don't love it so well, Clark, or it may be taken from you. Oh! dear boy, pray that whatever your sacrifice may be, it be not that."

When my aunt appeared on the morning after her arrival, she was still in a semi-somnambulant[5] state. She seemed not to realize that she was in the city where she had spent her youth, the place longed for hungrily half a lifetime. She had been so wretchedly train-sick throughout the journey that she had no recollection of anything but her discomfort, and, to all intents and purposes, there were but a few hours of nightmare between the farm in Red Willow County and my study on Newbury Street. I had planned a little pleasure for her that afternoon, to repay her for some of the glorious moments she had given me when we used to milk together in the straw-thatched cowshed and she, because I was more than usually tired, or because her husband had spoken sharply to me, would tell me of the splendid performance of the *Huguenots*[6] she had seen in Paris, in her youth. At two o'clock the Symphony Orchestra was to give a Wagner program, and I intended to take my aunt; though, as I conversed with her I grew

---

5. **somnambulant:** sleep-walking.

6. ***Huguenots:*** an opera about the French Protestants of the seventeenth century by Giacomo Meyerbeer (1791–1864).

The Museum of Modern Art, New York City.

though she was perfectly familiar with their respective situations, and had once possessed the piano score of *The Flying Dutchman*. I began to think it would have been best to get her back to Red Willow County without waking her, and regretted having suggested the concert.

From the time we entered the concert hall, however, she was a trifle less passive and inert, and for the first time seemed to perceive her surroundings. I had felt some trepidation least she might become aware of the absurdities of her attire, or might experience some painful embarrassment at stepping suddenly into the world to which she had been dead for a quarter of a century. But, again, I found how superficially I had judged her. She sat looking about her with eyes as impersonal, almost as stony, as those with which the granite Rameses in a museum watches the froth and fret[7] that ebbs and flows about his pedestal—separated from it by the lonely stretch of centuries. I have seen this same aloofness in old miners who drift into the Brown hotel at Denver, their pockets full of bullion, their linen soiled, their haggard faces unshaven; standing in the thronged corridors as solitary as though they were still in a frozen camp on the Yukon, conscious that certain experiences have isolated them from their fellows by a gulf no haberdasher[8] could bridge.

We sat at the extreme left of the first balcony, facing the arc of our own and the balcony above us, veritable hanging gardens, brilliant as tulip beds. The matinée audience was made up chiefly of women. One lost the contour of faces and figures, indeed any effect of line whatever, and there was only the color of bodices past counting, the shimmer of fabrics soft and firm, silky and sheer; red, mauve, pink, blue, lilac, purple, ecru, rose, yellow, cream, and white, all the colors that an impressionist finds in a sunlit landscape, with here and there the dead shadow of a frock coat. My Aunt Georgiana regarded them as though they had been so many daubs of tube-paint on a palette.

When the musicians came out and took their places, she gave a little stir of anticipation, and looked with quickening interest down over the rail at that invariable grouping, perhaps the first wholly familiar thing that had greeted her eye since she had left old Maggie and her weakling

doubtful about her enjoyment of it. Indeed, for her own sake, I could only wish her taste for such things quite dead, and the long struggle mercifully ended at last. I suggested our visiting the Conservatory and the Common before lunch, but she seemed altogether too timid to wish to venture out. She questioned me absently about various changes in the city, but she was chiefly concerned that she had forgotten to leave instructions about feeding half-skimmed milk to a certain weakling calf, "old Maggie's calf, you know, Clark," she explained, evidently having forgotten how long I had been away. She was further troubled because she had neglected to tell her daughter about the freshly opened kit of mackerel in the cellar, which would spoil if it were not used directly.

I asked her whether she had ever heard any of the Wagnerian operas, and found that she had not,

---

7. **fret:** agitations or worries.
8. **haberdasher:** someone who sells men's clothing. A men's clothing store used to be called a "haberdashery."

calf. I could feel how all those details sank into her soul, for I had not forgotten how they had sunk into mine when I came fresh from plowing forever and forever between green aisles of corn, where, as in a treadmill, one might walk from daybreak to dusk without perceiving a shadow of change. The clean profiles of the musicians, the gloss of their linen, the dull black of their coats, the beloved shapes of the instruments, the patches of yellow light thrown by the green shaded lamps on the smooth, varnished bellies of the cellos and the bass viols in the rear, the restless, wind-tossed forest of fiddle necks and bows—I recalled how, in the first orchestra I had ever heard, those long bow strokes seemed to draw the heart out of me, as a conjurer's stick reels out yards of paper ribbon from a hat.

The first number was the *Tannhauser* overture. When the horns drew out the first strain of the Pilgrim's chorus, my Aunt Georgiana clutched my coat sleeve. Then it was I first realized that for her this broke a silence of thirty years; the inconceivable silence of the plains. With the battle between the two motives, with the frenzy of the Venusberg theme and its ripping of strings, there came to me an overwhelming sense of the waste and wear we are so powerless to combat; and I saw again the tall, naked house on the prairie, black and grim as a wooden fortress; the black pond where I had learned to swim, its margin pitted with sun-dried cattle tracks; the rain-gullied clay banks about the naked house, the four dwarf ash seedlings where the dishcloths were always hung to dry before the kitchen door. The world there was the flat world of the ancients; to the east, a cornfield that stretched to daybreak; to the west, a corral that reached to sunset; between, the conquests of peace, dearer bought than those of war.

The overture closed, my aunt released my coat sleeve, but she said nothing. She sat staring at the orchestra through a dullness of thirty years, through the films made little by little by each of the three hundred and sixty-five days in every one of them. What, I wondered, did she get from it? She had been a good pianist in her day, I knew, and her musical education had been broader than that of most music teachers of a quarter of a century ago. She had often told me of Mozart's operas and Meyerbeer's, and I could remember hearing her sing, years ago, certain melodies of Verdi's. When I had fallen ill with a fever in her house she

used to sit by my cot in the evening—when the cool, night wind blew in through the faded mosquito netting tacked over the window and I lay watching a certain bright star that burned red above the cornfield—and sing ''Home to our mountains, O, let us return!'' in a way fit to break the heart of a Vermont boy near dead of homesickness already.

I watched her closely through the prelude to *Tristan and Isolde,* trying vainly to conjecture what that seething turmoil of strings and winds might mean to her, but she sat mutely staring at the violin bows that drove obliquely downward like the pelting streaks of rain in a summer shower. Had this music any message for her? Had she enough left to at all comprehend this power which had kindled the world since she had left it? I was in a fever of curiosity, but Aunt Georgiana sat silent upon her peak in Darien.[9] She preserved this utter immobility throughout the number from the *Flying Dutchman,* though her fingers worked mechanically upon her black dress, as though, of themselves, they were recalling the piano score they had once played. Poor old hands! They had been stretched and twisted into mere tentacles to hold and lift and knead with; the palm unduly swollen, the fingers bent and knotted—on one of them a thin, worn band that had once been a wedding ring. As I pressed and gently quieted one of those groping hands, I remembered with quivering eyelids their services for me in other days.

Soon after the tenor began the ''Prize Song,''[10] I heard a quick drawn breath and turned to my aunt. Her eyes were closed, but the tears were glistening on her cheeks, and I think, in a moment more, they were in my eyes as well. It never really died, then—the soul that can suffer so excruciatingly and so interminably; it withers to the outward eye only; like that strange moss which can lie on a dusty shelf half a century and yet, if placed in water, grows green again. She wept so throughout the development and elaboration of the melody.

During the intermission before the second half of the concert, I questioned my aunt and found that the ''Prize Song'' was not new to her. Some

9. **silent upon her peak in Darien:** an allusion to a poem by John Keats (1795–1821), which is about Keats's awe in the presence of a work of art. (The poem is ''On First Looking Into Chapman's Homer.'')
10. **''Prize Song'':** A beautiful aria from the third act of Wagner's opera *Die Meistersinger.*

years before there had drifted to the farm in Red Willow County a young German, a tramp cow puncher, who had sung the chorus at Beyruth, when he was a boy, along with other peasant boys and girls. Of a Sunday morning he used to sit on his gingham-sheeted bed in the hands' bedroom which opened off the kitchen, cleaning the leather of his boots and saddle, singing the "Prize Song," while my aunt went about her work in the kitchen. She had hovered about him until she had prevailed upon him to join the country church, though his sole fitness for this step, in so far as I could gather, lay in his boyish face and his possession of this divine melody. Shortly afterward he had gone to town on the Fourth of July, had drunk for several days, lost his money at a faro table, ridden a saddled Texan steer on a bet, and disappeared with a fractured collarbone. All this my aunt told me huskily, wanderingly, as though she were talking in the weak lapses of illness.

"Well, we have come to better things than the old *Trovatore*[11] at any rate, Aunt Georgie?" I queried, with a well-meant effort at jocularity.

Her lip quivered and she hastily put her handkerchief up to her mouth. From behind it she murmured, "And you have been hearing this ever since you left me, Clark?" Her question was the gentlest and saddest of reproaches.

The second half of the program consisted of four numbers from the *Ring,* and closed with Siegfried's funeral march. My aunt wept quietly, but almost continuously, as a shallow vessel overflows in a rainstorm. From time to time her dim eyes looked up at the lights which studded the ceiling, burning softly under their dull glass globes; doubtless they were stars in truth to her. I was still perplexed as to what measure of musical comprehension was left to her, she who had heard nothing but the singing of Gospel Hymns at Methodist services in the square frame schoolhouse on Section Thirteen for so many years. I was wholly unable to gauge how much of it had been dissolved in soapsuds, or worked into bread, or milked into the bottom of a pail.

The deluge of sound poured on and on; I never knew what she found in the shining current of it; I never knew how far it bore her or past what happy islands. From the trembling of her face I could well believe that before the last numbers

11. **Trovatore:** an opera by the Italian composer Giuseppe Verdi (1813–1901).

At the Opera by Mary Cassatt (1880). Oil.

Museum of Fine Arts, Boston.

she had been carried out where the myriad graves are, into the gray, nameless burying grounds of the sea; or into some world of death vaster yet, where, from the beginning of the world, hope has lain down with hope and dream with dream and, renouncing, slept.

The concert was over; the people filed out of the hall chattering and laughing, glad to relax and find the living level again, but my kinswoman made no effort to rise. The harpist slipped its green felt cover over his instrument; the flute players shook the water from their mouthpieces; the men of the orchestra went out one by one, leaving the stage to the chairs and music stands, empty as a winter cornfield.

I spoke to my aunt. She burst into tears and sobbed pleadingly. "I don't want to go, Clark, I don't want to go!"

I understood. For her, just outside the door of the concert hall, lay the black pond with the cattle-tracked bluffs; the tall, unpainted house, with weather-curled boards; naked as a tower, the crook-backed ash seedlings where the dishcloths hung to dry; the gaunt, moulting turkeys picking up refuse about the kitchen door.

Responding to the Story

Analyzing the Story

Identifying Details

1. Who is the narrator of the story? What message contained in the uncle's letter sets the action in motion?
2. Numerous **flashbacks** in the story provide information about Aunt Georgiana's life after she moved to Nebraska. Cite some of her hardships and disappointments.
3. Explain why the narrator feels he owed a great debt to Aunt Georgiana. What special treat has he planned for her in Boston?
4. Describe Aunt Georgiana's reactions to the concert.

Interpreting Meanings

5. What seems to be Clark's attitude toward his Uncle Howard? Locate the passage in which Cather hints at this attitude.
6. Georgianna says about music, "Don't love it so well, Clark, or it may be taken from you." How do you feel about this attitude toward life and its joys?
7. As she often does, Cather uses a male narrator to tell her story. Locate passages in which this first-person narrator actually acts as an **omniscient narrator.** How would you characterize Clark? Can you see any reason why Cather didn't use a woman's voice to tell her story?
8. Summarize in your own words what Clark "understands" at the end of the story.
9. The story contrasts the past and present lives of both Aunt Georgiana and her nephew. On the whole, what seems to be Cather's **theme** in the story? How does the central episode of the concert, reflected in the title, contribute to this theme?
10. Willa Cather was an accomplished musician, and the powerful attraction of music is a theme that often recurs in her fiction. Find the passage in which Cather describes the effect the music might have had on Georgiana's imagination and feelings. Does this story convey some of the emotional effects that anyone might experience in listening to music?
11. In contrast to the music and the music hall is the emotional effect of the Nebraska frontier, the **setting** we hear about over and over again in the story. How would you describe the feeling Cather wants us to have for this setting? What specific **images** create this feeling?
12. If this story were told by a Romantic, how would Aunt Georgiana's visit to Boston have turned out? How would a Romantic writer have described the Nebraska farm setting?

Writing About the Story

A Creative Response

1. **Describing a Character.** Write a paragraph describing a person's appearance in a way that reveals something about his or her character. Imitate Cather's techniques in the paragraph on page 543 beginning "But Mrs. Springer knew nothing of all this. . . ." Before you write, decide what characteristics you want to emphasize. Then list some aspects of clothing or appearance that suggest these characteristics.

A Critical Response

2. **Analyzing Imagery.** In a brief essay, contrast the most prominent images Cather uses in this story to describe farm life and city life. Describe the emotional impact of each set of images.
3. **Comparing Responses to Nature.** *Walden,* by Henry David Thoreau (page 207), expresses other feelings about the natural world and its relationship to the human world. In a brief essay, compare and contrast the experience of Cather's heroine with that of Thoreau. How would you account for the different feelings toward the natural world?

Analyzing Language and Style

Figures of Speech

In each figure of speech that follows, identify the two distinct parts of the comparison. Then tell what you think these different things have in common.

1. "We sat at the extreme left of the first balcony, facing the arc of our own and the balcony above us, veritable hanging gardens, brilliant as tulip beds." (Page 545)
2. ". . . the restless, wind-tossed forest of fiddle necks and bows . . ." (Page 546)
3. ". . . I recalled how, in the first orchestra I had ever heard, those long bow strokes seemed to draw the heart out of me, as a conjurer's stick reels out yards of paper ribbon from a hat." (Page 546)
4. ". . . she sat mutely staring at the violin bows that drove obliquely downward like the pelting streaks of rain in a summer shower." (Page 546)
5. "The deluge of sound poured on and on; I never knew what she found in the shining current of it . . ." (Page 547)
6. ". . . the men of the orchestra went out . . . , leaving the stage to the chairs and music stands, empty as a winter cornfield." (Page 547)

Thomas Wolfe
(1900–1938)

Thomas Wolfe is probably the most autobiographical of all American writers. Although his novels and short stories are peopled by fictional characters, the fiction actually chronicles the events of his Southern upbringing and his later life in New York and Europe.

Wolfe was born in the Smoky Mountains, in Asheville, North Carolina, the youngest of eight children. Much of his fiction centers on a character named Eugene Gant, the youngest child in a large Southern family, whose life parallels Wolfe's own.

When Wolfe was eight years old, his parents separated. His mother ran a boardinghouse, which she called My Old Kentucky Home; his father, given to bouts of violent drinking, lived only a few blocks away, behind his stone-cutting shop. The boy, very unhappy with the new situation, lived with his mother. The boardinghouse appears repeatedly in Wolfe's fiction, usually depicted in an unpleasant light.

Like his character Eugene Gant, Wolfe entered college when he was sixteen. At six feet six inches, he dominated any group he was a part of; his extraordinary height was one reason Wolfe was so self-conscious all his life.

After he graduated from the University of North Carolina in 1920, Wolfe studied playwriting at Harvard. In 1924, he moved to New York City, where he taught at New York University while trying unsuccessfully to have his plays produced. That same year, he made the first of seven trips to Europe. The time he spent abroad, like his childhood, became material for his fiction.

During this time, Wolfe became involved with Aline Bernstein, a woman much older than he was. They spent five years together, sometimes in England, sometimes in New York, where Wolfe continued to teach and to work on *Look Homeward, Angel*. Wolfe wrote extensively about this affair later in *The Web and the Rock*.

Look Homeward, Angel, his first and best novel, was completed in 1928. After it was rejected by several publishers, Scribner's showed interest. As a result, Wolfe began what would be

nearly a remarkable association with Maxwell Perkins, the famous editor who persuaded Wolfe to cut three hundred pages from his enormous story and saw the novel through to publication.

By 1935, Perkins felt that Wolfe's second novel, *Of Time and the River*, was ready for publication. This huge, sprawling book continues the story of Eugene Gant, the young Southern writer who moves to a northeastern city.

Wolfe eventually argued with Scribner's, and before his sudden death in 1938, he had signed up with Harper's, another publisher, and delivered to them enormous chunks of a new manuscript. Another editor labored over the mass of material and, after Wolfe's death, published it as several posthumous books, including *You Can't Go Home Again* (1940).

Some readers believe that his editors did not necessarily do Wolfe a service in reducing his manuscripts to manageable novel size. They think that Wolfe wanted to create one huge, epic work of fiction. If this is so, Wolfe's effort was much like Whitman's, though a failure. But, as William Faulkner said, Wolfe's greatness is measured by the magnitude of his failure; he dared what no other American novelist had attempted.

GATSBY'S PARTY

What so fascinates us about parties? For one thing, parties are charged with possibility. If we go, we may meet new people who may bring a welcome change to our lives—a new job, a new love, or simply a new experience of some kind. Parties are also hazardous. We may say the wrong thing, wear the wrong clothes, and reveal such an unattractive side of ourselves that we will never be asked again.

At one time in his life, Scott Fitzgerald cared very much about parties. Here in the third chapter of his novel *The Great Gatsby,* he describes one of the most famous parties in literature, surely the ultimate one of the Jazz Age. Nick Carraway, who tells us about it, has rented a modest cottage next door to Jay Gatsby's huge mansion in West Egg, on the north shore of Long Island.

Nick has just taken his first job as a securities salesman in New York. While he is knowledgeable about the world, he's an impressionable young man. And he's impressed with the mysterious Jay Gatsby.

There was music from my neighbor's house through the summer nights. In his blue gardens men and girls came and went like moths among the whisperings and the champagne and the stars. At high tide in the afternoon I watched his guests diving from the tower of his raft, or taking the sun on the hot sand of his beach while his two motorboats slit the waters of the Sound, drawing aquaplanes over cataracts of foam. On weekends his Rolls Royce became an omnibus, bearing parties to and from the city between nine in the morning and long past midnight, while his station wagon scampered like a brisk yellow bug to meet all trains. And on Mondays eight servants, including an extra gardener, toiled all day with mops and scrubbing brushes and hammers and garden shears, repairing the ravages of the night before.

Every Friday five crates of oranges and lemons arrived from a fruiterer in New York—every Monday these same oranges and lemons left his back door in a pyramid of pulpless halves. There was a machine in the kitchen which could extract the juice of two hundred oranges in half an hour if a little button was pressed two hundred times by a butler's thumb.

At least once a fortnight a corps of caterers came down with several hundred feet of canvas and enough colored lights to make a Christmas tree of Gatsby's enormous garden. On buffet tables, garnished with glistening hors d'oeuvre, spiced baked hams crowded against salads of harlequin designs and pastry pigs and turkeys bewitched to a dark gold. In the main hall a bar with a real brass rail was set up, and stocked with gins and liquors and with cordials so long forgotten that most of his female guests were too young to know one from another.

By seven o'clock the orchestra has arrived, no thin five-piece affair, but a whole pitful of oboes and trombones and saxophones and viols and cornets and piccolos, and low and high drums. The last swimmers have come in from the beach now and are dressing upstairs; the cars from New York are parked five deep in the drive, and already the halls and salons and verandas are gaudy with primary colors, and hair shorn in strange new ways, and shawls beyond the dreams of Castile. The bar is in full swing, and floating rounds of cocktails permeate the garden outside, until the air is alive with chatter and laughter, and casual innuendo and introductions forgotten on the spot, and enthusiastic meetings between women who never knew each other's names.

The lights grow brighter as the earth lurches away from the sun, and now the orchestra is playing yellow cocktail music, and the opera of voices pitches a key higher. Laughter is easier minute by minute, spilled with prodigality, tipped out at a cheerful world. The groups change more swiftly, swell with new arrivals, dissolve and form in the same breath; already there are wanderers, confident girls who weave here and there among the stouter and more stable, become for a sharp, joyous moment the center of a group, and then, excited with triumph, glide on through the sea

This picture and the one on page 560 are from
The Great Gatsby starring Robert Redford and Mia
Farrow and directed by Jack Clayton.

Paramount Pictures (1974).

change of faces and voices and color under the
constantly changing light.

Suddenly one of these gypsies, in trembling
opal, seizes a cocktail out of the air, dumps it
down for courage and, moving her hands like
Frisco, dances out alone on the canvas platform.
A momentary hush; the orchestra leader varies
his rhythm obligingly for her, and there is a burst
of chatter as the erroneous news goes around that
she is Gilda Gray's understudy from the *Follies*.
The party has begun.

I believe that on the first night I went to Gatsby's house I was one of the few guests who had
actually been invited. People were not invited—
they went there. They got into automobiles which
bore them out to Long Island, and somehow they
ended up at Gatsby's door. Once there they were
introduced by somebody who knew Gatsby, and
after that they conducted themselves according to
the rules of behavior associated with amusement
parks. Sometimes they came and went without
having met Gatsby at all, came for the party with
a simplicity of heart that was its own ticket of
admission.

I had been actually invited. A chauffeur in a
uniform of robin's-egg blue crossed my lawn early
that Saturday morning with a surprisingly formal
note from his employer: the honor would be entirely Gatsby's, it said, if I would attend his "little
party" that night. He had seen me several times,
and had intended to call on me long before, but a
peculiar combination of circumstances had pre-

vented it—signed Jay Gatsby, in a majestic hand.

Dressed up in white flannels I went over to his lawn a little after seven, and wandered around rather ill at ease among swirls and eddies of people I didn't know—though here and there was a face I had noticed on the commuting train. I was immediately struck by the number of young Englishmen dotted about; all well dressed, all looking a little hungry, and all talking in low, earnest voices to solid and prosperous Americans. I was sure that they were selling something: bonds or insurance or automobiles. They were at least agonizingly aware of the easy money in the vicinity and convinced that it was theirs for a few words in the right key.

As soon as I arrived I made an attempt to find my host but the two or three people of whom I asked his whereabouts stared at me in such an amazed way, and denied so vehemently any knowledge of his movements, that I slunk off in the direction of the cocktail table—the only place in the garden where a single man could linger without looking purposeless and alone.

I was on my way to get roaring drunk from sheer embarrassment when Jordan Baker came out of the house and stood at the head of the marble steps, leaning a little backward and looking with contemptuous interest down into the garden.

Welcome or not, I found it necessary to attach myself to someone before I should begin to address cordial remarks to the passers-by.

"Hello!" I roared, advancing toward her. My voice seemed unnaturally loud across the garden.

"I thought you might be here," she responded absently as I came up. "I remembered you lived next door to——"

She held my hand impersonally, as a promise that she'd take care of me in a minute, and gave ear to two girls in twin yellow dresses, who stopped at the foot of the steps.

"Hello!" they cried together. "Sorry you didn't win."

That was for the golf tournament. She had lost in the finals the week before.

"You don't know who we are," said one of the girls in yellow, "but we met you here about a month ago."

"You've dyed your hair since then," remarked Jordan, and I started, but the girls had moved casually on and her remark was addressed to the premature moon, produced like the supper, no doubt, out of a caterer's basket. With Jordan's slender golden arm resting in mine, we descended the steps and sauntered about the garden. A tray of cocktails floated at us through the twilight, and we sat down at a table with the two girls in yellow and three men, each one introduced to us as Mr. Mumble.

"Do you come to these parties often?" inquired Jordan of the girl beside her.

"The last one was the one I met you at," answered the girl, in an alert confident voice. She turned to her companion: "Wasn't it for you, Lucille?"

It was for Lucille, too.

"I like to come," Lucille said. "I never care what I do, so I always have a good time. When I was here last I tore my gown on a chair, and he asked me my name and address—inside of a week I got a package from Croirier's with a new evening gown in it."

"Did you keep it?" asked Jordan.

"Sure I did. I was going to wear it tonight, but it was too big in the bust and had to be altered. It was gas blue with lavender beads. Two hundred and sixty-five dollars."

"There's something funny about a fellow that'll do a thing like that," said the other girl eagerly. "He doesn't want any trouble with *any*body."

"Who doesn't?" I inquired.

"Gatsby. Somebody told me——"

The two girls and Jordan leaned together confidentially.

"Somebody told me they thought he killed a man once."

A thrill passed over all of us. The three Mr. Mumbles bent forward and listened eagerly.

"I don't think it's so much *that*," argued Lucille skeptically; "it's more that he was a German spy during the war."

One of the men nodded in confirmation.

"I heard that from a man who knew all about him, grew up with him in Germany," he assured us positively.

"Oh, no," said the first girl, "it couldn't be that, because he was in the American army during the war." As our credulity switched back to her she leaned forward with enthusiasm. "You look at him sometimes when he thinks nobody's looking at him. I'll bet he killed a man."

She narrowed her eyes and shivered. Lucille shivered. We all turned and looked around for Gatsby. It was testimony to the romantic speculation he inspired that there were whispers about him from those who had found little that it was necessary to whisper about in this world.

The first supper—there would be another one after midnight—was now being served, and Jordan invited me to join her own party, who were spread around a table on the other side of the garden. There were three married couples and Jordan's escort, a persistent undergraduate given to violent innuendo, and obviously under the impression that sooner or later Jordan was going to yield him up her person to a greater or lesser degree. Instead of rambling, this party had preserved a dignified homogeneity, and assumed to itself the function of representing the staid nobility of the countryside—East Egg condescending to West Egg, and carefully on guard against its spectroscopic gaiety.

"Let's get out," whispered Jordan, after a somehow wasteful and inappropriate half hour; "this is much too polite for me."

We got up, and she explained that we were going to find the host: I had never met him, she said, and it was making me uneasy. The undergraduate nodded in a cynical, melancholy way.

The bar, where we glanced first, was crowded, but Gatsby was not there. She couldn't find him from the top of the steps, and he wasn't on the veranda. On a chance we tried an important-looking door, and walked into a high Gothic library, paneled with carved English oak, and probably transported complete from some ruin overseas.

A stout, middle-aged man, with enormous owl-eyed spectacles, was sitting somewhat drunk on the edge of a great table, staring with unsteady concentration at the shelves of books. As we entered he wheeled excitely around and examined Jordan from head to foot.

"What do you think?" he demanded impetuously.

"About what?"

He waved his hand toward the book shelves.

"About that. As a matter of fact you needn't bother to ascertain. I ascertained. They're real."

"The books?"

He nodded.

"Absolutely real—have pages and everything. I thought they'd be a nice durable cardboard. Matter of fact, they're absolutely real. Pages and— Here! Lemme show you."

Taking our skepticism for granted, he rushed to the bookcases and returned with Volume One of the "Stoddard Lectures."

"See!" he cried triumphantly. "It's a bona fide piece of printed matter. It fooled me. This fella's a regular Belasco. It's a triumph. What thoroughness! What realism! Knew when to stop, too— didn't cut the pages.[1] But what do you want? What do you expect?"

He snatched the book from me and replaced it hastily on its shelf, muttering that if one brick was removed the whole library was liable to collapse.

"Who brought you?" he demanded. "Or did you just come? I was brought. Most people were brought."

Jordan looked at him alertly, cheerfully, without answering.

"I was brought by a woman named Roosevelt," he continued. "Mrs. Claud Roosevelt. Do you know her? I met her somewhere last night. I've been drunk for about a week now, and I thought it might sober me up to sit in a library."

"Has it?"

"A little bit, I think. I can't tell yet. I've only been here an hour. Did I tell you about the books? They're real. They're——"

"You told us."

We shook hands with him gravely and went back outdoors.

There was dancing now on the canvas in the garden; old men pushing young girls backward in eternal graceless circles, superior couples holding each other tortuously, fashionably, and keeping in the corners—and a great number of single girls dancing individualistically or relieving the orchestra for a moment of the burden of the banjo or the traps. By midnight the hilarity had increased. A celebrated tenor had sung in Italian, and a notorious contralto had sung in jazz, and between the numbers people were doing "stunts" all over the garden, while happy, vacuous bursts of laughter rose toward the summer sky. A pair of stage twins, who turned out to be the girls in yellow, did a baby act in costume, and champagne was served in glasses bigger than finger bowls. The moon had risen higher, and floating in the Sound was a triangle of silver scales, trembling a little to the stiff, tinny drip of the banjoes on the lawn.

I was still with Jordan Baker. We were sitting at a table with a man of about my age and a rowdy little girl, who gave way upon the slightest provocation to uncontrollable laughter. I was enjoying

---

1. In bookmaking, several pages are printed on large sheets of paper that are later folded and bound as a book. In days past, the first reader would have to cut the pages.

myself now. I had taken two finger bowls of champagne, and the scene had changed before my eyes into something significant, elemental, and profound.

At a lull in the entertainment the man looked at me and smiled.

"Your face is familiar," he said, politely. "Weren't you in the Third Division during the war?"

"Why, yes, I was in the Ninth Machine-Gun Battalion."

"I was in the Seventh Infantry until June nineteen-eighteen. I knew I'd seen you somewhere before."

We talked for a moment about some wet, gray little villages in France. Evidently he lived in this vicinity, for he told me that he had just bought a hydroplane, and was going to try it out in the morning.

"Want to go with me, old sport? Just near the shore along the Sound."

"What time?"

"Any time that suits you best."

It was on the tip of my tongue to ask his name when Jordan looked around and smiled.

"Having a gay time now?" she inquired.

"Much better." I turned again to my new acquaintance. "This is an unusual party for me. I haven't even seen the host. I live over there—" I waved my hand at the invisible hedge in the distance, "and this man Gatsby sent over his chauffeur with an invitation."

For a moment he looked at me as if he failed to understand.

"I'm Gatsby," he said suddenly.

"What!" I exclaimed. "Oh, I beg your pardon."

"I thought you knew, old sport. I'm afraid I'm not a very good host."

He smiled understandingly—much more than understandingly. It was one of those rare smiles with a quality of eternal reassurance in it, that you may come across four or five times in life. It faced—or seemed to face—the whole external world for an instant, and then concentrated on *you* with an irresistible prejudice in your favor. It understood you just as far as you wanted to be understood, believed in you as you would like to

believe in yourself, and assured you that it had precisely the impression of you that, at your best, you hoped to convey. Precisely at that point it vanished—and I was looking at an elegant young roughneck, a year or two over thirty, whose elaborate formality of speech just missed being absurd. Some time before he introduced himself I'd got a strong impression that he was picking his words with care.

Almost at the moment when Mr. Gatsby identified himself, a butler hurried toward him with the information that Chicago was calling him on the wire. He excused himself with a small bow that included each of us in turn.

"If you want anything just ask for it, old sport," he urged me. "Excuse me. I will rejoin you later."

When he was gone I turned immediately to Jordan—constrained to assure her of my surprise. I had expected that Mr. Gatsby would be a florid and corpulent person in his middle years.

"Who is he?" I demanded. "Do you know?"

"He's just a man named Gatsby."

"Where is he from, I mean? And what does he do?"

"Now *you're* started on the subject," she answered with a wan smile. "Well, he told me once he was an Oxford man."

A dim background started to take shape behind him, but at her next remark it faded away.

"However, I don't believe it."

"Why not?"

"I don't know," she insisted, "I just don't think he went there."

Something in her tone reminded me of the other girl's "I think he killed a man," and had the effect of stimulating my curiosity. I would have accepted without question the information that Gatsby sprang from the swamps of Louisiana or from the lower East Side of New York. That was comprehensible. But young men didn't—at least in my provincial inexperience I believed they didn't—drift coolly out of nowhere and buy a palace on Long Island Sound.

"Anyhow, he gives large parties," said Jordan, changing the subject with an urban distaste for the concrete. "And I like large parties. They're so intimate. At small parties there isn't any privacy."

There was the boom of a bass drum, and the voice of the orchestra leader rang out suddenly above the echolalia of the garden.

"Ladies and gentlemen," he cried. "At the request of Mr. Gatsby we are going to play for you

The Rocky Mountain Emigrants Crossing the Plains (1866). Lithograph by Currier and Ives.

struck a dirge at the burials on the great plains. Jody sat quietly watching Grandfather. The stern blue eyes were detached. He looked as though he were not very interested in the story himself.

When it was finished, when the pause had been politely respected as the frontier of the story, Billy Buck stood up and stretched and hitched his trousers. "I guess I'll turn in," he said. Then he faced Grandfather. "I've got an old powder horn and a cap and ball pistol down to the bunkhouse. Did I ever show them to you?"

Grandfather nodded slowly. "Yes, I think you did, Billy. Reminds me of a pistol I had when I was leading the people across." Billy stood politely until the little story was done, and then he said, "Good night," and went out of the house.

Carl Tiflin tried to turn the conversation then. "How's the country between here and Monterey? I've heard it's pretty dry."

"It is dry," said Grandfather. "There's not a drop of water in the Laguna Seca. But it's a long pull from '87. The whole country was powder then, and in '61 I believe all the coyotes starved to death. We had fifteen inches of rain this year."

"Yes, but it all came too early. We could do with some now." Carl's eye fell on Jody. "Hadn't you better be getting to bed?"

Jody stood up obediently. "Can I kill the mice in the old haystack, sir?"

"Mice? Oh! Sure, kill them all off. Billy said there isn't any good hay left."

Jody exchanged a secret and satisfying look with Grandfather. "I'll kill every one tomorrow," he promised.

Jody lay in his bed and thought of the impossible world of Indians and buffaloes, a world that had ceased to be forever. He wished he could have been living in the heroic time, but he knew he was not of heroic timber. No one living now, save possibly Billy Buck, was worthy to do the things that had been done. A race of giants had lived then, fearless men, men of a staunchness unknown in this day. Jody thought of the wide plains and of the wagons moving across like centipedes. He thought of Grandfather on a huge white horse, marshaling the people. Across his mind marched the great phantoms, and they marched off the earth and they were gone.

He came back to the ranch for a moment, then. He heard the dull rushing sound that space and silence make. He heard one of the dogs, out in the doghouse, scratching a flea and bumping his elbow against the floor with every stroke. Then the wind arose again and the black cypress groaned and Jody went to sleep.

He was up half an hour before the triangle sounded for breakfast. His mother was rattling the stove to make the flames roar when Jody went through the kitchen. "You're up early," she said. "Where are you going?"

"Out to get a good stick. We're going to kill the mice today."

"Who is 'we'?"

"Why, Grandfather and I."

"So you've got him in it. You always like to have someone in with you in case there's blame to share."

"I'll be right back," said Jody. "I just want to have a good stick ready for after breakfast."

He closed the screen door after him and went out into the cool blue morning. The birds were noisy in the dawn and the ranch cats came down from the hill like blunt snakes. They had been hunting gophers in the dark, and although the four cats were full of gopher meat, they sat in a semi-circle at the back door and mewed piteously for milk. Doubletree Mutt and Smasher moved sniffing along the edge of the brush, performing the duty with rigid ceremony, but when Jody whistled, their heads jerked up and their tails waved. They plunged down to him, wriggling their skins and yawning. Jody patted their heads seriously, and moved on to the weathered scrap pile. He selected an old broom handle and a short piece of inch-square scrap wood. From his pocket he took a shoelace and tied the ends of the sticks loosely together to make a flail. He whistled his new weapon through the air and struck the ground experimentally, while the dogs leaped aside and whined with apprehension.

Jody turned and started down past the house toward the old haystack ground to look over the field of slaughter, but Billy Buck, sitting patiently on the back steps, called to him, "You better come back. It's only a couple of minutes till breakfast."

Jody changed his course and moved toward the house. He leaned his flail against the steps. "That's to drive the mice out," he said. "I'll bet they're fat. I'll bet they don't know what's going to happen to them today."

"No, nor you either," Billy remarked philosophically, "nor me, nor anyone."

Jody was staggered by this thought. He knew it was true. His imagination twitched away from the mouse hunt. Then his mother came out on the back porch and struck the triangle, and all thoughts fell in a heap.

Grandfather hadn't appeared at the table when they sat down. Billy nodded at his empty chair. "He's all right? He isn't sick?"

"He takes a long time to dress," said Mrs. Tiflin. "He combs his whiskers and rubs up his shoes and brushes his clothes."

Carl scattered sugar on his mush. "A man that's led a wagon train across the plains has got to be pretty careful how he dresses."

Mrs. Tiflin turned on him. "Don't do that, Carl! Please don't!" There was more of threat than of request in her tone. And the threat irritated Carl.

"Well, how many times do I have to listen to the story of the iron plates, and the thirty-five horses? That time's done. Why can't he forget it, now it's done?" He grew angrier while he talked, and his voice rose. "Why does he have to tell them over and over? He came across the plains. All right! Now it's finished. Nobody wants to hear about it over and over."

The door into the kitchen closed softly. The four at the table sat frozen. Carl laid his mush spoon on the table and touched his chin with his fingers.

Then the kitchen door opened and Grandfather walked in. His mouth smiled tightly, and his eyes were squinted. "Good morning," he said, and he sat down and looked at his mush dish.

Carl could not leave it there. "Did—did you hear what I said?"

Grandfather jerked a little nod.

"I don't know what got into me, sir. I didn't mean it. I was just being funny."

Jody glanced in shame at his mother, and he saw that she was looking at Carl, and that she wasn't breathing. It was an awful thing that he was doing. He was tearing himself to pieces to talk like that. It was a terrible thing to him to retract a word, but to retract it in shame was infinitely worse.

Grandfather looked sidewise. "I'm trying to get right side up," he said gently. "I'm not being mad. I don't mind what you said, but it might be true, and I would mind that."

"It isn't true," said Carl. "I'm not feeling well this morning. I'm sorry I said it."

"Don't be sorry, Carl. An old man doesn't see things sometimes. Maybe you're right. The crossing Is finished. Maybe it should be forgotten, now it's done."

Carl got up from the table. "I've had enough to eat. I'm going to work. Take your time, Billy!" He walked quickly out of the dining room. Billy gulped the rest of his food and followed soon after. But Jody could not leave his chair.

"Won't you tell any more stories?" Jody asked.

"Why, sure I'll tell them, but only when—I'm sure people want to hear them."

"I like to hear them, sir."

"Oh! Of course you do, but you're a little boy. It was a job for men, but only little boys like to hear about it."

Jody got up from his place. "I'll wait outside for you, sir. I've got a good stick for those mice."

He waited by the gate until the old man came out on the porch. "Let's go down and kill the mice now," Jody called.

"I think I'll just sit in the sun, Jody. You go kill the mice."

"You can use my stick if you like."

"No, I'll just sit here a while."

Jody turned disconsolately away, and walked down toward the old haystack. He tried to whip up his enthusiasm with thoughts of the fat juicy mice. He beat the ground with his flail. The dogs coaxed and whined about him, but he could not go. Back at the house he could see Grandfather sitting on the porch, looking small and thin and black.

Jody gave up and went to sit on the steps at the old man's feet.

"Back already? Did you kill the mice?"

"No, sir. I'll kill them some other day."

The morning flies buzzed close to the ground and the ants dashed about in front of the steps. The heavy smell of sage slipped down the hill. The porch boards grew warm in the sunshine.

Jody hardly knew when Grandfather started to talk. "I shouldn't stay here, feeling the way I do." He examined his strong old hands. "I feel as though the crossing wasn't worth doing." His eyes moved up the sidehill and stopped on a motionless hawk perched on a dead limb. "I tell those old stories, but they're not what I want to tell. I only know how I want people to feel when I tell them."

"It wasn't Indians that were important, nor adventures, nor even getting out here. It was a whole bunch of people made into one big crawling beast. And I was the head. It was westering and westering. Every man wanted something for himself, but the big beast that was all of them wanted only westering. I was the leader, but if I hadn't been there, someone else would have been the head. The thing had to have a head.

"Under the little bushes the shadows were black at white noonday. When we saw the mountains at last, we cried—all of us. But it wasn't getting here that mattered, it was movement and westering.

"We carried life out here and set it down the way those ants carry eggs. And I was the leader. The westering was as big as God, and the slow steps that made the movement piled up and piled up until the continent was crossed.

"Then we came down to the sea, and it was done." He stopped and wiped his eyes until the rims were red. "That's what I should be telling instead of stories."

When Jody spoke, Grandfather started and looked down at him. "Maybe I could lead the people some day," Jody said.

The old man smiled. "There's no place to go. There's the ocean to stop you. There's a line of old men along the shore hating the ocean because it stopped them."

"In boats I might, sir."

"No place to go, Jody. Every place is taken. But that's not the worst—no, not the worst. Westering has died out of the people. Westering isn't a hunger anymore. It's all done. Your father is right. It is finished." He laced his fingers on his knee and looked at them.

Jody felt very said. "If you'd like a glass of lemonade I could make it for you."

Grandfather was about to refuse, and then he saw Jody's face. "That would be nice," he said. "Yes, it would be nice to drink a lemonade."

Jody ran into the kitchen where his mother was wiping the last of the breakfast dishes. "Can I have a lemon to make a lemonade for Grandfather?"

His mother mimicked—"And another lemon to make a lemonade for you."

"No, ma'am. I don't want one."

"Jody! You're sick!" Then she stopped suddenly. "Take a lemon out of the cooler," she said softly. "Here, I'll reach the squeezer down to you."

Responding to the Story

Analyzing the Story

Identifying Facts

1. Explain why Jody looks forward to his grandfather's visit. In contrast, how do his father and mother feel?
2. According to Mrs. Tiflin, why does her father still talk about leading the wagon train west?
3. What is the subject of Grandfather's stories? In what way was he the "leader of the people"?
4. Steinbeck uses an old fictional device when he has Grandfather overhear something that he was not intended to hear. How does Carl insult the old man, and how does this exchange between the two older men affect Jody?

Interpreting Meanings

5. What seems to have been the true significance of "the crossing" for Jody's grandfather?
6. Carl Tiflin is strongly intolerant of his father-in-law's oft-told stories. Do you think it is just boredom that provokes Carl's anger? Or could he be taking the stories as some reflection on his own life? What might that be?
7. Jody is the one character who can't get enough of his grandfather's old stories. Why does he have the appetite for them?
8. Given what he says and does and given the way other characters respond to him, how would you **characterize** Billy Buck? What do their actions with the moth (page 583) reveal about the characters of Billy and Carl?
9. How does Jody in the early part of the story show a streak of cruelty, perhaps like his father's? What is the significance of his decision to give up the mice hunt?
10. The story is full of **ironies**. How does Steinbeck ironically characterize the modern age by the use of the mice hunt?
11. There are several **conflicts** in "The Leader of the People,"—between Carl Tiflin and his wife, between Jody and his father, and between Jody's father and his grandfather. Describe the source of each conflict. Which interests you the most? Would you say this story is more about family relationships, or more about the changing attitudes of each new generation?
12. What would you say is the **theme** of this story? Do you believe, as Jody's grandfather does, that there are no longer any frontiers for young Americans? If you disagree, where would you look for modern frontiers?

Writing About the Story

A Creative Response

1. **Using Another Point of View.** What has Jody learned from his experience with Grandfather and his father? In a paragraph, write out Jody's thoughts as he looks back on this day ten years later. Write in the first person, using Jody's own voice.

A Critical Response

2. **Comparing and Contrasting Characters.** In an essay, compare and contrast the characters of Grandfather and Carl Tiflin. Consider what you are told about how the characters look, what they say, how they behave, and how other people feel about them. In your essay, use three adjectives to characterize each man.
3. **Comparing Themes.** In an essay, explain how at least two of the stories you have read in this unit touch on the theme of lost opportunities for heroism.

Analyzing Language and Style

Figures of Speech

Scholars have defined three hundred or more figures of speech, but most people are familiar with five types: (1) the **simile,** in which two dissimilar things are compared with the use of specific comparison words (such as *like, as, resembles*); (2) the **metaphor,** in which two dissimilar things are identified without the use of the specific comparison words; (3) **personification,** a type of metaphor in which something inanimate is described as if it is human or alive; (4) **oxymoron,** a combination of two words that seem to contradict each other (wise fool, death in life, sweet sorrow); and (5) **hyperbole,** in which exaggeration is used for special effect.

Following are some figures of speech from "The Leader of the People." See if you can identify the type of figures of speech being used; then paraphrase the figure of speech in your own words.

1. "lean March sunshine" (page 580)
2. "entangled him in her soft tone" (page 581)
3. "wind sang on the hilltops" (page 581)
4. "blue eyes were sternly merry" (page 581)
5. "a granite dignity" (page 582)
6. "how his insides were collapsed and empty" (page 583)
7. "wagons moving across like centipedes" (page 585)
8. "a whole bunch of people made into one big crawling beast" (page 587)

THE MIGRANT WAY TO THE WEST

This episode is Chapter 17 from *The Grapes of Wrath*. Here we see how Steinbeck creates sympathy for these depression-broken people. Watch how he reveals their feelings for the farms they have lost, and their mixture of hope and anxiety about their future in the promised land of California. As you read, notice how Steinbeck's language gives the journey an epic quality.

Migrants' cars on their way west.

The cars of the migrant people crawled out of the side roads onto the great cross-country highway, and they took the migrant way to the West. In the daylight they scuttled like bugs to the westward; and as the dark caught them, they clustered like bugs near to shelter and to water. And because they were lonely and perplexed, because they had all come from a place of sadness and worry and defeat, and because they were all going to a new mysterious place, they huddled together; they talked together; they shared their lives, their food, and the things they hoped for in the new country. Thus it might be that one family camped near a spring, and another camped for the spring and for company, and a third because two families had pioneered the place and found it good. And when the sun went down, perhaps twenty families and twenty cars were there.

In the evening a strange thing happened: the twenty families became one family, the children were the children of all. The loss of home became one loss, and the golden time in the West was one dream. And it might be that a sick child threw despair into the hearts of twenty families, of a hundred people; that a birth there in a tent kept a hundred people quiet and awestruck through the night and filled a hundred people with the birth-joy in the morning. A family which the night before had been lost and fearful might search its goods to find a present for a new baby. In the evening, sitting about the fires, the twenty were one. They grew to be units of the camps, units of the evenings and the nights. A guitar unwrapped

Drought refugees from Texas arrive at Exeter, California, 1936. Photograph by Dorothea Lange.

from a blanket and tuned—and the songs, which were all of the people, were sung in the nights. Men sang the words, and women hummed the tunes.

Every night a world created, complete with furniture—friends made and enemies established; a world complete with braggarts and with cowards, with quiet men, with humble men, with kindly men. Every night relationships that make a world, established; and every morning the world torn down like a circus.

At first the families were timid in the building and tumbling worlds, but gradually the technique of building worlds became their technique. Then leaders emerged, then laws were made, then codes came into being. And as the worlds moved westward they were more complete and better furnished, for their builders were more experienced in building them.

The families learned what rights must be observed—the right of privacy in the tent; the right to keep the past black hidden in the heart; the right to talk and to listen; the right to refuse help or to accept, to offer help or to decline it; the right of son to court and daughter to be courted; the right of the hungry to be fed; the rights of the pregnant and the sick to transcend all other rights.

And the families learned, although no one told them, what rights are monstrous and must be destroyed: the right to intrude upon privacy, the right to be noisy while the camp slept, the right of seduction or rape, the right of adultery and theft and murder. These rights were crushed, because the little worlds could not exist for even a night with such rights alive.

And as the worlds moved westward, rules became laws, although no one told the families. It is unlawful to foul near the camp; it is unlawful in any way to foul the drinking water; it is unlawful to eat good rich food near one who is hungry, unless he is asked to share.

And with the laws, the punishments—and there were only two—a quick and murderous fight or ostracism;[1] and ostracism was the worst. For, if one broke the laws his name and face went with him, and he had no place in any world, no matter where created.

In the worlds, social conduct became fixed and rigid, so that a man must say "Good morning" when asked for it, so that a man might have a willing girl if he stayed with her, if he fathered her children and protected them. But a man might not have one girl one night and another the next, for this would endanger the worlds.

The families moved westward, and the technique of building the worlds improved so that the people could be safe in their worlds; and the form was so fixed that a family acting in the rules knew it was safe in the rules.

There grew up government in the worlds, with leaders, with elders. A man who was wise found that his wisdom was needed in every camp; a man who was a fool could not change his folly with his world. And a kind of insurance developed in these nights. A man with food fed a hungry man, and thus insured himself against hunger. And when a baby died a pile of silver coins grew at the door flap, for a baby must be well buried, since it has had nothing else of life. An old man may be left in a potter's field,[2] but not a baby.

A certain physical pattern is needed for the building of a world—water, a river bank, a stream, a spring, or even a faucet unguarded. And there is needed enough flat land to pitch the tents, a little brush or wood to build the fires. If there is a garbage dump not too far off, all the better; for there can be found equipment—stove tops, a curved fender to shelter the fire, and cans to cook in and to eat from.

And the worlds were built in the evening. The people, moving in from the highways, made them with their tents and their hearts and their brains.

In the morning the tents came down, the canvas was folded, the tent poles tied along the running board, the beds put in place on the cars, the pots in their places. And as the families moved westward, the technique of building up a home in the evening and tearing it down with the morning light became fixed; so that the folded tent was packed in one place, the cooking pots counted in their box. And as the cars moved westward, each member of the family grew into his proper place, grew into his duties; so that each member, old and young, had his place in the car; so that in the weary, hot evenings, when the cars pulled into the camping places, each member had his duty and went to it without instruction: children to gather wood, to carry water; men to pitch the tents and

1. **ostracism:** social exclusion; banishment.

2. **potter's field:** a public burial place for people who cannot afford to pay funeral expenses.

John Steinbeck **591**

bring down the beds; women to cook the supper and to watch while the family fed. And this was done without command. The families, which had been units of which the boundaries were a house at night, a farm by day, changed their boundaries. In the long hot light, they were silent in the cars moving slowly westward; but at night they integrated with any group they found.

Thus they changed their social life—changed as in the whole universe only man can change. They were not farm men any more, but migrant men. And the thought, the planning, the long staring silence that had gone out to the fields, went now to the roads, to the distance, to the West. That man whose mind had been bound with acres lived with narrow concrete miles. And his thought and his worry were not any more with rainfall, with wind and dust, with the thrust of the crops. Eyes watched the tires, ears listened to the clattering motors, and minds struggled with oil, with gasoline, with the thinning rubber between air and road. Then a broken gear was tragedy. Then water in the evening was the yearning, and food over the fire. Then health to go on was the need and strength to go on, and spirit to go on. The wills thrust westward ahead of them, and fears that had once apprehended drought or flood now lingered with anything that might stop the westward crawling. . . .

Responding to the Chapter

Analyzing the Chapter

Identifying Facts

1. What economic conditions caused the migrants to move West?
2. We learn that the migrants developed a new social order and new rules of behavior on the road. What are some of these?

Interpreting Meanings

3. What specific words and comparisons in the first paragraph reveal that the journey of the migrants is not presented in romantic, heroic terms? Yet, in what ways does Steinbeck present the migrants as admirable?
4. Explain what Steinbeck means when he says these people changed "as only in the whole universe man can change" (page 592). Is this a positive or negative remark about people?
5. Do you think from this extract that Steinbeck saw people as essentially good and moral, or as essentially evil and corrupt? Support your answer with references to the chapter.
6. What are the differences and likenesses between the migrants' journey west and the westering described by Grandfather in "The Leader of the People" (page 579)?
7. What groups can you cite that separate and come together as the migrants do in this account? Explain the tie that keeps these groups "together."
8. On the basis of this chapter, explain why you believe *The Grapes of Wrath* was either an attack on, or an affirmation of, traditional American values.

Vernon Evans, a migrant to Oregon from South Dakota (1936).

The Library of Congress, Washington, D.C.

Writing About the Chapter

A Critical Response

Comparing Imagery. Grandfather in "The Leader of the People" says that "It wasn't the Indians that were important, nor adventures, nor even getting out here. It was a whole bunch of people made into one crawling beast." In an essay, explain how this chapter uses similar images to describe the migrants. What do you think this might reveal about how Steinbeck feels about the power of the individual versus the power of the group?

Primary Sources
Nobel Prize Acceptance Speech, 1962

"I thank the Swedish Academy for finding my work worthy of this highest honor. In my heart there may be doubt that I deserve the Nobel Award over other men of letters whom I hold in respect and reverence—but there is no question of my pleasure and pride in having it for myself.

"It is customary for the recipient of this award to offer scholarly or personal comment on the nature and the direction of literature. However, I think it would be well at this particular time to consider the high duties and the responsibilities of the makers of literature.

"Such is the prestige of the Nobel Award and of this place where I stand that I am impelled, not to squeak like a grateful and apologetic mouse, but to roar like a lion out of pride in my profession and in the great and good men who have practiced it through the ages.

"Literature was not promulgated by a pale and emasculated critical priesthood singing their litanies in empty churches—nor is it a game for the cloistered elect, the tinhorn mendicants of low-calorie despair.

"Literature is as old as speech. It grew out of human need for it and it has not changed except to become more needed. The skalds, the bards, the writers are not separate and exclusive. From the beginning, their functions, their duties, their responsibilities have been decreed by our species.

"Humanity has been passing through a gray and desolate time of confusion. My great predecessor, William Faulkner, speaking here, referred to it as a tragedy of universal physical fear, so long sustained that there were no longer problems of the spirit, so that only the human heart in conflict with itself seemed worth writing about. Faulkner, more than most men, was aware of human strength as well as of human weakness. He knew that the understanding and the resolution of fear are a large part of the writer's reason for being.

"This is not new. The ancient commission of the writer has not changed. He is charged with exposing our many grievous faults and failures, with dredging up to the light our dark and dangerous dreams for the purpose of improvement.

"Furthermore, the writer is delegated to declare and to celebrate man's proven capacity for greatness of heart and spirit—for gallantry in defeat, for courage, compassion and love. In the endless war against weakness and despair, these are the bright rally flags of hope and emulation. I hold that a writer who does not passionately believe in the perfectability of man has no dedication nor any membership in literature.

"The present universal fear has been the result of a forward surge in our knowledge and manipulation of certain dangerous factors in the physical world. It is true that other phases of understanding have not yet caught up with this great step, but there is no reason to presume that they cannot or will not draw abreast. Indeed, it is a part of the writer's responsibility to make sure that they do. With humanity's long, proud history of standing firm against all of its natural enemies, sometimes in the face of almost certain defeat and extinction, we would be cowardly and stupid to leave the field on the eve of our greatest potential victory.

"Understandably, I have been reading the life of Alfred Nobel; a solitary man, the books say, a thoughtful man. He perfected the release of explosive forces capable of creative good or of destructive evil, but lacking choice, ungoverned by conscience or judgment.

"Nobel saw some of the cruel and bloody misuses of his inventions. He may even have foreseen the end result of his probing—access to ultimate violence, to final destruction. Some say that he became cynical, but I do not believe this. I think he strove to invent a control—a safety valve. I think he found it finally only in the human mind and the human spirit.

"To me, his thinking is clearly indicated in the categories of these awards. They are offered for increased and continuing knowledge of man and of his world—for *understanding* and *communication,* which are the functions of literature. And they are offered for demonstrations of the capacity for peace—the culmination of all the others.

"Less than fifty years after his death, the door of nature was unlocked and we were offered the dreadful burden of choice. We have usurped many of the powers we once ascribed to God. Fearful and unprepared, we have assumed lordship over the life and death of the whole world of all living things. The danger and the glory and the choice rest finally in man. The test of his perfectibility is at hand.

"Having taken God-like power, we must seek in ourselves for the responsibility and the wisdom we once prayed some deity might have. Man himself has become our greatest hazard and our only hope. So that today, Saint John the Apostle may well be paraphrased: In the end is the *word,* and the word is *man,* and the word is *with* man."

—John Steinbeck

James Thurber
(1894–1961)

James Thurber is generally acknowledged to be the foremost American humorist of the twentieth century. He was a supremely gifted cartoonist and a writer of essays, sketches, and stories. For a 1956 collection of fables, he made fun of the puffery that characterizes biographies of literary figures and presented this self-portrait:

> James Thurber was born in Columbus, Ohio, where so many awful things happened to him, on 8 December 1894. He was unable to keep anything on his stomach until he was seven years old, but grew to six feet one and a half inches tall and to weigh a hundred and fifty-four pounds fully dressed for winter. He began to write when he was ten years old and to draw when he was fourteen. Quick to arouse, he is very hard to quiet and people often just go away. At Buckeye Lake, Ohio, in 1923, he won a canary bird throwing baseballs at dolls. He has never been taken at fan-tan.[1] He uses the Thurber overbidding convention and even the most skilled partners have no chance with him. He never listens when anybody else is talking, preferring to keep his mind a blank until they get through, so he can talk. His favorite book is *The Great Gatsby*. His favorite author is Henry James. He wears excellent clothes very badly and can never find his hat. He is Sagittarius with the moon in Aries and gets along fine with persons born between the 20th and the 24th of August.

Thurber did grow up in Columbus, Ohio, and he graduated from Ohio State University in 1919. He then worked as a reporter for the *Columbus Dispatch* and the *Chicago Tribune* for a number of years, before coming to New York City. In 1927, he went to work for *The New Yorker* magazine and remained a member of its staff for the rest of his life. In addition to many collections of stories, essays, and children's books, Thurber collaborated on a successful Broadway play called *The Male Animal* (1940).

His humor often turned on the chaos of contemporary American life. Thurber focused on the "little man," who cannot quite assert himself in a confusing world where women seem surer of their way. Thus, Walter Mitty, the anti-hero of Thurber's most famous story, seeks release in fantasy from a wife who overwhelms him.

While Thurber claimed to welcome the feminist movement, hoping it would seize power and prevent men from blowing the world to bits, he viewed women with a certain ambivalence—as intimidating to their mates, and as mother-figures rather than as partners. (Thurber's attitude toward women is comically revealed in his cartoons that illustrate Mitty's story.)

Thurber defined humor as "a kind of of emotional chaos told about calmly and quietly in retrospect." But humor is not subject to rational explanation. Perhaps this was in the mind of Thurber's friend, the writer Mark Van Doren, when he said of Thurber: "He was an extraordinary man . . . with so many quick changes: gentle and fierce, fascinating and boring, sophisticated and boorish, kind and cruel, broadminded and parochial. You can't explain Thurber."

---

1. **fan-tan:** a card game.

THE SECRET LIFE OF WALTER MITTY

The name Walter Mitty has entered our language as the epitome of the "little guy" who is dominated by an assertive wife. You might recognize both Mitty and the formidable Mrs. Mitty—they are character types that form the basis of many American situation comedies. Mitty is based on a stereotype of the henpecked husband, but Mitty himself is an original. Read the first paragraph and stop. Based on this paragraph, what does it seem as if this story is going to be about?

We're going through!" The Commander's voice was like thin ice breaking. He wore his full-dress uniform, with the heavily braided white cap pulled down rakishly over one cold gray eye. "We can't make it, sir. It's spoiling for a hurricane, if you ask me." "I'm not asking you, Lieutenant Berg," said the Commander. "Throw on the power lights! Rev her up to 8,500! We're going through!" The pounding of the cylinders increased: ta-pocketa-pocketa-pocketa-*pocketa-pocketa*. The commander stared at the ice forming on the pilot window. He walked over and twisted a row of complicated dials. "Switch on No. 8 auxiliary!" he shouted. "Switch on No. 8 auxiliary!" repeated Lieutenant Berg. "Full strength in No. 3 turret!" shouted the Commander. "Full strength in No. 3 turret!" The crew, bending to their various tasks in the huge, hurtling eight-engined Navy hydroplane, looked at each other and grinned. "The Old Man'll get us through," they said to one another. "The Old Man ain't afraid of Hell!" . . .

"Not so fast! You're driving too fast!" said Mrs. Mitty. "What are you driving so fast for?"

"Hmm?" said Walter Mitty. He looked at his wife, in the seat beside him, with shocked astonishment. She seemed grossly unfamiliar, like a strange woman who had yelled at him in a crowd. "You were up to fifty-five," she said. "You know I don't like to go more than forty. You were up to fifty-five." Walter Mitty drove on toward Waterbury in silence, the roaring of the SN202 through the worst storm in twenty years of Navy flying fading in the remote, intimate airways of his mind. "You're tensed up again," said Mrs. Mitty. "It's one of your days. I wish you'd let Dr. Renshaw look you over."

Walter Mitty stopped the car in front of the building where his wife went to have her hair done. "Remember to get those overshoes while I'm having my hair done," she said. "I don't need overshoes," said Mitty. She put her mirror back into her bag. "We've been all through that," she said, getting out of the car. "You're not a young man any longer." He raced the engine a little. "Why don't you wear your gloves? Have you lost your gloves?" Walter Mitty reached in a pocket and brought out the gloves. He put them on, but after she had turned and gone into the building and he had driven on to a red light, he took them off again. "Pick it up, brother!" snapped a cop as the light changed, and Mitty hastily pulled on his gloves and lurched ahead. He drove around the streets aimlessly for a time, and then he drove past the hospital on his way to the parking lot.

. . . "It's the millionaire banker, Wellington McMillan," said the pretty nurse. "Yes?" said Walter Mitty, removing his gloves slowly. "Who has the case?" "Dr. Renshaw and Dr. Benbow, but there are two specialists here, Dr. Remington from New York and Mr. Pritchard-Mitford from London. He flew over." A door opened down a long, cool corridor and Dr. Renshaw came out. He looked distraught and haggard. "Hello, Mitty," he said. "We're having the devil's own time with McMillan, the millionaire banker and close personal friend of Roosevelt. Obstreosis of the ductal tract. Tertiary. Wish you'd take a look at him." "Glad to," said Mitty.

In the operating room there were whispered introductions: "Dr. Remington, Dr. Mitty. Mr. Pritchard-Mitford, Dr. Mitty." "I've read your book on streptothricosis," said Pritchard-Mitford, shaking hands. "A brilliant performance, sir."

"Thank you," said Walter Mitty. "Didn't know you were in the States, Mitty," grumbled Remington. "Coals to Newcastle,[1] bringing Mitford and me up here for a tertiary." "You are very kind," said Mitty. A huge, complicated machine, connected to the operating table, with many tubes and wires, began at this moment to go pocketa-pocketa-pocketa. "The new anesthetizer is giving way!" shouted an intern. "There is no one in the East who knows how to fix it!" "Quiet, man!" said Mitty, in a low, cool voice. He sprang to the machine, which was now going pocketa-pocketa-queep-pocketa-queep. He began fingering delicately a row of glistening dials. "Give me a fountain pen!" he snapped. Someone handed him a fountain pen. He pulled a faulty piston out of the machine and inserted the pen in its place. "That will hold for ten minutes," he said. "Get on with the operation." A nurse hurried over and whispered to Renshaw, and Mitty saw the man turn pale. "Coreopsis has set in," said Renshaw nervously. "If you would take over, Mitty?" Mitty looked at him and at the craven figure of Benbow, who drank, and at the grave, uncertain faces of the two great specialists. "If you wish," he said. They slipped a white gown on him; he adjusted a mask and drew on thin gloves; nurses handed him shining . . .

"Back it up, Mac! Look out for that Buick!" Walter Mitty jammed on the brakes. "Wrong lane, Mac," said the parking lot attendant, looking at Mitty closely. "Gee. Yeh," muttered Mitty. He began cautiously to back out of the lane marked "Exit Only." "Leave her sit there," said the attendant. "I'll put her away." Mitty got out of the car. "Hey, better leave the key." "Oh," said Mitty, handing the man the ignition key. The attendant vaulted into the car, backed it up with insolent skill, and put it where it belonged.

They're so damn cocky, thought Walter Mitty, walking along Main Street; they think they know everything. Once he had tried to take his chains off, outside New Milford, and he had got them wound around the axles. A man had had to come out in a wrecking car and unwind them, a young, grinning garageman. Since then Mrs. Mitty always made him drive to a garage to have the chains taken off. The next time, he thought, I'll wear my right arm in a sling; they won't grin at me then.

"House and Woman."

Cartoon by James Thurber from *The Thurber Carnival* (1957).

I'll have my right arm in a sling and they'll see I couldn't possibly take the chains off myself. He kicked at the slush on the sidewalk. "Overshoes," he said to himself, and he began looking for a shoe store.

When he came out into the street again, with the overshoes in a box under his arm, Walter Mitty began to wonder what the other thing was his wife had told him to get. She had told him, twice, before they set out from their house for Waterbury. In a way he hated these weekly trips to town—he was always getting something wrong. Kleenex, he thought, Squibb's, razor blades? No. Toothpaste, toothbrush, bicarbonate, carborundum, initiative and referendum? He gave it up. But she would remember it. "Where's the what's-its-name?" she would ask. "Don't tell me you forgot the what's-its-name." A newsboy went by shouting something about the Waterbury trial.

. . . "Perhaps this will refresh your memory." The District Attorney suddenly thrust a heavy automatic at the quiet figure on the witness stand. "Have you ever seen this before?" Walter Mitty took the gun and examined it expertly. "This is my Webley-Vickers 50.80," he said calmly. An excited buzz ran around the courtroom. The Judge rapped for order. "You are a crack shot with any sort of firearms, I believe?" said the District Attorney, insinuatingly. "Objection!" shouted Mitty's attorney. "We have shown that the defendant could not have fired the shot. We have shown that

---

1. **Goals to Newcastle:** a proverbial expression referring to unnecessary effort. Newcastle, in England, produced coal itself.

he wore his right arm in a sling on the night of the fourteenth of July.'' Walter Mitty raised his hand briefly and the bickering attorneys were stilled. "With any known make of gun," he said evenly, "I could have killed Gregory Fitzhurst at three hundred feet *with my left hand.*" Pandemonium broke loose in the courtroom. A woman's scream rose above the bedlam and suddenly a lovely, dark-haired girl was in Walter Mitty's arms. The District Attorney struck at her savagely. Without rising from his chair, Mitty let the man have it on the point of the chin. "You miserable cur!" . . .

"Puppy biscuit," said Walter Mitty. He stopped walking and the buildings of Waterbury rose up out of the misty courtroom and surrounded him again. A woman who was passing laughed. "He said 'Puppy biscuit,' " she said to her companion. "That man said 'Puppy biscuit' to himself." Walter Mitty hurried on. He went into an A. & P., not the first one he came to but a smaller one farther up the street "I want some biscuit for small, young dogs," he said to the clerk. "Any special brand, sir?" The greatest pistol shot in the world thought a moment. "It says 'Puppies Bark for It' on the box," said Walter Mitty.

His wife would be through at the hairdresser's in fifteen minutes, Mitty saw in looking at his watch, unless they had trouble drying it; sometimes they had trouble drying it. She didn't like to get to the hotel first; she would want him to be there waiting for her as usual. He found a big leather chair in the lobby, facing a window, and he put the overshoes and the puppy biscuit on the floor beside it. He picked up an old copy of *Liberty*

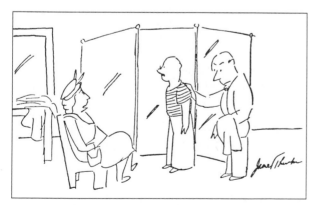

"I don't want him to be comfortable."

Cartoon by James Thurber from *The Thurber Carnival* (1957).

and sank down into the chair. "Can Germany Conquer the World Through the Air?" Walter Mitty looked at the pictures of bombing planes and of ruined streets.

. . . "The cannonading has got the wind up in young Raleigh, sir," said the sergeant. Captain Mitty looked up at him through tousled hair. "Get him to bed," he said wearily. "With the others. I'll fly alone." "But you can't, sir," said the sergeant anxiously. "It takes two men to handle that bomber and the Archies[2] are pounding hell out of the air. Von Richtman's circus[3] is between here and Saulier." "Somebody's got to get that ammunition dump," said Mitty. "I'm going over. Spot of brandy?" He poured a drink for the sergeant and one for himself. War thundered and whined around the dugout and battered at the door. There was a rending of wood and splinters flew through the room. "A bit of a near thing," said Captain Mitty carelessly. "The box barrage is closing in," said the sergeant. "We only live once, Sergeant," said Mitty, with his faint, fleeting smile. "Or do we?" He poured another brandy and tossed it off. "I never see a man could hold his brandy like you, sir," said the sergeant. "Begging your pardon, sir." Captain Mitty stood up and strapped on his huge Webley-Vickers automatic. "It's forty kilometers through hell, sir," said the sergeant. Mitty finished one last brandy. "After all," he said softly, "what isn't?" The pounding of the cannon increased; there was the rat-tat-tatting of machine guns, and from somewhere came the menacing pocketa-pocketa-pocketa of the new flamethrowers. Walter Mitty walked to the door of the dugout humming "Auprès de Ma Blonde."[4] He turned and waved to the sergeant. "Cheerio!" he said. . . .

Something struck his shoulder. "I've been looking all over this hotel for you," said Mrs. Mitty. "Why do you have to hide in this old chair? How did you expect me to find you?" "Things close in," said Walter Mitty vaguely. "What?" Mrs. Mitty said. "Did you get the what's-its-name? The puppy biscuit? What's in that box?" "Overshoes," said Mitty. "Couldn't you have put them on in the store?" "I was thinking," said Walter Mitty. "Does it ever occur to you that I am sometimes thinking?" She looked at him. "I'm

---

2. **Archies:** German antiaircraft gunners.
3. **circus:** a squadron of planes.
4. **"Auprès de Ma Blonde":** a French song whose title means "Near My Blonde."

going to take your temperature when I get you home," she said.

They went out through the revolving doors that made a faintly derisive whistling sound when you pushed them. It was two blocks to the parking lot. At the drugstore on the corner she said, "Wait here for me. I forgot something. I won't be a minute." She was more than a minute. Walter Mitty lighted a cigarette. It began to rain, rain with sleet in it. He stood up against the wall of the drugstore, smoking. . . . He put his shoulders back and his heels together. "To hell with the handkerchief," said Walter Mitty scornfully. He took one last drag on his cigarette and snapped it away. Then, with that faint, fleeting smile playing about his lips, he faced the firing squad; erect and motionless, proud and disdainful, Walter Mitty the Undefeated, inscrutable to the last.

"Well, who made the magic go out? . . ."

Cartoon by James Thurber from *The Thurber Carnival* (1957).

Responding to the Story

Analyzing the Story

Identifying Facts

1. Describe the **setting** of Walter Mitty's everyday life. In contrast, what are the settings of his secret life?
2. What errands is Mitty on in his real life? What deeds does he perform in his secret life?
3. Thurber makes use of a psychological technique known as **free association,** in which words and sounds from real life become associated with elements of Mitty's daydreams. How does each daydream begin, and what sends Mitty into it? What decidedly unheroic events snap Mitty out of his reveries?

Interpreting Meanings

4. What is the central **irony** of Mitty's life? Is this irony humorous, serious, or partly both? Explain.
5. **Parody** is the satirical imitation of someone's speech, manners, or ideas. Where does Thurber use parody in this story? Who or what are the targets of the satire? (Look at the **jargon** bandied about in the daydreams.)
6. Walter Mitty could be seen as one of a line of archetypal American characters that begins with Ben Franklin's "self-made man." What does Mitty's life reveal about the opportunities offered for heroism today? What is your opinion of Thurber's message here?
7. Could Mitty be a disappointed romantic? Explain.

Writing About the Story

A Critical Response

1. **Analyzing Characters.** Walter Mitty and the formidable Mrs. Mitty have by now become stock American character types. In an essay, analyze the characters of Walter and his spouse. In your analysis, tell how the character types of "Mrs. Mitty" and "Walter Mitty" are found in popular movies and TV shows today.
2. **Comparing Stories.** James Thurber has been accused of being "tough" on women, a criticism that has also been leveled against Washington Irving for his portrait of Dame Van Winkle (page 125). In an essay, compare and contrast these two American couples—Rip and his wife, and Walter and Mrs. Mitty. Consider the characters' strengths and weaknesses, the source of their conflicts, the way their conflicts are resolved, the relationships between husband and wife, and the tone of each story.

Primary Sources
The New Yorker's *Farewell*

Thurber's long-time associate on *The New Yorker,* E. B. White, wrote this parting tribute to his friend on November 11, 1961.

"I am one of the lucky ones; I knew him before blindness hit him, before fame hit him, and I tend always to think of him as a young artist in a small office in a big city, with all the world still ahead. It was a fine thing to be young and at work in New York for a new magazine when Thurber was young and at work, and I will always be glad that this happened to me.

"It was fortunate that we got on well; the office we shared was the size of a hall bedroom. There was just room enough for two men, two typewriters, and a stack of copy paper. The copy paper disappeared at a scandalous rate—not because our production was high (although it was) but because Thurber used copy paper as the natural receptacle for discarded sorrows, immediate joys, stale dreams, golden prophecies, and messages of good cheer to the outside world and to fellow workers. His mind was never at rest, and his pencil was connected to his mind by the best conductive tissue I have ever seen in action. The whole world knows what a funny man he was, but you had to sit next to him day after day to understand the extravagance of his clowning, the wildness and subtlety of his thinking, and the intensity of his interest in others and his sympathy for their dilemmas— dilemmas that he instantly enlarged, put in focus, and made immortal, just as he enlarged and made immortal the strange goings-on in the Ohio home of his boyhood. His waking dreams and his sleeping dreams commingled shamelessly and uproariously. Ohio was never far from his thoughts, and when he received a medal from his home state in 1953, he wrote, 'The clocks that strike in my dreams are often the clocks of Columbus.' It is a beautiful sentence and a revealing one.

"He was both a practitioner of humor and a defender of it. The day he died, I came on a letter from him, dictated to a secretary and signed in pencil with his sightless and enormous 'Jim.' 'Every time is a time for humor,' he wrote. 'I write humor the way a surgeon operates, because it is a livelihood, because I have a great urge to do it, because many interesting challenges are

A self-portrait of James Thurber and dog.

set up, and because I have the hope it may do some good.' Once, I remember, he heard someone say that humor is a shield, not a sword, and it made him mad. He wasn't going to have anyone beating his sword into a shield. That 'surgeon,' incidentally, is pure Mitty. During his happiest years, Thurber did not write the way a surgeon operates, he wrote the way a child skips rope, the way a mouse waltzes.

"Although he is best known for 'Walter Mitty' and *The Male Animal,* the book of his I like best is *The Last Flower.* In it you will find his faith in the renewal of life, his feeling for the beauty and fragility of life on earth. Like all good writers, he fashioned his own best obituary notice. Nobody else can add to the record, much as he might like to. And of all the flowers, real and figurative, that will find their way to Thurber's last resting place, the one that will remain fresh and wiltproof is the little flower he himself drew, on the last page of that lovely book."

—E. B. White

Katherine Anne Porter (1890–1980)

Katherine Anne Porter was born in a Texas log cabin in 1890, a distant cousin of the American short-story writer William Sidney Porter (better known as O. Henry). She was raised, mostly by her grandmother, as a member of a sprawling family on close terms with hardship and deprivation. Her schooling was fragmentary. In later life she tended to embroider these plain origins with a certain romantic opulence, as though her past could be revised like a novel-in-progress.

The first of her four marriages took place when she was sixteen. She was consistently impatient with lasting marital relationships, and yet she disliked being alone. Her early years were a struggle to define herself as an individual, as a Southern woman, as the beauty which she was, and as the writer which, so very slowly, she was becoming.

After her Texas youth, Porter traveled widely, living at various times in the West, in New York City's Greenwich Village, in New England, Washington, Mexico, Paris, and Berlin. She supported herself as a newspaper reporter and editor and as a translator of French and Spanish literature.

As a creative writer, she was largely self-taught. She became well-read and she had a natural talent for clear, flowing language. She could tell an effortless story in which a searching intelligence was interwoven with honesty, sound psychology, a flawless memory, and a vivid sense of scene. The grace of her objective style concealed the labor that went into it. Porter worked slowly and painstakingly, and she did not begin publishing until she was over thirty.

She produced her first book, *Flowering Judas,* in 1930. This collection of early stories won her a critical reputation as a stylist. The book grew out of Porter's recollections of her Mexican experience immediately after World War I. *Hacienda* (1934), was also set in Mexico, while *Noon Wine* (1937) presented a powerful tale of violence on a Texas farm.

Much of Porter's work presents Southern women characters caught up in a web of custom and obligation. Her main themes include the bur-den of past evil and the strain with which that evil holds us captive in the present. Miranda, the clearly autobiographical central figure of so many of her stories, is forever trying to separate the fictions of family legend from objective truth. She knows that people do not always tell the truth, and she is skeptical of the romance with which they disguise the realities of poverty and sexuality.

With the publication of her finest story collection, *Pale Horse, Pale Rider* (1939), Porter's growing audience eagerly awaited a promised novel. She began that novel in 1941. It told of the passage of the steamer *Vera* from Mexico to Germany in the summer of 1931, during the early days of Adolf Hitler's rise to power. The passengers are escaping their loneliness and are in search of fantasy, rather than friendship or love. The novel, entitled *Ship of Fools,* is really about the seeds of World War II—a bitter portrait of the Nazi state and the human race's capacity for cruelty. It did not appear until 1962, by which time many of her readers had abandoned hope for it. *Ship of Fools* enjoyed a wide popular success, and it led to the many tributes (including the National Book Award and the Pulitzer Prize) which embellished the final years of Porter's long life.

THE GRAVE

Some of Porter's most brilliant stories are about a young girl named Miranda, who grows up in the South at the turn of the century. Stories about growing up (also called coming-of-age stories) always involve a character who achieves new self-awareness as he or she prepares to take an adult's role in a particular society. Watch for the symbols that make this story of growing up particularly rich and even a bit mysterious.

The grandfather, dead for more than thirty years, had been twice disturbed in his long repose by the constancy and possessiveness of his widow. She removed his bones first to Louisiana and then to Texas as if she had set out to find her own burial place, knowing well she would never return to the places she had left. In Texas she set up a small cemetery in a corner of her first farm, and as the family connection grew, and oddments of relations came over from Kentucky to settle, it contained at last about twenty graves. After the grandmother's death, part of her land was to be sold for the benefit of certain of her children, and the cemetery happened to lie in the part set aside for sale. It was necessary to take up the bodies and bury them again in the family plot in the big new public cemetery, where the grandmother had been buried. At last her husband was to lie beside her for eternity, as she had planned.

The family cemetery had been a pleasant small neglected garden of tangled rose bushes and ragged cedar trees and cypress, the simple flat stones rising out of uncropped sweet-smelling wild grass. The graves were lying open and empty one burning day when Miranda and her brother Paul, who often went together to hunt rabbits and doves, propped their twenty-two Winchester rifles carefully against the rail fence, climbed over and explored among the graves. She was nine years old and he was twelve.

They peered into the pits all shaped alike with such purposeful accuracy, and looking at each other with pleased adventurous eyes, they said in solemn tones: "These were graves!" trying by words to shape a special, suitable emotion in their minds, but they felt nothing except an agreeable thrill of wonder: they were seeing a new sight, doing something they had not done before. In them both there was also a small disappointment at the entire commonplaceness of the actual spectacle. Even if it had once contained a coffin for years upon years, when the coffin was gone a grave was just a hole in the ground. Miranda leaped into the pit that had held her grandfather's bones. Scratching around aimlessly and pleasurably as any young animal, she scooped up a lump of earth and weighed it in her palm. It had a pleasantly sweet, corrupt smell, being mixed with cedar needles and small leaves, and as the crumbs fell apart, she saw a silver dove no larger than a hazel nut, with spread wings and a neat fan-shaped tail. The breast had a deep round hollow in it. Turning it up to the fierce sunlight, she saw that the inside of the hollow was cut in little whorls. She scrambled out, over the pile of loose earth that had fallen back into one end of the grave, calling to Paul that she had found something, he must guess what . . . His head appeared smiling over the rim of another grave. He waved a closed hand at her. "I've got something too!" They ran to compare treasures, making a game of it, so many guesses each, all wrong, and a final showdown with opened palms. Paul had found a thin wide gold ring carved with intricate flowers and leaves. Miranda was smitten at sight of the ring and wished to have it. Paul seemed more impressed by the dove. They made a trade, with some little bickering. After he had got the dove in his hand, Paul said, "Don't you know what this is? This is a screw head for a *coffin!* . . . I'll bet nobody else in the world has one like this!"

Miranda glanced at it without covetousness. She had the gold ring on her thumb; it fitted perfectly. "Maybe we ought to go now," she said, "maybe someone'll see us and tell somebody."

They knew the land had been sold, the cemetery was no longer theirs, and they felt like trespassers. They climbed back over the fence, slung their rifles loosely under their arms—they had been shooting at targets with various kinds of firearms since they were seven years old—and set out to look for the rabbits and doves or whatever small game might happen along. On these expeditions Miranda always followed at Paul's heels along the path, obeying instructions about handling her gun when going through fences; learning how to stand it up properly so it would not slip and fire unexpectedly; how to wait her time for a shot and not just bang away in the air without looking, spoiling shots for Paul, who really could hit things if given a chance. Now and then, in her excitement at seeing birds whizz up suddenly before her face, or a rabbit leap across her very toes, she lost her head, and almost without sighting she flung her rifle up and pulled the trigger. She hardly ever hit any sort of mark. She had no proper sense of hunting at all. Her brother would be often completely disgusted with her. "You don't care whether you get your bird or not," he said. "That's no way to hunt." Miranda could not understand his indignation. She had seen him smash his hat and yell with fury when he had missed his aim. "What I like about shooting," said Miranda, with exasperating inconsequence, "is pulling the trigger and hearing the noise."

"Then, by golly," said Paul, "whyn't you go back to the range and shoot at bulls-eyes?"

"I'd just as soon," said Miranda, "only like this, we walk around more."

"Well, you just stay behind and stop spoiling my shots," said Paul, who, when he made a kill, wanted to be certain he had made it. Miranda, who alone brought down a bird once in twenty rounds, always claimed as her own any game they got when they fired at the same moment. It was tiresome and unfair and her brother was sick of it.

"Now, the first dove we see, or the first rabbit, is mine," he told her. "And the next will be yours. Remember that and don't get smarty."

"What about snakes?" asked Miranda idly. "Can I have the first snake?"

Waving her thumb gently and watching her gold ring glitter, Miranda lost interest in shooting. She was wearing her summer roughing outfit: dark blue overalls, a light blue shirt, a hired-man's straw hat, and thick brown sandals. Her brother had the same outfit except his was a sober hickory-nut color. Ordinarily Miranda preferred her overalls to any other dress, though it was making rather a scandal in the countryside, for the year was 1903, and in the back country the law of female decorum had teeth in it. Her father had been criticized for letting his girls dress like boys and go careering around astride barebacked horses. Big sister Maria, the really independent and fearless one, in spite of her rather affected ways, rode at a dead run with only a rope knotted around her horse's nose. It was said the motherless family was running down, with the Grandmother no longer there to hold it together. It was known that she had discriminated against her son Harry in her will, and that he was in straits about money. Some of his old neighbors reflected with vicious satisfaction that now he would probably not be so stiffnecked, nor have any more high-stepping horses either. Miranda knew this, though she could not say how. She had met along the road old women of the kind who smoked corncob pipes, who had treated her grandmother with most sincere respect. They slanted their gummy old eyes sideways at the granddaughter and said, "Ain't you ashamed of yoself, Missy? It's against the Scriptures to dress like that. Whut yo Pappy thinkin about?" Miranda, with her powerful social sense, which was like a fine set of antennae radiating from every pore of her skin, would feel ashamed because she knew well it was rude and ill-bred to shock anybody, even bad-tempered old crones, though she had faith in her father's judgment and was perfectly comfortable in the clothes. Her father had said, "They're just what you need, and they'll save your dresses for school . . ." This sounded quite simple and natural to her. She had been brought up in rigorous economy. Wastefulness was vulgar. It was also a sin. These were truths; she had heard them repeated many times and never once disputed.

Now the ring, shining with the serene purity of fine gold on her rather grubby thumb, turned her feelings against her overalls and sockless feet, toes sticking through the thick brown leather straps. She wanted to go back to the farmhouse, take a good cold bath, dust herself with plenty of Maria's violet talcum powder—provided Maria was not present to object, of course—put on the thinnest, most becoming dress she owned, with a big sash, and sit in a wicker chair under the trees . . . These things were not all she wanted, of course; she had vague stirrings of desire for luxury and a grand way of living which could not take precise form in her imagination but were founded on family legend of past wealth and leisure. These immediate comforts were what she could have, and she wanted them at once. She lagged rather far behind Paul, and once she thought of just turning back without a word and going home. She stopped, thinking that Paul would never do that to her, and so she would have to tell him. When a rabbit leaped, she let Paul have it without dispute. He killed it with one shot.

When she came up with him, he was already kneeling, examining the wound, the rabbit trailing from his hands. "Right through the head," he said complacently, as if he had aimed for it. He took out his sharp, competent bowie knife and started to skin the body. He did it very cleanly and quickly. Uncle Jimbilly knew how to prepare the skins so that Miranda always had fur coats for her dolls, for though she never cared much for her dolls she liked seeing them in fur coats. The children knelt facing each other over the dead animal. Miranda watched admiringly while her brother stripped the skin away as if he were taking off a glove. The flayed flesh emerged dark scarlet, sleek, firm; Miranda with thumb and finger felt the long fine muscles with the silvery flat strips binding them to the joints. Brother lifted the oddly bloated belly. "Look," he said, in a low amazed voice. "It was going to have young ones."

Very carefully he slit the thin flesh from the center ribs to the flanks, and a scarlet bag appeared. He slit again and pulled the bag open, and there lay a bundle of tiny rabbits, each wrapped in a thin scarlet veil. The brother pulled these off and there they were, dark gray, their sleek wet down lying in minute even ripples, like a baby's head just washed, their unbelievably small delicate ears folded close, their little blind faces almost featureless.

Miranda said, "Oh, I want to *see*," under her breath. She looked and looked—excited but not frightened, for she was accustomed to the sight of animals killed in hunting—filled with pity and astonishment and a kind of shocked delight in the wonderful little creatures for their own sakes, they were so pretty. She touched one of them ever so carefully. "Ah, there's blood running over them," she said and began to tremble without knowing why. Yet she wanted most deeply to see and to know. Having seen, she felt at once as if she had

known all along. The very memory of her former ignorance faded, she had always known just this. No one had ever told her anything outright, she had been rather unobservant of the animal life around her because she was so accustomed to animals. They seemed simply disorderly and unaccountably rude in their habits, but altogether natural and not very interesting. Her brother had spoken as if he had known about everything all along. He may have seen all this before. He had never said a word to her, but she knew now a part at least of what he knew. She understood a little of the secret, formless intuitions in her own mind and body, which had been clearing up, taking form, so gradually and so steadily she had not realized that she was learning what she had to know. Paul said cautiously, as if he were talking about something forbidden: "They were just about ready to be born." His voice dropped on the last word. "I know," said Miranda, "like kittens. I know, like babies." She was quietly and terribly agitated, standing again with her rifle under her arm, looking down at the bloody heap. "I don't want the skin," she said. "I won't have it." Paul buried the young rabbits again in their mother's body, wrapped the skin around her, carried her to a clump of sage bushes, and hid her away. He came out again at once and said to Miranda, with an eager friendliness, a confidential tone quite unusual in him, as if he were taking her into an important secret on equal terms: "Listen now. Now you listen to me, and don't ever forget. Don't you ever tell a living soul that you saw this. Don't tell a soul. Don't tell Dad because I'll get into trouble. He'll say I'm leading you into things you ought not to do. He's always saying that. So now don't you go and forget and blab out sometime the way you're always doing . . . Now, that's a secret. Don't you tell."

Miranda never told, she did not even wish to tell anybody. She thought about the whole worrisome affair with confused unhappiness for a few days. Then it sank quietly into her mind and was heaped over by accumulated thousands of impressions, for nearly twenty years. One day she was picking her path among the puddles and crushed refuse of a market street in a strange city of a strange country, when without warning, plain and clear in its true colors as if she looked through a frame upon a scene that had not stirred nor changed since the moment it happened, the episode of that far-off day leaped from its burial place before her mind's eye. She was so reasonlessly horrified she halted suddenly staring, the scene before her eyes dimmed by the vision back of them. An Indian vendor had held up before her a tray of dyed sugar sweets, in the shapes of all kinds of small creatures: birds, baby chicks, baby rabbits, lambs, baby pigs. They were in gay colors and smelled of vanilla, maybe . . . It was a very hot day and the smell in the market, with its piles of raw flesh and wilting flowers, was like the mingled sweetness and corruption she had smelled that other day in the empty cemetery at home: the day she had remembered always until now vaguely as the time she and her brother had found treasure in the opened graves. Instantly upon this thought the dreadful vision faded, and she saw clearly her brother, whose childhood face she had forgotten, standing again in the blazing sunshine, again twelve years old, a pleased sober smile in his eyes, turning the silver dove over and over in his hands.

Responding to the Story

Analyzing the Story

Identifying Facts

1. When and where does the major incident of the story take place? How old are Miranda and Paul?
2. What are they hunting? How are their feelings about hunting different?
3. What does Miranda discover in the grave she explores? What does Paul find? What do they do with the things they find?
4. What does Miranda want to do about her clothing after she puts the ring on? (How does the ring make her think of her role as a woman?)
5. At first Miranda is excited by the discovery of the rabbit's young ones. What changes her feelings, so that she begins to tremble? How does Porter go on to describe what Miranda discovers about herself?
6. The **setting** of the story changes in the final paragraph. When and where does it take place. How is this scene connected with the incident involving the rabbit?

Interpreting Meanings

7. How do you think the incident with the rabbit relates to the discovery of the dove and the ring? (Think about where the dove and the ring had really come from, and whether the rabbit changed the children's feelings about their treasures, which they had initially regarded only with delight.)
8. Chart the changes in Miranda's feelings from the beginning to the end of this story. Be sure you are clear on what causes the changes.
9. Why do you think Paul insists that Miranda not tell their father about the rabbit he has killed?
10. What do you think Miranda and her brother discover about birth and life and death on that long-ago day?
11. How would you state the story's **theme**?

Writing About the Story

A Critical Response

Responding to a Critical Comment. Three critics said this about "The Grave":

> This matter of clothes, and the pressures of society, and the role of women in the society, powerfully affects the meaning of the story. For if it is about a rite of initiation into the meaning of life, what is at stake is no mere matter of biological maturity. Miranda's growing up cannot be separated from the context of the family and the larger society of which the family is a part.
>
> —Cleanth Brooks, R. W. B. Lewis, and Robert Penn Warren

In a three-paragraph essay, state your opinion on the critics' remarks. Quote passages from the story to support what you say.

Analyzing Language and Style

Imagery and Symbolism

Some critics compare this story to a lyric poem, which uses imagery and symbolism to create a state of mind, not to develop plot or create character.

1. What does the name *Miranda* mean? How is it a suitable name for the heroine of the story?
2. What symbolism can you suggest for the season of the year in which the children make their discoveries?
3. What does a dove usually symbolize? A wedding ring?
4. If this is a story about innocence and experience, does it end with an image of innocence or experience? How would you define innocence and experience?

William Faulkner
(1897–1962)

Yoknapatawpha County, Mississippi, is surely the hardest of American literary place names to pronounce. Still, it is wise to learn how (yäk'-nə·pə·tô'fə), for it is famous as the imagined world of William Faulkner, the scene of his most celebrated novels and stories. Debate will always rage about the position of figures in our literary pantheon, but critics are now unanimous in their opinion that Faulkner is one of the greatest of all American novelists.

Imaginary Yoknapatawpha is similar in many ways to the actual impoverished farmland, with its red clay hills, that rings Oxford, Mississippi, home of the state's university. It was there that William's father, Murray Falkner (William added the "u" to the family name), ran a livery stable and later became the university's business manager. William Faulkner lived and wrote there throughout most of his life.

Faulkner was a mediocre student and quit high school in the tenth grade, but he read widely, and he wrote poetry. At the outbreak of World War I, the U. S. Army rejected him because he failed to meet their height and weight requirements. However, he enlisted in the Canadian Air Force and trained for flight duty, only to see the war end before he was commissioned. Returning to Oxford after the war, he took some courses at the university and did poorly in English. With neither profession nor skill, and a marked distaste for regular employment, he seemed a moody and puzzling young man to his neighbors.

Faulkner took several short-lived jobs, among them that of postmaster for the university. Resigning from this job, he wrote, "I will be damned if I propose to be at the beck and call of every itinerant scoundrel who has two cents to invest in a postage stamp."

In 1924, he left Oxford for New Orleans, where he met Sherwood Anderson (page 525), who had attracted much attention with the publication of *Winesburg, Ohio* (1919), his study of small-town life. Impressed and encouraged by Anderson, Faulkner tried his hand at fiction. In six weeks he completed a first novel, *Soldiers'*

Pay, a self-conscious story about the lost generation. Thereafter Faulkner wrote with a tireless energy.

Within the next three years, Faulkner found his great theme: the American South as a microcosm for the universal themes of time, the passions of the human heart, and the destruction of the wilderness. Faulkner saw the South as a nation unto itself, with a strong sense of its noble past and an array of myths by which it clung to its pride, despite the humiliating defeat of the Civil War and the acceptance of the distasteful values of an industrial North. Faulkner started to explore these themes in 1929 with the publication of *Sartoris* and *The Sound and the Fury,* two novels published within months of each other. While *Sartoris* was a fairly conventional novel, it is notable because it was the first story set in mythical Yoknapatawpha, Faulkner's own "little postage stamp of native soil." *The Sound and the Fury* was a milestone in American literature, due to Faulkner's bold manipulation of point of view and of its stream-of-consciousness narrative technique.

In the decade which followed, Faulkner produced a succession of dazzling books: *As I Lay Dying* (1930), *Sanctuary* (1931), *Light in August* (1932), *Absalom! Absalom!* (1936)—considered by many readers to be his finest work—*The Unvanquished* (1938), and *The Hamlet* (1940). These works reveal Faulkner as equally skillful in the tragic and the comic modes. He portrayed the South accurately, perceptively, and with a poignant ambivalence—on the one hand affectionate, on the other critical. He once said of the South, "Well, I love it and I hate it."

Faulkner described his South through fictional families who often reappear from novel to novel. They resemble trees, attaining grandeur, casting much shade, and then growing old and dry, crumbling as the scrub of social change grows up around their fallen limbs and stumps.

There are the aristocratic Sartorises, who resemble Faulkner's own ancestors. Colonel Bayard Sartoris, for example, was patterned after Faulkner's great-grandfather, who rose from rural poverty to command the Second Mississippi Regiment, built a railroad, wrote a best-selling novel, and was murdered on the street by his business partner.

There are also the Compsons, who incorporate some characteristics of the author's immediate family. They form the centerpiece of *The Sound and the Fury,* which records the decline of a once great clan, and with it, the passing of a traditionally Southern world.

As I Lay Dying tells of the poor-white Bundren family and its efforts to bring the body of its matriarch, Addie, back to the town of Jefferson for burial. The novel reveals these humble people as more enduring than their social betters. *Light in August* also concerns the Burden family and explores the problem of racism through the character of the protagonist, Joe Christmas. Although he can pass as white, Joe is regarded as a mulatto; his failure to find a place in either white or black society leads to his murder.

And finally, there are the Snopeses—Faulkner's unforgettable portrayal of a sprawling clan of irresponsible, depraved, socially ambitious varmints, who rise from the dust and cheat their way to respectability and wealth, destroying the old values of aristocracy and peasantry alike.

Faulkner is admittedly a difficult writer, with uncommon methods of handling chronology and point of view. He often forces the reader to piece together events from a seemingly random and fragmentary series of impressions experienced by a variety of narrators. Faulkner's style often strains conventional syntax; he might pile up clause upon clause in an effort to capture the complexity of thought. In *The Sound and the Fury,* for example, he entrusts part of the narrative to the chaotic intelligence of the mentally handicapped son, Benjy Compson. But the efforts of patient readers are richly repaid, as they discover in book after book a mythical universe in which the moral dilemmas are the perennial mysteries of human existence.

By the time he received the Nobel Prize for literature in 1950, Faulkner's best work was behind him. After his richly productive period (1929–1942), he wrote many more stories and novels, including *Intruder in the Dust* (1948), *Requiem for a Nun* (1951), *A Fable* (1954), *The Town* (1957), *The Mansion* (1959), and *The Reivers* (1962). All these works displayed his characteristic virtuosity and willingness to experiment, but his powers were clearly diminished. His critics noted this and tended to underestimate his lasting importance.

Faulkner's writing surely diverged from that of his realist contemporaries—notably Ernest Hemingway, whom he put at the bottom of his own list of the best American contemporary writers. "Wolfe, Hemingway, Dos Passos, and myself," he once chose for his ladder of literary accomplishment. He then explained further: "I rated Wolfe first, myself second. I put Hemingway last. I said we were all failures. All of us had failed to match the dream of perfection. . . . I rated Hemingway last because he stayed within what he knew. He did it fine, but he didn't try for the impossible."

Of the novel itself, Faulkner said: "The only mistake with any novel is if it fails to create pleasure. That it is not true is irrelevant; a novel is to be enjoyed. A book that fails to create enjoyment is not a good one."

But there is no argument over William Faulkner's preeminence among Southern writers. As Flannery O'Connor once put it: "The presence alone of Faulkner in our midst makes a great difference in what the writer can and cannot permit himself to do. Nobody wants his mule and wagon stalled on the same track the Dixie Limited is roaring down."

SPOTTED HORSES

Here is critic Malcolm Cowley's account of the genesis of Flem Snopes, the central character in "Spotted Horses" and a character Faulkner used over and over again.

"Thirty or forty years after the Civil War, Flem Snopes appeared in the little community of Frenchman's Bend, in the southeastern corner of Faulkner's county. Flem was the son of a Civil War bushwhacker and horse thief. A lumpish and silent young man, with eyes the color of stagnant water, he never drank or smoked, but he sometimes chewed a nickel's worth of tobacco until the suption was out of it. 'Flem Snopes don't even tell himself what he is up to,' one of his neighbors said. 'Not if he was laying in bed with himself in the dark of the moon.'

"In his dark-of-the-moon fashion, Flem managed to get control of the general store, the cotton gin, and the blacksmith shop, the only three money-making enterprises in Frenchman's Bend; and one by one he introduced a horde of his relatives to take charge of them. Lump Snopes, the storekeeper; I. O. Snopes, the schoolmaster; Mink Snopes, the killer; Ike Snopes, the idiot boy who fell in love with a cow; Eck Snopes, the stupid and good-natured blacksmith: all together they descended on the community like field mice, devouring everything, cheating everybody, cheating one another; and when Flem had cheated even Ratliff, the sewing-machine agent, known as the shrewdest man in the county, they all moved on to Jefferson, like mice into an untouched field of grain."

The narrator of this wildly funny story about Flem Snopes is the sewing machine agent named Ratliff.

I

Yes, sir. Flem Snopes has filled that whole country full of spotted horses. You can hear folks running them all day and all night, whooping and hollering, and the horses running back and forth across them little wooden bridges ever now and then kind of like thunder. Here I was this morning pretty near half way to town, with the team ambling along and me setting in the buckboard about half asleep, when all of a sudden something come swurging[1] up outen the bushes and jumped the road clean, without touching hoof to it. It flew right over my team, big as a billboard and flying through the air like a hawk. It taken me thirty minutes to stop my team and untangle the harness and the buckboard and hitch them up again.

That Flem Snopes. I be dog if he ain't a case, now. One morning about ten years ago, the boys was just getting settled down on Varner's porch for a little talk and tobacco, when here come Flem out from behind the counter, with his coat off and his hair all parted, like he might have been clerking for Varner for ten years already. Folks all knowed him; it was a big family of them about five miles down the bottom.[2] That year, at least. Share-cropping. They never stayed on any place over a year. Then they would move on to another place, with the chap or maybe the twins of that year's litter. It was a regular nest of them. But Flem. The rest of them stayed tenant farmers, moving ever year, but here come Flem one day, walking out from behind Jody Varner's counter like he owned it. And he wasn't there but a year or two before folks knowed that, if him and Jody was both still in that store in ten years more, it would be Jody clerking for Flem Snopes. Why, that fellow could make a nickel where it wasn't but four cents to begin with. He skun[3] me in two trades, myself, and the fellow that can do that, I just hope he'll get rich before I do; that's all.

---

1. **swurging:** perhaps dialect for "surging."

2. **bottom:** for "bottom land," or low ground.
3. **skun:** skinned.

All right. So here Flem was, clerking at Varner's, making a nickel here and there and not
telling nobody about it. No, sir. Folks never
knowed when Flem got the better of somebody,
lessen[4] the fellow he beat told it. He'd just set
there in the store-chair, chewing his tobacco and
keeping his own business to hisself, until about a
week later we'd find out it was somebody else's
business he was keeping to hisself—provided the

fellow he trimmed was mad enough to tell it.
That's Flem.

We give him ten years to own ever thing Jody
Varner had. But he never waited no ten years. I
reckon you-all know that gal of Uncle Billy Varner's, the youngest one; Eula. Jody's sister. Ever
Sunday ever yellow-wheeled buggy and curried
riding horse in that country would be hitched to
Bill Varner's fence, and the young bucks setting
on the porch, swarming around Eula like bees
around a honey pot. One of these here kind of

---

4. **lessen:** unless.

big, soft-looking gals that could giggle richer than plowed new-ground. Wouldn't none of them leave before the others, and so they would set there on the porch until time to go home, with some of them with nine and ten miles to ride and then get up tomorrow and go back to the field. So they would all leave together and they would ride in a clump down to the creek ford and hitch them curried horses and yellow-wheeled buggies and get out and fight one another. Then they would get in the buggies again and go on home.

Well, one day about a year ago, one of them yellow-wheeled buggies and one of them curried saddle-horses quit this country. We heard they was heading for Texas. The next day Uncle Billy and Eula and Flem come into town in Uncle Bill's surrey,[5] and when they come back, Flem and Eula was married. And on the next day we heard that two more of them yellow-wheeled buggies had left the country. They mought have gone to Texas, too. It's a big place.

Anyway, about a month after the wedding, Flem and Eula went to Texas, too. They was gone pretty near a year. Then one day last month, Eula come back, with a baby. We figgured up, and we decided that it was as well-growed a three-months-old baby as we ever see. It can already pull up on a chair. I reckon Texas makes big men quick, being a big place. Anyway, if it keeps on like it started, it'll be chewing tobacco and voting time it's eight years old.

And so last Friday here come Flem himself. He was on a wagon with another fellow. The other fellow had one of these two-gallon hats and a ivory-handled pistol and a box of gingersnaps sticking out of his hind pocket, and tied to the tailgate of the wagon was about two dozen of them Texas ponies, hitched to one another with barbed wire. They was colored like parrots and they was quiet as doves, and ere a one of them would kill you quick as a rattlesnake. Nere a one of them[6] had two eyes the same color, and nere a one of them had ever see a bridle, I reckon; and when that Texas man got down offen the wagon and walked up to them to show how gentle they was, one of them cut his vest clean offen him, same as with a razor.

Flem had done already disappeared; he had went on to see his wife, I reckon, and to see if

that ere baby had done gone on to the field to help Uncle Billy plow maybe. It was the Texas man that taken the horses on to Mrs. Littlejohn's lot. He had a little trouble at first, when they come to the gate, because they hadn't never see a fence before, and when he finally got them in and taken a pair of wire cutters and unhitched them and got them into the barn and poured some shell corn into the trough, they durn nigh tore down the barn. I reckon they thought that shell corn was bugs, maybe. So he left them in the lot and he announced that the auction would begin at sunup tomorrow.

That night we was setting on Mrs. Littlejohn's porch. You-all mind the moon was nigh full that night, and we could watch them spotted varmints swirling along the fence and back and forth across the lot same as minnows in a pond. And then now and then they would all kind of huddle up against the barn and rest themselves by biting and kicking one another. We would hear a squeal, and then a set of hoofs would go Bam! against the barn, like a pistol. It sounded just like a fellow with a pistol, in a nest of cattymounts, taking his time.

II

It wasn't ere a man knowed yet if Flem owned them things or not. They just knowed one thing: that they wasn't never going to know for sho if Flem did or not, or if maybe he didn't just get on that wagon at the edge of town, for the ride or not. Even Eck Snopes didn't know, Flem's own cousin. But wasn't nobody surprised at that. We knowed that Flem would skin Eck quick as he would ere a one of us.

They was there by sunup next morning, some of them come twelve and sixteen miles, with seed-money tied up in tobacco sacks in their overalls, standing along the fence, when the Texas man come out of Mrs. Littlejohn's after breakfast and clumb onto the gate post with that ere white pistol butt sticking outen his hind pocket. He taken a new box of gingersnaps outen his pocket and bit the end offen it like a cigar and spit out the paper, and said the auction was open. And still they was coming up in wagons and a horse- and mule-back and hitching the teams across the road and coming to the fence. Flem wasn't nowhere in sight.

But he couldn't get them started. He begun to

---

5. **surrey:** a light carriage.
6. **nere a one of them:** not a one of them.

ther, with her hands across her middle, holding the rope. "I reckon I better," she says. Her and Henry went into the lot. The horses broke and run. Henry and Mrs. Armstid followed.

"Get him into the corner," Henry says. They got Henry's horse cornered finally, and Henry taken the rope, but Mrs. Armstid let the horse get out. They hemmed it up again, but Mrs. Armstid let it get out again, and Henry turned and hit her with the rope. "Why didn't you head him back?" Henry says. He hit her again. "Why didn't you?" It was about that time I looked around and see Flem Snopes standing there.

It was the Texas man that done something. He moved fast for a big man. He caught the rope before Henry could hit the third time, and Henry whirled and made like he would jump at the Texas man. But he never jumped. The Texas man went and taken Henry's arm and led him outen the lot. Mrs. Armstid come behind them and the Texas man taken some money outen his pocket and he give it into Mrs. Armstid's hand. "Get him into the wagon and take him on home," the Texas man says, like he might have been telling them he enjoyed his supper.

Then here come Flem. "What's that for, Buck?" Flem says.

"Thinks he bought one of them ponies," the Texas man says. "Get him on away, missus."

But Henry wouldn't go. "Give him back that money," he says. "I bought that horse and I aim to have him if I have to shoot him."

And there was Flem, standing there with his hands in his pockets, chewing, like he had just happened to be passing.

"You take your money and I take my horse," Henry says. "Give it back to him," he says to Mrs. Armstid.

"You don't own no horse of mine," the Texas man says. "Get him on home, missus."

Then Henry seen Flem. "You got something to do with these horses," he says. "I bought one. Here's the money for it." He taken the bill outen Mrs. Armstid's hand. He offered it to Flem. "I bought one. Ask him. Here. Here's the money," he says, giving the bill to Flem.

When Flem taken the money, the Texas man dropped the rope he had snatched outen Henry's hand. He had done sent Eck Snopes's boy up to the store for another box of gingersnaps, and he taken the box outen his pocket and looked into it.

It was empty and he dropped it on the ground. "Mr. Snopes will have your money for you tomorrow," he says to Mrs. Armstid. "You can get it from him tomorrow. He don't own no horse. You get him into the wagon and get him on home." Mrs. Armstid went back to the wagon and got in. "Where's that ere buckboard I bought?" the Texas man says. It was after sundown then. And then Mrs. Littlejohn come out on the porch and rung the supper bell.

IV

I come on in and et supper. Mrs. Littlejohn would bring in a pan of bread or something, then she would go out to the porch a minute and come back and tell us. The Texas man had hitched his team to the buckboard he had swapped them last two horses for, and him and Flem had gone, and then she told that the rest of them that never had ropes had went back to the store with I. O. Snopes to get some ropes, and wasn't nobody at the gate but Henry Armstid, and Mrs. Armstid setting in the wagon in the road, and Eck Snopes and that boy of hisn. "I don't care how many of them fool men gets killed by them things," Mrs. Littlejohn says, "but I ain't going to let Eck Snopes take that boy into that lot again." So she went down to the gate, but she come back without the boy or Eck neither.

"It ain't no need to worry about that boy," I says. "He's charmed." He was right behind Eck last night when Eck went to help feed them. The whole drove of them jumped clean over that boy's head and never touched him. It was Eck that touched him. Eck snatched him into the wagon and taken a rope and frailed the tar outen him.

So I had done et and went to my room and was undressing, long as I had a long trip to make next day; I was trying to sell a machine to Mrs. Bundren up past Whiteleaf; when Henry Armstid opened that gate and went in by hisself. They couldn't make him wait for the balance of them to get back with their ropes. Eck Snopes said he tried to make Henry wait, but Henry wouldn't do it. Eck said Henry walked right up to them and that when they broke, they run clean over Henry like a hay-mow breaking down. Eck said he snatched that boy of hisn out of the way just in time and that them things went through that gate like a creek flood and into the wagons and teams hitched side the road, busting wagon tongues and snapping harness like it was fishing-line, with Mrs. Armstid still setting in their wagon in the middle of it like something carved outen wood. Then they scattered, wild horses and tame mules with pieces of harness and single trees dangling offen them, both ways up and down the road.

"There goes ourn, paw!" Eck says his boy said. "There it goes, into Mrs. Littlejohn's house." Eck says it run right up the steps and into the house like a boarder late for supper. I reckon so. Anyway, I was in my room, in my underclothes, with one sock on and one sock in my hand, leaning out the window when the commotion busted out, and when I heard something run into the melodeon in the hall; it sounded like a railroad engine. Then the door to my room come sailing in like when you throw a tin bucket top into the wind and I looked over my shoulder and see something that looked like a fourteen-foot pinwheel a-blaring its eyes at me. It had to blare them fast, because I was already done jumped out the window.

I reckon it was anxious, too. I reckon it hadn't never seen barbed wire or shell corn before, but I know it hadn't never seen underclothes before, or maybe it was a *sewing-machine agent* it hadn't never seen. Anyway, it swirled and turned to run back up the hall and outen the house, when it met Eck Snopes and that boy just coming in, carrying a rope. It swirled again and run down the hall and out the back door just in time to meet Mrs. Littlejohn. She had just gathered up the clothes she had washed, and she was coming onto the back porch with a armful of washing in one hand a scrubbing-board in the other, when the horse skidded up to her, trying to stop and swirl again. It never taken Mrs. Littlejohn no time a-tall.

"Git outen here, you son," she says. She hit it across the face with the scrubbing-board; that ere scrubbing-board split as neat as ere a axe could have done it, and when the horse swirled to run back up the hall, she hit it again with what was left of the scrubbing-board, not on the head this time. "And stay out," she says.

Eck and that boy was half-way down the hall by this time. I reckon that horse looked like a pinwheel to Eck too. "Git to hell outen here, Ad!" Eck says. Only there wasn't time. Eck dropped flat on his face, but the boy never moved. The boy was about a yard tall maybe, in overhalls just

like Eck's; that horse swoared over his head without touching a hair. I saw that, because I was just coming back up the front steps, still carrying that ere sock and still in my underclothes, when the horse come onto the porch again. It taken one look at me and swirled again and run to the end of the porch and jumped the banisters and the lot fence like a hen-hawk and lit in the lot running and went out the gate again and jumped eight or ten upside-down wagons and went on down the road. It was a full moon then. Mrs. Armstid was still setting in the wagon like she had done been carved outen wood and left there and forgot.

That horse. It ain't never missed a lick. It was going about forty miles a hour when it come to the bridge over the creek. It would have had a clear road, but it so happened that Vernon Tull was already using the bridge when it got there. He was coming back from town; he hadn't heard about the auction; him and his wife and three daughters and Mrs. Tull's aunt, all setting in chairs in the wagon bed, and all asleep, including the mules. They waked up when the horse hit the bridge one time, but Tull said the first he knew was when the mules tried to turn the wagon around in the middle of the bridge and he seen that spotted varmint run right twixt the mules and run up the wagon tongue like a squirrel. He said he just had time to hit it across the face with his whip-stock, because about that time the mules turned the wagon around on that ere one-way bridge and that horse clumb across one of the mules and jumped down onto the bridge again and went on, with Vernon standing up in the wagon and kicking at it.

Tull said the mules turned in the harness and clumb back into the wagon, too, with Tull trying to beat them out again, with the reins wrapped around his wrist. After that he says all he seen was overturned chairs and womenfolks' legs and white drawers shining in the moonlight, and his mules and that spotted horse going on up the road like a ghost.

The mules jerked Tull outen the wagon and drug him a spell on the bridge before the reins broke. They thought at first that he was dead, and while they was kneeling around him, picking the bridge splinters outen him, here come Eck and that boy, still carrying the rope. They was running and breathing a little hard. "Where'd he go?" Eck says.

V

I went back and got my pants and shirt and shoes on just in time to go and help get Henry Armstid outen the trash in the lot. I be dog if he didn't look like he was dead, with his head hanging back and his teeth showing in the moonlight, and a little rim of white under his eyelids. We could still hear them horses, here and there; hadn't none of them got more than four-five miles away yet, not knowing the country, I reckon. So we could hear them and folks yelling now and then: "Whooey. Head him!"

We toted Henry into Mrs. Littlejohn's. She was in the hall; she hadn't put down the armful of clothes. She taken one look at us, and she laid down the busted scrubbing-board and taken up the lamp and opened a empty door. "Bring him in here," she says.

We toted him in and laid him on the bed. Mrs. Littlejohn set the lamp on the dresser, still carrying the clothes. "I'll declare, you men," she says. Our shadows was way up the wall, tiptoeing too; we could hear ourselves breathing. "Better get his wife," Mrs. Littlejohn says. She went out, carrying the clothes.

"I reckon we had," Quick says. "Go get her, somebody."

"Whyn't you go?" Winterbottom says.

"Let Ernest git her," Durley says. "He lives neighbors with them."

Ernest went to fetch her. I be dog if Henry didn't look like he was dead. Mrs. Littlejohn come back, with a kettle and some towels. She went to work on Henry, and then Mrs. Armstid and Ernest come in. Mrs. Armstid come to the foot of the bed and stood there, with her hands rolled into her apron, watching what Mrs. Littlejohn was doing, I reckon.

"You men git outen the way," Mrs. Littlejohn says. "Git outside," she says. "See if you can't find something else to play with that will kill some more of you."

"Is he dead?" Winterbottom says.

"It ain't your fault if he ain't," Mrs. Littlejohn says. "Go tell Will Varner to come up here. I reckon a man ain't so different from a mule, come long come short. Except maybe a mule's got more sense."

We went to get Uncle Billy. It was a full moon. We could hear them, now and then, four mile away: "Whooey. Head him." The country was full of them, one on ever wooden bridge in the land, running across it like thunder: "Whooey. There he goes. Head him."

We hadn't got far before Henry begun to scream. I reckon Mrs. Littlejohn's water had brung him to; anyway, he wasn't dead. We went on to Uncle Billy's. The house was dark. We called to him, and after a while the window opened and Uncle Billy put his head out, peart as a peckerwood, listening. "Are they still trying to catch them durn rabbits?" he says.

He come down, with his britches on over his night shirt and his suspenders dangling, carrying his horse-doctoring grip. "Yes, sir," he says, cocking his head like a woodpecker; "they're still a-trying."

We could hear Henry before we reached Mrs. Littlejohn's. He was going Ah-Ah-Ah. We stopped in the yard. Uncle Billy went on in. We could hear Henry. We stood in the yard, hearing them on the bridges, this-a-way and that: "Whooey. Whooey."

"Eck Snopes ought to caught hisn," Ernest says.

"Looks like he ought," Winterbottom said.

Henry was going Ah-Ah-Ah steady in the house; then he begun to scream. "Uncle Billy's started," Quick says. We looked into the hall. We could see the light where the door was. Then Mrs. Littlejohn come out.

"Will needs some help," she says. "You, Ernest. You'll do." Ernest went into the house.

"Hear them?" Quick said. "That one was on Four Mile bridge." We could hear them; it sounded like thunder a long way off; it didn't last long:

"Whooey."

We could hear Henry: "Ah-Ah-Ah-Ah-Ah."

"They are both started now," Winterbottom says. "Ernest too."

That was early in the night. Which was a good thing, because it taken a long night for folks to chase them things right and for Henry to lay there and holler, being as Uncle Billy never had none of this here chloryfoam to set Henry's leg with. So it was considerate in Flem to get them started early. And what do you reckon Flem's comment was?

That's right. Nothing. Because he wasn't there. Hadn't nobody see him since that Texas man left.

Sundown, Running Free by Millard Sheets (1978). Watercolor.   The Kennedy Galleries, New York City.

VI

That was Saturday night. I reckon Mrs. Armstid got home about daylight, to see about the chaps. I don't know where they thought her and Henry was. But lucky the oldest one was a gal, about twelve, big enough to take care of the little ones. Which she did for the next two days. Mrs. Armstid would nurse Henry all night and work in the kitchen for hern and Henry's keep, and in the afternoon she would drive home (it was about four miles) to see to the chaps. She would cook up a pot of victuals and leave it on the stove, and the gal would bar the house and keep the little ones quiet. I would hear Mrs. Littlejohn and Mrs. Armstid talking in the kitchen. "How are the chaps making out?" Mrs. Littlejohn says.

"All right," Mrs. Armstid says.

"Don't they git skeered at night?" Mrs. Littlejohn says.

"Ina May bars the door when I leave," Mrs. Armstid says. "She's got the axe in bed with her. I reckon she can make out."

I reckon they did. And I reckon Mrs. Armstid was waiting for Flem to come back to town; hadn't nobody seen him until this morning; to get her money the Texas man said Flem was keeping for her. Sho. I reckon she was.

Anyway, I heard Mrs. Armstid and Mrs. Littlejohn talking in the kitchen this morning while I was eating breakfast. Mrs. Littlejohn had just told Mrs. Armstid that Flem was in town. "You can ask him for that five dollars," Mrs. Littlejohn says.

"You reckon he'll give it to me?" Mrs. Armstid says.

Mrs. Littlejohn was washing dishes, washing them like a man, like they was made out of iron. "No," she says. "But asking him won't do no hurt. It might shame him. I don't reckon it will, but it might."

"If he wouldn't give it back, it ain't no use to ask," Mrs. Armstid says.

"Suit yourself," Mrs. Littlejohn says. "It's your money."

I could hear the dishes.

"Do you reckon he might give it back to me?" Mrs. Armstid says. "That Texas man said he would. He said I could get it from Mr. Snopes later."

"Then go and ask him for it," Mrs. Littlejohn says.

I could hear the dishes.

"He won't give it back to me," Mrs. Armstid says.

"All right," Mrs. Littlejohn says. "Don't ask him for it, then."

I could hear the dishes; Mrs. Armstid was helping. "You don't reckon he would, do you?" she says. Mrs. Littlejohn never said nothing. It sounded like she was throwing the dishes at one another. "Maybe I better go and talk to Henry about it," Mrs. Armstid says.

"I would," Mrs. Littlejohn says. I be dog if it didn't sound like she had two plates in her hands, beating them together. "Then Henry can buy another five-dollar horse with it. Maybe he'll buy one next time that will out and out kill him. If I thought that, I'd give you back the money, myself."

"I reckon I better talk to him first," Mrs. Armstid said. Then it sounded like Mrs. Littlejohn taken up all the dishes and throwed them at the cook-stove, and I come away.

That was this morning. I had been up to Bundren's and back, and I thought that things would have kind of settled down. So after breakfast, I went up to the store. And there was Flem, setting in the store-chair and whittling, like he might not have ever moved since he come to clerk for Jody Varner. I. O. was leaning in the door, in his shirt sleeves and with his hair parted too, same as Flem was before he turned the clerking job over to I. O. It's a funny thing about them Snopes: they all looks alike, yet there ain't ere a two of them that claims brothers. They're always just cousins, like Flem and Eck and Flem and I. O. Eck was there too, squatting against the wall, him and that boy, eating cheese and crackers outen a sack; they told me that Eck hadn't been home a-tall. And that Lon Quick hadn't got back to town, even. He followed his horse clean down to Samson's

Bridge, with a wagon and a camp outfit. Eck finally caught one of hisn. It run into a blind lane at Freeman's and Eck and the boy taken and tied their rope across the end of the lane, about three foot high. The horse come to the end of the lane and whirled and run back without ever stopping. Eck says it never seen the rope a-tall. He says it looked just like one of these here Christmas pinwheels. "Didn't it try to run again?" I says.

"No," Eck says, eating a bite of cheese offen his knife blade. "Just kicked some."

"Kicked some?" I says.

"It broke its neck," Eck says.

Well, they was squatting there, about six of them, talking, talking at Flem; never nobody knowed yet if Flem had ere a interest in them horses or not. So finally I come right out and asked him. "Flem's done skun all of us so much," I says, "that we're proud of him. Come on, Flem," I says, "how much did you and that Texas man make offen them horses? You can tell us. Ain't nobody here but Eck that bought one of them; the others ain't got back to town yet, and Eck's your own cousin; he'll be proud to hear, too. How much did you-all make?"

They was all whittling, not looking at Flem, making like they was studying. But you could a heard a pin drop. And I. O. He had been rubbing his back up and down on the door, but he stopped now, watching Flem like a pointing dog. Flem finished cutting the sliver offen his stick. He spit across the porch, into the road. "Twarn't none of my horses," he says.

I. O. cackled, like a hen, slapping his legs with both hands. "You boys might just as well quit trying to get ahead of Flem," he said.

Well, about that time I see Mrs. Armstid come outen Mrs. Littlejohn's gate, coming up the road. I never said nothing. I says, "Well, if a man can't take care of himself in a trade, he can't blame the man that trims him."

Flem never said nothing, trimming at the stick. He hadn't seen Mrs. Armstid. "Yes, sir," I says. "A fellow like Henry Armstid ain't got nobody but hisself to blame."

"Course he ain't," I. O. says. He ain't seen her, neither. "Henry Armstid's a born fool. Always is been. If Flem hadn't a got his money, somebody else would."

We looked at Flem. He never moved. Mrs. Armstid come on up the road.

"That's right," I says. "But, come to think of it, Henry never bought no horse." We looked at Flem; you could a heard a match drop. "That Texas man told her to get that five dollars back from Flem next day. I reckon Flem's done already taken that money to Mrs. Littlejohn's and give it to Mrs. Armstid."

We watched Flem. I. O. quit rubbing his back against the door again. After a while Flem raised his head and spit across the porch, into the dust. I. O. cackled, just like a hen. "Ain't he a beating fellow, now?" I. O. says.

Mrs. Armstid was getting closer, so I kept on talking, watching to see if Flem would look up and see her. But he never looked up. I went on talking about Tull, about how he was going to sue Flem, and Flem setting there, whittling his stick, not saying nothing else after he said they wasn't none of his horses.

Then I. O. happened to look around. He seen Mrs. Armstid. "Psssst!" he says. Flem looked up. "Here she comes!" I. O. says. "Go out the back. I'll tell her you done went in to town today."

But Flem never moved. He just set there, whittling, and we watched Mrs. Armstid come up onto the porch, in that ere faded sunbonnet and wrapper and them tennis shoes that made a kind of hissing noise on the porch. She come onto the porch and stopped, her hands rolled into her dress in front, not looking at nothing.

"He said Saturday," she says, "that he wouldn't sell Henry no horse. He said I could get the money from you."

Flem looked up. The knife never stopped. It went on trimming off a sliver same as if he was watching it. "He taken that money off with him when he left," Flem says.

Mrs. Armstid never looked at nothing. We never looked at her, neither, except that boy of Eck's. He had a half-et cracker in his hand, watching her, chewing.

"He said Henry hadn't bought no horse," Mrs. Armstid says. "He said for me to get the money from you today."

"I reckon he forgot about it," Flem said. "He taken that money off with him Saturday." He whittled again. I. O. kept on rubbing his back, slow. He licked his lips. After a while the woman looked up the road, where it went on up the hill, toward the graveyard. She looked up that way for a while, with that boy of Eck's watching her and I. O.

rubbing his back slow against the door. Then she turned back toward the steps.

"I reckon it's time to get dinner started," she says.

"How's Henry this morning, Mrs. Armstid?" Winterbottom says.

She looked at Winterbottom; she almost stopped. "He's resting, I thank you kindly," she says.

Flem got up, outen the chair, putting his knife away. He spit across the porch. "Wait a minute, Mrs. Armstid," he says. She stopped again. She didn't look at him. Flem went on into the store, with I. O. done quit rubbing his back now, with his head craned after Flem, and Mrs. Armstid standing there with her hands rolled into her dress, not looking at nothing. A wagon come up the road and passed; it was Freeman, on the way to town. Then Flem come out again, with I. O. still watching him. Flem had one of these little striped sacks of Jody Varner's candy; I bet he still owes Jody that nickel, too. He put the sack into Mrs. Armstid's hand, like he would have put it into a hollow stump. He spit again across the porch. "A little sweetening for the chaps," he says.

"You're right kind," Mrs. Armstid says. She held the sack of candy in her hand, not looking at nothing. Eck's boy was watching the sack, the half-et cracker in his hand; he wasn't chewing now. He watched Mrs. Armstid roll the sack into her apron. "I reckon I better get on back and help with dinner," she says. She turned and went back across the porch. Flem set down in the chair again and opened his knife. He spit across the porch again, past Mrs. Armstid where she hadn't went down the steps yet. Then she went on, in that ere sunbonnet and wrapper all the same color, back down the road toward Mrs. Littlejohn's. You couldn't see her dress move, like a natural woman walking. She looked like a old snag still standing up and moving along on a high water. We watched her turn in at Mrs. Littlejohn's and go outen sight. Flem was whittling. I. O. begun to rub his back on the door. Then he begun to cackle, just like a durn hen.

"You boys might just as well quit trying," I. O. says. "You can't git ahead of Flem. You can't touch him. Ain't he a sight, now?"

I be a dog if he ain't. If I had brung a herd of wild cattymounts into town and sold them to my neighbors and kinfolks, they would have lynched me. Yes, sir.

Responding to the Story

Analyzing the Story

Identifying Facts

1. In Section I, what facts do we learn about the **character** Flem Snopes? How long will it take Flem to gain control of Jody Varner's business?
2. Describe all those spotted horses. What comic **comparisons** does the writer use to help us visualize them? What details immediately establish the fact that the "spotted varmints" are dangerous?
3. In Section II, why doesn't Mrs. Armstid want her husband to buy one of the horses?
4. Who is Eck Snopes? How does he start the bidding at the auction?
5. Explain how the townspeople are swindled by the Texas man at the auction.
6. What problem is faced by Henry Armstid in Section III. What does the Texas man tell Mrs. Armstid?
7. Describe how Mrs. Littlejohn deals with the horse in her house in Section IV. What advice does she give Mrs. Armstid?
8. In Section VI, when Mrs. Armstid tries to collect her five dollars from Flem Snopes, how does Flem react? What does the generous Flem finally give her?

Interpreting Meanings

9. Describe the **character** of Flem Snopes, basing your answer on his words and actions, and on the comments of other characters, including the narrator. How do you know that Flem was really involved in the scam of the horses?
10. What sort of person is Mrs. Armstid? What does her way of rolling her hands in her dress tell us?
11. How do the citizens of Yoknapatawpha County view greed and the ability, so highly developed in Flem at "skunning" or "trimming" someone in a deal?
12. Reread the scene in which Mrs. Armstid and Mrs. Littlejohn are washing dishes in Section V. What details make this one of the story's funniest scenes?
13. Although the story deals mostly with men, the women are important characters. Are the women more or less admirable than the men? Who is more romantic and who is more realistic—the men or the women? Explain.
14. How did you feel about these characters? Are they universal types—that is, could the story have taken place in any part of the country, or world?
15. Which parts of the story could have been serious, or pathetic, if the story had been told by a writer with a serious theme in mind?

Writing About the Story

A Creative Response

1. **Writing a Tall Tale.** Take a character type from your own part of the world and write a tall tale showing this person in action.

A Critical Response

2. **Responding to a Critic.** The critic Malcolm Cowley, who has called "Spotted Horses" the culminating example of American backwoods humor, has written the following about William Faulkner:

> He is not so much a novelist, in the usual sense of being a writer who sets out to observe actions and characters, then fits them into the framework of a story, as he is an epic or bardic poet in prose, a creator of myths that he weaves together into a legend of the South.
>
> —Malcolm Cowley

In a brief essay, tell how you think this evaluation may or may not apply to "Spotted Horses." Are there any poetic or mythic elements in the story? Are the spotted horses "epical" in any way? (Are they larger-than-life?) Does this story have the ring of a legend?

3. **Comparing Two Writers.** If you read more of Faulkner, you'll see that he writes in two American traditions. Some of his stories are in the tradition of the psychological horror tale (as Poe's and Hawthorne's stories are). Others of his stories, like "Spotted Horses," are in the tradition of frontier humor (as many of Twain's stories are). In an essay, compare "Spotted Horses" with Twain's "The Raftsmen" (page 404). Before you write, gather your data in a chart, like the following. If you need help with any of these terms, check the Handbook of Literary Terms at the back of this book.

Frontier Humor Devices	Faulkner	Twain
The Trickster		
The boaster		
Exaggeration		
Comic descriptions		
Understatement		
Dialect		

Analyzing Language and Style

Dialect

No writer has ever been more aware of the freshness, vividness, and hilarity to be drawn from regional speech than William Faulkner.

What sly joy we get from hearing that Eula Varner was "one of these here kind of big, soft-looking gals that could giggle richer than plowed new-ground." What a delight to be told that something is "swurging up outen the bushes," or to hear that Tull "seen that spotted varmint run right twixt the mules and run up the wagon tongue like a squirrel."

Examine "Spotted Horses" for these uses of dialect:

1. Changes in the pronunciation of words (changes from standard English pronunciation).

2. Use of new dialect words (either brand new words that you have never heard before, or old words that are used in new ways. (Can you use the **context** to guess at the words' meanings?)

3. Changes in syntax—in the way words are arranged in the sentence.

4. Changes in grammar—in the singular and plural forms of nouns, in the agreement of nouns and verbs, in the tenses of verbs, in the forms of pronouns.

5. Use of colorful expressions.

To hear and enjoy the particular rhythms of this Mississippi dialect, select a passage from "Spotted Horses" and read it aloud. (For just one example, how do you think the storyteller would say the story's opening words, "Yes, sir"?)

Primary Sources
Nobel Prize Acceptance Speech, 1950

"I feel that this award was not made to me as a man but to my work—a life's work in the agony and sweat of the human spirit, not for glory and least of all for profit, but to create out of the materials of the human spirit something which did not exist before. So this award is only mine in trust. It will not be difficult to find a dedication for the money part of it commensurate with the purpose and significance of its origin. But I would like to do the same with the acclaim too, by using this moment as a pinnacle from which I might be listened to by the young men and women already dedicated to the same anguish and travail, among whom is already that one who will someday stand here where I am standing.

"Our tragedy today is a general and universal physical fear so long sustained by now that we can even bear it. There are no longer problems of the spirit. There is only the question: When will I be blown up? Because of this, the young man or woman writing today has forgotten the problems of the human heart in conflict with itself which alone can make good writing because only that is worth writing about, worth the agony and the sweat.

"He must learn them again. He must teach himself that the basest of all things is to be afraid; and, teaching himself that, forget it forever, leaving no room in his workshop for anything but the old verities and truths of the heart, the old universal truths lacking which any story is ephemeral and doomed—love and honor and pity and pride and compassion and sacrifice. Until he does so he labors under a curse. He writes not of love but of lust, of defeats in which nobody loses anything of value, of victories without hope and worst of all without pity and compassion. His griefs grieve on no universal bones, leaving no scars. He writes not of the heart but of the glands.

"Until he relearns these things he will write as though he stood among and watched the end of man. I decline to accept the end of man. It is easy enough to say that man is immortal simply because he will endure; that when the last ding-dong of doom has clanged and faded from the last worthless rock hanging tideless in the last red and dying evening, that even then there will still be one more sound: that of his puny inexhaustible voice, still talking. I refuse to accept this. I believe that man will not merely endure: he will prevail. He is immortal, not because he alone among creatures has an inexhaustible voice, but because he has a soul, a spirit capable of compassion and sacrifice and endurance. The poet's, the writer's, duty is to write about these things. It is his privilege to help man endure by lifting his heart, by reminding him of the courage and honor and hope and pride and compassion and pity and sacrifice which have been the glory of his past. The poet's voice need not merely be the record of man, it can be one of the props, the pillars to help him endure and prevail."

—William Faulkner

Flannery O'Connor (1925–1964)

Flannery O'Connor was born in Savannah, Georgia, in 1925 and spent her short life almost entirely in nearby Milledgeville, where her family had lived since before the Civil War. Although she limited herself to a rural, southern literary terrain and the body of her work was small, her place in twentieth-century American literature is secure.

She wrote steadily from 1948 until her death in 1964. For fourteen of those sixteen years she was plagued by lupus, a painful, wasting disease that she had inherited from her father and that kept her ever more confined and immobile. "I have never been anywhere but sick," she wrote. "In a sense sickness is a place, more instructive than a long trip to Europe, and it's always a place where there's no company, where nobody can follow. Sickness before death is a very appropriate thing and I think those who don't have it miss one of God's great mercies."

She graduated from the Women's College of Georgia in 1945. She then went off to the Writers' Workshop at the University of Iowa. Her first novel, *Wise Blood,* was published in 1952. She followed that novel with a short story collection, *A Good Man Is Hard to Find* (1953), a second novel, *The Violent Bear It Away* (1955), and a second collection of stories, *Everything That Rises Must Converge* (1965).

Always disciplined as a writer, O'Connor forced herself to sit at her desk without conscious distraction of any sort at the same time every day for two hours, even if no inspiration came. "Sometimes I work for months and have to throw everything away," she commented, "but I don't think any of that time was wasted. Something goes on that makes it easier when it does come well." While her central concern in her fiction was the abstract idea of good and evil, she felt compelled to confine herself to the concrete. "The peculiar problem of the short-story writer," she noted, "is how to make the action he describes reveal as much of the mystery of existence as possible. He has only a short space to do it in and he can't do it by statement. He has to do it by showing, not by saying, and by showing the concrete—so that his problem is how to make the concrete work double time for him."

From the first, she was recognized as a satirist of astonishing originality and vigor, whose targets were smugness, optimism, and self-righteousness. However, the essential element of Flannery O'Connor's life and work was that she was born a Roman Catholic and that she remained one without the slightest wavering of faith throughout her thirty-nine years. A thunder-and-lightning Christian belief pervades every story and novel she ever wrote. Her attraction to the grotesque and the violent puts off many critics and readers. They fail to appreciate that the violent motifs in her fiction grow from her passionate, Christian vision of our secular times.

What she wanted to tell us, in a voice that could not be ignored, was that in our rationality we had lost the one essential—a spiritual center for our lives. "Redemption is meaningless," O'Connor wrote, "unless there is cause for it in the actual life we live, and for the last few centuries there has been operating in our culture the secular belief that there is no such cause."

The title story of *A Good Man Is Hard to Find,* for example, concerns a family of six, all of whom are killed by an escaped convict, the Misfit. When the grandmother pleads with the Misfit to pray to Jesus for help, he replies: "I don't need no hep. I'm doing all right by myself." O'Connor seems to be saying that we have become so accustomed to the lack of God in our lives that a writer must use violent means to communicate the point. Her method is rather like that of the expert mule-trainer, who begins a school by smiting the animal on the head with a two-by-four, explaining "First you have to get their attention."

With all their peculiarities, O'Connor's characters are disturbingly familiar. They are homespun figures, worldly as any Georgia barnyard or roadside café, drawn with a kind of humor that balances on the edge of terror. Just as we are made to feel comfortable, enjoying the carnival show, the comedy is miraculously transcended, and we realize that the situation has a philosophical meaning. All the freaks and clowns have taken on God's meaning. God is here, and the devil is too. They are wholly in charge—the devil is tempting away, and, without waiting for the Day of Judgment, God is dishing out a terrible punishment to the wicked.

THE LIFE YOU SAVE MAY BE YOUR OWN

You won't have to read very far to discover that this story is both disturbing and funny. Pay special attention to the way the characters talk. Don't let the casual, down-home voice fool you, however. "The Life You Save May Be Your Own" is an exquisite piece of storytelling. There are three vivid characters here, each one a masterful portrait from the rural South. They find themselves in a situation that is both tragic and comic, and they act out a classic theme—that of innocence beset by evil.

You don't believe that by the story's end Mr. Shiftlet will avoid his punishment, do you? That's no ordinary, passing cloud in his path . . . is it?

The old woman and her daughter were sitting on their porch when Mr. Shiftlet came up their road for the first time. The old woman slid to the edge of her chair and leaned forward, shading her eyes from the piercing sunset with her hand. The daughter could not see far in front of her and continued to play with her fingers. Although the old woman lived in this desolate spot with only her daughter and she had never seen Mr. Shiftlet before, she could tell, even from a distance, that he was a tramp and no one to be afraid of. His left coat sleeve was folded up to show there was only half an arm in it and his gaunt figure listed slightly to the side as if the breeze were pushing him. He had on a black town suit and a brown felt hat that was turned up in the front and down in the back and he carried a tin tool box by a handle. He came on, at an amble, up her road, his face turned toward the sun which appeared to be balancing itself on the peak of a small mountain.

The old woman didn't change her position until he was almost into her yard; then she rose with one hand fisted on her hip. The daughter, a large girl in a short blue organdy dress, saw him all at once and jumped up and began to stamp and point and make excited speechless sounds.

Mr. Shiftlet stopped just inside the yard and set his box on the ground and tipped his hat at her as if she were not in the least afflicted; then he turned toward the old woman and swung the hat all the way off. He had long black slick hair that hung flat from a part in the middle to beyond the tips of his ears on either side. His face descended in forehead for more than half its length and ended suddenly with his features just balanced over a jutting steel-trap jaw. He seemed to be a young man but he had a look of composed dissatisfaction as if he understood life thoroughly.

"Good evening," the old woman said. She was about the size of a cedar fence post and she had a man's gray hat pulled down low over her head.

Post office in Nethers, Virginia (1935). Photograph by
Arthur Rothstein.

Courtesy of Mrs. Arthur Rothstein.

The tramp stood looking at her and didn't answer. He turned his back and faced the sunset. He swung both his whole and his short arm up slowly so that they indicated an expanse of sky and his figure formed a crooked cross. The old woman watched him with her arms folded across her chest as if she were the owner of the sun, and the daughter watched, her head thrust forward and her fat helpless hands hanging at the wrists. She had long pink-gold hair and eyes as blue as a peacock's neck.

He held the pose for almost fifty seconds and then he picked up his box and came on to the porch and dropped down on the bottom step. "Lady," he said in a firm nasal voice, "I'd give a fortune to live where I could see me a sun do that every evening."

"Does it every evening," the old woman said and sat back down. The daughter sat down too and watched him with a cautious sly look as if he were a bird that had come up very close. He leaned to one side, rooting in his pants pocket, and in a second he brought out a package of chewing gum and offered her a piece. She took it and unpeeled it and began to chew without taking her eyes off him. He offered the old woman a piece but she only raised her upper lip to indicate she had no teeth.

Mr. Shiftlet's pale sharp glance had already passed over everything in the yard—the pump near the corner of the house and the big fig tree that three or four chickens were preparing to roost in—and had moved to a shed where he saw the square rusted back of an automobile. "You ladies drive?" he asked.

"That car ain't run in fifteen year," the old woman said. "The day my husband died, it quit running."

"Nothing is like it used to be, lady," he said. "The world is almost rotten."

"That's right," the old woman said. "You from around here?"

"Name Tom T. Shiftlet," he murmured, looking at the tires.

"I'm pleased to meet you," the old woman said. "Name Lucynell Crater and daughter Lucynell Crater. What you doing around here, Mr. Shiftlet?"

He judged the car to be about a 1928 or '29 Ford. "Lady," he said, and turned and gave her his full attention, "lemme tell you something. There's one of these doctors in Atlanta that's taken a knife and cut the human heart—the human heart," he repeated, leaning forward, "out of a man's chest and held it in his hand," and he held his hand out, palm up, as if it were slightly weighted with the human heart, "and studied it like it was a day-old chicken, and lady," he said, allowing a long significant pause in which his head slid forward and his clay-colored eyes brightened, "he don't know no more about it than you or me."

"That's right," the old woman said.

"Why, if he was to take that knife and cut into every corner of it, he still wouldn't know no more than you or me. What you want to bet?"

"Nothing," the old woman said wisely. "Where you come from, Mr. Shiftlet?"

He didn't answer. He reached into his pocket and brought out a sack of tobacco and a package of cigarette papers and rolled himself a cigarette, expertly with one hand, and attached it in a hanging position to his upper lip. Then he took a box of wooden matches from his pocket and struck one on his shoe. He held the burning match as if he were studying the mystery of flame while it traveled dangerously toward his skin. The daughter began to make loud noises and to point to his hand and shake her finger at him, but when the flame was just before touching him, he leaned down with his hand cupped over it as if he were going to set fire to his nose and lit the cigarette.

He flipped away the dead match and blew a stream of gray into the evening. A sly look came over his face. "Lady," he said, "nowadays, people'll do anything anyways. I can tell you my name is Tom T. Shiftlet and I come from Tarwater, Tennessee, but you never have seen me before: how you know I ain't lying? How you know my name ain't Aaron Sparks, lady, and I come from Singleberry, Georgia, or how you know it's not George Speeds and I come from Lucy, Alabama, or how you know I ain't Thompson Bright from Toolafalls, Mississippi?"

"I don't know nothing about you," the old woman muttered, irked.

"Lady," he said, "people don't care how they lie. Maybe the best I can tell you is, I'm a man; but listen lady," he said and paused and made his tone more ominous still, "what is a man?"

The old woman began to gum a seed. "What you carry in that tin box, Mr. Shiftlet?" she asked.

"Tools," he said, put back. "I'm a carpenter."

"Well, if you come out here to work, I'll be able to feed you and give you a place to sleep but

I can't pay. I'll tell you that before you begin," she said.

There was no answer at once and no particular expression on his face. He leaned back against the two-by-four that helped support the porch roof. "Lady," he said slowly, "there's some men that some things mean more to them than money." The old woman rocked without comment and the daughter watched the trigger that moved up and down in his neck. He told the old woman then that all most people were interested in was money, but he asked what a man was made for. He asked her if a man was made for money, or what. He asked her what she thought she was made for but she didn't answer, she only sat rocking and wondered if a one-armed man could put a new roof on her garden house. He asked a lot of questions that she didn't answer. He told her that he was twenty-eight years old and had lived a varied life. He had been a gospel singer, a foreman on the railroad, an assistant in an undertaking parlor, and he come over the radio for three months with Uncle Roy and his Red Creek Wranglers. He said he had fought and bled in the Arm Service of his country and visited every foreign land and that everywhere he had seen people that didn't care if they did a thing one way or another. He said he hadn't been raised thataway.

A fat yellow moon appeared in the branches of the fig tree as if it were going to roost there with the chickens. He said that a man had to escape to the country to see the world whole and that he wished he lived in a desolate place like this where he could see the sun go down every evening like God made it to do.

"Are you married or are you single?" the old woman asked.

There was a long silence. "Lady," he asked finally, "where would you find you an innocent woman today? I wouldn't have any of this trash I could just pick up."

The daughter was leaning very far down, hanging her head almost between her knees watching him through a triangular door she had made in her overturned hair; and she suddenly fell in a heap on the floor and began to whimper. Mr. Shiftlet straightened her out and helped her get back in the chair.

"Is she your baby girl?" he asked.

"My only," the old woman said "and she's the sweetest girl in the world. I would give her up for nothing on earth. She's smart too. She can sweep the floor, cook, wash, feed the chickens, and hoe. I wouldn't give her up for a casket of jewels."

"No," he said kindly, "don't ever let any man take her away from you."

"Any man come after her," the old woman said, "I'll have to stay around the place."

Mr. Shiftlet's eye in the darkness was focused on a part of the automobile bumper that glittered in the distance. "Lady," he said, jerking his short arm up as if he could point with it to her house and yard and pump, "there ain't a broken thing on this plantation that I couldn't fix for you, one-arm jackleg or not. I'm a man," he said with a sullen dignity, "even if I ain't a whole one. I got," he said, tapping his knuckles on the floor to emphasize the immensity of what he was going to say, "a moral intelligence!" and his face pierced out of the darkness into a shaft of doorlight and he stared at her as if he were astonished himself at this impossible truth.

The old woman was not impressed with the phrase. "I told you you could hang around and work for food," she said, "if you don't mind sleeping in that car yonder."

"Why listen, lady," he said with a grin of delight, "the monks of old slept in their coffins!"

"They wasn't as advanced as we are," the old woman said.

The next morning he began on the roof of the garden house while Lucynell, the daughter, sat on a rock and watched him work. He had not been around a week before the change he had made in the place was apparent. He had patched the front and back steps, built a new hog pen, restored a fence, and taught Lucynell, who was completely deaf and had never said a word in her life, to say the word "bird." The big rosy-faced girl followed him everywhere, saying "Burrttddt ddbirrrttdt," and clapping her hands. The old woman watched from a distance, secretly pleased. She was ravenous for a son-in-law.

Mr. Shiftlet slept on the hard narrow back seat of the car with his feet out the side window. He had his razor and a can of water on a crate that served him as a bedside table and he put up a piece of mirror against the back glass and kept his coat neatly on a hanger that he hung over one of the windows.

In the evenings he sat on the steps and talked while the old woman and Lucynell rocked violently in their chairs on either side of him. The old woman's three mountains were black against the dark blue sky and were visited off and on by various planets and by the moon after it had left the chickens. Mr. Shiftlet pointed out that the reason he had improved this plantation was because he had taken a personal interest in it. He said he was even going to make the automobile run.

He had raised the hood and studied the mechanism and he said he could tell that the car had been built in the days when cars were really built. You take now, he said, one man puts in one bolt and another man puts in another bolt and another man puts in another bolt so that it's a man for a bolt. That's why you have to pay so much for a car: you're paying all those men. Now if you didn't have to pay but one man, you could get you a cheaper car and one that had had a personal interest taken in it, and it would be a better car. The old woman agreed with him that this was so.

Mr. Shiftlet said that the trouble with the world was that nobody cared, or stopped and took any trouble. He said he never would have been able to teach Lucynell to say a word if he hadn't cared and stopped long enough.

"Teach her to say something else," the old woman said.

"What you want her to say next?" Mr. Shiftlet asked.

The old woman's smile was broad and toothless and suggestive. "Teach her to say 'sugarpie,' " she said.

Mr. Shiftlet already knew what was on her mind.

The next day he began to tinker with the automobile and that evening he told her that if she would buy a fan belt, he would be able to make the car run.

The old woman said she would give him the money. "You see that girl yonder?" she asked, pointing to Lucynell who was sitting on the floor a foot away, watching him, her eyes blue even in the dark. "If it was ever a man wanted to take her away, I would say, 'No man on earth is going to take that sweet girl of mine away from me!' but if he was to say, 'Lady, I don't want to take her away, I want her right here,' I would say, 'Mister, I don't blame you none. I wouldn't pass up a chance to live in a permanent place and get the sweetest girl in the world myself. You ain't no fool,' I would say."

"How old is she?" Mr. Shiftlet asked casually.

"Fifteen, sixteen," the old woman said. The girl was nearly thirty but because of her innocence it was impossible to guess.

"It would be a good idea to paint it too," Mr. Shiftlet remarked. "You don't want it to rust out."

"We'll see about that later," the old woman said.

The next day he walked into town and returned with the parts he needed and a can of gasoline. Late in the afternoon, terrible noises issued from the shed and the old woman rushed out of the house, thinking Lucynell was somewhere having a fit. Lucynell was sitting on a chicken crate, stamping her feet and screaming, "Burrddttt! bddurrddtttt!" but her fuss was drowned out by the car. With a volley of blasts it emerged from the shed, moving in a fierce and stately way. Mr. Shiftlet was in the driver's seat, sitting very erect. He had an expression of serious modesty on his face as if he had just raised the dead.

That night, rocking on the porch, the old woman began her business, at once. "You want you an innocent woman, don't you?" she asked sympathetically. "You don't want none of this trash."

"No'm, I don't," Mr. Shiftlet said.

"One that can't talk," she continued, "can't sass you back or use foul language. That's the kind for you to have. Right there," and she pointed to Lucynell sitting cross-legged in her chair, holding both feet in her hands.

"That's right," he admitted. "She wouldn't give me any trouble."

"Saturday," the old woman said, "you and her and me can drive into town and get married."

Mr. Shiftlet eased his position on the steps.

"I can't get married right now," he said. "Everything you want to do takes money and I ain't got any."

"What you need with money?" she asked.

"It takes money," he said. "Some people'll do anything anyhow these days, but the way I think, I wouldn't marry no woman that I couldn't take on a trip like she was somebody. I mean take her to a hotel and treat her. I wouldn't marry the Duchesser Windsor," he said firmly, "unless I could take her to a hotel and giver something good to eat.

"I was raised thataway and there ain't a thing I can do about it. My old mother taught me how to do."

"Lucynell don't even know what a hotel is,"

the old woman muttered. "Listen here, Mr. Shiftlet," she said, sliding forward in her chair, "you'd be getting a permanent house and a deep well and the most innocent girl in the world. You don't need no money. Lemme tell you something: there ain't any place in the world for a poor disabled friendless drifting man."

The ugly words settled in Mr. Shiftlet's head like a group of buzzards in the top of a tree. He didn't answer at once. He rolled himself a cigarette and lit it and then he said in an even voice, "Lady, a man is divided into two parts, body and spirit."

The old woman clamped her gums together.

"A body and a spirit," he repeated. "The body, lady, is like a house: it don't go anywhere; but the spirit, lady, is like an automobile: always on the move, always . . ."

"Listen, Mr. Shiftlet," she said, "my well never goes dry and my house is always warm in the winter and there's no mortgage on a thing about this place. You can go to the courthouse and see for yourself. And yonder under that shed is a fine automobile." She laid the bait carefully. "You can have it painted by Saturday. I'll pay for the paint."

In the darkness, Mr. Shiftlet's smile stretched like a weary snake waking up by a fire. After a second he recalled himself and said, "I'm only saying a man's spirit means more to him than anything else. I would have to take my wife off for the weekend without no regards at all for cost. I got to follow where my spirit says to go."

"I'll give you fifteen dollars for a weekend trip," the old woman said in a crabbed voice. "That's the best I can do."

"That wouldn't hardly pay for more than the gas and the hotel," he said. "It wouldn't feed her."

"Seventeen-fifty," the old woman said. "That's all I got so it isn't any use you trying to milk me. You can take a lunch."

Mr. Shiftlet was deeply hurt by the word "milk." He didn't doubt that she had more money sewed up in her mattress but he had already told her he was not interested in her money. "I'll make that do," he said and rose and walked off without treating with her further.

On Saturday the three of them drove into town in the car that the paint had barely dried on and Mr. Shiftlet and Lucynell were married in the Ordinary's office while the old woman witnessed. As they came out of the courthouse, Mr. Shiftlet began twisting his neck in his collar. He looked morose and bitter as if he had been insulted while someone held him. "That didn't satisfy me none," he said. "That was just something a woman in an office did, nothing but paper work and blood tests. What do they know about my blood? If they was to take my heart and cut it out," he said, "they wouldn't know a thing about me. It didn't satisfy me at all."

"It satisfied the law," the old woman said sharply.

"The law," Mr. Shiftlet said and spit. "It's the law that don't satisfy me."

He had painted the car dark green with a yellow band around it just under the windows. The three of them climbed in the front seat and the old woman said, "Don't Lucynell look pretty? Looks like a baby doll." Lucynell was dressed up in a white dress that her mother had uprooted from a trunk and there was a Panama hat on her head with a bunch of red wooden cherries on the brim. Every now and then her placid expression was changed by a sly isolated little thought like a shoot of green in the desert. "You got a prize!" the old woman said.

Mr. Shiftlet didn't even look at her.

They drove back to the house to let the old woman off and pick up the lunch. When they were ready to leave, she stood staring in the window of the car, with her fingers clenched around the glass. Tears began to seep sideways out of her eyes and run along the dirty creases in her face. "I ain't ever been parted with her for two days before," she said.

Mr. Shiftlet started the motor.

"And I wouldn't let no man have her but you because I seen you would do right. Goodbye, Sugarbaby," she said, clutching at the sleeve of the white dress. Lucynell looked straight at her and didn't seem to see her there at all. Mr. Shiftlet eased the car forward so that she had to move her hands.

The early afternoon was clear and open and surrounded by pale blue sky. Although the car would go only thirty miles an hour, Mr. Shiftlet imagined a terrific climb and dip and swerve that went entirely to his head so that he forgot his morning bitterness. He had always wanted an automobile but he had never been able to afford one before. He drove very fast because he wanted to make Mobile by nightfall.

Occasionally he stopped his thoughts long enough to look at Lucynell in the seat beside him. She had eaten the lunch as soon as they were out of the yard and now she was pulling the cherries off the hat one by one and throwing them out the window. He became depressed in spite of the car. He had driven about a hundred miles when he decided that she must be hungry again and at the next small town they came to, he stopped in front of an aluminum-painted eating place called The Hot Spot and took her in and ordered her a plate of ham and grits. The ride had made her sleepy and as soon as she got up on the stool, she rested her head on the counter and shut her eyes. There was no one in The Hot Spot but Mr. Shiftlet and the boy behind the counter, a pale youth with a greasy rag hung over his shoulder. Before he could dish the food, she was snoring gently.

"Give it to her when she wakes up," Mr. Shiftlet said. "I'll pay for it now."

The boy bent over her and stared at the long pink-gold hair and the half-shut sleeping eyes. Then he looked up and and stared at Mr. Shiftlet. "She looks like an angel of Gawd," he murmured.

"Hitchhiker," Mr. Shiftlet explained. "I can't wait. I got to make Tuscaloosa."

The boy bent over again and very carefully touched his finger to a strand of the golden hair and Mr. Shiftlet left.

He was more depressed than ever as he drove on by himself. The late afternoon had grown hot and sultry and the country had flattened out. Deep in the sky a storm was preparing very slowly and without thunder as if it meant to drain every drop of air from the earth before it broke. There were times when Mr. Shiftlet preferred not to be alone. He felt too that a man with a car had a responsibility to others and he kept his eye out for a hitchhiker. Occasionally he saw a sign that warned: "Drive carefully. The life you save may be your own."

The narrow road dropped off on either side into dry fields and here and there a shack or a filling station stood in a clearing. The sun began to set directly in front of the automobile. It was a reddening ball that through his windshield was slightly flat on the bottom and top. He saw a boy in overalls and a gray hat standing on the edge of the road and he slowed the car down and stopped in front of him. The boy didn't have his hand raised to thumb the ride, he was only standing there, but he had a small cardboard suitcase and his hat was set on his head in a way to indicate that he had left somewhere for good. "Son," Mr. Shiftlet said, "I see you want a ride."

The boy didn't say he did or he didn't but he opened the door of the car and got in, and Mr. Shiftlet started driving again. The child held the suitcase on his lap and folded his arms on top of it. He turned his head and looked out the window away from Mr. Shiftlet. Mr. Shiftlet felt oppressed. "Son," he said after a minute, "I got the best old mother in the world so I reckon you only got the second best."

The boy gave him a quick dark glance and then turned his face back out the window.

"It's nothing so sweet," Mr. Shiftlet continued, "as a boy's mother. She taught him his first prayers at her knee, she give him love when no other would, she told him what was right and what wasn't, and she seen that he done the right thing. Son," he said, "I never rued a day in my life like the one I rued when I left that old mother of mine."

The boy shifted in his seat but he didn't look at Mr. Shiftlet. He unfolded his arms and put one hand on the door handle.

"My mother was a angel of Gawd," Mr. Shiftlet said in a very strained voice. "He took her from heaven and giver to me and I left her." His eyes were instantly clouded over with a mist of tears. The car was barely moving.

The boy turned angrily in the seat. "You go to the devil!" he cried. "My old woman is a fleabag and yours is a stinking polecat!" and with that he flung the door open and jumped out with his suitcase into the ditch.

Mr. Shiftlet was so shocked that for about a hundred feet he drove along slowly with the door still open. A cloud, the exact color of the boy's hat and shaped like a turnip, had descended over the sun, and another, worse looking, crouched behind the car. Mr. Shiftlet felt that the rottenness of the world was about to engulf him. He raised his arm and let it fall again to his breast. "Oh Lord!" he prayed. "Break forth and wash the slime from this earth!"

The turnip continued slowly to descend. After a few minutes there was a guffawing peal of thunder from behind and fantastic raindrops, like tin-can tops, crashed over the rear of Mr. Shiftlet's car. Very quickly he stepped on the gas and with his stump sticking out the window he raced the galloping shower into Mobile.

Responding to the Story

Analyzing the Story

Identifying Facts

1. Describe the improvements Mr. Shiftlet makes in the Craters' place during his first week there.
2. Explain how Mr. Shiftlet seems to want to exploit the Craters. How does the older Lucynell want to exploit Mr. Shiftlet?
3. What has become of young Lucynell and Mr. Shiftlet by the story's end?

Interpreting Meanings

4. In the opening pages of the story, what details of **setting,** of **characterization,** and of **dialogue** carry potentially ominous or menacing undertones?
5. What is the significance of the remarks made by the hitchhiker just before he leaps from the moving car? What are we to make of the fact that Mr. Shiftlet feels that "the rottenness of the world" is about to engulf him? What **irony** do you sense in Mr. Shiftlet's realization?
6. The ending of the story focuses on Mr. Shiftlet, rather than on the two Lucynells. Explain how you think the writer means us to regard him. Is he a prophet or a demon? Consider why O'Connor points out, early in the story, that Shiftlet's "figure formed a crooked cross" (page 623).
7. What is the significance of the peculiar clouds and the storm pursuing Mr. Shiftlet toward Mobile at the end of the story?
8. How would the story's **theme** and **effect** have changed if Mr. Shiftlet had returned to the café for Lucynell? How did you feel about the way the story ended?
9. Do you sense **irony** in the story's title? How would you state the story's **theme,** using the warning expressed in the title?
10. Can you see any relationship between Mr. Shiftlet and Flem Snopes in "Spotted Horses" (page 607). Explain.
11. Are there any heroes in this story? Do you think it is a story about innocence vs. evil? Or do you think it is a story about a world in which everyone is a rogue? Explain.
12. Think of this story in relation to other stories you have read. What is your response to O'Connor's characters and theme? What do you think of her **tone?**

Writing About the Story

A Creative Response

1. **Extending the Story.** What becomes of Lucynell, asleep in the Hot Spot? Write an ending to the story in which you account for Lucynell.

A Critical Response

2. **Expressing an Opinion.** Read O'Connor's comments about this story under "Primary Sources" (which follows). In a brief essay, tell (a) why you think the TV producers would change the story, (b) whether you think the story would be popular if it were dramatized on TV today, or made into a movie, and (c) why a textbook would omit the last paragraph.
3. **Analyzing the Story.** In an essay, state whether you think the story is an **ironic parody** of a **romance.** (See page 630.) If so, account for these ironic reversals of the typical romance story:

   a. The nurturing mother
   b. The beautiful, innocent young woman
   c. The charming prince who is the rescuer
   d. The romance setting in a fairy-tale kingdom

Analyzing Language and Style

Connotations

In addition to its literal meaning, a word may have **connotative** meanings—that is, associations and emotional overtones that have come to be attached to the word. In this story, O'Connor uses words with strong connotations to reveal an attitude toward the character of Mr. Shiftlet.

1. Skim the story to find four **figures of speech** used to describe Mr. Shiftlet's appearance or actions. What do you associate with each figure of speech? What feelings do the descriptive words arouse in you?
2. Find two words used to describe the cloud and thunder that pursue Mr. Shiftlet toward Mobile.
3. Taken all together, what do you think these six words or phrases reveal about Mr. Shiftlet and the way we are to regard him?
4. For the words *steel-trap, clay-colored, trigger, snake, turnips,* and *guffawed,* substitute words with completely different connotations. What happens to our view of the character of Mr. Shiftlet?

Primary Sources
The Adventures of Mr. Shiftlet

The following comments are from O'Connor's collection of letters called *The Habit of Being*.

"I am going to New York on the 30th to be, if you please, interviewed by Mr. Harvey Breit (on the 31st) on a program he is starting up over at NBC-TV [*Galley-Proof*]. They are also going to dramatize the opening scene from 'The Life You Save' etc. Do you reckon this is going to corrupt me? I already feel like a combination of Msgr. Sheen and Gorgeous George [a wrestler]. Everybody who has read *Wise Blood* thinks I'm a hillbilly nihilist, whereas I would like to create the impression over the television that I'm a hillbilly Thomist,[1] but I will probably not be able to think of anything to say to Mr. Harvey Breit but 'Huh?' and 'Ah dunno.' When I come back I'll probably have to spend three months day and night in the chicken pen to counteract these evil influences.

. . .

"I have just sold the television rights to 'The Life You Save May Be Your Own' to what I understand is called the General Electric Playhouse. All I know about television is hearsay but somebody told me that this was a production conducted by Ronald Regan (?). I don't know if this means RR will be Mr. Shiftlet or not. A staggering thought. Mr. Shiftlet and the idiot daughter will no doubt go off in a Chrysler and live happily ever after. Anyway, on account of this, I am buying my mother a new refrigerator. While they make hash out of my story, she and me will make ice in the new refrigerator.

. . .

"I have just learned via one of those gossip columns that the story I sold for a TV play is going to be put on in the spring and that a *tap-dancer* by the name of Gene Kelly is going to make his television debut in it. The punishment always fits the crime. They must be going to make a musical out of it

. . .

"... A letter from my agent today announces that 'The Life You Save' will be presented February 1 on the Schlitz Playhouse at 9:30 New York time. My eager beaver friend in NY keeps sending me clippings of gossip columns, one announcing that Kelly will star in Flannery O'Connor's 'backwoods love story.' Another saying Kelly says 'It's a kind of hillbilly thing in which I play a guy who *befriends* a deaf-mute girl in the hills of Kentucky. It gives me a great chance to do some straight acting, something I really have no opportunity to do in movies.' See? He ain't had the opportunity before. There'll be no singing & dancing, Kelly says. I think it's chanel 5 and people tell me you can't get it very good here, so I hope you will absolutely be in front of your set this time at the correct hour, as I must have some representative there to give Kelly a good leer every now and then for me. I don't know who his leading lady will be, but doubtless my NY friend will be providing that information before long. She thinks this is all hilariously funny and keeps writing me, 'Has dignity no value for you?' etc. It will probably be appropriate to smoke a corncob pipe while watching this. All my kinfolks are going to think that it is a great improvement over the original story.

. . .

"Someone has just called my attention to the fact that this . . . text which has 'The Life You Save' in it has it with the last paragraph omitted. I would be much obliged if you would call Harcourt [her publisher] and tell them. I think some kind of protest ought to be lodged. I suppose there is nothing that can be done about it now but I centainly don't like the idea of my story being in a text-book and the last paragraph omitted. . . ."

—Flannery O'Connor

---

1. **Thomist:** someone who follows the thinking of the thirteenth-century philosopher Thomas Aquinas.

THE FOUR "MODES" OF FICTION

According to some critics, all narrative literature can be more or less described in terms of four basic "modes," or story patterns. These modes are romance, tragedy, irony, and comedy. Tragedy and comedy are opposites, and so are romance and irony.

In the typical **romance** story, a hero or heroine undertakes a quest and is usually successful. In such a story (and we are all familiar with them from the fairy tales of our childhoods), beauty, innocence, and goodness prevail over evil, often with the help of magic or supernatural intervention.

In a typical **tragedy,** on the other hand, the hero or heroine is a noble, admirable character who falls from a position of some prominence to disaster or even death. This tragic hero is overcome by evil, but in the course of the struggle, he or she has also gained self-knowledge and wisdom. Our response to tragedy is often a kind of exhilaration. We have seen the best that human beings are capable of, especially in the face of overwhelming adversity.

Opposite to romance is **irony.** In the world of irony, there are no heroes and no triumphs. There are certainly no fairy godmothers and no magic wands. In some ironic stories, the world is a place where injustice, crime, and general foolishness are taken for granted. The characters who triumph in such a world are often crafty rascals and even con artists—people who learn how to manipulate the world for their own gain. In other forms of irony, the characters are ordinary human beings like ourselves, who are caught in a world that offers little opportunity for heroism. Unlike the great tragic heroes, these characters are all too human. Walter Mitty is an example of this type of character, one who longs for heroism but is limited to shopping for puppy biscuits in Waterbury, Connecticut. The characters in ironic fiction often find themselves in settings that are confining, that offer no opportunities for free choice. Such fiction is often actually set in prisons, totalitarian societies, or even madhouses.

Opposite to tragedy is **comedy.** In a comedy, the central characters are often two lovers who want to marry despite parental and societal obstacles. By the end of a comedy, the young lovers have triumphed over the forces blocking them and are to be married. At the end of many comedies, we even have a wedding, suggesting the renewal of life and love. Other comedies are about characters who triumph over the forces of tradition that are blocking their freedom in some way. At the end of such comedies, the characters are embarked on a new life, unhampered by the bonds that had blocked them earlier.

These are extremely simple descriptions of the complex modes used in narrative literature. You can see from the description of irony that O'Connor's story—and many of the other stories in this unit—can be seen as examples of the ironic mode.

What modes do you think the other stories in this unit are written in?

Eudora Welty
(1909–   )

Eudora Welty was born in the quintessentially Southern city of Jackson, Mississippi, and she has lived in Jackson almost her whole life. As the daughter of an insurance man and a school-teacher, she enjoyed a conventional girlhood. She recalls pleading with her brothers to teach her golf, sharing their enthusiasm for baseball, and bicycling to the library in *two* petticoats to forestall the librarian's caustic remark, "I can see straight through you."

Welty attended Mississippi State College for Women, graduated from the University of Wisconsin, and did graduate work at Columbia University, anticipating a career in advertising. However, the depression sent her home to Jackson with a belief, which did not fail her, that she would succeed as a writer of fiction.

Welty's widely recognized triumph is a painstaking accuracy in colloquial speech. The exactly right word always matters to her. She has always been fascinated by words, by the *way* people say things, by snatches of overheard dialogue. She was once delighted to hear a country woman confess to "a gnawing and a craving" for something. Telling a friend about it, Welty added, "Wasn't that a wonderful way of putting it? A gnawing and a craving!"

She greatly admires the work of Katherine Anne Porter (see page 600), who befriended her when she was sending out stories and getting back rejection slips. It was the literary agent Diarmuid Russell who shared Welty's belief in an ultimate success. He not only took her on as a client, but said of a certain Welty story that if the editor didn't accept it, "he ought to be horse-whipped." (The editor in question bought the story.)

Welty's first collections of stories, *A Curtain of Green* and *The Wide Net,* appeared in the

1940's. These were followed by *The Golden Apples* (1949), one of her best-known volumes of short stories. Then came a novella, *The Ponder Heart* (1954), which was made into a Broadway play. *Losing Battles,* Welty's fine comic novel about a family reunion in the rural South, was published in 1970. Two years later, Welty produced *The Optimist's Daughter,* a poignant short novel about family conflicts; this book won her the Pulitzer Prize. An autobiographical memoir entitled *One Writer's Beginnings,* based on lectures Welty gave at Harvard University, was published in 1983 to wide critical acclaim.

Welty admits to being blessed with a visual mind, and she says that this gift makes for "the best shorthand a writer can have." She once wrote, "To watch everything about me, I regarded grimly and possessively as a *need.*" Clearly, that need became an enviable, artistic vision.

A WORN PATH

The major character in this story is named Phoenix Jackson. Before you begin reading, look up the word *phoenix* in a dictionary. As you read, think about why Welty chose this name for her traveler. Phoenix makes her journey in rural Mississippi, late in the Depression era.

It was December—a bright frozen day in the early morning. Far out in the country there was an old Negro woman with her head tied in a red rag, coming along a path through the pinewoods. Her name was Phoenix Jackson. She was very old and small and she walked slowly in the dark pine shadows, moving a little from side to side in her steps, with the balanced heaviness and lightness of a pendulum in a grandfather clock. She carried a thin, small cane made from an umbrella, and with this she kept tapping the frozen earth in front of her. This made a grave and persistent noise in the still air, that seemed meditative like the chirping of a solitary little bird.

She wore a dark striped dress reaching down to her shoe tops, and an equally long apron of bleached sugar sacks, with a full pocket: all neat and tidy, but every time she took a step she might have fallen over her shoelaces, which dragged from her unlaced shoes. She looked straight ahead. Her eyes were blue with age. Her skin had a pattern all its own of numberless branching wrinkles and as though a whole little tree stood in the middle of her forehead, but a golden color ran underneath, and the two knobs of her cheeks were illumined by a yellow burning under the dark. Under the red rag her hair came down on her neck in the frailest of ringlets, still black, and with an odor like copper.

Now and then there was a quivering in the thicket. Old Phoenix said, "Out of my way, all you foxes, owls, beetles, jack rabbits, coons and wild animals! . . . Keep out from under these feet, little bobwhites. . . . Keep the big wild hogs out of my path. Don't let none of those come running my direction. I got a long way." Under her small black-freckled hand her cane, limber as a buggy whip, would switch at the brush as if to rouse up any hiding things.

On she went. The woods were deep and still. The sun made the pine needles almost too bright to look at, up where the wind rocked. The cones dropped as light as feathers. Down in the hollow was the mourning dove—it was not too late for him.

The path ran up a hill. "Seem like there is chains about my feet, time I get this far," she said, in the voice of argument old people keep to use with themselves. "Something always take a hold of me on this hill—pleads I should stay."

After she got to the top she turned and gave a full, severe look behind her where she had come. "Up through pines," she said at length. "Now down through oaks."

Her eyes opened their widest, and she started down gently. But before she got to the bottom of the hill a bush caught her dress.

Her fingers were busy and intent, but her skirts were full and long, so that before she could pull them free in one place they were caught in another. It was not possible to allow the dress to tear. "I in the thorny bush," she said. "Thorns, you doing your appointed work. Never want to let folks pass, no sir. Old eyes thought you was a pretty little *green* bush."

Finally, trembling all over, she stood free, and after a moment dared to stoop for her cane.

"Sun so high!" she cried, leaning back and looking, while the thick tears went over her eyes. "The time getting all gone here."

At the foot of this hill was a place where a log was laid across the creek.

"Now comes the trial," said Phoenix.

Putting her right foot out, she mounted the log and shut her eyes. Lifting her skirt, leveling her cane fiercely before her, like a festival figure in some parade, she began to march across. Then she opened her eyes and she was safe on the other side.

"I wasn't as old as I thought," she said.

But she sat down to rest. She spread her skirts on the bank around her and folded her hands over

her knees. Up above her was a tree in a pearly cloud of mistletoe. She did not dare to close her eyes, and when a little boy brought her a plate with a slice of marble cake on it she spoke to him. "That would be acceptable," she said. But when she went to take it there was just her own hand in the air.

So she left that tree, and had to go through a barbed-wire fence. There she had to creep and crawl, spreading her knees and stretching her fingers like a baby trying to climb the steps. But she talked loudly to herself: she could not let her dress be torn now, so late in the day, and she could not pay for having her arm or her leg sawed off if she got caught fast where she was.

At last she was safe through the fence and risen up out in the clearing. Big dead trees, like black men with one arm, were standing in the purple stalks of the withered cotton field. There sat a buzzard.

"Who you watching?"

In the furrow she made her way along.

"Glad this not the season for bulls," she said, looking sideways, "and the good Lord made his snakes to curl up and sleep in the winter. A pleasure I don't see no two-headed snake coming around that tree, where it come once. It took a while to get by him, back in the summer."

She passed through the old cotton and went into a field of dead corn. It whispered and shook and was taller than her head. "Through the maze now," she said, for there was no path.

Then there was something tall, black, and skinny there, moving before her.

At first she took it for a man. It could have been a man dancing in the field. But she stood still and listened, and it did not make a sound. It was as silent as a ghost.

"Ghost," she said sharply, "who be you the ghost of? For I have heard of nary death close by."

But there was no answer—only the ragged dancing in the wind.

She shut her eyes, reached out her hand, and touched a sleeve. She found a coat and inside that an emptiness, cold as ice.

"You scarecrow," she said. Her face lighted. "I ought to be shut up for good," she said with laughter. "My senses is gone. I too old. I the oldest people I ever know. Dance, old scarecrow," she said, "while I dancing with you."

She kicked her foot over the furrow, and with mouth drawn down, shook her head once or twice in a little strutting way. Some husks blew down and whirled in streamers about her skirts.

Then she went on, parting her way from side to side with the cane, through the whispering field. At last she came to the end, to a wagon track where the silver grass blew between the red ruts. The quail were walking around like pullets, seeming all dainty and unseen.

"Walk pretty," she said. "This the easy place. This the easy going."

She followed the track, swaying through the quiet bare fields, through the little strings of trees silver in their dead leaves, past cabins silver from weather, with the doors and windows boarded shut, all like old women under a spell sitting there. "I walking in their sleep," she said, nodding her head vigorously.

In a ravine she went where a spring was silently flowing through a hollow log. Old Phoenix bent and drank. "Sweet gum makes the water sweet," she said, and drank more. "Nobody know who made this well, for it was here when I was born."

The track crossed a swampy part where the moss hung as white as lace from every limb. "Sleep on, alligators, and blow your bubbles." Then the track went into the road.

Deep, deep the road went down between the high green-colored banks. Overhead the live oaks met, and it was as dark as a cave.

A black dog with a lolling tongue came up out of the weeds by the ditch. She was meditating, and not ready, and when he came at her she only hit him a little with her cane. Over she went in the ditch, like a little puff of milkweed.

Down there, her senses drifted away. A dream visited her, and she reached her hand up, but nothing reached down and gave her a pull. So she lay there and presently went to talking. "Old woman," she said to herself, "that black dog come up out of the weeds to stall you off, and now there he sitting on his fine tail, smiling at you."

A white man finally came along and found her—a hunter, a young man, with his dog on a chain.

"Well, Granny!" he laughed. "What are you doing there?"

"Lying on my back like a June bug waiting to be turned over, mister," she said, reaching up her hand.

He lifted her up, gave her a swing in the air, and set her down. "Anything broken, Granny?"

"No, sir, them old dead weeds is springy enough," said Phoenix, when she had got her breath. "I thank you for your trouble."

"Where do you live, Granny?" he asked, while the two dogs were growling at each other.

"Away back yonder, sir, behind the ridge. You can't even see it from here."

"On your way home?"

"No sir, I going to town."

"Why, that's too far! That's as far as I walk when I come out myself, and I get something for my trouble." He patted the stuffed bag he carried, and there hung down a little closed claw. It was one of the bobwhites, with its beak hooked bitterly to show it was dead. "Now you go on home, Granny!"

"I bound to go to town, mister," said Phoenix. "The time come around."

He gave another laugh, filling the whole landscape. "I know you old colored people! Wouldn't miss going to town to see Santa Claus!"

But something held old Phoenix very still. The deep lines in her face went into a fierce and different radiation. Without warning, she had seen with her own eyes a flashing nickel fall out of the man's pocket onto the ground.

"How old are you, Granny?" he was saying.

"There is no telling, mister," she said, "no telling."

Then she gave a little cry and clapped her hands and said, "Git on away from here, dog! Look! Look at that dog!" She laughed as if in admiration. "He ain't scared of nobody. He a big black dog." She whispered. "Sic him!"

"Watch me get rid of that cur," said the man. "Sic him, Pete! Sic him!"

Phoenix heard the dogs fighting, and heard the man running and throwing sticks. She even heard a gunshot. But she was slowly bending forward by that time, further and further forward, the lids stretched down over her eyes, as if she were doing this in her sleep. Her chin was lowered almost to her knees. The yellow palm of her hand came out from the fold of her apron. Her fingers slid down and along the ground under the piece of money with the grace and care they would have in lifting an egg from under a setting hen. Then she slowly straightened up, she stood erect, and the nickel was in her apron pocket. A bird flew by. Her lips moved. "God watching me the whole time. I come to stealing."

The man came back, and his own dog panted about them. "Well, I scared him off that time," he said, and then he laughed and lifted his gun and pointed it at Phoenix.

She stood straight and faced him.

"Doesn't the gun scare you?" he said, still pointing it.

"No, sir, I seen plenty go off closer by, in my day, and for less than what I done," she said, holding utterly still.

He smiled, and shouldered the gun. "Well, Granny," he said, "you must be a hundred years old, and scared of nothing. I'd give you a dime if I had any money with me. But you take my advice and stay home, and nothing will happen to you."

"I bound to go on my way, mister," said Phoenix. She inclined her head in the red rag. Then they went in different directions, but she could hear the gun shooting again and again over the hill.

She walked on. The shadows hung from the oak trees to the road like curtains. Then she smelled wood smoke, and smelled the river, and she saw a steeple and the cabins on their steep steps. Dozens of little black children whirled around her. There ahead was Natchez shining. Bells were ringing. She walked on.

In the paved city it was Christmas time. There were red and green electric lights strung and criss-crossed everywhere, and all turned on in the day-time. Old Phoenix would have been lost if she had not distrusted her eyesight and depended on her feet to know where to take her.

She paused quietly on the sidewalk where people were passing by. A lady came along in the crowd, carrying an armful of red-, green- and silver-wrapped presents; she gave off perfume like the red roses in hot summer, and Phoenix stopped her.

"Please, missy, will you lace up my shoe?" She held up her foot.

"What do you want, Grandma?"

"See my shoe," said Phoenix. "Do all right for out in the country, but wouldn't look right to go in a big building."

"Stand still then, Grandma," said the lady. She put her packages down on the sidewalk beside her and laced and tied both shoes tightly.

"Can't lace 'em with a cane," said Phoenix. "Thank you, missy. I doesn't mind asking a nice lady to tie up my shoe, when I gets out on the street."

Moving slowly and from side to side, she went into the big building, and into a tower of steps, where she walked up and around and around until her feet knew to stop.

She entered a door, and there she saw nailed up on the wall the document that had been stamped with the gold seal and framed in the gold frame, which matched the dream that was hung up in her head.

"Here I be," she said. There was a fixed and ceremonial stiffness over her body.

"A charity case, I suppose," said an attendant who sat at the desk before her.

But Phoenix only looked above her head. There was sweat on her face, the wrinkles in her skin shone like a bright net.

"Speak up, Grandma," the woman said. "What's your name? We must have your history, you know. Have you been here before? What seems to be the trouble with you?"

Old Phoenix only gave a twitch to her face as if a fly were bothering her.

"Are you deaf?" cried the attendant.

But then the nurse came in.

"Oh, that's just old Aunt Phoenix," she said. "She doesn't come for herself—she has a little grandson. She makes these trips just as regular as clockwork. She lives away back off the Old Natchez Trace." She bent down. "Well, Aunt Phoenix, why don't you just take a seat? We won't keep you standing after your long trip." She pointed.

The old woman sat down, bolt upright in the chair.

"Now, how is the boy?" asked the nurse.

Old Phoenix did not speak.

"I said, how is the boy?"

But Phoenix only waited and stared straight ahead, her face very solemn and withdrawn into rigidity.

"Is his throat any better?" asked the nurse. "Aunt Phoenix, don't you hear me? Is your grandson's throat any better since the last time you came for the medicine?"

With her hands on her knees, the old woman waited, silent, erect and motionless, just as if she were in armor.

"You mustn't take up our time this way, Aunt

Phoenix," the nurse said. "Tell us quickly about your grandson, and get it over. He isn't dead, is he?"

At last there came a flicker and then a flame of comprehension across her face, and she spoke.

"My grandson. It was my memory had left me. There I sat and forgot why I made my long trip."

"Forgot?" The nurse frowned. "After you came so far?"

Then Phoenix was like an old woman begging a dignified forgiveness for waking up frightened in the night. "I never did go to school, I was too old at the Surrender," she said in a soft voice. "I'm an old woman without an education. It was my memory fail me. My little grandson, he is just the same, and I forgot it in the coming."

"Throat never heals, does it?" said the nurse, speaking in a loud, sure voice to old Phoenix. By now she had a card with something written on it, a little list. "Yes. Swallowed lye. When was it?— January—two-three years ago—"

Phoenix spoke unasked now. "No, missy, he not dead, he just the same. Every little while his throat begin to close up again, and he not able to swallow. He not get his breath. He not able to help himself. So the time come around, and I go on another trip for the soothing medicine."

"All right. The doctor said as long as you came to get it, you could have it," said the nurse. "But it's an obstinate case."

"My little grandson, he sit up there in the house all wrapped up, waiting by himself," Phoenix went on. "We is the only two left in the world. He suffer and it don't seem to put him back at all. He got a sweet look. He going to last. He wear a little patch quilt and peep out holding his mouth open like a little bird. I remembers so plain now. I not going to forget him again, no, the whole enduring time. I could tell him from all the others in creation."

"All right." The nurse was trying to hush her now. She brought her a bottle of medicine. "Charity," she said, making a check mark in a book.

Old Phoenix held the bottle close to her eyes, and then carefully put it into her pocket.

"I thank you," she said.

"It's Christmas time, Grandma," said the attendant. "Could I give you a few pennies out of my purse?"

"Five pennies is a nickel," said Phoenix stiffly.

"Here's a nickel," said the attendant.

Phoenix rose carefully and held out her hand. She received the nickel and then fished the other nickel out of her pocket and laid it beside the new one. She stared at her palm closely, with her head on one side.

Then she gave a tap with her cane on the floor.

"This is what come to me to do," she said. "I going to the store and buy my child a little windmill they sells, made out of paper. He going to find it hard to believe there such a thing in the world. I'll march myself back where he waiting, holding it straight up in this hand."

She lifted her free hand, gave a little nod, turned around, and walked out of the doctor's office. Then her slow step began on the stairs, going down.

Responding to the Story

Analyzing the Story

Identifying Facts

1. Describe the purpose of Phoenix Jackson's journey. On her way to Natchez, what obstacles does she overcome?
2. Explain how Phoenix acquires the two nickels. How does she intend to spend them?
3. What is the result of Phoenix's long and perilous journey through the woods? Does she get what she wants? Explain.

Interpreting Meanings

4. Phoenix Jackson, the central figure of this story, is surely memorable. How do Welty's descriptions of her **appearance**, **speech**, and **behavior** identify her with the world of nature and with time itself?
5. Describe what her encounters with the little boy offering marble cake, with the buzzard, with the scarecrow, with the bramblebush, and finally with the hunter tell us about Phoenix's **character**.
6. Would you describe Phoenix as a heroine, in the traditional sense of the word? Why?

7. What do you suppose possessed the hunter to point his gun at the old woman? Do you think the hunter deliberately lies about not having any money? Or is there another explanation?

8. What is **ironic** about the reason the hunter suggests for Phoenix's long journey? Do many people treat Phoenix condescendingly? Why?

9. Explain the significance of Phoenix's name. Why is it an appropriate name for her?

10. Describe the story's seasonal **setting,** and explain its significance. Does Welty use the setting to make us feel **irony** in the nurses' attitude? Explain.

11. When the nurse gives Phoenix the medicine, she says, "Charity," and makes a check mark in her book. Given the character of Phoenix, what is **ironic** about the nurse's statement and action?

12. When you grasped the purpose of Phoenix's long journey to Natchez, what did you discover about her life? Is it a fulfilled one? Is it tragic? Explain.

13. What do you think is Welty's **theme** in "A Worn Path"? Put another way, what "worn path" is open to us all?

Writing About the Story

A Creative Response

1. **Extending the Story.** Read the essay by Welty that follows below. Then write your own ending for Phoenix's story.

A Critical Response

2. **Analyzing the Journey.** In her comment on the story that follows, Welty summarizes the purposes of the adventures she invented for her character. In an essay, identify the specific parts of the journey that could be categorized as:

   a. dreams
   b. harassments
   c. small triumphs
   d. some jolts to the traveler's pride
   e. some flights of fancy to console the traveler
   f. encounters to scare the traveler
   g. cause to be ashamed
   h. a moment to dance and preen

   In your essay, explain how Phoenix's journey takes on mythic significance—how is it like the quests taken by heroes like Odysseus?

3. **Responding to a Comment.** Welty says of her story, "The only certain thing at all is the worn path," and she identifies the path as a metaphor for the habit of love. In a paragraph, explain what Welty might mean by the "habit of love" and tell why this habit might be compared with a worn path (and not with a new road, or the shining path of a rocket, or a crystal stairway).

4. **Analyzing Character.** Does Phoenix change as a result of her experiences? Or is she essentially timeless? In an essay present your answers to these questions.

Primary Sources
"Is Phoenix Jackson's Grandson Really Dead?"

"A story writer is more than happy to be read by students; the fact that these serious readers think and feel something in response to his work he finds life-giving. At the same time he may not always be able to reply to their specific questions in kind. I wondered if it might clarify something, for both the questioners and myself, if I set down a general reply to the question that comes to me most often in the mail, from both students and their teachers, after some classroom discussion. The unrivaled favorite is this: 'Is Phoenix Jackson's grandson really *dead?*'

"It refers to a short story I wrote years ago called 'A Worn Path,' which tells of a day's journey an old woman makes on foot from deep in the country into town and into a doctor's office on behalf of her little grandson; he is at home, periodically ill, and periodically she comes for his medicine; they give it to her as usual, she receives it and starts the journey back.

"I had not meant to mystify readers by withholding any fact; it is not a writer's business to tease. The story is told through Phoenix's mind as she undertakes her errand. As the author at one with the character as I tell it, I must assume that the boy is alive. As the reader, you are free to think as you like, of course: the story invites you to believe that no matter what happens, Phoenix for as long as she is able to walk and can hold to her purpose will make her journey. The *possibility* that she would keep on even if he were dead is there in her devotion and its single-minded, single-track errand. Certainly the *artistic* truth, which should be good enough for the fact, lies in Phoenix's own answer to that question. When the nurse asks, 'He isn't dead, is he?' she speaks for herself: 'He still the same. He going to last.'

"The grandchild is the incentive. But it is the journey, the going of the errand, that is the story, and the question is not whether the grandchild is in reality alive or dead.

It doesn't affect the outcome of the story or its meaning from start to finish. But it is not the question itself that has struck me as much as the idea, almost without exception implied in the asking, that for Phoenix's grandson to be dead would somehow make the story 'better.'

"It's *all right,* I want to say to the students who write to me, for things to be what they appear to be, and for words to mean what they say. It's all right, too, for words and appearances to mean more than one thing—ambiguity is a fact of life. A fiction writer's responsibility covers not only what he presents as the facts of a given story but what he chooses to stir up as their implications; in the end, these implications, too, become facts, in the larger, fictional sense. But it is not all right, not in good faith, for things *not* to mean what they say.

"The grandson's plight was real and it made the truth of the story, which is the story of an errand of love carried out. If the child no longer lived, the truth would persist in the 'wornness' of the path. But his being dead can't increase the truth of the story, can't affect it one way or the other. I think I signal this, because the end of the story has been reached before old Phoenix gets home again: she simply starts back. To the question 'Is the grandson really dead?' I could reply that it doesn't make any difference. I could also say that I did not make him up in order to let him play a trick on Phoenix. But my best answer would be: '*Phoenix* is alive.'

"The origin of a story is sometimes a trustworthy clue to the author—or can provide him with the clue—to its key image; maybe in this case it will do the same for the reader. One day I saw a solitary old woman like Phoenix. She was walking; I saw her, at middle distance, in a winter country landscape, and watched her slowly make her way across my line of vision. That sight of her made me write the story. I invented an errand for her, but that only seemed a living part of the figure she was herself: what errand other than for someone else could be making her go? And her going was the first thing, her persisting in her landscape was the real thing, and the first and the real were what I wanted and worked to keep. I brought her up close enough, by imagination, to describe her face, make her present to the eyes, but the full-length figure moving across the winter fields was the indelible one and the image to keep, and the perspective extending into the vanishing distance the true one to hold in mind.

"I invented for my character, as I wrote, some passing adventures—some dreams and harassments and a small triumph or two, some jolts to her pride, some flights of fancy to console her, one or two encounters to scare her, a moment that gave her cause to feel ashamed, a moment to dance and preen—for it had to be a *journey,* and all these things belonged to that, parts of life's uncertainty.

"A narrative line is in its deeper sense, of course, the tracing out of a meaning and the real continuity of a story lies in this probing forward. The real dramatic force of a story depends on the strength of the emotion that has set it going. The emotional value is the measure of the reach of the story. What gives any such content to 'A Worn Path' is not its circumstances but its *subject:* the deep-grained habit of love.

"What I hoped would come clear was that in the whole surround of this story, the world it threads through, the only certain thing at all is the worn path. The habit of love cuts through confusion and stumbles or contrives its way out of difficulty, it remembers the way even when it forgets, for a dumbfounded moment, its reason for being. The path is the thing that matters.

"*Her* victory—old Phoenix's—is when she sees the diploma in the doctor's office, when she finds 'nailed up on the wall the document that had been stamped with the gold seal and framed in the gold frame, which matched the dream that was hung up in her head.' The return with the medicine is just a matter of retracing her own footsteps. It is the part of the journey, and of the story, that can now go without saying.

"In the matter of function, old Phoenix's way might even do as a sort of parallel to your way of work if you are a writer of stories. The way to get there is the all-important, all-absorbing problem, and this problem is your reason for undertaking the story. Your only guide, too, is your sureness about your subject, about what this subject is. Like Phoenix, you work all your life to find your way, through all the obstructions and the false appearances and the upsets you may have brought on yourself, to reach a meaning—using inventions of your imagination, perhaps helped out by your dreams and bits of good luck. And finally too, like Phoenix, you have to assume that what you are working in aid of is life, not death.

"But you would make the trip anyway—wouldn't you?—just on hope."

—Eudora Welty

THE AMERICAN LANGUAGE

Most people think of slang as a kind of corrupt English, the product of ignorance and laziness. They see slang as a sort of linguistic disease that flourishes in the poorest and worst-maintained neighborhoods of the language. Slang, they feel, should be stamped out for the health and well-being of the general public.

But slang or its equivalent is as old as language itself. In fact, many words that at one time were considered slang or were unacceptable later entered the language and are now used by all speakers.

Before the middle of the eighteenth century, the words for slang as we know it today were *cant* and *argot*. *Cant* referred to the specialized language of thieves and beggars. *Argot* referred to the specialized language of other occupations (sailors and farmers, for examples). Gradually, the word *slang* came to refer to any informal, nonstandard, specialized language. Slang today especially refers to a kind of colorful, lively language that quickly becomes popular and that often just as quickly drops out of use.

Slang has always been popular among the young. When writer Russell Baker explained why he was slow catching up with the word *wimp,* he expressed an age-old adult complaint: "By the time I learned what the latest kid-saying was," he wrote, "kids had stopped saying it."

Why Do We Use Slang?

Why do people use slang? Not usually out of ignorance, despite popular misconceptions. Most slang terms are substitutes for fairly common words or phrases. A waitress who calls in the order "Adam and Eve on a raft—wreck 'em," knows how to say "two scrambled eggs on toast." Looked at from this point of view, using slang is actually a lot of work. One has to learn new, usually unnecessary words, as well as the rules for using them. Moreover, since slang very often goes out of style quickly, this process has to be continually repeated. A lot of work, and to what end?

We ordinarily think of language as a means of communication. But anthropologists point out that it has a more subtle function as well—marking kinship. Members of a family or tribe reinforce their relatedness by their language. If you think about it for a moment, you will probably realize that your family does the same thing, through the use of some key words or particular "comic" pronunciations. This is the most important function of slang: it marks members of a group and asserts the group's relatedness. Slang is a group's playful, inventive, deliberately informal use of language; it helps to define the members of a group and keep them together.

"The group" can be of any size, and come from any social class.

American Slang

"Failure to do your homework on proper grammatical usage will result in a final grade of zero, zip, zilch . . ."

It can be a single family or a large and widespread profession. Teen-agers, athletes, actors, truck drivers, doctors, criminals, movie makers, and soldiers all have their own slang. People outside the group who try to use its slang almost always appear ridiculous. Think of how embarrassing it is to hear middle-aged parents try to use their teen-aged children's slang.

Various other theories have attempted to explain slang and its origins. Walt Whitman claimed that slang produced poets and poetry. This is an exaggeration, but it might point to another explanation for the persistence of slang. Slang may be used for the sheer pleasure of making sounds. It may also be a way to create new metaphors, sometimes just for the fun of it, sometimes to capture attention. Perhaps slang is used because as humans we have an impulse to be "word makers." If we look at *The American Thesaurus of Slang* (1953) we can see that people have persisted in making up new slang terms for concepts that already have more than enough terms to name them. Even over thirty years ago, we had 180 slang terms for "having no money"; 400 slang terms for "failing"; 200 slang terms for "getting angry." By now, who can tell how many new slang terms have been added to those lists?

The response to slang on the part of those who do not speak it is often highly critical. This is because some slang is vulgar, or is a pointless corruption of standard speech with no justification other than novelty. Slang can also be imprecise, and some people who use a great deal of popular slang have limited vocabularies. In fact, most slang disappears very quickly. The group being marked by a slang term is also apt to be fluid and hard to define, as the 1920's "flappers" and the later "valley girls" proved to be.

The Origins of American Slang

America has always been a fertile ground for the development of slang, especially since the 1830's, when informality was considered an almost essential aspect of democracy. The country's cowboys, railroad workers, politicians, and members of hundreds of new occupations introduced many slang terms, often to name things for which there were no existing words. The newspaper industry helped to popularize these terms; more recently, television, radio, and movies have done the same thing.

Slang words and phrases develop in exactly the same ways as additions to standard English.

1. Existing words may be given a new meaning. *Sack,* during World War II, became the almost universal slang word for "bed," and it helped to create countless new phrases for "sleep": *hit the sack, sack out, sack time, sack duty,* and *sack drill. Flaky* is a more recent example of a word that has been given a novel slang meaning.

2. Two or more words may be combined to form a new expression. Americans' love affair with cars, for example, gave us the marvelously inventive *rattle-trap* and the more recent *gas-guzzler.* One

"I said all those in favor say 'Aye.'"

From *The New Yorker,* September 14, 1987.

witty compound word, *rubberneck,* was once said to be the best slang word ever coined. The current computer craze has given us *user-friendly,* a personification that describes a program that is kind about your mistakes.

3. A word may be "clipped" to form a shortened word. The word *Jeep* was born in 1941, from "G.P.," or *general purpose vehicle.* Fan, as in *baseball fan,* was clipped from the word *fanatic.*

4. Words may also be borrowed from other languages. During the westward expansion, *bronco* was borrowed from the Spanish for "rough" and *mustang* from the Spanish for "stray." *Boob tube,* a recent slang example, borrows from the Spanish word *bobo,* "fool."

5. Some slang words are simply invented. Among American backwoodsmen of the nineteenth century, the wilder the invention, the better. If you had the *peedoodles,* you were nervous; if you were *puckerstoppled,* you were embarrassed; confusion was *conbobberation;* and a heavy blow, in a fight or from the weather, was a *sockdologer.* Those words have disappeared, but other inventions have remained. *Blizzard,* for example, was first invented to refer to a big windstorm, perhaps from the German word *blitz,* for "lightning." When *blizzard* was used in 1870 by an Iowa newspaper to describe a violent snowstorm, it was found to be so useful that it soon became standard English.

Nowadays, slang terms are spread by being printed, but in the past, informal language did not see print until it was well established. Vulgar slang terms were never printed. Thus, many slang terms lived and died unrecorded. One of the earliest recorders of American slang was Benjamin Franklin, who published a dictionary of slang terms referring to drunkenness in 1737 (as a warning about its dangers). He found 228 of them, all, as he wrote, "gathered . . . from the modern tavern conversations of tipplers." Almost all of them have disappeared today, including colorful phrases like *been to Barbados, got a brass eye,* and *as stiff as a ring bolt.* Two of them, though, *oiled* and *stewed,* are in current usage. (In 1960, *The Dictionary of American Slang* listed 327 slang synonyms for the same condition.)

"High Talk" by Roy Doty.

The New York Times, July 4, 1965.

From Slang to Standard English

Most slang terms die quickly. There is a constant turnover, especially among "in" words. *Lounge lizard, hootchie-kootchie,* and *goo-goo eyes* came and went as fast as *cool cat, squaresville, rap,* and *hep.* (*Hep's* offspring, *hip,* is still with us, however.) Terms which fill a need in standard English sometimes make the transition from slang to standard. *Plunder, fix, all right,* and *roughneck* all started as slang and were once condemned by one *highbrow* or another.

Who decides what is slang and what is standard usage? The easiest answer to this is that we all do. Native speakers of a language have a finely tuned sense of the distinction between formal and informal language. As some slang words achieve wide popular usage, though, that distinction may blur. For example, which of these words would you say are slang, and which are standard: *corny, scrumptious, pinhead?* You might say, "Look it up in the dictionary." But the answer depends on which dictionary you use. Dictionaries whose primary purpose is to *describe* the language are apt to provide fewer usage distinctions than dictionaries prepared by lexicographers who feel that it is important to *dictate* usage. Here are the verdicts of three popular American dictionaries on whether or not our three test words are slang:

	Corny	Scrumptious	Pinhead
Webster's Second International	No	Yes	No
Webster's Third International	No	No	No
American Heritage Dictionary	Yes	Yes	Yes

Obviously, lexicographers disagree on when a word becomes widely enough used to qualify as "standard." Some words, in fact, never make the jump at all. Terms which fill a real informal need often remain as slang for generations. Terms like *rubberneck, to squeal, baloney,* and *nifty* have endured, although regarded as slang for years. These words seem so informal that they resist incorporation into standard English, but they survive to remind us of our capacity for making poetry out of the commonplace.

Analyzing Language

1. We have said that *The American Thesaurus of Slang* lists hundreds of slang terms for common experiences or things. How many slang terms can you list for (a) *a car;* (b) *failing;* (c) *getting angry;* (d) *going to sleep?* Once you have your list, discuss the metaphors on which the slang terms are based.

2. Slang is often created by the same processes that create poetry. Slang uses **figurative language,** such as **metaphor** and **simile** (striking comparisons between two things that are dissimilar in most ways) and **hyperbole** (exaggeration). Identify the form of figurative language each of the following words or phrases is based on, and explain the comparisons used. Then provide another example of slang using the same kind of figure of speech.

chicken	to talk someone's ear off
stuffed shirt	tenderfoot
hit the ceiling	rubberneck
out like a light	to put on ice

3. Here are some clipped forms of words in current use. Use a dictionary to identify their full forms.

ad lib	flu	pep
bus	gas	prom
cello	gym	prop

4. Today's slang words might be tomorrow's standard English. All of the following standard words were once considered slang. Check the etymology of each one in a dictionary. Can you propose reasons why each word developed its current meanings?

bleachers	freshman	kidnap
bore	glib	tidy
club	handsome	trip

5. The American genius for creating new words or using old words in creative ways is displayed to advantage in the sports sections of our newspapers. Explain in plain English each of the italicized examples of "sports argot."

   a. Maryland Is 10–2 After *Winning Streak* Is *Snapped* (headline)
   b. Houston used five *fast-break* baskets to take a 17–7 lead.
   c. Susan Brown, *benched* her last game for the first time in three years, scored 25 points and *hauled down* a conference record 27 rebounds.
   d. Carl Furillo *popped out* to shortstop.
   e. Army *punched* its way to Notre Dame's one-yard line.

MAKING GENERALIZATIONS

Writing Assignment

Write a brief essay in which you discuss the theme of either William Faulkner's "Spotted Horses" (page 607) or Flannery O'Connor's "The Life You Save May Be Your Own" (page 621). In your essay, tell how you responded to the theme and to the story as a whole.

Background

What Is a Generalization?

A **generalization** is a statement about every member of a group. Most generalizations include a word such as *all, every, always, no, none,* or *never.* When you use a generalization in writng or speaking, stop to think of how much proof you have for it. The following generalization, for example, would be easy to prove:

> All of Shakespeare's plays are written in both prose and poetry.

That generalization happens to be true. You can prove it by examining all 38 of Shakespeare's plays. A generalization that is proven true is a **valid** generalization.

Other generalizations are not so easy to prove. Consider this one, for example:

> No playwright has created as many different characters as Shakespeare.

In order to prove this generalization, you would have to examine the works of every playwright who ever lived. If you cannot do this, the generalization is an invalid one.

Both of the generalizations you have just read are statements of fact: They can be proven to be true or false. Generalizations, however, often deal with opinions. Here are two examples:

1. All of Faulkner's characters are odd.
2. Flannery O'Connor never created an unbelievable character.

When you use a generalization to state an opinion, you should ask yourself two questions. First, are you familiar with *all* the members of the "group" you are generalizing about? Second, do you have enough examples to support your opinion?

If you can't answer *yes* to the first question, you should avoid using a generalization. Your sentence should include a qualifying word such as *many, most, often,* or *sometimes.*

Even if you can answer *yes* to the first question, think carefully about your supporting evidence. Do you have any doubt about being able to support an all-inclusive statement? If so, use a qualifying word and avoid being caught in error.

Tell whether each of the following generalizations is a statement of fact or opinion. Then explain what would be necessary to prove each statement. (Don't concern yourself with whether the statement is true or false.)

1. Twentieth-century poetry is easier to understand than eighteenth-century poetry.
2. More women than men write poetry.
3. Ernest Hemingway is the best American writer of the twentieth century.
4. Ernest Hemingway is the most popular American writer of the twentieth century.
5. Modern writers use symbols more frequently than writers of previous centuries did.

Theme as a Generalization

A story's **theme** is the central insight about life that the writer wants to communicate; it's the story's "meaning," its "controlling idea." Usually, the theme is not directly stated; it is left for you to figure out. This is not always an easy job, but if you enjoy thinking, it's an enormously pleasurable one.

The theme of a story is stated as a **generalization,** a statement that applies not just to the specific events and characters in the story, but to life in general or to a whole group of people. Remember that your statement of theme will differ from another reader's. Remember also that the theme is always a statement and always a generalization. That makes it different from the story's **subject** or from a **plot summary.** Compare the following statements about "The Leader of the People" by John Steinbeck (page 579).

Subject of the Story:
How old people feel and how they are treated; the end of the frontier; the loss of the heroic past.

Plot Summary of the Story:
After Jody's father hurts Grandfather's feelings by com-

plaining about his endless storytelling, Jody goes out of his way to be kind to his grandfather. But at the climax of the story, grandfather learns the truth about how Carl feels about his stories, and he admits that "Westering," and his own usefulness, is over.

Theme of the Story:

Many old people dwell on the past because they feel they have outlived their usefulness. To them, the past often seems more heroic, more exciting, more meaningful than the present. This can result in a clash of generations which can cause pain in a family; often it is only the very youngest members of a family who are patient with the old. At the same time, the story reveals another truth: that life is continually changing; that even as people grow old and change, so do countries and the people in them change. Just as the "leader of the people" of yesterday is merely today's garrulous "old man," so is the frontier of yesterday merely today's beach at Malibu.

Guidelines for Stating a Theme

1. Before you settle on a statement of theme, write out several possible statements. Then test each one on the story as a whole. If a statement of theme doesn't seem to cover all the important parts of a story, then you'll have to go back and revise it. Keep revising your statement of theme until you feel it adequately covers the story as a whole.
2. State the theme as a generalization, but be careful about using universal terms like *every, always,* and *all.* Most thematic statements should include qualifying words, such as *often, may,* and *sometimes.*
3. A theme can sometimes be stated in a single sentence, but this is rare. Avoid reducing the theme to a common saying or to a moral lesson. "It's hard to be old," for example, isn't an adequate statement of the theme of "The Leader of the People." You may need a paragraph or even a whole essay to state the theme of a complex story. A long story or a novel may have more than one theme.
4. Don't agonize over getting it exactly right. There's no single, correct way of stating a story's theme.
5. You don't have to agree with the writer's theme. Based on your own experiences and observations, you may decide that the story's theme just isn't "true."

Prewriting

This isn't an easy assignment; the stories are complex, and they deal with unusual characters. Look back over both stories, and decide which one you have the strongest feelings about. Then reread the story carefully. Take the time to write out the answers to each of the following questions.

1. What is the story's **subject**?
2. How can the **plot** be summarized in three or four sentences?
3. Who is the main **character** in the story? Does the character change? What does the main character learn as a result of the story's events?
4. Identify the scenes or passages in the story that you think are **key passages.** What makes these passages stand out from the rest of the story?
5. What does the story seem to reveal about human nature or human relationships? What does the story reveal about such things as innocence, evil, responsibility, love?
6. How did the story make you feel as you read it? How did you feel as you thought about it later?

Writing

Use your Prewriting notes to plan your essay. You might follow an organization like this one:

Paragraph 1: Cite the story's title, author, and subject. Summarize the plot in three or four sentences.
Paragraphs 2–3 (or as many paragraphs as you need): State the story's theme as precisely as you can. Cite specific details, characters, and events from the story to support your statement of theme.
Paragraph 4: Tell how you responded to the story and its theme. Tell whether you think the story's theme is valid or significant, or is it trite and overdone?

Revising and Proofreading

Use the guidelines in the section at the back of this book, called **Writing About Literature,** to revise and proofread your essay.

POETRY
VOICES OF AMERICAN CHARACTER

Threshing by John Stuart Curry (c. 1935). Oil. The Kennedy Galleries, Inc., New York.

UNIT EIGHT

American Poetry: 1890–1910

When Walt Whitman died in 1892, he was the nation's famous "good gray poet," but his true genius was as yet unrecognized. Whitman's great contemporary, Emily Dickinson, was still unpublished and unknown. In fact, her work would have been lost to the world were it not for the many packets of hand-written poems she had wrapped up and put away, with no thought that they would ever be published. By 1892, Dickinson had already been dead for six years—"an island in dishonored grass" on the green slopes of a little cemetery in Massachusetts. The magnitude of Whitman's and Dickinson's contributions to poetry would not be clear for years. But these two poets had indeed joined Poe, Melville, Hawthorne, Twain, and Henry James as writers unmistakably American in character and universal in appeal.

After the deaths of Whitman and Dickinson, American poetry went into a decline. But time would show that the comparatively uneventful period between 1890 and 1910 was but the trough of a wave that was about to break. The force of this wave, when it arrived, would be strong enough to wash away the last traces of British influence on American poetry and to carry our poets into their most dazzling period of variety and experimentation.

This period of experimentation began when droves of American poets began to explore the artistic life of Europe. This home-grown talent was invigorated by European influences, especially in Paris, where writers, artists, and composers from all over the world were absorbing the lessons of great painters like Pablo Picasso, Georges Braque, and Henri Matisse. These artists were exploring new ways of seeing and representing reality. The generation of writers that kept pace with them would produce not simply poetry, as the world had always understood it, but "modern poetry." Modernism would become the prevailing international style in poetry until midway into the twentieth century. (See Unit Nine.)

But a few individuals with American accents and American habits of looking at the world provided a powerful counterbalance to the cosmopolitan tendencies of some of their contemporaries. These were the poets of native character, those who ignored or defied the revolutionary new developments that led to modernism. Figuratively speaking, these writers stayed "at home," while almost all the artists they knew were actually on their way to Paris or felt themselves to be living spiritually in its surroundings.

These poets did not enlist in the reverse emigration that took many grandsons and granddaughters of Europeans back to Europe. Instead, they said what they had to say in plain American speech and without concern for their place in the modernist movement. Their poetry gave expression to voices of the American character.

Clarinet by Georges Braque (1913). Mixed media.

Museum of Modern Art, New York. Nelson A. Rockefeller Bequest.

Voices of New England

The greatest among the voices of American character was Robert Frost (page 670). Frost was a poet whose independence was grounded in his ability to handle ordinary New England speech and in his surprising skill in appropriating the most conventional poetic forms and giving them a twist all his own. In an era when "good" was equated with "new," the only new thing about Robert Frost was old: individual poetic genius. Using this gift to impose his own personality on the iambic line in verse, Frost created a poetic voice that was unique and impossible to imitate.

This Frostian "character" spoke folk wisdom with the serious-

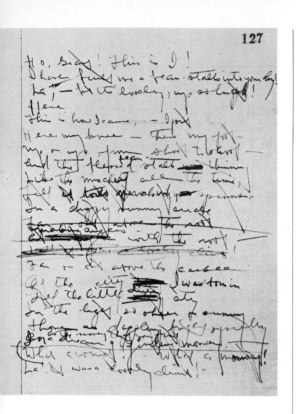

ness of a philosopher and philosophy with the simple eloquence of a New England farmer. His view of the world was dark because he found darkness in the workings of nature; yet this was the same world of nature which at times presented him with objects of beauty. Frost spent a great part of his life examining nature with curiosity and tenderness and recording his discoveries.

Before Robert Frost had arrived in New England to make it his home and poetic territory, another writer had already established himself as the region's unofficial poetic voice. Edwin Arlington Robinson (page 651) dealt with the daily life of his "Down East home"—Gardiner, Maine—by lightly disguising the place in his poems as Tilbury Town. In the citizens of Gardiner, he found characters like Miniver Cheevy and Richard Cory, each of whom represented an American "type." These characters came into his poems larger than life, and their fates were manifestations of their characters. Like Frost, Robinson tended to regard nature more as a threat than a comfort. He felt that it was our common lot to live in "the black and awful chaos of the night," looking for signs of order and promises of immortality, but seldom finding anything to justify our expectations.

Robinson chose to work in traditional forms. Yet, unlike Frost, he did not impose upon these forms the voice of a single personality. The voices we hear in Robinson's lyrics are varied: sometimes conversational and folksy, but more often touched with a high degree of literacy and controlled by emotional reserve. The most familiar voice in Robinson's work is that of an observer who absorbs everything in sight without disclosing his personal involvement with what he sees and reports.

Another poet with New England roots was Edna St. Vincent Millay (page 665), the child prodigy from a little town on the Maine coast. As an adult in New York City, she became the symbol of the liberated woman of her day. "Vincent," as she was known to her friends, created this role for herself by publishing poems in which women held the social, intellectual, and romantic prerogatives society had previously reserved for men. And once Millay had created this bold, carefree figure of a female Casanova, she was forced to live up to the expectations of her audience.

A national celebrity while she was still in her twenties, Millay was both the happy recipient of fame and its victim. The fame was based partly on her personal notoriety and partly on her finely crafted verse. She managed to persuade the reading public that her lyrics were cut from the same cloth as those of Shakespeare, Donne, and Keats. But while Millay could imitate these poets, she could not equal them. She was unable to find a modern equivalent for the imagination and craft that had made them great, not merely in their own time, but for all time.

At her best, however, Millay wrote highly emotional, sometimes ecstatic celebrations of nature and of the joy of being alive and young. Her romantic boldness and extravagance of spirit offered a refreshing change from the needlepoint prettiness of familiar "ladies' verse," and she charmed a generation with the unapologetic love of pleasure in her sonnets and quatrains.

Voices of the Middle West

Each of these New England poets of the early years of the century was a highly skilled composer of traditional verse. Their fellow poets in the Middle West were more adventuresome. They had begun to produce loose, colloquial lines and rough-hewn stanzas that would bring to the American heartland its own poetic identity.

One of these Middle Western poets put together a sort of mass biography that told the hidden story of the citizens of a small town. His name was Edgar Lee Masters (page 656), and his book was *Spoon River Anthology* (1915). Along with the stories by Sherwood Anderson (page 525) in *Winesburg, Ohio* (1919), this volume of portraits in verse broke new ground that would be explored by American writers for years to come. At a time when calendar artists were depicting American life as a perpetually sunny adventure, and when some writers were sentimentalizing everything from the good old summertime to the old mill stream, Masters offered a shocking view of small-town life. When he took the lid—the coffin lid, to be exact—off Spoon River and allowed the dead to speak for themselves, they uttered a litany of greed, frustration, and spiritual deprivation. The diction of his talking skeletons was plain, and they made their confessions in the colloquial cadences of free verse. Masters's best-selling collection received the same kind of interest Americans were beginning to give to Freudian case histories.

Voices of the Black Experience

In poetry, black culture found expression in two different ways. Most quickly accepted by white readers were the works of black poets who wrote in conventional forms. These metrically regular and rhymed verse forms made even the most urgent and desperate of black concerns seem undisturbing. The second form of black expression was poetry that based its rhythms on spirituals and jazz, its lyrics on songs known as the blues, and its diction on the street talk of the black ghettos. The conflict that all of this posed for gifted black poets of the nineteenth century can be most clearly seen in the frustrated career of Paul Laurence Dunbar (page 662).

Foremost among the lyricists were James Weldon Johnson (page 698), Claude McKay (page 704), Langston Hughes (page 706), and Countee Cullen (page 712). These poets brought literary distinction to the broad movement of artists known as the Harlem Renaissance. Geographically, the center of that movement was Harlem, the section of New York City that stands above 110th Street in Manhattan. Its spiritual center, however, was not a place on the map but a place in the consciousness of a people whose gifts had long been ignored, patronized as "quaint," or otherwise relegated to the margins of American art. But when, hand in hand with the music echoing from New Orleans, Memphis, and Chicago, black poetry became part of the Jazz Age, it was responsible for a new appreciation of the role of black talent in American culture.

Group Portrait in the Dark Tower by James Van Der Zee. Photograph.

The Dark Tower was a famous salon in a townhouse on West 136th Street in Harlem. Poems by Hughes and Cullen were painted on the walls.

Voices of the West

The most distinctive voice heard during the years when modernism was overtaking traditionalism in poetry was that of Robinson Jeffers (page 694). Jeffers steered a wavering course that kept him neither bound by convention nor committed to experiment. Working sometimes in meter and rhyme, more often in long and sinuous lines of free verse, Jeffers was less notable for his craftsmanship than for his unorthodox attitudes toward progress, religion, and the nature of humanity.

While his contemporaries were celebrating democracy and the rise of the common man, Jeffers took a very dim view of both. He looked at the scientific and political developments of the new century with a godlike remoteness and distaste. Isolating himself on the rocky shore of California's Monterey peninsula, he created metaphors of what he saw from the windows of the stone tower in which he wrote. Although Jeffers did nothing to promote himself or to rally converts to his dissident beliefs, his poetry gained a wide audience during his lifetime. After his death, his poems became an inspiration to the scene inhabited by the Beats and other West Coast literary groups of the 1960's.

Voices of the South

Most American poets of the early twentieth century were characterized by earnestness, sentiment, and simple, unadorned language. One exception was John Crowe Ransom (page 690). Ransom stood for wit, intellectual subtlety, and the mannerisms of another century. Genteel and courtly, he was the product both of the aristocratic Old South and of a classical education, begun at Vanderbilt University in Tennessee and continued as a Rhodes Scholar at Oxford in England. Going against the grain of the typical poetry of his generation, Ransom looked back to seventeenth-century England. The marks of poetic art at that time were formal grace and philosophical playfulness; the role of the poet was to provide witty entertainment for highly educated readers. Like his long-dead models, Ransom could deal with tragic matters without spilling a tear; he could deal with the comic aspects of life without forgetting that laughter and grief eventually join hands. His classical tone was intimidating to some readers. But others saw that his aristocratic genius was only a thin disguise for a gentle, generous nature and a passionate concern for the beauty and elegance of the English language.

If the American character is defined collectively by the voices that express it, we must conclude that "the American character" is an abstraction. But if we listen to individual voices as they speak for themselves, we become aware that American poetry reflects our national life in all its diversity. In this unit, you'll find American voices that reflect our freedom to criticize, to oppose, or to sing proudly of America's richness—from the smoky jazz clubs of Harlem to the spumey ledges of Big Sur in California.

Edwin Arlington Robinson (1869–1935)

By the 1890's, the vitality of the century seemed exhausted and the gathering forces of modernism were still scattered and obscure. Many poets between 1890 and 1910 were churning out the same old rhymes and meters of Romanticism. But in those two decades, one voice spoke with an authentic, contemporary American accent: that of Edwin Arlington Robinson.

The strengths that distinguish Robinson are his native voice and his wise and ironic view of human behavior. Robinson's bedrock realism informs even the most formal of his carefully wrought poems. In some of his poetic portraits of individuals, he anticipates by a decade the more loosely drawn portraits found in Edgar Lee Masters's *Spoon River Anthology*; and in his skill with meter, Robinson foreshadows Robert Frost's gift for bending the strictly counted line to accommodate the ease and flow of vernacular speech.

Robinson was a Yankee from the rocky coast of Maine. Born at Head Tide in 1869, he lived for the next twenty-seven years—except for the two years when he attended Harvard as a special student—in the town of Gardiner. Gardiner became the Tilbury Town of his poems, the home of some of his most famous characters. When he was in his late twenties, Robinson moved to New York City and published his first book. There he supported himself at menial jobs, including one as a timekeeper at the construction site of the new subway system.

After a year of this work, Robinson's fortunes took a surprising turn for the better. Among the young poet's readers was none other than the President of the United States, Theodore Roosevelt. When Roosevelt learned that the poet he admired was barely scraping by on a laborer's salary, he arranged to have him hired as a clerk by the New York Custom House, a position Robinson held for five years. Another form of assistance came in an invitation to the famous MacDowell Colony in Peterboro, New Hampshire. This was a center for composers, artists, and writers established by the widow of the American composer Edward MacDowell. There Robinson spent long working summers for the greater part of his life. Though he was a loner by temperament, he became a popular poet. Even in an increasingly modernist age, Robinson's poetry, which was traditional in form, continued to be read and admired, and he was awarded the Pulitzer Prize three times. At the time of his death, his reputation had survived the tide of modernism that had once threatened to wash it away.

One of the persistent themes of early twentieth-century American poetry is that the conventions of small-town life are a façade which often obscures unpleasant realities. In this famous poem, an unidentified speaker tells what happened to his fellow-citizen Richard Cory. Does the harsh surprise ending hint that the real story is the one that remains untold?

Richard Cory

Whenever Richard Cory went downtown,
    We people on the pavement looked at him:
He was a gentleman from sole to crown,
    Clean favored, and imperially slim.

5   And he was always quietly arrayed,
    And he was always human when he talked;
But still he fluttered pulses when he said,
    "Good morning," and he glittered when he walked.

And he was rich—yes, richer than a king—
10   And admirably schooled in every grace:
In fine, we thought that he was everything
    To make us wish that we were in his place.

So on we worked, and waited for the light,
    And went without the meat, and cursed the bread;
15   And Richard Cory, one calm summer night,
    Went home and put a bullet through his head.

Responding to the Poem

Analyzing the Poem

Identifying Details

1. What advantages does Richard Cory have that make the townspeople envy him?
2. What contrasting picture of their own lives is presented in the fourth stanza?
3. List all the details in the poem revealing that the townspeople regarded Richard Cory with awe and a sense of inferiority. How would you define the word *human* in line 6?

Interpreting Meanings

4. What is **ironic** in the fact that Richard Cory took his own life? What irony is there in the fact that the night was calm?

5. What aspects of Richard Cory's life are *not* mentioned? How might these hidden or overlooked areas account for his fate?
6. How would you describe the speaker's **tone**? Does the contrast between the tone of the speaker and the tragic nature of the story heighten the poem's emotional effect? Explain why or why not.
7. What **moral** or lesson might be found in the tale of Richard Cory? Do the poem and its moral have relevance to our experience today?
8. Read Robinson's own comments on "Richard Cory" on the opposite page. What do you think he means when he says there's a lot of "humanity" in the poem? Why do you think it made his correspondent feel "cold"? How do you respond to the poem?

Portrait of Jacques Emile Blanche Rouen by
John Singer Sargent (late 19th century). Oil.

Musee des Beaux Arts, Rouen, France.

Analyzing Language and Style

Connotations

Robinson never says it outright, but he implies that his townspeople see Richard Cory as a king. Robinson achieves this effect by using words with connotations of royalty. How do words get such **connotations,** or emotional overtones and associations? In general, connotations come from shared usage.

It would be hard, for example, for a writer to call a character a "lamb" without someone familiar with English making an immediate association with innocence and docility. This would be true even for readers who had never seen a lamb; they would only have to be familiar with the Bible or with nursery rhymes to recognize this archetypal use of the image of the lamb. On the other hand, what do you associate with the word *wolf*? With the word *lion*? Where do you think those associations come from?

1. Find at least five words or phrases in "Richard Cory" that suggest kingliness or royalty.
2. Replace each of these words with a neutral word— one that, in your opinion, has no strong connotations at all. How is the effect of the poem different?
3. What meanings can you suggest for the word *gentleman* in line 3? What associations do you make with that word?
4. Why is *downtown* (line 1) a better word than *uptown* in this poem?

Primary Sources
Robinson on "Richard Cory"

"I've written a nice little thing called 'Richard Cory'— 'Whenever Richard Cory went downtown, we people on the pavement looked at him . . . And Richard Cory, one calm summer night, went home and put a bullet through his head.' There isn't any idealism in it, but there's lots of something else—humanity, maybe."

. . .

"Why don't you like 'Richard Cory?' You say it makes you feel cold, but that statement doesn't seem to agree with my impression of your character. It can't be you are squeamish after all. If you are, don't read 'Reuben Bright' or he will knock you down. I used to read about clearness, force, and elegance in the rhetoric books, but I'm afraid I go in chiefly for force. So you will not be offended if I'm not always elegant. There are too many elegant men in the world just now, and they seem to be increasing."

. . .

"I don't have trances, furors, or ecstasies. My poetic spells are of the most prosaic sort. I just sit down and grind it out and use a trifle more tobacco than is good for me."

. . .

"You may call me anything you like—anything but Eddie. I had an aunt who called me Eddie and now she doesn't call me at all."

—from *Letters to Edith Brower,*
Edwin Arlington Robinson

The title of this poem is simply a man's name, yet it contains a clue to the poem's meaning. "Miniver" is the white fur trim, sometimes ermine, seen on the costumes of nobility in medieval and Renaissance portraits. The subjects of such portraits included rich and wicked members of the Medici family of Renaissance Italy.

Other references in the poem evoke heroic eras of the past. Camelot was the place where King Arthur presided over the Knights of the Round Table; Thebes was a city famous in the history of ancient Greece; and "Priam's neighbors" were those who lived near Troy, ruled by King Priam during the Trojan War.

Read the poem aloud. From its sound, would you expect it to be comic or tragic?

Miniver Cheevy

Miniver Cheevy, child of scorn,
    Grew lean while he assailed the seasons;
He wept that he was ever born,
    And he had reasons.

5 Miniver loved the days of old
    When swords were bright and steeds were
      prancing:
The vision of a warrior bold
    Would set him dancing.

Miniver sighed for what was not,
10   And dreamed, and rested from his labors;
He dreamed of Thebes and Camelot,
    And Priam's neighbors.

Miniver mourned the ripe renown
    That made so many a name so fragrant;
15 He mourned Romance, now on the town,°
    And Art, a vagrant.

Miniver loved the Medici,
    Albeit he had never seen one;
He would have sinned incessantly
20   Could he have been one.

Miniver cursed the commonplace
    And eyed a khaki suit with loathing;
He missed the medieval grace
    Of iron clothing.

25 Miniver scorned the gold he sought,
    But sore annoyed was he without it;
Miniver thought, and thought, and thought,
    And thought about it.

Miniver Cheevy, born too late,
30   Scratched his head and kept on thinking;
Miniver coughed, and called it fate,
    And kept on drinking.

15. **on the town:** on welfare.

Responding to the Poem

Analyzing the Poem

Identifying Details

1. Briefly summarize Miniver Cheevy's reasons for weeping that he was ever born.
2. "Romance" and "Art" are **personified** in the fourth stanza. According to Miniver, what has happened to Romance and Art in his own time?
3. How does the disappointed Miniver cope with his lot in life?

Interpreting Meanings

4. What does "child of scorn" mean?
5. Do Miniver's problems really stem from his having been "born too late"? Explain.
6. What is the effect of the abbreviated rhythm in the fourth line of each stanza?
7. Point out three details in the poem that make Miniver appear ridiculous. How would you describe the change in **tone** in the last stanza, and how does this change affect the poem's meaning?

The Sentimental Yearner by Grant Wood (1936).
Pencil and colored paper on tan paper.

Sotheby Parke-Bernet Galleries, Inc., New York.

8. Do you think "Miniver Cheevys" are found in contemporary life? What sorts of worlds do they mourn for?

9. Compare Walter Mitty (page 595) to Miniver Cheevy.

Writing About the Poems

A Creative Response

1. Using Another Point of View. Let Richard Cory tell his own story, in either prose or verse. Use the first person "I" and be sure to record what Cory thinks of the people who look up to him.

2. Answering a Speaker. Write a letter to Miniver Cheevy giving him advice on how to free himself from his nostalgic thoughts.

A Critical Response

3. Responding to the Poems. In a brief essay, tell how you responded to these two poems, and cite specific reasons for your response. You might respond to (a) the characterizations, (b) tone, (c) verse forms, (d) use of irony, or (e) view of life and human nature. Quote from the poems in explaining your response.

4. Comparing Characters. In a brief essay, compare and contrast the characters of Richard Cory and Miniver Cheevy. As the focus of your composition, quote a line from either Emerson (pages 187–203) or Thoreau (pages 204–225). Tell specifically how Robinson's characters are distortions of the ideals proposed by the two earlier writers.

Edgar Lee Masters
(1869–1950)

Edgar Lee Masters was born in Garnett, Kansas. Like his contemporary Carl Sandburg (page 747), he was a product of that part of the Middle West known as the "corn belt" or "Bible belt." Also like Sandburg, he found his own voice in the free verse that characterized the second decade of the twentieth century. But while Sandburg soon developed his own particular mode of expression and built a career upon it, Masters produced just one book in a spare style that served his homely subject matter. Then he reverted to a more conventionally "poetic" style: pretty, romantic, and wordy.

Yet this one book, *Spoon River Anthology* (1915), was a landmark in American literature, and it made Masters famous. It is a collection of more than two hundred epitaphs spoken by the inhabitants of a cemetery in the fictional town of Spoon River: drunkards, bankers, judges, poets, atheists, preachers, gamblers, druggists, and housewives.

The dramatic device of having the epitaphs spoken by the deceased subjects themselves served Masters brilliantly. Drawing upon his memories of Petersburg and Lewistown—the Illinois towns he knew during his first twenty years—he used the epitaphs to show the hidden underside of American life. Its victims, freed by death to talk without fear of consequences, tell their stories and, bit by bit, fill in a picture of small-town life vastly different from the magazine cover images. Against the sentimentality and folksiness of these images, Masters's voices from the grave made a heartfelt protest that hundreds of thousands of readers recognized as buried truth brought into the daylight.

Spoon River Anthology became one of the most widely read books in an age that was fascinated by psychology. Better than any scientific study, it revealed how the conventions of society warred with the real needs and beliefs of its members. By turning "case histories" into lyrics, Masters gave speech to the inarticulate and, at the same time, brought a new kind of realism to poetry.

Richard Bone, like many other departed citizens of the town, is troubled by his conscience. Bone confesses hypocrisy in quietly accepting false appearances. The name Masters gives this speaker is itself a clue to his profession and his nature. As a stonecutter in life, he engraved words that would identify skeletons; as a spokesman for his own conscience, he speaks words that "cut to the bone." Read the poem aloud to hear how it imitates real speech.

Richard Bone

When I first came to Spoon River
I did not know whether what they told me
Was true or false.
They would bring me the epitaph
5 And stand around the shop while I worked
And say "He was so kind," "He was wonderful,"
"She was the sweetest woman," "He was a consistent Christian."
And I chiseled for them whatever they wished,
All in ignorance of its truth.
10 But later, as I lived among the people here,
I knew how near to the life
Were the epitaphs that were ordered for them as they died.
But still I chiseled whatever they paid me to chisel
And made myself party to the false chronicles
15 Of the stones,
Even as the historian does who writes
Without knowing the truth,
Or because he is influenced to hide it.

Responding to the Poem

Analyzing the Poem

Identifying Details

1. What does Richard Bone come to realize about the town of Spoon River? Explain why he keeps on carving false sentiments.
2. What **analogy,** or comparison, does the speaker draw in the poem's last three lines?

Interpreting Meanings

3. In line 11, the speaker says he knew "how near to the life" were his epitaphs. How do you know he means "how *far* from the life"? Would the latter choice of words have been as effective? Why or why not?
4. What does Bone mean when he says he made himself "party to" the false chronicles of the stones?
5. Is Richard Bone making too much of his job? Or is there is a more universal message in this poem? Explain.

Writing About the Poem

A Creative Response

Inventing Names for Characters. Aside from hinting at the character's profession, the name Masters gave to Richard Bone suggests something about his personality. The same can be said about such characters as Miniver Cheevy (see page 654) and Willy Loman in Arthur Miller's play *Death of a Salesman.* Willy has no clout in the business world and few inner resources to fall back upon, and could thus be considered a *low man* in his society. With this in mind, invent a name for each of the fictional characters described below:

1. Someone with serious doubts about his or her abilities
2. Someone other people naturally follow
3. Someone who is very patriotic
4. Someone with no sense of humor

Among the many voices from the dead that echo through the pages of *Spoon River Anthology,* Lucinda Matlock's is unique in that it seems both to scold and to boast. The scolding is explicit. It is directed at "sons and daughters" whose lax attitudes toward the serious business of life are regarded as "degenerate." The boasting is implicit. It is something we pick up by reading between the lines. Do you agree that the speaker feels she is entitled to a kind of praise because, over a span of ninety-six years, she met the challenges of life in the raw Middle West and overcame them? (Masters based Lucinda Matlock on his grandmother, Lucinda Masters.)

Lucinda Matlock

I went to dances at Chandlerville,
And played snap-out at Winchester.
One time we changed partners,
Driving home in the moonlight of middle June,
5   And then I found Davis.
We were married and lived together for seventy years,
Enjoying, working, raising the twelve children,
Eight of whom we lost
Ere I had reached the age of sixty.
10   I spun, I wove, I kept the house, I nursed the sick,
I made the garden, and for holiday
Rambled over the fields where sang the larks,
And by Spoon River gathering many a shell,
And many a flower and medicinal weed—
15   Shouting to the wooded hills, singing to the green valleys.
At ninety-six I had lived enough, that is all,
And passed to a sweet repose.
What is this I hear of sorrow and weariness,
Anger, discontent, and drooping hopes?
20   Degenerate sons and daughters,
Life is too strong for you—
It takes life to love Life.

Responding to the Poem

Analyzing the Poem

Identifying Details

1. List the simple pleasures and pastimes the speaker mentions in describing her life. What hardships has she experienced?

Interpreting Meanings

2. Explain why the speaker feels that the younger generation is "degenerate." Is it fair for her to imply that their own lives could be as happy as hers? Or has she simply been lucky in the circumstances of her life?

3. The poem's **theme** is summed up in the last line. Explain the meaning of this final statement. What two meanings do you give to the word *life*?

4. What do you feel is Masters's own attitude toward Lucinda Matlock? Does he regard her as a judgmental old lady, or as a voice of wisdom? Give evidence from the poem to support your view.

5. If it were possible to ask the "sons and daughters" to speak in their own defense, what might they say?

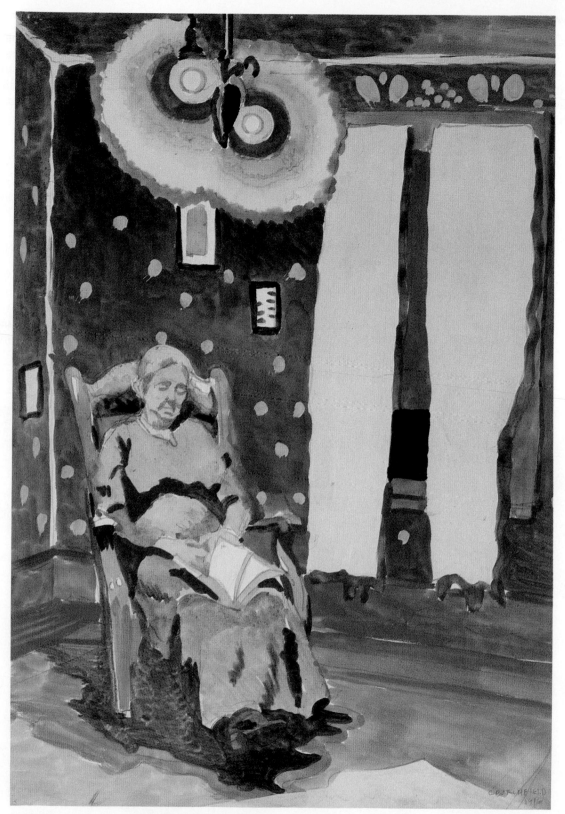

In the Parlor by Charles E. Burchfield (1916).
Watercolor and pencil on paper.

Christie's, New York.

Many of the stories told in *Spoon River Anthology* are interlocking. The villain of the whole book is Deacon Thomas Rhodes, who "ran the church as well as the store and the bank." We hear about Rhodes from a number of victims, including Butch Weldy.

Butch also refers to Jack the Fiddler, a blind man who is buried in the Spoon River cemetery. Jack was killed when Butch, who had been drinking, drove a carriage into a ditch. Read the first line of Butch's epitaph and think about what it implies about the speaker's life.

"Butch" Weldy

After I got religion and steadied down
They gave me a job in the canning works,
And every morning I had to fill
The tank in the yard with gasoline,
5 That fed the blowfires in the sheds
To heat the soldering irons.
And I mounted a rickety ladder to do it,
Carrying buckets full of the stuff.
One morning, as I stood there pouring,
10 The air grew still and seemed to heave,
And I shot up as the tank exploded,
And down I came with both legs broken,
And my eyes burned crisp as a couple
  of eggs
For someone left a blowfire going,
And something sucked the flame into
15 the tank.
The Circuit Judge said whoever did it
Was a fellow-servant of mine, and so
Old Rhodes' son didn't have to pay me.
And I sat on the witness stand as blind
20 As Jack the Fiddler, saying over and over,
"I didn't know him at all."

Responding to the Poem

Analyzing the Poem

Identifying Details

1. Describe Butch Weldy's accident.
2. When Butch talks about what happened to him, he produces a horrifying **simile**. What is it?
3. Explain why the Circuit Judge decided that Old Rhodes's son didn't have to compensate Butch for the accident.

Interpreting Meanings

4. When a person says that he has "steadied down," what is he implying about his former way of life? What **irony** do you feel when you consider that this horrible accident took place *after* Butch settled down?
5. How do you think Butch feels about the accident that ruined his life?
6. Do you think Masters shares Butch's feelings about the accident and about the decision made by the judge? Describe what you think Masters's own **tone** is in this poem.
7. *Spoon River Anthology* was published in 1915. Could something like Butch's accident happen today? What do you think a contemporary court of law would do for a victim like Butch?

Writing About the Poem

A Critical Resonse

Comparing and Contrasting Poems. In a paragraph, compare and contrast "Butch" Weldy with this poem:

> **Mrs. George Reece**
>
> To this generation I would say:
> Memorize some bit of verse of truth or beauty.
> It may serve a turn in your life.
> My husband had nothing to do
> 5   With the fall of the bank—he was only cashier.
> The wreck was due to the president, Thomas Rhodes.
> And his vain, unscrupulous son.
> Yet my husband was sent to prison,
> And I was left with the children,
> 10   To feed and clothe and school them.
> And I did it, and sent them forth
> Into the world all clean and strong,
> And all through the wisdom of Pope, the poet:
> "Act well your part, there all the honor lies."
>
> —Edgar Lee Masters

Primary Sources
The Genesis of Spoon River

[1914]

"About the 20th of May my mother came to visit us, and we had many long talks. . . . In our talks now we went over the whole past of Lewistown and Petersburg, bringing up characters and events that had passed from my mind. We traced these persons to their final fates, to the positions in life that they were then in. We had many sessions at this recalling of old days. . . .

"The psychological experience of this was truly wonderful. Finally on the morning she was leaving for Springfield we had a last and rather sobering talk. It was Sunday, too, and after putting her on the train at 53rd Street I walked back home full of strange pensiveness. The little church bell was ringing, but spring was in the air. I went to my room and immediately wrote 'The Hill,' and two or three of the portraits of *Spoon River Anthology*. Almost at once the idea came to me: Why not make this book the book I had thought about in 1906, in which I

should draw the macrocosm by portraying the microcosm? Why not put side by side the stories of two characters interlocked in fate, thus giving both misunderstood souls a chance to be justly weighed? . . .

"People ask me over and over where the town of Spoon River is located. As there is no such town, I have to answer that there is only a river. And what a river! What a small stream winding its way through flatlands, amid hills that only distance lifts into any beauty, through jungles of weeds and thickets and melancholy cottonwoods. It goes by little towns as ugly and lonely as the tin-roofed hamlets of Kansas. Yet this is the town, or one of the towns, and this is the river and the country from which I extracted whatever beauty there is in that part of *Spoon River Anthology* which relates to a village depiction, and is not concerned with a world view."

—from *Across Spoon River: An Autobiography,* Edgar Lee Masters

6. Explain how Dunbar's use of **meter, rhyme,** and **repetition** give his poem the effect of a traditional ballad. Why is this form especially appropriate, given the poem's content?

7. How would you describe the **tone** of the oak tree's story? Given the nature of the story, would you have expected a more bitter tone? Explain.

Writing About the Poem

A Creative Response

1. **Setting the Poem to Music.** If you are so inclined, try setting Dunbar's poem to music. Will you use a plaintive "ballad" sound, or something else?

A Critical Response

2. **Analyzing Imagery.** In a paragraph, discuss the use of concrete imagery in "The Haunted Oak." Give specific examples of imagery appealing to the senses of sight, hearing, and touch.

Analyzing Language and Style
Archaic Diction

Dictionaries describe *archaic* words as terms, or meanings of terms, that occur in older writings but are rarely used today. Sometimes writers deliberately use archaic diction to give their texts a certain old-fashioned flavor. Use a dictionary to check your answers to these questions about Dunbar's diction. You may have to go to the library for a large dictionary.

1. Find six words in the poem that are used in their archaic senses. Look especially at lines 1, 5, 11, 19, 20, and 23.

2. Are any of these words still used today in other senses? If so, use each word in a sentence to show its current meaning (or one of its meanings).

3. Substitute modern terms for each of the archaic words you have found. (You'll have to rewrite some lines to do so.) How do the new words change the poem's effect?

Primary Sources
Dunbar and Dialect Poetry

James Weldon Johnson (page 698) talked with Dunbar about the problem of dialect poetry. Dunbar was unwilling to continue writing in that style:

"We talked again and again about poetry. I told him my doubts regarding the further possibilities of stereotyped dialect. He was hardly less dubious than I. He said, 'You know, of course, that I didn't start as a dialect poet. I simply came to the conclusion that I could write it as well, if not better, than anybody else I knew of, and that by doing so I should gain a hearing, and now they don't want me to write anything but dialect.' There was a tone of self-reproach in what he said; and five years later, in his fatal illness, he sounded that same tone more deeply when he said to me, 'I've kept on doing the same things, and doing them no better. I have never gotten to the things I really wanted to do.'"

—James Weldon Johnson

Edna St. Vincent Millay (1892–1950)

Like Edwin Arlington Robinson, Edna St. Vincent Millay was born on the granite coast of Maine and established her poetic reputation in New York. Also like Robinson, she lived to see the day when, despite many honors and the devotion of a wide audience, she had to realize that her reputation had barely withstood the onslaught of modernism. Millay had much in common with exponents of modernism such as Pound, Eliot, and Hart Crane—except, ironically, a philosophy of poetry.

Millay achieved fame even before she graduated from Vassar College, with the publication of her first collection of verse, *Renascence and Other Poems* (1917). After World War I, she moved to Greenwich Village. This was an era when that section of New York City was not only a haven for artists, but also a place where women were as free as men to speak their minds, to live by their own rules, and to pursue careers—activities that most Americans still considered improper for women. Taking advantage of this liberated atmosphere, Millay became one of its leading voices—a free spirit who wrote saucy and slightly scandalous lyrics in a style that occasionally evoked Elizabethan verse. Millay's philosophy might best be described in her own words:

First Fig
My candle burns at both ends;
   It will not last the night;
But ah, my foes, and oh, my friends—
   It gives a lovely light!

Millay also became caught up in the radical dissent of the time, and she worked passionately, if vainly, to save the anarchists Sacco and Vanzetti, who were executed in Massachusetts in 1927 after a celebrated trial.

"Vincent," as she was familiarly known, was a skilled actress and speaker with the flair of a seasoned performer. Like Vachel Lindsay, she gave recitals during long, nationwide tours in which she won a degree of celebrity seldom associated with poets. Deliberately mannish in appearance, she wore her hair close-cut, and her costume derived from popular portraits of the English poet Lord Byron, which showed him dressed in black except for a broad white collar.

Both shocking and fascinating to her audiences, Millay grew in popularity even as her poetic achievements began to decline. Her most productive period was between the two World Wars, when she published seven collections of poetry, as well as a series of dramas written for the Provincetown Players in New York. In 1923, she became the first woman to win the Pulitzer prize for poetry, for *The Ballad of the Harp-Weaver*.

During World War II, Millay determined to write "public" poetry to contribute to the Allied cause. She produced scores of poems which, although widely read, proved that outrage and passion could not substitute for the verbal artistry that poetry demands. The lyricist had been overtaken by the propagandist.

One of the brightest literary stars of a generation was all but faded from sight when, in her fifty-eighth year, Edna St. Vincent Millay died alone at her home, Steepletop.

The title of the poem is a Spanish word meaning "remembrance" or "souvenir." The poet evokes a happy memory of youth: a carefree night spent riding one of the several ferry boats that once connected the island of Manhattan with its neighbors. Do you recognize the feeling described in the first line?

Recuerdo

We were very tired, we were very merry—
We had gone back and forth all night on the ferry.
It was bare and bright, and smelled like a stable—
But we looked into a fire, we leaned across a table,
5   We lay on a hill-top underneath the moon;
And the whistles kept blowing, and the dawn came soon.

We were very tired, we were very merry—
We had gone back and forth all night on the ferry;
And you ate an apple, and I ate a pear,
10   From a dozen of each we had bought somewhere;
And the sky went wan, and the wind came cold,
And the sun rose dripping, a bucketful of gold.

We were very tired, we were very merry,
We had gone back and forth all night on the ferry.
15   We hailed, "Good morrow, mother!" to a shawl-covered head,
And bought a morning paper, which neither of us read;
And she wept, "God bless you!" for the apples and pears,
And we gave her all our money but our subway fares.

Responding to the Poem

Analyzing the Poem

Identifying Details

1. What details describe what the speaker and her friend did this night?

Interpreting Meanings

2. Who do you think the "we" in the poem are? What do lines 4–5 suggest about their feelings for one another?
3. Why do you think they gave all their money to the "shawl-covered head"? What does this action say about the power of love?
4. Identify the **metaphor** in line 12. Describe what this image reveals about the speaker's feelings.

5. Read the poem aloud, using the tone and pacing of natural speech. Then describe the poem's **meter** and **rhyme scheme.** What use of repetition contributes to the poem's **mood**?

Analyzing Language and Style

Imagery and Feelings

Poetic imagery is not merely decorative; used skillfully, it can help the poet control the reader's responses and feelings. Imagery depends a great deal on the suggestive power of words—on their **connotations.** For example, the image in line 3 ("smelled like a stable") might, for someone who happened to despise the odor of stables, create

Band Playing on the Hudson by Reginald Marsh
(1932). Watercolor.

Sotheby Parke-Bernet Galleries, Inc., New York.

a feeling of distaste for this night on the ferry. But for many readers, the odor of a stable suggests something pleasant—earthiness, the warmth of animals, the coziness of a place protected from the out-of-doors.

If the poet had said that the ferry "smelled of manure," we'd have a different image and probably different feelings about the experience.

1. Think of at least one verb that could replace "blowing" (line 6) in order to create a negative or unpleasant feeling.

2. Think of at least three things other than a bucketful of gold to which the poet might have compared the rising sun (line 12) to suggest unpleasant connotations.

3. Think of the image suggested by the phrase "shawl-covered head." How might the poet have described the old woman to suggest something unpleasant or even threatening?

4. In what other ways might Millay have made the woman unpleasant?

In this dirge, or lament, the poet sets up the expectation that the speaker will eventually make some sort of peace with death and destiny. But that expectation is never fulfilled: The speaker maintains a note of stark, unqualified grief right to the end. Do you think Millay is questioning conventional attitudes toward death and loss? Is she perhaps defying the sentiments expressed by other poets and elegists throughout the centuries?

Dirge Without Music

I am not resigned to the shutting away of loving hearts in the hard
    ground.
So it is, and so it will be, for so it has been, time out of mind:
Into the darkness they go, the wise and the lovely. Crowned
With lilies and with laurel they go; but I am not resigned.

5   Lovers and thinkers, into the earth with you.
Be one with the dull, the indiscriminate dust.
A fragment of what you felt, of what you knew,
A formula, a phrase remains—but the best is lost.

The answers quick and keen, the honest look, the laughter, the love—
10   They are gone. They are gone to feed the roses. Elegant and curled
Is the blossom. Fragrant is the blossom. I know. But I do not approve.
More precious was the light in your eyes than all the roses in the world.

Down, down, down into the darkness of the grave
Gently they go, the beautiful, the tender, the kind;
15   Quietly they go, the intelligent, the witty, the brave.
I know. But I do not approve. And I am not resigned.

Responding to the Poem

Analyzing the Poem

Identifying Details

1. In the first stanza, the speaker mourns the loss of "the wise and the lovely." Whose loss does she mourn in stanza 2? Stanza 4?

Interpreting Meanings

2. What phrase best expresses the speaker's attitude toward death?
3. Explain what the speaker means by the statement in line 8 that "the best" is lost after death. What is "the best," in her opinion? Do you agree that "the best is lost" in death?
4. What comparison does the speaker make in lines 10–12? Explain her point here. How does the beauty and delicacy of the flower image help to drive home this point?
5. The last line almost echoes the sentiment of the first, except that the speaker adds another note when she states, "I do not approve." How does this new sentiment affect the **tone** and meaning of the poem?
6. Although this poem contains certain patterns of **rhythm** and **rhyme**, Millay tries not to allow these sound effects to create "music" for her dirge, or "lament."

Do you think she avoids creating a lilting, musical effect? Explain what you think *is* the effect of the poem's sound.

7. Describe what might have prompted Millay to write this poem.

8. Are this speaker's feelings about death widely shared? Explain.

Writing About the Poems

A Creative Response

1. **Writing a Conversation.** Write a conversation between the speakers in "Recuerdo" and "Dirge Without Music." Have the speakers discuss a topic that allows you to show their contrasting attitudes toward life.

A Critical Response

2. **Responding to the Poem.** In protesting against a natural process such as death, Millay risks sounding like someone who has not grown up (although she was in her fifties when she wrote this poem). In a brief essay, explain whether you feel that "Dirge Without Music" expresses an immature attitude toward death, or displays a wise and mature—if unexpected—view. Give reasons for your opinion.

3. **Comparing and Contrasting Poems.** In a brief essay, compare and contrast "Dirge" with "Thanatopsis" by William Cullen Bryant (page 142). Before you write, gather data for your essay by filling out a chart like the following one.

	Millay	Bryant
Speaker		
Subject		
Message		
Tone		
Rhythm		
Rhyme		

Primary Sources
"The brawny male sends his picture"

In 1912, one of the judges for a poetry contest remarked that "Renascence," the poem submitted by E. St. Vincent Millay, Esq., must surely be the work of a forty-five-year-old brawny male. When she heard of this remark, Edna St. Vincent Millay sent this letter.

[December 5, 1912]

"To Mr. Ficke and Mr. Bynner:

"Mr. Earle has acquainted me with your wild surmises. Gentlemen: I must convince you of your error; my reputation is at stake. I simply will not be a 'brawny male.' Not that I have an aversion to brawny males; *au contraire, au contraire.* But I cling to my femininity!

"Is it that you consider brain and brawn so inseparable? I have thought otherwise. Still, that is all a matter of personal opinion. But, gentlemen: When a woman insists that she is twenty, you must not, must not call her forty-five. That is more than wicked; it is indiscreet.

"Mr. Ficke, you are a lawyer. I am very much afraid of lawyers. Spare me, kind sir! Take into consideration my youth—for I am indeed but twenty—and my fragility—for 'I do protest I am a maid'—and—sleuth me no sleuths!

"Seriously: I thank you also for the compliment you have unwittingly given me. For tho I do not yet aspire to be forty-five and brawny, if my verse so represents me, I am more gratified than I can say. When I was a little girl, this is what I thought and wrote:

Let me not shout into the world's great ear
Ere I have something for the world to hear.
Then let my message like an arrow dart
And pierce a way into the world's great heart.

"You cannot know how much I appreciate what you have said about my 'Renascence.'

"If you should care to look up the April, 1907, number of *Current Literature,* you would find a review of my *Land of Romance* (near a review of Mr. Bynner's *Fair of My Fancy*). And you might be interested in Mr. Edward Wheeler's comment: "The poem which follows (by E. St. Vincent Millay) seems to me to be phenomenal. The author, whether boy or girl we do not know, is just fourteen years of age.

E. St. V. M.

"P.S. The brawny male sends his picture. I *have* to laugh."

Robert Frost
(1874–1963)

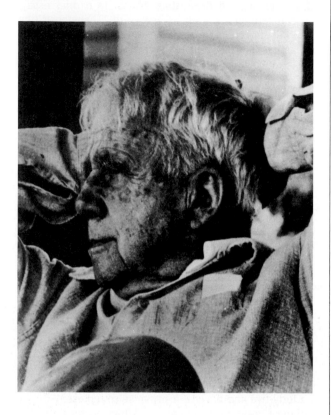

Although Robert Frost is the poet whom Americans most closely identify with New England, he was born in San Francisco, California. He was ten years old before he first saw the New England landscapes and knew the changing seasons that he would later describe with the familiarity of a native son. The boy's move across the country was the result of his father's early death and his mother's decision to settle in the industrial town of Lawrence, Massachusetts. After high school there, Frost entered Dartmouth College in New Hampshire. He decided after a few months that he was not yet ready for higher education, and he returned to Lawrence to work in the cotton mills and to write. His verses, however, found little favor with magazine editors.

In his early twenties, married and with a growing family, Frost finally began to feel the need for a more formal education than his random reading could provide. He took his family to Cambridge, Massachusetts, where he entered Harvard and stayed for only two years. He later wrote of his decision to leave: "Harvard had taken me away from the question of whether I could write or not."

Frost earned a living as a schoolteacher and as an editor before deciding to try farming. For ten years, Frost tilled the stony New Hampshire soil on thirty acres which his grandfather had bought for him. But he decided that the concentration demanded by writing poetry did not mix with the round-the-clock physical effort of working the land. Discouraged, he returned to teaching for a few years; then in 1912 he sought a complete change of scene by taking his family to England.

The move turned out to be a wise one. Stimulated by meeting English poets, Frost continued to write poetry, though he found his subjects in New England. In the three years he spent abroad, he completed the two volumes that would make him famous—*A Boy's Will* (1913) and *North of Boston* (1914). These collections included several poems that would stand among Frost's best-known works: "The Tuft of Flowers," "In Hardwood Groves," "Mending Wall," "The Death of the Hired Man," and "After Apple-Picking." These poems were marked by a flinty realism and an impressive mastery of iambic rhythm, narrative dialogue, and the dramatic monologue.

When Frost came back to New Hampshire in 1915, he was no longer an obscure scribbler intent on turning New England folkways into poetry; he was an accomplished writer who had already extended the scope and character of American literature into the twentieth century. In 1916, the publication of *Mountain Interval*—a collection that included such favorites as "The Road Not Taken," "Birches," and " 'Out, Out—' "—solidified his fame. Rewarded with many prizes (including four Pulitzer Prizes and a Congressional medal), numerous honorary degrees, and the faithful attention of a wide readership, Frost spent the rest of his life as a lecturer at a number of colleges, and as a public performer who, as he put it, liked to "say" rather than to recite his poetry.

On stage, Frost in his later years became a character of his creation—a lovable, fumbling old gent who could nevertheless pierce the minds and hearts of those able to see beyond his play-acting. In private, he was apt to put aside this guileless character and become a sometimes wicked commentator on the pretensions of rival poets; and he could be just as cutting to gushing devotees, who were unaware that he held in contempt the very flattery he demanded.

On Inaugural Day, 1961, standing bareheaded in a bright, cold wind beside President John F. Kennedy on the Capitol steps in Washington, D.C., Frost recited "The Gift Outright." His art with words had brought him not only the friendship of a president (who was half his age) but, by means of radio and television, the largest single audience in history for a poet.

In a period when poetry was being changed by verbal experiment and by exotic influences from abroad, Frost remained devoted to traditional forms and firmly rooted in American soil. If, at the time of his death, he seemed to belong more to the past than to the present, his reputation today is secure. Neither the cranky realism nor the homely philosophy of self-reliance and spiritual independence that mark his work has been forgotten. He was an artist who developed his talents with stubborn persistence, and he found a unique voice that remained unaffected by the clamor of modernism.

Robert Frost reading a poem at the inauguration of John F. Kennedy, January 20, 1961. Four American Presidents are shown in this photograph.

Frost was particularly proud of his sonnets, and he often expressed regret that more of them were not reprinted in the hundreds of anthologies in which his work appeared. "Design" reveals how densely packed with ideas his sonnets can be. Based on the very first line of the poem, what would you predict its tone is going to be? What words make you feel that way?

Design

I found a dimpled spider, fat and white,
On a white heal-all,° holding up a moth
Like a white piece of rigid satin cloth—
Assorted characters of death and blight
5   Mixed ready to begin the morning right,
Like the ingredients of a witches' broth—
A snowdrop spider, a flower like a froth,
And dead wings carried like a paper kite.

What had that flower to do with being white,
10   The wayside blue and innocent heal-all?
What brought the kindred spider to that height,
Then steered the white moth thither in the night?
What but design of darkness to appall?
If design govern in a thing so small.

2. **heal-all:** a flowering plant believed to have curative powers.

Responding to the Poem

Analyzing the Poem

Identifying Details

1. Identify the three "characters" discussed in the poem. What color is each one? What is happening to the three characters?
2. Identify each of the **similes** in the **octave** (first eight lines) of the sonnet.
3. Briefly stated, tell what questions the poet asks in the **sestet** (last six lines) of the sonnet.

Interpreting Meanings

4. Look up the word *character* in a dictionary. Which definitions of the word might Frost be applying in line 4? How does each definition affect the meaning of the line? What justifies the poet's description of these things as "characters of death and blight"?
5. In line 13, the poet answers his own questions with another question. In your own words, explain how this question answers the previous one.
6. In line 14, Frost qualifies his answer with a reservation, beginning with a crucial "if." What final question remains in his mind? How would you define a "design of darkness"?
7. How does the last line affect the whole **tone** and meaning of the poem?
8. Describe the **rhyme scheme** of the poem. In your view, how does Frost's use of a very limited number of rhymes affect the poem's **tone**?
9. How would a Puritan writer from Unit One have answered the questions Frost asks in the poem? How would the Rationalists from Unit Two, or a scientist, answer them?
10. Do you see any similarities between Frost's use of the color white in this poem and Melville's use of white in *Moby-Dick*? (See page 297.) Why do you think each writer chose this color?

Writing About the Poem

A Critical Response

1. **Responding to a Critic.** Laurence Perrine has made this comment about "Design":

> Frost's brief poem, like the wayside blue or white heal-all, seems from the outside innocent enough. But within its fourteen innocent-seeming lines, Frost chillingly poses the problem of evil.
>
> —Laurence Perrine

In an essay, explain your response to this comment on the poem. If you agree with it, give reasons why. If you disagree, be sure to state what *you* think is the central issue in the poem.

2. **Contrasting Three Selections.** In a brief essay, explain how these three writers use the image of a spider: Edward Taylor in "Upon a Spider Catching a Fly" (page 46); Jonathan Edwards in "Sinners in the Hands of an Angry God" (page 37); and Robert Frost in "Design." Remember that often the differences in the use of images and symbols are as interesting and important as the similarities.

3. **Comparing Poems.** In a brief essay, compare "Design" with one of the following poems:

   a. "To a Waterfowl" by William Cullen Bryant (page 139)
   b. "Upon a Spider Catching a Fly" by Edward Taylor (page 46)
   c. "The Rhodora" by Ralph Waldo Emerson (page 198)
   d. "On the Beach at Night" by Walt Whitman (page 343)
   e. "Apparently with no surprise" by Emily Dickinson (page 368)

Before you write, gather your data in a chart like the following one:

	"Design"	Other Poem
Rhyme		
Rhythm		
Figures of speech		
Tone		
Message of poem		

Before you read this poem, make a guess as to the meaning of Frost's puzzling title.

Neither Out Far Nor in Deep

The people along the sand
All turn and look one way.
They turn their back on the land.
They look at the sea all day.

5   As long as it takes to pass
A ship keeps raising its hull;
The wetter ground like glass
Reflects a standing gull.

The land may vary more;
10 But wherever the truth may be—
The water comes ashore,
And the people look at the sea.

They cannot look out far.
They cannot look in deep.
15 But when was that ever a bar
To any watch they keep?

Responding to the Poem

Analyzing the Poem

Identifying Details

1. What phenomenon of human behavior does the poet observe in the first stanza? According to line 9, why does this behavior seem surprising?
2. What is the one **simile** that gives an imaginative lift to the stark, flat landscape and seascape the poem depicts?

Interpreting Meanings

3. In what way are lines 11–12 tinged with **irony**?
4. On a literal level, why is it that the people in the poem can look neither "out far" nor "in deep"? What more general human limitations might be **symbolized** by our inability to probe the distance and depth of the sea?
5. What might the sea and the land **symbolize** in this poem? What larger meaning might the "watch" (line 16) take on?
6. Comment on the poet's **tone** in the last line. Does he admire the watchers for keeping their vigil in spite of all obstacles? Does he feel scorn or pity for their failure to recognize their limitations? Do you have some other interpretation? Explain.

Writing About the Poem

A Creative Response

1. **Revising the Poem.** Suppose Frost had used the pronoun *you* instead of *they* in the poem. How might the **tone** have differed? Rewrite the first or last stanza, changing *they* to *you*. Include any other changes you think should be made for the sake of consistency. Then write a paragraph explaining how your stanza differs from Frost's.
2. If you have musical talent, invent a melody for the poem.

A Critical Response

3. **Comparing Literary Works.** In a paragraph, compare Frost's message in this poem with Ishmael's reflections on the human response to the sea in the passage from Melville's *Moby-Dick* beginning on page 298. What does each passage suggest about its author's outlook?
4. **Comparing Poems.** In a paragraph, compare "Neither Out Far Nor in Deep" with Whitman's "On the Beach at Night Alone" (page 345). Consider the message in each poem, the form it is stated in, and the overall effect of the poem.

Sea Watchers by Edward Hopper (1952). Oil.

Collection of Mr. and Mrs. Ralph Ritter,
Kansas City, Missouri.

As spindly and awkward as a giraffe's legs, the birch trees of Robert Frost's New England have white bark ringed with black. Their trunks are remarkably pliable—a fact which gives this poem its realistic base.

To tell his parable about birch-swinging and to communicate his message, Frost chose blank verse—unrhymed iambic pentameter. The success of the poem depends on how well the poet can maintain the strict beat and, at the same time, sound as if there were no rules to obey but the rhythms of ordinary conversation.

Birches

When I see birches bend to left and right
Across the lines of straighter darker trees,
I like to think some boy's been swinging them.
But swinging doesn't bend them down to stay
5   As ice storms do. Often you must have seen them
Loaded with ice a sunny winter morning
After a rain. They click upon themselves
As the breeze rises, and turn many-colored
As the stir cracks and crazes their enamel.
10   Soon the sun's warmth makes them shed crystal shells
Shattering and avalanching on the snow crust—
Such heaps of broken glass to sweep away
You'd think the inner dome of heaven had fallen.
They are dragged to the withered bracken by the load,
15   And they seem not to break; though once they are bowed
So low for long, they never right themselves:
You may see their trunks arching in the woods
Years afterwards, trailing their leaves on the ground
Like girls on hands and knees that throw their hair
20   Before them over their heads to dry in the sun.
But I was going to say when Truth broke in
With all her matter of fact about the ice storm,
I should prefer to have some boy bend them
As he went out and in to fetch the cows—
25   Some boy too far from town to learn baseball,
Whose only play was what he found himself,
Summer or winter, and could play alone.
One by one he subdued his father's trees
By riding them down over and over again
30   Until he took the stiffness out of them,
And not one but hung limp, not one was left
For him to conquer. He learned all there was
To learn about not launching out too soon
And so not carrying the tree away
35   Clear to the ground. He always kept his poise
To the top branches, climbing carefully
With the same pains you use to fill a cup
Up to the brim, and even above the brim.
Then he flung outward, feet first, with a swish,

40 Kicking his way down through the air to the ground.
    So was I once myself a swinger of birches.
    And so I dream of going back to be.
    It's when I'm weary of considerations,
    And life is too much like a pathless wood
45 Where your face burns and tickles with the cobwebs
    Broken across it, and one eye is weeping
    From a twig's having lashed across it open.
    I'd like to get away from earth awhile
    And then come back to it and begin over.
50 May no fate willfully misunderstand me
    And half grant what I wish and snatch me away
    Not to return. Earth's the right place for love:
    I don't know where it's likely to go better.
    I'd like to go by climbing a birch tree,
55 And climb black branches up a snow-white trunk
    Toward heaven, till the tree could bear no more,
    But dipped its top and set me down again.
    That would be good both going and coming back.
    One could do worse than be a swinger of birches.

Responding to the Poem

Analyzing the Poem

Identifying Details

1. Describe the scenario that the speaker imagines when he sees birch trees. What realistic objection to his idea does he recognize in lines 4–5? What "matter of fact" does "Truth" break in with in lines 5–20?
2. In lines 48–49, what does the speaker say he would like to do? How does he relate this wish to swinging a birch tree?

Interpreting Meanings

3. Find at least three examples of **metaphor** and **onomatopoeia** in the poem.
4. Two strong **similes** give the poem a richness that is both imaginative and the result of close observation. What are these similes?
5. What does the playful activity of swinging birches seem to **symbolize** in the poem?
6. A **parable** is a short story in which an ordinary event from everyday life is used to teach a much wider moral or religious lesson. Summarize in your own words what you think the moral or message of Frost's parable is.
7. Describe the complex, conflicting attitudes toward life revealed through this parable about birch-swinging.

Writing About the Poem

A Creative Response

1. **Reading Nature.** Write a paragraph or a short poem in which you use an everyday sight or event to comment on a much larger subject.

A Critical Response

2. **Comparing Writings.** You have read how the Puritans and later the Romantics "read" lessons into nature. In a paragraph, tell whether or not you think Frost's poems "Design" and "Birches" are part of this same tradition. Explain why you believe Frost is more like the Puritans or the Romantics in his attitude.
3. **Comparing Attitudes.** Suppose a Puritan writer were to come upon the bent birches. What response might he or she have to the natural scene? Write out that response in a paragraph.
4. **Responding to the Poem.** In a famous remark about the nature of poetry, Frost once said that a poem "begins in delight and ends in wisdom." In a brief essay, show how this applies to "Birches." If you do *not* think it applies, give your reasons. Whichever point of view you take, be sure you define what you think *delight* and *wisdom* mean.

New Englanders and other people who live in cold climates are familiar with the way the ground heaves when it freezes. This annual occurrence dislocates stone walls and fences, cracks pavements, and squeezes underground stones and boulders out onto the landscape. This natural phenomenon is caused by the expansion of freezing water in the soil. Frost uses it as the starting point for "Mending Wall." Stop after you've read the first four lines of the poem; think about those lines, and describe the visual subject of the poem up to that point.

Mending Wall

Something there is that doesn't love a wall,
That sends the frozen-ground-swell under it
And spills the upper boulders in the sun,
And makes gaps even two can pass abreast.
5   The work of hunters is another thing:
I have come after them and made repair
Where they have left not one stone on a stone,
But they would have the rabbit out of hiding,
To please the yelping dogs. The gaps I mean,
10 No one has seen them made or heard them made,
But at spring mending time we find them there.
I let my neighbor know beyond the hill;
And on a day we meet to walk the line
And set the wall between us once again.
15 We keep the wall between us as we go.
To each the boulders that have fallen to each.
And some are loaves and some so nearly balls
We have to use a spell to make them balance:
"Stay where you are until our backs are turned!"
20 We wear our fingers rough with handling them.
Oh, just another kind of outdoor game,
One on a side. It comes to little more:
There where it is we do not need the wall:
He is all pine and I am apple orchard.
25 My apple trees will never get across
And eat the cones under his pines, I tell him.
He only says, "Good fences make good neighbors."
Spring is the mischief in me, and I wonder
If I could put a notion in his head:
30 "*Why* do they make good neighbors? Isn't it
Where there are cows? But here there are no cows.
Before I built a wall I'd ask to know
What I was walling in or walling out,
And to whom I was like to give offense.
35 Something there is that doesn't love a wall,
That wants it down." I could say "Elves" to him,
But it's not elves exactly, and I'd rather

He said it for himself. I see him there,
Bringing a stone grasped firmly by the top
40 In each hand, like an old-stone savage armed.
He moves in darkness as it seems to me,
Not of woods only and the shade of trees.
He will not go behind his father's saying,
And he likes having thought of it so well
45 He says again, "Good fences make good neighbors."

Responding to the Poem

Analyzing the Poem

Identifying Details

1. What makes the speaker say that "something" doesn't love a wall? Besides this "something," who else sometimes knocks down walls?
2. Describe what is happening in lines 13–16. According to the speaker, why is rebuilding the wall merely a game (lines 23–26)?
3. What question does the speaker think should be settled before building a wall, according to lines 32–34?
4. Why would the speaker say "Elves" (line 36)?
5. From whom did the neighbor get his saying "Good fences make good neighbors"?

Interpreting Meanings

6. In lines 23–27, what two different personality types or temperaments might be dramatized?
7. Why do you think the speaker would rather his neighbor said "Elves" (lines 37–38)?
8. The speaker says in lines 41–42 that the neighboring farmer moves in a "darkness" that is "not of woods only and the shade of trees." What else might this darkness be? Explain the significance of the **simile** in line 40.
9. What might the wall **symbolize**? In your view, what philosophies about human social relations does the poem explore?

10. How do you explain the fact that the man who doesn't see the need for a wall is the one who, every spring, is the first to call upon his neighbor and so make sure the wall is rebuilt? Might he want something more from his neighbor than merely a hand with repair work?
11. Which of these two men is in greater harmony with nature, in your opinion? Why do you think so?
12. When the speaker repeats his neighbor's statement in the poem's last line, does he mean to emphasize his neighbor's stubbornness? Or does he somewhat reluctantly mean to recognize that there's wisdom in the statement?
13. Do *you* believe that "good fences make good neighbors"? Why or why not?

Writing About the Poem

A Creative Response

1. **Changing the Poem's Voice.** Let the neighbor give his answer to this speaker's musings on the purpose of the wall.

A Critical Response

2. **Comparing Poems.** Do you think this poem has anything in common with Dickinson's "The soul selects her own society" (page 357)? Answer this question in a paragraph.

In the Bible, when God creates the world, He says "Let there be light." And after each stage of creation, we read "and God saw that it was good."

Keep these ideas in mind as you read Frost's vision of an event that is the opposite of creation.

Once by the Pacific

The shattered water made a misty din.
Great waves looked over others coming in,
And thought of doing something to the shore
That water never did to land before.
5 The clouds were low and hairy in the skies,
Like locks blown forward in the gleam of eyes.
You could not tell, and yet it looked as if
The shore was lucky in being backed by cliff,
The cliff in being backed by continent;
10 It looked as if a night of dark intent
Was coming, and not only a night, an age.
Someone had better be prepared for rage.
There would be more than ocean water broken
Before God's last *Put out the Light* was spoken.

Responding to the Poem

Analyzing the Poem

Identifying Details

1. Identify at least three examples of **personification** in the poem.

Interpreting Meanings

2. What does the scene remind the speaker of?
3. Explain what you think the speaker means by "a night of dark intent . . . not only a night, an age" (lines 10–11). Whose "intent" is he referring to?
4. Who do you think is the "someone" who "had better be prepared for rage" (line 12)? Whose "rage"?
5. Besides ocean water, what else might be "broken" during that rage?
6. *"Put out the light"* is something anyone might say on an ordinary evening at home. How does the use of this casual, domestic phrase make the poem's message even more chilling? What would you say that message is?
7. The poem's **title** suggests that Frost is describing a scene he once saw as he gazed at the Pacific Ocean. What larger "moment" might this scene **symbolize**?

8. Do you view this poem as a warning? Or do you think Frost is just expressing a certain philosophy of life? Explain what the warning might be, or discuss the philosophy.

Writing About the Poem

A Critical Response

Comparing Poems. In a brief essay, compare "Once by the Pacific" to Whitman's poem called "On the Beach at Night" (see page 343). Before you write, gather your data in a chart like the one following. Your essay does not have to include all the items in the chart.

	Whitman	Frost
Message in poem		
Use of symbols		
Tone		
Use of rhymes and rhythms		
Use of imagery		

This poem is a dramatic lyric—dramatic because it presents characters who speak in voices assigned to them by the poet, lyric because it is less concerned with describing events and actions than it is with revealing feelings. Most of the poem is a dialogue in blank verse. Its main character never speaks for himself, yet his presence dominates the poem. By the last line, we have heard as much about him as we need in order to understand his background, habits, and attitudes. And in gradually coming to know the "hired man," we also come to know the personalities of the husband and wife whose dialogue carries the drama.

Embedded in the poem is one of Frost's most famous sayings, one often quoted by many people who probably have no idea where it comes from:

"Home is the place where, when you have to go there,
They have to take you in."

The Death of the Hired Man

Oil Lamp by Andrew Wyeth (1945). Oil.

Sotheby Parke-Bernet Galleries, Inc., New York.

Mary sat musing on the lamp flame at the table,
Waiting for Warren. When she heard his step,
She ran on tiptoe down the darkened passage
To meet him in the doorway with the news
5 And put him on his guard. "Silas is back."
She pushed him outward with her through the door
And shut it after her. "Be kind," she said.
She took the market things from Warren's arms
And set them on the porch, then drew him down
10 To sit beside her on the wooden steps.

"When was I ever anything but kind to him?
But I'll not have the fellow back," he said.
"I told him so last haying, didn't I?
If he left then, I said, that ended it.
15 What good is he? Who else will harbor him
At his age for the little he can do?
What help he is there's no depending on.
Off he goes always when I need him most.
He thinks he ought to earn a little pay,
20 Enough at least to buy tobacco with,
So he won't have to beg and be beholden.
'All right,' I say, 'I can't afford to pay
Any fixed wages, though I wish I could.'
'Someone else can.' 'Then someone else will have to.'
25 I shouldn't mind his bettering himself
If that was what it was. You can be certain,
When he begins like that, there's someone at him
Trying to coax him off with pocket money—
In haying time, when any help is scarce.
30 In winter he comes back to us. I'm done."

"Sh! not so loud: He'll hear you," Mary said.

"I want him to: He'll have to soon or late."

"He's worn out. He's asleep beside the stove.
When I came up from Rowe's I found him here,
35 Huddled against the barn door fast asleep,
A miserable sight, and frightening, too—
You needn't smile—I didn't recognize him—
I wasn't looking for him—and he's changed.
Wait till you see."

                    "Where did you say he'd been?"

40 "He didn't say. I dragged him to the house,
And gave him tea and tried to make him smoke.
I tried to make him talk about his travels.
Nothing would do: He just kept nodding off."

"What did he say? Did he say anything?"

"But little."

45   "Anything? Mary, confess
He said he'd come to ditch the meadow for me."

"Warren!"

          "But did he? I just want to know."

"Of course he did. What would you have him say?
Surely you wouldn't grudge the poor old man
50 Some humble way to save his self-respect.
He added, if you really care to know,
He meant to clear the upper pasture, too.
That sounds like something you have heard before?
Warren, I wish you could have heard the way
55 He jumbled everything. I stopped to look
Two or three times—he made me feel so queer—
To see if he was talking in his sleep.
He ran on Harold Wilson—you remember—
The boy you had in haying four years since.
60 He's finished school, and teaching in his college.
Silas declares you'll have to get him back.
He says they two will make a team for work:
Between them they will lay this farm as smooth!
The way he mixed that in with other things.
65 He thinks young Wilson a likely lad, though daft
On education—you know how they fought
All through July under the blazing sun,
Silas up on the cart to build the load,
Harold along beside to pitch it on.''

70 "Yes, I took care to keep well out of earshot."

"Well, those days trouble Silas like a dream.
You wouldn't think they would. How some things linger!
Harold's young college-boy's assurance piqued him.
After so many years he still keeps finding
75 Good arguments he sees he might have used.
I sympathize. I know just how he feels
To think of the right thing to say too late.
Harold's associated in his mind with Latin.
He asked me what I thought of Harold's saying
80 He studied Latin, like the violin,
Because he liked it—that an argument!
He said he couldn't make the boy believe
He could find water with a hazel prong—
Which showed how much good school had ever done him.
85 He wanted to go over that. But most of all
He thinks if he could have another chance
To teach him how to build a load of hay——"

"I know, that's Silas' one accomplishment.
He bundles every forkful in its place,
90 And tags and numbers it for future reference,
So he can find and easily dislodge it
In the unloading. Silas does that well.
He takes it out in bunches like big birds' nests.
You never see him standing on the hay
95 He's trying to lift, straining to lift himself."

"He thinks if he could teach him that, he'd be
Some good perhaps to someone in the world.
He hates to see a boy the fool of books.
Poor Silas, so concerned for other folk,
100 And nothing to look backward to with pride,
And nothing to look forward to with hope,
So now and never any different."

Part of a moon was falling down the west,
Dragging the whole sky with it to the hills.
105 Its light poured softly in her lap. She saw it
And spread her apron to it. She put out her hand
Among the harplike morning-glory strings,
Taut with the dew from garden bed to eaves,
As if she played unheard some tenderness
110 That wrought on him beside her in the night.
"Warren," she said, "he has come home to die:
You needn't be afraid he'll leave you this time."

"Home," he mocked gently.

                    "Yes, what else but home?
It all depends on what you mean by home.
115 Of course he's nothing to us, anymore
Than was the hound that came a stranger to us
Out of the woods, worn out upon the trail."

"Home is the place where, when you have to go there,
They have to take you in."

                    "I should have called it
120 Something you somehow haven't to deserve."

Warren leaned out and took a step or two,
Picked up a little stick, and brought it back
And broke it in his hand and tossed it by.
"Silas has better claim on us you think
125 Than on his brother? Thirteen little miles
As the road winds would bring him to his door.
Silas has walked that far no doubt today.
Why doesn't he go there? His brother's rich,
A somebody—director in the bank."

To understand this little lyric, be sure you know two important accounts: that of the loss of Eden in Genesis, and, in Greek mythology, that of the loss of the Golden Age. When you first read the title of the poem, what do you think it's going to be about?

Nothing Gold Can Stay

Nature's first green is gold,
Her hardest hue to hold.
Her early leaf's a flower;
But only so an hour.
Then leaf subsides to leaf.
So Eden sank to grief,
So dawn goes down to day.
Nothing gold can stay.

Responding to the Poem

Analyzing the Poem

Identifying Details

1. Identify four specific things in the poem that cannot, or did not, "stay."

Interpreting Meanings

2. Think of what the very first buds of leaves look like in spring, and explain what line 1 means.
3. Explain the natural process described in line 5.
4. What Biblical event is **alluded** to in line 6? What state of mind or situation might "Eden" **symbolize** here?
5. "Gold" as used here is not the precious metal, but an idea. What different ideas might "gold" **symbolize**? Why can't "gold" stay—or do you disagree?
6. Show how its **rhymes** and **rhythm** contribute to this poem's compactness and completeness. How do **alliteration, slant rhyme,** and other **sound echoes** also contribute to the poem's tightly woven effect?
7. How would you describe the speaker's **tone**?

Writing About the Poem

A Creative Response

1. **Paraphrasing.** This poem is composed of only forty words. Try to paraphrase it as briefly as possible. Then read your paraphrase to see if you have left out anything important. Can you paraphrase it in fewer than forty words and still account for every idea?

A Critical Response

2. **Comparing Poems.** In a paragraph, tell how this poem is similar to or different from "Eldorado" by Edgar Allan Poe (page 248) or "Miniver Cheevy" by Edwin Arlington Robinson (page 654). Consider these elements of the poem:

   a. Use of gold as an image and symbol
   b. Message
   c. Tone
   d. Poetic form and technique

Primary Sources
"I must have the pulse beat of rhythm . . ."

These comments are from an interview held on October 21, 1923, with *New York Times* reporter Rose C. Feld. A month after the interview, Frost won his first Pulitzer Prize. Here, Frost has been talking about American poetry.

". . . We're still a bit afraid. America, for instance, was afraid to accept Walt Whitman when he first sang the songs of democracy. His influence on American poetry began to be felt only after the French had hailed him as a great writer, a literary revolutionist. Our own poet had to be imported from France before we were sure of his strength.

"Today almost every man who writes poetry confesses his debt to Whitman. Many have gone very much further than Whitman would have traveled with them. They are the people who believe in wide straddling.

"I, myself, as I said before, don't like it for myself. I do not write free verse; I write blank verse. I must have the pulse beat of rhythm, I like to hear it beating under the things I write.

"That doesn't mean I do not like to read a bit of free verse occasionally. I do. It sometimes succeeds in painting a picture that is very clear and startling. It's good as something created momentarily for its sudden startling effect; it hasn't the qualities, however, of something lastingly beautiful.

"And sometimes my objection to it is that it's a pose. It's not honest. When a man sets out consciously to tear up forms and rhythms and measures, then he is not interested in giving you poetry. He just wants to perform; he wants to show you his tricks. He will get an effect; nobody will deny that, but it is not a harmonious effect.

"Sometimes it strikes me that the free-verse people got their idea from incorrect proof sheets. I have had stuff come from the printers with lines half left out or positions changed about. I read the poems as they stood, distorted and half finished, and I confess I get a rather pleasant sensation from them. They make a sort of nightmarish half-sense."

—Robert Frost

This poem presents the very last part of a story. We will never know that story, yet we can tell that something has gone wrong; that things weren't supposed to end this way; that even as she dispatches her farewell letter, the woman in the case is ambivalent about what she has done. Except that this woman once had a father whose advice she listened to, we know nothing of what might have been a romance—or no more than a courtship.

Parting, Without a Sequel

She has finished and sealed the letter
At last, which he so richly has deserved,
With characters venomous and hatefully
    curved,
And nothing could be better.

5   But even as she gave it,
Saying to the blue-capped functioner of
    doom,
"Into his hands," she hoped the leering
    groom
Might somewhere lose and leave it.

Then all the blood
Forsook the face. She was too pale for
10   tears,
Observing the ruin of her younger years.
She went and stood

Under her father's vaunting oak
Who kept his peace in wind and sun, and
    glistened
15   Stoical in the rain; to whom she listened
If he spoke.

And now the agitation of the rain
Rasped his sere° leaves, and he talked low
    and gentle,
Reproaching the wan daughter by the lintel;
20   Ceasing, and beginning again.

Away went the messenger's bicycle,
His serpent's track went up the hill forever.
And all the time she stood there hot as
    fever
And cold as any icicle.

---

18. **sere:** dry

Day Dreams by Eastman Johnson (1877). Oil on paper board.

Private collection.

Responding to the Poem

Analyzing the Poem

Identifying Details

1. What decisive action has the poem's main character just taken?
2. The driving force in this poem is a **conflict** within the main character herself. What details reveal her anger? What evidence reveals that she has mixed feelings about her decision?

Interpreting Meanings

3. Identify the "blue-capped functioner of doom" in line 6. Why do you think he is described as "leering"?
4. Why do you think the main character hopes this person might lose her letter?
5. In what fashion does the oak tree "speak" to the daughter in the fifth stanza, and what message does the tree convey? What qualities associated with an oak tree might make it an appropriate **symbol** for the woman's father?
6. Why do you think the messenger's track is described as a "serpent's track" in line 22 instead of, for example, a snail's track or just a wheel track? In what sense does the track go on "forever"?
7. How could someone be "hot as fever" and "cold as any icicle" at the same time? What does this suggest the letter writer is feeling?
8. While **rhyme** can add music to poetry, it can also create wry humor. What ingenious and funny three-syllable rhyme ends the poem? Do you think the poet is making a comment by ending this serious, unhappy story on a slightly ridiculous note?
9. What is the significance of the poem's title? Do you think there usually *is* a "sequel" to stories of unrequited love?

Writing About the Poem

A Critical Response

1. **Comparing Poems.** Write a brief essay comparing "Bells for John Whiteside's Daughter" and James Russell Lowell's "She Came and She Went" (page 168). What emotions does each speaker express? What view of death does each poem reveal? Support your comparisons with specific references to the poems.
2. **Filling in Meanings.** Who is the letter writer in "Parting, Without a Sequel"? Is it a young girl who has fallen in love for the first time and been rejected? Or is it an older woman whose lover has rejected her, leaving her to contemplate a lonely old age? Does the main character really talk to the oak tree? Or is it her father who speaks? Is the poet sympathetic to his letter writer? Or is his tone slightly mocking and comical? Answer these questions in a brief essay, using details from the poem to support your interpretations. Then compare your answers in class. Do others agree or disagree, and why?
3. **Comparing Poems.** Compare "Parting, Without a Sequel" to Emily Dickinson's "Heart! We will forget him" (page 355). Consider these elements of the poems:

   a. Messages   c. Tones
   b. Speakers   d. Imagery

4. **Responding to a Critic.** One critic wrote that Ransom's poems emphasized such themes as

   > mortality and the fleetingness of youthful vigor and grace . . . and the disparity between the world as man would have it and as it actually is, between what people want and need emotionally and what is available for them . . .
   >
   > —Thomas Daniel Young

   Show how this comment is or is not supported by either or both of the poems you have just read. Support your opinion with references to the poems.

Analyzing Language and Style

Multiple Meanings of Words

1. *Characters* is a word that can mean (a) letters of the alphabet, (b) personal qualities, (c) reputations, (d) persons. Which meaning does the word have in line 3? Do you think Ransom is also suggesting something about his letter writer's feelings or even her character?
2. List the meanings the word *groom* can have. Which meaning specifically applies to line 7? Given the situation in the poem, do you think another meaning is echoed here?
3. Surprisingly, the archaic meaning of the word *wan* is "gloomy or dark." What is the common meaning of the word today? Which meaning does Ransom intend in line 19?
4. The word *sere* in line 18 sounds like *seer.* What does *seer* mean? Do you think Ransom is punning on the word?
5. What does the word *vaunting* mean here? Do you think the use of this word could suggest a slight mockery of the tree's wise advice?

Here is a sonnet in the form of an argument—a poet's argument with himself. In the course of the argument, he condemns his own inadequate efforts to write poetry, becomes content to settle for the simple powers of observation, and, ironically, ends up with a fine poem. What feelings does the image of a wild swan evoke for you?

Love the Wild Swan

"I hate my verses, every line, every word,
Oh pale and brittle pencils ever to try
One grass blade's curve, or the throat of one bird
That clings to twig, ruffled against white sky.
5   Oh cracked and twilight mirrors ever to catch
One color, one glinting flash, of the splendor of things.
Unlucky hunter, Oh bullets of wax,
The lion beauty, the wild-swan wings, the storm of the wings."
—This wild swan of a world is no hunter's game.
10   Better bullets than yours would miss the white breast,
Better mirrors than yours would crack in the flame.
Does it matter whether you hate your . . . self? At least
Love your eyes that can see, your mind that can
Hear the music, the thunder of the wings. Love the wild swan.

Responding to the Poem

Analyzing the Poem

Identifying Details

1. What complaint does the speaker make in the poem's first four lines?
2. What adjectives in lines 1–8 emphasize the speaker's feeling of weakness and failure?
3. What response is made to the speaker's complaint in the **sestet,** the last six lines of the sonnet?

Interpreting Meanings

4. What might "cracked and twilight mirrors" **symbolize** in line 5? Who is the "unlucky hunter," and what are his "bullets of wax"?
5. This sonnet's **sestet** presents an **extended metaphor** in which the world is compared to a wild swan. What details extend this metaphor? What attitude toward the world does this comparison suggest?
6. What might the "flame" in line 11 be? Why might "better mirrors" crack in it?
7. Why does the speaker hesitate in the middle of line 12? What other word than "self" might he be reaching for?

Writing About the Poems

A Creative Response

1. **Rephrasing a Poem.** Rewrite "Love the Wild Swan" in the form of a dialogue between two people. Include a brief description of each character.

A Critical Response

2. **Responding to the Poem.** "Shine, Perishing Republic" was published in 1930. In a brief essay, explain why you think Jeffers's view of the American condition is or is not still valid. First, summarize the view expressed in the poem. Then tell whether or not you think this view applies to contemporary America. Support your position with specific references to the poem and to contemporary life.

Analyzing Language and Style

Rhymes

Many words in the English language look as if they should rhyme, but don't (*dough/through/bough*). (Such words are called "eye rhymes.") Many other words look as if they don't rhyme, but they do (*dough/go/sew/blow*). **Exact rhymes** are rhymes that consist of the repetition of the accented vowel sound and all succeeding sounds in words (*bicycle/icicle*). **Slant rhymes** (also called **approximate** or **imperfect rhymes**) are sounds that are similar but not exactly the same (*blue/bled; yellow/willow*).

In "Love the Wild Swan," find examples of:

1. Two pairs of end rhymes that look as if they should rhyme exactly, but are actually slant rhymes
2. Two other end rhymes that look as if they should not rhyme at all, but that contain slant rhymes
3. Two other end rhymes that look as if they should not rhyme, but are actually perfect rhymes

THE HARLEM RENAISSANCE

James Weldon Johnson (1871–1938)

James Weldon Johnson—poet, teacher, and lawyer—was born in Jacksonville, Florida. He was educated at Atlanta University in Georgia and Columbia University in New York City. Throughout his career, Johnson was an energetic exponent of civil rights, and in his writing he constantly sought recognition for the contributions that blacks had made to American culture.

After serving as U.S. Consul to Nicaragua and Venezuela (1906–1913), Johnson became a field secretary of the National Association for the Advancement of Colored People (NAACP), and was later named the organization's executive secretary. In 1930, he became a professor at Fisk University. Eight years later, he died in an automobile accident.

Although some of Johnson's early poems are in dialect, he soon abandoned that style for standard English, which he felt was capable of greater variety and power. His principal theme was black pride, which he celebrated in such poems as "Fifty Years," written on the fiftieth anniversary of the Emancipation Proclamation, and "O Black and Unknown Bards," a tribute to the anonymous authors of Negro spirituals. With his brother, the composer John Rosamond Johnson, he wrote a number of songs and light operas, and the brothers collaborated in editing two collections of Negro spirituals.

Johnson was an important leader of the first phase of the Harlem Renaissance. His anthology, *The Book of American Negro Poetry* (1922) was

Portrait of James W. Johnson by Winold Reiss (1925). Pastel.

one of the earliest and most significant collections of poems by blacks. In addition to poetry, he wrote fiction (most notably *The Autobiography of an Ex-Colored Man,* published in 1912), nonfiction studies of black life, and an autobiography, *Along This Way* (1933).

This poem is one of eight "sermons" written by Johnson in the style of the old-time black preachers. He collected the sermons in a book called *God's Trombones*—the trombone being the preacher's voice, "the instrument possessing above all others the power to express the wide and varied range of emotions encompassed by the human voice." Johnson tells us that the man delivering this sermon would intone, moan, plead, blare, crash, and thunder. You should listen to the poem read aloud.

Go Down Death

A Funeral Sermon

Weep not, weep not,
She is not dead;
She's resting in the bosom of Jesus.
Heart-broken husband—weep no more;
5   Grief-stricken son—weep no more;
Left-lonesome daughter—weep no more;
She's only just gone home.

Day before yesterday morning,
God was looking down from his great, high heaven,
10   Looking down on all his children,
And his eye fell on Sister Caroline,
Tossing on her bed of pain.
And God's big heart was touched with pity,
With the everlasting pity.

15   And God sat back on his throne,
And he commanded that tall, bright angel standing at his
     right hand:
Call me Death!
And that tall, bright angel cried in a voice
That broke like a clap of thunder:
20   Call Death! Call Death!
And the echo sounded down the streets of heaven
Till it reached away back to that shadowy place,
Where Death waits with his pale, white horses.

And Death heard the summons,
25   And he leaped on his fastest horse,
Pale as a sheet in the moonlight.
Up the golden street Death galloped,
And the hoofs of his horse struck fire from the gold,
But they didn't make no sound.
30   Up Death rode to the Great White Throne,
And waited for God's command.

And God said: Go down, Death, go down,
Go down to Savannah, Georgia,
Down in Yamacraw,

Go Down Death by Aaron Douglas (1927). Oil on masonite.

35 And find Sister Caroline.
She's borne the burden and heat of the day,
She's labored long in my vineyard,
And she's tired—
She's weary—
40 Go down, Death, and bring her to me.

And Death didn't say a word,
But he loosed the reins on his pale, white horse,
And he clamped the spurs to his bloodless sides,
And out and down he rode,
45 Through heaven's pearly gates,
Past suns and moons and stars;
On Death rode,
And the foam from his horse was like a comet in the sky;
On Death rode,
50 Leaving the lightning's flash behind;
Straight on down he came.

While we were watching round her bed,
She turned her eyes and looked away,
She saw what we couldn't see;
55 She saw Old Death. She saw Old Death
Coming like a falling star.
But Death didn't frighten Sister Caroline;
He looked to her like a welcome friend.
And she whispered to us: I'm going home,
60 And she smiled and closed her eyes.

And Death took her up like a baby,
And she lay in his icy arms,
But she didn't feel no chill.
And Death began to ride again—
65 Up beyond the evening star,
Out beyond the morning star,
Into the glittering light of glory,
On to the Great White Throne.

And there he laid Sister Caroline
70 On the loving breast of Jesus.
And Jesus took his own hand and wiped away her tears,
And he smoothed the furrows from her face,
And the angels sang a little song,
And Jesus rocked her in his arms,
75 And kept a-saying: Take your rest,
Take your rest, take your rest.

Weep not—weep not,
She is not dead;
She's resting in the bosom of Jesus.

Responding to the Poem

Analyzing the Poem

Identifying Details

1. Where is God in stanza 2, and where is Death in stanza 3? According to stanza 5, where is Sister Caroline?
2. How does Sister Caroline respond to Death's arrival in stanza 7?
3. Point out at least three **similes** that help to suggest the power and magnificence of the workings of heaven.

Interpreting Meanings

4. Does the speaker portray God and Jesus as distant, forbidding figures, or as familiar, gentle ones? Point out at least four details that support your interpretation.
5. Death riding a pale horse is a legendary figure in literature and art. Sometimes referred to as the Grim Reaper, he is often pictured as a skeleton on horseback carrying a scythe (a tool used to cut down hay and grass). While most of these traditional representations of death are fearful, the one in this poem is not. How does the poet transform this conventionally horrifying image into an almost comforting one?
6. Johnson was a highly sophisticated writer. Why do you think he uses the informal language of folk tradition for this poem?
7. Why do you think Death rides a "pale" or white horse? Where else have you seen the color white used in a similar **symbolic** way?

Writing About the Poem

A Creative Response

1. **Extending the Poem.** Think about the character of Death as it is drawn in the poem. Write a speech that Death might make to the people addressed in the poem.

A Critical Response

2. **Comparing Sermons.** Extracts from another famous sermon in American literature are on page 37—Jonathan Edwards's "Sinners in the Hands of an Angry God." In a brief essay, compare and contrast Johnson's sermon with Edwards's. Consider these elements of each sermon:

   a. Imagery
   b. Figures of speech
   c. Message
   d. Tone
   e. Audience
   f. Purpose

3. **Comparing and Contrasting Poems.** Compare and contrast the attitudes toward death expressed in "Go Down Death" and Millay's "Dirge Without Music" (page 670). What emotions in the face of death does each speaker convey? What aspects of life—the pleasures or the hardships—does each speaker stress? What view does each take of what happens to human beings after death?

Analyzing Language and Style

Free Verse and the Orator's Style

Johnson and Paul Laurence Dunbar (page 664) had several discussions about poetry. Dunbar was essentially conservative in style, but Johnson was interested in experimenting. When Johnson was working on the poems that would eventually become *God's Trombones,* he talked with Dunbar:

> I showed Paul the things I had done under the sudden influence of Whitman. He read them through and, looking at me with a queer smile, said "I don't like them, and I don't see what you are driving at." He may have been justified, but I was taken aback. I got out my copy of *Leaves of Grass* and read him some of the things I admired most. There was, at least, some personal consolation in the fact that his verdict was the same on Whitman himself.
>
> —James Weldon Johnson

Examine "Go Down Death" and see if you can identify the influence of Whitman (page 326). Look for these elements of Whitman's style:

1. Repetition and parallel structure to create rhythm
2. The language of everyday conversation, including slang
3. Variation of lines, from very long to very short

Primary Sources
God's Trombones

In the preface to *God's Trombones,* Johnson describes the genesis of his poems.

"The old-time preacher was generally a man far above the average in intelligence; he was, not infrequently, a man of positive genius. The earliest of these preachers must have virtually committed many parts of the Bible to memory through hearing the scriptures read or preached from in the white churches which the slaves attended. They were the first of the slaves to learn to read, and their reading was confined to the Bible, and specifically to the more dramatic passages of the Old Testament. A text served mainly as a starting point and often had no relation to the development of the sermon. Nor would the old-time preacher balk at any text within the lids of the Bible. There is the story of one who after reading a rather cryptic passage took off his spectacles, closed the Bible with a bang and by way of preface said, 'Brothers and sisters, this morning—I intend to explain the unexplainable—find out the undefinable—ponder over the imponderable—and unscrew the inscrutable.' "

. . .

"The old-time Negro preacher of parts was above all an orator, and in good measure an actor. He knew the secret of oratory, that at bottom it is a progression of rhythmic words more than it is anything else. Indeed, I have witnessed congregations moved to ecstasy by the rhythmic intoning of sheer incoherencies. He was a master of all the modes of eloquence. He often possessed a voice that was a marvelous instrument, a voice he could modulate from a sepulchral whisper to a crashing thunder clap. His discourse was generally kept at a high pitch of fervency, but occasionally he dropped into colloquialisms and, less often, into humor. He preached a personal and anthropomorphic God, a sure-enough heaven and a red-hot hell. His imagination was bold and unfettered. He had the power to sweep his hearers before him; and so himself was often swept away. At such times his language was not prose but poetry. It was from memories of such preachers there grew the idea of this book of poems."

—James Weldon Johnson

Black preacher at the Fourth Street Church of Christ in Natchez, Mississippi.

Photograph by Eve Arnold (1983).

Claude McKay
(1890–1948)

Claude McKay was one of the most influential members of the Harlem Renaissance of the 1920's. He was born and raised on the Caribbean island of Jamaica, the child of poor farm workers. When he was six, he went to live with an older brother who was a schoolteacher, and his early education came chiefly from his brother's library. At nineteen, McKay became a policeman in Kingston, but he was also writing poetry in the Jamaican dialect. In 1912, two volumes of this poetry, *Songs of Jamaica* and *Constab Ballads,* appeared. These popular volumes brought him praise as the Robert Burns of Jamaica, and they won their author a prize which enabled him to travel to the United States. He studied here for two years, first at Tuskegee Institute in Alabama and then at Kansas State College. In 1914 he moved to Harlem, the center of black culture in the United States.

In Harlem, McKay supported himself with a variety of jobs, from longshoreman to handyman to waiter, while he continued to perfect his craft and to publish poetry in periodicals. In 1920, his third book, *Spring in New Hampshire,* was published. His most important book of poetry, *Harlem Shadows,* appeared in 1922.

By this time, McKay was a major figure in the Harlem Renaissance. He had served for a time as an editor of the radical newspapers, *The Liberator* and *The Masses.* Like many writers of the time, he was attracted to what was then thought of as the "noble experiment" of communism in the Soviet Union. In 1922 he went to Russia with one of the driving spirits of the American radical movement, Max Eastman. Together, they toured the country and met the architects of Russian communism, including Lenin and Trotsky.

For the next ten years, McKay lived abroad, principally in France. He wrote four novels, including the best-selling *Home to Harlem* (1928), an award-winning work about a black soldier's return from World War I.

Portrait of Claude McKay by Carl Van Vechten (1941).

The Studio Museum in Harlem.

In the early 1930's, McKay became disillusioned with communism, and, his productive years over, he wrote very little from then on. In 1942, he converted to Roman Catholicism and returned to the United States, where he spent the remainder of his life as a teacher in Catholic schools in Chicago.

Despite the use of Jamaican dialect early in his career, most of McKay's poetry is firmly traditional in form and style. His many sonnets were largely influenced by the English Romantic poets, especially Wordsworth, Keats, and Shelley. In subject matter, however, those sonnets were far from traditional; they express McKay's ambivalent and often defiant feelings about black life in America.

America

Although she feeds me bread of bitterness,
And sinks into my throat her tiger's tooth,
Stealing my breath of life, I will confess
I love this cultured hell that tests my
    youth!
5 Her vigor flows like tides into my blood,
Giving me strength erect against her hate.
Her bigness sweeps my being like a flood.

Yet as a rebel fronts a king in state,
I stand within her walls with not a shred
10 Of terror, malice, not a word of jeer.
Darkly I gaze into the days ahead,
And see her might and granite wonders
    there,
Beneath the touch of Time's unerring hand,
Like priceless treasures sinking in the sand.

Responding to the Poem

Analyzing the Poem

Identifying Details

1. In lines 1–3, what treatment does the poet say he receives from America?
2. What qualities of America cause the speaker to love her anyway?

Interpreting Meanings

3. America is **personified** in this poem as an entity both cruel and powerful. What **images** suggest America's cruelty and injustice? What images convey her power?
4. A rebel with "not a shred / Of terror, malice, not a word of jeer" might seem to be a rebel without a rebellion. How does the poem resolve this **paradox** or apparent contradiction?
5. What does the speaker see happening to America as he gazes into "the days ahead"? How would you explain this projected fate?
6. How does this speaker's attitude toward America compare with that of the speaker of "Shine, Perishing Republic" (page 695)?

Writing About the Poem

A Creative Response

1. **Capturing the Poet's Feelings.** Design a poster or write a bumper sticker that the speaker in this poem might display. Try to capture in a phrase or two the main idea expressed in the poem.

A Critical Response

2. **Comparing and Contrasting Poems.** The title of the following poem is the name of the Egyptian pharaoh Rameses II, who ruled in the thirteenth century B.C., and who left many monuments to himself. The poem is a comment on passing glory. Compare this poem, published in 1817 in England, to "America." Discuss the poems' similarities and differences in form, subject, point of view, and emotion.

Ozymandias

I met a traveler from an antique land
Who said: Two vast and trunkless legs of stone
Stand in the desert . . . Near them, on the sand,
Half sunk, a shattered visage lies, whose frown,
And wrinkled lip, and sneer of cold command,
Tell that its sculptor well those passions read
Which yet survive, stamped on these lifeless
    things,
The hand that mocked them, and the heart that
    fed:
And on the pedestal these words appear:
"My name is Ozymandias, king of kings:
Look on my works, ye Mighty, and despair!"
Nothing beside remains. Round the decay
Of that colossal wreck, boundless and bare
The lone and level sands stretch far away.

           —Percy Bysshe Shelley

Langston Hughes (1902–1967)

One evening in 1926, the poet Vachel Lindsay was eating dinner in the Wardman Park Hotel in Washington, D.C. The busboy, a shy twenty-four-year-old black man, left three or four poems near Lindsay's plate. Lindsay liked the poems so much that he read them in his performance that night. The next morning, Washington newspapers carried enthusiastic stories about "The Busboy Poet," and the young writer, Langston Hughes, found that he had been "discovered" overnight. The publicity and Lindsay's encouragement helped Hughes to publish his first volume of poems, *The Weary Blues,* and won him a scholarship to Lincoln University. By the time he graduated from college in 1929, the energetic young author had published a second volume of poetry and a novel.

The busboy who had so shyly approached Lindsay was no beginner. By 1926, Hughes had already published poems in the prestigious black magazine *Crisis,* and had been included in an anthology of the Harlem Renaissance, *The New Negro.* He spoke German and Spanish; had lived in Mexico, France, and Italy; and had worked his way to Africa and back as a crew member on a ship. He was ambitious and energetic, and he had learned early to rely on himself. During the career that followed his "overnight" success, Hughes wrote fifteen volumes of verse, six novels, three books of short stories, eleven plays, and a variety of nonfiction works.

Hughes was born in Joplin, Missouri. His parents were well-educated and ambitious. They separated when Langston was young, and for a number of years he lived with his maternal grandmother. When he was twelve, he moved with his mother and stepfather to Cleveland, where he attended high school. Here he read the great twentieth-century Midwestern poets—Edgar Lee Masters, Carl Sandburg, and Vachel Lindsay—and started writing poetry under their influence.

When Hughes graduated from high school in 1920, he went to Mexico to live with his father, a successful businessman. His father, Hughes later said, "had great contempt for poor people," and for this and other reasons the two men did not get along. When his father insisted that Langston study to become an engineer, he chose to go to Columbia University in New York, in order to see Harlem. But the attractions of Harlem did not compensate for Hughes's dislike of engineering; he dropped out of school and began to travel. Four years later, he was a busboy in that Washington hotel.

The most important early influence on Hughes's poetry was Carl Sandburg (page 747), who sought to express the voice of the people in free verse, unrestrained by the formal restrictions or stylistic demands of the past. Encouraged by Sandburg's example, Hughes tried to reproduce the voice of black people, especially the blacks of Harlem, the poor people for whom his father had so little sympathy.

Hughes often used jazz rhythms and the repetitive structure of the blues in his poems; toward the end of his career he wrote poems specifically for jazz accompaniment. He was also responsible for the founding of several black theater companies, and he wrote and translated a number of dramatic works. His work, he said, was an attempt to "explain and illuminate the Negro condition in America." It succeeded in doing that with both vigor and compassion.

Hughes wrote several poems called "Harlem." In this one, look for signs of the speaker's emotional state. Is he angry, amused, baffled? Can he be described by more than one of these adjectives?

Harlem

Here on the edge of hell
Stands Harlem—
Remembering the old lies,
The old kicks in the back,
5   The old "Be patient"
They told us before.

Sure, we remember.
Now when the man at the corner store
Says sugar's gone up another two cents,
10   And bread one,
And there's a new tax on cigarettes—
We remember the job we never had,
Never could get,
And can't have now
15   Because we're colored.

So we stand here
On the edge of hell
In Harlem
And look out on the world
20   And wonder
What we're gonna do
In the face of what
We remember.

The Block (detail) by Romare Beardon (1971). Oil.

Metropolitan Museum of Art, New York.

Responding to the Poem

Analyzing the Poem

Identifying Details

1. Name the specific hardships and injustices that the people of Harlem remember, according to the speaker in the poem.

Interpreting Meanings

2. What ideas about Harlem does the speaker suggest when he says that it is "on the edge of hell"?
3. Do you interpret the poem's final stanza as an expression of powerlessness, or as a threat? Defend your opinion.

Writing About the Poem

A Creative Response

1. **Writing a News Report.** Write the opening paragraph for a newspaper article or TV news special about the Harlem described in the poem. Include at least one of the points made by Hughes.

A Critical Response

2. **Comparing Poems.** Hughes's "Harlem" and McKay's "America" are poetic responses to oppression. In a brief essay, compare the two responses. Which poem do you find more effective as protest, and why?

I, Too

I, too, sing America.

I am the darker brother.
They send me to eat in the kitchen
When company comes,
5 But I laugh,
And eat well,
And grow strong.

Tomorrow,
I'll be at the table
10 When company comes.
Nobody'll dare
Say to me,
"Eat in the kitchen,"
Then.

15 Besides,
They'll see how beautiful I am
And be ashamed—

I, too, am America.

Responding to the Poem

Analyzing the Poem

Identifying Details

1. Where does the speaker say he is sent "when company comes"? What does he say his place will be "tomorrow"?

Interpreting Meanings

2. Who are "they" in line 3? What realization does the speaker predict will eventually cause "them" to feel shame?
3. This poem clearly describes the effects of racism, yet there is optimism and forgiveness in the speaker's **tone.** What details in the poem suggest a view of America as one family that will eventually realize the injustice of discrimination?
4. The poem's last line is almost an echo of its first. What change has been made in the last line? What message is highlighted by this change? How would the poem have been affected if these two lines were reversed?
5. Do you think the prophecy in this poem (written in 1922) has in any way come true? In what ways has it not come true?

The Builders-Family by Jacob Lawrence
(1974). Oil.

Among the great contributions of American culture to the world is the music produced by blacks: blues, ragtime, jazz, and all the musical expressions still developing out of them. Here Hughes tries both to report the experience of a "sad raggy tune" and to capture some of its rhythms in words.

The Weary Blues

Droning a drowsy syncopated tune,°
Rocking back and forth to a mellow croon,
   I heard a Negro play.
Down on Lenox Avenue° the other night
5 By the pale dull pallor of an old gas light
   He did a lazy sway . . .
   He did a lazy sway . . .
To the tune o' those Weary Blues.
With his ebony hands on each ivory key
10 He made that poor piano moan with melody.
   O Blues!
Swaying to and fro on his rickety stool
He played that sad raggy tune like a musical fool.
   Sweet Blues!
15 Coming from a black man's soul.
   O Blues!
In a deep song voice with a melancholy tone
I heard that Negro sing, that old piano moan—
   "Ain't got nobody in all this world,
20 Ain't got nobody but ma salf.
   I's gwine to quit ma frownin'
   And put ma troubles on the shelf."
Thump, thump, thump, went his foot on the floor.
He played a few chords then he sang some more—
25 "I got the Weary Blues
   And I can't be satisfied.
   Got the Weary Blues
   And can't be satisfied—
   I ain't happy no mo'
30 And I wish that I had died."
And far into the night he crooned that tune.
The stars went out and so did the moon.
The singer stopped playing and went to bed
While the Weary Blues echoed through his head.
35 He slept like a rock or a man that's dead.

1. **syncopated tune:** a melody in which normally unaccented beats are accented.

4. **Lenox Avenue:** a principal street in Harlem.

Jazz Musicians by Romare Beardon. Oil.

Cordier and Ekstrom Galleries, Inc., New York.

Responding to the Poem

Analyzing the Poem

Identifying Details

1. What are some of the words in the poem that help to create a slow, weary, melancholy **mood**?

Interpreting Meanings

2. How does the message of the blues singer's first verse contrast with that of his second?
3. Describe how the poem's structure suggests the rhythms of blues music. Point out examples of **alliteration** and **onomatopoeia** that also add to the poem's wailing, musical effect.
4. How would you describe the emotional effect of the **image** in line 32?
5. What **similes** in the poem's last line describe how the singer sleeps? What do you think are the implications of the last five words?

Writing About the Poems

A Creative Response

1. **Creating Music for a Poem.** If you are musically inclined, choose any passage in "The Weary Blues" and set it to music. If you can't write music, you might make up a melody for the passage by singing it.

A Critical Response

2. **Comparing the Voices in Two Poems.** Write a brief essay analyzing the attitudes of the speakers in "Harlem" and "I, Too." In what ways are the speakers similar? In what ways are they different?
3. **Comparing Poems.** Years earlier, Walt Whitman had written "I hear America singing" (page 331). He also wrote "I celebrate myself and sing myself" (page 332). In a brief essay, comment on how Hughes's poem echoes these lines and comments on them.

Countee Cullen
(1903–1946)

Countee Cullen grew up in New York City, the adopted son of a Methodist minister. He was a brilliant student, and during high school he was already writing accomplished poems in traditional forms. He graduated *magna cum laude* from New York University in 1925. In his senior year in college, Cullen won the Witter Bynner Award for poetry; that same year, *Color,* his first volume of verse, was published. This collection won a Harmon Gold award and established the young poet's reputation.

After receiving his Master's degree from Harvard in 1926, Cullen worked as an assistant editor of the important black magazine *Opportunity.* His poems were published in such influential periodicals as *Harper's, Poetry,* and *Crisis.* In 1927, he published *Copper Sun,* a collection of verse, and *Caroling Dusk,* an anthology of black poetry. *Caroling Dusk* was a significant contribution to the Harlem Renaissance, but the introduction Cullen wrote for the book was controversial. He called for black poets to write traditional verse and to avoid the restrictions of solely racial themes.

At the peak of his career, in 1928, Cullen married the daughter of the famous black writer W. E. B. Du Bois and published a third collection of poems, *The Ballad of the Brown Girl.* The following year he published a fourth volume, *The Black Christ.* Although he continued to write prose until the end of his life, this was his last collection of poetry. Like some of the Romantic poets he so much admired, Cullen spent his lyric talents early in his life. During the Great Depression of the 1930's, unable to make a living solely from writing, he began teaching in Harlem public schools, a job that he held until his early death.

Portrait of Countee Cullen by Winold Reiss (1925). Pastel.

Cullen's verse was most heavily influenced by the poetry of the English Romantics, especially John Keats. He thought of himself primarily as a lyric poet in the Romantic tradition, not as a black poet writing about social and racial themes. Nevertheless, Cullen found himself repeatedly drawn to such themes. He was aware of this conflict, and described it in a poem called "Uncle Jim." In the beginning of that poem, the young poet sneers at his uncle, whose heart is "walled up with bitterness" at white people. The poet would prefer to live in a Romantic world with a friend "Who drinks my joy as tipplers drain / Deep goblets filled with wine." But despite his efforts to achieve this ideal state, he finds himself brought back to the problems his uncle represents. "I wonder why," the poem concludes, "My mind should stray . . . / To muse on Uncle Jim."

Usually, "tableau" means a scene or an action stopped cold, like a still picture in a reel of film. Here we have a "tableau vivant"; that is, a little scene in which figures live and move, a moment caught and preserved.

Tableau

(For Donald Duff)

Locked arm in arm they cross the way,
    The black boy and the white,
The golden splendor of the day,
    The sable pride of night.

5   From lowered blinds the dark folk stare,
    And here the fair folk talk,
Indignant that these two should dare
    In unison to walk.

Oblivious to look and word
10   They pass, and see no wonder
That lightning brilliant as a sword
    Should blaze the path of thunder.

Responding to the Poem

Analyzing the Poem

Identifying Details

1. What **metaphors** describe the two boys in stanza 1?
2. How do the "dark folk" and "fair folk" feel about what the boys are doing?
3. How do the boys respond?

Interpreting Meanings

4. In stanza 3, who or what is the "lightning brilliant as a sword"? Who or what is the "path of thunder"?
5. Why should such a modest and commonplace thing as the friendship between two boys evoke such a dramatic statement? What larger topic is the poem really about?

Passengers by Raphael Soyer (1953). Oil.

Kennedy Galleries, Inc., New York.

Think about the title of this poem. Does it suggest something serious, or something relatively minor?

You might be disturbed by one word in this poem—imagine how it affected a child.

Incident

Once, riding in old Baltimore,
    Heart-filled, head-filled with glee,
I saw a Baltimorean
    Keep looking straight at me.

5   Now I was eight and very small,
    And he was no whit bigger,
And so I smiled, but he poked out
    His tongue, and called me "Nigger."

I saw the whole of Baltimore
    From May until December;
10 Of all the things that happened there
    That's all that I remember.

Responding to the Poem

Analyzing the Poem

Identifying Details

1. Which line reveals the speaker's mood at the beginning of the incident?
2. How many people are involved in the incident? Who are they?
3. What is the incident?

Interpreting Meanings

4. What might lead an eight-year-old boy to insult another child in the way described here? In what way might a child's prejudice be even more disturbing than an adult's?
5. What **ironic overtones** does the title have? Is this really only an "incident"?
6. The speaker never directly states his emotional response to the experience. How does the last stanza indirectly make clear the impression the event had on him?
7. How did the incident affect you?

Writing About the Poem

A Creative Response

1. **Writing Dialogue.** Write a conversation between the two boys who appear in "Tableau." Have them discuss what happens in "Incident."
2. **Planning a Screenplay.** Suppose you were going to do a short film based on the poem "Incident." Write a list of camera shots, in the order in which they would appear on the screen.
3. **Setting the Poem to Music.** If you can write music, create a melody for "Incident."

A Critical Response

4. **Comparing Poems.** Compare the diction and sentence structure in "Tableau" and "Incident." In a brief essay, show how the poet uses language to create two different effects in poems that are about very similar subjects.

THE AMERICAN LANGUAGE

American Dialects

James Fenimore Cooper, writing to a British audience in 1828, boasted about the absence of American dialects: "In America, while there are provincial or state peculiarities, in tone, and even in pronunciation and use of certain words, there is no patois [dialect]. An American may distinguish between the Georgian and the New England man, but you cannot." Americans, Cooper claimed, were too active and mobile for dialects to establish themselves—a point with which many other observers agreed.

Yet a little over fifty years later, another American writer claimed to be using no less than *seven* dialects from a fairly small region in a single novel, *Huckleberry Finn* (page 414). "In this book," Mark Twain wrote in an explanatory note, "a number of dialects are used, to wit: the Missouri Negro dialect; the extremest form of the backwoods South-Western dialect; the ordinary 'Pike-County' dialect; and four modified varieties of this last."

Unity or Variety?

Quite a bit had changed in America in that fifty years, but not enough to create a wholesale explosion of dialects where none had existed before. Even if Twain was exaggerating about his "four modified varieties" of the "Pike County dialect," *Huckleberry Finn* depends for part of its effect on its use of dialect. Who was right about American dialects—Cooper or Twain?

Cooper was looking at an America that he was contrasting with England—a young, unified, mobile, democratic country, in which, if there were differences, they were kept within the family. ("An American may distinguish . . . but you cannot.") Moreover, Cooper saw the country evolving toward even greater unity. "The distinctions in speech," he wrote in the same essay, "were far greater twenty years ago than they are now."

Twain was looking very closely at a particular region of America and at distinctions of race, education, upbringing, and geography, all of which had small but significant effects on speech. Moreover, he was looking at a country whose recent Civil War had underscored the disunity of its people.

What we might call the Cooper and the Twain views toward American dialects, then, really represent two ways of looking at America and American speech. The Cooper view saw America as a unified nation marked principally by its distinctness from England. Twain saw the nation in terms of regional distinctions.

The Cooper view was shared by people like Noah Webster. Webster's dream was to stamp out local dialects and further unify the country (page 173). He stated this attitude in this comparison between American and British language: "We are less infected with various dialects, the remains of the different conquerers of the English nation, than the inhabitants of England." A dialect in Webster's view was a weakness, an infection to be cured by education and spelling reform.

But Twain and other regional writers saw the local speech as one of the best ways of describing the inhabitants of a region. Dialect stories and poems, in fact, were very popular in the late nineteenth and early twentieth centuries. They were usually comic, and much of the humor derived from the funny pronunciations and peculiar local words. At the same time these stories and poems in regional dialect illustrated the wisdom of the common man.

A New Englander called Hosea Bigelow was a famous "common-sense" character created by James Russell Lowell in his *Bigelow Papers*. Here Hosea's New England speech patterns are shown, as he addresses recruiting officers for the Mexican War—a conflict which Hosea, in his common sense, strongly disapproved of.

> Ez fer war, I call it murder—
>   There you hev it plain an' flat;
> I don't want to go no furder
>   Than my Testament fer that;
> God hez sed so plump an' fairly,
>   It's ez long ez it is broad,
> An' you've gut to git up airly
>   Ef you want to take in God.
>
> —from *Bigelow Papers,*
> James Russell Lowell

What Is a Dialect?

In his novel *The Grapes of Wrath,* John Steinbeck records a conversation between migrant workers from different parts of the country. Here the Joads, from Oklahoma, meet Ivy Wilson, from Kansas:

> "We're Joads," said Pa. "We come from right near Sallisaw."
> "Well, we're proud to meet you folks," said Ivy Wilson. "Sairy, these is Joads."
> "I knowed you wasn't Oklahomy folks. You talk queer kinda—that ain't no blame, you understan'."
> "Ever'body says words different," said Ivy. "Arkansas folks says 'em different, and Oklahomy folks says 'em different. And we seen a lady from Massachusetts, an' she said 'em differentest of all. Couldn't hardly make out what she was sayin'."
>
> —from *The Grapes of Wrath,*
> John Steinbeck

The "queer" talk that makes these Americans so different in speech is, of course, what linguists call dialect. A **dialect** can be defined as the characteristic language habits of a particular speech community. A speech community can be looked at in a very broad

"There wuz Maw and me, surrounded by screamin' Frenchmen, our Michelin-book lost and our faithful Cook's tour-guide nowhar in sight! . . .

Analyzing Language

1. One of the characteristics of a dialect is its use of a particular vocabulary. The objects or activities named by the words in each group below are all the same, but people in different regions of the country give them different names. Which word do you use? Do all of your classmates agree?

   a. *Porch* or *veranda*?
   b. *Pail* or *bucket*?
   c. *Faucet, spigot,* or *tap*?
   d. *Sidewalk* or *pavement*?
   e. *Quarter to four, quarter till four,* or *quarter of four*?
   f. *Graduated college* or *graduated from college*?
   g. *Hero sandwich, hoagie, wedge,* or *submarine*?
   h. *Soda* or *pop*?
   i. *Spider, skillet,* or *frying pan*?
   j. *Stand in line* or *on line*?
   k. *Swimsuit* or *bathing suit*?
   l. *Neaten, tidy,* or *ready up a room*?

2. Read the following passages, which reproduce several American dialects. Then answer the questions that follow.

Missouri, 1840's

"I've done considerable in the doctoring way in my time. Layin' on o' hands is my best holt—for cancer, and paralysis, and sich things; and I k'n tell a fortune pretty good, when I've got somebody along to find out the facts for me. Preachin's my line, too; and workin' camp-meetin's; and missionaryin around."

—from *The Adventures of Huckleberry Finn,*
Mark Twain

Midwest, 1920's

Whoever had been settin' in that chair, why they'd get up when Jim come in and give it to him.

You'd of thought it was a reserved seat like they have sometimes in a theayter. Hod would generally always stand or walk up and down, or some Saturdays, of course, he'd be settin' in this chair part of the time, gettin' a haircut.

Well, Jim would set there a w'ile without openin' his mouth only to spit, and then finally he'd say to me, "Whitey"—my right name, that is, my right first name, is Dick, but everybody round here calls me Whitey—Jim would say, "Whitey, your nose looks like a rosebud tonight. You must of been drinkin' some of your aw de cologne."

—from "Haircut,"
Ring Lardner

Black, New York City, 1980's

"I'm axin you all a simple question. You keep talkin bout what's proper for a woman my age. How old am I anyhow?" And Joe Lee slams his eyes shut and squinches up his face to figure. And Task run a hand over his ear and stare into his glass like the ice cubes goin calculate for him. And Elo just starin at the top of my head like she goin rip the wig off any minute now.

—from "My Man Bovane,"
Toni Cade Bambara

Interstate Truckers, 1980's

"This is that Alabama Rebel, this is that Alabama Rebel, do I have a copy?"

"Ahh, 10–4 on that, Alabama Rebel."

"This is that Alabama Rebel westbound on 80, ah, what's your handle, buddy, and where you comin from?"

"This is that, ah, Toby Trucker, eastbound for that big O town, round about the 445 marker."

"I copy you clear, Toby Trucker. How's about that Smokey Bear situation up by that Lincoln town?"

"Ah, you'll have to hold her back a little through there. Alabama Rebel, ah, place is crawling with Smokies like usual. Saw three of em's lights up on the overpass just after the airport here."

—from "I-80 Nebraska,"
John Sayles

a. What variations from standard pronunciation do the spellings indicate?
b. Is each writer consistent in his or her spelling variations? Can you propose reasons for any inconsistencies?
c. What nonstandard or slang words and phrases are used by each speaker? What do these words mean?
d. Are the speakers ungrammatical at any points?
e. Do you find any examples of "eye-dialect"—a word spelled the way it is sounded in standard pronunciation? (An example would be *sez* for *says*.) Can you suggest any reasons why a writer would use eye-dialect?
f. Which passage reproduces the dialect of a group, not of a region?

INTERPRETING AND RESPONDING TO A POEM

Writing Assignment

Write a brief essay interpreting "Only the Polished Skeleton," by Countee Cullen. Include a discussion of the poem's meaning and of the feelings the poem evoked in you.

Background

When you **paraphrase** a work, you restate it in your own words, usually in simpler language. When you **interpret** a work, you explain what you think it means, and you tell how you reached that conclusion. In most cases, an essay of interpretation will include at least some paraphrasing.

The experience of reading a poem leaves us with two basic responses: we understand the poem's meaning and we feel an emotional reaction.

1. The **sense** or **meaning** of a poem is the idea the poet wants to convey. It is similar to the theme of a work of fiction. The meaning of a poem is rarely stated directly. It usually must be inferred by the reader.
2. Emotion is an important element in most poems. Poets evoke feelings in several ways, but you might concentrate on **connotations** and **imagery.**

   a. The **connotations** of a word are the emotions and associations attached to it, in addition to its strict dictionary definitions. The adjectives *determined* and *stubborn,* for example, have similar dictionary definitions, or denotations. Their connotations, however, are very different. Words with strong connotations are sometimes called "loaded words."

   In "The Haunted Oak" (page 663), for example, Dunbar uses connotations to arouse our emotions. What are the connotations of such loaded words as *dread, dried, weird,* and *pain*? What other words and phrases in the poem are loaded with connotations that are likely to create an emotional response?

   b. **Imagery** is the use of concrete, sensual details that appeal to our senses. Since imagery is an essential part of most poetry, your interpretation of a poem will almost certainly include a discussion of images. In "The Haunted Oak," the image of the oak tree is central to the meaning of the poem. What feelings do you associate with Dunbar's image?

Prewriting

Read the following poem several times. (One reading is never enough when you are going to write about a poem.) Try to read it aloud at least once, in order to appreciate its sound effects.

Only the Polished Skeleton

The heart has need of some deceit
    To make its pistons rise and fall;
For less than this it would not beat,
    Nor flush the sluggish vein at all.

5   With subterfuge and fraud the mind
        Must fend and parry thrust for thrust,
With logic brutal and unkind
    Beat off the onslaughts of the dust.

Only the polished skeleton
10   Of flesh relieved and pauperized,
Can rest at ease and think upon
    The worth of all it so despised.

          —Countee Cullen

Apply the following guidelines to the poem, and take notes on your answers. For questions that ask for examples, jot down examples (line numbers, words, and phrases).

Guidelines for Interpreting a Poem

1. What is the poem's **subject**? Does the poem describe an object or scene, an experience, or a character? Does the poet comment directly on the subject?
2. What **main idea** or meaning is the poet trying to convey? What lines or phrases give clues to the poem's meaning?
3. What would you say is the poem's **tone**—the poet's attitude toward the subject? How does the tone contribute to the total effect of the poem?
4. What **feeling** did you have after reading the poem? What specifically in the poem caused you to feel this way? (How did the imagery, connotations, figurative language, and sound effects affect the way the poem made you feel?)

Writing

You might follow this plan for organizing your paper:

Paragraph 1: Cite the title, author, and subject of the poem. Briefly paraphrase the poem.

Paragraph 2: Interpret the poem's meaning, or main idea. Tell how you arrived at this interpretation.

Paragraph 3: Discuss your emotional response to the poem—how did the poem make you feel? Tell what elements in the poem (imagery, word connotation, figurative language, etc.) evoked this response, referring to specific lines and phrases.

Paragraph 4: Summarize your response to the poem as a whole—whether you liked it or not, and why.

Here is an essay of interpretation and response for "The Haunted Oak" by Paul Laurence Dunbar.

In "The Haunted Oak" Paul Laurence Dunbar recalls the era in which lynch mobs seized men and hanged them. The poem uses an unusual point of view to tell about one lynching. The first stanza introduces the speaker in the poem. He asks an old oak tree's withered bough why it is bare. In the rest of the poem, the oak tree tells the story of the lynching, of the tree's sympathy for the victim, and of the effects of the victim's curses.	**Cites title, author, subject of poem.** **Points out unusual feature—point of view.** **Briefly paraphrases poem.**
In this poem, Dunbar expresses feelings about the injustice of the lynch mobs, who executed victims and escaped punishment for their crimes. Although he does not mention the victim's race, I know that historically most of the lynch victims were black.	**Interprets poem and poet's purpose.**
In ironic contrast to the people in the poem, Nature is personified and shown to be in sympathy with the victim. The tree bent "down to hear his sigh" (1. 9) and "trembled sore when they rode away" (1. 11). In the fourth stanza, a dog howls and the night wind moans—as if grieving for the victim.	**Points out irony.** **Cites lines and phrases from poem to support a point.**
But all who are guilty escape punishment for their crime, except for the judge who apparently allowed the lynching to take place and did not prosecute the lynchers. Even as he hunts an innocent deer, the judge is hunted by the guiltless victim, who "rides his soul / In the guise of a mortal fear" (11. 26-27). The victim's curses have other lasting effects: The ghost haunts the oak tree and withers the life from the bough on which he was hanged.	**Infers details about the judge.**
I felt sadness and anger at the murder of so many guiltless victims, and I felt horror at the way in which they were killed. I also felt a kind of spooky feeling from the images of the "weird" moonlight, the wailing wind, the howling dog, the ghost, and the tree.	**Discusses reader's emotional response.** **Cites specific images.**
Dunbar's tone is very restrained. We know how angry he must be, but he never comments directly on what happened. This makes the effect of the poem even more powerful.	**Discusses poet's tone.**
I liked "The Haunted Oak" very much. I think the unusual point of view, the mournful and spooky imagery, and the poet's tone all work together to create a powerful poem.	**Summarizes reader's response.**

Revising and Proofreading

Use the guidelines in the section at the back of this book, called **Writing About Literature,** to revise and proofread your essay.

IMAGISM AND SYMBOLISM

The Chrysler Building Under Construction
by Earl Horter (1931). Ink and watercolor
on paper.

The Whitney Museum of American Art,
New York City. Gift of Mrs. William
A. Marstellar

UNIT NINE

Make it new! Art is a joyous thing.

—Ezra Pound

Sometime in the early twentieth century, Americans awoke to a sense that their own national culture had come of age. This was true in poetry and in painting, in jazz music and in modern dance, even in the new architecture of the skyscraper. In all these fields, Americans could point to their own contributions to the art of the Western world.

Up to this point, American poets (except for Whitman and Dickinson, who were still barely recognized) had shown little success in breaking free of their British ties. Ironically, when the liberation came, American poets found their new inspiration in an unexpected place—the "exotic" atmosphere of Paris.

This is not to say that the new poets failed to reflect a sense of the promise and wonder of their own nation. Their work was, for the most part, deeply rooted in the American grain. But, inspired by the revolutionary literary movement in France, they were able to transcend the narrow aspects of their creative lives. Learning from the French poets, the Americans were able to produce a new type of poetry through which the true American genius could speak.

The Influence of Poe

This international adventure of modern American poetry began through the influence of a poet who was born in Boston and never set foot in France—Edgar Allan Poe (page 226). In 1847, the French poet Charles Baudelaire (1821–1867) discovered Poe's verse and his critical theories. Baudelaire was impressed to find that Poe was unlike most American poets of the time in one important respect: Poe had no patience with poetry as a sermon or as an argument for some cause. What most excited Baudelaire was Poe's conviction that poetry should be concerned with the revelation of beauty, both physical and spiritual.

Poe was a paradox. Although he lived in the century of expansion, he did not look to the vast geographical frontiers that lighted the imagination of many American writers. He was unlike Walt Whitman, whose broad vision ranged like the sun across the continent and who translated himself into the whole concept of "America." Instead, Poe looked inward for inspiration, to the frontiers of the human mind. There he heard voices that spoke sometimes in angelic tones and sometimes in demonic whispers. Where Whitman celebrated the daylight enterprise and variety of America, Poe dwelt in a twilight zone, where figures from the real world mingled with figures from dreams.

Poe's poems expressed a hidden side of America. They spoke for the America that struggled with the spiritual effects of a culture that was becoming increasingly urban and capitalistic, in which the life of the soul was being eroded by greed and the lust for power.

Poe's concerns were beauty and human psychology, and his work is filled with settings and objects intended to arouse the feelings of his readers. In these respects, he was a forerunner of the movement in France known as Symbolism. This movement was itself strongly influenced by the works of Poe's French admirer, Charles Baudelaire.

In France, Symbolism dominated literature roughly from 1875 to 1895, but its influence was not fully felt in America until the second decade of the twentieth century.

Symbolism is a form of expression in which the world of appearances is violently rearranged by artists who seek a different and more truthful version of reality. The Symbolist poets do not merely describe objects; instead, they try to portray the emotional effects that objects produce.

Don't be misled by the term *symbolism*. It does not deal with the religious, national, or psychological symbols we are all familiar with. In fact, the Symbolist movement was concerned with getting rid of such symbols. The first Symbolists believed that these symbols had been overused, to the point where they were so dull that they no longer had any value in poetry.

A key word in symbolism is **revelation.** The Symbolists tried to create poems that would allow the imagination to discover truths. Imagination is more reliable than reason, the Symbolists said, and just as precise. They insisted with almost religious fervor that mystery exists; that a part of our experience will always remain unexplained by logic and science; and that the task of the imagination is the penetration of the nonrational part of our makeup.

Symbolism vs. Romanticism

Symbolism was a new manifestation of the Romanticism that had swept over Europe and America in the nineteenth century. (See Units Three and Four.)

The Romantics had stressed the primacy of feeling and the independence of the individual, and they had made a great stand against the mechanization of human life. They respected science as a form of knowledge, but were suspicious of the ways science was being put to use. The Romantics did not celebrate the technological advances of an age of steam power and iron construction, of factories and planned cities. Instead, they found hope for the human race in a return to nature. In the natural world, the Romantics found messages that spoke to the soul and gave it strength.

Now, decades later, the pace of industrialization and mechanization had increased, but the natural world—the haven of the Romantics—had been stripped of much of its mystery. Nature itself had become the object of scientific classification and reinterpretation.

Symbolism: The Search for a New Reality

The Flatiron Building in New York City, under construction (1901–1902). The triangular building was designed by D. H. Burnham and Company, and for years was the world's most famous skyscraper.

I Saw the Figure 5 in Gold by Charles Demuth (1928). Oil.

The Metropolitan Museum of Art, New York City. Alfred Steiglitz Collection.

After the publication of Charles Darwin's *The Origin of Species* (1859), the individual who wandered in nature could no longer behave as its divinely ordained master. In fact, according to Darwin's investigations, the human species seemed to have evolved in the same way that the animals had: through survival of the fittest. In short, what faced the artist as the twentieth century opened was the onslaught of the modern world, with its combined victory of science and technology, with its spiritual debasement, and its wholesale impoverishment of masses of people. The Symbolist poets faced this world with a distaste amounting to outrage. They could not, as poets, transform or erase it, so their revolt was spiritual. They tried to reconstitute the sense of what it meant to be human in a time when materialism was rapidly replacing religion and when individualism was succumbing to the power of mass culture.

The result was a pessimism that strongly contrasted with the optimism of most Romantics. The Romantics believed that people and the world could become perfect. The Symbolists had little faith that a true change in social conditions could come about until people recovered the dignity that science and technology had taken away from them.

Americans and Symbolism

The two Americans who first came into close contact with Symbolism were Ezra Pound (page 729) and T. S. Eliot (page 758). Finding themselves in Europe at the outbreak of World War I, these two poets remained abroad for nearly all of their lives. But their physical absence from America did not diminish their influence. By their poetic practice and their critical writings, they brought the meanings and techniques of the French Symbolist movement into American poetry.

The most important single aspect of Symbolism that changed the texture of American poetry was a concern for the purification of language. With the help of several British poets, a group of Americans led by Pound founded a school perhaps better known and understood in America than Symbolism itself. This was the movement known as Imagism, dating from the years 1909–1917.

The **Imagists** were related to the Symbolists only in their conviction that poetry can be made purer by concentration on the precise, clear, unqualified image. Imagery alone, the Imagists believed, could carry a poem's emotion and message. It could do this almost instantly, without all the elaborate metrics and stanza patterns that were part of poetry's traditional mode. The Imagists—including Pound, Hilda Doolittle, and Amy Lowell—took on the role of reformers. They would rid poetry of its prettiness, sentimentality, and artificiality. They would concentrate on the raw power of the image to communicate feeling and thought.

The Imagists issued a "manifesto," or public declaration, proposing "to use the language of common speech," but to use "always the *exact* word, not merely the decorative word." In the same spirit, they called for poetry "hard and clear, never blurred or indefinite."

Aware that images are mostly associated with pictorial art, the Imagists declared: "We are not a school of painters, but we believe that poetry should render particulars exactly and not deal in vague generalities, however magnificent and sonorous." Some of the Imagists' inspiration was drawn from Eastern art forms, particularly the strict Japanese verse form known as **haiku**. In seventeen syllables a haiku juxtaposes two distinct images, and the reader is supposed to experience a moment of enlightenment on seeing how these images are related.

Pound defined an **image** as "that which presents an intellectual and emotional complex in an instant of time." Here is a famous Imagist poem that illustrates this concept:

In a Station of the Metro

The apparition of these faces in the crowd;
Petals on a wet, black bough.

—Ezra Pound

Imagism: "The Exact Word"

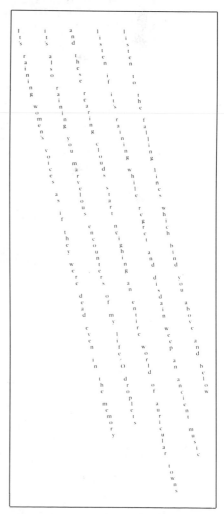

"It's Raining," a poem by French Symbolist Guillaume Apollinaire (1880–1918).

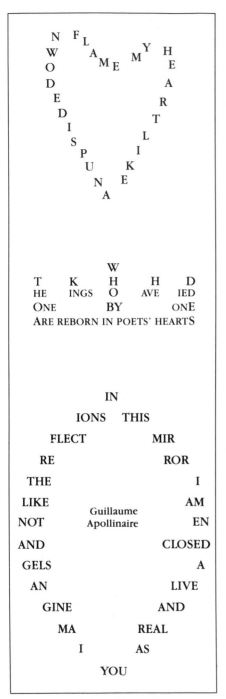

"Heart, Crown, and Mirror," a poem by French Symbolist Guillaume Apollinaire (1880–1918).

In this brief lyric, the "instant of time" is the moment the poet sees the faces in a crowd in a Paris subway station. Suddenly, the faces remind the observer of petals hanging from the wet bough of a tree. The "intellectual and emotional complex" is the moment when we realize that these faces are as fragile as the petals, soon to fall from the black tree.

Today, poems with this sort of imagistic technique are commonplace. But at the time the Imagists published their manifesto on poetry's nature and function, their theory created a great stir. It was disturbing partly because it insisted that the range of poetic subject matter might include the kitchen sink as well as the rising of the moon, the trash can as well as the Chinese porcelain vase.

But the strongest opposition to the Imagists was caused by their proposal "to create new rhythms—as the expression of new moods. . . . We do believe that the individuality of a poet may often be better expressed in free verse than in conventional forms." To tradition-minded poets, this **free verse** was deplorable. It meant a loosening of poetic standards and an assault on the very craft of poetry. The history of poetry in the following decades would prove that these poets were mistaken in their fears about the decline of poetic standards. They did not yet realize that successful free verse was at least as difficult to create as verse written in traditional forms.

While Imagism never became an important movement in itself, it gave rise to some of our finest talents. The reputations of some of the movement's early leaders have faded with time. But others in the forefront of Imagism went beyond the movement's limitations and expanded its insights. Besides Pound and Eliot, these included William Carlos Williams (page 735), Marianne Moore (page 742), E. E. Cummings (page 753), and Wallace Stevens (page 768).

Imagism came to stand for a whole new order of poetry in the United States. Most Americans became acquainted with the movement mainly as the school of "free verse." By this they meant simply poetry without regular rhyming and metrical patterns. But the Imagist program was not only a call for a new method of organizing lines and stanzas; it was an invitation to a new way of seeing the world.

As practiced by its masters, Imagism had much in common with the new art of film. Instead of following normal rules of logic, syntax, and grammar in presenting a subject, Imagists startled their readers. They used closeups, flashbacks, and montage—the film device of showing two or three images at once. Readers could no longer simply sit back and gradually take in a poem as it unrolled, because the connections provided by conventional poets were often omitted by the Imagists. Readers had to grasp on their own the logic of the back-to-back images. In other words, readers now had to participate in a poem in order to understand it. Those unwilling or unable to do this were quick to belittle the products of Imagism and to dismiss the movement as a fad. But modern American poetry, conceived in France by the Symbolist movement and nurtured in the cradle of Imagism, was here to stay.

Ezra Pound
(1885–1972)

Ezra Pound is remembered by many people as the man who was charged with treason during World War II and who spent many years in a mental institution. This notoriety, acquired toward the end of his life, has tended to obscure Pound's impact on American poetry. But his healthy influence is still apparent everywhere; the generations of poets who have come after him have confirmed it. They have kept alive a happier memory of a man whose career wavered between brilliance and episodic madness.

Pound was born in Hailey, Idaho, and grew up in Pennsylvania. After graduating from Hamilton College in Clinton, New York, he took the first steps toward a teaching career, first at the University of Pennsylvania and then at Wabash College in Indiana. Even as a young man, however, Pound was too unconventional in his thinking and behavior to fit into a conservative academic community.

In search of greater personal freedom and of contacts with European poets, Pound settled in London in 1908. There he became a leading spokesman for the new poetic movement known as Imagism. He also became a self-exiled critic of American life and torchbearer for any art that challenged the complacent middle class.

Pound—whose slogan was "Make it new!"— was a born teacher whose advice was sought by the most brilliant young writers of the period. T. S. Eliot (page 758) acknowledged Pound's valuable advice when he dedicated his great poem *The Waste Land* (1922) to Pound. For a time, Pound served as an unpaid secretary and mentor to the great Irish poet William Butler Yeats.

After World War I, Pound felt the need for even broader horizons than London offered him. He moved to Paris in 1920, the same year that he published *Hugh Selwyn Mauberley,* one of his most important poems. He spent time with artists from many countries whose innovations put them in the forefront of modernism. Pound also mingled with the American expatriate community—writers who had voluntarily left home to live and write in the headier atmosphere of France. These included Ernest Hemingway (page 566), Gertrude Stein, E. E. Cummings (page 753), and Archibald MacLeish.

In 1924, Pound moved to the town of Rapallo, Italy, overlooking the Tyrrhenian Sea. There he continued to write poetry and criticism. And now came a tragic turning point in Pound's life. His interest in economics and social theory led him to support Benito Mussolini, the Fascist dictator of Italy.

When World War II broke out, Mussolini's government allied itself with Hitler and became an enemy of the United States. Pound stayed in Italy, and in a terrible lapse of judgment turned propagandist for Mussolini's policies. In his radio broadcasts from Italy, Pound denounced the struggle of Great Britain, France, the United States, and the Soviet Union against Germany, Italy, and Japan. Some of these broadcasts were vicious with anti-Semitism.

When the American army advanced northward up the Italian peninsula in 1945, Pound, the notorious propagandist, was taken prisoner. He was confined to a cage on an airstrip near Pisa and eventually returned to the United States to be tried for treason. But psychiatrists judged him to be mentally incompetent, and the poet was committed to St. Elizabeth's, a hospital for the criminally insane, in Washington, D.C.

Twelve years later, he was released through the intercession of poets Archibald MacLeish and Robert Frost, who argued that his literary contributions outweighed his disastrous lack of judgment and his notorious bigotry. Pound lived out the ten years left to him in Rapallo and in Venice. He was a sad old man who rarely spoke. In his rare interviews, he seemed to try to penetrate the meanings of his own life, though he remained assertive and opinionated about poetry, economics, and the state of the world to the end.

During these years of exile, a reporter once asked Pound where he was living. "In hell," the old man answered. "Which hell?" the reporter asked. "Here," said Pound, pressing his heart. "Here."

When he died in Venice, Pound left behind a body of work extending from the delicate lyrics he wrote at the turn of the century to *The Cantos,* an enormous epic he did not complete until well over fifty years later. He also left a public record which still uncomfortably involves scholars and historians in that mystery known as "The Case of Ezra Pound."

The River-Merchant's Wife: A Letter

Li T'ai Po

While my hair was still cut straight across my forehead
Played I about the front gate, pulling flowers.
You came by on bamboo stilts, playing horse,
You walked about my seat, playing with blue plums.
5   And we went on living in the village of Chokan:
Two small people, without dislike or suspicion.

At fourteen I married My Lord you.
I never laughed, being bashful.
Lowering my head, I looked at the wall.
10   Called to, a thousand times, I never looked back.

Wang Hsi-chih Watching Geese by Ch'ien Hsuan (1235–1300).
Handscroll, ink color and gold on paper.

At fifteen I stopped scowling,
I desired my dust to be mingled with yours
Forever and forever and forever.
Why should I climb the lookout?

15   At sixteen you departed,
You went into far Ku-to-yen, by the river of swirling eddies,
And you have been gone five months.
The monkeys make sorrowful noise overhead.

You dragged your feet when you went out.
20   By the gate now, the moss is grown, the different mosses,
Too deep to clear them away!
The leaves fall early this autumn, in wind.
The paired butterflies are already yellow with August
Over the grass in the West garden;
25   They hurt me. I grow older.
If you are coming down through the narrows of the river Kiang,
Please let me know beforehand,
And I will come out to meet you
        As far as Cho-fu-Sa.

The Metropolitan Museum of Art, New York.

Responding to the Poem

Analyzing the Poem

Identifying Details

1. What events are referred to in stanzas 1–4?
2. In the last stanza, what does the wife promise to do?

Interpreting Meanings

3. How is the third stanza a turning point in the poem? In line 14, what is the wife indirectly expressing?
4. What **image** suggests that the husband was reluctant to leave home?
5. How is the season of the year appropriate to the **mood** of the poem?
6. What "hurts" the young wife in line 25, and why? Why does she say, after only five months, that she grows "older" (line 25)?
7. Why do you think the husband left? Do you think he is ever going to return? What may have delayed him?
8. Do you think this letter was ever sent?

Primary Sources
"A Few Don'ts by an Imagist"

Ezra Pound wrote the following "rules" for poets in an article in the March 1913 issue of *Poetry* magazine. Many of them are useful to all writers.

"It is better to present one Image in a lifetime than to produce voluminous words. . . .

"Pay no attention to the criticism of men who have never themselves written a notable work. Consider the discrepancies between the actual writing of the Greek poets and dramatists, and the theories of the Greco-Roman grammarians, concocted to explain their meters.

Language

"Use no superfluous word, no adjective, which does not reveal something.

"Don't use such an expression as 'dim lands of peace.' It dulls the image. It mixes an abstraction with the concrete. It comes from the writer's not realizing that the natural object is always the *adequate* symbol.

"Go in fear of abstractions. Don't retell in mediocre verse what has already been done in good prose. Don't think any intelligent person is going to be deceived when you try to shirk all the difficulties of the unspeakably difficult art of good prose by chopping your composition into line lengths. . . .

"Don't imagine that the art of poetry is any simpler than the art of music, or that you can please the expert before you have spent at least as much effort on the art of verse as the average piano teacher spends on the art of music.

"Be influenced by as many great artists as you can, but have the decency either to acknowledge the debt outright, or to try to conceal it.

Rhythm and Rhyme

"Let the neophyte know assonance and alliteration, rhyme immediate and delayed, simple and polyphonic, as a musician would expect to know harmony and counterpoint and all the minutiae of his craft. No time is too great to give to these matters or to any one of them, even if the artist seldom has need of them. . . .

"Consider the way of the scientists rather than the way of an advertising agent for a new soap.

"The scientist does not expect to be acclaimed as a great scientist until he has *discovered* something. He begins by learning what has been discovered already. He goes from that point onward. He does not bank on being a charming fellow personally. He does not expect his friends to applaud the results of his freshman class work. Freshmen in poetry are unfortunately not confined to a definite and recognizable classroom. They are 'all over the shop.' Is it any wonder 'the public is indifferent to poetry'?

"Don't chop your stuff into separate iambs. Don't make each line stop dead at the end, and then begin every next line with a heave. Let the beginning of the next line catch the rise of the rhythm wave, unless you want a definite longish pause. . . .

"If you are using a symmetrical form, don't put in what you want to say and then fill up the remaining vacuums with slush. . . ."

—Ezra Pound

THE OBJECTIVE CORRELATIVE

Throughout the poem on page 730, the letter writer's feelings are expressed more often by references to objects and activities than by direct statements. This is a method often practiced by Pound and identified by T. S. Eliot in a famous definition. Eliot said that the only valid way to express emotion in art is to find an **objective correlative.** He defined this term as "a set of objects, a situation, a chain of events which shall be the formula of that *particular* emotion."

The term "objective correlative" soon became a permanent part of the vocabulary of poetic analysis. Seven years earlier, however, Pound had anticipated the essence of the term, when he had referred to poetry as "a sort of inspired mathematics" that gives us "equations for the human emotions."

Eliot's definition became much more widely known. However, both men were getting at the same idea. Poetry, they believed, is a means of expressing emotion *indirectly* but precisely. Poetry does this by finding the images and actions that best embody a feeling.

This position led to a kind of poetic shorthand that eliminated everything but part of the equation (the objective correlative). In this shorthand, a reader would not find the connections that usually join the parts of an argument, a story, or even most poems. Readers are forced to supply these connections by themselves. In doing so, they will discover the logic of the poem. This kind of reading can be hard work, but many people also find it very satisfying.

"The River-Merchant's Wife" is a good example of this kind of poem. How many objective correlatives can you find? In other words, how many examples can you find in the poem where emotions are embodied in objects or actions, instead of being expressed directly?

Begin by concentrating on the ways in which the bride makes her courtship vivid. Then notice how her shy, modest character is established. Continue by finding the concrete equivalents of particular emotions. Think about the "lookout" in line 14 and the "river of swirling eddies" in line 16.

A note of caution: Not every poem deals in objective correlatives. Most poems, including many modern ones, have a logical or narrative sequence that is easy to recognize. But other poems will make no logical sense until *you* supply the connecting links. They are organized, not by a *logical* sequence, but by a *psychological* one. These are the poems that can be analyzed according to Eliot's definition of *objective correlative.*

Ezra Pound in the garden of his Paris studio (1923).

The Red Wheelbarrow

so much depends
upon

a red wheel
barrow

glazed with rain
water

beside the white
chickens.

A Comment on the Poem

This little poem at first glance seems to be very slight. But it has proved to have the leverage power that Archimedes spoke of when he said "Give me a place to stand, and I will move the world." Where William Carlos Williams stood was a place where ordinary things were *not* used as symbols or metaphors; they were simply ordinary things. The world he moved was the world of poetry, which, before him, saw things not as things in themselves, but objects to be used (to be compared, to be endowed with alien meaning, or to be played with); in themselves, things meant nothing.

How do we talk about this poem? When we consider analyzing it as a poem, where do we begin? Trying to answer these questions leads only to frustration. And that's exactly what Williams had in mind: a composition of words so complete and simple that it would deny all attempts to treat it as a poem.

And yet, there is the temptation to ask what happens in the brief course of the poem that has made it so durable. It was, after all, *composed* and not a typographical accident, so it can be talked about. But our talk must be concerned with the modest premises of the poem; we must not attempt to give it meanings that it does not claim.

The first line contains a vague but enormously suggestive phrase that leads the reader to expect an answer. (*What* depends on *what?*) But, except for the metaphorical lift of the word *glazed,* what the reader gets is only bare, flat reality—a moment captured as permanently as if it had been photographed. If the poem can be said to have some movement, some progress, from its first word to its last, it would be in what we call "reverse action." Our yearning toward what might be implicit in "so much depends" is quietly checked by the homely beauty of what *is*.

In many other poems like this one, Williams brought a realistic new dimension into American poetry. Williams showed us a way of recording the visible world without filtering it through the imagination.

Do you like or dislike this poem? Why?

The Great Figure

Among the rain
and lights
I saw the figure 5
in gold
5   on a red
fire truck
moving
tense
unheeded
10 to gong clangs
siren howls
and wheels rumbling
through the dark city.

Responding to the Poem

Analyzing the Poem

Interpreting Meanings

1. What one word is used **metaphorically** to describe the fire truck as if it's a person?
2. Which **images** recreate specific sights and sounds?

3. Did you think the "great figure" was going to be the number 5 on an ordinary old fire truck? What did you expect it to be? What is suggested by the term "great figure"?
4. How do you think the speaker feels about this brief scene?

A tract is a religious or political message aimed at converting its readers. In this verse tract, Williams describes the way a funeral should be conducted. And yet, by the time he has finished, we realize that "a funeral" is only his apparent subject. He is really talking about the conduct of life, and perhaps even about poetry.

"Tract" was first published in 1917, when horses were still used to draw milk wagons, bread wagons, and ornately decorated hearses. But the poet's comments on horse-drawn hearses could just as easily be applied to the limousines used in funerals today.

Tract

I will teach you my townspeople
how to perform a funeral—
for you have it over a troop
of artists—
5   unless one should scour the world—
you have the ground sense necessary.

See! the hearse leads.
I begin with a design for a hearse.
For Christ's sake not black—
10   nor white either—and not polished!
Let it be weathered—like a farm wagon—
with gilt wheels (this could be
applied fresh at small expense)
or no wheels at all:
15   a rough dray to drag over the ground.

Knock the glass out!
My God—glass, my townspeople!
For what purpose? Is it for the dead
to look out or for us to see
20   how well he is housed or to see
the flowers or the lack of them—
or what?
To keep the rain and snow from him?
He will have a heavier rain soon:
25   pebbles and dirt and what not.
Let there be no glass—
and no upholstery! phew!
and no little brass rollers
and small easy wheels on the bottom—
30   my townspeople what are you thinking of!

A rough plain hearse then
with gilt wheels and no top at all.
On this the coffin lies
by its own weight.
             No wreaths please—
35   especially no hothouse flowers.
Some common memento is better,

something he prized and is known by:
his old clothes—a few books perhaps—
God knows what! You realize
40   how we are about these things,
my townspeople—
something will be found—anything—
even flowers if he had come to that.
So much for the hearse.

45   For heaven's sake though see to the driver!
Take off the silk hat! In fact
that's no place at all for him
up there unceremoniously
dragging our friend out to his own dignity!
50   Bring him down—bring him down!
Low and inconspicuous! I'd not have him
      ride
on the wagon at all—damn him—
the undertaker's understrapper!
Let him hold the reins
55   and walk at the side
and inconspicuously too!

Then briefly as to yourselves:
Walk behind—as they do in France,
seventh class,° or if you ride
60   Hell take curtains! Go with some show
of inconvenience; sit openly—
to the weather as to grief.
Or do you think you can shut grief in?
What—from us? We who have perhaps
65   nothing to lose? Share with us
share with us—it will be money
in your pockets.
             Go now
I think you are ready.

---

59. **seventh class:** an exaggerated reference to first-, second-, and third-class travel on European trains and buses.

Funeral by Clementine Hunter (1956). House paint on cardboard.

Collection of Siri von Reis.

Responding to the Poem

Analyzing the Poem

Identifying Details

1. Name all the different aspects of a funeral mentioned by the speaker. What does he advise the townspeople to do about each aspect of the ritual?

Interpreting Meanings

2. When the speaker calls for "gilt wheels" in line 12 is he being inconsistent? What might such prominent wheels contribute to the funeral scene the speaker is describing?

3. What two kinds of rain is the speaker talking about in lines 23 and 24? In making his suggestions for a funeral, is the speaker exhibiting cruelty or disrespect toward the dead? What is his purpose in calling for all this plainness, and even pain and discomfort for the participants?

4. Assume that the speaker is talking about much more than funerals. What might the "rough plain hearse" represent? What might the driver in lines 45–56 represent? Why would the speaker get so angry when he's talking about the driver?

5. Throughout the poem, the speaker talks of simplicity and honest grief. Then he closes by saying, "share with us—it will be money in your pockets." Do you think this seemingly hard-boiled promise reflects cynicism on the part of the speaker? Or can the promise of "money in your pockets" be interpreted in more than one way?

6. Summarize this speaker's **main idea** about art, even about the way poetry should be written. Assuming that the poem is about poetry as well as about funerals, do you think Williams follows his own directions?

7. What do you think about this "tract"? Do you agree with its advice on ritual and art, or do you prefer richness rather than plainness?

Like many other poems by Williams, this one is about a process—a development, a transformation, or a condition at the point of change. Here the subject is the coming of spring, examined as if seen under a magnifying glass. The poet also examines the *feeling* of spring, in which changes in nature are reflected in someone who observes them. As you read, try to form mental images of the scene in the poem.

Spring and All

By the road to the contagious hospital°
under the surge of the blue
mottled clouds driven from the
northeast—a cold wind. Beyond, the
5   waste of broad, muddy fields
brown with dried weeds, standing and fallen

patches of standing water
the scattering of tall trees

All along the road the reddish
10   purplish, forked, upstanding, twiggy
stuff of bushes and small trees
with dead, brown leaves under them
leafless vines—

Lifeless in appearance, sluggish
15   dazed spring approaches—

They enter the new world naked,
cold, uncertain of all
save that they enter. All about them
the cold, familiar wind—

20   Now the grass, tomorrow
the stiff curl of wildcarrot leaf
One by one objects are defined—
It quickens: clarity, outline of leaf

But now the stark dignity of
25   entrance—Still, the profound change
has come upon them: rooted, they
grip down and begin to awaken

---

1. **contagious hospital:** for people with contagious diseases.

Responding to the Poem

Analyzing the Poem

Identifying Details

1. Describe the specific **images** the speaker sees by the road in the first three stanzas.

Interpreting Meanings

2. Is "the contagious hospital" merely incidental in the poem, since the poet would have gone there in the course of his daily rounds? Or does the reference contribute something important to the poem? What would have been lost if the poet had said "by the road to the library," for example?
3. The first three stanzas are about plants. The pronoun in line 16, however, may refer to more than plants. What broader meaning might the word *they* have?
4. Reread the last stanza. Which two meanings of the word *still* makes line 25 a **paradox?**
5. In the course of his career, Williams delivered thousands of babies. Can you see any connection between that fact and the last three stanzas of the poem? What

specific references would apply equally to the coming of spring and the birth of an infant?
6. In its treatment of spring, how does this poem differ from a typical Romantic poem?
7. What is the significance of the full title of the poem?

Writing About the Poems

A Creative Response

1. **Retitling Poems.** "The Red Wheelbarrow" and "The Great Figure" have titles that refer to concrete objects. Make up similar titles for "Tract" and "Spring and All." In each case, base your title on a concrete object that suggests the meaning of the poem.

A Critical Response

2. **Analyzing a Poem.** Select any one of the poems you have just read by Williams. In a brief essay, show how he uses concrete objects to make statements about people, art, or life in general.

Primary Sources
Williams Talks About Poetry

"I'll never forget the dream I had a few days after he [Williams's father] died, after a wasting illness, on Christmas Day, 1918. I saw him coming down a peculiar flight of exposed steps, steps I have since identified as those before the dais of Pontius Pilate in some well-known painting. But this was in a New York office building, Pop's office. He was bare-headed and had some business letters in his hand on which he was concentrating as he descended. I noticed him and with joy cried out, 'Pop! So, you're *not* dead!' But he only looked up at me over his right shoulder and commented severely, 'You know all that poetry you're writing. Well, it's no good.' I was left speechless and woke trembling.

. . .

"What were we seeking? No one knew consistently enough to formulate a 'movement.' We were restless and constrained, closely allied with the painters. Impressionism, dadaism, surrealism applied to both painting and the poem. What a battle we made of it merely getting rid

of capitals at the beginning of every line! The immediate image, which was impressionistic, sure enough, fascinated us all. We had followed Pound's instructions, his famous 'Don'ts,' eschewing inversions of the phrase. . . . Literary allusions, save in very attenuated form, were unknown to us. Few had the necessary reading.

"We were looked at askance by scholars and those who turned to scholarship for their norm. To my mind the thing that gave us most a semblance of a cause was not Imagism, as some thought, but the line: the poetic line and our hopes for its recovery from stodginess. I say recovery in the sense that one recovers a salt from solution by chemical action. We were destroyers, vulgarians, obscurantists to most who read; though occasionally a witty line, an unusual reference, or a wrench of the simile to force it into approximation with experience rather than reading—bringing a whole proximate 'material' into view—found some response from the alert."

—from *The Autobiography,*
William Carlos Williams

Marianne Moore
(1887–1972)

Marianne Moore is remembered by many people as the woman who wrote a poem in 1955 celebrating the only World Series the Brooklyn Dodgers ever won. Moore spent more than half her life in Brooklyn, where she became one of the most famous supporters of the local baseball team.

She was born in Kirkwood, a suburb of St. Louis, Missouri. She became a schoolteacher, a librarian, the editor of *The Dial* (a magazine that encouraged young writers), and one of the outstanding poets of her time.

Moore was a graduate of Bryn Mawr at a time when that college was still known as a school for "bluestockings" (highly educated and well-read women). She spent a good part of her life caring for her brother and mother. When her mother died, Moore lost her best friend—and her toughest critic. In 1929, she moved to Brooklyn. Among the literary celebrities in New York, she was easily identifiable by her antique capes and other eighteenth-century touches in costume.

Behind the costume, however, Moore was a quiet, conventional woman. Mixing with the *literati* did not mean that she endorsed their tolerance in matters of personal behavior or their embrace of anything in the arts that seemed new, or bold, or simply amusing.

The only thing "modern" about Moore was her poetry. Like a bird building a nest, she would carefully piece together in her poetry material gathered from her reading in social and natural history. It has been said of her that no one was ever more indebted to other writers for material and, at the same time, more original. Her poetry reflects some of the influence of the Imagists, and it also makes constant use of the

Portrait of Marianne Moore by George Platt Lynes.

concrete in the tradition of William Carlos Williams. Like the graphic artists of the twentieth century, Moore was able to join apparently unrelated elements of what she observed and bring them into a "picture" with a single focus.

In some of her poems, such as "The Steeple-Jack," Moore works like a painter whose nervous strokes and jagged edges capture a hundred details in one moment stopped in time. What she says in this poem might apply to readers approaching her work in general: "It is a privilege to see so much confusion."

An essentially visual poem, this one also has many thoughtful and playful moments. As Moore carefully paints a portrait of a coastal town, she emphasizes the little particular details, and renders them with the same exactness that we find in the paintings and engravings of Albrecht Dürer, the great German artist of the late fifteenth century. Each detail is important to the portrait of the town; some of them also indicate the character of the mind which so meticulously records them.

The Steeple-Jack

Dürer would have seen a reason for living
    in a town like this, with eight stranded whales
to look at; with the sweet sea air coming into your house
on a fine day, from water etched
5   with waves as formal as the scales
on a fish.

One by one in two's and three's, the seagulls keep
    flying back and forth over the town clock,
or sailing around the lighthouse without moving their wings—
10   rising steadily with a slight
    quiver of the body—or flock
mewing where

a sea the purple of the peacock's neck is
    paled to greenish azure as Dürer changed
15   the pine green of the Tyrol to peacock blue and guinea
gray. You can see a twenty-five-
    pound lobster; and fish nets arranged
to dry. The

whirlwind fife-and-drum of the storm bends the salt
20   marsh grass, disturbs stars in the sky and the
star on the steeple; it is a privilege to see so
much confusion. Disguised by what
    might seem the opposite, the sea-
side flowers and

25   trees are favored by the fog so that you have
    the tropics at first hand: the trumpet vine,
foxglove, giant snapdragon, a salpiglossis that has
spots and stripes; morning-glories, gourds,
    or moon-vines trained on fishing twine
30   at the back door:

cattails, flags, blueberries and spiderwort,
    striped grass, lichens, sunflowers, asters, daisies—
yellow and crab-claw ragged sailors with green bracts—toadplant,
petunias, ferns; pink lilies, blue
35   ones, tigers; poppies; black sweet peas.
The climate

is not right for the banyan, frangipani, or
    jack-fruit trees; or for exotic serpent
life. Ring lizard and snakesskin for the foot, if you see fit;
40   but here they've cats, not cobras, to
      keep down the rats. The diffident
little newt

with white pin-dots on black horizontal spaced-
    out bands lives here; yet there is nothing that
45   ambition can buy or take away. The college student
named Ambrose sits on the hillside
    with his not-native books and hat
and sees boats

at sea progress white and rigid as if in
50   a groove. Liking an elegance of which
the source is not bravado, he knows by heart the antique
sugar-bowl shaped summerhouse of
    interlacing slats, and the pitch
of the church

55   spire, not true, from which a man in scarlet lets
    down a rope as a spider spins a thread;
he might be part of a novel, but on the sidewalk a
sign says C. J. Poole, Steeple-Jack,
    in black and white; and one in red
60   and white says

Danger. The church portico has four fluted
    columns, each a single piece of stone, made
modester by whitewash. This would be a fit haven for
waifs, children, animals, prisoners,
65   and presidents who have repaid
sin-driven

senators by not thinking about them. The
    place has a schoolhouse, a post office in a
    store, fishhouses, henhouses, a three-masted
70   schooner on the stocks. The hero, the student,
    the steeple-jack, each in his way,
is at home.

It could not be dangerous to be living
75   in a town like this, of simple people,
who have a steeple-jack placing danger signs by the church
while he is gilding the solid-
    pointed star, which on a steeple
stands for hope.

Responding to the Poem

Analyzing the Poem

Identifying Details

1. In "The Steeple-Jack" (as in many of Moore's poems), conventional poetic meter and free verse are replaced by the strict count of **syllables.** Count the number of syllables in each line of the first stanza. Then do the same with the following stanzas. Is the pattern repeated? In which stanza does Moore introduce a new pattern of syllables?
2. The poem is unified by an unusual **rhyme scheme.** To discover what it is, find the two lines that rhyme in the first stanza. Then examine the following stanzas to see if you can find a pattern of rhyme.
3. What details in the poem suggest the location of the town?
4. List as many **images** as you can find that help you see, hear, and smell the town.
5. What does the speaker think of this town?

Interpreting Meanings

6. What role does Ambrose play in the poem?
7. Considering the poem's title, why would Moore take so long to bring in C. J. Poole? Why do you think the poem is named for him?
8. What is the nature of the confusion referred to in the fourth stanza? Why does Moore consider it a privilege to view this confusion?
9. Explain the significance of the fact that the hero, the student, and the steeple-jack are all "at home."
10. Explain what you think is the significance of the star at the poem's end.
11. How would you describe the **tone** of this poem? How did it make you feel about this town?

12. How does Moore's view of a small Maine town contrast with Edwin Arlington Robinson's character studies of people who live in another Maine town? (See pages 652 and 654.)

Writing About the Poem

A Creative Response

1. **Imitating the Poet's Technique.** Imitating Moore's technique of meticulously cataloging the town's sights, sounds, and smells, describe a place you know well and have some feeling for. Select images that will reveal your feelings for this scene. Try to use specific images. For example, Moore does not just say, "There were plants there"; she names twenty-two of them.

A Critical Response

2. **Comparing the Poem to a Prose Text.** How does Moore's vision of the ideal town contrast with Babbitt's view of what makes a perfect "burg"? (See page 535.) Write a paragraph in which you cite the differences between the two visions.

Analyzing Language and Style

Precise Meanings

Like most poets, Marianne Moore loved words and she knew a great number of them. Use a dictionary to be sure you know the precise meanings of *Tyrol, salpiglossis, lichens, bracts, banyan, portico, fluted.*

Primary Sources
Animals and Athletes

"Why an inordinate interest in animals and athletes? They are subjects of art and exemplars of it, are they not? minding their own business. Pangolins, hornbills, pitchers, catchers, do not pry or prey—or prolong the conversation; do not make us self-conscious; look their best when caring least; although in a Frank Buck documentary I saw a leopard insult a crocodile (basking on a river bank—head only visible on the bank), bat the animal on the nose and continue on its way without so much as a look back. Perhaps I really don't know. I do know that I don't know how to account for a person who could be indifferent to miracles of dexterity, a certain feat by Don Zimmer—a Dodger at the time—making a backhand catch, of a ball coming hard from behind on the left, fast enough to take his hand off."

—from *A Marianne Moore Reader*

Carl Sandburg
(1878–1967)

When he died in his ninetieth year, Carl Sandburg was already an American myth. Sandburg's deeply lined, leathery face and his boyish shock of hair had been familiar to his compatriots for more than five decades. As the author of two of the most famous poems of the century—"Chicago" (1914) and "Fog" (1916)—and of a six-volume biography of Abraham Lincoln (1926–1939), Sandburg had carved a place for himself in modern literature. As a poetic spokesman for the American worker in the toils of industrialization, he had become part of the folklore from which he drew his inspiration. While he seemed on the page to be the roughest of American poets, Sandburg was actually a gentle and contemplative man. He found his most characteristic voice in the vernacular—in slang, street talk, and common speech full of clichés and plain expressions.

A descendant of Swedes who had settled in Galesburg, Illinois, where he was born, Sandburg was not so much schooled in a classroom as in the proverbial "school of hard knocks." Before he was twenty, he had ranged the Middle West from Illinois to Nebraska, supporting himself with odd jobs. He thus came in contact with laborers in the fields and the factories that would one day provide his own poetic landscape. Sandburg volunteered to fight in the Spanish-American War that broke out in 1898, more from restlessness than patriotism, and he served in the first Puerto Rican campaign. When the war ended, he was finally ready to go back to school. He graduated from Lombard College in his hometown, where he was captain of the basketball team and editor of the college newspaper. It was at Lombard that Sandburg began to think of himself as a writer, particularly as a poet. But his first professional writing was in advertising, politics, and journalism.

Carl Sandburg photographed by Edward Steichen.

After a succession of jobs, Sandburg finally became known as a poet at the age of thirty-six when the influential magazine *Poetry* published some of his shorter poems, including "Chicago." Sandburg's audacious use of colloquialism and free verse (reflecting to some degree the influence of Walt Whitman) involved him in critical controversy and established his reputation as a major literary figure. The poet's affirmation of American democracy and of the inherent nobility of labor and the working person culminated in one of his best-known collections of poems, *The People, Yes* (1936), a Whitmanesque panorama of America that expressed its author's profound social faith. Besides his poetry and the monumental biography of Lincoln, Sandburg composed folk songs and ballads, autobiographical memoirs, and children's books.

Chicago by Louis Lozowick (1923). Oil.

Chicago

Hog Butcher for the World,
Tool Maker, Stacker of Wheat,
Player with Railroads and the Nation's Freight Handler;
Stormy, husky, brawling,
5   City of the Big Shoulders:

They tell me you are wicked and I believe them, for I
    have seen your painted women under the gas lamps
    luring the farm boys.
And they tell me you are crooked and I answer: Yes, it is
    true I have seen the gunman kill and go free to kill
    again.
And they tell me you are brutal and my reply is: On the
    faces of women and children I have seen the marks
    of wanton hunger.
And having answered so I turn once more to those who
    sneer at this my city, and I give them back the sneer
    and say to them:
Come and show me another city with lifted head singing
    so proud to be alive and coarse and strong and
10   cunning.
Flinging magnetic curses amid the toil of piling job on job,
    here is a tall bold slugger set vivid against the little
    soft cities;
Fierce as a dog with tongue lapping for action, cunning as
    a savage pitted against the wilderness,
    Bareheaded,
    Shoveling,
15   Wrecking,
    Planning,
    Building, breaking, rebuilding.
Under the smoke, dust all over his mouth, laughing with
    white teeth,
Under the terrible burden of destiny laughing as a young
    man laughs,
Laughing even as an ignorant fighter laughs who has never
20   lost a battle,
Bragging and laughing that under his wrist is the pulse,
    and under his ribs the heart of the people,
            Laughing!
Laughing the stormy, husky, brawling laughter of Youth,
    half-naked, sweating, proud to be Hog Butcher,
    Tool Maker, Stacker of Wheat, Player with Rail-
    roads and Freight Handler to the Nation.

Responding to the Poem

Analyzing the Poem

Identifying Details

1. Sandburg opens with a litany of **epithets,** or descriptive phrases, about Chicago. What does each of these epithets reveal about the city and the various activities that make up its economy?
2. What do people tell the speaker about Chicago? What is the speaker's answer to each of these comments about the city?

Interpreting Meanings

3. Many different images contribute to this portrait of Chicago, but its central **image** is never named. To what is Chicago really being compared? How is this image introduced and extended?
4. What are the city's main strengths and main weaknesses, according to Sandburg? On balance, what seems to be his attitude toward the city: Does he think it is boastful? Defensive? One-sided? Naive? Proud? Which attitude do you think the poet would most want to emphasize?
5. How does the long list in the last line help to unify the poem?
6. Find at least four examples of **parallelism** in the poem. How does this use of parallelism affect the poem's rhythm?
7. Which features of Chicago do you think have changed since this poem was written in 1914? Which features mentioned in the poem might still be part of the life of the city?
8. What would you say to those critics who have claimed that Sandburg's poetry is full of bluster and proclamations at the expense of thought?

Writing About the Poem

A Creative Response

1. **Writing an Apostrophe.** Think about the epithets Sandburg uses in addressing Chicago in his opening stanza. Then choose a city, town, or other area you know well. Write at least five epithets addressing the place you have chosen, using Sandburg's style as a model.

A Critical Response

2. **Comparing and Contrasting Poems.** Sandburg was one of the poets who followed Walt Whitman's lead toward a less formal mode of expression in poetry. Reread Whitman's "I Hear America Singing" (page 331). Then write a brief essay in which you compare and contrast that poem with Sandburg's "Chicago." Pay specific attention to the two poets' techniques and to their attitudes toward their subjects. Before you write, gather your data in a chart like the following one.

	Whitman	Sandburg
Subject		
Imagery		
Figures of speech		
Rhythm		
Catalogs of details		
Slang and colloquial language		
Tone		

In the time when railroad travel was common, a *limited* run was one that made fewer stops and charged a higher fare than other trains traveling the same route. A limited was therefore usually preferred by busy people who could afford the higher cost. As you read, look for one other meaning of the word *limited*.

Limited

I am riding on a limited express, one of the crack trains of the
    nation.
Hurtling across the prairie into blue haze and dark air go fifteen
    all-steel coaches holding a thousand people.
(All the coaches shall be scrap and rust and all the men and
    women laughing in the diners and sleepers shall pass to
    ashes.)
I ask a man in the smoker where he is going and he answers:
    "Omaha."

As Centuries Pass in the Night by William Foster
(early 20th century). Oil.

Edaville Railroad Collection.

Responding to the Poem

Analyzing the Poem

Identifying Details

1. Where is the speaker of the poem?
2. What does the speaker predict will happen to the train and its passengers?

Interpreting Meanings

3. What does the word *crack* mean in line 1?
4. What phrase in line 1 prepares the reader for the paradox, or self-contradiction, that underlies the whole poem?
5. In your own words state the **main idea** in this poem, using the word *limited*.
6. Do you think there is a double meaning in the speaker's question in line 4? If so, what **irony** do you sense in the other passenger's answer: ''Omaha''? (Where are he, and all ''riders,'' really going?)
7. What connections can you see between this poem and Robert Frost's ''Nothing Gold Can Stay'' on page 688?
8. How could the poem's details be up-dated?

Primary Sources
''Rhymes are iron fetters''

In his Notes for a Preface to *Complete Poems,* Carl Sandburg quoted another great American poet on rhyme:

''Oliver Wendell Holmes, skilled rhymester, told a young poet: 'When you write in prose you say what you mean. When you write in verse you say what you must.' Having said this to the young man, Holmes bethought himself and then wrote, 'I was thinking more especially of rhymed verse. Rhythm alone is a tether, and not a very long one. But rhymes are iron fetters; it is dragging a chain and ball to march under their incumbrance; it is a clog-dance you are figuring in when you execute your metrical *pas seul.*[1] . . . You want to say something about the heavenly bodies, and you have a beautiful line ending with the word stars. . . . You cannot make any use of cars, I will suppose; you have no occasion to talk about scars; 'the red planet Mars' has been used already; Dibdin has said enough about the gallant tars; what is there left for you but bars? So you give up your trains of thought, capitulate to necessity, and manage to lug in some kind of allusion, in place or out of place, which will allow you to make use of bars. Can there be imagined a more certain process for breaking up all continuity of thought, than this miserable subjugation of intellect to the clink of well or ill matched syllables?'

''The fact is ironic. A proficient and sometimes exquisite performer in rhymed verse goes out of his way to register the point that the more rhyme there is in poetry the more danger of its tricking the writer into something other than the urge in the beginning.''

—Carl Sandburg

---

1. **pas seul** (pä söl): French for a solo dance.

E. E. Cummings
(1894–1962)

E. E. Cummings (the initials stand for Edward Estlin) was born in Cambridge, Massachusetts, the son of a Unitarian minister. After a childhood spent within walking distance of Harvard, he attended the university at a time when aspiring writers were beginning to feel the impact of the two developments that would shape the character of American poetry for half a century. These new influences, sources of both inspiration and imitation, were French Symbolism and free verse. Like other poets, Cummings found in the Imagist manifesto guidelines that allowed him to break old rules and to try verbal experiments which would define his style.

If there is such a thing as "rugged individualism" in poetry, Cummings may be its prime example. All by himself, he altered conventional English syntax and made typography and the division of words part of the shape and meaning of a poem. And—in the age of celebration of the common man—he went against the grain by championing the virtues of elitism. "So far as I am concerned," he wrote, "poetry and every other art was and is and forever will be strictly and distinctly a question of individuality . . . poetry is being, not doing. If you wish to follow, even at a distance, the poet's calling . . . you've got to come out of the measurable doing universe into the immeasurable house of being. . . . Nobody else can be alive for you; nor can you be alive for anybody else."

Graduating from college in the midst of World War I, Cummings became part of the conflict well before American soldiers appeared on European battlefields in 1917. He volunteered for an ambulance corps privately financed by Americans and staffed by young men like himself. Crossing to Bordeaux on a French troop ship threatened by German U-Boats, Cummings had hardly begun his duties when a French censor, intercepting one of his typographically odd letters, imprisoned him on suspicion of espionage. Released within three months, and little the worse for wear, Cummings drew upon the experience to produce his first important book of prose, *The Enormous Room* (1922).

After World War I, Cummings returned to France. He was one of the American literary expatriates who found in Paris the freedom and inspiration they felt were denied them by the restrictive Puritanism of their own country. During this period, Cummings refined the eccentric shifts of syntax and typography that would become his trademark. In 1923, he published his first collection of verse, *Tulips and Chimneys*, which was followed by *&* (1925), *XLI Poems* (1925), and *is 5* (1926). His poetry is often marked by jubilant lyricism, as he celebrates love, nature's beauty, and an almost Transcendentalist affirmation of the individual. He reserved his mischievous wit for the satire of the "unman," by which he meant the unthinking, unfeeling temperament of urban "humans."

Cummings split his time between an apartment in Greenwich Village in New York City and a house in Silver Lake, New Hampshire. He died still believing that "when skies are hanged and oceans drowned, / the single secret will still be man."

Although this poem deals with destruction, it is an optimistic statement about people and the possibilities facing the human race. The syntax here is more difficult than that of the previous poem.

Read it through once or twice to get a general idea of what it is saying. Then read it carefully, line by line, noting where sentences and "thought groups" begin and end.

what if a much of a which of a wind

what if a much of a which of a wind
gives the truth to summer's lie;
bloodies with dizzying leaves the sun
and yanks immortal stars awry?
5 Blow king to beggar and queen to seem
(blow friend to fiend:blow space to time)
—when skies are hanged and oceans
   drowned,
the single secret will still be man

what if a keen of a lean wind flays
10 screaming hills with sleet and snow:
strangles valleys by ropes of thing
and stifles forests in white ago?

Blow hope to terror; blow seeing to blind
(blow pity to envy and soul to mind)
—whose hearts are mountains,roots are
15   trees,
it's they shall cry hello to the spring

what if a dawn of a doom of a dream
bites this universe in two,
peels forever out of his grave
20 and sprinkles nowhere with me and you?
Blow soon to never and never to twice
(blow life to isn't:blow death to was)
—all nothing's only our hugest home;
the most who die, the more we live

Pink Locusts and Windy Moon
by Charles Burchfield (1959). Watercolor.

Chase Manhattan Bank Collection, New York.

Responding to the Poem

Analyzing the Poem

Identifying Details

1. If the world is blown away, what will still survive?
2. Who "shall cry hello to the spring" if the world freezes over?
3. What will happen if the universe is blown up?
4. What **images** describe the seasons of the year in the first two stanzas? How does the third stanza deal with time on a different scale?
5. Describe the **rhyme scheme** of the poem. How does Cummings make use of **slant rhyme?**

Interpreting Meaning

6. What common human fears does Cummings refer to in the first six lines of each stanza? How does he comment on those fears in the last two lines of each stanza?
7. What is the effect of the direct reference to "me and you" in line 20?
8. What do you think Cummings means by the last two lines? Is he celebrating life or death? Explain.

Writing About the Poem

A Critical Response

1. **Comparing Poems.** In a paragraph, compare this poem to Whitman's "On the Beach at Night" on page 343. Consider the theme or message, imagery, tone, form, and structure of the poems before you write.
2. **Comparing the Poems to a Statement.** In the quotation that follows under "Primary Sources," from the intro-duction to his collection called *New Poems,* Cummings makes several statements about poetry and his audience, and at the same time reveals an attitude toward life itself. In a brief essay, tell whether you find any of these statements related to the messages in his poems. Use specific lines from the poems to support your opinions.

Analyzing Language and Style

Diction

In "nobody loses all the time," Cummings uses two words that would not be found in poetry of an earlier generation.

1. *Highfalootin* is listed in one dictionary as an Americanism—that is, a word that originated in America, or that is peculiar to American English. What does it mean?
2. *Splendiferous* is listed as colloquial, meaning that it would not be used in formal written English. What does it mean?
3. What words might a more conservative writer from a past era have used in place of each of these words?
4. What would be a more elegant and formal way of saying "we all cried like the Missouri"?
5. What does the diction of this poem reveal about its speaker? How does it help set the poem's tone?
6. In "what if a much of a which of a wind," Cummings uses verbs, adjectives, and adverbs as nouns. Find five examples. In each case, what does the word mean as a noun?

Primary Sources
"Miracles are to come"

"The poems to come are for you and for me and are not for mostpeople —it's no use trying to pretend that mostpeople and ourselves are alike. Mostpeople have less in common with ourselves than the squarerootofmi-nusone. You and I are human beings;mostpeople are snobs. . . .

"you and I are not snobs. We can never be born enough. We are human beings;for whom birth is a supremely welcome mystery,the mystery of growing:the mystery which happens only and whenever we are faithful to ourselves. You and I wear the dangerous looseness of doom and find it becoming. Life,for eternal us,is now; and now is much too busy being a little more than everything to seem anything,catastrophic included. . . .

"Miracles are to come. With you I leave a remembrance of miracles:they are by somebody who can love and who shall be continually reborn,a human being;somebody who said to those near him,when his fingers would not hold a brush 'tie it into my hand'—"

—E. E. Cummings

T. S. Eliot
(1888–1965)

At the time when he was regarded as America's most eminent living poet, T. S. Eliot announced that he was an "Anglo-Catholic in religion, a royalist in politics, and a classicist in literature." In 1927, Eliot gave up his American citizenship and became a subject of the King of England. The same year he was received into the Church of England. (By a kind of poetic justice, this loss to America was later to be made up for: W. H. Auden, the leading British poet of his time, became a naturalized American citizen in 1946.) But residence in an adopted country does not necessarily change the philosophy or the style of a poet. Eliot continued to speak in a voice first heard in the Puritan pulpits of Massachusetts. And Auden retained a British sense of language unaffected by the in-roads of American speech.

T. S. Eliot's family was rooted in New England, yet he was born in St. Louis, Missouri, where his father was the chancellor of Washington University. Eliot's childhood awareness of his native city would show itself in his poetry, but only after he had moved far away from St. Louis. He graduated from Harvard and went on to postgraduate work at the Sorbonne in Paris.

Just before the outbreak of World War I, Eliot took up residence in London, the city that would become his home for the rest of his life. There he worked for a time in a bank, suffered a nervous breakdown, married an emotionally troubled Englishwoman, and finally took up the business of literature. He became active as a publisher in the outstanding firm of Faber & Faber, and, on his own, edited *The Criterion,* a literary magazine. As a critic, he was responsible for reviving interest in many neglected poets, notably the seventeenth-century poet John Donne.

Long before he decided to live abroad permanently, Eliot had developed a taste for classical literature. He was as familiar with European and Eastern writings as he was with the masterpieces of English. But the most crucial influence upon his early work came from the late-nineteenth-century French poets who, as a group, came to be known as the Symbolists. When he was nine-

teen, Eliot came upon a book by the British critic Arthur Symons entitled *The Symbolist Movement in Literature.* "I myself owe Mr. Symons a great debt," wrote Eliot. "But for having read his book I should not . . . have heard of Laforgue and Rimbaud; I should probably not have begun to read Verlaine; and but for reading Verlaine, I should not have heard of Corbière. So the Symons book is one of those which have affected the course of my life."

The poets Eliot mentions were men of distinctly different talents. Yet they all believed in poetry as an art of suggestion rather than statement. They saw poetry as an art of recreating states of mind and feeling, as opposed to reporting or confessing them. These beliefs became the basis of Eliot's own poetic methods. When people complained that this poetic method of suggestion was complex and difficult to understand, Eliot retorted that poetry had to be complex to express the complexities of modern life. More or less ignoring the still undervalued contribution of Walt Whitman, Eliot and other American poets also believed that, divorced from British antecedents, they would once and for all bring the peculiar rhythms of their native speech into the mainstream of world literature. Eliot and these other poets are often referred to as Modernists.

Eliot had an austere view of poetic creativity; he disagreed with those who regarded a poem as a means of self-expression, as a source of comfort, or as a kind of spiritual pep talk. Practicing what he preached, Eliot startled his contemporaries in 1917 with "The Love Song of J. Alfred Prufrock" and "Portrait of a Lady." Then, in 1922, with the editorial advice and encouragement of Ezra Pound, Eliot published *The Waste Land,* a long work which would become the most significant poem of the early twentieth century. The poem was so influential that the word *wasteland* entered common usage from Eliot's work. The word suggests a civilization that is spiritually empty and paralyzed by indecision and anxiety.

Assembled in the manner of a painter's collage or a movie-maker's montage, *The Waste Land* proved that it was possible to write an epic poem of classical scope in the space of 434 lines. Critics pored over the poem's complex structure and its dense network of allusions to world literature, Oriental religion, and anthropology. A few years after *The Waste Land* appeared, Eliot published a series of notes identifying many of his key references. (He was dismayed to find that some of his more ardent admirers were more interested in the notes than in the poem itself.)

In 1925, Eliot published a kind of lyrical postscript to *The Waste Land* called *The Hollow Men,* with its somber conclusion:

> This is the way the world ends
> This is the way the world ends
> This is the way the world ends
> Not with a bang but a whimper.
> —from *The Hollow Men*

In *The Hollow Men,* Eliot repeats and expands some of the themes of his longer poem and arrives at that point of despair beyond which lie but two alternatives: renewal or annihilation.

For critics surveying Eliot's career, it has become commonplace to say that, after the spiritual dead-end of *The Hollow Men,* Eliot chose hope over despair, and faith over the world-weary cynicism that marked his early years. But there is much evidence in his later poems to indicate that, for Eliot, hope and faith were not conscious choices. Instead, they were the consequences of a submission, even a surrender, to that "peace which passeth understanding" referred to in the last line of *The Waste Land.*

His later poems include *Ash Wednesday* (1930), with its deeply religious spiritual explorations, and *Four Quartets,* which contain the philosophical conclusions of a lifetime (though always tentative).

Eliot spent the remainder of his poetic career in an extended meditation upon the limits of individual will and the limitless power of faith in the presence of grace.

Cited for his work as "a trail-blazing pioneer of modern poetry," Eliot was awarded the Nobel Prize for literature in 1948. In the decades that followed, he came frequently to the United States to lecture and to read his poems, sometimes to audiences so large he had to appear in football stadiums. Some of those who fought to buy tickets on the fifty-yard line were probably unaware of the irony in all of this: that a man once regarded as the most difficult and obscure poet of his era had achieved the drawing power of a rock star.

Ezra Pound (who called Eliot "Possum") wrote a few final words on the death of his old friend, ending with this passage:

"Am I to write 'about' the poet Thomas Stearns Eliot? Or my friend 'the Possum'? Let him rest in peace, I can only repeat, but with the urgency of fifty years ago: READ HIM."

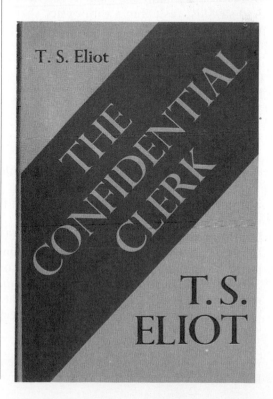

This poem is written as an interior monologue; it is all going on inside the head of a man named Prufrock. Sometimes Prufrock's line of reasoning is interrupted by an unexpected thought. You will often have to supply the missing connections in the speaker's stream of thoughts and associations.

The poem was published in 1917. As you read, think of how it reflects these ideas about Eliot's own time, and perhaps about ours as well:

1. The idea that people are spiritually empty.
2. The idea that contemporary life is unromantic and unheroic.

Read the poem through twice. Read it aloud, or listen to it being read aloud, at least once. Then answer the questions in the side-notes.

The Love Song of J. Alfred Prufrock

S'io credesse che mia risposta fosse
A persona che mai tornasse al mondo,
Questa fiamma staria senza piu scosse.
Ma perciocche giammai di questo fondo
Non torno vivo alcun, s'i'odo il vero,
Senza tema d'infamia ti rispondo.°

Let us go then, you and I,
When the evening is spread out against the sky
Like a patient etherized upon a table;
Let us go, through certain half-deserted streets,
5   The muttering retreats
Of restless nights in one-night cheap hotels
And sawdust restaurants with oyster shells:
Streets that follow like a tedious argument
Of insidious intent
10   To lead you to an overwhelming question . . .
Oh, do not ask, "What is it?"
Let us go and make our visit.

In the room the women come and go
Talking of Michelangelo.°

The yellow fog that rubs its back upon the window
15   panes,
The yellow smoke that rubs its muzzle on the window
        panes
Licked its tongue into the corners of the evening,
Lingered upon the pools that stand in drains,
Let fall upon its back the soot that falls from chimneys,
20   Slipped by the terrace, made a sudden leap,
And seeing that it was a soft October night,
Curled once about the house, and fell asleep.

And indeed there will be time
For the yellow smoke that slides along the street,
25   Rubbing its back upon the window panes;

Epigraph: This quotation is from Dante's great epic poem *The Divine Comedy*. Guido da Montefeltro, a man consigned to Hell for dispensing evil advice, speaks from a flame shaped like a tongue: "If I believed my answer were being made to someone who could return to the world, this flame would shake no more. But since (if what I hear is true) no one has ever returned alive from these depths, I will answer you without fear of disgrace." Think of Prufrock as speaking from another kind of hell—a hell of his own feelings.

3. *What is the evening compared with?*

7. *List the facts you know about where the speaker wants to take his companion.*

14. Michelangelo: the great artist of the Italian Renaissance.

22. *What details are you given about this setting? What season is it?*

Tea Leaves by William Paxton (1909). Oil.   The Metropolitan Museum of Art, New York.

we cannot understand: the bat
    holding on upside down or in quest of some-
        thing to

eat, elephants pushing, a wild horse taking a roll, a
      tireless wolf under
  a tree, the immovable critic twitching his skin like
      a horse that feels a flea, the base-
  ball fan, the statistician—
    nor is it valid
      to discriminate against "business documents
      and

school-books"; all these phenomena are important.
      One must make a distinction
  however: when dragged into prominence by half
      poets, the result is not poetry,
  nor till the poets among us can be
    "literalists of
    the imagination"—above
      insolence and triviality and can present

for inspection, imaginary gardens with real toads in
      them, shall we have
  it. In the meantime, if you demand on the one hand,
  the raw material of poetry in
    all its rawness and
    that which is on the other hand
      genuine, you are interested in poetry.

                                —Marianne Moore

Writing

The following two paragraphs are from one reader's analysis of "what if a much of a which of a wind" by E. E. Cummings (page 756). Notice how the writer gives a brief paraphrase of the poem, stanza by stanza, and then moves on to talk about form.

> The poem "what if a much of a which of a wind" by E. E. Cummings at first seems as confusing as its first-line title. The speaker in the poem seems to be wondering about the possibilities of doom that might befall the human race. In the first stanza the speaker thinks about the winds of autumn that give "the truth to summer's lie" (line 2) and might blow the immortal stars out of their places. The second stanza is about the winds of

winter that could possibly bring back the ice age ("and stifles forests in white ago," line 12). In the last stanza, the speaker wonders about "a dawn of a doom of a dream" that destroys the universe, maybe nuclear weapons ("bites this universe in two," line 18). In each stanza, the speaker envisions a time when human life is utterly changed, when all is terror and nothingness. But still, the last two lines in each stanza offer a very positive affirmation of life. Human life, Cummings seems to be saying, will endure the worst catastrophes that humans or nature can devise.

> One of the things I noticed about the poem is that, despite its eccentric punctuation, it does have a strict form. The stanzas repeat a complicated pattern. Each stanza begins with a four-line question about the wind, beginning with the words "what if." The fifth and sixth lines of each stanza tell what the wind blows, and most of the things blown are abstract. In each stanza, lines 7–8 offer a two-line resolution, or answer to the question at the beginning of the stanza. . . .

In succeeding paragraphs, this writer should talk about the other elements in the poem and how they contribute to its meaning. The last paragraph, following the instructions, should discuss the writer's response.

Revising and Proofreading

Use the guidelines in the section at the back of this book, called **Writing About Literature,** to revise and proofread your essay.

AMERICAN DRAMA

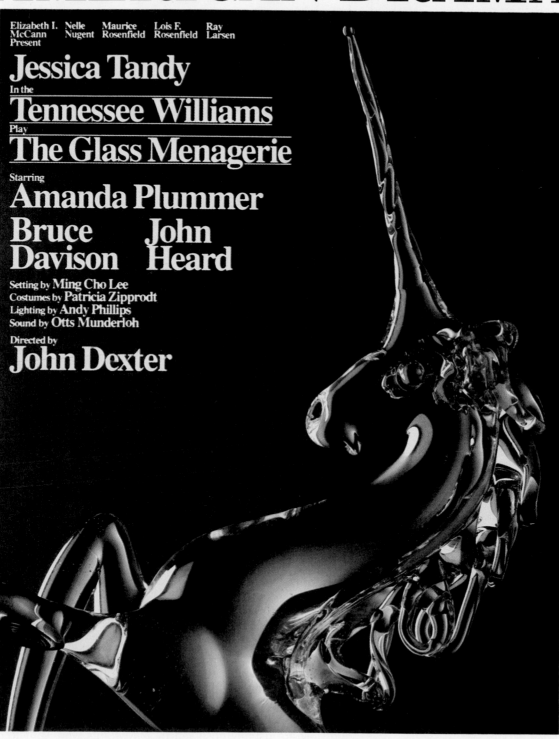

Elizabeth I. McCann, Nelle Nugent, Maurice Rosenfield, Lois F. Rosenfield, Ray Larsen Present

Jessica Tandy

In the

Tennessee Williams

Play

The Glass Menagerie

Starring

Amanda Plummer

Bruce Davison   John Heard

Setting by Ming Cho Lee
Costumes by Patricia Zipprodt
Lighting by Andy Phillips
Sound by Otts Munderloh

Directed by

John Dexter

UNIT TEN

The Elements of Drama

Theater is one of the most emotionally satisfying experiences imaginable. It touches our inner core, and gives insight into who we are.

—Theodore Mann

Drama is probably the most difficult form of writing; it certainly seems to take the longest to learn. According to a saying, young poets are eighteen, young novelists are twenty-four, and young playwrights are thirty.

George S. Kaufman, a noted American writer of comedies during the 1930's and 1940's, said that writing plays was not an art, but a trick. Art or trick, it is difficult, possibly because when a play is written, it is not finished in the same way that a poem or novel is. There remains the painful and pleasurable process of bringing the play to life on stage, with the help of a director, actors, set designer, costume designer, stagehands, musicians, electricians—and a responsive audience. Producing a play is a team effort, and much can go wrong. A beautifully written and acted scene, for example, can be ruined if the electrician dims the lights too rapidly.

Another difference between drama and other literary forms is that movement and gesture are essential elements in drama. Some of the high points in a play may even be nonverbal. In *The Diary of Anne Frank,* for example, Mr. Frank realizes that the Nazis are downstairs and that the family's hiding place is about to be discovered. He turns to his family and friends and spreads his hands in resignation. This heartbreaking moment is conceived by the playwright; but its achievement on the stage—the exact gesture—requires the close and creative cooperation of actor and director.

Young writers are often drawn to the stage by the theatrical trappings: the gestures, the colorful sets, and the magical effects that drama can achieve. But playwrights soon learn that theatrical effects are rarely enough in themselves. The effects and gestures are there only to serve a story, and it must be a story that engages the passions of the collaborators—the director, actors, and dozens of others who work to produce a play. Stage technicians may dazzle our senses with intricate and fascinating effects; but if a play doesn't have a significant story, we find nothing "moving" in the end, because our emotions have not been touched.

The Basic Principles of Drama

When a play goes wrong, it is almost always because the writer has failed to conceive the story in dramatic terms. There are, of course, some plays (such as Thornton Wilder's *Our Town*) that "work" in the theater even though they ignore the usual principles of drama. But over the centuries certain principles have developed, and they are usually observed by playwrights who want to catch, hold, and reward the attention of an audience.

Costume design for *Our Town* (detail) by Patricia Zipprodt.

Museum of the City of New York.

The analogy is slightly oversimplified, but we respond to a play in very much the way we respond to a sports event. Let's assume that one summer evening you go to a professional baseball game. For some reason, you take a liking to one of the pitchers. Then someone sitting next to you says that the pitcher has been out with an injured elbow for several weeks and is trying to make a comeback. If he fails in this game, he is finished. You start rooting for him. He gets some bad calls from the plate umpire, and you boo or whistle. Then your neighbor tells you that the pitcher is not pitching his best. Unless he stops protecting his injured elbow and starts putting more speed in his pitches, he will not win.

Most plays have more psychological complexity than this situation does. With a little imagination, however, we can add to the pitcher's problems. Suppose, for instance, that the pitcher's wife is afraid that if he throws too hard, he will ruin his elbow and be unable to play. She tells him that if he damages his elbow further, she will leave him; but, to him, the glory of winning transcends practical matters. To his wife, he is a ball-playing ''boy,'' careless and immature. And so forth. . . .

What has happened in this scenario is what happens in almost every play. Early on, the playwright organizes our emotions behind some character or group of characters: We are ''for'' them. The playwright has placed these characters in a situation involving **conflict,** and then has made us understand that it is not just any conflict: The character or characters have something vital at stake.

The History of American Drama

Eugene O'Neill (1888–1953) is generally considered the first important figure in American drama. It is significant that several decades after the 1920 production of his first full-length play, *Beyond the Horizon,* he is still regarded as the most important playwright America has produced.

American drama before O'Neill consisted mostly of shows and entertainments. These wildly theatrical spectacles often featured such delights as chariot races and burning cities, staged by means of special effects that dazzled audiences. Melodramas and farces were also written for famous actors, much as television shows today are created to display the personalities and talents of popular performers. In fact, O'Neill's own father, James, spent the better part of his life touring in a spectacular melodrama based on Alexander Dumas's *The Count of Monte Cristo.*

There was great theatrical activity in nineteenth-century America, a time when there were no movies, radio, or television. Every town of any size had its theater or "opera house" in which touring companies performed. Given the hunger for entertainment, one may wonder why no significant American drama was written in the century that produced, among others, Melville, Emerson, Whitman, Dickinson, and Twain.

Goodspeed Opera House in East Haddam, Connecticut. Photograph by Inge Morath.

Theater as a Social Art

One explanation for this is that theater has usually followed the other arts, rather than pointing the way toward new directions. Robert Sherwood, one of the group of notable American playwrights between 1920 and 1940, once said: "Drama travels in the caboose of literature." The theater seems to take up new attitudes, subject matter, and forms only after they have been explored in the other arts. For the most part, theater tends to dramatize accepted attitudes and values.

The reason for this is that theater is a social art, one we attend as part of a large group; we seem to respond to something new much more slowly as a group than we do as individuals. When you laugh or cry in the theater, your response is noticed. You are, in a sense, giving your approval, and this approval may be subject to criticism or condemnation by those sitting around you who are not laughing or crying. You may not be shocked to *read* about your secret thoughts, dreams, and desires; but when you *see* them shown on stage as you sit among a thousand people, you may refuse to respond, refuse to acknowledge them. You may even rise up and stalk out of the theater

Thus, the novel and to some extent the poetry of the nineteenth and early twentieth centuries were more daring than the theater in giving us a "record of experience," in showing us life as it *is* lived, not as it *should be* lived. During this period before O'Neill, American drama tended to be mild and sentimental, rarely questioning the life and attitudes it depicted, almost never challenging the accepted traditions of its times.

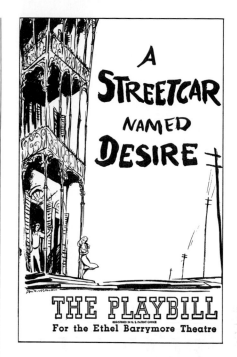

The Influence of Ibsen, Strindberg, and Chekhov

European drama, which was to influence modern American drama profoundly, "matured" in the last third of the nineteenth century with the achievements of three playwrights: the Norwegian Henrik Ibsen (1828–1906), the Swede August Strindberg (1849–1912), and the Russian Anton Chekhov (1860–1904). Ibsen deliberately tackled subjects such as guilt, sexuality, and mental illness— subjects which had never before been so realistically and disturbingly portrayed on stage. Strindberg brought to his characterizations an unprecedented level of psychological complexity. And Chekhov, along with Ibsen and Strindberg, shifted the subject matter of drama from wildly theatrical displays of external action to inner action and emotions and the concerns of everyday life. Chekhov once remarked, "People don't go to the North Pole and fall off icebergs. They go to the office and quarrel with their wives and eat cabbage soup."

These three great playwrights bequeathed to their American heirs plays about life as it is actually lived. They presented characters and situations more or less realistically, in what has been called the "slice of life" dramatic technique.

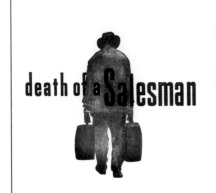

death of a **Salesman**

The **PLAYBILL** *for the Morosco Theatre*

the American business machine, which disposes of him when he has outlived his usefulness.

Miller is a writer of high moral seriousness, whether he is dealing with personal versus social responsibility, as in *All My Sons* (1947), or with witch hunts past and present, as in *The Crucible* (1953). Miller writes a plain and muscular prose that under the force of emotion often becomes eloquent, as in Linda Loman's famous speech in *Death of a Salesman,* where she talks to her two sons about their father:

> I don't say he's a great man. Willy Loman never made a lot of money. His name was never in the paper. He's not the finest character that ever lived. But he's a human being, and a terrible thing is happening to him. So attention must be paid. He's not to be allowed to fall into his grave like an old dog. Attention, attention must finally be paid to such a person.

> —from *Death of a Salesman,*
> Arthur Miller

Although Tennessee Williams was Miller's contemporary, his concern was not with social matters, but with personal ones. If Miller is often the playwright of our social conscience, then Williams was the playwright of our souls. In play after play, he probed the psychological complexities of his characters, especially of his women: Amanda and Laura in *The Glass Menagerie* (1944), Blanche in *A Streetcar Named Desire* (1947), and Alma in *Summer and Smoke* (1948).

In contrast to Miller's spare, plain language, Williams's writing is delicate and sensuous; it is often colored with lush imagery and evocative rhythms. Miller's characters are, by and large, ordinary people with whom we identify because they are caught up in the social tensions of our times. Williams's characters are often women who are "lost ladies," drowning in their own neuroses, but somehow mirroring a part of our own complex psychological selves.

The actual scenes in Williams's plays are usually purely realistic, even though these scenes may deal with colorful and "extreme" characters. But Williams usually theatricalized the realism with "music in the wings" or symbolic props, such as Laura's unicorn in *The Glass Menagerie* or the looming statue of Eternity in *Summer and Smoke.* He always conceived his plays in visually arresting, colorful, theatrical environments—an effort in which he was aided by the imaginative designer Jo Mielziner, who designed the sets for many of his plays.

The Revolt Against Realism

In the mid-nineteenth century, realism in drama was conceived as a revolt against crude theatricalism. Currently, there is a revolt against realism itself in American drama. Naturally, the movement is toward theatricalism again, with its emphasis on stage effects and imaginative settings. This revolt does not confine itself to a particular manner of staging; instead, it extends to the texture of language and plot in the scripts themselves.

The moral and religious certainties that once bound people together exert little or no force on many modern audiences. Some people believe that survival itself depends on a willingness to accept life as formless or meaningless.

Some American playwrights found this new outlook on life impossible to express in the orderly "beginning, middle, end" format of realism. They borrowed, again from Europe, a theater of fragmentation, impressions, and stream of consciousness that was called "expressionist." **Expressionist drama** aimed at the revelation of characters' interior consciousness without reference to a logical sequence of surface actions. Many writers who used expressionist techniques in drama came to be called playwrights of the Theater of the Absurd.

Samuel Beckett (born 1906) and Eugene Ionesco (born 1912) were among the founders of the Theater of the Absurd. The drama critic Martin Esslin has written this about the Absurdists:

> The action of a play of the Theater of the Absurd is not intended to tell a story but to communicate a pattern of poetic images. To give but one example: Things happen in [Samuel Beckett's] *Waiting for Godot* [1953], but these things do not constitute a plot or a story; they are an image of Beckett's intuition that *nothing really ever happens* in man's existence.

—Martin Esslin

The trouble with a static play that mirrors a static life is that it is static. It is an image, a picture; and a picture can absorb our interest for only so long because it lacks the progression and development of a dramatic story. We can observe a situation without development for about the length of a one-act play. Perhaps this is why so many of the so-called absurdist plays *are* only one act, such as Beckett's *Krapp's Last Tape* and Ionesco's *The Bald Soprano.*

The most significant Absurdist in America has been Edward Albee (born 1928). Albee is not a pure Absurdist, since, like all innovative playwrights, he experiments with many forms. From 1960 to 1970, Albee produced a play a year. These works ranged from his startling, one-act debut, *The Zoo Story* (1960), through the absurdist play *The American Dream* (1961) and the savage and electrifying domestic drama, *Who's Afraid of Virginia Woolf?* (1962), which made Albee world-famous.

Experimental drama has increased the options that are open to playwrights. Dramatists now have the freedom to express their deepest feelings in almost any form they choose—provided that their approach can be made comprehensible to an audience and touch their emotions. There are practically no conventions in the theater anymore; there is simply a stage and an audience. Playwrights are free to load the stage with scenery, lights, and special effects; but they are equally free—as the playwright was in the age of Shakespeare—to have an actor gesture toward one side of an utterly bare stage and say, "This is the Forest of Arden."

Scene from *Happy Days* by Samuel Beckett.

Tennessee Williams (1911–1983)

The Glass Menagerie has become an American classic. When it opened on Broadway in the spring of 1945, Mississippi-born Tennessee Williams was practically unknown; almost overnight, he became an international success.

Though Williams became known principally for his colorful women characters—Blanche in *A Streetcar Named Desire* (1947), Alma in *Summer and Smoke* (1948), Maggie in *Cat on a Hot Tin Roof* (1955)—he also created some great male characters, among them Stanley Kowalski in *A Streetcar Named Desire*. Marlon Brando's portrayal of Stanley in the original production, and in the movie, established a kind of mumbling, torn-Tee-shirt technique of acting that was to become popular with many of the younger male actors of the next decade.

The Glass Menagerie is a mixture of straightforward, realistic play construction and ''poetic,'' highly imaginative conception and language. Williams used this combination for most of his works. The structure of his plays is basically conventional; his vision, his ''voice,'' is imaginative and sensitive.

Because *The Glass Menagerie* is a memory play, its images are hazy. In production, when the curtain goes up, we see the apartment and the alley through a transparent gauze curtain called a ''scrim.'' The narrator speaks in a kind of poetic prose, and when the scrim rises, we see the set lit but with pools of light and shadow.

The characters, too, are poetically conceived and removed from the daily life of the Great Depression of the 1930's. In a few lines in the opening narration, Williams sets the social background of the period; but he is not really interested in the larger society. In all his plays, what interests him most is the psychological makeup of his characters. Laura Wingfield passes her life listening to phonograph records and rearranging her collection of glass animals. Tom wants to be a writer and to escape to the sea. Amanda lives in the past glories of being a Southern belle. In contrast to the Wingfield family, the gentleman caller is not poetic. He is from the real world,

and it is the touching confrontation of this real man with the withdrawn Laura that provides the climax of the play.

In December 1944, *The Glass Menagerie* was tried out in Chicago. It was ''dying'' until the influential drama critic Claudia Cassidy came to its rescue and demanded that people see the play. When it moved on to New York in the spring of 1945, it was an instant success.

Williams had two extraordinary collaborators. Amanda was originally played by one of the great actresses of the American stage, Laurette Taylor. She had been in retirement for some years for many reasons, one of which was that she had developed a drinking problem. She was lured out of retirement by Williams's play, and the natural drama of opening night was increased by the tension generated by the question, ''Would Laurette Taylor make it?'' She did make it. It was her greatest and her last performance in the theater.

Williams's other great collaborator was Jo Mielziner, the foremost stage designer of his day. Williams was only a young playwright, but he brought both these collaborators a play with a passionate and poetic expression of his feelings for his own sister (see page 829), and with a brilliantly conceived dramatic structure. All of Tennessee Williams's collaborators rose to new heights when they helped him realize on stage this small gem of a play.

THE GLASS MENAGERIE

Nobody, not even the rain, has such small hands.

—E. E. Cummings

The photographs that illustrate the play are from the Long Wharf
Theater Production, in New Haven, Connecticut, 1986.

The Characters

Amanda Wingfield (*the mother*)
A little woman of great but confused vitality clinging frantically to another time and place. Her characterization must be carefully created, not copied from type. She is not paranoiac, but her life is paranoia.[1] There is much to admire in Amanda, and as much to love and pity as there is to laugh at. Certainly she has endurance and a kind of heroism, and though her foolishness makes her unwittingly cruel at times, there is tenderness in her slight person.

Laura Wingfield (*her daughter*)
Amanda, having failed to establish contact with reality, continues to live vitally in her illusions, but Laura's situation is even graver. A childhood illness has left her crippled, one leg slightly shorter than the other, and held in a brace. This defect need not be more than suggested on the stage. Stemming from this, Laura's separation increases till she is like a piece of her own glass collection, too exquisitely fragile to move from the shelf.

Tom Wingfield (*her son*)
And the narrator of the play. A poet with a job in a warehouse. His nature is not remorseless, but to escape from a trap he has to act without pity.

Jim O'Connor (*the gentleman caller*)
A nice, ordinary, young man.

Scene 1

The Wingfield apartment is in the rear of the building, one of those vast hive-like conglomerations of cellular living-units that flower at warty growths in overcrowded urban centers of lower middle-class population and are symptomatic of the impulse of this largest and fundamentally enslaved section of American society to avoid fluidity and differentiation and to exist and function as one interfused mass of automatism.

The apartment faces an alley and is entered by a fire escape, a structure whose name is a touch of accidental poetic truth, for all of these huge buildings are always burning with the slow and implacable fires of human desperation. The fire escape is part of what we see—that is, the landing of it and steps descending from it.

The scene is memory and is therefore nonrealistic. Memory takes a lot of poetic license. It omits some details; others are exaggerated, according to the emotional value of the articles it touches, for memory is seated predominantly in the heart. The interior is therefore rather dim and poetic.

At the rise of the curtain, the audience is faced with the dark, grim rear wall of the Wingfield tenement. This building is flanked on both sides by dark, narrow alleys which run into murky canyons of tangled clotheslines, garbage cans, and the sinister latticework of neighboring fire escapes. It is up and down these side alleys that exterior entrances and exits are made during the play. At the end of TOM's *opening commentary, the dark tenement[2] wall slowly becomes transparent and reveals the interior of the ground-floor Wingfield apartment.*

Nearest the audience is the living room, which also serves as a sleeping room for LAURA, *the sofa unfolding to make her bed. Just beyond, separated from the living room by a wide arch or second proscenium with transparent faded portieres[3] (or second curtain), is the dining room. In an old-fashioned whatnot[4] in the living room are seen scores of transparent glass animals. A blown-up photograph of the father hangs on the wall of the living room, to the left of the archway. It is the face of a very handsome young man in a doughboy's First World War cap. He is gallantly smiling, ineluctably smiling, as if to say "I will be smiling forever."*

Also hanging on the wall, near the photograph, are a typewriter keyboard chart and a Gregg shorthand diagram. An upright typewriter on a small table stands beneath the charts.

---

1. **paranoia** (par′ə·noi′ə): behavior characterized by delusions, especially of being persecuted.

2. **tenement:** an apartment house in a poor neighborhood.
3. **portieres** (pôr·tyerz′): curtains covering a doorway, used instead of a door.
4. **whatnot:** open shelves for holding small objects ("whatnots").

The audience hears and sees the opening scene in the dining room through both the transparent fourth wall of the building and the transparent gauze portieres of the dining-room arch. It is during this revealing scene that the fourth wall slowly ascends, out of sight. This transparent exterior wall is not brought down again until the very end of the play, during TOM's *final speech.*

The narrator is an undisguised convention of the play. He takes whatever license with dramatic convention is convenient to his purposes.

[TOM *enters, dressed as a merchant sailor, and strolls across to the fire escape. There he stops and lights a cigarette. He addresses the audience.*]

Tom. Yes, I have tricks in my pocket, I have things up my sleeve. But I am the opposite of a stage magician. He gives you illusion that has the appearance of truth. I give you truth in the pleasant disguise of illusion.

To begin with, I turn back time. I reverse it to that quaint period, the thirties, when the huge middle class of America was matriculating in a school for the blind. Their eyes had failed them, or they had failed their eyes, and so they were having their fingers pressed forcibly down on the fiery Braille alphabet of a dissolving economy.

In Spain there was revolution. Here there was only shouting and confusion. In Spain there was Guernica. Here there were disturbances of labor, sometimes pretty violent, in otherwise peaceful cities such as Chicago, Cleveland, Saint Louis . . . This is the social background of the play.

[*Music begins to play.*]

The play is memory. Being a memory play, it is dimly lighted, it is sentimental, it is not realistic. In memory everything seems to happen to music. That explains the fiddle in the wings.

I am the narrator of the play, and also a character in it. The other characters are my mother, Amanda, my sister, Laura, and a gentleman caller who appears in the final scenes. He is the most

"I give you truth in the pleasant guise of illusion."

realistic character in the play, being an emissary from a world of reality that we were somehow set apart from. But since I have a poet's weakness for symbols, I am using this character also as a symbol; he is the long delayed but always expected something that we live for.

There is a fifth character in the play who doesn't appear except in this larger-than-life-size photograph over the mantel. This is our father who left us a long time ago. He was a telephone man who fell in love with long distances; he gave up his job with the telephone company and skipped the light fantastic out of town . . .

The last we heard of him was a picture postcard from Mazatlan, on the Pacific coast of Mexico, containing a message of two words: "Hello—Goodbye!" and no address.

I think the rest of the play will explain itself. . . .

[AMANDA's voice becomes audible through the portieres.]

[Legend on screen: "Ou sont les neiges?"[5]]

[TOM divides the portieres and enters the dining room. AMANDA and LAURA are seated at a drop-leaf table. Eating is indicated by gestures without food or utensils. AMANDA faces the audience. TOM and LAURA are seated in profile. The interior has lit up softly and through the scrim we see AMANDA and LAURA seated at the table.]

Amanda (calling). Tom?
Tom. Yes, Mother.
Amanda. We can't say grace until you come to the table!
Tom. Coming, Mother. (He bows slightly and withdraws, reappearing a few moments later in his place at the table.)
Amanda (to her son). Honey, don't push with your fingers. If you have to push with something, the thing to push with is a crust of bread. And chew—chew! Animals have secretions in their stomachs which enable them to digest food without mastication, but human beings are supposed to chew their food before they swallow it down. Eat food leisurely, son, and really enjoy it. A well-cooked meal has lots of delicate flavors that have to be held in the mouth for appreciation. So chew your food and give your salivary glands a chance to function!

[TOM deliberately lays his imaginary fork down and pushes his chair back from the table.]

Tom. I haven't enjoyed one bite of this dinner because of your constant directions on how to eat it. It's you that make me rush through meals with your hawk-like attention to every bite I take. Sickening—spoils my appetite—all this discussion of—animals' secretion—salivary glands—mastication!
Amanda (lightly). Temperament like a Metropolitan star!

[TOM rises and walks toward the living room.]

You're not excused from the table.
Tom. I'm getting a cigarette.
Amanda. You smoke too much.

[LAURA rises.]

Laura. I'll bring in the blanc mange.[6]

[TOM remains standing with his cigarette by the portieres.]

Amanda (rising). No, sister—you be the lady this time and I'll be the servant.
Laura. I'm already up.
Amanda. Resume your seat, little sister—I want you to stay fresh and pretty—for gentlemen callers!
Laura (sitting down). I'm not expecting any gentlemen callers.
Amanda (crossing out to the kitchenette, airily). Sometimes they come when they are least expected! Why, I remember one Sunday afternoon in Blue Mountain—

[She enters the kitchenette.]

Tom. I know what's coming!
Laura. Yes. But let her tell it.
Tom. Again?
Laura. She loves to tell it.

[AMANDA returns with a bowl of dessert.]

Amanda. One Sunday afternoon in Blue Mountain—your mother received—seventeen—gentle-

---

5. **"Ou sont les neiges"**: French, for "Where are the snows?" This is a reference to a famous line by the fifteenth-century French poet, François Villon. The complete line is a sad question about the passing of time: "But where are the snows of yesteryear?"

6. **blanc mange** (blə·mänj'): a dessert shaped in a mold.

men callers! Why, sometimes there weren't chairs enough to accommodate them all. We had to send the servant over to bring in folding chairs from the parish house.

Tom (*remaining at the portieres*). How did you entertain those gentlemen callers?

Amanda. I understood the art of conversation!

Tom. I bet you could talk.

Amanda. Girls in those days *knew* how to talk, I can tell you.

Tom. Yes?

[*Image on screen:* AMANDA *as a girl on a porch, greeting callers.*]

Amanda. They knew how to entertain their gentlemen callers. It wasn't enough for a girl to be possessed of a pretty face and a graceful figure—although I wasn't slighted in either respect. She also needed to have a nimble wit and a tongue to meet all occasions.

Tom. What did you talk about?

Amanda. Things of importance going on in the world! Never anything coarse or common or vulgar.

[*She addresses* TOM *as though he were seated in the vacant chair at the table though he remains by the portieres. He plays this scene as though reading from a script.*]

My callers were gentlemen—all! Among my callers were some of the most prominent young planters of the Mississippi Delta—planters and sons of planters!

[TOM *motions for music and a spot of light on* AMANDA. *Her eyes lift, her face glows, her voice becomes rich and elegiac.*]

[*Screen legend:* "Ou sont les neiges d'antan?"]

There was young Champ Laughlin who later became vice-president of the Delta Planters Bank. Hadley Stevenson who was drowned in Moon Lake and left his widow one hundred and fifty thousand in Government bonds. There were the Cutrere brothers, Wesly and Bates. Bates was one of my bright particular beaux! He got in a quarrel with that wild Wainwright boy. They shot it out on the floor of Moon Lake Casino. Bates was shot through the stomach. Died in the ambulance on his way to Memphis. His widow was also well provided-for, came into eight or ten thousand acres, that's all. She married him on the rebound—never loved her—carried my picture on

him the night he died! And there was that boy that every girl in the Delta had set her cap for! That beautiful, brilliant young Fitzhugh boy from Greene County!

Tom. What did he leave his widow?

Amanda. He never married! Gracious, you talk as though all of my old admirers had turned up their toes to the daisies!

Tom. Isn't this the first you've mentioned that still survives?

Amanda. That Fitzhugh boy went North and made a fortune—came to be known as the Wolf of Wall Street! He had the Midas touch, whatever he touched turned to gold! And I could have been Mrs. Duncan J. Fitzhugh, mind you! But—I picked your *father!*

Laura (*rising*). Mother, let me clear the table.

Amanda. No, dear, you go in front and study your typewriter chart. Or practice your shorthand a little. Stay fresh and pretty!—It's almost time for your gentlemen callers to start arriving. [*She flounces girlishly toward the kitchenette.*] How many do you supppose we're going to entertain this afternoon?

[TOM *throws down the paper and jumps up with a groan.*]

Laura (*alone in the dining room*). I don't believe we're going to receive any, Mother.

Amanda (*reappearing, airily*). What? No one—not one? You must be joking!

[LAURA *nervously echoes her laugh. She slips in a fugitive manner through the half-open portieres and draws them gently behind her. A shaft of very clear light is thrown on her face against the faded tapestry of the curtains. Faintly the music of "The Glass Menagerie" is heard as she continues lightly:*]

Not one gentleman caller? It can't be true! There must be a flood, there must have been a tornado!

Laura. It isn't a flood, it's not a tornado, Mother. I'm just not popular like you were in Blue Mountain. . . .

[TOM *utters another groan.* LAURA *glances at him with a faint, apologetic smile. Her voice catches a little:*]

Mother's afraid I'm going to be an old maid.

[*The scene dims out with "The Glass Menagerie" music.*]

Scene 2

On the dark stage the screen is lighted with the image of blue roses. Gradually LAURA's *figure becomes apparent and the screen goes out. The music subsides.*

LAURA *is seated in the delicate ivory chair at the small claw-foot table. She wears a dress of soft violet material for a kimono—her hair is tied back from her forehead with a ribbon. She is washing and polishing her collection of glass.* AMANDA *appears on the fire escape steps. At the sound of her ascent,* LAURA *catches her breath, thrusts the bowl of ornaments away, and seats herself stiffly before the diagram of the typewriter keyboard as though it held her spellbound. Something has happened to* AMANDA. *It is written in her face as she climbs to the landing: a look that is grim and hopeless and a little absurd. She has on one of those cheap or imitation velvety-looking cloth coats with imitation fur collar. Her hat, is five or six years old, one of those dreadful cloche[1] hats that were worn in the late Twenties, and she is clutching an enormous black patent-leather pocketbook with nickel clasps and initials. This is her full-dress outfit, the one she usually wears to the D.A.R.[2] Before entering she looks through the door. She purses her lips, opens her eyes very wide, rolls them upward and shakes her head. Then she slowly lets herself in the door. Seeing her mother's expression* LAURA *touches her lips with a nervous gesture.*

Laura. Hello, Mother, I was— *(She makes a nervous gesture toward the chart on the wall.* AMANDA *leans against the shut door and stares at* LAURA *with a martyred look.)*

Amanda. Deception? Deception? *(She slowly removes her hat and gloves, continuing the sweet suffering stare. She lets the hat and gloves fall on the floor—a bit of acting.)*

Laura *(shakily).* How was the D.A.R. meeting?

[AMANDA *slowly opens her purse and removes a dainty white handkerchief which she shakes out delicately and delicately touches to her lips and nostrils.*]

---

1. **cloche**: a close-fitting hat.
2. **D.A.R.**: Daughters of the American Revolution, a patriotic organization made up of descendants of those colonists who fought with the American patriots during the Revolutionary War.

Didn't you go to the D.A.R. meeting, Mother?

Amanda *(faintly, almost inaudibly).* —No.—No. *(then more forcibly:)* I did not have the strength— to go to the D.A.R. In fact, I did not have the courage! I wanted to find a hole in the ground and hide myself in it forever! *(She crosses slowly to the wall and removes the diagram of the typewriter keyboard. She holds it in front of her for a second, staring at it sweetly and sorrowfully—then bites her lips and tears it in two pieces.)*

Laura *(faintly).* Why did you do that, Mother?

[AMANDA *repeats the same procedure with the chart of the Gregg Alphabet.*]

Why are you—

Amanda. Why? Why? How old are you, Laura?

Laura. Mother, you know my age.

Amanda. I thought that you were an adult; it seems that I was mistaken. *(She crosses slowly to the sofa and sinks down and stares at* LAURA.*)*

Laura. Please don't stare at me, Mother.

[AMANDA *closes her eyes and lowers her head. There is a ten-second pause.*]

Amanda. What are we going to do, what is going to become of us, what is the future?

[*There is another pause.*]

Laura. Has something happened, Mother?

[AMANDA *draws a long breath, takes out the handkerchief again, goes through the dabbing process.*]

Mother, has—something happened?

Amanda. I'll be all right in a minute. I'm just bewildered—*(She hesitates.)*—by life. . . .

Laura. Mother, I wish that you would tell me what's happened!

Amanda. As you know, I was supposed to be inducted into my office at the D.A.R. this afternoon.

[*Screen image:* A swarm of typewriters.]

But I stopped off at Rubicam's Business College to speak to your teachers about your having a cold and ask them what progress they thought you were making down there.

Laura. Oh. . . .

Amanda. I went to the typing instructor and introduced myself as your mother. She didn't know who you were. "Wingfield," she said, "We don't have any such student enrolled at the school!" I assured her she did, that you had been going to classes since early in January. "I wonder," she said, "If you could be talking about that terribly shy little girl who dropped out of school after only a few days' attendance?" "No," I said, "Laura, my daughter, has been going to school every day for the past six weeks!" "Excuse me," she said. She took the attendance book out and there was your name, unmistakably printed, and all the dates you were absent until they decided that you had dropped out of school. I still said, "No, there must have been some mistake! There must have been some mix-up in the records!" And she said, "No—I remember her perfectly now. Her hands shook so that she couldn't hit the right keys! The first time we gave a speed test, she broke down completely—was sick at the stomach and almost had to be carried into the wash room! After that morning she never showed up any more. We phoned the house but never got any answer"— While I was working at Famous-Barr, I suppose, demonstrating those—

[*She indicates a brassiere with her hands*.]

Oh! I felt so weak I could barely keep on my feet! I had to sit down while they got me a glass of water! Fifty dollars' tuition, all of our plans—my hopes and ambitions for you—just gone up the spout, just gone up the spout like that.

[LAURA *draws a long breath and gets awkwardly to her feet. She crosses to the victrola*[3] *and winds it up*.]

What are you doing?
Laura. Oh! (*She releases the handle and returns to her seat.*)
Amanda. Laura, where have you been going when you've gone out pretending that you were going to business college?
Laura. I've just been going out walking.
Amanda. That's not true.
Laura. It is. I just went walking.
Amanda. Walking? Walking? In winter? Deliberately courting pneumonia in that light coat? Where did you walk to, Laura?
Laura. All sorts of places—mostly in the park.
Amanda. Even after you'd started catching that cold?
Laura. It was the lesser of two evils, Mother.

[*Screen image:* Winter scene in a park.]

---

3. **victrola:** record player.

I couldn't go back there. I—threw up—on the floor!
Amanda. From half past seven till after five every day you mean to tell me you walked around in the park, because you wanted to make me think that you were still going to Rubicam's Business College?
Laura. It wasn't as bad as it sounds. I went inside places to get warmed up.
Amanda. Inside where?
Laura. I went in the art museum and the bird houses at the Zoo. I visited the penguins every day! Sometimes I did without lunch and went to the movies. Lately I've been spending most of my afternoons in the Jewel Box, that big glass house where they raise the tropical flowers.
Amanda. You did all this to deceive me, just for deception?

[LAURA *looks down*.] Why?

Laura. Mother, when you're disappointed, you get that awful suffering look on your face, like the picture of Jesus' mother in the museum!
Amanda. Hush!
Laura. I couldn't face it.

[*There is a pause. A whisper of strings is heard. Legend on screen:* "The Crust of Humility."]

Amanda (*hopelessly fingering the huge pocketbook*). So what are we going to do the rest of our lives? Stay home and watch the parades go by? Amuse ourselves with the glass menagerie, darling? Eternally play those worn-out phonograph records your father left as a painful reminder of him? We won't have a business career—we've given that up because it gave us nervous indigestion! (*She laughs wearily.*) What is there left but dependency all our lives? I know so well what becomes of unmarried women who aren't prepared to occupy a position. I've seen such pitiful cases in the South—barely tolerated spinsters living upon the grudging patronage of sister's husband or brother's wife—stuck away in some little mousetrap of a room—encouraged by one in-law to visit another—little birdlike women without any nest—eating the crust of humility all their life!

Is that the future that we've mapped out for ourselves? I swear it's the only alternative I can think of! (*She pauses.*) It isn't a very pleasant alternative, is it? (*She pauses again.*) Of course—some girls *do marry*.

"He used to call me—Blue Roses."

[LAURA *twists her hands nervously.*]

Haven't you ever liked some boy?

Laura. Yes. I liked one once. *(She rises.)* I came across his picture a while ago.

Amanda *(with some interest).* He gave you his picture?

Laura. No, it's in the yearbook.

Amanda *(disappointed).* Oh—a high school boy.

[*Screen image:* Jim as the high school hero bearing a silver cup.]

Laura. Yes. His name was Jim. *(She lifts the heavy annual from the claw-foot table.)* Here he is in *The Pirates of Penzance*.[4]

Amanda *(absently).* The what?

---

4. *The Pirates of Penzance*: a comic operetta by Gilbert and Sullivan.

Laura. The operetta the senior class put on. He had a wonderful voice and we sat across the aisle from each other Mondays, Wednesdays, and Fridays in the Aud. Here he is with the silver cup for debating! See his grin?

Amanda (*absently*). He must have a jolly disposition.

Laura. He used to call me—Blue Roses.

[*Screen image:* Blue Roses.]

Amanda. Why did he call you such a name as that?

Laura. When I had that attack of pleurosis[5]—he asked me what was the matter when I came back. I said pleurosis—he thought that I said Blue Roses! So that's what he always called me after that. Whenever he saw me, he'd holler, "Hello, Blue Roses!" I didn't care for the girl that he went out with. Emily Meisenbach. Emily was the best-dressed girl at Soldan. She never struck me, though, as being sincere . . . It says in the Personal Section—they're engaged. That's—six years ago! They must be married by now.

Amanda. Girls that aren't cut out for business careers usually wind up married to some nice man. (*She gets up with a spark of revival.*) Sister, that's what you'll do!

[LAURA *utters a startled, doubtful laugh. She reaches quickly for a piece of glass.*]

Laura. But, Mother—

Amanda. Yes? (*She goes over to the photograph.*)

Laura (*in a tone of frightened apology*). I'm—crippled!

Amanda. Nonsense! Laura, I've told you never, never to use that word. Why, you're not crippled, you just have a little defect—hardly noticeable, even! When people have some slight disadvantage like that, they cultivate other things to make up for it—develop charm—and vivacity—and—*charm!* That's all you have to do! (*She turns again to the photograph.*) One thing your father had *plenty* of—was *charm!*

[*The scene fades out with music.*]

---

5. **pleurosis:** Laura means pleurisy, a lung infection.

Responding to the Play

Analyzing Scenes 1 and 2

Identifying Facts

1. Tom's opening speech sketches the social background of the play and introduces the main characters. What basic information does Tom provide in this speech about his family? About the gentleman caller? About the nature of the play itself?

2. In Scene 1, how do we know that there is tension among the family members? Who seems to cause the tension?

3. A play is put in motion by some element that upsets the situation at the beginning of the story. The new element here arrives in Scene 2. What is it? How does it upset the opening situation, and how does it set the play in motion?

4. In Scene 2, what does Laura say and do to reveal that she is "set apart" from the real world?

5. What is the significance of the "blue roses" that appear on the screen at the start of Scene 2?

Interpreting Meanings

6. At this point in the play, does Amanda seem to be a weak or a strong character? Does she arouse your sympathy, or do you think Williams wants you to dislike her? Explain.

7. How do we know that the boy in the yearbook was important to Laura? Why doesn't Amanda seem particularly interested in this young man?

8. In *The Glass Menagerie*, Tennessee Williams has created "theater poetry" by using various arts besides language. For example, he uses the two transparencies at the beginning of the play to enhance the idea that this is a memory play. Check through the stage directions and dialogue to find other uses of visual and sound effects which, combined with words, help to create "theater poetry." Do any of these effects add a touch of humor to the play?

9. Few people have Laura's specific physical handicap. Do you think most people can identify with her? Why or why not?

Scene 3

Legend on screen: "After the fiasco—"

TOM *speaks from the fire escape landing.*

Tom. After the fiasco at Rubicam's Business College, the idea of getting a gentleman caller for Laura began to play a more and more important part in Mother's calculations. It became an obsession. Like some archetype of the universal unconscious,[1] the image of the gentleman caller haunted our small apartment. . . .

[*Screen image:* A young man at the door of a house with flowers.]

An evening at home rarely passed without some allusion to this image, this specter, this hope. . . . Even when he wasn't mentioned, his presence hung in Mother's preoccupied look and in my sister's frightened, apologetic manner—hung like a sentence passed upon the Wingfields!

Mother was a woman of action as well as words. She began to take logical steps in the planned direction. Late that winter and in the early spring—realizing that extra money would be needed to properly feather the nest and plume the bird—she conducted a vigorous campaign on the telephone, roping in subscribers to one of those magazines for matrons called *The Homemaker's Companion,* the type of journal that features the serialized sublimations of ladies of letters who think in terms of delicate cuplike breasts, slim, tapering waists, rich, creamy thighs, eyes like wood smoke in autumn, fingers that soothe and caress like strains of music, bodies as powerful as Etruscan sculpture.

[*Screen image:* The cover of a glamor magazine.]

[AMANDA *enters with the telephone on a long extension cord. She is spotlighted in the dim stage.*]

Amanda. Ida Scott? This is Amanda Wingfield! We *missed* you at the D.A.R. last Monday! I said to myself: She's probably suffering with that sinus condition! How is that sinus condition? Horrors! Heaven have a mercy!—You're a Christian martyr, yes, that's what you are, a Christian martyr! Well, I just now happened to notice that your subscription to the *Companion's* about to expire! Yes, it expires with the next issue, honey!—just when that wonderful new serial by Bessie Mae Hopper is getting off to such an exciting start. Oh, honey, it's something that you can't miss! You remember how *Gone with the Wind* took everybody by storm? You simply couldn't go out if you hadn't read it. All everybody *talked* was Scarlett O'Hara. Well, this is a book that critics already compare to *Gone with the Wind.* It's the *Gone with the Wind* of the post-World-War generation!—What?—Burning?—Oh, honey, don't let them burn, go take a look in the oven and I'll hold the wire! Heavens—I think she's hung up!

[*The scene dims out.*]

[*Legend on screen:* "You think I'm in love with Continental Shoemakers?"]

[*Before the lights come up again, the violent voices of* TOM *and* AMANDA *are heard. They are quarreling behind the portieres. In front of them stands* LAURA *with clenched hands and panicky expression. A clear pool of light is on her figure throughout this scene.*]

Tom. What in hell am I—
Amanda *(shrilly).* Don't you use that—
Tom. —supposed to do!
Amanda. —expression! Not in my—
Tom. Ohhh!
Amanda. —presence! Have you gone out of your senses?
Tom. I have, that's true, *driven* out!
Amanda. What is the matter with you, you—big—big—IDIOT!
Tom. Look!—I've got *no thing,* no single thing—
Amanda. Lower your voice!
Tom. —in my life here that I can call my OWN! Everything is—
Amanda. Stop that shouting!
Tom. Yesterday you confiscated my books! You had the nerve to—
Amanda. I took that horrible novel back to the library—yes! That hideous book by that insane Mr. Lawrence.[2]

---

1. **archetype of the universal unconscious**: an image common to all people, one that has persisted in the human unconscious down through the ages.

2. **Mr. Lawrence**: D. H. Lawrence (1885–1930), an English novelist and poet, whose writing was once considered shockingly sexual.

[TOM *laughs wildly*.]

I cannot control the output of diseased minds or people who cater to them—

[TOM *laughs still more wildly*.]

BUT I WON'T ALLOW SUCH FILTH BROUGHT INTO MY HOUSE! No, no, no, no, no!
Tom. House, house! Who pays rent on it, who makes a slave of himself to—
Amanda *(fairly screeching)*. Don't you DARE to—
Tom. No, no, *I* mustn't say things! *I've* got to just—
Amanda. Let me tell you—
Tom. I don't want to hear any more!

[*He tears the portieres open. The dining-room area is lit with a turgid smoky red glow. Now we see* AMANDA; *her hair is in metal curlers and she is wearing a very old bathrobe, much too large for her slight figure, a relic of the faithless* MR. WINGFIELD. *The upright typewriter now stands on the drop-leaf table, along with a wild disarray of manuscripts. The quarrel was probably precipitated by* AMANDA's *interruption of* TOM's *creative labor. A chair lies overthrown on the floor. Their gesticulating shadows are cast on the ceiling by the fiery glow.*]

Amanda. You *will* hear more, you—
Tom. No, I won't hear more, I'm going out!
Amanda. You come right back in—
Tom. Out, out, out! Because I'm—
Amanda. Come back here, Tom Wingfield! I'm not through talking to you!
Tom. Oh, go—
Laura *(desperately)*. Tom!
Amanda. You're going to listen, and no more insolence from you! I'm at the end of my patience!

[*He comes back toward her.*]

Tom. What do you think I'm at? Aren't I supposed to have any patience to reach the end of, Mother? I know, I know. It seems unimportant to you, what I'm *doing*—what I *want* to do—having a little *difference* between them! You don't think that—
Amanda. I think you've been doing things that you're ashamed of. That's why you act like this. I don't believe that you go every night to the movies. Nobody goes to the movies night after night. Nobody in their right minds goes to the movies as often as you pretend to. People don't go to the movies at nearly midnight, and movies don't let out at two A.M. Come in stumbling. Muttering to yourself like a maniac! You get three hours' sleep and then go to work. Oh, I can picture the way you're doing down there. Moping, doping, because you're in no condition.
Tom *(wildly)*. No, I'm in no condition!
Amanda. What right have you got to jeopardize your job? Jeopardize the security of us all? How do you think we'd manage if you were—
Tom. Listen! You think I'm crazy about the *warehouse*? (*He bends fiercely toward her slight figure.*) You think I'm in love with the Continental Shoemakers? You think I want to spend fifty-five *years* down there in that—*celotex interior!* with—fluorescent—*tubes!* Look! I'd rather somebody picked up a crowbar and battered out my brains—than go back mornings! I *go!* Every time you come in yelling that damn *"Rise and Shine!" "Rise and Shine!"* I say to myself, "How *lucky dead* people are!" But I get up. I *go!* For sixty-five dollars a month I give up all that I dream of doing and being *ever!* and you say self—*self's* all I ever think of. Why, listen, if self is what I thought of, Mother, I'd be where he is—GONE! (*He points to his father's picture.*) As far as the system of transportation reaches! (*He starts past her. She grabs his arm.*) Don't grab at me, Mother!
Amanda. Where are you going?
Tom. I'm going to the *movies!*
Amanda. I don't believe that lie!

[TOM *crouches toward her, overtowering her tiny figure. She backs away, gasping*.]

Tom. I'm going to opium dens! Yes, opium dens, dens of vice and criminals' hangouts, Mother. I've joined the Hogan Gang, I'm a hired assassin, I carry a tommy gun in a violin case! I run a string of cat houses in the Valley! They call me Killer, Killer Wingfield, I'm leading a double-life, a simple, honest warehouse worker by day, by night a dynamic *czar* of the *underworld, Mother.* I go to gambling casinos, I spin away fortunes on the roulette table! I wear a patch over one eye and a false mustache, sometimes I put on green whiskers. On those occasions they call me—*El Diablo!* Oh, I could tell you many things to make you sleepless! My enemies plan to dynamite this place. They're going to blow us all sky-high some night! I'll be glad, very happy, and so will you! You'll go up, up on a broomstick, over Blue Mountain with seventeen gentlemen callers! You ugly—babbling old—*witch.* . . . *(He goes through a series of violent, clumsy movements, seizing his overcoat, lunging to the door, pulling it fiercely open. The women watch him, aghast. His arm catches in the sleeve of the coat as he struggles to pull it on. For a moment he is pinioned by the bulky garment. With an outraged groan he tears the coat off again, splitting the shoulder of it, and hurls it across the room. It strikes against the shelf of Laura's glass collection, and there is a tinkle of shattering glass. Laura cries out as if wounded.)*

[*Music.*]

[*Screen legend:* "The Glass Menagerie."]

Laura *(shrilly). My glass!*—menagerie. . . . *(She covers her face and turns away.)*

[*But* AMANDA *is still stunned and stupefied by the "ugly witch" so that she barely notices this occurrence. Now she recovers her speech.*]

Amanda *(in an awful voice).* I won't speak to you—until you apologize!

[*She crosses through the portieres and draws them together behind her.* TOM *is left with* LAURA. LAURA *clings weakly to the mantel with her face averted.* TOM *stares at her stupidly for a moment. Then he crosses to the shelf. He drops awkwardly on his knees to collect the fallen glass, glancing at* LAURA *as if he would speak but couldn't.*]

["The Glass Menagerie" *music steals in as the scene dims out.*]

"*You ugly—babbling old—witch . . .*"

Scene 4

The interior of the apartment is dark. There is a faint light in the alley. A deep-voiced bell in a church is tolling the hour of five.

TOM *appears at the top of the alley. After each solemn boom of the bell in the tower, he shakes a little noisemaker or rattle as if to express the tiny spasm of man in contrast to the sustained power and dignity of the Almighty. This and the unsteadiness of his advance make it evident that he has been drinking. As he climbs the few steps to the fire escape landing light steals up inside.* LAURA *appears in the front room in a nightdress. She notices that* TOM's *bed is empty.* TOM *fishes in his pockets for his door key, removes a motley assortment of articles in the search, including a shower of movie ticket stubs and an empty bottle. At last he finds the key, but just as he is about to insert it, it slips from his fingers. He strikes a match and crouches below the door.*

Tom (bitterly). One crack—and it falls through!

[LAURA *opens the door.*]

Laura. Tom! Tom, what are you doing?
Tom. Looking for a door key.
Laura. Where have you been all this time?
Tom. I have been to the movies.
Laura. All this time at the movies?
Tom. There was a very long program. There was a Garbo picture and a Mickey Mouse and a travelogue and a newsreel and a preview of coming attractions. And there was an organ solo and a collection for the Milk Fund—simultaneously—which ended up in a terrible fight between a fat lady and an usher!
Laura (innocently). Did you have to stay through everything?
Tom. Of course! And, oh, I forgot! There was a big stage show! The headliner on this stage show was Malvolio the Magician. He performed wonderful tricks, many of them, such as pouring water back and forth between pitchers. First it turned to wine and then it turned to beer and then it turned to whisky. I know it was whisky it finally turned into because he needed somebody to come up out of the audience to help him, and I came up—both shows! It was Kentucky Straight Bourbon. A very generous fellow, he gave souvenirs. (*He pulls from his back pocket a shimmering rainbow-colored scarf.*) He gave me this. This is his

magic scarf. You can have it, Laura. You wave it over a canary cage and you get a bowl of goldfish. You wave it over the goldfish bowl and they fly away canaries. . . . But the wonderfullest trick of all was the coffin trick. We nailed him into a coffin and he got out of the coffin without removing one nail. (*He has come inside.*) There is a trick that would come in handy for me—get me out of this two-by-four situation! (*He flops onto the bed and starts removing his shoes.*)
Laura. Tom—shhh!
Tom. What're you shushing me for?
Laura. You'll wake up Mother.
Tom. Goody, goody! Pay 'er back for all those "Rise an' Shines." (*He lies down, groaning.*) You know it don't take much intelligence to get yourself into a nailed-up coffin, Laura. But who ever got himself out of one without removing one nail?

(*As if in answer, the father's grinning photograph lights up. The scene dims out.*)

[*Immediately following, the church bell is heard striking six. At the sixth stroke the alarm clock goes off in* AMANDA's *room, and after a few moments we hear her calling: "Rise and Shine! Rise and Shine!* LAURA, *go tell your brother to rise and shine!"*]

Tom (sitting up slowly). I'll rise—but I won't shine.

[*The light increases.*]

Amanda. Laura, tell your brother his coffee is ready.

[LAURA *slips into the front room.*]

Laura. Tom!—It's nearly seven. Don't make Mother nervous.

[*He stares at her stupidly.*]

(Beseechingly). Tom, speak to Mother this morning. Make up with her, apologize, speak to her!
Tom. She won't to me. It's her that started not speaking.
Laura. If you just say you're sorry she'll start speaking.
Tom. Her not speaking—is that such a tragedy?
Laura. Please—please!
Amanda (calling from the kitchenette). Laura, are you going to do what I asked you to do, or do I have to get dressed and go out myself?

Laura. Going, going—soon as I get on my coat!

[*She pulls on a shapeless felt hat with a nervous, jerky movement, pleadingly glancing at* TOM. *She rushes awkwardly for her coat. The coat is one of* AMANDA'*s, inaccurately made-over, the sleeves too short for* LAURA.]

Butter and what else?

Amanda (*entering from the kitchenette*). Just butter. Tell them to charge it.

Laura. Mother, they make such faces when I do that.

Amanda. Sticks and stones can break our bones, but the expression on Mr. Garfinkel's face won't harm us! Tell your brother his coffee is getting cold.

Laura (*at the door*). Do what I asked you, will you, will you, Tom?

[*He looks sullenly away.*]

Amanda. Laura, go now or just don't go at all!

Laura (*rushing out*). Going—going!

[*A second later she cries out.* TOM *springs up and crosses to the door.* TOM *opens the door.*]

Tom. Laura?

Laura. I'm all right. I slipped, but I'm all right.

Amanda (*peering anxiously after her*). If anyone breaks a leg on those fire-escape steps, the landlord ought to be sued for every cent he possesses! (*She shuts the door. Now she remembers she isn't speaking to* TOM *and returns to the other room.*)

[*As* TOM *comes listlessly for his coffee, she turns her back to him and stands rigidly facing the window on the gloomy gray vault of the areaway. Its light on her face with its aged but childish features is cruelly sharp, satirical as a Daumier[1] print.*]

[*The music of "Ave Maria," is heard softly.*]

[TOM *glances sheepishly but sullenly at her averted figure and slumps at the table. The coffee is scalding hot; he sips it and gasps and spits it back in the cup. At his gasp,* AMANDA *catches her breath and half turns. Then she catches herself and turns back to the window.* TOM *blows on his coffee, glancing sidewise at his mother. She clears her throat.* TOM *clears his. He starts to rise, sinks back down again, scratches his head, clears his throat again.* AMANDA *coughs.* TOM *raises his cup in both hands to blow on it, his eyes staring over the rim of it at his mother for several moments. Then he slowly sets the cup down and awkwardly and hesitantly rises from the chair.*]

Tom (*hoarsely*). Mother. I—I apologize, Mother.

[AMANDA *draws a quick, shuddering breath. Her face works grotesquely. She breaks into childlike tears.*]

I'm sorry for what I said, for everything that I said, I didn't mean it.

Amanda (*sobbingly*). My devotion has made me a witch and so I make myself hateful to my children!

Tom. *No,* you *don't.*

Amanda. I worry so much, don't sleep, it makes me nervous!

Tom (*gently*). I understand that.

Amanda. I've had to put up a solitary battle all these years. But you're my right-hand bower![2] Don't fall down, don't fail!

Tom (*gently*). I try, Mother.

Amanda (*with great enthusiasm*). Try and you will *succeed!* (*The notion makes her breathless.*) Why, you—you're just *full* of natural endowments! Both of my children—they're *unusual* children! Don't you think I know it? I'm so—*proud!* Happy and—feel I've—so much to be thankful for but—promise me one thing, son!

Tom. What, Mother?

Amanda. Promise, son, you'll—never be a drunkard!

Tom (*turns to her grinning*). I will never be a drunkard, Mother.

Amanda. That's what frightened me so, that you'd be drinking! Eat a bowl of Purina!

Tom. Just coffee, Mother.

Amanda. Shredded wheat biscuit?

Tom. No. No, Mother, just coffee.

Amanda. You can't put in a day's work on an empty stomach. You've got ten minutes—don't gulp! Drinking too-hot liquids makes cancer of the stomach. . . . Put cream in.

Tom. No, thank you.

Amanda. To cool it.

Tom. No! No, thank you, I want it black.

Amanda. I know, but it's not good for you. We have to do all that we can to build ourselves up.

---

1. **Daumier** (dō·myā′): Honoré Daumier (1809–1879), a French artist and caricaturist.

2. **bower:** in certain card games, the two highest cards. The jack of trumps is the right bower, therefore the main support.

In these trying times we live in, all that we have to cling to is—each other. . . . That's why it's so important to—Tom, I—I sent out your sister so I could discuss something with you. If you hadn't spoken I would have spoken to you. (*She sits down.*)

Tom (*gently*). What is it, Mother, that you want to discuss?

Amanda. *Laura!*

[TOM *puts his cup down slowly.*]

[*Legend on screen:* "Laura." *Music:* "*The Glass Menagerie.*"]

Tom. —Oh.—Laura . . .

Amanda (*touching his sleeve*). You know how Laura is. So quiet but—still water runs deep! She notices things and I think she—broods about them.

[TOM *looks up.*]

A few days ago I came in and she was crying.

Tom. What about?

Amanda. You.

Tom. Me?

Amanda. She has an idea that you're not happy here.

Tom. What gave her that idea?

Amanda. What gives her any idea? However, you do act strangely. I—I'm not criticizing, understand *that!* I know your ambitions do not lie in the warehouse, that like everybody in the whole wide world—you've had to—make sacrifices, but—Tom—Tom—life's not easy, it calls for—Spartan endurance! There's so many things in my heart that I cannot describe to you! I've never told you but I—*loved* your father. . . .

Tom (*gently*). I know that, Mother.

Amanda. And you—when I see you taking after his ways! Staying out late—and—well, you *had* been drinking the night you were in that—terrifying condition! Laura says that you hate the apartment and that you go out nights to get away from it! Is that true, Tom?

Tom. No. You say there's so much in your heart that you can't describe to me. That's true of me, too. There's so much in my heart that I can't describe to *you!* So let's respect each other's—

Amanda. But, why—*why,* Tom—are you always so *restless?* Where do you *go* to, nights?

Tom. I—go to the movies.

Amanda. Why do you go to the movies so much, Tom?

Tom. I go to the movies because—I like adventure. Adventure is something I don't have much of at work, so I go to the movies.

Amanda. But, Tom, you go to the movies *entirely* too *much!*

Tom. I like a lot of adventure.

[AMANDA *looks baffled, then hurt. As the familiar inquisition resumes,* TOM *becomes hard and impatient again.* AMANDA *slips back into her querulous attitude toward him.*]

[*Image on screen:* A sailing vessel with Jolly Roger.]

Amanda. Most young men find adventure in their careers.

Tom. Then most young men are not employed in a warehouse.

Amanda. The world is full of young men employed in warehouses and offices and factories.

Tom. Do all of them find adventure in their careers?

Amanda. They do or they do without it! Not everybody has a craze for adventure.

Tom. Man is by instinct a lover, a hunter, a fighter, and none of those instincts are given much play at the warehouse!

Amanda. Man is by instinct! Don't quote instinct to me! Instinct is something that people have got away from! It belongs to animals! Christian adults don't want it!

Tom. What do Christian adults want, then, Mother?

Amanda. Superior things! Things of the mind and the spirit! Only animals have to satisfy instincts! Surely your aims are somewhat higher than theirs! Than monkeys—pigs—

Tom. I reckon they're not.

Amanda. You're joking. However, that isn't what I wanted to discuss.

Tom (*rising*). I haven't much time.

Amanda (*pushing his shoulders*). Sit down.

Tom. You want me to punch in red at the warehouse, Mother?

Amanda. You have five minutes. I want to talk about Laura.

[*Screen legend:* "Plans and Provisions."]

Tom. All right! What about Laura?

Amanda. We have to be making some plans and provisions for her. She's older than you, two years, and nothing has happened. She just drifts

"Down at the warehouse, aren't there some—nice young men?"

along doing nothing. It frightens me terribly how she just drifts along.

Tom. I guess she's the type that people call home girls.

Amanda. There's no such type, and if there is, it's a pity! That is unless the home is hers, with a husband!

Tom. What?

Amanda. Oh, I can see the handwriting on the wall as plain as I see the nose in front of my face! It's terrifying! More and more you remind me of your father! He was out all hours without explanation—Then *left! Goodbye!* And me with the bag to hold. I saw that letter you got from the Merchant Marine. I know what you're dreaming of. I'm not standing here blindfolded. *(She pauses.)* Very well, then. Then *do* it! But not till there's somebody to take your place.

Tom. What do you mean?

Amanda. I mean that as soon as Laura has got somebody to take care of her, married, a home of her own, independent—why, then you'll be free to go wherever you please, on land, on sea, whichever way the wind blows you! But until that time you've got to look out for your sister. I don't say me because I'm old and don't matter! I say for your sister because she's young and dependent.

I put her in business college—a dismal failure! Frightened her so it made her sick at the stomach. I took her over to the Young People's League at the church. Another fiasco. She spoke to nobody, nobody spoke to her. Now all she does is fool with

those pieces of glass and play those worn-out records. What kind of a life is that for a girl to lead?
Tom. What can I do about it?
Amanda. Overcome selfishness! Self, self, self is all that you ever think of!

[TOM *springs up and crosses to get his coat. It is ugly and bulky. He pulls on a cap with earmuffs.*]

Where is your muffler? Put your wool muffler on!

[*He snatches it angrily from the closet, tosses it around his neck and pulls both ends tight.*]

Tom! I haven't said what I had in mind to ask you.
Tom. I'm too late to—
Amanda (*catching his arm—very importunately; then shyly*). Down at the warehouse, aren't there some—nice young men?
Tom. No!
Amanda. There *must* be—*some* . . .
Tom. Mother—(*He gestures.*)
Amanda. Find out one that's clean-living—doesn't drink and ask him out for sister!
Tom. What?
Amanda. For *sister!* To *meet!* Get *acquainted!*
Tom (*stamping to the door*). Oh, my *go-osh!*
Amanda. Will you?

[*He opens the door. She says, imploringly:*]

Will you?

[*He starts down the fire escape.*]

Will you? *Will* you dear?
Tom (*calling back*). Yes!

[AMANDA *closes the door hesitantly and with a troubled but faintly hopeful expression.*]

[*Screen image:* The cover of a glamor magazine.]

[*The spotlight picks up* AMANDA *at the phone.*]

Amanda. Ella Cartwright? This is Amanda Wingfield! How are you, honey? How is that kidney condition?

[*There is a five-second pause.*]

Horrors!

[*There is another pause.*]

You're a Christian martyr, yes, honey, that's what you are, a Christian martyr! Well, I just now happened to notice in my little red book that your subscription to the *Companion* has just run out! I knew that you wouldn't want to miss out on the wonderful serial starting in this new issue. It's by Bessie Mae Hopper, the first thing she's written since *Honeymoon for Three*. Wasn't that a strange and interesting story? Well, this one is even lovelier, I believe. It has a sophisticated, society background. It's all about the horsey set on Long Island!

[*The light fades out.*]

Responding to the Play

Analyzing Scenes 3 and 4

Identifying Facts

1. In Scene 2, we saw that Amanda was in **conflict** with Laura. Who is in conflict in Scene 3? What starts the conflict, and what is it about?
2. Each of the Wingfields escapes from unpleasant reality into a comforting, private world. In Scene 1, Amanda escapes from her present circumstances by remembering and talking about her past youth, her beauty, and her romantic successes. How does Laura escape the real world? What does Tom do to escape from his unhappiness?
3. What part does Laura play in the angry argument between Tom and Amanda?
4. What does Amanda ask Tom to do?

Interpreting Meanings

5. In the conflict between Tom and Amanda in Scene 3, which character do you sympathize with, and why? What does Williams want us to feel about Amanda?
6. How is Laura's relationship with Tom different from her relationship with Amanda? How can we tell that Tom is truly fond of Laura?
7. Amanda often refers to her absent husband, and his grinning picture is highlighted at various points during the play. What does the photograph represent to Amanda? To Tom? How is the photo a constant threat to Amanda and Laura's survival?
8. The outburst of anger that ends Scene 3 marks the emotional peak of the play so far. How has the playwright prepared us for Tom's anger and Amanda's accusations?

Scene 5

Legend on the screen: "Annunciation."

Music is heard as the light slowly comes on.

It is early dusk of a spring evening. Supper has just been finished in the Wingfield apartment. AMANDA *and* LAURA, *in light-colored dresses, are removing dishes from the table in the dining room, which is shadowy, their movements formalized almost as a dance or ritual, their moving forms as pale and silent as moths.* TOM, *in white shirt and trousers, rises from the table and crosses toward the fire escape.*

Amanda (*as he passes her*). Son, will you do me a favor?

Tom. What?

Amanda. Comb your hair! You look so pretty when you hair is combed!

[TOM *slouches on the sofa with the evening paper. Its enormous headline reads: "Franco[1] Triumphs."*]

There is only one respect in which I would like you to emulate your father.

Tom. What respect is that?

Amanda. The care he always took of his appearance. He never allowed himself to look untidy.

[*He throws down the paper and crosses to the fire escape.*]

Where are you going?

Tom. I'm going out to smoke.

Amanda. You smoke too much. A pack a day at fifteen cents a pack. How much would that amount to in a month? Thirty times fifteen is how much, Tom? Figure it out and you will be astounded at what you could save. Enough to give you a night-school course in accounting at Washington U.! Just think what a wonderful thing that would be for you, son!

[TOM *is unmoved by the thought.*]

Tom. I'd rather smoke. (*He steps out on the landing, letting the screen door slam.*)

Amanda (*sharply*). I know! That's the tragedy of it. . . . (*Alone, she turns to look at her husband's picture.*)

[*Dance music: "The World Is Waiting for the Sunrise!"*]

Tom (*to the audience*). Across the alley from us was the Paradise Dance Hall. On evenings in Spring the windows and doors were open and the music came outdoors. Sometimes the lights were turned out except for a large glass sphere that hung from the ceiling. It would turn slowly about and filter the dusk with delicate rainbow colors. Then the orchestra played a waltz or a tango, something that had a slow and sensuous rhythm. Couples would come outside, to the relative privacy of the alley. You could see them kissing behind ash pits and telephone poles. This was the compensation for lives that passed like mine, without any change or adventure. Adventure and change were imminent in this year. They were waiting around the corner for all these kids. Suspended in the mist over Berchtesgaden,[2] caught in the folds of Chamberlain's umbrella. In Spain there was Guernica![3] But here there was only hot swing music and liquor, dance halls, bars, and movies, and sex that hung in the gloom like a chandelier and flooded the world with brief, deceptive rainbows. . . . All the world was waiting for bombardments!

[AMANDA *turns from the picture and comes outside.*]

Amanda (*sighing*). A fire escape landing's a poor excuse for a porch. (*She spreads a newspaper on a step and sits down, gracefully and demurely as if she were settling into a swing on a Mississippi veranda.*) What are you looking at?

Tom. The moon.

Amanda. Is there a moon this evening?

Tom. It's rising over Garfinkel's Delicatessen.

Amanda. So it is! A little silver slipper of a moon. Have you made a wish on it yet?

Tom. Um-hum.

---

1. **Franco:** General Francisco Franco, who led the rebel army in the Spanish Civil War and later became Fascist dictator of Spain.

2. **Berchtesgaden . . . Chamberlain's umbrella:** Neville Chamberlain, Britain's Prime Minister, always carried a large, black umbrella. He visited Adolf Hitler at his mountain retreat at Berchtesgaden, Germany, in 1938. At this meeting, the two statesmen agreed that Hitler would be given Czechoslovakia in exchange for a promise not to invade any more countries in Europe—a pledge that Hitler did not keep.

3. **Guernica** (ger·nē′kə): a small town in northern Spain which was fire-bombed by the Fascists during the Spanish Civil War.

Amanda. What did you wish for?

Tom. That's a secret.

Amanda. A secret, huh? Well, I won't tell mine either. I will be just as mysterious as you.

Tom. I bet I can guess what yours is.

Amanda. Is my head so transparent?

Tom. You're not a sphinx.

Amanda. No, I don't have secrets. I'll tell you what I wished for on the moon. Success and happiness for my precious children! I wish for that whenever there's a moon, and when there isn't a moon, I wish for it, too.

Tom. I thought perhaps you wished for a gentleman caller.

Amanda. Why do you say that?

Tom. Don't you remember asking me to fetch one?

Amanda. I remember suggesting that it would be nice for your sister if you brought home some nice young man from the warehouse. I think that I've made that suggestion more than once.

Tom. Yes, you have made it repeatedly.

Amanda. Well?

Tom. We are going to have one.

Amanda. *What?*

Tom. A gentleman caller!

[*The annunciation is celebrated with music.*]

[AMANDA *rises.*]

[*Image on screen:* A caller with a bouquet.]

Amanda. You mean you have asked some nice young man to come over?

Tom. Yep. I've asked him to dinner.

Amanda. You really did?

Tom. I did!

Amanda. You did, and did he—*accept?*

Tom. He did!

Amanda. Well, well—well, well! That's—lovely!

Tom. I thought that you would be pleased.

Amanda. It's definite then?

Tom. Very definite.

Amanda. Soon?

Tom. Very soon.

Amanda. For heaven's sake, stop putting on and tell me some things, will you?

Tom. What things do you want me to tell you?

Amanda. *Naturally* I would like to know when he's *coming!*

Tom. He's coming tomorrow.

Amanda. *Tomorrow?*

Tom. Yep. Tomorrow.

Amanda. But, Tom!

Tom. Yes, Mother?

Amanda. Tomorrow gives me no time!

Tom. Time for what?

Amanda. Preparations! Why didn't you phone me at once, as soon as you asked him, the minute that he accepted? Then, don't you see, I could have been getting ready!

Tom. You don't have to make any fuss.

Amanda. Oh, Tom, Tom, Tom, of course I have to make a fuss! I want things nice, not sloppy! Not thrown together. I'll certainly have to do some fast thinking, won't I?

Tom. I don't see why you have to think at all.

Amanda. You just don't know. We can't have a gentleman caller in a pigsty! All my wedding silver has to be polished, the monogrammed table linen ought to be laundered! The windows have to be washed and fresh curtains put up. And how about clothes? We have to *wear* something, don't we?

Tom. Mother, this boy is no one to make a fuss over!

Amanda. Do you realize he's the first young man we've introduced to your sister? It's terrible, dreadful, disgraceful that poor little sister has never received a single gentleman caller! Tom, come inside! (*She opens the screen door.*)

Tom. What for?

Amanda. I want to ask you some things.

Tom. If you're going to make such a fuss, I'll call it off, I'll tell him not to come!

Amanda. You certainly won't do anything of the kind. Nothing offends people worse than broken engagements. It simply means I'll have to work like a Turk! We won't be brilliant, but we will pass inspection. Come on inside.

[TOM *follows her inside, groaning.*]

Sit down.

Tom. Any particular place you would like me to sit?

Amanda. Thank heavens I've got that new sofa! I'm also making payments on a floor lamp I'll have sent out! And put the chintz covers on, they'll brighten things up! Of course I'd hoped to have these walls re-papered. . . . What is the young man's name?

Tom. His name is O'Connor.

Amanda. That, of course, means fish—tomorrow is Friday! I'll have that salmon loaf—with Durkee's dressing! What does he do? He works at the warehouse?

Tom. Of course! How else would I—

Amanda. Tom, he—doesn't drink?

Tom. Why do you ask me that?

Amanda. Your father *did*!

Tom. Don't get started on that!

Amanda. He *does* drink, then?

Tom. Not that I know of!

Amanda. Make sure, be certain! The last thing I want for my daughter's a boy who drinks!

Tom. Aren't you being a little bit premature? Mr. O'Connor has not yet appeared on the scene!

Amanda. But will tomorrow. To meet your sister, and what do I know about his character? Nothing! Old maids are better off than wives of drunkards!

Tom. Oh, my God!

Amanda. Be still!

Tom (*leaning forward to whisper*). Lots of fellows meet girls whom they don't marry!

Amanda. Oh, talk sensibly, Tom—and don't be sarcastic! (*She has gotten a hairbrush.*)

Tom. What are you doing?

Amanda. I'm brushing that cowlick down! (*She attacks his hair with the brush.*) What is this young man's position at the warehouse?

Tom (*submitting grimly to the brush and the interrogation*). This young man's position is that of a shipping clerk, Mother.

Amanda. Sounds to me like a fairly responsible job, the sort of a job *you* would be in if you just had more *get-up*. What is his salary? Have you any idea?

Tom. I would judge it to be approximately eighty-five dollars a month.

Amanda. Well—not princely, but—

Tom. Twenty more than I make.

Amanda. Yes, how well I know! But for a family man, eighty-five dollars a month is not much more than you can just get by on. . . .

Tom. Yes, but Mr. O'Connor is not a family man.

Amanda. He might be, mightn't he? Some time in the future?

Tom. I see. Plans and provisions.

Amanda. You are the only young man that I know of who ignores the fact that the future becomes the present, the present the past, and the past turns into everlasting regret if you don't plan for it!

Tom. I will think that over and see what I can make of it.

Amanda. Don't be supercilious with your mother! Tell me some more about this—what do you call him?

Tom. James D. O'Connor. The D. is for Delaney.

Amanda. Irish on *both* sides! *Gracious!* And doesn't drink?

Tom. Shall I call him up and ask him right this minute?

Amanda. The only way to find out about those things is to make discreet inquiries at the proper moment. When I was a girl in Blue Mountain and it was suspected that a young man drank, the girl whose attentions he had been receiving, if any girl *was,* would sometimes speak to the minister of his church, or rather her father would if her father was living, and sort of feel him out on the young man's character. That is the way such things are discreetly handled to keep a young woman from making a tragic mistake!

Tom. Then how did you happen to make a tragic mistake?

Amanda. That innocent look of your father's had everyone fooled! He *smiled*—the world was *enchanted*! No girl can do worse than put herself at the mercy of a handsome appearance! I hope that Mr. O'Connor is not too good-looking.

Tom. No, he's not too good-looking. He's covered with freckles and hasn't too much of a nose.

Amanda. He's not right-down homely, though?

Tom. Not right-down homely. Just medium homely, I'd say.

Amanda. Character's what to look for in a man.

Tom. That's what I've always said, Mother.

Amanda. You've never said anything of the kind and I suspect you would never give it a thought.

Tom. Don't be so suspicious of me.

Amanda. At least I hope he's the type that's up and coming.

Tom. I think he really goes in for self-improvement.

Amanda. What reason have you to think so?

Tom. He goes to night school.

Amanda (*beaming*). Splendid! What does he do, I mean study?

Tom. Radio engineering and public speaking!

Amanda. Then he has visions of being advanced in the world! Any young man who studies public speaking is aiming to have an executive job some day! And radio engineering? A thing for the future! Both of these facts are very illuminating. Those are the sort of things that a mother should know concerning any young man who comes to call on her daughter. Seriously or—not.

Tom. One little warning. He doesn't know about Laura. I didn't let on that we had dark ulterior motives. I just said, why don't you come and have dinner with us? He said okay and that was the whole conversation.

Amanda. I bet it was! You're eloquent as an oyster. However, he'll know about Laura when he gets here. When he sees how lovely and sweet and pretty she is, he'll thank his lucky stars he was asked to dinner.

Tom. Mother, you mustn't expect too much of Laura.

Amanda. What do you mean?

Tom. Laura seems all those things to you and me because she's ours and we love her. We don't even notice she's crippled any more.

Amanda. Don't say crippled! You know that I never allow that word to be used!

Tom. But face facts, Mother. She is and—that's not all—

Amanda. What do you mean "not all?"

Tom. Laura is very different from other girls.

Amanda. I think the difference is all to her advantage.

Tom. Not quite all—in the eyes of others—strangers—she's terribly shy and lives in a world of her own and those things make her seem a little peculiar to people outside the house.

Amanda. Don't say peculiar.

Tom. Face the facts. She is.

[*The dance hall music changes to a tango that has a minor and somewhat ominous tone.*]

Amanda. In what way is she peculiar—may I ask?

Tom (*gently*). She lives in a world of her own—a world of little glass ornaments, Mother. . . .

[*He gets up.* AMANDA *remains holding the brush, looking at him, troubled.*]

She plays old phonograph records and—that's about all—

[*He glances at himself in the mirror and crosses to the door.*]

Amanda (*sharply*). Where are you going?

Tom. I'm going to the movies. (*He goes out the screen door.*)

Amanda. Not to the movies, every night to the movies! (*She follows quickly to the screen door.*) I don't believe you always go to the movies!

[*He is gone.* AMANDA *looks worriedly after him for a moment. Then vitality and optimism return and she turns from the door, crossing to the portieres.*]

Laura! Laura!

[LAURA *answers from the kitchenette.*]

Laura. Yes, Mother.

Amanda. Let those dishes go and come in front!

[LAURA *appears with a dish towel.* AMANDA *speaks to her gaily.*]

Laura, come here and make a wish on the moon!

[*Screen image:* The Moon.]

Laura (*entering*). Moon—moon?

Amanda. A little silver slipper of a moon. Look over your left shoulder, Laura, and make a wish!

[LAURA *looks faintly puzzled as if called out of sleep.* AMANDA *seizes her shoulders and turns her at an angle by the door.*]

Now! Now, darling, *wish!*

Laura. What shall I wish for, Mother?

Amanda (*her voice trembling and her eyes suddenly filling with tears*). Happiness! Good fortune!

[*The sound of the violin rises and the stage dims out.*]

Scene 6

The light comes up on the fire escape landing. TOM *is leaning against the grill, smoking.*

[*Screen image:* The high school hero.]

Tom. And so the following evening I brought Jim home to dinner. I had known Jim slightly in high school. In high school Jim was a hero. He had tremendous Irish good nature and vitality with the scrubbed and polished look of white chinaware. He seemed to move in a continual spotlight. He was a star in basketball, captain of the debating club, president of the senior class and the glee club and he sang the male lead in the annual light operas. He was always running or bounding, never just walking. He seemed always at the point of defeating the law of gravity. He was shooting with such velocity through his adolescence that you would logically expect him to arrive at nothing short of the White House by the time he was thirty. But Jim apparently ran into more interference after his graduation from Soldan. His speed had definitely slowed. Six years after he left high school he was holding a job that wasn't much better than mine.

[*Screen image:* The Clerk.]

He was the only one at the warehouse with whom I was on friendly terms. I was valuable to him as someone who could remember his former glory, who had seen him win basketball games and the silver cup in debating. He knew of my secret practice of retiring to a cabinet of the washroom to work on poems when business was slack in the warehouse. He called me Shakespeare. And while the other boys in the warehouse regarded me with suspicious hostility, Jim took a humorous attitude toward me. Gradually his attitude affected the others, their hostility wore off and they also began to smile at me as people smile at an oddly fashioned dog who trots across their path at some distance.

I knew that Jim and Laura had known each other at Soldan, and I had heard Laura speak of his voice. I didn't know if Jim remembered her or not. In high school Laura had been as unobtrusive as Jim had been astonishing. If he did remember Laura, it was not as my sister; for when I asked him to dinner, he grinned and said, "You know, Shakespeare, I never thought of you as having folks!"

He was about to discover that I did. . . .

[*Legend on screen:* "The accent of a coming foot."]

[*The light dims out on* TOM *and comes up in the Wingfield living room—a delicate lemony light. It is about five on a Friday evening of late spring which comes "scattering poems in the sky."*]

[AMANDA *has worked in preparation for the gentleman caller. The results are astonishing. The new floor lamp with its rose silk shade is in place, a colored paper lantern conceals the broken light fixture in the ceiling, new billowing white curtains are at the windows, chintz covers are on the chairs and sofa, a pair of new sofa pillows make their initial appearance. Open boxes and tissue paper are scattered on the floor.*]

[LAURA *stands in the middle of the room with lifted arms while* AMANDA *crouches before her, adjusting the hem of a new dress, devout and ritualistic. The dress is colored and designed by memory. The arrangement of* LAURA's *hair is changed; it is softer and more becoming. A fragile unearthly prettiness has come out in* LAURA; *she is like a piece of translucent glass touched by light, given a momentary radiance, not actual, not lasting.*]

Amanda (*impatiently*). Why are you trembling?
Laura. Mother, you've made me so nervous!
Amanda. How have I made you nervous?
Laura. By all this fuss! You make it seem so important!
Amanda. I don't understand you, Laura. You couldn't be satisfied with just sitting home, and yet whenever I try to arrange something for you, you seem to resist it. (*She gets up.*) Now take a look at yourself. No, wait! Wait just a moment— I have an idea!
Laura. What is it now?

[AMANDA *produces two powder puffs which she wraps in handkerchiefs and stuffs in* LAURA's *bosom.*]

Laura. Mother, what are you doing?
Amanda. They call them "Gay Deceivers"!
Laura. I won't wear them!
Amanda. You will!
Laura. Why should I?
Amanda. Because, to be painfully honest, your chest is flat.
Laura. You make it seem like we were setting a trap.
Amanda. All pretty girls are a trap, a pretty trap, and men expect them to be.

[*Legend on screen:* "A pretty trap."]

Now look at yourself, young lady. This is the prettiest you will ever be! (*She stands back to admire* LAURA.) I've got to fix myself now! You're going to be surprised by your mother's appearance!

[AMANDA *crosses through the portieres, humming gaily.* LAURA *moves slowly to the long mirror and stares solemnly at herself. A wind blows the white curtains inward in a slow, graceful motion and with a faint, sorrowful sighing.*]

Amanda (*from somewhere behind the portieres*). It isn't dark enough yet.

[LAURA *turns slowly before the mirror with a troubled look.*]

[*Legend on screen:* "This is my sister: Celebrate her with strings!" *Music plays.*]

Amanda (*laughing, still not visible*). I'm going to show you something. I'm going to make a spectacular appearance!
Laura. What is it, Mother?
Amanda. Possess your soul in patience—you will see! Something I've resurrected from that old trunk! Styles haven't changed so terribly much after all. . . . (*She parts the portieres.*) Now just look at your mother! (*She wears a girlish frock of yellowed voile with a blue silk sash. She carries a bunch of jonquils—the legend of her youth is nearly revived. Now she speaks feverishly:*) This is the dress in which I led the cotillion. Won the cakewalk twice at Sunset Hill, wore one spring to the Governor's Ball in Jackson! See how I sashayed around the ballroom, Laura? (*She raises her skirt and does a mincing step around the room.*) I wore it on Sundays for my gentlemen callers! I had it on the day I met your father. . . . I had malaria fever all that spring. The change of climate from East Tennessee to the Delta—weakened resistance. I had a little temperature all the time—not enough to be serious—just enough to make me restless and giddy! Invitations poured in—parties all over the Delta! "Stay in bed," said Mother, "You have fever!"—but I just wouldn't. I took quinine but kept on going, going! Evenings, dances! Afternoons, long, long rides! Picnics—lovely! So lovely, that country in May—all lacy with dogwood, literally flooded with jonquils! That was the Spring I had the craze for jonquils. Jonquils became an absolute obsession. Mother said, "Honey, there's no more room for jonquils." And still I kept on bringing in more jonquils. Whenever, wherever I saw them, I'd say, "Stop! Stop! I see jonquils!" I made the young men help me gather the jonquils! It was a joke, Amanda and her jonquils. Finally there were no more vases to hold them, every available space was filled with jonquils. No vases to hold them? All right, I'll hold them myself! And then I—(*She stops in front of the picture. Music plays.*) met your father! Malaria fever and jonquils and then—this—boy. . . . (*She switches on the rose-colored lamp.*) I hope they get here before it starts to rain. (*She crosses the room and places the jonquils in a bowl on the table.*) I gave your brother a little extra change so he and Mr. O'Connor could take the service car home.

Laura (*with an altered look*). What did you say his name was?
Amanda. O'Connor.
Laura. What is his first name?
Amanda. I don't remember. Oh, yes, I do. It was—Jim!

[LAURA *sways slightly and catches hold of a chair.*]

[*Legend on screen:* "Not Jim!"]

Laura (*faintly*). Not—Jim!
Amanda. Yes, that was it, it was Jim! I've never known a Jim that wasn't nice!

[*The music becomes ominous.*]

Laura. Are you sure his name is Jim O'Connor?
Amanda. Yes. Why?
Laura. Is he the one that Tom used to know in high school?
Amanda. He didn't say so. I think he just got to know him at the warehouse.
Laura. There was a Jim O'Connor we both knew in high school—(*then, with effort*) If that is the one that Tom is bringing to dinner—you'll have to excuse me, I won't come to the table.
Amanda. What sort of nonsense is this?
Laura. You asked me once if I'd ever liked a boy. Don't you remember I showed you this boy's picture?
Amanda. You mean the boy you showed me in the yearbook?
Laura. Yes, that boy.
Amanda. Laura, Laura, were you in love with that boy?
Laura. I don't know, Mother. All I know is I couldn't sit at the table if it was him!
Amanda. It won't be him! It isn't the least bit likely. But whether it is or not, you will come to the table. You will not be excused.
Laura. I'll have to be, Mother.
Amanda. I don't intend to humor your silliness, Laura. I've had too much from you and your brother, both! So just sit down and compose yourself till they come. Tom has forgotten his key so you'll have to let them in, when they arrive.
Laura (*panicky*). Oh, Mother—*you* answer the door!
Amanda (*lightly*). I'll be in the kitchen—busy!
Laura. Oh, Mother, please answer the door, don't make me do it!

Amanda (*crossing into the kitchenette*). I've got to fix the dressing for the salmon. Fuss, fuss—silliness!—over a gentleman caller!

[*The door swings shut.* LAURA *is left alone.*]

[*Legend on screen:* ''Terror!'']

[*She utters a low moan and turns off the lamp—sits stiffly on the edge of the sofa, knotting her fingers together.*]

[*Legend on screen:* ''The Opening of a Door!'']

[TOM *and* JIM *appear on the fire escape steps and climb to the landing. Hearing their approach,* LAURA *rises with a panicky gesture. She retreats to the portieres. The doorbell rings.* LAURA *catches her breath and touches her throat. Low drums sound.*]

Amanda (*calling*). Laura, sweetheart! The door!

[LAURA *stares at it without moving.*]

Jim. I think we just beat the rain.
Tom. Uh-huh. (*He rings again, nervously.* JIM *whistles and fishes for a cigarette.*)
Amanda (*very, very gaily*). Laura, that is your brother and Mr. O'Connor! Will you let them in, darling?

[LAURA *crosses toward the kitchenette door.*]

Laura (*breathlessly*). Mother—you go to the door!

[AMANDA *steps out of the kitchenette and stares furiously at* LAURA. *She points imperiously at the door.*]

Laura. Please, please!
Amanda (*in a fierce whisper*). What is the matter with you, you silly thing?
Laura (*desperately*). Please, you answer it, *please!*
Amanda. I told you I wasn't going to humor you, Laura. Why have you chosen this moment to lose your mind?
Laura. Please, please, please, you go!
Amanda. You'll have to go to the door because I can't!
Laura (*despairingly*). I can't either!
Amanda. *Why?*
Laura. I'm *sick!*
Amanda. I'm sick too—of your nonsense! Why can't you and your brother be normal people? Fantastic whims and behavior!

[TOM *gives a long ring.*]

Preposterous goings on! Can you give me one reason—(*She calls out lyrically.*) Coming! Just one second!—why you should be afraid to open a door? Now you answer it, Laura!
Laura. Oh, oh, oh . . . (*She returns through the portieres, darts to the victrola, winds it frantically and turns it on.*)
Amanda. Laura Wingfield, you march right to that door!
Laura. *Yes—yes, Mother!*

[*A faraway, scratchy rendition of* ''Dardanella'' *softens the air and gives her strength to move through it. She slips to the door and draws it cautiously open.* TOM *enters with the caller,* JIM O'CONNOR.]

Tom. Laura, this is Jim. Jim, this is my sister, Laura.
Jim (*stepping inside*). I didn't know that Shakespeare had a sister!
Laura (*retreating, stiff and trembling, from the door*). How—how do you do?
Jim (*heartily, extending his hand*). Okay!

[LAURA *touches it hesitantly with hers.*]

Jim. Your hand's *cold*, Laura!
Laura. Yes, well—I've been playing the victrola.
Jim. Must have been playing classical music on it! You ought to play a little hot swing music to warm you up!
Laura. Excuse me—I haven't finished playing the victrola. . . . (*She turns awkwardly and hurries into the front room. She pauses a second by the victrola. Then she catches her breath and darts through the portieres like a frightened deer.*)
Jim (*grinning*). What was the matter?
Tom. Oh—with Laura? Laura is—terribly shy.
Jim. Shy, huh? It's unusual to meet a shy girl nowadays. I don't believe you ever mentioned you had a sister.
Tom. Well, now you know. I have one. Here is the *Post Dispatch*. You want a piece of it?
Jim. Uh-huh.
Tom. What piece? The comics?
Jim. Sports! (*He glances at it.*) Ole Dizzy Dean[4] is on his bad behavior.
Tom (*uninterested*). Yeah? (*He lights a cigarette and goes over to the fire escape door.*)

---

4. **Dizzy Dean:** major league pitcher (1932–1941) with the St. Louis Cardinals and the Chicago Cubs.

Jim. Where are *you* going?

Tom. I'm going out on the terrace.

Jim (*going after him*). You know, Shakespeare— I'm going to sell you a bill of goods!

Tom. What goods?

Jim. A course I'm taking.

Tom. Huh?

Jim. In public speaking! You and me, we're not the warehouse type.

Tom. Thanks—that's good news. But what has public speaking got to do with it?

Jim. It fits you for—executive positions!

Tom. Awww.

Jim. I tell you it's done a helluva lot for me.

[*Image on screen:* Executive at his desk.]

Tom. In what respect?

Jim. In every! Ask yourself what is the difference between you an' me and men in the office down front? Brains?—No!—Ability?—No! Then what? Just one little thing—

Tom. What is that one little thing?

Jim. Primarily it amounts to—social poise! Being able to square up to people and hold your own on any social level!

Amanda (*from the kitchenette*). Tom?

Tom. Yes, Mother?

Amanda. Is that you and Mr. O'Connor?

Tom. Yes, Mother.

Amanda. Well, you just make yourselves comfortable in there.

Tom. Yes. Mother.

Amanda. Ask Mr. O'Connor if he would like to wash his hands.

Jim. Aw, no—no—thank you—I took care of that at the warehouse. Tom—

Tom. Yes?

Jim. Mr. Mendoza was speaking to me about you.

Tom. Favorably?

Jim. What do you think?

Tom. Well—

Jim. You're going to be out of a job if you don't wake up.

Tom. I am waking up—

Jim. You show no signs.

Tom. The signs are interior.

[*Image on screen:* The sailing vessel with the Jolly Roger again.]

Tom. I'm planning to change. (*He leans over the fire escape rail, speaking with quiet exhilaration. The incandescent marquees and signs of the first-run movie houses light his face from across the alley. He looks like a voyager.*) I'm right at the point of committing myself to a future that doesn't include the warehouse and Mr. Mendoza or even a night-school course in public speaking.

Jim. What are you gassing about?

Tom. I'm tired of the movies.

Jim. Movies!

Tom. Yes, movies! Look at them— (*A wave toward the marvels of Grand Avenue.*) All of these glamorous people—having adventures—hogging it all, gobbling the whole thing up! You know what happens? People go to the *movies* instead of *moving!* Hollywood characters are supposed to have all the adventures for everybody in America, while everybody in America sits in a dark room and watches them have them! Yes, until there's a war. That's when adventure becomes available to the masses! *Everyone's* dish, not only Gable's! Then the people in the dark room come out of the dark room to have some adventures themselves— goody, goody! It's our turn now, to go to the South Sea Island—to make a safari—to be exotic, far-off! But I'm not patient. I don't want to wait till then. I'm tired of the *movies* and I am *about* to *move!*

Jim (*incredulously*). Move?

Tom. Yes.

Jim. When?

Tom. Soon!

Jim. Where? Where?

[*The music seems to answer the question, while* TOM *thinks it over. He searches in his pockets.*]

Tom. I'm starting to boil inside. I know I seem dreamy, but inside—well, I'm boiling! Whenever I pick up a shoe, I shudder a little thinking how short life is and what I am doing! Whatever that means, I know it doesn't mean shoes—except as something to wear on a traveler's feet! (*He finds what he has been searching for in his pockets and holds out a paper to* JIM.) Look—

Jim. What?

Tom. I'm a member.

Jim (*reading*). The Union of Merchant Seamen.

Tom. I paid my dues this month, instead of the light bill.

Jim. You will regret it when they turn the lights off.

Tom. I won't be here.

Jim. How about your mother?

Tom. I'm like my father. . . . Did you notice how

he's grinning in his picture in there? And he's been absent going on sixteen years!

Jim. You're just talking, you drip. How does your mother feel about it?

Tom. Shhh! Here comes Mother! Mother is not acquainted with my plans!

Amanda *(coming through the portieres).* Where are you all?

Tom. On the terrace, Mother.

[*They start inside. She advances to them.* TOM *is distinctly shocked at her appearance. Even* JIM *blinks a little. He is making his first contact with girlish Southern vivacity and in spite of the night-school course in public speaking is somewhat thrown off the beam by the unexpected outlay of social charm. Certain responses are attempted by* JIM *but are swept aside by* AMANDA's *gay laughter and chatter.* TOM *is embarrassed but after the first shock* JIM *reacts very warmly. He grins and chuckles, is altogether won over.*]

[*Image on screen:* Amanda as a girl.]

Amanda *(coyly smiling, shaking her girlish ringlets).* Well, well, well, so this is Mr. O'Connor. Introductions entirely unnecessary. I've heard so much about you from my boy. I finally said to him, Tom—good gracious!—why don't you bring this paragon[1] to supper? I'd like to meet this nice young man at the warehouse!—instead of just hearing him sing your praises so much! I don't know why my son is so stand-offish—that's not Southern behavior!

Let's sit down and—I think we could stand a little more air in here! Tom, leave the door open. I felt a nice fresh breeze a moment ago. Where has it gone to? Mmm, so warm already! And not quite summer, even. We're going to burn up when summer really gets started. However, we're having—we're having a very light supper. I think light things are better fo' this time of year. The same as light clothes are. Light clothes an' light food are what warm weather calls fo'. You know our blood gets so thick during th' winter—it takes a while fo' us to *adjust* ou'selves!—when the season changes . . . It's come so quick this year. I wasn't prepared. All of a sudden—heavens! Already summer! I ran to the trunk an' pulled out this light dress—terribly old! Historical almost! But feels so good—so good an' co-ol, y' know. . . .

Tom. Mother—

Amanda. Yes, honey?

Tom. How about—supper?

Amanda. Honey, you go ask Sister if supper is ready! You know that Sister is in full charge of supper! Tell her you hungry boys are waiting for it. *(To* JIM*)* Have you met Laura?

Jim. She—

Amanda. Let you in? Oh, good, you've met already! It's rare for a girl as sweet an' pretty as Laura to be domestic! But Laura is, thank heavens, not only pretty but also very domestic. I'm not at all. I never was a bit. I never could make a thing but angel-food cake. Well, in the South we had so many servants. Gone, gone, gone. All vestige of gracious living! Gone completely! I wasn't prepared for what the future brought me. All of my gentlemen callers were sons of planters and

---

1. **paragon** (par'ə·gän'): a model of excellence or perfection.

"I married no planter! I married . . . a telephone man who—fell in love with long-distance!"

so of course I assumed that I would be married to one and raise my family on a large piece of land with plenty of servants. But man proposes—and woman accepts the proposal! To vary that old, old saying a little bit[2]—I married no planter! I married a man who worked for the telephone company! That gallantly smiling gentleman over there! *(She points to the picture.)* A telephone man who—fell in love with long-distance! Now he travels and I don't even know where! But what am I going on for about my—tribulations? Tell me yours—I hope you don't have any! Tom?

Tom *(returning).* Yes, Mother?

Amanda. Is supper nearly ready?

Tom. It looks to me like supper is on the table.

---

2. **But man proposes . . . a bit**: Amanda is referring to the saying, "Man proposes, but God disposes."

Amanda. Let me look— *(She rises prettily and looks through the portieres.)* Oh, lovely! But where is Sister?

Tom. Laura is not feeling well and she says that she thinks she'd better not come to the table.

Amanda. What? Nonsense! Laura? Oh, Laura!

Laura *(from the kitchenette, faintly).* Yes, Mother.

Amanda. You really must come to the table. We won't be seated until you come to the table! Come in, Mr. O'Connor. You sit over there, and I'll. . . . Laura? Laura Wingfield! You're keeping us waiting, honey! We can't say grace until you come to the table!

[*The kitchenette door is pushed weakly open and* LAURA *comes in: She is obviously quite faint, her lips trembling, her eyes wide and staring. She moves unsteadily toward the table.*]

[*Screen legend:* "Terror!"]

[*Outside a summer storm is coming on abruptly. The white curtains billow inward at the windows and there is a sorrowful murmur from the deep blue dusk.*]

[LAURA *suddenly stumbles; she catches at a chair with a faint moan.*]

Tom. Laura!
Amanda. Laura!

[*There is a clap of thunder.*]

[*Screen legend:* "Ah!"]

(*Despairingly*) Why, Laura, you *are* ill, darling! Tom, help your sister into the living room, dear! Sit in the living room, Laura—rest on the sofa. Well! (*to* JIM *as* TOM *helps his sister to the sofa in the living room*) Standing over the hot stove made her ill! I told her that it was just too warm this evening, but—

[TOM *comes back to the table.*]

Is Laura all right now?
Tom. Yes.
Amanda. What *is* that? Rain? A nice cool rain has come up! (*She gives* JIM *a frightened look.*) I think we may—have grace—now . . .

(TOM *looks at her stupidly.*) Tom, honey—you say grace!
Tom. Oh . . . "For these and all thy mercies—"

[*They bow their heads,* AMANDA *stealing a nervous glance at* JIM. *In the living room* LAURA, *stretched on the sofa, clenches her hand to her lips, to hold back a shuddering sob.*]

God's Holy Name be praised—

[*The scene dims out.*]

Responding to the Play

Analyzing Scenes 5 and 6

Identifying Facts

1. In Scene 5, Tom displays an attitude toward his mother that we have not seen before. Describe that attitude, and find the lines of dialogue that reveal it. Cite two lines of dialogue from this scene that show that Amanda is also trying to behave differently toward Tom.
2. What does Amanda ask Tom to do at the end of this scene?
3. In Scene 6, we hear that the much-talked-about gentleman caller is finally about to arrive. Before we meet him, what information does Tom give us about him? How does Amanda react to this new information about the gentleman caller?
4. In Scene 5, Tom gives his mother two realistic warnings to counter Amanda's pleasant fantasy of the gentleman caller. What are these warnings? How does Amanda react to them?
5. How does Amanda transform herself for the gentleman caller? How is her attitude about their guest different from Laura's?
6. What is Laura's reaction when she learns the identity of the gentleman caller? How does Amanda respond to this reaction?

Interpreting Meanings

7. At the beginning of Scene 5, both Tom and Amanda try to make peace. Why do they begin to argue again?
8. The basic **dramatic situation** from which a play can grow involves a person or persons whom we care about, who are in more or less desperate situations with a great deal at stake. Such characters decide to act and then actually take steps to achieve their "wants." Discuss how these dramatic elements are used up to this point in *The Glass Menagerie*.
9. In most plays, suspense is preferable to surprise. If we reach the top of a hill and look down to see two trains at the moment they crash, it is a **surprise** and it is shocking. But dramatically, it would be more effective if, as we neared the top of the hill, we saw the trains approaching each other on the same track from perhaps a mile apart. This would be **suspense:** we are very anxious about what will happen next. How has Tennessee Williams used suspense in the play up to now?
10. We have seen that Amanda is a complex **character**— not easily described as either "good" or "bad." What aspect of her character do we see in Scene 6? Do you feel sympathetic toward her? Explain.
11. What are your feelings for the gentleman caller at this point in the play? How do you feel about Tom?

Scene 7

It is half an hour later. Dinner is just being finished in the dining room, LAURA *is still huddled upon the sofa, her feet drawn under, her head resting on a pale blue pillow, her eyes wide and mysteriously watchful. The new floor lamp with its shade of rose-colored silk gives a soft, becoming light to her face, bringing out the fragile, unearthly prettiness which usually escapes attention. From outside there is a steady murmur of rain, but it is slackening and soon stops; the air outside becomes pale and luminous as the moon breaks through the clouds. A moment after the curtain rises, the lights in both rooms flicker and go out.*

Jim. Hey, there, Mr. Light Bulb!

[AMANDA *laughs nervously.*]

[*Legend on screen:* "Suspension of a public service."]

Amanda. Where was Moses when the lights went out? Ha-ha. Do you know the answer to that one, Mr. O'Connor?
Jim. No, Ma'am, what's the answer?
Amanda. In the dark!

[JIM *laughs appreciatively.*]

Everybody sit still. I'll light the candles. Isn't it lucky we have them on the table? Where's a match? Which of you gentlemen can provide a match?
Jim. Here.
Amanda. Thank you, Sir.
Jim. Not at all, Ma'am!
Amanda (*as she lights the candles*). I guess the fuse has burnt out. Mr. O'Connor, can you tell a burnt-out fuse? I know I can't and Tom is a total loss when it comes to mechanics.

[*They rise from the table and go into the kitchenette, from where their voices are heard.*]

Oh, be careful you don't bump into something. We don't want our gentleman caller to break his neck. Now wouldn't that be a fine howdy-do?
Jim. Ha-ha! Where is the fuse-box?
Amanda. Right here next to the stove. Can you see anything?
Jim. Just a minute.
Amanda. Isn't electricity a mysterious thing? Wasn't it Benjamin Franklin who tied a key to a kite? We live in such a mysterious universe, don't we? Some people say that science clears up all the mysteries for us. In my opinion it only creates more! Have you found it yet?
Jim. No, Ma'am. All these fuses look okay to me.
Amanda. Tom!
Tom. Yes, Mother?
Amanda. That light bill I gave you several days ago. The one I told you we got the notices about?

[*Legend on screen:* "Ha!"]

Tom. Oh—yeah.
Amanda. You didn't neglect to pay it by any chance?
Tom. Why, I—
Amanda. Didn't! I might have known it!
Jim. Shakespeare probably wrote a poem on that light bill, Mrs. Wingfield.
Amanda. I might have known better than to trust him with it! There's such a high price for negligence in this world!
Jim. Maybe the poem will win a ten-dollar prize.
Amanda. We'll just have to spend the remainder of the evening in the nineteenth century, before Mr. Edison made the Mazda lamp!
Jim. Candlelight is my favorite kind of light.
Amanda. That shows you're romantic! But that's no excuse for Tom. Well, we got through dinner. Very considerate of them to let us get through dinner before they plunged us into everlasting darkness, wasn't it, Mr. O'Connor?
Jim. Ha-ha!
Amanda. Tom, as a penalty for your carelessness you can help me with the dishes.
Jim. Let me give you a hand.
Amanda. Indeed you will not!
Jim. I ought to be good for something.
Amanda. Good for something? (*Her tone is rhapsodic.*) *You?* Why, Mr. O'Connor, nobody, *nobody's* given me this much entertainment in years—as you have!
Jim. Aw, now, Mrs. Wingfield!
Amanda. I'm not exaggerating, not one bit! But Sister is all by her lonesome. You go keep her company in the parlor! I'll give you this lovely old candelabrum that used to be on the altar at the Church of the Heavenly Rest. It was melted a little out of shape when the church burnt down. Lightning struck it one Spring. Gypsy Jones was holding a revival at the time and he intimated that church was destroyed because the Episcopalians gave card parties.
Jim. Ha-ha.

Amanda. And how about you coaxing Sister to drink a little wine? I think it would be good for her! Can you carry both at once?

Jim. Sure. I'm Superman!

Amanda. Now, Thomas, get into this apron!

[JIM *comes into the dining room, carrying the candelabrum, its candles lighted, in one hand and a glass of wine in the other. The door of the kitchenette swings closed on* AMANDA'S *gay laughter; the flickering light approaches the portieres.* LAURA *sits up nervously as* JIM *enters. She can hardly speak from the almost intolerable strain of being alone with a stranger.*]

[*Screen legend:* "I don't suppose you remember me at all!"]

[*At first, before* JIM'S *warmth overcomes her paralyzing shyness,* LAURA'S *voice is thin and breathless, as though she had just run up a steep flight of stairs.* JIM'S *attitude is gently humorous. While the incident is apparently unimportant, it is to* LAURA *the climax of her secret life.*]

Jim. Hello there, Laura.

Laura *(faintly)*. Hello.

[*She clears her throat.*]

Jim. How are you feeling now? Better?

Laura. Yes. Yes, thank you.

Jim. This is for you. A little dandelion wine. *(He extends the glass toward her with extravagant gallantry.)*

Laura. Thank you.

Jim. Drink it—but don't get drunk!

[*He laughs heartily.* LAURA *takes the glass uncertainly; she laughs shyly.*]

Where shall I set the candles?

Laura. Oh—oh, anywhere . . .

Jim. How about here on the floor? Any objections?

Laura. No.

Jim. I'll spread a newspaper under to catch the drippings. I like to sit on the floor. Mind if I do?

Laura. Oh, no.

Jim. Give me a pillow?

Laura. What?

Jim. A pillow!

Laura. Oh . . . *(She hands him one quickly.)*

Jim. How about you? Don't you like to sit on the floor?

Laura. Oh—yes.

Jim. Why don't you, then?

Laura. I—will.

Jim. Take a pillow!

(LAURA *does. She sits on the floor on the other side of the candelabrum.* JIM *crosses his legs and smiles engagingly at her.*) I can't hardly see you sitting way over there.

Laura. I can—see you.

Jim. I know, but that's not fair, I'm in the limelight.

[LAURA *moves her pillow closer.*]

Good! Now I can see you! Comfortable?

Laura. Yes.

Jim. So am I. Comfortable as a cow! Will you have some gum?

Laura. No, thank you.

Jim. I think that I will indulge, with your permission. *(He musingly unwraps a stick of gum and holds it up.)* Think of the fortune made by the guy that invented the first piece of chewing gum. Amazing, huh? The Wrigley Building is one of the sights of Chicago—I saw it when I went up to the Century of Progress. Did you take in the Century of Progress?

Laura. No, I didn't.

Jim. Well, it was quite a wonderful exposition. What impressed me most was the Hall of Science. Gives you an idea of what the future will be in America, even more wonderful than the present time is! *(There is a pause.* JIM *smiles at her.)* Your brother tells me you're shy. Is that right, Laura?

Laura. I—don't know.

Jim. I judge you to be an old-fashioned type of girl. Well, I think that's a pretty good type to be. Hope you don't think I'm being too personal—do you?

Laura *(hastily, out of embarrassment)*. I believe I *will* take a piece of gum, if you—don't mind. *(clearing her throat)* Mr. O'Connor, have you—kept up with your singing?

Jim. Singing? Me?

Laura. Yes. I remember what a beautiful voice you had.

Jim. When did you hear me sing?

[LAURA *does not answer, and in the long pause which follows a man's voice is heard singing offstage.*]

VOICE:
O blow, ye winds, heigh-ho,
A-roving I will go!
 I'm off to my love
 With a boxing glove—
Ten thousand miles away!

Jim. You say you've heard me sing?
Laura. Oh, yes! Yes, very often . . . I don't suppose—you remember me—at all?
Jim (*smiling doubtfully*). You know I have an idea I've seen you before. I had that idea soon as you opened the door. It seemed almost like I was about to remember your name. But the name that I started to call you—wasn't a name! And so I stopped myself before I said it.
Laura. Wasn't it—Blue Roses?
Jim (*springing up, grinning*). Blue Roses! My gosh, yes—Blue Roses! That's what I had on my tongue when you opened the door! Isn't it funny what tricks your memory plays? I didn't connect you with high school somehow or other. But that's where it was; it was high school. I didn't even know you were Shakespeare's sister! Gosh, I'm sorry.
Laura. I didn't expect you to. You—barely knew me!
Jim. But we did have a speaking acquaintance, huh?
Laura. Yes, we—spoke to each other.
Jim. When did you recognize me?
Laura. Oh, right away!
Jim. Soon as I came in the door?
Laura. When I heard your name I thought it was probably you. I knew that Tom used to know you a little in high school. So when you came in the door—well, then I was—sure.
Jim. Why didn't you *say* something, then?
Laura (*breathlessly*). I didn't know what to say, I was—too surprised!
Jim. For goodness' sakes! You know, this sure is funny!
Laura. Yes! Yes, isn't it, though . . .
Jim. Didn't we have a class in something together?
Laura. Yes, we did.
Jim. What class was that?
Laura. It was—singing—chorus!
Jim. Aw!
Laura. I sat across the aisle from you in the Aud.
Jim. Aw.
Laura. Mondays, Wednesdays, and Fridays.
Jim. Now I remember—you always came in late.

Laura. Yes, it was so hard for me, getting upstairs. I had that brace on my leg—it clumped so loud!
Jim. I never heard any clumping.
Laura (*wincing at the recollection*). To me it sounded like—thunder!
Jim. Well, well, well, I never even noticed.
Laura. And everybody was seated before I came in. I had to walk in front of all those people. My seat was in the back row. I had to go clumping all the way up the aisle with everyone watching!
Jim. You shouldn't have been self-conscious.
Laura. I know, but I was. It was always such a relief when the singing started.
Jim. Aw, yes, I've placed you now! I used to call you Blue Roses. How was it that I got started calling you that?
Laura. I was out of school a little while with pleurosis. When I came back you asked me what was the matter. I said I had pleurosis—you thought I said *Blue Roses*. That's what you always called me after that!
Jim. I hope you didn't mind.
Laura. Oh, no—I liked it. You see, I wasn't acquainted with many—people. . . .
Jim. As I remember you sort of stuck by yourself.
Laura. I—I—never have had much luck at—making friends.
Jim. I don't see why you wouldn't.
Laura. Well, I—started out badly.
Jim. You mean being—
Laura. Yes, it sort of—stood between me—
Jim. You shouldn't have let it!
Laura. I know, but it did, and—
Jim. You were shy with people!
Laura. I tried not to be but never could—
Jim. Overcome it?
Laura. No, I—I never could!
Jim. I guess being shy is something you have to work out of kind of gradually.
Laura (*sorrowfully*). Yes—I guess it—
Jim. Takes time!
Laura. Yes—
Jim. People are not so dreadful when you know them. That's what you have to remember! And everybody has problems, not just you, but practically everybody has got some problems. You think of yourself as having the only problems, as being the only one who is disappointed. But just look around you and you will see lots of people as disappointed as you are. For instance, I hoped when I was going to high school that I would be further along at this time, six years later, than I

am now. You remember that wonderful write-up I had in *The Torch?*
Laura. Yes! *(She rises and crosses to the table.)*
Jim. It said I was bound to succeed in anything I went into!

[LAURA *returns with the high school year book.*]

Holy Jeez! *The Torch!*

[*He accepts it reverently. They smile across the book with mutual wonder.* LAURA *crouches beside him and they begin to turn the pages.* LAURA'*s shyness is dissolving in his warmth.*]

Laura. Here you are in *The Pirates of Penzance!*
Jim *(wistfully).* I sang the baritone lead in that operetta.
Laura *(raptly).* So—*beautifully!*
Jim *(protesting).* Aw—
Laura. Yes, yes—beautifully—beautifully!
Jim. You heard me?
Laura. All three times!
Jim. No!
Laura. Yes!
Jim. All three performances?
Laura *(looking down).* Yes.
Jim. Why?
Laura. I—wanted to ask you to—autograph my program. *(She takes the program from the back of the year book and shows it to him.)*
Jim. Why didn't you ask me to?
Laura. You were always surrounded by your own friends so much that I never had a chance to.
Jim. You should have just—
Laura. Well, I—thought you might think I was—
Jim. Thought I might think you was—what?
Laura. Oh—
Jim *(with reflective relish).* I was beleaguered by females in those days.
Laura. You were terribly popular!
Jim. Yeah—
Laura. You had such a—friendly way—
Jim. I was spoiled in high school.
Laura. Everybody—liked you!
Jim. Including you?
Laura. I—yes, I—did, too— *(She gently closes the book in her lap.)*
Jim. Well, well, well! Give me that program, Laura.

[*She hands it to him. He signs it with a flourish.*]

There you are—better late than never!
Laura. Oh, I—what a—surprise!

Jim. My signature isn't worth very much right now. But some day—maybe—it will increase in value! Being disappointed is one thing and being discouraged is something else. I am disappointed but I am not discouraged. I'm twenty-three years old. How old are you?
Laura. I'll be twenty-four in June.
Jim. That's not old age!
Laura. No, but—
Jim. You finished high school?
Laura *(with difficulty).* I didn't go back.
Jim. You mean you dropped out?
Laura. I made bad grades in my final examinations. *(She rises and replaces the book and the program on the table. Her voice is strained.)* How is—Emily Meisenbach getting along?
Jim. Oh, that kraut-head!
Laura. Why do you call her that?
Jim. That's what she was.
Laura. You're not still—going with her?
Jim. I never see her.
Laura. It said in the "Personal" section that you were—engaged!
Jim. I know, but I wasn't impressed by that—propaganda!
Laura. It wasn't—the truth?
Jim. Only in Emily's optimistic opinion!
Laura. Oh—

[*Legend:* "What have you done since high school?"]

[JIM *lights a cigarette and leans indolently back on his elbows smiling at* LAURA *with a warmth and charm which lights her inwardly with altar candles. She remains by the table, picks up a piece from the glass menagerie collection, and turns it in her hands to cover her tumult.*]

Jim *(after several reflective puffs on his cigarette).* What have you done since high school?

[*She seems not to hear him.*]

Huh?

[LAURA *looks up.*]

I said what have you done since high school, Laura?
Laura. Nothing much.
Jim. You must have been doing something these six long years.
Laura. Yes.
Jim. Well, then, such as what?

Laura. I took a business course at business college—

Jim. How did that work out?

Laura. Well, not very—well—I had to drop out, it gave me—indigestion—

[JIM *laughs gently*.]

Jim. What are you doing now?

Laura. I don't do anything—much. Oh, please don't think I sit around doing nothing! My glass collection takes up a good deal of time. Glass is something you have to take good care of.

Jim. What did you say—about glass?

Laura. Collection I said—I have one— (*She clears her throat and turns away again, acutely shy.*)

Jim (*abruptly*). You know what I judge to be the trouble with you? Inferiority complex! Know what that is? That's what they call it when someone low-rates himself! I understand it because I had it, too. Although my case was not so aggravated as yours seems to be. I had it until I took up public speaking, developed my voice, and learned that I had an aptitude for science. Before that time I never thought of myself as being outstanding in any way whatsoever! Now I've never made a regular study of it, but I have a friend who says I can analyze people better than doctors that make a profession of it. I don't claim that to be necessarily true, but I can sure guess a person's psychology, Laura! (*He takes out his gum.*) Excuse me, Laura. I always take it out when the flavor is gone. I'll use this scrap of paper to wrap it in. I know how it is to get it stuck on a shoe. (*He wraps the gum in paper and puts it in his pocket.*) Yep—that's what I judge to be your principal trouble. A lack of confidence in yourself as a person. You don't have the proper amount of faith in yourself. I'm basing that fact on a number of your remarks and also on certain observations I've made. For instance that clumping you thought was so awful in high school. You say that you even dreaded to walk into class. You see what you did? You dropped out of school, you gave up an education because of a clump, which as far as I know was practically non-existent! A little physical defect is what you have. Hardly noticeable even! Magnified thousands of times by imagination! You know what my strong advice to you is? Think of yourself as *superior* in some way!

Laura. In what way would I think?

Jim. Why, man alive, Laura! Just look about you a little, what do you see? A world full of common people! All of 'em born and all of 'em going to die! Which of them has one-tenth of your good points! Or mine! Or anyone else's, as far as that goes—gosh! Everybody excels in some one thing. Some in many! (*He unconsciously glances at himself in the mirror.*) All you've got to do is discover in *what!* Take me, for instance. (*He adjusts his tie at the mirror.*) My interest happens to lie in electro-dynamics. I'm taking a course in radio engineering at night school, Laura, on top of a fairly responsible job at the warehouse. I'm taking that course and studying public speaking.

Laura. Ohhhh.

Jim. Because I believe in the future of television! (*Turning his back to her.*) I wish to be ready to go up right along with it. Therefore I'm planning to get in on the ground floor. In fact I've already made the right connections and all that remains is for the industry itself to get under way! Full steam—(*His eyes are starry.*) Knowledge— Zzzzzp! Money—Zzzzzzp!—Power! That's the cycle democracy is built on!

[*His attitude is convincingly dynamic.* LAURA *stares at him, even her shyness eclipsed in her absolute wonder. He suddenly grins.*]

I guess you think I think a lot of myself!

Laura. No—o-o-o, I—

Jim. Now how about you? Isn't there something you take more interest in than anything else?

Laura. Well, I do—as I said—have my—glass collection—

[*A peal of girlish laughter rings from the kitchenette.*]

Jim. I'm not sure I know what you're talking about. What kind of glass is it?

Laura. Little articles of it, they're ornaments mostly! Most of them are little animals made out of glass, the tiniest little animals in the world. Mother calls them a glass menagerie! Here's an example of one, if you'd like to see it! This one is one of the oldest. It's nearly thirteen.

[*Music:* "The Glass Menagerie."]

[*He stretches out his hand.*]

Oh, be careful—if you breathe, it breaks!

Jim. I'd better not take it. I'm pretty clumsy with things.

Laura. Go on, I trust you with him! (*She places the piece in his palm.*) There now—you're holding

"Unicorns—aren't they extinct in the modern world?"

him gently! Hold him over the light, he loves the light! You see how the light shines through him?

Jim. It sure does shine!

Laura. I shouldn't be partial, but he is my favorite one.

Jim. What kind of a thing is this one supposed to be?

Laura. Haven't you noticed the single horn on his forehead?

Jim. A unicorn, huh?

Laura. Mmmm-hmmm!

Jim. Unicorns—aren't they extinct in the modern world?

Laura. I know!

Jim. Poor little fellow, he must feel sort of lonesome.

Laura (smiling). Well, if he does, he doesn't complain about it. He stays on a shelf with some horses that don't have horns and all of them seem to get along nicely together.

Jim. How do you know?

Laura (lightly). I haven't heard any arguments among them!

Jim (grinning). No arguments, huh? Well, that's a pretty good sign! Where shall I set him?

Laura. Put him on the table. They all like a change of scenery once in a while!

Jim. Well, well, well, well—(He places the glass piece on the table, then raises his arms and stretches.) Look how big my shadow is when I stretch!

Laura. Oh, oh, yes—it stretches across the ceiling!

Jim (crossing to the door). I think it's stopped raining. (He opens the fire-escape door and the background music changes to a dance tune.) Where does the music come from?

Laura. From the Paradise Dance Hall across the alley.

Jim. How about cutting the rug a little, Miss Wingfield?

Laura. Oh, I—

Jim. Or is your program filled up? Let me have a look at it. (He grasps an imaginary card.) Why, every dance is taken! I'll just have to scratch some out.

[Waltz music: "La Golondrina."]

Ahhh, a waltz! (He executes some sweeping turns by himself, then holds his arms toward LAURA.)

Laura (breathlessly). I—can't dance!

Jim. There you go, that inferiority stuff!

Laura. I've never danced in my life!

Jim. Come on, try!

Laura. Oh, but I'd step on you!

Jim. I'm not made out of glass.

Laura. How—how—how do we start?

Jim. Just leave it to me. You hold your arms out a little.

Laura. Like this?

Jim (taking her in his arms). A little bit higher. Right. Now don't tighten up, that's the main thing about it—relax.

Laura (laughing breathlessly). It's hard not to.

Jim. Okay.

Laura. I'm afraid you can't budge me.

Jim. What do you bet I can't? (He swings her into motion.)

Laura. Goodness, yes, you can!

Jim. Let yourself go, now, Laura, just let yourself go.

Laura. I'm—

Jim. Come on!

Laura. —trying!

Jim. Not so stiff—easy does it!

Laura. I know but I'm—

Jim. Loosen th' backbone! There now, that's a lot better.

Laura. Am I?

Jim. Lots, lots better! (He moves her about the room in a clumsy waltz.)

Laura. Oh, my!

Jim. Ha-ha!

Laura. Oh, my goodness!

Jim. Ha-ha-ha!

[They suddenly bump into the table, and the glass piece on it falls to the floor. JIM stops the dance.]

What did we hit on?

Laura. Table.

Jim. Did something fall off it? I think—

Laura. Yes.

Jim. I hope that it wasn't the little glass horse with the horn!

Laura. Yes. (She stoops to pick it up.)

Jim. Aw, aw, aw. Is it broken?

Laura. Now it is just like all the other horses.

Jim. It's lost its—

Laura. Horn! It doesn't matter. Maybe it's a blessing in disguise.

Jim. You'll never forgive me. I bet that that was your favorite piece of glass.

Laura. I don't have favorites much. It's no tragedy, Freckles. Glass breaks so easily. No matter how careful you are. The traffic jars the shelves and things fall off them.

Jim. Still I'm awfully sorry that I was the cause.

Laura *(smiling).* I'll just imagine he had an operation. The horn was removed to make him feel less—freakish!

[*They both laugh.*]

Now he will feel more at home with the other horses, the ones that don't have horns. . . .

Jim. Ha-ha, that's very funny! *(Suddenly he is serious.)* I'm glad to see that you have a sense of humor. You know—you're—well—very different! Surprisingly different from anyone else I know! *(His voice becomes soft and hesitant with a genuine feeling.)* Do you mind me telling you that?

[LAURA *is abashed beyond speech.*]

I mean it in a nice way—

[LAURA *nods shyly, looking away.*]

You make me feel sort of—I don't know how to put it! I'm usually pretty good at expressing things, but—this is something that I don't know how to say!

[LAURA *touches her throat and clears it—turns the broken unicorn in her hands. His voice becomes softer.*]

Has anyone ever told you that you were pretty?

[*There is a pause, and the music rises slightly.* LAURA *looks up slowly, with wonder, and shakes her head.*]

Well, you are! In a very different way from anyone else. And all the nicer because of the difference, too.

[*His voice becomes low and husky.* LAURA *turns away, nearly faint with the novelty of her emotions.*]

I wish that you were my sister. I'd teach you to have some confidence in yourself. The different people are not like other people, but being different is nothing to be ashamed of. Because other people are not such wonderful people. They're one hundred times one thousand. You're one times one! They walk all over the earth. You just stay here. They're common as—weeds, but—you—well, you're—*Blue Roses!*

[*Image on screen:* Blue Roses.]

[*The music changes.*]

Laura. But blue is wrong for—roses. . . .

Jim. It's right for you! You're—pretty!

Laura. In what respect am I pretty?

Jim. In all respects—believe me! Your eyes—your hair—are pretty! Your hands are pretty! *(He catches hold of her hand.)* You think I'm making this up because I'm invited to dinner and have to be nice. Oh, I could do that! I could put on an act for you, Laura, and say lots of things without being very sincere. But this time I am. I'm talking to you sincerely. I happened to notice you had this inferiority complex that keeps you from feeling comfortable with people. Somebody needs to build your confidence up and make you proud, instead of shy and turning away and—blushing. Somebody—ought to—*kiss* you, Laura!

[*His hand slips slowly up her arm to her shoulder as the music swells tumultuously. He suddenly turns her about and kisses her on the lips. When he releases her,* LAURA *sinks on the sofa with a bright, dazed look.* JIM *backs away and fishes in his pocket for a cigarette.*]

[*Legend on screen:* ''A souvenir.'']

Stumblejohn!

[*He lights the cigarette, avoiding her look. There is a peal of girlish laughter from* AMANDA *in the kitchenette.* LAURA *slowly raises and opens her hand. It still contains the little broken glass animal. She looks at it with a tender, bewildered expression.*]

Stumblejohn! I shouldn't have done that—that was way off the beam. You don't smoke, do you?

[*She looks up, smiling, not hearing the question. He sits beside her rather gingerly. She looks at him speechlessly—waiting. He coughs decorously and moves a little farther aside as he considers the situation and senses her feelings, dimly, with perturbation. He speaks gently.*]

Would you—care for a—mint?

[*She doesn't seem to hear him but her look grows brighter even.*]

Peppermint? Life Saver? My pocket's a regular drug store—wherever I go. . . . *(He pops a mint in his mouth. Then he gulps and decides to make a clean breast of it. He speaks slowly and gingerly.)* Laura, you know, if I had a sister like you,

"Somebody—ought to—kiss you, Laura!"

graphically what he thinks her methods and tone should be.)—you just sip your coffee, see, and say easy like that you been thinking 'bout that deal Walter Lee is so interested in, 'bout the store and all, and sip some more coffee, like what you saying ain't really that important to you— And the next thing you know, she be listening good and asking you questions and when I come home—I can tell her the details. This ain't no fly-by-night proposition, baby. I mean we figured it out, me and Willy and Bobo.

Ruth *(with a frown)*. Bobo?

Walter. Yeah. You see, this little liquor store we got in mind cost seventy-five thousand and we figured the initial investment on the place be 'bout thirty-thousand, see. That be ten thousand each. Course, there's a couple of hundred you got to pay so's you don't spend your life just waiting for them clowns to let your license get approved—

Ruth. You mean graft?

Walter *(frowning impatiently)*. Don't call it that. See there, that just goes to show you what women understand about the world. Baby, don't *nothing* happen for you in this world 'less you pay *somebody* off!

Ruth. Walter, leave me alone! *(She raises her head and stares at him vigorously—then says, more quietly.)* Eat your eggs, they gonna be cold.

Walter *(straightening up from her and looking off)*. That's it. There you are. Man say to his woman: I got me a dream. His woman say: Eat your eggs. *(Sadly, but gaining in power)* Man say: I got to take hold of this here world, baby! And a woman will say: Eat your eggs and go to work. *(Passionately now)* Man say: I got to change my life, I'm choking to death, baby! And his woman say—*(in utter anguish as he brings his fists down on his thighs)*—Your eggs is getting cold!

Ruth *(softly)*. Walter, that ain't none of our money.

Walter *(not listening at all or even looking at her)*. This morning, I was lookin' in the mirror and thinking about it . . . I'm thirty-five years old; I been married eleven years and I got a boy who sleeps in the living room—*(very, very quietly)*—and all I got to give him is stories about how rich white people live . . .

Ruth. Eat your eggs, Walter.

Walter. *Damn my eggs . . . damn all the eggs that ever was!*

Ruth. Then go to work.

Walter *(looking up at her)*. See—I'm trying to talk to you 'bout myself—*(shaking his head with the repetition)*—and all you can say is eat them eggs and go to work.

Ruth *(wearily)*. Honey, you never say nothing new. I listen to you every day, every night and every morning, and you never say nothing new. *(Shrugging)* So you would rather *be* Mr. Arnold than be his chauffeur. So—I would *rather* be living in Buckingham Palace.

Walter. That is just what is wrong with the colored woman in this world . . . Don't understand about building their men up and making 'em feel like they somebody. Like they can do something.

Ruth *(drily, but to hurt)*. There *are* colored men who do things.

Walter. No thanks to the colored woman.

Ruth. Well, being a colored woman, I guess I can't help myself none.

[*She rises and gets the ironing board and sets it up and attacks a huge pile of rough-dried clothes, sprinkling them in preparation for the ironing and then rolling them into tight fat balls.*]

Walter *(mumbling)*. We one group of men tied to a race of women with small minds.

[*His sister* BENEATHA *enters. She is about twenty, as slim and intense as her brother. She is not as pretty as her sister-in-law, but her lean, almost intellectual face has a handsomeness of its own. She wears a bright-red flannel nightie, and her thick hair stands wildly about her head. Her speech is a mixture of many things; it is different from the rest of the family's insofar as education has permeated her sense of English—and perhaps the Midwest rather than the South has finally—at last—won out in her inflection; but not altogether, because over all of it is a soft slurring and transformed use of vowels which is the decided influence of the Southside. She passes through the room without looking at either* RUTH *or* WALTER *and goes to the outside door and looks, a little blindly, out to the bathroom. She sees that it has been lost to the Johnsons. She closes the door with a sleepy vengeance and crosses to the table and sits down a little defeated.*]

Beneatha. I am going to start timing those people.

Walter. You should get up earlier.

Beneatha *(her face in her hands. She is still fighting the urge to go back to bed.)*. Really— would you suggest dawn? Where's the paper?

Walter *(pushing the paper across the table to her as he studies her almost clinically, as though he*

"*You know that check is coming tomorrow.*"

never going to start getting ahead till they start gambling on some different kinds of things in the world—investments and things.

Mama. What done got into you, girl? Walter Lee done finally sold you on investing.

Ruth. No. Mama, something is happening between Walter and me. I don't know what it is—but he needs something—something I can't give him any more. He needs this chance, Lena.

Mama (*frowning deeply*). But liquor, honey—

Ruth. Well—like Walter say—I spec people going to always be drinking themselves some liquor.

Mama. Well—whether they drinks it or not ain't none of my business. But whether I go into business selling it to 'em *is,* and I don't want that on my ledger this late in life. (*Stopping suddenly and studying her daughter-in-law*) Ruth Younger, what's the matter with you today? You look like you could fall over right there.

Ruth. I'm tired.

Mama. Then you better stay home from work today.

Ruth. I can't stay home. She'd be calling up the agency and screaming at them, "My girl didn't come in today—send me somebody! My girl didn't come in!" Oh, she just have a fit . . .

Mama. Well, let her have it. I'll just call her up and say you got the flu—

Ruth (*laughing*). Why the flu?

Mama. 'Cause it sounds respectable to 'em. Something white people get, too. They know 'bout the flu. Otherwise they think you been cut up or something when you tell 'em you sick.

Ruth. I got to go in. We need the money.

"Seem like God didn't see fit to give the black man nothing but dreams— but He did give us children to make them dreams worthwhile."

Mama. Somebody would of thought my children done all but starved to death the way they talk about money here late. Child, we got a great big old check coming tomorrow.

Ruth (sincerely, but also self-righteously). Now that's your money. It ain't got nothing to do with me. We all feel like that—Walter and Bennie and me—even Travis.

Mama (thoughtfully, and suddenly very far away). Ten thousand dollars—

Ruth. Sure is wonderful.

Mama. Ten thousand dollars.

Ruth. You know what you should do, Miss Lena? You should take yourself a trip somewhere. To Europe or South America or someplace—

Mama (throwing up her hands at the thought). Oh, child!

Ruth. I'm serious. Just pack up and leave! Go on away and enjoy yourself some. Forget about the family and have yourself a ball for once in your life—

Mama (drily). You sound like I'm just about ready to die. Who'd go with me? What I look like wandering 'round Europe by myself?

Ruth. Shoot—these here rich white women do it all the time. They don't think nothing of packing up they suitcases and piling on one of them big steamships and—swoosh!—they gone, child.

Mama. Something always told me I wasn't no rich white woman.

Ruth. Well—what are you going to do with it then?

Mama. I ain't rightly decided. (Thinking. She speaks now with emphasis.) Some of it got to be put away for Beneatha and her schoolin'—and ain't nothing going to touch that part of it. Nothing. (She waits several seconds, trying to make up her mind about something, and looks at RUTH a little tentatively before going on.) Been thinking that we maybe could meet the notes on a little old two-story somewhere, with a yard where Travis could play in the summertime, if we use part of the insurance for a down payment and everybody kind of pitch in. I could maybe take on a little day work again, few days a week—

Ruth (studying her mother-in-law furtively and concentrating on her ironing, anxious to encourage without seeming to). Well, Lord knows, we've put enough rent into this here rat trap to pay for four houses by now . . .

Mama (looking up at the words "rat trap" and then looking around and leaning back and sighing—in a suddenly reflective mood—). "Rat trap"—yes, that's all it is. (Smiling) I remember just as well the day me and Big Walter moved in here. Hadn't been married but two weeks and wasn't planning on living here no more than a year. (She shakes her head at the dissolved dream.) We was going to set away, little by little, don't you know, and buy a little place out in Morgan Park. We had even picked out the house. (Chuckling a little) Looks right dumpy today. But Lord, child, you should know all the dreams I had 'bout buying that house and fixing it up and making me a little garden in the back—(She waits and stops smiling.) And didn't none of it happen. (Dropping her hands in a futile gesture)

Ruth (keeps her head down, ironing). Yes, life can be a barrel of disappointments, sometimes.

Mama. Honey, Big Walter would come in here some nights back then and slump down on that couch there and just look at the rug, and look at me and look at the rug and then back at me—and I'd know he was down then . . . really down. (After a second very long and thoughtful pause; she is seeing back to times that only she can see.) And then, Lord, when I lost that baby—little Claude—I almost thought I was going to lose Big Walter too. Oh, that man grieved hisself! He was one man to love his children.

Ruth. Ain't nothin' can tear at you like losin' your baby.

Mama. I guess that's how come that man finally worked hisself to death like he done. Like he was fighting his own war with this here world that took his baby from him.

Ruth. He sure was a fine man, all right. I always liked Mr. Younger.

Mama. Crazy 'bout his children! God knows there was plenty wrong with Walter Younger—hardheaded, mean, kind of wild with women—plenty wrong with him. But he sure loved his children. Always wanted to have something—be something. That's where Brother gets all these notions, I reckon. Big Walter used to say, he'd get right wet in the eyes sometimes, lean his head back with the water standing in his eyes and say, "Seem like God didn't see fit to give the black man nothing but dreams—but He did give us children to make them dreams seem worthwhile." (She smiles.) He could talk like that, don't you know.

Ruth. Yes, he sure could. He was a good man, Mr. Younger.

Mama. Yes, a fine man—just couldn't never catch up with his dreams, that's all.

[BENEATHA *comes in, brushing her hair and looking up to the ceiling, where the sound of a vacuum cleaner has started up.*]

Beneatha. What could be so dirty on that woman's rugs that she has to vacuum them every single day?

Ruth. I wish certain young women 'round here who I could name would take inspiration about certain rugs in a certain apartment I could also mention.

Beneatha (*shrugging*). Well, good God, how much cleaning can a house need.

Mama (*not liking the Lord's name used thus*). Bennie!

Ruth. Just listen to her—just listen!

Beneatha. Oh, . . .

Mama. If you use the Lord's name just one more time—

Beneatha (*a bit of a whine*). Oh, Mama—

Ruth. Fresh—just fresh as salt, this girl!

Beneatha (*drily*). Well—if the salt loses its savor[3]—

Mama. Now that will do. I just ain't going to have you 'round here reciting the scriptures in vain—you hear me?

Beneatha. How did I manage to get on everybody's wrong side by just walking into a room?

Ruth. If you weren't so fresh—

Beneatha. Ruth, I'm twenty years old.

Mama. What time you be home from school today?

Beneatha. Kind of late. (*With enthusiasm*) Madeline is going to start my guitar lessons today.

[MAMA *and* RUTH *look up with the same expressions.*]

Mama. Your *what* kind of lessons?

Beneatha. Guitar.

Ruth. Oh, Father!

Mama. How come you done taken it in your mind to learn to play the guitar?

Beneatha. I just want to, that's all.

Mama (*smiling*). Lord, child, don't you know what to do with yourself? How long it going to be before you get tired of this now—like you got tired of that little play-acting group you joined last year? (*looking at* RUTH) And what was it the year before that?

---

3. **salt . . . savor:** Matthew 5:13: ". . . if the salt has lost its savor . . . it is thenceforth good for nothing, but to cast out. . . ."

Ruth. The horseback-riding club for which she bought that fifty-five-dollar riding habit that's been hanging in the closet ever since!

Mama (*to* BENEATHA). Why you got to flit so from one thing to another, baby?

Beneatha (*sharply*). I just want to learn to play the guitar. Is there anything wrong with that?

Mama. Ain't nobody trying to stop you. I just wonders sometimes why you has to flit so from one thing to another all the time. You ain't never done nothing with all that camera equipment you brought home—

Beneatha. I don't flit! I—I experiment with different forms of expression—

Ruth. Like riding a horse?

Beneatha. —People have to express themselves one way or another.

Mama. What is it you want to express?

Beneatha (*angrily*). Me! (MAMA *and* RUTH *look at each other and burst into raucous laughter.*) Don't worry—I don't expect you to understand.

Mama (*to change the subject*). Who you going out with tomorrow night?

Beneatha (*with displeasure*). George Murchison again.

Mama (*pleased*). Oh—you getting a little sweet on him?

Ruth. You ask me, this child ain't sweet on nobody but herself—(*Underbreath*) Express herself!

[*They laugh.*]

Beneatha. Oh—I like George all right, Mama. I mean I like him enough to go out with him and stuff, but—

Ruth (*for devilment*). What does *and stuff* mean?

Beneatha. Mind your own business.

Mama. Stop picking at her now, Ruth. (*A thoughtful pause, and then a suspicious sudden look at her daughter as she turns in her chair for emphasis.*) What *does* it mean?

Beneatha (*wearily*). Oh, I just mean I couldn't ever really be serious about George. He's—he's so shallow.

Ruth. Shallow—what do you mean he's shallow? He's *rich!*

Mama. Hush, Ruth.

Beneatha. I know he's rich. He knows he's rich, too.

Ruth. Well—what other qualities a man got to have to satisfy you, little girl?

Beneatha. You wouldn't even begin to understand. Anybody who married Walter could not possibly understand.

Mama (*outraged*). What kind of way is that to talk about your brother?

Beneatha. Brother is a flip—let's face it.

Mama (*to* RUTH, *helplessly*). What's a flip?

Ruth (*glad to add kindling*). She's saying he's crazy.

Beneatha. Not crazy. Brother isn't really crazy yet—he—he's an elaborate neurotic.

Mama. Hush your mouth!

Beneatha. As for George. Well. George looks good—he's got a beautiful car and he takes me to nice places and, as my sister-in-law says, he is probably the richest boy I will ever get to know and I even like him sometimes—but if the Youngers are sitting around waiting to see if their little Bennie is going to tie up the family with the Murchisons, they are wasting their time.

Ruth. You mean you wouldn't marry George Murchison if he asked you someday? That pretty, rich thing? Honey, I knew you was odd—

Beneatha. No I would not marry him if all I felt for him was what I feel now. Besides, George's family wouldn't really like it.

Mama. Why not?

Beneatha. Oh, Mama—The Murchisons are hon-est-to-God-real-*live*-rich colored people, and the only people in the world who are more snobbish than rich white people are rich colored people. I thought everybody knew that. I've met Mrs. Murchison. She's a scene!

Mama. You must not dislike people 'cause they well off, honey.

Beneatha. Why not? It makes just as much sense as disliking people 'cause they are poor, and lots of people do that.

Ruth (*a wisdom-of-the-ages manner; to* MAMA). Well, she'll get over some of this—

Beneatha. Get over it? What are you talking about, Ruth? Listen, I'm going to be a doctor. I'm not worried about who I'm going to marry yet—if I ever get married.

Mama and Ruth. *If!*

Mama. Now, Bennie—

Beneatha. Oh, I probably will . . . but first I'm going to be a doctor, and George, for one, still thinks that's pretty funny. I couldn't be bothered with that. I am going to be a doctor and everybody around here better understand that!

Mama (*kindly*). 'Course you going to be a doctor, honey, God willing.

Beneatha (*drily*). God hasn't got a thing to do with it.

Mama. Beneatha—that just wasn't necessary.

Beneatha. Well— I get sick of hearing about God.

Mama. Beneatha!

Beneatha. I mean it! I'm just tired of hearing about God all the time. What has He got to do with anything? Does he pay tuition?

Mama. You 'bout to get your fresh little jaw slapped!

Ruth. That's just what she needs, all right!

Beneatha. Why? Why can't I say what I want to around here, like everybody else?

Mama. It don't sound nice for a young girl to say things like that—you wasn't brought up that way. Me and your father went to trouble to get you and Brother to church every Sunday.

Beneatha. Mama, you don't understand. It's all a matter of ideas, and that is just one idea I don't accept. It's not important. I am not going out and be immoral or commit crimes because I don't believe in God. I don't even think about it. It's just that I get tired of Him getting credit for all the things the human race achieves through its own stubborn effort. There simply is no God in heaven—there is only man and it is he who makes miracles!

[MAMA *absorbs this speech, studies her daughter and rises slowly and crosses to* BENEATHA *and slaps her powerfully across the face. After, there is only silence and the daughter drops her eyes from her mother's face, and* MAMA *is very tall before her.*]

Mama. Now—you say after me, in my mother's house there is still God. (*There is a long pause and* BENEATHA *stares at the floor wordlessly.* MAMA *repeats the phrase with precision and cool emotion.*) In my mother's house there is still God.

Beneatha. In my mother's house there is still God. (*A long pause*)

Mama (*walking away from* BENEATHA, *too disturbed for triumphant posture; stopping and turning back to her daughter*). There are some ideas we ain't going to have in this house. Not long as I am at the head of this family.

Beneatha. Yes, ma'am.

[MAMA *walks out of the room.*]

Ruth (*almost gently, with profound understanding*). You think you a woman, Bennie—but you still a little girl. What you did was childish—so you got treated like a child.

Beneatha. I see. (*Quietly*) I also see that everybody thinks it's all right for Mama to be a tyrant. But all the tyranny in the world will never make her right!

[*She picks up her books and goes out.*]

Ruth (*goes to* MAMA's *door*). She said she was sorry.

Mama (*coming out, going to her plant*). They frightens me, Ruth. My children.

Ruth. You got good children, Lena. They just a little off sometimes—but they're good.

Mama. No—there's something come down between me and them that don't let us understand each other and I don't know what it is. One done almost lost his mind thinking 'bout money all the time and the other done commence to talk about things I can't seem to understand in no form or fashion. What is it that's changing, Ruth?

Ruth (*soothingly, older than her years*). Now . . . you taking it all too seriously. You just got strong-willed children and it takes a strong woman like you to keep 'em in hand.

Mama (*looking at her plant and sprinkling a little water on it*). They spirited all right, my children. Got to admit they got spirit—Bennie and Walter. Like this little old plant that ain't never had enough sunshine or nothing—and look at it . . .

[*She has her back to* RUTH, *who has had to stop ironing and lean against something and put the back of her hand to her forehead.*]

Ruth (*trying to keep* MAMA *from noticing*). You . . . sure . . . loves that little old thing, don't you? . . .

Mama. Well, I always wanted me a garden like I used to see sometimes at the back of the houses down home. This plant is close as I ever got to having one. (*She looks out of the window as she replaces the plant.*) Lord, ain't nothing as dreary as the view from this window on a dreary day, is there? Why ain't you singing this morning, Ruth? Sing that "No Ways Tired." That song always lifts me up so—(*She turns at last to see that* RUTH *has slipped quietly into a chair, in a state of semi-consciousness.*) Ruth! Ruth honey—what's the matter with you . . . Ruth!

Curtain

Scene 2

It is the following morning; a Saturday morning, and house cleaning is in progress at the YOUNGERS. *Furniture has been shoved hither and yon and* MAMA *is giving the kitchen-area walls a washing down.* BENEATHA, *in dungarees, with a handkerchief tied around her face, is spraying insecticide into the cracks in the walls. As they work, the radio is on and a Southside disk-jockey program is inappropriately filling the house with a rather exotic saxophone blues.* TRAVIS, *the sole idle one, is leaning on his arms, looking out of the window.*

Travis. Grandmama, that stuff Bennie is using smells awful. Can I go downstairs, please?

Mama. Did you get all them chores done already? I ain't seen you doing much.

Travis. Yes'm—finished early. Where did Mama go this morning?

Mama (*looking at* BENEATHA). She had to go on a little errand.

Travis. Where?

Mama. To tend to her business.

Travis. Can I go outside then?

Mama. Oh, I guess so. You better stay right in front of the house, though . . . and keep a good lookout for the postman.

Travis. Yes'm. (*He starts out and decides to give his* AUNT BENEATHA *a good swat on the legs as he passes her.*) Leave them poor little old cockroaches alone, they ain't bothering you none.

[*He runs as she swings the spray gun at him both viciously and playfully.* WALTER *enters from the bedroom and goes to the phone.*]

Mama. Look out there, girl, before you be spilling some of that stuff on the child!

Travis (*teasing*). That's right—look out now! (*He exits.*)

Beneatha (*drily*). I can't imagine that it would hurt him—it has never hurt the roaches.

Mama. Well, little boys' hides ain't as tough as Southside roaches.

Walter (*into phone*). Hello—Let me talk to Willy Harris.

Mama. You better get over there behind the bureau. I seen one marching out of there like Napoleon yesterday.

Walter. Hello, Willy? It ain't come yet. It'll be here in a few minutes. Did the lawyer give you the papers?

Beneatha. There's really only one way to get rid of them, Mama—

Mama. How?

Beneatha. Set fire to this building.

Walter. Good. Good. I'll be right over.

Beneatha. Where did Ruth go, Walter?

Walter. I don't know (*He exits abruptly.*)

Beneatha. Mama, where did Ruth go?

Mama (*looking at her with meaning*). To the doctor, I think.

Beneatha. The doctor? What's the matter? (*They exchange glances.*) You don't think—

Mama (*with her sense of drama*). Now I ain't saying what I think. But I ain't never been wrong 'bout a woman neither.

[*The phone rings.*]

Beneatha (*at the phone*). Hay-lo . . . (*Pause, and a moment of recognition*) Well—when did you get back! . . . And how was it? . . . Of course I've missed you—in my way . . . This morning? No . . . house cleaning and all that and Mama hates it if I let people come over when the house is like this . . . You *have*? Well, that's different . . . What is it— Oh, what the heck, come on over . . . Right, see you then. (*She hangs up.*)

Mama (*who has listened vigorously, as is her habit*). Who is that you inviting over here with this house looking like this? You ain't got the pride you was born with!

Beneatha. Asagai doesn't care how houses look, Mama—he's an intellectual.

Mama. *Who?*

Beneatha. Asagai—Joseph Asagai. He's an African boy I met on campus. He's been studying in Canada all summer.

Mama. What's his name?

Beneatha. Asagai, Joseph. Ah-sah-guy . . . He's from Nigeria.[1]

Mama. Oh, that's the little country that was founded by slaves way back . . .

Beneatha. No, Mama—that's Liberia.[2]

Mama. I don't think I never met no African before.

Beneatha. Well, do me a favor and don't ask him a whole lot of ignorant questions about Africans. I mean, do they wear clothes and all that—

---

1. **Nigeria:** largest and most populous country on the western coast of Africa. Nigeria was a British protectorate when this play opened, but gained its independence in 1960.
2. **Liberia:** nation on the west coast of Africa, established as a republic in 1847 by freed American slaves.

Mama. Well, now, I guess if you think we so ignorant 'round here maybe you shouldn't bring your friends here—

Beneatha. It's just that people ask such crazy things. All anyone seems to know about when it comes to Africa is Tarzan—

Mama (*indignantly*). Why should I know anything about Africa?

Beneatha. Why do you give money at church for the missionary work?

Mama. Well, that's to help save people.

Beneatha. You mean save them from *heathenism*—

Mama (*innocently*). Yes.

Beneatha. I'm afraid they need more salvation from the British and the French.

[RUTH *comes in forlornly and pulls off her coat with dejection. They both turn to look at her.*]

Ruth (*dispiritedly*). Well, I guess from all the happy faces—everybody knows.

Beneatha. You pregnant?

Mama. Lord have mercy, I sure hope it's a little old girl. Travis ought to have a sister.

[BENEATHA *and* RUTH *give her a hopeless look for this grandmotherly enthusiasm.*]

Beneatha. How far along are you?

Ruth. Two months.

Beneatha. Did you mean to? I mean did you plan it or was it an accident?

Mama. What do you know about planning or not planning?

Beneatha. Oh, Mama.

Ruth (*wearily*). She's twenty years old, Lena.

Beneatha. Did you plan it, Ruth?

Ruth. Mind your own business.

Beneatha. It is my business—where is he going to live, on the *roof*? (*There is silence following the remark as the three women react to the sense of it.*) Gee—I didn't mean that, Ruth, honest. Gee, I don't feel like that at all. I—I think it is wonderful.

Ruth (*dully*). Wonderful.

Beneatha. Yes—really.

Mama (*looking at* RUTH, *worried*). Doctor say everything going to be all right?

Ruth (*far away*). Yes—she says everything is going to be fine . . .

Mama (*immediately suspicious*). "She"— What doctor you went to?

[RUTH *folds over, near hysteria.*]

Mama (*worriedly hovering over* RUTH). Ruth honey—what's the matter with you—you sick?

[RUTH *has her fists clenched on her thighs and is fighting hard to suppress a scream that seems to be rising in her.*]

Beneatha. What's the matter with her, Mama?
Mama (*working her fingers in* RUTH'S *shoulder to relax her*). She be all right. Women gets right depressed sometimes when they get her way. (*Speaking softly, expertly, rapidly*) Now you just relax. That's right . . . just lean back, don't think 'bout nothing at all . . . nothing at all—
Ruth. I'm all right . . .

[*The glassy-eyed look melts and then she collapses into a fit of heavy sobbing. The bell rings.*]

Beneatha. Oh, . . . that must be Asagai.
Mama (*to* RUTH). Come on now, honey. You need to lie down and rest awhile . . . then have some nice hot food.

[*They exit,* RUTH'S *weight on her mother-in-law.* BENEATHA, *herself profoundly disturbed, opens the door to admit a rather dramatic-looking young man with a large package.*]

Asagai. Hello, Alaiyo—
Beneatha (*holding the door open and regarding him with pleasure*). Hello . . . (*Long pause*) Well—come in. And please excuse everything. My mother was very upset about my letting anyone come here with the place like this.
Asagai (*coming into the room*). You look disturbed too . . . Is something wrong?
Beneatha (*still at the door, absently*). Yes . . . we've all got acute ghetto-itus. (*She smiles and comes toward him, finding a cigarette and sitting.*) So—sit down! How was Canada?
Asagai (*a sophisticate*). Canadian.
Beneatha (*looking at him*). I've very glad you are back.
Asagai (*looking back at her in turn*). Are you really?
Beneatha. Yes—very.
Asagai. Why—you were quite glad when I went away. What happened?
Beneatha. You went away.
Asagai. Ahhhhhhhh.
Beneatha. Before—you wanted to be so serious before there was time.
Asagai. How much time must there be before one knows what one feels?

Beneatha (*stalling this particular conversation; her hands pressed together, in a deliberately childish gesture*). What did you bring me?
Asagai (*handing her the package*). Open it and see.
Beneatha (*eagerly opening the package and drawing out some records and the colorful robes of a Nigerian woman*). Oh, Asagai! . . . You got them for me! . . . How beautiful . . . and the records too! (*She lifts out the robes and runs to the mirror with them and holds the drapery up in front of herself.*)
Asagai (*coming to her at the mirror*). I shall have to teach you how to drape it properly. (*He flings the material about her for the moment and stands back to look at her.*) Ah—Oh-pay-gay-day, oh-gbah-mu-shay. (*a Yoruba[3] exclamation for admiration*) You wear it well . . . very well . . . mutilated hair and all.
Beneatha (*turning suddenly*). My hair—what's wrong with my hair?
Asagai (*shrugging*). Were you born with it like that?
Beneatha (*reaching up to touch it*). No . . . of course not.

[*She looks back to the mirror, disturbed.*]

Asagai (*smiling*). How then?
Beneatha. You know perfectly well how . . . as crinkly as yours . . . that's how.
Asagai. And it is ugly to you that way?
Beneatha (*quickly*). Oh, no—not ugly . . . (*More slowly, apologetically*) But it's so hard to manage when it's, well—raw.
Asagai. And so to accommodate that—you mutilate it every week?
Beneatha. It's not mutilation!
Asagai (*laughing aloud at her seriousness*). Oh . . . please! I am only teasing you because you are so very serious about these things. (*He stands back from her and folds his arms across his chest as he watches her pulling at her hair and frowning in the mirror.*) Do you remember the first time you met me at school? . . . (*He laughs.*) You came up to me and you said—and I thought you were the most serious little thing I had ever seen—you said: (*He imitates her.*) "Mr. Asagai—I want very much to talk with you. About Africa. You see, Mr. Asagai, I am looking for my *identity!*" (*He laughs.*)

---

3. **Yoruba:** a tribe living in southwestern Nigeria, and the language they speak.

Beneatha (*turning to him, not laughing*). Yes—(*Her face is quizzical, profoundly disturbed.*)

Asagai (*still teasing and reaching out and taking her face in his hands and turning her profile to him*). Well . . . it is true that this is not so much a profile of a Hollywood queen as perhaps a queen of the Nile—(*A mock dismissal of the importance of the question*) But what does it matter? Assimilationism[4] is so popular in your country.

Beneatha (*wheeling, passionately, sharply*). I am not an assimilationist!

Asagai (*The protest hangs in the room for a moment and* ASAGAI *studies her, his laughter fading*). Such a serious one. (*There is a pause.*) So—you like the robes? You must take excellent care of them—they are from my sister's personal wardrobe.

Beneatha (*with incredulity*). You—you sent all the way home—for me?

Asagai (*with charm*). For you—I would do much more . . . Well, that is what I came for. I must go.

Beneatha. Will you call me Monday?

Asagai. Yes . . . We have a great deal to talk about. I mean about identity and time and all that.

Beneatha. Time?

Asagai. Yes. About how much time one needs to know what one feels.

Beneatha. You never understood that there is more than one kind of feeling which can exist between a man and a woman—or, at least, there should be.

Asagai (*shaking his head negatively but gently*). No. Between a man and a woman there need be only one kind of feeling. I have that for you . . . Now even . . . right this moment . . .

Beneatha. I know—and by itself—it won't do. I can find that anywhere.

Asagai. For a woman it should be enough.

Beneatha. I know—because that's what it says in all the novels that men write. But it isn't. Go ahead and laugh—but I'm not interested in being someone's little episode in America or—(*with feminine vengeance*)—one of them! (ASAGAI *has burst into laughter again.*) That's funny . . . , huh!

Asagai. It's just that every American girl I have known has said that to me. White—black—in this you are all the same. And the same speech, too!

Beneatha (*angrily*). Yuk, yuk, yuk!

---

4. **Assimilationism** (ə·sim′ə lā′shəniz′m): the belief that minority groups should drop their ethnic, racial, and religious identities and be absorbed into the mainstream majority culture.

Asagai. It's how you can be sure that the world's most liberated women are not liberated at all. You all talk about it too much!

[MAMA *enters and is immediately all social charm because of the presence of a guest.*]

Beneatha. Oh—Mama—this is Mr. Asagai.

Mama. How do you do?

Asagai (*total politeness to an elder*). How do you do, Mrs. Younger. Please forgive me for coming at such an outrageous hour on a Saturday.

Mama. Well, you are quite welcome. I just hope you understand that our house don't always look like this. (*Chatterish*) You must come again. I would love to hear all about—(*not sure of the name*)—your country. I think it's so sad the way our American Negroes don't know anything about Africa 'cept Tarzan and all that. And all that money they pour into these churches when they ought to be helping you people over there drive out them French and Englishmen done taken away your land.

[*The mother flashes a slightly superior look at her daughter upon completion of the recitation.*]

Asagai (*taken aback by this sudden and acutely unrelated expression of sympathy*). Yes . . . yes . . .

Mama (*smiling at him suddenly and relaxing and looking him over*). How many miles is it from here to where you come from?

Asagai. Many thousands.

Mama (*looking at him as she would* WALTER). I bet you don't half look after yourself, being away from your mama either. I spec you better come 'round here from time to time and get yourself some decent home-cooked meals . . .

Asagai (*moved*). Thank you. Thank you very much. (*They are all quiet, then—*) Well . . . I must go. I will call you Monday, Alaiyo.

Mama. What's that he call you?

Asagai. Oh—"Alaiyo." I hope you don't mind. It is what you would call a nickname, I think. It is a Yoruba word. I am a Yoruba.

Mama (*looking at* BENEATHA). I—I thought he was from—

Asagai (*understanding*). Nigeria is my country. Yoruba is my tribal origin—

Beneatha. You didn't tell us what Alaiyo means . . . for all I know, you might be calling me Little Idiot or something . . .

Asagai. Well . . . let me see . . . I do not know how just to explain it . . . The sense of a thing can be so different when it changes languages.

Beneatha. You're evading.

Asagai. No—really it is difficult . . . *(Thinking)* It means . . . it means One for Whom Bread—Food—Is Not Enough. *(He looks at her.)* Is that all right?

Beneatha *(understanding, softly).* Thank you.

Mama *(looking from one to the other and not understanding any of it).* Well . . . that's nice . . . You must come see us again—Mr.—

Asagai. Ah-sah-guy . . .

Mama. Yes . . . Do come again.

Asagai. Goodbye. *(He exits.)*

Mama *(after him).* Lord, that's a pretty thing just went out here! *(Insinuatingly, to her daughter)* Yes, I guess I see why we done commence to get so interested in Africa 'round here. Missionaries my aunt Jenny! *(She exits.)*

Beneatha. Oh, Mama! . . .

[*She picks up the Nigerian dress and holds it up to her in front of the mirror again. She sets the headdress on haphazardly and then notices her hair again and clutches at it and then replaces the headdress and frowns at herself. Then she starts to wriggle in front of the mirror as she thinks a Nigerian woman might.* TRAVIS *enters and regards her.*]

Travis. You cracking up?

Beneatha. Shut up.

[*She pulls the headdress off and looks at herself in the mirror and clutches at her hair again and squinches her eyes as if trying to imagine something. Then, suddenly, she gets her raincoat and kerchief and hurriedly prepares for going out.*]

Mama *(coming back into the room).* She's resting now. Travis, baby, run next door and ask Miss Johnson to please let me have a little kitchen cleanser. This here can is empty as Jacob's kettle.

Travis. I just came in.

Mama. Do as you told. *(He exits and she looks at her daughter.)* Where you going?

Beneatha *(halting at the door).* To become a queen of the Nile!

[*She exits in a breathless blaze of glory.* RUTH *appears in the bedroom doorway.*]

Mama. Who told you to get up?

Ruth. Ain't nothing wrong with me to be lying in no bed for. Where did Bennie go?

Mama *(drumming her fingers).* Far as I could make out—to Egypt. *(RUTH just looks at her.)* What time is it getting to?

Ruth. Ten twenty. And the mailman going to ring that bell this morning just like he done every morning for the last umpteen years.

[TRAVIS *comes in with the cleanser can.*]

Travis. She say to tell you that she don't have much.

Mama *(angrily).* Lord, some people I could name sure is tight-fisted! *(Directing her grandson)* Mark two cans of cleanser down on the list there. If she that hard up for kitchen cleanser, I sure don't want to forget to get her none!

Ruth. Lena—maybe the woman is just short on cleanser—

Mama *(not listening).* —Much baking powder as she done borrowed from me all these years, she could of done gone into the baking business!

[*The bell sounds suddenly and sharply and all three are stunned—serious and silent—mid-speech. In spite of all the other conversations and distractions of the morning, this is what they have been waiting for, even* TRAVIS, *who looks helplessly from his mother to his grandmother.* RUTH *is first to come to life again.*]

Ruth *(to* TRAVIS*). Get down them steps, boy!*

[TRAVIS *snaps to life and flies out to get the mail.*]

Mama *(her eyes wide, her hand to her breast).* You mean it done really come?

Ruth *(excited).* Oh, Miss Lena!

Mama *(collecting herself).* Well . . . I don't know what we all so excited about 'round here for. We known it was coming for months.

Ruth. That's a whole lot different from having it come and being able to hold it in your hands . . . a piece of paper worth ten thousand dollars . . . *(TRAVIS bursts back into the room. He holds the envelope high above his head, like a little dancer, his face is radiant and he is breathless. He moves to his grandmother with sudden slow ceremony and puts the envelope into her hands. She accepts it, and then merely holds it and looks at it.)* Come on! Open it . . . Lord have mercy, I wish Walter Lee was here!

Travis. Open it, Grandmama!

"How many miles is it from here to where you come from?"

Walter. You just don't understand, Mama, you just don't understand.

Mama. Son—do you know your wife is expecting another baby? (WALTER *stands, stunned, and absorbs what his mother has said.*) That's what she wanted to talk to you about. (WALTER *sinks down into a chair.*) This ain't for me to be telling—but you ought to know. (*She waits.*) I think Ruth is thinking bout doing something to that child.

Walter (*slowly understanding*). No— no— Ruth wouldn't—

Mama. When the world gets ugly enough—a woman will do anything for her family. *The part that's already living.*

Walter. You don't know Ruth, Mama, if you think she would—

[RUTH *opens the bedroom door and stands there a little limp.*]

Ruth (*beaten*). Yes I would too, Walter. (*Pause*) . . .

[*There is total silence as the man stares at his wife and the mother stares at her son.*]

Mama (*presently*). Well— (*Tightly*) Well—son, I'm waiting to hear you say something . . . I'm waiting to hear how you be your father's son. Be the man he was . . . (*Pause*) Your wife say she don't want your child. And I'm waiting to hear you talk like him and say we a people who give children life, not destroys them—(*She rises.*) I'm waiting to see you stand up and look like your daddy and say we done give up one baby to poverty and that we ain't going to give up nary another one . . . I'm waiting.

Walter. Ruth—

Mama. If you a son of mine, tell her! (WALTER *turns, looks at her and can say nothing. She continues, bitterly.*) You . . . you are a disgrace to your father's memory. Somebody get me my hat.

Curtain

Responding to the Play

Analyzing Act One

Identifying Details

1. In the fourth speech of the play, the line "Check coming today?" arouses our interest and curiosity. Trace the development of the check in this act as it moves from something that arouses our curiosity to something that becomes the central plot issue of the play.
2. In a play, our attention is held by people in **conflict.** Look carefully at the opening scene through Walter's exit (page 839). Point out the number of subjects, large and small, over which the characters argue.
3. Walter expresses his "dream" in Scene 1. What does he want to do with Mama's money? How does his dream **conflict** with Beneatha's ambition?
4. At the end of Scene 2, why is Mama so angry with Walter?

Interpreting Meanings

5. It has been said that to enjoy a play we must believe what is happening and care about the characters. Is the action of the play believable so far? Explain your answer.

6. At the end of Act I, which character are you "rooting" for most, and why?
7. There has been a considerable build-up for Mama's entrance, which occurs late in Scene 1. What are we told about Mama before she appears? In a play, showing is better than telling. When she makes her entrance, Mama immediately shows us in small ways what kind of woman and mother she is. What does she do, and what do her actions reveal about her **character**?
8. It is important that we know the strength of Mama's religious beliefs because it is these beliefs that influence her decision not to give Walter the money. How does the playwright show us how strong Mama's beliefs are?
9. The character of Asagai, introduced in Scene 2, gives us a different perspective on life in the Younger household. What does Asagai represent? How is he contrasted with George Murchison, Benethea's other admirer?
10. What dramatic questions have been posed in this first act? What possible answers could each question have?

Act Two

Scene 1

Time: Later the same day.

At rise: RUTH *is ironing again. She has the radio going. Presently* BENEATHA's *bedroom door opens and* RUTH's *mouth falls and she puts down the iron in fascination.*

Ruth. What have we got on tonight!

Beneatha (*emerging grandly from the doorway so that we can see her thoroughly robed in the costume* ASAGAI *brought*). You are looking at what a well-dressed Nigerian woman wears—(*She parades for* RUTH, *her hair completely hidden by the headdress; she is coquettishly fanning herself with an ornate oriental fan, mistakenly more like Butterfly[1] than any Nigerian that ever was.*) Isn't it beautiful? (*She promenades to the radio and, with an arrogant flourish, turns off the good loud blues that is playing.*) Enough of this assimilationist junk! (RUTH *follows her with her eyes as she goes to the phonograph and puts on a record and turns and waits ceremoniously for the music to come up. Then, with a shout—*) OCOMOGO-SIAY![2]

[RUTH *jumps. The music comes up, a lovely Nigerian melody.* BENEATHA *listens, enraptured, her eyes far away—"back to the past." She begins to dance.* RUTH *is dumfounded.*]

Ruth. What kind of dance is that?

Beneatha. A folk dance.

Ruth (*Pearl Bailey[3]*). What kind of folks do that, honey?

Beneatha. It's from Nigeria. It's a dance of welcome.

Ruth. Who you welcoming?

Beneatha. The men back to the village.

Ruth. Where they been?

Beneatha. How should I know—out hunting or something. Anyway, they are coming back now . . .

Ruth. Well, that's good.

Beneatha (*with the record*).

---

1. **Butterfly:** Madame Butterfly, the heroine in the opera by Giacomo Puccini.
2. **Ocomogosiay:** a shout of triumph in battle. It is a coined word, combining syllables from the Yoruba, Swahili, and Zulu languages.
3. **Pearl Bailey:** an American entertainer, singer, and actress. Ruth is imitating her.

Alundi, alundi
Alundi alunya
Jop pu a jeepua
Ang gu sooooooooooo

Ai yai yae . . .
Ayehaye—alundi . . .[4]

[WALTER *comes in during this performance; he has obviously been drinking. He leans against the door heavily and watches his sister, at first with distaste. Then his eyes look off—"back to the past"—as he lifts both his fists to the roof, screaming.*]

Walter. YEAH . . . AND ETHIOPIA STRETCH FORTH HER HANDS AGAIN! . . .

Ruth (*drily, looking at him*). Yes—and Africa sure is claiming her own tonight. (*She gives them both up and starts ironing again.*)

Walter (*all in a drunken, dramatic shout*). Shut up! . . . I'm digging them drums . . . them drums move me! . . . (*He makes his weaving way to his wife's face and leans in close to her.*) In my *heart of hearts*—(*He thumps his chest.*)—I am much warrior!

Ruth (*without even looking up*). In your heart of hearts you are much drunkard.

Walter (*coming away from her and starting to wander around the room, shouting*). Me and Jomo[5] . . . (*Intently, in his sister's face. She has stopped dancing to watch him in this unknown mood.*) That's my man, Kenyatta. (*Shouting and thumping his chest*) FLAMING SPEAR! . . . (*He is suddenly in possession of an imaginary spear and actively spearing enemies all over the room.*) OCOMOGOSIAY . . . THE LION IS WAKING . . . OWIMOWEH![6] (*He pulls his shirt open and leaps up on a table and gestures with his spear. The bell rings.* RUTH *goes to answer.*)

Beneatha (*to encourage* WALTER, *thoroughly caught up with this side of him*). OCOMOGO-SIAY, FLAMING SPEAR!

Walter (*on the table, very far gone, his eyes pure glass sheets. He sees what we cannot, that he is a leader of his people, a great chief, a descendant*

---

4. **alundi . . . alundi:** a Yoruba harvest festival song. *Alundi* means "Happy holiday."
5. **Jomo:** Jomo Kenyatta (1894?–1978), leader and president of Kenya. *Jomo* means "flaming spear."
6. **Owimoweh:** variation of a Zulu word meaning "lion."

"OH, DO YOU HEAR, MY BLACK BROTHERS?"

of Chaka,[7] *and that the hour to march has come*). Listen, my black brothers—

Beneatha. OCOMOGOSIAY!

Walter. —Do you hear the waters rushing against the shores of the coastlands—

Beneatha. OCOMOGOSIAY!

Walter. —Do you hear the screeching of the cocks in yonder hills beyond where the chiefs meet in council for the coming of the mighty war—

Beneatha. OCOMOGOSIAY!

Walter. —Do you hear the beating of the wings of the birds flying low over the mountains and the low places of our land—

[RUTH *opens the door.* GEORGE MURCHISON *enters.*]

Beneatha. OCOMOGOSIAY!

Walter. —Do you hear the singing of the women, singing the war songs of our fathers to the babies in the great houses . . . singing the sweet war songs? OH, DO YOU HEAR, MY BLACK BROTHERS!

Beneatha (*completely gone*). We hear you, Flaming Spear—

Walter. Telling us to prepare for the greatness of the time—(*to* GEORGE) Black Brother!

[*He extends his hand for the fraternal clasp.*]

George. Black Brother, your Mother!

Ruth (*having had enough, and embarrassed for the family*). Beneatha, you got company—what's the matter with you? Walter Lee Younger, get down off that table and stop acting like a fool . . .

[WALTER *comes down off the table suddenly and makes a quick exit to the bathroom.*]

Ruth. He's had a little to drink . . . I don't know what her excuse is.

George (*to* BENEATHA). Look honey, we're going to the theater—we're not going to be *in* it . . . so go change, huh?

Ruth. You expect this boy to go out with you looking like that?

Beneatha (*looking at* GEORGE). That's up to George. If he's ashamed of his heritage—

George. Oh, don't be so proud of yourself, Bennie—just because you look eccentric.

Beneatha. How can something that's natural be eccentric?

George. That's what being eccentric means—being natural. Get dressed.

Beneatha. I don't like that, George.

Ruth. Why must you and your brother make an argument out of everything people say?

Beneatha. Because I hate assimilationist Negroes!

Ruth. Will somebody please tell me what assimila-whoever means!

George. Oh, it's just a college girl's way of calling people Uncle Toms—but that isn't what it means at all.

Ruth. Well, what does it mean?

Beneatha (*cutting* GEORGE *off and staring at him as she replies to* RUTH). It means someone who is willing to give up his own culture and submerge himself completely in the dominant, and in this case, *oppressive* culture!

George. Oh, dear, dear, dear! Here we go! A lecture on the African past! On our Great West African Heritage! In one second we will hear all about the great Ashanti[8] empires; the great Songhay[9] civilizations; and the great sculpture of Bénin[10]—and then some poetry in the Bantu[11]—and the whole monologue will end with the word *heritage!* (*Nastily*) Let's face it, baby, your heritage is nothing but a bunch of raggedy . . . spirituals and some grass huts!

Beneatha. *Grass huts!* (RUTH *crosses to her and forcibly pushes her toward the bedroom.*) See there . . . you are standing there in your splendid ignorance talking about people who were the first to smelt iron on the face of the earth! (RUTH *is pushing her through the door.*) The Ashanti were performing surgical operations when the English—(RUTH *pulls the door to, with* BENEATHA *on the other side, and smiles graciously at* GEORGE. BENEATHA *opens the door and shouts the end of the sentence defiantly at* GEORGE.)—

---

7. **Chaka:** Zulu chief and military leader (1787?–1828).

8. **Ashanti:** people in west Africa who had a powerful empire in the eighteenth and nineteenth centuries. Ashanti was once a British protectorate, and is now primarily in Ghana.
9. **Songhay:** west African empire in the sixteenth century.
10. **Bénin:** west African kingdom (c. 1400–1700) known for its beautiful sculpture, metalwork, and carved ivory.
11. **Bantu:** family of languages spoken in central and southern Africa, including Zulu and Swahili.

were still tatooing themselves with blue dragons . . . (*She goes back inside.*)

Ruth. Have a seat, George. (*They both sit.* RUTH *folds her hands rather primly on her lap, determined to demonstrate the civilization of the family.*) Warm, ain't it? I mean for September. (*Pause*) Just like they always say about Chicago weather: If it's too hot or cold for you, just wait a minute and it'll change. (*She smiles happily at this cliché of clichés.*) Everybody say its got to do with them bombs and things they keep setting off. (*Pause*) Would you like a nice cold beer?

George. No, thank you. I don't care for beer. (*He looks at his watch.*) I hope she hurries up.

Ruth. What time is the show?

George. It's an eight-thirty curtain. That's just Chicago, though. In New York standard curtain time is eight forty.

[*He is rather proud of this knowledge.*]

Ruth (*properly appreciating it*). You get to New York a lot?

George (*offhand*). Few times a year.

Ruth. Oh—that's nice. I've never been to New York.

[WALTER *enters. We feel he has relieved himself, but the edge of unreality is still with him.*]

Walter. New York ain't got nothing Chicago ain't. Just a bunch of hustling people all squeezed up together—being ''Eastern.''

[*He turns his face into a screw of displeasure.*]

George. Oh—you've been?

Walter. *Plenty* of times.

Ruth (*shocked at the lie*). Walter Lee Younger!

Walter (*staring her down*). Plenty! (*Pause*) What we got to drink in this house? Why don't you offer this man some refreshment. (*To* GEORGE) They don't know how to entertain people in this house, man.

George. Thank you—I don't really care for anything.

Walter (*feeling his head; sobriety coming*). Where's Mama?

Ruth. She ain't come back yet.

Walter (*looking* MURCHISON *over from head to toe, scrutinizing his carefully casual tweed sports jacket over cashmere V-neck sweater over soft eyelet shirt and tie, and soft slacks, finished off with white buckskin shoes*). Why all you college boys wear them funny-looking white shoes?

Ruth. Walter Lee!

[GEORGE MURCHISON *ignores the remark.*]

Walter (*to* RUTH). Well, they look crazy—white shoes, cold as it is.

Ruth (*crushed*). You have to excuse him—

Walter. No he don't! Excuse me for what? What you always excusing me for! I'll excuse myself when I needs to be excused! (*A pause*) They look as funny as them black knee socks Beneatha wears out of here all the time.

Ruth. It's the college *style*, Walter.

Walter. Style?!—She looks like she got burnt legs or something!

Ruth. Oh, Walter—

Walter (*an irritable mimic*). Oh, Walter! Oh, Walter! (*to* MURCHISON) How's your old man making out? I understand you all going to buy that big hotel on the Drive? (*He finds a beer in the refrigerator, wanders over to* MURCHISON, *sipping and wiping his lips with the back of his hand, and straddling a chair backwards to talk to the other man.*) Shrewd move. Your old man is all right, man. (*Tapping his head and half winking for emphasis*) I mean he knows how to operate. I mean he thinks *big*, you know what I mean, I mean for a *home*, you know? But I think he's kind of running out of ideas now. I'd like to talk to him. Listen, man, I got some plans that could turn this city upside down. I mean I think like he does. *Big*. Invest big, gamble big, shoot, lose *big* if you have to, you know what I mean. It's hard to find a man on this whole Southside who understands my kind of thinking—you dig? (*He scrutinizes* MURCHISON *again, drinks his beer, squints his eyes and leans in close, confidential, man to man.*) Me and you ought to sit down and talk sometimes, man. Man, I got me some ideas . . .

Murchison (*with boredom*). Yeah—sometimes we'll have to do that, Walter.

Walter (*understanding the indifference, and offended*). Yeah—well, when you get the time, man. I know you a busy little boy.

Ruth. Walter, please—

Walter (*bitterly, hurt*). I know ain't nothing in this world as busy as you colored college boys with your fraternity pins and white shoes . . .

Ruth (*covering her face with humiliation*). Oh, Walter Lee—

Walter. I see you all all the time—with the books tucked under your arms—going to your (*British A—a mimic*) ''clahsses.'' And for what! What in the world you learning over there? Filling up your heads—(counting off on his fingers)—with the sociology and the psychology—but they teaching you how to be a man? How to take over and run the world? They teaching you how to run a rubber plantation or a steel mill? Naw—just to talk proper and read books and wear white shoes . . .

George (looking at him with distaste, a little above it all). You're all wacked up with bitterness, man.

Walter (intently, almost quietly, between the teeth, glaring at the boy). And you—ain't you bitter, man? Ain't you just about had it yet? Don't you see no stars gleaming that you can't reach out and grab? You happy? You contented turkey—you happy? You got it made? Bitter? Man, I'm a volcano. Bitter? Here I am a giant—surrounded by ants! Ants who can't even understand what it is the giant is talking about.

Ruth (passionately and suddenly). Oh, Walter—ain't you with nobody!

Walter (violently). No! 'Cause ain't nobody with me! Not even my own mother!

Ruth. Walter, that's a terrible thing to say!

[BENEATHA enters, dressed for the evening in a cocktail dress and earrings.]

George. Well—hey, you look great.

Beneatha. Let's go, George. See you all later.

Ruth. Have a nice time.

George. Thanks. Good night. (To WALTER, sarcastically) Good night, Prometheus.[12]

[BENEATHA and GEORGE exit.]

Walter (to RUTH). Who is Prometheus?

Ruth. I don't know. Don't worry about it.

Walter (in fury, pointing after GEORGE). See there—they get to a point where they can't insult you man to man—they got to go talk about something ain't nobody never heard of!

Ruth. How do you know it was an insult? (to humor him) Maybe Prometheus is a nice fellow.

Walter. Prometheus! I bet there ain't even no such thing! I bet that simple-minded clown—

Ruth. Walter— (She stops what she is doing and looks at him.)

---

12. **Prometheus:** in Greek mythology, a Titan (giant) who stole fire from the gods and gave it to humans. Zeus, king of the gods, punished Prometheus by chaining him to a mountain, where each day a vulture ate out his liver. Each night, Zeus caused the liver to be renewed so that the torture was excruciating and endless. Prometheus was finally freed by Hercules.

Walter (yelling). Don't start!

Ruth. Start what?

Walter. Your nagging! Where was I? Who was I with? How much money did I spend?

Ruth (plaintively). Walter Lee—why don't we just try to talk about it . . .

Walter (not listening). I been out talking with people who understand me. People who care about the things I got on my mind.

Ruth (wearily). I guess that means people like Willy Harris.

Walter. Yes, people like Willy Harris.

Ruth (with a sudden flash of impatience). Why don't you all just hurry up and go into the banking business and stop talking about it!

Walter. Why? You want to know why? 'Cause we all tied up in a race of people that don't know how to do nothing but moan, pray and have babies!

[The line is too bitter even for him and he looks at her and sits down.]

Ruth. Oh, Walter . . . (Softly) Honey, why can't you stop fighting me?

Walter (without thinking). Who's fighting you? Who even cares about you?

[This line begins the retardation of his mood.]

Ruth. Well—(She waits a long time, and then with resignation starts to put away her things.) I guess I might as well go on to bed . . . (More or less to herself) I don't know where we lost it . . . but we have . . . (Then, to him) I—I'm sorry about this new baby, Walter. . . . I guess I just didn't realize how bad things was with us . . . I guess I just didn't really realize—(She starts out to the bedroom and stops.) You want some hot milk?

Walter. Hot milk?

Ruth. Yes—hot milk.

Walter. Why hot milk?

Ruth. 'Cause after all that liquor you come home with you ought to have something hot in your stomach.

Walter. I don't want no milk.

Ruth. You want some coffee then?

Walter. No, I don't want no coffee. I don't want nothing hot to drink. (Almost plaintively) Why you always trying to give me something to eat?

Ruth (standing and looking at him helplessly). What else can I give you, Walter Lee Younger?

[She stands and looks at him and presently turns to go out again. He lifts his head and watches her *going away from him in a new mood which began to emerge when he asked her "Who cares about you?"*]

Walter. It's been rough, ain't it, baby? *(She hears and stops but does not turn around he continues to her back.)* I guess between two people there ain't never as much understood as folks generally thinks there is. I mean like between me and you— *(She turns to face him.)* How we gets to the place where we scared to talk softness to each other. *(He waits, thinking hard himself.)* Why you think it got to be like that? *(He is thoughtful, almost as a child would be.)* Ruth, what is it gets into people ought to be close?

Ruth. I don't know, honey. I think about it a lot.

Walter. On account of you and me, you mean? The way things are with us. The way something done come down between us.

Ruth. There ain't so much between us, Walter . . . Not when you come to me and try to talk to me. Try to be with me . . . a little even.

Walter *(total honesty).* Sometimes . . . sometimes . . . I don't even know how to try.

Ruth. Walter—

Walter. Yes?

Ruth *(coming to him, gently and with misgiving, but coming to him).* Honey . . . life don't have to be like this. I mean sometimes people can do things so that things are better . . . You remember how we used to talk when Travis was born . . . about the way we were going to live . . . the kind of house . . . *(She is stroking his head.)* Well, it's all starting to slip away from us . . .

[MAMA *enters, and* WALTER *jumps and shouts at her.*]

Walter. Mama, where have you been?

Mama. My—them steps is longer than they used to be. Whew! *(She sits down and ignores him.)* How you feeling this evening, Ruth?

[RUTH *shrugs, disturbed some at having been prematurely interrupted and watching her husband knowingly.*]

Walter. Mama, where have you been all day?

Mama *(still ignoring him and leaning on the table and changing to more comfortable shoes).* Where's Travis?

Ruth. I let him go out earlier and he ain't come back yet. Boy, is he going to get it!

Walter. Mama!

Mama *(as if she has heard him for the first time).* Yes, son?

Walter. Where did you go this afternoon?

Mama. I went downtown to tend to some business that I had to tend to.

Walter. What kind of business?

Mama. You know better than to question me like a child, Brother.

Walter *(rising and bending over the table).* Where were you Mama? *(Bringing his fists down and shouting)* Mama, you didn't go do something with that insurance money, something crazy?

[*The front door opens slowly, interrupting him, and* TRAVIS *peeks his head in, less than hopefully.*]

Travis *(to his mother).* Mama, I—

Ruth. "Mama I" nothing! You're going to get it, boy! Get on in that bedroom and get yourself ready!

Travis. But I—

Mama. Why don't you all never let the child explain hisself.

Ruth. Keep out of it now, Lena.

[MAMA *clamps her lips together, and* RUTH *advances toward her son menacingly.*]

Ruth. A thousand times I have told you not to go off like that—

Mama *(holding out her arms to her grandson).* Well—at least let me tell him something. I want him to be the first one to hear . . . Come here, Travis. *(The boy obeys, gladly.)* Travis—*(She takes him by the shoulder and looks into his face.)*—you know that money we got in the mail this morning?

Travis. Yes'm—

Mama. Well—what you think your grandmama gone and done with that money?

Travis. I don't know, Grandmama.

Mama *(putting her finger on her nose for emphasis).* She went out and she bought you a house! *(The explosion comes from* WALTER *at the end of the revelation and he jumps up and turns away from all of them in a fury.* MAMA *continues, to* TRAVIS.*)* You glad about the house? It's going to be yours when you get to be a man.

Travis. Yeah—I always wanted to live in a house.

Mama. All right, gimme some sugar then— *(*TRAVIS *puts his arms around her neck as she watches her son over the boy's shoulder. Then, to* TRAVIS, *after the embrace.)* Now when you say

". . . it's all starting to slip away from us . . ."

your prayers tonight, you thank God and your grandfather—'cause it was him who give you the house—in his way.

Ruth *(taking the boy from* MAMA *and pushing him toward the bedroom).* Now you get out of here and get ready for your beating.

Travis. Aw, Mama—

Ruth. Get on in there—*(Closing the door behind him and turning radiantly to her mother-in-law)* So you went and did it!

Mama *(quietly, looking at her son with pain).* Yes, I did.

Ruth *(raising both arms classically). Praise God!* *(Looks at* WALTER *a moment who says nothing. She crosses rapidly to her husband.)* Please, honey—let me be glad . . . you be glad too. *(She has laid her hands on his shoulders, but he shakes himself free of her roughly, without turning to face her.)* Oh, Walter . . . a home . . . a home. *(She comes back to* MAMA.*)* Well—where is it? How big is it? How much it going to cost?

Mama. Well—

Ruth. When we moving?

Mama *(smiling at her).* First of the month.

Ruth *(throwing back her head with jubilance). Praise God!*

Mama *(tentatively, still looking at her son's back turned against her and* RUTH*).* It's—it's a nice house too . . . *(She cannot help speaking directly to him. An imploring quality in her voice, her manner, makes her almost like a girl now.)* Three bedrooms—nice big one for you and Ruth . . . Me and Beneatha still have to share our room, but Travis have one of his own—and *(with difficulty)* I figure if the—new baby—is a boy, we could get one of them double-decker outfits . . . And there's a yard with a little patch of dirt where I could maybe get to grow me a few flowers . . . And a nice big basement . . .

Ruth. Walter honey, be glad—

Mama *(still to his back, fingering things on the table).* 'Course I don't want to make it sound fancier than it is . . . It's just a plain little old house—but it's made good and solid—and it will be *ours.* Walter Lee—it makes a difference in a man when he can walk on floors that belong to *him* . . .

Ruth. Where is it?

Mama *(frightened at this telling).* Well—well—it's out there in Clybourne Park—

[RUTH's *radiance fades abruptly, and* WALTER *fi-*

nally turns slowly to face his mother with incredulity and hostility.]

Ruth. Where?

Mama *(matter-of-factly).* Four o six Clybourne Street, Clybourne Park.

Ruth. Clybourne Park? Mama, there ain't no colored people living in Clybourne Park.

Mama *(almost idiotically).* Well, I guess there's going to be some now.

Walter *(bitterly).* So that's the peace and comfort you went out and bought for us today!

Mama *(raising her eyes to meet his finally).* Son— I just tried to find the nicest place for the least amount of money for my family.

Ruth *(trying to recover from the shock).* Well— well—'course I ain't one never been 'fraid of no crackers, mind you—but—well, wasn't there no other houses nowhere?

Mama. Them houses they put up for colored in them areas way out all seem to cost twice as much as other houses. I did the best I could.

Ruth *(Struck senseless with the news, in its various degrees of goodness and trouble, she sits a moment, her fists propping her chin in thought, and then she starts to rise, bringing her fists down with vigor, the radiance spreading from cheek to cheek again).* Well—well!—All I can say is—if this is my time in life—*my time*—to say goodbye— *(and she builds with momentum as she starts to circle the room with an exuberant, almost tearfully happy release)*—to these . . . cracking walls!—(She pounds the walls.)—and these marching roaches!—(She wipes at an imaginary army of marching roaches.)—and this cramped little closet which ain't now or never was no kitchen! . . . then I say it loud and good, Hallelujah! and goodbye misery . . . I don't never want to see your ugly face again! (She laughs joyously, having practically destroyed the apartment, and flings her arms up and lets them come down happily, slowly, reflectively, over her abdomen, aware for the first time perhaps that the life therein pulses with happiness and not despair.)* Lena?

Mama *(moved, watching her happiness).* Yes, honey?

Ruth *(looking off).* Is there—is there a whole lot of sunlight?

Mama *(understanding).* Yes, child, there's a whole lot of sunlight.

[*Long pause*]

Ruth (*collecting herself and going to the door of the room* TRAVIS *is in*). Well—I guess I better see 'bout Travis. (*to* MAMA) Lord, I sure don't feel like whipping nobody today! (*She exits.*)

Mama (*The mother and son are left alone now and the mother waits a long time, considering deeply, before she speaks.*). Son—you—you understand what I done, don't you? (WALTER *is silent and sullen.*) I—I just seen my family falling apart today . . . just falling to pieces in front of my eyes . . . We couldn't of gone on like we was today. We was going backwards 'stead of forwards—talking 'bout not wanting babies and wishing each other was dead . . . When it gets like that in life—you just got to do something different, push on out and do something bigger . . . (*She waits.*) I wish you say something, son . . . I wish you'd say how deep inside you think I done the right thing—

Walter (*crossing slowly to his bedroom door and finally turning there and speaking measuredly*). What you need me to say you done right for? *You* the head of this family. You run our lives like you want to. It was your money and you did what you wanted with it. So what you need for me to say it was all right for? (*Bitterly, to hurt her as deeply as he knows is possible*) So you butchered up a dream of mine—you—who always talking 'bout your children's dreams . . .

Mama. Walter Lee—

[*He just closes the door behind him.* MAMA *sits alone, thinking heavily.*]

Curtain

Scene 2

Time: Friday night. A few weeks later.

At rise: Packing crates mark the intention of the family to move. BENEATHA *and* GEORGE *come in, presumably from an evening out again.*

George. O.K. . . . O.K., whatever you say . . . (*They both sit on the couch. He tries to kiss her. She moves away.*) Look, we've had a nice evening; let's not spoil it, huh? . . .

[*He again turns her head and tries to nuzzle in and she turns away from him, not with distaste but with momentary lack of interest; in a mood to pursue what they were talking about.*]

Beneatha. I'm *trying* to talk to you.

George. We always talk.

Beneatha. Yes—and I love to talk.

George (*exasperated; rising*). I know it and I don't mind it sometimes . . . I want you to cut it out, see—The moody stuff, I mean. I don't like it. You're a nice-looking girl . . . all over. That's all you need, honey, forget the atmosphere. Guys aren't going to go for the atmosphere—they're going to go for what they see. Be glad for that. Drop the Garbo[1] routine. It doesn't go with you. As for myself, I want a nice—(*groping*)—simple (*thoughtfully*)—sophisticated girl . . . not a poet—O.K.?

[*She rebuffs him again and he starts to leave.*]

Beneatha. Why are you angry?

George. Because this is stupid! I don't go out with you to discuss the nature of "quiet desperation"[2] or to hear all about your thoughts—because the world will go on thinking what it thinks regardless—

Beneatha. Then why read books? Why go to school?

George (*with artificial patience, counting on his fingers*). It's simple. You read books—to learn facts—to get grades—to pass the course—to get a degree. That's all—it has nothing to do with thoughts.

[*A long pause*]

Beneatha. I see. (*A longer pause as she looks at him*) Good night, George.

[GEORGE *looks at her a little oddly, and starts to exit. He meets* MAMA *coming in.*]

George. Oh—hello, Mrs. Younger.

Mama. Hello, George, how you feeling?

George. Fine—fine, how are you?

Mama. Oh, a little tired. You know them steps can get you after a day's work. You all have a nice time tonight?

George. Yes—a fine time. Well, good night.

Mama. Good night. (*He exits.* MAMA *closes the door behind her.*) Hello, honey. What you sitting like that for?

Beneatha. I'm just sitting.

---

1. **Garbo:** Greta Garbo (born 1905), Swedish star of American films, who was famous for her moodiness and for the line "I want to be alone."
2. **"quiet desperation":** George is referring to a line from Henry David Thoreau's *Walden* (see page 207): "The mass of men lead lives of quiet desperation."

in America around you. . . . All the great schools in the world! And—and I'll say, all right son—it's your seventeenth birthday, what is it you've decided? . . . Just tell me where you want to go to school and you'll *go*. Just tell me what it is you want to be—and you'll *be* it. . . . Whatever you want to be—Yessir! *(He holds his arms open for* TRAVIS.*)* You just name it, son . . . *(*TRAVIS *leaps into them.)* and I hand you the world!

[WALTER's *voice has risen in pitch and hysterical promise and on the last line he lifts* TRAVIS *high.]*

Blackout

Scene 3

Time: Saturday, moving day, one week later.

Before the curtain rises, RUTH's voice, a strident, dramatic church alto, cuts through the silence.

It is, in the darkness, a triumphant surge, a penetrating statement of expectation: "Oh, Lord, I don't feel no ways tired! Children, oh, glory hallelujah!"

As the curtain rises we see that RUTH is alone in the living room, finishing up the family's packing. It is moving day. She is nailing crates and tying cartons. BENEATHA enters, carrying a guitar case, and watches her exuberant sister-in-law.

"Just tell me what it is you want to be—and you'll be *it . . ."*

Ruth. Hey!

Beneatha (*putting away the case*). Hi.

Ruth (*pointing at a package*). Honey—look in that package there and see what I found on sale this morning at the South Center. (RUTH *gets up and moves to the package and draws out some curtains.*) Lookahere—hand-turned hems!

Beneatha. How do you know the window size out there?

Ruth (*who hadn't thought of that*). Oh— Well, they bound to fit something in the whole house. Anyhow, they was too good a bargain to pass up. (RUTH *taps her head, suddenly remembering something.*) Oh, Bennie—I meant to put a special note on that carton over there. That's your mama's good china and she wants 'em to be very careful with it.

Beneatha. I'll do it.

[BENEATHA *finds a piece of paper and starts to draw large letters on it.*]

Ruth. You know what I'm going to do soon as I get in that new house?

Beneatha. What?

Ruth. Honey—I'm going to run me a tub of water up to here . . . (*With her fingers practially up to her nostrils*) And I'm going to get in it—and I am going to sit . . . and sit . . . and sit in that hot water and the first person who knocks to tell *me* to hurry up and come out—

Beneatha. Gets shot at sunrise.

Ruth (*laughing happily*). You said it, sister! (*Noticing how large* BENEATHA *is absent-mindedly making the note*) Honey, they ain't going to read that from no airplane.

Beneatha (*laughing herself*). I guess I always think things have more emphasis if they are big, somehow.

Ruth (*looking up at her and smiling*). You and your brother seem to have that as a philosophy of life. Lord, that man—done changed so 'round here. You know—you know what we did last night? Me and Walter Lee?

Beneatha. What?

Ruth (*smiling to herself*). We went to the movies. (*Looking at* BENEATHA *to see if she understands*) We went to the movies. You know the last time me and Walter went to the movies together?

Beneatha. No.

Ruth. Me neither. That's how long it been. (*Smiling again*) But we went last night. The picture wasn't much good, but that didn't seem to matter. We went—and we held hands.

Beneatha. Oh, Lord!

Ruth. We held hands—and you know what?

Beneatha. What?

Ruth. When we come out of the show it was late and dark and all the stores and things was closed up . . . and it was kind of chilly and there wasn't many people on the streets . . . and we was still holding hands, me and Walter.

Beneatha. You're killing me.

[WALTER *enters with a large package. His happiness is deep in him; he cannot keep still with his new-found exuberance. He is singing and wiggling and snapping his fingers. He puts his package in a corner and puts a phonograph record, which he has brought in with him, on the record player. As the music comes up he dances over to* RUTH *and tries to get her to dance with him. She gives in at last to his raunchiness and in a fit of giggling allows herself to be drawn into his mood and together they deliberately burlesque an old social dance of their youth.*]

Beneatha (*Regarding them a long time as they dance, then drawing in her breath for a deeply exaggerated comment which she does not particularly mean.*). Talk about—olddddddddddd-fashioneddddddd—Negroes!

Walter (*stopping momentarily*). What kind of Negroes? (*He says this in fun. He is not angry with her today, nor with anyone. He starts to dance with his wife again.*)

Beneatha. Old-fashioned.

Walter (*as he dances with* RUTH). You know, when these *New Negroes* have their convention— (*pointing at his sister*)—that is going to be the chairman of the Committee on Unending Agitation. (*He goes on dancing, then stops.*) Race, race, race! . . . Girl, I do believe you are the first person in the history of the entire human race to successfully brainwash yourself. (BENEATHA *breaks up and he goes on dancing. He stops again, enjoying his tease.*) Shoot, even the N double A C P takes a holiday sometimes! (BENEATHA *and* RUTH *laugh. He dances with* RUTH *some more and starts to laugh and stops and pantomimes someone over an operating table.*) I can just see that chick someday looking down at some poor cat on an operating table before she starts to slice him, saying . . . (*pulling his sleeves back maliciously*) "By the way, what are your views on civil rights down there? . . ." (He laughs at her again and starts to dance happily. The bell sounds.)

Beneatha. Sticks and stones may break my bones, but . . . words will never hurt me!

[BENEATHA *goes to the door and opens it as WAL-TER and RUTH go on with the clowning. BE-NEATHA is somewhat surprised to see a quiet-looking middle-aged white man in a business suit holding his hat and a briefcase in his hand and consulting a small piece of paper.*]

Man. Uh—how do you do, miss. I am looking for a Mrs.—*(He looks at the slip of paper.)* Mrs. Lena Younger?

Beneatha *(smoothing her hair with slight embarrassment).* Oh—yes, that's my mother. Excuse me *(She closes the door and turns to quiet the other two.)* Ruth! Brother! Somebody's here. *(Then she opens the door. The man casts a curious quick glance at all of them.)* Uh—come in please.

Man *(coming in).* Thank you.

Beneatha. My mother isn't here just now. Is it business?

Man. Yes . . . well, of a sort.

Walter *(freely, the Man of the House).* Have a seat, I'm Mrs. Younger's son. I look after most of her business matters.

[RUTH *and* BENEATHA *exchange amused glances.*]

Man *(regarding WALTER, and sitting).* Well— My name is Karl Lindner . . .

Walter *(stretching out his hand).* Walter Younger. This is my wife—(RUTH *nods politely.)*—and my sister.

Lindner. How do you do.

Walter *(amiably, as he sits himself easily on a chair, leaning with interest forward on his knees and looking expectantly into the newcomer's face).* What can we do for you, Mr. Lindner!

Lindner *(some minor shuffling of the hat and briefcase on his knees).* Well—I am a representative of the Clybourne Park Improvement Association—

Walter *(pointing).* Why don't you sit your things on the floor?

Lindner. Oh—yes. Thank you. *(He slides the briefcase and hat under the chair.)* And as I was saying—I am from the Clybourne Park Improvement Association and we have had it brought to our attention at the last meeting that you people— or at least your mother—has bought a piece of

residential property at—*(He digs for the slip of paper again.)*—four o six Clybourne Street . . .

Walter. That's right. Care for something to drink? Ruth, get Mr. Lindner a beer.

Lindner *(upset for some reason).* Oh—no, really. I mean thank you very much, but no thank you.

Ruth *(innocently).* Some coffee?

Lindner. Thank you, nothing at all.

[BENEATHA *is watching the man carefully.*]

Lindner. Well, I don't know how much you folks know about our organization. *(He is a gentle man; thoughtful and somewhat labored in his manner.)* It is one of these community organizations set up to look after—oh, you know, things like block upkeep and special projects and we also have what we call our New Neighbors Orientation Committee . . .

Beneatha *(drily).* Yes—and what do they do?

Lindner *(Turning a little to her and then returning the main force to WALTER.).* Well—it's what you might call a sort of welcoming committee, I guess. I mean they, we, I'm the chairman of the committee—go around and see the new people who move into the neighborhood and sort of give them the lowdown on the way we do things out in Clybourne Park.

Beneatha *(with appreciation of the two meanings, which escape RUTH and WALTER).* Un-huh.

Lindner. And we also have the category of what the association calls—*(He looks elsewhere.)*— uh—special community problems . . .

Beneatha. Yes—and what are some of those?

Walter. Girl, let the man talk.

Lindner *(with understated relief).* Thank you. I would sort of like to explain this thing in my own way. I mean I want to explain to you in a certain way.

Walter. Go ahead.

Lindner. Yes. Well. I'm going to try to get right to the point. I'm sure we'll all appreciate that in the long run.

Beneatha. Yes.

Walter. Be still now!

Lindner. Well—

Ruth *(still innocently).* Would you like another chair—you don't look comfortable.

Lindner *(more frustrated than annoyed).* No, thank you very much. Please. Well—to get right to the point I—*(a great breath, and he is off at last)* I am sure you people must be aware of some of the incidents which have happened in various

"Today everybody knows what it means to be on the outside of something."

parts of the city when colored people have moved into certain areas—(BENEATHA *exhales heavily and starts tossing a piece of fruit up and down in the air.*) Well—because we have what I think is going to be a unique type of organization in American community life—not only do we deplore that kind of thing—but we are trying to do something about it. (BENEATHA *stops tossing and turns with a new and quizzical interest to the man.*) We feel— (*gaining confidence in his mission because of the interest in the faces of the people he is talking to*)—we feel that most of the trouble in this world, when you come right down to it—(*He hits his knee for emphasis.*)—most of the trouble exists because people just don't sit down and talk to each other.

Ruth (*nodding as she might in church, pleased with the remark*). You can say that again, mister.

Lindner (*more encouraged by such affirmation*). That we don't try hard enough in this world to

understand the other fellow's problem. The other guy's point of view.

Ruth. Now that's right.

[BENEATHA *and* WALTER *merely watch and listen with genuine interest.*]

Lindner. Yes—that's the way we feel out in Clybourne Park. And that's why I was elected to come here this afternoon and talk to you people. Friendly like, you know, the way people should talk to each other and see if we couldn't find some way to work this thing out. As I say, the whole business is a matter of *caring* about the other fellow. Anybody can see that you are a nice family of folks, hard working and honest I'm sure. (BENEATHA *frowns slightly, quizzically, her head tilted regarding him.*) Today everybody knows what it means to be on the outside of *something*. And of course, there is always somebody who is out to take the advantage of people who don't always understand.

Walter. What do you mean?

Lindner. Well—you see our community is made up of people who've worked hard as the dickens for years to build up that little community. They're not rich and fancy people; just hard-working, honest people who don't really have much but those little homes and a dream of the kind of community they want to raise their children in. Now, I don't say we are perfect and there is a lot wrong in some of the things they want. But you've got to admit that a man, right or wrong, has the right to want to have the neighborhood he lives in a certain kind of way. And at the moment the overwhelming majority of our people out there feel that people get along better, take more of a common interest in the life of the community, when they share a common background. I want you to believe me when I tell you that race prejudice simply doesn't enter into it. It is a matter of the people of Clybourne Park believing, rightly or wrongly, as I say, that for the happiness of all concerned that our Negro families are happier when they live in their *own* communities.

Beneatha (*with a grand and bitter gesture*). This, friends, is the Welcoming Committee!

Walter (*dumfounded, looking at* LINDNER). Is this what you came marching all the way over here to tell us?

Lindner. Well, now we've been having a fine conversation. I hope you'll hear me all the way through.

Walter (*tightly*). Go ahead, man.

Lindner. You see—in the face of all things I have said, we are prepared to make your family a very generous offer . . .

Beneatha. Thirty pieces and not a coin less![1]

Walter. Yeah?

Lindner (*putting on his glasses and drawing a form out of the briefcase*). Our association is prepared, through the collective effort or our people, to buy the house from you at a financial gain to your family.

Ruth. Lord have mercy, ain't this the living gall!

Walter. All right, you through?

Lindner. Well, I want to give you the exact terms of the financial arrangement—

Walter. We don't want to hear no exact terms of

no arrangements. I want to know if you got any more to tell us 'bout getting together?

Lindner (*taking off his glasses*). Well—I don't suppose that you feel . . .

Walter. Never mind how I feel—you got any more to say 'bout how people ought to sit down and talk to each other? . . . Get out of my house, man. (*He turns his back and walks to the door.*)

Lindner (*looking around at the hostile faces and reaching and assembling his hat and briefcase*). Well—I don't understand why you people are reacting this way. What do you think you are going to gain by moving into a neighborhood where you just aren't wanted and where some elements—well—people can get awful worked up when they feel that their whole way of life and everything they've ever worked for is threatened.

Walter. Get out.

Lindner (*at the door, holding a small card*). Well—I'm sorry it went like this.

Walter. Get out.

Lindner (*almost sadly regarding* WALTER). You just can't force people to change their hearts, son.

[*He turns and puts his card on a table and exits.* WALTER *pushes the door to with stinging hatred, and stands looking at it.* RUTH *just sits and* BENEATHA *just stands. They say nothing.* MAMA *and* TRAVIS *enter.*]

Mama. Well—this all the packing got done since I left out of here this morning. I testify before God that my children got all the energy of the dead. What time the moving men due?

Beneatha. Four o'clock. You had a caller, Mama. (*She is smiling, teasingly.*)

Mama. Sure enough—who?

Beneatha (*her arms folded saucily*). The Welcoming Committee.

[WALTER *and* RUTH *giggle.*]

Mama (*innocently*). Who?

Beneatha. The Welcoming Committee. They said they're sure going to be glad to see you when you get there.

Walter (*devilishly*). Yeah, they said they can't hardly wait to see your face.

[*Laughter*]

Mama (*sensing their facetiousness*). What's the matter with you all?

---

1. **Thirty . . . less:** a reference to the thirty pieces of silver Judas Iscariot received for betraying Jesus.

Walter. Ain't nothing the matter with us. We just telling you 'bout the gentleman who came to see you this afternoon. From the Clybourne Park Improvement Association.

Mama. What he want?

Ruth (*in the same mood as* BENEATHA *and* WALTER). To welcome you, honey.

Walter. He said they can't hardly wait. He said the one thing they don't have, that they just *dying* to have out there is a fine family of colored people! (*to* RUTH *and* BENEATHA) Ain't that right!

Ruth and Beneatha (*mockingly*). Yeah! He left his card in case—

[*They indicate the card, and* MAMA *picks it up and throws it on the floor—understanding and looking off as she draws her chair up to the table on which she has put her plant and some sticks and some cord.*]

Mama. Father, give us strength. (*Knowingly—and without fun*) Did he threaten us?

Beneatha. Oh—Mama—they don't do it like that anymore. He talked Brotherhood. He said everybody ought to learn how to sit down and hate each other with good Christian fellowship.

[*She and* WALTER *shake hands to ridicule the remark.*]

Mama (*sadly*). Lord, protect us . . .

Ruth. You should hear the money those folks raised to buy the house from us. All we paid and then some.

Beneatha. What they think we going to do—eat 'em?

Ruth. No honey, marry 'em.

Mama (*shaking her head*). Lord, Lord, Lord . . .

Ruth. Well—that's the way the crackers crumble. Joke.

Beneatha (*laughingly noticing what her mother is doing*). Mama, what are you doing?

Mama. Fixing my plant so it won't get hurt none on the way . . .

Beneatha. Mama, you going to take *that* to the new house?

Mama. Un-huh—

Beneatha. That raggedy-looking old thing?

Mama (*stopping and looking at her*). It expresses *me.*

Ruth (*with delight, to* BENEATHA). So there, Miss Thing!

[WALTER *comes to* MAMA *suddenly and bends down behind her and squeezes her in his arms with all his strength. She is overwhelmed by the suddenness of it and, though delighted, her manner is like that of* RUTH *and* TRAVIS.]

Mama. Look out now, boy! You make me mess up my thing here!

Walter (*his face lit, he slips down on his knees beside her, his arms still around her*). Mama . . . you know what it means to climb up in the chariot?

Mama (*gruffly, very happy*). Get on away from me now . . .

Ruth (*near the gift-wrapped package, trying to catch* WALTER'S *eye*). Psst—

Walter. What the old song say, Mama . . .

Ruth. Walter— Now? (*She is pointing at the package.*)

Walter (*speaking the lines, sweetly, playfully, in his mother's face*).

I got wings . . . you got wings . . .
All God's Children got wings . . .

Mama. Boy—get out of my face and do some work . . .

Walter.

When I get to heaven gonna put on my wings,
Gonna fly all over God's heaven . . .

Beneatha (*teasingly, from across the room*). Everybody talking 'bout heaven ain't going there!

Walter (*to* RUTH, *who is carrying the box across to them*). I don't know, you think we ought to give her that . . . Seems to me she ain't been very appreciative around here.

Mama (*eyeing the box, which is obviously a gift*). What is that?

Walter (*taking it from* RUTH *and putting it on the table in front of* MAMA). Well—what you all think? Should we give it to her?

Ruth. Oh—she was pretty good today.

Mama. I'll good you— (*She turns her eyes to the box again.*)

Beneatha. Open it, Mama.

[*She stands up, looks at it, turns and looks at all of them, and then presses her hands together and does not open the package.*]

Walter (*sweetly*). Open it, Mama. It's for you. (MAMA *looks in his eyes. It is the first present in her life without its being Christmas. Slowly she opens her package and lifts out, one by one, a brand-new sparkling set of gardening tools.* WAL-

"To our own Mrs. Miniver . . ."

TER *continues, prodding.*) Ruth made up the note—read it . . .

Mama (*picking up the card and adjusting her glasses*). "To our own Mrs. Miniver[2]—Love from Brother, Ruth, and Beneatha." Ain't that lovely . . .

Travis (*tugging at his father's sleeve*). Daddy, can I give her mine now?

Walter. All right, son. (TRAVIS *flies to get his gift.*) Travis didn't want to go in with the rest of us, Mama. He got his own. (*Somewhat amused*) We don't know what it is . . .

Travis (*racing back in the room with a large hatbox and putting it in front of his grandmother*). Here!

Mama. Lord have mercy, baby. You done gone and bought your grandmother a hat?

Travis (*very proud*). Open it!

[*She does and lifts out an elaborate, but very elaborate, wide gardening hat, and all the adults break up at the sight of it.*]

Ruth. Travis, honey, what is that?

Travis (*who thinks it is beautiful and appropriate*). It's a gardening hat! Like the ladies always have on in the magazines when they work in their gardens.

Beneatha (*giggling fiercely*). Travis—we were trying to make Mama Mrs. Miniver—not Scarlett O'Hara![3]

Mama (*indignantly*). What's the matter with you all! This here is a beautiful hat! (*Absurdly*) I always wanted me one just like it!

[*She pops it on her head to prove it to her grandson, and the hat is ludicrous and considerably oversized.*]

Ruth. Hot dog! Go, Mama!

Walter (*doubled over with laughter*). I'm sorry, Mama—but you look like you ready to go out and chop you some cotton sure enough!

[*They all laugh except* MAMA, *out of deference to* TRAVIS's *feelings.*]

Mama (*gathering the boy up to her*). Bless your heart—this is the prettiest hat I ever owned— (WALTER, RUTH, *and* BENEATHA *chime in—*

noisily, festively, and insincerely congratulating TRAVIS *on his gift.*) What are we all standing around here for? We ain't finished packin' yet. Bennie, you ain't packed one book.

[*The bell rings.*]

Beneatha. That couldn't be the movers . . . it's not hardly two good yet—

[BENEATHA *goes into her room.* MAMA *starts for door.*]

Walter (*turning, stiffening*). Wait—wait—I'll get it. (*He stands and looks at the door.*)

Mama. You expecting company, son?

Walter (*just looking at the door*). Yeah—yeah . . .

[MAMA *looks at* RUTH, *and they exchange innocent and unfrightened glances.*]

Mama (*not understanding*). Well, let them in, son.

Beneatha (*from her room*). We need some more string.

Mama. Travis—you run to the hardware and get me some string cord.

[MAMA *goes out and* WALTER *turns and looks at* RUTH. TRAVIS *goes to a dish for money.*]

Ruth. Why don't you answer the door, man?

Walter (*suddenly bounding across the floor to her*). 'Cause sometimes it hard to let the future begin! (*Stooping down in her face*)

> I got wings! You got wings!
> All God's children got wings!

[*He crosses to the door and throws it open. Standing there is a very slight little man in a not too prosperous business suit and with haunted frightened eyes and a hat pulled down tightly, brim up, around his forehead.* TRAVIS *passes between the men and exits.* WALTER *leans deep in the man's face, still in his jubilance.*]

> When I get to heaven gonna put on my wings,
> Gonna fly all over God's heaven . . .

[*The little man just stares at him.*]

> Heaven—

(*Suddenly he stops and looks past the little man into the empty hallway.*) Where's Willy, man?

Bobo. He ain't with me.

Walter (*not disturbed*). Oh—come on in. You know my wife.

---

2. **Mrs. Miniver:** a genteel English heroine of a movie by that name, played by Greer Garson.
3. **Scarlett O'Hara:** flamboyant heroine of *Gone With the Wind,* a novel about the South and the Civil War.

Bobo (*dumbly, taking off his hat*). Yes—h'you, Miss Ruth.

Ruth (*quietly, a mood apart from her husband already, seeing* BOBO). Hello, Bobo.

Walter. You right on time today . . . Right on time. That's the way! (*He slaps* BOBO *on his back.*) Sit down . . . lemme hear.

[RUTH *stands stiffly and quietly in back of them, as though somehow she senses death, her eyes fixed on her husband.*]

Bobo (*his frightened eyes on the floor, his hat in his hands*). Could I please get a drink of water, before I tell you about it, Walter Lee?

[WALTER *does not take his eyes off the man.* RUTH *goes blindly to the tap and gets a glass of water and brings it to* BOBO.]

Walter. There ain't nothing wrong, is there?

Bobo. Lemme tell you—

Walter. Man—didn't nothing go wrong?

Bobo. Lemme tell you—Walter Lee. (*Looking at* RUTH *and talking to her more than to* WALTER) You know how it was. I got to tell you how it was. I mean first I got to tell you how it was all the way . . . I mean about the money I put in, Walter Lee . . .

Walter (*with taut agitation now*). What about the money you put in?

Bobo. Well—it wasn't much as we told you—me and Willy—(*He stops.*) I'm sorry, Walter. I got a bad feeling about it. I got a real bad feeling about it . . .

Walter. Man, what you telling me about all this for? . . . Tell me what happened in Springfield . . .

Bobo. Springfield.

Ruth (*like a dead woman*). What was supposed to happen in Springfield?

Bobo (*to her*). This deal that me and Walter went into with Willy— Me and Willy was going to go down to Springfield and spread some money 'round so's we wouldn't have to wait so long for the liquor license . . . That's what we were going to do. Everybody said that was the way you had to do, you understand, Miss Ruth?

Walter. Man—what happened down there?

Bobo (*a pitiful man, near tears*). I'm trying to tell you, Walter.

Walter (*screaming at him suddenly*). THEN TELL ME . . . DAMMIT . . . WHAT'S THE MATTER WITH YOU?

Bobo. Man . . . I didn't go to no Springfield, yesterday.

Walter (*halted, life hanging in the moment*). Why not?

Bobo (*the long way, the hard way to tell*). 'Cause I didn't have no reasons to . . .

Walter. Man, what are you talking about!

Bobo. I'm talking about the fact that when I got to the train station yesterday morning—eight o'clock like we planned . . . Man—*Willy didn't never show up.*

Walter. Why . . . where was he . . . where is he?

Bobo. That's what I'm trying to tell you . . . I don't know . . . I waited six hours . . . I called his house . . . and I waited . . . six hours . . . I waited in that train station six hours . . . (*Breaking into tears*) That was all the extra money I had in the world . . . (*Looking up at* WALTER *with the tears running down his face*) Man, *Willy is gone.*

Walter. Gone, what you mean Willy is gone? Gone where? You mean he went by himself. You mean he went off to Springfield by himself—to take care of getting the license—(*Turns and looks anxiously at* RUTH) You mean maybe he didn't want too many people in on the business down there? (*Looks to* RUTH *again, as before*) You know Willy got his own ways. (*Looks back to* BOBO) Maybe you was late yesterday and he just went on down there without you. Maybe—maybe—he's been callin' you at home tryin' to tell you what happened or something. Maybe—maybe—he just got sick. He's somewhere—he's got to be somewhere. We just got to find him—me and you got to find him. (*Grabs* BOBO *senselessly by the collar and starts to shake him*) We got to!

Bobo (*in sudden angry, frightened agony*). What's the matter with you, Walter! *When a cat take off with your money he don't leave you no maps!*

Walter (*turning madly, as though he is looking for* WILLY *in the very room*). Willy! . . . Willy . . . don't do it . . . Please don't do it . . . Man, not with that money . . . Man, please, not with that money . . . Oh, God, . . . Don't let it be true . . . (*He is wandering around, crying out for* WILLY *and looking for him or perhaps for help from God.*) Man . . . I trusted you . . . Man, I put my life in your hands . . . (*He starts to crumple down on the floor as* RUTH *just covers her face in horror.* MAMA *opens the door and comes into the room, with* BENEATHA *behind her.*) Man . . . (*He starts to pound the floor with his fists, sobbing wildly.*) *That money is made out of my father's flesh . . .*

Bobo *(standing over him helplessly).* I'm sorry, Walter . . . *(Only* WALTER's *sobs reply.* BOBO *puts on his hat.)* I had my life staked on this deal, too . . . *(He exits.)*

Mama *(to* WALTER*).* Son—*(She goes to him, bends down to him, talks to his bent head.)* Son . . . Is it gone? Son, I give you sixty-five hundred dollars. Is it gone? All of it? Beneatha's money too?

Walter *(lifting his head slowly).* Mama . . . I never . . . went to the bank at all . . .

Mama *(not wanting to believe him).* You mean . . . your sister's school money . . . you used that too . . . Walter? . . .

Walter. Yessss! . . . All of it . . . It's all gone . . .

[There is total silence. RUTH *stands with her face covered with her hands;* BENEATHA *leans forlornly against a wall, fingering a piece of red ribbon from the mother's gift.* MAMA *stops and looks at her son without recognition and then, quite without thinking about it, starts to beat him senselessly in the face.* BENEATHA *goes to them and stops it.]*

Beneatha. Mama!

*[*MAMA *stops and looks at both of her children and rises slowly and wanders vaguely, aimlessly away from them]*

Mama. I seen . . . him . . . night after night . . . come in . . . and look at the rug . . . and then look at me . . . the red showing in his eyes . . . the veins moving in his head . . . I seen him grow thin and old before he was forty . . . working and working and working like somebody's old horse . . . killing himself . . . and you—you give it all away in a day . . .

Beneatha. Mama—

Mama. Oh, God . . . *(She looks up to Him.)* Look down here—and show me the strength.

Beneatha. Mama—

Mama *(folding over).* Strength . . .

Beneatha *(plaintively).* Mama . . .

Mama. Strength!

Curtain

Responding to the Play

Analyzing Act Two

Identifying Details

1. In Scene 1, how does Walter react to Beneatha's version of an African dance and chant? How does George Murchison react to both Walter and Beneatha?

2. At the end of Scene 1, we find out what Mama has done with the insurance money. What is Ruth's reaction to Mama's news? What hints have we had earlier that this is what Ruth wanted all along?

3. How does Walter react to Mama's announcement? What is the problem with the new house?

4. In Scene 2, what does Mama say and do that makes Walter feel differently about his future? In Scene 3, what are we told and shown that convinces us that Walter has changed?

5. What is the purpose of Mr. Lindner's visit to the Younger family? How does Walter react when he realizes what Mr. Lindner really wants?

6. What bad news does Bobo bring to the family at the end of Scene 3?

Interpreting Meanings

7. In Scene 1, why does George address Walter as "Prometheus"?

8. Walter asks Ruth, "What is it gets into people ought to be close?" When they try to talk about why they are having such problems, they reach no conclusion. What do you think the playwright wants us to understand as the cause of their problems?

9. Beneatha is a serious character, but she also becomes comic through her excesses. Discuss how she can be seen as a comic **character.** Is she a convincing character, or a stereotype? Explain.

10. To which character does Mama first reveal her news in Scene 1? Why?

11. Scene 3 is full of **reversals,** in which sudden shifts take place in the fortunes of the main characters. Discuss the reversals in this scene. What is the mood at the beginning of this scene and at the end?

12. How do you feel about the various characters at this point in the play? Are you rooting for any particular character? Have your sympathies switched from one character to another? Explain.

Act Three

An hour later.

At curtain, there is a sullen light of gloom in the living room, gray light not unlike that which began the first scene of Act One. At left we can see WALTER *within his room, alone with himself. He is stretched out on the bed, his shirt out and open, his arms under his head. He does not smoke, he does not cry out, he merely lies there, looking up at the ceiling, much as if he were alone in the world.*

In the living room BENEATHA *sits at the table, still surrounded by the now almost ominous packing crates. She sits looking off. We feel that this is a mood struck perhaps an hour before, and it lingers now, full of the empty sound of profound disappointment. We see on a line from her brother's bedroom the sameness of their attitudes. Presently the bell rings and* BENEATHA *rises without ambition or interest in answering. It is* ASAGAI, *smiling broadly, striding into the room with energy and happy expectation and conversation.*

Asagai. I came over . . . I had some free time. I thought I might help with the packing. Ah, I like the look of packing crates! A household in preparation for a journey! It depresses some people . . . but for me . . . it is another feeling. Something full of the flow of life, do you understand? Movement, progress . . . It makes me think of Africa.

Beneatha. Africa!

Asagai. What kind of a mood is this? Have I told you how deeply you move me?

Beneatha. He gave away the money, Asagai . . .

Asagai. Who gave away what money?

Beneatha. The insurance money. My brother gave it away.

Asagai. Gave it away?

Beneatha. He made an investment! With a man even Travis wouldn't have trusted.

Asagai. And it's gone?

Beneatha. Gone!

Asagai. I'm very sorry . . . And you, now?

Beneatha. Me? . . . Me? . . . Me I'm nothing . . . Me. When I was very small . . . we used to take our sleds out in the wintertime and the only hills we had were the ice-covered stone steps of some houses down the street. And we used to fill them in with snow and make them smooth and slide down them all day . . . and it was very dangerous you know . . . far too steep . . . and sure enough one day a kid named Rufus came down too fast and hit the sidewalk . . . and we saw his face just split open right there in front of us . . . And I remember standing there looking at his bloody open face thinking that was the end of Rufus. But the ambulance came and they took him to the hospital and they fixed the broken bones and they sewed it all up . . . and the next time I saw Rufus he just had a little line down the middle of his face . . . I never got over that . . .

[WALTER *sits up, listening on the bed. Throughout this scene it is important that we feel his reaction at all times, that he visibly respond to the words of his sister and* ASAGAI.]

Asagai. What?

Beneatha. That that was what one person could do for another, fix him up—sew up the problem, make him all right again. That was the most marvelous thing in the world . . . I wanted to do that. I always thought it was the one concrete thing in the world that a human being could do. Fix up the sick, you know—and make them whole again. This was truly being God . . .

Asagai. You wanted to be God?

Beneatha. No—I wanted to cure. It used to be so important to me. I wanted to cure. It used to matter. I used to care. I mean about people and how their bodies hurt . . .

Asagai. And you've stopped caring?

Beneatha. Yes—I think so.

Asagai. Why?

[WALTER *rises, goes to the door of his room and is about to open it, then stops and stands listening, leaning on the door jamb.*]

Beneatha. Because it doesn't seem deep enough, close enough to what ails mankind—I mean this thing of sewing up bodies or administering drugs. Don't you understand? It was a child's reaction to the world. I thought that doctors had the secret to all the hurts. . . . That's the way a child sees things—or an idealist.

Asagai. Children see things very well sometimes—and idealists even better.

Beneatha. I know that's what you think. Because you are still where I left off—you still care. This is what you see for the world, for Africa. You with the dreams of the future will patch up all Africa—you are going to cure the Great Sore of colonialism with Independence——

Asagai. Yes!

Beneatha. Yes—and you think that one word is the penicillin of the human spirit: "Independence!" But then what?

Asagai. That will be the problem for another time. First we must get there.

Beneatha. And where does it end?

Asagai. End? Who even spoke of an end? To life? To living?

Beneatha. An end to misery!

Asagai (*smiling*). You sound like a French intellectual.

Beneatha. No! I sound like a human being who just had her future taken right out of her hands! While I was sleeping in my bed in there, things were happening in this world that directly concerned me—and nobody asked me, consulted me—they just went out and did things—and changed my life. Don't you see there isn't any real progress, Asagai, there is only one large circle that we march in, around and around, each of us with our own little picture—in front of us—our own little mirage that we think is the future.

Asagai. That is the mistake.

Beneatha. What?

Asagai. What you just said—about the circle. It isn't a circle—it is simply a long line—as in geometry, you know, one that reaches into infinity. And because we cannot see the end—we also cannot see how it changes. And it is very odd but those who see the changes are called "idealists"—and those who cannot, or refuse to think, they are the "realists." It is very strange, and amusing too, I think.

Beneatha. You—you are almost religious.

Asagai. Yes . . . I think I have the religion of doing what is necessary in the world—and of worshiping man—because he is so marvelous, you see.

Beneatha. Man is foul! And the human race deserves its misery!

Asagai. You see: *you* have become the religious one in the old sense. Already, and after such a small defeat, you are worshiping despair.

Beneatha. From now on, I worship the truth—and the truth is that people are puny, small, and selfish. . . .

Asagai. Truth? Why is it that you despairing ones always think that only you have the truth? I never thought to see *you* like that. You! Your brother made a stupid, childish mistake—and you are grateful to him. So that now you can give up the ailing human race on account of it. You talk about what good is struggle; what good is anything? Where are we all going? And why are we bothering?

Beneatha. *And you cannot answer it!* All your talk and dreams about Africa and Independence. Independence and then what? What about all the crooks and petty thieves and just plain idiots who will come into power to steal and plunder the same as before—only now they will be black and do it in the name of the new Independence— You cannot answer that.

Asagai (*shouting over her*). *I live the answer!* (*Pause*) In my village at home it is the exceptional man who can even read a newspaper . . . or who ever *sees* a book at all. I will go home and much of what I will have to say will seem strange to the people of my village . . . But I will teach and work and things will happen, slowly and swiftly. At times it will seem that nothing changes at all . . . and then again . . . the sudden dramatic events which make history leap into the future. And then quiet again. Retrogression even. Guns, murder, revolution. And I even will have moments when I wonder if the quiet was not better than all that death and hatred. But I will look about my village at the illiteracy and disease and ignorance and I will not wonder long. And perhaps . . . perhaps I will be a great man . . . I mean perhaps I will hold on to the substance of truth and find my way always with the right course . . . and perhaps for it I will be butchered in my bed some night by the servants of empire . . .

Beneatha. *The martyr!*

Asagai. . . . or perhaps I shall live to be a very old man, respected and esteemed in my new nation . . . And perhaps I shall hold office and this is what I'm trying to tell you, Alaiyo; perhaps the things I believe now for my country will be wrong and outmoded, and I will not understand and do terrible things to have things my way or merely to keep my power. Don't you see that there will be young men and women, not British soldiers then, but my own black countrymen . . . to step out of the shadows some evening and slit my then useless throat? Don't you see they have always been there . . . that they always will be. And that such a thing as my own death will be an advance? They who might kill me even . . . actually replenish me!

Beneatha. Oh, Asagai, I know all that.

Asagai. Good! Then stop moaning and groaning and tell me what you plan to do.

Beneatha. Do?

Asagai. I have a bit of a suggestion.

Beneatha. What?

Asagai *(rather quietly for him)*. That when it is all over—that you come home with me—

Beneatha *(slapping herself on the forehead with exasperation born of misunderstanding)*. Oh—Asagai—at this moment you decide to be romantic!

Asagai *(quickly understanding the misunderstanding)*. My dear, young creature of the New World—I do not mean across the city—I mean across the ocean; home—to Africa.

Beneatha *(slowly understanding and turning to him with murmured amazement)*. To—to Nigeria?

Asagai. Yes! . . . *(Smiling and lifting his arms playfully)* Three hundred years later the African Prince rose up out of the seas and swept the maiden back across the middle passage over which her ancestors had come—

Beneatha *(unable to play)*. Nigeria?

Asagai. Nigeria. Home. *(Coming to her with genuine romantic flippancy)* I will show you our mountains and our stars; and give you cool drinks from gourds and teach you the old songs and the ways of our people—and, in time, we will pretend that—*(very softly)*—you have only been away for a day—

[*She turns her back to him, thinking. He swings her around and takes her full in his arms in a long embrace which proceeds to passion.*]

Beneatha *(pulling away)*. You're getting me all mixed up—

Asagai. Why?

Beneatha. Too many things—too many things have happened today. I must sit down and think. I don't know what I feel about anything right this minute.

[*She promptly sits down and props her chin on her fist.*]

Asagai *(charmed)*. All right, I shall leave you. No—don't get up. *(Touching her, gently, sweetly)* Just sit awhile and think . . . Never be afraid to sit awhile and think. *(He goes to door and looks at her.)* How often I have looked at you and said, "Ah—so this is what the New World hath finally wrought . . ."

[*He exits.* BENEATHA *sits on alone. Presently* WALTER *enters from his room and starts to rummage through things, feverishly looking for something. She looks up and turns in her seat.*]

Beneatha *(hissingly)*. Yes—just look at what the New World hath wrought! . . . Just look! *(She gestures with bitter disgust.)* There he is! *Monsieur le petit bourgeois noir*[1]—himself! There he is—Symbol of a Rising Class! Entrepreneur! Titan[2] of the system! (WALTER *ignores her completely and continues frantically and destructively looking for something and hurling things to floor and tearing things out of their place in his search.* BENEATHA *ignores the eccentricity of his actions and goes on with the monologue of insult.)* Did you dream of yachts on Lake Michigan, Brother? Did you see yourself on that Great Day sitting down at the Conference Table, surrounded by all the mighty bald-headed men in America? All halted, waiting, breathless, waiting for your pronouncements on industry? Waiting for you—Chairman of the Board? (WALTER *finds what he is looking for—a small piece of white paper—and pushes it in his pocket and puts on his coat and rushes out without ever having looked at her. She shouts after him.)* I look at you and I see the final triumph of stupidity in the world!

[*The door slams and she returns to just sitting again.* RUTH *comes quickly out of* MAMA's *room.*]

Ruth. Who was that?

Beneatha. Your husband.

Ruth. Where did he go?

Beneatha. Who knows—maybe he has an appointment at U.S. Steel.

Ruth *(anxiously, with frightened eyes)*. You didn't say nothing bad to him, did you?

Beneatha. Bad? Say anything bad to him? No—I told him he was a sweet boy and full of dreams and everything is strictly peachy keen, as the ofay kids say!

[MAMA *enters from her bedroom. She is lost, vague, trying to catch hold, to make some sense of her former command of the world, but it still eludes her. A sense of waste overwhelms her gait; a measure of apology rides on her shoulders. She goes to her plant, which has remained on the table, looks at it, picks it up and takes it to the window sill and sits it outside, and she stands and looks at it a long moment. Then she closes the*

---

1. **Monsieur le petit bourgeois noir:** "Mister black lower middle class." The *petit bourgeois* are owners of shops and small business.
2. **Titan:** In Greek mythology, the Titans were a race of giants.

window, straightens her body with effort and turns around to her children.]

Mama. Well—ain't it a mess in here, though? (*A false cheerfulness, a beginning of something*) I guess we all better stop moping around and get some work done. All this unpacking and everything we got to do. (RUTH *raises her head slowly in response to the sense of the line; and* BENEATHA *in similar manner turns very slowly to look at her mother.*) One of you all better call the moving people and tell 'em not to come.

Ruth. Tell 'em not to come?

Mama. Of course, baby. Ain't no need in 'em coming all the way here and having to go back. They charges for that too. (*She sits down, fingers to her brow, thinking.*) Lord, ever since I was a little girl, I always remembers people saying, "Lena—Lena Eggleston, you aims too high all the time. You needs to slow down and see life a little more like it is. Just slow down some." That's what they always used to say down home—"Lord, that Lena Eggleston is a high-minded thing. She'll get her due one day!"

Ruth. No, Lena . . .

Mama. Me and Big Walter just didn't never learn right.

Ruth. Lena, no! We gotta go. Bennie—tell her . . . (*She rises and crosses to* BENEATHA *with her arms outstretched.* BENEATHA *doesn't respond.*) Tell her we can still move . . . the notes ain't but a hundred and twenty-five a month. We got four grown people in this house—we can work . . .

Mama (*to herself*). Just aimed too high all the time—

Ruth (*turning and going to* MAMA *fast—the words pouring out with urgency and desperation*). Lena—I'll work . . . I'll work twenty hours a day in all the kitchens in Chicago . . . I'll strap my baby on my back if I have to and scrub all the floors in America and wash all the sheets in America if I have to—but we got to move . . . We got to get out of here . . .

[MAMA *reaches out absently and pats* RUTH's *hand.*]

Mama. No—I sees things differently now. Been thinking 'bout some of the things we could do to fix this place up some. I seen a secondhand bureau over on Maxwell Street just the other day that could fit right there. (*She points to where the new furniture might go.* RUTH *wanders away from her.*) Would need some new handles on it and then a little varnish and then it look like something brand-new. And—we can put up them new curtains in the kitchen . . . Why this place be looking fine. Cheer us all up so that we forget trouble ever came . . . (*To* RUTH) And you could get some nice screens to put up in your room round the baby's bassinet . . . (*She looks at both of them, pleadingly.*) Sometimes you just got to know when to give up some things . . . and hold on to what you got.

[WALTER *enters from the outside, looking spent and leaning against the door, his coat hanging from him.*]

Mama. Where you been, son?

Walter (*breathing hard*). Made a call.

Mama. To who, son?

Walter. To The Man.

Mama. What man, baby?

Walter. The Man, Mama. Don't you know who The Man is?

Ruth. Walter Lee?

Walter. *The Man.* Like the guys in the streets say—The Man. Captain Boss—Mistuh Charley . . . Old Captain Please Mr. Bossman . . .

Beneatha (*suddenly*). Lindner!

Walter. That's right! That's good. I told him to come right over.

Beneatha (*fiercely, understanding*). For what? What do you want to see him for!

Walter (*looking at his sister*). We going to do business with him.

Mama. What you talking 'bout, son?

Walter. Talking 'bout life, Mama. You all always telling me to see life like it is. Well—I laid in there on my back today . . . and I figured it out. Life just like it is. Who gets and who don't get. (*He sits down with his coat on and laughs.*) Mama, you know it's all divided up. Life is. Sure enough. Between the takers and the "tooken." (*He laughs.*) I've figured it out finally. (*He looks around at them.*) Yeah. Some of us always getting "tooken." (*He laughs.*) People like Willy Harris, they don't never get "tooken." And you know why the rest of us do? 'Cause we all mixed up. Mixed up bad. We get to looking 'round for the right and the wrong; and we worry about it and cry about it and stay up nights trying to figure out 'bout the wrong and the right of things all the time . . . And all the time, man, them takers is out there operating, just taking and taking. Willy Harris? Shoot—Willy Harris don't even count. He don't even count in the big scheme of things. But I'll say one thing for old Willy Harris . . . he's taught me something. He's taught me to keep my eye on what counts in this world. Yeah—*(Shouting out a little)* Thanks, Willy!

Ruth. What did you call that man for, Walter Lee?

Walter. Called him to tell him to come on over to the show. Gonna put on a show for the man. Just what he wants to see. You see, Mama, the man came here today and he told us that them people out there where you want us to move—well they so upset they willing to pay us not to move out there. *(He laughs again.)* And—and oh, Mama—you would of been proud of the way me and Ruth and Bennie acted. We told him to get out . . . Lord have mercy! We told the man to get out. Oh, we was some proud folks this afternoon, yeah. *(He lights a cigarette.)* We were still full of that old-time stuff . . .

Ruth *(coming toward him slowly)*. You talking 'bout taking them people's money to keep us from moving in that house?

Walter. I ain't just talking 'bout it, baby—I'm telling you that's what's going to happen.

Beneatha. Oh, God! Where is the bottom! Where is the real honest-to-God bottom so he can't go any farther!

Walter. See—that's the old stuff. You and that boy that was here today. You all want everybody to carry a flag and a spear and sing some marching songs, huh? You wanna spend your life looking into things and trying to find the right and the wrong part, huh? Yeah. You know what's going to happen to that body someday—he'll find himself sitting in a dungeon, locked in forever—and the takers will have the key! Forget it, baby! There ain't no causes—there ain't nothing but taking in this world, and he who takes most is smartest—and it don't make a bit of difference *how.*

Mama. You making something inside me cry, son. Some awful pain inside me.

Walter. Don't cry, Mama. Understand. That white man is going to walk in that door able to write checks for more money than we ever had. It's important to him and I'm going to help him . . . I'm going to put on the show, Mama.

Mama. Son—I come from five generations of people who was slaves and sharecroppers—but ain't nobody in my family never let nobody pay 'em no money that was a way of telling us we wasn't fit to walk the earth. We ain't never been that poor.

(Raising her eyes and looking at him) We ain't never been that dead inside.

Beneatha. Well—we are dead now. All the talk about dreams and sunlight that goes on in this house. All dead.

Walter. What's the matter with you all! I didn't make this world! It was given to me this way! Lord, yes, I want me some yachts someday! Yes, I want to hang some real pearls 'round my wife's neck. Ain't she supposed to wear no pearls? Somebody tell me—tell me, who decides which woman is suppose to wear pearls in this world. I tell you I am a *man*—and I think my wife should wear some pearls in this world!

[*This last line hangs a good while and* WALTER *begins to move about the room. The word "Man" has penetrated his consciousness; he mumbles it to himself repeatedly between strange agitated pauses as he moves about.*]

Mama. Baby, how you going to feel on the inside?

Walter. Fine! . . . Going to feel fine . . . a man . . .

Mama. You won't have nothing left then, Walter Lee.

Walter *(coming to her)*. I'm going to feel fine, Mama. I'm going to look that man in the eyes and say—*(He falters.)*—and say, "All right, Mr. Lindner—*(He falters even more.)*—that's your neighborhood out there. You got the right to keep it like you want. You got the right to have it like you want. Just write the check and—the house is yours." And, and I am going to say—*(His voice almost breaks.)* And you—you people just put the money in my hand and you won't have to live next to this bunch of stinking . . . *(He straightens up and moves away from his mother, walking around the room.)* Maybe—maybe I'll just get down on my black knees . . . *(He does so;* RUTH *and* BENNIE *and* MAMA *watch him in frozen horror.)* Captain, Mistuh, Bossman. *(He starts crying.)* A-hee-hee-hee! *(Wringing his hands in profoundly anguished imitation)* Yassssssuh! Great White Father, just gi' ussen de money, fo' God's sake, and we's ain't gwine come out deh and dirty up yo' white folks neighborhood . . .

[*He breaks down completely, then gets up and goes into the bedroom.*]

Beneatha. That is not a man. That is nothing but a toothless rat.

Mama. Yes—death done come in this here house. *(She is nodding, slowly, reflectively.)* Done come walking in my house. On the lips of my children. You what supposed to be my beginning again. You—what supposed to be my harvest. *(To BE-NEATHA)* You—you mourning your brother?

Beneatha. He's no brother of mine.

Mama. What you say?

Beneatha. I said that that individual in that room is no brother of mine.

Mama. That's what I thought you said. You feeling like you better than he is today? *(BENEATHA does not answer.)* Yes? What you tell him a minute ago? That he wasn't a man? Yes? You give him up for me? You done wrote his epitaph too—like the rest of the world? Well, who give you the privilege?

Beneatha. Be on my side for once! You saw what he just did, Mama! You saw him—down on his knees. Wasn't it you who taught me—to despise any man who would do that. Do what he's going to do.

Mama. Yes—I taught you that. Me and your daddy. But I thought I taught you something else too . . . I thought I taught you to love him.

Beneatha. Love him? There is nothing left to love.

Mama. There is always something left to love. And if you ain't learned that, you ain't learned nothing. *(Looking at her)* Have you cried for that boy today? I don't mean for yourself and for the family 'cause we lost the money. I mean for him; what he been through and what it done to him. Child, when do you think is the time to love somebody the most; when they done good and made things easy for everybody? Well then, you ain't through learning—because that ain't the time at all. It's when he's at his lowest and can't believe in hisself 'cause the world done whipped him so. When you starts measuring somebody, measure him right, child, measure him right. Make sure you done taken into account what hills and valleys he come through before he got to wherever he is.

[TRAVIS *bursts into the room at the end of the speech, leaving the door open.*]

Travis. Grandmama—the moving men are downstairs! The truck just pulled up.

Mama *(turning and looking at him)*. Are they, baby? They downstairs?

[*She sighs and sits.* LINDNER *appears in the doorway. He peers in and knocks lightly, to gain attention, and comes in. All turn to look at him.*]

Lindner *(hat and briefcase in hand)*. Uh—hello . . . (RUTH *crosses mechanically to the bedroom door and opens it and lets it swing open freely and slowly as the lights come up on* WALTER *within, still in his coat, sitting at the far corner of the room. He looks up and out through the room to* LINDNER.)

Ruth. He's here.

[*A long minute passes and* WALTER *slowly gets up.*]

Lindner *(coming to the table with efficiency, putting his briefcase on the table and starting to unfold papers and unscrew fountain pens)*. Well, I certainly was glad to hear from you people. (WALTER *has begun the trek out of the room, slowly and awkwardly, rather like a small boy, passing the back of his sleeve across his mouth from time to time.)* Life can really be so much simpler than people let it be most of the time. Well—with whom do I negotiate? You, Mrs. Younger, or your son here? (MAMA *sits with her hands folded on her lap and her eyes closed as* WALTER *advances.* TRAVIS *goes close to* LINDNER *and looks at the papers curiously.)* Just some official papers, sonny.

Ruth. Travis, you go downstairs.

Mama *(opening her eyes and looking into* WAL-TER'*s)*. No. Travis, you stay right here. And you make him understand what you doing, Walter Lee. You teach him good. Like Willy Harris taught you. You show where our five generations done come to. Go ahead, son—

Walter *(looks down into his boy's eyes.* TRAVIS *grins at him merrily and* WALTER *draws him beside him with his arm lightly around his shoulders.)*. Well, Mr. Lindner. (BENEATHA *turns away.)* We called you—*(There is a profound, simple groping quality in his speech.)*—because, well, me and my family *(He looks around and shifts from one foot to the other.)* Well—we are very plain people . . .

Lindner. Yes—

Walter. I mean—I have worked as a chauffeur most of my life—and my wife here, she does domestic work in people's kitchens. So does my mother. I mean—we are plain people . . .

Lindner. Yes, Mr. Younger—

Walter *(really like a small boy, looking down at his shoes and then up at the man)*. And—uh—well, my father, well, he was a laborer most of his life.

"*. . . this is—this is my son, who makes the sixth generation of our family in this country . . .*"

Lindner (*absolutely confused*). Uh, yes—

Walter (*looking down at his toes once again*). My father almost beat a man to death once because this man called him a bad name or something, you know what I mean?

Lindner. No, I'm afraid I don't.

Walter (*finally straightening up*). Well, what I mean is that we come from people who had a lot of pride. I mean—we are very proud people. And that's my sister over there and she's going to be a doctor—and we are very proud—

Lindner. Well—I am sure that is very nice, but—

Walter (*starting to cry and facing the man eye to eye*). What I am telling you is that we called you over here to tell you that we are very proud and that this is—this is my son, who makes the sixth generation of our family in this country, and that we have all thought about your offer and we have decided to move into our house because my father—my father—he earned it. (MAMA *has her eyes closed and is rocking back and forth as though she were in church, with her head nodding the amen yes.*) We don't want to make no trouble for nobody or fight no causes—but we will try to be good neighbors. That's all we got to say. (*He looks the man absolutely in the eyes.*) We don't want your money. (*He turns and walks away from the man.*)

Lindner (*looking around at all of them*). I take it then that you have decided to occupy.

Beneatha. That's what the man said.

Lindner (*to* MAMA *in her reverie*). Then I would like to appeal to you, Mrs. Younger. You are older and wiser and understand things better I am sure . . .

Mama (*rising*). I am afraid you don't understand. My son said we was going to move and there ain't nothing left for me to say. (*Shaking her head with double meaning*) You know how these young folks is nowadays, mister. Can't do a thing with 'em. Goodbye.

Lindner (*folding up his materials*). Well—if you are that final about it . . . There is nothing left for me to say. (*He finishes. He is almost ignored by the family, who are concentrating on* WALTER LEE. *At the door* LINDNER *halts and looks around.*) I sure hope you people know what you're doing. (*He shakes his head and exits.*)

Ruth (*looking around and coming to life*). Well, for God's sake—if the moving men are here— LET'S GET THIS BLESSED FAMILY OUT OF HERE!

3. Now you can move on to **evaluating** each element. Don't be timid about making your judgments; trust your instincts. Pretend you're reviewing the play for people who are eager to know your opinion.

Measure the play against each of the criteria listed under **Guidelines.** You might measure each criterion on a scale of 1 to 10 or 0 to 4 stars. Or you can rate each criterion on a scale like this one:

VERY POOR WEAK FAIR AVERAGE GOOD GREAT

4. Next, look over your evaluation of each element and come to some evaluation of the play as a whole. Do you think it's a good play? A great play? Do you think it will still be meaningful a hundred or two hundred years from now? Write a **thesis statement** that expresses your overall evaluation of the play.
5. Now organize your ideas, and decide what you'll include in your essay. Think of the body of your essay as providing support or evidence to back up the opinion that you've expressed in your thesis statement. You probably won't be able to discuss all of the criteria we have suggested; include the ones that give the strongest support to your thesis statement.
6. Find specific examples (incidents, quotations, characters) to support what you plan to say about the play. Jot down scene numbers, page numbers, line numbers, quotations, etc.

Writing

You might use the following plan for organizing your essay. Before you begin writing, make a rough outline of what you'll include in Paragraphs 2-6:

Paragraph 1: Introduction, thesis statement, overall evaluation of play.
Paragraph 2: Evaluation of the play's **characters.**
Paragraph 3: Evaluation of the **plot.**
Paragraph 4: Evaluation of the **theme.** Discuss whether or not you agree with the playwright's "message."
Paragraph 5: Evaluation of the **setting.**
Paragraph 7: Concluding paragraph, giving your subjective response to the play and reasons for that response.

Revising and Proofreading

Use the guidelines in the section at the back of this book, called **Writing About Literature,** to revise and proofread your essay.

Additional Writing Assignment

Pretend you are a TV or movie critic writing for your school newspaper. Write an evaluation of a television drama or series or a movie you have seen recently. Use the criteria here to discuss the elements of the drama or movie. Write at least three paragraphs.

FICTION
1945 TO THE PRESENT

Interior with Doorway by Richard Diebenkorn (1962). Oil.   The Pennsylvania Academy of the Fine Arts, Philadelphia. Henry Gilpin Fund.

UNIT ELEVEN

At all times, an old world is collapsing and a new world arising; we have better eyes for the collapse than the rise, for the old one is the world we know. The artist, in focusing on his own creation, finds, and offers, relief from the tension and sadness of being burdened not just with consciousness but with historical consciousness. . . .

—from *Hugging the Shore*,
John Updike

Literature in the Atomic Age

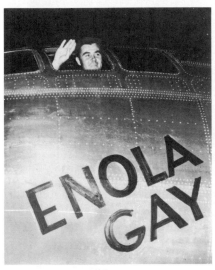

Enola Gay, the airplane that dropped the atomic bomb on Hiroshima.

On August 6, 1945, at 8:15 A.M., an atomic bomb was dropped upon the Japanese city of Hiroshima from the U.S. Air Force plane *Enola Gay.* Within seconds, the center of Hiroshima had disappeared. Though the bomb in effect ended World War II, its mushroom cloud has cast a shadow over each generation since.

The bomb is the dramatic symbol of the last half of the twentieth century. Its infamous mushroom cloud represents the proliferation of science and technology, the purpose of which was, ironically enough, to benefit humankind, to make life richer and easier for all of us.

In many ways, science and technology have fulfilled their promise. They have increased our life spans and fed and housed us better. They have moved us faster from place to place—even allowing a few of us to stroll on the surface of the moon.

But at the same time, science and technology have standardized and "assembly-lined" our lives. They have diminished Emerson's rugged individual. Now people often feel they are only a number on a computer disk or credit card. Even their thoughts seem to be shaped or controlled by mass advertising, mass journalism, and mass entertainment. Some people even predict that our new technologies threaten to deliver the planet itself back to lower organisms—to the cockroaches and turtles, perhaps—who may survive the nuclear holocaust which might one day engulf us.

Although many Americans disapproved of the use of the atomic bomb to end World War II, most Americans agreed with the purpose of the war itself. They were fighting against tyranny, against regimes that would destroy the American way of life. Only twenty years later, however, the United States became deeply involved in another overseas war—this time in Vietnam—that would sharply divide the nation. Many Americans could see no purpose in this war, and began to protest American involvement. Perhaps it was this atmosphere of rebellion, or maybe just a sense of the increasing precariousness of existence, that produced the "Sixties generation." Some of these young people used drugs to escape from the real world's uncertainties. Others began to challenge the accepted ideas of American society. Demonstrations, both peaceful and violent, became commonplace.

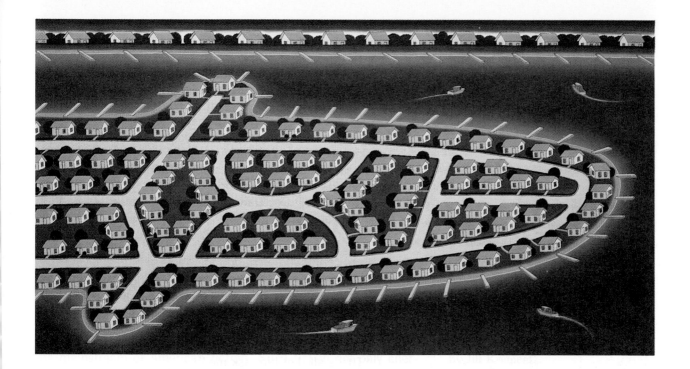

The New Voices in Fiction

To some writers, such as Kurt Vonnegut, the madness of the world was an inescapable condition of modern life, and the only appropriate response was hard-edged laughter at life's tragic ironies. The term "black humor" was coined to describe his work, as well as that of Joseph Heller, Terry Southern, and others. Heller's novel *Catch-22* (1962) is set in World War II, but the absurdities it describes belong to post-War life. In *Catch-22,* madness and war are inextricably mixed, not because madness is a result of war but because war is a result of our madness. The novel's protagonist, Yossarian, is a pilot who wants to get out of flying any more combat missions:

> It was a horrible joke, but Doc Daneeka didn't laugh until Yossarian came to him one mission later and pleaded again, without any real expectation of success, to be grounded. Doc Daneeka snickered once and was soon immersed in problems of his own, which included Chief White Halfoat, who had been challenging him all that morning to Indian wrestle, and Yossarian, who decided right then and there to go crazy.
> "You're wasting your time," Doc Daneeka was forced to tell him.
> "Can't you ground someone who's crazy?"
> "Oh, sure. I have to. There's a rule saying I have to ground anyone who's crazy."
> "Then why don't you ground me? I'm crazy. Ask Clevinger."
> "Clevinger? Where *is* Clevinger? You find Clevinger and I'll ask him."

Nassau County: A Time-Photo Alteration by Roger Brown (c. 1980). Oil.

Hirshhorn Museum and Sculpture Garden, Washington, D.C.

The Search for Transcendence

The English novel has from its beginnings concerned itself with the depiction of social life, but American fiction has often dealt with larger questions, such as the nature of good and evil and the search for transcendent spiritual values in the natural world. These are principal themes of our greatest nineteenth-century writers, of thinkers like Emerson and Thoreau and of writers of fiction like Melville, Hawthorne, and Poe. And much of the best fiction since World War II—including the work of such varied authors as Saul Bellow, Norman Mailer, Joan Didion, and John Updike—has dealt with these same themes.

Updike's characters, for example, seek spiritual revelations in ordinary life. "The invariable mark of wisdom," Emerson wrote, "is to find the miraculous in the common." This is the wisdom Updike's characters are searching for. Harry "Rabbit" Angstrom, for example, the protagonist of *Rabbit, Run* (1960), is burdened by what he sees as the "fraud" of modern life. Rabbit tries to deal with his many problems—a dead-end job, an unhappy marriage to an alcoholic wife, and the feeling that his best years are long over—by running from them. Yet despite these evasions, he continues to search for some higher meaning. Driving with a minister one day, for example, Rabbit describes his spiritual feelings: " 'Well, I don't know all this about theology, but I'll tell you. I *do*

John Updike

THE CENTAUR

"Heaven is the creation inconceivable to man, earth the creation conceivable to him. He himself is the creature on the boundary between heaven and earth."
KARL BARTH

Alfred A. Knopf   New York
1963

1942–1945	1945	1945	1947–1948
Physicist Enrico Fermi succeeds in splitting the atom, 1942 \n\n 6 million Jews murdered in concentration camps in Europe, 1939–1945	War ends in Europe May 8, 1945 \n\n Atomic bomb dropped over Hiroshima, August 6, 1945	**Hersey wins the Pulitzer Prize for *A Bell for Adano*, 1945** \n\n **Wright publishes *Black Boy*, 1945**	**Robert Lowell wins the Pulitzer Prize for Poetry, 1947** \n\n **Eliot receives Nobel Prize for Literature, 1948**
1953	**1954**	**1954–1955**	**1957–1958**
Joseph McCarthy investigates Communist influence in the government, 1953–1955 \n\n **James Baldwin publishes *The Fire Next Time*, 1953**	Segregation of races in public schools declared illegal, 1954 \n\n **Hemingway wins the Nobel Prize for Literature, 1954**	**Roethke wins the Pulitzer Prize for Poetry, 1954** \n\n **Wallace Stevens wins the Pulitzer Prize for Poetry, 1955**	**Wilbur wins the Pulitzer Prize for Poetry, 1957** \n\n **Hansberry's *A Raisin in the Sun* opens on Broadway, 1958**
1969	**1973**	**1976–1977**	**1978**
Momady wins the Pulitzer Prize for Fiction, 1969 \n\n American astronauts land on moon, 1969	**Welty wins the Pulitzer Prize for Fiction, 1973** \n\n Watergate Investigation begins in Washington, 1973 \n\n Vietnam ceasefire, 1973	U.S. celebrates its Bicentennial, 1976 \n\n **James Merrill wins the Pulitzer Prize for Poetry, 1977**	**James McPherson wins the Pulitzer Prize for Nonfiction, 1978** \n\n **Isaac Bashevis Singer receives Nobel Prize for Literature, 1978**

feel, I guess, that somewhere behind all this'—he gestures outward at the scenery; they are passing the housing development this side of the golf course, half-wood half brick one-and-a-half-stories in little flat bulldozed yards with tricycles and spindly three-year-old trees, the un-grandest landscape in the world—'there's something that wants me to find it.' "

It is more difficult to find transcendent spiritual values in the cheap clutter of modern life than it was in the woods around Emerson's Concord, but Updike's characters continue the search. "I find myself circling back to man's religious nature," Updike has written of his own work, "and the real loss to man and art alike when that nature has nowhere to plug itself in . . ." These words could serve to describe the work of a great variety of recent writers whose intellectual roots can be traced to the Transcendentalists of the nineteenth century, and even further back to those hardy, practical Puritans who braved a two-month voyage in a tiny wooden boat in order to find an outlet for their own religious natures.

1949	1950	1951–1952	1952–1960
Faulkner receives Nobel Prize for Literature, 1949	**Gwendolyn Brooks wins the Pulitzer Prize for Poetry, 1950**	**J.D. Salinger publishes** *The Catcher in the Rye,* **1951**	**Marianne Moore wins the Pulitzer Prize for Poetry, 1952**
Mao Tse-tung's Communists conquer China, 1949	U.N. forces enter Korean Conflict, 1950–1953	**Ralph Ellison publishes** *The Invisible Man,* **1952**	The Eisenhower Years, 1953–1960

1961–1962	1962–1963	1963–1965	1967–1968
Soviet Union (1961) and U.S. (1962) resume nuclear tests, 1961	**Saul Bellow receives Nobel Prize for Literature, 1962**	President John F. Kennedy assassinated, 1963	**Sexton wins the Pulitzer Prize for Poetry, 1967**
First troops sent into Vietnam, 1962	**William Carlos Williams wins the Pulitzer Prize for Poetry, 1963**	Civil Rights Act prohibits discrimination, 1964	**Malamud wins the Pulitzer Prize for Fiction, 1967**
		Berryman wins the Pulitzer Prize for Poetry, 1965	Martin Luther King, Jr., murdered, April 14, 1968

1979	1982	1983	
Russell Baker wins the Pulitzer Prize for Commentary, 1979	**Updike wins the Pulitzer Prize for Fiction, 1982**	**Baker wins the Pulitzer Prize for Autobiography, 1983**	
Mob in Iran seizes U.S. Embassy and takes 53 hostages, 1979	**Plath wins the Pulitzer Prize for Poetry, 1982**	**Walker wins the Pulitzer Prize for Fiction, 1983**	

Isaac Bashevis Singer (1904–   )

To say of Isaac Bashevis Singer that he is the greatest living writer in Yiddish is hardly an extravagant claim. Yiddish is a language derived from Medieval High German and written in Hebrew. It was once common in New York City, but as the old generation of European immigrants dies out, their language is dying out as well.

Despite the small Yiddish-speaking audience, Singer has reached many readers through translation. He has been praised in the most prestigious literary circles, and in 1978 he was awarded the Nobel Prize for Literature.

Singer was born in Poland, the son and grandson of rabbis. He was intended for the rabbinate himself, but he decided that the religious life was too confining. "I began to doubt not the power of God, but all the traditions and dogmas," he has said. Secular writing did appeal to him. "I often met situations which baffled me and from the moment I knew there was such a thing as literature I thought how wonderful it would be to describe such things."

Alarmed by the rise of anti-Semitism and the Nazis in Europe, Singer left for America in 1935, joining his older brother, who was also a writer. In New York, he went to work for the city's Yiddish newspaper, *The Jewish Daily Forward*. Soon, besides newspaper articles, he was publishing his first fiction pieces.

Singer's style is spare, almost Biblical in its apparent simplicity. "When I tell a story, I tell a story," he says. "I don't try to discuss, criticize, or analyze my characters." However, his explicitness seems to be a cloak for the real power of his storytelling, which lies in the poetry of his language and in the mystical quality of his themes. Beneath the surface of the most ordinary circumstances in his stories, supernatural forces—both divine and demonic—are at work.

"I really believe there are spirits in this world," Singer has said, "and that man has a soul and that the soul is not the only spiritual entity in the world. . . . I find it very easy to believe in reincarnation, possession by devils, and other such things. We have many proofs that such things exist."

In 1978 Singer was awarded the Nobel Prize for Literature. Among his best-known works are his novel *The Family Moskat* (1950) and his short-story collections *Gimpel the Fool* (1957), *The Spinoza of Market Street* (1961), *Enemies* (1970), and *A Crown of Feathers* (1973). He has also written volumes of memoirs and books for children. In 1982, his *Collected Stories* was published.

For all his success, Singer lives simply (still in New York City) and speaks humbly. "When I began to write I was fifteen and I never heard of anybody making a living from writing. I am still surprised every time I get a check for a story."

THE KEY

This story is set in the Upper West Side of New York City—a neighborhood that Singer himself has lived in for many years. Many people like Bessie can be seen there today—old people who live alone in a city that seems to ignore them. But Singer is a writer who is interested in redemption. He is also a writer who does not limit himself to realism. Watch what happens to Bessie.

1.

At about three o'clock in the afternoon, Bessie Popkin began to prepare to go down to the street. Going out was connected with many difficulties, especially on a hot summer day: first, forcing her fat body into a corset, squeezing her swollen feet into shoes, and combing her hair, which Bessie dyed at home and which grew wild and was streaked in all colors—yellow, black, gray, red; then making sure that while she was out her neighbors would not break into her apartment and steal linen, clothes, documents, or just disarrange things and make them disappear.

Besides human tormentors, Bessie suffered from demons, imps, Evil Powers. She hid her eyeglasses in the night table and found them in a slipper. She placed her bottle of hair dye in the medicine chest; days later she discovered it under the pillow. Once, she left a pot of borsch[1] in the refrigerator, but the Unseen took it from there and after long searching Bessie came upon it in her clothes closet. On its surface was a thick layer of fat that gave off the smell of rancid tallow.

What she went through, how many tricks were played on her and how much she had to wrangle in order not to perish or fall into insanity, only God knew. She had given up the telephone because racketeers and degenerates called her day and night, trying to get secrets out of her. . . . The errand boy from the grocery store attempted to burn her belongings with a cigarette. To evict her from the rent-controlled apartment where she had lived for thirty-five years, the company and the superintendent infested her rooms with rats, mice, cockroaches.

Bessie had long ago realized that no means were adequate against those determined to be spiteful—not the metal door, the special lock, her letters to the police, the mayor, the FBI, and even the President in Washington. But while one breathed one had to eat. It all took time: checking the windows, the gas vents, securing the drawers. Her paper money she kept in volumes of the encyclopedia, in back copies of the *National Geographic*, and in Sam Popkin's old ledgers. Her stocks and bonds Bessie had hidden among the logs in the fireplace, which was never used, as well as under the seats of the easy chairs. Her jewels she had sewn into the mattress. There was a time when Bessie had safe-deposit boxes at the bank, but she long ago convinced herself that the guards there had passkeys.

At about five o'clock, Bessie was ready to go out. She gave a last look at herself in the mirror—small, broad, with a narrow forehead, a flat nose, and eyes slanting and half closed, like a Chinaman's. Her chin sprouted a little white beard. She wore a faded dress in a flowered print, a misshapen straw hat trimmed with wooden cherries and grapes, and shabby shoes. Before she left, she made a final inspection of the three rooms and the kitchen. Everywhere there were clothes, shoes, and piles of letters that Bessie had not opened. Her husband, Sam Popkin, who had died almost twenty years ago, had liquidated his real estate business before his death, because he was about to retire to Florida. He left her stocks, bonds, and a number of passbooks from savings banks, as well as some mortgages. To this day, firms wrote to Bessie, sent her reports, checks. The Internal Revenue Service claimed taxes from her. Every few weeks she received announcements from a funeral company that sold plots in an "airy cemetery." In former years, Bessie used to answer

---

1. **borsch** (bôrsh): (also spelled *borscht*) a Russian beet soup, eaten hot or cold.

letters, deposit her checks, keep track of her income and expenses. Lately she had neglected it all. She even stopped buying the newspaper and reading the financial section.

In the corridor, Bessie tucked cards with signs on them that only she could recognize between the door and the door frame. The keyhole she stuffed with putty. What else could she do—a widow without children, relatives, or friends? There was a time when the neighbors used to open their doors, look out, and laugh at her exaggerated care; others teased her. That had long passed. Bessie spoke to no one. She didn't see well, either. The glasses she had worn for years were of no use. To go to an eye doctor and be fitted for new ones was too much of an effort. Everything was difficult—even entering and leaving the elevator, whose door always closed with a slam.

Bessie seldom went farther than two blocks from her building. The street between Broadway and Riverside Drive became noisier and filthier from day to day. Hordes of urchins ran around half naked. Dark men with curly hair and wild eyes quarreled in Spanish with little women whose bellies were always swollen in pregnancy. They talked back in rattling voices. Dogs barked, cats meowed. Fires broke out and fire engines, ambulances, and police cars drove up. On Broadway, the old groceries had been replaced by supermarkets, where food must be picked out and put in a wagon and one had to stand in line before the cashier.

God in heaven, since Sam died, New York, America—perhaps the whole world—was falling apart. All the decent people had left the neighborhood and it was overrun by a mob of thieves, robbers, whores. Three times Bessie's pocketbook had been stolen. When she reported it to the police, they just laughed. Every time one crossed the street, one risked one's life. Bessie took a step and stopped. Someone had advised her to use a cane, but she was far from considering herself an old woman or a cripple. Every few weeks she painted her nails red. At times, when the rheumatism left her in peace, she took clothes she used to wear from the closets, tried them on, and studied herself in the mirror.

Opening the door of the supermarket was impossible. She had to wait till someone held it for her. The supermarket itself was a place that only the Devil could have invented. The lamps burned with a glaring light. People pushing wagons were likely to knock down anyone in their path. The shelves were either too high or too low. The noise was deafening, and the contrast between the heat outside and the freezing temperature inside! It was a miracle that she didn't get pneumonia. More than anything else, Bessie was tortured by indecision. She picked up each item with a trembling hand and read the label. This was not the greed of youth but the uncertainty of age. According to Bessie's figuring, today's shopping should not have taken longer than three quarters of an hour, but two hours passed and Bessie was still not finished. When she finally brought the wagon to the cashier, it occurred to her that she had forgotten the box of oatmeal. She went back and a woman took her place in line. Later, when she paid, there was new trouble. Bessie had put the bill in the right side of her bag, but it was not there. After long rummaging, she found it in a small change purse on the opposite side. Yes, who could believe that such things were possible? If she told someone, he would think she was ready for the madhouse.

When Bessie went into the supermarket, the day was still bright; now it was drawing to a close. The sun, yellow and golden, was sinking toward the Hudson, to the hazy hills of New Jersey. The buildings on Broadway radiated the heat they had absorbed. From under gratings where the subway trains rumbled, evil-smelling fumes arose. Bessie held the heavy bag of food in one hand, and in the other she grasped her pocketbook tightly. Never had Broadway seemed to her so wild, so dirty. It stank of softened asphalt, gasoline, rotten fruit, the excrement of dogs. On the sidewalk, among torn newspapers and the butts of cigarettes, pigeons hopped about. It was difficult to understand how these creatures avoided being stepped on in the crush of passers-by. From the blazing sky a golden dust was falling. Before a storefront hung with artificial grass, men in sweated shirts poured papaya juice and pineapple juice into themselves with haste, as if trying to extinguish a fire that consumed their insides. Above their heads hung coconuts carved in the shapes of Indians. On a side street, black and white children had opened a hydrant and were splashing naked in the gutter. In the midst of that heat wave, a truck with microphones drove around blaring out shrill songs and deafening

The Sitter by Larry Rivers (1956). Oil.

Metropolitan Museum of Art, New York City.

Another time, she wakened to see a ball of fire, a kind of lit-up soap bubble, soar from one roof to another and sink behind it. She was aware that what she saw was the spirit of someone who had just died.

Bessie had fallen asleep. She woke up with a start. It was daybreak. From the side of Central Park the sun rose. Bessie could not see it from here, but on Broadway the sky became pink and reddish. On the building to the left, flames kindled in the windows; the panes ran and blinked like the portholes of a ship. A pigeon landed nearby. It hopped on its little red feet and pecked into something that might have been a dirty piece of stale bread or dried mud. Bessie was baffled. How do these birds live? Where do they sleep at night? And how can they survive the rains, the cold, the snow? I will go home, Bessie decided. People will not leave me in the streets.

Gettng up was a torment. Her body seemed glued to the step on which she sat. Her back ached and her legs tingled. Nevertheless, she began to walk slowly toward home. She inhaled the moist morning air. It smelled of grass and coffee. She was no longer alone. From the side streets men and women emerged. They were going to work. They bought newspapers at the stand and went down into the subway. They were silent and strangely peaceful, as if they, too, had gone through a night of soul-searching and come out of it cleansed. When do they get up if they are already on their way to work now, Bessie marveled. No, not all in this neighborhood were gangsters and murderers. One young man even nodded good morning to Bessie. She tried to smile at him, realizing she had forgotten that feminine gesture she knew so well in her youth; it was almost the first lesson her mother had taught her.

She reached her building, and outside stood the Irish super, her deadly enemy. He was talking to the garbage collectors. He was a giant of a man, with a short nose, a long upper lip, sunken cheeks, and a pointed chin. His yellow hair covered a bald spot. He gave Bessie a startled look. "What's the matter, Grandma?"

Stuttering, Bessie told him what had happened to her. She showed him the handle of the key she had clutched in her hand all night.

"Mother of God!" he called out.

"What shall I do?" Bessie asked.

"I will open your door."

"But you don't have a passkey."

"We have to be able to open all doors in case of fire."

The super disappeared into his own apartment for a few mintues, then he came out with some tools and a bunch of keys on a large ring. He went up in the elevator with Bessie. The bag of food still stood on the threshold, but it looked depleted. The super busied himself at the lock. He asked, "What are these cards?"

Bessie did not answer.

"Why didn't you come to me and tell me what happened? To be roaming around all night at your age—my God!" As he poked with his tools, a door opened and a little woman in a housecoat and slippers, her hair bleached and done up in curlers, came out. She said, "What happened to you? Every time I opened the door, I saw this bag. I took out your butter and milk and put them in my refrigerator."

Bessie could barely restrain her tears. "Oh, my good people," she said. "I didn't know that . . ."

The super pulled out the other half of Bessie's key. He worked a little longer. He turned a key and the door opened. The cards fell down. He entered the hallway with Bessie and she sensed the musty odor of an apartment that has not been lived in for a long time. The super said, "Next time, if something like this happens call me. That's what I'm here for."

Bessie wanted to give him a tip, but her hands were too weak to open her bag. The neighbor woman brought in the milk and butter. Bessie went into her bedroom and lay down on the bed. There was a pressure on her breast and she felt like vomiting. Something heavy vibrated up from her feet to her chest. Bessie listened to it without alarm, only curious about the whims of the body; the super and the neighbor talked, and Bessie could not make out what they were saying. The same thing had happened to her over thirty years ago when she had been given anesthesia in the hospital before an operation—the doctor and the nurse were talking but their voices seemed to come from far away in a strange language.

Soon there was silence, and Sam appeared. It was neither day nor night—a strange twilight. In her dream, Bessie knew that Sam was dead but that in some clandestine way he had managed to get away from the grave and visit her. He was feeble and embarrassed. He could not speak. They wandered through a space without a sky, without earth, a tunnel full of debris—the wreckage of a nameless structure—a corridor dark and winding, yet somehow familiar. They came to a region where two mountains met, and the passage between shone like sunset or sunrise. They stood there hesitating and even a little ashamed. It was like that night of their honeymoon when they went to Ellenville in the Catskills and were let by the hotel owner into their bridal suite. She heard the same words he had said to them then, in the same voice and intonation: "You don't need no key here. Just enter—and *mazel tov*."[2]

—Translated by the author and Evelyn Torton Beck

---

2. **mazel tov** (mä′zəl·tôv): Yiddish for "good luck."

Responding to the Story

Analyzing the Story

Identifying Facts

1. Describe the ways in which Bessie Popkin has isolated herself from her neighbors. Find the details that reveal that Bessie sees her **setting** as hostile and inhuman.
2. Describe Bessie's **conflicts.**
3. The key to the turning point of the story is an actual key. Explain how Bessie's suspicions shut her out of even her own home. What is she now forced to do?
4. Describe the miraculous signs from another world that Bessie sees during the night.
5. As Bessie goes home in the morning, how does the storyteller let us know that she is "cleansed," that she now sees the world in a new light?
6. What happens to Bessie at the end of the story

Interpreting Meanings

7. As Bessie puts her head to the door on page 898, she hears a murmur. What is the sound? How does this **foreshadow** the ending?
8. As part 2 opens, Bessie awakens on the church steps. The first sign of a figurative "awakening" occurs when we read that she "gaped [because] she had almost forgotten that there was a sky, a moon, stars. Years had passed and she never looked up—always down." What does this last statement mean literally? Given what you know of Bessie, explain what it means **figuratively.**
9. We generally think of **comedies** as stories with happy endings. But comedy can also encompass many other kinds of plots. One critic, Northrop Frye, says that the theme of comedy is the integration of society: By the end of most comedies, a character is incorporated into a community. Given this theory, do you think Singer's story qualifies as an example of comedy? Explain why or why not.

10. How does Singer seem to feel about his characters—would you say he is sympathetic to them, or does he view them with irony and amusement? How do you feel about the people in "The Key"?

Writing About the Story

A Creative Response

1. **Adopting Another Point of View.** Although this story is told by an **omniscient narrator,** the **point of view** is limited to that of a single character. What observations might some of the other characters make about Bessie and her problems? (Include animals as characters in the story.) Write two or three paragraphs in which you relate specific incidents from the story, using the first-person point of view of another character.

A Critical Response

2. **Analyzing the Theme.** When Bessie sits on the steps, she remembers the Yiddish proverb, "If one lives without a reckoning, one dies without confession." Write an essay explaining what you think the proverb means and how it supports the main **theme** of Singer's story. Before you write, think about the following questions: What is a reckoning? In what way has Bessie lived without one? What is the symbolic meaning of the story's title? What confession does Bessie make?
3. **Relating the Speech to the Story.** In a brief essay, cite at least three points in Singer's Nobel lecture (see "Primary Sources," page 902 that relate to "The Key."
4. **Comparing Stories.** In a paragraph, explain how this story is like Eudora Welty's story "A Worn Path" (page 632) in at least two ways. Before you write, consider how each story uses these elements:

    a. Character
    b. A perilous journey
    c. A triumphant resolution
    d. A theme involving love

Analyzing Language and Style

Imagery

To help us imagine Bessie's urban setting, Singer uses many **images**—words or combinations of words that appeal to our senses of sight, smell, hearing, taste, or touch.

1. Look at the passage beginning "Never had Broadway seemed to her so wild, so dirty," on page 896. Read the rest of this passage, and list the images according to their sensory connection: sight, smell, hearing, taste, or touch.

2. Imagery is not merely decoration for a story; imagery can help a writer control the reader's feelings. After reading this passage, what feeling do you have for Bessie's setting?

3. In this story, the imagery is especially interesting because it reflects what the main character, Bessie, thinks of her setting. How would you describe Bessie's feelings about her neighborhood? Does the writer necessarily share these feelings?

Primary Sources
Nobel Prize Acceptance Speech, 1978

"The storyteller and poet of our time, as in any other time, must be an entertainer of the spirit in the full sense of the word, not just a preacher of social or political ideals. There is no paradise for bored readers and no excuse for tedious literature that does not intrigue the reader, uplift his spirit, give him the joy and the escape that true art always grants. Nevertheless, it is also true that the serious writer of our time must be deeply concerned about the problems of his generation. He cannot but see that the power of religion, especially belief in revelation, is weaker today than it was in any other epoch in human history. More and more children grow up without faith in God, without belief in reward and punishment, in the immortality of the soul, and even in the validity of ethics. The genuine writer cannot ignore the fact that the family is losing its spiritual foundation. All the dismal prophecies of Oswald Spengler have become realities since the Second World War. No technological achievements can mitigate the disappointment of modern man, his loneliness, his feeling of inferiority, and his fear of war, revolution, and terror. Not only has our generation lost faith in Providence, but also in man himself, in his institutions, and often in those who are nearest to him.

"In their despair a number of those who no longer have confidence in the leadership of our society look up to the writer, the master of words. They hope against hope that the man of talent and sensitivity can perhaps rescue civilization. Maybe there is a spark of the prophet in the artist after all.

"As the son of a people who received the worst blows that human madness can inflict, I have many times resigned myself to never finding a true way out. But a new hope always emerges, telling me that it is not yet too late for all of use to take stock and make a decision. I was brought up to believe in free will. Although I came to doubt all revelation, I can never accept the idea that the universe is a physical or chemical accident, a result of blind evolution. Even though I learned to recognize the lies, the cliches, and the idolatries of the human mind, I still cling to some truths which I think all of us might accept someday. There must be a way for man to attain all possible pleasures, all the powers and knowledge that nature can grant him, and still serve God—a God who speaks in deeds, not in words, and whose vocabulary is the universe.

"I am not ashamed to admit that I belong to those who fantasize that literature is capable of bringing new horizons and new perspectives—philosophical, religious, esthetical, and even social. In the history of old Jewish literature there was never any basic difference between the poet and the prophet. Our ancient poetry often became law and a way of life.

"Some of my cronies in the cafeteria near the *Jewish Daily Forward* in New York call me a pessimist and a decadent, but there is always a background of faith behind resignation. I found comfort in such pessimists and decadents as Baudelaire, Verlaine, Edgar Allan Poe, and Strindberg. My interest in psychic research made me find solace in such mystics as your Swedenborg and in our own Rabbi Nachman Bratzlaver, as well as in a great poet of my time, my friend Aaron Zeitlin, who died a few years ago and left a spiritual inheritance of high quality, most of it in Yiddish.

"The pessimism of the creative person is not decadence, but a mighty passion for the redemption of man. While the poet entertains he continues to search for eternal truths, for the essence of being. In his own fashion he tries to solve the riddle of time and change, to find an answer to suffering, to reveal love in the very abyss of cruelty and injustice. Strange as these words may sound, I often play with the idea that when all the social theories collapse and wars and revolutions leave humanity in utter gloom, the poet—whom Plato banned from his Republic—may rise up to save us all."

—Isaac Bashevis Singer

Bernard Malamud
(1914–1986)

Bernard Malamud was one of the principal figures in the group of Jewish writers whose work has enriched American literature in the second half of the twentieth century. Yet Malamud preferred not to be so easily pigeon-holed. He did indeed write *about* Jews, but he wrote *for* all people.

Malamud's characters are usually discovered at some barren level of bare subsistence. Though we may feel compassion for them, they themselves do not display the least self-pity. If their plight is sad, it is also triumphant, because they are surviving in heroic fashion against the odds all humans face.

"As you are grooved, so you are grieved," Malamud once wrote as preamble to an account of his own bleak upbringing. He was the older of two sons of a Russian immigrant storekeeper. His mother died when he was fourteen. He grew up in Brooklyn in a household without books, music, or pictures on the wall. During the Great Depression, he worked at the census office and at a yarn factory to help support his family, but he felt these youthful deprivations were important to him as a writer. Getting down to essential needs and "turning inward," Malamud believed, are the best preparation for a career of making fiction.

It was the suffering of European Jews during World War II that convinced Malamud he had something to say as a writer. "I for one believe that not enough has been made of the tragedy of the destruction of six million Jews," he has said. "Somebody has to cry—even if it's a writer, twenty years later."

Malamud's unique drama is spun out of the commonplace, the tragicomedy of survival in a brutal world. But his stories are always informed by love and, indeed, his characters are largely redeemed by human love.

When he received the 1958 National Book Award for his collection of short stories called *The Magic Barrel*, Malamud spoke up for the contemporary individual: "I am quite tired of the colossally deceitful devaluation of man in this day. . . . Whatever the reason, his fall from grace in his eyes is betrayed by the words he has invented to describe himself as he is now: fragmented, abbreviated, other-directed, organizational. . . . The devaluation exists because he accepts it without protest."

Malamud taught English in New York City high schools and fiction at Oregon State University and Bennington College in Vermont. His first novel, *The Natural* (1952), whose central character is a baseball player, was made into a popular film in 1984. His other well-known books are *The Assistant* (1957), which some critics consider his best work, *The Fixer* (1966), and *The Tenants* (1971). He won, over the course of his career, the Pulitzer Prize and National Book Awards.

Malamud was a firm believer in the power of story and plot. "Writers who can't invent stories," he once said, "often pursue other strategies, even substituting style for narrative. I feel that story is the basic element of fiction, though that ideal is not popular with disciples of the 'new novel.' They remind me of the painter who couldn't paint people, so he painted chairs. The story will be with us as long as man is. You know that, in part, because of its effect on children. It's through story that they learn that mystery won't kill them. Through story they learn they have a future."

THE MAGIC BARREL

Within the community of this story, a young person (or even an old person) wanting to marry might ask for the help of a matchmaker. For a fee, the matchmaker would produce a suitable mate. As you read the story, notice how Malamud helps you to picture these characters and their urban setting, and to hear the particular quality of their speech.

Birthday by Marc Chagall (1915). Oil on cardboard.

Museum of Modern Art, New York City.
Lillie P. Bliss Bequest.

Not long ago there lived in uptown New York, in a small, almost meager room, though crowded with books, Leo Finkle, a rabbinical student in the Yeshiva University. Finkle, after six years of study, was to be ordained in June and had been advised by an acquaintance that he might find it easier to win himself a congregation if he were married. Since he had no present prospects of marriage, after two tormented days of turning it over in his mind, he called in Pinye Salzman, a marriage broker whose two-line advertisement he had read in the *Forward*.[1]

The matchmaker appeared one night out of the dark fourth-floor hallway of the graystone rooming house where Finkle lived, grasping a black, strapped portfolio that had been worn thin with use. Salzman, who had been long in the business, was of slight but dignified build, wearing an old hat, and an overcoat too short and tight for him. He smelled frankly of fish, which he loved to eat, and although he was missing a few teeth, his presence was not displeasing, because of an amiable manner curiously contrasted with mournful eyes. His voice, his lips, his wisp of beard, his bony fingers were animated, but give him a moment of repose and his mud blue eyes revealed a depth of sadness, a characteristic that put Leo a little at ease although the situation, for him, was inherently tense.

He at once informed Salzman why he had asked him to come, explaining that his home was in Cleveland, and that but for his parents, who had married comparatively late in life, he was alone in the world. He had for six years devoted himself almost entirely to his studies, as a result of which, understandably, he had found himself without time for a social life and the company of young women. Therefore he thought it the better part of trial and error—of embarrassing fumbling—to call in an experienced person to advise him on these matters. He remarked in passing that the function of the marriage broker was ancient and honorable, highly approved in the Jewish community, because it made practical the necessary without hindering joy. Moreover, his own parents had been brought together by a matchmaker. They had made, if not a financially profitable marriage— since neither had possessed any worldly goods to speak of—at least a successful one in the sense of their everlasting devotion to each other. Salzman listened in embarrassed surprise, sensing a sort of apology. Later, however, he experienced a glow of pride in his work, an emotion that had left him years ago, and he heartily approved of Finkle.

The two went to their business. Leo had led Salzman to the only clear place in the room, a table near a window that overlooked the lamp-lit city. He seated himself at the matchmaker's side but facing him, attempting by an act of will to suppress the unpleasant tickle in his throat. Salzman eagerly unstrapped his portfolio and removed a loose rubber band from a thin packet of much-handled cards. As he flipped through them, a gesture and sound that physically hurt Leo, the student pretended not to see and gazed steadfastly out the window. Although it was still February, winter was on its last legs, signs of which he had for the first time in years begun to notice. He now observed the round white moon, moving high in the sky through a cloud menagerie, and watched with half-open mouth as it penetrated a huge hen, and dropped out of her like an egg laying itself. Salzman, though pretending through eyeglasses he had just slipped on, to be engaged in scanning the writing on the cards, stole occasional glances at the young man's distinguished face, noting with pleasure the long, severe scholar's nose, brown eyes heavy with learning, sensitive yet ascetic lips, and a certain, almost hollow quality of the dark cheeks. He gazed around at shelves upon shelves of books and let out a soft, contented sigh.

When Leo's eyes fell upon the cards, he counted six spread out in Salzman's hand.

"So few?" he asked in disappointment.

"You wouldn't believe me how much cards I got in my office," Salzman replied. "The drawers are already filled to the top, so I keep them now in a barrel, but is every girl good for a new rabbi?"

Leo blushed at this, regretting all he had revealed of himself in a curriculum vitae[2] he had sent to Salzman. He had thought it best to acquaint him with his strict standards and specifications, but in having done so, felt he had told the marriage broker more than was absolutely necessary.

---

1. *Forward:* the *Jewish Daily Forward*, a Yiddish newspaper in New York City.

2. **curriculum vitae** (vīt'ē): a resumé.

Responding to the Story

Analyzing the Story

Identifying Facts

1. Almost like an old folk tale, this story opens with a paragraph that summarizes the problem. According to this paragraph, who is the story's protagonist, what does he want, and what steps does he take to get what he wants?
2. Another character—Pinye Salzman—is introduced in the second paragraph. Find the descriptive details that seem to hint that there is something tragic in Salzman's past.
3. From his reactions to Salzman's clients, what do you discover about the kind of woman Finkle wants to marry? Explain what Finkle discovers about himself after the experience with Lily.
4. Explain why Finkle falls in love with the woman in the photograph. What clues hint at her identity?

Interpreting Meanings

5. What do you think caused Stella's father to regard her as dead?
6. Finkle confesses to Lily, "I came to God not because I loved Him, but because I did not." How would you explain this **paradox**, or seeming contradiction? How does Finkle's confession support the **theme** of the story as a whole?
7. Why do you think Finkle pictures in Stella his own redemption? What does he want to be redeemed *from*?
8. What do you think of the last scene in the story? Do you think Salzman arrangd a marriage for Finkle after all? Explain.
9. What seasons open and close the story? In terms of the story's **plot**, what significance can you see in these seasonal settings?
10. Explain the story's title.

Writing About the Story

A Creative Response

1. **Extending the Story.** In a paragraph, describe what the characters in this story are doing twenty years after the story ends. Are Leo and Stella in love? Whether they are in love or not, are they still together? Has Salzman forgiven his daughter?

A Critical Response

2. **Comparing Two Stories.** Write an essay comparing "The Magic Barrel" to Singer's "The Key" (page 895). Base your comparison on at least two of the elements listed below:

   a. A comic plot that ends with the character uniting with someone.
   b. The use of visions and dreams
   c. An isolated character who is redeemed by love
   d. A setting that is transformed by love

3. **Responding to a Critic.** Select one of the following comments about Malamud's fiction and write a paragraph responding to it. Tell whether or not the comment has to do with the plot, characters, or theme of "The Magic Barrel."

   a. "Malamud has always had a fondness for telling tales arranged for the purpose of a specific moral lesson." (Alan Lelchuk)
   b. "What it is to be human, and to be humane, is his deepest concern." (Philip Roth)

John Updike
(1932–   )

John Updike grew up in the small town of Shillington in rural Pennsylvania. Gifted with what seems a total recall of what it is like to grow up in the American middle class, Updike also displays a skill with language that can evoke our responses to even the most ordinary and familiar events. In short, his talent is for taking our common daily experience and endowing it with both substance and importance.

In his boyhood memoir, *The Dogwood Tree*, Updike portrays his youthful ambition as artistic: ". . . riding a thin pencil line out of Shillington, out of time altogether, into an infinity of unseen and even unborn hearts." He describes returning to Shillington as a mature, successful writer and confronting a picture of himself as this ambitious boy. He senses disappointment: "Like some phantom conjured by this child from a glue bottle, I have executed his commands; acquired pencils, paper, and an office. Now I wait apprehensively for his next command, or at least a nod of appreciation, and he smiles through me as if I am already transparent with failure."

Graduating *summa cum laude* from Harvard College in 1954, Updike studied drawing in England for a year, and on his return to the United States went to work for *The New Yorker*. After two years there, he made the courageous decision to support his young family entirely by writing. He left New York for Massachusetts, and he has since produced a shelf full of impressive novels, stories, poems, and critical essays.

From the first, Updike's stories had a freshness and honesty that brought them regularly into *The New Yorker's* pages. They have since been collected under such titles as *Pigeon Feathers* (1962) and *The Music School* (1966). His novels have brought Updike further acclaim. Among the most successful have been the three tales in the Rabbit series: *Rabbit, Run* (1960), *Rabbit Redux* (1971), and *Rabbit Is Rich* (1981), for which Updike was awarded a Pulitzer Prize.

These novels chronicle the life of Harry "Rabbit" Angstrom, who lives, as his creator might have, an outwardly conventional life in a small Pennsylvania town. In revealing Rabbit's yearnings and disappointments, the uncertain course of his heart, and the dismaying fluctuations of his relationships with family and friends, Updike gives us a remarkably accurate portrait of the 1960's and 1970's in the United States. Here are Americans like ourselves, reacting to changing attitudes about national, social, and moral behavior. As always with an Updike novel, readers enjoy the feel of life—the sights, smells, and sounds that bring life into focus.

Two of Updike's other widely read novels are *The Centaur* (1963) and *A Month of Sundays* (1975). Of *The Centaur*, Updike notes that it is the only place he could ever say he loved his father. The second novel Updike calls *The Scarlet Letter* in modern dress. Besides his prose and poetry, Updike's essays rank with some of the most perceptive criticism of our day. Several of his critical essays have been collected in a volume entitled *Hugging the Shore* (1983).

In accepting the American Book Award in 1982, Updike said to young writers: "Have faith. May you surround yourselves with parents, editors, mates, and children as supportive as mine have been. But the essential support and encouragement of course come from within, arising out of the mad notion that your society needs to know what only you can tell it."

SON

This story deals with several different generations in the same family, so the title has more meanings than you might at first expect. As you begin each section, read slowly to make sure you know which "son" the narrator is talking about. In view of the subject of the story, it might be of interest to know that Updike's older son has become a writer too; like those of his father, David Updike's stories are also appearing in *The New Yorker*. They give yet another perspective on some of the same family situations that have served his father as subject matter.

He is often upstairs, when he has to be home. He prefers to be elsewhere. He is almost sixteen, though beardless still, a man's mind indignantly captive in the frame of a child. I love touching him, but don't often dare. The other day, he had the flu, and a fever, and I gave him a back rub, marveling at the symmetrical knit of muscle, the organic tension. He is high-strung. Yet his sleep is so solid he sweats like a stone in the wall of a well. He wishes for perfection. He would like to destroy us, for we are, variously, too fat, too jocular, too sloppy, too affectionate, too grotesque and heedless in our ways. His mother smokes too much. His younger brother chews with his mouth open. His older sister leaves unbuttoned the top button of her blouses. His younger sister tussles with the dogs, getting them overexcited, avoiding doing her homework. Everyone in the house talks nonsense. He would be a better father than his father. But time has tricked him, has made him a son. After a quarrel, if he cannot go outside and kick a ball, he retreats to a corner of the house and reclines on the beanbag chair in an attitude of strange, infantile or leonine, torpor.[1] We exhaust him, without meaning to. He takes an interest in the newspaper now, the front page as well as the sports, in this tiring year of 1973.

He is upstairs, writing a musical comedy. It is a Sunday in 1949. Somehow, he has volunteered to prepare a high school assembly program; people will sing. Songs of the time go through his head, as he scribbles new words. *Up in de mornin', down at de school, work like a debil for my grades.* Below him, irksome voices grind on, like machines working their way through tunnels. His parents each want something from the other. "Marion, you don't understand that man like I do; he has a heart of gold." This father's charade is very complex: The world, which he fears, is used as a flail[2] on his wife. But from his cringing attitude he would seem to an outsider the one being flailed. With burning red face, the woman accepts the role of aggressor as penance for the fact, the incessant shameful fact, that *he* has to wrestle with the world while she hides here, in solitude, on this farm. This is normal, but does not seem to them to be so. Only by convolution have they arrived at the dominant submissive relationship society has assigned them. For the man is maternally kind and with a smile hugs to himself his jewel, his certainty of being victimized; it is the mother whose tongue is sharp, who sometimes strikes. "Well, he gets you out of the house, and I guess that's gold to you." His answer is "Duty calls," pronounced mincingly. "The social contract is a balance of compromises." This will infuriate her, the son knows; as his heart thickens, the downstairs overflows with her hot voice. *"Don't* wear that smile at me! And *take* your hands off your hips; you look like a sissy!" Their son tries not to listen. When he does, visual details of the downstairs flood his mind: the two antagonists, circling with their coffee cups; the shabby mismatched furniture; the hopeful books; the docile framed photographs of the dead, docile and still as cowed students. This matrix of pain that bore him—he

---

1. **torpor** (tôr′pôr): sluggishness; apathy.

2. **flail:** a tool used to thresh grain; here, used metaphorically to mean a whip.

feels he is floating above it, sprawled on the bed as on a cloud, stealing songs as they come into his head (*Across the hallway from the guidance room/Lives a French instructor called Mrs. Blum*), contemplating the brown meadow from the upstairs window (last summer's burdock[3] stalks like the beginnings of an alphabet, an apple tree holding three rotten apples as if pondering why they failed to fall), yearning for Monday, for the ride to school with his father, for the bell that calls him to homeroom, for the excitements of class, for Broadway, for fame, for the cloud that will carry him away, out of this, out.

He returns from his paper-delivery route and finds a few Christmas presents for him on the kitchen table. I must guess at the year. 1913? Without opening them, he knocks them to the floor, puts his head on the table, and falls asleep. He must have been consciously dramatizing his plight: His father was sick, money was scarce, he had to work, to win food for the family when he was still a child. In his dismissal of Christmas, he touched a nerve: his love of anarchy, his distrust of the social contract. He treasured this moment of proclamation; else why remember it, hoard a memory

3. **burdock:** a coarse, hairy weed with large leaves, prickley, and purple flowers.

so bitter, and confide it to his son many Christmases later? He had a teaching instinct, though he claimed that life miscast him as a schoolteacher. I suffered in his classes, feeling the confusion as a persecution of him, but now wonder if his rebellious heart did not court confusion, not as Communists do, to intrude their own order, but, more radical still, as an end pleasurable in itself, as truth's very body. Yet his handwriting (an old pink permission slip recently fluttered from a book where it had been marking a page for twenty years) was always considerately legible, and he was sitting up doing arithmetic the morning of the day he died.

And letters survive from that yet prior son, written in brown ink, in a tidy tame hand, home to his mother from the Missouri seminary where he was preparing for his vocation. The dates are 1887, 1888, 1889. Nothing much happened: He missed New Jersey, and was teased at a church social for escorting a widow. He wanted to do the right thing, but the little sheets of faded penscript exhale a dispirited calm, as if his heart already knew he would not make a successful minister, or live to be old. His son, my father, when old, drove hundreds of miles out of the way to visit the Missouri town from which those letters had been sent. Strangely, the town had not changed; it looked

Mario Suarez
(1925–   )

Mario Suarez, who grew up in Tucson, Arizona, and attended the University of Arizona, often writes about his childhood in Tucson and the people he knew in the barrio—the Spanish-speaking part of the city. Suarez has been writing since his years in college. He now teaches at the California State Polytechnic College of Pomona. He has described in an essay the sprawling downtown section of Tucson known as El Hoyo, the setting of "Maestria"

Perhaps El Hoyo, its inhabitants, and its essence can best be explained by telling you a little bit about a dish called *capirotada*. Its origin is uncertain. But it is made of old, new, stale, and hard bread. It is sprinkled with water, and then it is cooked with raisins, olives, onions, tomatoes, peanuts, cheese, and general leftovers of that which is good and bad. It is seasoned with salt, sugar, pepper, and sometimes chili or tomato sauce. It is fired with tequila or sherry wine. It is served hot, cold, or just "on the weather," as they say in El Hoyo. The Garcías like it one way, the Quevedos another, the Trilos another, and the Ortegas still another. While in general appearance it does not differ much from one home to another, it tastes different everywhere. Nevertheless, it is still *capirotada*. And so it is with El Hoyo's Chicanos. While many seem to the undiscerning eye to be alike, it is only because collectively they are referred to as Chicanos. But like *capirotada*, fixed in a thousand ways and served on a thousand tables, which can only be evaluated by individual taste, the Chicanos must be so distinguished.

MAESTRIA

This story centers on the sport of cockfighting, in which trained roosters are put inside a ring to fight while observers bet on the outcome. Many people consider this a gruesome form of entertainment, but it was once very popular in some parts of the United States. Cockfighting has since been outlawed in most states, due mostly to the efforts of groups favoring humane treatment of animals. The title of this story means, "the quality of being a *maestro*." The story opens with an explanation of the word *maestro*. You will find the story is less about cockfighting and more about loss.

Whenever a man is referred to as a *maestro*, it means that he is master of whatever trade, art, or folly he practices. If he is a shoemaker, for example, he can design, cut, and finish any kind of shoe he is asked for. If he is a musician, he knows composition, direction, execution, and thereby plays Viennese waltzes as well as the bolero. If he is a thief, he steals thousands, for he would not damn his soul by taking dimes. That is *maestria*. It is applied with equal honor to a painter, tailor, barber, printer, carpenter, mechanic, bricklayer, window washer, ditchdigger, or bootblack if his ability merits it. Of course, when a man is graying and has no apparent trade or usefulness, out of courtesy people may forget he is a loafer and will call him a *maestro*. Whether he is or not is of no importance. Calling him a *maestro* hurts no one.

During the hard times of Mexico's last revolution[1] many *maestros* left Mexico with their families with the idea of temporarily making a living north of the Rio Grande. But the revolution lasted for such a long time that when it finally came to an end, the *maestros*, now with larger families, remained here in spite of it. During the hard times of the last depression they opened little establishments on West Broad Street and North Pike where they miraculously made a dollar on some days and as many as two or three on others—always putting on, because they were used to hard times, a good face. When good times returned, most of the *maestros* closed up their little establishments and went to work for the larger concerns which came back in business. Some left for the increasing number of factory jobs in California. But some, enjoying their long independence and believing that it is better to be a poor lord than a rich servant, kept their little establishments open.

Gonzalo Pereda, for example, was a *maestro* who kept a little saddle shop open on West Broad Street. Being a great conversationalist, he was not against having company at all hours. Being easy with his money, he was always prey for those that told him of need in their homes. And easier prey still for those that often talked him into closing up his establishment so that they might gossip of old times over a bottle of beer. Being a good craftsman, therefore, had never helped to give the *maestro* more than enough with which to provide for his family.

But if there were men in the world who worried about their work after being through for the day, as far as the *maestro* was concerned, they deserved to die young. It certainly was not so with Gonzalo Pereda. Life, he figured, was too short anyway. When he closed up in the afternoon, he rid his mind completely of jobs pending and overhead unpaid. He simply hurried home to feed his stable of fighting roosters and to eat supper with his family. Even before taking off his hat he made his way to the back yard to see that his roosters had fresh water and that their cages were clean. That the *maestro* did all of this before going to greet his family does not mean that he liked the roosters better. But the family, now grown up and with its own affairs, could wait. The roosters, dependent on his arrival for their care, could and should not.

One day when the *maestro* came home, he

---

1. **Mexico's last revolution:** in 1910, the dictator Porfirio Díaz was ousted and a more democratic government was established. The revolution lasted seven years.

Burro and Peddler by Milton Avery (1946). Oil. Grace Borgenicht Gallery, New York City.

found a little cage in his back yard. Attached to the top of it was a tag which read, "A present from your friend Bernabe Lerda. Chihuahua, Mexico." In the cage was a red rooster. The *maestro* stuck his finger through an opening and had to jerk it out immediately when the rooster picked at it with a bill which seemed to be made of steel. The *maestro* took a thin leather strip from his pocket, opened the cage, and tied it to the rooster's leg. Then he took the rooster out in order to examine him carefully. The *maestro* looked closely at the rooster's long thick legs, at his tail, which by its length might have belonged to a peacock, at the murder in both of his eager eyes; and the *maestro* knew that this rooster would assassinate any unfortunate fowl pitted against him.

After gazing around a bit the little rooster stretched and strutted. He flapped his wings a few times, and then he crowed. The *maestro* was amazed. How could it be, he asked himself, that an animal could possess such pomp? How was it that he knew he was a better rooster than any other that had ever emerged from a hen's egg and therefore strutted about like a racehorse confident of winning the Kentucky Derby? How did he know he was such a handsome example of chickenhood that he, without doubt, could be the Valentino of any chicken yard? Well, it was unbelievable, but it was so. And the *maestro* was sure that this rooster, being from Mexico, no less, would slash his way to thirty victories once they put him in the pit. A few minutes later, when one of the *maestro*'s sons saw the rooster, both decided that he must have a worthy name: They decided to call him *Killer*.

So great a stir did Killer cause that the *maestro*

forgot all about eating supper that night. While he watched admiringly, Killer took his time about eating his grain and drinking his cool water. One would have thought that the *maestro* could aliment[2] himself by merely gazing at the conceited rooster as he strutted about. The *maestro* said, "The minute he goes into the pit, the other rooster will drop dead from fright. Just look at the beautiful creature."

And so it was. The following Sunday afternoon the *maestro* burst in through the front door with Killer. Killer was still hot under the wings from having chased the other rooster and then having slashed it to ribbons. He was still kicking inside the cage as if asking for all the roosters who ever sported a gaff[3] to take him on. "You should have seen him," said the *maestro* to his wife. "Killer is the greatest rooster that ever lived." Then he took Killer to the back yard to cool off.

During the night there was a big commotion in the yard. Killer had gotten out of his cage and was attacking the other roosters through the wire fronts of their cages. Already, in a minute or so, there was blood in front of the cage belonging to a rooster named General, who had retreated to the back of his cage for safety. Killer was squaring off, with his neck feathers ruffled, at another cage, in an effort to pick out the eyes of a rooster named Diablo. "He is really cute, isn't he?" asked the *maestro*. Then he took Killer, and holding him said, "Well, I guess it is only natural for him to want to fight. He had no competition this afternoon." When Killer was put in another cage, the *maestro* and his son went back to bed.

After the Killer's second fight, the following Sunday, the *maestro* once again came in through the front door with Killer. This time Killer had disposed of his adversary in less than two minutes. The *maestro* was happy. "I am convinced," he said, "that Killer is a butcher if there ever was one." And in victory the *maestro* brought Killer through the front door after the third, fourth, and fifth fights. Now, of course, Killer traveled to and from the pit in style. His was a big cage, made and designed to give him a lot of comfort, with letters reading "Killer."

On the Sunday that Killer won his sixth fight, the *maestro* was so happy when he brought Killer

through the front door for his wife to admire that tears came from his eyes as he said, "Every rooster that sees this champion can say that the devil has taken him." And on that day Killer established himself firmly as the best rooster that had ever come to fall into the *maestro*'s possession. This Sunday, after all, had been a great one for the *maestro*, financially speaking and otherwise.

The following Sunday the *maestro* got up very early. Before his daughter left for church, he had her take out the camera in order to photograph Killer. The picture that came out best would be sent away to *Hook and Gaff*, a magazine dedicated to cockfights and poultry. They photographed Killer from various angles. In the arms of the *maestro*. Perched on top of a pole. Looking into a hen roost.

But that afternoon, after the fight, the *maestro* did not storm through the front door to tell how Killer had all put peeled and removed the entrails from the opposing rooster. The *maestro* hurried around the side of the house to the back yard with Killer in his hands. Killer, the invincible one, had met his match. After six battles had come his Waterloo. The reason that Killer was not dead was because the *maestro* had stopped the fight and forfeited his bet. But Killer seemed more dead than alive. His bill was open as if to force breath into his lungs. One of his wings was almost torn off. His back was deeply gashed. One of his eyes was closed. The *maestro* worked frantically to keep Killer alive. He put flour under the torn wing. He took a damp rag and wiped the blood off Killer's head. The *maestro* looked as though he had lost his best friend.

For many days the Killer did not eat. He only stood, and weakly, on his long, thick legs. The *maestro* came home many times to take care of him. He brought Killer some baby-chicken feed in order that he might eat something when he recuperated enough to open his eyes. But to no avail. The *maestro*'s gladiator still seemed close to death.

Then, of a sudden, Killer got better. He began to pick at the baby-chicken feed. And the *maestro* was overwhelmed with joy. Killer did not strut as before, or crow, or flap his wings; but he would, in time. Many things, the *maestro* often said, were fixed by time alone.

Towards the end of Killer's convalescence the *maestro* felt proud of the job he had done in rescuing the Killer from death. As a finishing touch

---

2. **aliment:** supply with food; nourish.
3. **gaff:** metal spur attached to the leg of a gamecock during a cockfight.

he decided to give the rooster, who was beginning to act somewhat like the Killer of old, some little pieces of liver. These would give him more blood. So while the *maestro*'s son opened Killer's bill, the *maestro* pushed a little piece of liver down Killer's throat. But the second piece caused Killer to gurgle, to kick momentarily, and then suddenly to die in the *maestro*'s hands. With tears in his eyes the *maestro* stroked his beloved Killer, bit his lip as he wrapped the limp body of his Spartan in a newspaper, and tenderly put it in the garbage can. Then, without supper, the *maestro* went to bed. His beloved Killer was gone.

Like Killer's plight, it might be added, is the plight of many things the *maestros* cherish. Each year they hear their sons talk English with a rapidly disappearing accent, that accent which one early accustomed only to Spanish never fails to have. Each year the *maestros* notice that their sons' Spanish loses fluency. But perhaps it is natural. The *maestros* themselves seem to forget about bulls and bullfighters, about guitars and other things so much a part of the world that years ago circumstances forced them to leave behind. They hear instead more about the difference between one baseball swing and another. Yes, perhaps it is only natural.

Ofttimes when *maestros* get together, they point out the fact that each year there are less and less of their little establishments around. They proudly say that the old generation was best; that the new generation knows nothing. They point out, for example, that there are no shoemakers anymore. They say that the new generation of so-called shoemakers are nothing but repairers of cheap shoes in need of half soles. They say that the musicians are but accompanists who learned to play an instrument in ten lessons and thus take money under false pretenses. Even the thieves, they tell you, are nothing but two-bit clips. The less said about other phases of *maestria*, they will add, the better.

When one of the *maestros* dies, all the other *maestros* can be counted upon to mourn him. They dust off the dark suits they seldom wear, and offer him, with their calloused hands folded in prayer, a rosary or two. They carry his coffin to and from the church. And they help fill his grave with the earth that will cover him thereafter. Then they silently know the reason why there are not so many of the little establishments as before. Perhaps it is natural. There are not so many *maestros* anymore.

Responding to the Story

Analyzing the Story

Identifying Facts

1. What is a *maestro*? What examples in the first paragraph illustrate the powerful meaning of the word?
2. What is Gonzalo Pereda's trade? Is he more serious about his trade or about his roosters? Explain.
3. Ironically, how does Pereda's prize rooster perish?
4. How is the plight of the *maestros* like that of Killer?

Interpreting Meanings

5. How do the last three sentences of the first paragraph prepare the reader for the comic **tone** of the story?
6. The story's **tone** is also revealed in some of the *maestro*'s remarks about his rooster. Why is it comically **ironic** that Pereda should call Killer "cute"? What is ironic about the words "His beloved Killer"?

7. All in all, do you think the writer seems to share the old men's feelings about *maestria*? Explain.

Writing About the Story

A Creative Response

1. **Describing a Character.** Write a brief description of someone—real or imagined—who deserves to be called a *maestro*, based on the way Suarez explains the word in the first paragraph.

A Critical Response

2. **Analyzing the Story.** Reread the last three paragraphs of the story. Then write a brief essay explaining the significance of Killer's death, in relation to the old men who cherish *maestria*.

Donald Barthelme (1931–   )

Donald Barthelme is an experimenter in fiction, a true member of the avant-garde, sometimes known as a "post-modernist." He is widely regarded as one of the ablest and most versatile stylists at work today—witty, adventurous, and profound.

In the broadest terms, Barthelme's premise is that while literature of the past has functioned to revitalize the imagination, storytelling has now largely lost the power to inspire, persuade, or even entertain us. He feels that our language has gone bankrupt. Since words no longer effectively communicate feelings, he says, they have lost the power to move us. Like the promotional and professional jargon that bombards us, contemporary langauge is thick with sludge and stuffing. Its use of clichés and its verbosity often obscure truth rather than reveal it. As Snow White, the title character of Barthelme's 1967 novel, says, "Oh I wish there were some words in the world that were not the words I always hear!"

But it is not the corruption of our language alone that troubles Barthelme. He sees the problems with language as a reflection of a contemporary society so dehumanized, so lacking in quality, that it can no longer sustain the kind of myths that once gave us our identity. Thus, he feels, the whole point of storytelling is lost.

In his fiction, Barthelme deliberately sets out to create a banal world that fails to make distinctions of quality in people, things, and ideas. Then, since he feels it is no longer possible to write about real life or the real world, he takes writing itself for his subject—the art of making art out of language. Barthelme uses language distinctively. As his interest lies in the form and sound of language, he tends to play with words, to make art out of fragments, much as contemporary painters make art out of everyday junk and pop artists make art out of cartoon figures.

Barthelme's plots are also unconventional. They are episodic, a clutter of styles, absurdities, and slapstick. "The only forms I trust," he has said, "are fragments." His characters are types, two-dimensional parodies of themselves, rather than fully developed individuals.

In Barthelme's hands, a myth is likely to turn into realism, and realism into absurdity; readers can lose their way in Barthelme's fiction, trying to identify with the proceedings and wondering about the writer's point. Barthelme has explained to those who are puzzled by his work: "Art is not difficult because it wishes to be difficult, rather because it wishes to be art. However much the writer might long to be, in his work, simple, honest, straightforward, these virtues are no longer available to him. He discovers that in being simple, honest, straightforward, nothing much happens . . . we are looking for the as yet unspeakable, the as yet unspoken."

Barthelme was born in Philadelphia and raised and educated in Texas. After serving with the U.S. Army in the Orient, he worked as a reporter on the *Houston Post*, as a museum director, as the editor of an art and literature review, as a professor of English at the City University of New York, and, most recently, as a teacher of creative writing at the University of Texas at Houston. He is a regular contributor to *The New Yorker*. Collections of his stories include *Come Back, Dr. Caligari* (1964), *Unspeakable Practices, Unnatural Acts* (1968), from which "Game" is taken, and *Overnight to Many Distant Cities* (1983).

TAMAR

This story takes place in London, just before the outbreak of World War II. The story presumes that the reader is aware of the Holocaust—the killing of six million Jewish men, women, and children by the Nazis during World War II. Hel- prin's narrative here is slow and roundabout. The character named in the title doesn't even appear until halfway through the story. Be patient. Hel- prin has a reason for telling the story the way he does.

Refugees photographed by N. R. Farbman. Life Magazine.

Courtesy Time, Inc.

Before the War, in London, I was trying to arrange a system whereby the Jews of Germany and Austria could sell their paintings and other works of art without depressing demand. It was very serious business, for our primary aim was to require that twenty-five percent of each sale go into an escape fund to provide transport for those who could not make it on their own. We thought that we could exact this price if we managed to keep market values steady. But all of Europe was on edge about the political situation, and no one was in the mood to buy anything. And then, after *Kristallnacht*,[1] every Jew in Germany came forward, wanting to sell precious objects.

At the time of our greatest hope, my job was to set up fronts for selling what we expected would be a flood of art coming from Middle Europe. If it had appeared that English collectors were opening their storerooms to take advantage of a favorable market, the excitement might well have pushed values upward. So we tried to get the cooperation of those prominent collectors who had the foresight to see what was about to happen on the Continent and were in sympathy with our cause. Excepting a very few, these were Jews. The others simply were not interested, and, anyway, we did not want to divulge the plan in too many places.

Soon I found myself deeply involved in the high society of Jews in London and in their great houses throughout the countryside. My conviction was then, as it is now, that it is not possible for Jews to be in "society" but that their efforts to be so are (except when immoderate or in bad taste) courageous, for the mechanisms of high social status are encouragements of vulnerability, safe only for those who can afford to lose themselves in pursuits superficial and deep and not fear that their fundamental positions will drop out from under them as a result of their inattention. My attitudes toward the Jewish peers and the Jewish upper class in general was mixed, and had complex roots. I admired their bravery while occasionally chafing at their blindness. I knew that, in spite of their learning and culture, they were isolated in such a way as to make me—a young man

of thirty-two—far better a judge of certain things than were they. I had been in the ghetto in Warsaw not a month before, and the people there had confided to me that they felt the end was near. They said, "Tell them, in England, that in Poland they are killing Jews." I had been in Berlin, Munich, Vienna, and Prague. I had passed through Jewish villages from Riga to Bucharest,[2] where I had seen a temple about to fall. How misty and beautiful it was, that autumn. I cannot describe the quiet. It was as if the nineteenth century—indeed, all the past—were in hiding and feared to give itself away. The whole world of the Jews in Central Europe looked outward with the saddest eyes. What could *I* do? I tried my best. I was working for the Jewish Agency, and had just come from two years in Palestine, in the desert, and thought that my responsibility was to save the Jews of Europe. Like all young men, I was full of speeches that I could not deliver. Somehow, I imagined that the art scheme would be everything. I have since forgiven myself.

Visions of the Jews in the forests, in green pine valleys as sharp as chevrons,[3] in villages marked by silent white ribbons of wood smoke, never left me as I undertook to master the intricacies of the London social season. I cannot remember when I have enjoyed myself more. Sometimes I became as lost and trusting as my hosts, and, even when I did not, the contrast between the Eastern European *Heimat*[4] and the drawing rooms of modern London was incalculably enlivening. I was suspended between two dream-worlds.

Just before Christmas, that time in all capitals when the city flares most brightly, I was oppressed with invitations. I had a blue pad upon which I listed my engagements, and one terrible, lovely week it had sixteen entries. I met so many dukes, duchesses, M.P.s,[5] industrialists, and academics that my eyes began to cross. But we had begun to succeed in hammering out a network for art sales, and I was confident and happy.

Then a magical power in the Jewish Agency must have decided that these several score dinners had made me into a diplomat, for I received an invitation to a dinner party on the twenty-first at the house of the most eminent Jew in all the Brit-

---

1. *Kristallnacht:* German for "the night of the broken windows." On the night of November 9, 1938, Nazi forces brutally attacked the Jews and their places of business throughout Germany and Austria. After Kristallnacht, there could be little doubt as to the fate in store for European Jews.

2. **Riga . . . Bucharest:** the capitals of Latvia and Rumania, respectively.
3. **chevrons:** a military insignia, consisting of a V-shaped bar.
4. *Heimat:* German for "motherland."
5. **M.P.s:** in Britain, Members of Parliament.

ish Empire. Only that summer, I had scrubbed pots, guarded at night, and lived in a tent, in a collective settlement in the Negev.[6] Now I ballooned with pride. The entire seventeenth century could not have produced enough frills to clothe the heavy monster of my pomposity. Sure that all my troubles were over forever, I spent every bit of my money on the most beautiful three-piece suit in London. When the tailor—who was himself a knight—heard where I was going, he set his men to work, and they finished it in three days. London became, for me, the set of a joyous light opera.

On the night of the twentieth, just twenty-four hours before what I assumed would be my apotheosis[7] (it was said that the Prime Minister would be there, and I imagined myself declaring to him a leaden diplomatic précis along the lines of the Magna Carta or the Treaty of Vienna[8]), I had yet another engagement, this one at the house of a Jewish art dealer whom I had recently regarded as a big fish. I was so overconfident that I left my hotel without his address, thinking that I would manage to find it anyway, since I knew its approximate location in Chelsea.[9]

I was due at six-thirty. For an hour and a half I rushed through Chelsea in this direction and that, trying to find the house. Everyone, it seemed, was having a dinner party, and all the buildings looked alike. When, finally, I arrived at the right square, I stood in a little park and stared at the house. It was five stories tall and it was lit like a theater. Through the sparkling windows came firelight, candlelight, and glimpses of enormous chandeliers—while the snow fell as if in time to sad and troubling music. Red and disheveled from running about, I stood in my splendid suit, frightened to go in. In that square, the coal smoke was coiling about like a great menagerie of airborne snakes, and occasionally it caught me and choked me in its unbearable fumes. But I remember it with fondness, because it was the smell of Europe in the winter; and, though it was devilish and foul, it seemed to say that, underneath everything, another world was at work, that the last century was alive in its clumsiness and warmth, signaling that all was well and that great contexts remained unbroken.

I was afraid to go in, because I was so late and because I knew what a fool I had been in judging these people according to the hierarchy in which they believed, and thus underrating them in comparison to the plutocrats[10] of the next night. But I took hold of myself and rang their bell. I heard conversation stop. A servant came to the door. Each of his steps shot through the wood like an X-ray. I was taken upstairs to a magnificent room in which were five tables of well-dressed people completely motionless and silent, like a group of deer surprised by a hunter. Every eye was upon me. Though frightened of fainting, I remained upright and seemingly composed. My host stood to greet me. Then he took me about like a roast, and introduced me to each and every guest, all of whom had a particular smile that can be described only as simultaneously benevolent, sadistic, and amused. I don't know why, but I broke into German, though my German was not the best. They must have been thinking, Who is this strange red-faced German who does not speak his own language well? Or perhaps they thought that I was confused as to my whereabouts. I suppose I was.

Then Herr Dennis, as I called him, took me by the arm and explained that, since they had readjusted the seating in my absence, I (who, the next day, would be waltzing with the Prime Minister) would have to sit at the children's table. It was a very great blow, especially since the poor children were bunched up all by themselves in a little ell of the room that led to the kitchen. I was in no position to protest; in fact, I was, by that time, quite numb.

As he led me, in a daze, toward the children's table, I imagined myself sitting with five or ten infants in bibs, staring down at them as if from a high tower, eating sullenly like a god exiled from Olympus. But when we rounded the corner of the ell, I discovered that the children were adolescents; and their charm arose to envelop me. First, there were four red-headed girl cousins, all in

---

6. **Negev:** a desert region in southern Israel.
7. **apotheosis** (a·po·thē·ō′sis): glorification; utmost happiness.
8. **Magna Carta . . . Vienna:** the Magna Carta was the great charter guaranteeing English liberties, signed by King John and the English barons in 1215; the Treaty of Vienna concluded the Napoleonic wars in 1815.
9. **Chelsea:** a district of London.

10. **plutocrats:** people whose health gives them power.

white. They were from thirteen to sixteen; they had between them several hundred million freckles; and they were so disturbed by my sudden arrival that they spent the next half hour swallowing, darting their eyes about, clearing their throats, and adjusting fallen locks of hair. They spoke as seriously as very old theologians, but even so much more delicately; they pieced together their sentences with great care, the way new skaters skate, and when they finished they breathed in relief, not unlike students of a difficult Oriental language, who must recite in class. At the end of these ordeals, they looked at each other with the split-second glances common to people who are very familiar. Then, there was a boy with dark woolly hair and the peculiarly adolescent animal-lost-out-on-the-heath expression common to young men whose abilities greatly exceed their experience. At my appearance, he lowered his horns, knowing that he was going to spend the rest of the evening bashing himself against a castle wall. I admired his courage; I liked him; I remembered. Next to him was a fat boy who wanted to be an opera singer. He was only fourteen, and when he saw that the threat presented by the woolly-haired boy was neutralized, he went wild with excitement, blooming at the four cousins with a gregariousness of which he had probably never been aware.

I liked these children. They seemed somewhat effete,[11] and sheltered, but I knew that this was because I was used to the adolescents of our collective, who were much older than their years, and that these young people were the products of an ultra-refined system of schooling. I knew that, if protected during this vulnerability, they might emerge with unmatched strength. I had been through the same system, and had seen my schoolmates undergo miraculous transformations. I knew as well that they were destined for a long and terrible war, but, then again, so were we all. Yes, I liked these children, and I enjoyed the fact that I had left those years behind.

I have not described everyone at that table. One remains. She was the daughter of my host, the eldest, the tallest, the most beautiful. Her name was Tamar, and as I had turned the corner she had seemed to rise in the air to meet me, while the others were lost in the dark. Tamar and I had faced one another in a moment of silence that I

---

11. **effete** (ə·fēt′): overrefined and delicate.

will not ever forget. Sometimes, on a windy day, crosscurrented waves in the shallows near a beach will spread about, trapped in a caldron of bars and brakes, until two run together face to face and then fall back in shocked tranquillity. So it was with Tamar. It was as if I had run right into her. I was breathless, and I believe that she was, too.

I immediately took command of myself, and did not look at her. In fact, I studied every face before I studied hers—black eyes; black hair; her mouth and eyes showing her youth and strength in the way they were set, in the way they moved, not ever having been tried or defeated or abused. She wore a rich white silk blouse that was wonderfully open at the top, and a string of matched pearls. For a moment, I was convinced that she was in her twenties, but when she smiled I saw a touching thin silver wire across her upper teeth, and I knew that she was probably no more than seventeen. She *was* seventeen, soon to be eighteen, soon to take off the wire, soon (in fact) to become a nurse with the Eighth Army in Egypt. But at that time she was just on the verge of becoming a woman, and she virtually glowed with the fact.

As soon as I saw the wire, I felt as if I could talk with her in a way that could be managed, and I did. Unlike the four red-headed cousins, she was fearless and direct. She laughed out loud without the slightest self-consciousness, and I felt as if in our conversation we were not speaking but dancing. Perhaps it was because she was so clear of voice, so alert, and so straightforward. She was old enough to parry, and she did, extraordinarily well.

"Tamar is going to Brussels next year," volunteered one of the red-haired girls, in the manner of a handmaiden at court, "to study at the Royal Laboratory for Underzek and Verpen."

"No, no, no," said Tamar. "What you're thinking of, Hannah, is called the Koninklijk Laboratorium voor Onderzoek van Voorwerpen van Kunst en Wetenschap, and it's in The Hague." She glided over the minefield of Dutch words without hesitation and in a perfect accent.

"Does Tamar speak Dutch?" I asked, looking right at her.

"Yes," she answered, "Tamar speaks Dutch, because she learnt it at her Dutch grandmother's knee—Daddy's mother. But," she continued, shaking a finger gently at Hannah, though really speaking to me, "I'm going to Brussels, to study restoration at the Institut Central des Beaux-Arts, or, if Fascism flies out the window in Italy between now and next year, to the Istituto Nazionale per il Restauro, in Rome.''

When she realized that her recitation of the names of these formidable institutes, each in its own language, might have seemed ostentatious, she blushed.

Emboldened nearly to giddiness, the fat boy interjected, ''We went to Rome. We ate shiski ba there, and the streets are made of water.''

''That's *Venice, stupid,*'' said one of the red-haired girls. ''And what is shiski ba?''

''Shiski ba,'' answered the fat boy, guilelessly, ''is roasted meat on a stick. The Turks sell it in the park.''

''Bob,''[12] I offered, by way of instruction. A silence followed, during which the poor boy looked at me blankly.

''Richard,'' he said, sending the four cousins (who knew him well) into a fit of hysteria. Tamar tried not to laugh, because she knew that he hung on her every gesture and word.

To change the subject, I challenged Tamar. ''Do you really think,'' I said, ''that you will be able to study on the Continent?''

She shrugged her shoulders and smiled in a way that belied her age. ''I'll do the best I can,'' she answered. ''Even if there is a war, it will have an end. I'll still be young, and I'll start again.''

My eyes opened at this. I don't know exactly why; perhaps it was that I imagined her in the future and became entranced with the possibility that I might encounter her then—in some faraway place where affection could run unrestrained. But I wanted to steer things away from art, war, and love.

So, while constantly fending off the quixotic[13] charges of the woolly-haired boy (without ever really looking at him), I told a long story about Palestine. Because they were children, more or less, I told them anything I wanted to tell them. Until long after the adults had left for the living room, I spoke of impossible battles between Jews and Bedouins,[14] of feats of endurance which made me reel merely in imagining them, of horses that flew, and golden shafts of light, pillars of fire,

A Nazi squadron rounds up Jewish survivors of the Warsaw Ghetto, December 27, 1945.

miracles here and there, the wonders of spoken Hebrew, and the lions that guarded the banks and post offices of Jerusalem—in short, anything which seemed as if it might be believed.

Tamar alternated between belief and disbelief with the satisfying rhythm of a blade turning back and forth over a whetstone.[15] She was weaving soft acceptance and sparkling disdain together in a tapestry which I feared she would throw right over my head. She did this in a most delicate cross-examination, the object of which was to

12. **Bob:** the narrator corrects the boy's pronunciation of *shish kebab.*
13. **quixotic:** idealistic to an impractical degree (like Don Quixote in Cervantes's novel).
14. **Bedouins:** nomadic tribes of Arabs who roam the desert.

15. **whetstone:** stone used for sharpening tools.

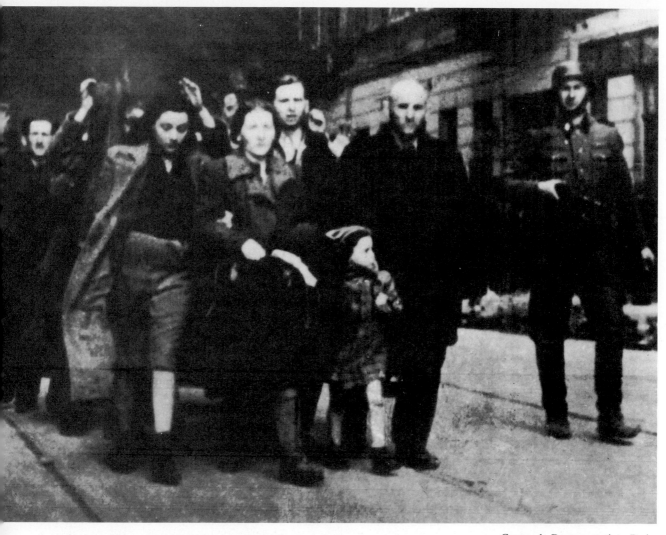

draw out more of the tale for the sake of the children, to satisfy her own curiosity, to mock me gently, and to continue—by entrapment and release—the feeling we had that, though we were still, we were dancing.

"Why," she asked, "did you not get water from the Bedouins that you captured, if you had already gone without it for ten days?"

"Ah!" I said, holding up my finger in the same way she had done with Hannah. "I was only able to capture them because they themselves had run out of water, and were thirstier than I was. And I did not capture them with a gun but by giving a graphic dissertation on European fountains; they were especially taken with my description of the Diana fountain in Bushy Park, and I believe that

they would have followed me anywhere after I told them what goes on in the Place de la Concorde."[16]

"What is it like to be a British Jew in Palestine?" asked Hannah, earnestly, and with such *Weltschmerz*[17] that it was as if an alpine storm cloud had rolled over the table.

"What is it like? It's like being an Italian Negro in Ethiopia, or"—I looked at Tamar—"like living in a continuous production of 'Romeo and Juliet.' " I had meant the allusion to "Romeo and Juliet" to be purely illustrative, but with a life of

---

16. **Place de la Concorde:** one of the principal squares in Paris.
17. *Weltschmerz:* a German expression meaning "sentimental melancholy over the state of the world."

its own it turned Tamar as red as a throbbing coal, and I, a generation apart, nearly followed suit. I was caught in my own springe,[18] enchanted—yet never really in danger, for not only did her father come to fetch me back into the world of adults but I had run those rapids before, and knew the still and deep water at their end.

I recall exactly how the children were sitting when I left them, poised to explode in gossip as soon as I had disappeared—it is likely that in my absence I was cut to ribbons by the woolly-haired boy, and perhaps deservedly so. As Tamar's father and I climbed a broad staircase to the library, where we would discuss business, I remembered the opera singer with whom I had once fallen in love. Her voice was like liquid or a jewel. I have not since heard such a beautiful voice. But she was, oddly enough, almost unknown. I went to Covent Garden[19] to find out in what productions she would sing. Her name was Erika, and when I inquired of the old man at the ticket office I found that he, too, was in love with her.

"I'm too old," he said, "and you're too young." I knew that this was true, and I must have looked pained, because he grabbed me through the ticket window and said, "Don't you see, it's much better that way!"

"I see nothing," I said. "If that's better, then I'm sorry to be alive."

"Wait," he said, and laughed. "You'll see. It's sweeter, much sweeter."

I went to the opera that season two dozen times just to see and hear Erika of the liquid voice. I

---

18. **springe:** a snare, often used to catch birds.
19. **Covent Garden:** London's principal opera house.

wanted, despite the fact that I was fifteen, to marry her immediately, to run away to Brazil or Argentina, to take her with me to the South Seas, etc., etc., etc. It had been unspeakable torture to watch her on a brilliantly lighted stage, singing in a way that fired up all my emotions.

But by the time I met Tamar, I knew that a lighted stage is often best left untouched, and I knew, further, that all connections are temporary, and, therefore, can be enjoyed in their fullness even after the most insubstantial touch—if only one knows how. I was, that night, in a dream within a dream. I was young again in a room of bright colors and laughter; and all the time the dark image of a smoky continent called me away and threatened to tear me apart. I did not know then that there is no contradiction in such contradictions; they are made for one another; without them, we would have nothing to lose and nothing to love.

Tamar was the most lovely girl—and had it not been for that delicate and slim bit of silver wire, I might not have known her as well as I did. Her father agreed to the scheme, but then the scheme collapsed, and the world collapsed soon after. Six years of war. Most of the Jews did not survive. Most of the paintings did. In six years of war, there was probably not a day when I did not think of the time when I had had to sit at the children's table, in a world of vulnerable beauty. Perhaps things are most beautiful when they are not quite real; when you look upon a scene as an outsider, and come to possess it in its entirety and forever; when you live the present with the lucidity and feeling of memory; when, for want of connection, the world deepens and becomes art.

Responding to the Story

Analyzing the Story

Identifying Facts

1. Explain why the narrator is in London at the beginning of the story, and what he is hoping to do.
2. Find passages that reveal his attitude toward the well-to-do Jews in London society. What does he think they have failed to understand?

3. What do you learn about Tamar's appearance, her age, and her dreams? What effect does the thin silver wire have on the narrator?

Interpreting Meanings

4. How would you explain Tamar's attraction to the narrator? What can we infer when Tamar blushes at the reference to Romeo and Juliet?

5. What does Erika, the opera singer, have to do with the story of Tamar?
6. What effect does Helprin achieve by wrapping the story of Tamar inside an account of the Nazis and the war? What passages of the story remind us, ironically, of what is about to happen in Europe?
7. What larger group of people might be represented by Herr Dennis and his family and friends? What do you think the children's table itself stands for in the narrator's memory?
8. The narrator uses a number of **paradoxes,** or apparent contradictions to sum up the story in the last two paragraphs. Identify each paradox.
9. What does "the world deepens and becomes art" mean? Explain the outlook on life that the narrator seems to be describing in the last passage. What is your response to what he says here?
10. Is this a romantic love story? Or is it a story about the redemptive power of beauty and art? Explain.

Writing About the Story

A Creative Response

1. **Writing a Journal Entry.** Imagine that Tamar kept a journal. Write an entry she might have recorded on the day she met the narrator at the dinner party.

A Critical Response

2. **Explaining a Statement.** On page 933, at the end of a paragraph describing how he felt about the Jews of London and Europe, and explaining how he came to be doing what he was doing, the narrator says, "I have since forgiven myself." In a paragraph, explain what you think this statement means. Before you write, look for other passages in the story that reveal how the narrator feels about that time in London.
3. **Responding to a Title.** In a brief essay, explain why Helprin chose the title "Tamar" for this story. In your essay, include your response to the title: Do you think it's a good one? Before you write, decide how the character of Tamar might be central to the point of Helprin's story.

Analyzing Language and Style

Figurative Language

Helprin's writings are distinguished by a style that is rich in descriptive detail and figurative language—the language of metaphors, similes, and personification.

1. "Visions of the Jews in the forests, in green pine valleys as sharp as chevrons. . . ."

   a. Describe the image created by this **simile**.
   b. What is significant about the choice of the word *chevron* in this particular context?

2. "The entire seventeenth century could not have produced enough frills to clothe the heavy monster of my pomposity."

   a. What is *pomposity*?
   b. How is it **personified** here?
   c. What does this image reveal about the narrator's feelings about himself?

3. "London became, for me, the set of a joyous light opera."

   a. What does this **metaphor** reveal about the narrator's feelings for London?
   b. Why is this image **ironic,** considering the narrator's purpose in London?

4. "It [the house] was five stories tall and it was lit like a theater."

   a. What does the comparison with a theater suggest, beyond an image of a brightly lit place?
   b. How would the effect have been different if the house had been compared with "a church full of candles" or with "a brightly lit palace"?

5. ". . . the snow fell as if in time to sad and troubling music." (Page 934)

   a. What is the emotional effect of this **simile**?
   b. Think of at least two other ways the snowfall might have been described to suggest other moods.

6. ". . . the coal smoke was coiling about like a great menagerie of airbone snakes. . . ." (Page 934)

   a. What is the emotional effect of this **simile**?
   b. In "The Love Song of J. Alfred Prufrock" (page 760), what is the same smoke compared with, and to what effect?

7. ". . . well-dressed people completely motionless and silent, like a group of deer surprised by a hunter." (Page 934) In light of what we know is going to happen to the Jews of Europe, why is this **simile** tragically appropriate?

8. "Then he took me about like a roast. . . ." (Page 934)

   a. Describe the picture this **simile** puts in your mind.
   b. What does the choice of comparison reveal about the narrator's attitude toward himself?

9. Find three comparisons describing the cousins at the children's table on page 934. What feeling for the children is revealed in each comparison?
10. The most significant figure of speech in the story might be the long extended **simile** describing the narrator's meeting with Tamar. Find the simile and explain in your own words what it reveals about the significance of this encounter.

Tim O'Brien
(1946–   )

Tim O'Brien was born in Austin, Minnesota, and graduated from Macalester College. In 1968, he was drafted and served with the U.S. Army in Vietnam, where he attained the rank of sergeant. Returning from the war, he went to Harvard for graduate work in English. A summer internship on the *Washington Post* led to a job as national affairs reporter for that newspaper.

O'Brien had been writing stories since childhood, and even in the midst of his academic work, he knew he wanted to write full-time. It was his military experience in Vietnam that provided the material for his fiction and personal narratives. *If I Die in a Combat Zone, Box Me Up and Send Me Home* (1973) is a collection of anecdotes and observations of his duty in Vietnam. The book drew widespread approval, particularly from veterans, as an authentic re-creation of the footsoldiers' experience in an unpopular war.

"I started writing fiction," O'Brien has said, "to get away from the whole idea of aping reality. I was tired of echoing what reality is and I was more interested in questions of what might be, what might have happened, what could have happened."

O'Brien's first novel, *Northern Lights*, appeared in 1974 and dealt with a veteran returned to civilian life. A second novel, *Going After Cacciato*, followed in 1978. This novel returned to the jungle war to give a soldier's fantasy of quitting the battle and walking off across the mountains to find Paris. *Cacciato* was acclaimed

as one of the few novels to have captured the essence of the Vietnam experience, and it won the National Book Award in 1979.

"*Cacciato* was an imagined novel," O'Brien has said. "It was a novel of psychology. I didn't want to tell the events of Vietnam again. I'd already done that once. I didn't want to say here's what it's like to get shot, and see people shot. I wanted to get into the head of a human being, a character, and write about terror and questions of courage and obligation to duty, and conscience."

SPEAKING OF COURAGE

Before he published the full novel about Cacciato, O'Brien published portions of it as short stories in various magazines. This story, which later appeared in the novel, was named as one of the O. Henry Prize Stories of 1978.

The novel about Cacciato is told through the eyes and sensibilities of a young soldier from Iowa named Paul Berlin. In this story, Paul has recently returned from battle duty in Vietnam. Like many veterans of that war, he is confused over the meaning of his experience. He is also vaguely dissatisfied with his performance.

The war was over, and there was no place in particular to go. Paul Berlin followed the tar road in its seven-mile loop around the lake, then he started all over again, driving slowly, feeling safe inside his father's big Chevy, now and again looking out onto the lake to watch the boats and waterskiers and scenery. It was Sunday and it was summer, and things seemed pretty much the same. The lake was the same. The houses were the same, all low-slung and split level and modern, porches and picture windows facing the water. The lots were spacious. On the lake side of the road, the houses were handsome and set deep in, well-kept and painted, with docks jutting out into the lake, and boats moored and covered with canvas, and gardens, and sometimes even gardeners, and stone patios with barbecue spits and grills, and wooden shingles saying who lived where. On the other side of the road, to his left, the houses were also handsome, though less expensive and on a smaller scale and with no docks or boats or wooden shingles. The road was a sort of boundary between the affluent and the almost affluent, and to live on the lake side of the road was one of the few natural privileges in a town of the prairie—the difference between watching the sun set over cornfields or over the lake.

It was a good-sized lake. In high school he'd driven round and round and round with his friends and pretty girls, talking about urgent matters, worrying eagerly about the existence of God and theories of causation, or wondering whether Sally Hankins, who lived on the lake side of the road, would want to pull into the shelter of Sunset Park. Then, there had been a war. But there had always been the lake. It had been dug out by the southernmost advance of the Wisconsin glacier. Fed by neither springs nor streams, it was a tepid, algaed lake that depended on fickle prarie rains for replenishment. Still, it was the town's only lake, the only one in twenty-six miles, and at night the moon made a white swath across its waters, and on sunny days it was nice to look at, and that evening it would dazzle with the reflections of fireworks, and it was the center of things from the very start, always there to be driven around, still mesmerizing and quieting and a good audience for silence, a seven-mile flat circumference that could be traveled by slow car in twenty-five minutes. It was not such a good lake for swimming. After college, he'd caught an ear infection that had almost kept him out of the war. And the lake had drowned Max Arnold, keeping him out of the war entirely. Max had been one who liked to talk about the existence of God. "No, I'm not saying *that*," he would say carefully against the drone of the engine. "I'm saying it is possible as an idea, even necessary as an idea, a final cause in the whole structure of causation." Now he knew, perhaps. Before the war, they'd driven around the lake as friends, but now Max was dead and most of the others were living in Des Moines or Sioux City, or going to school somewhere, or holding down jobs. None of the girls was left. Sally Hankins was married. His father would not talk. His father had been in another war, so he knew the truth already, and he would not talk about it, and there was no one left to talk with.

He turned on the radio. The car's big engine fired machinery that blew cold air all over him. Clockwise, like an electron spinning forever around its nucleus, the big Chevy circled the lake, and he had little to do but sit in the air conditioning, both hands on the wheel, letting the car carry

STEPHEN E HENDRICKS · EDWARD J KAPUSTA · FRANCIS F THORPE ·

DENNY RAY EASTER · ROBERT D HERTZ · HAROLD E CARR · BILLY RAY PRICE II · ROBERT

DONALD W SMITH · RUDOLPH C THOMAS · EDGAR T WEST Jr · JERRY LEE MOFFETT · ROBE

DANIEL F COX · JOSEPH W GAA Jr · JAMES A HARWOOD · BILLY RAY ANDERSON · DAV

WILLIAM A MALENFANT · CURTIS W MOORE · WILLIAM NANI III · DELBERT R PORTER · BRIAN

ROBERT F SHARPE · WILLIAM R ZEYEN · FEET BARNETT Sr · CHARLES R BESS · DEWAINE

PAUL DARBY · JOHN E DAVIS · DONALD G DIETRICK · CHARLES R BESS · DEWAINE

HERBERT S HINSON · ROGER G HOILER · MARTIN JIM II · PAUL E LEARY Jr · CARLTON

TERRY F MEZERA · EARL NELSON · REINALDO REIN RODRIGUEZ · ROY RODRIGUEZ SALINAS · BELL

LEE D STUART Jr · CHARLES D StCLAIR · WILLIAM L THIGPEN · JOHNNY N WARD II · JOH

WILLIAM B BLACKMON Jr · ALBERT L BROWN · DAVID W DOON · JOHN L DOBROSKI · DANIEL

JOHN H GEDDINGS · MALCOLM LYONS · ROBERT T MIRRES · JESSE NIXON · JAMES

PERRY M SMITH · CECIL W SOUTHERLAND · JOSEPH S STOWELL · WILLIAM E AARONSON IV

JOSHUA M DANIELS · EUGENE C GILMORE · BILLY JOE PLASTER Jr · CARD FORGE · WILLIE

GLENN R ETHINGTON · JESUS A GONZALES · STEPHEN A AUSCHATH · RONALD D ROWSEY · WD

JAMES C THAMES · JESSIE A BROOKS · JAMES R CARTER · TOMMY DOSS · ROBER

ARTHUR A NABBEN · RONALD D STEPHENSON · LOUIS W TRAVERS · RONALD M GARRISON · RON

GREGORY S KARGER · EUGENE H VICKERS · STEVEN W VOGL · BART NEWBOLD Jr · SAMUE

RONNIE G VAUGHAN · LARRY D DEAN · FRANK A CELANO · ROY JOHNSON · KENNE

HUGH D OPPERMAN · GREGORY L PEFFER · MICHAEL H PETTY · DENNIS A SCHLOSSOW · WILLIAM

DONALD L SENTI · FREDERICK A VIGIL · ALFONSO A BRITO · JERRY A COTTON · GEO

RONALD J REVIS · JAMES L COLWYE · STEPHEN L ENDSLEY · CALVIN E MUACK · WILLIAM

RICHARD C PORTER · MERRELL E BRUMLEY Jr · WILLIAM O CREECH II · JUAN C GONZALES · GERS

JAMES P MARKEY Jr · WILLIAM D NICODEMUS · GEORGE L ROBERTSON · ROBERT G EGNAS · IC

DEWIGHT E NORTON · STEVEN J OLCOTT · WILLIAM F REICHERT · JAMES E WEATHERSBY · GARNSY

DEAN A HARRIS · RONALD M RIGDON · ARTHUR A SMITH · MICHAEL E WILLIAMS · HAROLD E

DAVID I MIXTER · ROBERT L PULLIAM · JEFFREY L BARLOW · HAROLD E BIRKY · JAME

ALLEN C ELL · RAFAEL GARCIAPAGAN · RONALD W WAUSLEY · RONALD N JASINSK

JOHN R MILLER · ROBERT A SISK · JOHNNY C SPEARS · JOHNNY E TINLIN · PATRICK G CARTWRIGHT · L

JOSEPH W CASINO · CLYDE W COBLE · GORDON E CRAWFORD · JAMES C HARRIS · LORI

KEITH M JACKSON · WALTER X MENDEZ · THOMAS C APPLEBY · STEPHEN A MOORE · STEPHE

RICHARD D RANDOLPH · KEITH A STODDARD · MICHAEL P AUSTIN · DARRELL W COWAN · ROB

FRANK S McCUTCHEON III · FLOYD RICHARDSON II · JOHN C STRAUSER · PHILIPP R

LUTHER N BAGNAL III · MARTIN J BURNS · MILFRED R GREEN · LENNART G LANGHORNE · THOM

ROBERT L STANDERWICK Sr · JOSEPH L STONE · WALLIS W WEBB · TERRENCE W WELDON · ROBER

JACKIE LEE DENNY · SAMUEL H EBERHART · GREGORY S SOMERS · LARRY H MARSHALL · DAV

ANDRES LOPEZ RAMON · NELSON G RICHARDSON · DANIEL PAUL · STEPHEN M TRAYNOR · PATR

CLIFTON E CALLAHAN · DAVID C JOHNSON · CLIFTON G NEWCOMB · JAMES LACKRIDGE

CARL M WOOD · LARRY A WOODBURN · RICHARD A AARON · DAVID L ALEXANDER · KEN

FRANK J GASPERICH Jr · AMBERS A HAMILTON · ROBERT J JACQUES · MICHAEL

WILLIAM B RHODES · ROBERT J ROGERS · JOSEPH A TERESINSKI · CURTIS L WILLIAMS · THEO

BRIAN R FOLEY · THOMAS P B KING · RICHARD S KOTWICKI · WILLIAM L ARCHER

RUSSELL G BLOCHER · DONALD L MEEHAN Jr · CHARLES L PEACE · JOSE MARIE ROCHA · DOUGLAS

LEWIS R YATES · ROLAND D TROYANO · BRUCE A VANDYKE · GERRITT E WITHERSPOON · HARRY

THOMAS A SONY · RAFAEL RIVERA BENITEZ · CHARLES G ROBO · TYRONE C BRADLEY · DAVID

him in orbit. It was a lazy Sunday. The town was small. Out on the lake, a man's motorboat had stalled, and the fellow was bent over the silver motor with a wrench and a frown, and beyond him there were waterskiers and smooth July waters and two mud hens.

The road curved west. The sun was low in front of him, and he figured it was close to five o'clock. Twenty after, he guessed. The war had taught him to figure time. Even without the sun, waking from sleep, he could usually place it within fifteen minutes either way. He wished his father were there beside him, so he could say, "Well, looks about five-twenty," and his father would look at his watch and say, "Hey! How'd you do that?" "One of those things you learn in the war," he would say. "I know exactly what you mean," his father would then say, and the ice would be broken, and then they would be able to talk about it as they circled the lake.

He drove past Slater Park and across the causeway and past Sunset Park. The radio announcer sounded tired. He said it was five-thirty. The temperature in Des Moines was eighty-one degrees, and "All you on the road, drive carefully now, you hear, on this fine Fourth of July." Along the road, kicking stones in front of them, two young boys were hiking with knapsacks and toy rifles and canteens. He honked going by, but neither boy looked up. Already he'd passed them six times, forty-two miles, nearly three hours. He watched the boys recede in his rearview mirror. They turned purply colored, like clotted blood, before finally disappearing.

"How many medals did you win?" his father might have asked.

"Seven," he would have said, "though none of them were for valor."

"That's all right," his father would have answered, knowing full well that many brave men did not win medals for their bravery, and that others won medals for doing nothing. "What are the medals you won?"

And he would have listed them, as a kind of starting place for talking about the war: the Combat Infantryman's Badge, the Air Medal, the Bronze Star (without a V-device for valor), the Army Commendation Medal, the Vietnam Campaign Medal, the Good Conduct Medal, and the Purple Heart, though it wasn't much of a wound, and there was no scar, and it didn't hurt and never had. While none of them was for valor, the dec-

orations still looked good on the uniform in his closet, and if anyone were to ask, he would have explained what each signified, and eventually he would have talked about the medals he did not win, and why he did not win them, and how afraid he had been.

"Well," his father might have said, "that's an impressive list of medals, all right."

"But none were for valor."

"I understand."

And that would have been the time for telling his father that he'd almost won the Silver Star, or maybe even the Medal of Honor.

"I almost won the Silver Star," he would have said.

"How's that?"

"Oh, it's just a war story."

"What's wrong with war stories?" his father would have said.

"Nothing, except I guess nobody wants to hear them."

"Tell me," his father would have said.

And then, circling the lake, he would have started the story by saying what a crazy hot day it had been when Frenchie Tucker crawled like a snake into the clay tunnel and got shot in the neck, going on with the story in great detail, telling how it smelled and what the sounds had been, everything, then going on to say how he'd almost won the Silver Star for valor.

"Well," his father would have said, "that's not a very pretty story."

"I wasn't very brave."

"You have seven medals."

"True, true," he would have said, "but I might have had eight," but even so, seven medals was pretty good, hinting at courage with their bright colors and heavy metals. "But I wasn't brave," he would have admitted.

"You weren't a coward, either," his father would have said.

"I might have been a hero."

"But you weren't a coward," his father would have insisted.

"No," Paul Berlin would have said, holding the wheel slightly right of center to produce the constant clockwise motion, "no, I wasn't a coward, and I wasn't brave, but I had the chance." He would have explained, if anyone were there to listen, that his most precious medal, except for the one he did not win, was the Combat Infantryman's Badge. While not strictly speaking a genuine medal—more an insignia of soldierdom—the CIB meant that he had seen the war as a real soldier, on the ground. It meant he'd had the opportunity to be brave, it meant that. It meant, too, that he'd seen Frenchie Tucker crawl into the tunnel so that just his feet were left showing, and heard the sound when he got shot in the neck. With its crossed rifles and silver and blue colors, the CIB was really not such a bad decoration, not as good as the Silver Star or Medal of Honor, but still evidence that he'd once been there with the chance to be very brave. "I wasn't brave," he would have said, "but I might have been."

The road descended into the outskirts of town, turning northwest past the junior college and tennis courts, then past the city park where tables were spread with sheets of colored plastic as picnickers listened to the high school band, then past the municipal docks where a fat woman stood in pedal-pushers and white socks, fishing for bullheads.[1] There were no other fish in the lake, excepting some perch and a few worthless carp. It was a bad lake for swimming and fishing both.

He was in no great hurry. There was no place in particular to go. The day was very hot, but inside the Chevy the air was cold and oily and secure, and he liked the sound of the big engine and the radio and the air conditioning. Through the windows, as though seen through one-way glass, the town shined like a stop-motion photograph, or a memory. The town could not talk, and it would not listen, and it was really a very small town anyway. "How'd you like to hear about the time I almost won the Silver Star for valor?" he might have said. The Chevy seemed to know its way around the lake.

It was late afternoon. Along an unused railway spur, four men were erecting steel launchers for the evening fireworks. They were dressed alike in khaki trousers, work shirts, visored caps, and black boots. They were sweating. Two of them were unloading crates of explosives from a city truck, stacking the crates near the steel launchers. They were talking. One of them was laughing. "How'd you like to hear about it?" he might have murmured, but the men did not look up. Later they would blow color into the sky. The lake would be like a mirror, and the picnickers would sigh. The colors would open wide. "Well, it was

1. **bullheads:** a type of freshwater fish with a spiny head and wide mouth.

this crazy hot day," he would have said to anyone who asked, "and Frenchie Tucker took off his helmet and pack and crawled into the tunnel with a forty-five and a knife, and the whole platoon stood in a circle around the mouth of the tunnel to watch him go down. 'Don't get blowed away,' said Stink Harris, but Frenchie was already inside and he didn't hear. You could see his feet wiggling, and you could smell the dirt and clay, and then, when he got shot through the neck, you could smell the gunpowder and you could see Frenchie's feet jerk, and that was the day I could have won the Silver Star for valor."

The Chevy rolled smoothly across the old railroad spur. To his right, there was only the open lake. To his left, the lawns were scorched dry like October corn. Hopelessly, round and round, a rotating sprinkler scattered water into Doctor Mason's vegetable garden. In August it would get worse. The lake would turn green, thick with bacteria and decay, and the golf course would dry up, and dragonflies would crack open for lack of good water. The summer seemed permanent.

The big Chevy curled past the A&W and Centennial Beach, and he started his seventh revolution around the lake.

He followed the road past the handsome low-slung houses. Back to Slater Park, across the causeway, around to Sunset Park, as though riding on tracks.

Out on the lake, the man with the stalled motorboat was still fiddling with the engine.

The two boys were still trudging on their hike. They did not look up when he honked.

The pair of mud hens floated like wooden decoys. The waterskiers looked tan and happy, and the spray behind them looked clean.

It was all distant and pretty.

Facing the sun again, he figured it was nearly six o'clock. Not much later the tired announcer in Des Moines confirmed it, his voice seeming to rock itself into a Sunday afternoon snooze.

Too bad, he thought. If Max were there, he would say something meaningful about the announcer's fatigue, and relate it to the sun low and red now over the lake, and the war, and courage. Too bad that all the girls had gone away. And his father, who already knew the difficulties of being brave, and who preferred silence.

Circling the lake, with time to talk, he would have told the truth. He would not have faked it. Starting with the admission that he had not been truly brave, he would have next said he hadn't been a coward, either. "I almost won the Silver Star for valor," he would have said, and, even so, he'd learned many important things in the war. Like telling time without a watch. He had learned to step lightly. He knew, just by the sound, the difference between friendly and enemy mortars, and with time to talk and with an audience, he could explain the difference in great detail. He could tell people that the enemy fired 82-millimeter mortar rounds, while we fired 81's, and that this was a real advantage to the enemy since they could steal our rounds and shoot them from their own weapons. He knew many lies. Simple, unprofound things. He knew it is a lie that only stupid men are brave. He knew that a man can die of fright, literally, because it had happened just that way to Billy Boy Watkins after his foot had been blown off. Billy Boy had been scared to death. Dead of a heart attack caused by fright, according to Doc Peret, who would know. He knew, too, that it is a lie, the old saying that you never hear the shot that gets you, because Frenchie Tucker was shot in the neck, and after they dragged him out of the tunnel he lay there and told everyone his great discovery; he'd heard it coming the whole way, he said excitedly; and then he raised his thumb and bled through his mouth, grinning at the great discovery. So the old saying was surely a lie, or else Frenchie Tucker was lying himself, which under the circumstances was hard to believe. He knew a lot of things. They were not new or profound, but they were true. He knew that he might have won a Silver Star, like Frenchie, if he'd been able to finish what Frenchie started in the foul tunnel. He knew many war stories, a thousand details, smells and the confusion of the senses, but nobody was there to listen, and nobody knew a damn about the war because nobody believed it was really a war at all. It was not a war for war stories, or talk of valor, and nobody asked questions about the details, such as how afraid you can be, or what the particular sounds were, or whether it hurts to be shot, or what you think about and hear and see on ambush, or whether you can really tell in a firefight which way to shoot, which you can't, or how you become brave enough to win the Silver Star, or how it smells of sulfur against your cheek after firing eighteen fast rounds, or how you crawl on hands and knees without knowing direction, and how, after crawling into the red-mouthed tunnel, you close your eyes like a mole and follow the tunnel walls and smell Frenchie's fresh blood and know a bullet cannot miss in there, and how there is nowhere to go but forward or backward, eyes closed, and how you can't go forward, and lose all sense, and are dragged out by the heels, losing the Silver Star. All the details, without profundity, simple and age old, but nobody wants to hear war stories because they are age old and not new and not profound, and because everyone knows already that it hadn't been a war like other wars. If Max or his father were ever to ask, or anybody, he would say. "Well, first off, it was a war the same as any war," which would not sound profound at all, but which would be the truth. Then he would explain what he meant in great detail, explaining that, right or wrong or win or lose, at root it had been a real war, regardless of corruption in high places or politics or sociology or the existence of God. His father knew it already, though. Which was why he didn't ask. And Max could not ask. It was a small town, but it wasn't the town's fault, either.

He passed the sprawling ranch-style homes. He lit a cigarette. He had learned to smoke in the war. He opened the window a crack but kept the air conditioner going full, and again he circled the lake. His thoughts were the same. Out on the lake, the man was frantically yanking the cord to his stalled outboard motor. Along the causeway, the two boys marched on. The pair of mud hens sought sludge at the bottom of the lake, heads under water and tails bobbing.

Six-thirty, he thought. The lake had divided into two halves. One half still glistened. The other was caught in shadow. Soon it would be dark. The crew of workers would shoot the sky full of color, for the war was over, and the town would celebrate independence. He passed Sunset Park once again, and more houses, and the junior college and tennis courts, and the picnickers and the high school band, and the municipal docks where the fat woman patiently waited for fish.

Already, though it wasn't quite dusk, the A&W was awash in neon lights.

He maneuvered his father's Chevy into one of the parking slots, let the engine idle, and waited. The place was doing a good holiday business. Mostly kids in their fathers' cars, a few farmers in for the day, a few faces he thought he remembered, but no names. He sat still. With the sound of the engine and air conditioning and radio, he could not hear the kids laughing, or the cars coming and going and burning rubber. But it didn't matter, it seemed proper, and he sat patiently and watched while mosquitoes and June bugs swarmed off the lake to attack the orange-colored lighting. A slim, hipless, deft young blonde delivered trays of food, passing him by as if the big Chevy were invisible, but he waited. The tired announcer in Des Moines gave the time, seven o'clock. He could trace the fall of dusk in the orange lights which grew brighter and sharper. It was a bad war for medals. But the Silver Star would have been nice. Nice to have been brave. The tactile, certain substance of the Silver Star, and how he could have rubbed his fingers over it, remembering the tunnel and the smell of clay in his nose, going forward and not backward in simple bravery. He waited patiently. The mosquitoes were electrocuting themselves against a Pest-Rid machine. The slim young carhop ignored him, chatting with four boys in a Firebird, her legs in nylons even in mid-summer.

He honked once, a little embarrassed, but she did not turn. The four boys were laughing. He could not hear them, or the joke, but he could see their bright eyes and the way their heads moved. She patted the cheek of the driver.

He honked again, twice. He could not hear the sound. The girl did not hear, either.

He honked again, this time leaning on the horn. His ears buzzed. The air conditioning shot cold air into his lap. The girl turned slowly, as though hearing something very distant, not at all sure. She said something to the boys, and they laughed, then she moved reluctantly toward him. EAT MAMA BURGERS said the orange and brown button on her chest. "How'd you like to hear about the war," he whispered, feeling vengeful. "The time I almost won the Silver Star."

She stood at the window, straight up so he could not see her face, only the button that said, EAT MAMA BURGERS. "Papa Burger, root beer, and french fries," he said, but the girl did not move or answer. She rapped on the window.

"Papa Burger, root beer, and french fries," he said, rolling it down.

She leaned down. She shook her head dumbly. Her eyes were as lovely and fuzzy as cotton candy.

"Papa Burger, root beer, and french fries," he said slowly, pronouncing the words separately and distinctly for her.

She stared at him with her strange eyes. "You blind?" she chirped suddenly. She gestured toward an intercom attached to a steel post. "You blind or something?"

"Papa Burger, root beer, and french fries."

"Push the button," she said, "and place your order." Then, first punching the button for him, she returned to her friends in the Firebird.

"Order," commanded a tinny voice.

"Papa Burger, root beer, and french fries."

"Roger-dodger," the voice said. "Repeat: one Papa, one beer, one fries. Stand by. That's it?"

"Roger," said Paul Berlin.

"Out," said the voice, and the intercom squeaked and went dead.

"Out," said Paul Berlin.

When the slim carhop brought him his tray, he ate quickly, without looking up, then punched the intercom button.

"Order," said the tinny voice.

"I'm done."

"That's it?"

"Yes, all done."

"Roger-dodger, over n' out," said the voice.

"Out."

On his ninth revolution around the lake he passed the hiking boys for the last time. The man with the stalled motorboat was paddling toward shore. The mud hens were gone. The fat woman was reeling in her line. The sun had left a smudge of watercolor on the horizon, and the bandshell was empty, and Doctor Mason's sprinkler went round and round.

On his tenth revolution, he switched off the air conditioning, cranked open a window and rested his elbow comfortably on the sill, driving with one hand. He could trace the contours of the tunnel. He could talk about the scrambling sense of being lost, though he could not describe it even in his thoughts. He could talk about the terror, but he could not describe it or even feel it anymore. He could talk about emerging to see sunlight, but he could not feel the warmth, or see the faces of the men who looked away, or talk about his shame. There was no one to talk to, and nothing to say.

On his eleventh revolution, the sky went crazy with color.

He pulled into Sunset Park and stopped in the shadow of a picnic shelter. After a time, he got out and walked down to the beach and stood with his arms folded and watched the fireworks. For a small town, it was a pretty good show.

Responding to the Story

Analyzing the Story

Identifying Facts

1. Describe the story's **setting**. In contrast, what sights, sounds, and smells does Paul remember from his time in Vietnam?
2. What does Paul wish his father would do?
3. List the things Paul has learned as a result of the war. According to Paul, why don't people want to hear about the war?
4. Explain what Frenchie Tucker did in Vietnam. What happened to him as a result?
5. What does Paul wish he had done in Vietnam? What does he want to tell his father?

Interpreting Meanings

6. Why do you think it is so difficult for Paul and his father to talk? What does Paul mean when he says that his father "knew the truth already"? What *truth* does his father know? How does he know it?
7. Discuss the **symbolic** meaning of the repeated circular action in the story, and of the repeated references to time.
8. What is the **symbolic** meaning of the date in the story's context?
9. Given his experiences, what is **ironic** about the military language in Paul's conversation with the disembodied voice on the drive-in's intercom system?
10. Find the passages where Paul mentions conversations about God. What purpose do you think these passages serve?
11. Do you think Paul's **internal conflict** has been resolved by the end of the story? Explain.
12. Do you think Paul is or is not a courageous person? Explain your answer.
13. Could Paul's feelings be the same for any soldier, in any war? Or do you think the Vietnam war was different? Explain.

Writing About the Story

A Creative Response

1. **Inventing an Interview.** Imagine that a TV reporter approaches Paul Berlin for an interview about Vietnam for that night's July 4 newscast. Write a dialogue made up of the reporter's questions and Berlin's answers.

A Critical Response

2. **Comparing Stories.** Both "Speaking of Courage" and Mark Helprin's "Tamar" (page 932) deal indirectly with the trauma of warfare. In a brief essay, explain how both stories use **contrast** to deal with their themes on this subject. In planning your essay, consider how contrast is evident in each story's setting, characterization, and tone of voice.
3. **Comparing and Contrasting Stories.** In an essay, show how O'Brien's story is similar to yet different from "The End of Something" (page 574), Ernest Hemingway's story about a young man who has returned home from another war. Before you write, fill out a chart like the following to help you determine where the stories are alike and where they differ.

	O'Brien	Hemingway
Setting		
Main character's conflict		
Resolution of problem		
Tone		
Theme		

James Alan McPherson (1943–   )

Born in Savannah, Georgia, James Alan Mc-Pherson recalls growing up in a lower-class black neighborhood, going to segregated schools, and knowing no white people socially. Looking back on his early years, he sees himself as the beneficiary of a series of contracts between the United States government and various institutions of society. One of these contracts helped him to enroll at Morris Brown College in Atlanta. Another contract helped him get a part-time job as a dining-car waiter for the Great Northern Railway.

A creative writing contest sponsored by the *Reader's Digest* started him writing fiction, and he sold his first story to *The Atlantic Monthly* in 1965. He continued to write while attending Harvard Law School and working as a janitor in a Cambridge apartment house. This job, he said later, gave him the solitude to write, and thus was probably the best contract he ever made.

McPherson's first collection of stories, *Hue and Cry*, appeared in 1969 and was widely praised for transcending stereotypes in both black and white characters. McPherson believes Americans need to find a basis other than race (which tends to erect walls between people) to deal with complex relationships in a society that is becoming more democratic and more offended by racial stereotypes.

"Those of us who are black," McPherson says, "and who have had to defend our humanity, should be obliged to continue defending it, on higher and higher levels, not of power, which is a kind of tragic trap, but on higher levels of consciousness."

In *Elbow Room,* a second collection of stories published in 1977, McPherson was aiming to present his hope for an America in which each citizen would contain the diversity of all, "carry the mainstream of the culture inside himself. As an American, . . . he would be a synthesis of high and low, black and white, city and country, provincial and universal. If he could live with these contradictions he would be simply a representative American." *Elbow Room* won the Pulitzer Prize in 1978.

McPherson has been a professor at the Writers' Workshop of the University of Iowa. He has also taught at the University of Virginia, Morgan State University, the University of California at Santa Cruz, and Harvard.

"Why I Like Country Music" first appeared in *The Harvard Advocate*.

WHY I LIKE COUNTRY MUSIC

Despite its title, this story is more about an important childhood experience than about country music. The music, however, plays a major role in the experience. As you read, pay careful attention to the tone of voice in which the story is told. Try to imagine that you are listening to the narrator as he talks aloud. You should be able to hear a very distinctive voice, similar to that of a subtle comedian beguiling an audience with a tale based on real life.

No one will believe that I like country music. Even my wife scoffs when told such a possibility exists. "Go on!" Gloria tells me. "I can see blues, bebop, maybe even a little buckdancing. But not bluegrass." Gloria says, "Hillbilly stuff is not just music. It's like the New York Stock Exchange. The minute you see a sharp rise in it, you better watch out."

I tend to argue the point, but quietly, and mostly to myself. Gloria was born and raised in New York; she has come to believe in the stock exchange as the only index of economic health. My perceptions were shaped in South Carolina; and long ago I learned there, as a waiter in private clubs, to gauge economic flux by the tips people gave. We tend to disagree on other matters too, but the thing that gives me most frustration is trying to make her understand why I like country music. Perhaps it is because she hates the South and has capitulated emotionally to the horror stories told by refugees from down home. Perhaps it is because Gloria is third generation Northern-born. I do not know. What I do know is that, while the two of us are black, the distance between us is sometimes as great as that between Ibo and Yoruba.[1] And I do know that, despite her protestations, I like country music.

"You are crazy," Gloria tells me.

I tend to argue the point, but quietly, and mostly to myself.

Of course I do not like all country stuff; just pieces that make the right connections. I like banjo because sometimes I hear ancestors in the strumming. I like the fiddle-like refrain in "Dixie" for the very same reason. But most of all I like square dancing—the interplay between fiddle and caller, the stomping, the swishing of dresses, the strutting, the proud turnings, the laughter. Most of all I like the laughter. In recent months I have wondered why I like this music and this dance. I have drawn no general conclusions, but from time to time I suspect it is because the square dance is the only dance form I ever mastered.

"I wouldn't say that in public," Gloria warns me.

I agree with her, but still affirm the truth of it, although quietly, and mostly to myself.

Dear Gloria: This is the truth of how it was:

In my youth in that distant country, while others learned to strut, I grew stiff as a winter cornstalk. When my playmates harmonized their rhythms, I stood on the sidelines in atonic[2] detachment. While they shimmied, I merely jerked in lackluster imitation. I relate these facts here, not in remorse or self-castigation, but as a true confession of my circumstances. In those days, down in our small corner of South Carolina, proficiency in dance was a form of storytelling. A boy could say, "I traveled here and there, saw this and fought that, conquered him and made love to her, lied to them, told a few others the truth, just so I could come back here and let you know what things out there are really like." He could communicate all this with smooth, graceful jiggles of

---

1. **Ibo and Yoruba** (ē′bō; yə·rōō′bə): two separate and distinct West African tribes in Nigeria.

2. **atonic:** weak; languid.

his round bottom, synchronized with intricately coordinated sweeps of his arms and small, unexcited movements of his legs. Little girls could communicate much more.

But sadly, I could do none of it. Development of these skills depended on the ministrations of family and neighbors. My family did not dance; our closest neighbor was a true-believing Seventh Day Adventist. Moreover, most new dances came from up North, brought to town usually by people returning to riff[3] on the good life said to exist in those far Northern places. They prowled our dirt streets in rented Cadillacs; paraded our brick sidewalks exhibiting styles abstracted from the fullness of life in Harlem, South Philadelphia, Roxbury, Baltimore, and the South Side of Chicago. They confronted our provincial clothes merchants with the arrogant reminder, "But people ain't wearin' this in New Yo*kkk!*" Each of their movements, as well as their world-weary smoothness, told us locals meaningful tales of what was missing in our lives. Unfortunately, those of us under strict parental supervision, or those of us without Northern connections, could only stand at a distance and worship these envoys of culture. We stood on the sidelines—styleless, gestureless, danceless, doing nothing more than an improvised one-butt shuffle—hoping for one of them to touch our lives. It was my good fortune, during my tenth year on the sidelines, to have one of these Northerners introduce me to the square dance.

My dear, dear Gloria, her name was Gweneth Lawson:

She was a pretty, chocolate brown little girl with dark brown eyes and two long black braids. After all these years, the image of these two braids evokes in me all there is to remember about Gweneth Lawson. They were plaited across the top of her head and hung to a point just above the back of her Peter Pan collar. Sometimes she wore two bows, one red and one blue, and these tended to sway lazily near the place on her neck where the smooth brown of her skin and the white of her collar met the ink-bottle black of her hair. Even when I cannot remember her face, I remember the rainbow of deep, rich colors in which she lived. This is so because I watched them, every weekday, from my desk directly behind hers in our fourth-grade class. And she wore the most magical

---

3. **riff:** improvise, as a jazz musician does.

perfume, or lotion, smelling just slightly of fresh-cut lemons, that wafted back to me whenever she made the slightest movement at her desk. Now I must tell you this much more, dear Gloria: Whenever I smell fresh lemons, whether in the market or at home, I look around me—not for Gweneth Lawson, but for some quiet corner where I can revive in private certain memories of her. And in pursuing these memories across such lemony bridges, I rediscover that I loved her.

Gweneth was from the South Carolina section of Brooklyn. Her parents had sent her south to live with her uncle, Mr. Richard Lawson, the brick mason, for an unspecified period of time. Just why they did this I do not know, unless it was their plan to have her absorb more of South Carolina folkways than conditions in Brooklyn would allow. She was a gentle, soft-spoken girl; I recall no condescension in her manner. This was all the more admirable because our unrestrained awe of a Northern-born black person usually induced in him some grand sense of his own importance. You must know that in those days older folks would point to someone and say, "He's from the North," and the statement would be sufficient in itself. Mothers made their children behave by advising that, if they led exemplary lives and attended church regularly, when they died they would go to New York. Only someone who understands what London meant to Dick Whittington, or how California and the suburbs function in the national mind, could appreciate the mythical dimensions of this Northlore.

But Gweneth Lawson was above regional idealization. Though I might have loved her partly because she was a Northerner, I loved her more because of the world of colors that seemed to be suspended about her head. I loved her glowing forehead and I loved her bright, dark brown eyes; I loved the black braids, the red and blue and sometimes yellow and pink ribbons; I loved the way the deep, rich brown of her neck melted into the pink or white cloth of her Peter Pan collar; I loved the lemony vapor on which she floated and from which on occasion, she seemed to be inviting me to be buoyed up, up, up into her happy world; I loved the way she caused my heart to tumble whenever, during a restless moment, she seemed about to turn her head in my direction; I loved her more, though torturously, on the many occasions when she did not turn. Because I was a shy

boy, I loved the way I could love her silently, at least six hours a day, without ever having to disclose my love.

My platonic[4] state of mind might have stretched onward into a blissful infinity had not Mrs. Esther

4. **platonic** (plə·ton'ik): not sensual, but purely spiritual.

Clay Boswell, our teacher, made it her business to pry into the affair. Although she prided herself on being a strict disciplinarian, Mrs. Boswell was not without a sense of humor. A round, full-breasted woman in her early forties, she liked to amuse herself, and sometimes the class as well, by calling the attention of all eyes to whoever of us violated the structure she imposed on classroom activities. She was particularly hard on people like me who could not contain an impulse to daydream, or those who allowed their eyes to wander too far away from lessons printed on the blackboard. A black and white sign posted under the electric clock next to the door summed up her attitude toward this kind of truancy: NOTICE TO ALL CLOCKWATCHERS, it read, TIME PASSES, WILL YOU? Nor did she abide timidity in her students. Her voice booming, "Speak up, boy!" was more than enough to cause the more emotional among us, including me, to break into convenient flows of warm tears. But by doing this we violated yet another rule, one on which depended our very survival in Mrs. Esther Clay Boswell's class. She would spell out this rule for us as she paced before her desk, slapping a thick, homemade ruler against the flat of her brown palm. "There ain't no *babies* in here," she would recite. *Thaap!* "Anybody thinks he's still a *baby* . . ." *Thaap!* ". . . should crawl back home to his mama. . . ." *Thaap!* "You little bunnies shed your *last water* . . ." *Thaap!* ". . . the minute you left home to come in here." *Thaap!* "From now on, you g'on do all your *cryin'* . . ." *Thaap!* ". . . *in church!*" *Thaap!* Whenever one of us compelled her to make this speech it would seem to me that her eyes paused overlong on my face. She would seem to be daring me, as if suspicious that, in addition to my secret passion for Gweneth Lawson, which she might excuse, I was also in the habit of throwing fits of temper.

She had read me right. I was the product of too much attention from my father. He favored me, paraded me around on his shoulder, inflated my ego constantly. . . . This, along with my father's generous attentions, made me selfish and used to having my own way. I *expected* to have my own way in most things, and when I could not, I tended to throw tantrums calculated to break through any barrier raised against me.

Mrs. Boswell was also perceptive in assessing the extent of my infatuation with Gweneth Lawson. Despite my stealth in telegraphing emissions of affection into the back part of Gweneth's brain, I could not help but observe, occasionally, Mrs. Boswell's cool glance pausing on the two of us. But she never said a word. Instead, she would settle her eyes momentarily on Gweneth's face and then pass quickly to mine. But in that instant she seemed to be saying, "Don't look back now, girl, but I *know* that bald-headed boy behind you has you on his mind." She seemed to watch me daily, with a combination of amusement and absolute detachment in her brown eyes. And when she stared, it was not at me but at the normal focus on my attention: the end of Gweneth Lawson's black braids. Whenever I sensed Mrs. Boswell watching I would look away quickly, either down at my brown desktop or across the room to the blackboard. But her eyes could not be eluded this easily. Without looking at anyone in particular, she could make a specific point to one person in a manner so general that only long afterward did the real object of her attention realize it had been intended for him.

"Now you little brown bunnies," she might say, "and you black buck rabbits and you few cottontails mixed in. . . ." And here, it sometimes seemed to me, she allowed her eyes to pause casually on me before resuming their sweep of the entire room. "Now I know your mamas already made you think life is a bed of roses, but in *my* classroom you got to know the footpaths through the *sticky* parts of the rosebed." It was her custom during this ritual to prod and goad those of us who were developing reputations for meekness and indecision; yet her method was Socratic[5] in that she compelled us, indirectly, to supply our own answers by exploiting one person as the walking symbol of the error she intended to correct. Clarence Buford, for example, an oversized but good-natured boy from a very poor family, served often as the helpmeet in this exercise.

"Buford," she might begin, slapping the ruler against her palm, "how does a tongue-tied country boy like you expect to get a wife?"

"I don't want no wife," Buford might grumble softly.

Of course the class would laugh.

"Oh yes you do," Mrs. Boswell would respond. "All you buck rabbits want wives." *Thaap!* "So how do you let a girl know you not just a bump on a log?"

"I know! I know!" a high voice might call from a seat across from mine. This, of course, would be Leon Pugh. A peanut-brown boy with curly hair, he seemed to know everything. Moreover, he seemed to take pride in being the only one who knew answers to life questions and would wave

---

5. **Socratic** (sō·kra′tik): referring to the Greek philosopher Socrates (469–399 B.C.), whose method of teaching involved asking questions that would lead to the correct answer.

his arms excitedly whenever our attentions were focused on such matters. It seemed to me his voice would be extra loud and his arms waved more strenuously whenever he was certain that Gweneth Lawson, seated across from him, was interested in an answer to Mrs. Esther Clay Boswell's question. His eager arms, it seemed to me, would be reaching out to grasp Gweneth instead of the question asked.

"Buford, you twisted-tongue, bunion-toed country boy," Mrs. Boswell might say, ignoring Leon Pugh's hysterical arm-waving, "you gonna let a cottontail like Leon get a girlfriend before you?"

"I don't want no girlfriend," Clarence Buford would almost sob. "I don't like no girls."

The class would laugh again while Leon Pugh manipulated his arms like a flight navigator under battle conditions. "I know! I know! I swear to *God* I know!"

When at last Mrs. Boswell would turn in his direction, I might sense that she was tempted momentarily to ask me for an answer. But as in most such exercises, it was the worldly-wise Leon Pugh who supplied this. "What do *you* think Leon?" she would ask inevitably, but with a rather lifeless slap of the ruler against her palm.

"My daddy told me . . ." Leon would shout, turning slyly to beam at Gweneth, ". . . my daddy and my big brother from the Bronx New York told me that to git *anythin'* in this world you gotta learn how to blow your own horn."

"Why, Leon?" Mrs. Boswell might ask in a bored voice.

"Because," the little boy would recite, puffing out his chest, "because if you don't blow your own horn ain't nobody else g'on blow it for you. That's what my daddy said."

"What do you think about that, Buford?" Mrs. Boswell would ask.

"I don't want no girlfriend anyhow," the puzzled Clarence Buford might say.

And then the cryptic lesson would suddenly be dropped.

This was Mrs. Esther Clay Boswell's method of teaching. More than anything written on the blackboard, her questions were calculated to make us turn around in our chairs and inquire in guarded whispers of each other, and especially of the wise and confident Leon Pugh, "What does she mean?" But none of us, besides Pugh, seemed able to comprehend what it was we ought to know but did not know. And Mrs. Boswell, plump brown fox that she was, never volunteered any more in the way of confirmation than was necessary to keep us interested. Instead, she paraded around us, methodically slapping the homemade ruler against her palm, suggesting by her silence more depth to her question, indeed, more implications in Leon's answer, than we were then able to perceive. And during such moments, whether inspired by selfishness or by the peculiar way Mrs. Boswell looked at me, I felt that finding answers to such questions was a task she had set for me, of all the members of the class.

Of course Leon Pugh, among other lesser lights, was my chief rival for the affections of Gweneth Lawson. All during the school year, from September through the winter rains, he bested me in my attempts to look directly into her eyes and say a simple, heartfelt, "hey." This was my ambition, but I never seemed able to get close enough to her attention. At Thanksgiving I helped draw a bounteous yellow cornucopia[6] on the blackboard, with fruits and flowers matching the colors that floated around Gweneth's head; Leon Pugh made one by himself, a masterwork of silver paper and multicolored crepe, which he hung on the door. Its silver tail curled upward to a point just below the face of Mrs. Boswell's clock. At Christmas, when we drew names out of a hat for the exchange of gifts, I drew the name of Queen Rose Phipps, a fairly unattractive squash-yellow girl of absolutely no interest to me. Pugh, whether through collusion with the boy who handled the lottery or through pure luck, pulled forth from the hat the magic name of Gweneth Lawson. He gave her a set of deep purple bows for her braids and a basket of pecans from his father's tree. Uninterested now in the spirit of the occasion, I delivered to Queen Rose Phipps a pair of white socks. Each time Gweneth wore the purple bows she would glance over at Leon and smile. Each time Queen Rose wore my white socks I would turn away in embarrassment, lest I should see them pulling down into her shoes and exposing her skinny ankles.

After class, on wet winter days, I would trail along behind Gweneth to the bus stop, pause near the steps while she entered, and follow her down the aisle until she chose a seat. Usually, however, in clear violation of the code of conduct to which

---

6. **cornucopia** (kôr·noo·kō′pē·ə): a horn of plenty.

all gentlemen were expected to adhere, Leon Pugh would already be on the bus and shouting to passers-by, "Move off! Get away! This here seat by me is reserved for the girl from Brooklyn New York." Discouraged but not defeated, I would swing into the seat next nearest her and cast calf-eyed glances of wounded affection at the back of her head or at the brown, rainbow profile of her face. And at her stop, some eight or nine blocks from mine, I would disembark behind her along with a crowd of other love-struck boys. There would then follow a well-rehearsed scene in which all of us, save Leon Pugh, pretended to have gotten off the bus either too late or too soon to wend our proper paths homeward. And at slight cost to ourselves we enjoyed the advantage of being able to walk close by her as she glided toward her uncle's green-frame house. There, after pausing on the wooden steps and smiling radiantly around the crowd like a spring sun in that cold winter rain, she would sing, "Bye, y'all," and disappear into the structure with the mystery of a goddess. Afterward I would walk away, but slowly, much slower than the other boys, warmed by the music and light in her voice against the sharp, wet winds of the February afternoon.

I loved her, dear Gloria, and I danced with her and smelled the lemony youth of her and told her that I loved her, all this in a way you would never believe:

You would not know or remember, as I do, that in those days, in our area of the country, we enjoyed a pleasingly ironic mixture of Yankee and Confederate folkways. Our meals and manners, our speech, our attitudes toward certain ambiguous areas of history, even our acceptance of tragedy as the normal course of life—these things and more defined us as Southern. Yet the stern morality of our parents, their toughness and penny-pinching and attitudes toward work, their covert allegiance toward certain ideals, even the directions toward which they turned our faces, made us more Yankee than Cavalier. Moreover, some of our schools were named for Confederate men of distinction, but others were named for the stern-faced believers who had swept down from the North to save a people back, back long ago, in those long forgotten days of once upon a time. Still, our schoolbooks, our required classroom songs, our flags, our very relation to the statues and monuments in public parks, negated the story that these dreamers from the North had ever

come. We sang the state song, memorized the verses of homegrown poets, honored in our books the names and dates of historical events both before and after that Historical Event which, in our region, supplanted even the division of the millennia introduced by the followers of Jesus Christ. Given the silent circumstances of our cultural environment, it was ironic, and perhaps just, that we maintained a synthesis of two traditions no longer supportive of each other. Thus it became traditional at our school to celebrate the arrival of spring on May first by both the ritual plaiting of the Maypole and square dancing.

On that day, as on a few others, the Superintendent of Schools and several officials were likely to visit our schoolyard and stand next to the rusty metal swings, watching the fourth, fifth, and sixth graders bob up and down and behind and before each other, around the gaily painted Maypoles. These happy children would pull and twist long runs of billowy crepe paper into wondrous, multicolored plaits. Afterward, on the edges of thunderous applause from teachers, parents and visiting dignitaries, a wave of elaborately costumed children would rush out onto the grounds in groups of eight and proceed with the square dance. "Dog*gone!*" the Superintendent of Schools was heard to exclaim on one occasion. "Y'all do it so good it just makes your *bones* set up and take notice."

Such was the schedule two weeks prior to May first, when Mrs. Boswell announced to our class that as fourth graders we were now eligible to participate in the festivities. The class was divided into two general sections of sixteen each, one group preparing to plait the pole and a second group, containing an equal number of boys and girls, practicing turns for our part in the square dance. I was chosen to square dance; so was Leon Pugh. Gweneth Lawson was placed with the pole plaiters. I was depressed until I remembered, happily, that I could not dance a lick. I reported this fact to Mrs. Boswell just after drawing, during recess, saying that my lack of skill would only result in our class making a poor showing. I asked to be reassigned to the group of Maypole plaiters. Mrs. B. looked me over with considerable amusement tugging at the corners of her mouth. "Oh, you don't have to *dance* to do the square dance," she said. "That's a dance that was made up to mock folks that couldn't dance." She paused a second before adding thoughtfully: "The worse you are at dancing, the better you can square dance. It's just about the best dance in the world for a stiff little bunny like you."

"I want to plait the Maypole," I said.

"You'll square dance or I'll grease your little butt," Mrs. Esther Clay Boswell said.

"I ain't gonna do *nothin'!*" I muttered. But I said this quietly, and mostly to myself, while walking away from her desk. For the rest of the day she watched me closely, as if she knew what I was thinking.

The next morning I brought a note from my father. "Dear Mrs. Boswell:" I had watched him write earlier that morning, "My boy does not square dance. Please excuse him as I am afraid he will break down and cry and mess up the show. Yours truly . . ."

Mrs. Boswell said nothing after she had read the note. She merely waved me to my seat. But in the early afternoon, when she read aloud the lists of those assigned to dancing and Maypole plaiting, she paused as my name rolled off her tongue. "You don't have to stay on the square dance team," she called to me. "You go on out in the yard with the Maypole team."

I was ecstatic. I hurried to my place in line some three warm bodies behind Gweneth Lawson. We prepared to march out.

"Wait a minute," Mrs. Boswell called. "Now it looks like we got seventeen bunnies on the Maypole team and fifteen on the square dance. We have to even things up." She made a thorough examination of both lists, scratching her head. Then she looked carefully up and down the line of stomping Maypoleites. "Miss Gweneth Lawson, you cute little cottontail you, it looks like you gonna have to go over to the square dance team. That'll give us eight sets of partners for the square dance . . . but now we have another problem." She made a great display of counting the members of the two squads of square dancers. "Now there's sixteen square dancers all right, but when we pair them off we got a problem of higher mathematics. With nine girls and only seven *boys,* looks like we gotta switch a girl from square dancing to Maypole and a boy from Maypole to square dancing."

I waited hopefully for Gweneth Lawson to volunteer. But just at that moment the clever Leon Pugh grabbed her hand and began jitterbugging as though he could hardly wait for the record player to be turned on and the dancing to begin.

"What a cute couple," Mrs. Boswell observed absently. "Now which one of you other girls wants to join up with the Maypole team?"

Following Pugh's example, the seven remaining boys grabbed the girls they wanted as partners. Only skinny Queen Rose Phipps and shy Beverly Hankins remained unclaimed. Queen Rose giggled nervously.

"Queen Rose," Mrs. B. called, "I know you don't mind plaiting the Maypole." She waved her ruler in a gesture of casual dismissal. Queen Rose raced across the room and squeezed into line.

"*Now,*" Mrs. Boswell said, "I need a boy to come across to the square dancers."

I was not unmindful of the free interchange of partners involved in square dancing, even though Leon Pugh had beat me in claiming the partner of my choice. All I really wanted was one moment swinging Gweneth Lawson in my arms. I raised my hand slowly.

"Oh, not *you,* little bunny," Mrs. Boswell said. "You and your daddy claim you don't like to square dance." She slapped her ruler against her palm. *Thaap! Thaap!* Then she said, "Clarence Buford, I *know* a big-footed country boy like you can square dance better than anybody. Come on over here and kiss cute little Miss Beverly Hankins."

"I don't like no girls *noway,*" Buford mumbled. But he went over and stood next to the giggling Beverly Hankins.

"Now!" said Mrs. B. "March on out in that yard and give that pole a good plaiting!"

We started to march out. Over my shoulder, as I reached the door, I glimpsed the overjoyed Leon Pugh whirling lightly on his toes. He sang in a confident tone:

"*I saw the Lord give Moses a pocketful of roses.*
I skid Ezekiel's wheel on a ripe banana peel.
I rowed the Nile, flew over a stile,
Saw Jack Johnson pick his teeth
With toenails from Jim Jeffries' feets . . ."

"Grab your partners!" Mrs. Esther Clay Boswell was saying as the oak door slammed behind us.

I had been undone. For almost two weeks I was obliged to stand on the sidelines and watch Leon Pugh allemande[7] left and do-si-do my be-

---

7. **allemande** (al·lə·mônd'): a dance step in a square dance.

loved Gweneth. Worse, she seemed to be enjoying it. But I must give Leon proper credit: He was a dancing fool. In a matter of days he had mastered, and then improved on, the various turns and bows and gestures of the square dance. He leaped while the others plodded, whirled each girl through his arms with lightness and finesse, chattered playfully at the other boys when they tumbled over their own feet. Mrs. Boswell stood by the record player calling, "Put some *strut* in it, Buford, you big potato sack. Watch Leon and see how *he* does it." I leaned against the classroom wall and watched the dancers, my own group having already exhausted the limited variations possible in matters of Maypole plaiting.

At home each night I begged my father to send another note to Mrs. Boswell, this time stating that I had no interest in the Maypole. But he resisted my entreaties and even threatened me with a whipping if I did not participate and make him proud of me. The real cause of his irritation was the considerable investment he had already made in purchasing an outfit for me. Mrs. Boswell had required all her students, square dancers and Maypole plaiters alike, to report on May first in outfits suitable for square dancing. My father had bought a new pair of dungarees, a blue shirt, a red and white polka-dot bandanna and a cowboy hat. He was in no mood to bend under the emotional weight of my demands. As a matter of fact, early in the morning of May first he stood beside my bed with the bandanna in his left hand and his leather belt in his right hand, just in case I developed a sudden fever.

I dragged myself heavily through the warm, blue spring morning toward school, dressed like a carnival cowboy. When I entered the classroom I sulked against the wall, being content to watch the other children. And what happy buzzings and jumping and excitement they made as they compared costumes. Clarence Buford wore a Tom Mix hat and a brown vest over a green shirt with red sixshooter patterns embossed on its collar. Another boy, Paul Carter, was dressed entirely in black, with a fluffy white handkerchief puffing from his neck. But Leon Pugh caught the attention of all eyes. He wore a red and white checkered shirt, a loose green bandanna clasped at his throat by a shining silver buffalo head, brown chaps sewed onto his dungarees, and shiny brown cowboy boots with silver spurs that clanked each time he moved. In his hand he carried a carefully

creased brown cowboy hat. He announced his fear that it would lose its shape and planned to put it on only when the dancing started. He would allow no one to touch it. Instead, he stood around clanking his feet and smoothing the crease in his fabulous hat and saying loudly, "My daddy says it pays to look good no matter what you put on."

The girls seemed prettier and much older than their ages. Even Queen Rose Phipps wore rouge on her cheeks that complemented her pale color. Shy Beverly Hankins had come dressed in a blue and white checkered bonnet and a crisp blue apron; she looked like a frontier mother. But Gweneth Lawson, my Gweneth Lawson, dominated the group of girls. She wore a long red dress with sheaves and sheaves of sparkling white crinoline belling it outward so it seemed she was floating. On her honey-brown wrists golden bracelets sparkled. A deep blue bandanna enclosed her head with the wonder of a summer sky. Black patent leather shoes glistened like half-hidden stars beneath the red and white of her hemline. She stood smiling before us and we marveled. At that moment I would have given the world to have been able to lead her about on my arm.

Mrs. Boswell watched us approvingly from behind her desk. Finally, at noon, she called, "Let's go on out!" Thirty-two living rainbows cascaded toward the door. Pole plaiters formed one line. Square dancers formed another. Mrs. Boswell strolled officiously past us in review. It seemed to me she almost paused while passing the spot where I stood on line. But she brushed past me, straightening an apron here, applying spittle and a rub to a rouge cheek there, waving a wary finger at an over-anxious boy. Then she whacked her ruler against her palm and led us out into the yard. The fifth and sixth graders had already assembled. On one end of the playground were a dozen or so tall painted poles with long, thin wisps of green and blue and yellow and rust-brown crepe floating lazily on the sweet spring breezes.

"Maypole teams *up!*" called Mr. Henry Lucas, our principal, from his platform by the swings. Beside him stood the white Superintendent of Schools (who said later of the square dance, it was reported to all the classes, "Lord y'all square dance so *good* it makes me plumb *ashamed* us white folks ain't takin' better care of our art stuff."). "Maypole teams up!" Mr. Henry Lucas shouted again. Some fifty of us, screaming shrilly, rushed to grasp our favorite color crepe. Then, to the music of "Sing Praise for All the Brightness and the Joy of Spring," we pulled and plaited in teams of six or seven until every pole was twisted as tight and as colorfully as the braids on Gweneth Lawson's head. Then, to the applause of proud teachers and parents and the whistles of the Superintendent of Schools, we scattered happily back under the wings of our respective teachers. I stood next to Mrs. Boswell, winded and trembling but confident I had done my best. She glanced down at me and said in a quiet voice, "I do believe you are learning the rhythm of the thing."

I did not respond.

"Let's *go!*" Leon Pugh shouted to the other kids, grabbing Gweneth Lawson's arm and taking a few clanking steps forward.

"Wait a minute, Leon," Mrs. Boswell hissed. "Mr. Lucas has to change the record."

Leon sighed. "But if we don't git out there first, all them other teams will take the best spots."

"Wait!" Mrs. Boswell ordered.

Leon sulked. He inched closer to Gweneth. I watched him swing her hand impatiently. He stamped his feet and his silver spurs jangled.

Mrs. Boswell looked down at his feet. "Why, Leon," she said, "you can't go out there with razors on your shoes."

"These ain't razors," Leon muttered. "These here are spurs my brother in Bronx New York sent me just for this here dance."

"You have to take them off," Mrs. Boswell said.

Leon growled. But he reached down quickly and attempted to jerk the silver spurs from the heels of his boots. They did not come off. "No time!" he called, standing suddenly. "Mr. Lucas done put the record on."

"Leon, you might *cut* somebody with those things," Mrs. Boswell said. "Miss Gweneth Lawson's pretty red dress could get caught in those things and then she'll fall as surely as I'm standin' here."

"I'll just go out with my boots off," Leon replied.

But Mrs. Boswell shook her head firmly. "You just run on to the lunchroom and ask cook for some butter or mayo. That'll help 'em slip off." She paused, looking out over the black dirt playground. "And if you miss the first dance, why there'll be a second and maybe even a third. We'll get a Maypole plaiter to sub for you."

My heart leaped. Leon sensed it and stared at me. His hand tightened on Gweneth's as she stood radiant and smiling in the loving spring sunlight. Leon let her hand drop and bent quickly, pulling at the spurs with the fury of a Samson.

"Square dancers *up!*" Mr. Henry Lucas called. . . .

The fifth and sixth graders were screaming and rushing toward the center of the yard. Already the record was scratching out the high, slick voice of the caller. . . . Leon moaned.

Mrs. Boswell looked directly at Gweneth, standing alone and abandoned next to Leon. "Miss Gweneth Lawson," Mrs. Boswell said in a cool voice, "it's a cryin' shame there ain't no prince to take you to that ball out there."

I do not remember moving, but I know I stood with Gweneth at the center of the yard. What I did there I do not know, but I remember watching the movements of others and doing what they did just after they had done it. Still, I cannot remember just when I looked into my partner's face or what I saw there. The scratchy voice of the caller bellowed directions and I obeyed:

"Allemande left with your left hand
Right to your partner with a right and left grand
. . ."

Although I was told later that I made an allemande right instead of left, I have no memory of the mistake.

"When you get to your partner pass her by
And pick up the next girl on the sly . . ."

Nor can I remember picking up any other girl. I only remember that during many turns and do-si-dos I found myself looking into the warm brown eyes of Gweneth Lawson. I recall that she smiled at me. I recall that she laughed on another turn. I recall that I laughed with her an eternity later.

". . . promenade that dear old thing
Throw your head right back and sing be-*cause,*
just be-*cause . . ."*

I do remember quite well that during the final promenade before the record ended, Gweneth stood beside me and I said to her in a voice much louder than that of the caller, "When I get up to Brooklyn I hope I see you." But I do not remember what she said in response. I want to remember that she smiled.

I know I smiled, dear Gloria. I smiled with the

YOUR PLACE IS EMPTY

This story deals with a common situation among young married couples—the strain resulting from an extended visit by a parent. In this case, the situation also involves a clash of cultures, since it is an Iranian mother who is staying with her son and his American wife. The story is told in the third person, and the opening section sets the scene. Once the mother is introduced, everything is revealed from her point of view.

Early in October, Hassan Ardavi invited his mother to come from Iran for a visit. His mother accepted immediately. It wasn't clear how long the visit was to last. Hassan's wife thought three months would be a good length of time. Hassan himself had planned on six months, and said so in his letter of invitation. But his mother felt that after such a long trip six months would be too short, and she was counting on staying a year. Hassan's little girl, who wasn't yet two, had no idea of time at all. She was told that her grandmother was coming but she soon forgot about it.

Hassan's wife was named Elizabeth, not an easy word for Iranians to pronounce. She would have been recognized as American the world over—a blond, pretty girl with long bones and an ungraceful way of walking. One of her strong points was an ability to pick up foreign languages, and before her mother-in-law's arrival she bought a textbook and taught herself Persian. "*Salaam aleikum*,"[1] she told the mirror every morning. Her daughter watched, startled, from her place on the potty-chair. Elizabeth ran through possible situations in her mind and looked up the words for them. "Would you like more tea? Do you take sugar?" At suppertime she spoke Persian to her husband, who looked amused at the new tone she gave his language, with her flat, factual American voice. He wrote his mother and told her Elizabeth had a surprise for her.

Their house was a three-story Colonial, but only the first two stories were in use. Now they cleared the third of its trunks and china barrels and *National Geographics*, and they moved in a few pieces of furniture. Elizabeth sewed flowered curtains for the window. She was unusually careful with them; to a foreign mother-in-law, fine seams might matter. Also, Hassan bought a pocket compass, which he placed in the top dresser drawer. "For her prayers," he said. "She'll want to face Mecca.[2] She prays three times a day."

"But which direction is Mecca from here?" Elizabeth asked.

Hassan only shrugged. He had never said the prayers himself, not even as a child. His earliest memory was of tickling the soles of his mother's feet while she prayed steadfastly on; everyone knew it was forbidden to pause once you'd started.

Mrs. Ardavi felt nervous about the descent from the plane. She inched down the staircase sideways, one hand tight on the railing, the other clutching her shawl. It was night, and cold. The air seemed curiously opaque. She arrived on solid ground and stood collecting herself—a small, stocky woman in black, with a kerchief over her smooth gray hair. She held her back very straight, as if she had just had her feelings hurt. In picturing this moment she had always thought Hassan would be waiting beside the plane, but there was no sign of him. Blue lights dotted the darkness behind her, an angular terminal loomed ahead, and an official was herding the passengers toward a plate-glass door. She followed, entangled in a web of meaningless sounds such as those you might hear in a fever dream.

Immigration. Baggage Claims. Customs. To all she spread her hands and beamed and shrugged,

---

1. *Salaam aleikum:* Persian for "Peace be with you."

2. **Mecca:** the holiest shrine of Islam, located in modern Saudi Arabia. Moslems throughout the world turn to face the direction of Mecca when they pray.

Dagney's Room by Barbara Kassel (1984). Oil.

showing she spoke no English. Meanwhile her fellow-passengers waved to a blur of faces beyond a glass wall. It seemed they all knew people here; she was the only one who didn't. She had issued from the plane like a newborn baby, speechless and friendless. And the customs official didn't seem pleased with her. She had brought too many gifts. She had stuffed her bags with them, discarding all but the most necessary pieces of her clothing so that she would have more room. There were silver tea sets and gold jewelry for her daughter-in-law, and for her granddaughter a doll dressed in the complicated costume of a nomad tribe, an embroidered sheepskin vest, and two religious medals on chains—one a disc inscribed with the name of Allah, the other a tiny gold Koran,[3] with a very effective prayer for long life folded up within it. The customs official sifted gold through his fingers like sand and frowned at the Koran. "Have I done something wrong?" she asked. But of course he didn't understand her. Though you'd think, really, that if he would just *listen* hard

enough, just meet her eyes once . . . it was a very simple language, there was no reason why it shouldn't come through to him.

For Hassan, she'd brought food. She had gathered all his favorite foods and put them in a drawstring bag embroidered with peacocks. When the official opened the bag he said something under his breath and called another man over. Together they unwrapped tiny newspaper packets and sniffed at various herbs. "Sumac," she told them. "Powder of lemons. Shambahleh." They gazed at her blankly. They untied a small cloth sack and rummaged through the kashk she had brought for soup. It rolled beneath their fingers and across the counter—hard white balls of yogurt curd, stuck with bits of sheep hair and manure. Some peasant had labored for hours to make that kashk. Mrs. Ardavi picked up one piece and replaced it firmly in the sack. Maybe the official understood her meaning: She was running out of patience. He threw up his hands. He slid her belongings down the counter. She was free to go.

Free to go where?

Dazed and stumbling, a pyramid of knobby parcels and bags, scraps of velvet and brocade and tapestry, she made her way to the glass wall. A

---

3. **Allah . . . Koran:** Allah is God, the supreme deity of Islam. The Koran is the Islamic holy book, consisting of visions and regulations recorded by the prophet Mohammed.

door opened out of nowhere and a stranger blocked her path. "Khanoum Jun," he said. It was a name that only her children would use, but she passed him blindly and he had to touch her arm before she would look up.

He had put on weight. She didn't know him. The last time she'd seen him he was a thin, stoop-shouldered medical student disappearing into an Air France jet without a backward glance. "Khanoum Jun, it's me," this stranger said, but she went on searching his face with cloudy eyes. No doubt he was a bearer of bad news. Was that it? A recurrent dream had warned her that she would never see her son again—that he would die on his way to the airport, or had already been dead for months but no one wanted to break the news; some second or third cousin in America had continued signing Hassan's name to his cheerful, anonymous letters. Now here was this man with graying hair and a thick mustache, his clothes American but his face Iranian, his eyes sadly familiar, as if they belonged to someone else. "Don't you believe me?" he said. He kissed her on both cheeks. It was his smell she recognized first—a pleasantly bitter, herblike smell that brought her the image of Hassan as a child, reaching thin arms around her neck. "It's you, Hassan," she said, and then she started crying against his gray tweed shoulder.

They were quiet during the long drive home. Once she reached over to touch his face, having wanted to do so for miles. None of the out-of-focus snapshots he'd sent had prepared her for the way he had aged. "How long has it been?" she asked. "Twelve years?" But both of them knew to the day how long it had been. All those letters of hers: "My dear Hassan, ten years now and still your place is empty." "Eleven years and still . . .'

Hassan squinted through the windshield at the oncoming headlights. His mother started fretting over her kerchief, which she knew she ought not to have worn. She'd been told so by her youngest sister, who had been to America twice. "It marks you," her sister had said. But that square of silk was the last, shrunken reminder of the veil she used to hide beneath, before the previous Shah[4] had banished such things. At her age, how could she expose herself? And then her teeth; her teeth were a problem too. Her youngest sister had said,

"You ought to get dentures made, I'm sure there aren't three whole teeth in your head." But Mrs. Ardavi was scared of dentists. Now she covered her mouth with one hand and looked sideways at Hassan, though so far he hadn't seemed to notice. He was busy maneuvering his car into the right-hand lane.

This silence was the last thing she had expected. For weeks she'd been saving up stray bits of gossip, weaving together the family stories she would tell him. There were three hundred people in her family—most of them related to each other in three or four different ways, all leading intricate and scandalous lives she had planned to discuss in detail, but instead she stared sadly out the window. You'd think Hassan would ask. You'd think they could have a better conversation than this, after such a long time. Disappointment made her cross, and now she stubbornly refused to speak even when she saw something she wanted to comment on, some imposing building or unfamiliar brand of car sliding past her into the darkness.

By the time they arrived it was nearly midnight. None of the houses were lit but Hassan's—worn brick, older than she would have expected. "Here we are," said Hassan. The competence with which he parked the car, fitting it neatly into a small space by the curb, put him firmly on the other side of the fence, the American side. She would have to face her daughter-in-law alone. As they climbed the front steps she whispered, "How do you say it again?"

"Say what?" Hassan asked.

"Her name. Lizabet?"

"Elizabeth. Like Elizabeth Taylor. *You* know."

"Yes, yes, of course," said his mother. Then she lifted her chin, holding tight to the straps of her purse.

Elizabeth was wearing blue jeans and a pair of fluffy slippers. Her hair was blond as corn silk, cut short and straight, and her face had the grave, sleepy look of a child's. As soon as she had opened the door she said, "*Salaam aleikum.*" Mrs. Ardavi, overcome with relief at the Persian greeting, threw her arms around her and kissed both cheeks. Then they led her into the living room, which looked comfortable but a little too plain. The furniture was straight-edged, the rugs uninteresting, though the curtains had a nice figured pattern that caught her eye. In one corner sat a shiny red kiddie car complete with license plates. "Is that the child's?" she asked.

---

4. **Shah:** before the Iranian revolution, the ruler of Iran.

"Hilary's?" She hesitated over the name. "Could I see her?"

"*Now?*" said Hassan.

But Elizabeth told him, "That's all right." (Women understood these things.) She beckoned to her mother-in-law. They climbed the stairs together, up to the second floor, into a little room that smelled of milk and rubber and talcum powder, smells she would know anywhere. Even in the half-light from the hallway, she could tell that Hilary was beautiful. She had black, tumbling hair, long black lashes, and skin of a tone they called wheat-colored, lighter than Hassan's. "There," said Elizabeth. "Thank you," said Mrs. Ardavi. Her voice was formal, but this was her first grandchild and it took her a moment to recover herself. Then they stepped back into the hallway. "I brought her some medals," she whispered. "I hope you don't mind."

"Medals?" said Elizabeth. She repeated the word anxiously, mispronouncing it.

"Only an Allah and a Koran, both very tiny. You'll hardly know they're there. I'm not used to seeing a child without a medal. It worries me."

Automatically her fingers traced a chain around her neck, ending in the hollow of her collarbone. Elizabeth nodded, looking relieved. "*Oh* yes. Medals," she said.

"Is that all right?"

"Yes, of course."

Mrs. Ardavi took heart. "Hassan laughs," she said. "He doesn't believe in these things. But when he left I put a prayer in his suitcase pocket, and you see he's been protected. Now if Hilary wore a medal, I could sleep nights."

"Of course," Elizabeth said again.

When they re-entered the living room, Mrs. Ardavi was smiling, and she kissed Hassan on the top of his head before she sat down.

American days were tightly scheduled, divided not into morning and afternoon but into 9:00, 9:30, and so forth, each half hour possessing its own set activity. It was marvelous. Mrs. Ardavi wrote her sisters: "They're more organized here. My daughter-in-law never wastes a minute." How terrible, her sisters wrote back. They were all in Teheran, drinking cup after cup of tea and idly guessing who might come and visit. "No, you misunderstand," Mrs. Ardavi protested. "I like it this way. I'm fitting in wonderfully." And to her youngest sister she wrote, "You'd think I was

American. No one guesses otherwise." This wasn't true, of course, but she hoped it would be true in the future.

Hassan was a doctor. He worked long hours, from six in the morning until six at night. While she was still washing for her morning prayers she could hear him tiptoe down the stairs and out the front door. His car would start up, a distant rumble far below her, and from her bathroom window she could watch it swing out from beneath a tatter of red leaves and round the corner and disappear. Then she would sigh and return to her sink. Before prayers she had to wash her face, her hands, and the soles of her feet. She had to draw her wet fingers down the part in her hair. After that she returned to her room, where she swathed herself tightly in her long black veil and knelt on a beaded velvet prayer mat. East was where the window was, curtained by chintz and misted over. On the east wall she hung a lithograph of the Caliph Ali and a color snapshot of her third son, Babak, whose marriage she had arranged just a few months before this visit. If Babak hadn't married, she never could have come. He was the youngest, spoiled by being the only son at home. It had taken her three years to find a wife for him. (One was too modern, one too lazy, one so perfect she had been suspicious.) But finally the proper girl had turned up, modest and well-mannered and sufficiently wide of hip, and Mrs. Ardavi and the bridal couple had settled in a fine new house on the outskirts of Teheran. Now every time she prayed, she added a word of thanks that at last she had a home for her old age. After that, she unwound her veil and laid it carefully in a drawer. From another drawer she took thick cotton stockings and elastic garters; she stuffed her swollen feet into opentoed vinyl sandals. Unless she was going out, she wore a housecoat. It amazed her how wasteful Americans were with their clothing.

Downstairs, Elizabeth would have started her tea and buttered a piece of toast for her. Elizabeth and Hilary ate bacon and eggs, but bacon of course was unclean and Mrs. Ardavi never accepted any.[5] Nor had it even been offered to her, except once, jokingly, by Hassan. The distinctive, smoky smell rose to meet her as she descended the stairs. "What does it taste like?" she always asked. She was dying to know. But Elizabeth's vocabulary didn't cover the taste of bacon; she

---

5. The Koran forbids Moslems to eat pork.

only said it was salty and then laughed and gave up. They had learned very early to travel a well-worn conversational path, avoiding the dead ends caused by unfamiliar words. "Did you sleep well?" Elizabeth always asked in her funny, childish accent, and Mrs. Ardavi answered, "So-so." Then they would turn and watch Hilary, who sat on a booster seat eating scrambled eggs, a thin chain of Pesian gold crossing the back of her neck. Conversation was easier, or even unnecessary, as long as Hilary was there.

In the mornings Elizabeth cleaned house. Mrs. Ardavi used that time for letter writing. She had dozens of letters to write, to all her aunts and uncles and her thirteen sisters. (Her father had had three wives, and a surprising number of children even for that day and age.) Then there was Babak. His wife was in her second month of pregnancy, so Mrs. Ardavi wrote long accounts of the American child-rearing methods. "There are some things I don't agree with," she wrote. "They let Hilary play outdoors by herself, with not even a servant to keep an eye on her." Then she would trail off and gaze thoughtfully at Hilary, who sat on the floor watching a television program called "Captain Kangaroo."

Mrs. Ardavi's own childhood had been murky and grim. From the age of nine she was wrapped in a veil, one corner of it clenched in her teeth to hide her face whenever she appeared on the streets. Her father, a respected man high up in public life, used to chase servant girls through the halls and trap them, giggling, in vacant bedrooms. At the age of ten she was forced to watch her mother bleed to death in childbirth, and when she screamed the midwife had struck her across the face and held her down till she had properly kissed her mother goodbye. There seemed no connection at all between her and this little overalled American. At times, when Hilary had one of her temper tantrums, Mrs. Ardavi waited in horror for Elizabeth to slap her and then, when no slap came, felt a mixture of relief and anger. "In Iran—" she would begin, and if Hassan was there he always said, "But this is not Iran, remember?"

After lunch Hilary took a nap, and Mrs. Ardavi went upstairs to say her noontime prayers and take a nap as well. Then she might do a little laundry in her bathtub. Laundry was a problem here. Although she liked Elizabeth, the fact was that the girl was a Christian, and therefore unclean; it would never do to have a Christian wash a Moslem's clothes. The automatic dryer was also unclean, having contained, at some point, a Christian's underwear. So she had to ask Hassan to buy her a drying rack. It came unassembled. Elizabeth put it together for her, stick by stick, and then Mrs. Ardavi held it under her shower and rinsed it off, hoping that would be enough to remove any taint. The Koran didn't cover this sort of situation.

When Hilary was up from her nap they walked her to the park—Elizabeth in her eternal blue jeans and Mrs. Ardavi in her kerchief and shawl, taking short painful steps in small shoes that bulged over her bunions. They still hadn't seen to her teeth, although by now Hassan had noticed them. She was hoping he might forget about the dentist, but then she saw him remembering every time she laughed and revealed her five brown teeth set wide apart.

At the park she laughed a great deal. It was her only way of communicating with the other women. They sat on the benches ringing the playground, and while Elizabeth translated their questions Mrs. Ardavi laughed and nodded at them over and over. "They want to know if you like it here," Elizabeth said. Mrs. Ardavi answered at length, but Elizabeth's translation was very short. Then gradually the other women forgot her, and conversation rattled on while she sat silent and watched each speaker's lips. The few recognizable words—"telephone," "television," "radio"—gave her the impression that American conversations were largely technical, even among women. Their gestures were wide and slow, disproving her youngest sister's statement that in America everyone was in a hurry. On the contrary, these women were dreamlike, moving singly or in twos across wide flat spaces beneath white November skies when they departed.

Later, at home, Mrs. Ardavi would say, "The red-haired girl, is she pregnant? She looked it, I thought. Is the fat girl happy in her marriage?" She asked with some urgency, plucking Elizabeth's sleeve when she was slow to answer. People's private lives fascinated her. On Saturday trips to the supermarket she liked to single out some interesting stranger. "What's the matter with that *jerky*-moving man? That girl, is she one of your dark-skinned people?" Elizabeth answered too softly, and never seemed to follow Mrs. Ardavi's pointing finger.

Supper was difficult; Mrs. Ardavi didn't like American food. Even when Elizabeth made something Iranian, it had an American taste to it—the vegetables still faintly crisp, the onions transparent rather than nicely blackened. "Vegetables not thoroughly cooked retain a certain acidity," Mrs. Ardavi said, laying down her fork. "This is a cause of constipation and stomachaches. At night I often have heartburn. It's been three full days since I moved my bowels." Elizabeth merely bent over her plate, offering no symptoms of her own in return. Hassan said, "At the table, Khanoum? At the table?"

Eventually she decided to cook supper herself. Over Elizabeth's protests she began at three every afternoon, filling the house with the smell of dill-weed and arranging pots on counters and cabinets and finally, when there was no more space, on the floor. She squatted on the floor with her skirt tucked between her knees and stirred great bowls of minced greens while behind her, on the gas range, four different pots of food bubbled and steamed. The kitchen was becoming more home-like, she thought. A bowl of yogurt brewed beside the stove, a kettle of rice soaked in the sink, and the top of the dishwasher was curlicued with the yellow dye from saffron. In one corner sat the pudding pan, black on the bottom from the times she had cooked down sugar to make a sweet for her intestines. "Now, this is your rest period," she always told Elizabeth. "Come to the table in three hours and be surprised." But Elizabeth only hovered around the kitchen, disturbing the serene, steam-filled air with clatter and slams as she put away pots, or pacing between stove and sink, her arms folded across her chest. At supper she ate little; Mrs. Ardavi wondered how Americans got so tall on such small suppers. Hassan, on the other hand, had second and third helpings. "I must be gaining five pounds a week," he said. "None of my clothes fit."

"That's good to hear," said his mother. And Elizabeth added something but in English, which Hassan answered in English also. Often now they broke into English for paragraphs at a time—Elizabeth speaking softly, looking at her plate, and Hassan answering at length and sometimes reaching across the table to cover her hand.

At night, after her evening prayers, Mrs. Ardavi watched television on the living room couch. She brought her veil downstairs and wrapped it around her to keep the drafts away. Her shoes lay on the rug beneath her, and scattered down the length of the couch were her knitting bag, her sack of burned sugar, her magnifying glass, and *My First Golden Dictionary*. Elizabeth read novels in an easy chair, and Hassan watched TV so that he could translate the difficult parts of the plot. Not that Mrs. Ardavi had much trouble. American plots were easy to guess at, particularly the Westerns. And when the program was boring—a documentary or a special news feature—she could pass the time by talking to Hassan. "Your cousin Farah wrote," she said. "Do you remember her? A homely girl, too dark. She's getting a divorce and in my opinion it's fortunate; he's from a lower class. Do you remember Farah?"

Hassan only grunted, his eyes on the screen. He was interested in American politics. So was she, for that matter. She had wept for President Kennedy, and carried Jackie's picture in her purse. But these news programs were long and dry, and if Hassan wouldn't talk she was forced to turn at last to her *Golden Dictionary*.

In her childhood, she had been taught by expensive foreign tutors. Her mind was her great gift, the compensation for a large, plain face and a stocky figure. But now what she had learned seemed lost, forgotten utterly or fogged by years, so that Hassan gave a snort whenever she told him some fact that she had dredged up from her memory. It seemed that everything she studied now had to penetrate through a great thick layer before it reached her mind. "Tonk you," she practiced. "Tonk you. Tonk you." "Thank you," Hassan corrected her. He pointed out useful words in her dictionary—grocery store words, household words—but she grew impatient with their wood-enness. What she wanted was the language to display her personality, her famous courtesy, and her magical intuition about the inside lives of other people. Nightly she learned "salt," "bread," "spoon," but with an inner sense of dullness, and every morning when she woke her English was once again confined to "thank you" and "NBC."

Elizabeth, meanwhile, read on, finishing one book and reaching for the next without even glancing up. Hassan chewed a thumbnail and watched a senator. He shouldn't be disturbed, of course, but time after time his mother felt the silence and the whispery turning of pages stretching her nerves until she had to speak. "Hassan?"

"Hmm."

"My chest seems tight. I'm sure a cold is coming on. Don't you have a tonic?"

"No," said Hassan.

Interpreting Meanings

6. In what ways is the **conflict** in this story the result of a clash of cultures? In what ways is it a clash of generations?

7. Describe the difference in **tone** between the beginning of the story and its end. How does this contrast comment on Mrs. Ardavi's visit?

8. What does Mrs. Ardavi mean when she writes to her son, "Your place is empty"? What additional meaning does this take on as the story ends?

9. How would you describe the relationship between Hassan and his mother? Which character do you feel most sympathy for in this story? Do you think the writer "stacks the deck" for or against any of the characters? Explain.

10. What would you say is the **theme** of this story? Is the story about a universal human experience, or is it only about people at this time, and in this place? Explain.

Writing About the Story

A Creative Response

1. **Taking Another Point of View.** Narrate the events of one incident in the story from Elizabeth's point of view. The incident should happen exactly as it is narrated in the story now; but shift the point of view from the limited third-person with its focus on Mrs. Ardavi, to the limited third-person with its focus on Elizabeth.

A Critical Response

2. **Comparing Two Stories.** Write a brief essay comparing this story with Updike's "Son" (page 916). What parent-child tensions do both stories deal with?

3. **Responding to the Story.** Can you see some advantages to Mrs. Ardavi's ways over the ways of her Americanized son and his wife? In a brief essay, discuss the differences in cultures revealed in this story, and how you respond to them.

Primary Sources
"Still Just Writing"

"I was standing in the schoolyard waiting for a child when another mother came up to me. 'Have you found work yet?' she asked. 'Or are you still just writing?'

"Now, how am I supposed to answer that?

"I could take offense, come to think of it. Maybe the reason I didn't is that I halfway share her attitude. They're *paying* me for this? For just writing down untruthful stories? I'd better look around for more permanent employment. For I do consider writing to be a finite job. I expect that any day now, I will have said all I have to say; I'll have used up all my characters, and then I'll be free to get on with my real life. When I make a note of new ideas on index cards, I imagine I'm clearing out my head, and that soon it will be empty and spacious. I file the cards in a little blue box, and I can picture myself using the final card one day—ah! through at last!—and throwing the blue box away. I'm like a dentist who continually fights tooth decay, working toward the time when he's conquered it altogether and done himself out of a job.

But my head keeps loading up again; the little blue box stays crowded and messy. Even when I feel I have no ideas at all, and can't possibly start the next chapter, I have a sense of something still bottled in me, trying to get out. . . .

"I spent my adolescence planning to be an artist, not a writer. After all, books had to be about major events, and none had ever happened to me. All I knew were tobacco workers, stringing the leaves I handed them and talking up a storm. Then I found a book of Eudora Welty's short stories in the high school library. She was writing about Edna Earle, who was so slow-witted she could sit all day just pondering how the tail of the *C* got through the loop of the *L* on the Coca-Cola sign. Why, I knew Edna Earle. You mean you could *write* about such people? I have always meant to send Eudora Welty a thank-you note, but I imagine she would find it a little strange."

—from "Still Just Writing,"
Anne Tyler

Andrea Lee
(1953–　　　)

Andrea Lee grew up in Yeadon, a prosperous Philadelphia suburb favored by black professionals. It was a place where grounds were well kept, children were sent off to good schools, and prejudice was something you learned about from books and television.

"Yeadon was as solid a repository of American virtues and American flaws as any other close-knit suburban community," she has said. "It had, and still has, its own peculiar flavor—a lively mixture of materialism, idealism, and ironic humor that prevents the minds of its children from stagnating."

In 1978, Lee went to Russia with her husband, a graduate student in Russian history, for eight months' study at Moscow State University and for another two months in Leningrad. The young Americans stood in lines and rode the subways with ordinary Russians. This year-long trip resulted in a series of articles which were collected in her much-praised book *Russian Journal*.

Lee's first novel was published in 1984. The heroine, Sarah Phillips, shares with Lee a prosperous upbringing and a Harvard education. Sarah is the daughter of a black minister who combines old-fashioned Baptist charisma with a

contemporary dedication to the civil rights movement.

Lee is now a staff writer for *The New Yorker* and currently lives in Rome.

NEW AFRICAN

Before reading this story, you might review the section on Puritan beliefs in Unit One (page 6). This story, set in Philadelphia in 1963, deals with a Baptist church whose members believe that baptism should be given only to those people who ask for it after receiving a special call from God.

On a hot Sunday morning in the summer of 1963, I was sitting with my mother, my brother Matthew, and my Aunts Lily, Emma, and May in a central pew of the New African Baptist Church. It was mid-August, and the hum of the big electric fans at the back of the church was almost enough to muffle my father's voice from the pulpit; behind me I could hear Mrs. Gordon, a stout, feeble old woman who always complained of dizziness, remark sharply to her daughter that at the rate the air-conditioning fund was growing it might as well be for the next century. Facing the congregation, my father—who was Reverend Ashley to the rest of the world—mopped his brow with a handkerchief and drank glasses of ice water from the heavy old-fashioned pitcher on the table by his side. He was still reading the text. Next, he'd do the sermon, then the baptism, and it would be an hour, maybe two, before the service was over. I rubbed my chin and then idly began to snap the elastic band that held my red straw hat in place over two stiff shoulder-length braids.

What I really wanted to do, I decided, was to go home, put on my shorts, and climb up into the tree house I'd built the day before with Matthew. We'd nailed an old bushel basket high in the branches of the big maple tree that stretched above the sidewalk in front of the house; it made a crow's nest where you could sit comfortably, except for a few splinters, and read or peer through the dusty leaves at the cars that passed down the quiet suburban road. There was shade and wind and a feeling of adventure in a treetop, where the air seemed to vibrate with the dry rhythm of the cicadas; it was as different as possible from church, where trolleys[1] passing in the city street outside set the stained-glass windows rattling and the packed congregation sat in a near-visible miasma of emotion and cologne.

I slouched between Mama and Aunt Lily and felt myself going limp with lassitude and boredom, as if the heat had melted my bones; the only thing about me with any character seemed to be my firmly starched eyelet dress. Below the scalloped hem, my legs were skinny and wiry, the legs of a ten-year-old amazon,[2] scarred from violent adventures with bicycles and skates. A fingernail tapped my wrist; it was Aunt Emma, reaching across Aunt Lily to press a piece of butterscotch into my hand. When I slipped the candy into my mouth, it tasted faintly of Arpège;[3] my mother and her three sisters were monumental women, ample of bust and slim of ankle, with a weakness for elegant footwear and French perfume. As they leaned back and forth to exchange discreet bits of gossip, they fanned themselves and me with fans from the Byron J. Wiggins Funeral Parlor. The fans, which were fluttering throughout the church, bore a depiction of the Good Shepherd: a hollow-eyed blond Christ holding three fat pink-cheeked children. This Christ resembled the Christ who stood among apostles on the stained-glass windows of the church. Deacon Wiggins, a thoughtful man, had also provided New African with a few dozen fans bearing the picture of a black child praying, but I rarely saw these in use.

There was little that was new or very African about the New African Baptist Church: The original congregation had been formed in 1813 by three young men from Philadelphia's large community of free blacks, and before many generations had passed it had become spiritual home to

---

1. **trolleys:** mass-transit vehicles that run along tracks set into the street. Trolleys used to be a common sight in American cities.

2. **amazon:** term for a strong, athletic woman, from the Amazons of Greek mythology, who were a race of female warriors.
3. **Arpège:** a brand of perfume.

974   Fiction: 1945 to the Present

I didn't listen to the words; what I noticed was the music of the whole—how the big voice darkened and lightened in tone, and how the grand architecture of the Biblical sentences ennobled the voice. The story, of course, was about Jesus, and John the Baptist. One phrase struck me newly each time: "This is my beloved son, in whom I am well pleased!" Daddy sang out those words in a clear, triumphant voice, and the choir echoed him. Ever since I could understand it, this phrase had made me feel melancholy; it seemed to expose a hard knot of disobedience that had always lain within me. When I heard it, I thought enviously of Matthew, for whom life always seemed to be a sedate and ordered affair; he, not I, was a child in whom a father could be well pleased.

Daddy beckoned to Billy Price, the first baptismal candidate in line, and Billy, ungainly in his white robe, descended the flight of steps into the pool. In soft, slow voices, the choir began to sing:

> Wade in the water,
> Wade in the water, children,
> Wade in the water, children.
> God gonna trouble
> The water.

In spite of Jordan Grimes's efforts, the choir swayed like a gospel chorus as it sang this spiritual; the result was to add an eerie jazz beat to the minor chords. The music gave me gooseflesh. Daddy had told me that this was the same song that the slaves had sung long ago in the South, when they gathered to be baptized in rivers and streams. Although I cared little about history, and found it hard to picture the slaves as being any ancestors of mine, I could clearly imagine them coming together beside a broad muddy river that wound away between trees drooping with strange vegetation. They walked silently in lines, their faces very black against their white clothes, leading their children; the whole scene was bathed in the heavy golden light that meant age and solemnity, the same light that seemed to weigh down the Israelites in illustrated volumes of Bible stories, and that shone now from the baptismal pool, giving the ceremony the air of a spectacle staged in a dream.

All attention in the darkened auditorium was now focused on the pool, where between the red curtains my father stood holding Billy Price by the shoulders. Daddy stared into Billy's face, and the boy stared back, his lips set and trembling. "And now, by the power invested in me," said Daddy, "I baptize you in the name of the Father, the Son, and the Holy Ghost." As he pronounced these words, he conveyed a tenderness as efficient and impersonal as a physician's professional manner; beneath it, however, I could see a strong private gladness, the same delight that transformed the contours of his face when he preached a sermon. He paused to flick a drop of water off his forehead, and then, with a single smooth, powerful motion of his arms, he laid Billy Price back into the water as if he were putting an infant to bed. I caught my breath as the boy went backward. When he came up, sputtering, two church mothers helped him out of the pool and through a doorway into a room where he would be dried and dressed. Daddy shook the water from his hands and gave a slight smile as another child entered the pool.

One by one, the baptismal candidates descended the stairs. Sue Anne Ivory began to cry, and had to be comforted. Caroline Piggee blushed and looked up at my father with such a coquettish air that I jealously wondered how he could stand it. After a few baptisms, my attention wandered, and I began to gnaw the edge of my thumb and to peer at the pale faces of the visiting college students. Then I thought about Matthew, who had punched me in the arm that morning and had shouted, "No punchbacks!" I also thought about a collection of horse chestnuts I meant to assemble in the fall, and about two books, one whose subject was adults and divorces, and another, by E. Nesbit, that continued the adventures of the Bastable children.

After Wendell Cullen had left the water (glancing uneasily back at the wet robe trailing behind him), Daddy stood alone among the curtains and the mirrors. The moving reflections from the pool made the stuffed dove hanging over him seem to flutter on its string. "Dear Lord," said Daddy, as Jordan Grimes struck a chord. "Bless these children who have chosen to be baptized in accordance with your teaching, and who have been reborn to carry out your work. In each of them, surely, you are well pleased." He paused, staring out into the darkened auditorium. "And if there is anyone out there—man, woman, child—who wishes to accept Christ today, and to be baptized next month, let him come forward now." He glanced around eagerly. "Oh, do come forward and give Christ your heart and give me your hand!"

Just then, Aunt Bessie gave me a little shake and whispered sharply, "Go on up and accept Jesus!"

I stiffened, and dug my bitten fingernails into my palms. The last clash of wills I had had with Aunt Bessie had been when she, crazily set in her old Southern attitudes, had tried to make me wear an enormous straw hat, as her "white children" did, when I played outside in the sun; the old woman had driven me to madness, and I had ended up spanked and sullen, crouching moodily under the dining room table. But this was different, outrageous, none of her business. I shook my head violently, and she took advantage of the darkness in the church to seize both of my shoulders and jounce me with considerable roughness, whispering, "Now, listen, young lady! Your daddy up there is calling you to Christ. Your big brother has already given his soul to the Lord. Now Daddy wants his little girl to step forward."

"No he doesn't." I glanced at the baptismal pool, where my father was clasping the hand of a strange man who had come up to him. I hoped that this would distract Aunt Bessie, but she was tireless.

"Your mama and your Aunt Lily and your Aunt May all want you to answer the call. You're hurting them when you say no to Jesus."

"No I'm not!" I spoke out loud, and I saw the people nearby turn to look at me. At the sound of my voice, Daddy, who was a few yards away, faltered for a minute in what he was saying and glanced over in my direction.

Just then, Aunt Bessie seemed to lose her head. She stood up, pulling me with her, and while I was still frozen in a dreadful paralysis tried to drag me down the aisle toward my father. The two of us began a brief struggle that could not have lasted more than a few seconds but that seemed an endless mortal conflict—my slippery patent leather shoes braced against the floor, my straw hat sliding cockeyed and lodging against one ear, my right arm twisting and twisting in the iron circle of the old woman's grip, my nostrils full of the dead-leaf smell of her powder and black skirts. In an instant, I had wrenched my arm free and darted up the aisle toward Mama, my aunts, and Matthew. As I slipped past the darkened pews, I imagined that I could feel eyes on me and hear whispers. "What'd you do, dummy?" whispered Matthew, tugging on my sash as I reached our pew, but I pushed past him without answering. Although it was hot in the church, my teeth were chattering: It was the first time I had won a battle with a grown-up, and the earth seemed to be about to cave in beneath me. I squeezed in between Mama and Aunt Lily just as the lights came back on in the church. In the baptismal pool, Daddy raised his arms for the last time. "The Lord bless you and keep you," came his big voice. "The Lord be gracious unto you, and give you peace."

What was curious was how uncannily subdued my parents were when they heard of my skirmish with Aunt Bessie. Normally, they were swift to punish Matthew and me for misbehavior in church and breaches in politeness toward adults; this episode combined the two, and smacked of sacrilege besides. Yet once I had made an unwilling apology to the old woman (as I kissed her she shot me such a vengeful look that I realized that forever after it was to be war to the death between the two of us), I was permitted, after we had driven home, to climb up into the green shade of the big maple tree. In those days, more than now, I fell away into a remote dimension whenever I opened a book; that afternoon, as I sat with rings of sunlight and shadow moving over my arms and legs, and winged yellow seeds plopping down onto the pages of "The Story of the Treasure Seekers," I felt a vague uneasiness—a sense of having misplaced something, of being myself misplaced. I was holding myself quite aloof from considering what had happened, as I did with most drastic events, but through the adventures of the Bastables I kept remembering the way my father had looked when he'd heard what happened. He had looked not severe or angry but merely puzzled, and he had regarded me with the same puzzled expression, as if he'd just discovered that I existed and didn't know what to do with me. "What happened, Sairy?" he asked, using an old baby nickname, and I said, "I didn't want to go up there." I hadn't cried at all, and that was another curious thing.

After that Sunday, all pressure on me to accept baptism ceased. I turned twelve, fifteen, then eighteen without being baptized, a fact that scandalized some of the congregation, but my parents,

EVALUATING A STORY'S ENDING

Writing Assignment

Write an essay in which you analyze the ending of one story in this unit. Discuss the various elements that make the story and its ending either effective or not effective, in your opinion.

Background

When you read a story, your mind often jumps ahead of what you are reading, as you try to guess what will happen next. **Predicting outcomes** provides some of the pleasure in reading fiction. The more you read, the more skilled you become at spotting clues worked into the narrative. One reason you continue reading a story is to feel the satisfaction of learning how close you came to predicting the right outcome.

Many modern stories, including some in this unit, do not end with a climax or resolution which gives you a sense of closure. Instead, they end with one or more conflicts unresolved, one or more questions unanswered, or one or more loose ends still untied.

In evaluating a short story, you have to balance your own expectations with the intent of the writer. If a story does not end with a neat, compact solution, it is possible that the writer wanted to leave you with more questions than answers.

Bernard Malamud and O. Henry, for example, both wrote short stories. But the two writers did not have the same view of the world, and their stories reflect the differences. O. Henry's typical surprise endings might cause you to smile as you instantly perceive the "lesson" of his story. Malamud is more likely to leave you with many unanswered questions, as you wonder whether there are any lessons at all to be learned from human experience.

Prewriting

Reread the story you have chosen to write about. As you read the story, try to answer each of the following questions. Write your answers in the form of notes, which you will use later for your essay.

Questions for Evaluating the Ending of a Short Story

1. The first time you read the story, what did you think was going to happen? Were you correct?
2. What was your original response to the ending of the story? Did you find it satisfying or not? Can you explain why?
3. Do you feel the writer cheated you out of a scene he or she had led you to expect?
4. Were there clues in the story that **foreshadowed** its end? Were the clues consistent with the outcome of the story? Did the writer drop any false clues?
5. Does the ending seem logical, given the nature of the characters? Does it seem inevitable? Can you imagine other endings that would be consistent with the rest of the story?
6. How did the ending contribute to the theme of the story? What is that theme?

Writing

Using your notes, prepare your essay. You might follow this plan:

Paragraph 1: Mention the title, the author, and the subject of the story; summarize the story's ending.
Paragraph 2: Explain why you think the ending was or was not logical and inevitable. Did the writer foreshadow the outcome of the story?
Paragraph 3: Evaluate the ending in terms of the theme and characterization. Discuss one or more alternative endings and explain why they would have been more or less satisfying.
Paragraph 4: Discuss your emotional response to the ending of the story.

Revising and Proofreading

To revise and proofread your essay, refer to the guidelines in the section at the back of the book called **Writing About Literature.**

MODERN NONFICTION

A Lawn Sprinkler by David Hockney (1967). Acrylic on canvas.   Collection of the artist.

UNIT TWELVE

Shortly after five o'clock I remembered that we had been invited out to dinner that night and realized that if I were to dose a pig there was no time to lose. The dinner date seemed a familiar conflict: I move in a desultory society and often a week or two will roll by without my going to anybody's house to dinner or anyone's coming to mine, but when an occasion does arise, and I am summoned, something usually turns up (an hour or two in advance) to make all human intercourse seem vastly inappropriate. I have come to believe that there is in hostesses a special power of divination, and that they deliberately arrange dinners to coincide with pig failure or some other sort of failure. At any rate, it was after five o'clock and I knew I could put off no longer the evil hour.

When my son and I arrived at the pigyard, armed with a small bottle of castor oil and a length of clothesline, the pig had emerged from his house and was standing in the middle of his yard, listlessly. He gave us a slim greeting. I could see that he felt uncomfortable and uncertain. I had brought the clothesline thinking I'd have to tie him (the pig weighed more than a hundred pounds), but we never used it. My son reached down, grabbed both front legs, upset him quickly, and when he opened his mouth to scream I turned the oil into his throat—a pink, corrugated area I had never seen before. I had just time to read the label while the neck of the bottle was in his mouth. It said Puretest. The screams, slightly muffled by oil, were pitched in the hysterically high range of pig-sound, as though torture were being carried out, but they didn't last long: It was all over rather suddenly, and, his legs released, the pig righted himself.

In the upset position the corners of his mouth had been turned down, giving him a frowning expression. Back on his feet again, he regained the set smile that a pig wears even in sickness. He stood his ground, sucking slightly at the residue of oil; a few drops leaked out of his lips while his wicked eyes, shaded by their coy little lashes, turned on me in disgust and hatred. I scratched him gently with oily fingers and he remained quiet, as though trying to recall the satisfaction of being scratched when in health, and seeming to rehearse in his mind the indignity to which he had just been subjected. I noticed, as I stood there, four or five small dark spots on his back near the tail end, reddish brown in color, each about the size of a housefly. I could not make out what they were. They did not look troublesome but at the same time they did not look like mere surface bruises or chafe marks. Rather they seemed blemishes of internal origin. His stiff white bristles almost completely hid them and I had to part the bristles with my fingers to get a good look.

Several hours later, a few mintues before midnight, having dined well and at someone else's expense, I returned to the pighouse with a flashlight. The patient was asleep. Kneeling, I felt his ears (as you might put your hand on the forehead of a child) and they seemed cool, and then with the light made a careful examination of the yard and the house for sign that the oil had worked. I found none and went to bed.

We had been having an unseasonable spell of weather—hot, close days, with the fog shutting in every night, scaling for a few hours in midday, then creeping back again at dark, drifting in first over the trees on the point, then suddenly blowing across the fields, blotting out the world and taking possession of houses, men, and animals. Everyone kept hoping for a break, but the break failed to come. Next day was another hot one. I visited the pig before breakfast and tried to tempt him with a little milk in his trough. He just stared at it, while I made a sucking sound through my teeth to remind him of past pleasures of the feast. With very small, timid pigs, weanlings, this ruse is often quite successful and will encourage them to eat; but with a large, sick pig the ruse is senseless and the sound I made must have made him feel, if anything, more miserable. He not only did not crave food, he felt a positive revulsion to it. I found a place under the apple tree where he had vomited in the night.

At this point, although a depression had settled over me, I didn't suppose that I was going to lose my pig. From the lustiness of a healthy pig a man derives a feeling of personal lustiness; the stuff that goes into the trough and is received with such enthusiasm is an earnest[3] of some later feast of his own, and when this suddenly comes to an end and the food lies stale and untouched, souring in the sun, the pig's imbalance becomes the man's, vicariously, and life seems insecure, displaced, transitory.

As my own spirits declined, along with the pig's, the spirits of my vile old dachshund rose. The frequency of our trips down the footpath through

---

3. **earnest:** a proof, or a sign.

the orchard to the pigyard delighted him, although he suffers greatly from arthritis, moves with difficulty, and would be bedridden if he could find anyone willing to serve him meals on a tray.

He never missed a chance to visit the pig with me, and he made many professional calls on his own. You could see him down there at all hours, his white face parting the grass along the fence as he wobbled and stumbled about, his stethoscope dangling—a happy quack, writing his villainous prescriptions and grinning his corrosive grin. When the enema bag appeared, and the bucket of warm suds, his happiness was complete, and he managed to squeeze his enormous body between the two lowest rails of the yard and then assumed full charge of the irrigation. Once, when I lowered the bag to check the flow, he reached in and hurriedly drank a few mouthfuls of the suds to test their potency. I have noticed that Fred will feverishly consume any substance that is associated with trouble—the bitter flavor is to his liking. When the bag was above reach, he concentrated on the pig and was everywhere at once, a tower of strength and inconvenience. The pig, curiously enough, stood rather quietly through this colonic[4] carnival, and the enema, though ineffective, was not as difficult as I had anticipated.

I discovered, though, that once having given a pig an enema there is no turning back, no chance of resuming one of life's more stereotyped roles. The pig's lot and mine were inextricably bound now, as though the rubber tube were the silver cord. From then until the time of his death I held the pig steadily in the bowl of my mind; the task of trying to deliver him from his misery became a strong obsession. His suffering soon became the embodiment of all earthly wretchedness. Along toward the end of the afternoon, defeated in physicking, I phoned the veterinary twenty miles away and placed the case formally in his hands. He was full of questions, and when I casually mentioned the dark spots on the pig's back, his voice changed its tone.

"I don't want to scare you," he said, "but when there are spots, erysipelas[5] has to be considered."

Together we considered erysipelas, with frequent interruptions from the telephone operator, who wasn't sure the connection had been established.

---

4. **colonic:** having to do with the colon.
5. **erysipelas:** an acute inflammation of the skin.

"If a pig has erysipelas can he give it to a person?" I asked.

"Yes, he can," replied the vet.

"Have they answered?" asked the operator.

"Yes, they have," I said. Then I addressed the vet again. "You better come over here and examine this pig right away."

"I can't come myself," said the vet, "but McFarland can come this evening if that's all right. Mac knows more about pigs than I do anyway. You needn't worry too much about the spots. To indicate erysipelas they would have to be deep hemorrhagic infarcts."

"Deep hemorrhagic what?" I asked.

"Infarcts," said the vet.

"Have they answered?" asked the operator.

"Well," I said, "I don't know what you'd call these spots, except they're about the size of a housefly. If the pig has erysipelas I guess I have it, too, by this time, because we've been very close lately."

"McFarland will be over," said the vet.

I hung up. My throat felt dry and I went to the cupboard and got a bottle of whiskey. Deep hemorrhagic infarcts—the phrase began fastening its hooks in my head. I had assumed that there could be nothing much wrong with a pig during the months it was being groomed for murder; my confidence in the essential health and endurance of pigs had been strong and deep, particularly in the health of pigs that belonged to me and that were part of my proud scheme. The awakening had been violent, and I minded it all the more because I knew that what could be true of my pig could be true also of the rest of my tidy world. I tried to put this distasteful idea from me, but it kept recurring. I took a short drink of the whiskey and then, although I wanted to go down to the yard and look for fresh signs, I was scared to. I was certain I had erysipelas.

It was long after dark and the supper dishes had been put away when a car drove in and McFarland got out. He had a girl with him. I could just make her out in the darkness—she seemed young and pretty. "This is Miss Owen," he said. "We've been having a picnic supper on the shore, that's why I'm late."

McFarland stood in the driveway and stripped off his jacket, then his shirt. His stocky arms and capable hands showed up in my flashlight's gleam as I helped him find his coverall and get zipped up. The rear seat of his car contained an astonishing amount of paraphernalia, which he soon overhauled, selecting a chain, a syringe, a bottle of oil, a rubber tube, and some other things I couldn't identify. Miss Owen said she'd go along with us and see the pig. I led the way down the warm slope of the orchard, my light picking out the path for them, and we all three climbed the fence, entered the pighouse, and squatted by the pig while McFarland took a rectal reading. My flashlight picked up the glitter of an engagement ring on the girl's hand.

"No elevation," said McFarland, twisting the thermometer in the light. "You needn't worry about erysipelas." He ran his hand slowly over the pig's stomach and at one point the pig cried out in pain.

"Poor piggledy-wiggledy!" said Miss Owen.

The treatment I had been giving the pig for two days was then repeated, somewhat more expertly, by the doctor, Miss Owen and I handing him things as he needed them—holding the chain that he had looped around the pig's upper jaw, holding the syringe, holding the bottle stopper, the end of the tube, all of us working in darkness and in comfort, working with the instinctive teamwork induced by emergency conditions, the pig unprotesting, the house shadowy, protecting, intimate. I went to bed tired but with a feeling of relief that I had turned over part of the responsibility of the case to a licensed doctor. I was beginning to think, though, that the pig was not going to live.

He died twenty-four hours later, or it might have been forty-eight—there is a blur in time here, and I may have lost or picked up a day in the telling and the pig one in the dying. At intervals during the last day I took cool fresh water down to him, and at such times as he found the strength to get to his feet he would stand with head in the pail and snuffle his snout around. He drank a few sips but no more; yet it seemed to comfort him to dip his nose in water and bobble it about, sucking in and blowing out through his teeth. Much of the time, now, he lay indoors half buried in sawdust. Once, near the last, while I was attending him I saw him try to make a bed for himself but he lacked the strength, and when he set his snout into the dust he was unable to plow even the little furrow he needed to lie down in.

He came out of the house to die. When I went down, before going to bed, he lay stretched in the yard a few feet from the door. I knelt, saw that he was dead, and left him there: His face had a mild look, expressive neither of deep peace nor of deep suffering, although I think he had suffered a good deal. I went back up to the house and to bed, and cried internally—deep hemorrhagic intears. I didn't wake till nearly eight the next morning, and when I looked out the open window the grave was already being dug, down beyond the dump under a wild apple. I could hear the spade strike against the small rocks that blocked the way. Never send to know for whom the grave is dug, I said to myself, it's dug for thee. Fred, I well knew, was supervising the work of digging, so I ate breakfast slowly.

It was a Saturday morning. The thicket in which I found the gravediggers at work was dark and warm, the sky overcast. Here, among alders and young hackmatacks, at the foot of the apple tree, Lennie had dug a beautiful hole, five feet long, three feet wide, three feet deep. He was standing in it, removing the last spadefuls of earth while Fred patrolled the brink in simple but impressive circles, disturbing the loose earth of the mound so that it trickled back in. There had been no rain in weeks and the soil, even three feet down, was dry and powdery. As I stood and stared, an enormous earthworm which had been partially exposed by the spade at the bottom dug itself deeper and made a slow withdrawal, seeking even remoter moistures at even lonelier depths. And just as Lennie stepped out and rested his spade against the tree and lit a cigarette, a small green apple separated itself from a branch overhead and fell into the hole. Everything about this last scene seemed overwritten—the dismal sky, the shabby woods, the imminence of rain, the worm (legendary bedfellow of the dead), the apple (conventional garnish of a pig).

But even so, there was a directness and dispatch[6] about animal burial, I thought, that made it a more decent affair than human burial: There was no stopover in the undertaker's foul parlor, no wreath nor spray; and when we hitched a line to the pig's hind legs and dragged him swiftly from his yard, throwing our weight into the harness and leaving a wake of crushed grass and smoothed rubble over the dump, ours was a businesslike procession, with Fred, the dishonorable pallbearer, staggering along in the rear, his perverse

---

6. **dispatch:** speed.

bereavement showing in every seam in his face; and the post mortem performed handily and swiftly right at the edge of the grave, so that the inwards that had caused the pig's death preceded him into the ground and he lay at last resting squarely on the cause of his own undoing.

I threw in the first shovelful, and then we worked rapidly and without talk, until the job was complete. I picked up the rope, made it fast to Fred's collar (he is a notorious ghoul), and we all three filed back up the path to the house, Fred bringing up the rear and holding back every inch of the way, feigning unusual stiffness. I noticed that although he weighed far less than the pig, he was harder to drag, being possessed of the vital spark.

The news of the death of my pig traveled fast and far, and I received many expressions of sympathy from friends and neighbors, for no one took the event lightly and the premature expiration of a pig is, I soon discovered, a departure which the community marks solemnly on its calendar, a sorrow in which it feels fully involved. I have written this account in penitence and in grief, as a man who failed to raise his pig, and to explain my deviation from the classic course of so many raised pigs. The grave in the woods is unmarked, but Fred can direct the mourner to it unerringly and with immense good will, and I know he and I shall often revisit it, singly and together, in seasons of reflection and despair, on flagless memorial days of our own choosing.

Responding to the Essay

Analyzing the Essay

Identifying Facts

1. Why does the narrator want to write about the pig? In the second paragraph, what comparison does he use to describe the process of raising a pig?
2. How does the narrator come to regard the pig's suffering and death? Find the passage where he identifies with the pig.

Interpreting Meanings

3. How often does Fred the dachshund appear? What is Fred's importance in the essay?
4. Find the passages where Fred is described as if he were human. White refers to his pet as a "vile" dachshund. Does White really dislike Fred? How would you describe his feelings toward his nosy dog?
5. Why were White's feelings about life—its sorrows and uncertainties—shaken by the death of his pig? What examples of **hyperbole** (exaggeration) does he use to illustrate his shaken feelings?
6. Why do you think White and Fred will visit the grave? What will they learn there?
7. Where does White explain his **purpose** in writing this essay? How would you explain this statement of purpose?
8. What passage or sentences would you say are key to this essay and its **theme**?
9. How did you respond to the essay—to its animal and its human characters?

Writing About the Essay

A Creative Response

1. **Imitating White's Technique.** Write a real or imagined recollection of an animal. Give the animal a human personality.

A Critical Response

2. **Analyzing Style.** In an essay, analyze White's essay to show how he creates humor. Before you write, consider how White uses these elements of humor:

   a. Comic metaphors
   b. Comic images
   c. Irony
   d. Exaggeration
   e. Puns

3. **Describing a Character.** In a brief essay, describe the character of Fred the dachshund as White creates it. Describe Fred's appearance, interests, and responses to the pig's problems.
4. **Explaining Allusion.** When, on page 998, White says "Never send to know for whom the grave is dug, . . . it's dug for thee," he is alluding to Meditation 17, written in 1623 by the English poet John Donne. (It is sometimes printed in part and called "No Man Is an Island.") Locate Donne's poem, and in an essay explain (a) why White uses the line at this point in his essay, and (b) what it adds to the essay's themes.

Lewis Thomas
(1913–   )

Scientists and imaginative writers—poets, dramatists, storytellers—were not always thought of as belonging to different groups. For hundreds of years, educated people assumed that they could and *should* master the fundamentals of both the arts and the sciences. Those who studied the "liberal arts" assumed that they could easily learn to grasp the basic principles of how the world was put together. But in the twentieth century, science no longer seems so accessible to even the college-educated reader; as a result, writers have been reluctant to discuss theories their audiences can only dimly understand. How many of us can state, clearly and succinctly, the current state of knowledge in biology? Physics? Astronomy? At best, most people may recognize familiar catchwords, such as black hole, quasar, DNA, gene-splicing, $E = mc^2$; but they would be hard-pressed to explain their meaning.

As writers have moved away in ignorance and frustration from discussing science and what its theories imply, they have retreated into the private sphere of life: families, personal relationships, individual careers and problems. In an essay called "Poetry in a Discouraging Time," critic Christopher Clausen discusses what has happened to the art of poetry. "Nearly everyone agrees," he writes, "that poetry in the twentieth century—at least in English-speaking countries—is not so highly honored nor widely read as it once was. Few doubt that the rise of science has had something to do with displacing it as a publicly important vehicle for those truths that people accept as being centrally important."

The separation of science from art has worried scientists as well. C. P. Snow, a British scientist and novelist, described this division of intellectuals into two distinct communities in a famous lecture, "The Two Cultures and the Scientific Revolution," delivered in 1959 at Cambridge University in England. Decrying the increasing gulf separating the two cultures, he proposed educational reforms that might bridge the gap. Snow began a debate that still continues, and variations of his ideas still haunt college and university administrators.

Snow was a rarity in being a scientist who could write for a general audience. If an average reader picks up a professional scientific journal, he or she is unlikely to find it either comprehensible or illuminating, let alone entertaining. Yet many readers hunger to be told something about advances in science; they want to share the excitement they can sense happening there. And as more people realize that technological advances are transforming their lives—and perhaps threatening their existence as a species—they need to know how and why things happen. Otherwise, how can ordinary citizens make informed decisions about the space program, nuclear weapons, pollution control, or genetic engineering?

So when a scientist appears who can write not only clearly, but wittily and profoundly, he or she is eagerly welcomed. It is a select company: Stephen Jay Gould, Roger B. Swain, Isaac Asimov, Carl Sagan, Loren Eisely, among others. In a slightly different company are a handful of doctors who have written skillfully and movingly about their professional experiences, like surgeons William Nolen and Richard Selzer. Among these scientists who see themselves also as humanists, physician Lewis Thomas has won a pre-eminent place.

Born in New York and educated at Princeton and Harvard, Thomas became a research pathologist. He served as a professor of pediatric research at the University of Minnesota, as dean at New York University-Bellevue Medical Center and at the Yale Medical School, and as president and then chancellor at Memorial Sloan-Kettering Cancer Center in New York.

Thomas's first book, *The Lives of a Cell* (1974), a collection of essays originally published in *The New England Journal of Medicine*, won the National Book Award. Two other collections followed: *The Medusa and the Snail* (1979) and *Late Night Thoughts on Listening to Mahler's Ninth Symphony* (1983). He also published a memoir of his life as a doctor, *The Youngest Science* (1983).

His interest is not merely technical. Thomas is deeply concerned with whether the human race will survive, although he continues to feel hope and optimism. Novelist John Updike wrote that Thomas's "willingness to see possibility where others see only doom is tonic and welcome."

Thomas has written, "There is a deeper need to teach science to those who will be needed for thinking about it, and this means pretty nearly everyone else. . . . And the poets, on whose shoulders the future rests, might, late nights, thinking things over, begin to see some meanings that elude the rest of us." Thomas finds scientific mysteries both exciting and heartening.

CETI

Thomas's essays typically combine detailed scientific fact, wit, and a humane theme. In "Ceti," Thomas begins with the relatively common speculation that there may be life on other worlds. His uncommon approach to this possibility is that we ought to consider carefully what our first messages to such life would be. Specialized scientific words are footnoted, but you should examine content clues and word structures to see if you can figure out what these words (and others) mean.

Tau Ceti is a relatively nearby star that sufficiently resembles our sun to make its solar system a plausible candidate for the existence of life. We are, it appears, ready to begin getting in touch with Ceti, and with any other interested celestial body in more remote places, out to the edge. CETI is also, by intention, the acronym of the First International Conference on Communication with Extraterrestrial Intelligence, held in 1972 in Soviet Armenia under the joint sponsorship of the National Academy of Sciences of the United States and the Soviet Academy which involved eminent physicists and astronomers from various countries, most of whom are convinced that the odds for the existence of life elsewhere are very high, with a reasonable probability that there are civilizations, one place or another, with technologic mastery matching or exceeding ours.

On this assumption, the conferees thought it likely that radioastronomy would be the generally accepted mode of interstellar communication, on grounds of speed and economy. They made a formal recommendation that we organize an international cooperative program, with new and immense radio telescopes, to probe the reaches of deep space for electromagnetic signals making sense. Eventually, we would plan to send out messages on our own and receive answers, but at the outset it seems more practical to begin by catching snatches of conversation between others.

So, the highest of all our complex technologies in the hardest of our sciences will soon be engaged, full scale, in what is essentially biologic research—and with some aspects of social science, at that.

The earth has become, just in the last decade, too small a place. We have the feeling of being confined—shut in; it is something like outgrowing a small town in a small county. The views of the dark, pocked surface of Mars, still lifeless to judge from the latest photographs, do not seem to have extended our reach; instead, they bring closer, too close, another unsatisfatory feature of our local environment. The blue noonday sky, cloudless, has lost its old look of immensity. The word is out that the sky is not limitless; it is finite. It is, in truth, only a kind of local roof, a membrane under which we live, luminous but confusingly refractile[1] when suffused with sunlight; we can sense its concave surface a few miles over our heads. We know that it is tough and thick enough so that when hard objects strike it from the outside they burst into flames. The color photographs of the earth are more amazing than anything outside: We live inside a blue chamber, a bubble of air blown by ourselves. The other sky beyond, absolutely black and appalling, is wide-open country, irresistible for exploration.

Here we go, then. An extraterrestrial embryologist, having a close look at us from time to time, would probably conclude that the morphogenesis[2] of the earth is coming along well, with the beginnings of a nervous system and fair-sized ganglions[3] in the form of cities, and now with specialized, dish-shaped sensory organs, miles across, ready to receive stimuli. He may well wonder, however, how we will go about responding. We are evolving into the situation of a Skinner pigeon in a Skinner box,[4] peering about in all directions, trying to make connections, probing.

When the first word comes in from outer space, finally, we will probably be used to the idea. We can already provide a quite good explanation for the origin of life, here or elsewhere. Given a moist planet with methane, formaldehyde, ammonia, and some usable minerals, all of which abound, exposed to lightning or ultraviolet irradiation at the right temperature, life might start off almost anywhere. The tricky, unsolved thing is how to get the polymers[5] to arrange in membranes and invent replication.[6] The rest is clear going. If they follow our protocol, it will be anaerobic[7] life at first, then photosynthesis and the first exhalation of oxygen, then respiring life and the great burst of variation, then speciation[8] and, finally, some kind of consciousness. It is easy, in the telling.

I suspect that when we have recovered from the first easy acceptance of signs of life from elsewhere, and finished nodding at each other, and finished smiling, we will be in for shock. We have had it our way, relatively speaking, being unique all these years, and it will be hard to deal with the thought that the whole, infinitely huge, spinning, clocklike apparatus around us is itself animate, and can sprout life whenever the conditions are right. We will respond, beyond doubt, by making connections after the fashion of established life, floating out our filaments, extending pili,[9] but we will end up feeling smaller than ever, as small as a single cell, with a quite new sense of continuity. It will take some getting used to.

The immediate problem, however, is a much more practical, down-to-earth matter, and must be giving insomnia to the CETI participants. Let us assume that there is, indeed, sentient life in one or another part of remote space, and that we will be successful in getting in touch with it. What on earth are we going to talk about? If, as seems likely, it is a hundred or more light years away, there are going to be some very long pauses. The barest amenities, on which we rely for opening conversations—Hello, are you there? from us, followed by Yes, hello, from them—will take two hundred years at least. By the time we have our party we may have forgotten what we had in mind.

We could begin by gambling on the rightness of our technology and just send out news of ourselves, like a mimeographed Christmas letter, but we would have to choose our items carefully, with durability of meaning in mind. Whatever information we provide must still make sense to us two centuries later, and must still seem important, or the conversation will be an embarrassment to all concerned. In two hundred years it is, as we have found, easy to lose the thread.

---

1. **refractile:** appearing to be or capable of being bent.
2. **morphogenesis:** development of an organism.
3. **ganglions:** masses of nerve cells.
4. **Skinner box:** an enclosure in which small animals are conditioned to obey certain stimuli. The box is named for its inventor, the American psychologist B. F. Skinner.
5. **polymers:** compounds of the same chemical elements.
6. **replication:** duplication; reproduction.

7. **anaerobic:** able to live without air or oxygen.
8. **speciation:** formation of new and different biological species.
9. **pili:** hairlike structures.

Perhaps the safest thing to do at the outset, if technology permits, is to send music. This language may be the best we have for explaining what we are like to others in space, with least ambiguity. I would vote for Bach, all of Bach, streamed out into space, over and over again. We would be bragging, of course, but it is surely excusable for us to put the best possible face on at the beginning of such an acquaintance. We can tell the harder truths later. And, to do ourselves justice, music would give a fairer picture of what we are really like than some of the other things we might be sending, like *Time*, say, or a history of the UN or Presidential speeches. We could send out our science, of course, but just think of the wincing at this end when the polite comments arrive two hundred years from now. Whatever we offer as today's items of liveliest interest are bound to be out of date and irrelevant, maybe even ridiculous. I think we should stick to music.

Perhaps, if the technology can be adapted to it, we should send some paintings. Nothing would better describe what this place is like, to an outsider, than the Cézanne[10] demonstrations that an apple is really part fruit, part earth.

What kinds of questions should we ask? The choices will be hard, and everyone will want his special question first. What are your smallest particles? Did you think yourselves unique? Do you have colds? Have you anything quicker than light? Do you always tell the truth? Do you cry? There is no end to the list.

Perhaps we should wait a while, until we are sure we know what we want to know, before we get down to detailed questions. After all, the main question will be the opener: Hello, are you there? If the reply should turn out to be Yes, hello, we might want to stop there and think about that, for quite a long time.

---

10. **Cézanne:** Paul Cézanne (1839–1906), French post-Impressionist painter.

Responding to the Essay

Analyzing the Essay

Identifying Facts

1. What does the essay's title refer to?
2. What technique has recently been proposed for human communication with life outside the solar system?
3. What practical problem will have to be faced by the CETI participants in such communication?
4. How does Thomas suggest that this problem could be solved?

Interpreting Meanings

5. In what kind of **tone** does Thomas close the essay?
6. When Thomas says we should beam Bach into outer space, he adds, "We would be bragging, of course." What does he mean?
7. What different aspects of our humanity does Thomas suggest in the questions he thinks we might ask, such as "Do you always tell the truth? Do you cry?" What do these questions reveal about our nature?
8. Think of the other essayists you have read: Franklin, Emerson, and Thoreau, for example. Would you describe Thomas as a rationalist, like Franklin, or as a Romantic idealist, like Emerson and Thoreau? Or is it impossible to categorize this essay?
9. Would you take issue with any of Thomas's points in this essay?

Writing About the Essay

A Creative Response

1. **Expressing Your Point of View.** Suppose you had to formulate the questions we might ask of sentient life in another part of remote space. In one paragraph, write out the questions you would ask. In a second paragraph, explain what "news of ourselves" you would send: Music? Newspapers? Technological contraptions? Art? In a third paragraph, tell what "harder truths" we might have to tell these beings later.

A Critical Response

2. **Evaluating the Essay.** Suppose this were a chapter in a high-school science textbook. How would you evaluate it? What is its main topic? What does it "teach"? Write out your evaluation in a paragraph.

Russell Baker
(1925–   )

Russell Baker is usually classified as a "humorist," but such a label is far too limiting. In his regular column written for the *New York Times* since 1962, Baker has commented on human foibles and follies, sometimes lightly, sometimes with seriousness, but almost always with a wit that provides a lesson. In "School vs. Education," reprinted here, Baker's attack on the American educational system is sharpened, rather than softened, by the humor of his exaggerations. "Little Red Riding Hood Revisited," has an entirely different target—the deterioration of the English language. Yet Baker can write a column with equal zest about the quality of the food he and his wife find at a truckstop. He observes whatever is going on around him, and American eating habits sometimes interest him as much as the philosophical basis of education.

Writing a column for more than twenty-five years requires not only stamina, but also irrepressible curiosity and unflagging interest in the details and happenings of daily life. Henry James once remarked that a writer should be someone "on whom nothing is lost." He probably meant that a writer watches, listens, picks up vibrations, sees the significance of small details, and interprets the meaning of events no one else notices. Russell Baker has these gifts. Critic R. Z. Sheppard has described how he uses them: "At his best, Baker fills his allotted space opposite the editorial page with bizarre, often bleak fantasies about human foolishness. At his second best, he holds a funhouse mirror up to the nature of the consumer state."

Baker has told the story of his childhood during the Great Depression in a best-selling autobiography, *Growing Up*. The book is a poignant, sometimes ambivalent tribute to the resilience and toughness of his mother, who was widowed when Russell was only five.

Baker casually describes his seventh-grade decision to become a writer. After he failed dismally as a magazine salesman, his mother saw an "A" on his seventh-grade composition on "my summer vacation." She immediately suggested that perhaps he could be a writer:

I clasped the idea to my heart. I had never met a writer, had shown no previous urge to write, and hadn't a notion of how to become a writer, but I loved stories and thought that making up stories must surely be almost as much fun as reading them. Best of all, though, and what really gladdened my heart, was the ease of a writer's life. Writers did not have to trudge through the town peddling from canvas bags, defending themselves against angry dogs, being rejected by surly strangers. Writers did not have to ring doorbells. So far as I could make out, what writers did couldn't even be classified as work.

Born in Virginia, Baker remained an Easterner. He graduated from Johns Hopkins University in Baltimore in 1947, joined the staff of the *Baltimore Sun*, and for the first two years covered a news beat. He didn't write a word himself, but phoned in his information to "rewrite" editors. He says:

I spent those years prowling the slums of Baltimore, studying the psychology of cops, watching people's homes burn, deciphering semiliterate police reports of dented fenders and suicides, and hanging around accident wards listening to people die. One night, sitting in a West Baltimore police station, patiently hating a skinny little clerk but forcing a smile nevertheless as he described for the hundredth time the pleasures he derived from attending hangings, I saw a cop come in with his ear in one hand and the man who had bitten it off gripped firmly in the other.

Baker is seldom grim or intense for long, however. He turns his phrases so that recognition arrives with laughter, and sometimes he writes a column that sounds as if he is simply enjoying his own exuberance. This essentially good-tempered point of view may be necessary for the sanity and long-term success of a newspaper columnist.

Not all humorists share that attitude, of course. Essayist Fran Leibowitz, whose sharp, biting humor has won her an admiring following, was once quoted as saying that all humor is basically abrasive and negative. But, she continued, if you disparage the mass audience, you have no readers, so that's one of the reasons there's not much good humor on the market today. The other reason for the lack of humor in books today, according to the ascerbic Leibowitz, is that "people are morons."

As his essay "Little Red Riding Hood Revisited" shows, Baker is not afraid to "disparage" a mass audience. Nor does he believe, as "School vs. Education" shows, that people are morons.

LITTLE RED RIDING HOOD REVISITED

As the British writer George Orwell pointed out in a famous essay he wrote in the 1940's, the use of language to confuse or suppress critical thinking has emerged as one of the fundamental dangers of our century. Orwell drew his examples from politics. Here, Russell Baker uses a familiar folk tale to satirize jargon, overinflated rhetoric, and other abuses of language in our time. See how many different types of abuses you can recognize in "the modern American language," as Baker presents it. What tone does Baker set in his very first sentence?

In an effort to make the classics accessible to contemporary readers, I am translating them into the modern American language. Here is the translation of *Little Red Riding Hood:*

Once upon a point in time, a small person named Little Red Riding Hood initiated plans for the preparation, delivery, and transportation of foodstuffs to her grandmother, a senior citizen residing at a place of residence in a wooded area of indeterminate dimension.

In the process of implementing this program, her incursion into the area was in mid-transportation process when it attained interface with an alleged perpetrator. This individual, a wolf, made inquiry as to the whereabouts of Little Red Riding Hood's goal, as well as inferring that he was de-

sirous of ascertaining the contents of Little Red Riding Hood's foodstuffs basket, and all that.

"It would be inappropriate to lie to me," the wolf said, displaying his huge jaw capability. Sensing that he was a mass of repressed hostility intertwined with acute alienation, she indicated.

"I see you indicating," the wolf said, "but what I don't see is whatever it is you're indicating at, you dig?"

Little Red Riding Hood indicated more fully, making one thing perfectly clear—to wit, that it was to her grandmother's residence and with a consignment of foodstuffs that her mission consisted of taking her to and with.

At this point in time the wolf moderated his rhetoric and proceeded to grandmother's resi-

SCHOOL VS. EDUCATION

Baker often begins his humorous essays with a premise, or assumption, that seems perfectly serious. In the first paragraph of "School vs. Education," for example, it seems as if he is promising us a serious survey of the skills that children have mastered at the age of six. But the second paragraph begins to make clear that Baker has used the word "skills" ironically. Before you read, discuss the title: Is there a difference between "school" and "education"?

By the age of six the average child will have completed the basic American education and be ready to enter school. If the child has been attentive in these preschool years, he or she will already have mastered many skills.

From television, the child will have learned how to pick a lock, commit a fairly elaborate bank holdup, prevent wetness all day long, get the laundry twice as white, and kill people with a variety of sophisticated armaments.

From watching his parents, the child, in many cases, will already know how to smoke, how much soda to mix with whiskey, what kind of language to use when angry, and how to violate the speed laws without being caught.

At this point, the child is ready for the second stage of education, which occurs in school. There, a variety of lessons may be learned in the very first days.

The teacher may illustrate the economic importance of belonging to a strong union by closing down the school before the child arrives. Fathers and mothers may demonstrate to the child the social cohesion that can be built on shared hatred by demonstrating their dislike for children whose pigmentation displeases them. In the latter event, the child may receive visual instruction in techniques of stoning buses, cracking skulls with a nightstick, and subduing mobs with tear gas. Formal education has begun.

During formal education, the child learns that life is for testing. This stage lasts twelve years, a period during which the child learns that success comes from telling testers what they want to hear.

Early in this stage, the child learns that he is either dumb or smart. If the teacher puts intelligent demands upon the child, the child learns he is smart. If the teacher expects little of the child, the child learns he is dumb and soon quits bothering to tell the testers what they want to hear.

At this point, education becomes more subtle. The child taught by school that he is dumb observes that neither he, she, nor any of the many children who are even dumber, ever fails to be promoted to the next grade. From this, the child learns that while everybody talks a lot about the virtue of being smart, there is very little incentive to stop being dumb.

What is the point of school, besides attendance? the child wonders. As the end of the first formal stage of education approaches, school answers this question. The point is to equip the child to enter college.

Children who have been taught they are smart have no difficulty. They have been happily telling testers what they want to hear for twelve years. Being artists at telling testers what they want to hear, they are admitted to college joyously, where they promptly learn that they are the hope of America.

Children whose education has been limited to adjusting themselves to their schools' low estimates of them are admitted to less joyous colleges which, in some cases, may teach them to read.

At this stage of education, a fresh question arises for everyone. If the point of lower education was to get into college, what is the point of college? The answer is soon learned. The point of college is to prepare the student—no longer a child now—to get into graduate school. In college, the student learns that it is no longer enough simply to tell the testers what they want to hear. Many are tested for graduate school; few are admitted.

Those excluded may be denied valuable certificates to prosper in medicine, at the bar, in the corporate boardroom. The student learns that the race is to the cunning and often, alas, to the unprincipled.

Thus, the student learns the importance of destroying competitors and emerges richly prepared to play his role in the great simmering melodrama of American life.

Afterward, the former student's destiny fulfilled, his life rich with Oriental carpets, rare porcelain, and full bank accounts, he may one day find himself with the leisure and the inclination to open a book with a curious mind, and start to become educated.

Responding to the Essay

Analyzing the Essay

Identifying Facts

1. What does Baker claim is "the point" of lower education in America? Of higher education? Of graduate school?

Interpreting Meanings

2. Baker remarks **satirically** on the so-called "skills" a preschooler receives. What are these skills, and what do they say about the society in which the child is growing up? Do you agree with Baker's points? Why or why not?
3. Much of Baker's humor derives from his gift for **hyperbole**, or exaggeration for effect. What are some examples of comic hyperbole in this essay? Do you think these points would be more effectively made in a serious essay? Why or why not?
4. What is the significance of the essay's title? How would you state Baker's main **theme**, or message?
5. According to Baker, what do American schoolchildren *not* learn during their formal education? Do you agree with him? Why or why not?

Writing About the Essay

A Creative Response

1. **Answering the Writer.** This essay originally appeared in a newspaper column. Write a letter to the editor telling what you think of it.

A Critical Response

2. **Supporting an Assertion with Examples.** Take one or more of the main points in "School vs. Education" and give some supporting examples from your experience. If you disagree with Baker's main points, give examples from your own experiences to refute them.

The Jack Paar Show. Photograph taken by Cornell Capa, 1959.

Analyzing Language and Style

Irony

1. What is ironic (or unexpected and inappropriate) about what the child learns from his or her parents?
2. What is ironic about what Baker calls "formal education" in paragraph 5?
3. What is ironic about what the child learns about success on tests?

Richard Wright (1908–1960)

Richard Wright was a writer with a gift for making people intensely uncomfortable—which is one measure of his power. He is typically described as the first black writer to expose American racism to a large white audience. But this cool academic assessment fails to capture the angry, relentless drive of his most famous novel, *Native Son* (1940), or of his autobiography, *Black Boy* (1945).

Black writers who followed Wright have had to emerge from his shadow; one of the most eloquent, James Baldwin (page 1027), even wrote an essay that repudiated Wright's influence, arguing that Wright had ignored some of the strengths of black life and had absorbed too completely white fantasies about black revenge. (But in a bow toward Wright, Baldwin called his own first book of essays *Notes of a Native Son*.)

In explaining Wright, critics have had to deal with his temporary membership in the Communist Party and with his eventual self-exile in Paris, where he lived for the last thirteen years of his life. Full of contradictions, Wright is hard to label. His early death at fifty-two cut off any connection to the generation of black writers who came of age in the 1960's and 1970's. These black writers—Baldwin, Ralph Ellison, Eldridge Cleaver, Toni Morrison, Maya Angelou, Alice Walker—have almost eclipsed Wright, just as his naturalistic style might sound out-of-date in a literary world that increasingly values elaborately intellectual technique, intricate narrative structures, and bleakly objective voices.

But Wright has not been forgotten. When the University of Mississippi organized a symposium on Wright and his work in 1985, it was front-page news in the *New York Times*. Part of the poignancy of such posthumous recognition comes from the fact that Wright had remembered his home state of Mississippi with "ambivalence." It is interesting to speculate on how he might have reacted to an authority on Southern culture who told the *Times*: "Faulkner is considered the top Mississippi writer, but I would put Wright with Eudora Welty and Tennessee Williams in their international reputation."

Wright's life began in poverty. His father, a sharecropper on a Mississippi farm, abandoned his family when Wright was five; when the boy was twelve, his mother could no longer support the family. Raised by various relatives, Wright early learned the bitter lessons of survival on ghetto streets. He remembers becoming familiar with alcohol at the age of six, working in a disreputable hotel while still a child, living with "the sustained expectation of violence." By borrowing a white man's library card, he was finally able to gain access to books. He wrote later that "it had been only through books—at best, no more than vicarious cultural transfusions—that I had managed to keep myself alive."

At seventeen, he fled the South forever, moving to Chicago and then to New York. In Chicago he found encouragement to continue his self-education and to write. He joined the WPA Writers Project, a Depression-era government organization that provided livelihood for many unemployed writers. He began to explore Marxism and eventually joined the Communist Party, at a time when many people thought it offered hope for a more equitable reorganization of society (and before the horrors of the Stalinist purges became public knowledge). Eventually disillusioned, Wright left the Party in 1942.

Wright achieved his first real recognition in 1940 with *Native Son*, a violent tale of a victimized black man, Bigger Thomas, who accidentally kills once, then murders again to avoid betrayal.

Black Boy secured Wright's fame. Some readers regard it as Wright's masterpiece; as one commented, "the truly 'created' self in an autobiography is more rare than the successful character in fiction." *Black Boy* became a best-seller, topping all the lists. But in the fifteen years following its publication, Wright, then living abroad, never wrote a book that equaled its success. He tried to understand the historical and cultural place of black people in modern life, visiting Africa and recording his observations in books like *Black Power* (1954) and *White Man, Listen!* (1957). But he felt as much an alien in Africa as anywhere else. He died in Paris, where he had found as much of a home as he could.

FROM **BLACK BOY**

In this excerpt from the early part of Wright's autobiography, the images of "home" are mainly those of physical and emotional hunger. The prose is spare and bitter, as if it reflected the gaunt look of a ghost that the boy feels standing by his bed at night. Yet after his memories of his irresponsible and uncaring father, Wright arrives at a final view of the old man that is rich in detail and emotional complexity.

One day my mother told me that we were going to Memphis on a boat, the *Kate Adams*, and my eagerness thereafter made the days seem endless. Each night I went to bed hoping that the next morning would be the day of departure.

"How big is the boat?" I asked my mother.

"As big as a mountain," she said.

"Has it got a whistle?"

"Yes."

"Does the whistle blow?"

"Yes."

"When?"

"When the captain wants it to blow."

"Why do they call it the *Kate Adams*?"

"Because that's the boat's name."

"What color is the boat?"

"White."

"How long will we be on the boat?"

"All day and all night."

"Will we sleep on the boat?"

"Yes, when we get sleepy, we'll sleep. Now, hush."

For days I had dreamed about a huge white boat floating on a vast body of water, but when my mother took me down to the levee on the day of leaving, I saw a tiny, dirty boat that was not at all like the boat I had imagined. I was disappointed and when time came to go on board I cried and my mother thought that I did not want to go with her to Memphis, and I could not tell her what the trouble was. Solace came when I wandered about the boat and gazed at Negroes throwing dice, drinking whiskey, playing cards, lolling on boxes, eating, talking, and singing. My father took me down into the engine room and the throbbing machines enthralled me for hours.

In Memphis we lived in a one-story brick tenement. The stone buildings and the concrete pavements looked bleak and hostile to me. The absence of green, growing things made the city seem dead. Living space for the four of us—my mother, my brother, my father, and me—was a kitchen and a bedroom. In the front and rear were paved areas in which my brother and I could play, but for days I was afraid to go into the strange city streets alone.

It was in this tenement that the personality of

my father first came fully into the orbit of my concern. He worked as a night porter in a Beale Street drugstore and he became important and forbidding to me only when I learned that I could not make noise when he was asleep in the day-time. He was the lawgiver in our family and I never laughed in his presence. I used to lurk tim-idly in the kitchen doorway and watch his huge body sitting slumped at the table. I stared at him with awe as he gulped his beer from a tin bucket, as he ate long and heavily, sighed, belched, closed his eyes to nod on a stuffed belly. He was quite fat and his bloated stomach always lapped over his belt. He was always a stranger to me, always somehow alien and remote. . . .

Hunger stole upon me so slowly that at first I was not aware of what hunger really meant. Hunger had always been more or less at my elbow when I played, but now I began to wake up at night to find hunger standing at my bedside, staring at me gauntly. The hunger I had known before this had been no grim, hostile stranger; it had been a nor-mal hunger that had made me beg constantly for bread, and when I ate a crust or two I was satis-fied. But this new hunger baffled me, scared me, made me angry and insistent. Whenever I begged for food now my mother would pour me a cup of tea which would still the clamor in my stomach for a moment or two; but a little later I would feel hunger nudging my ribs, twisting my empty guts until they ached. I would grow dizzy and my vi-sion would dim. I became less active in my play, and for the first time in my life I had to pause and think of what was happening to me.

"Mama, I'm hungry," I complained one after-noon.

"Jump up and catch a kungry," she said, trying to make me laugh and forget.

"What's a *kungry*?"

"It's what little boys eat when they get hun-gry," she said.

"What does it taste like?"

"I don't know."

"Then why do you tell me to catch one?"

"Because you said that you were hungry," she said, smiling.

I sensed that she was teasing me and it made me angry.

"But I'm hungry. I want to eat."

"You'll have to wait."

"But I want to eat now."

"But there's nothing to eat," she told me.

"Why?"

"Just because there's none," she explained.

"But I want to eat," I said, beginning to cry.

"You'll just have to wait," she said again.

"But why?"

"For God to send some food."

"When is He going to send it?"

"I don't know."

"But I'm hungry!"

She was ironing and she paused and looked at me with tears in her eyes.

"Where's your father?" she asked me.

I stared in bewilderment. Yes, it was true that my father had not come home to sleep for many days now and I could make as much noise as I wanted. Though I had not known why he was absent, I had been glad that he was not there to shout his restrictions at me. But it had never oc-curred to me that his absence would mean that there would be no food.

"I don't know," I said.

"Who brings food into the house?" my mother asked me.

"Papa," I said. "He always brought food."

"Well, your father isn't here now," she said.

"Where is he?"

"I don't know," she said.

"But I'm hungry," I whimpered, stomping my feet.

"You'll have to wait until I get a job and buy food," she said.

As the days slid past the image of my father became associated with my pangs of hunger, and whenever I felt hunger I thought of him with a deep biological bitterness.

My mother finally went to work as a cook and left me and my brother alone in the flat each day with a loaf of bread and a pot of tea. When she returned at evening she would be tired and dispir-ited and would cry a lot. Sometimes, when she was in despair, she would call us to her and talk to us for hours, telling us that we now had no father, that our lives would be different from those of other children, that we must learn as soon as possible to take care of ourselves, to dress our-selves, to prepare our own food; that we must take upon ourselves the responsibility of the flat while she worked. Half frightened, we would promise solemnly. We did not understand what had happened between our father and our mother and the most that these long talks did to us was to make us feel a vague dread. Whenever we asked why father had left, she would tell us that we were too young to know.

One evening my mother told me that thereafter I would have to do the shopping for food. She took me to the corner store to show me the way. I was proud; I felt like a grown-up. The next afternoon I looped the basket over my arm and went down the pavement toward the store. When I reached the corner, a gang of boys grabbed me, knocked me down, snatched the basket, took the money, and sent me running home in panic. That evening I told my mother what had happened, but she made no comment; she sat down at once, wrote another note, gave me more money, and sent me out to the grocery again. I crept down the steps and saw the same gang of boys playing down the street. I ran back in to the house.

"What's the matter?" my mother asked.

"It's those same boys," I said. "They'll beat me."

"You've got to get over that," she said. "Now, go on."

"I'm scared," I said.

"Go on and don't pay any attention to them," she said.

I went out of the door and walked briskly down the sidewalk, praying that the gang would not molest me. But when I came abreast of them someone shouted.

"There he is!"

They came toward me and I broke into a wild run toward home. They overtook me and flung me to the pavement. I yelled, pleaded, kicked, but they wrenched the money out of my hand. They yanked me to my feet, gave me a few slaps, and sent me home sobbing. My mother met me at the door.

"They b-beat m-me," I gasped. "They t-t-took the m-money."

I started up the steps, seeking the shelter of the house.

"Don't you come in here," my mother warned me.

I froze in my tracks and stared at her.

"But they're coming after me," I said.

"You just stay right where you are," she said in a deadly tone. "I'm going to teach you this night to stand up and fight for yourself."

She went into the house and I waited, terrified, wondering what she was about. Presently she returned with more money and another note; she also had a long heavy stick.

"Take this money, this note, and this stick," she said. "Go to the store and buy those groceries. If those boys bother you, then fight."

I was baffled. My mother was telling me to fight, a thing that she had never done before.

"But I'm scared," I said.

"Don't you come into this house until you've gotten those groceries," she said.

"They'll beat me; they'll beat me," I said.

"Then stay in the streets; don't come back here!"

I ran up the steps and tried to force my way past her into the house. A stinging slap came on my jaw. I stood on the sidewalk, crying.

"Please, let me wait until tomorrow," I begged.

"No," she said. "Go now! If you come back into this house without those groceries, I'll whip you!"

She slammed the door and I heard the key turn in the lock. I shook with fright. I was alone upon the dark, hostile streets and gangs were after me. I had the choice of being beaten at home or away from home. I clutched the stick, crying, trying to reason. If I were beaten at home, there was absolutely nothing that I could do about it; but if I were beaten in the streets, I had a chance to fight and defend myself. I walked slowly down the sidewalk, coming closer to the gang of boys, holding the stick tightly. I was so full of fear that I could scarcely breathe. I was almost upon them now.

"There he is again!" the cry went up.

They surrounded me quickly and began to grab for my hand.

"I'll kill you!" I threatened.

They closed in. In blind fear I let the stick fly, feeling it crack against a boy's skull. I swung again, lamming another skull, then another. Realizing that they would retaliate if I let up for but a second, I fought to lay them low, to knock them cold, to kill them so that they could not strike back at me. I flayed with tears in my eyes, teeth clenched, stark fear making me throw every ounce of my strength behind each blow. I hit again and again, dropping the money and the grocery list. The boys scattered, yelling, nursing their heads, staring at me in utter disbelief. They had never seen such frenzy. I stood panting, egging them on, taunting them to come on and fight. When they refused, I ran after them and they tore out for their homes, screaming. The parents of the boys rushed into the streets and threatened me, and for the first time in my life I shouted at grown-ups, telling them that I would give them the same if they bothered me. I finally found my grocery list and the money and went to the store. On my way back I kept my stick poised for instant use, but there was not a single boy in sight. That night I won the right to the streets of Memphis. . . .

After my father's desertion, my mother's ardently religious disposition dominated the household and I was often taken to Sunday school where I met God's representative in the guise of a tall, black preacher. One Sunday my mother invited the tall, black preacher to a dinner of fried chicken. I was happy, not because the preacher was coming but because of the chicken. One or two neighbors also were invited. But no sooner had the preacher arrived than I began to resent him, for I learned at once that he, like my father, was used to having his own way. The hour for dinner came and I was wedged at the table between talking and laughing adults. In the center of the table was a huge platter of golden-brown fried chicken. I compared the bowl of soup that sat before me with the crispy chicken and decided in favor of the chicken. The others began to eat their soup, but I could not touch mine.

"Eat your soup," my mother said.

"I don't want any," I said.

"You won't get anything else until you've eaten your soup," she said.

The preacher had finished his soup and had asked that the platter of chicken be passed to him. It galled me. He smiled, cocked his head this way and that, picking out choice pieces. I forced a spoonful of soup down my throat and looked to see if my speed matched that of the preacher. It did not. There were already bare chicken bones on his plate, and he was reaching for more. I tried eating my soup faster, but it was no use; the other people were now serving themselves chicken and the platter was more than half empty. I gave up and sat staring in despair at the vanishing pieces of fried chicken.

"Eat your soup or you won't get anything," my mother warned.

I looked at her appealingly and could not answer. As piece after piece of chicken was eaten, I was unable to eat my soup at all. I grew hot with anger. The preacher was laughing and joking and the grown-ups were hanging on his words. My growing hate of the preacher finally became more important than God or religion and I could no longer contain myself. I leaped up from the table, knowing that I should be ashamed of what I was doing, but unable to stop, and screamed, running blindly from the room.

"That preacher's going to eat *all* the chicken!" I bawled.

The preacher tossed back his head and roared with laughter, but my mother was angry and told me that I was to have no dinner because of my bad manners.

When I awakened one morning my mother told me that we were going to see a judge who would make my father support me and my brother. An hour later all three of us were sitting in a huge crowded room. I was overwhelmed by the many faces and the voices which I could not understand. High above me was a white face which my mother told me was the face of the judge. Across the huge room sat my father, smiling confidently, looking at us. My mother warned me not to be fooled by my father's friendly manner; she told me that the judge might ask me questions, and if he did I must tell him the truth. I agreed, yet I hoped that the judge would not ask me anything.

For some reason the entire thing struck me as being useless; I felt that if my father were going to feed me, then he would have done so regardless of what a judge said to him. And I did not want my father to feed me; I was hungry, but my thoughts of food did not now center about him. I waited, growing restless, hungry. My mother gave me a dry sandwich and I munched and stared, longing to go home. Finally I heard my mother's name called; she rose and began weeping so copiously that she could not talk for a few moments; at last she managed to say that her husband had deserted her and two children, that her children were hungry, that they stayed hungry, that she worked, that she was trying to raise them alone. Then my father was called; he came forward jauntily, smiling. He tried to kiss my mother, but she turned away from him. I only heard one sentence of what he said.

"I'm doing all I can, Your Honor," he mumbled, grinning.

It had been painful to sit and watch my mother

Domino Players (detail) by Horace Pippin (1943).
Oil on composition board.

The Phillips Collection, Washington, D.C.

crying and my father laughing and I was glad when we were outside in the sunny streets. Back at home my mother wept again and talked complainingly about the unfairness of the judge who had accepted my father's word. After the court scene, I tried to forget my father; I did not hate him; I simply did not want to think of him. Often when we were hungry my mother would beg me to go to my father's job and ask him for a dollar, a dime, a nickel . . . But I would never consent to go. I did not want to see him.

My mother fell ill and the problem of food became an acute, daily agony. Hunger was with us always. Sometimes the neighbors would feed us or a dollar bill would come in the mail from my grandmother. It was winter and I would buy a dime's worth of coal each morning from the corner coalyard and lug it home in paper bags. For a time I remained out of school to wait upon my mother,

then Granny came to visit us and I returned to school.

At night there were long, halting discussions about our going to live with Granny, but nothing came of it. Perhaps there was not enough money for railroad fare. Angered by having been hauled into court, my father now spurned us completely. I heard long, angrily whispered conversations between my mother and grandmother to the effect that "that woman ought to be killed for breaking up a home." What irked me was the ceaseless talk and no action. If someone had suggested that my father be killed, I would perhaps have become interested; if someone had suggested that his name never be mentioned, I would no doubt have agreed; if someone had suggested that we move to another city, I would have been glad. But there was only endless talk that led nowhere and I began to keep away from home as much as possible, preferring the simplicity of the streets to the worried, futile talk at home.

Finally we could no longer pay the rent for our dingy flat; the few dollars that Granny had left us before she went home were gone. Half sick and in despair, my mother made the rounds of the charitable institutions, seeking help. She found an orphan home that agreed to assume the guidance of me and my brother provided my mother worked and made small payments. My mother hated to be separated from us, but she had no choice.

The orphan home was a two-story frame building set amid trees in a wide, green field. My mother ushered me and my brother one morning into the building and into the presence of a tall, gaunt, mulatto woman who called herself Miss Simon. At once she took a fancy to me and I was frightened speechless; I was afraid of her the moment I saw her and my fear lasted during my entire stay in the home.

The house was crowded with children and there was always a storm of noise. The daily routine was blurred to me and I never quite grasped it. The most abiding feeling I had each day was hunger and fear. The meals were skimpy and there were only two of them. Just before we went to bed each night we were given a slice of bread smeared with molasses. The children were silent, hostile, vindictive, continuously complaining of hunger. There was an overall atmosphere of nervousness and intrigue, of children telling tales upon others, of children being deprived of food to punish them.

The home did not have the money to check the growth of the wide stretches of grass by having it mown, so it had to be pulled by hand. Each morning after we had eaten a breakfast that seemed like no breakfast at all, an older child would lead a herd of us to the vast lawn and we would get on our knees and wrench the grass loose from the dirt with our fingers. At intervals Miss Simon would make a tour of inspection, examining the pile of pulled grass beside each child, scolding or praising according to the size of the pile. Many mornings I was too weak from hunger to pull the grass; I would grow dizzy and my mind would become blank and I would find myself, after an interval of unconsciousness, upon my hands and knees, my head whirling, my eyes staring in bleak astonishment at the green grass, wondering where I was, feeling that I was emerging from a dream . . .

During the first days my mother came each night to visit me and my brother, then her visits stopped. I began to wonder if she, too, like my father, had disappeared into the unknown. I was rapidly learning to distrust everything and everybody. When my mother did come, I asked her why had she remained away so long and she told me that Miss Simon had forbidden her to visit us, that Miss Simon had said that she was spoiling us with too much attention. I begged my mother to take me away; she wept and told me to wait, that soon she would take us to Arkansas. She left and my heart sank.

Miss Simon tried to win my confidence; she asked me if I would like to be adopted by her if my mother consented and I said no. She would take me into her apartment and talk to me, but her words had no effect. Dread and distrust had already become a daily part of my being and my memory grew sharp, my senses more impressionable; I began to be aware of myself as a distinct personality striving against others. I held myself in, afraid to act or speak until I was sure of my surroundings, feeling most of the time that I was suspended over a void. My imagination soared; I dreamed of running away. Each morning I vowed that I would leave the next morning, but the next morning always found me afraid.

One day Miss Simon told me that thereafter I was to help her in the office. I ate lunch with her and, strangely, when I sat facing her at the table, my hunger vanished. The woman killed something in me. Next she called me to her desk where she sat addressing envelopes.

"Step up close to the desk," she said. "Don't be afraid."

I went and stood at her elbow. There was a wart on her chin and I stared at it.

"Now, take a blotter from over there and blot each envelope after I'm through writing on it," she instructed me, pointing to a blotter that stood about a foot from my hand.

I stared and did not move or answer.

"Take the blotter," she said.

I wanted to reach for the blotter and succeeded only in twitching my arm.

"Here," she said sharply, reaching for the blotter and shoving it into my fingers.

She wrote in ink on an envelope and pushed it toward me. Holding the blotter in my hand, I stared at the envelope and could not move.

"Blot it," she said.

I could not lift my hand. I knew what she had said; I knew what she wanted me to do; and I had heard her correctly. I wanted to look at her and say something, tell her why I could not move; but my eyes were fixed upon the floor. I could not summon enough courage while she sat there looking at me to reach over the yawning space of twelve inches and blot the wet ink on the envelope.

"Blot it!" she spoke sharply.

Still I could not move or answer.

"Look at me!"

I could not lift my eyes. She reached her hand to my face and I twisted away.

"What's wrong with you?" she demanded.

I began to cry and she drove me from the room. I decided that as soon as night came I would run away. The dinner bell rang and I did not go to the table, but hid in a corner of the hallway. When I heard the dishes rattling at the table, I opened the door and ran down the walk to the street. Dusk was falling. Doubt made me stop. Ought I go back? No; hunger was back there, and fear. I went on, coming to concrete sidewalks. People passed me. Where was I going? I did not know. The farther I walked the more frantic I became. In a confused and vague way I knew that I was doing more running *away* from than running *toward* something. I stopped. The streets seemed dangerous. The buildings were massive and dark. The moon shone and the trees loomed frighteningly. No, I could not go on. I would go back. But I had walked so far and had turned too many corners and had not kept track of the direction. Which way led back to the orphan home? I did not know. I was lost.

I stood in the middle of the sidewalk and cried. A "white" policeman came to me and I wondered if he was going to beat me. He asked me what was the matter and I told him that I was trying to find my mother. His "white" face created a new fear in me. I was remembering the tale of the "white" man who had beaten the "black" boy. A crowd gathered and I was urged to tell where I lived. Curiously, I was too full of fear to cry now. I wanted to tell the "white" face that I had run off from an orphan home and that Miss Simon ran it, but I was afraid. Finally I was taken to the police station where I was fed. I felt better. I sat in a big chair where I was surrounded by "white" policemen, but they seemed to ignore me. Through the window I could see that night had completely fallen and that lights now gleamed in the streets. I grew sleepy and dozed. My shoulder was shaken gently and I opened my eyes and looked into a "white" face of another policeman who was sitting beside me. He asked me questions in a quiet, confidential tone, and quite before I knew it he was not "white" anymore. I told him that I had run away from an orphan home and that Miss Simon ran it.

It was but a matter of minutes before I was walking alongside a policeman, heading toward the home. The policeman led me to the front gate and I saw Miss Simon waiting for me on the steps. She identified me and I was left in her charge. I begged her not to beat me, but she yanked me upstairs into an empty room and lashed me thoroughly. Sobbing, I slunk off to bed, resolved to run away again. But I was watched closely after that.

My mother was informed upon her next visit that I had tried to run away and she was terribly upset.

"Why did you do it?" she asked.

"I don't want to stay here," I told her.

"But you must," she said. "How can I work if I'm to worry about you? You must remember that you have no father. I'm doing all I can."

"I don't want to stay here," I repeated.

"Then, if I take you to your father . . ."

"I don't want to stay with him either," I said.

"But I want you to ask him for enough money for us to go to my sister's in Arkansas," she said.

Again I was faced with choices I did not like, but I finally agreed. After all, my hate for my father was not so great and urgent as my hate for the orphan home. My mother held to her idea and one night a week or so later I found myself standing in a room in a frame house. My father and a strange woman were sitting before a bright fire that blazed in a grate. My mother and I were standing about six feet away, as though we were afraid to approach them any closer.

"It's not for me," my mother was saying. "It's for your children that I'm asking you for money."

"I ain't got nothing," my father said, laughing.

"Come here, boy," the strange woman called to me.

I looked at her and did not move.

"Give him a nickel," the woman said. "He's cute."

"Come here, Richard," my father said, stretching out his hand.

I backed away, shaking my head, keeping my eyes on the fire.

"He is a cute child," the strange woman said.

"You ought to be ashamed," my mother said to the strange woman. "You're starving my children."

"Now, don't you-all fight," my father said, laughing.

"I'll take that poker and hit you!" I blurted at my father.

He looked at my mother and laughed louder.

"You told him to say that," he said.

"Don't say such things, Richard," my mother said.

"You ought to be dead," I said to the strange woman.

The woman laughed and threw her arms about my father's neck. I grew ashamed and wanted to leave.

"How can you starve your children?" my mother asked.

"Let Richard stay with me," my father said.

"Do you want to stay with your father, Richard?" my mother asked.

"No," I said.

"You'll get plenty to eat," he said.

"I'm hungry now," I told him. "But I won't stay with you."

"Aw, give the boy a nickel," the woman said.

My father ran his hand into his pocket and pulled out a nickel.

"Here, Richard," he said.

"Don't take it," my mother said.

"Don't teach him to be a fool," my father said. "Here, Richard, take it."

I looked at my mother, at the strange woman, at my father, then into the fire. I wanted to take the nickel, but I did not want to take it from my father.

"You ought to be ashamed," my mother said, weeping. "Giving your son a nickel when he's hungry. If there's a God, He'll pay you back."

"That's all I got," my father said, laughing again and returning the nickel to his pocket.

We left. I had the feeling that I had had to do with something unclean. Many times in the years after that the image of my father and the strange woman, their faces lit by the dancing flames, would surge up in my imagination so vivid and strong that I felt I could reach out and touch it; I would stare at it, feeling that it possessed some vital meaning which always eluded me.

A quarter of a century was to elapse between the time when I saw my father sitting with the strange woman and the time when I was to see him again, standing alone upon the red clay of a Mississippi plantation, a sharecropper, clad in ragged overalls, holding a muddy hoe in his gnarled, veined hands—a quarter of a century during which my mind and consciousness had become so greatly and violently altered that when I tried to talk to him I realized that, though ties of blood made us kin, though I could see a shadow of my face in his face, though there was an echo of my voice in his voice, we were forever strangers, speaking a different language, living on vastly distant planes of reality. That day a quarter of a century later when I visited him on the plantation—he was standing against the sky, smiling toothlessly, his hair whitened, his body bent, his eyes glazed with dim recollection, his fearsome aspect of twenty-five years ago gone forever from him—I was overwhelmed to realize that he could never understand me or the scalding experiences that had swept me beyond his life and into an area of living that he could never know. I stood before him, poised, my mind aching as it embraced the simple nakedness of his life, feeling how completely his soul was imprisoned by the slow flow of the seasons, by wind and rain and sun, how fastened were his memories to a crude and raw past, how chained were his actions and emotions to the direct, animalistic impulses of his withering body . .

From the white landowners above him there had not been handed to him a chance to learn the meaning of loyalty, of sentiment, of tradition. Joy was as unknown to him as was despair. As a creature of the earth, he endured, hearty, whole, seemingly indestructible, with no regrets and no hope. He asked easy, drawing questions about me, his other son, his wife, and he laughed, amused, when I informed him of their destinies. I forgave him and pitied him as my eyes looked past him to the unpainted wooden shack. From far beyond the horizons that bound this bleak plantation there had come to me through my living the knowledge that my father was a black peasant who had gone to the city seeking life, but who had failed in the city; a black peasant whose life had been hopelessly snarled in the city, and who had at last fled the city—that same city which had lifted me in its burning arms and borne me toward alien and undreamed-of shores of knowing.

Responding to the Autobiography

Analyzing the Autobiography
Identifying Facts

1. In most of this excerpt, Wright works in swift strokes to draw sharp **images** or pictures of his life. One such picture, for example, shows the boy and his mother confronting his father in court. Another shows the boy standing by Miss Simon's desk in the orphanage. What other important pictures are created in these extracts from the autobiography?
2. What details does Wright use to make the reader feel the hunger he experienced as a boy?
3. Why did Richard associate his father with his pangs of hunger?
4. How did Richard win the right to the streets of Memphis?
5. Wright speaks of how "the personality of my father first came fully into the orbit of my concern" (page 1011). What *is* that personality? How does his father behave in the courtroom scene and in the later confrontation with Richard, his mother, and the strange woman?
6. What does Wright realize about his father in the last passage? How was the city's effect on his father different from its effect on Wright himself?

Interpreting Meanings

7. When his mother gives Richard a heavy stick and sends him back to confront the street bullies, what lesson is she trying to teach him? Do you think she was right? Was there anything else she could have done instead?
8. Why can't Richard eat his soup when the preacher is devouring the fried chicken? What does this detail reveal about the boy's **character**?
9. What sad events finally forced Richard's mother to send her sons to an orphanage? If Wright had been living in a contemporary city, what might have happened to him and his family?
10. One of the most painful **images** in this excerpt is the one of the young boy pulling grass at the orphanage. Wright makes no direct comment on this scene, except to describe his physical sensations. What might he have said? Do you wish he had said it, or do you think it wasn't necessary? What feelings does this scene evoke in you?
11. Remembering his father and the strange woman, "their faces lit by the dancing flames," Wright says that he felt that in later life this scene "possessed some vital meaning which always eluded me." What do you think he means?

Writing About the Autobiography
A Creative Response

1. **Experimenting with Point of View.** Write a monologue from Richard's mother's point of view, in which she tells her feelings and memories about the time she sent Richard back to the streets with a stick. Or, write a series of paragraphs in which all the different characters "remember" Richard Wright from their own perspective: Miss Simon, the policeman, the judge, the strange woman, the father, the mother.

A Critical Response

2. **Comparing and Contrasting Two Writers.** In a short essay, compare the **style** and the **themes** of Wright's story with those in Mark Twain's *The Adventures of Huckleberry Finn* (page 414) or in Susan Toth's *Ivy Days* (page 1040). In your comments on style, consider sentence structure, dialogue, the use of detail, and tone of voice. How did each piece of writing affect you?

Analyzing Language and Style
Dialogue

We often think of **dialogue**, or the directly quoted words of conversation between two or more people, as the property of drama or fiction. But dialogue can also play a significant role in nonfiction. In this excerpt from Wright's autobiography, for example, almost every scene is dramatized through dialogue.

Wright might easily have chosen a different approach. For instance, instead of quoting the conversation between himself and his mother in the first scene, he might have simply described his eagerness to see the *Kate Adams*, his speculations about the boat's size, its whistle, and its name. But by recalling and presenting his conversation with his mother, Wright *shows*, rather than describes, his feelings. At the same time, he creates a vivid and touching character portrait of his mother.

Select one scene from this excerpt that includes dialogue, and examine the conversation carefully. Then write a paragraph in which you describe what the situation would be like *without* the use of dialogue. Answer these questions in your paragraphs.

1. What specific contributions do you think the dialogue makes to the scene's total effect and to Wright's characterizations?
2. Would the scene have been as effective if the dialogue had been omitted?

N. Scott Momaday
(1934–   )

Among the voices of the American past, one of the most poignant and powerful to make itself heard at last has been that of the Native American, or the American Indian. In the past, the American Indian appeared in literature and the other arts in the baldest of stereotypes, either as a noble, primitive warrior or as a fearsome, ignorant savage. One has only to look at Western movies from the 1940's or 1950's to see how blatant these stereotypes were. Even in American history, textbooks seldom questioned the popular view that the white settlers' gradual "winning of the West" was a virtuous struggle against the unwarranted resistance of the Indians. Few Americans gave much thought either to the moral basis on which the United States expanded, or to the history of Native Americans.

When the civil rights movement of the late 1950's brought the plight of American blacks to the public, other minority groups began to demand their fair share of attention, too. Native Americans spoke loudly and clearly of loss, injustice, and prejudice. Among many books telling their story have been popular historian Dee Brown's *Bury My Heart at Wounded Knee* (1970), Vine Deloria's novel *Custer Died for Your Sins* (1969), Lynn Andrews's novel *Medicine Woman* (1983), Louise Erdrich's novel *Love Medicine* (1984), and the works of N. Scott Momaday.

Momaday was born in Lawton, Oklahoma, of Kiowa ancestry on his father's side, and part Cherokee on his mother's. After receiving a B.A. degree from New Mexico State University, Momaday studied creative writing at Stanford University, where he received his Ph.D. in 1963. He taught at the University of California at Santa Barbara for several years, then at Berkeley and at New Mexico State.

But Momaday broke loose from the standard academic mold with two works grounded in his knowledge of American Indian life: a Pulitzer-Prize-winning novel, *House Made of Dawn* (1968), and two memoirs, *The Way to Rainy Mountain* (1969) and *The Names* (1976). *The Way to Rainy Mountain* is part legend, part history, and part poetry, with an unusual artistic addition of striking illustrations by Momaday's father. Following the introduction, Momaday describes the Kiowas' history in a form that is associative and imagistic; it works on the reader's imagination in subtle ways that do not depend on a straightforward narrative. On one page, he sets down a Kiowa legend; on the facing page, he places a short excerpt from a traditional history and then a personal memory of his own. The inner truth blends with the outer; emotion mixes with fact.

The Kiowas' journey to Rainy Mountain begins in the hidden mists of time, when a tribe of unknown origin descends from the headwaters of the Yellowstone River eastward to the Black Hills (now in South Dakota) and south to the Wichita Mountains. It ends in a cemetery where many of Momaday's Kiowa kinfolk are buried. Momaday says that "the journey is an evocation of three things in particular: a landscape that is incomparable, a time that is gone forever, and the human spirit, which endures."

The incomparable landscape is the Great Plains, wind-swept and lonely, in turn brilliant with summer sun and buried in winter snows. Momaday's love of the land where he grew up suffuses everything he writes. He reminds us of both the spiritual richness and the rigors of living close to the land, under a wide, open sky, in harmony with the changing seasons. In his work, Momaday has looked at his own particular landscape from so many angles that his pictures often shimmer like a prism.

FROM THE WAY TO RAINY MOUNTAIN

An American Portrait by Fritz Scholder (1979). Oil.

The Anschutz Collection.

AUTOBIOGRAPHICAL NOTES

Baldwin begins this essay with a factual account of his youth, adolescence, and young manhood. But he soon lives up to his statement that "part of **the business of the writer is to examine attitudes," by probing his own outlook more deeply. The essay was published in 1955.**

I was born in Harlem thirty-one years ago. I began plotting novels at about the time I learned to read. The story of my childhood is the usual bleak fantasy, and we can dismiss it with the restrained observation that I certainly would not consider living it again. In those days my mother was given to the exasperating and mysterious habit of having babies. As they were born, I took them over with one hand and held a book with the other. The children probably suffered, though they have since been kind enough to deny it, and in this way I read *Uncle Tom's Cabin* and *A Tale of Two Cities* over and over and over again; in this way, in fact, I read just about everything I could get my hands on—except the Bible, probably because it was the only book I was encouraged to read. I must also confess that I wrote—a great deal—and my first professional triumph, in any case, the first effort of mine to be seen in print, occurred at the age of twelve or thereabouts, when a short story I had written about the Spanish revolution won some sort of prize in an extremely short-lived church newspaper. I remember the story was censored by the lady editor, though I don't remember why, and I was outraged.

Also wrote plays, and songs, for one of which I received a letter of congratulations from Mayor La Guardia,[1] and poetry, about which the less said, the better. My mother was delighted by all these goings-on, but my father wasn't; he wanted me to be a preacher. When I was fourteen I became a preacher, and when I was seventeen I stopped. Very shortly thereafter I left home. For God knows how long I struggled with the world of commerce and industry—I guess they would

say they struggled with *me*—and when I was about twenty-one I had enough done of a novel to get a Saxton Fellowship. When I was twenty-two the fellowship was over, the novel turned out to be unsalable, and I started waiting on tables in a Village[2] restaurant and writing book reviews—mostly, as it turned out, about the Negro problem, concerning which the color of my skin made me automatically an expert. Did another book, in company with photographer Theodore Pelatowski, about the storefront churches in Harlem. This book met exactly the same fate as my first—fellowship, but no sale (It was a Rosenwald Fellowship.) By the time I was twenty-four I had decided to stop reviewing books about the Negro problem—which, by this time, was only slightly less horrible in print than it was in life—and I packed my bags and went to France, where I finished, God knows how, *Go Tell It on the Mountain*.

Any writer, I suppose, feels that the world into which he was born is nothing less than a conspiracy against the cultivation of his talent—which attitude certainly has a great deal to support it. On the other hand, it is only because the world looks on his talent with such a frightening indifference that the artist is compelled to make his talent important. So that any writer, looking back over even so short a span of time as I am here forced to assess, finds that the things which hurt him and the things which helped him cannot be divorced from each other; he could be helped in a certain way only because he was hurt in a certain way; and his help is simply to be enabled to move from one conundrum[3] to the next—one is tempted

---

1. **Mayor La Guardia:** Fiorello La Guardia (1882–1947), mayor of New York City, 1934–1945.

2. **Village:** Greenwich Village, a district of Manhattan.
3. **conundrum** (kə·nun′drəm): riddle; puzzling problem.

to say that he moves from one disaster to the next. When one begins looking for influences one finds them by the score. I haven't thought much about my own, not enough anyway; I hazard that the King James Bible, the rhetoric of the storefront church, something ironic and violent and perpetually understated in Negro speech—and something of Dickens' love for bravura[4]—have something to do with me today; but I wouldn't stake my life on it. Likewise, innumerable people have helped me in many ways; but finally, I suppose, the most difficult (and most rewarding) thing in my life has been the fact that I was born a Negro and was forced, therefore, to effect some kind of truce with this reality. (Truce, by the way, is the best one can hope for.)

One of the difficulties about being a Negro writer (and this is not special pleading, since I don't mean to suggest that he has it worse than anybody else) is that the Negro problem is written about so widely. The bookshelves groan under the weight of information, and everyone therefore considers himself informed. And this information, furthermore, operates usually (generally, popularly) to reinforce traditional attitudes. Of traditional attitudes there are only two—For or Against—and I, personally, find it difficult to say which attitude has caused me the most pain. I am speaking as a writer; from a social point of view I am perfectly aware that the change from ill will to good will, however motivated, however imperfect, however expressed, is better than no change at all.

But it is part of the business of the writer—as I see it—to examine attitudes, to go beneath the surface, to tap the source. From this point of view the Negro problem is nearly inaccessible. It is not only written about so widely; it is written about so badly. It is quite possible to say that the price a Negro pays for becoming articulate is to find himself, at length, with nothing to be articulate about. ("You taught me language," says Caliban to Prospero, "and my profit on't is I know how to curse.")[5] Consider: The tremendous social activity that this problem generates imposes on whites and Negroes alike the necessity of looking forward, of working to bring about a better day.

This is fine, it keeps the waters troubled; it is all, indeed, that has made possible the Negro's progress. Nevertheless, social affairs are not generally speaking the writer's prime concern, whether they ought to be or not; it is absolutely necessary that he establish between himself and these affairs a distance which will allow, at least, for clarity, so that before he can look forward in any meaningful sense, he must first be allowed to take a long look back. In the context of the Negro problem neither whites nor blacks, for excellent reasons of their own, have the faintest desire to look back; but I think that the past is all that makes the present coherent, and further, that the past will remain horrible for exactly as long as we refuse to assess it honestly.

I know, in any case, that the most crucial time in my own development came when I was forced to recognize that I was a kind of bastard of the West; when I followed the line of my past I did not find myself in Europe but in Africa. And this meant that in some subtle way, in a really profound way, I brought to Shakespeare, Bach, Rembrandt, to the stones of Paris, to the cathedral at Chartres, and to the Empire State Building, a special attitude. These were not really my creations, they did not contain my history; I might search in them in vain forever for any reflection of myself. I was an interloper; this was not my heritage. At the same time I had no other heritage which I could possibly hope to use—I had certainly been unfitted for the jungle or the tribe. I would have to appropriate these white centuries, I would have to make them mine—I would have to accept my special attitude, my special place in this scheme—otherwise I would have no place in *any* scheme. What was the most difficult was the fact that I was forced to admit something I had always hidden from myself, which the American Negro has had to hide from himself as the price of his public progress; that I hated and feared white people. This did not mean that I loved black people; on the contrary, I despised them, possibly because they failed to produce Rembrandt. In effect, I hated and feared the world. And this meant, not only that I thus gave the world an altogether murderous power over me, but also that in such a self-destroying limbo I could never hope to write.

One writes out of one thing only—one's own experience. Everything depends on how relentlessly one forces from this experience the last drop, sweet or bitter, it can possibly give. This is

---

4. **bravura** (brə·voor′ə): daring; a dashing display.
5. Caliban is a rough creature of nature whom Prospero tries to civilize. See *The Tempest* by William Shakespeare, Act I, Scene 2, line 363.

Labor Day parade. Photograph taken by Eve Arnold, 1983.

ing to the wire mesh. Now I ran across the boys' yard clear to the Cyclone fence and thought about the hair that I had seen sticking out of the canvas. It was going to be summer soon, so you could feel that freedom coming on too.

I ran back into the girls' yard, and there was the quiet sister all by herself. I ran past her, and she followed me into the girls' lavatory. My footsteps rang hard against cement and tile because of the taps I had nailed into my shoes. Her footsteps were soft, padding after me. There was no one in the lavatory but the two of us. I ran all around the rows of twenty-five open stalls to make sure of that. No sisters. I think we must have been playing hide-and-go-seek. She was not good at hiding by herself and usually followed her sister; they'd hide in the same place. They must have gotten separated. In this growing twilight, a child could hide and never be found.

I stopped abruptly in front of the sinks, and she came running toward me before she could stop herself, so that she almost collided with me. I walked closer. She backed away, puzzlement, then alarm in her eyes.

"You're going to talk," I said, my voice steady and normal, as it is when talking to the familiar, the weak, and the small. "I am going to make you talk, you sissy-girl." She stopped backing away and stood fixed.

I looked into her face so I could hate it close up. She wore black bangs, and her cheeks were pink and white. She was baby-soft. I thought that I could put my thumb on her nose and push it bonelessly in, indent her face. I could poke dimples into her cheeks. I could work her face around like dough. She stood still, and I did not want to look at her face anymore; I hated fragility. I walked around her, looked her up and down the way the Mexican and Negro girls did when they fought, so tough. I hated her weak neck, the way it did not support her head but let it droop; her head would fall backward. I stared at the curve of her nape. I wished I was able to see what my own neck looked like from the back and sides. I hoped it did not look like hers; I wanted a stout neck. I grew my hair long to hide it in case it was a flower-stem neck. I walked around to the front of her to hate her face some more.

I reached up and took the fatty part of her cheek, not dough, but meat, between my thumb and finger. This close, and I saw no pores. "Talk," I said. "Are you going to talk?" Her skin was fleshy, like squid out of which the glassy blades of bones had been pulled. I wanted tough skin, hard brown skin. I had callused my hands; I had scratched dirt to blacken the nails, which I cut straight across to make stubby fingers. I gave her face a squeeze. "Talk." When I let go, the pink rushed back into my white thumbprint on her skin. I walked around to her side. "Talk!" I shouted into the side of her head. Her straight hair hung, the same all these years, no ringlets or braids or permanents. I squeezed her other cheek. "Are you? Huh? Are you going to talk?" She tried to shake her head, but I had hold of her face. She had no muscles to jerk away. Her skin seemed to stretch. I let go in horror. What if it came away in my hand? "No, huh?" I said, rubbing the touch of her off my fingers. "Say 'No,' then," I said. I gave her another pinch and a twist. "Say 'No.' " She shook her head, her straight hair turning with her head, not swinging side to side like the pretty girls'. She was so neat. Her neatness bothered me. I hated the way she folded the wax paper from her lunch; she did not wad her brown paper bag and her school papers. I hated her clothes—the blue pastel cardigan, the white blouse with the collar that lay flat over the cardigan, the home-made flat, cotton skirt she wore when everybody else was wearing flared skirts. I hated pastels; I would wear black always. I squeezed again, harder, even though her cheek had a weak rubbery feeling I did not like. I squeezed one cheek, then the other, back and forth until the tears ran out of her eyes as if I had pulled them out. "Stop crying," I said, but although she habitually followed me around, she did not obey. Her eyes dripped; her nose dripped. She wiped her eyes with her papery fingers. The skin on her hands and arms seemed powdery-dry, like tracing paper, onion paper. I hated her fingers. I could snap them like breadsticks. I pushed her hands down. "Say 'Hi,' " I said. " 'Hi'. Like that. Say your name. Go ahead. Say it. Or are you stupid? You're so stupid, you don't know your own name, is that it? When I say, 'What's your name?' you just blurt it out, O.K.? What's your name?" Last year the whole class had laughed at a boy who couldn't fill out a form because he didn't know his father's name. The teacher sighed, exasperated and was very sarcastic, "Don't you notice things? What does your mother call him?" she said. The class laughed at how dumb he was not to notice things. "She calls him father of me," he said. Even we laughed although we knew that his mother did not call his father by name, and a son does not know his father's name. We laughed and were relieved that our parents had had the foresight to tell us some names we could give the teachers. "If you're not stupid," I said to the quiet girl, "what's your name?" She shook her head, and some hair caught in the tears; wet black hair stuck to the side of the pink and white face. I reached up (she was taller than I) and took a strand of hair. I pulled it. "Well, then, let's honk your hair," I said. "Honk. Honk." Then I pulled the other side—"ho-o-n-k"—a long pull; "ho-o-n-n-nk"—a longer pull. I could see her little white ears, like white cutworms curled underneath the hair. "Talk!" I yelled into each cutworm.

I looked right at her. "I know you talk," I said. "I've heard you." Her eyebrows flew up. Something in those black eyes was startled, and I pursued it. "I was walking past your house when you didn't know I was there. I heard you yell in English and in Chinese. You weren't just talking. You were shouting. I heard you shout. You were saying, 'Where are you?' Say that again. Go ahead, just the way you did at home." I yanked harder on the hair, but steadily, not jerking. I did not want to pull it out. "Go ahead. Say, 'Where are you?' Say it loud enough for your sister to come. Call her. Make her come help you. Call her name. I'll stop if she comes. So call. Go ahead."

She shook her head, her mouth curved down, crying. I could see her tiny white teeth, baby teeth. I wanted to grow big strong yellow teeth. "You do have a tongue," I said. "So use it." I pulled the hair at her temples, pulled the tears out of her eyes. "Say, 'Ow' " I said. "Just 'Ow.' Say, 'Let go.' Go ahead. Say it. I'll honk you again if you don't say, 'Let me alone.' Say, 'Leave me alone,' and I'll let you go. I will. I'll let go if you say it. You can stop this anytime you want to, you know. All you have to do is tell me to stop. Just say, 'Stop.' You're just asking for it, aren't you? You're just asking for another honk. Well then, I'll have to give you another honk. Say, 'Stop.' " But she didn't. I had to pull again and again.

Sounds did come out of her mouth, sobs, chokes, noises that were almost words. Snot ran out of her nose. She tried to wipe it on her hands, but there was too much of it. She used her sleeve. "You're disgusting," I told her. "Look at you, snot streaming down your nose, and you won't say a word to stop it. You're such a nothing." I

moved behind her and pulled the hair growing out of her weak neck. I let go. I stood silent for a long time. Then I screamed, "Talk!" I would scare the words out of her. If she had had little bound feet, the toes twisted under the balls, I would have jumped up and landed on them—crunch!—stomped on them with my iron shoes. She cried hard, sobbing aloud. "Cry, 'Mama,' " I said. "Come on. Cry, 'Mama.' Say, 'Stop it.' "

I put my finger on her pointed chin. "I don't like you. I don't like the weak little toots you make on your flute. Wheeze. Wheeze. I don't like the way you don't swing at the ball. I don't like the way you're the last one chosen. I don't like the way you can't make a fist for tetherball. Why don't you make a fist? Come on. Get tough. Come on. Throw fists." I pushed at her long hands; they swung limply at her sides. Her fingers were so long, I thought maybe they had an extra joint. They couldn't possibly make fists like other people's. "Make a fist," I said. "Come on. Just fold those fingers up; fingers on the inside, thumbs on the outside. Say something. Honk me back. You're so tall, and you let me pick on you.

"Would you like a hanky? I can't get you one with embroidery on it or crocheting along the edges, but I'll get you some toilet paper if you tell me to. Go ahead. Ask me. I'll get it for you if you ask." She did not stop crying. "Why don't you scream, 'Help'?" I suggested. "Say, 'Help.' Go ahead." She cried on. "O.K. O.K. Don't talk. Just scream, and I'll let you go. Won't that feel good? Go ahead. Like this." I screamed not too loudly. My voice hit the tile and rang it as if I had thrown a rock at it. The stalls opened wider and the toilets wider and darker. Shadows leaned at angles I had not seen before. I was very late. Maybe a janitor had locked me in with this girl for the night. Her black eyes blinked and stared, blinked and stared. I felt dizzy from hunger. We had been in this lavatory together forever. My mother would call the police again if I didn't bring my sister home soon. "I'll let you go if you say just one word," I said. "You can even say 'a' or 'the,' and I'll let you go. Come on. Please." She didn't shake her head anymore, only cried steadily, so much water coming out of her. I could see the two duct holes where the tears welled out. Quarts of tears but no words. I grabbed her by the shoulder. I could feel bones. The light was coming in queerly through the frosted glass with the chicken wire embedded in it. Her crying was like an animal's—a seal's—

and it echoed around the basement. "Do you want to stay here all night?" I asked. "Your mother is wondering what happened to her baby. You wouldn't want to have her mad at you. You'd better say something." I shook her shoulder. I pulled her hair again. I squeezed her face. "Come on! Talk! Talk! Talk!" She didn't seem to feel it anymore when I pulled her hair. "There's nobody here but you and me. This isn't a classroom or a playground or a crowd. I'm just one person. You can talk in front of one person. Don't make me pull harder and harder until you talk." But her hair seemed to stretch; she did not say a word. "I'm going to pull harder. Don't make me pull anymore, or your hair will come out and you're going to be bald. Do you want to be bald? You don't want to be bald, do you?"

Far away, coming from the edge of town, I heard whistles blow. The cannery was changing shifts, letting out the afternoon people, and still we were here at school. It was a sad sound—work done. The air was lonelier after the sound died.

"Why won't you talk?" I started to cry. What if I couldn't stop, and everyone would want to know what happened? "Now look what you've done," I scolded. "You're going to pay for this. I want to know why. And you're going to tell me why. You don't see I'm trying to help you out, do you? Do you want to be like this, dumb (do you know what dumb means?), your whole life? Don't you ever want to be a cheerleader? Or a pompon girl? What are you going to do for a living? Yeah, you're going to have to work because you can't be a housewife. Somebody has to marry you before you can be a housewife. And you, you are a plant. Do you know that? That's all you are if you don't talk. If you don't talk, you can't have a personality. You'll have no personality and no hair. You've got to let people know you have a personality and a brain. You think somebody is going to take care of you all your stupid life? You think you'll always have your big sister? You think somebody's going to marry you, is that it? Well, you're not the type that gets dates, let alone gets married. Nobody's going to notice you. And you have to talk for interviews, speak right up in front of the boss. Don't you know that? You're so dumb. Why do I waste my time on you?" Sniffling and snorting. I couldn't stop crying and talking at the same time. I kept wiping my nose on my arm, my sweater lost somewhere (probably not worn because my mother said to wear a sweater). It

seemed as if I had spent my life in that basement, doing the worst thing I had yet done to another person. "I'm doing this for your own good," I said. "Don't you dare tell anyone I've been bad to you. Talk. Please talk."

I was getting dizzy from the air I was gulping. Her sobs and my sobs were bouncing wildly off the tile, sometimes together, sometimes alternating. "I don't understand why you won't say just one word," I cried, clenching my teeth. My knees were shaking, and I hung on to her hair to stand up. Another time I'd stayed too late, I had had to walk around two Negro kids who were bonking each other's head on the concrete. I went back later to see if the concrete had cracks in it. "Look. I'll give you something if you talk. I'll give you my pencil box. I'll buy you some candy. O.K.? What do you want? Tell me. Just say it, and I'll give it to you. Just say, 'yes,' or, 'O.K.,' or, 'Baby Ruth.' " But she didn't want anything.

I had stopped pinching her cheek because I did not like the feel of her skin. I would go crazy if it came away in my hands. "I skinned her," I would have to confess.

Suddenly I heard footsteps hurrying through the basement, and her sister ran into the lavatory calling her name. "Oh, there you are," I said. "We've been waiting for you. I was only trying to teach her to talk. She wouldn't cooperate, though." Her sister went into one of the stalls and got handfuls of toilet paper and wiped her off. Then we found my sister, and we walked home together. "Your family really ought to force her to speak," I advised all the way home. "You mustn't pamper her."

The world is sometimes just, and I spent the next eighteen months sick in bed with a mysterious illness. There was no pain and no symptoms, though the middle line in my left palm broke in two. Instead of starting junior high school, I lived like the Victorian recluses I read about. I had a rented hospital bed in the living room, where I watched soap operas on TV, and my family cranked me up and down. I saw no one but my family, who took good care of me. I could have no visitors, no other relatives, no villagers. My bed was against the west window, and I watched the seasons change the peach tree. I had a bell to ring for help. I used a bedpan. It was the best year and a half of my life. Nothing happened.

But one day my mother, the doctor, said, "You're ready to get up today. It's time to get up

Mademoiselle would have approved. Although dates appeared on Fridays through Sundays, popping up on lawns, porches, and living room carpets like rare and short-lived jack-in-the-pulpits, those of us left on campus pretended not to notice. "Studying this weekend," we determinedly remained as we were, wrinkled and defiantly grundgy in our everyday skirts and stained cardigans.

Although in my four years at Smith, I never really felt I had the right wardrobe—or was sure I could successfully wear it if I did—I was eventually able to achieve the rumpled, dirty look that I thought was my only alternative to Green Street. Late in my junior year, I found a trench coat on sale in downtown Northampton. Although it was not just like everyone else's in style and color—too creamy white, no epaulets—it was my first trench coat, and I loved it. Soon it acquired a patina of smudges, smears, and studied neglect. With it I wore my "tennies,"[4] also gradually soiled to a satisfactory gray.

---

4. **"tennies"**: slang for tennis sneakers.

On the sunny spring morning of my senior year when I knew I might receive an award at honors chapel—I had read about one for which I was a logical candidate—I deliberately dressed in jeans, sweatshirt, gray tennies, and my battered trench coat. Hands jammed casually in my pockets, belt looped around my waist, collar turned up, I strode happily up the stage stairs to accept the certificate for the Victoria Louise Schrager Prize from the outstretched hand of President Mendenhall. It was for a senior who had made an outstanding contribution in academics and extracurricular activities, and it meant to me that at last I had made it. Yet I was almost as proud of how I looked: not beautiful, not striking, but absolutely authentic. I remember wiggling my bare toes in my threadbare sneakers, secure in the knowledge that my stark ankles (though rubbed rawish red at the back) looked much more sophisticated than if I'd worn socks. For a brief while at Smith we had a word, plain but oddly transformed, that meant "with it," "cool," or "neat." That low-keyed and powerful word was "shoe." For those moments on the stage, I felt "shoe." Finally I was dressed right.

Responding to the Memoir

Analyzing the Memoir

Identifying Details

1. Before she came to Massachusetts, where had Sue Allen gotten her ideas about the East?
2. What did she think was the "Eastern look"?
3. The writer says she finally achieved a "dirty, rumpled look" that she felt was her only alternative to "Green Street." What details describe these two alternatives?

Interpreting Meanings

4. Why does this section (the first chapter in the book) begin with a description of Posture Pictures? What is the emotional effect of the opening paragraph?
5. Although the writer talks about clothes, she is trying to convey some of her feelings about her first days at college. What were these feelings? Do you think they are fairly universal?
6. Why was it so important to Sue Allen that she look like the "Eastern girls"? What does this reveal about her **character** at this stage of her life?
7. Groups have different ways of identifying who belongs, who is "in" and who is "out." What are some of the different groups you see in your school, and how are they identified?
8. This passage also talks about **stereotypes**—fixed ideas about people and events that allow for no individuality. Stereotypes are often based on racial or religious prejudice. What are these stereotypes? What pictures do you have about areas of the United States you have never seen—the East, West, North, or South? For example, what do you see in your mind's eye when someone talks about Nashville? New York? San Francisco? New Orleans? Gary, Indiana? Where do you think such stereotypes come from?
9. Do you think the memoir is about something important, or do you think clothing is essentially a trivial subject? (Is clothing the real topic of the memoir?)

Writing About the Memoir

A Creative Response

1. **Imitating Toth's Technique.** Belonging, or not belonging, is a painful subject. But much good writing comes from examining pain. (Philip Roth, a celebrated American novelist, once said, "We writers are lucky: Nothing truly bad can happen to us. It's all material.") If you can stand it, write a description of a time when you desperately wanted to belong to something—and couldn't.

2. **Changing the Point of View.** Select an incident from this memoir and rewrite it from another point of view. How might the **tone** of the account change as the interpretation of events changes?

A Critical Response

3. **Developing a Statement.** "Clothes were a language I understood." Write a short essay explaining what this sentence means and whether you think most people would agree with it.

4. **Evaluating Objectivity.** In the extract from an article that follows (under "Primary Sources"), Susan Toth talks about the accuracy of memory. In a brief essay, evaluate her memoir in terms of its objectivity. Do you think the writer has been honest? Do you think she has reported facts in an unbiased way? Do you think that someone else reporting on some of these same events might view them differently?

Primary Sources
"The Importance of Being Remembered"

Several years after the publication of her two memoirs, Susan Allen Toth wrote an article about the responses she had received to her books.

"The importance of feeling remembered—of having one's everyday life, pleasures and sorrows set down in the semipermanence of print—came home poignantly at another book-signing gathering. My former high school drama coach, whom I had respected and loved, appeared with an urgent question. I had written in *Blooming* about the death of his small daughter and its effect on me 23 years before. I had changed names and a few identifying facts, as I did with anyone easily recognizable. Although her real name was Susie—like mine, so I had never forgotten it—I had called her Mary. After grasping my hand and congratulating me on my book, he paused. Looking intently into my eyes, his face strained and shadowed by that old and terrible loss, he said, 'I have to know one thing. You called her Mary in the book. Did you remember her real name?' I assured him I had, and his face eased.

"Not all my audience was convinced that I *did* remember my facts correctly. 'Weren't you making up the Mystery Farm of the Week?' more than one person at public readings asked suspiciously, referring to a popular newspaper feature I'd mentioned. Some who had grown up in small towns, with the confidence of those who have detasseled corn or cheered at a high school basketball tournament, rose indignantly to my defense on this and other matters. Young people—meaning those under 40—often could not believe the innocence I claimed for those of us

who grew up in the 1950's in that Iowa town or a little later in Northampton, Massachusetts. 'Could *anyone* have been that naïve?' they asked. I could only attest that I had told the truth as scrupulously as I could."

—Susan Allen Toth

John Hersey
(1914–   )

John Hersey was born in China, where he lived until he was eleven. He graduated from Yale and studied at Cambridge University in England, served as private secretary to the novelist Sinclair Lewis, and reported from the South Pacific and the Mediterranean during World War II for *Time* and *Life* magazines.

But "journalism" (if that means objective factual reporting) could not contain Hersey's passionate concern about contemporary events. In 1945 he won the Pulitzer Prize for his novel *A Bell for Adano*, based on what he had seen of American military government in Italy. Some critics saw this novel as a troubling examination of democracy, its ideals, and the difficulties of putting it into practice. A year later, Hersey followed this success with *Hiroshima*. Combining the techniques of a novel and the factual air of journalism to describe a real event, *Hiroshima* began what some critics call the genre of the "nonfiction novel." Hersey took an almost incomprehensible fact, the dropping of an atomic bomb on a civilian population, and showed how it affected the lives of six survivors. Through their eyes, Americans could experience this catastrophe as if it were happening to them and to their friends and neighbors. Through Hersey's vivid narrative and his gift for characterization, the unimaginable became horrifyingly real.

Hiroshima became a national event, a precursor of the kind of "celebrity" status best-sellers often enjoy today, with attention paid to the authors on talk shows and in interviews in magazines and newspapers. *Hiroshima* first appeared in *The New Yorker*, which devoted its entire issue to the book—a startling commitment for a magazine. Critic Sam Girgus reported that Albert Einstein ordered one thousand copies of it, the American Broadcasting Company had the book read aloud on its radio stations, and the Book-of-the-Month Club distributed free copies, on the grounds that nothing else in print "could be of more importance at this moment to the human race." *Hiroshima* has been called the most significant piece of reportage of modern times.

After *Hiroshima*, Hersey became famous as a writer who could make history understandable. He continued to dramatize issues and events, dealing with the Holocaust, racism, fascism, narrow utilitarian education, and other evils of modern life. He called his type of fiction "the novel of contemporary history" and wrote that "this kind of novel should make anyone who reads it better able to meet life in his generation—whenever that generation may be." He has produced books at markedly steady intervals from the 1940's to the 1980's. These include the highly acclaimed novel *The Wall* (1950), about the annihilation of Polish Jews in the Warsaw ghetto, and *Blues* (1987), a brilliant "meditation" on Hersey's favorite sport, fishing (which, of course, turns out to be about much more than fly-casting and trolling).

However, none of Hersey's work in the past three decades has had the impact of *Hiroshima*. Whether *Hiroshima*'s impact was "literary" or "social," whether it has lasting significance or whether it will not be read fifty years from now, no one can say for sure. There is no doubt, however, that the book still continues to force readers to face the horrifying realities of nuclear war. In almost half a century, no book on nuclear warfare has come close to *Hiroshima*'s impact on our moral and ethical sensibilities.

A NOISELESS FLASH

Hiroshima after the atomic blast.

At exactly fifteen minutes past eight in the morning, on August 6, 1945, Japanese time, at the moment when the atomic bomb flashed above Hiroshima, Miss Toshiko Sasaki, a clerk in the personnel department of the East Asia Tin works, had just sat down at her place in the plant office and was turning her head to speak to the girl at the next desk. At that same moment, Dr. Masakazu Fujii was settling down cross-legged to read the Osaka *Asahi* on the porch of his private hospital, overhanging one of the seven deltaic rivers which divide Hiroshima; Mrs. Hatsuyo Nakamura, a tailor's widow, stood by the window of her kitchen, watching a neighbor tearing down his house because it lay in the path of an air-raid-defense fire lane; Father Wilhelm Kleinsorge, a German priest of the Society of Jesus, reclined in his underwear on a cot on the top floor of his order's three-story mission house, reading a Jesuit magazine, *Stimmen der Zeit;*[1] Dr. Terufumi Sasaki, a young member of the surgical staff of the city's large, modern Red Cross Hospital, walked along one of the hospital corridors with a blood specimen for a Wassermann test[2] in his hand; and the Reverend Mr. Kiyoshi Tanimoto, pastor of the Hiroshima Methodist Church, paused at the door of a rich man's house in Koi, the city's western suburb, and prepared to unload a handcart full of things he had evacuated from town in fear of the massive B-29 raid which everyone expected Hiroshima to suffer. A hundred thousand people were killed by the atomic bomb, and these six were among the survivors. They still wonder why they lived when so many others died. Each of them counts many small items of chance or volition—a step taken in time, a decision to go indoors, catching one streetcar instead of the next—that spared him. And now each knows that in the act of survival he lived a dozen lives and saw more death than he ever thought he would see. At the time, none of them knew anything.

The Reverend Mr. Tanimoto got up at five o'clock that morning. He was alone in the parsonage, because for some time his wife had been commuting with their year-old baby to spend nights with a friend in Ushida, a suburb to the north. Of all the important cities of Japan, only two, Kyoto and Hiroshima, had not been visited in strength by *B-san*, or Mr. B, as the Japanese, with a mixture of respect and unhappy familiarity, called the B-29; and Mr. Tanimoto, like all his neighbors and friends, was almost sick with anxiety. He had heard uncomfortably detailed accounts of mass raids on Kure, Iwakuni, Tokuyama, and other nearby towns; he was sure Hiroshima's turn would come soon. He had slept badly the night before, because there had been several air raid warnings. Hiroshima had been getting such warnings almost every night for weeks, for at that time the B-29s were using Lake Biwa, northeast of Hiroshima, as a rendezvous point, and no matter what city the Americans planned to hit, the Superfortresses streamed in over the coast near Hiroshima. The frequency of the warnings and the continued abstinence of Mr. B with respect to Hiroshima had made its citizens jittery; a rumor was going around that the Americans were saving something special for the city.

Mr. Tanimoto is a small man, quick to talk, laugh, and cry. He wears his black hair parted in the middle and rather long; the prominence of the frontal bones just above his eyebrows and the smallness of his mustache, mouth, and chin give him a strange, old-young look, boyish and yet wise, weak and yet fiery. He moves nervously and fast, but with a restraint which suggests that he is a cautious, thoughtful man. He showed, indeed, just those qualities in the uneasy days before the bomb fell. Besides having his wife spend the nights in Ushida, Mr. Tanimoto had been carrying all the portable things from his church, in the close-packed residential district called Nagaragawa, to a house that belonged to a rayon manufacturer in Koi, two miles from the center of town. The rayon man, a Mr. Matsui, had opened his then unoccupied estate to a large number of his friends and acquaintances, so that they might evacuate

---

1. *Stimmen der Zeit:* German for "Voices of the Time."
2. **Wassermann test:** a test used to identify syphilis.

whatever they wished to a safe distance from the probable target area. Mr. Tanimoto had had no difficulty in moving chairs, hymnals, Bibles, altar gear, and church records by pushcart himself, but the organ console and an upright piano required some aid. A friend of his named Matsuo had, the day before, helped him get the piano out to Koi; in return, he had promised this day to assist Mr. Matsuo in hauling out a daughter's belongings. That is why he had risen so early.

Mr. Tanimoto cooked his own breakfast. He felt awfully tired. The effort of moving the piano the day before, a sleepless night, weeks of worry and unbalanced diet, the cares of his parish—all combined to make him feel hardly adequate to the new day's work. There was another thing, too: Mr. Tanimoto had studied theology at Emory College, in Atlanta, Georgia; he had graduated in 1940; he spoke excellent English; he dressed in American clothes; he had corresponded with many American friends right up to the time the war began; and among a people obsessed with a fear of being spied upon—perhaps almost obsessed himself—he found himself growing increasingly uneasy. The police had questioned him several times, and just a few days before, he had heard that an influential acquaintance, a Mr. Tanaka, a retired officer of the Toyo Kisen Kaisha steamship line, an anti-Christian, a man famous in Hiroshima for his showy philanthropies and notorious for his personal tyrannies, had been telling people that Tanimoto should not be trusted. In compensation, to show himself publicly a good Japanese, Mr. Tanimoto had taken on the chairmanship of his local *tonarigumi*, or Neighborhood Association, and to his other duties and concerns this position had added the business of organizing air raid defense for about twenty families.

Before six o'clock that morning, Mr. Tanimoto started for Mr. Matsuo's house. There he found that their burden was to be a *tansu*, a large Japanese cabinet, full of clothing and household goods. The two men set out. The morning was perfectly clear and so warm that the day promised to be uncomfortable. A few minutes after they started, the air raid siren went off—a minute-long blast that warned of approaching planes but indicated to the people of Hiroshima only a slight degree of danger, since it sounded every morning at this time, when an American weather plane came over. The two men pulled and pushed the handcart through the city streets. Hiroshima was a fan-shaped city, lying mostly on the six islands formed by the seven estuarial rivers that branch out from the Ota River; its main commercial and residential districts, covering about four square miles in the center of the city, contained three-quarters of its population, which had been reduced by several evacuation programs from a wartime peak of 380,000 to about 245,000. Factories and other residential districts, or suburbs, lay compactly around the edges of the city. To the south were the docks, an airport, and the island-studded Inland Sea. A rim of mountains runs around the other three sides of the delta. Mr. Tanimoto and Mr. Matsuo took their way through the shopping center, already full of people, and across two of the rivers to the sloping streets of Koi, and up them to the outskirts and foothills. As they started up a valley away from the tight-ranked houses, the all-clear sounded. (The Japanese radar operators, detecting only three planes, supposed that they comprised a reconnaissance.[3]) Pushing the handcart up to the rayon man's house was tiring, and the men, after they had maneuvered their load into the driveway and to the front steps, paused to rest awhile. They stood with a wing of the house between them and the city. Like most homes in this part of Japan, the house consisted of a wooden frame and wooden walls supporting a heavy tile roof. Its front hall, packed with rolls of bedding and clothing, looked like a cool cave full of fat cushions. Opposite the house, to the right of the front door, there was a large, finicky rock garden. There was no sound of planes. The morning was still; the place was cool and pleasant.

Then a tremendous flash of light cut across the sky. Mr. Tanimoto has a distinct recollection that it traveled from east to west, from the city toward the hills. It seemed a sheet of sun. Both he and Mr. Matsuo reacted in terror—and both had time to react (for they were 3,500 yards, or two miles, from the center of the explosion). Mr. Matsuo dashed up the front steps into the house and dived among the bedrolls and buried himself there. Mr. Tanimoto took four or five steps and threw himself between two big rocks in the garden. He bellied up very hard against one of them. As his face was against the stone, he did not see what happened. He felt a sudden pressure, and then splinters and pieces of board and fragments of tile fell on him. He heard no roar. (Almost no one in Hiroshima

---

3. **reconnaissance** (ri·kän'ə·zənts): an exploratory mission.

Michael Herr
(1940–   )

In a preface to *Dispatches* (1977), based on his experiences as a war correspondent in Vietnam, Michael Herr acknowledges permission to quote lyrics from a long list of songs. The songs are not at all like tunes from the two world wars, boisterous marching songs like "As the Caissons Go Rolling Along" or mournful love lyrics like "Lili Marlene." What Herr recalls from Vietnam are the pounding rhythms of rock and roll, country music, hard rock, the Beatles, Mick Jagger, Keith Richards, and Bob Dylan. Those voices are often harsh, dissonant, bitter, and accusatory. They insist on making themselves heard. That is the same tone in which Herr reports on the war.

For several years after the formal fighting ended in Vietnam, no major books appeared about America's longest and most unpopular war. It was also a war America had not won, and one which many Americans had vehemently opposed. No one seemed to want to talk about what had gone wrong and why. Many Americans preferred to forget it.

But in the late 1970's, the silence ended. Just as insistently as the voices in the songs Herr remembers, novelists, poets, dramatists, screenwriters, and journalists have begun to try to capture some sense from a seemingly senseless war. Important nonfiction books have included Ronald Gasser's *365 Days*; Philip Caputo's *A Rumor of War* (1977); Ron Kovic's *Born on the Fourth of July* (1976); Frances Fitzgerald's *Fire in the Lake*; Tim O'Brien's *If I Die in a Combat Zone, Box Me Up and Ship Me Home* (1973). In 1978, O'Brien (see page 940), a veteran of Vietnam, won the National Book Award for his novel *Going After Cacciato*, a complicated and powerful tale of a soldier fleeing the Vietnam battlefield. Other significant novels are Robert Stone's *Dog Soldiers* (1973), Steven Smith's *American Boys* (1975), and James Webb's *Fields of Fire* (1978).

What may strike a reader of the following excerpt from Herr's *Dispatches* is how different it seems in tone and intent from John Hersey's third-person narrative in *Hiroshima* (page 1052).

Herr's voice is intensely personal, with sudden sharp emphasis, angry asides, and moments of black humor. Herr himself is very much present in these dispatches, which are news bulletins from the front; we see him as one of his own characters, jumping in and out of "choppers," interviewing a colonel, eating in a mess hall with the soldiers. Spewing out information in a breathless rush, he hurries through his story, sometimes flashing forward to new scenes, sometimes backward to old ones, tossing in images and song lyrics, introducing characters and anecdotes with the speed of snapshots, and then moving on. The effect is compelling: Herr catches the prose rhythm of a war that has no center, no beginning, and no end.

Other writers about Vietnam have admired Herr's work. Playwright David Rabe (*Streamers, The Basic Training of Pavlo Hummel, Sticks and Bones*) commented:

> Michael Herr is the only writer I've read who has written in the mad-pop-poetic / bureaucratically camouflaged language in which Vietnam was lived. The trees take up attack postures, sanity defoliates before your eyes, and the generals spin out theories like Macbeth's witches. He gets very close to taking you all the way over.
>
> —David Rabe

FROM DISPATCHES

Just as the terrain of the Vietnam Highlands possessed a nightmarish, disorienting quality, so the experiences and memories of the war that Herr describes seem fragmented, jagged, discontinuous. To mirror this theme, the author structures his narrative around a series of anecdotes, rather than in a conventional chronological framework. It is up to you, the reader, to interpret these anecdotes as you would interpret a mosaic, judging for yourself what each fragment contributes to the whole picture.

U. S. Highway 1 (panel) by Allan D'Arcangelo (1963). Acrylic on canvas.   Virginia Museum of Fine Arts.

old-time travelers—road men in a day when cars had running boards and lunchroom windows said AIR COOLED in blue letters with icicles dripping from the tops—those travelers have told me the golden legends of seven-calendar cafes.

To the rider of back roads, nothing shows the tone, the voice of a small town more quickly than the breakfast grill or the five-thirty tavern. Much of what the people do and believe and share is evident then. The City Cafe in Gainesboro had three calendars that I could see from the walk. Inside were no interstate refugees with full bladders and empty tanks, no wild-eyed children just released from the glassy cell of a station wagon back seat, no long-haul truckers talking in CB numbers.[1] There were only townspeople wearing overalls, or catalog-order suits with five-and-dime ties, or uniforms. That is, here were farmers and mill hands, bank clerks, the dry goods merchant, a policeman, and chiropractor's receptionist. Because it was Saturday, there were also mothers and children.

I ordered my standard on-the-road breakfast: two eggs up, hash browns, tomato juice. The waitress, whose pale, almost translucent skin shifted hue in the gray light like a thin slice of mother of pearl, brought the food. Next to the eggs was a

---

1. **CB numbers:** identifying numbers for users of citizens' band radios, or CB's.

biscuit with a little yellow Smiley button stuck in it. She said, "You from the North?"

"I guess I am." A Missourian gets used to Southerners thinking him a Yankee, a Northerner considering him a cracker, a Westerner sneering at his effete Easternness, and the Easterner taking him for a cowhand.

"So whata you doin' in the mountains?"

"Talking to people. Taking some pictures. Looking mostly."

"Lookin' for what?"

"A three-calendar cafe that serves Smiley buttons on the biscuits."

"You needed a smile. Tell me really."

"I don't know. Actually, I'm looking for some jam to put on this biscuit now that you've brought one."

She came back with grape jelly. In a land of quince jelly, apple butter, apricot jam, blueberry preserves, pear conserves, and lemon marmalade, you always get grape jelly.

"Whata you lookin' for?"

Like anyone else, I'm embarrassed to eat in front of a watcher, particularly if I'm getting interviewed. "Why don't you have a cup of coffee?"

"Cain't right now. You gonna tell me?"

"I don't know how to describe it to you. Call it harmony."

She waited for something more. "Is that it?" Someone called her to the kitchen. I had managed almost to finish by the time she came back. She sat on the edge of the booth. "I started out in life not likin' anything, but then it grew on me. Maybe that'll happen to you." She watched me spread the jelly. "Saw your van." She watched me eat the biscuit. "You sleep in there?" I told her I did. "I'd love to do that, but I'd be scared spitless."

"I don't mind being scared spitless. Sometimes."

"I'd love to take off cross country. I like to look at different license plates. But I'd take a dog. You carry a dog?"

"I don't know if I got directions for where you're goin'," the ambulance driver said. "I *think* there's a Nameless down the Shepardsville Road."

"When I get to Shepardsville, will I have gone too far?"

"Ain't no Shepardsville."

"How will I know when I'm there?"

"Cain't say for certain."

"What's Nameless look like?"

"Don't recollect."

"Is the road paved?"

"It's possible."

Those were the directions. I was looking for an unnumbered road named after a nonexistent town that would take me to a place called Nameless that nobody was sure existed.

Clumps of wild garlic lined the country highway that I hoped was the Shepardsville Road. It scrimmaged with the mountain as it tried to stay on top of the ridges; the hillsides were so steep and thick with oak, I felt as if I were following a trail through the misty treetops. Chickens, doing more work with their necks than legs, ran across the road, and, with a battering of wings, half leapt and half flew into the lower branches of oaks. A vicious pair of mixed-breed German shepherds raced along trying to eat the tires. After miles, I decided I'd missed the town—assuming there truly *was* a Nameless, Tennessee. It wouldn't be the first time I'd qualified for the Ponce de Leon[2] Believe Anything Award.

I stopped beside a big man loading tools in a pickup. "I may be lost."

"Where'd you lose the right road?"

"I don't know. Somewhere around nineteen sixty-five."

"Highway fifty-six, you mean?"

"I came down fifty-six. I think I should've turned at the last junction."

"Only thing down that road's stumps and huckleberries, and the berries ain't there in March. Where you tryin' to get to?"

"Nameless. If there is such a place."

"You might not know Thurmond Watts, but he's got him a store down the road. That's Nameless at his store. Still there all right, but I might not vouch you that tomorrow." He came up to the van. "In my Army days, I wrote Nameless, Tennessee, for my place of birth on all the papers, even though I lived on this end of the ridge. All these ridges and hollers got names of their own. That's Steam Mill Holler over yonder. Named after the steam engine in the gristmill. Miller had him just one arm but done a good business."

"What business you in?"

"I've always farmed, but I work in Cookeville now in a heatin' element factory. Bad back made

---

2. **Ponce de Leon:** Spanish explorer (1460–1521) who, according to legend, was looking for the Fountain of Youth.

moving picture in the United States and later shortened to *movie.* (*Flick,* from the flickering that movies used to be plagued with, is probably a newspaper invention.)

The *telephone* was invented in 1876 and the *phonograph* in 1877 (*phono* is Greek for "voice"). The technology for wireless communication led to the *radiotelegraph* in the late nineteenth century. In 1906 this was shortened to *radio,* although it was not until the 1920's that commercial radio became popular.

The television achieved popular commercial success in the late 1940's. The British shortened *television* to *telly,* while Americans abbreviated it to *TV.* (This was a period, as we shall see, when initials and acronyms were especially popular in the United States.)

Acronyms: Convenient Abbreviations

One method of forming new words, now so popular that it threatens to overwhelm us, is the use of acronyms. (The word *acronym* is probably an Americanism, although the practice is ancient.) The term comes from the Greek words for "tip" and "name," and refers to a word formed from the combination of the first letters of the words in a phrase. *Radar* was a technological acronym (from "*ra*dio *de*tecting *an*d *r*anging") and it quickly knocked out the British candidate, *radiolocator. Sonar* ("sound navigation and ranging") followed, as did, much later, *laser* ("light amplification by stimulated emission of radiation").

The acronym device was not the sole property of scientists and technologists. In the twentieth century, wars and bureaucracy have bred many of these conveniently shortened words, from AWOL ("absent without leave"), coined in the First World War, to UNICEF ("United Nations International Children's Emergency Fund"). The Second World War saw the growth of a great many more alphabetical designations, such as POW ("prisoner of war"), and also a great many acronyms, such as WAVE and WAC ("Women Accepted for Volunteer Emergency Service" and "Women's Army Corps"). WAVE is an example of the now common practice of first inventing the acronym and then finding a phrase to justify it. A term like AWOL, on the other hand, grew into an acronym. In its early days the letters were pronounced separately, while now it is common to pronounce it "ay wall." Why do you think the pronunciation of POW didn't make a similar shift?

The Airplane

The airplane had an effect on American culture in the twentieth century similar to the effect of the railroad in the nineteenth. *Aeroplane* originally referred to the plane of the wing, which provides the lift, but the word quickly came to refer to the entire craft. The word had been spelled *airplane* in the United States since the 1870's. When the Wright Brothers patented their flying machine in 1906, the word was already there, waiting for them. The new technology of *aeronautics* borrowed part of its name from sailing technology (*nautes* is Greek for "sailor"), and it borrowed a number of technical terms from sailing as well. *Cockpit, cabin, stewardess, steward, rudder,* and many other terms were adapted from the ocean liners that the airplane was shortly to drive almost to extinction. New words and combinations, like *barnstorm, tailspin,* and *Mayday* (from the French *m'aidez*—"help me"), came into common usage as a result of the airplane.

Nautes, by the way, connects the ancient and the modern worlds in a strikingly direct way. The *Argonauts* sailed with Jason in a ship called the *Argo* in search of the Golden Fleece in Greek mythology. The *astronauts* ("star sailors") sailed to the moon in the twentieth century. (The *Astros* play in Houston, long associated with the space program, and the first artificial turf, *Astroturf,* was developed for their stadium. Thus the stars found their way into the fabric of the national pastime.)

Space and Computer Jargon

The space program brought together experts in several advanced technologies, from military pilots to civil engineers and scientists. Americans heard their jargon on television and adopted some of it. Terms like *countdown, blast-off, malfunction,* and *put on hold* are all familiar to us from the astronauts' jargon. Flyers had long had a number of terms for an unexplained malfunction. The word *gremlin* was common during World War II, to be replaced by *bug,* which is still in use. The word the astronauts probably use most often, though, is *glitch,* a term immediately taken over by computer experts.

The language associated with computers is often highly technical, and much of it will probably never enter standard usage. *RAM, ROM,* and *DOS,* acronyms for "Random Access Memory," "Read Only Memory," and "Disk Operating System," are all familiar to computer users, but they seem to have little application outside their technical uses. Computer people have adapted many standard English words to technical uses, though, and a number of these are edging back into the non-computer world with slightly different meanings.

The most notable of these are nouns that have been changed to verbs. *Access, format,* and *program* are being used as verbs with some frequency today, although some purists object to such usages as unfamiliar and unattractive. (*Program* has already produced an offspring, *deprogram,* referring to "reverse brainwashing.") *Interface* (both as a noun and a verb) has also had an inhospitable reception from purists and other people who are sensitive to language. It remains to be seen whether *interface* and other terms will enter standard English or fade back into the pages of technical dictionaries. If such terms survive, it will be because they are perceived to fill a real need in the language.

Computer slang is often lively and whimsical. If a programmer interferes with someone else's program, for example, he is said to

"You've learned to respond to verbal commands. Now let's test your computer literacy."

Here is a portion of an evaluation of a biography of James Madison, a central figure in the framing of the Constitution and President of the United States from 1809–1817. The review was published in a newspaper.

Robert Allen Rutland, a professor of history at the University of Tulsa, is an experienced specialist in the history of the American Revolution, the founding of the Republic, and the struggle to maintain the Federal Union during its fragile youth. In *James Madison*, he makes a strong case for Madison as *the* Founding Father, surpassing all others. Opinions on this conclusion may differ, but the author's evidence is impressive.

Mr. Rutland uses voluminous quotations from letters, speeches, and other sources to set forth Madison's views on republicanism, individual liberty, the balance (or division) of power among the branches of government, financial honesty, and slavery. The reader is left in no doubt as to Madison's importance as an effective republican leader at a time when post-Revolution America cried out for organization and leadership. . . .

In his preface, Mr. Rutland states that his book is for the reader who does not want to face Irving Brant's six-volume biography, also entitled *James Madison* (1941–1961). That is a commendable aim, and this book fulfills the writer's purpose admirably. But the length of a scholarly work is only part of the picture. The manner of the writing is something different, and here Mr. Rutland runs into difficulty. Although there are bright passages in which the reader can almost see the action and sense the atmosphere of the time, there are also many pages filled with quotations from documents (properly footnoted) where the reading is hard slogging.

Madison's life was filled with intellectual dueling, expressed in the roundabout language of his day. He was a man of thought and of ideals, a soft-spoken, low-key intellectual whose life was busy but hardly colorful. So it requires dedication to Madison for the reader to concentrate steadily on this book in order to reap the benefits of the author's considerable scholarship. . . .

—Alden Todd

Prewriting

Choose a selection that you feel strongly about, and re-read it carefully with the guidelines in mind. Take notes as you read.

Before you write, jot down your responses to each of the guidelines cited above. Use all these notes as the rough draft of your evaluation.

Be sure you have formulated a thesis statement before you begin writing. Before you write, test your thesis statement: Does it apply to all the points you'll make in your essay? You might find that you have to revise it slightly, or even heavily.

Writing

In your opening paragraph, cite the title and author of the piece you are evaluating. It will help to keep your topic in focus if you state your thesis statement in the first paragraph also.

In each succeeding paragraph, cite evidence from the selection to support your opinions. Open each succeeding paragraph with a topic statement.

In your concluding paragraph, summarize your evaluation.

Revising and Proofreading

Use the guidelines in the section at the back of this book, called **Writing About Literature,** to revise and proofread your essay.

POETRY IN A TIME OF DIVERSITY

Double Talk by Inez Storer (1987). Oil.

Rena Bransten Gallery, San Francisco.

UNIT THIRTEEN

Theodore Roethke (1908–1963)

Theodore Roethke was born in Saginaw, Michigan, where his father owned the largest greenhouse complex in the state. His childhood was spent close to nature, nurturing cuttings and small plants and walking in the vast acres of woodlands owned by his family. This childhood world would provide the foundation for much of his poetry, which often looks at the smallest aspects of nature—worms, snails, tiny seedlings—through the eyes of a child. "I have a genuine love of nature," he wrote when he was a sophomore in college. "When I get alone under an open sky where man isn't too evident—then I'm tremendously exalted and a thousand vivid ideas and sweet visions flood my consciousness." Later, he said "Everything that lives is holy: I call upon these holy forms of life."

Roethke studied law and wrote advertising copy for some time after graduating from college, but his desire to become a writer finally led him to graduate school. He began a teaching career at the University of Pennsylvania (where he also coached the tennis team); and from 1947 until his death he taught at the University of Washington. Roethke was a passionate and dedicated teacher who brought the same energy to the classroom that he brought to poetry. He sought in teaching the same rewards he sought in his writing: transcendence and illumination. "Most teaching is visceral," he wrote, "and the general uproar that constitutes a verse class, especially so. It is as ephemeral as the dance. . . . [Teaching] is what is left after all the reading and thinking and reciting: the residue, the illumination."

The search for illumination and ecstasy was a fundamental concern for Roethke in life as well as in poetry. This search brought with it a psychological imbalance that he tried to face openly and employ honestly in his verse. "My heart keeps open house," he wrote in an early poem.

> My truths are all foreknown,
> This anguish self-revealed.
> I'm naked to the bone,
> With nakedness my shield.
> —from "Open House"

Between 1947 and 1958 Roethke published four volumes and received a number of honors, including the Pulitzer Prize, the National Book Award, and the Bollingen Award. A poet of both pain and joy, the dark and the light, Roethke tried to find in both extremes the same transcendent moment, "a consciousness beyond the mundane," as he once put it, "a purity, a final innocence."

In this poem, a sensitive and caring man who is "neither father nor lover" inevitably shares some of the feelings of both. The poet writes an elegy for a young woman who probably never realized that, in the eyes of her teacher, she was not just a name on a class list, but a precious human being.

Elegy for Jane

My Student, Thrown by a Horse

I remember the neckcurls, limp and damp as tendrils,
And her quick look, a sidelong pickerel smile;
And how, once startled into talk, the light syllables leaped for her,
And she balanced in the delight of her thought,
5   A wren, happy, tail into the wind,
Her song trembling the twigs and small branches.
The shade sang with her;
The leaves, their whispers turned to kissing;
And the mold sang in the bleached valleys under the rose.

10 Oh, when she was sad, she cast herself down into such a pure depth,
Even a father could not find her:
Scraping her cheek against straw;
Stirring the clearest water.

My sparrow, you are not here,
15 Waiting like a fern, making a spiny shadow.
The sides of wet stones cannot console me,
Nor the moss, wound with the last light.

If only I could nudge you from this sleep,
My maimed darling, my skittery pigeon.
20 Over this damp grave I speak the words of my love:
I, with no rights in this matter,
Neither father nor lover.

Responding to the Poem

Analyzing the Poem

Identifying Details

1. Count the number of times in the poem when the dead girl, or something about her, is compared to a plant or animal.

Interpreting Meanings

2. What do the comparisons to plants and animals tell us about the speaker's personality?

3. What, in your opinion, is the effect of the speaker's saying he has "no rights in this matter" (line 21)?

Writing About the Poem

A Critical Response

Comparing Poems. Compare the treatment of death and mourning in "Elegy for Jane" and John Crowe Ransom's "Bells for John Whiteside's Daughter" (page 693). Consider the poems' **figures of speech** and **tones**.

Robert Hayden (1913–1980)

Born and raised in a slum district of Detroit, Robert Hayden graduated from Wayne State University and received his M.A. from the University of Michigan. There, in Michigan, Hayden formed friendships with young poets of his own age. These friendships were based on shared poetic tastes and upon enthusiastic readings of the American and British writers who were united by anti-Fascist sentiment and by the political optimism that flourished until the outbreak of the Spanish Civil War in 1936. (The Spanish war made it clear that the emergent democracies in Europe would be opposed to the death by the military power of the old regimes.)

His university associations greatly enhanced Hayden's understanding of the poetic techniques developed in the early twentieth century and of the ways in which poetry could serve as the voice of political consciousness. But Hayden was unprepared for the eruption of the loosely joined poetry written by his younger black contemporaries who came to prominence in the racially troubled 1960's.

Hayden was as deeply committed to the same causes and to the same demands for equality and liberation as they were; but he was temperamentally unable to abandon the standards of the art of poetry as he understood them in order to transform his work into what he saw as propaganda, however righteously motivated. He was also reluctant to accept the notion that poetry by blacks should be judged only on the basis of its immediate impact and momentary relevance.

Hayden's career as a college teacher began at Fisk University in Tennessee and was crowned by his acceptance of a distinguished professorship at the University of Michigan—the same institution where, as a poor freshman, he lived in a segregated rooming house. His notable collections of verse include *Heart-Shape in the Dust* (1940); *The Lion and the Archer* (1948); *Figures of Time: Poems* (1955); *Words in the Mourning Time: Poems* (1970); and *The Night-Blooming Cereus* (1972). His style in these collections ranges from the strictly traditional form of the sonnet to the effective use of free verse in dramatic and narrative poems. Hayden was a member of the American Academy and Institute of Arts and Letters. Just before his death, he served as Consultant in Poetry to the Library of Congress, the first black poet ever to hold that position.

The title is part of the first line of a famous song from George Gershwin's and Du Bose Heyward's opera *Porgy and Bess* (1935). To complete the line, we add, "is easy," and so we have the touchstone of the poem—a statement combining irony with simple fact.

The substance of the poem is what "he [the poet] recalls." As a child in Detroit, Hayden lived in a black ghetto: not the Catfish Row of Charleston, South Carolina, the setting of the opera.

"Trees of heaven" (line 6) is a reference to the sumac trees that flourish even in the concrete and asphalt of crowded cities. "Mosaic eyes" (line 20) are the eyes of the Old Testament prophet and deliverer Moses. Jack Johnson (line 29) was the first black heavyweight boxing champion, a man who became rich and lived in the flamboyant high style identified with the "roaring twenties." If his limousine was not literally cut from a diamond, it was flashy enough to make people think of it as a dazzling jewel. "Ethiopia" in line 32 refers to a black homeland famous in history.

"Summertime and the Living . . ."

Nobody planted roses, he recalls,
but sunflowers gangled° there sometimes,
tough-stalked and bold
and like the vivid children there unplanned.
5   There circus-poster horses curveted°
in trees of heaven
above the quarrels and shattered glass,
and he was bareback rider of them all.

No roses there in summer—
10   oh, never roses except when people died—
and no vacations for his elders,
so harshened after each unrelenting day
that they were shouting-angry.
But summer was, they said, the poor folks' time
15   of year. And he remembers
how they would sit on broken steps amid

The fevered tossings of the dusk, the dark,
wafting hearsay with funeral-parlor fans
or making evening solemn by
20   their quietness. Feels their Mosaic eyes
upon him, though the florist roses
that only sorrow could afford
long since have bidden them Godspeed.

Oh, summer summer summertime—

25   Then grim street preachers shook
their tambourines and Bibles in the face
of tolerant wickedness;
then Elks parades and big splendiferous
Jack Johnson in his diamond limousine
30   set the ghetto burgeoning
with fantasies
of Ethiopia spreading her gorgeous wings.

2. **gangled:** gathered, clustered.

5. **curveted:** leaped upward.

Responding to the Poem

Analyzing the Poem

Identifying Details

1. What **images** does the poet use in the first three stanzas to describe the ghetto of his youth?
2. Roses are mentioned three times in the poem. Identify these contexts, and explain what the speaker connects with roses in each instance.
3. What does the speaker remember in the last stanza?

Interpreting Meanings

4. What is the implied contrast between the "grim street preachers" (line 25) and Jack Johnson?
5. In the first stanza, what do the "sunflowers" (line 2) and the "vivid children" (line 4) have in common?
6. How did the boy react to the circus poster (line 5)? How does the **image** of the circus poster contrast with the boy's all-too-real setting?
7. "Burgeoning" (line 30) means "suddenly growing or developing." What does the use of this word in this context suggest?

8. In what way is the poem's title **ironic**?
9. How does the **tone** of the last five lines echo the tone of the first stanza?

Writing About the Poem

A Creative Response

1. **Giving an Oral Reading.** Find an instrumental recording of "Summertime." (It has been recorded by hundreds of performers.) Listen to it several times as you read Hayden's poem. Then prepare an oral reading for your class, using the recording as background music.

A Critical Response

2. **Analyzing the Poem.** It could be argued that "Summertime and the Living . . ." expresses mixed feelings about the poet's youth. In a brief essay, discuss the use of ambiguity in this poem, paying particular attention to the treatment of material and spiritual values.

Elizabeth Bishop
(1911–1979)

A "poet's poet," Elizabeth Bishop has been the acknowledged master of both the highest art and most meticulous craft for many of the important poets of her time. She has also been an unacknowledged inspiration for many others still trying to solve the mystery of her impenetrable simplicity.

Born in Worcester, Massachusetts, she spent her early years in a Nova Scotia village—a childhood marked by the early death of her father and darkened by the long illness of her mother. These circumstances, in effect, made her an orphan whose upbringing was entrusted to the care of relatives.

At the time of her mother's death in a psychiatric hospital, Bishop was a student at Vassar College. After graduation, she embarked on a career quietly devoted to poetry and, by means of a private income, to travels. During these travels, she discovered two places congenial enough to detain her for years—Key West and Rio de Janeiro. *Questions of Travel,* the title she gave to one of her last books, might serve as an index to the story of a life told in poems that are always "letters from abroad." In these poems, places, near or far, provide merely temporary settings for an endless inquiry into the nature of perception and reality. In 1955 her *Poems: North and South—A Cold Spring* was awarded the Pulitzer Prize.

In the final years of her life, Bishop lived on the Boston waterfront in an apartment on Lewis Wharf and spent her summers on an island off the coast of Maine. These changes of scene came about when her close friend Robert Lowell became ill and Harvard University invited her to take over the classes he had been scheduled to teach. She continued to teach at Harvard until her death.

A shy woman with a taste for the exotic as well as a love of the ordinary, Bishop surrounded herself with artifacts acquired in the course of her travels. She conducted herself with a scrupulous conventionality much at odds with the audacity and profundity of her imagination. Her poems most truly reveal her character: a combination of the conservatism and moral rectitude associated with "the north" and the casual sensuousness and cheerfully untidy sprawl associated with nature and the everyday outdoor life of "the south." For Elizabeth Bishop, geography was less a matter of maps and place names than of states of mind and areas of feeling.

The death here is "first" only because it was the event in Elizabeth Bishop's childhood that first acquainted her with mortality.

If the setting (Nova Scotia) were not named in this poem's title, certain details might be puzzling. The "chromographs," or tinted photographs, of the British royal family indicate Canada's place in the British Empire at that time. "The Maple Leaf (Forever)" refers to the Canadian national anthem and to the image of a maple leaf on the Cana-dian flag. In a Nova Scotian parlor, a "stuffed loon"—or any other bird from the lakes or shores of the province—was a common decorative item.

In those days, people who had died were "laid out" at home—that is, their coffins were brought into the family parlor or living room, and for one to three days, members of the family and friends came to pay their last respects. Anyone who remembers this ritual from childhood knows that it is an occasion one never forgets.

First Death in Nova Scotia

Winter, New Hampshire by Peter Blume. Oil.

Museum of Fine Arts, Boston.
Bequest of John Spaulding.

In the cold, cold parlor
my mother laid out Arthur
beneath the chromographs:
Edward, Prince of Wales,
5   with Princess Alexandra,
and King George with Queen Mary.
Below them on the table
stood a stuffed loon
shot and stuffed by Uncle
10   Arthur, Arthur's father.

Since Uncle Arthur fired
a bullet into him,
he hadn't said a word.
He kept his own counsel
15   on his white, frozen lake,
the marble-topped table.
His breast was deep and white,
cold and caressable;
his eyes were red glass,
20   much to be desired.

"Come," said my mother,
"Come and say goodbye
to your little cousin Arthur."
I was lifted up and given
25   one lily of the valley

to put in Arthur's hand.
Arthur's coffin was
a little frosted cake,
and the red-eyed loon eyed it
30   from his white, frozen lake.

Arthur was very small.
He was all white, like a doll
that hadn't been painted yet.
Jack Frost had started to paint him
35   the way he always painted
the Maple Leaf (Forever).
He had just begun on his hair,
a few red strokes, and then
Jack Frost had dropped the brush
40   and left him white, forever.

The gracious royal couples
were warm in red and ermine;
their feet were well wrapped up
in the ladies' ermine trains.
45   They invited Arthur to be
the smallest page at court.
But how could Arthur go,
clutching his tiny lily,
with his eyes shut up so tight
50   and the roads deep in snow?

Responding to the Poem

Analyzing the Poem

Identifying Details

1. Describe the situation in the poem.
2. What **images** help you picture the parlor?
3. What does the speaker imagine the royal family has invited Arthur to be?

Interpreting Meanings

4. How can you tell that this poem is written from the perspective of a child?
5. What do you think the stuffed loon contributes to the meaning of this poem?
6. Find all the **images** in the poem that have to do with cold or snow. Why are they appropriate?

7. The poem ends with a **rhetorical question**—one that does not call for an answer. How does this question affect the emotional content of the poem?
8. Suppose the speaker in the poem were Arthur's mother. How would that change the **tone** of the poem? Are the sentiments in the poem appropriate to the person who is expressing them? Explain.

Since the title of this poem gives us no indication as to what its subject is, we have to assume that it calls attention to the poet's method of composing her poem. This method might be described as taking notes and making observations about a thunderstorm. But you'll soon be aware that these are not the sort of eyewitness details we'd expect from a reporter. Instead, they amount to a series of little pictures in the poet's mind, pictures she would like us to think about.

Little Exercise

Think of the storm roaming the sky uneasily
like a dog looking for a place to sleep in,
listen to it growling.

Think how they must look now, the mangrove keys°
5   lying out there unresponsive to the lightning
in dark, coarse-fibered families,

where occasionally a heron may undo his head,
shake up his feathers, make an uncertain comment
when the surrounding water shines.

10   Think of the boulevard and the little palm trees
all stuck in rows, suddenly revealed
as fistfuls of limp fish-skeletons.

It is raining here. The boulevard
and its broken sidewalks with weeds in every crack,
15   are relieved to be wet, the sea to be freshened.

Now the storm goes away again in a series
of small, badly lit battle-scenes,
each in "Another part of the field."°

Think of someone sleeping in the bottom of a rowboat
20   tied to a mangrove root or the pile of a bridge;
think of him as uninjured, barely disturbed.

4. **mangrove keys:** small islands created by dirt and other matter collecting around the roots of a mangrove tree, which grows in shallow waters.

18. **"Another . . . field":** a stage direction used in battle scenes of Shakespearean plays.

Responding to the Poem

Analyzing the Poem

Identifying Details

1. Geographically, where does the poem occur? Name the clues that support your sense of its locale.
2. The movement of the poem has much in common with that of a documentary movie. A series of quick shots, one after the other, tell a story in pictures. Describe the "shots" you see.

3. In a poem full of comparisons of one thing with another, two are full-fledged **similes.** Where are they?
4. What uses of **personification** can you identify in the poem?

Interpreting Meanings

5. The only human being in this poem is "someone" who does not make an appearance until the very end. Who might this person be? What might the poet want to

In a Florida Jungle by Winslow Homer (1886). Watercolor.   Worcester Art Museum, Worcester, Massachusetts.

suggest by telling us to think of this person as "un-injured, barely disturbed"?

6. By calling her poem "Little Exercise," Elizabeth Bishop seems to make light of her verse, as though it were no more than a skillful assemblage of observations about a storm. But perhaps her light-hearted approach disguises deeper meanings. What might at least one of these meanings be?

Writing About the Poems

A Creative Response

1. **Imitating the Writer's Technique.** Write a series of notes of your own, or a poem, called "Little Exercise." Concentrate on a scene of action or a setting and write down at least five vivid images that you notice in it. Open with the words "Think of. . . ."

A Critical Response

2. **Comparing Poems.** Like Marianne Moore, Bishop creates her artistry from the accumulation of vivid de-

tails. Select one of Bishop's poems, and in a brief essay, compare and contrast her use of details with the method used by Marianne Moore in "The Steeple-Jack" (page 743).

Analyzing Language and Style

Multiple Meanings

Poets sometimes use a word with multiple meanings, intending to make us think about the two (or more) meanings at once.

1. What meanings does the word *manners* have? Could several meanings apply to the poem here?
2. What various meanings can the word *frosted* have? Can it have more than one meaning in line 28 of "First Death in Nova Scotia"?
3. What are the various meanings of *exercise*? Could more than one meaning apply to the title?
4. What meanings can the word *disturbed* have? In what sense or senses is the word used in the last line of "Little Exercise"?

Randall Jarrell
(1914–1965)

One of the most careful and erudite readers of contemporary poetry, Randall Jarrell was, at the same time, both an abrasive critic and a generous promoter of the art.

Born in Nashville, Tennessee, Jarrell was brought up in California. His childhood experiences included close observation of the gaudy remnants of the "old" Hollywood, a personal acquaintance with the MGM lion, and an apprehension of the difference between fantasy and fact, between life and myths about life, that would provide him with themes for poetry for years to come.

After graduating from Vanderbilt University in his native city, Jarrell began a career that led to membership in the English departments of many colleges and universities, from Texas to New York. In 1942, he joined the Army Air Corps, served for a time as a pilot and then, for a longer time, as Celestial Navigation Trainer of pilots assigned to fly the famous B-29 bombers of World War II. Out of this experience came two notable books of poetry, *Little Friend, Little Friend* (1945) and *Losses* (1948). In the regard of many critics, these books have not been surpassed as American contributions to the literature of World War II.

A man of extraordinary wit, Jarrell gave full play to his gifts in his often caustic and devastating critical articles and essays, particularly in *A Sad Heart at the Supermarket* (1962). In poetry, however, his faculty for contemptuous criticism is kept under wraps. His wit shows itself only in mellow good humor ("I feel like the

first men who read Wordsworth. / It's so simple I can't understand it.") and in a resigned toleration of the more absurd aspects of American life.

Struck by a car while walking on a North Carolina highway in 1965, Jarrell's tragic death raised some questions. But of his loss to American letters and to the poets who had counted upon him to explain, judge, and celebrate their art, there was no question at all.

The Death of the Ball Turret Gunner

From my mother's sleep I fell into the State,
And I hunched in its belly till my wet fur froze.
Six miles from earth, loosed from its dream of life,
I woke to black flak and the nightmare fighters.
When I died they washed me out of the turret with a hose.

Responding to the Poem

Analyzing the Poem

Responding to Details

1. What is the temperature like in the ball turret?
2. How far from earth does the bomber ascend? What happens at that altitude?
3. What happens to the gunner?

Interpreting Meanings

4. "Belly" here can be read on two levels. What two bellies could the speaker be talking about? How is the ball turret like a womb?
5. How do you know that the speaker didn't enter the army as a result of a rational decision?
6. What is the speaker's "wet fur"? Why do you think he compares himself to an animal?
7. How does the grisly process described in the final line fit in with the rest of the poem?

8. While the speaker is not around to receive a medal, he *is* a hero. Why do you think he shows no awareness of that fact?
9. What, in the long run, is this poem about? Is it about political dissent? Is it a statement about the way things in the world are regimented and mechanized? Is it about the destruction of the innocent?

Writing About the Poem

A Creative Response

Writing from Another Point of View. Find a newspaper article about someone who has died. Then write a paragraph or a short poem from the imagined point of view of the dead person. Imitate, as closely as you can, the style of "The Death of the Ball Turret Gunner."

Primary Sources
The Ball Turret

"A ball turret was a plexiglass sphere set into the belly of a B-17 or B-24, and inhabited by two .50 caliber machine guns and one man, a short small man. When this gunner tracked with his machine guns a fighter attacking his bomber from below, he revolved with the turret; hunched upsidedown in his little sphere, he looked like the fetus in the womb. The fighters which attacked him were armed with cannon firing explosive shells. The hose was a steam hose."

—Randall Jarrell

Gwendolyn Brooks
(1917–   )

Gwendolyn Brooks established her credentials early, in two volumes of poetry (one of which was awarded the Pulitzer Prize in 1949) that demonstrated her skill in the conventional poetic forms. After this, Brooks began to turn to more open forms and to a more extensive use of common speech. This transition was sparked by two developments. One was the insistence of young black poets that their poetry should not only reflect their own special experience, but that it should also be based in the speech rhythms and the vernacular of urban black culture. The other development was the expansion of black consciousness and black power in the embattled years of the 1950's and 1960's, when the triumphs of the civil rights movement gave new cohesion and pride to the followers of Martin Luther King, Jr.

Kansas-born, Gwendolyn Brooks grew up in Chicago and has been identified with that city and its enormous black community for most of her life. Much honored by her city and her state, she has won an illustrious place in both. Brooks has been honored not only because of her literary achievements, but also because of her efforts in behalf of young black writers, to whom she has given practical advice and encouragement. For many of these young writers, Brooks, in her role as teacher and editor, has opened doors to self-realization and to professional careers.

Brooks's works include the short novel *Maud Martha* (1953), an autobiographical work called *Report from Part One* (1972), and her poetry, collected in books called *Annie Allen* (1949) and *Family Pictures* (1970).

With borrowings from the spiritual "Swing Low, Sweet Chariot," Gwendolyn Brooks writes a poem that also has the rhythm of a song. Part of this rhythm is due to her use of the trochee—a metrical foot in which an accented syllable is followed by one that is not accented. From the title, we know that De Witt Williams is dead. Although the poem provides few details, we are nevertheless asked to imagine what the life of this "plain black boy" was like. "The L" refers to Chicago's elevated railway. "Forty-seventh Street" and "Northwest Corner, Prairie" are part of the south side. You should read the poem aloud.

Of De Witt Williams on His Way to Lincoln Cemetery

He was born in Alabama.
He was bred in Illinois.

He was nothing but a
Plain black boy.

5 Swing low swing low sweet sweet chariot.
Nothing but a plain black boy.

Drive him past the Pool Hall.
Drive him past the Show.
Blind within his casket,
10 But maybe he will know.

Down through Forty-seventh Street:
Underneath the L,
And Northwest Corner, Prairie,
That he loved so well.

15 Don't forget the Dance Halls—
Warwick and Savoy,
Where he picked his women, where
He drank his liquid joy.

Born in Alabama.
20 Bred in Illinois.
He was nothing but a
Plain black boy.

Swing low swing low sweet sweet chariot.
Nothing but a plain black boy.

Responding to the Poem

Analyzing the Poem

Interpreting Meanings

1. On the basis of the details given about the route of his funeral procession, how would you characterize De Witt Williams?
2. What is the effect of the word "maybe" in line 10?
3. With a background so humble, why do you think De Witt Williams is important enough to be the inspiration for a poem?
4. "De Witt" and "Lincoln" are both prominent names in American history. Do you think the poet wants us to accept them as merely incidental facts? Or do you think she intends a touch of **irony** here?

5. How would you describe the **tone** of this elegy?

Writing About the Poem

A Creative Response

Preparing a Choral Reading. Get together with two or more classmates. Plan and rehearse a reading of the poem that alternates between single and multiple voices. Then perform the reading for the class. If you were to have background music for the recitation, what music would you choose?

Robert Lowell
(1917–1977)

Of all the poets who came to maturity in the years immediately after World War II, none displayed greater ability or exerted more influence than Robert Lowell. From virtually the beginning of his career, Lowell was a central figure in American poetry, earning the admiration of his peers and the recognition of the literary establishment. His first published volume, *Lord Weary's Castle,* won the Pulitzer Prize in 1946; from then until his death more than thirty years later, he was a major figure in modern literature.

Lowell was born into an aristocratic Boston family whose ancestors went back to the *Mayflower.* Among them were well-known ministers, judges, politicians, educators, and literary figures. Nineteenth-century poet James Russell Lowell (page 167) was his great-uncle; Amy Lowell, the poet who helped promote the cause of Imagism (page 724), was his cousin.

This rich heritage was both blessing and burden to Lowell. He grew up with American history in his veins. "In some ways you are the luckiest poet I know!" his friend Elizabeth Bishop once wrote to Lowell, explaining that in writing about his family he was also automatically writing about American history. "All you have to do is put down the names," she said. At the same time, though, his family's conservative, traditional, Beacon Hill background was suffocating to the young poet. Much of Lowell's adolescence and early adulthood consisted of rebellious acts intended to carve out his own identity as an individual and as a poet.

One early act of rebellion against his family was to leave Harvard after two years and transfer to Kenyon College in Ohio, where poet John Crowe Ransom (page 692) was teaching. The summer before he enrolled at Kenyon, Lowell lived in a tent on poet Allen Tate's lawn in Nashville, Tennessee, soaking up all he could learn from Tate about writing poetry. Tate and Ransom were both supporters of what was called the New Criticism. They admired (and wrote) densely packed, "formal, difficult poems," as Lowell later put it, and Lowell also began writing in this manner.

He graduated from Kenyon in 1940, married novelist Jean Stafford, and started what would be a distinguished career of teaching and writing. A year later, in what was at least partially another rebellious act against his family's Protestant roots, he converted to Roman Catholicism.

In the early days of World War II, Lowell tried to enlist in the Navy several times, but was rejected for his poor eyesight. By 1943, appalled at the destruction caused by American bombing in Europe, he refused induction into the Army and was sentenced to prison for a year and a day. "I was a fire-breathing Catholic C.O. [conscientious objector]," he later wrote in a poem called "Memories of West Street and Lepke," "and made my manic statement, / telling off the state and president."

The poems that emerged from this period, in volumes like *Land of Unlikeness, Lord Weary's Castle,* and *The Mills of the Kavanaughs,* were tight, formal, and intellectually challenging. They often combined a dark view of American history with symbols drawn from Catholic doctrine, and they usually presented a grim vision of a world about to end. Their complex diction and many-leveled puns sometimes obscured their meaning. When *Lord Weary's Castle* was published, the Boston *Globe* exclaimed that Lowell was the "most promising poet in a hundred years." But his own father was quoted in the same article as saying, "Poets seem to see more in his work than most other people." That was also true.

Lowell had great natural ability, but he also revised and rewrote obsessively, often going through twenty or thirty drafts of a poem before he was happy with it.

In the 1950's, Lowell's style and subject matter gradually changed, although he never gave up his habit of endlessly revising his work. At poetry readings with writers like Allen Ginsberg, whose loose, free-wheeling style was instantly communicable to audiences, Lowell began simplifying some of his own poems as he read them. "I'd make little changes just impromptu," he later said. "I began to have a certain disrespect for the tight forms. If you could make it easier just by changing syllables, then why not?" As a result, Lowell began consciously writing a looser, freer verse. Paradoxically, writing more formally was more natural for Lowell, and he would thus often "translate" tight, rhymed couplets into free verse as he revised.

Lowell's subject matter in these poems became more personal than in his earlier work. All of his life, he suffered great bouts of mental instability, and, until medication succeeded in stabilizing his condition, he sometimes had to be hospitalized. In these poems, which were eventually published together with a prose memoir in *Life Studies* (1959), Lowell wrote frankly about his situation as a "Mayflower screwball." His tone was not self-pitying or self-indulgent. Instead, he usually described his suffering with light irony intended to keep things in perspective. "What use is my sense of humor?" he asked in "Waking in the Blue," a poem about a period he spent in a psychiatric hospital. The implicit answer was that his sense of humor helped him to tolerate a painful situation.

Life Studies was one of the most influential works of poetry written after World War II. It helped to make acceptable the highly personal poetry being written by a number of younger poets, many of whom were Lowell's students: Sylvia Plath (page 1115) and Anne Sexton (page 1118). These poets, along with others such as John Berryman (page 1120), are sometimes referred to as "confessional poets" because of the intimate details in their poems.

In the 1960's, Lowell became more and more of a public figure. Like many writers of the time, he expressed opposition to the war in Vietnam in his writing and speeches, and, on one well-publicized occasion, he refused an invitation to participate in a White House Festival of the Arts. His poetry of this period remained personal, and he wrote a great many unrhymed sonnets, first published as *Notebooks* in 1969 and then in revised form as *History* in 1973. In addition to poetry, Lowell wrote a number of well-received dramas during this period, most notably *The Old Glory* (1965), which adapted stories by Herman Melville and Nathaniel Hawthorne.

In 1977, returning to New York from London, he died of a heart attack in a taxi coming from the airport.

"They gave up everything to serve the Republic," says the Latin inscription preceding this poem. "They" are all the Union soldiers who served during the Civil War. But, more specifically, "they" are the members of the first regiment of black soldiers from a free state, in this case Massachusetts. Under a white commander, Robert Gould Shaw, this regiment stormed Fort Wagner, South Carolina, in an assault resulting in many deaths, including that of the commander himself.

The subject of the poem is not that event, however, but its memorial—the bronze monument by the great sculptor Augustus Saint-Gaudens, which stands in Boston Common, the park directly across from the State House.

Today, Boston has a new aquarium that is a major tourist attraction. In 1959, when "For the Union Dead" was written, an older aquarium in South Boston—empty, deserted, and dilapidated—provided just the right image to set up the relationship between past and present.

Because this is a difficult poem, you should read it at least twice. A comment follows the poem.

For the Union Dead

"Relinquunt Omnia Servare Rem Publicam."

The old South Boston Aquarium stands
in a Sahara of snow now. Its broken windows are boarded.
The bronze weathervane cod has lost half its scales.
The airy tanks are dry.

5   Once my nose crawled like a snail on the glass;
my hand tingled
to burst the bubbles
drifting from the noses of the cowed, compliant fish.

My hand draws back. I often sigh still
10   for the dark downward and vegetating kingdom
of the fish and reptile. One morning last March,
I pressed against the new barbed and galvanized
fence on the Boston Common. Behind their cage,
yellow dinosaur steam shovels were grunting
15   as they cropped up tons of mush and grass
to gouge their underworld garage.

Parking spaces luxuriate like civic
sand piles in the heart of Boston.
A girdle of orange, Puritan-pumpkin colored girders
20   braces the tingling Statehouse,

shaking over the excavations, as it faces Colonel Shaw
and his bell-cheeked Negro infantry
on St. Gaudens' shaking Civil War relief,
propped by a plank splint against the garage's earthquake.

25   Two months after marching through Boston,
half the regiment was dead;
at the dedication,
William James could almost hear the bronze Negroes breathe.

Their monument sticks like a fishbone
30   in the city's throat.
Its Colonel is as lean
as a compass-needle.

He has an angry wrenlike vigilance,
a greyhound's gentle tautness;
35   he seems to wince at pleasure,
and suffocate for privacy.

He is out of bounds now. He rejoices in man's lovely,
peculiar power to choose life and die—
when he leads his black soldiers to death,
40   he cannot bend his back.

On a thousand small town New England greens,
the old white churches hold their air
of sparse, sincere rebellion; frayed flags
quilt the graveyards of the Grand Army of the Republic.

45   The stone statues of the abstract Union Soldier
grow slimmer and younger each year—
wasp-waisted, they doze over muskets
and muse through their sideburns . . .

Shaw's father wanted no monument
50   except the ditch,
where his son's body was thrown
and lost with his "niggers."

The ditch is nearer.
There are no statues for the last war° here;
55   on Boylston Street, a commercial photograph
shows Hiroshima boiling

over a Mosler Safe, the "Rock of Ages"
that survived the blast. Space is nearer.
When I crouch to my television set,
60   the drained faces of Negro schoolchildren rise like balloons.

Colonel Shaw
is riding on his bubble,
he waits
for the blesséd break.

65   The Aquarium *is* gone. Everywhere,
giant finned cars nose forward like fish;
a savage servility
slides by on grease.

---

54. **the last war:** that is, World War II.

A Comment on the Poem

A good poem can withstand anything said about it, whether it is interpretation or criticism. Understanding "For the Union Dead" depends upon the knowledge the reader brings to it as much as it depends upon what the poem itself offers. After you read this poem, you should try to paraphrase it, in order to clarify some of its references and allusions and to open possibilities of interpretation. When your paraphrase ends, the poem will not. Instead, it will invite you to go back to the first line and, newly equipped, begin an emotional and intellectual adventure. Looking at the ruined aquarium on its desert of snow, the poet remembers how, as a child, he used to press his nose right up against the glass of the great fish tanks; he recalls how his hand itched to get inside the tanks and play with the rising bubbles and all the marvelous sea-creatures that swam in them. But he is no longer a child. He draws back his hand, even though something in his nature still hungers to explore another order of life—that subconscious region where all beings in the "vegetating kingdom" had their beginnings.

The grown man won't press his nose against the glass. Instead, he presses himself against the fence that makes a "cage" in which steam shovels are gouging out space for an underground parking garage. The tremors of excavation work are so thunderous that both the State House and the bronze monument facing it have to be braced for protection. The jeopardy in which "progress" has placed both State House and monument brings the poet's central subject—the black regiment—into focus.

Having paraded through Boston as heroes on their way to the battlefield, half of these soldiers were dead within two months. When the monument to them was dedicated in 1897, the memory of these men was so much alive, and their faces and figures so faithfully rendered in bronze, that the great American psychologist William James felt that they almost breathed.

But now the poet observes that the monument "sticks like a fishbone in the city's throat," meaning that it is an irritant. Ironically, Boston is not only the city where the abolitionist movement was stronger than anywhere else; it is also, like many places in the United States, a place where racism has persisted. The poet compares Colonel Shaw, the regiment's leader, to the needle on a compass; this characterization suggests that Shaw pointed the way, a way in which whites and blacks united might become part of a nation's most honorable history.

Then follows a more detailed description of Colonel Shaw, in which certain features are regarded as evidence of a great character. This makes him "out of bounds" in a time and place where his special kind of vision and integrity are conspicuously lacking.

Then, instantaneously, like a change of scene in a movie, the poet's eye suddenly "pans" over the New

Robert Gould Shaw Memorial by Augustus Saint-Gaudens (1894–1897). Bronze. Beacon Hill, Boston, Massachusetts.

England landscape (line 41). Churches on village greens remind him of the Revolutionary War; cemeteries with their "quilt" of ragged flags recall the Civil War; the young soldiers of the Union, "stone statues" all alike, remain young and slim as their nation grows older and fatter.

Colonel Shaw's father, we learn, felt that the monument to his son was unnecessary; people had only to remember the ditch where the young commander's body was thrown with those of his soldiers. "The ditch," that common boneyard of blacks and whites, "is nearer," says the poet. Why? Because nuclear holocaust threatens a world more preoccupied with sales and profits than with its own survival. The annihilation of the Japanese city of Hiroshima by an atom bomb is used by the manufacturers of Mosler Safes to hustle their product. An advertisement shows the safe's "survival factor," and even compares it with the "Rock of Ages," or the cross of Christ.

The bubbles that rose in the fish tanks of the old aquarium return at the end of the poem. They are now "balloons" which the poet compares to the "drained faces" of black youngsters. They also appear as the buried dream of Colonel Shaw which, like a bubble, may still "break" when idealism explodes into reality.

The old aquarium and everything it stood for in the speaker's childhood imagination no longer exist. "Finned" luxury cars now "slide by," just as the marvelous fish once glided through the bubbly depths of their tanks. To the speaker, the chrome-laden automobiles represent a "savage servility." They move "on grease," the byproduct of the oil that supplies the modern world's energy, and the end-product and sludgy residue of the world's great power.

Responding to the Poem

Analyzing the Poem

Identifying Details

1. What **images** describe the old South Boston Aquarium?
2. What **images** describe what the speaker saw on Boston Common? What **metaphor** describes the steam shovels?
3. What **images** describe the St. Gaudens monument? How many things is the colonel compared with?
4. What do the frayed flags in the graveyards remind the speaker of?
5. What details tell you what happened to Colonel Shaw and his men?
6. What **image** in the last stanza reminds us of the scene described in the second stanza?

Interpreting Meanings

7. What does the poet mean by saying Colonel Shaw "rejoices in man's lovely, / peculiar power to choose life and die" (lines 37–38)?
8. What historical events in Boston and other American cities might the poet be referring to with the mention of the "drained faces" of black children on television (line 60)?
9. What do you think is the "savage servility" mentioned in the last stanza?
10. Explain how the title of the poem could have at least two meanings.
11. How does the speaker feel about what he sees in his city? How would you describe the poem's **tone**: Is it ironic, nostalgic, or sarcastic? Explain.

Writing About the Poem

A Creative Response

1. **Writing a Description.** Choose a building, preferably an old one that you have seen often. Write a paragraph or a short poem describing the building as it is now, and as it once was. Does the change in the building reflect a wider change in society, or in your town?
2. **Comparing and Contrasting Poems.** In 1867, Henry Timrod (1828–1867) wrote the following poem for the commemoration of the graves of the Confederate dead at Magnolia Cemetery in Charleston, South Carolina. In an essay, explain how this poem is like or unlike Lowell's in terms of (a) **theme** or **message**, (b) **tone**, (c) **diction**, and (d) **form**.

Ode on the Confederate Dead

SUNG AT THE OCCASION OF DECORATING
THE GRAVES AT MAGNOLIA CEMETERY,
CHARLESTON, S.C., 1867

Sleep sweetly in your humble graves,
  Sleep, martyrs of a fallen cause;
Though yet no marble column craves
  The pilgrim here to pause.

5 In seeds of laurel in the earth
    The blossom of your fame is blown,
And somewhere, waiting for its birth,
    The shaft is in the stone!°

Meanwhile, behalf the tardy years
10   Which keep in trust your storied tombs,
Behold! your sisters bring their tears,
    And these memorial blooms.

Small tributes! but your shades will smile
    More proudly on these wreaths today,
15 Than when some cannon-molded pile
    Shall overlook this bay.

Stoop, angels, hither from the skies!
    There is no holier spot of ground
Than where defeated valor lies,
20   By mourning beauty crowned!

---

8. An allusion to the Arthurian legend. Arthur proved he was the rightful king by pulling a sword out of a stone.

Richard Wilbur
(1921–   )

New York City was his birthplace, but Richard Wilbur grew up in suburban New Jersey. He attended Amherst College in Massachusetts, served with combat troops in Europe during World War II, and went to graduate school at Harvard. There he prepared for the illustrious teaching career that has taken him to long-term appointments at Wellesley, Wesleyan (Connecticut), and Smith.

From the moment his first book, *The Beautiful Changes* (1947), arrived on the poetic scene, Wilbur was recognized as the most graceful and technically adept poet in the younger generation. His poetry is reminiscent of the meters and natural speech of Robert Frost and of the metaphysical elegance and emotional reticence of Wallace Stevens.

But the influences of Frost and Stevens are merely overtones. Wilbur's poetic character is forged of his own unassertive religious devotion, his political liberalism, and his irrepressible delight in "the things of this world." Wilbur writes at a time when poetry has often been marked by self-exploitation and formlessness, as well as by uneasy borrowings from the paintings of minimalists and surrealists. But Wilbur has continued to write lyrics demanding scrupulous care and skill. His inward vision of delight finds expression in measured speech and indelible metaphor.

Wilbur's famous English translation of Moliere's comedy *The Misanthrope* has been followed in recent years by other translations from the great French playwright.

When Wilbur is not embarked on reading tours that take him across the breadth of the continent, he divides his time between Cummington, Massachusetts, the Berkshire village where he lives within a stone's throw of the homestead of William Cullen Bryant, and Key West, Florida. There his house is almost adjacent to the residences of his fellow poets John Ciardi and James Merrill.

Wilbur's collection *Things of This World* (1956) won the Pulitzer Prize and the National Book Award. In 1987 he was named America's Poet Laureate.

This title presents us with an ambiguity: Does it mean that our idea of what is beautiful is subject to change? Or does it suggest that the poem is about changes, or with beautiful transformations? As we learn almost at once, the poem erases these distinctions by uniting them: The beautiful *does* change, and changes can be beautiful.

"Queen Anne's Lace" is a common weed. Its flower looks like a crocheted doily with a tiny ruby at its center. "Lucernes" is a reference to the glacier-fed Alpine *Lac Lucerne* in Switzerland.

The Beautiful Changes

One wading a Fall meadow finds on all sides
The Queen Anne's Lace lying like lilies
On water; it glides
So from the walker, it turns
5   Dry grass to a lake, as the slightest shade of you
Valleys my mind in fabulous blue Lucernes.

The beautiful changes as a forest is changed
By a chameleon's tuning his skin to it;
As a mantis, arranged
10 On a green leaf, grows
Into it, makes the leaf leafier, and proves
Any greenness is deeper than anyone knows.

Your hands hold roses always in a way that says
They are not only yours; the beautiful changes
15 In such kind ways,
Wishing ever to sunder
Things and things' selves for a second finding, to lose
For a moment all that it touches back to wonder.

Responding to the Poem

Analyzing the Poem

Identifying Details

1. What does the Queen Anne's Lace do to the dry grass? What does the thought of "you" do to the speaker?
2. What do the chameleon and the mantis in stanza 2 have in common?
3. What does the beautiful do in the last stanza?

Interpreting Meanings

4. With great delicacy, the final stanza makes a strong statement. **Paraphrase** that statement.
5. In your own words explain the two meanings expressed by the title. Does the poem as a whole support one meaning or the other, or both?
6. Is this a love poem? Pick out the lines that support your answer.

Time is the name we give to an idea. "More time, more time," says Richard Wilbur. He speaks for us all in a poem concerned with a moment that includes eternity. The occasion is New Year's Eve, when the bells that tell time are "wrangling" with the snow that marks time, as if there were something uneasy and still unresolved in the relationship of a minute of time to all time.

The first two stanzas give us pictures of time present. In the third and fourth stanzas, time past is made vivid by what has survived: the outlines of million-year-old ferns as they are found pressed into stone; the huge prehistoric beasts called mammoths—some of which, buried in the ice of polar regions, are still visible; and the famous little dog perfectly preserved in the same volcanic ashes that suffocated the great city of Pompeii nearly two thousand years ago.

Year's End

Now winter downs the dying of the year,
And night is all a settlement of snow;
From the soft street the rooms of houses show
A gathered light, a shapen atmosphere,
5   Like frozen-over lakes whose ice is thin
And still allows some stirring down within.

I've known the wind by water banks to shake
The late leaves down, which frozen where they fell
And held in ice as dancers in a spell
10   Fluttered all winter long into a lake;
Graved on the dark in gestures of descent,
They seemed their own most perfect monument.

Six O'Clock by Charles Burchfield (1936). Watercolor.

Everson Museum of Art, Syracuse, New York.

There was perfection in the death of ferns
Which laid their fragile cheeks against the stone
15   A million years. Great mammoths overthrown
Composedly have made their long sojourns,
Like palaces of patience, in the gray
And changeless lands of ice. And at Pompeii

The little dog lay curled and did not rise
20   But slept the deeper as the ashes rose
And found the people incomplete, and froze
The random hands, the loose unready eyes
Of men expecting yet another sun
To do the shapely thing they had not done.

25   These sudden ends of time must give us pause.
We fray into the future, rarely wrought
Save in the tapestries of afterthought.
More time, more time. Barrages of applause
Come muffled from a buried radio.
30   The New-year bells are wrangling with the snow.

Responding to the Poem

Analyzing the Poem

Identifying Details

1. At what time of year is the speaker expressing his thoughts?
2. In line 1, what two different meanings of the word *down* are suggested?
3. What examples does the poet use in the third and fourth stanzas to illustrate the "sudden ends of time"?
4. What does the poet compare people to in lines 26 and 27?

Interpreting Meanings

5. Why does the speaker ask for "more time"? (line 28)
6. Why do you think the radio is "buried"? (line 29)
7. What is the **problem,** or tension, that the speaker presents in this poem? How does the **image** in the last line concisely express that tension?
8. Do you agree that we "fray into the future"? Explain.

Writing About the Poems

A Critical Response

Analyzing the Poems. In both "The Beautiful Changes" and "Year's End," Wilbur gently challenges common assumptions about beauty, love, and death. In a brief essay, show how Wilbur attempts to persuade us of an unusual, even **paradoxical** (seemingly contradictory) way of considering these subjects.

Analyzing Language and Style

Sound Effects

Wilbur's poems often have the effect of free verse, but they are written with the most careful attention to metrics and rhyme.

1. What is the **rhyme scheme** of "Year's End"?
2. Can you find any **internal rhymes**?
3. What basic **meter** is the poem written in?
4. What variations does the poet introduce to keep the meter from sounding sing-song and the rhymes from sounding mechanical?
5. How many examples of **alliteration** can you find? Of **assonance**?
6. What sounds in the poem seem to echo the poem's sense, or contribute to its mood?

James Dickey
(1923–   )

One of the most robust and resourceful of American poets, James Dickey was born in Atlanta, Georgia, and educated at Vanderbilt University in Nashville, Tennessee. He has exemplified the modern spirit of his native state ever since, at the comparatively late age of thirty-seven, he published his first collection of poems. This volume announced the arrival of a talent independent of poetic "schools," or even of the bookish life styles to which most young poets are drawn. A high-school football player, a fighter pilot in World War II and in the Korean War, as well as an enthusiastic hunter (sometimes with bow and arrow), Dickey comes to poetry as a man of action. His deepest philosophical concerns have to do with conscious man and woman and unconscious nature, and the endless lessons to be learned from their interaction.

At his best, Dickey is a poet of situations gravely posed, of situations dramatized by moral alternatives or made urgent by haunting questions of guilt, regret, and human culpability.

Dickey's story-telling talent is matched by the vigor and skill of his "open" poetic techniques. But though he dispenses with conventional forms, he does not abandon the rigid control they demand. Dickey depends on his own innate sense of balance and spacing to achieve what other poets can achieve only by more formal means.

Dickey has been much in the public eye since the success of his novel *Deliverance* (1970) and the motion picture based on it (in which he appeared in the role of a sheriff). Dickey is also remembered as the only poet besides Robert Frost whose friendship with a President—in his case, with fellow Georgian Jimmy Carter—has become part of the literary lore of the century.

As in all dreams, the details are photographically exact, and yet the meaning is elusive. To share his funeral march, the poet asks us to share the dream that he had—at least insofar as he can re-create it in words.

Sled Burial, Dream Ceremony

Cross by the Sea, Canada
by Georgia O'Keeffe
(1932). Oil.

The Currier Gallery of Art,
Manchester, New Hampshire.

While the south rains, the north
Is snowing, and the dead southerner
Is taken there. He lies with the top of his casket
Open, his hair combed, the particles in the air
5 Changing to other things. The train stops

In a small furry village, and men in flap-eared caps
And others with women's scarves tied around their heads
And business hats over those, unload him,
And one of them reaches inside the coffin and places
10 The southerner's hand at the center

Of his dead breast. They load him onto a sled,
An old-fashioned sled with high-curled runners,
Drawn by horses with bells, and begin
To walk out of town, past dull red barns
15   Inching closer to the road as it snows

Harder, past an army of gunny-sacked bushes,
Past horses with flakes in the hollows of their swaybacks,
Past round faces drawn by children
On kitchen windows, all shedding basic-shaped tears.
20   The coffin top still is wide open;

His dead eyes stare through his lids,
Not fooled that the snow is cotton. The woods fall
Slowly off all of them, until they are walking
Between rigid little houses of ice-fishers
25   On a plain which is a great plain of water

Until the last rabbit track fails, and they are
At the center. They take axes, shovels, mattocks,
Dig the snow away, and saw the ice in the form
Of his coffin, lifting the slab like a door
30   Without hinges. The snow creaks under the sled

As they unload him like hay, holding his weight by ropes.
Sensing an unwanted freedom, a fish
Slides by, under the hole leading up through the snow
To nothing, and is gone. The coffin's shadow
35   Is white, and they stand there, gunny-sacked bushes,

Summoned from village sleep into someone else's dream
Of death, and let him down, still seeing the flakes in the air
At the place they are born of pure shadow
Like his dead eyelids, rocking for a moment like a boat
40   On utter foreignness, before he fills and sails down.

Responding to the Poem

Analyzing the Poem

Identifying Details

1. Briefly summarize what happens to the southerner.
2. What is the dead person compared to in lines 39–40?

Interpreting Meanings

3. The phrase "gunny-sacked bushes" appears twice. What is compared to the wrapped-up bushes in each **metaphor**?

4. What new **simile** is introduced in the last stanza? Do you think this could suggest that one kind of journey may lead to the beginning of another? If so, what could that other journey be?
5. This is a dream meditation on death. Why do you think the poet chose to make the dead man from the South and to situate his burial spot in the North?
6. What lines in the poem seem appropriate to the perception of events in a dream?
7. Do you think this poem has anything in common with Williams's poem "Tract" (page 738)? Explain.

James Merrill
(1926–)

The most urbane and learned of contemporary American poets, James Merrill was born in New York City, the son of one of the nation's most eminent businessmen. He spent his childhood in New York and on the eastern shore of Long Island before he was sent to Lawrenceville Academy in New Jersey. Following in his father's footsteps, Merrill attended Amherst College. After living for extensive periods in Paris and Rome, he took up a semi-permanent residence in Athens, which lasted for more than two decades. But Merrill's life abroad was not one of self-imposed exile or—as in the case of the famous expatriate writers of the 1920's—based on a desire to escape the parochialism of American culture. Merrill returned to his own country often. He held short-term teaching positions at several colleges, gave hundreds of public readings, and maintained many close friendships in the academic and literary communities.

Merrill's talent was full-blown and distinctive by the time he reached the age of twenty—a fact that marks him as a prodigy. He was one of those people—rare among writers, but not among musicians and painters—whose earliest works show signs of precocious mastery. Beginning as a lyricist, Merrill published nine volumes of increasingly impressive work before turning his attention to the slow and artful composition of an epic, *The Changing Light at Sandover*. No doubt the longest poem in recent years, this poem is also regarded by many critics and scholars as one of the greatest works of epic dimension in this century. It was published in three separate books that were, each in its own way, so extraordinarily brilliant that they brought Merrill almost every award and prize that poetry is capable of garnering. *The Changing Light at Sandover* appeared as one volume in 1981. Some reviewers and academics hailed it as one of the supreme products of American genius. But others in literary and academic professions took the poem as an affront. It was a prodigious performance, which disturbed minds with settled views and forced them to consider what they could not comfortably ignore.

Merrill was aware of the controversial reception of his masterpiece, but he was not involved in either its defense or its promotion. Merrill soon returned to lyrics that annotate his engagement with life as it is lived between his permanent home in the seaside village of Stonington, Connecticut, and his winter residence in the historically designated "old town" of Key West, Florida.

Imagine this poem as being set in the nineteenth century. Try to hear the difference between the parson's words and the words of the speaker of the poem.

Kite Poem

"One is reminded of a certain person,"
Continued the parson, settling back in his chair
With a glass of port, "who sought to emulate
The sport of birds (it was something of a chore)
5   By climbing up on a kite. They found his coat
Two counties away; the man himself was missing."

His daughters tittered: it was meant to be a lesson
To them—they had been caught kissing, or some such nonsense,
The night before, under the crescent moon.
10   So, finishing his pheasant, their father began
This thirty-minute discourse, ending with
A story improbable from the start. He paused for breath,

Having shown but a few of the dangers. However, the wind
Blew out the candles and the moon wrought changes
15   Which the daughters felt along their stockings. Then,
Thus persuaded, they fled to their young men
Waiting in the sweet night by the raspberry bed,
And kissed and kissed, as though to escape on a kite.

Responding to the Poem

Analyzing the Poem

Identifying Details

1. What story does the parson tell his daughters? Why does he tell it?
2. How do the daughters react to his instructive tale?
3. What do the daughters do later?
4. How many **internal rhymes,** approximate rhymes, and examples of **alliteration,** can you find in the poem?

Interpreting Meanings

5. The poem begins with a little story containing a moral. When it ends, that moral has been forgotten and replaced by another. What is the moral we are left with?

6. The parson stands for one thing; the moon for another. How would you state the difference?
7. Why does the poet call this "Kite Poem"?

Writing About the Poem

A Creative Response

Taking Another Point of View. Write the daughters' response to the parson. Have them explain the moral they took from his story (which was not the moral he intended).

Adrienne Rich
(1929–   )

Adrienne Rich was born in Baltimore, Maryland. She attended Radcliffe College and published her first volume of poems, *A Change of World,* in 1951, the year she graduated. Poet W. H. Auden selected the volume for the prestigious Yale University Press Younger Poets Series. In his introduction, he wrote that Rich's poems ''are neatly and modestly dressed, speak quietly but do not mumble, respect their elders but are not cowed by them.''

Rich later saw these poems as too heavily influenced by her ''elders,'' especially by British modernist poets like W. B. Yeats and Auden himself. Their tightly constructed forms, she felt, had gotten in the way of the personal and political subject matter she had wanted to deal with but had been unable to write about directly. ''Formalism,'' she wrote of these poems, ''was part of the strategy—like asbestos gloves, it allowed me to handle materials I couldn't pick up barehanded.''

In her later volumes, especially those published after the mid-1960's, Rich strove to break away from the tight craftsmanship of her early poems, and her work became more feminist and political in content. She had come to see, she later wrote, that ''politics was not something 'out there' but something 'in here' and of the essence of my condition.'' As she examined her own situation as a woman, Rich was also addressing larger questions of personal and political relationships.

Like Robert Lowell (page 1098) and Sylvia Plath (page 1115), Rich presented herself as a representative of her times; the less rigid and

less traditional forms that she later adopted allowed her to handle such subject matter ''barehanded.'' Her later poems, collected in such volumes as *The Will to Change* (1971), *Diving into the Wreck* (1973), and *A Wild Patience Has Taken Me This Far* (1981), became somewhat less ''neatly and modestly dressed,'' but they also became more direct and more urgent. She was ''diving into the wreck,'' as she wrote in one poem, ''to see the damage that was done / and the treasures that prevail.''

With the assistance of her husband, Polish-born Marie Curie (1867–1934) discovered radium, the radioactive element that made X-rays, nuclear fission, and nuclear weapons possible. Twice awarded the Nobel Prize, once for physics and once for chemistry, she remains the most honored woman scientist in history. But, like many of the survivors of the atomic bomb dropped on Hiroshima, Marie Curie died of the effects of radiation. In her case, the deadly emanations came not from a bomb dropped from the sky, but from the substances stored in her own laboratory.

Power

Living   in the earth-deposits   of our history

Today a backhoe divulged   out of a crumbling flank of earth
one bottle   amber   perfect   a hundred-year-old
cure for fever   or melancholy   a tonic
5   for living on this earth   in the winters of this climate

Today I was reading about Marie Curie:
she must have known she suffered   from radiation sickness
her body bombarded for years   by the element
she had purified
10   It seems she denied to the end
the source of the cataracts on her eyes
the cracked and suppurating skin   of her finger-ends
till she could no longer hold   a test-tube or a pencil

She died   a famous woman   denying
15   her wounds
denying
her wounds   came   from the same source as her power

Responding to the Poem

Analyzing the Poem

Identifying Details

1. What accidental discovery, described in the first stanza, is the occasion for the poem?

Interpreting Meanings

2. How would you state directly the grim **ironies** of this poem?
3. Can you think of other situations in which "wounds" might come from the same source as "power"?
4. Do you think this is a political poem? If so, give your reasons.

Writing About the Poem

A Critical Response

Analyzing the Poem. The poem is concerned with two discoveries. In an essay, tell what you think they have in common, and what is their essential difference.

Sylvia Plath
(1932–1963)

Until her tragic death in 1963, Sylvia Plath's existence was, from most appearances, a model of achievement. She was born in Boston and spent her early years in the nearby seaside town of Winthrop. Both her parents were immigrants—her father, a professor of biology at Boston University, from Poland, and her mother, a teacher of secretarial skills, from Austria. A key event in Sylvia's life was the death of her father from diabetes, when she was only eight years old.

Plath started writing stories and poems while she was still in grammar school. Even at the earliest stages of her career, she was persistent: she received forty-five rejection slips from *Seventeen* magazine before finally publishing a story there in 1950. She won a scholarship to Smith College, where she flourished. She was active in campus activities, went off to Yale and Harvard for parties and dances, and continued to write poems and stories. She won a much-coveted fiction prize at *Mademoiselle* magazine in her junior year at Smith, and spent that summer as a guest editor in the magazine's New York office.

The first serious sign of the dangerous turbulence in her emotional life came at the end of that storybook summer, when she was overcome by depression and attempted suicide. After a period of psychiatric treatment and electro-shock therapy—"the agony of slow rebirth and psychic regeneration," as she called it—she returned to college and her promising career. But she was ill with manic depression, years before drug therapy was available.

After graduating *summa cum laude* from Smith, Plath went to Cambridge University in England on a Fulbright fellowship. At Cambridge, she met English poet Ted Hughes, whom she married in 1956. They lived in Boston during the late 1950's, and in early 1960 they moved to London, where Plath's first book of poetry, *The Colossus,* was published. In April of that year, their daughter Frieda was born. A second child, Nicholas, was born in 1962. The following year, Plath's autobiographical novel, *The Bell Jar,* was published.

During 1962 and the first weeks of 1963, in London, Plath wrote poetry at a furious pace—sometimes two or three poems a day. The subject matter and style of these poems, published in a volume called *Ariel* three years after her death, were significantly different from her earlier work. Most of the poems in *The Colossus* were relatively restrained and formal, displaying the influence of a number of poets, from the classicism of John Crowe Ransom (page 692) to the exuberance of Theodore Roethke (page 1084). But the *Ariel* poems, especially the bitter poems about her father and about her own attempts at suicide, showed a violence and a frankness that no reader of her earlier work would have anticipated. As Robert Lowell wrote in his foreword to the book, "These poems are playing Russian roulette with six cartridges in the cylinder, a game of 'chicken,' the wheels of both cars locked and unable to swerve." The poems were, he said, an "appalling and triumphant fulfillment" of her talents, but they came at an unbearably high price. By 1963, Plath was separated from her husband and caring for two babies in an unheated London flat. In February, during the coldest London winter in a hundred and fifty years, Plath's depression returned. She attempted suicide again, and this time she succeeded.

The word *spinster* is an uncomplimentary term for a woman, usually an older one, who has never married. In this poem, the psychology of one spinster who chose to remain unmarried is explained in terms of order and disorder, safety and jeopardy, and their counterparts in the actual and symbolic aspects of winter and spring. This poem is from Plath's first collection, *The Colossus*.

Spinster

Now this particular girl
During a ceremonious April walk
With her latest suitor
Found herself, of a sudden, intolerably struck
5   By the birds' irregular babel
And the leaves' litter.

By this tumult afflicted, she
Observed her lover's gestures unbalance the air,
His gait stray uneven
10   Through a rank wilderness of fern and flower.
She judged petals in disarray,
The whole season, sloven.

How she longed for winter then!—
Scrupulously austere in its order
15   Of white and black
Ice and rock, each sentiment within border,
And heart's frosty discipline
Exact as a snowflake.

But here—a burgeoning
20   Unruly enough to pitch her five queenly wits
Into vulgar motley—
A treason not to be borne. Let idiots
Reel giddy in bedlam spring:
She withdrew neatly.

25   And round her house she set
Such a barricade of barb and check
Against mutinous weather
As no mere insurgent man could hope to break
With curse, fist, threat
30   Or love, either.

Responding to the Poem

Analyzing the Poem

Identifying Details

1. Describe the situation in the first stanza. What sounds and sights so upset the girl?
2. What increases the girl's sense of affliction in the second stanza?
3. What aspects of winter in the third stanza contrast with the aspects of April that the girl observes on her walk?
4. What does the girl do in the fourth and fifth stanzas? What is she trying to "keep out" in the fifth stanza?

Interpreting Meaning

5. *Bedlam,* in stanza 4, is the archaic word for an insane asylum. It is drawn from the name *Bethlehem,* the name of the famous "madhouse" in the city of London. How can "spring" be regarded as a kind of "bedlam" or "chaos"? Why would anyone "fear" spring?
6. The fifth stanza is about the defenses put up by "this particular girl" once she has withdrawn from April, her suitor, and the normal expectations of society. What are these defenses? Do you think they are actual defenses, or are they more **symbolic**? Explain.
7. How might the poem be read not only as a comment on a particular kind of female psychology, but also as a series of **metaphors** that illuminate a kind of temperament that is not necessarily female?

Analyzing Language and Vocabulary

Multiple Meanings

1. In stanza 4, *burgeoning* means, literally, "to come into flower," as in the case of buds, leaves, and blossoms. *Burgeoning* can also refer to "the sudden manifestation of a feeling or an idea." How, in this stanza, are both meanings of *burgeoning* suggested?
2. "Motley" in stanza 4 refers to a kind of multicolored costume worn by clowns and jesters. Used as an adjective, it can also mean "made up of different elements." When the girl's "five *queenly* wits" (that is, her five senses) are pitched "into *vulgar* motley," what do you picture happening? What—psychologically speaking—is also happening?

Emily Dickinson and the Raven by Will Barnet (1980). Oil.

The Kennedy Galleries, New York City.

John Berryman
(1914–1972)

Like his friend Robert Lowell, John Berryman started his career in the 1940's by writing tight, complex poems influenced by the great poets of the early twentieth century. The major influence for Lowell was T. S. Eliot; for Berryman, it was the Irish poet William Butler Yeats. Both Lowell and Berryman changed their styles drastically in the late 1950's and early 1960's. Lowell shifted to the looser, more relaxed verse of *Life Studies.* Berryman moved to a quirky, nervous, eighteen-line form that he used in his long work, *The Dream Songs* (1969), published in segments over a thirteen-year period. One volume of this work won the Pulitzer Prize in 1964.

In *The Dream Songs,* Berryman created a character he called Henry. Through Henry, the poet dealt with a vast number of subjects, public and private, in an eccentric style that sometimes baffled critics. The book was a personal record of the poet's turbulent life, and his responses to events, especially the deaths of his poet friends.

John Berryman was born John Smith in McAlester, Oklahoma. His father was a banker and his mother was a schoolteacher. When John was ten, the family moved to Tampa, Florida. His parents' marriage was stormy and unstable, and a few months before John's twelfth birthday his father shot himself to death outside the boy's window.

John's mother moved to New York and re-married, and the boy took on his stepfather's name. He graduated from Columbia University in New York City and spent two years at Cambridge University in England. When he returned to the United States, he began teaching and writing. During his career, he taught at a number of schools, including Harvard, Princeton, and the University of Minnesota.

In 1948, Berryman published his first volume, *The Dispossessed.* Some of these poems dealt indirectly with his father's death, others with World War II. The sense of dispossession, of being "put out of one's own," as Berryman later referred to it, pervades much of his early work. Berryman felt personally dispossessed by the loss of his father, and publicly dispossessed by the actions of governments during the war.

In 1956, Berryman published *Homage to Mistress Bradstreet,* an unusual, book-length poem about the Colonial poet Anne Bradstreet and the alienation he imagined she experienced. Here too, Berryman's sense of loss and dispossession is strong: "Both of our worlds unhanded us," Berryman says to the Colonial poet at one point.

This poem is partly an interpretation of *Hunters in the Snow,* a painting by the great sixteenth-century Flemish artist Pieter Brueghel (see opposite). It is also an independent discourse on time, history, and the nature of art. The poem's twenty-five lines make up a single sentence. Notice how skillfully the strict iambic rhythm flows from beginning to end.

Winter Landscape

The three men coming down the winter hill
In brown, with tall poles and a pack of hounds
At heel, through the arrangement of the trees,
Past the five figures at the burning straw,
5   Returning cold and silent to their town,

Returning to the drifted snow, the rink
Lively with children, to the older men,
The long companions they can never reach,
The blue light, men with ladders, by the church
10   The sledge and shadow in the twilit street,

Hunters in the Snow by Pieter Brueghel the Elder (1565). Oil on wood.

Kunsthistoriches Museum, Vienna.

John Berryman   1121

Are not aware that in the sandy time
To come, the evil waste of history
Outstretched, they will be seen upon the brow
Of that same hill: when all their company
15   Will have been irrecoverably lost,

These men, this particular three in brown
Witnessed by birds will keep the scene and say
By their configuration with the trees,
The small bridge, the red houses and the fire,
20   What place, what time, what morning occasion

Sent them into the wood, a pack of hounds
At heel and the tall poles upon their shoulders,
Thence to return as now we see them and
Ankle-deep in snow down the winter hill
25   Descend, while three birds watch and the fourth flies.

Responding to the Poem

Analyzing the Poem

Identifying Details

1. Describe the scene in the painting that Berryman uses as the basis for the poem.
2. What details emphasize that the scene has been frozen in time?

Interpreting Meanings

3. In stanza 1, what does the word *arrangement* suggest? What are the implications of this word for both a poet and a painter?
4. In the second stanza, the statement about the "older men" in lines 6 and 7 has to do with both life and art. In terms of life, what does this statement suggest? What does it say about art?
5. What are the implications of the word *sandy* in line 11? In what ways might history be considered an "evil waste"?
6. In the fourth stanza, what word echoes *arrangement* in line 3? How does this word remind us that art does not merely record life, but manipulates it?

Writing About the Poem

A Creative Response

Imitating the Poet's Technique. Either continue to write about Brueghel's winter landscape, or take another painting from this book and describe what you think the original scene was like. Describe what will "never happen" in that painting.

James Wright (1927–1980)

James Wright, the son of a factory worker, was born in Martins Ferry, Ohio, that part of the country that was once considered the crossroads of the industrial North and the rural South. Early on, Wright came to know the sooty hills and blast furnaces of his hometown. His knowledge of the men and women whose existence was governed by job lay-offs and the ups and downs of the economy remained with him all his life and became an important source of his poetry.

While he was attending a vocational high school in Martins Ferry, two of Wright's teachers became aware of his unusual writing ability and encouraged him to develop his talent. He went on to study at Kenyon College in Ohio with John Crowe Ransom (page 692), the eminent poet and teacher. He spent a year in Vienna and returned to do graduate work at the University of Washington. There he came under the good influence of another famous poet-teacher, Theodore Roethke (page 1084). Wright's own distinction as a poet was recognized at once when, at the age of thirty, he published his first book, *The Green Wall* (1957).

For most of his adult life, Wright taught literature and creative writing at the University of Minnesota, at Macalester College in St. Paul, Minnesota, and finally at Hunter College in New York City, where he died at the age of fifty-two.

Wright's lyricism is based on a clear-eyed sense of the gritty realities of a seam of American life that is more often sung about in country music than in poetry. His sympathetic concern for the poor and the inarticulate gives his work a strong emotional focus. But he avoids the predictable sentimental pitfalls through the elegance and economy of his style.

Wright said, toward the end of his life, "I have written about the things I am deeply concerned with—crickets outside my window, cold and hungry old men, ghosts in the twilight, horses in a field, a red-haired child in her mother's arms, a feeling of desolation in the fall, some cities I've known. I try and say how I love my country and how I despise the way it is treated. I try and speak of the beauty and again of the ugliness in the lives of the poor and neglected."

Horses at a Mountain Stream by Frederic Remington. Oil.   The Kennedy Galleries, New York City.

A simple everyday incident leads to a moment of transcendence—an experience in which actuality falls away and the spirit is released into a state of being for which most people can find no words. Here a poet describes that state as one in which he feels as though he might "break into blossom."

A Blessing

Just off the highway to Rochester, Minnesota,
Twilight bounds softly forth on the grass.
And the eyes of those two Indian ponies
Darken with kindness.
5 They have come gladly out of the willows
To welcome my friend and me.
We step over the barbed wire into the pasture
Where they have been grazing all day, alone.
They ripple tensely, they can hardly contain their happiness
10 That we have come.
They bow shyly as wet swans. They love each other.
There is no loneliness like theirs.
At home once more,
They begin munching the young tufts of spring in the darkness.
15 I would like to hold the slenderer one in my arms,
For she has walked over to me
And nuzzled my left hand.
She is black and white,
Her mane falls wild on her forehead,
20 And the light breeze moves me to caress her long ear
That is delicate as the skin over a girl's wrist.
Suddenly I realize
That if I stepped out of my body I would break
Into blossom.

Responding to the Poem

Analyzing the Poem

Identifying Details

1. In one sense, the poem is a progression from a road in Minnesota to a "place" that exists only in the realm of feeling. Trace the steps by which the speaker is led from a spot on the map to a "place" with no physical location.
2. **Anthropomorphism** is a term used to describe the tendency of human beings to read their own feelings into nonhuman objects. In how many places in this poem does the author ascribe human feelings to the ponies?

Interpreting Meanings

3. What is the significance of the poem's title?
4. What do you think the author means by the phrase, "There is no loneliness like theirs" (line 12)?
5. In Greek mythology, human beings often undergo marvelous transformations called **metamorphoses**. What metamorphosis ends this poem? Do you think it is a good one to describe a particular feeling?

Writing About the Poem

Comparing Two Writers. In an essay, identify all the points of comparison you can find between this poem and the prose extract from *Nature* by Emerson on page 191.

Julia Alvarez
(1950–   )

Born in New York City, Julia (pronounced
"hoolia") Alvarez spent her early childhood in
the Dominican Republic. She has been a scholar
at the Breadloaf Writer's Conference in Vermont
and has won the American Academy of Poetry
Prize. Linda Pastan, also a poet, has said of Alvarez's work: "Searching for the secret meanings of what has been known as woman's work,
Julia Alvarez in this promising first book is also
searching for the secret meanings of her womanhood." Other critics have noticed that she explores her ambivalent relations to the lost
Caribbean heritage she inherited from her
mother.

Alvarez's first book of poetry, called *Homecoming* (1984), includes many poems on domestic subjects (such as "Dusting," "Making Our
Beds," and the poem that follows). Alvarez
teaches creative writing at George Washington
University.

You won't read far in this poem before you discover allusions to the war in Vietnam. Read
aloud, to hear how the poet manages to make a
poem written with concern for meter and rhyme
sound like everyday conversation.

How I Learned to Sweep

My mother never taught me sweeping. . . .
One afternoon she found me watching
TV. She eyed the dusty floor
boldly, and put a broom before
5   me, and said she'd like to be able
to eat her dinner off that table,
and nodded at my feet, then left.
I knew right off what she expected
and went at it. I stepped and swept;
10   the TV blared the news; I kept
my mind on what I had to do,
until in minutes, I was through.
Her floor was as immaculate
as a just-washed dinner plate.
15   I waited for her to return
and turned to watch the President,
live from the White House, talk of war:
in the Far East our soldiers were
landing in their helicopters
20   into jungles their propellers

swept like weeds seen underwater
while perplexing shots were fired
from those beautiful green gardens
into which these dragonflies
25   filled with little men descended.
I got up and swept again.
as they fell out of the sky.
I swept all the harder when
I watched a dozen of them die . . .
30   as if their dust tell through the screen
upon the floor I had just cleaned.
She came back and turned the dial;
The screen went dark. *That's beautiful,*
she said, and ran her clean hand through
35   my hair, and on, over the window-
sill, coffee table, rocker, desk,
and held it up—I held my breath—
That's beautiful, she said, impressed,
she hadn't found a speck of death.

Responding to the Poem

Analyzing the Poem

Identifying Details

1. What was on TV the afternoon the speaker learned to sweep?
2. According to the speaker, why was her mother impressed with her work?
3. Where does this poet use **rhymes**? How would you describe the poem's **meter**? Give reasons for your answers.

Interpreting Meanings

4. What are the dragonflies in line 24? Why do you think the speaker sweeps all the harder as they fall out of the sky?
5. What do you think she is trying to clean, in addition to her mother's dusty floor?

6. What is the significance of the last line, in light of what the speaker has seen on TV? Explain.
7. Is this poem about sweeping, or is it really about something else? Explain your opinion.

Writing About the Poem

A Critical Response

1. **Analyzing an Image.** In a brief essay, trace the use of the image of dust in this poem. What do you think the dust might mean in the poem? Why do you think the writer uses the word *dust* instead of the word *dirt* or *grit*?
2. **Comparing Poems.** In a brief essay, compare and contrast the imagery used in Alvarez's and Ginsberg's poems. What aspect of modern life does each poet draw his or her imagery from?

Allen Ginsberg
(1926–   )

The son of Louis Ginsberg, a schoolteacher and poet of conventional tendencies and modest reputation, Allen Ginsberg was born in Newark, New Jersey, and brought up in nearby Paterson. Paterson is the industrial town given literary prominence by William Carlos Williams, the poet who came to be young Ginsberg's spiritual father and poetic master. Like Williams, Ginsberg was at first attracted to the great poets of England. But in what amounted to a hundred and eighty degree turn in his thought and practice, Ginsberg soon became one of the staunchest promoters of the American idiom and of poetry that echoed the rhythms of American speech.

While still at Columbia College, from which he graduated in 1948, Ginsberg became associated with the novelist Jack Kerouac and with other young writers who would eventually constitute the literary movement known as the Beat Generation. In footloose travels abroad and "on the road" across the United States, Ginsberg typefied the restless and alienated nature of the Beat Generation and its sub-culture. When, at the age of thirty, he published his long poem *Howl,* Ginsberg became the Beats' most famous spokesman.

Ginsberg and other members of his Beat Generation eventually joined forces, so to speak, with Lawrence Ferlinghetti, Gary Snyder, and other writers with similar ideologies or techniques and established a group known as the San Francisco Renaissance. Ginsberg's influence broadened, and his role as a kind of literary and philosophical *guru* made him the standard-bearer of dissent in the conduct of life, as well as in the practice of his art.

In the open forms in which he writes, Ginsberg has explored Eastern and Western mysticism from Buddha to William Blake. Even though he has been preoccupied with the human psyche, Ginsberg has also called for realistic action against war, against the abuse of nature, and against all curbs on freedom.

This poem has a double meaning (pollution and politics) and a single point of view. The speaker is impatient with those powers that spoil the natural world and with those that contribute to the world's turmoil. Most of its references are the commonplace stuff of newspaper headlines. As you read, you might think of the poem as a series of exaggerated visual cartoons.

Homework

Homage Kenneth Koch

If I were doing my Laundry I'd wash my dirty Iran
I'd throw in my United States, and pour on the Ivory Soap, scrub up Africa,
   put all the birds and elephants back in the jungle,
I'd wash the Amazon river and clean the oily Carib & Gulf of Mexico,
Rub that smog off the North Pole, wipe up all the pipelines in Alaska,
Rub a dub dub for Rocky Flats and Los Alamos, Flush that sparkly Cesium
5   out of Love Canal
Rinse down the Acid Rain over the Parthenon & Sphinx, Drain the Sludge
   out of the Mediterranean basin & make it azure again,
Put some blueing back into the sky over the Rhine, bleach the little Clouds
   so snow return white as snow,
Cleanse the Hudson Thames & Neckar, Drain the Suds out of Lake Erie
Then I'd throw big Asia in one giant Load & wash out the blood & Agent Orange,
Dump the whole mess of Russia and China in the wringer, squeeze out the
10   tattletail Gray of U.S. Central American police state,
& put the planet in the drier & let it sit 20 minutes or an Aeon till it came
   out clean.

Responding to the Poem

Analyzing the Poem

Identifying Details

1. This poem refers to a number of social and environmental ills in the modern world. Identify as many of these situations as you can.
2. In the last line, how long does the speaker say he will wait for the wash to come "out clean"?
3. List the verbs in the poem that give it a sense of action. Do all the verbs have to do with doing a laundry?

Interpreting Meanings

4. What underlying **metaphor** pervades the poem?
5. Characterize the **tone** of the poem. How does Ginsberg mingle amusing and serious elements?
6. What significances can you identify in the poem's **title**?
7. What is Ginsberg's **main idea**? What do you think of his specific choices for the wash?

U.N. Painting by Larry Rivers (1959). Oil.

Writing About the Poem

A Creative Response

1. **Imitating the Writer's Technique.** Write a poem in which you describe, as Ginsberg does, what you would "wash" in the world if you could. Open with the line "If I were doing my laundry, I'd wash . . ." Imitate Ginsberg's technique and use proper names.

A Critical Response

2. **Evaluating the Poem.** In a brief essay, explain what elements qualify this piece of writing as a poem. Consider these elements of poetry: **repetition, rhythm, rhyme,** and **figurative language.**

EVALUATING A POEM

Writing Assignment
Write a brief essay in which you analyze and evaluate one of the following poems.

That Gull

That gull, for instance,
a clam in his straw beak
like a growth, or a black snout—
see how he loops it in toward shore
5 & with a rough
egg-breaking guess, drops it,
then swoops to gargle the soft stuff.

Observe how he leaves
his dishes broken & unwashed,
10 goes scissoring up & windward
—like the soul on its aëry ladders—
there to tilt & soar.
One more simile aloft, *n'est-ce pas,*°
in the vast metaphor?

—John Malcolm Brinnin

13. **n'est-ce pas** (nes pä'): French for "Right?" or "Isn't that so?"

Washyuma Motor Hotel

Beneath the cement foundations
of the motel, the ancient spirits
of the people conspire sacred tricks.
They tell stories and jokes and laugh
5 and laugh.

The American passersby
get out of their hot, stuffy cars
at evening, pay their money wordlessly,
and fall asleep without benefit of dreams.
10 The next morning, they get up,
dress automatically, brush their teeth,
get in their cars and drive away.
They haven't noticed that the cement
foundations of the motor hotel
15 are crumbling, but by bit.

The ancient spirits tell stories
and jokes and laugh and laugh.

—Simon J. Ortiz

Background
How can you evaluate the quality of a poem? When you evaluate something, you make judgments based on objective standards, or criteria. You can use the following guidelines to evaluate any poem. (You may want to add a few criteria of your own to this list.)

Guidelines for Evaluating a Poem
1. Do you **respond** in some way to the poem? Does it affect your emotions or make you think? Does it remind you of anything in your own experience?
2. What is the controlling **idea** in the poem? Is it an important idea, or an overworked idea?
3. Is every **word** in the poem necessary? Do the words express ideas precisely, or are they vague and inexact?
4. Does the poem contain fresh **images** and **figures of speech?** Or are they trite and clichéd?
5. Does the poem use **sound** effectively? Does the sound of the poem support the poem's meaning?

Prewriting

Before you write, be sure you have read the poem carefully several times. Read it at least once aloud. Be sure you can explain the figures of speech in the poem. (What is compared with what?) Be sure you understand all the words and allusions.

Then use the guidelines to take notes. Use your notes as the raw material for your essay.

Here are a few sample notes taken by a reader who was about to evaluate the poem "Homework" by Allen Ginsberg:

1. **Response:** poem made me laugh and then made me think about the whole idea of renewing the world. It also put very comical images in my head.
2. **Controlling idea:** that sometimes we dream of being so god-like that we could just scrub the world down so that it shines innocent and clean again. (A neat idea and an important one)
3. **Words:** many precise names and precise actions (name some verbs).
4. **Figures of speech:** best part of the poem. (Etc.)

Writing

Now write your evaluation of one of the poems here. Write at least four paragraphs.

Guidelines for Writing an Evaluation

1. In your opening paragraph, include a **thesis statement** that expresses your overall evaluation of the poem. Use the rest of your essay to present "evidence" to support this evaluation.
2. Organize your essay carefully. Present your ideas in the best possible order. You might want to save your most important point for last; or, you might want to start off with it.
3. Express your ideas in the clearest possible way. Get rid of excess wordiness.
4. Support every judgment with one or two examples. Quote phrases from the poem. Be sure to give the line number for each citation.

Revising and Proofreading

Reread your first draft several times. Make changes in wording and organization until you are satisfied. Be sure that you've supported your opinions or generalizations.

Use the guidelines in the section at the back of this book, called **Writing About Literature,** to revise and proofread your essay.

INDEX

1. E. B. White writes
2. Longfellow born
3. Bowdoin College
4. Millay born
5. E. A. Robinson writes
6. J. D. Salinger writes
7. Cummings lives
8. Frost's farm
9. Bradford writes
10. Rowlandson taken captive
11. Edwards's church
12. Bradstreet writes
13. Taylor's church
14. Bryant born
15. Whittier boyhood
16. Holmes born
17. James Russell Lowell born
18. Emerson born
19. Dickinson home
20. Walden Pond
21. Sexton born
22. Robert Lowell and Plath born
23. Algonquian myths and legends
24. Webster writes dictionary
25. Merrill lives
26. Knight travels
27. Stevens lives
28. Whitman writes
29. Melville born
30. Cullen writes
31. Singer writes
32. Hughes writes
33. Hersey writes
34. Herr writes
35. Helprin boyhood
36. Harte born
37. Crane born
38. Paine writes
39. Wilbur boyhood
40. Franklin writes
41. Andrea Lee born
42. Updike born
43. Jeffers born
44. Fitzgerald home
45. Douglass boyhood
46. Rich born
47. Byrd writes
48. Patrick Henry born
49. Jefferson born
50. Poe boyhood
51. Russell Baker born
52. Pearl S. Buck born
53. Thomas Wolfe born
54. O. Henry born
55. Henry Timrod born
56. O'Connor born
57. McPherson born
58. Walker born
59. James Weldon Johnson born
60. Tennessee Williams lives
61. Bishop lives
62. McKay studies (Tuskegee Inst.)
63. Jarrell born
64. Ransom teaches (Vanderbilt)
65. Dickey educated
66. Robert Penn Warren born
67. Dreiser born
68. Dunbar born
69. Bierce born
70. Thurber born
71. Sherwood Anderson's Winesburg
72. James Wright born
73. Roethke born
74. Hayden born
75. Thornton Wilder born
76. Tim O'Brien born
77. Sandburg born
78. Masters's Spoon River
79. Hansberry born
80. Sinclair Lewis born
81. Fitzgerald born
82. Toth girlhood
83. Twain boyhood
84. Eliot born
85. Moore born
86. Least Heat Moon writes
87. Williams's dramas
88. K.A. Porter born
89. Barthelme teaches
90. Berryman born
91. Brooks born
92. Masters born
93. Cather's stories
94. Chippewa and Sioux myths and legends
95. Momaday's Devils Tower
96. K.A. Porter writes
97. Momaday writes
98. Thornton Wilder writes
99. Navaho myths and legends
100. Pound born
101. Hemingway buried
102. Twain stories and sketches
103. Steinbeck stories
104. Frost born
105. Malamud teaches
106. Roethke teaches
107. Cheyenne myths and legends
108. Jack London stories
109. Kingston writes
110. Faulkner stories
111. Welty home
112. Richard Wright born
113. Jeffers writes

WRITING ABOUT LITERATURE

Writing Answers to Essay Questions

Most units in this book are followed by Exercises in Critical Thinking and Writing, which include step-by-step instruction in using the writing process for answering questions about literature. These exercises are listed in the index in the back of this book. The following strategies will give you additional help in organizing and writing your essays.

1. Read the essay question carefully. Make sure you understand exactly what the question is asking and note how much evidence is required. Look for these *key verbs*:

• **Analyze:** This verb means ''to break something down into its elements,'' so you can see its true nature.

EXAMPLE: *Analyze the character of Rip Van Winkle.*
STRATEGY: Review the ways a writer can create character (see page 1141). Then make a list of what you know about Rip and how you know it. Use your list to make a generalization about Rip's character.

• **Compare:** This means ''to point out similarities.'' **Contrast** means ''to point out differences.''

EXAMPLE: *Contrast ''Annabel Lee'' with ''Bells for John Whiteside's Daughter.''*
STRATEGY: Make a chart listing the differences in the poems. Focus on the elements of poetry: sound effects, form, figures of speech, imagery, tone, and main idea.

• **Describe:** This means you should tell how something looks, sounds, smells, tastes, or feels.

EXAMPLE: *Describe Jay Gatsby, as he is portrayed in ''Gatsby's Party.''*
STRATEGY: Reread the excerpt and list all the details describing Gatsby's appearance and manner. Look for details telling how Gatsby looks, acts, and speaks, and how he affects other people.

• **Discuss:** This means you should comment in a general way.

EXAMPLE: *Discuss the use of imagery in three poems by William Carlos Williams.*
STRATEGY: Make a list of the images and note where they are drawn from: nature, city, etc. Are the images important to the meaning and tone of the poems? What emotions do they carry?

• **Evaluate:** This means ''to judge how effective something is.''

EXAMPLE: *Evaluate the play* The Glass Menagerie.
STRATEGY: Think about the elements of drama and evaluate the way they are used in this particular play. Is the plot consistent and logical? Are the characters credible? Is the theme important and not trite? Is the language fresh and original?

• **Illustrate:** You should provide examples to support an idea or statement.

EXAMPLE: *Illustrate the use of dialect in Mark Twain's works.*
STRATEGY: First, define dialect. Then list the examples of dialectical pronunciations, vocabulary, and syntax in Twain's work. In your essay, cite a few examples of dialect that are most interesting, or funny, or convincing.

• **Interpret:** You must explain the meaning or importance of something.

EXAMPLE: *Interpret the theme of Malamud's story ''The Magic Barrel.''*
STRATEGY: First, reread the story carefully, and then write down several statements that might serve as the story's theme. Review the story to see which statement best covers all the key elements in the story. Cite incidents and key passages that support your statement of theme.

• **Respond:** This asks that you give your personal reactions to a work. (This is a ''subjective'' assignment.)

EXAMPLE: *Explain your response to Andrea Lee's story ''New African.''*
STRATEGY: Write down your immediate response: Tell whether you liked or disliked the story, how it made you feel, what it made you think about. Whenever possible, write down reasons for your response. Then review the main elements of the story (plot, character, theme, point of view, setting, tone) and write down your response to the way the writer used each element.

2. Write a thesis statement stating the main idea of your essay. Be sure to gather evidence to support your thesis statement. Do a rough outline that includes two or three main points to support the main idea. You may want to write several thesis statements and test each one out. Select the one that best covers all your main points.

3. Write one paragraph for each point you wish to make. Include topic sentences; try to express each topic as clearly and simply as you can.

4. End with a paragraph that summarizes or restates your main points. Try to conclude your essay with a good ''clincher sentence.''

Writing and Revising a Research Paper

You may be asked to choose your own topic for a research report about a literary work. This means that your essay should include information from three or more outside sources (sources in addition to the story, poem, play, essay, or novel you are writing about).

Prewriting

1. Choose a limited topic that you can cover adequately. In a report of 500–700 words, for example, you can't possibly cover all of Henry Wadsworth Longfellow's life or discuss all of his poetry. But you can discuss and interpret one poem, or you can compare and contrast two poems.

2. In the library, look for information about your topic, and take notes. You will find information in the card catalogue listed under the author's name. Your librarian will direct you to other reference works available in your particular library. As you take notes, use notecards, and be sure to include the source (title of book or magazine article, author, publisher, and date of copyright) and page reference on each card. You may have several different cards (on different topics) from a single source. For example, from one article about Longfellow's poetry, you might have one notecard on the various themes he wrote about and another separate card with comments on his imagery.

3. Write several thesis statements. Eventually you will select one that best covers your topic.

4. Develop a working outline. List two or three important ideas that will develop or support your thesis statement. To support each of these ideas, use quotations, specific details, and examples from the work you are writing about. (The work you are writing about is known as the *primary source*. You might also refer to other works, letters, and journals by the same writer. The quotations and information from books, articles, and reviews about the work or its writer are known as *secondary sources*.) Once you've arranged your main ideas and quotations in the order that seems most logical to you, you'll have an informal working outline.

Writing

The draft of your essay should include the following parts:

1. Introduction. The first paragraph should catch the audience's interest and tell what the essay will be about. Your thesis statement should begin or end the opening paragraph.

2. Body. The body of your essay should develop your thesis statement. Each paragraph in the body of your essay should include a topic sentence and supporting evidence.

3. Conclusion. The final paragraph may restate the thesis statement, summarize the main ideas, or give your personal response to the work.

Revising

Reread your first draft at least once for content and at least once for style.

1. Content. Check to see that you've supported your thesis statement with enough strong evidence. Make sure you have documented information from three or more sources.

2. Style. To make your essay read smoothly, you may need to combine some choppy sentences or break up long sentences into shorter ones. Cut unnecessary or repetitive words and phrases. Make sure your ideas are clear and easy to follow. You'll find revision is easier if you try to listen to your words, as if you are reading the essay aloud.

Proofreading

Remember that the titles of poems, short stories, and essays should be enclosed in quotation marks. The titles of plays, novels, and other book-length works should be in italics. (In handwriting and typing, italics are indicated by underlining.) Use the following proofreader's symbols to correct errors in spelling and punctuation.

Symbol	Example	Meaning of Symbol
$\equiv$	Sarah knight	Capitalize a lower-case letter.
/	A Farewell To Arms	Change a capital letter to lower case.
$\wedge$	Great The Gatsby	Insert a word or phrase.

∧	High Non	Insert a letter.
⊙	⊙Scott Fitzgerald	Add a period.
⌄	"I,Too"	Add a comma.
⌄/⌄	⌄Elegy for Jane⌄	Insert quotation marks.
—	From <u>Black Boy</u>	Set in italics.
∼	Ar∼Tyler	Change the order of the letters.
⌿	Emily Dickins⌿on	Delete and close up space.
¶	¶William Faulkner died in 1962.	Begin a new paragraph.

A Model Essay

The following essay is a comment on "Divina Commedia I" by Henry Wadsworth Longfellow. The essay shows revisions that the writer made in the first draft.

Oft have I seen at some cathedral door
  A laborer, pausing in the dust and heat,
  Lay down his burden, and with reverent feet
  Enter, and cross himself, and on the floor
5 Kneel to repeat his paternoster° o'er;
  Far off the noises of the world retreat;

  The loud vociferations of the street
  Become an undistinguishable roar.
So, as I enter here from day to day,
10 And leave my burden at this minster gate,°
  Kneeling in prayer, and not ashamed to pray,
The tumult of the time disconsolate
  To inarticulate murmurs dies away,
  While the eternal ages watch and wait.
          —Henry Wadsworth Longfellow

---

5. **paternoster** (pät'ər nôs'tər): the Lord's Prayer (*pater noster* is "our father" in Latin).

10. **minster gate:** church gate.

INTRODUCTORY PARAGRAPH

Catches reader's interest.

Thesis statement.

BODY

Topic statement.

"Divina Commedia I" by Henry Wadsworth Longfellow

You can read ^understand^ a poem without knowing anything about ~~it~~ the writer's life, but sometimes, if you don't know the biographical details, you miss a lot. To understand "Divina Commedia I" by Henry Wadsworth Longfellow, it is helpful to know some details about Longfellow's life and about his poetry in general.

The details of Longfellow's life that relate to "Divina Commedia I" are tragic. After his wife's ~~tragic~~ death in 1861, Longfellow used to begin each day translating some of Dante's [epic] poem, <u>The Divine Comedy,</u> into English. (Wagen knecht, 209) "Divina Commedia I" is the first of six sonnets that Longfellow wrote ~~to serve~~ as prefaces to Dante's epic. Three years before this particular sonnet was written, Longfellow's wife was burned to death in her home, when some sealing wax fell on the cloth of her light dress and ignited it. Longfellow himself [was badly burned] ~~almost died of the burns he received~~ when he tried to beat out the flames with his bare hands. The "burden" referred to in the sonnet [(line 10)] must refer to the [is] burden of sadness the poet carries with him.

[of knowing] Some [of] Longfellow's ~~theories of poetry~~ [poetic techniques] also help[s] to illumine this sonnet. According to William Charvat, Longfellow's poems tend to teach austere lessons: "We are to work for work's sake. We are to accept life's labors, deprivals, and sorrows." [(Charvat, 432) The] ~~This sonnet illustrates this~~ [belief] ~~lesson~~. For Longfellow, the work of translation helped [lessen] ~~to accept~~ life's sorrows. This is an optimistic, almost Puritantic belief; it seemed to have worked with Longfellow.

[n] Aother charac[t]eristic [+] of Long[f]ellow's poetry [is revealed in this] ~~helps to the~~ poem. According to Leonard Unger, Longfellow's lyric and meditative poems have a characteristic development. They mov[e]ing from "image to analogy to statement." [(Unger, 498)] This is the pattern of ~~Longfellow's poem~~ ["Divina Comedia I."] The poem begins with [the] ~~an~~ image of a laborer l[a]ying down his burden (probably his tools) and praying in a [cathedral] ~~church~~ (lines 1-8). While he prays, the street noises retreat. With the words "So, I enter . . ." [(line 9),] the speaker makes an analogy between the laborer's act [as] and his own act ~~of lying~~ [He too lays] down his ~~own~~ [and kneels] burden to pray. [The speaker's] His burden is not a physical one, but a [mental]

Supporting details.

Cites secondary source.

Cites from the poem.

Topic statement.

Supporting details.

Cites secondary source.

Topic statement.

Cites secondary source.

Supporting details.

Cites from poem.

CONCLUSION

~~mental burden,~~ but the prayer has the same effect on him that it has on the laborer. For the poet, ~~it connects him~~ *prayer is a connection* with eternity. *The disconsolate present time dies away, to reveal the waiting ages of eternity."*

If Before I knew
~~Without knowing~~ that the poet at the time was mourning ~~over~~ the

Summarizes topic.

I thought
loss of his wife, the poem ~~would be more~~ puzzling. Once ~~you~~ *I* kn~~o~~*e*w ~~the~~

sought
~~reasons~~ why Longfellow ~~had for seeking~~ comfort in prayer, ~~then~~ the

a much
poem bec~~o~~mes more powerful. *and spoke to a feeling I could share⊙*

Documenting Sources

Find out which method of documentation your teacher prefers: parenthetical citations, footnotes, or end notes.

1. **Parenthetical citations** give brief information in parentheses immediately after a quotation or other reference. More detailed information about each source is given in the bibliography. This simplified method of documenting sources is recommended by the MLA (Modern Language Association).

For a quotation from a prose passage by a writer who is identified in the text: *page number*.

In "Rip Van Winkle," Washington Irving explains that Rip has a "foolish and well-oiled disposition" (page 128).

For a quotation by a writer whose name is *not* mentioned in the text: *Author's last name, page number*.

The first arrivals to Cape Cod saw "a hideous and desolate wilderness" (Bradford, 14).

For a quotation from a play: *Act, Scene*.

When she has announced that she has bought a house with the insurance money, Mama tells Walter that the family ". . . couldn't of gone on like we was today. We was going backwards 'stead of forwards. . . ." (Act II, Scene 1).

For a quotation from a poem: *line number*.

Robinson begins his poem by calling Miniver Cheevy a "child of scorn" (line 1).

---

2. **Footnotes** are placed at the bottom of the page on which the reference appears. A raised number at the end of the reference within the essay indicates a footnote[1]. Footnotes are generally numbered consecutively within a work.

[1] Wagenknecht, Edward, *Henry Wadsworth Longfellow* (New York: Oxford University Press, 1966).

[2] Charvat, William, "Henry Wadsworth Longfellow" in *Major Writers of America, Shorter Edition*, edited by Perry Miller *et al.* (New York: Harcourt Brace Jovanovich, 1966).

Check a writing handbook, or ask your teacher for the style for footnoting poems, magazine articles, interviews, and books with more than one author.

3. **End notes** are identical to footnotes except that they are listed on a separate page entitled "Notes" at the end of a paper. End notes are numbered consecutively.

4. A **bibliography** should be included at the end of your essay. This is an alphabetical list of all the sources you consulted in researching your essay, even if they don't appear in your footnotes. Bibliography entries are listed alphabetically by the author's last name. Here is a bibliography that lists the sources for the model essay on Longfellow's "Divina Commedia I."

Bibliography

Charvat, William, "Henry Wadsworth Longfellow" in *Major Writers of America, Shorter Edition*, edited by Perry Miller *et al.* (New York: Harcourt Brace Jovanovich, 1966).

Unger, Leonard, editor-in-chief, *American Writers: A Collection of Literary Biographies* (New York: Charles Scribner's Sons).

Wagenknecht, Edward, *Henry Wadsworth Longfellow* (New York: Oxford University Press, 1966).

HANDBOOK OF LITERARY TERMS

You will find more information about the terms in this Handbook at the pages given at the ends of the entries. To learn more about **Allegory,** for example, turn to pages 39, 232, and 246 in this book.

Cross-references at the ends of some entries refer to other entries in the Handbook containing related information. For instance, at the end of **Antagonist** you are referred to **Protagonist.**

ALLEGORY A story or poem in which characters, settings, and events stand for other people or events or for abstract ideas or qualities. An allegory can be read on one level for its literal meaning and on a second level for its symbolic, or allegorical, meaning. The most famous allegory in the English language is *The Pilgrim's Progress* (1678) by Puritan writer John Bunyan, in which Pilgrim, in his journey to the Celestial City, meets such personages as Mr. Worldly Wiseman, Hopeful, and Giant Despair and travels to such places as the Slough of Despond, the Valley of Humiliation, and Doubting Castle. All Puritans were trained to see their own lives as allegories of Biblical experiences. Nathaniel Hawthorne's and Edgar Allan Poe's fictions are often called allegorical.

See pages 30, 232, 246.

ALLITERATION The repetition of the same or similar consonant sounds in words that are close together. Alliteration is used to create musical effects and to establish mood. In the following line from "The Tide Rises, the Tide Falls" by Henry Wadsworth Longfellow, the repetition of the "s" sound is an example of alliteration:

The sea, the sea in the darkness calls

See pages 254, 262, 333, 553.

ALLUSION A reference to someone or something that is known from history, literature, religion, politics, sports, science, or some other branch of culture. T. S. Eliot drew on his knowledge of the Bible when he alluded to the raising of Lazarus from the dead in "The Love Song of J. Alfred Prufrock" on page 760. The title of Robert Hayden's poem "Summertime and the Living . . ." on page 1087 is an allusion to a song from the opera *Porgy and Bess*.

You won't understand the following cartoon unless you recognize the fairy tale it alludes to.

"They're offering a deal—you can pay court costs and damages, they drop charges of breaking and entering."

Drawing by Maslin. © 1988 The New Yorker Magazine, Inc.

See pages 30, 91, 160, 170, 232, 254, 318, 392, 688, 767, 999.

AMBIGUITY A technique by which a writer deliberately suggests two or more different, and sometimes conflicting, meanings in a work. Nathaniel Hawthorne's "Rappaccini's Daughter" on page 275 has an ambiguous ending; the title of Richard Wilbur's "The Beautiful Changes" on page 1105 is also deliberately ambiguous.

See page 509.

ANALOGY A comparison made between two things to show how they are alike. In "The Crisis" on page 94 Thomas Paine draws an analogy between a thief breaking into a house and the King of England interfering in the affairs of the American colonies.

See pages 99, 657.

ANAPEST A metrical foot that has two unstressed syllables followed by one stressed syllable. The word coexist is an example of an anapest.

ANECDOTE A very brief story, told to illustrate a point or serve as an example of something. In Benjamin Franklin's *Autobiography* (page 74), the account of the speckled ax is an anecdote.

See page 80.

ANTAGONIST The opponent who struggles against or blocks the hero, or protagonist, in a story. In Mark Twain's *The Adventures of Huckleberry Finn*, Miss Watson is one of Huck's many antagonists. In Herman Melville's *Moby-Dick*, the white whale is Ahab's antagonist.

See also *Protagonist*.

ANTHROPOMORPHISM Attributing human characteristics to an animal or inanimate object. E. B. White creates humor by anthropomorphizing his dog Fred in his essay "Death of a Pig" (page 994).

See page 1125.

APHORISM A brief, cleverly worded statement that makes a wise observation about life. Benjamin Franklin's *Poor Richard's Almanack* (page 84) is a book of aphorisms. Ralph Waldo Emerson's style is **aphoristic**—he incorporates many pithy sayings into his essays (which is why he is so quotable).

See page 202.

APOSTROPHE A technique by which a writer addresses an inanimate object, an idea, or a person who is either dead or absent. William Cullen Bryant apostrophizes a bird in "To a Waterfowl" (page 139). Ralph Waldo Emerson apostrophizes a flower in "The Rhodora" (page 198). Oliver Wendell Holmes apostrophizes a shell and his soul in "The Chambered Nautilus" (page 164).

See pages 196, 199.

ARGUMENT A form of persuasion that appeals to reason (instead of emotion) to convince an audience to think or act in a certain way. The *Declaration of Independence* provides some famous examples of argument.

See pages 99, 107.
See also *Persuasion*.

ASSONANCE The repetition of similar vowel sounds followed by different consonant sounds, especially in words that are close together. Notice the repeated sound of "i" in the following lines by Henry Wadsworth Longfellow:

> The tide rises, the tide falls,
> The twilight darkens, the curlew calls

See page 333.
See also *Alliteration, Onomatopoeia, Rhyme.*

AUTOBIOGRAPHY An account of the writer's own life. Benjamin Franklin's autobiography (page 74) is one of the most famous autobiographies in American literature. A selection from Richard Wright's autobiography, *Black Boy*, is on page 1011.

See pages 74, 1011.

BALLAD A song or poem that tells a story. The typical ballad tells a tragic story in the form of a monologue or dialogue. Ballads usually have a simple, steady rhythm, a rhyme pattern, and a refrain, all of which make them easy to memorize. Ballads composed by unknown singers and passed on orally from one generation to the next are called **folk ballads. Literary ballads** are written to imitate the sounds and subjects of folk ballads. A strong tradition of folk ballads and of literary ballads exists in the United States. Country-and-western music, for example, frequently features songs written to imitate the old ballads.

BIOGRAPHY An account of someone's life written by another person. The most famous biography in American literature is Carl Sandburg's multivolume life of Abraham Lincoln.

BLANK VERSE Poetry written in unrhymed iambic pentameter. Blank verse has a long history in English literature. It was used notably by such poets as Shakespeare and Milton in the sixteenth and seventeenth centuries and by Robert Frost in the twentieth.

See pages 144, 687.
See also *Iambic Pentameter.*

CADENCE The natural, rhythmic rise and fall of a language as it is normally spoken. Cadence is different from **meter,** in which the stressed and unstressed syllables of a poetic line are carefully counted to conform to a regular pattern. Walt Whitman was a master at imitating the cadences of spoken American English in his free verse.

See pages 324, 333, 335, 349.
See also *Free Verse, Meter, Rhythm.*

CAESURA A pause or break within a line of poetry. Some pauses are indicated by punctuation; others are suggested by phrasing or meaning. In these lines, the caesuras are marked by double vertical lines. These pauses are indicated by punctuation:

> Announced by all the trumpets of the sky,
> Arrives the snow, ‖ and, ‖ driving o'er the fields,
> Seems nowhere to alight: ‖ the whited air
> Hides hills and woods . . .

—from "The Snow-Storm,"
Ralph Waldo Emerson

CATALOGUE A list of things, people, or events. Cataloging was a favorite device of Walt Whitman, who included lists throughout *Leaves of Grass*.

> See pages 324, 337, 345, 349, 413.

CHARACTER An individual in a story or play. A character always has human traits, even if the character is an animal, as in Aesop's fables, or a god, as in the Greek and Roman myths.

The process by which the writer reveals the personality of a character is called **characterization.** A writer can reveal a character in the following ways:

1. By telling us directly what the character is like: sneaky, generous, mean to pets, and so on.
2. By describing how the character looks and dresses.
3. By letting us hear the character speak.
4. By revealing the character's private thoughts and feelings.
5. By revealing the character's effect on other people— showing how other characters feel or behave toward the character.
6. By showing the character in action.

The first method of revealing a character is called **direct characterization.** When a writer uses this method, we do not have to figure out what a character's personality is like—the writer tells us directly. The other five methods of revealing a character are known as **indirect characterization.** When a writer uses these methods, we have to exercise our own judgment, putting clues together to figure out what a character is like—just as we do in real life when we are getting to know someone.

Characters are often classified as static or dynamic. A **static character** is one who does not change much in the course of a story. A **dynamic character,** on the other hand, changes in some important way as a result of the story's action. Characters can also be classified as flat or round. **Flat characters** have only one or two personality traits. They are one-dimensional, like a piece of cardboard; they can be summed up by a single phrase. In contrast, **round characters** have more dimensions to their personalities— they are complex, just as real people are.

> See pages 80, 136, 274, 292, 301, 304, 309, 413, 564, 588, 618, 852, 873, 883.

CLICHÉ A word or phrase, often a figure of speech, that has become lifeless because of overuse. Some examples of clichés are: "green with envy," "quiet as a mouse," and "pretty as a picture." Russell Baker mocks the use of clichés in his essay "Little Red Riding Hood Revisited" (page 1005).

> See pages 540, 1007.

CLIMAX That point in a plot that creates the greatest intensity, suspense, or interest. The climax is usually the point at which the conflict in the story is resolved.

> See pages 232, 292, 507, 828, 883.

COMEDY In general, a story that ends with a happy resolution of the conflicts faced by the main character or characters. In many comedies, the conflict is provided when a young couple that wishes to marry is blocked by adult figures. In many comedies, the main character at the end has moved into a world of greater freedom; this is the kind of comedy we see in Washington Irving's "Rip Van Winkle." Some comedies are humorous; some are not.

> See pages 630, 901.

CONCEIT An elaborate metaphor that compares two things that are startlingly different. Often a conceit is also a very lengthy comparison. The poems of Edward Taylor (pages 46 and 49) and of Emily Dickinson (pages 355–369) are known for their conceits. T. S. Eliot, in more recent literary history, also used conceits (see page 760).

> See page 48.

CONCRETE POEM A poem in which the words are arranged on a page to suggest a visual representation of the subject. In English poetry in the seventeenth century, poets wrote concrete poems in the shapes of such things as crosses, altars, and wings; today poets write concrete poems in the shapes of waves, hearts, cats, flowers.

> See pages 727, 728.

CONFESSIONAL POETRY A twentieth-century term used to describe poetry that uses intimate material from the poet's life. The material is usually painful, disturbing, or sad. In twentieth-century American literature, some of the leading Confessional poets have been Robert Lowell, John Berryman, Anne Sexton, and Sylvia Plath.

> See page 1083.

CONFLICT The struggle between opposing forces or characters in a story. A conflict can be **internal,** involving opposing forces within a person's mind. James Thurber's "The Secret Life of Walter Mitty" (page 595), for example, deals with a man who has a comical internal conflict between his desire for heroism and his cowardice in the face of a formidable spouse. **External** conflicts can exist between two people, between a person and nature or a machine, or between a person and a whole society. In "Your Place Is Empty" (page 960), for example, Anne Tyler shows two characters (or two cultures) coming into conflict. Many stories have both types of conflict.

> See pages 137, 588, 778, 828, 852, 901, 929, 947, 971, 982.

CONNOTATION **The associations and emotional overtones that have become attached to a word or phrase, in addition to its strict dictionary definition.** The words *determined, firm, rigid, stubborn,* and *pigheaded* have similar dictionary definitions, but widely varying connotations, or overtones of meaning. *Determined* and *firm* both suggest an admirable kind of resoluteness; *rigid* suggests an inability to bend and a kind of mindless refusal to change. (It calls to mind a rigid board.) *Stubborn* and *pigheaded,* on the other hand, have strongly negative connotations. *Stubborn* has associations with a mule, and *pigheaded* with the pig, which, wrongly or not, is an animal often associated with stupidity. Here are some other words that are more or less synonymous but which have vastly different connotations: *fastidious* and *fussy; day-dreamer* and *escapist; scent, odor,* and *stink.* Words with strong connotations are often called **loaded words.**

See pages 83, 163, 201, 232, 247, 249, 293, 628, 653, 666.

CONSONANCE **The repetition of the same or similar final consonant sounds on accented syllables or in important words.** The expressions *tick-tock* and *ping-pong* contain examples of consonance. Some modern poets use consonance in place of rhyme.

COUPLET **Two consecutive rhyming lines of poetry.** If the two rhyming lines express a complete thought, they are called a **closed couplet.** The following lines are from a poem built on a series of closed couplets.

> If ever wife was happy in a man,
> Compare with me, ye women, if you can.
>
> —from "To My Dear and Loving Husband,"
> Anne Bradstreet

See page 44.

DACTYL **A metrical foot of three syllables in which the first syllable is stressed and the next two are unstressed.** The word téndĕncў is a dactyl.

DENOUEMENT (dā·nōō·män′) **The conclusion (or resolution) of a story.** In French, the word means "unraveling." At this point in a story, all the mysteries are unraveled, the conflicts are resolved, and all the questions raised by the plot are answered. Much modern fiction ends before the denouement, so that the story leaves us with a sense of incompleteness.

DESCRIPTION **A form of discourse that uses language to create a mood or emotion.** Description does this by the use of words that appeal to our senses: sight, hearing, touch, sound, taste.

See page 428.

DIALECT **A way of speaking that is characteristic of a certain social group or of the inhabitants of a certain geographical area.** Dialects may differ from one another in vocabulary, pronunciation, and grammar. As in most countries, one dialect has become dominant in America, and it is known as Standard English. This is the dialect used most often on national radio and television news broadcasts. Many writers try to capture dialects to give their stories local color, humor, or an air of authenticity. Among the writers in this book who make skilled use of dialect are Mark Twain, Eudora Welty, Flannery O'Connor, William Faulkner, and Langston Hughes.

See pages 404, 413, 462, 619, 664, 716–720.

DICTION **A speaker or writer's choice of words.** Diction can be formal, informal, colloquial, full of slang, poetic, ornate, plain, abstract, concrete, etc. Diction is dependent on the writer's subject, purpose, and audience. Some words, for example, are suited to informal conversations, but are inappropriate in a formal speech. Diction has a powerful effect on the **tone** of a piece of writing. Russell Baker mocks the diction of Washington bureaucrats in his essay "Little Red Riding Hood Revisited" (page 1005).

See pages 58, 349, 370, 664, 757.

DRAMATIC MONOLOGUE **A poem in which a character speaks to one or more listeners.** The reactions of the listener must be inferred by the reader. From the speaker's words, the reader learns about the setting, the situation, the identity of the other characters, and the personality of the speaker. The outstanding dramatic monologue in American literature is T. S. Eliot's "The Love Song of J. Alfred Prufrock" (page 760). The poems in Edgar Lee Masters's *Spoon River Anthology* are also dramatic monologues.

ELEGY **A poem of mourning, usually about someone who has died.** Most elegies are written to mark a person's death, but some extend their subject to reflect on life, death, and the fleeting nature of beauty. The elegies in this book include William Cullen Bryant's "Thanatopsis" (page 142), John Crowe Ransom's "Bells for John Whiteside's Daughter" (page 691), and Theodore Roethke's "Elegy for Jane" (page 1085).

See pages 770, 1026.

EPIC **A long narrative poem, written in heightened language, which recounts the deeds of a heroic character who**

embodies the values of a particular society. Epics in English include *Beowulf* (c. 700) and John Milton's *Paradise Lost* (1667). Some critics view Walt Whitman's *Leaves of Grass* as an American epic, in which the hero is the questing poet.

See page 329.

EPITHET A descriptive word or phrase that is frequently used to characterize a person or thing. The epithet "the father of his country" is often used to characterize George Washington. New York City's popular epithet, "the Big Apple," is frequently used by advertisers. Epics such as Homer's *Odyssey* and *Iliad* frequently use **stock epithets** over and over again to describe certain characters or places: "patient Penelope," "wily Odysseus," "earth-shaker" (for Poseidon).

ESSAY A short piece of nonfiction prose in which the writer discusses some aspect of a subject. The word *essay* comes from the French *essai,* meaning "to try," a derivation that suggests that the essay form is not an exhaustive treatment of a subject. Essays are sometimes classified as formal or informal, or as formal or personal (or familiar). The form has been especially popular in the twentieth century, particularly among American writers. Some famous American essayists of the past include Thomas Paine (page 93), Ralph Waldo Emerson (page 187), and Henry David Thoreau (page 204). More recent essayists include E. B. White (page 993), Lewis Thomas (page 1001), Russell Baker (page 1004), James Baldwin (page 1027), Joan Didion, Alice Walker, and Edward Abbey.

See Unit Twelve.

EXPOSITION One of the four major forms of discourse, in which something is explained or "set forth." Exposition is most commonly used in nonfiction. The word *exposition* also refers to that part of a plot in which the reader is given important background information on the characters, their setting, and their problems. Such exposition is usually provided at the opening of a story or play. A good example is Tom's opening speech in Tennessee Williams's *The Glass Menagerie* (see page 789).

See page 778.

FABLE A very short story told in prose or poetry that teaches a practical lesson about how to succeed in life. In many fables, the characters are animals that behave like people. The most ancient fabulist is the Greek Aesop; the most famous American fabulist is James Thurber (page 594), who produced two collections: *Fables for Our Time* and *Further Fables for Our Time.*

FARCE A type of comedy in which ridiculous and often stereotyped characters are involved in silly, far-fetched situations. The humor in a farce is often physical and slapstick, with characters being hit in the face with pies or running into open doors. American movies have produced many farces, including those starring Laurel and Hardy, Abbott and Costello, and the Marx brothers.

FIGURE OF SPEECH A word or phrase that describes one thing in terms of another and that is not meant to be taken literally. Figures of speech always involve a comparison of two things that are basically very dissimilar. Hundreds of figures of speech have been identified by scholars; the most common ones are **simile, metaphor, personification, and symbol.** Figurative language is also basic to everyday speech. Statements like "She is a tower of strength" and "He is a pain in the neck" use figures of speech.

See pages 40, 62, 148, 195, 293, 304, 359, 428, 548, 553, 588, 1026.
See also *Metaphor, Simile, Personification, Symbol.*

FLASHBACK A scene that interrupts the normal chronological sequence of events in a story to depict something that happened at an earlier time. Although the word was coined to describe a technique used by movie makers, the technique itself is at least as old as ancient Greek literature. Much of Homer's epic poem the *Odyssey* is a flashback. Willa Cather uses frequent flashbacks to reveal the past of her heroine in "A Wagner Matinée" (page 542).

See pages 438, 548.

FOIL A character who acts as a contrast to another character. In Nathaniel Hawthorne's "Rappaccini's Daughter," the sane physician Signor Baglioni is a foil to the mad scientist Rappaccini.

See page 292.

FOOT A metrical unit of poetry. A foot always contains at least one stressed syllable, and, usually, one or more unstressed syllables. An **iamb** is a common foot in English poetry: It consists of an unstressed syllable followed by a stressed syllable (‿ˊ).

See also *Anapest, Dactyl, Iamb, Spondee, Trochee.*

FORESHADOWING The use of hints and clues to suggest what will happen later in a plot. A writer might use foreshadowing to create suspense or to prefigure later events. In "The End of Something," for example, Hemingway foreshadows the conclusion of his story by placing hints in the dialogue between Nick and Marjorie as they pass the ruins of the old mill.

See pages 301, 309, 400, 548, 564.

FORMS OF DISCOURSE A system of classifying writing according to purpose. The four main forms of discourse are **description**, **narration**, **exposition**, and **persuasion**.

FREE VERSE Poetry that does not conform to a regular meter or rhyme scheme. Poets who write in free verse try to reproduce the natural rhythms of the spoken language. Free verse uses the traditional poetic elements of **imagery**, **figures of speech**, **repetition**, **internal rhyme**, **alliteration**, and **onomatopoeia**. The first American practitioner of free verse was Walt Whitman (page 326). Some of Whitman's heirs are William Carlos Williams (page 735), Carl Sandburg (page 747), and Allen Ginsberg (page 1127).

See pages 324, 333, 702, 707, 728.

HYPERBOLE A figure of speech that uses an incredible exaggeration, or overstatement, for effect. In *The Adventures of Huckleberry Finn*, Mark Twain has Huck use hyperbole for comic effect, as in this passage, in which Huck explains what he thinks he knows about kings:

My, you ought to seen old Henry the Eight when he was in bloom. He *was* a blossom. He used to marry a new wife every day, and chop off her head next morning. And he would do it as indifferent as if he was ordering up eggs. "Fetch up Nell Gwynn," he says. They fetch her up. Next morning, "Chop off her head!" And they chop it off. . . . "Ring up fair Rosamun." Fair Rosamun answers the bell. Next morning, "Chop off her head."

—from *The Adventures of Huckleberry Finn*, Mark Twain

See pages 413, 588, 999, 1009.

IAMB A metrical foot in poetry that has an unstressed syllable followed by a stressed syllable, as in the word protéct.
See pages 44, 144.

IAMBIC PENTAMETER A line of poetry that contains five iambic feet. The iambic pentameter line is the most common in English and American poetry. Shakespeare and John Milton, among others, used iambic pentameter in their major works. So did such American poets as William Cullen Bryant, Ralph Waldo Emerson, Robert Frost, and Wallace Stevens. Here, for example, are the opening lines of a poem by Emerson:

In Máy, whĕn séa wĭnds pierćed oŭr sólĭtudĕs,
Ĭ fóund thĕ frésh Rhŏdóră ĭn thĕ wóods

—from "The Rhodora,"
Ralph Waldo Emerson

See pages 145, 199.

IMAGERY The use of language to evoke a picture or a concrete sensation of a person, a thing, a place, or an experience. Although most images appeal to the sense of sight, they also sometimes appeal to the senses of taste, smell, hearing, and touch as well.

See pages 40, 51, 99, 145, 151, 160, 166, 168, 193, 232, 246, 260, 316, 335, 340, 344, 356, 357, 359, 413, 428, 491, 507, 564, 569, 604, 666, 1038.

IMAGISM A twentieth-century movement in European and American poetry which advocated the creation of hard, clear images, concisely written in everyday speech. The leading Imagist poets in America were Ezra Pound, Amy Lowell, Hilda Doolittle, and William Carlos Williams.

See page 727.

IMPRESSIONISM A nineteenth-century movement in literature and art which advocated a recording of the artist's personal impressions of the world, rather than a strict representation of reality. Some of the famous American Impressionists in art were Mary Cassatt, Maurice Prendergast, and William Merritt Chase. Stephen Crane wrote *The Red Badge of Courage*, in an impressionistic style.

See pages 442, 462, 509.

INCONGRUITY The deliberate joining of opposites or of elements that are not appropriate to each other. T. S. Eliot's famous opening simile in "The Love Song of J. Alfred Prufrock" joins two incongruous elements: a sunset and a patient knocked out by ether on an operating table. Incongruity can also be used for humor; we laugh at the sight of an elephant dressed in a pink tutu because the two elements are incongruous. Writers also use incongruity for dramatic effect. In Donald Barthelme's "Game" (page 926), the childish actions of the characters are in sharp contrast with the nuclear war they can start by turning a key.

See pages 171, 413, 569.

INTERNAL RHYME Rhyme that occurs within a line of poetry or within consecutive lines. The first line of the following pair includes an internal rhyme.

And so, all the nighttide, I lie down by the side
Of my darling—my darling—my life and my bride
                    —from ''Annabel Lee,''
                    Edgar Allan Poe

See also *Rhyme*.

INVERSION The reversal of the normal word order in a sentence or phrase. An English sentence normally is built on subject-verb-complement, in that order. An inverted sentence reverses one or more of those elements. In poetry written many years ago, writers often inverted word order as a matter of course, in order to have the words conform to the meter, or to create rhymes. The poetry of Anne Bradstreet (page 42) contains many inversions, as in the first line of the poem on the burning of her house:

In silent night when rest I took

In prose, inversion is often used for emphasis, as when Patrick Henry, in his fiery speech to the Virginia Convention, said ''Suffer not yourselves to be betrayed with a kiss'' (instead of ''Do not suffer [allow] yourselves, etc.''

See pages 43, 145, 166, 199.

IRONY In general, a discrepancy between appearances and reality. There are three main types of irony: (1) **Verbal irony** occurs when someone says one thing but really means something else. When Benjamin Franklin refers to the Native Americans as ''savages'' in his essay on page 81, he is using irony. He really means that their oppressors are savage and that the Native Americans are highly civilized. (2) **Situational irony** takes place when there is a discrepancy between what is expected to happen, or what would be appropriate to happen, and what really does happen. A famous use of situational irony is in Edwin Arlington Robinson's poem ''Richard Cory,'' in which a man in an enviable position, with every advantage, takes his own life. (3) **Dramatic irony** is so called because it is often used on stage. In this kind of irony, a character in the play or story thinks one thing is true, but the audience or reader knows better. When Emily Dickinson writes ''Success is counted sweetest by those who ne'er succeed,'' we sense a kind of dramatic irony: We know, but the poet did not, that she would in fact be counted as enormously successful by later generations.

See pages 163, 292, 318, 362, 365, 384, 401, 413, 477, 491, 540, 564, 588, 628, 630, 637, 652, 755, 1009, 1059.

LOCAL COLOR A term applied to fiction or poetry which tends to place special emphasis on a particular setting, including its customs, clothing, dialect, and landscape. Local color flourished in the United States after the Civil War. The most famous local colorists are Bret Harte (West), Sarah Orne Jewett (Maine), Joel Chandler Harris (Georgia), Kate Chopin (Louisiana), James Whitcomb Riley (Indiana), Hamlin Garland (Middle West), and O. Henry (New York City).

See *Regionalism*.

LYRIC POEM A poem that does not tell a story but expresses the personal feelings or thoughts of a speaker. Lyric poems in this text range from the philosophic ''Thanatopsis'' by William Cullen Bryant to the satiric ''Homework'' by Allen Ginsberg.

See Units Five, Eight, Nine, and Thirteen.

METAPHOR A figure of speech that makes a comparison between two unlike things without the use of such specific words of comparison as *like, as, than,* or *resembles*. There are several kinds of metaphor:

   1. A **directly stated metaphor** states the comparison explicitly: ''Fame is a bee'' (Emily Dickinson).
   2. An **implied metaphor** does not state explicitly the two terms of the comparison: ''I like to see it lap the miles'' (Emily Dickinson) is an implied metaphor in which the verb *lap* implies a comparison between ''it'' (which is a train) and some animal that ''laps'' up water.
   3. An **extended metaphor** is a metaphor that is extended or developed as far as the writer wants to take it. Dickinson's poem beginning ''Fame is a bee'' is an extended metaphor: The comparison between fame and a bee is extended through four lines. (See also page 766.)
   4. A **dead metaphor** is a metaphor that has been used so often that the comparison is no longer vivid: ''The head of the house,'' ''the seat of government,'' ''a knotty problem'' are all dead metaphors.
   5. A **mixed metaphor** is a metaphor that has gotten out of control and mixes its terms so that they are visually or imaginatively incompatible. If you say, ''The President is a lame duck who is running out of gas,'' you've lost control of your metaphor and have produced a statement that is ridiculous (ducks do not run out of gas).

See pages 35, 44, 47, 91, 99, 145, 151, 163, 166, 195, 219, 309, 357, 360, 367, 390, 413, 462, 588, 1073.

METER A pattern of stressed and unstressed syllables in poetry. The meter of a poem is commonly indicated by using the symbol (′) for stressed syllables and the symbol (◡) for unstressed syllables. This is called **scanning** the poem. The following lines from Edward Arlington Robinson's ''Richard Cory'' are scanned.

Meter is described as **iambic, trochaic, dactylic,** or **anapestic.** These lines from ''Richard Cory'' are iambic because they are built on iambs—an unstressed syllable followed by a stressed syllable.

$$\breve{~}\,\acute{~}\,\breve{~}\,\acute{~}\,\breve{~}\,\breve{~}\acute{~}\,\breve{~}\,\acute{~}$$
And he was always quietly arrayed
$$\breve{~}\,\acute{~}\,\breve{~}\,\acute{~}\,\breve{~}\,\acute{~}\,\breve{~}\,\acute{~}$$
And he was always human when he talked;

See pages 249, 252, 260, 357, 360.

METONYMY A figure of speech in which a person, place, or thing is referred to by something closely associated with it. Referring to a king as ''the crown'' is an example of metonymy, as is calling a car ''wheels.''

MODERNISM A term for the bold new experimental styles and forms that swept the arts during the first third of the twentieth century. Modernism called for changes in subject matter, in fictional styles, in poetic forms, and in attitudes. T. S. Eliot and Ezra Pound are associated with the Modernist movement in poetry. Their aim was to rid poetry of its nineteenth-century ''prettiness'' and sentimentality.

See pages 758, 1082.
See also *Imagism, Symbolism.*

MOTIVATION The reasons for a character's behavior. In order for us to understand why characters act the way they do, their motivation has to be believable, at least in terms of the story. At times, a writer will directly reveal motivation; in subtler fiction, we have to use details from the story to infer motivation.

See also *Character.*

NARRATIVE The form of discourse that tells about a series of events. Narration is used in all kinds of literature: fiction, nonfiction, and poetry. Usually a narrative is told in **chronological order**—in the order in which the events occurred. The other three major forms of discourse are **description, exposition,** and **persuasion.**

NATURALISM A nineteenth-century literary movement that was an extension of realism and that claimed to portray life exactly as it was. The Naturalists relied heavily on the new fields of psychology and sociology, and they tended to dissect human behavior with complete objectivity, the way a scientist would dissect a specimen in the laboratory. The Naturalists were also influenced by Darwinian theories of the survival of the fittest. Naturalists believed that human behavior is determined by heredity and environment; they felt that people have no recourse to supernatural forces and that human beings, like the animals, are subject to laws of nature beyond their control.

The outstanding Naturalists among American writers are Theodore Dreiser, Stephen Crane (see page 439), and Frank Norris. Some people consider John Steinbeck's *The Grapes of Wrath* (page 589) a Naturalistic novel, in which characters are the pawns of economic conditions.

See page 383.
See also *Realism.*

OBJECTIVE CORRELATIVE An object, a situation, or a chain of events which serves as the formula for a specific emotion. The term was first used by T. S. Eliot in an essay.

See page 733.

OCTAVE An eight-line poem, or the first eight lines of a Petrarchan sonnet.

See also *Sonnet.*

ODE A lyric poem, usually long, on a serious subject and written in dignified language. In ancient Greece and Rome, odes were written to be read in public at ceremonial occasions. In modern literature, odes tend to be more private, informal, and reflective. Robert Lowell's ''For the Union Dead'' (page 1100) and Henry Timrod's ''Ode on the Confederate Dead'' (page 1103) are examples of the personal, meditative ode.

ONOMATOPOEIA The use of sounds that echo their sense. The word *buzz*, for example, is an onomatopoeic word because it imitates the sound it names. Onomatopoeia is an important element in most poetry.

See pages 141, 154, 262, 333, 337, 553.

OXYMORON A figure of speech that combines opposite or contradictory terms in a brief phrase. ''Sweet sorrow,'' ''deafening silence,'' and ''living death'' are common oxymorons. (Some jokesters claim that phrases like ''jumbo shrimp,'' ''congressional leadership,'' and ''limited nuclear war'' are also oxymorons.)

See page 588.

PARABLE A relatively short story that teaches a moral, or lesson, about how to lead a good life. The most famous parables are those told by Jesus in the Gospels.

See pages 47, 266, 274, 677.

PARADOX A statement that appears self-contradictory, but that reveals a kind of truth. Many writers like to use paradox because it allows them to express the complexity of life by showing how opposing ideas can be both contradictory and true. Emily Dickinson often used paradoxes, as in this line: ''I taste a liquor never brewed.''

See pages 48, 171, 193, 224, 705, 741, 752, 1119.

PARALLEL STRUCTURE (also called parallelism) The repetition of words or phrases that have similar grammatical structures. In his Gettysburg Address, Lincoln used several memorable examples of parallel structure, as when he refers to "government of the people, by the people, for the people."

Four score and seven years ago our fathers brought forth on this continent a new nation, conceived in liberty, and dedicated to the proposition that all men are created equal.

Now we are engaged in a great civil war, testing whether that nation, or any nation so conceived and so dedicated, can long endure. We are met on a great battlefield of that war. We have come to dedicate a portion of that field as a final resting place for those who here gave their lives that that nation might live. It is altogether fitting and proper that we should do this.

But, in a larger sense, we cannot dedicate—we cannot consecrate—we cannot hallow—this ground. The brave men, living and dead, who struggled here, have consecrated it far above our poor power to add or detract. The world will little note nor long remember what we say here, but it can never forget what they did here. It is for us the living, rather, to be dedicated here to the unfinished work which they who fought here have thus far so nobly advanced. It is rather for us to be here dedicated to the great task remaining before us—that from these honored dead we take increased devotion to that cause for which they gave the last full measure of devotion—that we here highly resolve that these dead shall not have died in vain—that this nation, under God, shall have a new birth of freedom—and that government of the people, by the people, for the people, shall not perish from the earth.

—"The Gettysburg Address,"
Abraham Lincoln

See pages 107, 333, 337, 750.

PARODY A work that makes fun of another work by imitating some aspect of the writer's style. Parodies often achieve their effects by humorously exaggerating certain features in the original work. Russell Baker's "Little Red Riding Hood Revisited" parodies the jargon of bureaucrats (page 1005) by using language that makes the old fairy tale practically incomprehensible.

See pages 309, 598, 628.

PERSONIFICATION A figure of speech in which an object or animal is given human feelings, thoughts, or attitudes. Personification is a type of metaphor in which two dissimilar things are compared. In "To the Fringed Gentian," Bryant personifies a flower by giving it an eye and eyelashes:

Then doth thy sweet and quiet eye
Look through its fringes to the sky.

See pages 145, 154, 199, 201, 247, 316, 365, 368, 491, 588, 654.
See also *Anthropomorphism, Apostrophe.*

PERSUASION One of the four forms of discourse, which uses reason and emotional appeals to convince a reader to think or act in a certain way. Persuasion is used in the Declaration of Independence (page 101), in Patrick Henry's "Give me liberty or give me death" speech (page 88), and in Thomas Paine's "The Crisis" (page 94). Persuasion is almost exclusively used in nonfiction, particularly in essays and speeches.

See page 92.

PLAIN STYLE A way of writing that stresses simplicity and clarity of expression. The plain style was favored by most Puritan writers, who avoided unnecessary ornamentation in all phases of their lives, including church ritual. In general, the plain style is characterized by simple sentences, by the use of everyday words from common speech, and by clear and direct statements. The plain style eliminates elaborate figures of speech and imagery. One of the chief exponents of the plain style in later American literature was Ernest Hemingway (page 566).

See pages 9, 22, 577.

PLOT The series of related events in a story or play, sometimes called the *storyline.* Most short-story plots contain the following elements: **exposition,** which tells us who the characters are and introduces their conflict; **complications,** which arise as the characters take steps to resolve their conflicts; the **climax,** that exciting or suspenseful moment when the outcome of the conflict is imminent; and a **resolution** or **denouement,** when the story's problems are all resolved, and the story ends.

The plots of dramas and novels are somewhat more complex because of their length. A schematic representation of a typical dramatic plot follows. It is based on a "pyramid" developed by the nineteenth-century German critic Gustav Freitag. The **rising action** refers to all the actions that take place before the **turning point** (sometimes called the **crisis**). This is the point at which the hero or heroine experiences a reversal of fortune; in a comedy, things begin to work out well, in a tragedy they get worse and worse. (In Shakespeare's plays, the turning point takes place in the third act. In *Romeo and Juliet,* for example, after he kills Mercutio in the third act, Romeo experiences one disaster after another.) All the action after the turning point is called **falling action** because it is leading to the final resolution (happy or unhappy) of the conflict. The major **climax** in most plays and novels takes place just before the ending; in Shakespeare's plays, it takes place in the fifth and last act. (In *Romeo and Juliet*, the major climax takes place when the two young people kill themselves.)

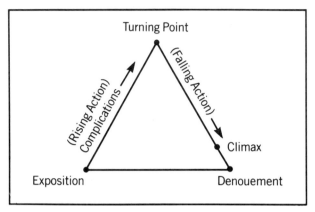

See page 914.

POINT OF VIEW The vantage point from which the writer tells a story. In broad terms, there are four main points of view: **first-person, third-person limited, omniscient,** and **objective.**

1. In the **first-person point of view,** one of the characters in the story tells the story, using first-person pronouns such as *I* and *we*. With this point of view, we can know only what the narrator knows. Mark Twain's novel *The Adventures of Huckleberry Finn* is told from the first-person point of view, by the novel's main character, a boy named Huck Finn. One of the great pleasures of that novel, in fact, is that its point of view allows us to hear Huck's very distinct voice and dialect.

2. In the **third-person limited point of view,** an unknown narrator (usually thought of as the author) tells the story, but this narrator zooms in to focus on the thoughts and feelings of only one character. (This point of view gets its name because the narrator refers to all the characters as *he, she,* and *they;* this narrator does not use the first-person pronoun *I.*) Like the first-person point of view, however, this point of view also limits us to the perceptions of one character, but in this case the narrator can tell us many things about the character, things that the character himself (or herself) might be unaware of. For example, Eudora Welty tells "A Worn Path" (page 632) from the third-person limited point of view of her heroine, an old woman named Phoenix Jackson. At one point, Welty's narrator tells us that Phoenix was "like an old woman begging a dignified forgiveness."

3. In the **omniscient point of view,** an omniscient (or "all-knowing") narrator tells the story, also using the third-person pronouns. However, this narrator, instead of focusing on one character only, often tells us everything about many characters: their motives, weaknesses, hopes, childhoods, and sometimes even their futures. This narrator can also comment directly on the character's actions. Washington Irving's "Rip Van Winkle" (page 125) is told from the omniscient point of view.

4. In the **objective point of view,** a narrator who is totally impersonal and objective tells the story, with no comment on any characters or events. The objective point of view is like the point of view of a movie camera; it is totally impersonal, and what we know is only what the camera might see. This narrator never gives any direct revelation of the characters' thoughts or motives. Ernest Hemingway (page 556) uses this objective point of view, which is why his stories often seem so puzzling to readers. "What happened?" we ask. The *reader* must infer what happens in Hemingway's stories, just as in real life we have to infer the motives, thoughts, and feelings of people we meet.

See pages 246, 301, 309, 438, 491, 548.

PROTAGONIST The central character in a story, the one who initiates or drives the action. The protagonist might or might not be the story's hero; some protagonists are actually the villains in the story.

See page 778.
See also *Antagonist.*

PUN A "play on words" based on the multiple meanings of a single word or on words that sound alike but mean different things. An example of the first type of pun is a singer explaining her claim that she was locked out of an audition because she couldn't find the right key. The second kind of pun can be found in the opening lines of Shakespeare's *Julius Caesar,* where a carpenter claims to be a mender of men's souls. Puns are often used as humor, but some puns are a serious element in poetry.

See pages 368, 734.

QUATRAIN A poem consisting of four lines, or four lines of a poem that can be considered as a unit. The typical ballad stanza, for example, is a quatrain.

RATIONALISM A movement that began in Europe in the seventeenth century, which held that we can arrive at truth by using our reason rather than relying on the authority of the past, on the authority of the Church, or on intuition. The Rationalists believed that all people were born with an innate ethical sense and had the ability to regulate and improve their own lives.

See page 68.

REALISM A style of writing, developed in the nineteenth century, that attempts to depict life accurately without idealizing or romanticizing it. Instead of writing about the long ago or far away, the realists concentrate often on contemporary life and on middle- and lower-class lives in particular. Among the outstanding realistic novelists in America are Stephen Crane (page 439), Willa Cather (page 541), and John Steinbeck (page 578).

See page 384.
See also *Naturalism, Romanticism.*

REFRAIN A word, phrase, line, or group of lines that is repeated, for effect, several times in a poem. Refrains are often used in ballads and other narrative poems. "And the tide rises, the tide falls" is a refrain in Longfellow's lyric (page 152), as is "in this kingdom by the sea" in Poe's "Annabel Lee" (page 250).

See page 168.

REGIONALISM Literature that emphasizes a specific geographic setting and that reproduces the speech, behavior, and attitudes of the people who live in that region. Among the great regional writers of the twentieth century are Sinclair Lewis (Midwest); John Steinbeck (California); and William Faulkner, Flannery O'Connor, and Eudora Welty (the South).

See page 381.

RESOLUTION The conclusion of a story, when all or most of the conflicts have been settled; often called the *dénouement.*

RHETORICAL QUESTION A question asked for an effect, and not actually requiring an answer. In his speech to the Virginia Convention, Patrick Henry asks several rhetorical questions. Such questions presume the audience agrees with the speaker on the answers.

See pages 91, 1091.

RHYME The repetition of vowel sounds in accented syllables and all succeeding syllables. *Listen* and *glisten* rhyme, as do *decay* and *away.* When words within the same line of poetry have repeated sounds, we have an example of **internal rhyme. End rhyme** refers to rhyming words at the ends of lines.

The pattern of rhymes in a poem is called a **rhyme scheme.** Rhyme scheme is commonly indicated with letters of the alphabet, each rhyming sound represented by a different letter of the alphabet. For example, the rhyme scheme of the following lines is *abab.*

Tell me not, in mournful numbers,	a
Life is but an empty dream!—	b
For the soul is dead that slumbers,	a
And things are not what they seem.	b

—from "A Psalm of Life,"
Henry Wadsworth Longfellow

Approximate rhymes (also called **off-rhymes, half rhymes, imperfect rhymes,** or **slant rhymes**) are words that have some correspondence in sound but not an exact one. Examples of approximate rhymes are often found in Emily Dickinson's poems. *Flash* and *flesh* are approximate rhymes, as are *stream* and *storm,* and *early* and *barley.* Approximate rhyme has the effect of catching the reader off guard: Where you expect a perfect rhyme, you get only an approximation. The emotional effect is something like that of the sound of a sharp or flat note in music.

See pages 47, 252, 254, 260, 262, 360, 697, 752.

RHYTHM A rise and fall of the voice produced by the alternation of stressed and unstressed syllables in language. When rhythm is tightly controlled and the stressed and unstressed syllables fall into a pattern, it is called **meter.**

See pages 340, 371, 689.
See also *Cadence, Meter.*

ROMANCE In general, a story in which an idealized hero or heroine undertakes a quest and is successful. In a romance, beauty, innocence, and goodness usually prevail over evil. In the past, romances were often set in the distant past and they used a great deal of fantasy. The laws of nature are often suspended in a romance, so that the hero or heroine often has supernatural powers, as we see in the adventures of King Arthur and his knights. Stories set in the American West are in the romance mode, except that the supernatural elements are eliminated (though the sheriff-hero usually has a nearly magical skill with his gun). Today we also use the word *romance* to refer to a kind of popular "potboiler" love story, which often takes place in an exotic setting.

See pages 628, 630.

ROMANTICISM A revolt against Rationalism that affected literature and the other arts, beginning in the late eighteenth century and remaining strong throughout most of the nineteenth century. Romanticism is marked by these characteristics: (1) a conviction that intuition, imagination, and emotion are superior to reason; (2) a conviction that poetry is superior to science; (3) a belief that contemplation of the natural world is a means of discovering the truth that lies behind mere reality; (4) a distrust of industry and city life and an idealization of rural life and of the wilderness; (5) an interest in the more "natural" past and in the supernatural. Romanticism affected so many creative people that it was bound to take many different forms; the result is that it is difficult to define the word in a way that includes everyone who might be called a Romantic. In the nineteenth century, for example, Romantics were outspoken in their love of nature and contempt for technology. In this century, however, as nature has been taken over by developers and highways, some writers have taken a romantic view of machines, buildings, and other products of technology.

See pages 118, 725.

SATIRE A type of writing that ridicules the shortcomings of people or institutions in an attempt to bring about a change. Satire can cover a wide range of tones, from gentle spoofing to savage mockery. In "A Fable for Critics," for example, James Russell Lowell pokes good-natured fun at his literary contemporaries (page 170). In *Babbitt* (page 535), Sinclair Lewis presents a vicious portrait of a small-town businessman. Satire is always intensely moral. Mark Twain, in *The Adventures of Huckleberry Finn* (page 414), satirizes a whole spectrum of American life, but the thrust of the novel is moral: Twain is making us see things that should not be permitted to exist (slavery is one of them).

See pages 83, 136, 170, 330, 540, 1007.

SCANNING The analysis of a poem to determine its meter. When you scan a poem, you describe the pattern of stressed and unstressed syllables in each line. Stresses or accents are indicated by the symbol (′) and unstressed syllables by the symbol (˘).

> To him who in the love of Nature holds
> Communion with her visible forms, she speaks
> A various language: for his gayer hours
> She has a voice of gladness, and a smile
>
> —from "Thanatopsis,"
> William Cullen Bryant

See pages 44, 370.
See also *Iambic Pentameter, Meter.*

SESTET Six lines of poetry, especially the last six lines of a Petrarchan sonnet.

See also *Sonnet.*

SETTING The time and location where a story takes place. Setting can have several functions in fiction: (1) Setting is often used to create **conflict.** In the purest and often simplest form of story, a character is in conflict with some element of a setting: The outcasts of Poker Flat in Bret Harte's story on page 394 are in conflict with a blizzard (the blizzard wins). (2) Often the setting helps to create **atmosphere** or **mood,** as does Edgar Allan Poe's setting of a decaying mansion in "The Fall of the House of Usher" (page 234). (3) Setting can also create and delineate **character:** Bessie Popkin's disorderly and locked-up apartment in Singer's story "The Key" (page 895) reflects Bessie's own isolation and emotional chaos.

See pages 136, 246, 292, 349, 438, 507, 548, 569, 573, 604.

SIMILE A figure of speech that makes an explicit comparison between two unlike things, using a word such as *like, as, than,* or *resembles*.

> Helen, thy beauty is to me
> Like those Nicéan barks of yore
>
> —from "To Helen,"
> Edgar Allan Poe

See pages 151, 168, 219, 254, 304, 359, 363, 491, 588, 661.
See also *Figure of Speech, Metaphor.*

SOLILOQUY A long speech made by a character in a play while no other characters are on stage. A soliloquy is different from a monologue in that the speaker appears to be thinking aloud, not addressing a listener. In *The Glass Menagerie* (page 787), Tom's periodic speeches are examples of soliloquies.

SONNET A fourteen-line lyric poem, usually written in iambic pentameter, that has one of two basic structures. The **Petrarchan sonnet,** also called the **Italian sonnet,** is named after the fourteenth-century Italian poet Petrarch. Its first eight lines, called the **octave,** ask a question or pose a problem. These lines have a rhyme scheme of *abba, abba.* The last six lines, called the **sestet,** respond to the question or problem. These lines have a rhyme scheme of *cde, cde.*

The form used to such perfection by William Shakespeare is known as the **English** or **Shakespearean sonnet.** It has three four-line units, or **quatrains,** and it concludes with a **couplet.** The most common rhyme scheme for the Shakespearean sonnet is *abab, cdcd, efef, gg.*

Longfellow, whose sonnet "The Cross of Snow" is on page 147, wrote many sonnets, as did Edna St. Vincent Millay (page 665), Robert Frost (page 670), and E. E. Cummings (page 753).

See pages 148, 673.

SPONDEE A metrical foot consisting of two syllables, both of which are stressed. The words *trueblue* and *nineteen* are made of spondees. When Whitman wrote "Beat! beat! drums" he used spondees. Spondaic feet are rarely used extensively because of their "thump-thump" sound. However, poets sometimes use spondees to provide a brief change from an iambic or trochaic beat, or to provide emphasis.

STEREOTYPE A fixed idea or conception of a character or an idea which does not allow for any individuality, often based on religious, social, or racial prejudices. Some common stereotypes are the unsophisticated farmer, the socially inept honor student, the dumb athlete, and the lazy teen-ager. Stereotypes are often deliberately used in comedies and in melodramas, where they receive instant recognition from the audience and make genuine characterization unnecessary. Babbitt in Sinclair Lewis's novel (page 535) has given rise to a whole range of unfair stereotypes based on the insensitive businessman—though at the time, Babbitt was an original.

See pages 137, 1044.

STREAM OF CONSCIOUSNESS A style of writing that portrays the inner (often chaotic) workings of a character's mind. The stream-of-consciousness technique usually consists of a recording of the random flow of ideas, memories, associations, images, and emotions, as they arise spontaneously in a character's mind. William Faulkner, in his great novel *The Sound and the Fury*, used a stream-of-consciousness technique. Two of the other great writers that used a stream-of-consciousness technique are the Irish writer James Joyce and the English writer Virginia Woolf.

See page 521.

STYLE The distinctive way in which a writer uses language. Styles can be plain, ornate, metaphorical, spare, descriptive, and so on. Style is determined by such factors as sentence length and complexity, syntax, use of figurative language and imagery, and diction.

See page 577.
See *Plain Style, Ornate Style, Stream of Consciousness.*

SURREALISM A movement in art and literature that started in Europe during the 1920's. Surrealists wanted to replace conventional realism with the full expression of the unconscious mind, which they considered to be more real than the "real" world of appearances. Surrealists, influenced by the psychoanalytic theories of Sigmund Freud, tried not to censor the images that came from their dreams or to impose logical connections on these images. This resulted in surprising combinations of "inner" and "outer" reality—a "suprareality." Surrealism affected writers as different as T. S. Eliot (page 758) and Donald Barthelme (page 925). Two famous Surreal artists are Salvador Dali and Marc Chagall. (See pages 904 and 913.)

SUSPENSE A feeling of uncertainty and curiosity about what will happen next in a story. A key element in fiction and drama, suspense is one of the "hooks" a writer uses to keep the readers or audience interested.

See pages 814, 884.

SYMBOL A person, place, thing, or event that has meaning in itself and that also stands for something more than itself. We can distinguish between **public** and **personal symbols.** The dove, for example, is a public symbol of peace—that is, it is widely accepted the world over as such a symbol. Uncle Sam is a public symbol that stands for the United States; a picture of a skull and crossbones is a public symbol of death; two snakes coiled around a staff are a widely accepted symbol of the medical profession.

Most symbols used in literature are personal symbols; even though a symbol may be widely used, a writer will usually adapt it in some imaginative, personal way so that it can suggest not just one, but a myriad of meanings. One of the most commonly used symbols in literature, for example, is the journey, which can stand for a search for truth, for redemption from evil, or for discovery of the self and freedom. The journey of Huck Finn and Jim down the Mississippi River has been interpreted to symbolize all of these concepts, and more.

Many writers, particularly those known as the Symbolists, have tried to find new symbols by which to express the complexities of experience.

See pages 141, 163, 232, 247, 249, 260, 274, 292, 316, 344, 428, 507, 532, 663, 680, 688, 772, 828.

SYMBOLISM A literary movement that originated in late-nineteenth-century France, in which writers rearranged the world of appearances in order to reveal a more truthful version of reality. The Symbolists believed that direct statements of feeling were inadequate; instead they called for new and striking symbols to evoke complexities of meaning and mood. The French Symbolists were influenced by the poetry and critical writings of the American Edgar Allan Poe (page 226). The poetry of Ezra Pound (page 729), T. S. Eliot (page 758), and Wallace Stevens (page 768) is in the Symbolist tradition.

See pages 604, 725.

SYNECDOCHE A figure of speech in which a part represents the whole. The capital city of a nation, for example, is often spoken of as though it were the government: "Washington and Teheran are both claiming popular support for their positions." In "The Love Song of J. Alfred Prufrock," T. S. Eliot writes, "And I have known the arms already. . . ." In that line, the word *arms* stands for the women he has known.

TALL TALE An outrageously exaggerated, humorous story that is obviously unbelievable. Tall tales are part of the folk literature of many countries, including America. Perhaps the most famous tall tale in American literature is Mark Twain's "The Celebrated Jumping Frog of Calaveras County." The bragging of the raftsmen in Twain's *Life on the Mississippi* (page 404) also provides examples of tall tales. William Faulkner's "Spotted Horses" (page 607) is a brilliant example of a tall tale turned into high art.

See page 618.

THEME The insight about human life that is revealed in a literary work. Themes are rarely stated directly in literature. Most often, a reader has to infer the theme of a work after considerable thought. Theme is different from **subject.** A story's subject might be stated as "growing up," "love," "heroism," or "fear." The theme is the statement the writer wants to make about that subject: "For most young people, growing up is a process that involves the pain of achieving self-knowledge." Theme must be stated in at least one sentence; most themes are complex enough to require several sentences, or even an essay.

See pages 136, 141, 232, 274, 368, 401, 532, 548, 564, 573, 577, 588, 604, 628.

TONE The attitude a writer takes toward the subject of a work, the characters in it, or the audience. In speaking, we use voice inflections to show how we feel about what we are saying. Writers manipulate language in an attempt to achieve the same effect. For example, John Hersey takes an objective tone in telling about the nuclear explosion in "A Noiseless Flash" (page 1051). In contrast, Michael Herr's tone toward the Vietnam war in "Dispatches" (page 1061) is subjective, confused, even fearful. Tone is dependent on **diction** and **style**, and we cannot say we have understood any work of literature until we have sensed the writer's tone. Tone can be described in a single word: objective, solemn, playful, ironic, sarcastic, critical, reverent, irreverent, philosophical, cynical, and so on.

See pages 35, 80, 136, 145, 151, 249, 274, 335, 340, 355, 362, 363, 365, 428, 507, 654, 661, 673.

TRAGEDY In general, a story in which a heroic character either dies or comes to some other unhappy end. In most tragedies, the main character is in an enviable, even exalted position when the story begins (in classical tragedies and in Shakespeare, the tragic hero is a king or queen, prince or princess). This character may bring about his or her own downfall because of an error in judgment or because of a personality failure known as a **tragic flaw** (Creon's stubbornness in *Antigone*, Hamlet's indecision). Or, the downfall may result from forces totally outside the character's control (Job in the Bible is the tragic victim of a wager between God and Satan). The tragic character has usually gained wisdom at the end of the story, in spite of suffering defeat, or even death. Our feeling on reading or viewing a tragedy is usually exaltation—despite the unhappy ending—because we have witnessed the best that human beings are capable of.

See page 630.
See also *Comedy.*

TRANSCENDENTALISM A nineteenth-century movement in the Romantic tradition, which held that every individual can reach ultimate truths through spiritual intuition, which transcends reasons and sensory experience. The Transcendental movement was centered in Concord, Massachusetts, the home of its leading exponents, Ralph Waldo Emerson and Henry David Thoreau. The basic tenets of the Transcendentalists were (1) a belief that God is present in every aspect of Nature, including every human being; (2) the conviction that everyone is capable of apprehending God through the use of intuition; (3) the belief that all of nature is symbolic of the spirit. A corollary of these beliefs was an optimistic view of the world as good and evil as nonexistent.

See pages 183, 316.

TROCHEE A metrical foot made up of an accented syllable followed by an unaccented syllable, as in the word taxi. A trochee is the opposite of an iamb and is sometimes used to vary the rhythm of an iambic poem.

See pages 151, 262, 333.

UNDERSTATEMENT A statement that says less than what is meant. Understatement, paradoxically, can make us recognize the truth of something by saying that just the opposite is true. If you sit down to a dinner plate that contains only a peanut-butter sandwich and you say, "A feast for a king," you are using understatement to emphasize how little, in fact, is on your plate. Understatement is often used to make an ironic point; it can also be used for humor.

See page 569.
See also *Hyperbole.*

VERNACULAR The language spoken by the people who live in a particular locality.

See also *Dialect.*

GLOSSARY

The glossary below is an alphabetical list of words found in the selections in this book. Use this glossary just as you use a dictionary—to find out the meanings of unfamiliar words. (A few technical, foreign, or more obscure words in this book are not listed here but are defined instead for you in the footnotes that accompany each selection.)

Many words in the English language have more than one meaning. This glossary gives the meanings that apply to the words as they are used in the selections in this book. Words closely related in form and meaning are usually listed together in one entry (*delta* and *deltaic*), and the definition is given for the first form.

The following abbreviations are used:

adj., adjective   **n.,** noun   **v.,** verb
adv., adverb   **pl.,** plural form

Unless a word is very simple to pronounce, its pronunciation is given in parentheses. A guide to the pronunciation symbols appears at the bottom of each right-hand glossary page.

For more information about the words in this glossary, or about words not listed here, consult a dictionary.

abate (ə·bāt′) *v.* To diminish; lessen.
abeyance (ə·bā′əns) *n.* Temporary suspension.
abhor (əb·hôr′) *v.* To detest; hate.
abominable (ə·bäm′ə·nə·b′l) *adj.* Nasty and disgusting.
abreast (ə·brest′) *adj.* Side by side.
absolve (əb·zälv′) *v.* To free from guilt or blame.
abyss (ə·bis′) *n.* Bottomless gulf or pit; anything too deep for measurement.
acclivity (ə·kliv′ə·tē) *n.* An upward slope of ground.
accrue (ə·krōō′) *v.* To come as a natural growth, advantage, or right to.
acrimonious (ak′rə·mō′nē·əs) *adj.* Bitter; harsh.
acronym (ak′rə·nim) *n.* A word formed from the first, or the first few, letters of a series of words, such as *radar,* from *ra*dio *d*etecting *a*nd *ra*nging.
adversary (ad′vər·ser·ē) *n.* Opponent; enemy.
affliction (ə·flik′shən) *n.* Anything causing pain, suffering, or distress.

affluent (af′loo·wənt) *adj.* Wealthy.
aghast (ə·gast′) *adj.* Terrified; feeling great horror.
airs (erz) *n. pl.* Melodies.
akimbo (ə·kim′bō) *adj.* With hands on hips and elbows bent outward.
alight (ə·līt′) *v.* To come down after flight; descend and settle.
allay (ə·lā′) *v.* To quiet; calm; put (fears) to rest.
aloft (ə·lôft′) *adv.* In the air; high up.
amenities (ə·men′ə·tēz) *n. pl.* Things that add to one's comfort; conveniences.
anemia (ə·nē′mē·ə) *n.* Lack of vigor or vitality; lifelessness.
anguish (aŋ′gwish) *n.* Great suffering; agony.
anon (ə·nän′) *adv.* Soon.
antagonist (an·tag′ə·nist) *n.* Opponent; competitor.
apotheosis (ə·päth′ē·ō′sis) *n.* Glorification of a person or thing.
apparition (ap′ə·rish′ən) *n.* A strange figure appearing suddenly and thought to be a ghost.
appropriate (ə·prō′prē·āt′) *v.* To take for one's own or exclusive use; take improperly, without permission.
arching (är′chiŋ) *adj.* Curving or bending.
arduous (är′joo·wəs) *adj.* Difficult to do; strenuous.
arrogant (ar′ə·gənt) *adj.* Full of pride and self-importance.
articulate (är·tik′yə·lāt′) *v.* To express clearly.
assail (ə·sāl′) *v.* To attack.
assent (ə·sent′) *n.* Agreement; approval.
audacity (ô·das′ə·tē) *n.* Shameless boldness; insolence.
auspicious (ôs·pish′əs) *adj.* Favorable; suggesting a good future.
automatism (ô·täm′ə·tiz′m) *n.* Automaton; an apparatus that automatically performs certain actions without thought or understanding.
avert (ə·vʉrt′) *v.* To prevent; keep from happening.
awry (ə·rī′) *adv.* Out of shape or out of normal order.

bedlam (bed′ləm) *n.* A situation characterized by noise and confusion.
beholden (bi·hōld′ən) *adj.* Indebted; obliged to feel grateful.
benign (bi·nīn′) *adj.* Favorable; beneficial; causing no harm.
bequeath (bi·kwēth′) *v.* To leave to someone in a will.

bier (bir) *n.* A platform on which a coffin or corpse is placed.

bliss (blis) *n.* Great joy or happiness.

blithe (blīth) *adj.* Cheerful; carefree.

borne (bôrn) *v.* Carried. (Past participle of *bear*.)

brash (brash) *adj.* Hasty and reckless; rash.

brittle (brit″l) *adj.* Easily broken because it is hard and not flexible.

burgeon (bur′jən) *v.* To sprout; expand; flourish.

calamity (kə·lam′ə·tē) *n.* Extreme misfortune; disaster.

camaraderie (käm′ə·räd′ər·ē) *n.* Warm feeling among friends.

cater-cornered (kat′ē·kôr′nərd) *adj.* Diagonal.

caterwaul (kat′ər·wôl′) *v.* To make a shrill, howling sound.

censure (sen′shər) *n.* An official expression of disapproval.

chafe (chāf) *v.* To irritate or make sore by rubbing.

chromograph (krō′mə·graf′) *n.* A tinted photograph.

circumspect (sur′kəm·spekt′) *adj.* Cautious; careful to consider all details before acting or judging.

clamor (klam′ər) *n.* A loud, sustained noise.

claxon (klak′s′n) *n.* An electric horn with a loud, shrill sound. (A variant spelling of *klaxon*.)

cohesion (kō·hē′zhən) *n.* The tendency to stick together.

comport (kəm·pôrt′) *v.* **1.** To agree with. **2.** To behave in a specified manner.

conglomeration (kən·gläm′ə·rā′shən) *n.* A mixture or mass of miscellaneous things.

conjecture (kən·jek′chər) *v.* To guess.

connubial (kə·nōō′bē·əl) *adj.* Having to do with marriage.

consign (kən·sīn′) *v.* To hand over or deliver; put into the care of another.

constrain (kən·strān′) *v.* To hold back; restrain; confine.

convivial (kən·viv′ē·əl) *adj.* Sociable; jovial.

countenance (koun′tə·nəns) *n.* Facial features or expressions.

cow (kou) *v.* To fill with fear; intimidate.

craven (krā′vən) *adj.* Cowardly.

credulous (krej′ōō·ləs) *adj.* Easily convinced; tending to believe too readily.

croon (krōōn) *v.* To sing or hum in a low, gentle tone.

dauntless (dônt′lis) *adj.* Fearless.

dearness (dir′nis) *n.* High price; great expense.

decadence (dek′ə·dəns) *n.* Deterioration; decay.

decorum (di·kôr′əm) *n.* Propriety and good taste in speech, manners, dress, etc.

deferential (def′ə·ren′shəl) *adj.* Respectful; extremely courteous.

delirium (di·lir′ē·əm) *n.* A temporary state of extreme mental excitement, marked by restlessness, confused speech, and hallucinations.

delta (del′tə) *n.* A deposit of sand and soil that forms at the mouth of a river. *adj.* **Deltaic.**

descry (di·skrī′) *v.* To catch sight of.

desultory (des″l·tôr′ē) *adj.* Passing from one thing to another in an aimless way; disconnected; not methodical.

diagnostic (dī′əg·näs′tik) *adj.* Of or constituting a diagnosis, a decision on the nature of a disease after a careful examination of symptoms.

dilemma (di·lem′ə) *n.* A problem that can be solved only by choosing between equally unpleasant alternatives.

din (din) *n.* A loud, continuous noise.

dirge (durj) *n.* A song, poem, or musical composition that expresses mourning.

discern (di·surn′) *v.* To perceive or recognize; make out clearly.

discernment (di·surn′mənt) *n.* Keen perception or judgment; insight.

disdain (dis·dān′) *n.* Contempt; scorn.

disjointed (dis·joint′id) *adj.* Disconnected; without unity.

dismal (diz′m′l) *adj.* Gloomy; bleak; depressing.

disparate (dis′pər·it) *adj.* Distinct or different in some essential way.

dissertation (dis′ər·tā′shən) *n.* A long, formal written or spoken presentation on some topic.

dissuade (di·swād′) *v.* To advise or persuade against.

divest (də·vest′) *v.* To get rid of something unwanted.

divulge (də·vulj′) *v.* To reveal.

dowry (dou′rē) *n.* The money or property that a woman brings to her husband at marriage.

dumbly (dum′lē) *adv.* Silently.

eccentric (ik·sen′trik) *adj.* Odd; unconventional; out of the ordinary.

eddies (ed′ēz) *n. pl.* Currents of air or water that move against the main current and form whirlpools or whirlwinds.

egress (ē′gres) *n.* The act of going out; a way out; exit.

eloquence (el′ə·kwəns) *n.* Skill in speaking or writing.

elude (i·lōōd′) *v.* To avoid or escape by means of skill.

emanate (em′ə·nāt′) *v.* To send forth; emit; issue.

embrasure (im·brā′zhər) *n.* An opening, as for a door or window.

eminent (em′ə·nənt) *adj.* Outstanding; noteworthy.

emissary (em′ə·ser′ē) *n.* An agent sent on a specific mission.

encumbrance (in·kum′brəns) *n.* Something that hinders or obstructs; burden.

enfeeble (in·fē′b′l) *v.* To weaken.

enmity (en′mə·tē) *n.* Hatred.

entreat (in·trēt′) *v.* To plead with; beg.

epitaph (ep′ə·taf′) *n.* A short composition written in memory of a dead person; an inscription on a tombstone.

epoch (ep′ək) *n.* A period in history considered important because of certain events, developments, or people.

equable (ek′wə·b'l) *adj.* Not easily upset; uniform; steady.

erratic (i·rat′ik) *adj.* Irregular; random; wandering.

exasperate (ig·zas′pə·rāt′) *v.* To irritate or annoy.

execrable (ek′si·krə·b'l) *adj.* Detestable; hateful.

execration (ek′si·krā′shən) *n.* A curse; the act of calling down evil upon.

exemplary (ig·zem′plə·rē) *adj.* Worth imitating; serving as a model or example.

expedient (ik·spē′dē·ənt) *n.* Something useful or convenient.

expunge (ik·spunj′) *v.* To erase or remove completely.

extort (ik·stôrt′) *v.* To take by violence or threats of violence.

extricate (eks′trə·kāt′) *v.* To disentangle; set free or release.

exultance (ig·zul′t'ns) *n.* An expression of joy or triumph.

facilitate (fə·sil′ə·tāt′) *v.* To make easy.

feeble (fē′b'l) *adj.* Weak; without force or effectiveness.

fiasco (fē·as′kō) *n.* A project that ends in total failure.

fissure (fish′ər) *n.* A long, narrow crack or opening; a dividing into parts.

flak (flak) *n.* The fire of antiaircraft guns.

fleeting (flēt′iŋ) *adj.* Passing swiftly; not lasting.

fluidity (floo·wid′ə·tē) *n.* Ease of movement.

forbearance (fôr·ber′əns) *n.* Self-control; patient restraint.

formidable (fôr′mə·də·b'l) *adj.* Hard to overcome; impressive in size, excellence, etc.

founder (foun′dər) *v.* To break down; collapse; fail.

frugality (froo·gal′ə·tē) *n.* The quality of being not wasteful; thrift; economy.

gait (gāt) *n.* Manner of walking or running.

gaunt (gônt) *adj.* Thin and hollow-eyed, as from great hunger or age.

genial (jēn′yəl) *adj.* Cheerful, friendly, and sympathetic.

gesticulate (jes·tik′yə·lāt′) *v.* To gesture with the hands or arms.

harangue (hə·raŋ′) *v.* To scold repeatedly.

harry (har′ē) *v.* To force or push along.

hedonistic (hēd′'n·is′tik) *adj.* Devoted to the pursuit of pleasure.

heretofore (hir′tə·fôr′) *adv.* Until now.

hobgoblin (häb′gäb′lin) *n.* A frightening hallucination.

hostile (häs′t'l) *adj.* Not friendly.

hypocrisy (hi·päk′rə·sē) *n.* The pretense of feeling what one does not feel or of being what one is not.

hypothesis (hī·päth′ə·sis) *n.* An unproved theory temporarily accepted to explain certain facts.

illumine (i·loo′min) *v.* To light.

imminence (im′ə·nəns) *n.* The quality of being likely to happen without delay; threatening.

impart (im·pärt′) *v.* To make known; tell; reveal.

impassiveness (im·pas′iv·nis) *n.* The quality of not feeling or not showing emotion.

impede (im·pēd′) *v.* To obstruct; hinder the progress of.

impel (im·pel′) *v.* To force; push forward.

imperious (im·pir′ē·əs) *adj.* **1.** Urgent; imperative. **2.** Acting in a dictatorial manner; overbearing and arrogant.

impertinence (im·pur′t'n·əns) *n.* Disrespect; insolence.

impervious (im·pur′vē·əs) *adj.* Not affected.

impetuous (im·pech′oo·wəs) *adj.* Acting with little or no thought; rash.

impious (im′pē·əs) *adj.* Lacking reverence for God.

implacable (im·plak′ə·b'l) *adj.* Relentless; not likely to be appeased or satisfied.

importunity (im′pôr·toon′ə·tē) *n.* Persistence in making a request or a demand.

impromptu (im·prämp′too) *adj.* Without preparation; spur-of-the-moment; unrehearsed.

impropriety (im′prə·prī′ə·tē) *n.* The quality of being improper or inappropriate.

inalienable (in·āl′yən·ə·b'l) *adj.* Not capable of being taken away or transferred.

incessantly (in·ses′'nt·lē) *adv.* Without interruption.

inconceivable (in′kən·sē′və·b'l) *adj.* Not able to be thought of, understood, imagined, or believed.

indiscreet (in′dis·krēt′) *adj.* Unwise; without thought or judgment.

indiscriminate (in′dis·krim′ə·nit) *adj.* Not making careful choices or distinctions.

indolent (in′də·lənt) *adj.* Lazy; idle.

indubitably (in·doo′bi·tə·blē) *adv.* Beyond doubt; unquestionably.

inebriate (in·e′brē·āt′) *v.* To make drunk; intoxicate.

inert (in·urt′) *adj.* Inactive; not moving.

inestimable (in·es′tə·mə·b'l) *adj.* Too great or valuable to be properly measured.

inevitable (in·ev′ə·tə·b'l) *adj.* Unavoidable.

infallible (in·fal′ə·b'l) *adj.* Unable to make an error. *n.* **Infallibility.**

---

fat, āpe, cär; ten, ēven; is, bīte; gō, hôrn, tool, look; oil, out; up, fur; get; joy; yet; chin; she; thin, **then**; zh, leisure; ŋ, ring; ə for *a* in *ago*, *e* in *agent*, *i* in *sanity*, *o* in *comply*, *u* in *focus*; ′ as in *able* (ā′b'l).

…uation (in·fach′oo·wā′shən) *n.* State of being carried away by foolish love or affection.

infidel (in′fə·d′l) *n.* Someone who does not believe in a particular religion.

ingress (in′gres) *n.* The act of going in; a way in; entrance.

iniquity (in·ik′wə·tē) *n.* Wickedness; evil; sin.

innuendo (in′yoo·wen′dō) *n.* An indirect remark or reference that implies something belittling or insulting; an insinuation.

insidious (in·sid′ē·əs) *adj.* Characterized by treachery or slyness; more dangerous than seems apparent.

insoluble (in·säl′yoo·b′l) *adj.* Without a solution.

insular (in′sə·lər) *adj.* Having the form of an island.

insuperable (in·soo′pər·ə·b′l) *adj.* Not able to be overcome or passed by.

insurgent (in·sur′jənt) *n.* Someone who rises up against established authority; a rebel.

interfuse (in′tər·fyooz′) *v.* To combine by mixing, blending, or fusing together.

interminable (in·tur′mi·nə·b′l) *adj.* Endless.

intermittent (in′tər·mit′′nt) *adj.* Stopping and starting at intervals; periodic.

internecine (in′tər·nē′sin) *adj.* Mutually destructive or harmful; deadly or harmful to both sides of a conflict.

intimate (in′tə·māt′) *v.* To make known indirectly; hint or imply.

intuition (in′too·wish′ən) *n. pl.* The faculty that enables one to learn without the conscious use of reasoning.

invective (in·vek′tiv) *n.* A violent, abusive verbal attack.

iteration (it′ə·rā′shən) *n.* Repetition.

itinerant (ī·tin′ər·ənt) *adj.* Traveling from place to place.

jargon (jär′gən) *n.* **1.** Specialized terminology used by a particular group of people. **2.** Obscure and often pretentious language.

jaunty (jônt′ē) *adj.* Sprightly; perky; having an easy confidence.

laborious (lə·bôr′ē·əs) *adj.* Involving much hard work; difficult.

lament (lə·ment′) *v.* To express deep sorrow; mourn.

leonine (lē′ə·nīn′) *adj.* Like a lion.

loathsome (lō*th*′səm) *adj.* Disgusting; detestable.

loll (läl) *v.* **1.** To droop. **2.** To lounge about in a lazy, relaxed manner.

loquacity (lō·kwas′ə·tē) *n.* A tendency to talk excessively.

magnitude (mag′nə·tood′) *n.* Greatness in size, extent, or influence.

manifestation (man′ə·fes·tā′shən) *n.* Demonstration or expression.

manifold (man′ə·fōld′) *adj.* Having many forms or parts.

maritime (mar′ə·tīm′) *adj.* Having to do with the sea.

martial (mär′shəl) *adj.* Military; having to do with war.

mean (mēn) *adj.* Low in quality, value, or importance.

meditative (med′ə·tāt′iv) *adj.* Inclined to reflect upon and think deeply about ideas.

mesmerize (mez′mər·īz′) *v.* To hypnotize; put in a trance.

mete (mēt) *v.* To give out measured portions; distribute.

meticulous (mə·tik′yoo·ləs) *adj.* Excessively careful about details; finicky.

mirth (murth) *n.* Joyfulness; merriment.

motley (mät′lē) *adj.* Made up of many different, often clashing, elements.

mottled (mät′′ld) *adj.* Marked with streaks or blots.

multitudes (mul′tə·toodz′) *n. pl.* Vast numbers.

murky (mur′kē) *adj.* Heavy with smoke or mist; dark and gloomy.

myriad (mir′ē·əd) *adj.* Of an indefinitely large number; innumerable.

nimble (nim′b′l) *adj.* Marked by quick light movement; marked by mental alertness.

nomadic (nō·mad′ik) *adj.* Characteristic of a wanderer who has no fixed home.

norms (nôrmz) *n. pl.* Standards or models for a group.

oblivious (ə·bliv′ē·əs) *adj.* Unmindful of; completely unaffected by.

obnoxious (əb·näk′shəs) *adj.* Very unpleasant; objectionable; offensive.

obsequious (əb·sē′kwē·əs) *adj.* Much too willing to serve or obey; overly submissive.

obstinancy (äb′stə·nə·sē) *n.* Stubbornness.

obtrude (əb·trood′) *v.* To thrust forward; push out.

occult (ə·kult′) *adj.* Beyond human understanding; mysterious.

ominous (äm′ə·nəs) *adj.* Threatening; sinister; having the character of a prediction of evil.

opulent (äp′yə·lənt) *adj.* Rich; luxurious; abundant.

orb *n.* A sphere.

ordeal (ôr·dēl′) *n.* A difficult or painful experience.

oscillate (äs′ə·lāt′) *v.* To swing or move regularly back and forth.

ostentatious (äs′tən·tā′shəs) *adj.* Characterized by a showy display of wealth, knowledge, etc.

pagan (pā′gən) *n.* A person who is not a Christian, a Moslem, or a Jew.

pallid (pal′id) *adj.* Pale; faint in color.

pallor (pal′ər) *n.* Paleness; lack of color.

paraphernalia (par′ə·fər·nāl′yə) *n.* Gear; equipment; any collection of things used in a certain activity.

pedestrian (pə·des′trē·ən) *adj.* Ordinary; dull.

pending (pen′diŋ) *adj.* Not yet decided or established.

pensive (pen′siv) *adj.* Thoughtful.

perturbation (pur′tər·bā′shən) *n.* Disturbance; great annoyance.

pickerel (pik′ər·əl) *n.* A small freshwater fish.

pigmentation (pig′mən·tā′shən) *n.* Coloration in plants or animals.

pique (pēk) *v.* To annoy.

placid (plas′id) *adj.* Calm; quiet.

plausible (plô′zə·b′l) *adj.* Seemingly true; believable.

plunder (plun′dər) *n.* Goods taken by force or fraud; loot.

politic (päl′ə·tik) *adj.* Having practical wisdom; shrewd; diplomatic.

pompous (päm′pəs) *adj.* Pretentious in speech or behavior; self-important.

portfolio (pôrt·fō′lē′ō′) *n.* A flat, portable case for carrying loose sheets of paper; a briefcase.

precedence (pres′ə·dəns) *n.* Priority; the act or right of preceding in importance.

precept (prē′sept) *n.* A rule of action or conduct.

premonitory (pri·män′ə·tôr′ē) *adj.* Relating to a feeling that something bad will soon happen.

preoccupied (prē·äk′yə·pīd′) *adj.* Wholly absorbed in one's thoughts.

presage (pri·sāj′) *v.* To give a warning of future evil.

prevail (pri·vāl′) *v.* To gain the advantage or mastery; be victorious; triumph.

prevalent (prev′ə·lənt) *adj.* Generally practiced or accepted.

prodigal (präd′i·gəl) *adj.* Wasteful.

profane (prə·fān′) *adj.* Showing disrespect or contempt for sacred things.

prostrate (präs′trāt) *adj.* Lying with the face down, in demonstration of great humility.

protocol (prōt′ə·kôl′) *n.* **1.** Any set of rules governing behavior, natural or artificial. **2.** The code of ceremonial rites and courtesies accepted as proper in official dealings.

provoke (prə·vōk′) *v.* To anger, irritate, or annoy; stir up.

prudent (prōōd′′nt) *adj.* Cautious; capable of sound judgment.

pulverize (pul′və·rīz′) *v.* To crush or grind into a powder or dust.

quail (kwāl) *v.* To draw back in fear.

quell (kwel) *v.* To quiet; put an end to.

querulous (kwer′ə·ləs) *adj.* Inclined to find fault; full of complaint.

rakish (rā′kish) *adj.* Dashing, careless.

ravening (rav′′n·iŋ) *adj.* Greedily or wildly hungry.

realm (relm) *n.* Region or area.

reconnoiter (rē′kə·noit′ər) *v.* To make a survey or careful examination of an area.

rectify (rek′tə·fī′) *v.* To correct; set right.

remonstrance (ri·män′strəns) *n.* A protest or complaint.

remote (ri·mōt′) *adj.* Far away; secluded.

rend (rend) *v.* To tear or rip.

repose (ri·pōz′) *n.* Rest; sleep; freedom from worry.

reprobate (rep′rə·bāt′) *v.* To disapprove of strongly; condemn.

repugnant (ri·pug′nənt) *adj.* Distasteful; offensive; disagreeable.

revere (ri·vir′) *v.* To regard with deep respect or love.

revery (rev′ər·ē) *n.* Daydream.

robust (rō·bust′) *adj.* Strong and healthy.

row (rou) *n.* A noisy quarrel or disturbance.

ruse (rōōz) *n.* A trick meant to deceive someone.

sage (sāj) *n.* A wise person respected for experience and judgment.

scoff (skôf) *v.* To make fun of by showing contempt or scorn.

scrupulous (skrōō′pyə·ləs) *adj.* Demanding precision, care, and exactness.

scuttle (skut′′l) *v.* To run quickly away from danger or trouble.

sentience (sen′shəns) *n.* Capacity for feeling or perceiving; consciousness.

sentinel (sen′ti·n′l) *n.* A guard set to protect a group.

skein (skān) *n.* Thread or yarn, wound in a coil.

skulk (skulk) *v.* To move in a sneaky or sinister manner.

slough (slou) *n.* A swamp.

slovenly (sluv′ən·lē) *adj.* Careless in appearance or habits.

smote (smōt) *v.* Hit or struck hard. (Past tense of *smite*.)

solace (säl′is) *n.* An easing of grief, loneliness, or discomfort.

spasm (spaz′m) *n.* A sudden, violent, temporary activity.

speckled (spek′′ld) *adj.* Covered with small marks of contrasting colors.

spy (spī) *v.* To notice.

squabble (skwäb′′l) *n.* A noisy, petty quarrel or dispute.

stanchion (stan′chən) *n.* An upright bar, beam, or post used as a support.

starkly (stärk′lē) *adv.* In an unsoftened or unembellished way.

stoicism (stō′i·siz′m) *n.* Unemotional acceptance of both pleasure and pain.

stolid (stäl′id) *adj.* Having or showing little or no emotion or sensitivity.

---

fat, āpe, cär; ten, ēven; is, bīte; gō, hôrn, tōōl, look; oil, out; up, fur; get; joy; yet; chin; she; thin, then; zh, leisure; ŋ, ring; ə for a in *ago*, e in *agent*, i in *sanity*, o in *comply*, u in *focus*; ′ as in *able* (ā′b′l).

submissive (səb·mis′iv) *adj.* Obedient; yielding; tending to give in without resistance.

suffused (sə·fyōozd′) *adj.* Filled with a glow or color.

sundry (sun′drē) *adj.* Various; miscellaneous.

supinely (sōo·pīn′lē) *adv.* Lying on the back, face upward.

symmetrical (si·met′ri·k′l) *adj.* Having the same form or arrangement on each side.

symptomatic (simp′tə·mat′ik) *adj.* Showing symptoms or signs of.

tactile (tak′t′l) *adj.* Able to be perceived by the sense of touch.

taunt (tônt) *v.* To tease in scornful or sarcastic language.

tedious (tē′dē·əs) *adj.* Tiresome; boring.

temporal (tem′pər·əl) *adj.* Worldly, not spiritual.

tendrils (ten′drəlz) *n. pl.* Threadlike parts of a climbing plant that coil around an object.

tentatively (ten′tə·tiv·lē) *adv.* Timidly; with hesitation or uncertainty.

tepid (tep′id) *adj.* Lukewarm; lacking warmth of feeling or enthusiasm.

till (til) *v.* To cultivate, in order to raise crops.

transfixed (trans·fikst′) *adj.* Made motionless, as if fastened to a spot.

translucent (trans·lōo′s′nt) *adj.* Allowing light to pass through.

travail (trav′āl) *n.* Intense pain; agony.

travesty (trav′is·tē) *v.* To make fun of by doing an exaggerated imitation; ridicule.

trepidation (trep′ə·dā′shən) *n.* Fearful uncertainty; anxiety.

tumultuous (too·mul′choo·wəs) *adj.* Wild and noisy; greatly agitated.

turgid (tʉr′jid) *adj.* Overstated in a self-important way; pompous.

turmoil (tʉr′moil) *n.* Commotion; uproar; confusion.

unseemly (un·sēm′lē) *adj.* Improper; indecent.

upbraid (up·brād′) *v.* To scold severely or bitterly.

utilitarian (yōo·til′ə·ter′ē·ən) *adj.* Stressing usefulness over beauty and other values.

vain (vān′) *adj.* **1.** Futile; ineffectual. **2.** Conceited.

vanquish (vaη′kwish) *v.* To defeat.

velocity (və·läs′ə·tē) *n.* Speed.

venerable (ven′ər·ə·b′l) *adj.* Worthy of respect or reverence.

venomous (ven′əm·əs) *adj.* Poisonous; intended to harm.

vex (veks) *v.* To annoy; irritate.

vigilance (vij′ə·ləns) *n.* Watchfulness; alertness.

vindictive (vin·dik′tiv) *adj.* Revengeful in spirit; seeking revenge.

vivacity (vi·vas′ə·tē) *n.* Liveliness of spirit; animation.

vivid (viv′id) *adj.* Forming clear or striking mental images; strong; active.

volition (vō·lish′ən) *n.* A conscious or deliberate decision or choice.

vulnerability (vul′nər·ə·bil′ə·tē) *n.* Openness to attack or criticism; a condition of being easily hurt.

wanton (wän′t′n) *adj.* Unprovoked and unjustifiable; deliberately hurtful.

wax (waks) *v.* To become.

waylay (wā′lā′) *v.* To ambush; wait for and attack.

wrench (rench) *v.* To twist, pull, or jerk suddenly and violently.

wrest (rest) *v.* To take by force or violence.

yawp (yôp) *n.* Rough, vigorous language.

zealous (zel′əs) *adj.* Fervent; enthusiastic; devoted to a purpose or mission.

INDEX OF SKILLS

LANGUAGE AND STYLE SKILLS

Most of the page numbers listed below refer to discussions that appear in the **Analyzing Language and Style** exercises. Additional page references for some terms may also be found in the Literary Skills index.

Trochaic meter 151, 1152
Words with multiple meanings 693, 1093, 1117

SPEAKING AND LISTENING SKILLS

Evaluating the sound of a poem 654
Giving an oral reading 1088
Identifying different voices in a poem 142, 663
Inventing an interview 947
Listening to dialects 404
Listening to form a picture of the character 298
Listening to how a poem imitates real speech 657
Listening to onomatopoeia 318
Listening to poetry 699, 760
Preparing a choral reading 1097
Reading aloud and identifying run-on lines and mid-line pauses 142
Reading aloud to compare and contrast cadence and trochaic tetrameter 333
Reading aloud to identify cadences 333
Reading aloud to identify patterns of stressed and unstressed syllables 262
Reading aloud to identify rhymes and rhythm 250
Reading aloud to identify rhythm and sound effects 152, 721
Reading dialect aloud 404, 414, 619
Reading poetry aloud 46, 164, 253, 355, 754, 756, 760, 773, 1097, 1130, 1132
Reading prose aloud 94
Scanning a poem 370, 687

COMPOSITION AND CRITICAL THINKING SKILLS

Writing: A Creative Response

Analyzing contemporary maxims 85
Applying meanings 390
Applying the poem to other situations 163
Casting a film 401, 715
Changing the poem 47, 674, 680, 696
Creating an image 734, 1026
Creating a setting 260, 564, 573
Creating epithets 750
Creating metaphors 413
Describing a character 924, 959

Describing a scene 151
Extending the play 828, 884
Extending the poem 687, 702
Extending the story 137, 292, 508, 628, 637, 914, 929
Imitating the writer's technique 252, 260, 428, 438, 508, 577, 746, 755, 766, 919, 982, 999, 1007, 1045, 1049, 1093, 1122, 1128
Inventing names for characters 657
Making a poem out of an essay 342
Paraphrasing the poem 688
Preparing a choral reading of a poem 1097
Reading the poem orally 1088
Responding to a character 540, 655
Responding to the writer 1009, 1030
Retitling a poem 741
Rewriting dialect 413
Setting the poem to music 664, 674, 711, 715
Staging the story 232
Updating the character 540
Updating the sermon 40
Using another point of view 21, 30, 40, 166, 219, 225, 246, 274, 316, 533, 588, 655, 901, 972, 1003, 1019, 1045, 1095, 1112
Using nature to communicate a message 677
Writing a description 1103
Writing a dialogue 669, 715, 766
Writing a firsthand account 99
Writing a free-verse poem 350
Writing a journal entry 35, 219, 428, 939
Writing a letter 145, 197
Writing an essay 195, 1065, 1073
Writing a newspaper article 91
Writing a news report 707
Writing an opening sentence 232
Writing a stanza 392
Writing a tall tale 618
Writing quatrains 370

Writing: A Critical Response

Analyzing a character 35, 316, 509, 598, 637, 687, 766, 884, 958, 982, 1038
Analyzing a code song 392
Analyzing a conflict 137, 533, 828
Analyzing allusions 392, 999

Analyzing a story's conclusion 988
Analyzing historical references 58
Analyzing humor 958, 999
Analyzing imagery and meaning 145, 548, 637, 664, 734, 1130
Analyzing persuasion 107, 113
Analyzing point of view 515
Analyzing rhetoric in persuasive writing 321
Analyzing setting 1026
Analyzing suspense 438, 1059
Analyzing theme 508, 573, 643, 901, 1049
Analyzing the poem 141, 199, 260, 350, 370, 693, 773, 1089, 1107, 1114, 1131
Analyzing the poem's appeal 160, 166
Analyzing the poem's message 166, 772
Analyzing the poet's statement 350, 757
Analyzing the precise meanings of words 63
Analyzing the story 247, 628, 924
Analyzing the story's effect 246
Analyzing the story's Romantic elements 292, 428
Analyzing the use of lights in a play 828
Analyzing the writer's attitude 44, 919
Analyzing the writer's personality 1065, 1073
Describing a character 999
Describing Biblical parallels 51, 292, 342
Developing a topic 219
Comparing and contrasting characters 588, 655, 767, 972
Comparing and contrasting descriptions 193, 553
Comparing and contrasting imagery 592, 673, 677
Comparing and contrasting philosophies 199, 540, 674, 711
Comparing and contrasting poems 47, 145, 168, 201, 252, 260, 320, 342, 345, 346, 350, 373, 661, 669, 673, 677, 680, 681, 688, 693, 702, 705, 707, 711, 715, 750, 755, 757, 772, 1085, 1093, 1103, 1130
Comparing and contrasting poetry to prose 350, 508, 746
Comparing and contrasting sermons 702

CRITICAL THINKING EXERCISES

The following is a list of the two-page exercises that follow each unit, in which critical thinking skills are taught step-by-step following the stages of the writing process. Additional exercises calling for critical thinking skills, including the skill of synthesis, are found in the composition assignments indexed on the previous page. The following critical thinking exercises are listed in the order in which they appear in the text.

INDEX OF COMMENTARIES

AN ORGANIZATION OF CONTENTS BY THEME

A core work for each theme is cited first, in bold type.

The Perilous Journey and the Quest

Of Plymouth Plantation, William Bradford
The Autobiography, Benjamin Franklin
Moby-Dick, Herman Melville
Song of Myself, Walt Whitman
The Adventures of Huckleberry Finn, Mark Twain
The Red Badge of Courage, Stephen Crane
"Because I could not stop for Death," Emily Dickinson
"The Leader of the People," John Steinbeck
"The Migrant Way West," John Steinbeck
"A Worn Path," Eudora Welty
Blue Highways, William Least Heat Moon
The Way to Rainy Mountain, N. Scott Momaday

O Brave New World: A New Society

The Declaration of Independence, Thomas Jefferson
"The Gettysburg Address," Abraham Lincoln
"America," Claude McKay
"I, Too," Langston Hughes
"Chicago," Carl Sandburg
"Shine, Perishing Republic," Robinson Jeffers
"The Steeple-Jack," Marianne Moore

The Individual and Society

Walden, Henry David Thoreau
"The Crisis," Thomas Paine
"Rip Van Winkle," Washington Irving
"Resistance to Civil Government," Henry David Thoreau
"Self-Reliance," Ralph Waldo Emerson
"The Outcasts of Poker Flat," Bret Harte
"Richard Cory," Edwin Arlington Robinson
"'Butch' Weldy," Edgar Lee Masters
"Mending Wall," Robert Frost
"The Garden," Ezra Pound
"The Key," Isaac Bashevis Singer
"Her Kind," Anne Sexton

Illusions and Visions

The Glass Menagerie, Tennessee Williams
A Raisin in the Sun, Lorraine Hansberry
"Gatsby's Party," F. Scott Fitzgerald
"Miniver Cheevy," Edwin Arlington Robinson
"Birches," Robert Frost
"Love the Wild Swan," Robinson Jeffers
"Summertime and the Living . . . ," Robert Hayden
"Sled Burial: Dream Ceremony," James Dickey

Generations

"The Leader of the People," John Steinbeck

Look Homeward, Angel, Thomas Wolfe
"Son," John Updike
"Your Place Is Empty," Anne Tyler
"New African," Andrea Lee
"Kite Poem," James Merrill

Loss and Renewal

"Ode on the Confederate Dead," Henry Timrod
"The Cross of Snow," Henry Wadsworth Longfellow
"Heart! We will forget him!" Emily Dickinson
"Success is counted sweetest," Emily Dickinson
"The End of Something," Ernest Hemingway
"Dirge Without Music," Edna St. Vincent Millay
"Death of the Hired Man," Robert Frost
"Parting, Without a Sequel," John Crowe Ransom
"Limited," Carl Sandburg
"Nothing Gold Can Stay," Robert Frost
"Death of a Soldier," Wallace Stevens
"Death of a Pig," E. B. White
"For the Union Dead," Robert Lowell
"Year's End," Richard Wilbur

The Triumph of Love

"A Worn Path," Eudora Welty
"Why I Like Country Music," James Alan McPherson
"Lucinda Matlock," Edgar Lee Masters

INDEX OF AUTHORS AND TITLES